Lecture Notes in Computer Science 5795

Lecture Notes in Computer Science 5795

Commenced Publication in 1973
Founding and Former Series Editors:
Gerhard Goos, Juris Hartmanis, and Jan van Leeuwen

Andy Schürr Bran Selic (Eds.)

Model Driven Engineering Languages and Systems

12th International Conference, MODELS 2009
Denver, CO, USA, October 4-9, 2009
Proceedings

Volume Editors

Andy Schürr
Technische Universität Darmstadt, Fachgebiet Echtzeitsysteme
Merckstraße 25, 64283, Darmstadt, Germany
E-mail: andy.schuerr@es.tu-darmstadt.de

Bran Selic
Malina Software Corporation
10 Blueridge Court, Nepean, Ontario, K2J 2J3, Canada
E-mail: selic@acm.org

Library of Congress Control Number: 2009934110

CR Subject Classification (1998): D.2, D.3, K.6.3, D.2.9, D.1, D.2.2

LNCS Sublibrary: SL 2 – Programming and Software Engineering

ISSN 0302-9743
ISBN-10 3-642-04424-7 Springer Berlin Heidelberg New York
ISBN-13 978-3-642-04424-3 Springer Berlin Heidelberg New York

springer.com

Printed in Germany

Typesetting: Camera-ready by author, data conversion by Scientific Publishing Services, Chennai, India
Printed on acid-free paper SPIN: 12760060 06/3180 5 4 3 2 1 0

Preface

The pioneering organizers of the first $\ll$ UML $\gg$ workshop in Mulhouse, France in the summer of 1998 could hardly have anticipated that, in little over a decade, their initiative would blossom into today's highly successful MODELS conference series, the premier annual gathering of researchers and practitioners focusing on a very important new technical discipline: model-based software and system engineering. This expansion is, of course, a direct consequence of the growing significance and success of model-based methods in practice. The conferences have contributed greatly to the heightened interest in the field, attracting much young talent and leading to the gradual emergence of its corresponding scientific and engineering foundations. The proceedings from the MODELS conferences are one of the primary references for anyone interested in a more substantive study of the domain.

The 12th conference took place in Denver in the USA, October 4–9, 2009 along with numerous satellite workshops and tutorials, as well as several other related scientific gatherings. The conference was exceptionally fortunate to have three eminent, invited keynote speakers from industry: Stephen Mellor, Larry Constantine, and Grady Booch.

A distinguishing feature of this year's conference was the inclusion, for the first time, of a dedicated "Empirical Results" papers category. The objective was to provide a specific forum for publishing significant results, from both industry and research, of the innovative application of model-based methods in practice, so that the broader community could be better informed of the capabilities and successes of this relatively young discipline. Consequently, a significant proportion of accepted papers belong to this category, indicating an accumulation of pent up high-quality scientific and technical work, which lacked a proper venue in the past and also demonstrating the increasing importance of model-based approaches in practice.

The program committee received 248 submissions from 33 countries. A number of papers were co-authored by researchers from different institutions in different countries, indicating a very healthy trend towards scientific collaboration unhampered by institutional and geographic borders. Of these the committee selected 45 full papers and 13 short papers, giving an acceptance rate of 18% and 5%, respectively.

As is customary, the program committee selected a small number of exceptional full-paper submissions that received the "Most Distinguished ACM SIGSOFT Paper Award". In addition, the best MODELS 2009 submission was chosen for the "Springer Best Paper Award". Last but certainly not least, from the papers published in the proceedings of the $\ll$ UML $\gg$ (MODELS) conference, the steering committee selected the one that, in their opinion, had had the greatest impact for the "Ten-Year Most Influential Paper Award" also provided by Springer.

We would like to thank everyone who submitted papers as well as proposals for workshops and tutorials. We would also like to express our gratitude to the large number of volunteers who contributed to the success of the conference. As in the past, special kudos are due to Richard van de Stadt, for his unfailing and always timely support of the highly versatile CyberChairPRO system. Last but not least, we would like to thank our sponsors, ACM, Aerospace, IEEE Computer Society, and Springer for their support of the MODELS 2009 conference.

October 2009

Andy Schürr
Bran Selic
Rob Pettit
Sudipto Ghosh

Organization

General Co-chairs

Robert Pettit	The Aerospace Corporation, USA
Sudipto Ghosh	Colorado State University, USA

Program Chairs

Andy Schürr (Scientific Paper Category)	Technische Universität Darmstadt, Germany
Bran Selic (Empirical Results Paper Category)	Malina Software, Canada

Registration Chair

Kathy Krell	Colorado State University, USA

Publicity Co-chairs

Arnor Solberg	SINTEF, Norway
Emanuel Grant	University of North Dakota, USA

Workshops Chair

James M. Bieman	Colorado State University, USA

Panels Chair

Øystein Haugen	University of Oslo, Norway

Tutorials Chair

Thomas Weigert	Missouri University of Science and Technology, USA

Doctoral Symposium Chair

Juergen Dingel	Queen's University, Canada

Educator's Symposium Co-chairs

Robert B. France	Colorado State University, USA
Martin Gogolla	University of Bremen, Germany

Scientific Papers Program Committee

Aditya Agrawal	The Mathworks Inc., USA
Egidio Astesiano	Università di Genova, Italy
Hernan Astudilo	Universidad Tecnica Federico Santa Maria, Chile
Balasubramanian Krishnakumar	The MathWorks Inc., USA
Laurent Balmeli	IBM, Japan
Don Batory	University of Texas, USA
Benoit Baudry	INRIA, France
Jean Bézivin	Université de Nantes, INRIA, France
Xavier Blanc	LIP6, France
Ruth Breu	University of Innsbruck, Austria
Lionel Briand	Simula Research Lab and University of Oslo, Norway
Jean-Michel Bruel	Université de Toulouse, France
Tony Clark	Thames Valley University, UK
Krzysztof Czarnecki	University of Waterloo, Canada
Juan de Lara	Universidad Autónoma de Madrid, Spain
Jens Dietrich	Massey University, New Zealand
Juergen Dingel	Queen's University, Canada
Stephane Ducasse	INRIA Lille, France
Keith Duddy	Queensland University of Technology, Australia
Alexander Egyed	Johannes Kepler University, Austria
Gregor Engels	University of Paderborn, Germany
Jean-Marie Favre	University of Grenoble, France
Franck Fleurey	SINTEF, Norway
Robert B. France	Colorado State University, USA
David Frankel	SAP, USA
Lidia Fuentes	University of Malaga, Spain
Harald Gall	University of Zurich, Switzerland
Dragan Gasevic	Athabasca University, Canada
Geri Georg	Colorado State University, USA
Sébastien Gérard	CEA LIST, France
Holger Giese	Hasso Plattner Institute at the University of Potsdam, Germany
Tudor Girba	University of Bern, Switzerland
Martin Gogolla	University of Bremen, Germany
Susanne Graf	VERIMAG, France
Emanuel Grant	University of North-Dakota, USA

Jeff Gray	University of Alabama at Birmingham, USA
John Grundy	University of Auckland, New Zealand
Esther Guerra	Universidad Carlos III de Madrid, Spain
Jun Han	Swinburne University of Technology, Australia
Øystein Haugen	SINTEF, Norway
Zhenjiang Hu	National Institute of Informatics, Japan
Heinrich Hussmann	Universität München, Germany
Jan Jurjens	Open University and MSRC, UK
Audris Kalnins	University of Latvia, Latvia
Gerti Kappel	Vienna University of Technology, Austria
Gabor Karsai	Vanderbilt University, USA
Ingolf Krüger	UC San Diego, USA
Jochen Kuester	IBM Research, Switzerland
Thomas Kühne	Victoria University of Wellington, New Zealand
Ralf Laemmel	University of Koblenz-Landau, Germany
Michele Lanza	University of Lugano, Switzerland
Michal Lawley	The Australian e-Health Research Centre, Australia
Timothy C. Lethbridge	University of Ottawa, Canada
Tom Maibaum	McMaster University, Canada
Tiziana Margaria	University of Potsdam, Germany
Radu Marinescu	Politechnic University of Timisoara, Romania
Dragan Milicev	University of Belgrade, Serbia
Birger Møller-Pedersen	University of Oslo, Norway
Ana Moreira	Universidade Nova de Lisboa, Portugal
Pierre-Alain Muller	Université de Haute-Alsace, France
Ileana Ober	IRIT, France
Richard Paige	University of York, UK
Dorina C. Petriu	Carleton University, Canada
Alfonso Pierantonio	Università degli Studi dell Aquila, Italy
Claudia Pons	University of La Plata, Argentina
Ivan Porres	bo Akademi University, Finland
Alexander Pretschner	Fraunhofer IESE and TU Kaiserslautern, Germany
Gianna Reggio	Università di Genova, Italy
Arend Rensink	University of Twente, The Netherlands
Bernhard Rumpe	TU Braunschweig, Germany
Bernhard Schätz	TU München, Germany
Andy Schürr	Technische Universität Darmstadt, Germany
Arnor Solberg	SINTEF, Norway
Bran Selic	Malina Software, Canada
Michal Smialek	Warsaw University of Technology, Poland
Perdita Stevens	University of Edinburgh, UK
Harald Störrle	University of Munich, Germany
Juha-Pekka Tolvanen	MetaCase, Finland
Laurence Tratt	Bournemouth University, UK

Axel Uhl	SAP AG, Germany
Antonio Vallecillo	Universidad de Málaga, Spain
Pieter Van Gorp	Technical University of Eindhoven, The Netherlands
Dániel Varró	Budapest University of Technology and Economics, Hungary
Eelco Visser	Technical University of Delft, The Netherlands
Andrzej Wasowski	IT University of Copenhagen, Denmark
Jon Whittle	Lancaster University, UK
Andreas Winter	Universiy of Koblenz-Landau, Germany

Empirical Results Program Committee

Robert Baillargeon	Panasonic Automotive Systems, USA
Francis Bordeleau	Canada
Murray Cantor	IBM Rational Software, USA
Tony Clark	Thames Valley University, UK
Diarmuid Corcoran	Ericsson AB, Sweden
Andy Evans	Xactium, UK
Geri Georg	Colorado State University, USA
Øystein Haugen	SINTEF, Norway
Steven Kelly	MetaCase, Finland
Jana Koehler	IBM Zurich Research Laboratory, Switzerland
Vinay Kulkarni	Tata Consultancy Services, India
Nikolai Mansourov	KDM Analytics, Canada
Stephen Mellor	UK
Ed Merks	itemis AG, Canada
Dragan Milicev	University of Belgrade, Serbia
Juan Carlos Molina	CARE Technologies, S.A., Spain
Pierre-Alain Muller	Université de Haute-Alsace, France
Nicolas Rouquette	Jet Propulsion Laboratory, Caltech, USA
Ina Schieferdecker	Fraunhofer FOKUS, Germany
Richard Soley	Object Management Group, USA
Ingo Stürmer	Model Engineering Solutions GmbH, Germany
Francois Terrier	CEA-LIST, France
Laurence Tratt	Bournemouth University, UK
Markus Voelter	Voelter, Germany
Michael von der Beeck	BMW Group, Germany
Ben Watson	Lockheed Martin Corporation, USA
Thomas Weigert	Missouri University of Science and Technology, USA
Frank Weil	Hengsoft, USA
Jon Whittle	Lancaster University, UK

Steering Committee

Heinrich Hussmann (Chair)
Geri Georg (Vice Chair)
Thomas Baar
Jean Bezivin
Lionel Briand
Jean-Michel Bruel
Steve Cook
Krzysztof Czarnecki
Gregor Engels
Rob Pettit
Jean-Marc Jézéquel
Stuart Kent
Chris Kobryn
Ana Moreira
Pierre-Alain Muller
Oscar Nierstrasz
Gianna Reggio
David Rosenblum
Doug Schmidt
Andy Schürr
Perdita Stevens
Jon Whittle

Sponsors

ACM (http://www.acm.org/)
Springer (http://www.springer.com/lncs)
IEEE Computer Society (www.computer.org)
Aerospace (http://www.aero.org/)

Additional Reviewers

Anantha Narayanan
Daniel Balasubramanian
Mauricio Alférez
Michal Antkiewicz
Gabriela Arevalo
Martin Assmann
Alberto Bacchelli
Omar Bahy Badreldin
András Balogh
Olivier Barais
Jorge Barreiros
Maria Cecilia Bastarrica
Basil Becker
Nicolas Belloir
Reda Bendraou
Gábor Bergmann
Selcuk Beyhan
Amancio Bouza
Petra Brosch
Benedikt Burgstaller
Jordi Cabot
Asma Charfi
Wassim El Hajj Chehade
Antonio Cicchetti
Robert Clarisó
Duc-Hanh Dang
Barry Demchak
Zekai Demirezen
Birgit Demuth
Simon Denier
Zinovy Diskin
Zinvy Diskin
Fred Doucet
Nikos Drivalos
Hubert Dubois
Cedric Dumoulin
Marina Egea
Huascar Espinoza
Louis Féraud
Claudiu Farcas
Emilia Farcas
Daniel Mendez Fernandez
Bernd Finkbeiner
Beat Fluri

Frederic Fondement
Andrew Forward
Gregor Gabrysiak
Nadia Gamez
Xiaocheng Ge
Christian Gerth
Giacomo Ghezzi
Roxana Giandini
Mike Giddings
Emanuel Giger
Mario Gleirscher
László Gönczy
Hans Groenniger
Roy Grønmo
Lindsay Groves
Yi Guo
Tormod Vaksvik Haavaldsrud
Lars Hamann
Zef Hemel
Frank Hermann
Markus Herrmannsdoerfer
Matthias Hert
Anders Hessellund
Stephan Hildebrandt
Berthold Hoffmann
Florian Hölzl
Ákos Horváth
Christian Huemer
Jerónimo Irazábal
Markus Kaiser
Jan Karstens
Lennart Kats
Amogh Kavimandan
Jacques Klein
Dimitrios Kolovos
Dagmar Koss
Stein Krogdahl
Mirco Kuhlmann
Uirá Kulesza
Thomas Kurpick
Fadoi Lakhal
Philip Langer
Jannik Laval
Hervé Leblanc
Jaejoon Lee
László Lengyel
Adrian Lienhard
Johan Lilius
Rafael Lotufo
Markus Luckey
Torbjörn Lundkvist
Naouel Moha
Chris McLaughlin
Massimiliano Menarini
Marius Minea
Maarten de Mol
Jesus J. Garcia Molina
Alix Mougenot
Chokri Mraidha
Freddy Munoz
Shiva Nejati
Stefan Neumann
Iulian Ober
Fernando Olivero
Carlos Parra
Ekaterina Pek
Gabriela Pérez
Luigia Petre
Rolf-Helge Pfeiffer
Monica Pinto
Fiona Polack
Damien Pollet
Claudia Pons
Ernesto Posse
Andreas Prinz
Ansgar Radermacher
Alek Radjenovic
István Ráth
Lukman Ab. Rahim
Daniel Ratiu
Y. Raghu Reddy
Dirk Reiss
Holger Rendel
Lukas Renggli
Jorge Ressia
Filippo Ricca
Taylor Riche
Jan O. Ringert
Jose E. Rivera
Sylvain Robert

Louis Rose
Ragnhild Kobro Runde
Davide Di Ruscio
Mehrdad Sabetzadeh
Joo Santos
Martin Schindler
Wolfgang Schubert
Martina Seidl
Maria Semenyak
Sagar Sen
Steven She
Devon Simmonds
Christian Soltenborn
Mark Stein
Yu Sun
Andreas Svendsen
Robert Tairas
Dragos Truscan
Gergely Varró
German Vega
Andres Vignaga
Hagen Voelzer
Thomas Vogel
Horst Voigt
Ksenia Wahler
Bo Wang
Ingo Weisemüller
Jules White
Manuel Wimmer
Michael Wuersch
Andreas Wübbeke
Yingfei Xiong
Eduardo Zambon
Vadim Zaytsev
Xiaorui Zhang
Tewfik Ziadi
Maria Zimakova
Steffen Zschaler
Jonas Zuberbuehler
Karolina Zurowska
Damien Pollet
Lukas Renggli

Table of Contents

Keynote 1

(Meta-)Model Modeling and Management

Quantitative Modeling with UML

Model Transformations and Constraints

Model Management

UML in Practice and Quality Assurance

Formalization of Model Transformations

Scenario Modeling

Business Application Development

Model Synchronisation and Change Propagation

Keynote 2

Language Specification and Annotation

Domain-Specific Languages

Model-Based Analysis

Model (De-)Composition and Abstractio

Distributed Software Development

Service and Business Process Integration

Keynote 3

Genericity and Constraints

Variability Management

Model Transformation Engineering

Symposium

Models. Models. Models. So What?

Stephen J. Mellor

Project Technology, Inc
StephenMellor@StephenMellor.com

Abstract. In 1985, in an interview for some then-popular magazine, I was asked when models and model-driven development would become commonplace. "In three years time," I replied confidently. In 1987, I was asked the same question, and my answer remained the same. And 1989. And '91. Were you to ask me the same question today, I would answer it in the same way. Perhaps I should have gone surfing instead.

While my answer has the virtue of consistency, how could I–how could we?–have been so wrong? Of course, we didn't have the technology back then. And we didn't have the computer power that could allow us to ignore certain inefficiencies introduced by abstraction. But have things really changed that much in nearly a quarter of a century? Our tools and computers are certainly better, but it is clear that we have failed to convert the great unwashed to the benefits and wonders of models and model-driven engineering.

This keynote will take a personal view of why we have (let's be positive, shall we?) yet to succeed. It will explore several technical, business and marketing issues that have impeded our progress. And because a keynote is intended to be positive, leaving delegates upbeat and energized, we shall also examine some encouraging indicators that could lead to model-driven engineering soon becoming commonplace. In, oh, let's say, three years?

A. Schürr and B. Selic (Eds.): MODELS 2009, LNCS 5795, p. 1, 2009.

Modeling Modeling

Pierre-Alain Muller[1], Frédéric Fondement[1], and Benoît Baudry[2]

[1] Université de Haute-Alsace, Mulhouse, France
{pierre-alain.muller,frederic.fondement}@uha.fr
[2] IRISA / INRIA Rennes, Rennes, France
benoit.baudry@irisa.fr

Abstract. Model-driven engineering and model-based approaches have permeated all branches of software engineering; to the point that it seems that we are using models, as Molière's Monsieur Jourdain was using prose, without knowing it. At the heart of modeling, there is a relation that we establish to represent something by something else. In this paper we review various definitions of models and relations between them. Then, we define a canonical set of relations that can be used to express various kinds of representation relations and we propose a graphical concrete syntax to represent these relations. Hence, this paper is a contribution towards a theory of modeling.

1 Introduction

Many articles have already been written about modeling, offering definitions at various levels of abstraction, introducing conceptual frameworks or pragmatic tools, describing languages or environments, discussing practices and processes. It is amazing to observe in many calls for papers how modeling is now permeating all fields of software engineering. It looks like a lot of people are using models, as Monsieur Jourdain [22] was using prose, without knowing it.

While much has already been written on this topic, there is however neither precise description about what we do when we model, nor rigorous description of the relations among modeling artifacts. Therefore we propose to focus on the very heart of modeling, straight on the relation that we establish to represent something by something else, when we say that we model. Interestingly, the nature of these (some)things does not have to be defined for thinking about the relations between them. We will show how we can focus on the nature of relations, or on the patterns of relations that we may discover between these things.

This paper is a contribution towards a theory of modeling. Whilst focused on modeling in software development and model-management, the presented material may apply to models in general, and in other disciplines. We define a canonical set of relations that can be used to ease and structure reasoning about modeling. This canonical set contains 5 representation relations that may be refined with nature (analytical/synthetical) and causality (correctness/validity).

A. Schürr and B. Selic (Eds.): MODELS 2009, LNCS 5795, pp. 2–16, 2009.

The paper proceeds as follows: after this introduction, section 2 (related works) summarizes what several authors have said about models, section 3 defines a set of primitive representation relations based on the analysis of these various points of views, section 4 illustrates the use of the notation via several examples excerpted from the software engineering field, and finally section 5 draws some final conclusions and outlines future works.

This paper is the result of numerous informal discussions we have had with so many people that it is almost impossible to enumerate them all here. We would like to especially thank a few of them: including Jean-Marie Favre, Thomas Kuehne, Colin Atkinson, Marc Pantel, and Christophe Gaston. We would also like to acknowledge the invaluable comments of anonymous reviewers of an earlier version of this paper.

Table 1. Summary of model definitions

Bézivin	"*A **model** is a simplification of a system built with an intended goal in mind. The model should be able to answer questions in place of the **actual system**.*" [2]
Brown	"***Models** provide **abstractions** of a physical system that allow engineers to reason about that system by ignoring extraneous details while focusing on the relevant ones.*" [3]
Jackson	"*Here the word '**Model**' means **a part of the Machine's local storage** or database that it keeps in a more or less synchronised correspondence with **a part of the Problem Domain**. The Model can then act as a **surrogate** for the Problem Domain, providing information to the Machine that can not be conveniently obtained from the Problem Domain itself when it is needed.* " [4]
Kuehne	"*A **model** is an **abstraction** of a (real or language based) **system** allowing predictions or inferences to be made.*" [5]
Ludewig	"***Models** help in developing **artefacts** by providing **information about the consequences of building those artefacts** before they are actually made.*" [1]
OMG	"*A **model** of a system is a **description** or **specification** of that system and its environment for some certain purpose.*" [6]
Seidewitz	"*A **model** is a set of statements about some **system under study** (SUS).*" [7]
Selic	"*Engineering **models** aim to reduce risk by helping us better understand **both a complex problem and its potential solutions** before undertaking the expense and effort of a full implementation.*" [8]
Steinmüller	A model is information: on something (content, meaning), created by someone (sender), for somebody (receiver), for some purpose (usage context). [9]

2 Related Works

Much has already been written on modeling. In this section we will examine related works, and start to classify what authors have said about models. The following table contains a summary of model definitions, even if Jochen Ludewig states in [1] that "*nobody can just define what a model is, and expect that other people will accept this definition; endless discussions have proven that there is no consistent common understanding of models*".

Features of Models

According to Stachowiak [10] a model needs to posses the following three features:

- **Mapping feature.** A model is based on an original.
- **Reduction feature.** A model only reflects a (relevant) selection of an original's properties
- **Pragmatic feature.** A model needs to be usable in place of an original with respect to some purpose.

According to Bran Selic [8] an engineering model must posses the following five characteristics:

- **Abstraction.** A model is always a reduced rendering of the system that it represents.
- **Understandability.** A model must remain in a form that directly appeals to our intuition.
- **Accuracy.** A model must provide a true-to-life representation of the modeled system's features of interest.
- **Predictiveness.** A model must correctly predict the interesting but nonobvious properties of the modeled system.
- **Inexpensiveness.** A model must be significantly cheaper to construct and analyse than the modeled system.

Different Kinds of Models

Ed Seidewitz classifies models in two categories: descriptions and specifications. "*A model may be used* ***to describe*** *a SUS (System Under Study). In this case, the model is considered correct if all statements made in the model are true for the SUS. Alternatively, a model may be used as* ***a specification*** *for a SUS, or for a class of SUS. In this case, a specific SUS is considered valid relative to this specification if no statement in the model is false for the SUS.*" [7].

Jean-Marie Favre, reminds us that systems have the truth, not models: "*Making the distinction between* ***specification models*** *and* ***descriptive models*** *is useful to express who, of the model or the system, has the truth*" [11]. Jochen Ludewig further states that in order to make our models more useful we have to compare them with reality: "*The reality is always right and the model is always wrong*" [1]. This is also acknowledged by Michael Jackson: "*The model is not the reality*" [4]. Wolfgang Hesse, stresses the fact that in software engineering models often play a double role: they may be either *prescriptive* or *descriptive*, depending on whether it is there *earlier* or *later* than its original [12]. He coins this the *Janus View*. This is close to the opinion of Bran Selic, in [8] where he states that the models may be developed as a precursor to implementing the physical system, or they may be derived from an existing system or a system in development as an aid to understanding its behavior.

Kuehne, going back to Peirce's (1839-1914) seminal work about semiotic, also distinguishes between token and type models [5]. He gives the following definitions:

- **Token models.** "*Elements of a token model capture* ***singular*** *(as opposed to universal)* ***aspects*** *of the original's elements, i.e., they model individual properties of the elements in the system.*"
- **Type models.** "*Most models used in model driven engineering are type models. In contrast to token models, type models capture the* ***universal*** *aspects of a system's elements by means of* ***classification***."

Another classification of models is provided by Mellor and his colleagues in [13] taking yet another perspective on models. The distinction is made between three kinds of models, depending on their level of precision. A model can be considered as a *Sketch*, as a *Blueprint*, or as an *Executable*. Fowler suggests in [14] a similar distinction based on three levels of models, namely *Conceptual Models*, *Specification Models* and *Implementation Models*.

Definition of Relations between Models

In [15] Bézivin identifies two fundamental relations coined *RepresentationOf* and *ConformantTo*. Jean-Marie Favre shows in [16] that the *ConformantTo* relation is actually a short-cut for a pattern of *RepresentationOf* and *ElementOf* relations. In Jean-Marie Favre's view (called mega-model), further expressed in [17], all MDE artifacts can be described with 4 (+1 derived) basic relations (*RepresentationOf*, *ElementOf*, *DecomposedIn*, *IsTransformedIn*, and the derived *ConformsTo*).

Ed Seidewitz also identifies two relations [7], named *interpretation* (the relationship of the model to the thing being modeled) and *theory of the modeling language* (the relationship of a given model to other models derivable from it).

3 Towards a Model of Modeling

In this section we will define a model of modeling along with a notation to represent relations between modeling artifacts. By a model of modeling (hence the title of this paper: *modeling modeling*) we designate a representation of what we manipulate when we use modeling techniques. Our target domain is software development; therefore, all our examples will be drawn from the software engineering field.

We will use a very simple language to build this representation, based on "things" and "arrows" between them, such as the "objects" and "morphisms" found in Category Theory [18]. Things can be anything (this includes what other authors have called models and systems), and nothing has to be known about the internal structure of these things (which therefore do not have to be collections of "elements"). Conversely, arrows do not need to be functions between sets (thus arrows cannot be applied to "elements" but only composed with other arrows).

We do not want to come up with a brand new interpretation of what a model is. In our mind, the model of modeling that we are defining should reflect (or encompass) the various points of views which have already been expressed by the authors cited in the related works. To this end, we will first analyze these points of view, and next use our simple notation to synthesize them all into one single representation.

Let's start by modeling the fact that we have things which represent others things. As stated by Bran Selic [8], we first have to find a tradeoff between abstraction and understandability; therefore we will depart from the single *System class* view of Jean-Marie Favre [11], and distinguish between a *source* thing (that many authors call the model) and a *target* thing (called *original* by Stachowiak [10]), although we understand that being a source thing or a target thing is relative to a given arrow, and does not imply anything about a given thing. This is represented in Figure 1, where the source is named X, the target Y, and the *RepresentationOf* relation μ.

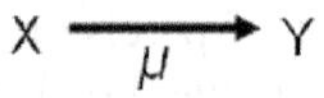

$$X \xrightarrow[\mu]{} Y$$

Fig. 1. X is a representation of Y

We are using on purpose a very simple graphic concrete syntax for representing modeling relations. Our notation is based on arrows, and is intended to be easy to draw by hand (on blackboard and napkins).

Intention

Neither things nor representations of things are built in isolation. As said by Steinmüller, both exist for a given purpose, exhibit properties, are built for some given stakeholders [9].

We can think about this as the *intention* of a thing. Intentional modeling [19] answers questions such as who and why, not what. The intention of a thing thus represents the reason why someone would be using that thing, in which context, and what are the expectations vs. that thing. It should be seen as a mixture of requirements, behavior, properties, and constraints, either satisfied or maintained by the thing.

As already said earlier, the "category theory kind" of thinking that we take in this paper does not require a description of the internals of the modeling artifacts (nor their intentions). Hence, it is enough to say that artifacts have an intention. The intentional flavor of models has also been used by Kuehne [23] in his description of metamodeling and by Gasevic et al. in their extension of Favre's megamodel [24]. The consequences of intentional thinking applied to modeling can be understood and represented using Venn diagrams [20]. The following table summarizes how the μ-relation may be specialized:

Table 2. Variations of the μ-relation, and graphical notation

	Intention	Description	Notation
a)	I(X) I(Y)	X and Y have totally different intentions. This usually denotes a shift in viewpoints.	X ⋯⋯▸ Y (μ)
b)	I(X) I(Y)	X and Y share some intention. X and Y can be partially represented by each other. The representation is both partial and extended.	X ↝ Y (μ)
c)	I(X) I(Y)	X is a partial representation of Y. Everything which holds for X makes sense in the context of Y. Y can be partially represented by X.	X ↝ Y (μ)
d)	I(X) I(Y)	X and Y share the same intention. They can represent each other. This usually denotes a shift in linguistic conformance.	X → Y (μ)
e)	I(X) I(Y)	X covers the intention of Y; X can represent Y, but X has additional properties. It is an extended representation.	X ↦ Y (μ)

All authors agree to say that the power of models stems from the fact they can be used in place of what they model, at least for some given purposes. This is what Stachowiak [10] calls the *pragmatic* feature of models. In practice it is convenient to work with a subset of the intention, and to consider that the μ-relation is a complete representation of that given subset: hence the μ/I notation below, which means that X is a representation of Y (for a given subset of the intention). The I sign can then be used elsewhere in a diagram, to show that a given pattern holds for that subset of the intention. If intention is constant throughout the diagram, it can be omitted as a notation shortcut.

Table 3. Notation shortcut. X is a complete representation of Y, for a given subset of the intention (in a given context).

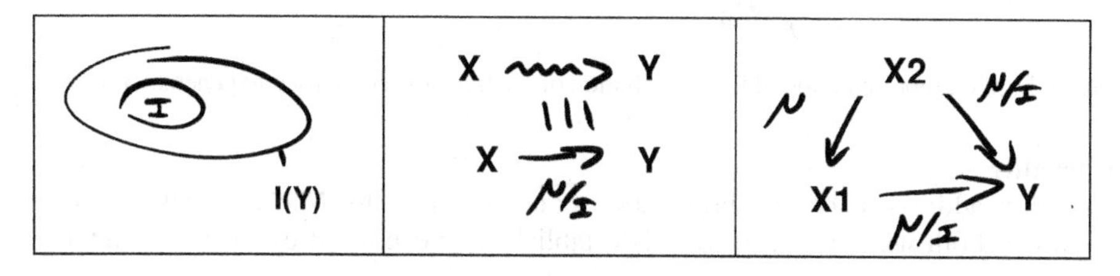

Analytical vs. Synthetical Nature of Representations

As seen earlier, several authors make a distinction between analytical models and synthetical models (respectively descriptive and specification models in the sense of Seidewitz [7] and Favre [11]).

An analytical representation relation states that the source expresses something about the target. We define the analytical representation (represented μ_α) as:

$$X \xrightarrow[\mu_\alpha]{} Y : \exists T_\alpha \mid X = T_\alpha(Y)$$

where T_α is a relation such as X can be derived (or abstracted) from Y. In model-driven parlance T_α could denote a model-transformation. Interestingly, intentions of source and target do not necessarily have to overlap (notice that for convenience we use here a simple arrow as a placeholder for the different kinds of relations that we have defined in table 2). In terms of truth (as coined by Favre), truth is held by the target in case of μ_α representation.

A synthetical representation relation explains that the target is generated from the source. We define the synthetical representation (represented μ_γ) as:

$$X \xrightarrow[\mu_\gamma]{} Y : \exists T_\gamma \mid Y = T_\gamma(X)$$

where T_γ is a relation such as Y can be derived (or generated) from X. In model-driven parlance T_γ could again denote a model-transformation. In terms of truth, truth is held by the source in case of μ_γ representation. If we talk in terms of intentions, this means that the intention of Y can be generated (synthesized) from the intention of X, or at least be driven by the intention of X, as Y is actually the result of T_γ applied to X. Quantifying the respective contributions of X and T_γ to the synthesis of Y is out of the scope of this paper.

However, if one wants to represent that the transformation significantly contributes to the target's intention, it is possible to use an explicit representation such as in Figure 2. Y is partially generated from X (for the S part of the intention). The complement (the S' part) is provided by T_γ. This could typically be used to represent that X is a PIM (Platform Independent Model), and Y a PSM (Platform Specific Model), with the specifics of the platform being introduced in Y by the T_γ transformation.

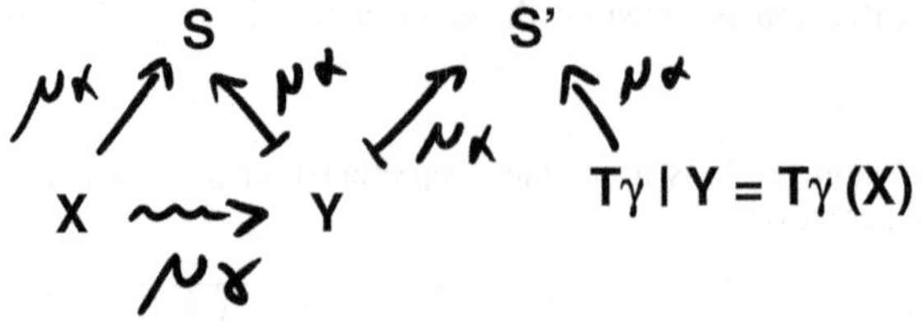

S S'

$T\gamma \mid Y = T\gamma(X)$

X Y

Fig. 2. Explicit representation of the contribution of the transformation used to generate Y from X

Causality

Causality addresses the synchronization concern raised by Michael Jackson [4]; it expresses both *when* the μ-relation is established, and *how* (if ever) it is maintained over time. Causality is either continuous (the relation is always enforced) or discrete (the relation is enforced at some given points in time). Causality is also tightly coupled with the truth of Favre [11]; actually, causality is a concern about whether a representation is still meaningful when the truth has changed. Going back to the definition of *correctness* and *validity* given by Ed Seidewitz [7], causality states:

- for an analytical representation, when X is *correct* wrt. Y.
- for a synthetical representation, when Y is *valid* wrt. X.

For computer based systems, causality is typically discrete, and making the models meaningful requires adherence to results of information theory such as Nyquist-Shannon sampling theorem [21]. Causality can be used to re-visit the definition given by Wolfgang Hesse, who makes an amalgam between analytical/synthetical representation, and earlier/later existence, when he proposes to distinguish between descriptive and prescriptive "*depending on whether it is (the model) there earlier or later than its original*" [12]. A way to lift this ambiguity is to separate clearly between nature (analytical/synthetical) and causality (correctness/validity) of the representation relation. In Figure 3 the model is a causal analytical representation of the system. If the system changes, the causal μ_α relation implies that the model is updated. In turn, as the model is also a causal μ_γ representation of the program, the program is updated to remain an analytical representation of the system.

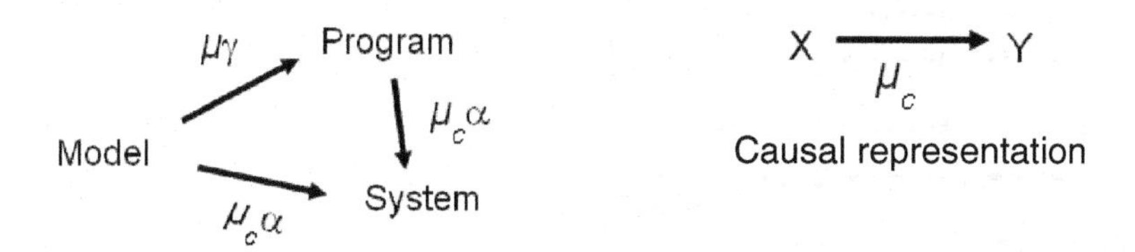

Fig. 3. Causality implies maintaining the representations over time

Transitivity

Transitivity addresses the composition properties of μ-relations of the same nature. Transitivity is realized when the intention of a composed μ-μ-relation contains the intention of a μ-relation. If transitivity holds, then it is possible to use the model of a model of a thing, in place of the model of that thing.

In some cases, there is only one possible result for the composition of relations. For example, on the third line of Table 4, if X is an extended representation of Y and if Y has the same intention as Z, then X is an extended representation of Z. In some cases there are 2 or 3 possible results when composing relations. For example, Figure 4 illustrates the two situations that can occur when X is an extended and partial representation of Y and Y is an extended and partial representation of Z. In case a, the intention that X shares with Y does not overlap at all with the intention that Y shares with Z, this means that X and Z have two completely different intentions. In case b, the intention that X shares with Y overlaps with the intention that Y shares with Z, this means that X is an extended and partial representation of Z.

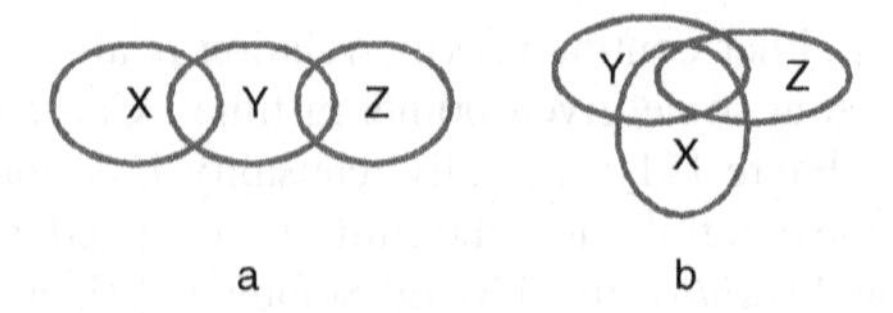

Fig. 4. Intention overlapping when composing partial extended relations

Table 4. Composition law for representations

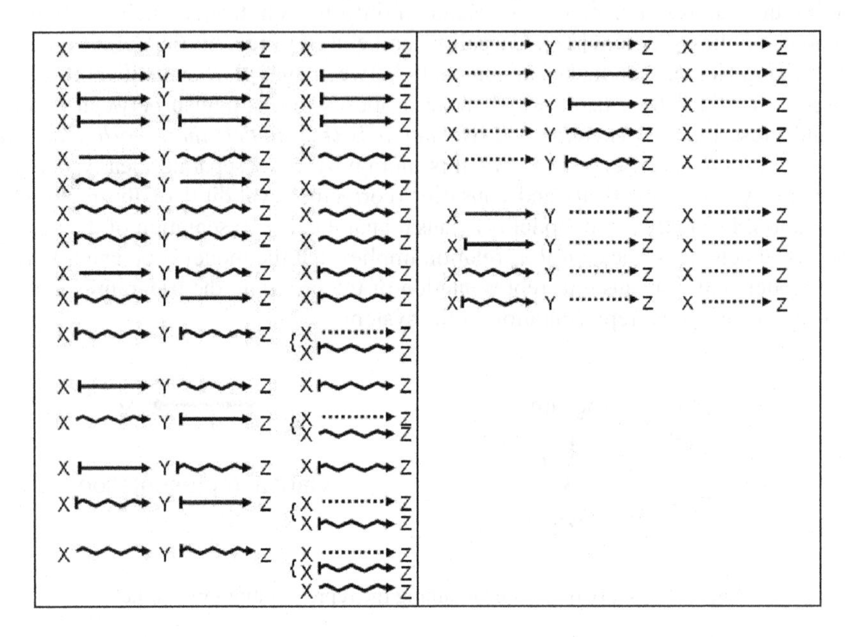

4 Examples

4.1 This Is Not a Pipe

Let's examine the already classic example inspired from Magritte's painting. The picture is a μ_α representation of the pipe. The picture and the pipe share some intention. In addition, the real pipe could be used to smoke, while the picture could be used to show the pipe remotely. This is represented by an extended partial μ_α representation.

In the following example, the distribution of colors plays the role of an analytical model, providing information about the picture from which it is generated. It does not share intention either with the picture or with the pipe (this is modeled by the dashed arrow); however it may be used to have an idea of the color of the real world pipe (transitively following the μ_α relations).

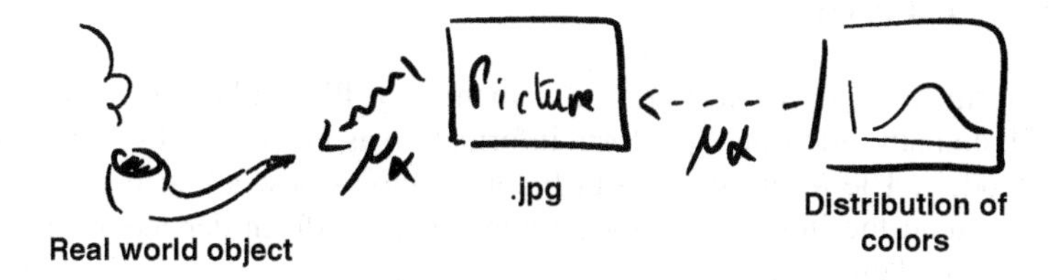

Fig. 5. Example of μ_α relations

4.2 Jackson'sProblem Domain and Machine

In table 2, the c) case represents the fact that the target (in our case generated) thing contains the intention of the source thing. This is especially interesting in case the source was itself in a μ_α relation with a third thing. Figure 6 shows such situation. M stands for model, S for system, and R for representation (with the idea that R is a computerized representation, in other words a program which implements S).

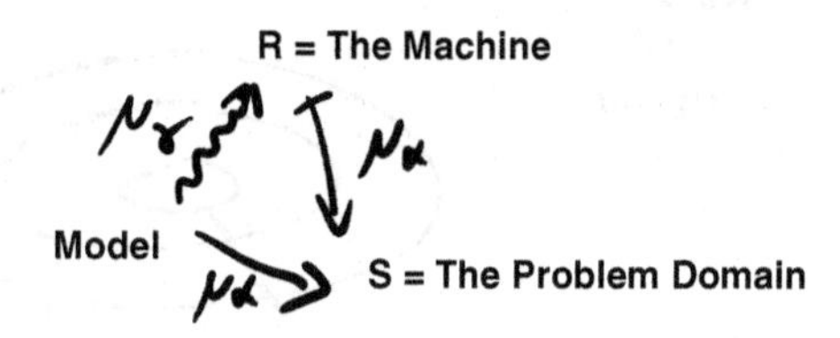

Fig. 6. Generated machine implementing a μ_α representation

This is the typical case for modeling, such as described for instance by Michael Jackson. S is the problem domain. R is what Jackson calls the machine. The μ_α relation from R to S is what Jackson calls the "*'model' which is part of the local storage or database that it keeps in a more or less synchronized correspondence with a part of the problem domain*" [4]. This view is also in line with Bran Selic, who states: "*the model eventually becomes the system that it was modeling*" [8].

The partial μ_γ and the extended μ_α relations express the fact that R is "richer" than M (and thus S) in terms of intention, because R contains additional information required for execution. The intention of the model can also be seen as the intersection of the intensions of the machine and the problem domain. The grayed part represents the additional intension required to "implement" the intention of the problem domain. This is what we name *platform dependence* in Figure 7.

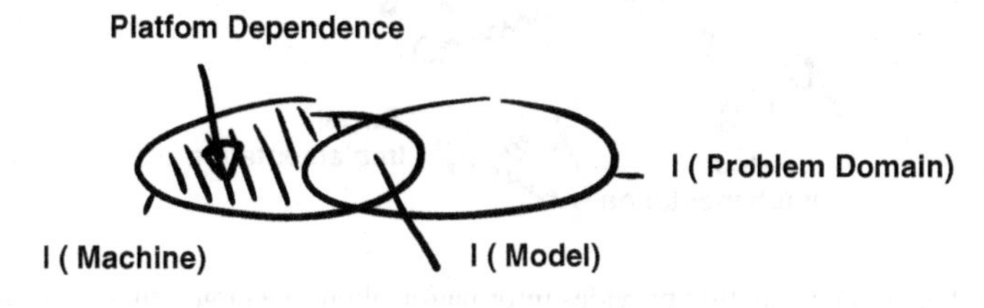

Fig. 7. The machine implements the subset of intention of the problem domain, represented by the model

4.3 PIM, PSM and PDM

A PSM (Platform Specific Model) is a refinement of a PIM (Platform Independent Model), which contains additional platform information as given by a PDM (Platform Description Model). The Venn diagram in Figure 8 shows how all successive levels of refinement extend the intention of the System, with platform dependent information required for implementation.

We also see here how the previous example (the triad System-Model-Representation) may be used as a meta-modeling pattern, by replacing M (the model) by PIM and R (the representation) by PSM (PDM was left unexpressed in the pattern).

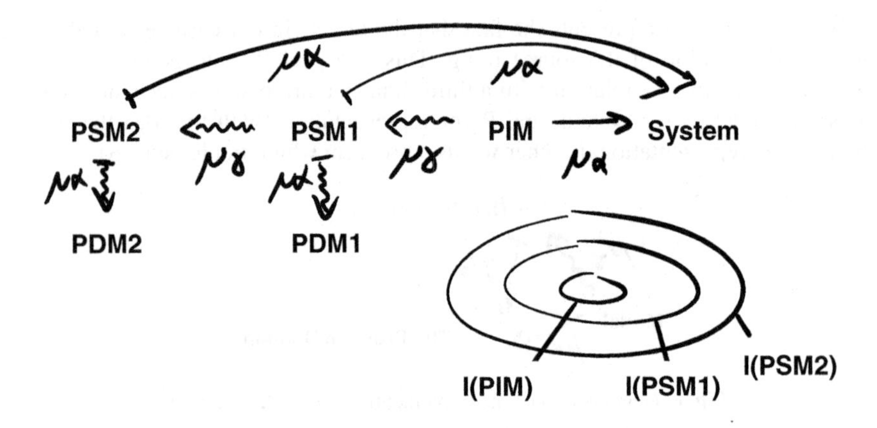

Fig. 8. Refinement of PIM into PSM, with platform specific information

4.4 Host-Target Development

In host-target development, the same program (here the model) is compiled both for a host machine (typically a workstation) and a target machine (typically some embedded computer). This allows early problem detection, even before the final hardware machine is available. Therefore, the host implementation can be considered as a partial analytical model of the target implementation (it may also be extended by host specific concerns).

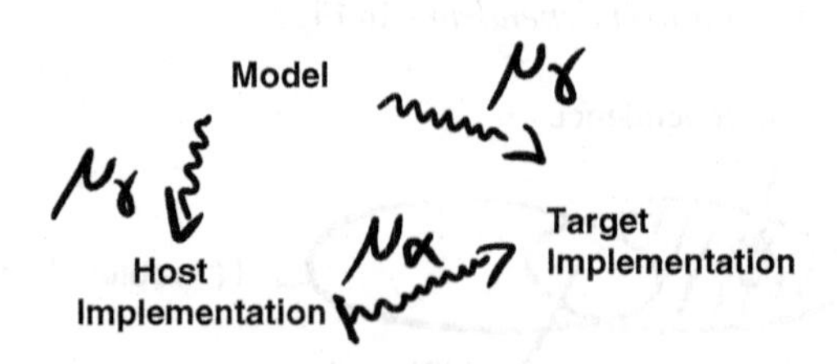

Fig. 9. The host implementation provides information about the target implementation

4.5 Round-Trip Engineering

Code skeletons are generated from UML class diagrams (represented by the μ_γ). Then, developers extend the skeletons by hand. If developers change the structure of the final program (and therefore also the structure of the skeletons which get updated at the same time as they live in the same file), then the class diagram has to be changed accordingly. We model this with a causal μ_α relation between class diagrams and Java skeletons. The causal nature of the relation implies that the model is always up-to-date.

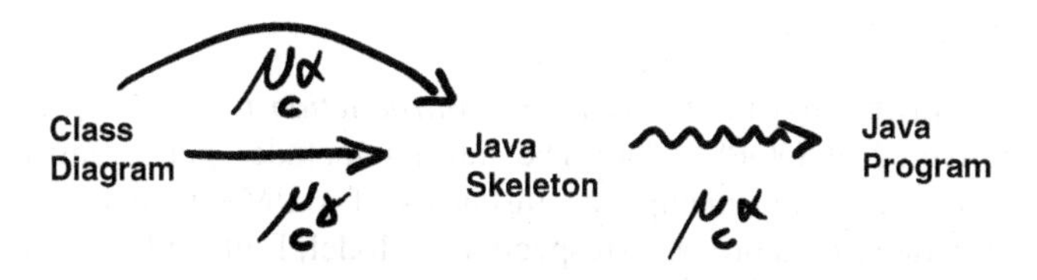

Fig. 10. Using causality to model round-trip engineering

4.6 Model-Based Testing

Model-based testing is performed by generating test cases that can be used to test the program. As represented in Figure 11, the model and the program are developed on one side while the test cases are developed separately. Then, testing consists in checking the consistency between these two views on the system. When an inconsistency is detected, an error has been found.

The test model is a partial representation of the system, with an additional intention of testing (looking for errors) that is not present in the system. The test model is also a partial representation of the model that shares intentions with the model (the concepts manipulated by these representations are the same), but again the test model has this additional test intention. Symmetrically, the model is a representation of the system. The model is then used to generate parts of the program.

When the test model is rich enough, test cases can be automatically synthesized from this model, according to a test adequacy criterion. Thus there exists a μ_γ relation

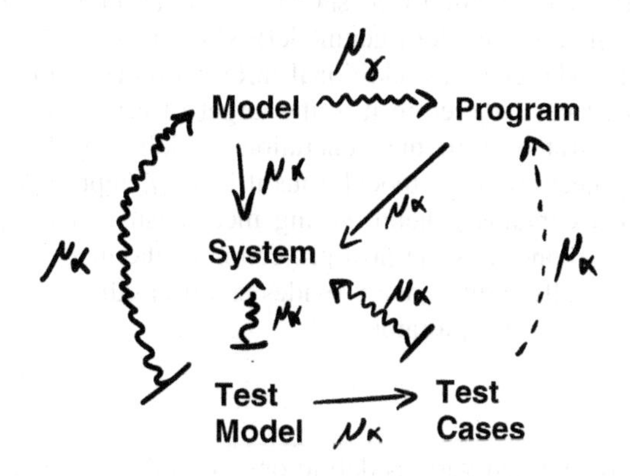

Fig. 11. Model-based testing

between these things. This particular relation also implies that the μ_α relation between the test model and the system is propagated to the test cases that are thus also representations of the system.

The last interesting relationship that appears on the figure is that test cases are representations of the program since they can provide information to analyze the presence of errors in the program. However, these two things do not share any intention since test cases aim at detecting errors in the program while the program aims at providing functionalities to some user.

4.7 Eclipse EMF

This example is drawn from the tutorial T38 "*Introduction to the Eclipse Modeling Framework*" delivered at OOPSLA'06. The tutorial includes generating a working graphical editor to create and manipulate instances of a UML model. The editor is made of three generated Java projects (respectively Model, Edit, and Editor).

The process starts with an XML file that contains a schema which represents a purchase order system. The various modeling artifacts are represented in Figure 12.

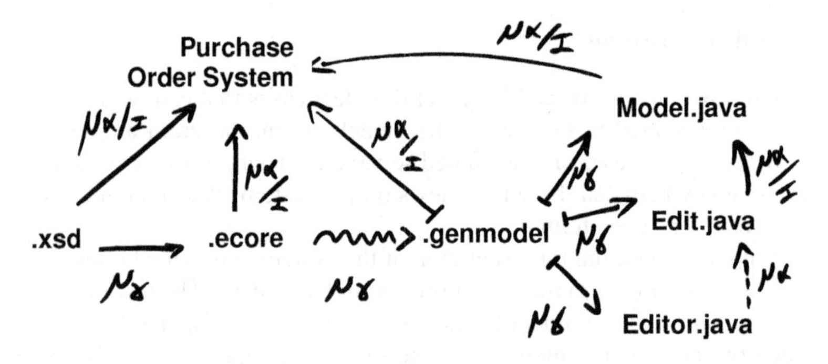

Fig. 12. Purchase order Eclipse EMF tutorial

The XML schema (.xsd file) is a μ_α representation of the system (wrt. a given intention I). The schema is used to generate an EMF model (.ecore file). The model and the schema share the same intention I, as shown by μ_α/I relations. The model is then used to generate a generation model (.genmodel) which is also in a μ_α relation with the system. The .genmodel contains additional information (wrt. the model) to drive the code generation process; therefore it is the target of a partial μ_γ relation. Three Java projects are generated from the generation model: model, edit, and editor. Edit.java is a Java projection of the model, thus it is a μ_α/I representation of the system as well. Edit.java contains general editing mechanisms (not dependent on the graphical user interface) and uses the java projection of the model (represented with another μ_α relation). Finally, Editor.java provides end-user editing facilities to visualize models, using a tree-based explorator.

5 Conclusion

In this paper we have analysed various definitions of models, as found in the related works, and we have proposed a modeling language which can be used as a foundation to represent the various representation relations between models, metamodels and languages.

Our language focuses on representation relations between modeling artifacts, without actually trying to understand the nature of these artifacts. Ignoring the details of their internal structure appears to be very effective because it magnifies the fact that modeling is a matter of relations and roles, and not intrinsic to the artifacts.

We have identified 5 variations of the representation relation (based on their intention), two natures (analytical and synthetical), and taken causal dependencies and transitivity into account. We have illustrated our approach with several simple examples, drawn from the software engineering domain.

From a practical point of view, we hope that this step toward a better understanding of representation relations will serve as a basis for rigorous metamodeling tools, in the same way as relational algebra triggered the development of efficient databases.

References

[1] Ludewig, J.: Models in software engineering - an introduction. SoSyM 2(3), 5–14 (2003)

[2] Bézivin, J., Gerbé, O.: Towards a Precise Definition of the OMG/MDA Frame-work. Presented at ASE, Automated Software Engineering (November 2001)

[3] Brown, A.W.: Model driven architecture: Principles and practice. SoSyM 3(3), 314–327 (2004)

[4] Jackson, M.: Some Basic Tenets of Description. Software and Systems Modeling 1(1), 5–9 (2002)

[5] Kuehne, T.: Matters of (meta-) modeling. SoSyM 5(4) (2006)

[6] OMG, Model Driven Architecture, Electronic Source: Object Management Group, `http://www.omg.org/mda/`

[7] Seidewitz, E.: What models means. IEEE Software 20(5), 26–32 (2003)

[8] Selic, B.: The pragmatics of Model-Driven Development. IEEE Software 20(5), 19–25 (2003)

[9] Steinmüller, W.: Informationstechnologie und Gesellschaft: Einführung in dieAngewandte Informatik, Wissenschaftliche Buchgesellschaft, Darmstadt (1993)

[10] Stachowiak, H.: Allgemeine Modelltheorie. Springer, Wien (1973)

[11] Favre, J.-M.: Foundations of Model (Driven) (Reverse) Engineering: Models - Epi-sode I: Stories of The Fidus Papyrus and of The Solarus. Presented at Dagstuhl Seminar 04101 on Language Engineering for Model-Driven Software Development, Dagsthul, Germany, February 29-March 5 (2004)

[12] Hesse, W.: More matters on (meta-)modeling: remarks on Kuehne's "matters". SoSyM 5(4), 387–394 (2006)

[13] Mellor, S.J., Scott, K., Uhl, A., Weise, D.: MDA Distilled: Principle of Model Driven Architecture. Addison Wesley, Reading (2004)

[14] Fowler, M., Scott, K., Booch, G.: UML distilled, Object Oriented series, 179 p. Addison-Wesley, Reading (1999)

[15] Bézivin, J.: In Search of a Basic Principle for Model-Driven Engineering. Novatica Journal, vol. Special Issue March-April 2004 (2004)

[16] Favre, J.-M.: Foundations of the Meta-pyramids: Languages and Metamodels - Epi-sode II, Story of Thotus the Baboon. Presented at Dagstuhl Seminar 04101 on Lan-guage Engineering for Model-Driven Software Development, Dagsthul, Germany, February 29-March 5 (2004)

[17] Favre, J.-M.: Towards a Megamodel to Model Software Evolution Through Software Transformation. In: Proceedings of the Workshop on Software Evolution through Transformation, SETRA 2004, Rome, Italy, October 2, vol. 127 (2004)
[18] Fokkinga, M.M.: A Gentle Introduction to Category Theory - The calculational approach, University of Twente (1994)
[19] Yu, E., Mylopoulos, J.: Understanding "Why" in Software Process Modelling, Analysis, and Design". In: Proceedings of the 16th International Conference on Soft-ware Engineering (ICSE), Sorrento, Italy, May 16-21, pp. 159–168 (1994)
[20] Venn, J.: On the Diagrammatic and Mechanical Representation of Propositions and Reasonings. Dublin Philosophical Magazine and Journal of Science 9(59), 1–18 (1880)
[21] Shannon, C.E.: Communication in the presence of noise. Proc. Institute of Radio Engineers 37(1), 10–21 (1949)
[22] Molière. Le Bourgeois gentilhomme (1607)
[23] Kuehne, T.: Matters of (Meta-) Modeling. Software and Systems Modeling 5(4), 369–385 (2006)
[24] Gasevic, D., Kaviani, N., Hatala, M.: On Metamodeling in Megamodels. In: Engels, G., Opdyke, B., Schmidt, D.C., Weil, F. (eds.) MODELS 2007. LNCS, vol. 4735, pp. 91–105. Springer, Heidelberg (2007)

Representation and Traversal of Large Clabject Models

Thomas Aschauer, Gerd Dauenhauer, and Wolfgang Pree

C. Doppler Laboratory Embedded Software Systems, University of Salzburg,
Jakob-Haringer-Str. 2, 5020 Salzburg, Austria
firstname.lastname@cs.uni-salzburg.at

Abstract. Multi-level modeling using so-called clabjects has been proposed as an alternative to UML for modeling domains that feature more than one classification level. In real-world applications, however, this modeling formalism has not yet become popular, because it is a challenge to efficiently represent large models, and providing fast access to all information spread across the meta-levels at the same time. In this paper we present the model representation concept that relies on a permanent condensed view of the model, the corresponding traversal algorithms, and their implementations that proved adequate for model-driven engineering of industrial automation systems consisting of hundreds of thousands of model elements.

Keywords: Clabject, Multi-Level Modeling, Efficient Representation.

1 Introduction

For the development of software intensive systems, model-driven engineering (MDE) is a promising approach for handling their inherent complexity. For real-world applications, MDE requires adequate means for describing the system's essential properties. In particular for domains that feature more than one classification-level, also known as meta-level, prominent modeling languages such as UML [1] fall short and workarounds are required [2]. Multi-level modeling, as an alternative to UML, is able to handle multiple domain meta-levels within a uniform framework [3]. Advantages of such a modeling approach have been shown by several contributions [2, 4, 5].

In real-world applications, however, multi-level modeling has been barely applied. Major hurdles for adopting a multi-level formalism are the lack of (1) available modeling environments that allow rapid prototyping, (2) real-world applications that corroborate the benefits of multi-level modeling, and (3) efficient implementations that are capable of handling large models. This paper focuses on (3) and briefly touches (2). Examples of (1) are described e.g. by Gutheil et al. [4].

We have applied multi-level modeling for automation systems in the domain of combustion engine development. There we use MDE to generate configuration parameters for the automation system. As it turned out in practice, the classification hierarchy supported by multi-level modeling is crucial for building and maintaining concise models. For the model transformations and for end-user views, however, it is often necessary to have a "condensed" view such that for a certain model element all

A. Schürr and B. Selic (Eds.): MODELS 2009, LNCS 5795, pp. 17–31, 2009.

structural properties are easily accessible, rather than having to traverse the whole meta-level hierarchy to collect that information. What makes matters even more complicated is that this condensed view in practice is not only used for read access, but is also modified. This implies that a method is needed for transparently mapping modification operations on the condensed view to the classification hierarchy.

This paper shows how to efficiently store and traverse a multi-level model, which is also capable of handling modification operations. Together with an efficient representation, we are able to provide a permanent condensed view of the model, which turned out to be the preferred access method for end-users. Since our models typically are large, that is, in the order of hundreds of thousands of model elements, we validate our performance goals by using sufficiently large test models.

In the following we present the basics of multi-level models in our domain and key requirements for their representation and retrieval. We then describe our representation method and a traversal algorithm. Finally, we evaluate our implementation.

2 Multi-Level Modeling with Clabjects

Automation systems in our domain are inherently complex for various reasons. They are usually built individually and comprise a large number of ready made parts, which are often customized. They also integrate sophisticated measurement devices that are software intensive systems by themselves. In this section we briefly describe the multi-level modeling approach that was employed to cope with that complexity [5].

Multi-level modeling is an alternative approach to conventional modeling that is able to overcome the limited support for modeling domain metalevels. The basic idea of multi-level modeling is to explicitly represent the different abstraction levels of model elements. Assume, for example, that we have to model concrete combustion engines, but also families of combustion engines from different vendors that specify the properties of the individual engines, in UML. Conceptually, engine is an instantiation of its family. Since instantiation is not directly supported at the M1 layer [1], workarounds such as the type-object pattern are required [2].

Different flavors of multi-level modeling have been proposed as solutions. Atkinson and Kühne, for example, propose a uniform notion of *classes* and *objects*, known as a *clabject* [2], that allows for an arbitrary number of classification levels; its advantages are well documented [3, 2, 4]. In principle, a clabject is a modeling entity that has a so-called *type facet* as well as an *instance facet*. It thus can be an instance of a clabject from a higher level, and at the same time it can be the type for another clabject instance at a lower level. Figure 1 shows the clabject model of our combustion engine example. The notation used here is similar to that of the original clabject concept, that is, a combination of UML notations for classes and objects [2, 6]. Each model element has a compartment for the name, and a combined compartment for the type facet and the instance facet. The arrows between the levels represent the "instance of" relationship. At the domain metatype level, the types Engine, Diesel Engine and Otto Engine are modeled like a conventional class hierarchy. Their *fields*, which are the equivalent of attributes in multi-level modeling [2], such as Inertia and Preheat_Time, are part of the corresponding clabject's type facet.

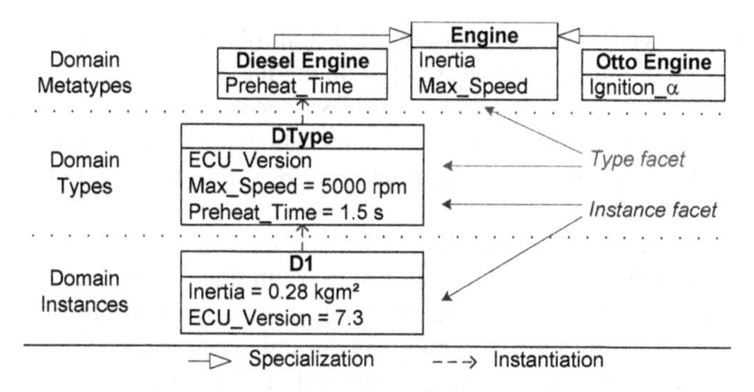

Fig. 1. Clabject-based engine model

Specified at the domain type level, the clabject DType is an instance of Diesel Engine. It provides values for the fields Max_Speed and Preheat_Time, which are part of DType's instance facet, and introduced a new field ECU_Version, which is part of DType's type facet. The domain instance D1 in turn instantiates DType and provides values for Inertia and ECU_Version. Note that D1's type facet is empty. By definition, the clabjects at the top-level only have a type facet, whereas the clabjects at the bottom level only have an instance facet.

3 Model Representation and Traversal Requirements

Analyzing the intended uses of our models, we can identify a number of requirements and assumptions regarding the usage of the models and expected performance and space requirements. This guides the design and implementation of the actual internal representation as well as the traversal algorithms.

(I) Large models. Due to the inherent complexity of the domain, we expect the models to be large, that is, consisting of more than 100,000 elements. This implies that we have to be able to represent models of considerable size in a memory-efficient way.

(II) Structural similarity. Automation systems in our domain typically are usually built individually of ready made parts, which are often customized. A substantial amount of these ready made parts, however, have similar structural information and share the same field values. For example, most temperature sensors are of the same type and thus the internal structure of their models is equivalent, except for some customization such as an additional plug. As an example, consider figure 2.

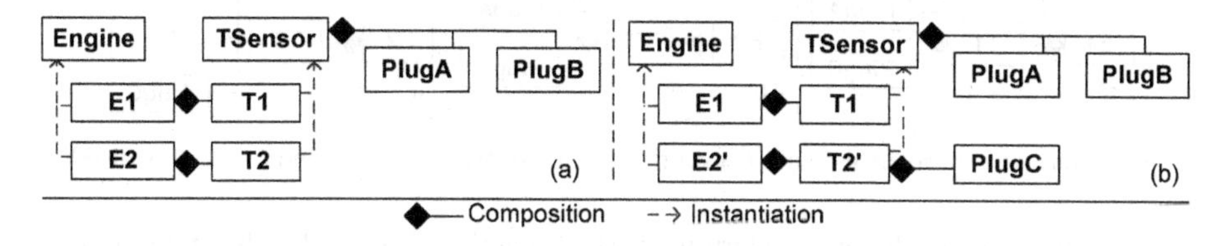

Fig. 2. Multiple usage of sensor type: (a) unmodified, (b) with modification

Here the sensor type TSensor is instantiated multiple times. In case (a) the sensor type TSensor is used within the context of both, engine E1 as clabject T1, and engine E2 as clabject T2. In case (b) the sensor type TSensor is instantiated twice, but with a modification: in T2' the element PlugC is added. The rest of the information modeled in TSensor, i.e. the containment of PlugA and PlugB, is the same for both instances.

(III) Model traversal. The prospective users of models are either the end users, building or exploring the model in a graphical user interface, or the model transformation system, analyzing the model and applying transformations. In both cases, the main method for accessing model elements is through traversal, starting at the root of the containment hierarchy, and visiting connected and contained model elements. In contrast to random access, one does not access contained model elements directly. So in our example in figure 2 (b) PlugC is not accessed directly, but only by navigating from E2' to T2' and then to PlugC.

We can distinguish two different ways of traversing a model: First, we can follow the *connectors*, which are the equivalent of associations in multi-level modeling [2]; for our example this corresponds to navigating from E2' via T2' to PlugC. Second, we can follow the instantiation and the generalization relationships; for the same example, this corresponds to navigating from E2' to Engine or from T2' to TSensor. Both traversals reveal essential information. Since for some uses, such as the model transformation, the complete model has to be traversed, it is crucial that the traversal of large models can be done in a reasonable amount of time.

(IV) Condensed traversal. The model transformation, for example, focuses on the structure of a particular model element. It does not matter whether the structure is modeled at a certain model element itself, or whether is received via inheritance or instantiation. In other words, this requires a traversal by following the connectors, but also by incorporating the connectors that are instantiated or inherited. For users performing this kind of "mixed" traversal, i.e. following connectors and also the instantiation and inheritance relationships, it is necessary to transparently "flatten" the classification hierarchy during traversal to provide a *condensed view* on the model.

As an example, consider the model shown in figure 2 (a). When the model transformation performs a condensed traversal, the information that both engines E1 and E2 use the same definition of TSensor is not relevant. What is relevant is the fact that both engines have a sensor with two plugs. So for the model transformation, all structural information modeled in TSensor appears as if it was modeled directly in E1 and E2. In the end, the result of the traversal looks like each engine defines its own sensor, as shown in figure 3 (a) and (b).

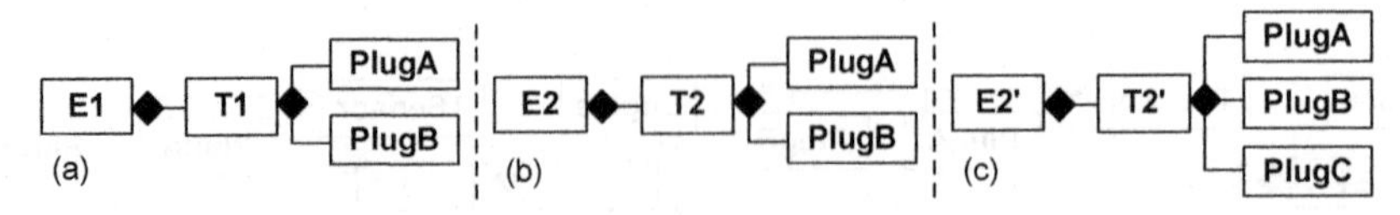

Fig. 3. Transparent traversal result: (a) starting at E1, (b) starting at E2, and (c) starting at E2'

When we traverse the model starting at E1 we get the associated clabject T1, and in turn the clabjects associated with T1, i.e. PlugA and PlugB. Starting the traversal at

E2 yields an analogous result. Note that although in the model PlugA only appears within the definition of TSensor, in the overall traversal result the same plug appears twice: within E1, and within E2. In both occurences, however, PlugA represents different real-world elements and thus actually has different identities, stemming from the semantics of the composition aggregation. The information about the classification, however, is not lost but available on request for each model element. For the elements T1 and T2, for example, it is possible to retrieve their types, i.e. TSensor. For both appearances of PlugA the retrieved type is the PlugA contained in TSensor.

For the case when the instantiation of TSensor is accompanied by a modification, as presented in figure 2 (b), we get the traversal result as shown in figure 3 (a) and (c). Again, starting the traversal at E1 yields the same result as described above. Starting the traversal at E2', however, yields a different result: First we get the associated clabject T2', and in turn the associated clabjects PlugA, PlugB, and PlugC. Note that PlugC appears in the traversal result in the same way as PlugA and PlugB do.

The algorithms necessary for condensed traversals could, of course, be implemented by the model transformation itself. It turns out, however, that this kind of traversal is also required by our user interface, so the modeling environment supports condensed traversal as the default.

(V) Modifiable traversal result. When a user traverses the model, the traversal result has to be modifiable, independent of the kind of traversal performed. While this is straightforward for the traversals following either connectors, or instantiation and inheritance, it is more difficult for the condensed traversal method. Assume, for example, that a user traverses the model shown in figure 2 (a), which leads to the condensed traversal result show in figure 3 (a) and (b). Further assume that the user adds a plug named PlugC to T2. Performing this operation on the traversal result implies that the modeling environment has to store the difference between the original element, which is TSensor, and its modified usage, which is T2. The expected effect on the traversal result is that the plug is retrieved additionally to the plugs already defined in the original sensor, which is exactly what we have already seen in figure 3 (c). Technically this requires determining the involved classification level and adding the modified elements there, such that we get the model as shown in figure 2 (b).

4 Implementation

The goals for moderate memory consumption (I) and good traversal performance (III) are contradicting, as keeping hundreds of thousands of individual elements in memory does not scale. So we have to trade memory for traversal speed. It turns out that the structural similarity in real-models (II) is a property that can be used to save memory, since we have to store structural information only once and reference that information when similar structures are modeled. For traversing the model in order to get the condensed view (IV), however, the saved memory implies some performance penalty since we have to reconstruct the structure of a clabject from the instantiation and inheritance relationships. Since the elements retrieved by the traversal have to be modifiable (V), we must add certain information such that the link between the classification hierarchy and the condensed view does not get lost, as shown in the sequel.

4.1 Language Representation

The modeling environment has to provide the language models are built of. As such it must be capable of representing arbitrary models, model elements, their fields, and relationships between them. Furthermore, multiple classification levels have to be supported, so means for expressing instantiation and generalization have to be provided. The basic entities of our modeling language are Clabject, Connector, Field, and Data Type; they are shown in figure 4.

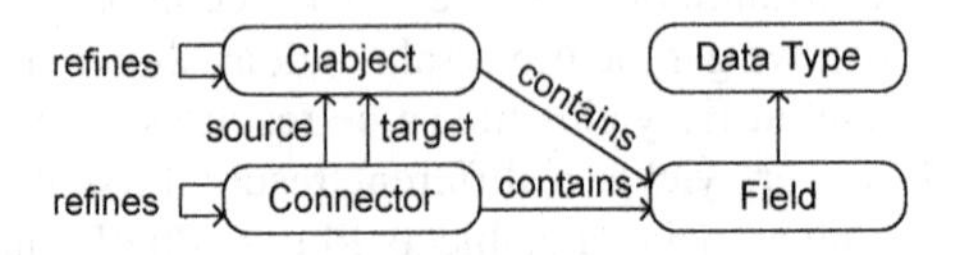

Fig. 4. Representation of language elements

The elements Clabject, Field and Connector are typical for clabject-based modeling languages [7]. What is unique by our solution is that the representation uses one single *refines*-relationship to represent both, instantiation as well as inheritance, for clabjects and connectors. We denote an element that is the source of a refinement relationship, i.e. a type or a generalization, as *refined clabject*, and the target of a refinement relationship, i.e. an instance or a specialization, as *refining clabject*. By using this single relationship we do not claim that the semantics of instantiation and inheritance are similar [8]. For the sole purpose of representing large models in memory and traversing them, however, a uniform treatment is beneficial, as we will see.

4.2 Permanent Condensed View

It is important to note that the language as described above is the interface of the modeling environment, i.e. model elements are represented as clabjects, connectors, and fields. Due to the traversal requirements as outlined earlier, we know that condensed traversal is the primary access method. Thus in our implementation condensed traversal is not just another way of exploring the model, but it is built in as foundation of the modeling environment. Its realization, however, requires some optimized data structures to be able to provide the condensed view within reasonable bounds of runtime and memory consumption. This, however, can be hidden from the users of the modeling environment.

4.3 Traversal of Refinements without Modifications

The simplest case of refinement (remember, this is either instantiation or inheritance) is refining an element without adding any additional information, neither additional structural information, nor any values for fields. An example of non-modifying refinement is shown in figure 2 (a).

Let C be the set of all clabjects and $x_0 \in C$ be a refining clabject that refines $x_1 \in C$, which in turn refines $x_2 \in C$, etc., such that we get the sequence of refined elements (x_1, x_2, …, x_n), where $x_n \in C$ is an element that is not refined from any other element. Since neither inheritance nor instantiation allows circularity, n denotes the depth of the refinement path and is a finite integer with $n \geq 0$. Further let R be the mapping of a clabject to the sequence of refined elements, e.g. $R(x_0)= (x_1, x_2, \ldots, x_n)$.

The basic scheme for the traversal is to visit the clabject at the root of the containment hierarchy, all its contained clabjects, and subsequently all clabjects in the refinement path. For compositions of refined clabjects we have to take special care since the contained elements can appear several times in the traversal result. An example is the double occurrence of PlugA in figure 3 (a) and (b). The identity of these elements is not only defined by their refined element, but also by the "context" in which they appear. Since the refinement depth can be greater than one, the context is given by the sequence of refining elements. In figure 3 (a) the context for PlugA is given by the sequence *(T1)*; in figure 3 (b) the context is given by the sequence *(T2)*.

Since such clabjects actually do not exist, but appear only in the traversal result, we call them "virtual" clabjects. Virtual clabjects are temporarily represented by lightweight placeholder objects that are created on the fly during traversal. The garbage collector can dispose of them after the traversal has finished. We get the following algorithm for determining the condensed traversal:

traverseClabject(*x*, *ctx*) performs a condensed traversal for the clabject *x* with context *ctx*, which is a list of clabjects, by visiting the clabject itself and then subsequently all clabjects along the refinement hierarchy. For a non-refining clabject the context *ctx* is the empty list. The *add...*–calls denote that a node in the traversal is reached and that it should be added to the traversal result. The symbol ↻ denotes recursion.

1. Visit the clabject; note that for virtual clabjects the context defines its identity:
   a) *addClabject(x, ctx).*
2. Visit fields, including that of refined clabjects:
   a) *field a* $\in$ *getFields(x):*
   b) *addField (a).*
3. Visit contained clabjects, including that of refined clabjects:
   a) $\forall$ *(connector r, context c)* $\in$ *getCompositions(x, ctx):*
   b) *addConnector(r).*
   c) ↻ *traverseClabject(r.target, c).*

getFields(*x*) collects all fields of clabject *x* by following the refinement path. The result is a list of fields. The symbol || denotes concatenation of lists.

1. Iterate over the refinement path, including x, to find fields of refined clabjects.
   a) $\forall$ *clabject* $q \in x \,||\, R(x)$ *:*
   b) *set result* ← *result* || *q. Fields.*

getCompositions(*x*, *ctx*) collects all compositions of clabject *x* with context *ctx* along the refinement path. Returns a list of pairs of the composition and the context.

1. Iterate over the refinement path, including x, to find compositions.
   a) $\forall$ *clabject* $q \in x \,||\, R(x)$ *:*
   b) $\forall$ *connector r, r.source* $= q \wedge$ *r.kind = Composition*

   Add the composition to the result; remember that the context of a refined clabject is the sequence of the refining clabjects in the current refinement path:

c) *set result ← result || (r, cxt || R(x).firstUntil(q)).*

(The list returned *by firstUntil(q)* does not include *q*, and is empty if $q \notin R(x)$.)

4.4 Modification and Materialization

The second case of refinement occurs when a refining element adds further information. The example of figure 2 (b) shows that the refining element T2' adds a plug to the structure of the refined clabject TSensor. Representing this case is straightforward since all the information about the modification is located at the refining element. More complicated is the situation where the information about the modification is not located in the refining element. Consider the example of figure 5.

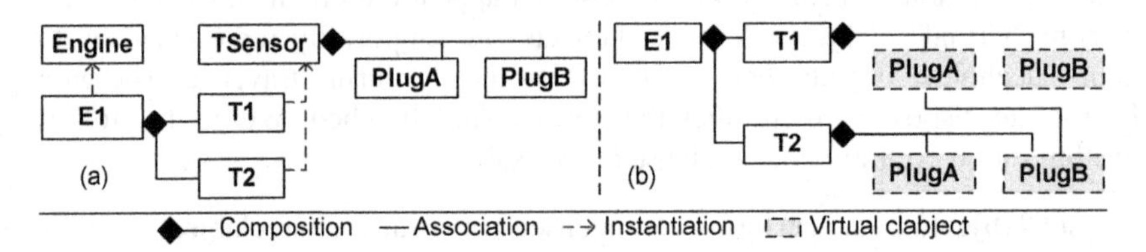

Fig. 5. Engine with two sensors: (a) model and (b) condensed view

The left hand side (a) shows the model of an engine E1 that contains two instances of TSensor, namely T1 and T2. The right hand side (b) shows the condensed view containing the virtual clabjects for both sensors. Now assume that we want to connect PlugA of T1 with PlugB of T2. Since neither of these two plugs exists as a clabject, i.e. both are virtual clabjects in the condensed view, we have to transparently create some sort of *proxy* elements that can be endpoints of connectors. We call this process "materialization", and figure 6 shows how it works.

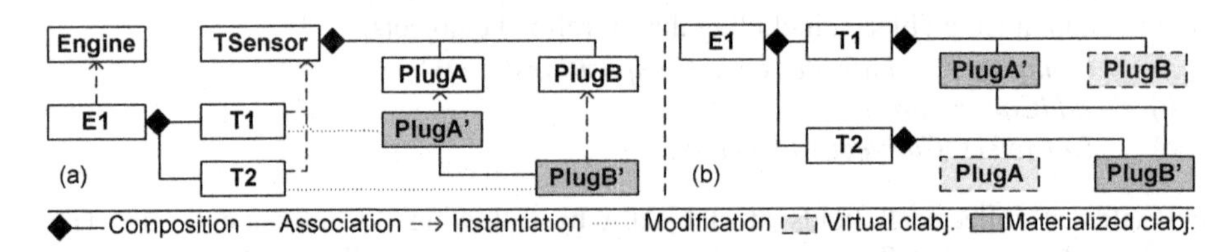

Fig. 6. Materialization: (a) model and (b) condensed view

In order to be able to connect the two plugs, we first have to create the materialized representation of the corresponding virtual clabjects, as shown on the left hand side (a): PlugA of T1 is materialized as PlugA', and PlugB of T2 is materialized as PlugB'. Now PlugA' and PlugB' are instances of the corresponding plugs of TSensor. Thus during materialization we create refinements. These refinements, however, until now do not contain any information except their identity, so they do not use much memory. After materialization, we can create a connector between PlugA' and PlugB'. In the condensed view, as shown on the right hand side (b), we then also get the condensed view of both materialized clabjects.

A materialized clabject, similar to a virtual clabject, only needs to keep track of the refined clabject and the context, which is a list of references to other clabjects, to be uniquely identifiable. In addition, it only stores the difference information to the refined clabject, so a materialized clabject also is a lightweight element.

4.5 Traversal of Refinements with Modifications

Traversing a model with simple modifications, i.e. additional contained elements directly at a refining clabject, is similar to traversing a model without modifications, but we also have to follow the additional compositions. It is easy to see that *traverse-Clabject* can already handle this case.

For refinements with materialized clabjects, as shown in figure 6, a materialized clabject is reached indirectly by traversing its refined clabject since we follow only compositions. Consider the traversal order E1, T1, TSensor, and PlugA. Our algorithm fails here since we expect to have PlugA' in the traversal result, and not PlugA. To resolve that situation, we have to follow the refinement relationship in the reverse direction, since then we can transparently skip PlugA in the traversal and instead visit PlugA'. To prevent an exhaustive search for determining the inverse of the refinement relationship, we use a dictionary *rmap* that maps the refined elements to the refining elements. This map includes the elements that are depicted by the "Modification"-relationship in the figure. In our implementation each clabject stores its own *rmap*, so we get the following traversal algorithm:

traverseMaterializedClabject(*x, ctx*) performs a condensed traversal for the clabject *x* with context *ctx*; can handle clabjects as well as materialized clabjects.

1. Visit the clabject; note that for virtual clabjects the context defines its identity:
   a) addClabject(x, ctx).
2. Visit fields, including that of refined clabjects:
   a) ∀ *field a* ∈ *getFields(x):*
   b) addField (a).
3. Visit contained clabjects, including that of refined clabjects:
   a) ∀ *(connector r, clabject y, context c)* ∈ *getMaterializedCompositions(x, ctx):*
   b) addConnector(r).
   c) ↻ *traverseMaterializedClabject(y, c).*

getMaterializedCompositions(*x, ctx*) collects all compositions of clabject *x* with context *ctx*. Returns a list of triples with: composition, target clabject, and context.

1. Iterate over the refinement path, including x, to find compositions:
   a) ∀ *clabject q* ∈ *x* || *R(x):*
   b) rmaps ← *rmaps* || *q.rmap.* (*q.rmap* retrieves the *rmap* of clabject *q*)
   c) ∀ *connector r, r.source = q* ∧ *r.kind = Composition:*

   When there is a materialized clabject for the target, take that instead of the target:

   d) if ∃ *m, m* ∈ *rmaps: m.contains(r.target) then*
   e) set result ← *result* || *(r, m.get(r.target), cxt* || *R(x).firstUntil(q)).*
   f) else
   g) set result ← *result* || *(r, r.target, cxt* || *R(x).firstUntil(q)).*

Traversing Non-Composition Connectors. Until now we have only considered compositions for traversal. For implementing the function *getConnectors(x, ctx)* that retrieves all connectors for a given clabject, we have to distinguish several cases. Consider figure 7.

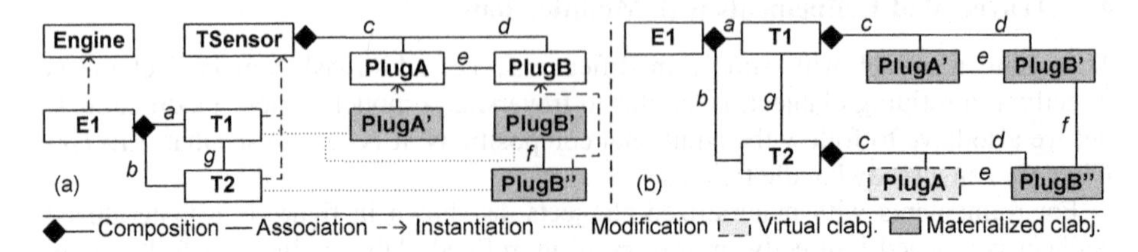

Fig. 7. Connectors and materialization: (a) model and (b) condensed view

Following the connector *g* in analogous to following compositions such *a* and *b*. For following direct connectors between materialized clabjects, such as *f*, we also have all information that we need. For following indirect connectors, i.e. connectors that stem from refined elements, between materialized clabjects such as *e* in the context of T1, additional information is required. Assume that during traversal we are at PlugA'. Following the refinement leads to PlugA, in turn to *e*, and further to PlugB. Now, however, we cannot resolve to PlugB'. Having the *rmap* of T1 enables us to resolve that materialization, and in the general case we have to use the whole context for resolution. Thus the context becomes an essential part of every materialized clabject. A similar case is following an indirect connector from a virtual clabject to a materialized clabject, such as *e* in the context to T2. Here we also need to resolve the materialized clabject by inspecting the context. Since virtual clabjects cannot have direct connectors (they must be materialized first), we have no further cases to consider.

Connector Refinement. Besides refining clabjects, also connectors can be refined. Handling these refinements requires resolving the refined connectors when we visit a connector during a traversal step. Analogously to refining clabjects, this only requires that we store the reverse refinement information at the corresponding clabject's *rmap*.

Field Refinement. Refining clabjects is not done as an end in itself, but typically is used to either provide field values in case of an instantiation, or to add new fields in case of a specialization. Thus the refinement relationship between two clabjects also relates their fields. Consider, for example, figure 7. Let TSensor declare the field Range. The instantiation of TSensor as T1 demands that we provide a range, e.g. from 0 to 100. Thus we can say that the field Range of T1 refines the field Range of TSensor. Extending *getFields* of our traversal algorithm is similar to extending *getCompositions* to *getMaterializedCompositions*.

Refinement Path. The presentation of the algorithms above used the function *R*, mapping a clabject to the sequence of refined elements. In our actual implementation we do not maintain a global map, but rather at each clabject and materialized clabject we store a reference to the refined clabject only. While this is beneficial for the performance, it is also necessary for the self-contained storage of the model parts, e.g. for building libraries of model elements. This, however, is out of scope for this paper.

4.6 Modifying the Condensed View

Since the condensed view is permanently available in our environment, we have to ensure that for any element that is visited via traversal, modification is possible. Modification for clabjects and materialized clabjects is straightforward, since these are exactly the places where we store the modification information. For modification of virtual clabjects, we first have to materialize them. Since for each virtual clabject the context is known, we already have all information that is needed to create the materialized clabject. So with our representation we have ensured that modifying the condensed view is possible, and moreover, that only local information is required.

5 Performance Evaluation

In order to demonstrate the feasibility of the internal representation and the traversal algorithm presented in the previous section, we performed measurements on test data.[1] We decided to use perfect n-ary trees in our tests. Informally, a perfect n-ary tree is a tree where all leaf nodes are at the same depth and each inner node, i.e. non-leaf node, has exactly n children. This decision to use such trees is based on the fact that we wanted to have (a) test structures of varying size, with (b) varying refinement depth. Furthermore, (c) the implementation of the condensed view does not depend on associations between model elements. In addition, we (d) want to use the same kind of test data for evaluating future extensions of the language. In our particular case, we used m trees, where each was a perfect quaternary tree of depth d. This test data construction simulates the existence of m top-level nodes in the model. The choice for quaternary trees is backed by the informal analysis of several models created with an earlier prototypical version of the modeling environment. Our tests use $m = 3$ and d ranging from five to nine, resulting in 4,095 to 1,048,575 clabjects.

Tests are performed for two principal cases: (a) trees without clabject refinement, and (b) trees where clabjects are refined to reuse structural information. In case (a), all clabjects are individually created. Thus in the traversal we do not encounter any virtual clabjects. In case (b), the structure of the lowest one or two levels is reused. If one level is reused, a clabject containing n leaves is created upfront. This is then reused for all clabjects at level $d - 1$. These clabjects thus contain n virtual clabjects each. In a subsequent test, we materialize them prior to traversal. Figure 8 shows the structure for both cases.

The example on the left hand side represents case (a): a binary tree consisting of individually created elements. The example on the right hand side represents case (b): clabject A is created upfront, and is refined multiple times in the tree, resulting in virtual cjabjects as e.g. contained in A'. These virtual clabjects can be materialized, e.g. simply by renaming them to "x" and "y".

[1] All measurements were performed on a Dell Precision M65 Mobile Workstation, equipped with an Intel® Core™2 CPU operating at 2GHz and with 2 GB of main memory, and running Windows XP Professional. The runtime environment was Microsoft .NET 3.0. Tests were executed as individual processes to prevent side effects of e.g. the garbage collector.

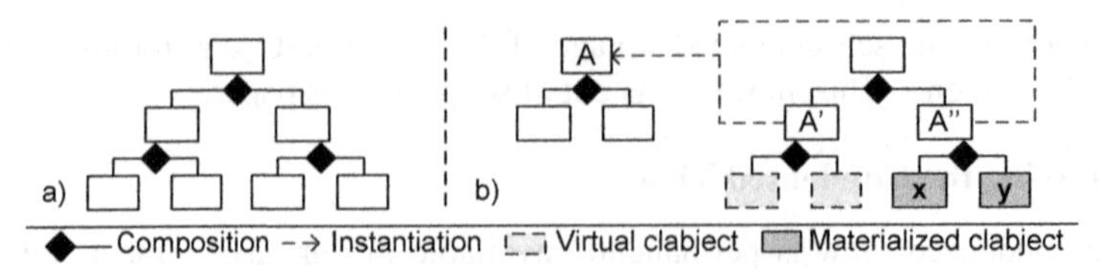

Fig. 8. Test data used for the measurements

If two levels are reused, a similar element is created upfront, but containing *n* clabjects which in turn refine from a clabject containing *n* leaves. While in principle it is possible to create even deeper reuse-hierarchies, we restricted the reuse depth in our test cases since we think this is a realistic measure for real world models.

5.1 Traversal Performance

As outlined in section 3, the model transformation code is one of the use cases for our models. In order to verify the feasibility of our modeling approach with respect to the performance requirements, we performed traversal tests of the whole model. Traversal is done recursively on the condensed view, depth first, without performing any additional code besides book-keeping, such as counting the number of visited clabjects. The time is measured using .Net's built in *System.Stopwatch* class. Case (a), i.e. a model without reuse, is taken as baseline. Traversal times for case (b), i.e. the models with element reuse, are expected to be slightly slower, since according to the implementation described in section 4, the traversal has to create virtual leaf elements on the fly for each reused element. Traversal also has to keep track of the context information. Table 1 shows the corresponding measurement results.

Table 1. Model traversal performance

		Iteration Time [s]				
		No Clabject Refinement	Refining Clabjects at			
			1 Level		2 Levels	
Tree Depth	Number of Clabjects		Virtual	Materialized	Virtual	Materialized
5	4,095	0.02	0.02	0.02	0.03	0.02
6	16,393	0.05	0.06	0.06	0.08	0.07
7	65,535	0.14	0.24	0.24	0.31	0.29
8	262,143	0.53	0.92	0.93	1.19	1.12
9	1,048,575	2.15	3.53	3.65	4.74	4.54

Somewhat unexpected, traversing the tree with virtual clabjects is roughly equally fast as traversing the tree with materialized clabjects. We interpret the result in that it shows that the dynamic creation of virtual clabject on the fly is fast, while maintaining the context for virtual and materialized clabjects is an overhead. The time used for visiting one individual clabject does not increase with growing model size. More important, the numbers also show that our reuse approach is reasonable fast, both for interactive use at modeling time, where only small parts are traversed, and for use by the model transformation.

5.2 Memory Consumption

Besides traversal performance, memory consumption of the models is one of our main requirements. Another series of tests was thus performed, measuring the impact of creating models on the total memory used by the process. Memory consumption is measured by using .Net's built in *System.GarbageCollector* class before and after creating the model. The measured numbers thus represent the net size of the models. Case (a) again is the baseline. Models of case (b) are expected to consume significantly less memory than in case (a), since according to the implementation described in section 4, virtual clabjects require no memory except for the context information, and even materialized clabjects need to represent only incremental information. Table 2 shows the corresponding measurement results.

Models for case (a), i.e. without reuse, require significant amounts of memory. In our example, up to 868.28 MB are necessary even for a model containing only simple clabjects with basic fields such as a name. In contrast, models for case (b), which reuse clabjects, require significantly less memory. For elements with one reuse-level, all leaves of the tree are virtual clabjects and do not require memory except for the context information. As expected, e.g. the tree of depth 9 with virtual clabjects as leaves, requires about the same amount of memory as the similar tree of depth 8, consisting of individually created clabject only. Analogously, the tree of depth 9 with two levels of reuse requires about the same amount of memory as the similar tree of depth 7 without reuse.

Table 2. Model memory consumption

		Memory Consumption [MB]				
	Number	No	Refining Clabjects at			
Tree	of	Clabject	1 Level		2 Levels	
Depth	Clabjects	Refinement	Virtual	Materialized	Virtual	Materialized
5	4,095	3.37	0.85	1.90	0.22	1.67
6	16,393	13.23	3.42	7.31	0.85	6.36
7	65,535	53.54	13.42	29.52	3.42	25.78
8	262,143	215.01	54.30	119.26	13.43	103.23
9	1,048,575	868.28	218.02	478.94	54.30	415.23

The measurement was also performed where *all* virtual clabjects were materialized and thus exist as objects in memory. The memory consumption is still significantly lower than for the models containing individually created clabjects. In real world models, however, we expect only a fraction of the virtual clabjects to be materialized, so this additional memory consumption is expected to be negligible. While memory consumption for models without reuse *is* problematic, we can see that our reuse approach keeps the memory consumption within practicable bounds.

6 Related Work

Handling of large models is a common requirement for the application of modeling environments in practice. The definition of "large", however, actually depends on the kind of models and on the subject domain. A natural border case is a model that barely fits into main memory. For the Eclipse Modeling Framework [9], for example, this problem also arises and is solved by dynamically loading and unloading model parts, transparently performed by the persistency layer [10]. EMF or MOF-based modeling approaches [11], however, do not support multi-level modeling with clabjects. In our implementation, we could exploit the property of structural similarity, which allows incorporating the space-efficient representation right at the implementation of modeling elements, so we can represent sufficiently large models without reaching memory limits.

The idea of unifying classes and objects has a long tradition in object-oriented programming languages, namely in prototype-based languages such as SELF [12]. A SELF-object consists of named slots that can carry values, which in turn are references to other objects. SELF uses an "inherits from"-relationship that unifies instantiation and specialization. Chambers et al. report on a similar assumption as we do: "Few SELF objects have totally unique format and behavior", since most objects are slightly modified clones [12]. They use so-called "maps" for representing common slots, such that individually created objects only have to store difference information. The basic idea is quite similar to ours, the implementation of a programming language, however, certainly differs from that of a modeling environment.

An early report by Batory and Kim on the quite complex domain of VLSI CAD applications also explores the structural similarity of model elements [13]. They describe an implementation based on a relational database that employs copying of data to achieve good retrieval performance. Their system, however, only supports one single classification level.

Gutheil et al. describe an effort to build a multi-level modeling tool that is also based on the clabject-idea [4]. They give some fundamental principles for coping with connectors in such an environment, e.g. for their graphical representation. It is however not reported how industry-sized models are handled.

7 Conclusion

This paper describes how core features of a clabject-based modeling environment can be implemented in practice. We describe the traversal algorithm for a condensed model view and how to reduce memory consumption of a condensed view. Based on the theoretical part, we evaluated our approach with test models of varying size. The results show that our concepts and their implementations are efficient both with respect to traversal time and memory consumption. The resulting clabject-based modeling environment meets the requirements for a real-world application, and thus demonstrates that multi-level modeling can indeed be used for large industrial applications.

Acknowledgements

The authors thank Stefan Preuer for his excellent implementation of the clabject representation code and the traversal algorithms.

References

1. Management Group: Unified Modeling Language Infrastructure, v 2.1.2 (2007)
2. Atkinson, C., Kühne, T.: Reducing accidental complexity in domain models. Software and Systems Modeling 7(3), 345–359 (2007)
3. Atkinson, C., Kühne, T.: The Essence of Multilevel Metamodeling. In: Gogolla, M., Kobryn, C. (eds.) UML 2001. LNCS, vol. 2185, pp. 19–33. Springer, Heidelberg (2001)
4. Gutheil, M., Kennel, B., Atkinson, C.: A Systematic Approach to Connectors in a Multilevel Modeling Environment. In: Czarnecki, K., Ober, I., Bruel, J.-M., Uhl, A., Völter, M. (eds.) MODELS 2008. LNCS, vol. 5301, pp. 843–857. Springer, Heidelberg (2008)
5. Aschauer, T., Dauenhauer, G., Pree, W.: Multi-Level Modeling for Industrial Automation Systems. In: 35th Euromicro SEAA Conference (to appear, 2009)
6. Object Management Group: Unified Modeling Language Superstructure, v 2.1.2 (2007)
7. Atkinson, C., Gutheil, M., Kennel, B.: A Flexible Infrastructure for Multi-Level Language Engineering (to appear, 2009)
8. Kühne, T.: Contrasting Classification with Generalisation. In: Proceedings of the Sixth Asia-Pacific Conference on Conceptual Modelling, New Zealand (2009)
9. Eclipse Foundation, Eclipse Modeling Framework, `http://www.eclipse.org/modeling/emf/`
10. Stepper, E.: Scale, Share and Store your Models with CDO 2.0. Talk at eclipseCON (2009)
11. Object Management Group, Meta Object Facility (MOF) 2.0 Core Specification (2004)
12. Chambers, C., Ungar, D., Lee, E.: An efficient implementation of SELF, a dynamically-typed object-oriented language based on prototypes. Lisp Symb. Comput. 4(3), 243–281 (1991)
13. Batory, D.S., Kim, W.: Modeling concepts for VLSI CAD objects. ACM Transactions on Database Systems 10(3), 322–346 (1985)

Meta-model Pruning*

Sagar Sen, Naouel Moha, Benoit Baudry, and Jean-Marc Jézéquel

INRIA Rennes-Bretagne Atlantique, Campus universitaire de beaulieu,
35042 Rennes Cedex, France
{ssen,moha,bbaudry,jezequel}@irisa.fr

Abstract. Large and complex meta-models such as those of UML and its profiles are growing due to modelling and inter-operability needs of numerous stakeholders. The complexity of such meta-models has led to coining of the term *meta-muddle*. Individual users often exercise only a small view of a meta-muddle for tasks ranging from model creation to construction of model transformations. What is the *effective meta-model* that represents this view? We present a flexible *meta-model pruning* algorithm and *tool* to extract effective meta-models from a meta-muddle. We use the notion of *model typing* for meta-models to verify that the algorithm generates a *super-type* of the large meta-model representing the meta-muddle. This implies that all programs written using the effective meta-model will work for the meta-muddle hence preserving backward compatibility. All instances of the effective meta-model are also instances of the meta-muddle. We illustrate how pruning the original UML meta-model produces different effective meta-models.

Keywords: Meta-model pruning, GPML, DSML, UML, Kermeta, effective modelling domain, test input domain.

1 Introduction

Development of complex software systems using *modelling languages* to specify *models* at high-levels of abstraction is the philosophy underlying Model-Driven Engineering (MDE). There are two schools of thought that advocate the development of such modelling languages : *general-purpose modelling* and *domain-specific modelling*. General-purpose modelling is leveraged by modelling languages such as the Unified Modelling Language (UML)[1] with a large number of classes and properties to model various aspects of a software system using the same language. The UML superstructure consists of subsets of visual modelling languages such as UML use case diagrams, activity diagrams, state machines, and class diagrams to specify models of software systems. UML is also extensible using the *profiles mechanism* [2] to provide modelling elements from specific domains such as services, aerospace systems, software radio, and data distribution [3]. One

* The research leading to these results has received funding from the European Communitys Seventh Framework Programme FP7/2007-2013 under grant agreement 215483 (S-Cube).

A. Schürr and B. Selic (Eds.): MODELS 2009, LNCS 5795, pp. 32–46, 2009.

of the primary advantages of the UML standard and its profiles is *inter-operability* between related domains in software development. On the other hand, domain-specific modelling promotes the construction of pure domain-specific modelling languages (DSMLs) [4]. One of the main disadvantages of a DSML is finding the ideal scope for its long term use. Identifying the scope involves abstracting DSML concepts in very early stages of its development. This leaves little room for adding concepts later in the lifetime of DSML. Despite the existence of several DSMLs general-purpose modelling languages (GPMLs) such as UML and its profiles are widely used to model complex software systems.

A major disadvantage of GPMLs such as the UML is its ever growing complexity and size. The widely accepted modelling language UML 2.0 has a specification document of about 1000 pages. The UML 2.0 *meta-model* used to specify the language contains 246 classes and 583 properties. The large number of classes and properties with several complex dependencies between them has led to the coining of the censorious term *meta-muddle* [5] to characterize huge GPMLs such as the UML. This criticism of UML can be attributed to the fact that it is an over-specification of the real *modelling domain* for a given application. For instance, if we intend to generate code from UML state machines there is no need to expose modelling elements for activity diagrams, or use case diagrams to the code generator. In practice, each application of the UML utilizes a subset of classes and properties in the UML. What is the *effective meta-model* that contains these required classes and properties and all its mandatory dependencies? This is the question that intrigues us and for which we provide a solution.

In this paper, we present a *meta-model pruning algorithm* that takes as input a large meta-model and a set of required classes and properties, to generate a target *effective meta-model*. The effective meta-model contains the required set of classes and properties. The term *pruning* refers to removal of unnecessary classes and properties. From a graph-theoretic point of view, given a large input graph (large input meta-model) the algorithm removes or prunes unnecessary nodes (classes and properties) to produce a smaller graph (effective meta-model). The algorithm determines if a class or property is unnecessary based on a set of rules and options. One such rule is removal of properties with lower bound multiplicity 0 and who's type is not a required type. We demonstrate using the notion of model typing that the generated effective meta-model, a subset of the large meta-model from a set-theoretic point of view, is a *super-type*, from a type-theoretic point of view, of the large input meta-model. This means that all programs written using the effective meta-model can also be executed for models of the original large meta-model. The pruning process preserves the meta-class names and meta-property names from the large input meta-model in the effective meta-model. This also implies that all instances (models) of the effective meta-model are also instances of the initial large input meta-model. All models of the effective meta-model are exchangeable across tools that use the large input meta-model as a standard. The extracted effective meta-model is very much like a transient DSML with necessary concepts for a problem domain at a given time. For example, we present an application of our algorithm to generate an effective meta-model to specify test models for a model transformation. The model transformation is developed by the French Spatial Agency (CNES) to transform UML models to code for embedded systems.

The paper is organized as follows. In Section 2 we present the motivation for our work. We present related work in Section 3 that attempt to solve problems discussed in motivation. In Section 4 we present the meta-model pruning algorithm. We introduce model typing in Section 5 to show that the effective meta-model is indeed a super-type of the large meta-model. In Section 6 we present the application of meta-model pruning to obtain an effective meta-model for develop test models for a model transformation. We conclude and present future work in Section 7.

2 Motivation

The motivation for us to develop a meta-model pruning algorithm comes from observations made by us and others in various phases of the MDE process. We categorize our observations in the form of scenarios:

Scenario 1: Input Domain of Model Transformations. A large meta-model such as that of UML is the de facto input meta-model for a large number of model transformations or model processing programs/tools. However, many of these model transformations manipulate only a subset of the concepts defined in the input meta-model. There is a sparse usage of concepts in the input meta-model. For instance, code generators from UML state machines [6] normally use only the UML class diagram and UML state machine modelling elements. Therefore, often the *large meta-model is not the real input meta-model* of a model transformation. We illustrate this scenario in Figure 1 (a) where meta-model MM_{large} specifies a large set of models but a model transformation MT is developed to process only a subset of this large set.

Scenario 2: Chain of Model Transformations. A consequence of not defining the real input domain of a model transformation is the non-compatibility/mismatch of outputs and inputs between transformations in chain. Consider a sequence of model transformations as shown in Figure 1 (b). The output meta-model MM_o^a of model transformation MT_a is also the input meta-model MM_i^b for the next model transformation MT_b. However, we do not know if all models generated by MT_a can be processed by the model transformation MT_b as the concepts manipulated by the model transformations may be different. In [7], we identify this issue as one of the barriers to validate model transformations. Not identifying and dealing with this mismatch between the real input meta-model and real output meta-model can lead to serious software faults.

Scenario 3: Testing Model Transformations. Creating a model that conforms to a large meta-model does not always require all the concepts in the meta-model. For instance, if you want to create a model to test a model transformation of the large meta-model you may need to use only a small number of concepts. The entire large meta-model does not serve the purpose of creating test models for a certain sub-domain of the input meta-model. The large

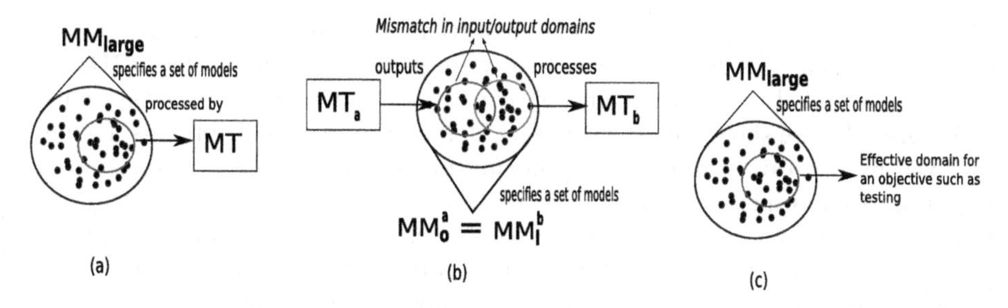

Fig. 1. Effective Meta-model Scenarios in Model Transformation Development

meta-model could pose a problem for a test model developer as she/he can be confused by the large number of concepts in the meta-model. In the context of automated testing, if you want to generate test models (such as using the tool Cartier [8] [9]) then you would want to transform the smallest possible input meta-model to a formal language for constraint satisfaction. Transforming the entire meta-model to a formal language will lead to a enormous constraint satisfaction problem. These large constraint satisfaction problems are often intractable. Solving smaller constraint satisfaction problems obtained from a small set of concepts and subsequently with fewer variables is relatively feasible.

Scenario 4: Software Process Modelling. Software process models contain several workflows. However, each workflow in a software process uses different sub-domains of a single shared meta-model such as the the UML. These workflows are often realized by different people and at different times. There are several software process methodologies that use the UML as the shared modelling language. The most popular of them is the Rational Unified Process (RUP) [10].

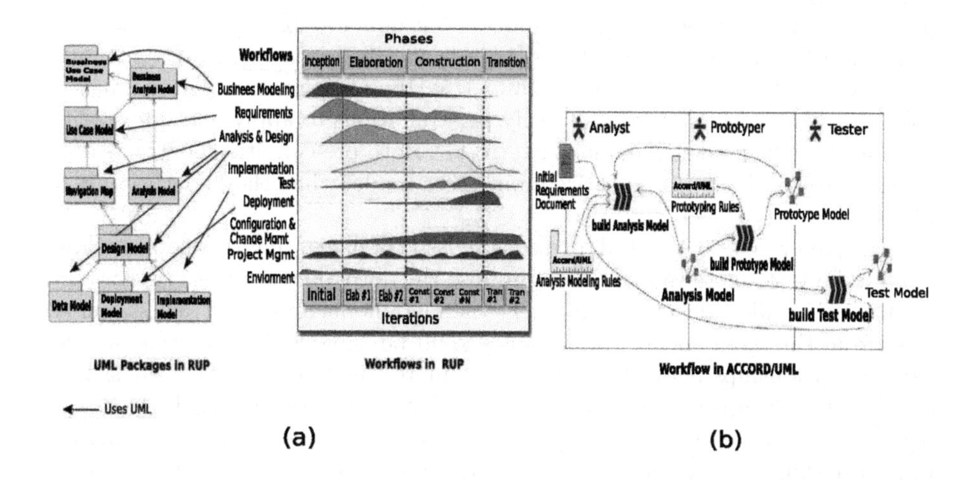

Fig. 2. (a) Workflows in RUP and its usage of UML (b) Workflow of ACCORD and its use of UML

Figure 2(a) shows the different workflows of RUP and the use of different subsets of UML for each workflow. Dedicated software processes such as ACCORD [11] use UML extended with domain-specific constructs to develop real-time systems. In Figure 2(b), we show the use of subsets UML in the ACCORD process. People involved in a certain workflow of a software process are exposed to concepts in the entire shared meta-model such as the UML instead of a subset of UML that represents their real work area. The access to unnecessary modelling elements to an engineer of a workflow could lead to errors in the software process.

The above scenarios are only some of the many possible scenarios where a large meta-model defines the modelling domain while only a sub-domain is in use.

3 Related Work

There has always been a need to define the effective modelling domain for a given objective in MDE. This is true especially in the case of using large GPMLs such as UML. In this section we present related work that deal with the problem of obtaining and using the effective modelling domain. We also pinpoint our contributions in this work.

Consider a fundamental task in MDE: Creating a model in a model editor such as in the Eclipse [12] environment. A popular editor for UML models is TOPCASED [13]. The tool can be used to create UML models such as class diagrams, state machines, activity diagrams, and use-case diagrams. If a modeller chooses to create class diagrams the tool presents the user with modelling elements for class diagrams such as classes and associations but not UML state machine modelling elements such as states and transitions. Therefore, the tool inherently prevents the modeller from using an unnecessary part of the UML meta-model. The *hard-coded* user interface in TOPCASED in fact presents the modeller with an effective modelling domain.

Model transformations on GPMLs such as UML are built for specific tasks and can process only a sub-domain of its huge input domain. To filter the input to a model transformation *pre-conditions* [14] are specified in a constraint language such as Object Constraint Language (OCL) [15] [16]. Graph transformation based model transformation languages specify pre-conditions to apply a graph rewriting rule on a left-hand side model pattern [17]. Both pre-condition contracts and patterns are specified on the entire input meta-model while they refer to only a sub-domain.

In the paper [5] Solberg et al. present the issue of navigating the meta-muddle notably the UML meta-model. They propose the development of Query/Extraction tools that allow developers to query the metamodel and to extract specified views from the metamodel. These tools should be capable of extracting simple derived relationships between concepts and more complex views that consist of derived relationships among many concepts. They mention the need to extract such views for different applications such as to define the domain of a model transformation and extracting a smaller metamodel from the concepts used in a model. Meta-modelling tools such as those developed by Xactium [18] and Adaptive Software [19] possess some of these abilities. The authors of [5] propose the use of *aspects* to extract such views. However, the authors do not elaborate on the objectives behind generating such views.

In this paper, we present the following contributions emerging from our observations in MDE and survey of previous work:

- **Contribution 1:** We present a meta-model pruning algorithm to extract an effective meta-model from a large meta-model.
- **Contribution 2:** We present an application of model typing to *verify* that an effective meta-model is indeed a super-type of the large input meta-model. All programs written using the effective meta-model are valid also for the original large meta-model. Our approach preserves meta-concept names in the effective meta-model from the large meta-model and hence all instances of the effective meta-model are instances of the large input meta-model.

4 Meta-model Pruning Algorithm

This section presents the *meta-model pruning algorithm* to transform a input meta-model to a pruned target meta-model. We acknowledge the fact there can be an entire family of pruning algorithms that can be used to prune a large meta-model to give various effective meta-models. In this paper, we present a *conservative* meta-model pruning algorithm to generate effective meta-models. Our initial motivation to develop the algorithm was to help scale a formal method for test model generation [8] in the case of large input meta-models. Therefore, given a set of required classes and properties the rationale for designing the algorithm was to remove a maximum number of classes and properties facilitating us to scale a formal method to solve constraints from a relatively small input meta-model. The set of required classes and properties are inputs that can come from either static analysis of a transformation, an example model, an objective function, or can be manually specified. Given these initial inputs we automatically identify mandatory dependent classes and properties in the meta-model and remove the rest. For instance, we remove all properties which have a multiplicity 0..* and with a type not in the set of required class types. However, we also add some flexibility to the pruning algorithm. We provide options such as those that preserve properties (and their class type) in a required class even if they have a multiplicity 0..*. In our opinion, no matter how you choose to design a pruning algorithm the final output effective meta-model should be a supertype of the large input meta-model. The pruning algorithm must also preserve identical meta-concept names such that all instances of the effective meta-model are instances of the large input meta-model. These final requirements ensure backward compatibility of the effective meta-model with respect to the large input meta-model.

4.1 Algorithm Overview

In Figure 3, we present an overview of the meta-model pruning algorithm. The inputs to the algorithm are: (1) A source meta-model $MM_s = MM_{large}$ which is also a large meta-model such as the meta-model for UML with about 246 Classes and 583 properties (in Ecore format) (2) A set of required classes C_{req} (3) A set of required properties P_{req}, and (4) A boolean array consisting of parameters to make the algorithm flexible for different pruning options.

The set of required classes C_{req} and properties P_{req} can be obtained from various sources as shown in Figure 3: (a) A static analysis of a model transformation can reveal which classes and properties are used by a transformation (b) The sets can be directly specified by the user (c) A test objective such as a set of partitions of the meta-model [20] is a specified on different properties which can be source for the set P_{req}. (d) A model itself uses objects of different classes. These classes and their properties can be the sources for C_{req} and P_{req}.

The output of the algorithm is a pruned effective meta-model $MM_t = MM_{effective}$ that contains all classes in C_{req}, all properties in P_{req} and their associated dependencies. Some of the dependencies are mandatory such as all super classes of a class and some are optional such as properties with multiplicity 0..* and whose class type is not in C_{req}. A set of parameters allow us to control the inclusion of these optional properties or classes in order to give various effective meta-models for different applications. The output meta-model $MM_{effective}$ is a subset and a super-type of MM_s.

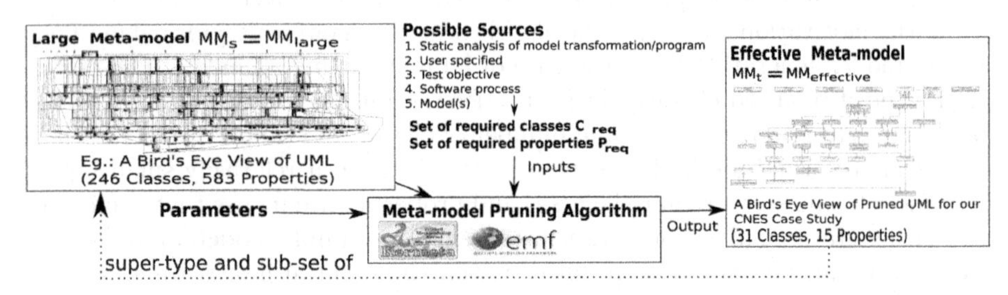

Fig. 3. The Meta-model Pruning Algorithm Overview

4.2 General Definitions

We present some general definitions we use for describing the meta-model pruning algorithm:

Definition 1. A primitive type b is an element in the set of primitives: $b \in \{String, Integer, Boolean\}$.

Definition 2. An enumeration type e is a 2-tuple $e := (name, L)$, where $name$ is a $String$ identifier, L is a finite set of enumerated literals.

Definition 3. A class type c is a 4-tuple $c := (name, P_c, Super, isAbstract)$, where $name$ is a $String$ identifier, P_c is a finite set of properties of class c, class c inherits properties of classes in the finite of classes $Super$ and $isAbstract$ is a $Boolean$ that determines if c is abstract.

Definition 4. A meta-model MM is a 2-tuple $MM := (T, P, Inv)$, where T is a finite set of class, primitive, and enumeration types, P is a set of properties, Inv is a finite set of invariants.

Type Operations: The operations on types used in this paper are: (a) $t.isInstanceOf(X)$ that returns true if t is of type X or inherits from X. (b) $t.allSuperClasses()$, if $t.isInstanceOf(Class)$, returns the set of all its super classes $t.Super$ including the super classes of its super classes and so on (multi-level).

Definition 5. A property p is a 7-tuple $p := (name, oC, type, lower, upper, opposite, isComposite)$, where $name$ is a $String$ identifier, oC is a reference to the owning class type, $type$ is a reference to the property type, $lower$ is a positive integer for the lower bound of the multiplicity, $upper$ is the a positive integer for the upper bound of the multiplicity, $opposite$ is a reference to an opposite property if any, and $isComposite$ determines if the objects referenced by p are composite (No other properties can contain these objects).

Property Operations: The operations on properties in this paper is $p.isConstrained()$ which returns $true$ if constrained by any invariant i such that $p \in i.P_I$. This is checked for all invariants $i \in MM.Inv$.

Definition 6. An invariant I is a 3-tuple $c := (T_I, P_I, Expression)$, where T_I is the set of types used in the invariant I and P_I is the set of properties used in I. An $Expression$ is a function of T_I and P_I that has a boolean value. The $Expression$ is often specified in a constraint language such as OCL [15].

Note: Throughout the section, we use the *relational dot-operator* to identify an element of a tuple. For example, we want to refer to the set of all types in a meta-model we use the expression $MM.T$,or $MM.P$ to refer to the set of all properties. Also, we do not consider user-defined meta-model *operations* or its argument signatures in our approach.

4.3 The Algorithm

The meta-model pruning algorithm (shown in Algorithm 1 has four inputs: (a) A source meta-model MM_s (b) Initial set of required types T_{req} (c) Initial set of required properties P_{req} (d) The top-level container class type C_{top}. (e) $Parameter$ which is a Boolean array. Each element in the array corresponds to an option to add classes or properties to the required set of classes and properties. In this paper, we consider three such options giving us a $Parameter$ vector of size 3.

The output of the algorithm is the pruned target meta-model MM_t. We briefly go through the working of the algorithm. The target meta-model MM_t is initialized with the source meta-model MM_s. The algorithm is divided into three main phases: (1) Computing set of all required types T_{req} in the meta-model, (2) Set of all required properties P_{req} in the meta-model (3) Removing all types and properties not that are not in T_{req} and P_{req}.

The first phase of the algorithm involves the computation of the entire set of required types T_{req}. The initial set T_{req} is passed as a parameter to the algorithm. We add the top-level container class C_{top} of MM_s to the set of required types T_{req} as shown in Step 2. In Step 3, we add the types of all required properties P_{req} to the set of required types T_{req}. In Step 4, we add types of all mandatory properties to T_{req}. Types of all properties with *lower bound greater than zero* are added to the set of required types T_{req} (Step 4.1). Similarly, if a property is constrained by an invariant in $MM.Inv$ then its type is included in T_{req} as shown in Step 4.2. If a property has an opposite type then we include the type of the opposite property, the owning class of the opposite property, and the type of the property to T_{req} in Step 4.3. The algorithm provides three options to add types of properties with lower multiplicity zero and are of type Class, PrimitiveType, and Enumeration respectively. The inclusion of these types is depicted in Steps 4.4, 4.5, and 4.6. The truth values elements of the *Parameter* array determine if these options are used. These options are only examples of making the algorithm flexible. The *Parameter* array and the options can be extended with general and user-specific requirements for generating effective meta-models. After obtaining T_{req} we add all its super classes across all levels to the set T_{req} as shown in Step 5.

The second phase of the algorithm consists of computing the set of all required properties P_{req}. Inclusion of mandatory properties are depicted from Step 6.1 through Step 6.5. In Step 6.1, we add all properties whose type are in T_{req} to P_{req}. In Step 6.2 we add all properties whose owning class are in T_{req} to P_{req}. In Step 6.3, we add properties with lower multiplicity greater than zero to P_{req}. If a property is constrained by a constraint in $MM.Inv$ we add it to P_{req} as depicted in Step 6.4. We add the opposite property of a required property to P_{req}. Finally, based on the options specified in the *Parameter* array, the algorithm adds properties to P_{req} with lower multiplicity zero and other characteristics.

In the third phase of the algorithm we remove types and properties from MM_t. In Step 7, we remove all properties that are not in P_{req} (Step 7.1) and all properties who's types are not in T_{req} (Step 7.2). In Step 8, we remove all types not in T_{req}. The result is an effective meta-model in MM_t. In Section 5, we present *model typing* for meta-models to show that MM_t is a super-type of MM_s. As a result, any program written with MM_t can be executed using models of MM_s.

4.4 Implementation

The meta-model pruning algorithm has been implemented in Kermeta [21]. Kermeta is a language for specifying metamodels, models, and model transformations that are compliant to the Meta Object Facility(MOF) standard [22]. The tool supports input meta-models in the Eclipse Modelling Framework's (EMF) [12] Ecore meta-modelling standard. The tool with usage instructions is available for download [23].

Algorithm 1. metamodelPruning(MM_s , T_{req}, P_{req}, C_{top}, $Parameter$)

1. Initialize target meta-model MM_t
$MM_t \leftarrow MM_s$
2. Add top-level class into the set of required types
$T_{req} \leftarrow T_{req} \cup C_{top}$
3. Add types of required properties to set of required types
$P_{req}.each\{p|T_{req} \leftarrow T_{req} \cup p.type\}$
4. Add types of obligatory properties
$MM_t.P.each\{p|$
4.1 $(p.lower > 0) \implies \{T_{req} \leftarrow T_{req} \cup p.type\}$
4.2 $(p.isConstrained(MM_t.Inv)) \implies \{T_{req} \leftarrow T_{req} \cup p.type\}$
4.3 $(p.opposite! = \phi) \implies \{T_{req} \leftarrow T_{req} \cup p.type, T_{req} \leftarrow T_{req} \cup p.opposite.type, T_{req} \leftarrow T_{req} \cup p.opposite.oC\}$
Option 1: Property of type Class with lower bound 0
if $Parameter[0] == True$ **then**
  4.4 $(p.lower == 0\, and\, p.type.isInstanceOf(Class)) \implies \{T_{req} \leftarrow T_{req} \cup p.type\}$
end if
Option 2: Property of type PrimitiveType with lower bound 0
if $Parameter[1] == True$ **then**
  4.5 $(p.lower == 0\ and\ p.type.isInstanceOf(PrimitiveType)) \implies \{T_{req} \leftarrow T_{req} \cup p.type\}$
end if
Option 3: Property of type Enumeration with lower bound 0
if $Parameter[2] == True$ **then**
  4.6 $(p.lower == 0 and p.type.isInstanceOf(Enumeration)) \implies \{T_{req} \leftarrow T_{req} \cup p.type\}\}$
end if
5. Add all multi-level super classes of all classes in T_{req}
$MM_t.T.each\{t \mid t.isInstanceOf(Class) \implies t.allSuperClasses.each\ \{s|T_{req} \leftarrow T_{req} \cup s\}\}$
6. Add all required properties to P_{req}
$MM_t.P.each\{p|$
6.1 $(p.type \in T_{req}) \implies \{P_{req} \leftarrow P_{req} \cup p\}$
6.2 $(p.oC \in T_{req}) \implies \{P_{req} \leftarrow P_{req} \cup p\}$
6.3 $(p.lower > 0) \implies P_{req} \leftarrow P_{req} \cup p\}$
6.4 $(p.isConstrained(MM_t.Inv)) \implies \{P_{req} \leftarrow P_{req} \cup p\}$
6.5 $(p.opposite! = \phi) \implies \{P_{req} \leftarrow P_{req} \cup p, P_{req} \leftarrow P_{req} \cup p.opposite\}$
Option 1: Property of type Class with lower bound 0
if $Parameter[0] == True$ **then**
  6.6 $(p.lower == 0\, and\, p.type.isInstanceOf(Class)) \implies \{P_{req} \leftarrow P_{req} \cup p\}$
end if
Option 2: Property of type PrimitiveType with lower bound 0
if $Parameter[1] == True$ **then**
  6.7 $(p.lower == 0\ and\ p.type.isInstanceOf(PrimitiveType)) \implies \{P_{req} \leftarrow P_{req} \cup p\}$
end if
Option 3: Property of type Enumeration with lower bound 0
if $Parameter[2] == True$ **then**
  6.8 $(p.lower == 0 and p.type.isInstanceOf(Enumeration)) \implies \{P_{req} \leftarrow P_{req} \cup p\}\}$
end if
7. Remove Properties
$MM_t.P.each\{p|$
7.1 $p \notin P_{req} \implies (t.P \leftarrow t.P - p)$
7.2 $p.type \notin T_{req} \implies (t.P \leftarrow t.P - p)\}$
}
8. Remove Types
$MM_t.T.each\{t|t \notin T_{req} \implies MM_t.T \leftarrow MM_t.T - t\}$

5 Model Typing

In the section we describe the notion of *model typing*. We use model typing to verify that meta-model pruning algorithm indeed generates a super-type of the input meta-model. Model typing corresponds to a simple extension to object-oriented typing in a model-oriented context [24]. A model typing is a strategy for typing models as collections of interconnected objects while preserving type conformance, used as a criterion of substitutability.

The notion of model type conformance (or substitutability) has been adapted and extended to model types based on Bruce's notion of type groups and type group matching [25]. The matching relation, denoted <#, between two meta-models defines a function of the set of classes they contain according to the following definition:

> Metamodel *M'* matches another metamodel *M* (denoted *M'* <# *M*) iff for each class *C* in *M*, there is one and only one corresponding class *C'* in *M'* such that every property *p* and operation *op* in *M.C* matches in *M'.C'* respectively with a property *p'* and an operation *op'* with parameters of the same type as in *M.C*.

This definition is adapted from [24] and improved here by relaxing the constraint related of the name-dependent conformance on properties and operations.

Let's illustrate model typing with two metamodels *M* and *M'* given in Figures 4 and 5. These two metamodels have properties and references that have different names. The metamodel *M'* has additional elements compared to the metamodel *M*.

> *C1* <# *COne* because for each property *COne.p* of type *D* (namely, *COne.name* and *COne.aCTwo*), there is a matching property *C1.q* of type *D'* (namely, *C1.id* and *C1.aC2*), such that *D'* <# *D*.
>
> Thus, *C1* <# *COne* requires *D'* <# *D*:
>
> - *COne.name* and *C1.id* are both of type *String*.
> - *COne.aCTwo* is of type *CTwo* and *C1.aC2* is of type *C2*, so *C1* <# *COne* requires *C2* <# *CTwo*. And, *C2* <# *CTwo* is true because *CTwo.element* and *C2.elem* are both of type *String*.

Thus, matching between classes may depend on the matching of their related dependent classes. As a consequence, the dependencies involved when evaluating model type matching are heavily cyclical [26]. The interested reader can find the details of matching rules used for model types in [26].

In Section 6, we illustrate the use of model typing integrated in the model transformation language Kermeta. We show that transformations written using the effective meta-model are also valid for models of the original large meta-model.

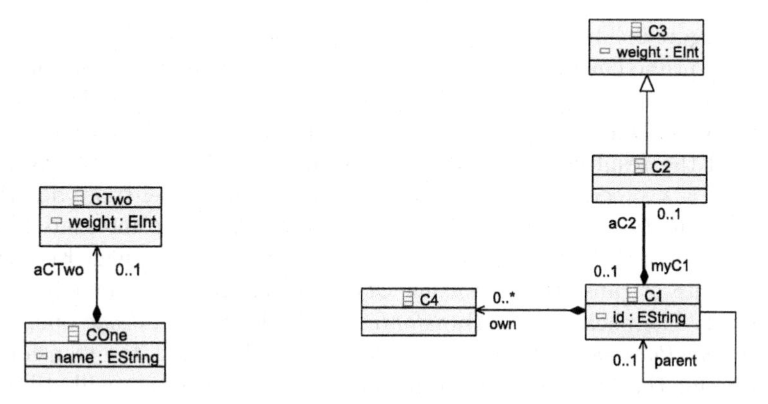

Fig. 4. Metamodel *M*

Fig. 5. Metamodel *M'*

6 Application

We apply the meta-model pruning algorithm to generate an effective meta-model to specify test models for model transformations. The model transformation in our case study is from the French National Space Agency (CNES) to generate embedded systems code from a set of input models. The project is sponsored by the DOMINO project of ANR. We do not discuss the transformation in detail in this paper. We, however, highlight that the transformation uses a subset of UML Activity diagram models. Our algorithm extracts an effective meta-model with the ultimate objective of testing the transformation. Testing can be done either by manually specifying test models or automatically generating them based on the technique in [8]. We do not elaborate on the testing phase in this paper.

```
package cnesTransfoMain;
require "http://www.eclipse.org/uml2/2.1.2/UML"
class Main {
    operation main() : Void is do
        var rep : EMFRepository init EMFRepository.new
        var res : kermeta::persistence::EMFResource
        res ?= rep.getResource("model.uml")
        var inputModel : uml::Model   //Input UML Model
        model ?= res.one
        var transfo : cnesPackage::Transfo<uml::UmlMM>
                        init cnesPackage::Transfo<uml::UmlMM>.new
        transfo.generateCode(inputModel)
     end }
-----------------------------------
package cnesPackage;
require UMLCNES;
class Transfo<MT : UMLCNES> { // Code generator ...
    operation generateCode( source : MT::Model) : Void is do
    ... end }
```

Listing 1. Kermeta Transformation to Demonstrate use of Effective Meta-model

The result of executing the algorithm with *no options* (no parameter specified) is the bare-minimum effective meta-model shown in Figure 6. A bare minimum effective meta-model , in our case, is sufficient to specify input models for the transformation. The meta-model is generated using an initial set of required classes C_{req}. All elements of C_{req} are provided as input the the pruning algorithm in the set T_{req} such that $C_{req} \in T_{req}$. The classes in C_{req} are shown within red boxes in Figure 6. The top-level class $C_{top} = Model$ is specified in a green-dashed box. In the pruned meta-model we observe that all disjoint subgraphs of the UML meta-model are removed such as UML State Machines, UML Class Diagrams, and UML Use Case Diagrams preserving only a subset of UML Activity diagram.

We call the resulting $MM_{effective}$ of UML, UMLCNES. We can verify that UMLCNES is a *super-type* of UML using the notion of model types described in Section 5. The type checking rules for model types has been integrated into the typing system of the modelling and model transformation language Kermeta [21]. We can write a transformation using UMLCNES as the input domain as shown in listing 1. The package *cnesTransfoMain* calls the *generateCode* operation (in package *cnesPackage*) with an UML input model. However, the transformation is defined for the UMLCNES meta-model. The transformation will still execute since UMLCNES is a super-type of UML. Test models can also be developed as instances of UMLCNES and transformed to UML without loss of information.

The pruning algorithm is *flexible.* We briefly illustrate this by pruning UML for the different options presented in the paper. In Table 1 we summarize the number of classes and properties for the different options of the meta-model pruning algorithm. The algorithm can be used to generate different effective meta-models with various applications. For example, another option that is not dealt with in this paper could be inclusion of all possible containers of a property to the set of required types. Options can be used to relax or tighten the pruning for applications where model transformations may evolve and use more concepts that initially perceived.

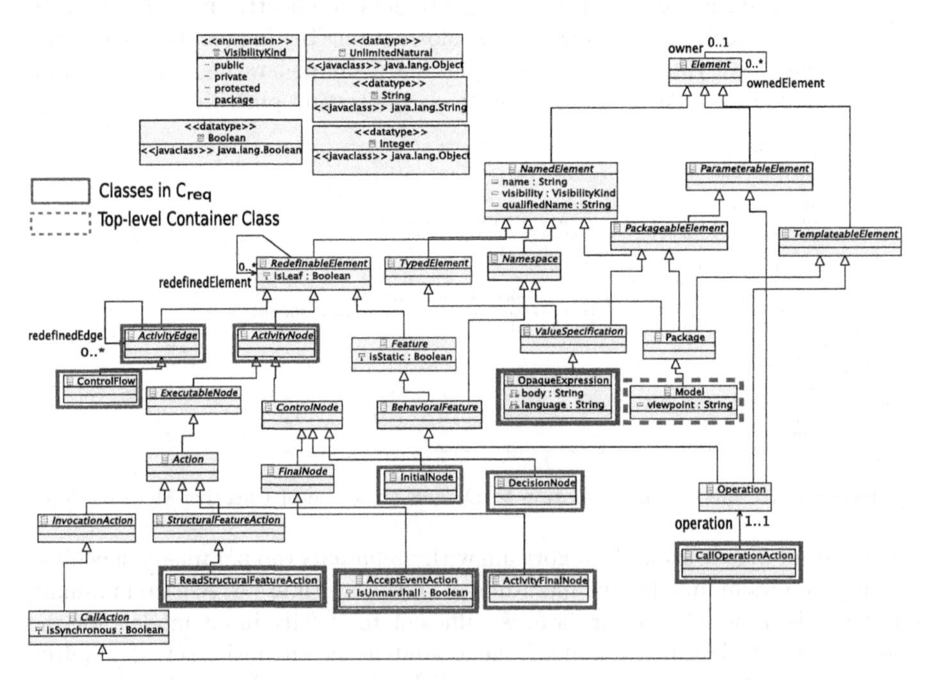

Fig. 6. The Effective UML Activity Diagram Meta-model for the CNES Case Study

Table 1. Meta-model Pruning Results for Options

	Original Uml	No Option	Option 1	Option 2	Option 3
Number of Classes	246	31	31	31	31
Number of Properties	583	15	26	30	30

7 Conclusion

Deriving effective modelling domains is an ubiquitous need in MDE. There are several existing ways such as invariants, pre-conditions and hard-coded knowledge in model editors such as TOPCASED to obtain some form of an effective modelling domain. Most of these approaches patch up the modelling domain with constraints or code to obtain a constrained or effective modelling domain. In this paper, we present an algorithm to extract an effective meta-model from a large meta-model via pruning the large meta-model. Very much like extracting the meta-model of a transient DSML. The input to the algorithm includes the large meta-model and a set of required classes and properties. The algorithm finds all mandatory dependencies between these required concepts. It then prunes the large meta-model such that only the required concepts and its mandatory dependencies are preserved. The flexible algorithm also allows inclusions of non-mandatory properties. The effective meta-model typically has fewer classes and properties compared to the input meta-model and is a super-type of the input meta-model. Therefore, any program written for the effective meta-model will also accept models of the large meta-model. In the future, we would like to integrate the meta-model pruning algorithm to dynamically generate an effective meta-model in MDE tool chains such as editors and transformations. There is also scope for adding more options to control the generation of an effective meta-model for various objectives.

References

1. OMG: UML 2.0 Specfication, `http://www.omg.org/spec/UML/2.0/`
2. Fuentes-Fernández, L., Vallecillo-Moreno, A.: An introduction to uml profiles. UPGRADE, European Journal for the Informatics Professional 5(2), 5–13 (2004)
3. OMG: UML Profile Catalog, `http://www.omg.org/technology/documents/profile_catalog.htm`
4. van Deursen, A., Klint, P., Visser, J.: Domain-specific languages: an annotated bibliography. SIGPLAN Not. 35(6), 26–36 (2000)
5. Solberg, A., France, R., Reddy, R.: Navigating the metamuddle. In: Proceedings of the 4th Workshop in Software Model Engineering, Montego Bay, Jamaica (2005)
6. Niaz, I.A., Tanaka, J.: Code generation from uml statecharts. In: Proc. 7 th IASTED International Conf. on Software Engineering and Application (SEA 2003), Marina Del Rey, pp. 315–321 (2003)
7. Baudry, B., Ghosh, S., Fleurey, F., France, R., Traon, Y.L., Mottu, J.M.: Barriers to systematic model transformation testing. Communications of the ACM (2009)
8. Sen, S., Baudry, B., Mottu, J.M.: On combining mullti-formalism knowledge to select test models for model transformaion testing. In: ACM/IEEE International Conference on Software Testing, Lillehammer, Norway (April 2008)

9. Sen, S., Baudry, B., Mottu, J.M.: Automatic model generation strategies for model transformation testing. In: Paige, R.F. (ed.) ICMT 2009. LNCS, vol. 5563, pp. 148–164. Springer, Heidelberg (2009)
10. Kruchten, P.: The Rational Unified Process: An Introduction, 3rd edn. Addison-Wesley Professional, Reading
11. Phan, T.H., Gerard, S., Terrier, F.: Real-time system modeling with accord/uml methodology: illustration through an automotive case study. In: Languages for system specification: Selected contributions on UML, systemC, system Verilog, mixed-signal systems, and property specification from FDL 2003, pp. 51–70 (2004)
12. Frank, B.: Eclipse Modeling Framework. The Eclipse Series, vol. 1. Addison-Wesley, Reading (2004)
13. Farail, P., Gaufillet, P., Canals, A., Le Camus, C., Sciamma, D., Michel, P., Crégut, X., Pantel, M.: The TOPCASED project: a toolkit in open source for critical aeronautic systems design. In: Embedded Real Time Software (ERTS), Toulouse, February-May (2006)
14. Sendall, S., Kozaczynski, W.: Model transformation: The heart and soul of model-driven software development. IEEE Softw. 20(5), 42–45 (2003)
15. OMG: The Object Constraint Language Specification 2.0, OMG Document: ad/03-01-07 (2007)
16. Lagarde, F., Terrier, F., André, C., Gérard, S.: Extending ocl to ensure model transformations, pp. 126–136 (2007)
17. Taentzer, G., Ehrig, K., Guerra, E., de Lara, J., Lengyel, L., Levendovszky, T., Prange, U., Varró, D., Varró-Gyapay, S.: Model transformation by graph transformation: A comparative study. In: ACM/IEEE 8th International Conference on Model Driven Engineering Languages and Systems, Montego Bay, Jamaica (October 2005)
18. Limited, X.: Language driven development and xmf-mosaic. Whitepaper (2005)
19. Inc., A.: `http://www.adaptive.com/`
20. Fleurey, F., Baudry, B., Muller, P.A., Traon, Y.L.: Towards dependable model transformations: Qualifying input test data. Journal of Software and Systems Modeling, SoSyM (2007)
21. Muller, P.A., Fleurey, F., Jezequel, J.M.: Weaving executability into object-oriented meta-languages. In: Briand, L.C., Williams, C. (eds.) MoDELS 2005. LNCS, vol. 3713, pp. 264–278. Springer, Heidelberg (2005)
22. OMG: Mof 2.0 core specification. Technical Report formal/06-01-01, OMG (April 2006) OMG Available Specification
23. Sen, S.: Meta-model pruning kermeta implementation, `https://www.irisa.fr/triskell/softwares-fr/protos/metamodelpruner/`
24. Steel, J., Jézéquel, J.M.: On model typing. Journal of Software and Systems Modeling (SoSyM) 6(4), 401–414 (2007)
25. Bruce, K.B., Vanderwaart, J.: Semantics-driven language design: Statically type-safe virtual types in object-oriented languages. Electronic Notes in Theoretical Computer Science 20, 50–75 (1999)
26. Steel, J.: Typage de modèles. PhD thesis, Université de Rennes 1 (April 2007)

A UML/MARTE Model Analysis Method for Detection of Data Races in Concurrent Systems

Marwa Shousha[1], Lionel C. Briand[2], and Yvan Labiche[1]

[1] Carleton University, Software Quality Engineering Lab, 1125 Colonel By Drive Ottawa, ON K1S 5B6, Canada
{mshousha,labiche}@sce.carleton.ca
[2] Simula Research Laboratory & University of Oslo, P.O. Box 134, Lysaker, Norway
briand@simula.no

Abstract. The earlier concurrency problems are identified, the less costly they are to fix. As larger, more complex concurrent systems are developed, early detection of problems is made increasingly difficult. We have developed a general approach meant to be used in the context of Model Driven Development. Our approach is based on the analysis of design models expressed in the Unified Modeling Language (UML) and uses specifically designed genetic algorithms to detect concurrency problems. Our main motivation is to devise practical solutions that are applicable in the context of UML design of concurrent systems without requiring additional modeling. All relevant concurrency information is extracted from UML models that comply with the UML Modeling and Analysis of Real-Time and Embedded Systems (MARTE) profile. Our approach was shown to work for both deadlocks and starvation. The current paper addresses data race detection, further illustrating how our approach can be tailored to other concurrency issues. Results on a case study inspired from the Therac-25 radiation machine show that our approach is effective in the detection of data races.

Keywords: MDD, data races, model analysis, concurrent systems, UML, MARTE, genetic algorithms.

1 Introduction

Concurrency problems should be identified early in the design process when they are less costly to fix. This is made increasingly difficult as larger and more complex concurrent systems are being developed. With the recent trend towards Model Driven Development (MDD) [15], the choice of using Unified Modeling Language (UML) models and their extensions as a source of concurrency information at the design level is natural and practical. However, the analysis of concurrency properties should not require additional modeling or a high learning curve on the part of the designers, or should at least minimize it. When the UML notation is not enough to completely model a system, the notation is extended via profiles. The Modeling and Analysis of Real-Time and Embedded Systems (MARTE) profile [19] addresses domain specific aspects of real-time, concurrent system modeling. Our aim is to develop a general

A. Schürr and B. Selic (Eds.): MODELS 2009, LNCS 5795, pp. 47–61, 2009.

automated approach that can be tailored to several types of concurrency errors (such as deadlocks, starvation, data races and data flow problems), and that can be easily integrated into a Model Driven Architecture (MDA) approach, the UML-based MDD standard by the OMG [15]. Our approach relies on a genetic algorithm (GA) that is tailored to different types of concurrency errors.

In previous works, we have tailored a GA for the detection of deadlocks [23] and starvation [13]. This paper is a continuation of these works, where we adapt the approach to the detection of data races. It differs from its predecessors in three areas: 1. A different UML profile is used. Instead of the SPT profile in [23], which was the standard at the time, we use the MARTE profile; 2. We have different GA components. a.) A different chromosome representation (our previous structure of genes [23, 13] contained lock information, which is not needed in the current paper). Since the chromosomes are different, the genetic operators of mutation and crossover are also different (though the principles remain the same, the realizations are different). b.) We use a different fitness function. We used fitness functions specifically designed to detect deadlocks and starvation, respectively [23, 13]. Here, we provide a fitness function geared towards data races; 3. We improve performance comparison. In both previous works, we measured performance against random search only. Here, we also compare our approach with a hill climbing search. Performance of each type of error naturally entails different case studies, each geared towards the respective problem being examined.

We next provide an overview about data races, highlighting the information needed as input to our approach. Sections 3 and 4 provide details of our tailored GA, and tool support. Section 5 describes a case study inspired from the Therac-25 radiation machine, along with results comparing random, hill climbing and GA searches. Related work is presented in Section 6 and we conclude in Section 7.

2 Background

Here we describe data races and aspects of relevance in the MARTE profile.

2.1 Data Races

Concurrency introduces the need for communication between executing *threads* [7]. Threads may communicate via a *shared memory location* during various *access times* for a defined *execution time*. These access and execution times may be specified as ranges, probability distributions, or definite values, although ranges are probably more common due to uncertainty at design time.

The term race condition has been generally used to describe situations where unsynchronized concurrent accesses result in unpredictable program states and behavior [1]. Data races, a specific type of race conditions, are quite common in concurrent systems [1]. These types of faults are due to unsynchronized access to a same memory location. Threads may access a shared location as either *reader threads* or *writer threads*. Problems then arise due to the order of execution of events [1]. While many times unsynchronized access to shared resources is due to errors on the part of the designer, it may also be on purpose to satisfy performance constraints. If undetected, data races can be disastrous in life-critical systems; such was the case with Therac-25

[4]. In general, three conditions must be met before a data race occurs: 1. Two or more threads access the same memory location concurrently, 2. At least one thread accesses the memory location for writing, 3. Thread access to the memory location is unsynchronized. When these three conditions are met, a writer and reader thread may execute concurrently within the shared memory, resulting in inconsistent data.

To proceed with our approach, we must first map the data race concepts, in particular those appearing in italics in this section, to UML and MARTE concepts, as they form the inputs of the GA.

2.2 MARTE Profile to Data Race Mapping

In UML, active objects have their own thread of control, and can be regarded as concurrent threads [12]. Only extensions of the UML standard, such as the MARTE profile [19], provide mechanisms to model detailed information pertaining to concurrency. The MARTE profile is a replacement of the SPT profile [24]. MARTE is geared towards both the real-time and embedded system domains. The profile is roughly divided into three major sub-divisions: 1. MARTE foundation (containing the basis for real-time and embedded system modeling. It defines time concepts and use of concurrent resources), 2. MARTE design model (specializes the foundation, allowing modeling of various features of real-time and embedded systems) 3. MARTE analysis model (allows the annotation of models for system analysis purposes). Much like SPT, the MARTE profile is modular in structure, allowing users to choose the appropriate subsets needed for their applications. We next describe the aspects of the profile that are relevant to our work.

In the MARTE design model, The Software Resource Modeling (SRM) sub-profile presents mechanisms for designing multitasking applications. SRM is subdivided into four packages: SW_ResourceCore (which contains all the basic resource concepts), SW_Concurrency (which contains concurrent execution concepts), SW_Interaction (which deals with communication and synchronization resources) and SW_Brokering (which deals with resource management). In the SW_Concurrency package, concurrently executing entities competing for resources are depicted with the `<<SwConcurrentResource>>` stereotype. As aforementioned, concurrency is also depicted in standard UML, but `<<SwConcurrentResource>>` enhances concurrent execution modeling due to its associated attributes, such as priorityElements, which is used to determine the priority of the associated thread. In the SW_Interaction package, shared resources are identified as `<<SharedDataComResource>>`.

The Generic Quantitative Analysis Modeling (GQAM) sub-profile - part of the MARTE analysis model - defines stereotype `<<saStep>>` (that extends stereotype `<<gaStep>>`) which is used when decisions about the allocation of system resources is made. Its tags include `priority` (the priority of the action on the host processor), `interOccTime` (interval between multiple initiations of the action), and `execTime` (the execution time of the action). Execution times can be specified as maximum and minimum time ranges. In the Timed Constraints subprofile, part of the MARTE foundation model, timed constraints can be specified on the occurrence of an event, on the duration of an execution, or on the temporal distance between two events. These are stereotyped with `<<TimedConstraint>>`.

The High-Level Application Modeling (HLAM) sub-profile from the MARTE design model introduces `<<RtService>>`, a specialized service with specific real-time constraints. It contains several attributes. A particular attribute, `concPolicy`, can be used to determine the type of concurrency policy used for the real-time service. Defined types include `reader` and `writer`.

This overview of MARTE illustrates that the input to our approach (the concepts presented in italics in Section 2.1) can be retrieved from a UML/MARTE design model. The mappings between those concepts and the profile are summarized in Table 1. It is then clear that the information used by our approach can be automatically retrieved from UML/MARTE models, in particular from sequence diagrams where those stereotypes and tags are used.

Table 1. Concept to MARTE Mapping

Concept	MARTE Stereotype/Tag	MARTE sub-profile
Thread	<<SwConcurrentResource>>	SRM::SW_Concurrency
Unprotected resource	<<SharedDataComResource>>	SRM::SW_Interaction
Reader	<<RtService>>/concPolicy = reader	HLAM
Writer	<<RtService>>/concPolicy = writer	HLAM
Thread exec. time in res.	<<gaStep>>/execTime	GQAM:: GQAM_Workload
Thread access time of res.	<<gaStep>>/interOccTime | <<gaStep>>/execTime	GQAM:: GQAM_Workload
Time constraints	<<TimedConstraint>>	TimedConstraints

2.3 Genetic Algorithms

GAs are a means of solving optimization problems. They are based on concepts adopted from genetic and evolutionary theories [10]. A GA first randomly creates an initial population of solutions, called chromosomes, then selects a number of these solutions and performs various genetic operators (mutation and crossover) to create new solutions. The measure of goodness of each solution, called fitness, is compared with other solutions, with only the fittest solutions retained. The process of selection, crossover and mutation, fitness comparison and replacement continues until the stopping criterion, such as a maximum number of generations [10], is reached.

3 Tailored Genetic Algorithm

To use a GA to detect the presence of data races, we must first tailor it by defining the chromosome representation, mutation and crossover operators as well as the fitness function, which we discuss next.

3.1 Chromosome Representation

A chromosome is composed of *genes* and models a solution to the optimization problem. The values to be optimized during data race detection are the access times of threads to a resource, such that the number of threads accessing a resource simultaneously is maximized. These access times are the values that will be altered by the GA to try to reach a data race situation. The access times must reflect schedulable scenarios. In other words, we need to ensure that all execution sequences represented by chromosomes are schedulable. This entails meeting system specifications of periods, minimum arrival times, and so on (see Sections 3.23.3 below). Thus, we need to encode threads (`<<SwConcurrentResource>>`), resources (`<<SharedDataComResource>>`), read and write operations (`<<RtService>>/ concPolicy = read`, `<<RtService>>/concPolicy = write`) and access times (`<<gaStep>> / interOccTime` or `<<gaStep>> / execTime`), which are available in the input model (Table 1).

Since, by definition, a data race involves multiple accesses to the same shared memory location, we consider only one resource at a time. Hence, the gene does not need to contain encoding of the resource, and can be depicted as a 2-tuple (T, a), where *T* is a thread and *a* is *T*'s access time of the resource. A tuple represents the execution of a thread when accessing the resource. Tuples are defined for a user specified time interval during which the designer wants to study the system's behavior. A heuristic for determining an appropriate time interval is given in Section 3.4. A special value of -1 is used to depict access times that lie outside this interval: (T, -1) represents a thread access that does not occur.

Because a chromosome models a solution to the optimization problem, it needs to be large enough to model all schedulable scenarios during the time interval. Hence, the chromosome size (its number of genes) is equal to the total number of times all threads attempt to access the resource in the given time interval. A thread can appear more than once in the chromosome if it accesses the resource multiple times.

Three constraints must be met for the formation of valid chromosomes and to simplify the crossover operation discussed below. 1.) All genes within the chromosome are ordered according to increasing thread identifiers, then increasing access times. 2.) Thread access times of the resource must fall within the specified time interval or are set to -1. 3.) Consecutive genes for the same thread must have access time differences equal to at least the minimum and at most the maximum access time range of the associated thread, if start and end times are defined as ranges.

Consider, for example, the set of three threads accessing a resource named MEOS: T1 (access range [1 325] time units, repeats every 399 time units), T2 (access range [325 398], repeats 400) and T3 (access range [327 392], repeats 400). In a time interval of [0 350] time units, the chromosome length would be three since each of the threads can access the resource at most once during this time interval. The following is then a valid chromosome: (T1, 324) (T2, 340) (T3, -1) where T1 accesses the resource at time unit 324, T2's access is at time 340 and T3 does not access the resource before time 350.

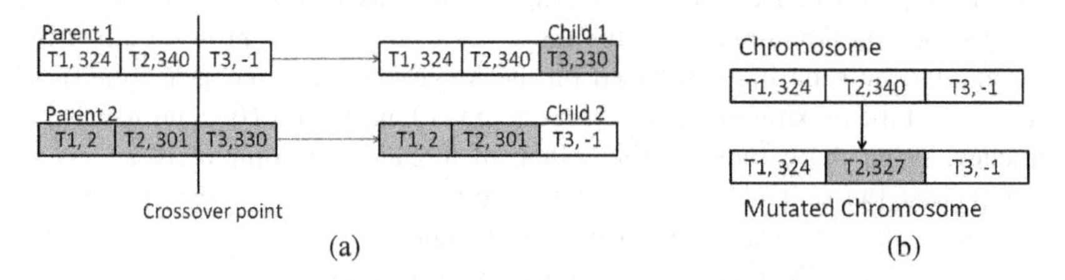

Fig. 1. (a) Crossover example. (b) Mutation example.

3.2 Crossover Operator

Crossover is the means by which desirable traits are passed from parent chromosomes to their offspring [10]. We use a one-point, sexual crossover operator: two parents are randomly split at the same location into two parts which are alternated to produce two children. For example in

Figure 1a, the two parents on the left produce the offspring on the right. If, after crossover, any two consecutive genes of the same thread no longer meet their access time requirements (constraint 3 is violated), the second gene's access time is randomly changed such that constraint 3 is met. This is repeated until all occurrences of this situation satisfy constraint 3.

3.3 Mutation Operator

Mutation introduces new genetic information, hence further exploring the search space, while aiding the GA in avoiding getting caught in local optima [10]. Mutation proceeds as follows: each gene in the chromosome is mutated based on a mutation probability and the resulting chromosome is evaluated for its new fitness. Our mutation operator mutates a gene by altering its access time. The rationale is to move access times along the specified time interval, with the aim of finding the optimal times at which these access times will be more likely to result in data races. When a gene is chosen for mutation, a new timing value is randomly chosen from the range of possible access range values. If the value chosen lies outside the time interval, the timing information is set to -1 to satisfy constraint 2. Similar to the crossover operator, if, after mutation, two consecutive genes no longer meet their access time requirements, the affected genes are altered such that the requirements are met. For the example of Figure 1b with access times [1 325], [325 398] and [327 392] in a time interval of [0 350], assume Parent 1's second gene is chosen for mutation. A new value (say, 327) is chosen from its access time range [325 398], as shown in Figure 1b.

3.4 Fitness Function

The fitness function determines the merit of a chromosome. Recall that data races occur when at least two threads share a resource and at least one is a writer thread. For the fitness function to be effective, the time interval over which it is defined must be adequate: it should be long enough for data races to occur, but not too long as it may hinder the performance of the search algorithm. This varies from system to system and depends on the amount of time resources available. We propose a heuristic for determining the time interval based on the longest thread execution time in the resource (*lt*) and the maximum resource access time of all threads (*lr*). Our heuristic is to guarantee, using these two variables, that all threads can completely access the resource at least twice. Therefore, the time interval equals: [0 $(lt+lr)*2$]. This is a minimum interval, as having threads access the resource just once may not be enough to uncover a data race. Designers can opt for a larger interval.

We define the following fitness function:

$$f(c) = \min_{i=startTime\,to\,endTime} \begin{cases} |W_i - N(W_i)| & if\#W_i \geq 1 \\ endTime & if\#W_i = 0 \end{cases} \quad (1)$$

StartTime and *endTime* are the starting and ending times of the time interval. W_i is the time unit i during which a writer thread accesses the shared resource. $N(W_i)$ is the time unit i of the nearest executing thread to W_i within the resource. W_i and $N(W_i)$ are in the range [*startTime endTime*]. $\#W_i$ is the total number of writer threads that access the resource during the time unit i. N, W_i and $\#W_i$ are obtained after scheduling.

The fitness function of equation (1) is a minimizing function; hence, it gives lower values to fitter individuals. Essentially, the fitness function minimizes the difference of resource access times between writer threads and any other thread (reader or writer). The smaller the difference, the closer the overlapping execution of a writer thread with another thread. A fitness value of zero indicates the presence of a data race, whereby the writer thread is executing within the resource at the same time unit as another thread, hence a data race. This is one of the properties of the function that guides the search towards situations where data races are possible and increasingly likely. The fitness function also ensures that scenarios where data races are possible (two threads executing and at least one is a writer) are always rewarded over situations where no data races are possible (when zero or one thread is executing, regardless of its type).

Let us consider the scheduling of the mutated chromosome in Figure 1b, where T1 is a writer thread and all other threads are readers. The time interval is assumed to be [0 350]. Using equation (1) for Figure 2, we examine the time units for resource R1:

At time units 321, 322, and 323: $\#W_i = 0$, min = 350

At time unit 324: $\#W_i = 1$, $W_i = 324$, $N(W_i) = 327$, absolute difference = 3, min = 3

At time unit 325, 326, and 327: $\#W_i = 0$, min = 350

then, f(c) = 3.

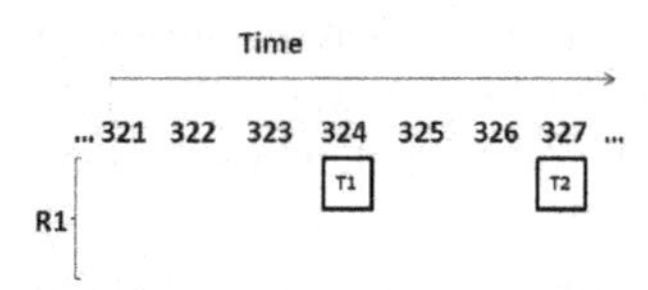

Fig. 2. Fitness function example

4 Tool and GA Parameters

We have built a prototype tool, Concurrency Fault Detector (CFD), for detection of data races using our approach. CFD is an automated system that identifies concurrency errors in any concurrent application modeled with the UML/MARTE notation. Currently, it can help identify deadlock, starvation [23, 13] and data race errors. CFD involves a sequence of steps. Users first input three categories of information: (1) UML/MARTE sequence diagrams for the analyzed system, (2) the execution time interval during which the system is to be analyzed, and (3) the type of concurrency error targeted: data race, deadlock or starvation. In the latter case, the target thread and target lock are also inputted. CFD then extracts the required information from the inputted UML/MARTE model (mainly from its sequence diagrams) and feeds it to the appropriate GA.

CFD is decomposed into two modular portions: a scheduler and a genetic algorithm. This modularity ensures that modifications can seamlessly be adapted to meet a wider set of requirements. Modifications to the scheduling strategy would only require altering the scheduler. Hence, the scheduler does not affect the applicability of our approach as it is merely a black box that aides in the calculation of the fitness function. It emulates single processor execution as it tracks all thread executions.

In the GA for data races, if a data race is detected, CFD outputs the sequence resulting in the data race as well as the time unit at which the data race occurs and a textual depiction of the threads executing within the resource at that time. If no such sequence is found, CFD terminates after 1000 generations, outputting the execution sequence with the lowest fitness value (since it is a minimization function). This does not guarantee that no data races exist. However, one can still feel more confident that such a case is unlikely (i.e., rare in the search space).

Since collecting input data is easy to automate from a UML case tool, and all the other phases are automated, CFD is meant to be used interactively: the user is expected to fix the design of the system when CFD terminates with a detected deadlock, data race, or starvation. This is the main reason why we developed a strategy that only reports one concurrency fault scenario at a time, i.e., per run of CFD, allowing designers to fix the system's design before running the modified design again on CFD.

Though various parameters of the GA must be specified, we can fortunately rely on a substantial literature reporting empirical results and making recommendations. Parameters include the type of GA used, population size, mutation and crossover rates and selection operator. We use a steady state GA, with a replacement percentage of 100%. The population size we apply is 200. This is higher than the size suggested in [10], but works more effectively for larger search spaces. The selection operator is rank selector, whereby chromosomes with higher fitness are more likely to be chosen than ones with lower fitness [18]. Mutation and crossover rates are $1.75/\gamma\sqrt{l}$ (where γ denotes the population size and l is the length of the chromosome) and 0.8, respectively. Both are based on the findings in [16] and [10], respectively.

All parameter values are based on findings reported in the literature, except population size, which was fine tuned after some experimentation. These parameter values have worked exceedingly well in all our case studies when considering both the detection rate and execution time to find a concurrency error. The same parameter values can be used for different systems designs, though further empirical investigation is required to ensure the generality of these parameter values. In the worst case, if one wants to be on the safe side and ensure fully optimal results, the parameters can be fine tuned once for each new system design: when the system design being checked is first analyzed. For further design modifications of the same system, the parameters need not be fine tuned.

We have used CFD on the case study presented next to assess our approach.

5 Case Study: Therac-25 (Therac)

The case study we use was inspired from the Therac-25 machine. The infamous Therac-25 was a computer controlled radiation therapy machine that was responsible for overdosing six patients. Investigations into the causes behind the overdoses

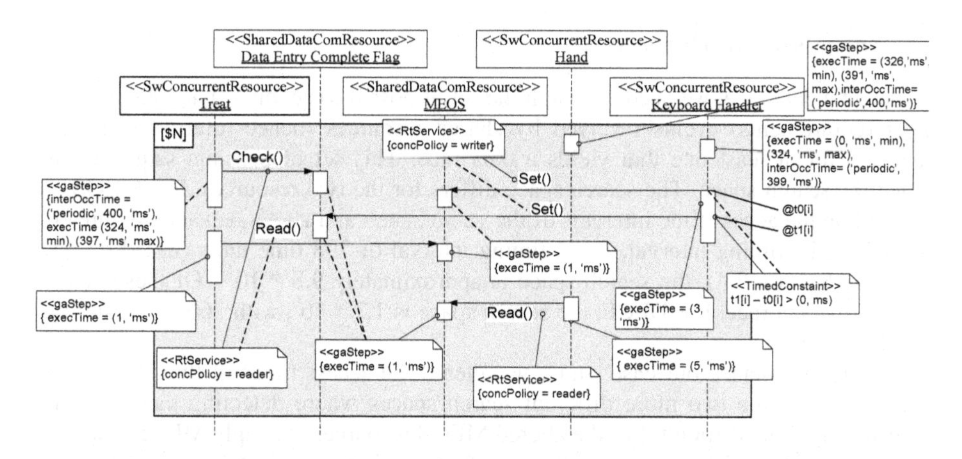

Fig. 3. Therac sequence diagram

revealed faults due to race conditions, whereby the high power electronic beam was activated (instead of the low power one), without the beam spreader plate rotated into place [4]. The original design of the Therac-25 system—or simply Therac—has been altered here, whereby access times of threads to resources have been increased to provide a larger search space, thus reflecting more realistic situations.

5.1 Therac Extended with MARTE

Figure 3 shows the UML/MARTE sequence diagram of the shared resources in Therac. The treatment monitor task, `Treat`, controls the phases of radiation treatment. It uses a control variable to determine which phase of the treatment is to be executed next. In the first phase, a check is performed to see whether the required radiation levels have been inputted. This check is performed by reading a variable named data entry complete flag (DECF), which is set by the keyboard handler task, where the operator of Therac enters radiation level information. DECF is set whenever the cursor is moved to the command line. Information about the radiation level specified by the operator is encoded into a two byte variable named MEOS (Mode/Energy offset). The higher byte of MEOS is used by `Treat` to set various parameters. The lower byte is used by `Hand`, which rotates the turntable according to the inputted energy and mode.

In the figure, two resources, MEOS and DECF, are shared as indicated by `<<SharedDataComResource>>`. The former is read and set by the three available threads designated with the `<<SwConcurrentResource>>` stereotype. The latter resource is only read and set by the `Treat` and `KeyboardHandler` threads. `Treat` periodically reads DECF between [324 397] and repeats at 400 ms. `KeyboardHandler` is a writer thread on the same resource. The same thread also sets MEOS. However, the write access to MEOS occurs before the write access to DECF; there is at least a one ms interval. The `Hand` thread periodically reads MEOS between [327 392] ms interval and repeats every 400 milliseconds.

5.2 Analysis of Search Space

To detect a data race, we need to search the set of possible (i.e. ones that adhere to the input requirements) events received by shared resources (hence referred to as sequences) for at least one that yields a data race. This set of possible sequences is called the search space. The search space differs for the two resources. For MEOS, it is based on the access time intervals of the `Treat`, `Hand` and `KeyboardHandler` threads as well as the timing interval. For a timing interval of 798 time units (based on our heuristic, Section 3.4), the search space is approximately $9.8 * 10^{12}$. Of these, $4.1 * 10^{8}$ yield a data race. For DECF, the search space is $1.7 * 10^{9}$, with 360,750 resulting in a data race.

To further enhance our case study, we altered the access times of threads in both resources to create two more different search spaces where detecting data races is significantly more difficult. For the altered MEOS resource, or simply MEOS2, with a timing interval of 2500 time units, the search space[1] is approximately $4.7 * 10^{9}$, with 4510 yielding a data race. For the altered DECF, or simply DECF2, with a timing interval of 800, the search space is $1.0 * 10^{7}$, with 99 resulting in a data race. We can then better assess how the performance of search techniques is affected by the difficulty of the search.

A search space is further characterized by its complexity. Points in the search space that result in data races are called global optima, whereas local optima are ones where all surrounding points have worse fitness, but the point itself is not an instance of a data race. The more local optima in the search space, the more complex it is. In both MEOS resources, the search space is complex, with many local optima. For DECF and DECF2, the search space has a few local optima, thus simplifying the search.

5.3 Case Study Design

We begin by describing the different techniques used, then relating how the case study was set up.

Description

We use three different techniques to detect data races: random generation, hill climbing and our GA approach. Both random and hill climbing are simpler techniques that are often suggested as benchmarks to justify the need for a GA search [25].

In random generation, a point in the search space (representing a sequence of resource accesses by various threads) is randomly chosen and checked for a data race. Running a random search involves running a pre-determined, usually large number of points in the search space.

For hill climbing, one random point is generated, then neighboring points are examined, with the one better than the current point replacing it. This continues until a point is reached that has no better neighbor. For Therac, a neighbor is one that differs by just one access value from the current point. For example, consider three threads, T1, T2 and T3, accessing a shared resource during the access time intervals [1 2], [3 5] and [6 7],

---

[1] Here, the search spaces are smaller than that of MEOS and DECF because thread access times are longer.

respectively. If the current point is (T1, 2) (T2, 3) (T3, 6), one valid neighbor would be: (T1, 1) (T2, 3) (T3, 6) which differs in only one access value from the current point.

Fairness of Comparisons

Because each of the three techniques proceeds differently, we generated the same number of sequences for other techniques as the GA to ensure a fair comparison. As GAs are a heuristic optimization technique, variance occurs in the results they produce. To account for this variability, we ran our case study 50 times on an Intel Core 2 2.0 GHz processor. Random generation and hill climbing were also run 50 times, with each run generating the same number of sequences as the number created and evaluated by a GA run. In the original design, with a timing interval of 802, a GA run generates on average 5184 sequences for MEOS and 4640 for DECF. In the altered design, the GA generates 6786 sequences on average for MEOS2 in a timing interval of 2500, and it generates 11681 sequences on average for DECF2 in a timing interval of 800. In all cases, for random, hill climbing and the GA, when a data race is detected, execution stops and a new run of the 50 is executed.

5.4 Results

Results of the detection rate of data races are presented in Table 2. All three techniques are capable of detecting data races in both MEOS and DECF, but with very different probabilities. Hill climbing does not fare very well in the former case. It appears to be oftentimes caught in local optima: 96% of the time, it is unable to detect a data race. This empirically suggests that the search space for MEOS is complex. We observe that our GA does better: 34% detection rate for MEOS. This confirms that where the search space is large and complex, GAs are known to yield much better results than the two other techniques [17]. Complexity is not an issue in random search because information about the landscape of the search space is not used during the search. However, random search performs poorly in MEOS due to the small percentage of sequences leading to a data race: only 0.004% of the search space yields a data race.

Table 2. Comparison of Performance

		MEOS	DECF	MEOS2	DECF2
	Search Space Size	$9.8 * 10^{12}$	$1.7 * 10^{9}$	$4.7 * 10^{9}$	$1.0 * 10^{7}$
	% of Data Race Sequences	0.004	0.02	$9.5 * 10^{-5}$	$9.5 * 10^{-4}$
Random	#Detections/#Runs	3/50	10/50	0/50	2/50
	Total Runtime (min:sec:ms)	01:07::281	00:44:324	04:29:819	01:52:818
	Detection rate	6%	20%	0%	4%
GA	#Detections/#Runs	17/50	49/50	4/50	43/50
	Total Runtime (min:sec:ms)	01:34:255	01:01:80	05:40:749	02:46:760
	Detection rate	34%	98%	8%	86%
Hill Climbing	# Detections /#Runs	2/50	50/50	1/50	50/50
	Total Runtime (min:sec:ms)	00:53:980	0:12:862	04:38:062	00:14:087
	Detection rate	4%	100%	2%	100%

On the other hand, in the case of the simpler DECF search space, hill climbing does exceedingly well, detecting data races in all runs. Here too, random search performs relatively well, owing to the higher percentage of sequences leading to a data race (0.02%). A GA is therefore of no benefit in this case, although it too performs well.

For MEOS2 and DECF2, the search spaces are of similar complexity as MEOS and DECF, respectively, but with smaller sizes and lower percentage of sequences leading to a data race. For MEOS2, the search space is large and complex, with $9.5 * 10^{-5}\%$ of sequences leading to a data race. Both random and hill climbing perform very poorly. The GA, while performing worse than for MEOS, still manages to detect data races four times as much as hill climbing. In DECF2, random performs worse because of the lower percentage of data race sequences ($9.5 * 10^{-4}\%$). The GA too performs worse than for DECF. Hill climbing remains unaffected by the size of the search space and changes in data race probabilities, probably due to the simplicity of the search space (few local optima).

In all MEOS cases, the GA far outperforms both random and hill climbing techniques. This confirms that it fares much better in large, complex search spaces, and is therefore a better option in many practical cases where such characteristics are likely to be present. As expected, the execution time of the GA is longer than the other techniques, yet in complex search spaces (MEOS) the difference with hill climbing is of the order of 20-30%. For both cases of DECF, where the search space is smaller and less complex, the GA detection rate is somewhat comparable to hill climbing, which is designed for such search spaces.

In large, complex search spaces, where few sequences yield data races, the GA yields significantly higher detection probabilities than other techniques. Because these probabilities for a run can still remain low, the GA must be run as many times as possible, given time constraints, to obtain the highest possible overall probability of detecting data races. Using the most complex case (MEOS2) as an example, with an 8% probability of data race detection, 50 GA runs results in a probability of less than 2% (0.92^{50}) not to detect a data race in at least one run, with a bit more than five minutes of execution time. Such execution times can of course be brought down significantly with faster hardware and parallel computing. Even when in practice the complexity of the search space is not known and it is not clear what percentage of this space results in a data race, using the GA will in the worst case yield comparable detection rates to hill climbing.

6 Related Work

In the context of detecting data races in concurrent systems, a number of works exist. Some [8, 9, 11, 14], do so using the code of the system under test. Kahlon et al. [14] begin by statically detecting the presence of shared variables in the code, before proceeding to output warnings about the presence of data races. Chugh et al. [20] also use a form of static analysis. In their work, they use program code to develop a data flow analysis for the system under test. They combine this with an independent race detection engine to return a version of the analysis that is suitable for concurrent threads. Both approaches necessitate putting off the detection of data races until the system under test is implemented. This has the disadvantage that any data races that are found due to design faults are very costly to fix. Furthermore, data races due to dynamically allocated shared resources might go undetected. Other works, such as Savage et al., tackle this point. They also use system code in their Eraser tool, but do so dynamically (at run time). In so doing, they ensure that dynamically allocated shared variables involved in data races are also detected [21]. There are limitations to their technique, however, the most important of which is that they are limited to examining paths that are triggered by their test cases. If the test cases chosen are not sufficient to visit a particular path where data races occur, the data race will remain undetected.

Model checking has been used to detect data races in concurrent systems, such as in the Java Path Finder [22]. The aim here is the same as our aim: to detect problems arising from system models. However, what differs is the context: our approach is meant to be used in the context of MDD, specifically MDA. As such, we rely on UML extended with profiles, rather than temporal logic specifications.

Of particular interest is the work by Lei, Wang and Li [2]. Here, the authors use a model-based approach for the detection of data races. Data races are identified by checking the state transitions of shared resources at runtime. The corresponding test scenarios leading to the race are then identified using UML activity diagrams extended with data operation tags. This extension is necessary as UML activity diagrams provide no means to model data sharing. Hence, the authors extend them with stereotypes to depict data sharing. The extended UML diagrams can then serve as an oracle for verifying execution traces. They also serve to ensure that both code and design are consistent. Lei, Wang and Li present results for two case studies. In the online store system, they discover five instances of data races. In the elevator system, they discover none. The authors note that they use random testing for comparison, but do not report results for it. They also do not provide execution times for their approach [2].

With the current trend towards MDD [15], models are regarded as the essence of system development. While their development may be time consuming, they can be used to partially automate other activities. The approach we propose is meant to be used in the context of the OMG's MDA, hence our reliance on the UML standard and MARTE profile, thereby reusing existing design models instead of developing specific models (as in the work by Lei et al.) or waiting until the system is implemented to execute its code. As all information required by our approach can be incorporated in the UML model of a system, this eliminates the need for additional modeling activities (e.g., using temporal logic). Use of the standard MARTE extension also eliminates the need for haphazard additions (e.g., extensions for modeling data sharing by Lei et al.). Furthermore, standard profiles tend to be implemented within commercial tools, once the profile has been approved (Rational Rhapsody 7.5 already includes the MARTE profile). While the sequence diagrams required by CFD may not be as detailed as required when the system is initially designed, adding information to these pre-existing diagrams for testing purposes is probably easier than working with a different model, such as in the case of Java Path Finder. In essence, our approach can be thought of as a guided random search to be used in the context of MDA.

In the context of MDD, a number of works utilize MARTE's predecessor: the SPT profile. Such works mostly focus on performance analysis rather than the analysis of model properties [3]. Other works use the MARTE profile, but with other aims than uncovering concurrency faults [6, 5]. In [6], the profile is used to create an approach for real-time embedded system modeling along with transformations to execute those models. In [5], the authors aim at probing the capabilities of MARTE by applying it to a case study.

7 Conclusions

Concurrency abounds in many software systems, where threads typically access many shared resources. If not handled properly, such accesses can lead to errors, and serious system failures. The earlier any such problem is detected during the design process, the better. In this paper, we describe an approach, based on a tailored GA search, for detecting data races. The approach is based on the analysis of design representations in UML completed with the MARTE profile. Since our goal is to provide an automated approach that can be applied in the context of model-driven, UML-based development, the choice of UML/MARTE was natural as it is the de facto standard for the object-oriented modeling of concurrent, real-time applications. This is also practical as it reduces the need for complex tooling and training, while reusing models already required for UML-based development. Our findings suggest that the GA has much higher chances than simpler alternatives (e.g., hill climbing) to detect data races when the search space is large and complex and few sequences lead to a data race, a situation we expect to be increasingly common in the design of industrial concurrent systems. Results also show that in our most complex case the probability of not detecting a data race is less than 2%, using a bit more than five minutes of execution time. Our current work focuses on providing a general framework that can be easily adapted to different types of concurrency problems.

References

1. Chen, L.: The Challenge of Race Conditions in Parallel Programming. Sun Developer Network, Sun Microsystems, http://developers.sun.com/solaris/articles/raceconditions.html
2. Lei, B., Wang, L., Li, X.: UML Activity Diagram Based Testing of Java Concurrent Programs for Data Race and Inconsistency. In: 1st International Conference on Software Testing, Verification and Validation, pp. 200–209. IEEE Press, Los Alamitos (2008)
3. Petriu, D.C.: Performance analysis with the SPT profile. In: Gerard, S., Babau, J., Champeau, J. (eds.) Model-Driven Engineering of Distributed and Embedded Systems, pp. 205–224. Wiley-ISTE (2005)
4. Leveson, N.: Safeware: System Safety and Computers. Addison-Wesley, Reading (1995)
5. Demathieu, S., Thomas, F., Andre, C., Gerard, S., Terrier, F.: First experiments using the UML profile for MARTE. In: 11th IEEE International Symposium on Object Oriented Real-Time Distributed Computing, pp. 50–57. The Printing House (2008)
6. Mradiha, C., Tanguy, Y., Jouvray, C., Terrier, F., Gerard, S.: An execution framework for MARTE-based models. In: 13th IEEE International Conference on Engineering of Complex Computer Systems, pp. 222–227. The Printing House (2008)
7. Downey, A.B.: The Little Book of Semaphores, 2nd edn. Green Tea Press (2005)

8. Flanagan, C., Freund, S.N.: Type-Based Race Detection for Java. ACM SIGPLAN Notices 35(5), 219–232 (2000)
9. Flanagan, C., Rustan, K., Leino, M., Lillibridge, M., Nelson, G., Saxe, J.B., Stata, R.: Extended Static Checker for Java. ACM SIGPLAN Notices 37(5), 234–245 (2002)
10. Haupt, R.L., Haupt, S.E.: Practical genetic algorithms. Wiley, Chichester (1998)
11. Abadi, M., Flanagan, C., Freund, S.N.: Types for Safe Locking: Static Race Detection for Java. ACM TOPLAS 28(2), 207–255 (2006)
12. OMG: Unified Modeling Language (UML). Version 2.1.2, `http://www.omg.org/cgi-bin/doc?formal/09-02-02.pdf`
13. Shousha, M., Briand, L.C., Labiche, Y.: A UML/MARTE Model Analysis Methodology for Detection of Starvation and Deadlocks in Concurrent Systems. Technical Report SCE-09-01. Carleton University, Canada (2009)
14. Kahlon, V., Yang, Y., Sankaranarayanan, S., Gupta, A.: Fast and Accurate Static Data-Race Detection for Concurrent Programs. In: Damm, W., Hermanns, H. (eds.) CAV 2007. LNCS, vol. 4590, pp. 226–239. Springer, Heidelberg (2007)
15. Kleppe, A., Warmer, J., Bast, W.: MDA Explained - The Model Driven Architecture: Practice and Promise. Addison-Wesley, Reading (2003)
16. Back, T.: Self-adaptation in genetic algorithms. In: Proceedings of European Conference on Artificial Life, pp. 263–271. MIT Press, Cambridge (1992)
17. Mahfoud, S.W., Goldberg, D.E.: Parallel recombinative simulated annealing: a genetic algorithm. Parallel Computing 21(1), 1–28 (1995)
18. Koza, J.R.: Genetic programming: on the programming of computers by means of natural selection. MIT Press, Cambridge (1992)
19. OMG: UML Profile for Modeling and Analysis of Real-time and Embedded Systems, `http://www.omg.org/cgi-bin/apps/doc?ptc/08-06-08.pdf`
20. Chugh, R., Voung, J.W., Jhala, R., Lerner, S.: Dataflow Analysis for Concurrent Programs Using Datarace Detection. In: ACM PLDI, pp. 316–326. ACM, New York (2008)
21. Savage, S., Burrows, M., Nelson, G., Sobalvarro, P., Anderson, T.: Eraser: A Dynamic Data Race Detector for Multithreaded Programs. ACM TOCS 15(4), 391–411 (1997)
22. Brat, G., Havelund, K., Park, S., Visser, W.: Java Pathfinder Second Generation of a Java Model Checker. In: Proceedings of Workshop on Advances in Verification (2000)
23. Shousha, M., Briand, L., Labiche, Y.: A UML/SPT model analysis methodology for concurrent systems based on genetic algorithms. In: Czarnecki, K., Ober, I., Bruel, J.-M., Uhl, A., Völter, M. (eds.) MODELS 2008. LNCS, vol. 5301, pp. 475–489. Springer, Heidelberg (2008)
24. OMG: UML Profile for Schedulability, Performance and Time Specification, `http://www.omg.org/docs/formal/05-01-02.pdf`
25. Ali, S., Briand, L.C., Hemmati, H., Panesar-Walawege, R.K.: A Systematic Review of the Application and Empirical Investigation of Search-based Test-Case Generation. Technical Report Simula. SE. 293. Simula Research Laboratory, Norway (2009)

Model Driven Performance Measurement and Assessment with MoDePeMART*

Marko Bošković[1] and Wilhelm Hasselbring[2]

[1] Athabasca University, Canada
marko.boskovic@athabascau.ca
[2] Software Engineering Group, University of Kiel, Germany
wha@informatik.uni-kiel.de

Abstract. Software performance is one of important software Quality of Service attributes. For this reason, several approaches integrate performance prediction in Model Driven Engineering(MDE). However, MDE still lacks a systematic approach for performance measurement and metrics assessment. This paper presents MoDePeMART, an approach for Model Driven Performance Measurement and Assessment with Relational Traces. The approach suggests declarative specification of performance metrics in a domain specific language and usage of relational databases for storage and metric computation. The approach is evaluated with the implementation of a UML Profile for UML Class and State diagrams and transformations from profile to a commercial relational database management system.

Keywords: Software Performance Measurement and Assessment, Model Driven Engineering, Transformational and Reactive Systems.

1 Introduction

Increasing dependency on software systems, and consequences of their failures, raises the question of software system trustworthiness [1]. In order to use software systems as dependable systems, means for quantification, verification, and contractual trust of those systems are being invented.

Means of quantification, verification, and contractual trust have to be done for both, functional and non-functional requirements. Functional requirements define functionality which is the objective of the system. Non-functional requirements are constraints on system's functionality offered by the system like security, privacy, reliability, timeliness etc [2]. They are characteristics of functionality design and implementation, and often are called quality requirements [1].

Some of the non-functional properties of a service, of particular interest to users, are often specified with the Quality of Service (QoS). Performance, is one of the QoS attributes. In this paper, performance is defined as degree to which

* This work is supported by the German Research Foundation(DFG), grant GRK 1076/1.

A. Schürr and B. Selic (Eds.): MODELS 2009, LNCS 5795, pp. 62–76, 2009.

objectives for timeliness are met [3]. It describes timing behavior of a software system and it is measured with metrics like throughput and response time.

Significance of meeting non-functional requirements in trustworthy software systems development, requires addressing them in the early design phases, in parallel to functional requirements. For this reason, research in meting performance requirements in Model Driven Engineering (MDE) was mostly dedicated to performance predictions with analytical modeling and simulation, e.g. [4]. Performance measurement and empirical assessment of predicted values are left to be done with profiling tools, or various techniques of manual insertions of code for data collection and metrics computation. There is still not a model driven approach for performance measurement and assessment.

This paper shows an approach for **Mo**del **D**riven **Pe**rformance **M**easurement and **A**ssessment with **R**elational **T**races) called ***MoDePeMART***. The essence of the approach is: (1) declarative specification of measurement points and metrics in a domain specific language, (2) automatic generation of code for data collection, storage, and metrics computation, and (3) usage of Relational Database Management Systems (RDBMS) for performance data storage and computation.

The paper is structured as follows. Section 2 explains the need for a model driven approach for performance measurement and assessment. Measurement and assessment with **MoDePeMART** is depicted in Section 3. The metamodel which enables declarative specification of measurements and metrics computation is described in Section 4. The evaluation of the approach through the implementation as a UML Profile for UML Class and State diagrams and transformations to MySQL RDBMS is shown in Section 5. Section 6 contains the comparative analysis of the approach with other approaches for performance measurement and assessment. The limitations (assumptions) of the approach are specified in Section 7. Section 8 gives an outlook of the approach and the directions for the future work.

2 Motivation

MDE is a software engineering paradigm which suggests using models as the primary artifacts of software development. It relies on two basic principles [5]: abstraction and automation.

Abstraction suggests usage of Domain Specific Modeling Languages (DSMLs). DSMLs are specialized modeling languages for solving classes of domain problems. Users of DSMLs are experts of that domain. Accordingly, DSMLs contain concepts used by domain experts. With DSMLs domain experts specify solutions to domain problems without being distracted by implementation details.

Automation handles implementation. It suggests transformations of DSML models to implementations. This principle can be seen as one more level of compilation.

In such a development process performance analyst faces several problems when trying to measure and assess performance. First, the modeling language used for software functionality development might not support constructs needed

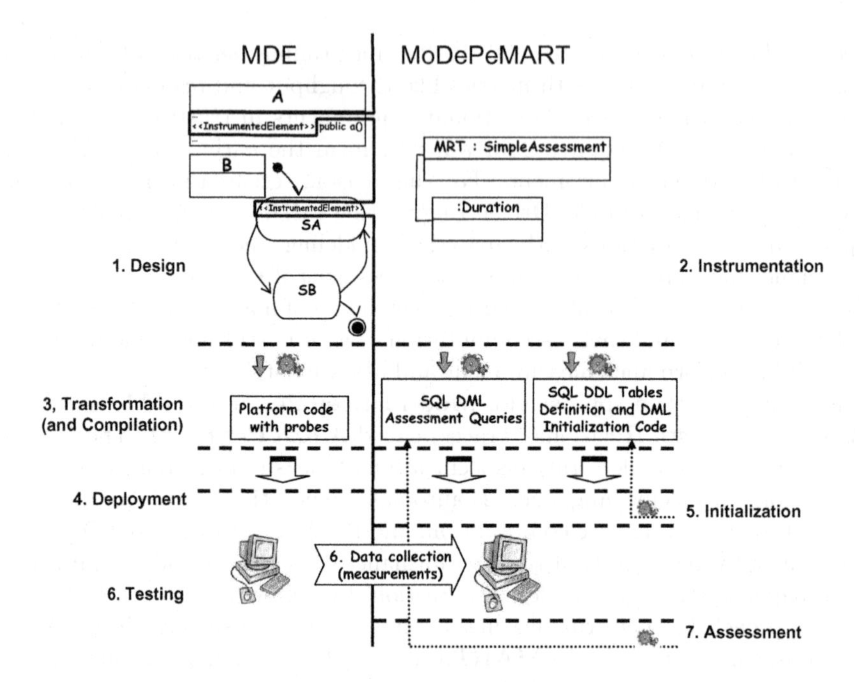

Fig. 1. Performance Measurement and Assessment in MDE with MoDePeMART

for the performance measurement and assessment, such as routines for obtaining time. Second, even if it does, a performance analyst is not an expert in that modeling language, and it might be difficult for him to use it. Finally, data collection and assessment at the platform level can be error-pronouns. In order to do it a performance analyst would have to know how the domain specific constructs are transformed to the platform. To remove these problems we suggest declarative specification of metrics of interest in DSML and automatic instrumentation and code generation, facilitated with the **MoDePeMART** approach and depicted in the next section.

3 MoDePeMART: Model Driven Performance Measurement and Assessment with Relational Traces

MoDePeMART integrates performance measurement and assessment in MDE, in such a way that it is transparent to the developer. The example on UML is described in Figure 1.

After the design model is finalized (1), the instrumentation (2) takes place. Here, measurement points are specified in the model. Furthermore, also are specified metrics of interest. Finally, the context of the service is specified. More on context is explained in Subsection 3.1. Measurement points, metrics, and context are specified in the DSML defined in Section 4.

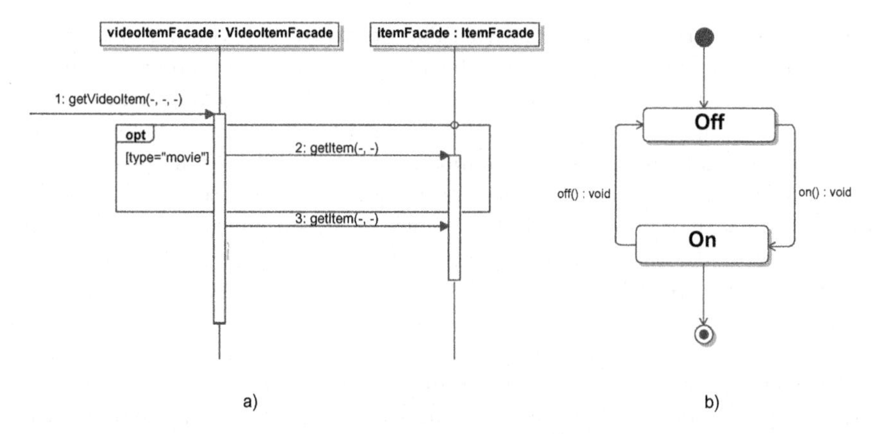

Fig. 2. Transformational (a) and reactive (b) behavior in **getVideoItem** method invocation

From the design and performance measurement and assessment model transformation (3) generates software code with integrated code for performance data collection, and code for performance data storage and metrics computation. The generated code for performance data storage and metrics computation is SQL DDL code for tables needed for data storage, and SQL DML code for initial table entries required for metrics computation. The transformation is followed by compilation of the platform code.

After the deployment (5) of the generated code, RDBMS for storing and metrics computation is initialized (6). Next, execution of test cases takes place during which data about software execution are collected(7). Finally, to compute performance metrics SQL DML queries are executed (8).

MoDePeMART approach is language independent approach. However, it assumes some characteristics of modeling languages and systems. These characteristics and performance assessment in such systems are discussed in the next section.

3.1 Transformational and Reactive Software Systems and Performance Assessment

MoDePeMART assumes that a modeling language for software development facilitates modeling of two subsystems: transformational and reactive. Transformational [6] systems are systems which take some input value and transform them to some output value through the set of steps specified by some algorithm. For the same input value, they will always go through the same steps. An example of transformational software system is in Figure 2 a).

The **getVideoItem** method is a method for obtaining video items in a small electronic items management application. Two kinds of items are obtained from the database with this method: a movie and a music video item. When user requests a movie, the value of the variable **type** is “movie” and the user gets two files: a movie trailer and the movie. The **getItem** invocation 2 obtains the trailer and the invocation 3 obtains the movie. When user requests a music video item, the value of **type** is not "movie" and only the **getItem** invocation 3 executes. This invocation obtains a music video file from the database.

Transformational programs are composed of [7]: simple commands (e.g. assigning a value to a variable), composite commands (e.g. a command block), guarded command (e.g. a UML option block or *if* statement), guarded command set (e.g. UML alternatives or the **C** *switch* statement), and loops. These commands are composed with two relations [7]: invocation (one uses another one) and sequential composition (one executes before another one).

Reactive software systems are systems which receive stimuli from environment and either change internal state, or produce some action in environment. The behavior depends on both stimulus and current system state. The reactive subsystem of the **ItemFacade** manages the data compression in database and the **getItem** method communication. When the state is **On**, the data is compressed in the DBMS and decompressed at the **ItemFacade** side. When **Off**, there is no compression.

The context of the service execution has to be taken into account when assessing performance. Inappropriate context specification can lead to inappropriate performance assessment. In systems with interwoven transformational and reactive part, both, transformational and reactive context have to be taken into account. Transformational context is the sequence of method (non)executions before and after the required service. For example, let us assume that it is of interest the response time of the **getItem** method when obtaining a movie file. If only the execution of the **getItem** would be considered without any specification of previous executions, the computed response time would also include executions of the **getItem** outside of the **getVideoItem** method. One more attempt without the specification of context is to consider the time between the invocation of the 3. **getItem** method from the **getVideoItem** method and the arrival of it's return value. However, in this case the final response time includes obtaining movies and music videos. The solution is in specification that the response time is computed for **getItem** method invoked from the **getVideoItem** and that the optional block did not execute before the **getItem** execution.

Reactive context is the state of the system. The state can have a diverse impact on response time. For example, if the communication in the previous example is compressed, obtaining a movie response time can be reduced. However, the response time of obtaining a trailer can be increased. Due to the small size of the trailer the compression, transfer of compressed data, and decompression can take more time than transfer of non-compressed data.

4 The Metamodel for Performance Measurement and Assessment

In previous section it is explained that the **MoDePeMART** suggest declarative specification of performance measurements and metrics computation with a

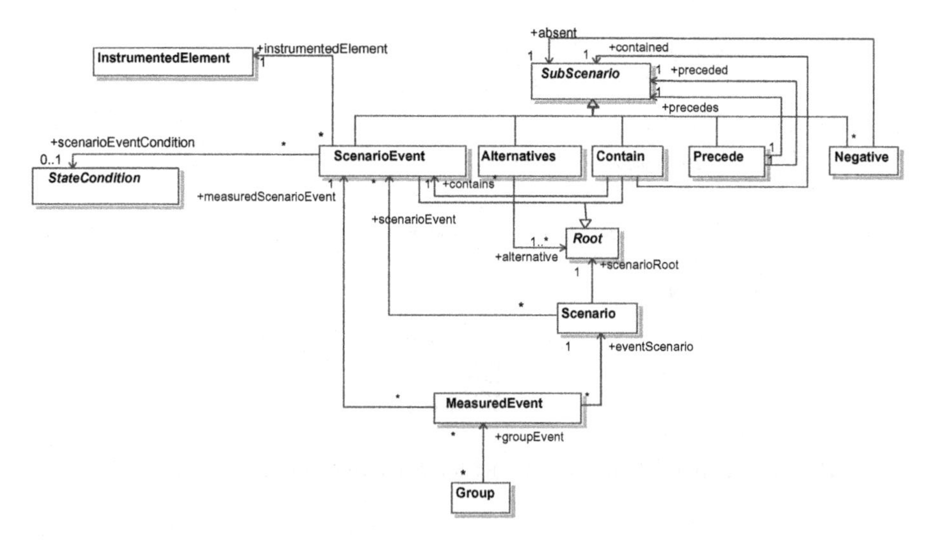

Fig. 3. The part of the metamodel for transformational context specification

DSML. For this reason, the DSML defining metamodel facilitates the declarative specification of: execution context, and metric computation.

The declarative specification of transformational execution context is enabled with the part of the metamodel in Figure 3.

The measurement points of a model are specified with instances of the **InstrumentedElement** metaclass. Instrumented elements can be either simple commands or statement block.

Transformational context can be specified with instances of **Scenario**, **Root**, **ScenarioEvent**, **Alternatives**, **Contain**, **Precede**, **Negation** and **SubScenario** metaclasses. A transformational context is encapsulated in the **Scenario** metaclass, and consists of it's **ScenarioEvent**s, and interrelations between them. A scenario event is an instrumented element and its reactive context. One instrumented element in the same reactive context can find itself several times in a scenario and each time it is a different **ScenarioEvent** instance. For example, **getItem** invocations in Figure 2 are specified with two **ScenarioEvent** instances.

Interrelations form a tree composed of **ScenarioEvent**, **Alternatives**, **Contain**, **Precede**, **Negation** and **SubScenario** metaclasses. A transformational context starts with root invocation. A root can be either an instance of **ScenarioEvent** for the scenario containing only one event, or an instance of ***Contain*** for more complex scenarios. Metaclasses **Contain** and **Precede** enable specification of invocation and sequential composition, respectively. The metaclass **Alternatives** supports specification of guarded command sets. Simple commands are being specified with **ScenarioEvent**. Composite command specified with the usage of **SubScenario** and all other metaclasses mentioned in this paragraph. Guarded commands specification is made possible with the **Negation** and **Precede**, as explained on the example in Subsection 3.1. Finally, loop

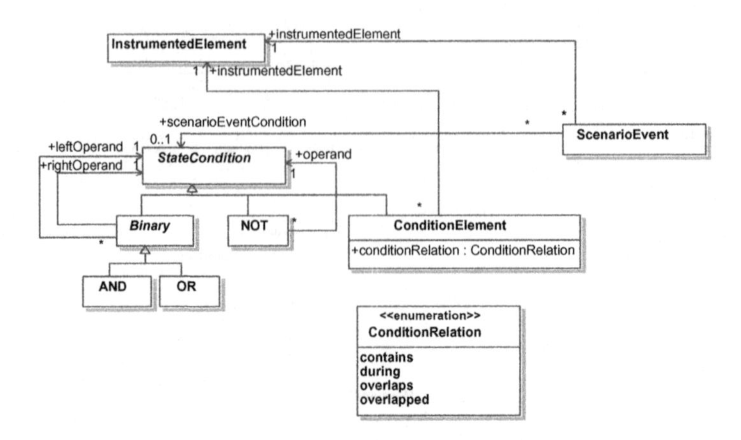

Fig. 4. The part of the metamodel for reactive context specification

can be considered as a statement block and it can be specified either as an instrumented element or a composite command.

The metamodel part shown in Figure 4 enables the reactive context specification.

Reactive context is specified with a boolean algebra of active states during the scenario event execution. Furthermore, the interrelation of active states and the scenario event is also taken into account. The boolean algebra is specified with **StateCondition**, **Binary**, **AND**, **OR**, **NOT** metaclasses, and **ConditionElement** metaclass. The possible interrelations are specified in the enumeration **ConditionRelation** enumeration. Based on the assumptions/limitations of the approach, explained in Section 7, and on the ontology of the interval interrelations identified in [8], four possible interrelations are identified: **contains**, **during**, **overlaps**, and **overlapped**. **Contains** is the interrelation between a state and a scenario event where a state starts before and ends after the execution of the scenario event. **Overlaps** is the interrelation in which a state starts before the start of the scenario event execution, but ends before the end of the scenario event execution. **During** and **overlapped** are inverse to **contains** and **overlaps**, respectively.

The **MeasuredEvent** metaclass is used after the context specification for the definition of an event of interest. It contains a context in the ***eventScenario*** attribute, and the event of interest in **measuredScenarioEvent** attribute. Finally, in some cases there is a need for treating several events as one. For example, if a performance analyst would like to measure throughput of a component, he would have to group all methods of that component, and then specify computation of throughput. The **Group** metaclass facilitates grouping of events for which metrics are computed.

The specification of events of interest is followed by specification of desired metrics and time intervals for which they are computed. The metrics metamodel part facilitating metrics specification is presented in Figure 5.

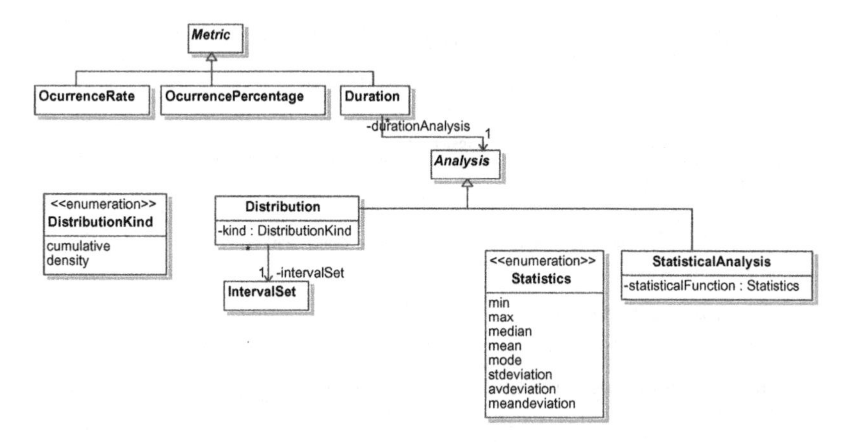

Fig. 5. The part of the metamodel for performance metrics specification

Metrics for performance assessment defined in this metamodel correspond to performance definition in Section 1, and UML SPT [9] and MARTE [10] standard metrics. **Duration** and **OccurrenceRate** metaclasses correspond to response time and throughput, respectively. **OccurrencePercentage** is used for verification of execution probabilities of different alternatives in branching.

Duration of a program construct is being characterized with some statistical functions. Those statistical functions are generalized with the **Analysis** metaclass. Statistical functions are divided into two groups. One group are **distribution functions**, **cumulative** and **density**, defined with instances of **Distribution** and **IntervalSet** metaclasses. Distribution functions are computed as histograms and **IntervalSet** instance defines withs of bars in histograms. The second group of functions are statistical functions which summarize a set of durations in one value. Such metrics' computation is being defined with **StatisticalAnalysis** metaclass instances. Examples of these metrics are mean, median, standard deviation, skewness and so on, and they are defined in the **Statistics** enumeration. This set can be extended. The only requirement is that each function in this enumeration has the corresponding function in the target RDBMS.

Values of all metrics vary over the time. For example, during the peek periods of day response time is higher than in the rest of the day. For this reason, the assessment has to address issues of varying performance metrics values. This is facilitated with the metamodel part in Figure 6.

SimpleAssessment metaclass enables separation of performance assessment time intervals into sub intervals. For example, let the assessment be for a time interval of one day and the metric of interest mean duration. With a **SimpleAssessment** instance and an instance of **TimeIntervalSet** it can be specified that mean duration is computed for each hour of the day. The **TimeIntervalSet** instance defines subintervals for which the metric is computed, here each hour of a day.

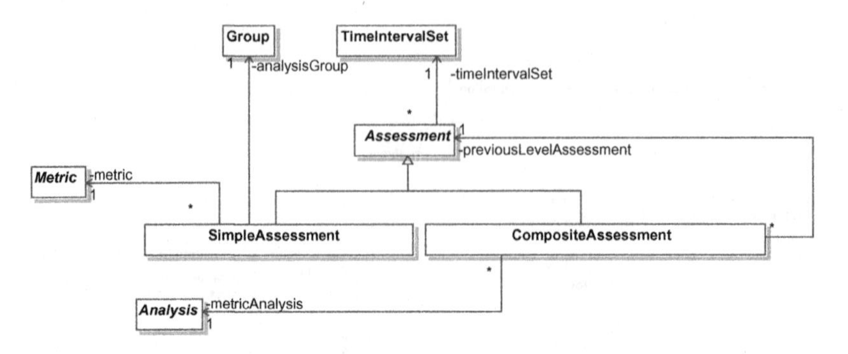

Fig. 6. The metamodel part for specification of time varying metrics observations

CompositeAssessment metaclass enables further statistical analysis of the simple assessment values. For example, with **CompositeAssessment** it can be specified a computation of density distribution of previously mentioned one hour mean durations. Furthermore, for example the standard deviation of one hour mean durations for six hours time intervals can be computed. The time subintervals for composite assessment are also specified with **TimeIntervalSet** instances.

5 Evaluation

The approach is evaluated with an implementation of a UML Profile, and transformations from the profile to Java with RMI and MySQL RDBMS. The UML profile is entitled **PeMA**: The UML Profile for **Pe**rformance **M**easurement and **A**ssessment, and it is, at the present moment, suited only for UML Class and State diagrams. The implementaion in MagicDraw 15.1 Community Edition can be seen in Figure 7.

For these two diagram types the only measurement elements which can be instrumented are operations in Class diagrams and states in State diagrams. The rest of the metamodel is implemented as a model library.

UML Class and State diagrams are transformed into client-server Java RMI applications. For denotation of UML classes modeling client functionality is defined a stereotype ≪Client≫. A corresponding Java class is generated for each class with the ≪Client≫ stereotype. Furthermore, generated are proxies of server classes whose methods are directly invoked by clients.

Server classes are classes without the ≪Client≫ stereotype. For each server class are generated a corresponding Java functionality implementation class and it's instances pool class. Pool classes facilitate concurrent execution defined in Section 7. When a client connects to the server immediately are allocated from pools instances of Java functionality classes to serve to the client. Dispatching between clients and corresponding instances is performed by generated RMI server object class. State charts at the client and server side are implemented with State pattern [11]. These transformations are out of this paper's scope.

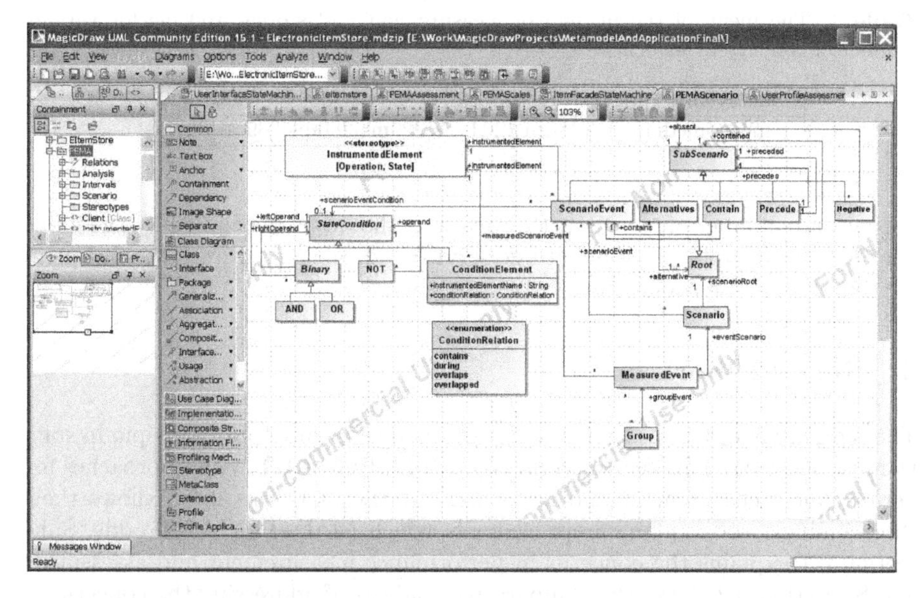

Fig. 7. The implementation UML Profile for **Pe**rformance **M**easurement and **A**ssessment in MagicDraw 15.1 CE. Figure shows the context specification part.

Used RDBMS for performance data storage and metrics computation is MySQL 5.2. JDBC MySQL Connector/J driver version 5.1.5 was used as a database driver for performance data storage. Transformations from measurement and assessment part to SQL code for initialization and metrics computation are out of scope of this paper.

Experiments on measuring the duration of the performance data storage procedure were conducted to depict the impact of the measurements to the overall performance. The application was running on the Intel Pentium 4 3.00 GHZ hyperthreaded processor (two virtual cores), 1GB of physical memory, and GNU/Linux 2.6.17.13. The observed value in the experiment was the duration of the performance measurement and data storage routine. Furthermore, it is analyzed with different number of concurrent service requests. For each number of concurrent requests, the experiment was repeated 10 times. Each repetition contained the complete restart of the server, in order to approximate the impact of the distribution of server software over working memory pages.

The experiment was conducted to show the central tendency of the duration of the routine. This should serve as orientation to the performance analyst of how long might the routine last. For this reason was computed the median of the duration routine. Then, in order to approximate the value of the data collection and storage routine median, it is computed the mean for all 10 repetitions. The results can be seen in Table 1.

The results show that the performance data collection and storage routine increases with the number of concurrent service requests. In order to obtain the right values of the response times the resulting values from Table 1 for the

Table 1. The mean of the median of measurement and storage routine for various number of concurrent invocations

Concurrent requests	1	10	20	30	60	100
mean(median)	192ms	204 ms	229ms	260ms	289ms	327ms

appropriate number of concurrent invocations should be multiplied by the number of the measurement points at one service and subtracted from the complete measured service response time.

6 Related Work

The measurement and assessment of performance is an important topic in software engineering. This section compares **MoDePeMART** with approaches for performance measurement and assessment at the platforms level, shows their shortcomings, and explains improvements which **MoDePeMART** adds. Subsection 6.1 explains the concerns in performance measurement and assessment and Subection 6.2 shows the comparative analysis of addressing the concerns.

6.1 Comparative Analysis Criteria

One of the major concerns is facilitating statistical analysis of response time. Different kinds of system require different statistical analysis. Furthermore, the parallel analysis of response time and throughput is also needed for validation of meeting SLAs with different number of users. Moreover, workload characteristics observations are important for validation of correspondence of prediction assumptions with test cases. Workload is described with the number, request rate, and arrival pattern.

Characteristics of paths are also of significant interest in measurement and assessment. Path characteristics, such as probability of execution and number of iterations are used in performance predictions.

Not all business tasks are of the same importance in systems, and the most important have to be met in any conditions. Ability of their isolation is of great importance. Furthermore, identification of execution context for critical business tasks is as important as identification of critical tasks themselves.

Performance analysis of software systems has to be done for representative time periods. For example, mean response time of whole day usage must not be the same as during the peek usage period.

Instrumentation transparency is also of great importance in measurement. Additional code for measurement can make the code for business logic more complex and hard to understand. Furthermore, reduction of measurement points is also one of the major concerns. It reduces measurement induced system overhead and saves space and time in metrics computation.

Finally, for avoiding assessment failures, keeping consistency between the data structures of collected data and for analysis is also of significant importance.

Table 2. Comparative analysis of related work ((+) facilitated, (-) not facilitated, (o) partially facilitated)

Measurement and Assessment Concern / Approach	Response time statistical analysis	Throughput	Workload characteristics (number of requests, request rate, pattern)	Path characteristics (probability in branching, loop iteration numbers)	Isolation of critical business tasks	Specification of execution context (transformational and reactive)	Metrics validity period specification	Instrumentation transparency	Measurement and metric computation data types consistency	Measurement points reduction
Klar et al. [12]	+	-	---	--	o	o-	-	+	+	+
Liao and Cohen [13]	+	-	+--	o-	o	o-	-	+	+	+
Hollingsworth et al. [14]	+	+	++-	o-	o	o-	-	+	+	+
The Open Group [15]	-	-	---	--	o	+-	-	-	+	-
Marenholz et al. [16]	-	-	---	--	o	o-	-	+	-	+
Debusman and Geihs [17]	-	-	---	--	o	o-	-	+	+	+
Diaconescu et al. [18]	+	+	---	--	o	--	-	+	+	-
MoDePeMART	+	+	++-	+-	+	+	+	+(o)	+(o)	+

6.2 The Comparative Analysis

The results of the comparative analysis can be seen in Table 2.

Klar et al. [12] introduced the idea of relating design models and instrumentation. Their approach enabled statistical analysis of durations. The instrumentation is done at the model level, and instrumentation and metrics computation automatically generated. However, there is no possibility of throughput and workload characteristics assessment. Furthermore, there is no negation of an occurrence. For this reason transformational context specification and isolation of business critical task is only partially supported. Reactive context and specification of metrics computation for various intervals is also not supported.

Liao and Cohen [13] and Hollingsworth et al. [14] introduced languages for performance assessment and monitoring. The major shortcomings of these languages are: lack of the reactive context analysis and inability to specify metrics computation for time intervals. Furthermore, due to the lack of the sequence not execution construct the business task isolation, and transformational context specification are only partially supported. Finally, Liao and Cohen [13] do not enable throughput assessment.

Application Response Measurement (ARM) standard is an attempt of standardization of data types in performance analysis. This standard addresses the questions of transformation context specification and the consistency of data in measurements and metrics computation. Aspect orientation, on the other hand, e.g. Marenholz et al. [16] solves only the problems of transparent instrumentation. Debusman and Geihs [17] combine AOP and ARM.

Diaconescu et al. [18] add a transparent software layer between components and middleware. Instrumentation is done at component interface, which is not sufficient for context and critical business instrumentation.

MoDePeMART approach manages all of the previous mentioned concern except for number of loop iterations analysis. Workload arrival pattern recognition is still not supported.

7 Limitations

MoDePeMART can be used in software systems with the next assumptions.

Measurement and assessment is possible only in systems with concurrency without intercommunication. In the execution model it is assumed that there are no concurrent executions which interfere. Moreover, the or invoker of a scenario is not aware of concurrent execution. Such approach is implemented in, for example, JEE Session Beans.

Synchronous communication. At the present time **MoDePeMART** supports only performance measurement and assessment for the systems communicating synchronously. Synchronous communication is the one where the caller of an operation is blocked and waits until the callee returns a result. After the caller gets the result it continues the execution [19].

There is no support for specification of measurement and metrics computation of loopbacks. A loopback is when in a scenario execution control flow reenters the method whose body already executes. The simplest loopback is recursion.

Granularity of timing mechanism is large enough so that execution of each instrumented element occurs in different chronon. Chronon is the smallest unit of time supported by the discrete time model. The granularity is defined with the smallest time units supported by the timing mechanism, such as milliseconds or nanoseconds. The assumption of this approach is that each instrumented element execution with the same sequence identifier executes in different chronon.

Job flow is assumed in the composite occurrence rate assessment. The system should be fast enough to handle the service requests, and thus the competition rate equals the arrival rate.

Finally, **the approach can be used only for verifying response time and throughput of services**. Verifying the equivalence between assumptions on workload, data, and loop iteration numbers in predictions and measurements and in execution is not facilitated.

8 Outlook and Future Work

This paper presents the **MoDePeMART** an approach for model driven performance measurement and assessment. This approach introduces an idea of raising the abstraction level of measurement and assessment in two ways. First, measurement and assessment is specified in the terms of modeling and not in the terms of implementation constructs. Second, it suggests a DSML for metrics specification and computation. Moreover, it suggests usage of relational database management systems for performance metrics storage and computation. The metamodel for the performance measurement and assessment DSML and a validation as a UML

Profile are presented in this paper. With the comparative analysis it is shown that the major benefits of this approach are specification of performance metrics interval computation and the isolation of critical business tasks. However, there are several possible improvements of the metamodel.

The metamodel could be extended in several ways. It could be extended to support performance measurement and assessment of asynchronous communication. Furthermore, the metamodel could be extended to support measurement and assessment of resources utilization. Moreover, the characterization of data used as parameters in services could also be added to the metamodel. Additionally, computation of iteration loop numbers could also be added. This is often needed when assessing the service characteristics. Finally, workload patterns are of great importance for service performance assessment. Extension of the metamodel for workload patterns assessment would be of great usefulness to performance analyst.

Current **PeMA** profile used only State and Class diagrams and both of them are not suited for specification of measurement context. It could be explored usage of activity and sequence diagrams for specification of execution scenario of interest. These diagrams are usually used for control flow description/prescription. This qualifies them as a good basis for transformational context specification. However, still remains the problem of finding the appropriate elements for state context, metrics, and the assessment part of the metamodel. Furthermore, application of the profile to other diagrams could be explored. In extending the profile for application to other diagrams the major challenge is the development of the stereotypes denotating instrumented elements. For example, in the UML metamodel body of activity diagram ***ConditionalNode*** is specified as an attribute. For this reason, it can not be directly annotated as an instrumented element.

The **MoDePeMART** currently facilitates only assessment of services performance. However, it offers a several promising extension directions. With previously mentioned metamodel extension, it could be made very useful in performance debugging or even continuous monitoring. Such language could be support for specification of automatic system adaptation based on the captured runtime performance characteristics.

References

1. Hasselbring, W., Reussner, R.: Toward Trustworthy Software Systems. IEEE Computer 39(4), 91–92 (2006)
2. Sommerville, I.: Software Engineering, 8th edn. Pearson/Addison Wesley, London (2007)
3. Smith, C.U., Williams, L.G.: Performance Solutions: A Practical Guide to Creating Responsive, Scalable Software. Addison-Wesley, MA (2001)
4. Balsamo, S., Di Marco, A., Inverardi, P., Simeoni, M.: Model-Based Performance Prediction in Software Development: A Survey. IEEE Transactions on Software Engineering 30(5), 295–310 (2004)
5. Selic, B.: A Short Course on MDA Specifications. In: INFWEST Seminar on Model Driven Software Engineering, Pirkkala, Tampere, Finland (2006)

6. Wieringa, R.J.: Design Methods for Reactive Systems: Yourdon, Statemate, and the UML. Morgan Kaufmann Publishers, San Fransisco (2003)
7. Dijkstra, E.W.: A Discipline of Programming. Prentice Hall PTR, Englewood Cliffs (1976)
8. Allen, J.F.: Maintaining Knowledge About Temporal Intervals. Communications of ACM 26(11), 832–843 (1983)
9. Object Management Group. UML Profile for Schedulability, Performance, and Time Specification, OMG document formal/05-01-02 (January 2005a), `http://www.omg.org/cgibin/apps/doc?formal/05-01-02.pdf` (accessed May 2009)
10. Object Management Group. A UML Profile for MARTE: Modeling and Analyzing Real-Time and Embedded Systems, Beta 2, OMG Adopted Spec., OMG document ptc/2008-06-09 (June 2008), `http://www.omgmarte.org/Documents/Specifications/08-06-09.pdf` (accessed May 2009)
11. Gamma, E., Helm, R., Johnson, R., Vlissides, J.: Design Patterns: Elements of Reusable Object-oriented Software. Addison-Wesley, Boston (1995)
12. Klar, R., Quick, A., Soetz, F.: Tools for a Model-driven Instrumentation for Monitoring. In: The 5th Int'l. Conf. on Modeling Techniques and Tools for Comp. Perf. Evaluation, pp. 165–180. Elsevier Science Publisher B.V., Amsterdam (1991)
13. Liao, Y., Cohen, D.: A Specificational Approach to High Level Program Monitoring and Measuring. IEEE Trans. on Soft. Engineering 18(11), 969–978 (1992)
14. Hollingsworth, J.K., Niam, O., Miller, B.P., Xu, Z., Goncalves, M.J.R., Zheng, L.: MDL: A Language and a Compiler for Dynamic Program Instrumentation. In: Proc. of the 1997 Int. Con. on Parallel Architectures and Compiler Techniques, pp. 201–213. IEEE Computer Society, Washington (1997)
15. The Open Group. Application Response Measurement (ARM)(1998), `http://www.opengroup.org/tech/management/arm` Technical Standard, Version 2, Issue 4.1 (accessed May 2009)
16. Mahrenholz, D., Spinczyk, O., Schroeder-Preikschat, W.: Program Instrumentation for Debugging and Monitoring with AspectC++. In: Proc. of the 5th IEEE Int. Symp. on Object-Oriented Real-Time Distributed Computing, pp. 249–256. IEEE Computer Society, Washington (2002)
17. Debusmann, M., Geihs, K.: Efficient and Transparent Instrumentation of Application Components using an Aspect-oriented Approach. In: Brunner, M., Keller, A. (eds.) DSOM 2003. LNCS, vol. 2867, pp. 209–220. Springer, Heidelberg (2003)
18. Diaconescu, A., Mos, A., Murphey, J.: Automatic Performance Management in Component Based Systems. In: 1st International Conference on Autonomic Computing (ICAC 2004), pp. 214–221. IEEE Computer Society, Washington (2004)
19. Object Management Group. UML 2.0 Specification: Superstructure, OMG document ptc/05- 07-04 (November 2004), `http://www.omg.org/cgi-bin/doc?formal/05-07-04` (accessed May 2009)

Security Analysis of a Biometric Authentication System Using UMLsec and JML*

John Lloyd[1] and Jan Jürjens[2]

[1] Atos Origin UK
[2] Open University (UK) and Microsoft Research, Cambridge
john.lloyd@atosorigin.com
http://jurjens.de/jan

Abstract. Quality assurance for security-critical systems is particularly challenging: many systems are developed, deployed, and used that do not satisfy their security requirements. A number of software engineering approaches have been developed over the last few years to address this challenge, both in the context of model-level and code-level security assurance. However, there is little experience so far in using these approaches in an industrial context, the challenges and benefits involved and the relative advantages and disadvantages of different approaches. This paper reports on experiences from a practical application of two of these security assurance approaches. As a representative of model-based security analysis, we considered the UMLsec approach and we investigated the JML annotation language as a representative of a code-level assurance approach. We applied both approaches to the development and security analysis of a biometric authentication system and performed a comparative evaluation based on our experiences.

Keywords: Security analysis, JML, UMLsec, biometric authentication.

1 Introduction

Designing and verifying security-critical software is very difficult because of the complexity of these mechanisms and of industrial systems, the interaction with adversaries and the ways in which systems use security mechanisms. The traditional industrial approach is to describe security requirements textually, design security features as an add-on to the system design, then patch flaws found or exposed after deployment - called 'penetrate and patch'. However this approach is lengthy, imprecise and difficult to check, which risks leaving security vulnerabilities that might result in major loss or damage before discovery. Removing vulnerabilities found in operational systems can be complex, time consuming and error-prone.

Researchers have developed formal methods for specifying a system in such a way that properties of the specification can be mathematically verified for correctness. However formal methods have not been widely adopted because the complexity of

* Empirical results category paper.

A. Schürr and B. Selic (Eds.): MODELS 2009, LNCS 5795, pp. 77–91, 2009.

both the languages and the systems modeled mean that staff need considerable skill, training and time to produce specifications and proofs, which incurs high costs.

To increase industry acceptance of formal methods, an approach is needed that integrates security requirements specification and verification with a method and language that can be used by general software designers. The UMLsec approach [1] addresses this by expressing security requirements within a system specification using the Unified Modeling Language (UML) and then using analysis tools to verify these requirements for correctness.

UMLsec is an approach based on a formal foundation but it aims to be easier for general software designers to use than traditional formal methods because the UMLsec language is simpler and integrated with UML. This aims to reduce the very high training and usage costs that have marginalised the use of formal methods. This approach also aims to be less expensive than the traditional 'penetrate and patch' approach as it could be applied at an early stage in system development when the cost of change would be low. The practical application reported in this paper therefore evaluated how easy it was to specify security requirements using UMLsec and how difficult it then was to implement a system from this UMLsec specification.

Even though the security requirements specification might have been verified, security flaws may be introduced during the design and implementation of the system or in subsequent changes. We therefore investigated using the Java Modeling Language (JML) to relate the implemented system back to its UMLsec security specification and verify that it is correct in relation to this specification.

We investigated these approaches by implementing a biometric authentication system adapted from a proposal by Viti and Bistarelli [2]). Biometrics are an attractive security mechanism for authentication because they are an inherent feature of a person and so cannot be lost or easily changed. We used this practical application to evaluate the model-level UMLsec security assurance approach and the code level JML assurance approach. We here compare their advantages and disadvantages, describe specific practical experiences with the two approaches and their combination in particular, discuss lessons learned and suggest possible improvements.

Although there is traditionally a lack of practical validation of software engineering research, it is increasingly being realised that this is an important component of such research, leading to increasing activity in this area. The work presented here is different from earlier reports of industrial applications of model-based security in that it focuses on security analysis on the code rather than the model level.

In the next section, we summarise the UMLsec and JML approaches. We then give an overview of the biometric authentication system in Section 3. Our security assurance using a combination of UMLsec and JML is described in Section 4. We cover lessons learned from the UMLsec and JML approaches in Section 5 and we end with a summary and suggestions for further work.

2 Software Security Assurance

In this section, we first discuss the practical challenges involved in providing assurance for security critical software and we then summarise the two approaches in our application: UMLsec for the model-level assurance and JML for the code-level assurance.

2.1 Challenges for Security Assurance

In practice, security is compromised most often not by breaking dedicated mechanisms such as encryption or security protocols, but by exploiting weaknesses in the way they are being used. Thus it is not enough to ensure the correct functioning of security mechanisms used. They cannot be 'blindly' inserted into a security-critical system, but the overall system development must take security aspects into account in a coherent way. While functional requirements are generally analyzed carefully in systems development, security considerations often arise after the fact. Adding security as an afterthought, however, often leads to problems and security engineers get little feedback about the secure functioning of their products in practice, since security violations are often kept secret for fear of harming a company's reputation.

In practice, the traditional strategy for security assurance has been 'penetrate and patch'. It has been accepted that deployed systems contain vulnerabilities: whenever a penetration of the system is noticed and the exploited weakness can be identified, the vulnerability is removed. For many systems, this approach is not ideal: each penetration may already have caused significant damage before the vulnerability can be removed. For systems that offer strong incentives for attack, such as financial applications, the prospect of being able to exploit a weakness even only once may be enough motivation to search for such a weakness. System administrators are often hesitant to apply patches because of disruption to the service. Having to create and distribute patches costs money and leads to loss of customer confidence. It would thus be preferable to consider security aspects more seriously in earlier phases of the system lifecycle, before a system is deployed, or even implemented, because late correction of requirements errors can be significantly more expensive than early correction.

2.2 Model-Based Security Using UMLsec

UMLsec is an extension of UML for secure systems development. Recurring security requirements, such as *secrecy*, *integrity*, and *authenticity* are offered as specification elements by the UMLsec extension. These properties and its associated semantics are used to evaluate UML diagrams of various kinds and indicate possible security vulnerabilities. One can thus verify that the desired security requirements, if fulfilled, enforce a given security objective. One can also ensure that the requirements are actually met by the given UML specification of the system (design solution). UMLsec encapsulates knowledge on prudent security engineering and thereby makes it available to developers who may not be experts in security. The extension is given in the form of a UML profile using the standard UML extension mechanisms. *Stereotypes* are used together with *tags* to formulate security requirements and assumptions on the system environment. *Constraints* give criteria that determine whether the requirements are met by the system design (design solution), by referring to a precise semantics mentioned below.

The tags defined in UMLsec represent a set of desired properties. For instance, "freshness" of a value means that an attacker cannot guess what its value was. Moreover, to represent a profile of rules that formalize the security requirements, the following are some of the stereotypes that are used: *«critical»*, *«high»*, *«integrity»*, *«internet»*, *«encrypted»*, *«LAN»*, *«secrecy»*, and *«secure links»*. The definition of the stereotypes allows for model checking and tool support. As an example consider *«secure links»*. This stereotype is used to ensure that security requirements on the communication are met by the physical layer: when attached to a UML subsystem, the constraint enforces that for each dependency *d* with a stereotype s representing a certain security requirement, the physical architecture of the system should support that security requirement at the given communication link.

A detailed explanation of the tags and stereotypes defined in UMLsec can be found in [1]. The extension has been developed based on experiences on the model-based development of security-critical systems in industrial projects involving German government agencies and major banks, insurance companies, smart card and car manufacturers, and other companies. There have been several applications of UMLsec in industrial development projects [3,4,5]. UMLsec supports automatic verification of security properties using the UMLsec tool-support [1] as well as IT security risk assessment [6].

2.3 The Java Modeling Language

The JML is a behavioural interface specification language which describes method pre- and post-conditions. It is based on the design-by-contract approach [7] that describes a requirement for a client to guarantee that agreed pre-conditions hold before calling a method defined by a class; in return, the class guarantees that agreed post-conditions will hold after the call. For example, a client calling a square root function would guarantee that the argument was a positive number and the class would guarantee that the result was approximately equal to the square root of the argument.

[8], [9] describe the basic features of the language and these papers are complemented by the reference manual [10]. JML is written as annotation comments beginning with `//@` within Java code. A `requires` clause specifies the method's pre-condition and ensures clause specifies normal and exception post-conditions. For example, the annotation `//@ requires x>= 0.0` specifies the pre-condition of the square root function. The client code calling this function must then ensure that this function is only called with a positive number argument. As the contracts expressed in JML are compiled into executable code, any run-time violation of them can be immediately detected, such as a negative argument in this function call.

3 The Biometric Authentication System

3.1 Context

The implemented biometric authentication system consists of a controlling PC with a combined scanner/smart card reader. The PC is connected to a server application that authenticates the user. The user firstly inserts a smart card containing a fingerprint biometric template into the USB port of the smart card reader. He then enters a PIN at the controlling host PC to activate the card, and places a finger on the scanner. The host then compares the scan to the fingerprint template; if they match, the host encrypts a nonce sent from the server with the user's private key stored on the smart card and returns it to the server. The server authenticates the user by decrypting the received nonce with the user's public key and confirming that it matches the nonce originally sent. This then completes user authentication by three factors: possession of a smart card; a PIN; and a biometric.

3.2 Specification Modeling Using UMLsec

The host-smart card and host–scanner protocols incorporate protocol fragments described in [11], [12]. The host establishes a shared symmetric key with the smart card and scanner which is then used to encrypt messages over the un-trusted connection between them. The system uses misuse counters to limit the numbers of PIN entries, biometric scans and server connection attempts.

The server connection uses the HTTPS protocol (HTTP over a Secure Sockets Layer (SSL)) to authenticate the server using its digital certificate and request client authentication using the user's digital certificate stored on the smart card.

We specified requirements using UML deployment, class and sequence diagrams. The deployment diagram describes the physical hardware and connections in the system. The class diagram describes the four main classes modeling the smart card, host PC, scanner and server in terms of their attributes and operations, plus secrecy, integrity, freshness and authenticity security requirements described using UMLsec. The sequence diagrams describe the interaction with the system user and the protocol of messages between the host and the smart card, scanner and the server. These protocols use cryptographic data and functions, and again we use UMLsec to express security requirements.

The system's software architecture is a software-only implementation of the host, scanner and smart card classes where the host is invoked by a user through a browser. Each message in the protocols between these classes is constructed, passed as an argument in a method call to the receiving object and then processed. The object's reply is handled as a method return value to retain the host's overall control of the dialogue.

The system uses the Java Cryptography Architecture (JCA) to encrypt and decrypt message data, the Java security package to implement nonces, message authentication codes and digital signatures, and the Java Secure Sockets Extension (JSSE) to provide the HTTPS server connection.

4 Security Assurance

4.1 JML Contracts

We implemented the software components of the system using about 1,300 lines of Java 6 code. We then used JML to try to verify parts of the system's code against its UMLsec specification. We had described system operations using the Object Constraint language (OCL) that is part of the UML notation, but we did not use it to formally describe all system constraints because we found OCL difficult to use for this task due to its complexity. This did not cause any development problems in our particular application because the designer and developer were the same person, but in a larger-scale project, where these roles are usually separate, more formal constraint documentation would be needed to communicate information. Also, an earlier decision to use JML at the design modeling stage would have helped structure the code during the implementation phase to increase the effectiveness of using JML. In particular, an early decision on the implementation language would allow a specific specification language like JML to be used rather than the generic OCL.

As an example of a method-level JML contract that we added, we now consider a method that compares the Message Authentication Code (MAC) calculated from a received message with the MAC in the message. The method handles different message types with different lengths. It was difficult to write a JML contract since neither the message type nor the return code were expressed as arguments as the method was an addition during implementation to consolidate a number of blocks of similar code. We eventually verified the check in JML by comparing each byte of the two MACs using a JML `\forall` expression:

```
//@ ensures (\forall int x; 0 <= x &&
//@   x <  mac.getMacLength();
//@   calcMac[x].compareTo(receivedMac[x])==0);
```

This example demonstrates that JML can be difficult to apply unless the method has been designed with JML verification in mind. A similar comment would apply when using another notation instead of JML (such as OCL). This is also in line with the intuitive idea that security contracts can be easier to specify if we can take advantage of the algebraic properties of the data involved.

We also used the finite state machine model proposed in [13] to verify that messages are sent in the correct sequence by the host. For this, static integers are declared defining the messages sent before the start and end of each method, thus:

```
//@ public static final ghost int
//@ INITIAL = 1,
//@ RESET = 2,
//@ ASKZ = 3,
//@ public ghost int state = INITIAL;
```

The JML ghost field state is assigned one of these values at the end of each method, for example: `//@ set state = ASKZ`.

The JML contract for the method can then test the relevant pre- and post-condition using this variable. For example, for a method which must begin after an `ASKZ` has been set and must end by sending an `ACK`, we defined the following:

```
/*@ public normal_behavior
  @       requires state == ASKZ;
  @       assignable \everything;
  @       ensures state == ACK;
  @*/
```

However, since each method handles several messages, we could not use JML to fully verify the correct message sequence, since JML can only check the state before the start and after termination of each method. Had these methods been written at a lower level of granularity to each handle only one message exchange then this would have been possible. We refactored several methods to confirm this. This example demonstrates that the software to be verified using JML should be designed in a style consistent with the use of JML to gain most value from its use.

The JML `\fresh` expression asserts that objects are freshly allocated and were not allocated in the pre-state. This contributes to the freshness security requirements implemented by nonces in the system in a useful way. For example:

```
//@ ensures \fresh (zSc);
```

verifies that the object `zSc` that stores a random number is freshly generated. Note that this check does not aim to guarantee that the pseudo-random algorithm used to generate the random number is itself secure. It does however make sure that an existing random number object is not reused accidentally or maliciously, which does prevent a certain class of fresh value security flaws.

We investigated using JML to verify that a message has been encrypted. There is no JML expression to support this directly and the cipher Java class does not have a method to return the encrypted or decrypted state to which it has been set. We could have rewritten the encryption code as a separate method and added an attribute that is set to the current cipher state; a JML or Java `assert` statement could then test this attribute value when each message is sent. However this would not directly test the encryption of the message. We therefore chose to test that the cipher text was different to the plain text by using a JML assert statement of the form:

```
//@ assert (\forall int x; 0 <= x &&
//@        x < plainText.length();
//@        plainText[x] != cipherText[x]);
```

after each message send. Again, this check does not aim to enforce, for example, that the used encryption algorithm is secure, but does make sure that the application of the encryption algorithm is not simply left out accidentally or maliciously.

Note that this example shows that it is important to distinguish the kind of property we would like to specify from what we can specify in a verifiable manner: The intended property refers to how hard it is for someone who does not have access to the encryption key to retrieve the original message. This is a property that cannot be expressed directly as a pre/post/invariant condition.

We also intended to specify in JML that methods called from outside the smart card methods could not read or assign to the field containing the PIN. This turned out to be relatively cumbersome because there is no JML keyword with the direct meaning 'not accessible'. Instead, one needs to add a JML to every method to specify all the fields that are accessible by each method.

4.2 JML Specification Patterns for Security

Warnier [14] proposes JML specification patterns for confidentiality and integrity. As part of our application, we investigated their usefulness for identifying security flaws. Warnier defines confidentiality as non-interference between variables of different security levels: the values of all non-confidential (low security) fields in the post state should be independent of the values of all confidential (high-security) fields in the pre-state. He defines a similar JML specification pattern for integrity where the values of high security variables in the post-state are required to be independent of low security variable values.

Although using specification patterns is a good idea in principle, in our experience, they were difficult to apply because many of the system's methods were rather large and therefore too complex to investigate using these patterns; they would have been more useful when applied to smaller methods. Also, there was a difficulty in applying the confidentiality pattern in cryptography which is common to information-flow type definitions of confidentiality: given a high-security plain-text, its encryption would be considered low-security (because it can only be decrypted by trusted parties, so the cipher text can be communicated publically). Thus, the encryption function itself would be considered to violate confidentiality according to this definition, although that is clearly not the case in reality.

4.3 Security Specifications in JML

Agarwal *et al.* [13] have written JML specifications for some security-relevant Java classes, although only a few are cryptography classes. These specifications aim to provide a more precise understanding of the behaviour of the classes than *javadoc* comments. This might reduce security flaws caused by using these classes incorrectly, for example with invalid pre-conditions or handling post-conditions incorrectly, and it might identify such errors during run-time assertion checking.

To investigate this potential, we compared the JML specifications of four methods of the `Signature` Java class used to support digital signature processing in the system to the *javadoc* comments for these methods. Overall, the JML specifications were somewhat more precise than *javadoc* but they required significantly more time to understand. Also, only three cryptography classes currently have JML specifications. The ability to automatically check JML contracts at run-time checking is of limited use for these specifications since nearly all pre-conditions are also handled by Java exception handling. The post-conditions could be relied on as the Java methods are rather unlikely to contain errors, being part of a standard library implementations that has been extensively tested and used already. We therefore found JML specifications for Java classes to be mainly a useful supplement to *javadoc* comments, which are not always completely precise and unambiguous.

4.4 Manual UMLsec / Code Validation Check

We manually checked the consistency of each UMLsec security requirement with its implementation in the prototype to examine whether and how it could be verified using JML. This was done in two stages: UMLsec to protocol; and protocol to code where each protocol component should map to code in the prototype. This protocol-to-code mapping check would have been easier had the protocol been implemented using one method to process each message in each class. Such a consistent structure would be essential for cost-effective manual checking by someone not already familiar with the code. If the contract for each method is then written in JML, it can be automatically checked statically and at runtime to complement a manual check.

This mapping check revealed several issues, which were examined as to how easily they could be detected using JML. Firstly, a MAC check had been omitted. This could be detected by coding a suitable JML contract on the Java code level. Secondly, the system deliberately did not implement secure storage of the smart card PIN or biometric template to protect their confidentiality or integrity because of insufficient development time. This could not be easily detected by a JML contract since the methods are either missing or return correct values.

The MAC and encryption cipher both use the same key, which is weak since if the key is broken then the whole system is insecure: different keys should be used for different types of cryptographic operations. This is a design weakness in the sequence diagram specification, which specifies usage of the same key. The code implementation actually correctly uses different keys here, so this would not have been revealed by a code-level check. This weakness is an example of a model-level security design check which could be very usefully added to the UMLsec verification tool framework.

There was initially an omission on the UMLsec specification level compared to the textual specification [2] regarding the generation of a new session key: Viti's protocol generates a session key from a combination of two nonces and a key stored in the smart card, but the UMLsec specification initially omitted the smart card key. This model-level inconsistency was revealed when coding, with the help of both the textual and the UMLsec specification. This example demonstrates the usefulness of performing assurance on both the model and the code level since the added redundancy further increases the trustworthiness of the resulting system.

An initial version of the implementation did not enforce the implied integrity requirements for the smart card ID in the smart card and host classes as there was no MAC check. This was a deliberate omission based on the erroneous assumption of the implementer that it would not lead to a security weakness. This is an example of a change by a developer with the intention of improving the protocol that actually introduces a security flaw. That this variation is insecure would have been revealed by the UMLsec model-level security analysis tools for verifying crypto-protocols. The inconsistency of the implementation with the UMLsec model can be revealed by JML contracts based on the UMLsec model if the change alters the interface or behaviour of methods (as it does in this example).

These issues reflect common issues occurring in industrial development: security specialists leave inconsistencies and flaws in specifications, and developers sometimes do not fully implement requirements because they forget, they make mistakes or they deliberately omit them to meet development deadlines. The success of our manual check in detecting these flaws is in line with earlier findings on the effectiveness of code reviews [15]. It argues for a rigorous manual code review against the specification as well as JML contracts, although this is time consuming. Further automated support to facilitate this check would therefore be very beneficial indeed.

4.5 JML Tools

JML aims to be supported by a range of open-source tools for statically checking assertions, checking assertions at runtime, unit testing support, and generating specifications and documentation [16]. The *jmlc* compiler and runtime assertion checker tests for violations of the JML assertions when the Java code is run. There are several static checkers, such as *ESC/Java*, that parse and type check JML, and statically check the consistency of the Java code against the JML specification.

We used the *ESC/Java 2* plug-in for the *Eclipse* workbench to statically check our JML and highlight syntax errors in the source code. The tool was easy to install and use, but had limited documentation. It identified some JML errors but not all warnings could be eliminated because of the missing explanatory documentation. Because of problems with installing the *JMLEclipse* runtime assertion checker plug-in, we could not investigate its usefulness towards verifying the system. We did however install the latest version of the common JML tools project [17], which are not yet integrated with *Eclipse*, and used the *jmlc* compiler to parse and type check the source code. This identified ten additional errors in the JML annotation previously missed by *ESC/Java 2*, although none revealed new security flaws. We then repeated the check using *ESC/Java 2* after installing the latest JML tools (including the latest version of the *jmlc* compiler) and it additionally reported errors in core Java classes within each prototype class. The likely causes of these errors are new language features of Java 6 in which the biometric authentication system is coded, since *ESC/Java 2* only supports earlier Java versions.

5 Lessons Learned

5.1 Evaluation of UMLsec

We found UMLsec and the associated cryptographic notation adequate for describing the system's security requirements since only three requirements could not easily be described: connection timeout value, protocol termination and types of communications links. Although the UMLsec notation is aimed to be extensible by the user in a given application, it would be very useful to have a process which would feed these ad-hoc extensions back into the standard UMLsec notation. Also, the meanings of some UMLsec stereotypes were not immediately easy to understand.

The UMLsec approach defines a threat model describing different kinds of adversaries. We had initially assumed a default adversary with no access to the trusted wire link between the smart card reader/scanner and host. However, vendors commonly implement a cryptographic protocol over this link, implying it is un-trusted. We therefore changed our assumption to an insider adversary that was able to delete, read or insert messages on this link, which required a substantial change to design and implement a cryptographic protocol within the biometric authentication system to preserve the security requirements. This emphasises the value of UMLsec's threat model in forcing attention on the nature of the security threat.

The associated cryptographic notation is succinct and unambiguous but not easy to understand without substantial study. It therefore requires a complementary summary textual description for the non-specialist reader, although we recognise the risk of the text becoming inconsistent with the diagrams if any changes are not applied consistently to both.

One could use general-purpose graphics software for the UML diagrams but this insufficiently supports the growing complexity of these diagrams and their consistency, and would not allow one to use the security analysis tool framework available for UMLsec. It is therefore important to create the UMLsec models in a general-purpose UML editor that allows the UML diagrams be imported as XMI files into the

UMLsec tool framework. It would also be very useful if these UML editors could be extended with the ability to highlight or filter out layers of information, although this is beyond the scope of the UMLsec tool framework since it assumes the use of a general-purpose UML editor.

The value of UMLsec diagrams is diminished if they are not maintained beyond the specification stage. Errors and omissions may be introduced into systems during changes after initial design, since the focus is often then on the detail of each change rather than on the effect on other aspects of the system, such as security. In industrial applications, changes are often not applied back to system specification documentation because of time, manpower or budgetary pressure. A project must commit to updating the system specification and UMLsec notation for every subsequent change if it is to fully benefit from its investment in applying the UMLsec approach in initial design. It would also be very useful to have automated tool-support that automatically reflects back changes on the implementation level to the model level. Some steps in this direction are documented in [6].

The analysis used version 1.5 of UML because most of the source material used this version. However UML is continually being enhanced. [1] assesses the effect of UML 2.0 on UMLsec as minor because the new version is sufficiently conservative to the previous diagram types and the new model elements are not needed in security engineering. For UML to have a long-lasting and deep impact in practice, the Object Management Group will need to ensure that future versions of UML continue to be conservative extensions of the previous ones, if organisations are to have confidence that an investment in adopting UML will provide long-term benefits.

UMLsec allows one to specify and automatically analyse security requirements and security design models but it does not prescribe how to create the design so that it will then be shown to satisfy the security requirements using the UMLsec analysis tools.. Thus, this input from a security designer is still needed. UMLsec also does not describe the level of security to be specified at the implementation level. For example the designer is not given explicit guidance on the cryptographic algorithms or key strengths necessary. This would again be a very useful addition to the current UMLsec notation and tools.

The UMLsec specification was a sound basis for design and code implementation, particularly the sequence diagrams as they were at a level of abstraction from which they could be directly coded.

5.2 Evaluation of the JML Approach

The value of using JML to verify the prototype code was limited because it was applied after, rather than during code development. Most of the methods were too large, which made it difficult to check many conditions using JML. JML was of limited value for small helper methods because they were not designed with clear pre- and post-conditions that JML could easily check. JML would therefore be more valuable if applied earlier starting in the design phase.

There was insufficient time to fully evaluate JML tool support. The *jmlc* compiler identified many syntax and type JML errors but *ESC/Java 2* was less useful, probably because it has not been maintained for newer versions of Java. Industry will be reluctant to adopt JML without some assurance of tool maintenance since it would constrain their ability to use new language versions. The new common JML tools are open source which would allow significant users in industry to update the tools to newer version of Java themselves, but most industrial users will not have the resources to do this themselves and will expect a commercial support package.

Although JML does not directly support message or storage confidentiality or integrity verification, we were able to code contracts to indirectly check these security requirements. However JML patterns for confidentiality and integrity were difficult to apply because many system methods were too large and complex; these patterns would have been more useful with smaller methods. Some guidance on the use of JML patterns during design is therefore needed.

JML's current support for verifying that messages are sent in the correct sequence using a finite state machine is somewhat cumbersome and error prone, so we would endorse proposals for a JML call sequence clause to specify the method protocol more succinctly.

JML specifications for a few Java cryptography classes provide to some extent a more precise description of class behaviour than the *javadoc* documentation but they take time to understand. They complement the *javadoc* documentation but are not a substitute for it being made more precise.

Using JML, we identified six instances of requirement implementation and integrity check omissions, and Java code errors. However a subsequent manual check of the prototype's code against the UML specification successfully identified a further 13 security flaws, inconsistencies and weaknesses, some of which were discussed in Section 4.4. Writing JML contracts thus effectively enforces parts of the security check by focusing attention on the code and specification, but it does not reveal all the flaws and specification inconsistencies present It would require considerable time and a good knowledge of the specification, application code and security to thoroughly manually check code, which might not be feasible in an industrial situation with time and cost pressures. However a check could be made by following design and coding style guidelines, and by using a checklist, which would help ensure that important areas were covered and act as documentation of the quality review.

JML will not detect security flaws contained in products, design features not implemented in code, associated business and operational processes, and infrastructure.

JML verifies code against a derivation of the UML specification rather than the specification itself: security flaws might also be missed if this derivation was not complete.

JML contracts impose a code structure if they are written during design. If these contracts are written by software or protocol designers then the developers' role is reduced to implementing and testing each defined method. Developers might regard this as diminishing their role and so resist its introduction. To avoid this, they could be asked to write the JML contracts from specifications produced by the protocol designer, although an independent reviewer should confirm the consistency of the JML with the specification during a code walkthough (and it would also be very useful to have automated tools that would check this).

JML is not dependent on UMLsec or UML; JML contracts could be written from any specification that described requirements in a clear and unambiguous way. An organisation could therefore introduce JML and UMLsec separately to avoid overloading the organisation with change.

The use of JML would increase development timescales and costs: JML requires time to learn and apply since the literature is still academically-focused, and it is not sufficiently comprehensive to reduce normal system testing. An organisation adopting JML would therefore need to develop a software specification style guide for JML, and to train designers and developers. However it would contribute to reducing security flaws in the system, which would reduce costs because of fewer subsequent fixes, and it would reduce the risk of loss and reputational damage from the exploitation of security flaws. JML would be easiest to justify in areas where this cost reduction and these risks were highest; biometric authentication protocols would be one such area because of the impracticality of resolving errors in applications on issued smart cards.

5.3 Reflections on This Experience

In this subsection, we summarise our views on this application experience.

How much effort was involved? About 56 person days (pd), comprising: 11 pd creating the design model of the protocol; 15 pd on the technical design of the software architecture; 11 pd for coding and testing the prototype; and 19 pd for verification of the prototype using JML and the manual check.

Were there ways in which the application of UMLsec and JML did not go as expected? The UMLsec approach was effective in specifying security requirements succinctly and precisely, and the threat model was particularly useful in clarifying the extent of an adversary's access to the system. Only three requirements could not be easily described and the meaning of one UMLsec stereotype was unclear to the given user so it was not used. It was difficult to check many conditions using JML because most of the application's methods were too large.

Did the approaches have to be changed or adapted to work properly and, if so, in what way? The UMLsec analysis tools had been used to verify the correctness of the specification in earlier work [3], which therefore did not have to be repeated in the current application. After using JML to verify the code, we carried out an additional manual check for security flaws to examine the effectiveness of the approach. Apart from that, the approaches were not changed.

Did the method reveal interesting or unexpected results? The process of manually applying UMLsec identified two security weaknesses, even though we did not use the automated UMLsec analysis tools (which had been applied in earlier work [11]). JML helped to verify system code by focusing attention on the consistency of the code with its UMLsec specification, which revealed a number of unexpected security flaws and weaknesses.

Did it not pick up issues that you expected it would? JML did not identify some security flaws, design weaknesses and inconsistencies in the UMLsec specification because the implementation was not suitably structured. However some of these would probably not have been easily revealed by JML even if it had been fully applied.

How did its use differ from previous uses? To our knowledge, this was the first combined application of UMLsec and JML to a biometric authentication system.

Can you say anything specific about the security of the application now that you have done the modeling? We investigated in some detail the correctness of the application against its security specification but we cannot completely prove this correctness since JML verifies code against a derivation of the UML specification rather than the specification itself. Future research might develop a tool to generate draft JML specifications from UMLsec sequence diagrams to both improve JML coding efficiency and reduce the risk of omissions.

How can you be sure that you have applied the method correctly or even optimally? The value of JML was limited in so far as it was applied after code development to an implementation that was not entirely structured in a suitable way. It would have been more useful to have used it to specify methods already during the design phase.

6 Summary

This paper describes the application of the UMLsec and JML assurance approaches to a biometric authentication system, with the focus on the use of JML to verify the code against its UMLsec specification. UMLsec was effective in specifying security requirements, in particular in modeling threat levels. The implementation was straightforward as the UMLsec protocol was unambiguous and on the same level of abstraction as the code. JML helped to verify the code by focusing attention on its consistency with the specification, revealing a number of security flaws. However, its value was limited in so far as it was used after code development on an implementation with an unsuitable structure.

A tool to generate draft JML conditions from UMLsec would improve the value of JML in this context. Other research might map UMLsec to features of implementation language frameworks, develop UMLsec and JML security patterns, evaluate other JML tools in a security requirements context and integrate these techniques within a coherent security systems development method.

Acknowledgements. Many thanks to Jonathan Stephenson for advice and guidance during this analysis, to Atos Origin UK for sponsorship, and to the reviewers for providing constructive feedback which helped improving the paper.

References

1. Jürjens, J.: Secure Systems Development with UML. Springer, Heidelberg (2005)
2. Viti, C., Bistarelli, S.: Study and development of a remote biometric authentication protocol, Technical Report IIT B4-04/2003, Consiglio Nazionale delle Ricerche,Istituto di Informatica e Telematica (September 2003)
3. Grünbauer, J., Hollmann, H., Jürjens, J., Wimmel, G.: Modelling and Verification of Layered Security Protocols: A Bank Application. In: Anderson, S., Felici, M., Littlewood, B. (eds.) SAFECOMP 2003. LNCS, vol. 2788, pp. 116–129. Springer, Heidelberg (2003)
4. Deubler, M., Grünbauer, J., Jürjens, J., Wimmel, G.: Sound Development of Secure Service-based Systems. In: 2nd International Conference on Service Oriented Computing (ICSOC 2004), pp. 115–124. ACM, New York (2004)

5. Best, B., Jürjens, J., Nuseibeh, B.: Model-based Security Engineering of Distributed Information Systems using UMLsec. In: 29th International Conference on Software Engineering (ICSE 2007), pp. 581–590. ACM, New York (2007)
6. Houmb, S., Georg, G., France, R., Bieman, J., Jürjens, J.: Cost-Benefit Trade-Off Analysis Using BBN for Aspect-Oriented Risk-Driven Development, Engineering of Complex Computer Systems. In: 10th IEEE International Conference on Engineering of Complex Computer Systems (ICECCS 2005), pp. 195–204 (2005)
7. Leavens, G., Cheon, Y.: Design by Contract with JML (2006), `ftp://ftp.cs.iastate.edu/pub/leavens/JML/jmldbc.pdf`
8. Leavens, G., Baker, A., Ruby, C.: JML: A Notation for Detailed Design. In: Behavioral Specifications of Businesses and Systems, ch. 12, pp. 175–188. Kluwer, Dordrecht (1999)
9. Leavens, G., Baker, A., Ruby, C.: Preliminary Design of JML: A Behavioural Interface Specification Language for Java. ACM SIGSOFT Software Engineering Notes 31(3) (May 2006)
10. Leavens, G., Poll, E., Clifton, C., Cheon, Y., Ruby, C., Cok, D., Muller, P., Kiniry, J., Chalin, P.: JML Reference Manual, DRAFT, Release 1.210, 2007/7/01 Ames, Iowa State University
11. Schmidt, R.: Modellbasierte Sicherheitsanalyse mit UMLsec: ein Biometrisches Zugangskontrollsystem (Model-based Security Analysis with UMLsec: a Biometric Access Control System) Ludwig-Maxim. Univ. München (2004)
12. Jürjens, J.: Model-based Security Engineering with UML. In: Aldini, A., Gorrieri, R., Martinelli, F. (eds.) FOSAD 2005. LNCS, vol. 3655, pp. 42–77. Springer, Heidelberg (2005)
13. Agarwal, P., Rubio-Medrano, C., Cheon, Y., Teller, P.: A Formal Specification in JML of the Java Security Package. Computer, Information, and Systems Sciences and Engineering, December 4–14 (2006)
14. Warnier, M.: Language Based Security for Java and JML, PhD thesis, Radboud University Nijmegen (2006)
15. Glass, R.: Inspections - Some Surprising Findings. Commun. ACM 42(4), 17–19 (1999)
16. Burdy, L., Cheon, Y., Cok, D., Ernst, M., Kiniry, J., Leavens, G., Rustan, K., Leino, M., Poll, E.: An overview of JML tools and applications. STTT 7(3), 212–232 (2005)
17. JML common tools, December 10 (2007), `http://sourceforge.net/projects/jmlspecs/`
18. Yu, Y., Jürjens, J., Mylopoulos, J.: Application of Traceability to Maintenance of Secure Software. In: Int. Conf. for Software Maintenance (ICSM). IEEE, Los Alamitos (2008)

Automatically Discovering Hidden Transformation Chaining Constraints

Raphaël Chenouard[1] and Frédéric Jouault[2]

[1] LINA, CNRS, Université de Nantes, France
[2] AtlanMod (INRIA & EMN), France
raphael.chenouard@univ-nantes.fr, frederic.jouault@inria.fr

Abstract. Model transformations operate on models conforming to precisely defined metamodels. Consequently, it often seems relatively easy to chain them: the output of a transformation may be given as input to a second one if metamodels match. However, this simple rule has some obvious limitations. For instance, a transformation may only use a subset of a metamodel. Therefore, chaining transformations appropriately requires more information.

We present here an approach that automatically discovers more detailed information about actual chaining constraints by statically analyzing transformations. The objective is to provide developers who decide to chain transformations with more data on which to base their choices. This approach has been successfully applied to the case of a library of endogenous transformations. They all have the same source and target metamodel but have some hidden chaining constraints. In such a case, the simple metamodel matching rule given above does not provide any useful information.

1 Introduction

One of the main objectives of Model-Driven Engineering (MDE) is to automatize software engineering tasks such as: the production of code from abstract models in forward engineering scenarios, the production of abstract models from code in reverse engineering scenarios, or a combination of the two previous cases in modernization scenarios. To achieve this automation, MDE relies on precisely defined models that can be processed by a computer. Each model conforms to a metamodel that defines concepts as well as relations between them. For instance, a Java metamodel has the concept of Java class, with the corresponding single-valued superclass relation (i.e., a class can only extend one other class). Similarly, the UML metamodel defines the concept of a UML class, with a multi-valued generalization relation (i.e., a class may extend several other classes). Many software engineering tasks such as those mentioned above can be performed by model transformations.

In order to reduce the effort of writing these transformations, complex tasks are generally not performed by complex transformations but rather by chains of simpler transformations. A model transformation chain is formed by feeding

A. Schürr and B. Selic (Eds.): MODELS 2009, LNCS 5795, pp. 92–106, 2009.

the output of a first transformation as input to second one. Complex chains can consist of a large number of transformations. For instance, in order to analyze a Java model with a Petri net tool, a first transformation may operate from Java to UML, and a second one from UML to Petri net.

Model transformations are reusable. In our previous example, if a different target formalism is to be used, the Java to UML transformation may be reused, while the second one is replaced. Some model transformation libraries such as [1] are already available to leverage this possibility. Typically, each entry specifies the name of the transformation as well as its source and target metamodels. Some documentation may also be available. A model-driven engineer confronted to a model transformation problem may first lookup for existing transformations. If no pre-existing transformation exactly performs the required task, some pieces may be used to form a chain into which only simpler new transformations need to be inserted. Source and target metamodel information may be used to chain transformations. A transformation from B to C may for instance be attached at the output of a transformation from A to B.

However, chaining transformations properly is generally a more complex task in practice. Knowing the source and target metamodels of a transformation is not enough. For instance, a transformation may only target a subset of its declared target metamodel. Feeding its output to a second transformation that takes a different subset of the same metamodel as input will typically not yield correct results. Computing a class dependency graph from a Java model by reusing a transformation that takes UML Class diagrams as input may not be possible with the Java to UML transformation targeting Petri nets used in the previous example. While this new transformation requires the class structure to be retrieved from the Java model, the initial transformation may have been limited to the generation of the Activity diagrams required for the generation of Petri nets.

The case of endogenous transformations is even more problematic. Because these transformations have the same source and target metamodel, they can in theory be inserted in a chain anywhere this metamodel appears. A collection of such transformations operating on the same metamodel could also be chained in any order. In practice, this may not lead to correct results (e.g., because a transformation may remove an element from the model that is required for another transformation to perform correctly).

Chaining transformations actually requires more precise knowledge about the individual transformations. For instance, if transformation t_1 relies on some information that is dropped by transformation t_2 then t_1 cannot be applied after t_2. This knowledge may be available in a documentation of some sort, but this is not always the case. One may also look at the insides of a transformation (i.e., its implementation), but this requires knowledge of the transformation language (there are several languages, and not everybody is an expert in all of them).

The situation would be simplified if each transformation clearly identified the subset of a metamodel it considers. But this is not always enough. For instance, some endogenous transformations have a fixed point execution semantics (i.e., they need to be executed again and again until the resulting model is not changed any more). In such a case, the metamodel subset generated by each iteration may be different (especially the last iteration when compared to the previous ones for transformations that remove elements one at a time).

The purpose of the work presented here is to automatically discover information about what model transformations actually do. The resulting data may be used to help the engineer decide how to chain transformations, and may complement what is in the documentation of the transformation if there is one. A Higher-Order Transformation [19] that takes as input the transformations to analyze produces a model containing the analysis results. This model may then be rendered to various surfaces using other transformations.

We have applied this approach to the case of a set of endogenous transformations that are used for the translation between constraint programming languages. All transformations take the same pivot metamodel as source and target metamodel and are written in ATL [12,11,9] (AtlanMod Transformation Language). However, different subsets of this metamodel are actually consumed and produced by each transformation. By statically analyzing these transformations we have been able to discover what they do, and infer chaining constraints from this knowledge.

The reminder of the paper is organized as follows. Section 2 presents a scenario involving a number of endogenous transformations operating on a single metamodel. Our transformation analysis approach is described in Section 3, and its application is presented in Section 4. The results are discussed in Section 5. Finally, Section 6 concludes.

2 Motivating Example

2.1 Interoperability of Constraint Programming Languages

In Constraint Programming (CP), one of the main goals is to define problems based on variables, domains and constraints such that a CP solver can compute their solutions [16]. In CP, various kinds of languages are used to state problems. For instance, the language of the ECL^{i}PS^e solver [2] is based on logic and Prolog, whereas OPL [8] (Optimization Programming Language) is a solver-independent language based on high-level modeling constructs. Some solvers have only programming APIs like ILOG Solver [14] or Gecode [17]. More recently, the definition of high-level modeling languages is becoming a hot topic in CP [15]. Then, new modeling languages have been developed such as Zinc and MiniZinc [13], Essence [7] and s-COMMA [18]. In these three cases, the high-level modeling language is translated into existing CP solver languages by using a flat intermediary language to ease the translation process and to increase the reusability of most transformations and reformulation tasks. This process is mainly achieved by hand-written translators using parsers and lexers.

In a recent work [4], model engineering was used to carry out this process from s-COMMA models to some solver languages. Then, this approach has been extended to get more freedom in the choice of the user modeling language [5]

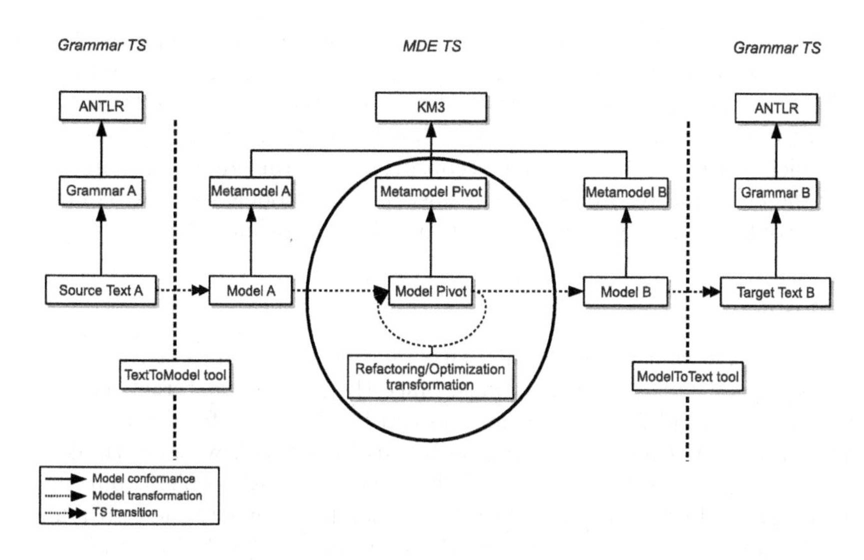

Fig. 1. A generic transformation process to translate CP models

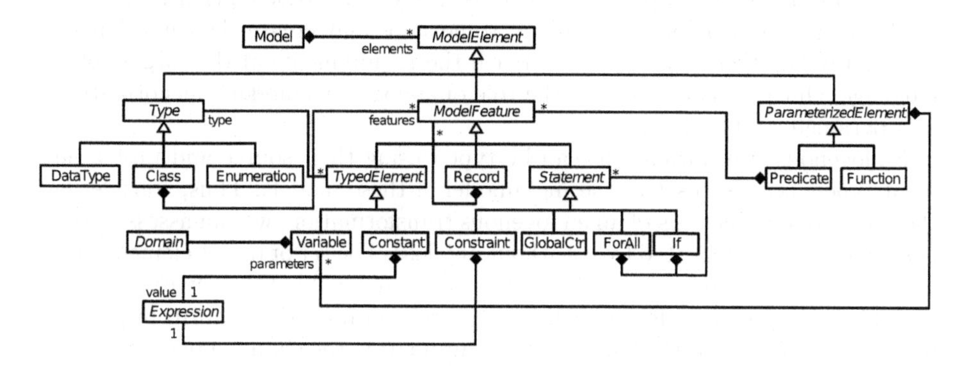

Fig. 2. Generic pivot metamodel for CP (excerpt)

(see Figure 1). A flexible pivot CP metamodel was introduced, on which several transformations are performed to achieve generic and reusable reformulation or optimization steps. The transformation chain from a language A to a language B is composed of three main steps: from A to pivot, pivot refactoring and pivot to B. Steps on pivot models may remove some structural features not authorized by the target solver language. Thus, objects, if or loop statements may be removed and replaced by an equivalent available structure, i.e. objects are flattened, if are expressed as boolean expressions and loops are unrolled. All these refactoring steps are not mandatory when considering a CP modeling language and a CP solver language, since loop or if statements may be available in most CP solvers. Since no existing model engineering tool exists to automate the chaining of these model transformations according to a source and a target metamodel, the user must build chains by hand without any verification process.

The main part of the generic CP pivot metamodel introduced in [5] is shown on Figure 2. Indeed, CP models are composed of a set of constraints, variables and domains. They are classified in an inheritance hierarchy, with abstract concepts such as `Statement` that corresponds to all kinds of constraint declarations. High-level model constructs are defined according to existing modeling languages, such as the class and record concepts. Most of pivot models will only contained elements conforming only to a subset of the whole pivot metamodel.

2.2 Problem

In this paper, we want to tackle the issues relating to the efficient management of a set of endogenous transformations. Since the source and target metamodels are similar, no additional information can be extracted from the header of an ATL transformation. Considering only this knowledge, we may think that endogenous transformations can be chained without any problem, but this is not true. The solution proposed by [21] is therefore not sufficient to address this problem because it only considers the signature (or header) of transformations. As shown in the motivating example, endogenous transformations achieve model reformulation or optimization steps. They have to be efficiently and correctly chained to avoid useless steps — some steps may create elements that are removed by another step — and to reach the requirements of the target solver language. Our goal is to discover the role of endogenous model transformations in a parameterizable chain.

Endogenous transformations can be typed using their source and target element types, i.e. a sub-set of the metamodel of these models. Thus, considering the set of source elements of an endogenous transformation, we can assess the set of source models supported by it without any loss. The set of target elements also allows us to type generated models. Then, we may be able to verify endogenous transformation chains. Moreover, using a search/optimization algorithm we may be able to find the "best" chain and thus automating the chaining of endogenous transformations according to an input metamodel and to an output metamodel corresponding to a high-level exogenous transformation.

3 Transformation Analysis

3.1 Identifying Domains and Codomains

In order to correctly chain model transformations it is necessary to have a certain understanding of what they do. Although it is not enough, source and target metamodels information is essential. The model M_B produced by a given transformation t_1 conforms to its target metamodel MM_B. It may only be fed as input to another transformation t_2 with the same metamodel MM_B as source metamodel.

This constraint may be expressed in functional terms as shown in [21]: transformations are considered as functions, and metamodels type their parameters in the case of simple transformations (Higher). For instance, if the source metamodel of t_1 is MM_A, and the target metamodel of t_2 is MM_C then: $t_1 : MM_A \rightarrow MM_B$ and $t_2 : MM_B \rightarrow MM_C$. In this notation the name of a metamodel is used to identify the set of models that conform to it. Thus, transformation t_1 is considered as a function of domain the set of models conforming to MM_A, and of codomain the set of models conforming to MM_B. In this example, if t_2 is total then it may be applied to the output of t_1 because the codomain of t_1 is also the domain of t_2.

In practice, model transformations are often partial functions: they do not map every element of their declared domain to an element of their codomain. For instance, t_2 may only work for a subset $MM'_B \subset MM_B$. If t_1 is surjective (i.e., it can produce values over its whole codomain) then t_2 cannot be applied to all output models that t_1 can produce. This shows that problems can arise when the domain of transformations (i.e., their source metamodels) is underspecified (i.e., too broad). If codomains (or target metamodels) are also underspecified, then there may not be any actual problem. For instance, if t_1 only produces results over $MM''_B \subseteq MM'_B$ then t_2 may be chained to t_1. Therefore, precisely identifying the actual domain and codomain of a transformation (i.e., definition domain and its image) would be an improvement over the current practice.

However, doing so is often complex because it requires deep analysis of transformations (e.g., not only source elements of transformation rules but also every navigation over source elements). Moreover, the semantics of a specific metamodel or transformation may make the problem harder. For instance, some endogenous transformations have a fixed point semantics and are called until a given type of element has been eliminated. Each intermediate step produces elements of this type except the last one. An example of such a transformation would eliminate for loops from a constraint program one nesting level at a time.

The objective of this paper is to provide a solution applicable with the current state of the art: actual domains and codomains cannot currently be 1) precisely computed, and 2) automatically checked. Therefore, if an approximation (because of 1)) is computed it must be represented in a simple form that the user may understand quickly (because of 2): the user has to interpret it). An example of such a simplification is the list of concepts (i.e., model element types coming from the metamodels) that are taken as input or produced as output of a transformation. This is the first analysis that has been applied to the motivating example presented in Section 2 with relatively poor results if considered alone.

3.2 Abstracting Rules

Other kinds of information may be used to better understand what a transformation does. ATL transformations are composed of rules that match source elements according to their type and some conditions (these form the source pattern of the rule), and that produce target elements of specific types (these form the target pattern of the rule). A transformation analyzer may produce an abstract representation of a set of transformation rules. This simplified description may take several forms.

One may think of representing the mapping between source and target metamodel concepts defined by the rules. Model weaving may be used for this purpose as shown in [6,11]. However, such a representation would be relatively verbose: there are as many mappings as rules, and the number of rules is typically close to the number of source or target concepts.

An additional simplification may be devised in the case of endogenous transformations in which elements are either copied (same target and source type) or mutated (different target and source types). These actions may be applied on every element of a given type, or only under certain conditions. Moreover, ATL lazy rules that are only applied if explicitly referenced (i.e., this is a kind of lazy evaluation) may also be used. Table 1 summarizes this classification of endogenous transformation rules. The first dimension (in columns) is the kind of action (copy or mutation) that is performed by the rule. The second dimension (in rows) corresponds to the cases in which the action is taken: always, under specific conditions, or lazily. Corresponding examples of rules taken from the motivating example are given below. No example of always or lazy mutation is given because there is no such case in the transformations of the motivating example.

Table 1. Classification of endogenous rules

	Copy	Mutation
Always		
Conditionally		
Lazily		

Listing 1 gives a rule that always copies data types. The target type (line 5) of such a rule is the same as its source type (line 3). It is concept *DataType* of the *CPPivot* metamodel in this listing. Moreover, it also copies all properties (e.g., source element name is copied to target element name at line 6). However, property-level information is not always so simple to identify. In many cases some properties are copied while others are recomputed. In order to keep the information presented to the user simple, property-level information is ignored in the current implementation of the transformation analyzer.

Listing 1. *Always copy* rule example

```
1 rule DataType {
2     from
3         s : CPPivot!DataType
4     to
5         t : CPPivot!DataType(
6             name <- s.name
7         )
8 }
```

A conditional copy happens when a copy rule has a filter or guard (i.e., a boolean expression that conditions the execution of the rule). The rule of Listing 2 is similar to the rule presented above in Listing 1 but has a guard specified at line 4. This rule performs a conditional copy.

Listing 2. *Conditionally copy* rule example

```
1 rule SetDomain {
2     from
3         s : CPPivot!SetDomain (
4             not s.parent.oclIsTypeOf(CPPivot!IndexVariable)
5         )
6     to
7         t : CPPivot!SetDomain (
8             values <- s.values
9         )
10 }
```

Listing 3 contains a lazy copy rule similar to the two previous rules of Listings 1 and 2 but starting with keyword *lazy* at line 1. Additionally, the rule presented here extends another rule via rule inheritance. This information is currently ignored during the abstraction process.

Listing 3. *Lazily copy* rule example

```
1 lazy rule lazyBoolVal extends lazyExpression {
2     from
3         b : CPPivot!BoolVal
4     to
5         t : CPPivot!BoolVal(
6             value <- b.value
7         )
8 }
```

An example of conditional mutation is given in Listing 4. This rule is a mutation because the target type *IntVal* (line 7) is different from the source type *VariableExpr* (line 3). It is conditional because there is a filter at line 4.

Listing 4. *Conditional mutation* rule example

```
1 rule VariableExpr2IntVal {
2     from
3         s : CPPivot!VariableExpr(
4             s.declaration.oclIsTypeOf(CPPivot!EnumLiteral)
5         )
6     to
7         t : CPPivot!IntVal(
8             value <- s.declaration.getEnumPos
9         )
10 }
```

3.3 Implementing Transformation Analysis

Transformation analysis is a case of Higher-Order Transformation [19] (HOT): it is a transformation that takes as input another transformation to be analyzed, and produces as output a model containing the analysis result. This HOT uses OCL expressions over the ATL metamodel, which is the metamodel of the language in which the transformations to analyze are written. These expressions recognize the patterns presented in Section 3.2. Then, an analysis model is created that relates concepts of the pivot metamodel to recognized patterns.

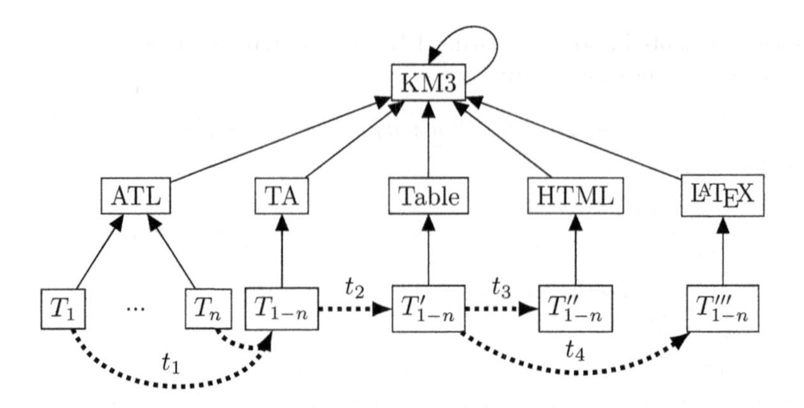

Fig. 3. Transformation analysis and results rendering

The main objective is to deliver a result that a user may understand and interpret. Consequently, special care was given to the rendering of the results. Figure 3 shows how the whole process is implemented. It starts from a collection of n ATL transformations T_1 to T_n conforming to the ATL metamodel. Transformation t_1 is applied to these transformations in order to obtain model T_{1-n} conforming to the TA (for Transformation Analysis) metamodel. This model contains the raw results of the analysis.

Then, transformation t_2 is applied in order to obtain model T'_{1-n} that conforms to a generic Table metamodel. This model may then be rendered to concrete display surfaces like HTML using transformation t_3, or LaTeXusing transformation t_4. The HTML rendering leverages the metamodels and transformation presented in [20], and available from Eclipse.org. The LaTeXrendering was specifically developed for the work presented in this paper. The tables given as example in Section 4 below have been generated automatically using the process depicted here. All metamodels conform to the KM3 [10] (Kernel MetaMeta-Model) metametamodel.

Although other techniques could have been used for the implementation, the whole transformation analysis and rendering process is defined in terms of models, metamodels, and transformations. This is an example of the unification power of models [3].

4 Experiments

4.1 Application to the Motivating Example

In the motivating example presented in Section 2 (see Figure 2), we consider five endogenous transformations achieving the following reformulation tasks:

- **Class and objects removal.** This complex endogenous transformation is decomposed in two steps. The first step removes classes and does not copy their features. Variables with a class type are mutated in an untyped record

definition that is a duplication of the class features. Other variables — with a primitive type like integer, real or boolean — are simply copied like other elements not being contained in a class declaration. The second step flattens record elements to get only variables with a primitive type.
- **Enumeration removal.** Some CP solvers do not accept symbolic domains. Thus, variables with a type being an enumeration are replaced by integer variables with a domain ranging from 1 to the possible number of symbolic values.
- **Useless If removal.** Boolean expressions used as tests in conditional if statements can be constant. In this case, it can be simplified, by removing conditional if elements and keeping only the relevant collection of statements.
- **For loops removal.** This reformulation task is implemented as a fixed point transformation followed by the useless if removal transformation. In the fixed point, each step removes only the deepest loops, i.e. loops that do not contain other loops. To ease the loops removing task, this composite element is replaced by another composite one being a conditional statement with an always true boolean test (i.e., a block).

We have applied on this example the HOT presented in the previous section. The results are detailed in the two following tables, which were automatically generated.

First, Table 2 presents the names of ignored in and out concrete concepts for each analysed transformation. These concepts are defined as concrete in the pivot metamodel, but they do not appear in any OCL expression of transformations. We can see, there is only one in ignored concept considering the record removal step. Indeed, this transformation was written with the assumption of being launched after the class instantiation transformation. Looking at the generated models, several concepts are missing, such as Class and Record for the record removal transformation.

Second, Table 3 gives more details on what endogenous transformations really do. Each line corresponds to an endogenous transformation analysis. Each column details the characteritics — always, conditionally and lazily — of none, one, several, or all other concepts. These characteristics are detailed for copy and mutation rules.

4.2 Interpreting the Results

Typing source and target models. The results given by Table 2 can be used to finely type authorized source and target models of the transformation. The set of authorized element types can be obtained by computing the difference between the set of all metamodel concepts and those presented in Table 2. It must be noted that looking only at the concepts in source patterns is not enough, since OCL navigation expressions can be used to explore and grab the elements contained in one being removed. Moreover, this information is only an approximation of the actual domain and codomain of the transformations, as described in Section 3.

Inferring partial transformation meaning. Considering Table 3, we can try to interprete the discovered knowledge to infer the transformation meaning. In the case of the class instantiation transformation, we can see that the only concept never copied and never mutated is the class concept. Since it is not in Table 2, it appears within OCL expressions, but it never appears within source patterns. It seems logical, since the aim of this transformation is to remove class statements by expanding their features. Then, variable elements are conditionally copied and conditionally mutated. Indeed, variable types are checked to know if they must be copied (i.e., their type is a primitive type) or if they must be mutated into record elements. Several concepts are always copied and never mutated. They correspond to type definitions or the root model concept, i.e. all concepts that can not be contained in a class. Finally all other concepts are conditionally copied and never mutated. It is checked they do not appear in a class before copying them.

Table 2. Experimental results: ignored elements

Transformation	Ignored in metaelements	Ignored out metaelements
classInstantiation		Class
enumRemoval		EnumLiteral, Enumeration
forallRemoval		
recordRemoval	Class	Class, Record
uselessIfRemoval		

Considering this knowledge, we can deduce that this transformation eliminates class elements, even if they are used within OCL navigation expressions. Variables are copied or mutated, whereas other elements are copied (some of them under a condition). So, this transformation mainly act on two types of elements: class and variable. We may use the set of element types occurring in the target patterns to know the sub-metamodel to which generated models conform.

Looking at the useless if removal transformation, we can easily infer its meaning. Indeed, only the if statements are conditionnally copied, while all other elements are always copied. Then, only some if statements are processed and might be removed.

Discovering fixed point transformations. A transformation having a fixed point semantics may have its codomain equal to its domain. It may focus only on a few concepts to conditionally mutate and to conditionally copy. All other concepts may be only copied. This pattern may allow us to detect whether an endogenous transformation could be applied in a fixed point scheme. In Tables 2 and 3 we see that the forall removal transformation matches this pattern. Looking only at Table 3, we may think that the enumeration removal transformation is also a fixed point transformation processing variables. However, Table 2 shows that its main goal is to remove enumerations, because its domain and its codomain are not equal (i.e., it removes all enumerations in one step).

Table 3. Experimental results: referenced elements

Copy	**lazily, cond.**	**never**	**lazily, cond.**	**cond.**	**never**	**always**	**cond.**
Mutation	**cond.**	**never**	**never**	**cond.**	**cond.**	**never**	**never**
classInstantiation	NONE	Class	NONE	Variable	NONE	EnumLiteral, Predicate, Enumeration, DataType, Model	ALL OTHER
enumRemoval	NONE	EnumLiteral, Enumeration	NONE	Variable, VariableExpr	NONE	ALL OTHER	NONE
forallRemoval	Forall, VariableExpr	NONE	ALL OTHER	IndexVariable	NONE	EnumLiteral, Predicate, Enumeration, Constant, DataType, Variable, Record, Class, Model, Array	SetDomain, IntervalDomain
recordRemoval	NONE	Record	NONE	NONE	PropertyExpr	EnumLiteral, Predicate, IndexVariable, Constraint, Enumeration, Constant, DataType, If, Model, Forall	ALL OTHER
uselessIfRemoval	NONE	NONE	NONE	NONE	NONE	ALL OTHER	If

5 Discussions

5.1 Application to Exogenous Transformations

The approach presented in this paper could be extended to support exogenous transformations. Thus, looking at the source patterns and all OCL expressions, we can define the refined type of source models of a transformation (i.e., a more precise definition of its domain). To get the refined type of target models (i.e., a more precise definition of the codomain), we just have to collect the set of concepts occurring in target patterns.

Moreover, we can consider most endogenous transformations as exogenous transformations between two sub-metamodels of the same metamodel. Then, the chaining of endogenous transformations can be transformed into a problem of chaining exogenous transformations. Inferring the meaning of an endogenous transformation may not be necessary (in most cases), since its main task may be to remove or add elements of a given type. However, more complex endogenous transformations may be more difficult to finely chained, since their meaning is necessary to understand how to use them. The knowledge collected in Table 3 is an attempt at achieving this goal with high-level characteristics on concepts. However, this knowledge does not focus on how matchings are performed in rules. Using a more detailed analysis, we could generate weaving models relating to model transformations and then analyze them. However, these models would be more verbose than Table 3. We could also try to analyse OCL expressions and mappings in transformation rules. Although, the cost and the difficulty of our approach is almost negligible when compared to these deeper analysis.

5.2 Debugging Transformations

The knowledge discovered through our analysis transformation can be used in debugging model transformations (exogenous or endogenous). Indeed, when a metamodel contains many concepts, a software engineer may forget to define all the corresponding rules. Thus the results from Table 2 can be directly used, but also the column of Table 3 that corresponds to elements never copied and never mutated. Other columns may also be useful to check that concepts are well classified and no copy or mutation rule are missing.

The data in Table 3 can also be used to discover mistakes in naming metamodel concepts in some rules or helpers. Indeed, some concepts of a metamodel may rarely have instances in models, and rules dealing with them may not be called. Thus, no error occurs even if the transformation contains some careless mistakes. In the case of our motivating example, we discovered several ill-written rules and helpers dealing with specific CP concepts that do not occur in our CP models.

6 Conclusion

In this paper, we addressed the problem of chaining model transformations. This problem is illustrated on a pivot metamodel for Constraint Programming (CP) that is used for translations between CP languages. Several issues are tackled in order to safely chain transformations. Thus, a higher-order transformation is proposed to statically analyze model transformations. It focuses on source and target concepts, thus defining refined metamodels to which models conform (i.e., more precise definitions of domains and codomains of model transformations). It also extracts some knowledge on how source concepts are processed and assigns characteristics to each concept: always copied, conditionally copied, lazily copied, never copied, always mutated, etc. Considering these characteristics, we are able to find element types that are mainly processed. This process is not accurate enough to exactly infer the meaning of model transformations (it is an abstraction), but it allows us to assert some constraints on how to chain several endogenous transformations. The contributions of this paper are of a different nature and complementary to the results presented in [21]. That paper focuses on a type system for transformation chains, and considers that declared types are good enough, whereas in this paper we have investigated the problem of imprecise transformation typing.

A possible extension of the work presented in this paper would be to go beyond the discovery of hidden chaining constraints and to fully automatize transformation chaining. This automation process could be performed using Artificial Intelligence techniques. An optimization problem can be defined to transform models from a source metamodel to another. The problem naturally comes to find a path in a graph corresponding to a model of the transformations and their types. Some heuristics can be defined to choose the best paths, which may contain as few redundant and as few useless steps as possible.

References

1. ATLAS Transformation Language (ATL) Library (2009), `http://www.eclipse.org/m2m/atl/atlTransformations/`
2. Apt, K.R., Wallace, M.: Constraint Logic Programming using Eclipse. Cambridge University Press, New York (2007)
3. Bézivin, J.: On the unification power of models. Software and System Modeling 4(2), 171–188 (2005)
4. Chenouard, R., Granvilliers, L., Soto, R.: Model-Driven Constraint Programming. In: Proceedings of ACM SIGPLAN PPDP, Valencia, Spain, pp. 236–246. ACM Press, New York (2008)
5. Chenouard, R., Granvilliers, L., Soto, R.: Rewriting Constraint Models with Metamodels. In: Proceedings of SARA2009. AAAI Press, Menlo Park (2009)
6. Didonet Del Fabro, M., Bézivin, J., Jouault, F., Valduriez, P.: Applying generic model management to data mapping. In: Proceedings of the Journées Bases de Données Avancées, BDA 2005 (2005)
7. Frisch, A.M., Grum, M., Jefferson, C., Hernández, B.M., Miguel, I.
8. Van Hentenryck, P.: The OPL Optimization Programming Language. The MIT Press, Cambridge (1999)
9. Jouault, F., Allilaire, F., Bézivin, J., Kurtev, I.: Atl: a model transformation tool. Science of Computer Programming 72(3), 31–39 (2008); Special Issue on Second issue of experimental software and toolkits (EST)

10. Jouault, F., Bézivin, J.: Km3: a dsl for metamodel specification. In: Gorrieri, R., Wehrheim, H. (eds.) FMOODS 2006. LNCS, vol. 4037, pp. 171–185. Springer, Heidelberg (2006)
11. Jouault, F., Kurtev, I.: On the architectural alignment of atl and qvt. In: Proceedings of the, ACM Symposium on Applied Computing (SAC 2006), Dijon, France, pp. 1188–1195. ACM Press, New York (2006)
12. Jouault, F., Kurtev, I.: Transforming models with atl. In: Bruel, J.-M. (ed.) MoDELS 2005. LNCS, vol. 3844, pp. 128–138. Springer, Heidelberg (2006)
13. Marriott, K., Nethercote, N., Rafeh, R., Stuckey, P.J., de la Banda, M.G., Wallace, M.: The Design of the Zinc Modelling Language. Constraints 13(3), 229–267 (2008)
14. Puget, J.-F.: A C++ Implementation of CLP. In: Proceedings of SPICIS 1994, Singapore (1994)
15. Puget, J.-F.: Constraint Programming Next Challenge: Simplicity of Use. In: Wallace, M. (ed.) CP 2004. LNCS, vol. 3258, pp. 5–8. Springer, Heidelberg (2004)
16. Rossi, F., van Beek, P., Walsh, T.: Handbook of Constraint Programming (Foundations of Artificial Intelligence). Elsevier Science Inc., New York (2006)
17. Schulte, C., Tack, G.: Views and Iterators for Generic Constraint Implementations. In: Hnich, B., Carlsson, M., Fages, F., Rossi, F. (eds.) CSCLP 2005. LNCS (LNAI), vol. 3978, pp. 118–132. Springer, Heidelberg (2006)
18. Soto, R., Granvilliers, L.: The Design of COMMA: An Extensible Framework for Mapping Constrained Objects to Native Solver Models. In: Proceedings of ICTAI, pp. 243–250. IEEE Computer Society, Los Alamitos (2007)
19. Tisi, M., Jouault, F., Fraternali, P., Ceri, S., Bézivin, J.: On the use of higher-order model transformations. In: Proceedings of the Fifth European Conference on Model-Driven Architecture Foundations and Applications (ECMDA), pp. 18–33 (2009)
20. Vépa, E., Bézivin, J., Brunelière, H., Jouault, F.: Measuring model repositories. In: Proceedings of the Model Size Metrics Workshop at the MoDELS/UML 2006 conference, Genoava, Italy (2006)
21. Vignaga, A., Jouault, F., Bastarrica, M.C., Brunelière, H.: Typing in Model Management. In: Proceedings of ICMT 2009, Zurich, Switzerland, pp. 197–212 (2009)

CSP(M): Constraint Satisfaction Problem over Models*

Ákos Horváth and Dániel Varró

Budapest University of Technology and Economics,
Department of Measurement and Information Systems,
H-1117 Magyar tudósok krt. 2, Budapest, Hungary
{ahorvath,varro}@mit.bme.hu

Abstract. Constraint satisfaction programming (CSP) has been successfully used in model-driven development (MDD) for solving a wide range of (combinatorial) problems. In CSP, declarative constraints capture restrictions over variables with finite domains where both the number of variables and their domains are required to be a priori finite. However, the existing formulation of constraint satisfaction problems can be too restrictive to support dynamically evolving domains and constraints necessitated in many MDD applications as the graph nature of the underlying models needs to be encoded with variables of finite domain. In the paper, we reformulate the constraint satisfaction problem directly on the model-level by using graph patterns as constraints and graph transformation rules as labeling operations. This allows expressing problems composed of dynamic model manipulation and complex graph structural constraints in an intuitive way. Furthermore, we present a prototype constraint solver for the domain of graph models built upon the VIATRA2 model transformation framework, and provide an initial evaluation of its performance.

Keywords: Constraint satisfaction programming, graph transformation.

1 Introduction

In artificial intelligence, the constraint satisfaction problem (CSP) is to find a solution to a set of constraints that impose conditions which has to be satisfied by a set of variables. Each variable typically takes its value from a finite domain. A solution is one (or all) assignment of variables which satisfy each constraint.

Constraint satisfaction techniques have been successfully applied for various problems of model-driven engineering for applying design patterns [1], to support domain-specific modeling [2] or in the context of model transformations [3]. As a commonality, all these approaches translate high-level models to an existing (off-the-shelf) constraint solver (like e.g. [4, 5]) to provide embedded design intelligence for modeling.

However, advanced constraint solvers typically apply certain restrictions for the CSP problem. For instance, the domains of variables are frequently required to be (a priori) finite, moreover, many approaches disallow the dynamical addition or retraction of constraints. Furthermore, mapping graph-like models obtained in model-driven engineering to variables with finite domain can be a non-trivial task, especially, when considering

* This work was partially supported by the EC FP6 DIANA (AERO1-030985) European Project.

A. Schürr and B. Selic (Eds.): MODELS 2009, LNCS 5795, pp. 107–121, 2009.

the evolution of models. While recent research initiatives in CSP have started to better address dynamic constraints [6], no efficient solvers are available for structural constraints over graph-like models.

In this paper, we investigate how advanced model transformation technology can contribute to solving dynamic constraint satisfaction problems with global constraints over the domain of model graphs. We extend the definition of constraint satisfaction problems by using *graph patterns to define structural (first-order logic) constraints*, and *graph transformation rules [7] as labeling operations*. Informally, all graph pattern constraints need to be satisfied by the underlying model when searching for a specific goal. However, instead of simple variable substitution, the labeling phase applies graph transformation rules to carry out model manipulations on the underlying graph domain.

As an analogy, our approach allows to (i) dynamically add/remove constraints from the problem domain, (ii) modify the domain of the variables during search and (iii) define structural constraints in a more natural way.

Furthermore, we developed a prototype constraint solver on top of the VIATRA2 [8] model transformation framework by using incremental constraint evaluation and various search strategies and heuristics. An initial evaluation of the solver is carried out using an allocation problem taken from critical systems.

The rest of the paper is structured as follows. In Sec. 2 we briefly introduce the concept of metamodeling, graph transformation and constraint satisfaction problems. Sec. 3 proposes our graph pattern and transformation based constraint solver. Related work is assessed in Sec. 5, and finally, Sec. 6 concludes the paper.

2 Background

In order to introduce our approach this section briefly outlines the basics of graph transformation and gives a motivating example from the avionics domain.

2.1 Running Example: Allocation of an IMA System

As a motivating example, let us assume an integrated modular avionics (IMA) system composed of *Jobs* (also referred as applications), *Partitions*, *Modules* and *Cabinets*. *Jobs* are the atomic software blocks of the system defined by their memory requirement. Based on their criticality level jobs are separated into two sets: *critical* and *simple* (non-critical). For critical jobs double or triple modular redundancy is applied while for simple ones only one instance is allowed. *Partitions* are complex software components composed of jobs with a predefined free memory space. Jobs can be allocated to the partition as long as they fit into its memory space. *Modules* are SW components capable of hosting partitions. Finally, *Cabinets* are storages for maximum

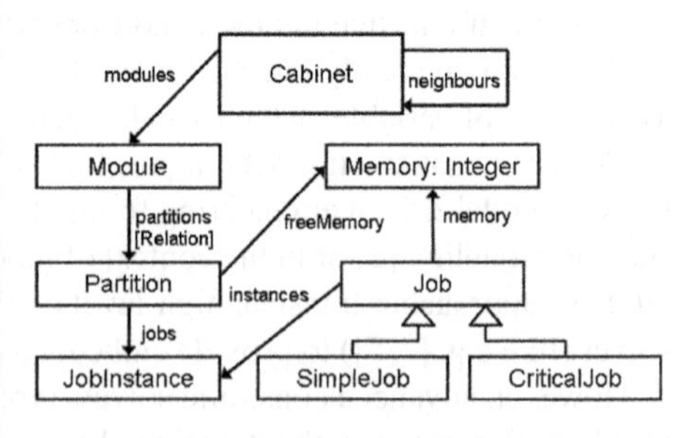

Fig. 1. Metamodel of an IMA architecture

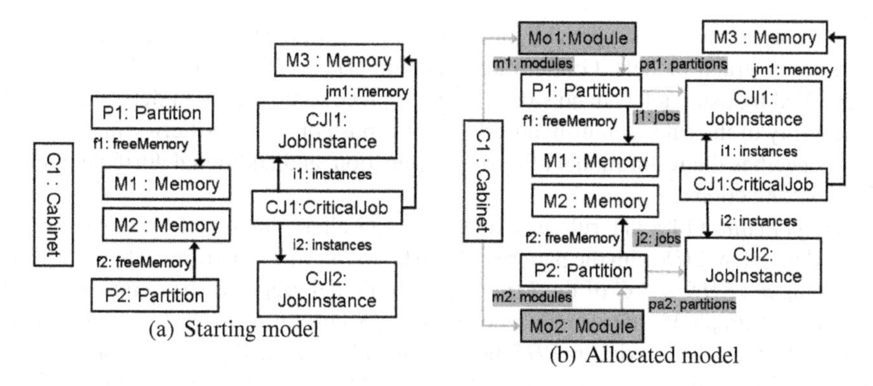

(a) Starting model (b) Allocated model

Fig. 2. Example IMA system

(in our example) up to two modules used to physically distribute elements of the system. Additionally a certain number of safety related requirements will also have to be satisfied: (i) a partition can only host jobs of one criticality level and (ii) instances of a certain critical job can not be allocated to the same partition and module. The task is to allocate an IMA system defined by its jobs and partitions over a predefined cabinet structure and to minimize the number of *modules* used.

A sample system composed of a critical job with two instances and two partitions with a single cabinet is shown in Fig. 2(a) with a possible allocation depicted in Fig. 2(b) defined over the metamodel captured in the VPM formalism [9] in Fig. 1. Newly created elements are highlighted in grey. Throughout the paper we will use this example to demonstrate the technicalities of our constraint satisfaction technique over models.

2.2 Graph Patterns and Graph Transformation

Graph patterns (*GP*) are frequently considered as the atomic units of model transformations [8]. They represent conditions that have to be fulfilled by a part of the instance model. The VIATRA2 notation in particular, describes them as a disjunction of pattern bodies $GP = \vee PB_i$, where a pattern is fulfilled if at least one of its pattern body is fulfilled. *Pattern bodies* $PB = (SC, AC, NAC_j)$ consist of (i) *structural conditions SC* prescribing the existence of nodes and edges of a given type, (ii) *attribute conditions* (*AC*) allowing term evaluation over the attributes of the matched elements (marked by the check keyword) and (iii) arbitrary number of negative application conditions. A *negative application condition* $NAC = \neg GP$, defined by a negative subpattern, prescribes contextual conditions for the original pattern which are forbidden in order to find a successful match. Negative conditions can be embedded into each other in an arbitrary depth (e.g. negations of negations), where the expressiveness of such patterns converges to first order logic [10].

A *match m* for a graph pattern *GP* in a instance model *M* denoted by $m : GP \longrightarrow M$ means that (i) $m : PB_i \mapsto M, (\exists PB_i \in GP)$ there exists an injective, type conformant total morphism *m* from one of its pattern bodies $PB_i = (SC_i, AC_i, NAC_{i,j})$ to the instance model; (ii) $m' : NAC_{i,j} \mapsto M, (\nexists NAC_{i,j})$ if no matches exist for any embedded NACs of that pattern body PB_i and (iii) all attribute conditions AC_i are fulfilled by *m*.

Graph transformation. [7] provides a high-level rule and pattern-based manipulation language for graph models. Graph transformation $GT = (LHS, RHS, AMA)$ rules can be specified by using a left-hand side – LHS (or precondition) pattern determining the applicability of the rule, a right-hand side – RHS (postcondition) pattern which declaratively specifies the result model after rule application, and additional attribute manipulation AMA actions .

The *application* of a GT rule to a host model G alters the model by replacing the pattern defined by LHS with the pattern defined by RHS. This is performed by (i) finding a matching $m : LHS \longrightarrow G$ of the LHS pattern in model graph G; (ii) removing a part of the model graph M that can be mapped to LHS but not to RHS; (iii) adding new elements to the which exist in RHS but not in LHS and finally (iv) performing the attribute manipulation operations described in AMA. A *graph transformation* step is denoted formally as $G \overset{r,m}{\Longrightarrow} H$, where H is the resulting model; r and m denote the applied rule and the matching, respectively.

Example. Sample graph patterns and transformation rules are depicted in Fig. 3. The jobInstancewithoutPartition pattern matches an input parameter JobInstance JIns which is not already allocated to a Partition P by the j1 jobs relation (elements of the NAC are encapsulated by the NEG rectangle).

The allocateJobInstance GT rule allocates the JobInstance JI to the Partition P1 (by the jobs j1 relation) if it is not already allocated to the P2 Partition and decreases the MP free memory attribute of the P1 partition by the memory requirement of Job J captured in MJ. We use a combined representation that jointly defines the left hand side (LHS) of the graph transformation rule, and the model manipulation operations to be carried out where newly created elements and attribute manipulation operations are tagged with an add and set keywords, respectively.

3 Constraint Satisfaction Programming

In this section, we provide a detailed description of our constraint satisfaction framework and its conceptual foundations and demonstrate how to apply it on the IMA system allocation problem introduced in Sec. 2.1.

3.1 Constraint Problem Specification

Constraint Satisfaction Problem for Variables of Finite Domain. A CSP(FD) is a problem composed of a finite set of variables, each of which is associated with a finite domain, and a set of constraints that restricts the values the variables can simultaneously take. In a more precise way a constraint satisfaction problem is a triple: (Z, D, C) where Z is a finite set of variables $x_1, x_2, ..., x_n$; D is a function which maps every variable in Z to a set of objects of arbitrary type; and C is a finite (possibly empty) set of constraints on an arbitrary subset of variables in Z. The task is to assign a value to each variable satisfying all the constraints. Solutions to CSPs are usually found by (i) *constraint propagation* a reasoning technique to explicitly forbid values or domains for variables by predicting future subsequent constraint violations and (ii) *variable labeling* searching through the possible assignments of values to variables already restricted by the (propagated) constraints.

Planner Algorithms. Planner algorithms [11] are hierarchical problem solving procedures subdividing the original problem into smaller parts. A planner $(I,E,O) \rightarrow P$, is a structure where I is a logic formula of the initial state, E is the logic formula of the goal state, while O is the set of permitted operations. The output P is a sequence of operations (called plan) providing a trajectory from the initial to the goal state. An operation $o = (C,A)$ is a pair where C stands for a precondition defined in first order logic and A for actions. Preconditions must hold before performing its specific operation.

3.2 CSP(M): Constraint Satisfaction Problem over Models

We now define constraint satisfaction problems over models (CSP(M)) by combining *CSP for finite domains* and *planner algorithms* (see in Sec. 3.1). In principle, our approach generalizes planner algorithms with the definition of *global constraints* that can additionally restrict certain trajectories of the search space and extends traditional CSP(FD) by introducing *labeling rules* to define and solve constraint problems over models even with dynamic model manipulation such as element creation and deletion.

A CSP(M) consist of an *initial model*; a *goal* that have to be satisfied by the *solution model* to be searched; *global constraints* that need to be satisfied by all models traversed during the search and finally a set of *labeling rules* capturing the permitted operations. Formally a CSP(M) $(M_0,C,G,L) : M_s$ is a structure where: M_0 is the initial model; C is a set of global constraints; G is a set of subgoals which together in conjunction form the goal and L is a set of labeling rules. The output M_s is the solution model satisfying:

- (i) $M_0 \rightsquigarrow M_s$; there exists a trajectory $M_o \xrightarrow{l_1} M_1 \xrightarrow{l_2} .. \xrightarrow{l_n} M_n$ where $i = 1..n : l_i \in L$. Meaning that M_s is reachable from M_0 through a sequence of applied labeling rules.
- (ii) $\forall G_i \in G : M_s \models G_i$; M_s satisfies all subgoals G_i
- (iii) $\forall C_i \in C : M_s \models C_i$; M_s also satisfies all global constraints C_i
- (iv) $\forall M_i, \forall C_j \in C : M_0 \rightsquigarrow M_i \wedge M_i \rightsquigarrow M_s \wedge M_i \models C_j$; along the trajectory from the initial to the solution model all visited model M_i satisfies each global constraint.

As models in MDD are usually described as graphs we instantiate our formalism on graph transformation using the VIATRA2 [8] language. This way models are captured by typed graphs over a given metamodel while subgoals and global constraints are defined using graph patterns and finally labeling rules are described as graph transformation rules. However, this formalism can also be incorporated into other modeling approaches such as MOF models, OCL constraints and QVT rules.

Goal and Global constraints. Both subgoals and global constraints are defined by graph patterns. The goal G is the conjunction of subgoals where a subgoal (graph pattern) is a disjunction of alternate pattern bodies.

A subgoal or global constraint C described by the graph pattern GP is either a *positive* or *negative* constraint. A negative constraint is satisfied by a model ($M \models C$) if it does not have a match in M, formally $m : GP \longrightarrow M$, $(\nexists m)$. While a positive constraint is satisfied if its representing graph pattern has a match in M; $m : GP \longrightarrow M$, $(\exists m)$. A further restriction on positive constraints can be formulated by stating that they are satisfied iff their representing graph pattern has a *predefined* positive number ($Cardinality$) of matches, formally $|\{m : GP \longrightarrow M\}| = Cardinality$. In our running example all patterns are considered as *negative constraints*.

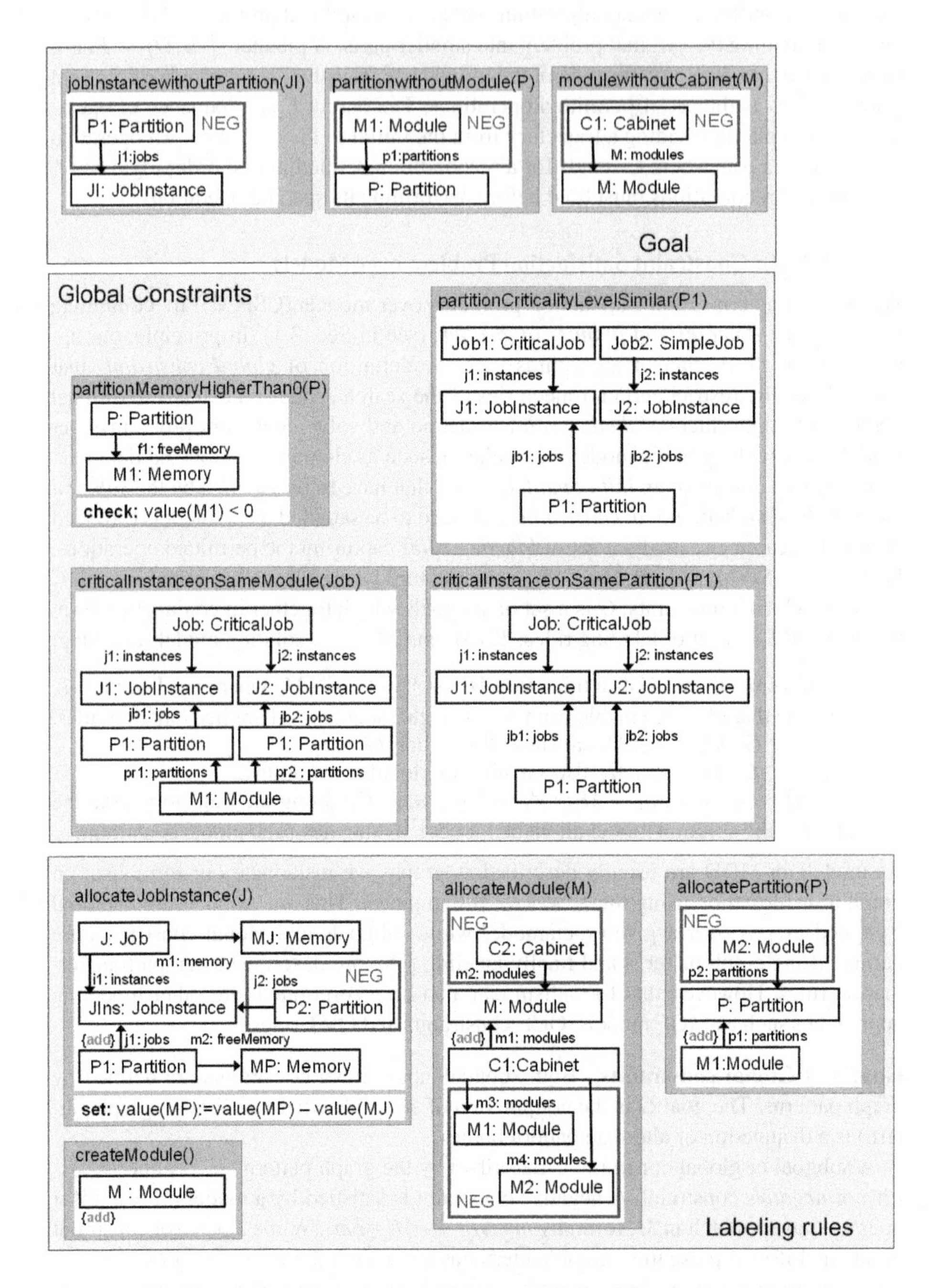

Fig. 3. Goals, Labeling rules and Global constraints of the running example

Labeling rules. Labeling rules are described as graph transformation rules. A labeling rule l is enabled when the precondition LHS_l of its representing graph transformation rule is applicable to the underlying model M, formally $m : LHS_l \longrightarrow M, (\exists m)$. However, additional properties are used to refine the execution order and semantics of an enabled rule application:

- *Priority (integer: 0..100)*: Defines a precedence relation on labeling rules. It organizes the labeling rules into sets based on their priorities. In each state the solver selects its next step from the set with the highest priority. In our running example we use the same priority for all labeling literals.
- *Execution mode (forall — choose)*: Defines whether a rule is simultaneous applied at all possible matches (forall) (as a single transition) or only once on a randomly selected single matching (choose). In the running example all labeling rules are using choose type execution mode.

Example. Our running example formalized as a CSP(M) problem is depicted in Fig. 3. The jobInstancewithoutPartition, partitionwithoutModule and modulewithoutCabinet subgoals formulating the *goal* describe that in a solution model each JobInstance, Partition and Module is allocated to a corresponding Partition, Module and Cabinet, respectively. For example, the jobInstancewithoutPartition subgoal captures its requirement using a double negation (NAC and negative constraint) stating that there are *no unallocated* job instance JI in the solution model. Similar double negation is used in case of the other two subgoals.

Global constraints formulate the safety and memory requirements. The partitionMemoryHigherThan0 pattern captures the simple memory constraint that all partitions must have higher than zero free memory. The safety requirement stating that a partition can only host jobs of one criticality level is captured by the partitionCriticalityLevelSimilar pattern. As it is a *negative constraint* it describes the (positive) case where the P1 partition holds two job instances J1 and J2 of a simple and a critical job Job1 and Job2, respectively. The criticalInstanceonSamePartition and criticalInstanceonSameModule patterns restrict in a similar way that no job instances J1 and J2 of a critical job Job can be allocated to the same partition P1 or module M1.

Finally, *labeling rules* describe the allocation operations. The allocatePartition graph transformation rule defines how a partition P can be allocated to a module M1. As a common technique in graph transformation based approaches, a negative application condition stating that the partition is not already allocated is used to indicate that the rule should only be used for unallocated partitions. On top of that the allocateModule rule uses an additional NAC to forbid allocation of module M to cabinet C1 when two other modules M1 and M2 are already presented on C1, while the allocateJobInstance defines an additional attribute operation to decrease the free memory value MP of partition P1 by the required memory MJ of the allocated job J. The createModule rule simply creates a module M without any precondition.

Although not demonstrating in our ongoing example, our constraint framework is able to dynamically add and remove subgoals and labeling rules during the traversal of the state space in response to changes made in the original formulation of the problem. This allows to address problems which can change over time and solutions are relying on already made decisions such as reconfiguration of system components. In this case the requirement of the provided QoS (e.g., at least three service nodes must be running) by the system can vary over time and reconfiguration needs to be applied on the actual system state.

3.3 Solving CSP over Models

To traverse the search space of a constraint program introduced in Sec. 3.2, we define the solver as a virtual machine that maintains a 4-tuple (CG, CS, AM, LS) as a state. CG is called the *current goal*; CS is the *constraint store*; AM is the *actual model*; and finally LS is the *labeling store*. The (i) *current goal* stores the subgoals that still need to be satisfied; the (ii) *constraint store* holds all constraints the solver has satisfied so far while the (iii) *actual model* represents the underlying actual model and finally the (iv) *labeling store* contains all enabled labeling rules. An element in the labeling store is a pair (l, m), where l is a labeling rule and m is a valid match of its precondition LHS_l in AM; formally $m : LHS_l \longrightarrow AM$.

Initially, the CG, CS and LS are initialized with the *goal*, *global constraints* and the enabled *labeling rules* of the CSP(M) problem, respectively, while AM is set to the initial model. The solver proceeds by selecting an enabled *labeling rule* (l, m) and applies it to AM resulting in AM'. After each *labeling rule* application (and after initialization) CS is checked for consistency. In principle, whenever (i) a *global constraint* in CS is violated the solver backtracks, (ii) a *subgoal* in CG is satisfied by M it is moved to CS and (iii) vica-versa moved from CS to CG if it becomes unsatisfied and finally (iv) a successful termination is reached when CG becomes empty.

Formally, a transition in the search space is a pair of 4-tuples of $(CG, CS, AM, LS) \rightarrow (CG', CS', AM', LS')$, which describes a step between the two states. A transition is possible iff $\exists(l, m) \in LS$ where $AM \stackrel{l,m}{\Longrightarrow} AM'$ i.e., a labeling rule can be applied on the actual model for a certain match. A goal G can be proved if there exists a trajectory of individual steps $(CG, CS, M_0, LS) \rightsquigarrow (\emptyset, CS', M_s, LS)$ for a satisfiable constraint store CS. In other words, a solution model is found if there exists a sequence of labeling rule applications, that lead to an empty CG and satisfiable CS.

Example. Let us consider that our running example is in the initial state S_0 depicted in Fig. 4. The actual model is the initial model M_0 (detailed in Fig. 2(a)); the current goal CG contains the jobInstancewithoutPartition and the partitionwithoutModule subgoals; the constraint store CS holds all global constraints and the modulewithoutCabinet subgoal while the labeling store LS holds the following pairs: (allocateJobInstance, CJI1), (allocateJobInstance, CJI2) and (createModule, ∅). The solver has three enabled labeling rules (transitions) $t1, t2, t3$ resulting in states $S1, S2, S3$. For example, $S1$ is traversed by applying the allocateJobInstance labeling rule on the critical job instance CJI1. In S_1 the actual model changed with an additional j1 jobs relation (highlighted in grey) between partition P1 and job instance CJI1; the current goal and constraint store did not change and contains the same elements as in S_0 while the labeling store changed to: (allocateJobInstance, CJI2) and (createModule, ∅). For easier readability, actual models of the states are depicted in Fig. 4 in a simplified way without type information e.g., the element CJI1: JobInstance is denoted as CJI1.

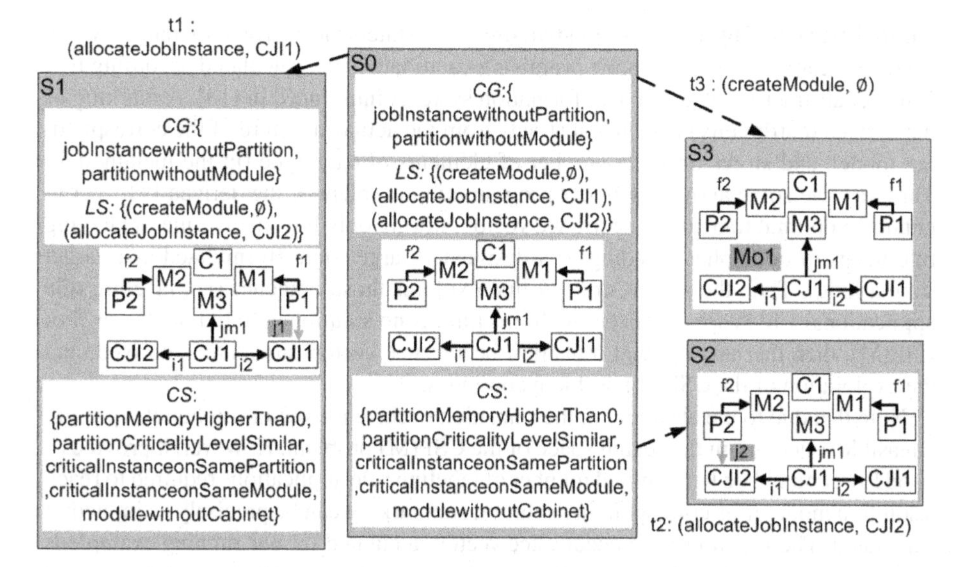

Fig. 4. Example State Space

3.4 Search Strategies

Most algorithms for solving CSPs systematically traverse the possible search space. Such algorithms are guaranteed (in case of finite search space) to find a solution, if one exists, or to prove that the problem is irresolvable.

The most common algorithm for performing systematic search is *backtracking* based on depth-first search. Backtracking incrementally builds candidates to the solutions, and abandons each partial candidate ("backtracks") as soon as it determines that it cannot possibly be completed to a valid solution. In our case it means that in the actual state a global constraint is violated or its labeling store is empty, thus backtracks the last applied step and continue with a different one. One of the main drawbacks of the simple backtracking algorithm is *thrashing*; i.e. repeated failure due to the same reason. Thrashing occurs because the backtracking algorithm does not identify the root cause of a conflict, i.e., the unsatisfiable global constraint or subgoal leading to a dead-end. Therefore, search in different parts of the search space keeps failing for the same reason.

In order to overcome trashing we implemented two additional search strategies:

Random Backjumping is a backtracking strategy based on the assumption that a traversal might be in a dead-end if no solution was found within a certain amount of time (deadline). When the solver exceeds this deadline, it jumps back to a state at least as high as the half of the actual depth of the search space tree. This way the solver can restart the traversal from an earlier state and continue on different random transitions. However, to keep the completeness of the traversal we implemented a simple policy introduced in [12] that is to increase the height of the backjump each time it is used. This approach is obviously not effective to prove unsatisfiability because all the runs except the last are wasted but has a good average performance in certain real scenarios.

Guided traversal by Petri net abstraction is a state space traversal strategy which conducts search towards the most promising candidate paths calculated according to a Petri net abstraction of graph transformation systems introduced in [13]. A marking of the derived (cardinality) Petri net abstracts from the actual structure of the corresponding model, and stores only the number of elements of each type (in the metamodel). This way, we solve an integer linear programming problem of the derived Petri net to obtain an optimal transition occurrence vector (storing only how many times a labeling rule needs to be applied) leading to a designated target state (formulated as a target submarking). Then the search strategy first explores those branches (i.e. labeling rule applications) which are consistent with this hint. If no solution is found on the level of CSP(M), then the next optimal transition occurrence vector candidate is derived, and the exploration of the CSP(M) problem continues.

Note that due to the abstraction, the transition occurrence vector might not represent a feasible trajectory in the search space of the CSP(M) problem. However, it provides a good lower bound on the minimal number of labeling rule applications required to reach a solution model if its corresponding solution submarking can be precisely estimated or calculated. The first transition occurrence vector calculated for our running example is $(2,1,1,1)$ meaning that to achieve a solution submarking derived from a solution model where all job instances and partitions are allocated, the allocateJobInstance rule has to be applied twice while the other three only once.

3.5 Optimization

To further reduce the size of the traversed state space we introduce two additional optimization techniques that complement our search strategies described in Sec. 3.4.

Look-ahead pattern. Additional restrictions on the applicability of labeling rules can be formulated by incorporating a subset of global constraints called *look-ahead* constraints into the precondition (LHS) of rules. These constraints are validated in the precondition of labeling rules to prevent unnecessary steps which would violate these constraints. Currently, this is a manual hint by the designer, but in the future, we plan to automate this task by applying critical pair analysis [14] or transformations of graph constraints to preconditions [15].

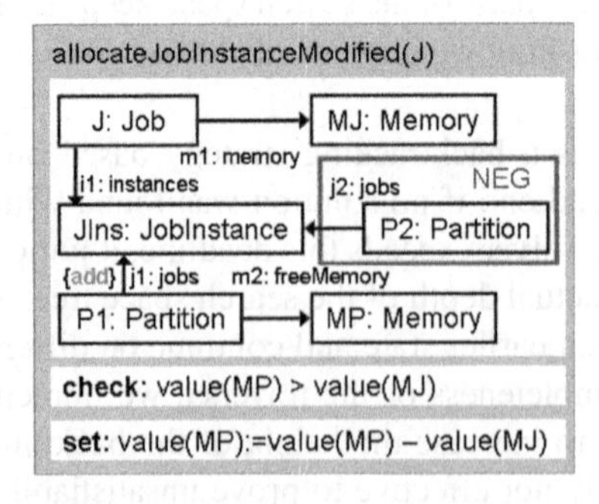

Fig. 5. Modified allocateJobInstance rule

In our running example the *allocateJobInstance* rule can be further restricted regarding the memory consumption of the JIns job instance making the *partitionsMemoryHigherThan* global (look-ahead) constraint obsolete. Its modified version with the extra check condition on the required and available memory is depicted in Fig. 5.

Exception priority. In order to explicitly restrict the number of application of labeling rules along a trajectory we introduced a priority class called *exception*. *Exception* rules have the lowest priority and will only be selected when no other labeling rules are enabled. In any trajectory if the number of applications of an exception rule exceeds its predefined value the solver backtracks and continues along another transition. Exception rules are used as hints by the solver to avoid state space explosion especially, when the Petri net based abstraction cannot predict the number of labeling rule applications for *element creation* rules without preconditions such as the createModule rule in the running example.

3.6 Implementation

We implemented an experimental solver for CSP(M) including all the techniques above on top the VIATRA2 model transformation framework, which offers efficient rule- and pattern-based manipulation of graph models by the means of graph transformation. In order to implement the solver using graph based state representation we had to address the problems of *constraint evaluation*, *typed graph comparison* and *backtracking*.

For effective *evaluation* of constraint satisfiability we rely upon the incremental pattern matcher component [16] of the framework. In case of incremental pattern matching, the matches of a pattern are stored to be readily available in constant time, and they are incrementally updated when the model changes. As matches of patterns are cached, this reduces the evaluation of constraints and preconditions of labeling rules to a simple check. This way, the solver has an incrementally maintained up-to-date view of its constraint store and enabled labeling rules. Furthermore, incrementality provides an efficient *constraint propagation* technique to immediately detect constraints violations after a labeling rule is fired.

As for *backtracking* between states, we implemented a simple transaction mechanism that saves the atomic model manipulation operations applied on the model in an undo stack. This stack not only allows us to backtrack the manipulations but also ease the computation of difference between neighbour states. This feature is also useful in problems that require solutions that are "nearest" to a given initial model (e.g. for reconfiguration rules).

For *comparison of graphs* we adapted the DSMDIFF [17] algorithm, which relies on (i) signatures (for nodes and edges) composed of type and name information and (ii) containment relation between nodes of the graph. It is also important to mention that to keep the memory consumption low, we serialized *already visited states* as strings and applied the algorithm directly on them.

The introduced solver is already in use in the context of the DIANA [18] European project as its underlying allocation engine for a system-level integration scenario.

4 Evaluation

To evaluate the performance of our CSP(M) solver, we carried out experiments[1] based on our running IMA allocation example. We assume that we have to allocate different software workloads (functionalities) on a system of three modules (which corresponds to the avionics architecture used in the DIANA project).

Each row in Table 1 defines a software workload allocation test case. The *Simple Job*, *Critical Job*, and *Partition* rows define the actual number of software components to be allocated where critical jobs are separated based on their redundancy scheme into double (DMR) and triple (TMR) modular redundancy. *All Job Instances* represents the total number of job instances to be allocated. For our initial measurement (denoted by *ATTR*) we assume that each job requires the same amount of memory (30 units) and each partition offers the same free memory (300 units).

Table 1. Runtime performance of the IMA allocation problem

	Simple job #	Critical Job		Partition #	All Job instances	Completed Allocation (out of 10)	Runtime [msec]			Traversed States #		
		DMR	TMR				min	max	avg	min	max	avg
ATTR.	3	2	4	4	19	10	1078	196469	66991	64	13984	4802
	5	2	5	5	24	6	4212	145823	81689	146	12632	8296
	16	2	5	5	35	1	-	50678	-	-	237	-
NON ATTR.	5	2	5	5	24	10	879	156322	41274	72	17639	4278
	16	2	5	5	35	4	12023	195672	57837	174	1311	404
	20	5	7	7	51	1	-	102452	-	-	276	-

Due to the random strategy of our solver we considered an allocation *completed* if a solution was found within 200 seconds. In each case we executed the solver ten times and present the number of *Completed Allocations*. *Runtime* performance and traversed *State Space* size of the completed allocations are also presented by their minimum (*min*), maximum (*max*) and average (*avg*) values for each test case.

During the analysis and profiling of our implementation we have discovered that the performance bottleneck in our system is mainly related to the model management component of the underlying VIATRA2 transformation framework (which is obviously not optimized for constraint solving purposes). In almost all cases we have observed that core attribute manipulation functions (e.g., setValue) are the most time consuming. This is due to the low-level notification mechanism that keeps the incremental pattern matcher up-to-date after changes in the model space, which is more effective for graph manipulations rather than attribute changes.

Therefore we also evaluated our approach without attribute manipulation (i.e., memory requirements) on the running example denoted by *NON ATTR.*. In order to solve a conceptually similar problem we defined an additional global constraint stating that a partition can not affiliate more than ten job instances. Results show that (i) in both cases solutions were found traversing only a small number of states compared to the size of the problem, (ii) the *NON ATTR.* implementation scales almost up to twice the size in

[1] For our experiments, we used a average PC with Core Duo@1.8 GHz and 2GB RAM running Windows XP and Java SDK 1.6.

the number of job instances to allocate and (iii) due to the heuristic character of the state space traversal the runtime performances can vary up to two order of magnitudes.

Our measurement shows that our constraint solver based upon incremental pattern matching is able to solve non-trivial problems of model oriented constraints. On the other hand further investigations have to be directed to combine them with constraints over regular attributes.

5 Related Work

Applications of CSP in MDD. While constraint satisfaction techniques have been successfully applied in the context of MDD. [19] proposes an approach for partial model completion based on constraint logic programming. [2] support efficient domain specific modeling by transforming constraints to a Prolog representation. In [1], poor design patterns are detected by using off-the-shelf CSP techniques and tools. [20] defines an interactive guided derivation algorithm to assist model designers by providing hints about valid editing operations that maintain global correctness of models.

In the context of model transformations, [21] proposes constraint solving as a graph pattern matching strategy. [3] proposes Constraint Relation Transformation an extension of QVT Relations with numerical constraints by integrating local numerical constraint solving (over attributes of model elements).

Recent approaches like [22, 23, 24] aim at automatically creating instance models, which conform to a given metamodel and a set of constraints. This model generation problem is solved by existing back-end tools like Alloy, or by a dedicated theorem prover for Horn-like clauses as in [24]. This problem can also be interpreted as a special (restricted) CSP problem without numeric constraints on attributes.

In all these papers, constraint satisfaction techniques are used to assist model-driven development. The main innovation of our work is just the opposite: it investigates how model transformation techniques can contribute to solve complex constraint satisfaction problems over complex structural constraints and dynamic labeling rules.

State Space Exploration for GT. There are several state space exploration approaches [25, 26] to analyze graph transformation systems. Common in these solutions that they store system states as graphs and directly apply transformation rules to explore the state space similar to our approach. Their main difference is that they use an exhaustive state space exploration to verify certain conditions in the graph transformation system, while our approach rely on guided traversals.

CSP-specific. Research in the field of constraint satisfaction programming has been conducted towards flexible and dynamic constraints [27, 6]. Our approach shows similarities with both approaches as (i) it also allows to add (or remove) additional constraints during the solution process as defined in the dynamic extension, and (ii) can give support for cost based optimization defined over the constraint (flexible) even in the case of complex structural constraints.

6 Conclusion and Future Work

In the current paper, we have presented a novel approach defining constraint problems directly over models (denoted shortly as *CSP(M)*) using graph transformation rules and graph patterns. As a distinctive feature from a CSP point of view, we extended traditional labeling by using model manipulation as provided by graph transformation to dynamically create and delete model elements. Furthermore, not demonstrated in the current paper but our framework also allows to *dynamically add/remove* subgoals and labeling rules to alter the constraint problem to address problems defined in dynamic constraint satisfaction programming [27].

We have also built (and initially evaluated) a prototype solver implementation on top of the VIATRA2 model transformation framework using incremental pattern matching that provides an efficient *constraint propagation* technique to immediately detect constraint violation. Moreover, the solver integrates various strategy (e.g. random backjumping, directed search) to guide the state space traversal.

As the main innovation, we argued that model transformation technology can efficiently contribute to formulate and solve constraint satisfaction problems with complex structural constraints and dynamic labeling rules.

In the future, we plan to investigate (i) how can traditional constraint programming concepts can be combined with our approach to effectively handle constraints over attributes, (ii) further state space optimization by automatic detection of look-ahead pattern based on critical pair analysis and finally (iii) other structural constraint based frameworks such as Alloy for a detailed comparison.

References

1. El-Boussaidi, G., Mili, H.: Detecting patterns of poor design solutions using constraint propagation. In: Czarnecki, K., Ober, I., Bruel, J.-M., Uhl, A., Völter, M. (eds.) MODELS 2008. LNCS, vol. 5301, pp. 189–203. Springer, Heidelberg (2008)
2. White, J., Schmidt, D., Nechypurenko, A., Wuchner, E.: Introduction to the generic eclipse modelling system. Eclipse Magazine (6), 11–18 (2007)
3. Petter, A., Behring, A., Mühlhäuser, M.: Solving constraints in model transformation. In: Paige, R.F. (ed.) ICMT 2009. LNCS, vol. 5563, pp. 132–147. Springer, Heidelberg (2009)
4. Intelligent Systems Laboratory, Swedish Institute of Computer Science: Sicstus Users manual (2009), http://www.sics.se/sicstus/docs/latest4/pdf/sicstus.pdf
5. Official website of ILOG Solver, http://www.ilog.com/products/cp/
6. Miguel, I., Shen, Q.: Dynamic flexible constraint satisfaction. Applied Intelligence 13(3), 231–245 (2000)
7. Algebraic Approaches to Graph Transformation. In: Rozenberg, G. (ed.) Handbook of Graph Grammars and Computing by Graph Transformations. Foundations, vol. 1. World Scientific, Singapore (1997)
8. Varró, D., Balogh, A.: The Model Transformation Language of the VIATRA2 Framework. Science of Computer Programming 68(3), 214–234 (2007)
9. Varró, D., Pataricza, A.: VPM: A visual, precise and multilevel metamodeling framework for describing mathematical domains and UML. Journal of Software and Systems Modeling 2(3), 187–210 (2003)
10. Rensink, A.: Representing first-order logic using graphs. In: Ehrig, H., Engels, G., Parisi-Presicce, F., Rozenberg, G. (eds.) ICGT 2004. LNCS, vol. 3256, pp. 319–335. Springer, Heidelberg (2004)
11. Weld, D.S.: An introduction to least commitment planning. AI Magazine 15(4), 27–61 (1994)

12. Baptista, L., Margues-Silva, J.: Using randomization and learning to solve hard real-world instances of satisfiability. In: Dechter, R. (ed.) CP 2000. LNCS, vol. 1894, pp. 489–494. Springer, Heidelberg (2000)
13. Varró-Gyapay, S., Varró, D.: Optimization in graph transformation systems using petri net based techniques. Electronic Communications of the EASST 2 (2006)
14. Heckel, R., Küster, J.M., Taentzer, G.: Confluence of typed attributed graph transformation systems. In: Corradini, A., Ehrig, H., Kreowski, H.-J., Rozenberg, G. (eds.) ICGT 2002. LNCS, vol. 2505, pp. 161–176. Springer, Heidelberg (2002)
15. Ehrig, H., Ehrig, K., Habel, A., Pennemann, K.H.: Theory of constraints and application conditions: From graphs to high-level structures. Funda. Inf. 74(1), 135–166 (2006)
16. Bergmann, G., Ökrös, A., Ráth, I., Varró, D., Varró, G.: Incremental pattern matching in the VIATRA transformation system. In: GRaMoT 2008, 3rd Int. Workshop on Graph and Model Transformation (2008)
17. Lin, Y., Gray, J., Jouault, F.: Dsmdiff: A differentiation tool for domain-specific models. European Journal of Information Systems, Special Issue on Model-Driven Systems Development 16(4), 349–361 (2007)
18. Official website of the Distributed equipment Independent environment for Advanced avioNics Applications (DIANA) European project, http://diana.skysoft.pt
19. Sen, S., Baudry, B., Precup, D.: Partial model completion in model driven engineering using constraint logic programming. In: INAP 2007: International Conference on Applications of Declarative Programming and Knowledge Management, Würzburg, Germany (2007)
20. Janota, M., Kuzina, V., Wasowski, A.: Model construction with external constraints: An interactive journey from semantics to syntax. In: Czarnecki, K., Ober, I., Bruel, J.-M., Uhl, A., Völter, M. (eds.) MODELS 2008. LNCS, vol. 5301, pp. 431–445. Springer, Heidelberg (2008)
21. Rudolf, M.: Utilizing constraint satisfaction techniques for efficient graph pattern matching. In: Ehrig, H., Engels, G., Kreowski, H.-J., Rozenberg, G. (eds.) TAGT 1998. LNCS, vol. 1764, pp. 238–252. Springer, Heidelberg (2000)
22. Anastasakis, K., Bordbar, B., Georg, G., Ray, I.: On challenges of model transformation from UML to Alloy. Software and Systems Modeling (2009)
23. Winkelmann, J., Taentzer, G., Ehrig, K., Küster, J.M.: Translation of restricted ocl constraints into graph constraints for generating meta model instances by graph grammars. Electron. Notes Theor. Comput. Sci. 211, 159–170 (2008)
24. Jackson, E., Sztipanovits, J.: Constructive techniques for meta and model level reasoning. In: Engels, G., Opdyke, B., Schmidt, D.C., Weil, F. (eds.) MODELS 2007. LNCS, vol. 4735, pp. 405–419. Springer, Heidelberg (2007)
25. Rensink, A.: The GROOVE simulator: A tool for state space generation. In: Pfaltz, J.L., Nagl, M., Böhlen, B. (eds.) AGTIVE 2003. LNCS, vol. 3062, pp. 479–485. Springer, Heidelberg (2004)
26. König, B., Kozioura, V.: Counterexample-guided abstraction refinement for the analysis of graph transformation systems. In: Hermanns, H., Palsberg, J. (eds.) TACAS 2006. LNCS, vol. 3920, pp. 197–211. Springer, Heidelberg (2006)
27. Schiex, T.: Solution reuse in dynamic constraint satisfaction problems. In: Proceedings of the 12th National Conference on Artificial Intelligence, pp. 307–312. AAAI Press, Menlo Park (1994)

Parsing SBVR-Based Controlled Languages*,**

Mathias Kleiner[1], Patrick Albert[2], and Jean Bézivin[1]

[1] INRIA - EMN, Atlanmod team, Nantes 44000, France
[2] ILOG S.A, 9 rue de Verdun, 94253 Gentilly, France
mathias.kleiner@inria.fr

Abstract. Conceptual schemas (CS) are core elements of information systems knowledge. A challenging issue in the management processes is to allow decision makers, such as business people, to directly define and refine their schemas using a pseudo-natural language. The recently published Semantics for Business Vocabulary and Rules (SBVR) is a good candidate for an intermediate layer: it offers an abstract syntax able to express a CS, as well as a concrete syntax based on structured English. In this article, we propose an original method for extracting a SBVR terminal model out of a controlled English text and then transform it into a UML class diagram. We describe a model-driven engineering approach in which constraint-programming based search is combined with model transformation. The use of an advanced resolution technique (configuration) as an operation on models allows for non-deterministic parsing and language flexibility. In addition to the theoretical results, preliminary experiments on a running example are provided.

Keywords: Controlled languages, parsing, SBVR, model-driven engineering, constraints, configuration, model search.

1 Introduction

Conceptual schemas (CS) are widely used in industry as formal representations of information systems knowledge. A CS is often the central element on which relies a set of operations. The UML/OCL combination is the de-facto standard for specifying a CS. However, designing, maintaining and refining a CS currently requires important technical skills. Stakeholders thus rely on experts to model their requirements. A recent trend in software engineering (requirements engineering) is to discover ways to facilitate this communication, by allowing decision makers to express their needs in a comprehensive language which can then be transformed into a formal representation.

In the business context, the Object Management Group (OMG) has recently published the SBVR (Semantics for Business Vocabulary and Rules) recommendation. SBVR provides a metamodel for business concepts and statements which can be used to define a CS. The specification also proposes a structured English

* Empirical results category paper.
** Work partially funded by the French ANR IdM++ project.

A. Schürr and B. Selic (Eds.): MODELS 2009, LNCS 5795, pp. 122–136, 2009.

form for a model that is easily understood by business people. However parsing the proposed structured English into a SBVR model is a difficult problem. In particular, the different interpretations that can be made for one sentence disqualifies the existing model driven engineering (MDE) tools (such as ATL[1] or QVT[2]) that are based on deterministic algorithms. If one wishes to keep this freedom in the language then the problem requires to *search for* a solution using advanced AI technics.

This article describes an automatic translation of SBVR structured English into a SBVR concrete model and a UML model of the described CS. The originality of our approach is that it combines constraint programming techniques with model transformation tools in a MDE framework. It is composed of three main operations. The first task is a syntactical and grammatical analysis of the text, which is directly related to the well-known and challenging field of (controlled) language parsers: we describe a SBVR parser based on an advanced constraint programming technique known as configuration. The second task is the transformation of the resulting model into a SBVR model. The third task is the transformation of the SBVR model into a UML model of the CS. The integration of constraint programming in MDE as an advanced transformation tool is an important and innovating contribution of this work.

Plan of article. Section 2 briefly introduces each technology used in our approach. We also present an overview of the whole process and a running example. Section 3 introduces the controlled language parser. Section 4 shows how the resulting model is transformed into a SBVR model. Section 5 proposes a transformation from SBVR to UML. Validation, implementation and experiments are presented in Section 6. Finally, we discuss related work in Section 7 and conclude.

2 Context of the Work

2.1 Brief Introduction to SBVR

SBVR is an OMG standard [3] intended to be the basis of the description of business activities in natural languages. SBVR attempts to build the bridge between Business Users and software artifacts, enabling non-IT specialists to parameterize and evolve the business logic embedded into applications. SBVR standardizes a set of concepts enabling the definitions of business specific Controlled Languages (declarative languages, whose grammar and lexicon have been limited in order to eliminate part of the ambiguity. See [4] as a historical paper, or more recently [5]). Business Rules Systems such as for example ILOG JRules[6] or Drools[7] are popular controlled languages used to explicitely model the business logic in a growing number of applications.

We will not describe SBVR exhaustively in this article. However a look at the Figures 1 and 2 might provide a feeling about the sophistication of the meta-model and about the approach that separates logical formulations from meanings.

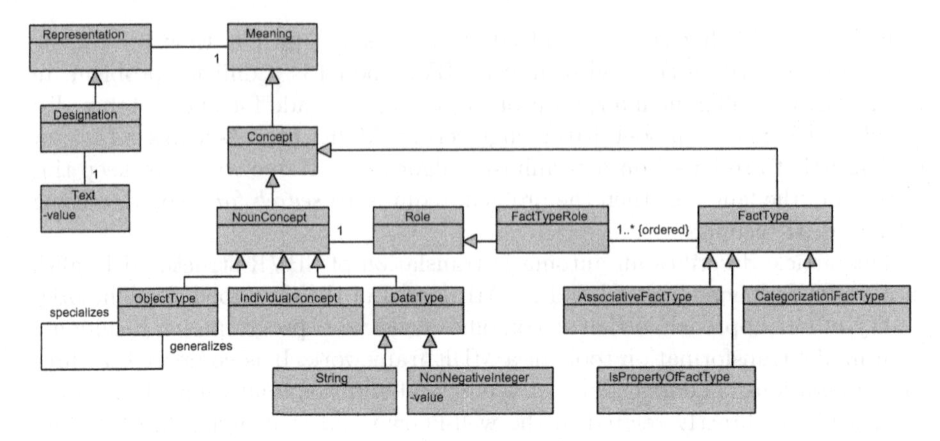

Fig. 1. Extract of the SBVR metamodel: meanings

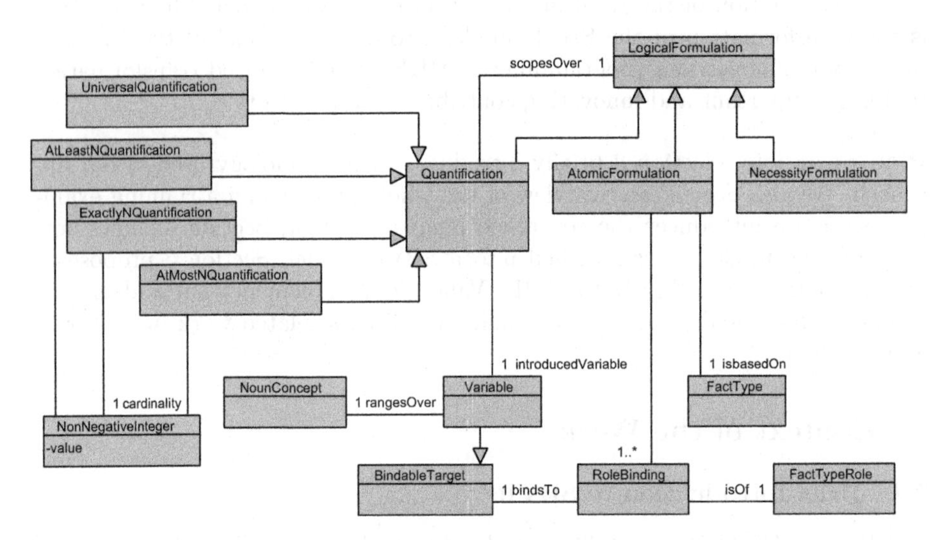

Fig. 2. Extract of the SBVR metamodel: logical formulations

2.2 Brief Introduction to Configuration

Configuring is the task of composing a complex system out of generic components [8]. Components, also called objects or model elements, are defined by their types, attributes, and known mutual relations. The acceptable systems are further constrained by the request: a set of problem-specific and/or user-specific requirements, represented by a fragment of the desired system (i.e. interconnected objects). From a knowledge representation perspective, configuration can be viewed as the problem of finding a graph (i.e. a set of connected objects) obeying the restrictions of an object model under constraints. From a model driven approach, it can be viewed as the problem of finding a finite model that conforms to a metamodel. More precisely, we consider the process as a model transformation where the source model is the request and the target model is the solution. The configuration model acts as the target metamodel. A *relaxed* version of this metamodel acts as the source metamodel. This relaxed metamodel is obtained by the removal of all constraints: minimum cardinalities are set to zero, attributes are optionals and OCL constraints are removed. The request, which is a set of target model elements with incomplete knowledge (for instance linked elements and attribute values are usually undefined), is therefore conformant to the source metamodel. In this context, the configurator *searches* for a target model, completing the source and creating all necessary model elements so that the result (if any) is conformant to the target metamodel.

Various formalisms or technical approaches have been proposed to handle configuration problems: extensions of the Constraint Satisfaction Problem paradigm [9,10,11], knowledge-based approaches [12], logic programming [13], and object-oriented approaches [14,15]. Configuration has traditionnaly been used with success in a number of industry applications such as manufacturing or software engineering. More recently, the expressive power of configuration formalisms has proven its usefulness for artificial intelligence tasks such as language parsing [16]. A deeper introduction to configuration can be found in [8].

In the sequel we propose to use Ilog JConfigurator [15] as a controlled language parser for SBVR. In this model-oriented approach, a configuration model (in our context, the target metamodel) is well-defined as a set of classes, relations and constraints. The UML/OCL language combination may be used to this purpose [17].

2.3 Brief Introduction to MDE and Model Transformation

Model Driven Engineering is a research area that considers the main software artifacts as graphs. This comes from an industrial need to have a regular and homogeneous organization where different facets of a software system may be easily separated or combined.

In MDE, models are considered as the unifying concept. The MDE community has been using the concepts of terminal model, metamodel, and metametamodel for quite some time. A terminal model is a representation of a system. It captures some characteristics of the system and provides knowledge about it. MDE tools act on terminal models expressed in precise modeling languages. The abstract syntax of a modeling language, when expressed as a model, is called a metamodel. A language definition is given by an abstract syntax (a metamodel), one or more concrete syntaxes, and a definition of its semantics. The relation between a model expressed in a language and the metamodel of this language is called conformsTo. This should not be confused with the representationOf relation holding between a terminal model and the system it represents. Metamodels are in turn expressed in a modeling language called metamodeling language. Its conceptual foundation is itself captured in a model called metametamodel. Terminal models, metamodels, and metametamodel form a three-level architecture with levels respectively named M1, M2, and M3. A formal definition of these concepts may be found in [18]. The principles of MDE may be implemented in several standards. For example, OMG proposes a standard metametamodel called Meta Object Facility (MOF).

The main way to automate MDE is by providing transformation facilities. The production of model Mb from model Ma by a transformation Mt is called a model transformation. In this work we use ATL (AtlanMod Transformation Language), a QVT-like model transformation language [1] allowing a declarative expression of a transformation by a set of rules.

2.4 Process Overview

Figure 3 sketches the overall process in a model-driven engineering framework. The input is a text in the form of structured English as has been proposed in the SBVR specification [3]. The text is injected into a model thanks to a simple metamodel for sentences and words annotating the position of words in the text. A second simple transformation uses a lexicon to label each word with a set of possible syntactical categories. We have then defined a metamodel, called *Syntax*, where we adapted configuration grammars[16] to SBVR and the model-driven engineering context. The text (as labeled words) is fed into a constraint-based configurator using the relaxed version of Syntax. The result of the configuration process, acting as a syntax and grammar analysis, is a finite model that conforms to the Syntax metamodel. This model is then transformed with a usual model transformation tool (here, ATL) to a model conforming to the SBVR metamodel through a set of rules using the grammatical dependencies found during configuration. This SBVR terminal model may then be processed again with ATL to obtain a corresponding UML model.

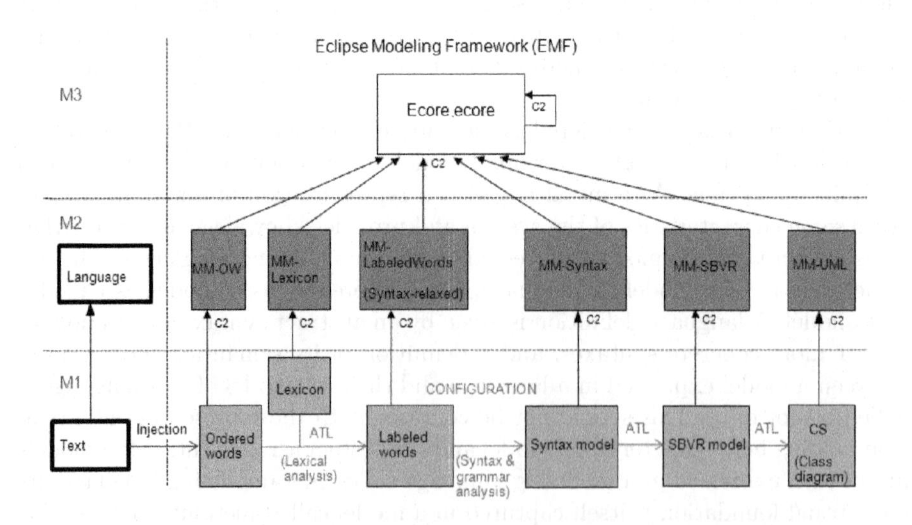

Fig. 3. Process overview

2.5 Running Example

An example will be used throughout the paper to illustrate the approach. The considered text is composed of three sentences defining a simple CS:

(1) Each company sells at least one product.
(2) Each product is sold by exactly one company.
(3) A software is a product.

This relatively simple example still embeds many important concepts. From the language parsing viewpoint it uses nouns, active and passive verbs, as well as different quantifiers. From the modelling viewpoint it shows the notions of classes, inheritance and relations with cardinalities. In the following Sections, we will show how each main task is applied on those sentences.

3 Parsing a Controlled Language for SBVR

Parsing natural languages is one of the major challenges of AI. Considering the difficulty of the task, many efforts have been focused on the more accessible field of controlled languages (CL) [19]. Among the existing approaches, [16] shows how property grammars [20] can be captured into a configuration model in order to parse a subset of French with a constraint-based configurator. The resulting parser does not inherit the deterministic behaviour of most CL parsers and is designed to be adapted to different grammars. We have modified and extended this method to the form of structured English proposed in the SBVR specification [3]. In our MDE approach, the proposed configuration model is defined as a metamodel called Syntax.

3.1 Syntax Metamodel

A fragment of this metamodel (most classes and relations) is presented in Figure 4. Syntax captures three main informations from the input text: syntactical categories, grammatical dependencies and SBVR semantics.

Syntactical Categorization. In order to obtain a syntactic tree from a sentence, we have adapted the property grammar model from [16] to English. The main class of the model is *Cat*, which denotes a syntactical category. A category is *terminal* when it is directly associated to a single word. Such categories include *NCat* (noun), *VCat* (verb) or *DCat* (determiner). Those categories may be further specialized: a verb is either transitive (*TVCat*) or intransitive (*ITVCat*). The possible categories of a given word are obtained with the lexicon in the previous transformation. A category is *non-terminal* when it is composed of other categories. *SentenceCat* (sentence), *NPCat* (noun phrase), *VPCat* (verb phrase) are the main non-terminal categories. A set of constraints further defines the acceptable categorizations. Such constraints involve for instance the categories

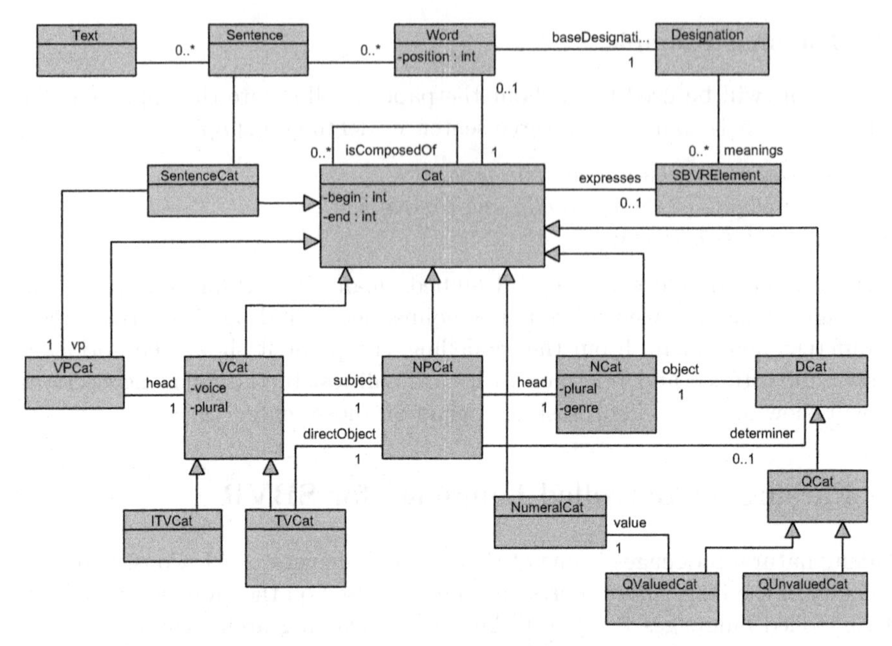

Fig. 4. Extract of the Syntax metamodel: syntax and grammar

constituents, or relative positions in the sentence. Here are some example constraints specified in OCL:

- *Each verb phrase for which the heading verb is transitive is composed of at least one noun phrase.* This constraint applies to the relation *isComposedOf* of a category:

```
context VPCat
inv: head.oclIsTypeOf(TVCat)
    implies isComposedOf->
     exists( elt.oclIsTypeOf(NPCat) )
```

- *A verb phrase is always preceeded by a noun phrase.* The constraint applies to the attributes "begin" and "end" of categories, which are obtained from their associated word(s):

```
context SentenceCat
inv: isComposedOf->exists(
    elt.oclIsTypeOf(NPCat)
    and elt.end < vp.begin )
```

Grammatical Dependencies. We have extended the syntactic model so that grammatical dependencies appear as explicit relations between categories. Similary to the syntactical part, a set of constraints defines the acceptable constructions. Here are some example constraints specified in OCL:

- *The subject of an active verb occurs before the verb phrase*:

```
context VPCat
inv: (head.voice = 'active')
    implies head.subject.end < begin
```

– *The head of a verb's subject shares the same plural*:

```
context VCat
inv: plural = subject.head.plural
```

SBVR Semantics. We have extended the metamodel with the main concepts of the SBVR metamodel. SBVR semantics are assigned to syntactical categories through the "expresses" relation. Again, a set of constraints governs the possible assignments. Here are some examples:

– *A transitive verb expresses a fact type.*:

```
context TVCat
inv: not expresses.oclIsUndefined()
    and expresses.oclIsKindOf(FactType)
```

– *The head of a subject of a verb expresses either an object type or an individual concept*:

```
context VCat
inv: subject.head.expresses.
      oclIsKindOf(ObjectType)
    or subject.head.expresses.
      oclIsKindOf(IndividualConcept)
```

About SBVR concepts singularity. A critical issue in assigning SBVR semantics to categories is the one of concepts singularity. More precisely, the same SBVR concept may be expressed in different sentences (or even in the same sentence). Consider for instance the first two sentences of our running example: the concepts "Company", "Product" and "To sell" are expressed multiple times. We obviously wish to avoid creating duplicate SBVR elements in the resulting model. A set of constraints forces the uniqueness of SBVR elements based on an equivalency statement. In the case of elements of class *ObjectType*, the disambiguation is done on the word's base designation. It can be formalized in OCL as follows:

```
inv: NCat.allInstances()->
    forAll(n1,n2 : NCat |
    (n1.word.baseDesignation =
     n2.word.baseDesignation)
   = (n1.expresses = n2.expresses))
```

Note that since the base designation is used, different forms of the same word are still recognized (i.e. "products" and "product" are matched). The same principle is applied to other SBVR elements such as fact types.

3.2 Parsing Process and Result

As explained previously, the input of the configuration process is a model of a relaxed version of the target metamodel. In our context, the input text is transformed into a set of interconnected configuration objects of type Text, Sentence, Words and Designations. For each word, the preceeding transformation, using the lexicon, has provided its properties (plural, voice, etc.), base designation

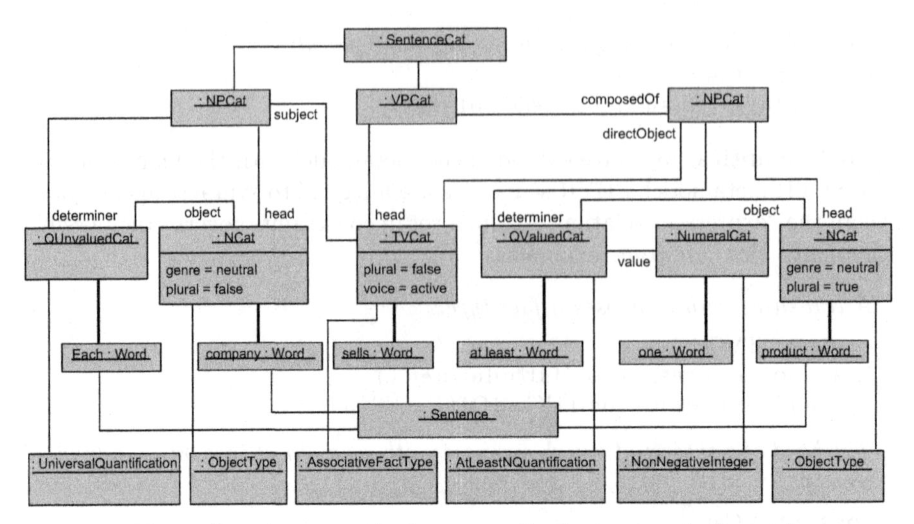

Fig. 5. Running example: fragment of a Syntax terminal model

(the base designation of the word "has" is "to have"), and candidate syntactical categories (the word "one" may be a noun, a numeral or an adjective).

The result of the configuration process is one (or more) terminal model(s) satisfying the configuration model constraints, when such a model exists. For instance, Figure 5 shows (a fragment of) the syntactical and grammatical part of a generated model for the sentence "Each company sells at least one product". It should be noted that this parsing process is not deterministic: due to language ambiguities, multiple solutions may be valid for the same request. For instance, consider the sentence "MyCode is a software". Without other sentences or lexicon information, it is not be possible to decide whether the *NounConcept* "MyCode" is an *ObjectType* (a specialization of Software) or an *IndividualConcept* (an instance of Software). Rather than arbitrary deciding on one model, search allows to generate all valid solutions which can be later compared, or even to optimize the target model based on some preferences. In this regard, our approach offers a high flexibility.

4 Transforming the Resulting Model into a SBVR Model

The model obtained during the parsing process exhibits the SBVR semantics expressed by (groups of) words. Using this information together with grammatical dependencies between elements, we are able to construct a complete SBVR model corresponding to the input text. This is achieved with model transformation using the ATL language [1]. Presenting each rule of the transformation in details is outside the scope of this article. However we propose an overview of its main principles.[1]

[1] Source code and documentation of all presented transformations have been submitted as a contribution to the Eclipse ATL project and are available on http://www.eclipse.org/m2m/atl/

4.1 Mapping Overview

A first straightforward mapping is obvious: each SBVRElement of the Syntax metamodel has its counterpart in the SBVR metamodel and therefore implies the creation of the target model element. However the relations between SBVR model elements are not exhibited in the source model and may require additional (intermediate) SBVR elements. A set of rules therefore allows to derive them from the grammatical relations of the source model.

As an example, consider the following rule that generates a (binary) AssociativeFactType and its roles from a transitive verb, its subject and direct object. It may be informally expressed as follows: "For an AssociativeFactType B expressed by a verb V in the source model, create an AssociativeFactType B' in the target model, with two roles R1 and R2, where R1's nounConcept is the target NounConcept of V's subject, and R2's nounConcept is the target NounConcept of V's direct object". The rule creates intermediate elements (the roles) and uses them to relate SBVR elements. Note that some of these elements (target NounConcepts of the subject and direct object) are created by a different rule.

Moreover, the transformation allows to create attribute values from a source information having a different datatype. Indeed, consider the word "one" in the first sentence of our running example. In the source model, the word is associated to the category "NumeralCat", expressing a non-negative integer in SBVR semantics. The rule that creates the target model element is able to assign a value to the attribute "value" of type "Integer", using the OCL construct "toInteger()" on the word's designation.

4.2 Transformation Process and Result

Once the transformation is complete, we obtain a model that conforms to SBVR, leaving aside the syntactical and grammatical information of the text. Figure 6 shows a fragment of the generated SBVR model for our running example, which corresponds to the sentence "Each company sells at least one product".

5 Transforming the Resulting Model into a UML Model

Once a valid SBVR model has been generated, it is possible to transform it into a corresponding UML (class diagram) model of the CS using ATL. Again, we do not detail each rule but present an overview of the mapping.

5.1 Mapping Overview

Some examples of the mapped concepts are presented in Table 1 where the dotted notation is used to navigate classes attributes and relations. The correspondance between concepts is quite natural: an ObjectType becomes a Class, an AssociativeFactType becomes an Association, a CategorizationFactType denotes inheritance (Generalization in UML), an IsPropertyOfFactType refers to an attribute,

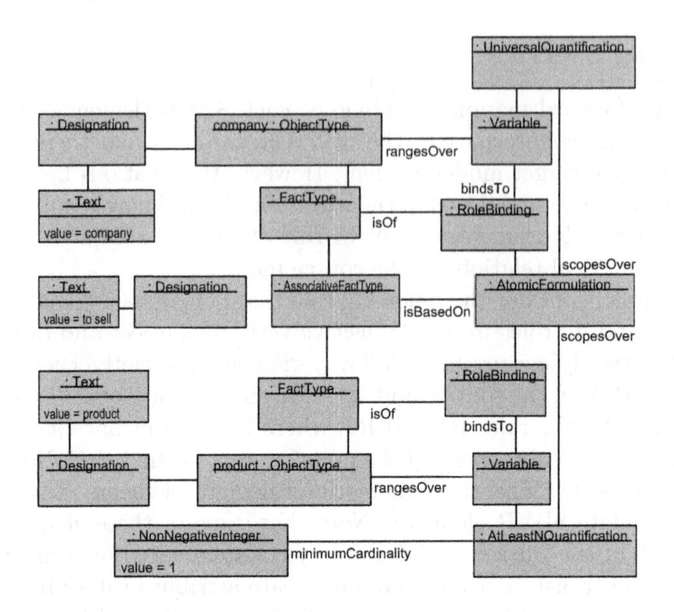

Fig. 6. Running example: fragment of the SBVR terminal model

Table 1. Excerpt of the mapping from SBVR concepts to UML concepts

SBVR concept	UML Concept
ObjectType	Class
ObjectType.Designation.Text.value	Class.name
DataType	DataType
IndividualConcept	InstanceSpecification
AssociativeFactType	Association
AssociativeFactType.Designation.Text.value	Association.name
AssociativeFactType.FactTypeRole	Property (Association.memberEnd)
AssociativeFactType.FactTypeRole.nounConcept	Property.classifier
CategorizationFactType	Generalization
CategorizationFactType.FactTypeRole#1	Generalization.general
AtLeastNQuantification.minimumCardinality.value	Property.lowerValue
AtMostNQuantification.maximumCardinality.value	Property.upperValue

an IndividualConcept becomes an InstanceSpecification, etc. Linked concepts and values are also quite explicit. However, most of the rules do not realize a straight one-to-one mapping but imply additional conditions, target elements from other rules, etc. For instance, consider the mapping for the SBVR concept *AtLeastNQuantification*. The *Property* for which *lowerValue* is assigned is the one obtained by transforming the *AssociativeFactType* that is target of the relation *AtLeastNQuantification.scopesOver.isBasedOn*. Ordered relations also play an important role: the first role of a categorization denotes the general class, whereas the second one refers to the specific class.

5.2 Transformation Process and Result

Once the transformation is complete, we obtain a UML specification of the CS. Figure 7 shows a UML terminal model obtained for our running example.

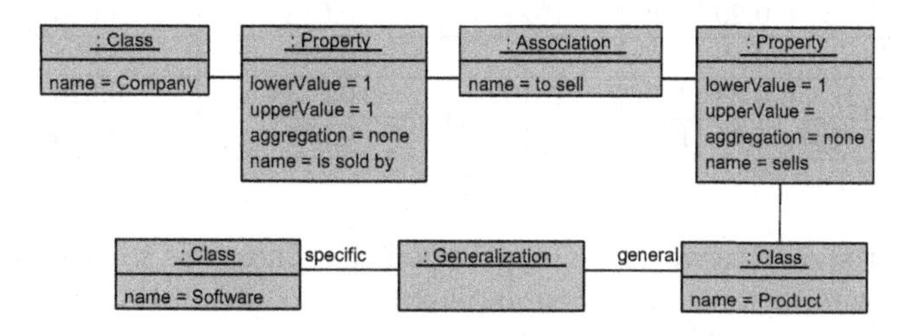

Fig. 7. Running example: fragment of the UML model

6 Implementation and Experiments

6.1 Implementation

The proposed approach has been integrated into an Eclipse-based model-driven engineering framework. To those aims, each presented metamodel has been written using the KM3 metamodelling language [18], which offers an automatic conversion to the EMF's ECore format [21]. These ECore metamodels are source and target metamodels of the proposed ATL transformations. The configuration tool JConfigurator has its own modelling language and currently offers only XML inputs and outputs. Therefore the Syntax metamodel is also defined directly within the tool as the configuration model. At runtime, the configuration request model is projected to XML in order to be parsed, and the XML representation of the solution is then injected into a model. This model (in XMI format) is passed over to the remaining ATL transformations.

6.2 Experiments

Experiments on the running example were conducted on a Core2Duo 3Ghz with 3GB of RAM. Table 2 shows the results. We first parsed each sentence separatly and then multiple sentences at once.

Parsing is efficient for separated sentences but the time required for the search task quickly increases with the whole text. This is due to the size of the source model which directly impacts the search space of the configurator whereas the ATL transformations are able to handle bigger models. Splitting the tasks is positive for performance and could be investigated further so as to reduce the configuration model to the minimum required for syntactical analysis. We currently focused on a straightforward integration of the configurator with a configuration model covering the whole Syntax metamodel. Future steps are, on the one hand, to extract the combinatorial core of the metamodel, and on the other hand, to allow a further specified request through different relaxation levels of the source

Table 2. Experiments on the running example (times in seconds)

sentence(s)	Text to Syntax			*Syntax to SBVR*	*SBVR to UML*
	Time	*Vars*	*Constraints*	*Time*	*Time*
(1)	0.26	527	1025	0.018	0.018
(2)	0.20	526	1022	0.018	0.016
(3)	0.19	475	885	0.015	0.018
(1)+(2)	0.38	973	2819	0.035	0.020
(1)+(2)+(3)	1.41	1328	5312	0.082	0.025

metamodel. It should however be emphasized that these are early experimental results. No optimizations have been applied to the configuration engine such as heuristics or symmetry breaking techniques, which are known to drastically reduce the computation times. Another alternative envisionned is to perform an incremental parsing of the text, sentence by sentence, using the ATL multiple source capabilities to unify the resulting SBVR models. The successful parsing of our non-trivial example however proves the feasability of the approach.

7 Related Work

In [22], a procedure for performing the reverse transformation is described: from a UML/OCL description of a CS, the authors show how it can be transformed into a SBVR terminal model using ATL, and then paraphrased with structured English text. Combining the two approaches is thus promising. Indeed, designing a CS often requires several discussions between stakeholders for refinements, and maintaining a CS leads to frequent evolutions. The combination would allow to switch from one representation to another automatically.

There has been previous research on using constraint programming technics in MDE, mostly about animation of relational specifications or model verification. [23] transforms UML/OCL specifications into a constraint satisfaction problem in order to check satisfiability. [24] proposes a similar method, although the underlying solver (Alloy [25]) is based on SAT. Both approaches inherit the limitations of the target formalism in which specifications must be translated. The configuration paradigm is expressive enough as self and thus avoids the translation phase. Moreover, to the best of our knowledge, this is the first time that a constraint-based search is embedded in MDE as a transformation tool. With respect to the domain of natural or controlled language parsers, our approach differs from most existing methods (such as ACE[4]). Indeed these parsers do not accept ambiguous grammars (i.e. not context-free), whereas we are able to parameterize the level of accepted ambiguities, thus allowing to define a trade-off between language coverage and computation efficiency.

8 Conclusion and Future Work

We have described a method which allows to parse a CS specification expressed in structured English into a UML class diagram. To those aims, we proposed

SBVR as an intermediate layer. The originality of our approach is the use of an advanced constraint-programming search technique (configuration) as a model transformation tool integrated in a MDE environment. Early experiments are provided as a proof-of-concept. Moreover, the proposed parser is flexible with respect to language coverage and disambiguation. There are many perspectives to this work. First, the metamodels can be extended to capture an increased portion of SBVR. The expressed meanings will then probably require to generate OCL constraints in addition to UML. Other target formalisms can also be considered such as OWL or Rule Systems. The experiments clearly show that there is a need for performance improvement in the search-based transformation. The leading direction is to reduce the search space by isolating the metamodel's combinatorial core, thus further decomposing the problem. Finally, the described configuration-based tool could benefit to other complex transformations that require searching for a target model instead of applying deterministic rules to the source model.

References

1. Jouault, F., Kurtev, I.: Transforming Models with ATL. In: Bruel, J.-M. (ed.) MoDELS 2005. LNCS, vol. 3844, pp. 128–138. Springer, Heidelberg (2006)
2. Object Management Group: Meta Object Facility (MOF) 2.0 Query/View/Transformation (QVT) Specification, version 1.0 (2008)
3. Semantics of Business Vocabulary and Business Rules (SBVR) 1.0 specification (2008), `http://www.omg.org/spec/SBVR/1.0/`
4. Schwitter, R., Fuchs, N.E.: Attempto controlled english (ace) a seemingly informal bridgehead in formal territory. In: JICSLP, p. 536 (1996)
5. Kaljurand, K.: Ace view - an ontology and rule editor based on controlled english. In: International Semantic Web Conference (Posters & Demos). CEUR Workshop Proceedings, vol. 401, CEUR-WS.org (2008)
6. JRules (2009), `http://www.ilog.fr/products/jrules/`
7. Drools (2009), `http://www.jboss.org/drools/`
8. Junker, U.: 26. In: Configuration. Volume Handbook of Constraint Programming. Elsevier, Amsterdam (2006)
9. Mittal, S., Falkenhainer, B.: Dynamic constraint satisfaction problems. In: Proceedings of AAAI 1990, pp. 25–32 (1990)
10. Stumptner, M., Haselböck, A.: A generative constraint formalism for configuration problems. In: Advances in Artificial Intelligence: Proceedings of AI*IA 1993, pp. 302–313. Springer, Heidelberg (1993)
11. Sabin, D., Freuder, E.C.: Composite constraint satisfaction. In: AI and Manufacturing Research Planning Workshop, pp. 153–161 (1996)
12. Stumptner, M.: An overview of knowledge-based configuration. AI Communications 10(2), 111–125 (1997)
13. Soininen, T., Niemela, I., Tiihonen, J., Sulonen, R.: Representing configuration knowledge with weight constraint rules. In: Proceedings of the AAAI Spring Symp. on Answer Set Programming, pp. 195–201 (2001)
14. Mailharro, D.: A classification and constraint-based framework for configuration. AI in Engineering, Design and Manufacturing (12), 383–397 (1998)

15. Junker, U., Mailharro, D.: The logic of (j)configurator: Combining constraint programming with a description logic. In: IJCAI 2003. Springer, Heidelberg (2003)
16. Estratat, M., Henocque, L.: Parsing languages with a configurator. In: Proceedings of the European Conference for Artificial Intelligence ECAI 2004, August 2004, pp. 591–595 (2004)
17. Felfernig, A., Friedrich, G., Jannach, D., Zanker, M.: Configuration knowledge representation using uml/ocl. In: Jézéquel, J.-M., Hussmann, H., Cook, S. (eds.) UML 2002. LNCS, vol. 2460, pp. 49–62. Springer, Heidelberg (2002)
18. Jouault, F., Bézivin, J.: Km3: A dsl for metamodel specification. In: Gorrieri, R., Wehrheim, H. (eds.) FMOODS 2006. LNCS, vol. 4037, pp. 171–185. Springer, Heidelberg (2006)
19. Kittredge, R.I.: Sublanguages and controlled languages. Oxford Press (2003)
20. Blache, P., Balfourier, J.-M.: Property grammars: a flexible constraint-based approach to parsing. In: IWPT. Tsinghua University Press (2001)
21. EMF (2009), `http://www.eclipse.org/modeling/emf/`
22. Cabot, J., Pau, R., Raventós, R.: From uml/ocl to sbvr specifications: a challenging transformation. In: Information Systems. Elsevier, Amsterdam (2009)
23. Cabot, J., Clarisó, R., Riera, D.: Umltocsp: a tool for the formal verification of uml/ocl models using constraint programming. In: ASE, pp. 547–548. ACM, New York (2007)
24. Dinh-Trong, T.T., Ghosh, S., France, R.B.: A systematic approach to generate inputs to test uml design models. In: ISSRE, pp. 95–104. IEEE Computer Society, Los Alamitos (2006)
25. Jackson, D.: Automating first-order relational logic. In: SIGSOFT FSE, pp. 130–139 (2000)

SLIM—A Lightweight Environment for Synchronous Collaborative Modeling

Christian Thum, Michael Schwind, and Martin Schader

University of Mannheim, D-68131 Mannheim, Germany
{thum,schwind,schader}@uni-mannheim.de
http://www.uni-mannheim.de

Abstract. UML diagrams have become the de-facto standard for the visual modeling of software systems. The creation and discussion of these diagrams is a critical factor impacting the quality of the artifacts under development. Traditionally, facilitating the collaboration of globally distributed team members with heterogeneous system environments has been a costly and time-consuming endeavor. This paper aims to advance the state-of-the-art of model-based development by providing a collaboration environment, which supports the synchronous distributed creation and manipulation of UML diagrams and also lowers the technical entry barriers for participating in the modeling process. We present a prototypical implementation of a collaborative editor for synchronous lightweight modeling (SLIM). Applying innovative techniques, which only rely on functionality natively supported by modern web browsers, technical issues impeding clients to be integrated into the collaborative environment are avoided and ad hoc collaboration is facilitated.

Keywords: Collaborative Modeling, Web 2.0, Real-Time Editor.

1 Introduction

Collaborative software development is a research paradigm, which has emerged in the broader concept of Computer Supported Collaborative Work (CSCW) and describes the involvement of multiple participants in the software development process across organizational, geographical, or socio-cultural boundaries. As a consequence of the increased dynamics in the economic environment and evolving organizational structures (e.g., virtual and network organizations), there is a strong need to support effective team collaboration. The increasing number of outsourcing and offshoring projects requires organizations to coordinate the work of geographically distributed team members. The success of software development projects does not only depend on organizational aspects like management support and the choice of an adequate software development process. Also technical aspects, like the development tools employed to support these processes are of vital importance. It is in this context that Jacobson, Booch, and Rumbaugh explain the reciprocal relationship between processes and tools [1]. They argue that, on the one hand, processes determine the functionality of tools but

A. Schürr and B. Selic (Eds.): MODELS 2009, LNCS 5795, pp. 137–151, 2009.

that innovative tools, on the other hand, are needed to allow for the development of new processes. The modeling and design phases fall into this process category. Due to their complexity, they generally have not been considered being suitable for support by lightweight collaboration tools. The development of software design diagrams is inherently a collaborative activity. It comprises contributions from multiple developers and establishes a common understanding of project goals. The involvement of domain experts and other stakeholders in the early development stages is an important prerequisite for improving the quality of software deliverables and artifacts. In the next section, we discuss selected requirements that a lightweight environment for collaborative modeling should meet. In section 3, we briefly discuss related work in the field of collaborative software engineering with regard to these requirements. The main part of the paper then describes the design and implementation of the SLIM environment with special emphasis on platform independence, simultaneously tackling the challenge of synchronizing client states. The paper concludes with an outlook on future developments and their potential impact on existing software development processes.

2 Design Aspects of a Lightweight Modeling Environment

The integration of distributed team members is subject to several challenges, which can serve as a basis for deriving requirements and design principles for a lightweight modeling environment. Globally distributed software developers usually are equipped with different client systems constituting a heterogeneous system landscape. Traditional approaches to interconnecting distributed developer teams require the installation, configuration, and maintenance of the same software on all client systems, which is time-consuming and costly. Ideally, collaboration partners should be able to participate in the modeling process regardless of the hardware and software equipment they use. Hence, ad hoc availability and straightforward accessibility can be identified as important non-functional requirements for collaboration software. Comprehensive web-based development platforms like SourceForge[1] or CodeBeamer[2] serve to support collaborative work at all stages of the software development process. They form the central infrastructure for coordinating, documenting, scheduling, and monitoring project tasks and activities. Therefore, they provide project management support as well as development tools that span the entire lifecycle, making integration into existing web-based development platforms an important aspect to be considered. Whitehead examines existing collaboration tools in the context of software engineering and derives possible future directions. He points out the need for tight integration of new and existing web-based and desktop-based environments, respectively [2]. Interoperability with established modeling environments increases the acceptance of innovative tools, since developers can continue using their preferred applications. In many cases, multiple modeling tools have to be used because

[1] `http://sourceforge.net`

[2] `http://www.intland.com`

not all modeling needs are met by a single tool. In summary, flexible access, ad hoc availability, integration into existing web-based development platforms, and interoperability with existing desktop-based tools have been identified as the central non-functional requirements crucial for the aptitude of a collaborative UML modeling tool. The first stage of our research mainly focuses on the technical feasibility of a lightweight approach that runs in unmodified browser environments. Therefore, the functional requirements the prototype is based on are very similar to those of a desktop modeling environment. Currently, the main intention is to support the development of a common understanding of a system's design in agile, distributed environments. For the time being, the environment will be limited to supporting UML class diagrams. Challenges arising from support for multiple diagram types are neglected for now and will be subject to further research.

3 Related Work

Distributed collaborative modeling has its roots in diverse industries, such as automotive [3] or building and construction [4], where it has already been established. In the software engineering domain, various commercial applications as well as research prototypes exist, which aim to support the collaborative development and discussion of diagrams. For example, Poseidon for UML Enterprise Edition [5] is a complex desktop application. It enables multiple collaborators to concurrently work on a shared diagram. Changes are reflected in real-time and the view on the shared diagram is synchronized between all clients. To enable the collaboration functionality, Java RMI is used [6]. With regard to the design aspect of flexible access this is a significant disadvantage. In order for RMI to function across organizational boundaries, certain ports have to be open. Different hardware and software environments on client systems as well as corporate firewalls form a barrier for the collaboration functionality of many desktop-based applications. Mehra et al. address this issue and state that none of the current collaborative systems are interoperable across heterogeneous and autonomous systems [7]. They point out that the reliance on proprietary protocols and technologies restricts systems to a particular platform and hence limits the ability to collaborate with others. To solve this problem, they show how collaborative software design can be supported with a web service-based architecture. Since web services use standard HTTP(S) ports for communication, firewall-related problems caused by proprietary technologies are not an issue. One major drawback of Mehra's desktop-based approach is the need to install a web server on each client system. This contradicts the requirement of ad hoc availability, as client systems have to be modified before collaboration can commence. Solutions that retain the advantage of being interoperable across heterogeneous systems and increase accessibility and availability at the same time use a browser-based (plug-ins allowed) or a browser-native approach (no plug-ins allowed). Relying only on functionality natively supported by modern web browsers reduces the system requirements towards clients intending to engage in collaborative activities. Based on the HTTP protocol, a cost-effective location and platform independent solution can be provided. Whereas browser-native tools minimize deployment effort (i.e., installation, configuration, and maintenance costs) they are often limited with regard to their functionality. The research prototype eEEL [8] can serve as a typical example. It provides a browser-based interface, which can be easily accessed. However, the tool only allows the automated visualization of diagrams from a textual representation but does not support collaborative editing of these diagrams. Campbell adds that there is a great variety of graphical group editors, none of which enables the creation of formal diagrams with a defined syntax [9]. This view is affirmed by Qi et al. They argue that many tools can be used as collaborative whiteboards or communication aids but not for the development of UML diagrams in a software engineering context [10]. As an alternative to specific solutions, generic network meeting tools such as WebEx[3] or Adobe Connect[4] could be applied to enable collaboration support for existing desktop based applications. Employing such generic meeting tools has to be evaluated critically with regard to the design aspect of ad hoc availability in highly dynamic loosely coupled environments (downloads or plug-ins are required). Furthermore, generic tools do not allow for simultaneous work on the same diagram. Typically only one user can have input control at a time, hence team productivity is limited.

4 Technologies Impact Tools

Jacobson, Booch, and Rumbaugh state that "*Tools impact Process*" [1]. Keeping this in mind, the conclusion "*Technologies impact Tools*" seems reasonable. This becomes evident particularly in the domain of software engineering. Browser-based applications have long been characterized by a lack of user interface interactivity. Thus, graphics or editing intensive UML tools were not considered suitable for the web and were implemented as desktop applications [2]. In order to create innovative tools, which influence existing processes, new technologies or a novel combination of existing technologies are needed. Markus et al. argue that, as technologies advance, new kinds of systems and methods are created [11]. In this context, the possibilities of the web [12] and especially the possibilities of the Web 2.0 [13] are often referred to as "*enabling technology.*" A recent McKinsey study [14] underpins this argument with empirical evidence: "*[...] companies are not only using more [Web 2.0] technologies but also leveraging them to change management practices and organizational structures.*" It is with this idea in mind that the technologies used for realizing the prototypical implementation of the SLIM environment are outlined in the following sections.

5 The SLIM Environment

In this section, we elaborate on the design aspects outlined above. Starting with a short discussion of the most adequate system architecture, the section embraces

[3] `http://www.webex.com`

[4] `http://www.adobe.com/products/acrobatconnectpro/`

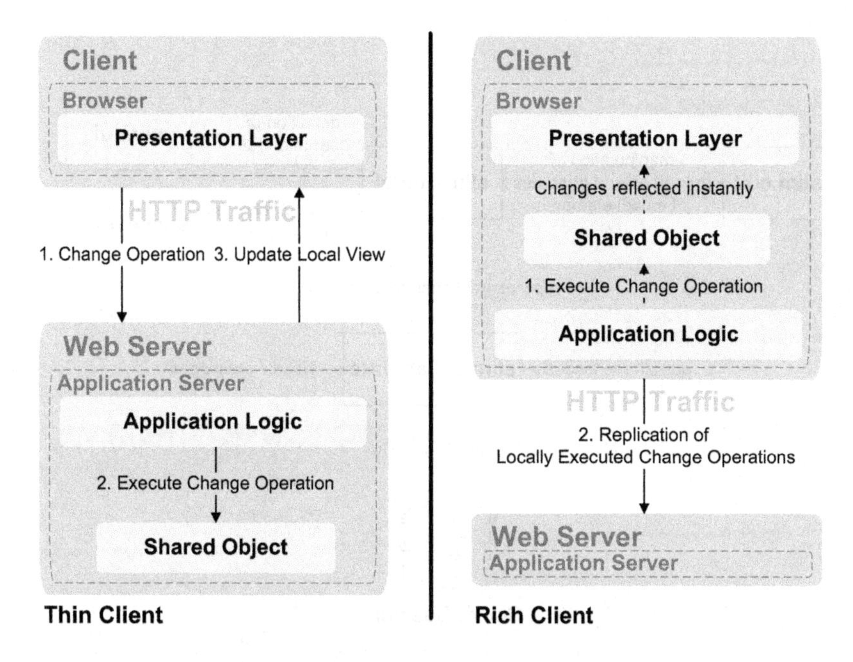

Fig. 1. Architecture alternatives

the realization of the interactive diagram editor and the collaboration functionality. The goal was to design an architecture, which provides a solid foundation to appropriately support high interactivity during synchronous collaboration sessions. One design decision that had to be made was whether change operations on the shared diagram are to be executed locally or on a central server. Fig. 1 visualizes these alternatives. In a thin client architecture, client functionality is limited to input and output operations. After each modification, clients have to update their local view with the server. The advantage of this approach is that changes are performed at a central location, making consistency control easier. Although change requests can be sent using AJAX requests without interrupting user activity, this approach negatively affects the system's responsiveness, due to the delay between sending change requests (1.) and receiving the updated view (3.). An alternative strategy is the use of decentralized updates or a replication approach in a rich client architecture. Here, the business logic completely resides on the client side. When a collaborative session starts, every client is initialized with a copy of the shared artifact representing the current session state. All change operations can then be executed locally, minimizing network traffic and guaranteeing a quicker response to user events. Since the server is only needed as a mediator forwarding messages between clients, the modeling tool can also be used for single-user sessions in offline mode. Lukosch and Schümmer recommend the use of a replication approach[5] when the degree of interactivity is high and the collaboration partners frequently invoke change operations on the shared artifact

[5] They distinguish between *decentralized updates* and *decentralized objects*.

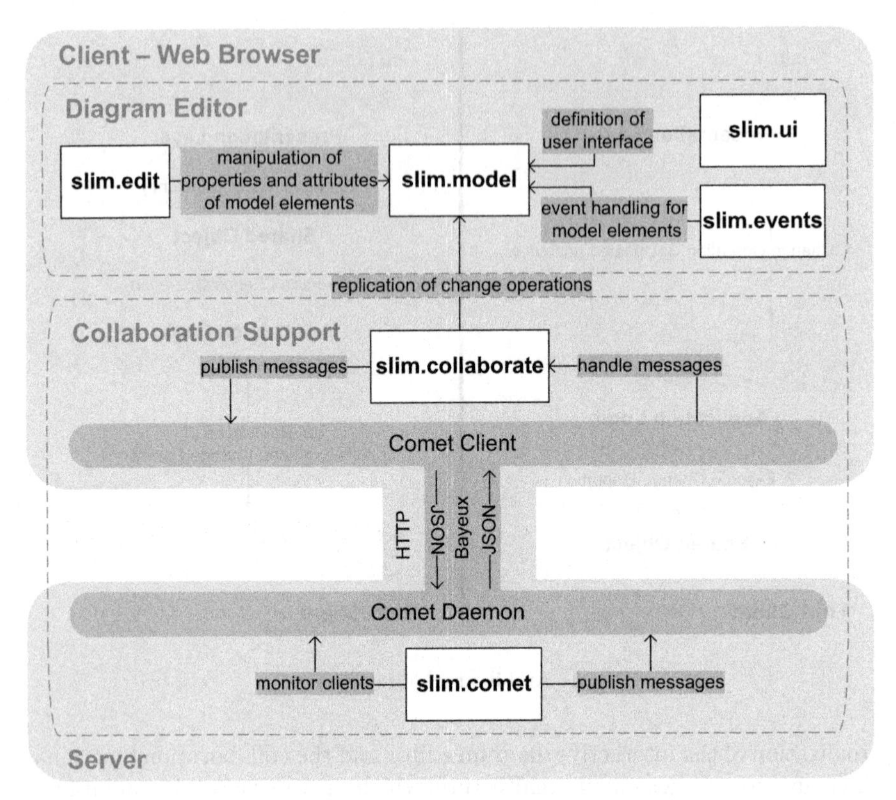

Fig. 2. System architecture

[15]. The SLIM environment is built upon this approach to achieve low latency and high responsiveness. Having discussed the general aspects pertaining to the rich client architecture design, we now present the components that constitute the system. Given the decentralized replication approach in which the server's primary role is that of a mediator, we elaborate on the client-side application logic in particular. Fig. 2 illustrates the components of the system architecture. To provide a better overview, the components of the diagram editor and those supporting collaboration are marked with a dashed line. In the following, the technical challenges for realizing the diagram editor and the collaboration support on the browser-native architecture are discussed. On the basis of the proposed solutions we present selected implementation details.

5.1 Diagram Editor

While the user interface can be implemented using HTML and CSS, the visualization of the graphical notation of UML elements requires the functionality of a 2D graphics library. Drawing interactive graphics on web pages has been difficult to achieve for a long time. Previous solutions have involved browser plug-ins or Java applets. As it was our goal to facilitate ad hoc collaboration by minimizing the entry requirements necessary to engage in collaboration, none of these solutions were suitable. Keeping this in mind, there were three possible ways of displaying the model elements in the browser-native environment: the emulation of vector graphics via HTML Div-Elements[6], the HTML 5 Canvas element[7], or SVG (Scalable Vector Graphics) and VML (Vector Markup Language)[8], respectively. The low performance paired with high memory consumption compared to other approaches [16] disqualify the emulation approach. The availability of the Canvas element in modern browsers goes along with support for SVG, which qualified usage of the Canvas element as a feasible solution. Being based on the XML format and with regard to existing use cases in the area of modeling, SVG, however, seemed to be the most appropriate choice. Especially in the field of UML modeling, SVG is a frequently used lightweight file format for creating resolution-independent graphics, which can be displayed natively by a wide range of browsers. Hritcu, Dumutriu, and Girdea show how to transform XMI data to SVG through XSL Transformations [18]. Microsoft's Internet Explorer does not support SVG but uses the proprietary VML. Since Internet Explorer is currently the most commonly used browser [19], relying on SVG would enforce the installation of a specific browser on the client systems. To address this issue and to abstract from browser specifics, we chose the graphics library of the Dojo Toolkit [20], which provides a uniform programming interface on top of SVG and VML. Hence, for realizing a cross-browser visualization of UML model elements, a combination of SVG and VML was used. For the implementation of an interactive diagram editor, a cross-browser procedure to handle events for graphical elements is needed. This is a basic prerequisite for responding to mouse gestures like selection, moving, and scaling of UML model elements. Although SVG and VML generally provide interfaces for event handling, browser support is limited. Fig. 3 illustrates the approach chosen for solving this problem. To be able to respond to events, the bounding box for each graphical element is determined. The coordinates of this bounding box are used to add a transparent Div-Element as an extra layer on top of the graphical element. Due to the event propagation mechanism in the Document Object Model, the Div-Element can register event handling routines for all underlying elements, particularly for the vector graphics. As Div-Elements are a part of the HTML standard supported by every web browser, a cross-browser way of responding to mouse gestures has been created. By adding child nodes into the document tree of the overlaying Div-Element, additional reusable event decorators for selecting, moving (2.1), resizing (2.2), and for creating connectors to other graphical elements (2.3) can be generated.

---

[6] Libraries based on this approach are the High Performance JavaScript Vector Graphics Library by Walter Zorn [16] and Draw2D by Andreas Herz [17].

[7] The Canvas element was introduced by Apple in 2004 and was included in the working draft of the HTML 5 standard by the W3C in 2008. Mozilla, Opera, and Safari support the Canvas element while the Internet Explorer does not.

[8] SVG and VML are declarative languages that allow modeling of 2D vector graphics using XML syntax. SVG is based on a recommendation of the W3C and is supported natively by many commonly used browsers (e.g., Mozilla, Opera, Safari).

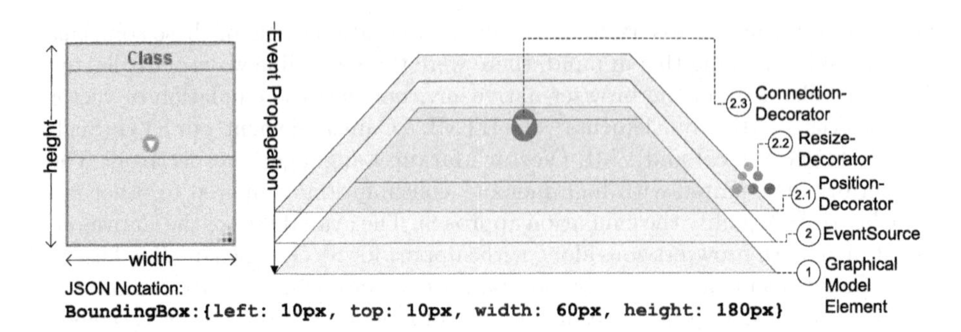

Fig. 3. Event handling

User Interface. As mentioned above, there is a trend towards moving development tools to the web. Integrated platforms like SourceForge provide user interfaces and tools that can be accessed via a web browser. Consequently, the interface of a collaborative modeling tool should also be accessible from a browser. The user interface should meet all functional requirements necessary to allow for the creation as well as the manipulation of diagrams. An essential difference between single and multiuser applications is the need to inform the participants about all events, which occur as a result of the multi-user collaboration activity. This information is needed for each participant to coordinate their own activities. The exchange of status and context information is referred to as "workspace awareness." With regard to the SLIM environment, this implies that each user should be able to notice that others access shared artifacts and to perceive the modifications they carry out. Implicit and explicit communication as well as a list of all meeting attendees is essential. For this reason, a notification service enabling implicit information exchange between the attendees has been implemented. This service informs all team members of operations conducted and makes it easier for all participants to perceive the changes made. All diagram elements currently selected for manipulation are visually highlighted. Some authors advocate the replication of mouse pointers of all users onto the screens of other participants. With an increasing number of participants, this will become confusing, easily. This view is shared by Stefik et al. [21], whose argument seems appropriate: "*The WYSIWIS display of cursors from multiple users is unacceptably distracting.*" To supplement implicit communication, a chat has been implemented as an additional means of exchanging information between participants.

Interoperability and Metadata Exchange. We already mentioned interoperability as a crucial design goal. The emphasis is on the exchange of UML metadata with other modeling tools. The XMI standard [22] specifies the data to be exchanged and how it should be encoded using XML. For the implementation of the prototype, the decision had to be made whether the functionality for serializing and deserializing UML diagrams should be implemented on the client or on the server side. On the server side, XMI frameworks such as the XMI handler of the Eclipse Modeling Framework (EMF) can be used. An advantage of this approach lies in the encapsulation of the serialization process. On the other hand, the use of a predefined framework implies an overhead compared to a direct serialization on the client side. First, the local representation of the UML diagram would have to be converted into the Ecore format, sent to the server, and then converted to XMI. A more direct approach—serializing UML models on the client side—seemed more appropriate. The format can then be used for the state transfer between collaborating clients. This represents an advantage of the implementation on the client side.

5.2 Collaboration Support

Due to its complexity, distributed modeling is generally executed as an integrative process implying intense coordination and communication within the development team. A typical challenge in collaborative multi-user applications is the synchronization of local states on all clients and the preservation of the shared objects' consistency. Therefore, the exchange of messages between clients is necessary. Previous suggestions have involved Flash XML Sockets or Java RMI. Realizing collaboration functionality on the basis of the stateless HTTP protocol, optimized for client requests, is not trivial. To be applicable in the context of synchronous collaborative modeling, the HTTP protocol must allow for the server to send notifications to the clients. In order to implement the strategy designed for synchronization of local states, it is necessary to propagate locally executed user actions to other clients. The HTTP protocol, which is used as the transport layer for communication, is built upon the request/response paradigm. All communication has to be initiated by the client. Although interactivity has increased in Web 2.0 applications, there is no simple way of sending events from the server to the clients. Because of this limitation, the HTTP protocol was not used for implementing synchronous collaboration. In his paper concerning the challenges of web-based collaboration, Dix states: "*HTTP is certainly not suited to real-time conversations!*" [23]. There is a variety of approaches that aim to overcome this limitation and enable the server to send notifications to the clients. Scalability and the latency between events on the server and the reception of a notification on the client are important criteria for assessing the efficiency of those approaches. One approach that is common due to its ease of implementation is polling. The client continuously sends requests to the server. Upon receiving the response from the server, the connection is closed and a new request is issued by the client. However, polling has serious drawbacks. In the worst case, a server-side event occurs immediately after sending a response. In this case, latency equals the sum of the length of the polling interval plus the time that passes until the HTTP response of the last polling request has reached the client. Recently, the term "Comet" has been coined, subsuming all techniques that allow the server to initiate client notification and send event notifications over HTTP to clients with negligible latency. These notifications can be sent in response to occurring events without explicit polling. There are two major ways of implementing server-side client notifications with low latency: streaming and long-polling. Both techniques can be used as transport type in a Comet architecture. Streaming uses a so-called forever response. In contrast to polling, the connection is not closed after sending a message from the server. This way, several messages can be send in a data stream over a single connection HTTP connection (multi-part/chunked response). With this approach, latency is minimal because different polling clients can be notified immediately after the event has occurred. The lag is solely comprised of the time needed for the HTTP response to reach the client. One significant disadvantage of streaming is that it is not possible to determine whether a given client is still receiving messages. Since the HTTP response is sent in parts there is a risk that messages received are delayed, because they might be buffered by proxy servers. This might result in a state, where the server is still sending messages although the client has already disconnected. A compromise between polling and streaming is long-polling. This approach utilizes a so-called persistent or long-lived HTTP connection. Connections to the server are kept open until either a server-side event or a timeout occurs. In both cases, the client has to send a new HTTP request to the server after receiving the response. Using this strategy, long-polling preserves the low latency of the HTTP streaming approach and at the same time avoids many disadvantages of both streaming and traditional polling, respectively. The frequency of sending empty responses is reduced because the server does not send responses immediately after receiving a request. By forcing the client to send a new request after receiving a message, it can be ensured that all clients are still active. Fig. 4 illustrates the Comet architecture as it has been used for implementing SLIM. The figure abstracts from technical details such as the transport layer used for sending messages on the basis of the HTTP protocol as described above. Event notifications are managed by three basic components, the Comet Client, the Comet Event Bus, and the server-side event processor. After initializing the connection, messages can be delivered from client to server (1.1–1.2–1.3) or vice versa (2.1–2.2–2.3). The Comet architecture serves as a solid foundation for the implementation of SLIM. Due to the thread-per-request model used by traditional web servers [25], the Comet approach is not scalable and thus cannot be used for collaborative sessions with many participants. As a solution, modern web servers implement asynchronous request processing. They allow to suspend processing of an HTTP request without blocking resources. The thread can then be used to process another request. Thus, a request can be suspended and resumed when an asynchronous event or a timeout occur. For the prototypical implementation of the SLIM environment, the Jetty Comet Daemon was used.

Synchronization of Local States. Typical challenges in collaborative multi-user applications involve synchronizing local states on all clients and preserving consistency of shared objects. In order to minimize network traffic, only incremental changes in form of the corresponding user operations are replicated between clients via the mediating server. The client executing a change operation on the shared diagram has to notify the server of the actions carried out. The server subsequently propagates the message to all participating clients. In the final step all clients replicate the change operations on their local copy of the shared diagram.

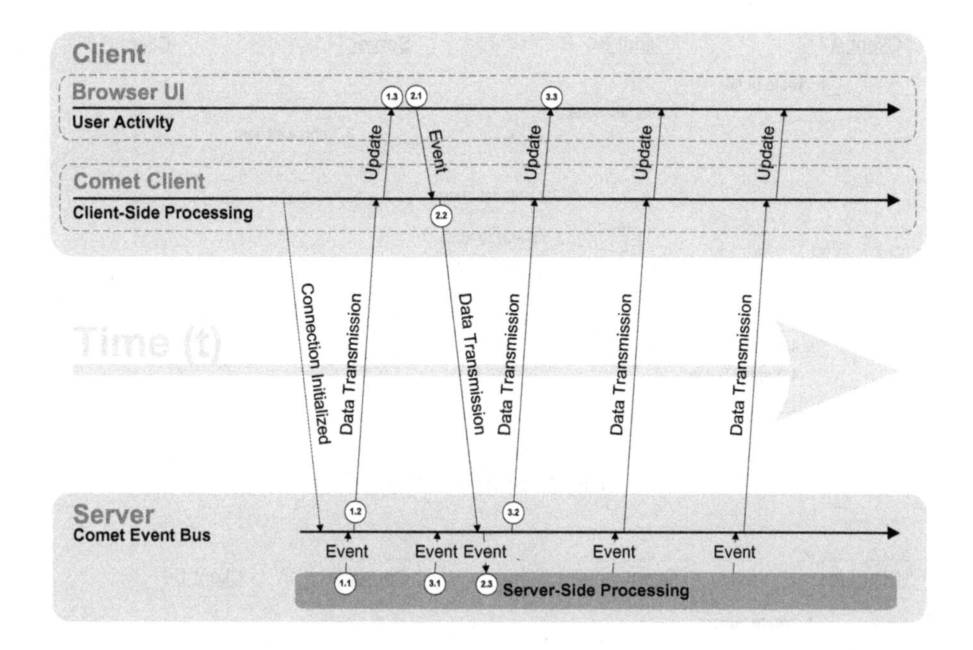

Fig. 4. Comet event processing [24]

This replication strategy requires having the local state pushed to each new client joining a running session. The local state comprises not only the current state of the shared artifact but also additional collaboration-related information such as elements being locked by users. This information has to be serialized and sent to the joining client. Based on the replication of user operations, all local states can be assumed to be synchronous; therefore, it does not matter which client is chosen to provide the state. With collaborative modeling, the current state of the shared artifact is represented by the UML model and can be serialized via XMI. The sequence diagram in Fig. 5 illustrates the conceptual design. Depicted is the case where client A joins an existing session of client B and client C. Client A creates a buffer (1.), in order to cache arriving messages for the duration of the state request. This is to ensure that no user operation is lost between request (2.) and receipt (3.) of the current state. To provide a better insight, this case is depicted in a second diagram. Upon receiving a state request (2.), the server randomly chooses a participating client (3.1) and forwards the request (3.2). Now the randomly selected client B (3.3) serializes its local state and sends it back to the server (3.4). The server eventually forwards the serialized state to the joining client (4.1). The client then updates its local state by deserializing the received data and then processing the buffer of cached user operations (4.2). Using server-initiated event notification as described above is one of the technical challenges; it has been implemented using browser-native functionality only. Passing messages through the server as a mediator is necessary, since client-to-client communication is not possible via the HTTP protocol. Direct communication between "*client systems*" could be realized by installing web servers on each client system [7], however, this approach would

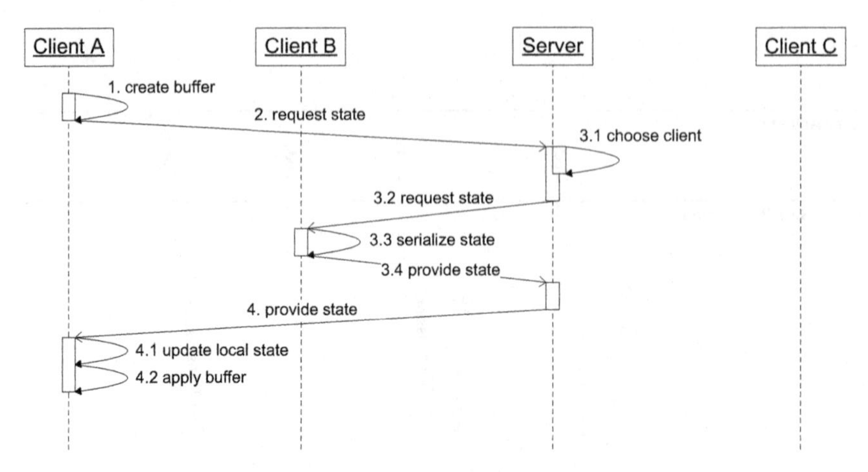

Fig. 5. State transfer

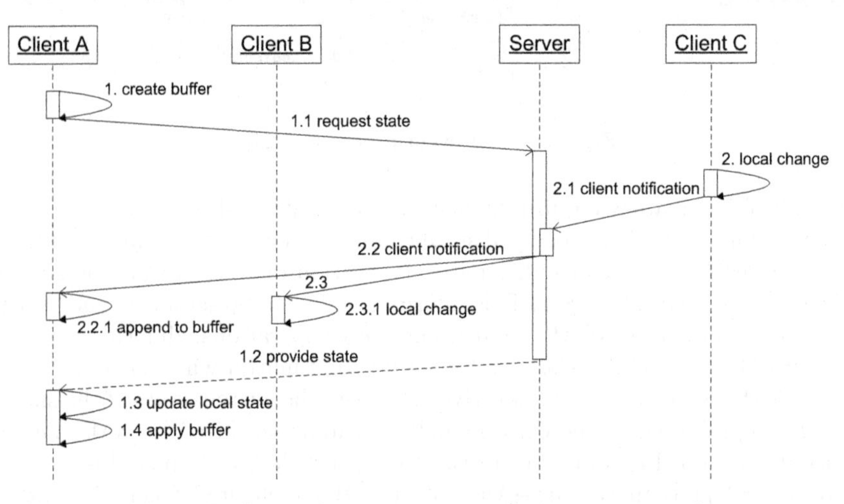

Fig. 6. Buffering change operations during state transfer

contradict the objective of providing a lightweight, easy to deploy, and flexible architecture. Complementary to the previous sequence diagram, Fig. 6 illustrates the use of the buffer, which caches the change operations received during request and receipt of the session state (2.1–2.2). Having received the updated state (1.2), client A can reconstruct, which change operations contained in the buffer are not yet reflected within the local state and can update the state accordingly (1.4).

Concurrency Control. One fundamental challenge of coordinating access to shared artifacts in real-time editors is ensuring that each user action yields the desired result on all clients. If editing is unconstrained, interference between clients is inevitable. Mechanisms aiming to avoid or resolve such conflicts are discussed in papers concerning Concurrency Control. Because of the novelty of the web

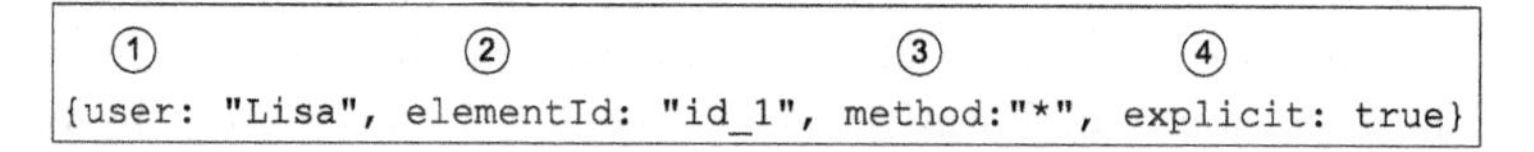

Fig. 7. JSON data set used for locking

technologies used, design patterns rather than predefined frameworks have been applied. For implementing concurrency control in the SLIM environment, the locking pattern was chosen. Locking is a design pattern, which restricts access to those parts of the diagram currently being edited. Before a participant can access a shared element it is checked whether the element has been locked by another user. The granularity level chosen determines the efficiency of this approach. If it is too coarse the number of activities that can be conducted in parallel is reduced. Fine-granular locking increases the number of parallel activities possible but increases the need for lock requests that have to be sent over the network. To reduce network load but still allow for a high degree of parallel work, locking at the element level seemed appropriate. Once elements are selected by a user they are locked for exclusive access. In case exclusive access to a larger part of the diagram is required, elements can be explicitly locked, so they remain locked even when they are deselected. When a collaborative session starts, every client is initialized with the local state which also comprises a list of currently locked elements. The synchronization of this list is done similarly to the synchronization of user operations described above. For publishing information concerning locked elements a JSON data structure is created, as depicted in Fig. 7. A lock comprises information pertaining to the name of the user setting the lock (1), the unique identifier of the element to be locked (2), and the operation to be locked (3). An additional flag indicates whether the lock is set implicitly or explicitly. The prototype uses a wildcard "*" for locking all methods affecting the state of a model element. However, the prototype can be extended to support finer granularity of locking single methods. For example, one user may request the single write permission to the attributes of a class element—the wildcard then has to be replaced by the appropriate method name (e.g., `setAttributes`). Using this approach, the number of operations that can be executed concurrently is increased by allowing users to access different properties of a model element without interfering with each other. Before a user is able to select an element it is checked if it is already locked by another user. If it is, selection is denied and a corresponding message is displayed in the status area. Otherwise, selection is completed successfully and access is locked for other users.

6 Conclusion

In this paper, we have shown the feasibility of a lightweight browser-native tool that supports the modeling process in distributed software engineering processes. Solutions to problems that previously prevented the implementation of graphical interactive editors on the sole basis of a web browser have been described. In particular, it has been shown that it is possible to provide a fully functional modeling tool with minimal requirements towards the client systems to be integrated. The high degree of flexibility and interoperability distinguishes SLIM from existing tools and collaborative environments. By leveraging the benefits of web technologies, tools can be created, which considerably reduce the barriers of engaging in collaborative work. Using such tools allows for quick and dynamic coupling between all stakeholders. In particular, the dependence of the distributed team members on the availability and capability of their IT department is reduced. Future research will target several important aspects: a deeper insight into organizational and UML-related challenges in collaborative usage scenarios will have to be gained. So far, the focus has been on the technical feasibility of a lightweight browser-native approach and support for different UML diagram types is limited to UML class diagrams. Additionally, SLIM will be integrated with a traceability and versioning system. Further information on the SLIM environment, including screenshots, can be found on the SLIM website[9].

References

1. Jacobson, I., Booch, G., Rumbaugh, J.: The Unified Software Development Process. Addison-Wesley, Boston (1999)
2. Whitehead, J.: Collaboration in software engineering: A roadmap. In: Future of Software Engineering (FOSE 2007), Minneapolis, Minnesota, USA, pp. 214–225 (2007)
3. Kong, S.H., Noh, S.D., Han, Y.G., Kim, G., Lee, K.I.: Internet-based collaboration system: Press-die design process for automobile manufacturer. The International Journal of Advanced Manufacturing Technology 20(9), 701–708 (2002)
4. East, E.W., Kirby, J.G., Perez, G.: Improved design review through web collaboration. Journal of Management in Engineering 20(2), 51–55 (2004)
5. Gentleware AG: Poseidon for UML (2008), `http://www.gentleware.com/editions.html`
6. Fragemann, P., Graham, E., Tietjens, J.: Poseidon for UML enterprise edition instalation guide (2008), `http://www.gentleware.com/fileadmin/media/pdfs/installguides/InstallGuide_Enterprise_quickstart.pdf`
7. Mehra, A., Grundy, J., Hosking, J.: Supporting collaborative software design with a plug-in, web services-based architecture. In: Workshop on Directions in Software Engineering Environments (WoDiSEE) at the 26th International Conference on Software Engineering (ICSE 2004), Edinburgh, Scotland. IEEE, Los Alamitos (2004)
8. Palaniappan, S., Ling, L.: A novel SVG application in UML system modelling. In: 6th SVG Open Conference, Nuremberg, Deutschland (2008)
9. Campbell, J.D.: Multi-user collaborative visual program development. In: IEEE 2002 Symposia on Human Centric Computing Languages and Environments, Arlington, Virginia, USA, pp. 122–130 (2002)
10. Qi, C., Grundy, J., Hosking, J.: An e-whiteboard application to support early design-stage sketching of UML diagrams. In: IEEE Symposium on Human Centric Computing Languages and Environments, Auckland, New Zealand, pp. 219–226 (2003)

[9] `http://www.wifo.uni-mannheim.de/~slim/`

11. Markus, M.L., Majchrzak, A., Gasser, L.: A design theory for systems that support emergent knowledge processes. MIS Quarterly 26(3), 179–212 (2002)
12. Bentley, R., Horstmann, T., Trevor, J.: The world wide web as enabling technology for CSCW: The case of BSCW. Computer Supported Cooperative Work (CSCW) 6(2), 111–134 (1997)
13. Hill, C., Yates, R., Jones, C., Kogan, S.L.: Beyond predictable workflows: Enhancing productivity in artful business processes. IBM Systems Journal 45(4), 663–682 (2006)
14. Bughin, J., Manyika, J., Miller, A.: Building the web 2.0 enterprise (2008)
15. Schmmer, T., Lukosch, S.: Patterns for Computer-Mediated Interaction. John Wiley & Sons, Chichester (2007)
16. Zorn, W.: High performance javascript vector graphics library (2006), http://www.walterzorn.com/jsgraphics/jsgraphics_e.htm
17. Herz, A.: Draw2D (2009), http://draw2d.org/
18. Hritcu, C., Dumitriu, S., Girdea, M.: UML2SVG (2007), http://uml2svg.sourceforge.net/
19. W3Schools: Browser statistics - web statistics and trends (2009), http://www.w3schools.com/browsers/browsers_stats.asp
20. Lazutkin, E., Xi, K.: dojox.gfx documentation (2008), http://docs.google.com/View?docid=d764479_1hnb2tn
21. Stefik, M., Bobrow, D.G., Foster, G., Lanning, S., Tatar, D.: Wysiwis revised: Early experiences with multiuser interfaces. ACM Transactions on Office Information Systems 5(2), 147–167 (1987)
22. OMG: MOF 2.0 / XMI mapping specification v2.1.1 (2007), http://www.omg.org/technology/documents/formal/xmi.htm
23. Dix, A.: Challenges for cooperative work on the web: An analytical approach. Computer Supported Cooperative Work (CSCW) 6(2), 135–156 (1997)
24. Russell, A.: Comet: Low latency data for the browser (2006), http://alex.dojotoolkit.org/?p=545
25. Wilkins, G.: Jetty continuations (2007), http://docs.codehaus.org/display/JETTY/Continuations

Language-Independent Change Management of Process Models

Christian Gerth[1,2,3], Jochen M. Küster[1], and Gregor Engels[3]

[1] IBM Zurich Research Laboratory, Säumerstr. 4,
8803 Rüschlikon, Switzerland
{cge,jku}@zurich.ibm.com
[2] Intern. Graduate School of Dynamic Intelligent Systems
[3] Department of Computer Science, University of Paderborn, Germany
{gerth,engels}@upb.de

Abstract. In model-driven development approaches, process models are used at different levels of abstraction and are described by different languages. Similar to other software artifacts, process models are developed in team environments and underlie constant change. This requires reusable techniques for the detection of changes between different process models and the computation of dependencies and conflicts between changes. In this paper, we propose a framework for the construction of process model change management solutions that provides generic techniques for the detection of differences and the computation of dependencies and conflicts between changes. The framework contains an abstract representation for process models that serves as a common denominator for different process models. In addition, we show how the framework is instantiated exemplarily for BPMN.

Keywords: Process model change management, process model differences.

1 Introduction

In recent years, the role of process models in the development of enterprise software systems has increased continuously. Today, process models are used at different levels in the development process. For instance, in Service-Oriented Architectures (SOA) [1], high-level business process models become input for the development of IT systems, and in running IT systems executable process models describe choreographies of Web Services [2]. A key driver behind this development is the necessity for a closer alignment of business and IT requirements [3], to reduce the reaction times in software development to frequent changes in competitive markets.

Typically in these scenarios, process models are developed, refined, and transformed in a team environment by several stakeholders that are often from different business units, resulting in different versions. These process model versions reflect the different views of the stakeholders involved. To obtain integrated process models comprising the changes applied to different versions, the versions need to be consolidated by means of process model change management.

Change management for process models consists of the following major activities: detection of differences, computation of dependencies and conflicts between differences, and resolution of differences. In general, change management is a language-dependent

A. Schürr and B. Selic (Eds.): MODELS 2009, LNCS 5795, pp. 152–166, 2009.

problem, i.e., a solution for a particular modeling language cannot be reused easily for another language, because of different syntax and semantics of the languages.

Existing approaches to model change management are either limited to a particular process modeling language [4] or focus mainly on structural models [5,6,7,8], such as class diagrams. In contrast to structural models, process models have a certain execution order, specified in the form of control-flow, data-flow, or even both. Moreover, process models have to fulfill further criteria, such as reachability or soundness (with respect to deadlocks, lack of synchronization) that are irrelevant for structural models. These criteria have to be considered when it comes to the consolidation of process models.

In our recent work [9], we have proposed an approach to difference detection and resolution between process models in the absence of a change log that makes use of a hierarchical decomposition of process models into fragments and compound change operations. In [10], we have addressed the computation of dependencies and conflicts between change operations.

In this paper, we generalize our recent results in terms of a framework for change management of process models. We introduce the concept of an intermediate representation for process models. This intermediate representation is an abstraction of specific process models that focuses on common semantical core concepts for the modeling of workflow in process models. Based on the intermediate representation, we compute differences between process models as well as dependencies and conflicts between them generically. Thereby, we make major components for process model change management reusable.

The remainder of this paper is organized as follows: Section 2 introduces a typical model-driven development scenario, in which we point out the particular problems for process model change management. As a solution, we propose an intermediate representation for process models embedded in a framework in Section 3. In Section 4, we show how the framework is instantiated exemplarily for BPMN. In Section 5, we present prototypic instantiations of the framework for the consolidation of BPMN process models and BPEL processes in IBM® WebSphere® products as proof of concept. Finally, we conclude with a discussion of related work and an outlook on future work.

2 Motivation

Software development approaches, such as service-oriented approaches, increasingly focus on a closer alignment of the business and IT side [3]. Figure 1 illustrates such an approach that consists of several phases.

In the *Model* phase, a business case is modeled in terms of a process model that represents the business needs and requirements for an IT solution. Then, in the *Develop* phase, the process model is stepwise refined and transformed into an executable IT solution, which is integrated and deployed in an existing environment (*Deploy* phase). In the *Monitor* phase, the IT solution is monitored and evaluated, to check whether all requirements have been met. Finally, in the *Analyze & Adapt* phase, the IT solution is adapted and modified until a desired behavior is reached and all requirements are fulfilled.

Typically, in such development approaches, different process models are used. On the business side, business cases are modeled in terms of high-level process models that specify necessary tasks together with an execution order and are understandable by a large group of stakeholders involved in the development process. Preferred modeling languages on the business side are, e.g., Business Process Modeling Notation (BPMN) [11], UML Activity Diagrams (UML-AD) [12], or Event-driven Process Chains (EPC) [13]. However, on the IT side, executable models are needed that specify implementation details. For modeling executable process models, the Business Process Execution Language (BPEL) [14] is a de facto standard.

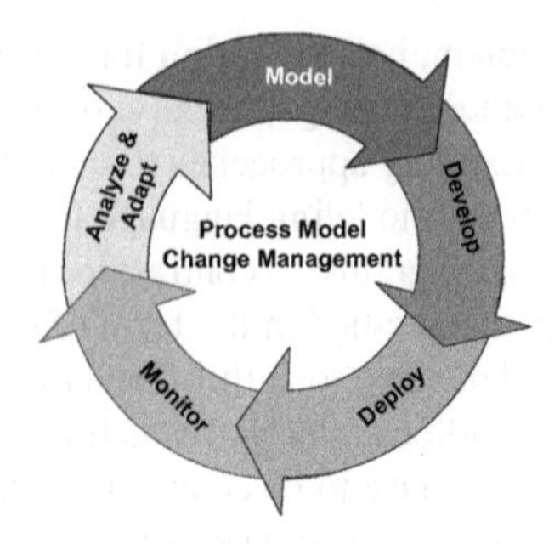

Fig. 1. Business-Driven Development [3]

Similar to other software artifacts process models are developed in distributed environments, i.e., different process models are created independently by different people. Figure 2 illustrates such a scenario, which may occur in the *Model* and the *Analyze & Adapt* phase. There, a source process model V_0 is independently refined into two versions, V_1 and V_2. At a certain point in time, the necessity arises to consolidate the different versions to obtain a unique input (V_3) for the next phase (e.g., the *Develop* phase). For that purpose, the differences between V_1 and V_0 as well as between V_2 and V_0 are computed[1]. In addition, dependencies and conflicts between differences need to be detected.

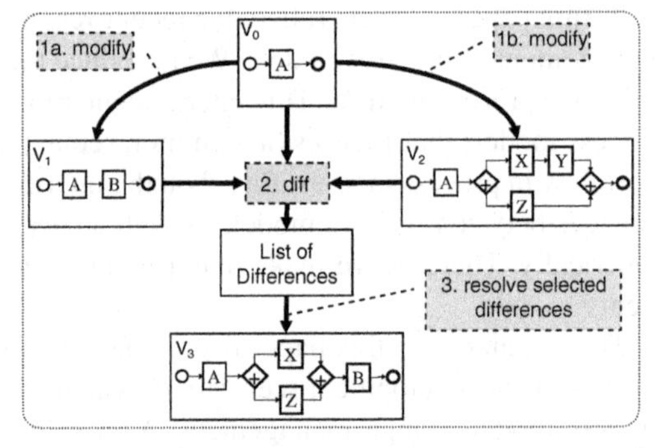

Fig. 2. Change Management within Language Boundaries

In such scenarios, where process models potentially exist in different representations (e.g., high-level or executable) and are developed in a distributed environment resulting in different versions, process model change management is required. Similar to concurrent versioning systems for textual documents, change management for process models provides means for the detection of differences between process models, the computation of dependencies and conflicts, and the resolution of differences.

The common purpose of all business process models is to describe all activities that are necessary to achieve a certain business case and to define an order in which the tasks have to be applied. With regards to change management, this means that it is necessary to identify inserted or removed tasks and changes to the execution order.

However, a generic approach to change management is difficult to realize because of the huge variety of different process modeling languages. First of all, different languages have different syntax and semantics. For instance: Some languages [11,12] use edges to define the execution order of tasks, whereas others define the execution order

[1] If V_1 and V_2 do not have a common ancestor, differences are detected between V_1 and V_2.

by nesting basic control elements [14], such as sequence, concurrency, and alternative. The former languages are also called graph-oriented and the latter ones block-oriented [15]. Even within one language, different ways to model one and the same concept exist, e.g., a control-flow split can be modeled either implicitly using pins and pin sets or explicitly using control nodes, such as decision or fork.

Figure 3 illustrates different ways to model control flow splits and joins. Here, the process models in Figure 3 (a) and (b) use explicit control flow splits and joins to specify parallel (a) and alternative (b) behavior. The process models given in the lower part of Figure 3 also specify parallel (c) and alternative (d) behavior. However, there the behavior is modeled by implicit control flow splits and joins or by a mixture of implicit and explicit elements. The ability to deal with syntactically different process models that are semantically equivalent (Figure 3 (a), (c) and (b), (d)) is crucial for change management solutions.

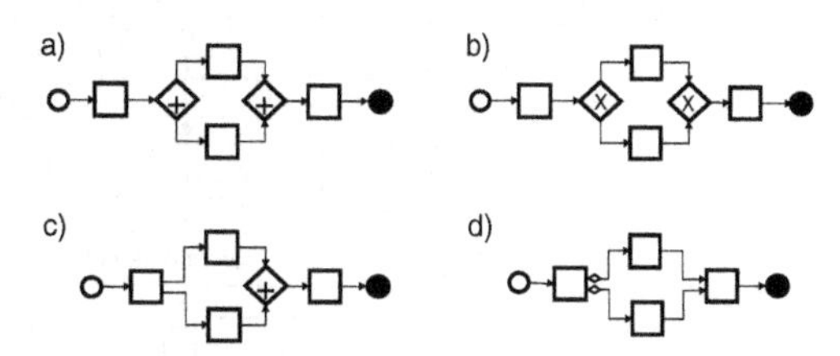

Fig. 3. Different ways to model parallel and alternative behavior

In general, the consolidation of process models in different languages requires individual implementations for change management. This means that change management techniques implemented for a concrete modeling language cannot be easily reused for another process modeling language. In the next section, we address this problem and propose a generic approach to process model change management.

3 A Framework for Process Model Change Management

In this section, we propose a generic approach to process model change management using a framework that contains generic components for the detection of differences and the computation of dependencies between the differences.

3.1 Generic Approach to Process Model Change Management

Figure 4 sketches our approach using the framework. The process model versions introduced in Figure 2 are abstracted to an intermediate representation (IR). Based on the IR, differences, dependencies, and conflicts are computed[2], which are captured in a difference model. Finally, IR differences are translated into differences for the concrete modeling language of the original process models and can then be applied to resolve differences.

An obvious advantage of this approach is that the framework can be instantiated for models in different process modeling languages and that only one implementation

[2] Computation of differences between process models requires a matching, in order to find corresponding elements. Model matching is an area of research in its own right with quite a lot of interest [6,5,16] and is not in the scope of this paper. For the remainder of this paper, we assume that a matching is given, e.g., by relating elements that have the same unique ID.

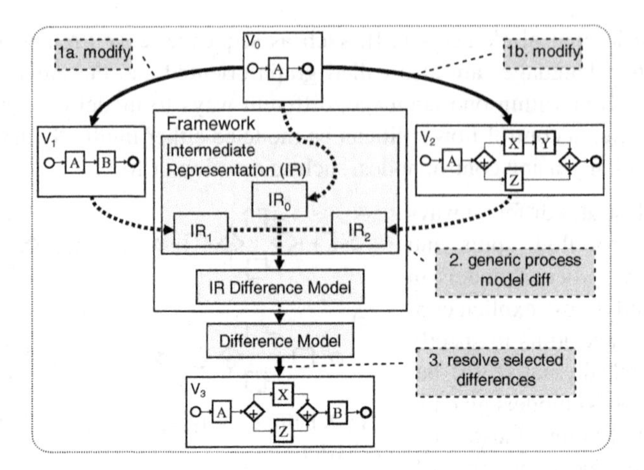

Fig. 4. Generic Approach to Process Model Change Management

for detection of differences, dependencies, and conflicts is required, as these computations are based on the IR. In addition, the approach can be easily extended by further languages. For instance, to support change management between models in another modeling language, say L, an abstraction of models in L into models in the IR needs to be defined and a translation of IR differences to L differences needs to be specified.

In the following, we introduce the main components of the framework in more detail.

3.2 Intermediate Representation (IR)

The IR is an abstraction and normalization of individual process models based on generic workflow graphs (WFG) [17,18,19] describing the actual workflow of process models in terms of a directed graph with nodes connected by edges. The graphs are further decomposed into fragments [19]. Thereby, the IR serves as a common denominator of process models at different levels of abstraction or in different languages, and enables a generic approach to process model change management. Figure 5 shows a reference meta model for the IR.

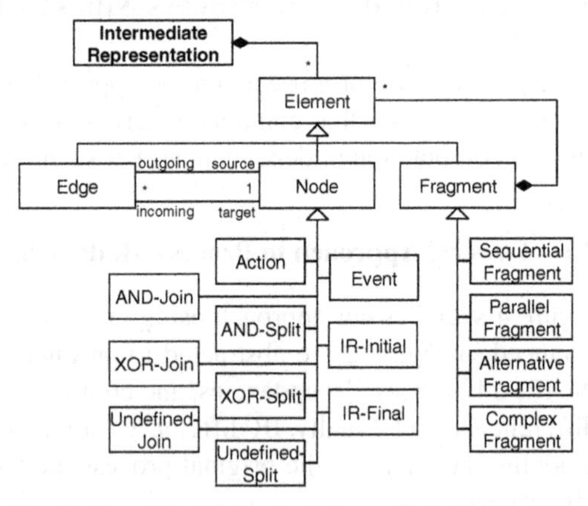

Fig. 5. Meta Model for the Intermediate Representation

The IR covers the semantics of syntactical elements that model the execution order of activities in a process model, such as *AND/XOR/Undefined – Splits* and *AND/XOR/Undefined – Joins*. These elementary, syntactical elements are supported by nearly all process modeling languages and enable the modeling of sequential, parallel, alternative, and complex behavior such as loops. In block-structured languages, such as BPEL, elementary splits and joins are not modeled directly, but are instead supported by composed model elements (blocks), e.g., a BPEL *Switch* structure models alternative behavior. However, such composed model elements can be reduced to pairs of elementary splits and joins.

Figure 6 (a) shows a process model in the intermediate representation decomposed into fragments. *IR – Initial* and *IR – Final* constitute unique start and end nodes of an IR, which are required for a decomposition into fragments. The fragments f_Z, f_X, and f_W are sequential fragments, and f_Y is an alternative fragment. The fragments form a hierarchy that is represented by the process structure tree [19] in Fig. 6 (b).

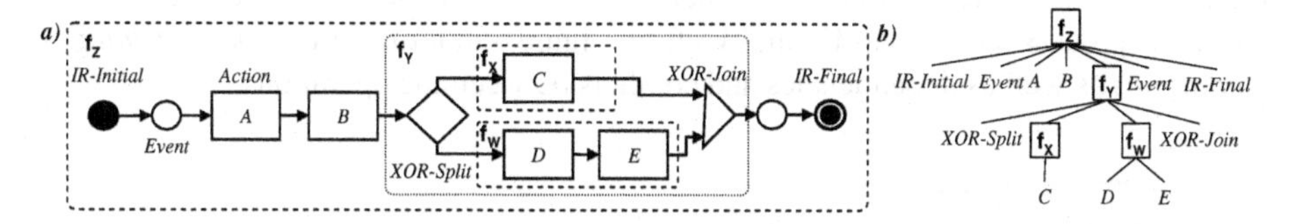

Fig. 6. Process Model in the Intermediate Representation (IR) and its Process Structure Tree (PST)

We define the semantics of the IR similar to the semantics of Petri nets [20] in terms of token flow. The nodes of the IR represent the transitions of a Petri net, and the edges are the places of the Petri net. A state of the IR can then be described as the number of tokens carried by the edges of an IR. In Figure 7, we informally describe the behavior of important elements of the IR following mainly the semantics defined in [21].

Syntax	Semantics
IR-Initial IR-Final	An *IR-Initial* can fire if none of the edges carries a token (i.e. initial state of the *IR*). When it executes, a single token is added to its outgoing edge. An *IR-Final* can fire if its incoming edge carries at least one token. Firing of an *IR-Final* removes all token from all edges in an *IR*.
Action Event AND-Split & Join	*Actions, Events,* and *AND-Splits* can fire if a token is on their incoming edge. *AND-Joins* require at least one token on each incoming edge, before they can fire. When an *Action*, an *Event*, or an *AND-Split/Join* fires, the number of tokens on each incoming edge is decreased by one and one token is added on each outgoing edge.
XOR-Split & Join	An *XOR-Split* can fire whenever a token is on its incoming edge. When a split fires, one token is taken from its incoming edge and exactly one of its outgoing edges is selected to which the token is added. The selection of the outgoing edge is nondeterministic. An *XOR-Join* can fire if at least one of its incoming edges carries a token. When a join fires, an incoming edge that carries at least one token is selected nondeterministically. One token is taken from this incoming edge and added to the outgoing edge of the *XOR-Join*.
? ? Undefined-Split & Join	The behavior of *Undefined-Splits* or *Joins* is not further specified. These elements are used to represent gateways in a concrete language, whose behavior is unknown or does not match to *AND/XOR* logic of the gateways presented above. An *Undefined-Split* or *Join* is always enclosed by a *Complex Fragment*.

Fig. 7. Syntax and Semantics of the Intermediate Representation

3.3 Difference Model

In this section, we introduce the difference model of our framework. Differences between two process models are represented in terms of *CompoundChangeOperations* that are composed of several element-based changes and automate the reconnection of control flow in the process model. An advantage of describing differences in terms of operations is that the operations can be directly applied to resolve the differences they describe. In addition, *CompoundChangeOperations* turned out to be more intuitive to human users and also ensure that a model is transformed from one consistent state into a new consistent state. More detailed information can be found in [9].

Figure 8 (a) visualizes the meta model for differences between process models. In Figure 8 (b) a concrete difference model is shown that captures the differences between the process models V_0, V_1, and V_2 from Figure 4 in terms of *CompoundChange-Operations* as well as dependencies and conflicts between the operations.

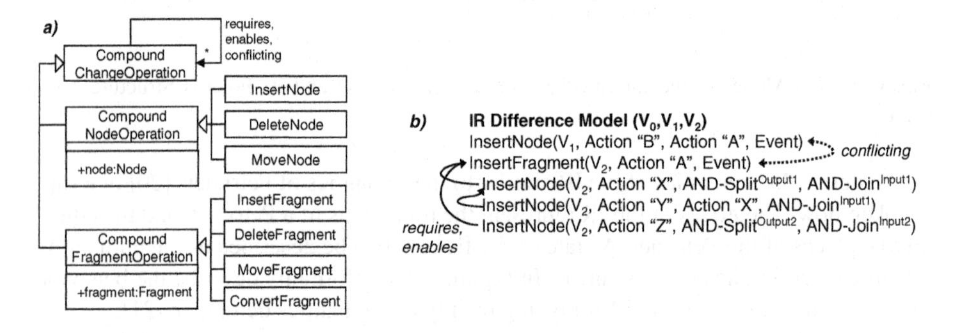

Fig. 8. (a) Meta Model of the IR Difference Model together with (b) an Instantiation Capturing the Differences between the Process Models V_0, V_1, and V_2 from Figure 4

Dependent Operations: Dependencies determine the order in which operations can be applied and ensure that process models stay in a connected and well-formed state. For instance, the insertion of a model element into a branch of a fragment, requires that the fragment (and its branches) were inserted before. Using the difference model, a dependency between two operations op_i and op_j can be defined using the associations *enables* and *requires*. In Figure 8 (b) the lower left arrows represent the *requires* association (the opposite direction represents the *enables* association).

Conflicting Operations: Two operations are in conflict if the application of one operations renders the other operation inapplicable. In the difference model, conflicting operations are represented by the association *conflicting*. For instance, the insertion of *Action B* in V_1 and the insertion of the fragment in V_2 in Figure 8 (b) are conflicting because their position parameter overlap. In [10] we have addressed the computation of dependencies and conflicts between change operations.

Having introduced our framework for process model change management, we show how it can be used in the next section.

4 Using the Framework

In this section, we show how the framework is instantiated exemplarily for change management of BPMN process models. We will first give an overview of the steps required for the instantiation. Then, we show how BPMN process models are abstracted into the IR and how change operations based on the IR can be translated to concrete change operations for BPMN.

4.1 Overview

To instantiate the framework, we propose the following six steps, as illustrated in Figure 9. Here, a typical merge scenario is presented, in which two BPMN process models shall be consolidated. The first and the last step are language-specific, whereas steps two to five are based on the IR and are independent of the modeling language. Before we discuss the language-specific steps in detail in Sections 4.2 and 4.3, we will briefly give an overview. More detailed informations about steps two to five can be found in [9].

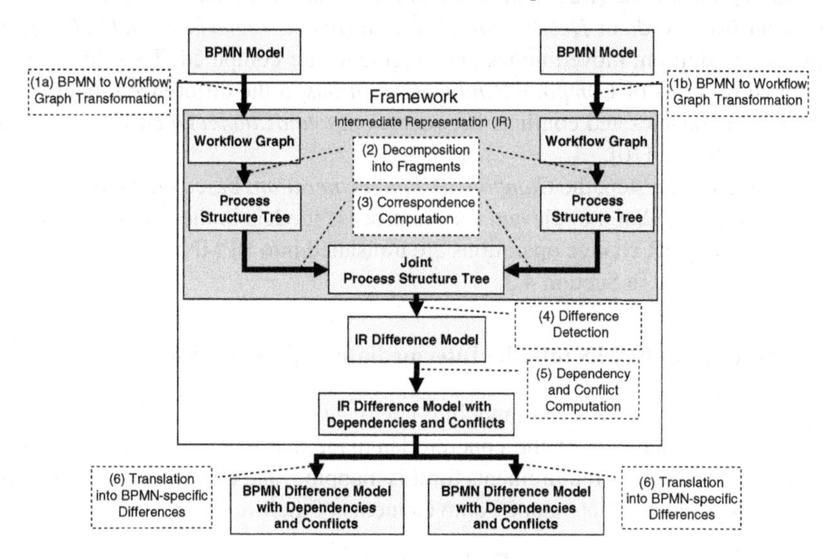

Fig. 9. BPMN Process Model Change Management using the Framework described in this Paper

In the first step, the BPMN process models need to be abstracted into the IR, resulting in a workflow graph for each BPMN process model. For this step a mapping between elements of a concrete modeling language (here BPMN) and the elements of the IR is required. How this mapping can be established for BPMN is discussed in Section 4.2. Using the mapping, a BPMN model can be abstracted to an IR model, and each IR model element stores a link to its corresponding concrete BPMN model element[3]. This link is later used to translate IR-based changes into BPMN changes.

[3] If an IR element does not have a directly corresponding BPMN element, the IR element corresponds to the corresponding element of either its predecessor or its successor. For instance, an IR *AND – Split* representing an implicit control flow split in BPMN (*Task* with multiple outgoing edges) has no directly corresponding BPMN element. Then, the corresponding concrete element of the IR *AND – Split* is the BPMN *Task* that implies the control flow split.

In the second step, the workflow graphs are decomposed into fragments as introduced in [19], resulting in a process structure tree (PST). In general, fragments enclose subgraphs of a workflow graph that have a single entry and a single exit node. Fragments are used to render the correlation between entry and exit nodes explicit and to derive *CompoundChangeOperations* for fragments. For instance, the relation between a newly inserted *AND – Split* and an *AND – Join* forming a parallel fragment can be obtained easily by a decomposition, because these two nodes are the entry and exit of a new fragment.

Before differences between the two workflow graphs can be detected, a matching of the graphs is required [6,5,16] to detect corresponding elements. In the following we assume that correspondences between corresponding elements are given. Using these correspondences between elements and the two PSTs obtained in the second step, we can compute a Joint-PST [9] by overlapping corresponding elements and fragments.

Based on this Joint-PST, we compute in the fourth step differences between the models. Generally, each node (fragment) without a counterpart in the other process model results in an *InsertNode* or *DeleteNode* operation (*InsertFragment* or *DeleteFragment* operation). In addition, moved nodes and fragments are computed. These differences are captured in terms of *CompoundChangeOperations* in the difference model. In the fifth step, dependencies and conflicts between *CompoundChangeOperations* are computed as described in [10].

Finally, in the sixth step, the *CompoundChangeOperations* based on the IR are translated into operations that are relevant for the process models in the concrete modeling language. Thereby, IR change operations are translated into BPMN change operations. This step is discussed in Section 4.3.

4.2 Abstraction of BPMN into the Intermediate Representation

For the abstraction of a concrete modeling language into the IR, we have to define a mapping between elements of the concrete language and elements of the IR. In the following, we first discuss requirements for this mapping, and then illustrate how a core subset of BPMN elements is mapped onto elements of the IR.

1. Requirement (Completeness): Each model in a concrete modeling language is mapped to a model in the intermediate representation.

2. Requirement (Syntactic Redundancy Elimination): Different syntactical ways to express semantically equivalent concepts (according to Fig. 7) are mapped to the same syntactical element(s) in the intermediate representation.

The first requirement can be fulfilled in an inductive way by mapping each element of a concrete language to the IR. In trivial cases this can be done one-by-one, e.g., a BPMN *Task* is mapped to an IR *Action*. In other cases, single elements cannot be mapped in isolation, because a group of model elements corresponds to an IR element or a group of IR elements corresponds to a concrete element. Then, those groups of elements need to be mapped together. In addition, for the second requirement, we have to take care that concrete model elements that are semantically equivalent are mapped to the same IR element.

For the abstraction of BPMN models into IR models, we consider a core subset of BPMN elements that covers fundamental activities, such as *Task*, *Subprocess*, and *Loop*, events, such as *Start* and *End*, as well as gateways, such as *AND*, *IOR*, *XOR*, and *Complex* logic. The elements are connected by BPMN *Sequence Flow* or *Message Flow*. Figure 10 illustrates how BPMN atomic activities, events, and connections are mapped onto the corresponding IR elements. BPMN *Tasks* are mapped to IR actions. BPMN *Start* and *End* events are abstracted to the IR event element, and BPMN *Sequence Flow* and *Message Flow* are abstracted to IR edges.

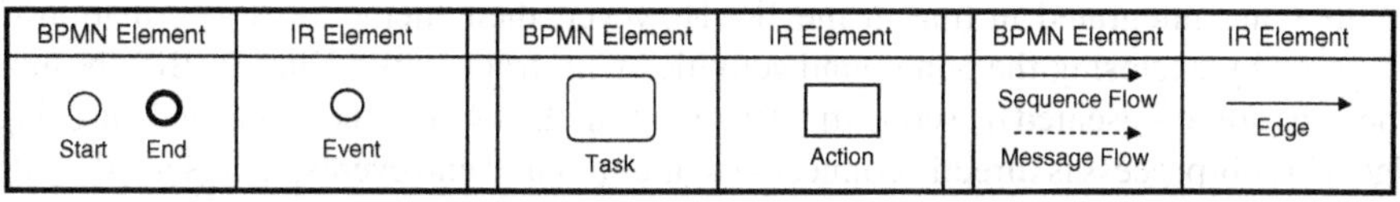

BPMN Element	IR Element	BPMN Element	IR Element	BPMN Element	IR Element
Start End	Event	Task	Action	Sequence Flow Message Flow	Edge

Fig. 10. Mapping of BPMN Task, Start, End, Connections to IR Elements

The mapping of BPMN gateways is shown in Figure 11. BPMN *inclusive* gateways and *complex* gateways are abstracted to *Undefined – Split/Join* elements of the IR. The mapping of BPMN *exclusive* and *parallel* gateways is straightforward. Two or more incoming (outgoing) edges of a BPMN element that is not a gateway, represent an implicit *Parallel – Fork* (*Exclusive – Merge*). These implicit gateways are syntactically different from explicit *exclusive* and *parallel* gateways (see Figure 3), but semantically equivalent. According to *Requirement 2.*, we map semantically equivalent implicit and explicit gateways to the same IR elements, as illustrated in the bottom row of Figure 11.

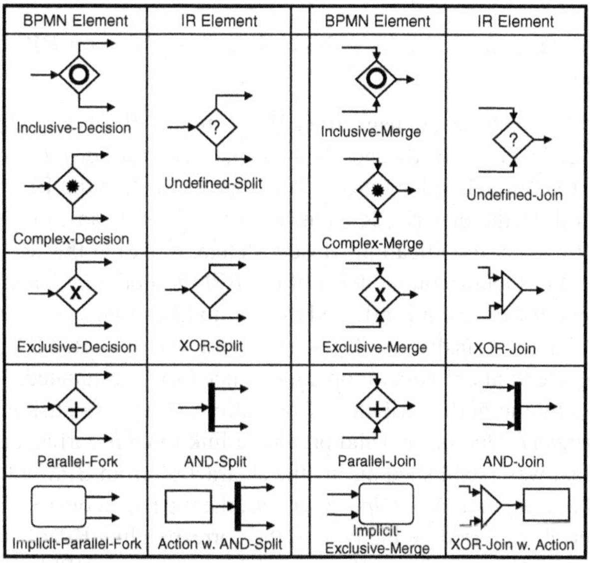

BPMN Element	IR Element	BPMN Element	IR Element
Inclusive-Decision Complex-Decision	Undefined-Split	Inclusive-Merge Complex-Merge	Undefined-Join
Exclusive-Decision	XOR-Split	Exclusive-Merge	XOR-Join
Parallel-Fork	AND-Split	Parallel-Join	AND-Join
Implicit-Parallel-Fork	Action w. AND-Split	Implicit-Exclusive-Merge	XOR-Join w. Action

Fig. 11. Mapping between BPMN Gateways and IR Splits and Joins

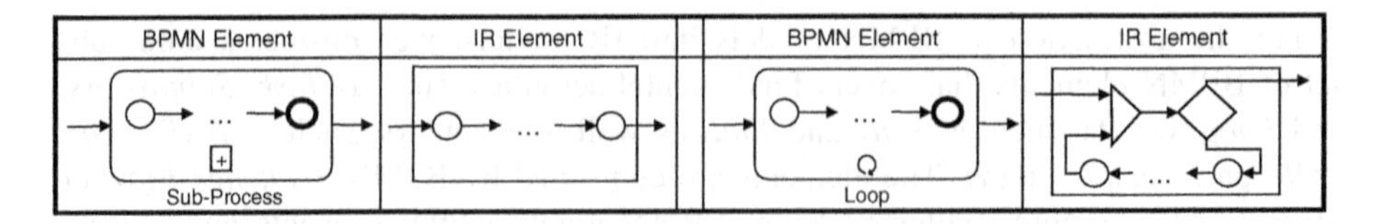

Fig. 12. Mapping of BPMN Sub-processes and Loops to IR Elements

Finally, BPMN compound activities, such as sub-processes and loops, are mapped as illustrated in Figure 12. The compound activities are flattened during the abstraction, i.e., they are integrated in-line in the IR. However, their hierarchical information is preserved by enclosing the compound activities with fragments in the IR. BPMN sub-processes are represented by sequential fragments in the IR. The incoming and outgoing edge of a sub-process is directly connected to the start and end events, represented by IR events. BPMN loops are abstracted into a combination of IR $XOR-Join$ and $XOR-Split$ that is enclosed by a alternative fragment as shown in Figure 12. The $XOR-Split$ takes the decision whether the loop is repeated or the loop is exited.

The mapping defined fulfills the requirements for an abstraction of a concrete language in the IR, because each element of the core subset of BPMN is mapped to the IR (Completeness). In addition, the second requirement (Syntactic Redundancy Elimination) is fulfilled, because different syntactical ways that model the same semantical concept (e.g. implicit/explicit BPMN *Parallel Fork*) are abstracted to the same IR element (IR $AND-Split$). Using the mapping, models in the core subset of BPMN can be abstracted to IR models. Then, differences between IR models are computed, using given correspondences between original elements, and stored in terms of *CompoundChangeOperations* in the difference model. In the following, we discuss how these changes based on the IR can be translated into BPMN change operations.

4.3 Translation of Generic Change Operations into Concrete BPMN Change Operations

The abstraction of a concrete language to the IR is a trade-off between changes that can be detected on the level of the IR and changes that need further interpretation on the level of the concrete modeling language. For instance, we map the BPMN event types *Start* and *End* both to the generic IR element *Event*. That means, on the level of the IR, we are able to detect modifications (insert, delete, move) to the IR element *Event*. However, we have to identify on the level of the BPMN modeling language whether a BPMN *Start* event or *End* event is affected by the modification.

Accordingly, for the translation of generic operations into BPMN change operations, underlying elements of generic operations need to be evaluated. Underlying elements are given by the node attributes of operations (fragment attributes in the case of *CompoundFragmentOperations*) and provide a link to their corresponding concrete model element that was established during the abstraction from BPMN to IR.

In the case of a *CompoundNodeOperation* op_n, the type of a concrete BPMN change operation is determined based on the type of the corresponding BPMN model element of op_n. For instance, a generic *InsertNode* operation inserting a BPMN *Task* activity is translated into a concrete *InsertTask* operation, as shown in Figure 13.

IR: InsertNode(V_2, Action "X", AND-Split^{Output1}, AND-Join^{Input1})

BPMN: InsertTask(V_2, "X", Parallel-Fork^{Output1}, Parallel-Join^{Input1})

Fig. 13. Translation of an IR Change Operation into a BPMN Change Operation

In the case of a *CompoundFragmentOperation* op_f, the type of the underlying fragment determines the type of the concrete BPMN change operation, e.g., a generic *InsertFragment* operation op_{IF} with an $AND-Split$ as entry, $AND-Join$ as exit and no further gateways as children is translated into a BPMN *InsertParallelFragment* operation. Note that a concrete change operation for fragments must take care that also all comprised operations of a *CompoundFragmentOperation* are applied. That means, in the case of the *InsertFragment* operation op_{IF}, the insertions of the fragments entry node and exit node also need to be executed by the BPMN *InsertParallelFragment* operation.

Finally, position parameters of generic insert and move operations that specify predecessor and successor of newly inserted or moved elements are translated by substituting generic *Node* elements with their corresponding concrete BPMN element.

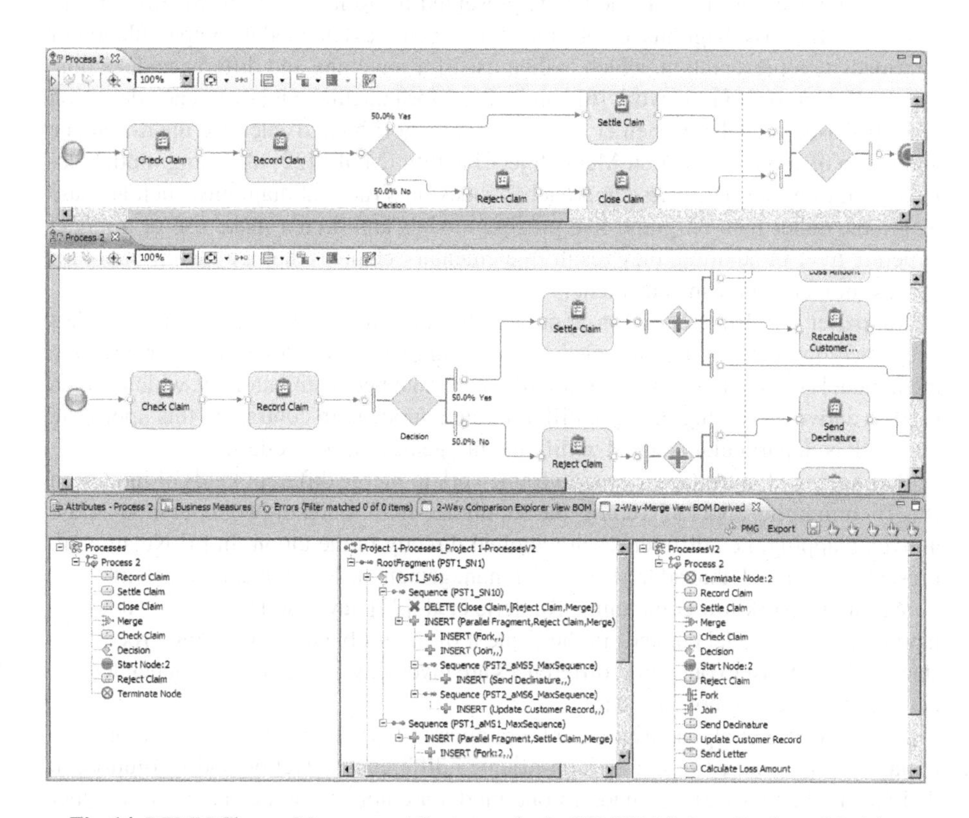

Fig. 14. BPMN Change Management Prototype in the IBM WebSphere Business Modeler

5 Tool Support

As proof of concept we have implemented the framework for process model change management. Figure 14 shows a prototype obtained by instantiating our framework for the IBM WebSphere Business Modeler in action. Two BPMN process models are shown together with a difference view. The difference view is divided into three columns. The left- and right-hand columns show the two BPMN process models in a tree structure that abstracts from control flow. The middle column of the difference view displays *CompoundChangeOperations* according to the structure of the two process models that need to be applied to transform one version of the BPMN process model in an other.

After defining the BPEL-to-IR mapping and a translation of generic, IR-based operations into BPEL operations the change management framework can be used in the IBM WebSphere Integration Developer for the consolidation of BPEL process models.

6 Related Work

In the area of difference detection of models, several approaches exist that can roughly be divided into generic approaches that can deal with different models and approaches that are limited to models in a specific language. A generic approach for matching and difference detection of UML models is presented by Kelter et al. in [5]. In their approach, UML class diagrams are abstracted to a generic data model comparable to our intermediate representation, which is then used for matching and difference detection. The EMF-Compare Framework [6] can be used for matching and difference detection of EMF-based models. Alanen et al. [7] present algorithms to calculate the difference and union of models based on Meta Object Facility (MOF) [22] assuming model elements with unique IDs. These approaches focus on structural diagrams, such as class diagrams, rather than on graph-like process models and do not make use of a model structure tree. In addition, they result in elementary changes that are inconvenient for process model change management [10].

Kappel et al. [16] propose an approach that provides means to exchange models between different tools. The approach has a strong focus on ontology engineering: First, meta models of concrete languages are lifted and mapped to an ontology, which is then used to derive a bridging between different meta models. In contrast to this approach, our work is in particular adapted to diff and merge of process models.

Pottinger et al. introduce a generic framework to merge different kinds of models in [8]. Their merging approach returns the "duplicate-free" union of two input models and a given mapping, i.e., differences are applied directly in the union. In [4] Nejati et al. present an approach that addresses model management of hierarchical Statecharts.

Within the workflow community, Rinderle et al. [23] have studied disjoint and overlapping process model changes in the context of the problem of migrating process instances. In contrast to our work, differences are given in a change log and dependencies between changes are not considered.

In [24], Giese et al. use triple graph grammars to synchronize models in a bidirectional way. In contrast to our session-oriented difference detection and resolution, in their work changes that are made to one model are applied immediately to the other model.

In consistency management of models, Egyed [25] has studied the detection of choices for fixing inconsistencies in UML models, which could be applied to conflict resolution of process models.

7 Conclusion and Future Work

In model-driven development approaches, process models are used at different levels of abstraction and in different languages. Similar to other software artifacts, process models are developed in team environments and underlie constant change. This requires reusable techniques for the detection of changes between different process models and the computation of dependencies between changes.

In this paper, we have presented a generic approach to process model change management based on a framework consisting of an intermediate representation and a difference model. We have then introduced a methodology of how the framework is used and have shown how BPMN can be abstracted to the IR and how generic change operation are translated into BPMN change operations. As proof of concept, the instantiation of the framework for BPMN and BPEL shows the general applicability of our approach.

There are several directions for future work. We would like to validate our approach also for other behavioral models, such as statecharts, which are used in the development of mechatronic systems. This includes a mapping of statecharts to the IR as well the definition of a translation of generic changes into statechart-specific changes. Future work will also include support for change management across language boundaries. In those scenarios, a (partial) mapping between the meta models of different modeling languages is required for the matching of process models and for the translation of changes.

References

1. Erl, T.: Service-Oriented Architecture: Concepts, Technology, and Design. Prentice Hall PTR, Upper Saddle River (2005)
2. Zimmermann, O., Tomlinson, M.R., Peuser, S.: Perspectives on Web Services: Applying SOAP, WSDL and UDDI to Real-World Projects (Springer Professional Computing). Springer, Heidelberg (2003)
3. Koehler, J., Hauser, R., Küster, J., Ryndina, K., Vanhatalo, J., Wahler, M.: The Role of Visual Modeling and Model Transformations in Business-Driven Development. In: Proceedings of GT-VMT 2006, pp. 1–12 (2006)
4. Nejati, S., Sabetzadeh, M., Chechik, M., Easterbrook, S.M., Zave, P.: Matching and Merging of Statecharts Specifications. In: ICSE 2007, pp. 54–64. IEEE Computer Society, Los Alamitos (2007)
5. Kelter, U., Wehren, J., Niere, J.: A Generic Difference Algorithm for UML Models. In: Liggesmeyer, P., Pohl, K., Goedicke, M. (eds.) Software Engineering 2005. LNI, vol. 64, pp. 105–116. GI (2005)
6. Eclipse Foundation: EMF Compare, `http://www.eclipse.org/modeling/emft/?project=compare`
7. Alanen, M., Porres, I.: Difference and Union of Models. In: Stevens, P., Whittle, J., Booch, G. (eds.) UML 2003. LNCS, vol. 2863, pp. 2–17. Springer, Heidelberg (2003)

8. Pottinger, R., Bernstein, P.A.: Merging Models Based on Given Correspondences. In: VLDB, pp. 826–873 (2003)
9. Küster, J.M., Gerth, C., Förster, A., Engels, G.: Detecting and Resolving Process Model Differences in the Absence of a Change Log. In: Dumas, M., Reichert, M., Shan, M.-C. (eds.) BPM 2008. LNCS, vol. 5240, pp. 244–260. Springer, Heidelberg (2008)
10. Küster, J.M., Gerth, C., Engels, G.: Dependent and Conflicting Change Operations of Process Models. In: Paige, R.F., Hartman, A. (eds.) ECMDA 2009. LNCS, vol. 5562, pp. 158–173. Springer, Heidelberg (2009)
11. Object Management Group (OMG): Business Process Modeling Notation (BPMN), http://www.omg.org/spec/BPMN/1.2
12. Object Management Group (OMG): Unified Modeling Language (UML): Superstructure (2005), http://www.uml.org
13. Keller, G., Nüttgens, M., Scheer, A.W.: Semantische Prozeßmodellierung auf der Grundlage Ereignisgesteuerter Prozeßketten (EPK). Technical Report 89 (January 1992)
14. Organization for the Advancement of Structured Information Standards (OASIS): Web Services Business Process Execution Language (WS-BPEL) Version 2.0., http://docs.oasis-open.org/wsbpel/2.0/OS/wsbpel-v2.0-OS.html
15. Mendling, J., Lassen, K.B., Zdun, U.: Transformation Strategies between Block-Oriented and Graph-Oriented Process Modelling Languages. In: Multikonferenz Wirtschaftsinformatik 2006. Band 2, pp. 297–312. GITO-Verlag (2006)
16. Kappel, G., Kapsammer, E., Kargl, H., Kramler, G., Reiter, T., Retschitzegger, W., Schwinger, W., Wimmer, M.: Lifting Metamodels to Ontologies: A Step to the Semantic Integration of Modeling Languages. In: [26], pp. 528–542 (2006)
17. van der Aalst, W.M.P., Hirnschall, A., Verbeek, H.M.W.: An Alternative Way to Analyze Workflow Graphs. In: Pidduck, A.B., Mylopoulos, J., Woo, C.C., Ozsu, M.T. (eds.) CAiSE 2002. LNCS, vol. 2348, pp. 535–552. Springer, Heidelberg (2002)
18. Sadiq, W., Orlowska, M.E.: Analyzing Process Models Using Graph Reduction Techniques. Inf. Syst. 25(2), 117–134 (2000)
19. Vanhatalo, J., Völzer, H., Leymann, F.: Faster and More Focused Control-Flow Analysis for Business Process Models Through SESE Decomposition. In: Krämer, B.J., Lin, K.-J., Narasimhan, P. (eds.) ICSOC 2007. LNCS, vol. 4749, pp. 43–55. Springer, Heidelberg (2007)
20. Murata, T.: Petri nets: Properties, analysis and applications. Proceedings of the IEEE 77(4), 541–580 (1989)
21. Vanhatalo, J., Völzer, H., Leymann, F., Moser, S.: Automatic Workflow Graph Refactoring and Completion. In: Bouguettaya, A., Krueger, I., Margaria, T. (eds.) ICSOC 2008. LNCS, vol. 5364, pp. 100–115. Springer, Heidelberg (2008)
22. Object Management Group (OMG): Meta Object Facility, http://www.omg.org/mof/
23. Rinderle, S., Reichert, M., Dadam, P.: Disjoint and Overlapping Process Changes: Challenges, Solutions, Applications. In: Meersman, R., Tari, Z. (eds.) OTM 2004. LNCS, vol. 3290, pp. 101–120. Springer, Heidelberg (2004)
24. Giese, H., Wagner, R.: Incremental Model Synchronization with Triple Graph Grammars. In: [26], pp. 543–557 (2006)
25. Egyed, A.: Fixing Inconsistencies in UML Design Models. In: ICSE 2007, pp. 292–301. IEEE Computer Society, Los Alamitos (2007)
26. Nierstrasz, O., Whittle, J., Harel, D., Reggio, G. (eds.): MoDELS 2006. LNCS, vol. 4199. Springer, Heidelberg (2006)

Requirements for Practical Model Merge – An Industrial Perspective*

Lars Bendix[1] and Pär Emanuelsson[2]

[1] Department of Computer Science, Lund Institute of Technology, Box 118, S-221 00 Lund, Sweden
bendix@cs.lth.se
[2] Ericsson AB, S-583 30 Linköping, Sweden
par.emanuelsson@ericsson.com

Abstract. All the support tools that developers are used to must be in place, if the use of model-centric development in companies has to take off. Industry deals with big models and many people working on the same model. Collaboration in a team inevitably leads to parallel work creating different versions that eventually will have to be merged together. However, our experience is that at present the support for model merge is far from optimal. In this paper, we put forward a number of requirements for practical merge tools, based on our analysis of literature, merge tool evaluations, interviews with developers, and a number of use cases for concurrent development of models. We found future work to do for both tool vendors and academic research. Fortunately we also uncovered a few tips and tricks that companies using model-centric development can implement on the short term while waiting for better times.

Keywords: Model merge, diff, version control, parallel work, team coordination, industrial experience.

1 Introduction

In industry, the use of models in development is gaining momentum. However, from our experience there are still a number of obstacles that have to be overcome before the use of model-driven development can really take off. Models can be used in many different ways ranging from simple visualization of code to a pure model-centric approach where the model is the sole focus of attention and executable code is generated directly from the model and never looked at or manipulated. For the past couple of years Ericsson AB has started to use the model-centric approach on more and more of its projects and has had some successful experience, but has also suffered from being an early adopter of a "technology" that for some aspects is still not fully mature.

Industrial use of model-driven development means not just creating big and complex models, but more importantly also the involvement of many people working on the same model. A key factor in the adoption of model-centric development is the presence of mature tools that can support the developers when they carry out their

* Empirical results category paper.

A. Schürr and B. Selic (Eds.): MODELS 2009, LNCS 5795, pp. 167–180, 2009.

tasks. The most basic set of tools necessary consists of a model editor and a model compiler. This will allow the single developer to create and manipulate a model and to compile it into running code. However, this will not scale to an industrial project where many people are involved. Effective collaboration in a team requires that people can share information and the existence of groupware that can help groups communicate, collaborate and coordinate their activities [11].

On a more traditional development project where textual programming languages like C, Python or Java are used, version control tools and functionality often work as the groupware that helps a team manage its coordination. They will address problems like "shared data", "simultaneous update" and "double maintenance" [4] that are intrinsic parts of team collaboration and cannot be avoided, but instead have to be managed to allow the team to work efficiently and without making mistakes. The version control tool supplies a workspace to manage the "shared data" problem and concurrency detection to help manage the "simultaneous update" problem. Merge functionality – that may or may not be part of the version control tool – helps manage the "double maintenance" problem by allowing for easy conflict detection and resolution. Finally, diff functionality allows the developer to get information about how two versions in the repository – or a version in the repository and the version in the workspace – differ.

Our experience at Ericsson AB was that the version control support worked pretty well, though not optimal, when working on model-centric projects. However, the merge/diff tool support was far from optimal. From an informal tool evaluation we did in early 2007, it emerged that even for extremely simple examples, the merge results could often be counterintuitive or downright wrong – in some cases the merge result produced would not even load in the model editor. In a different study covering more tools the authors even went so far as to conclude that the "state of model merge tools is abysmal" [5]. It was decided to investigate more carefully the maturity of model merge with three objectives. First, to find solutions that could be implemented immediately by developers and projects. Second, to discover results from research that could be integrated in the tools provided by vendors. Third, to distinguish and define problems that need to be researched to provide more mature support for model merge.

In a previous paper, we reported on our results from an initial literature survey of academic research on model merge and an initial analysis of similarities and differences between text merge and model merge [6]. In a later paper, we proposed and discussed the consequences of a number of use cases for text and model merge, based on problems and suggestions that emerged from interviews with developers at more sites within Ericsson AB [7]. In this paper, we first present the context for the experience reported and clarify the terminology we have chosen to use. Then we give a more thorough analysis of relevant use cases from [7] with the aim to distil a number of requirements for a practical model merge tool. These requirements are then grouped into related themes that are discussed in more detail, and finally we draw our conclusions. This paper is based on a recent more thorough evaluation of model merge tools [18] and further interviews with developers.

2 Background

In this chapter, we will first describe the context in which we have obtained the experience we report, then we give a brief review of previous work done in this field followed by a clarification of the terminology that we use in this paper and finally the delimitations that will hold for the subsequent analysis and discussion.

Context. Ericsson AB has developed several large systems with millions of lines of code using UML in a model-centric way. This means that executable code is generated directly from the models and only models are considered for work, whereas generated code is never looked at or manipulated. We are able to obtain good reliability of systems and execution speed and code volume is acceptable. Furthermore, we have seen positive effects on code comprehension and on system complexity. As such the use of model technology has proved a success for industrial use and Ericsson AB would like to continue.

However, there are still a number of unresolved problems on the collaborative level because of the immaturity of tool support. We often work in big projects with up to 100 people working on the same model. On some projects people are even distributed on more than one site, making collaboration even more difficult without proper tool support. Without this support people resort to doing manual merges using three screens for the two alternatives and the result; instead of having tool-supported 3-way merge. Or they use a text merge tool on the textual representation of the model; which works in some cases, but requires knowledge of the representation format.

These "solutions" make it possible for the project teams to survive the use of model-centric development, but we would like to see better direct support from tools and processes.

Previous work. For textual documents there has long been mature merge tool support and early on the software configuration management (SCM) research community started to look at widening merge support. Early attempts were on structured documents in the context of structure-oriented environments [22] and syntax-directed editors [3]. However, since neither structure-oriented environments nor syntax-directed editors caught on that line of research died out. Interest has more recently resurfaced with the widespread use of structured texts and documents and thus the need to be able to provide support for collaboration for such structures. One line of research focuses on hypertext systems [17] whereas another line looks at models in general and UML models in particular [19].

People from outside the SCM community have also shown interest in looking at how to support the collaborative work on models. Early research focused on the detection and visualization of differences [23], [13] of diagrams to allow people to understand and analyze the evolution of changes to diagrams. More recently this has been extended to include merging of diagrams [14], [24] to support also the reconciliation of parallel work. This interest from the model community has grown into two lines of interesting workshops – one that looks more specifically at the technical versioning aspects of models [9], [10] and one that treats more general aspects of model evolution [15], [16].

Terminology. Reading through the literature from the model community we encountered some problems with terminology that made it difficult to know precisely what was being talked about and caused us some initial confusion. To avoid similar confusion in the readers of this paper, we find it proper to clarify the terminology we use here. There is a line of research on model merge that has a much more theoretical and mathematical approach [1], [2], [21], [20] and [8] than the more technical approaches mentioned above. Most of that work – though not all – focus on merge of different types of models and not of different versions of the same model. They "borrow" much from the mathematical world and work on defining and using the algebraic properties of operators on models. So we end up with many operators that sometimes have different meanings for the same operator. Here we define our meaning of four of these operators:

diff vs. *compare*: diff computes the differences between two versions of the same type of model (eg. class diagram); compare computes the differences between two models of different types (eg. class diagram and sequence diagram)

merge vs. *union*: merge integrates two (parallel) versions of the same type of model (eg. class diagram) and usually (in this paper) is a 3-way merge with a common ancestor; union integrates two models of different type (eg. class diagram and sequence diagram) and usually is 2-way without a common ancestor

Premise. What we present in this paper does not pretend to be general. It is based on the experience from one company – though from several independent branches – and the analysis and discussions are targeted at the specific needs of that company. However, since we believe that model-centric development and its problems do not vary much from company to company, we are confident that most of our findings – even with the delimitations below – will be generally applicable and of interest also to a wider audience.

In this paper, we treat *diff* and *merge* only as we are interested in working on different versions of the same type model. We detail only (mostly) merge as we consider diff to be a part of and a pre-requisite for a merge and therefore it shares similar problems. We have version control of models so historic versions are available and 3-way merge always possible. We talk about UML – and not models in general – and we can (and do) have UUIDs. All people on a team will use the same tools and processes and we value tools that integrate with other tools over integrated frameworks because that allows for more flexibility in setting up a working environment. Finally, we have a bias for feature-oriented development, which means that more feature teams will have to modify the same (parts of a) model at the same time.

3 From Use Cases to Requirements

In this chapter, we analyse a number of the use cases that were presented in [7]. We use them to distil more detailed requirements for practical model merge support. We briefly describe and motivate each use case. This is followed by an analysis of the use case, where we relate the model case with the traditional support in the text case. Finally we state and briefly discuss the use case's consequential requirements.

At this point we do not discriminate between requirements that are targeted at the version control tool, the model merge tool, the model language or the model work process. A more detailed discussion of the interrelations and dependencies between and the consequences of the requirements will be given in chapter 4 below. The use cases are intended to give the context in which model merge will have to live and as such hints at how it should work and what the requirements are if there is to be the same support for model merge as for text merge.

Some of the use cases from [7] are not used here for several reasons. Use case 3.1.b: *Work in isolation*, because it was meant to highlight collaboration in general and is not relevant to a specific analysis of merge support. It is part of what is supplied by the version control tool through the concept of a workspace – the consequence of which is that we may need to merge the parallel work done in more workspaces. Use case 3.1.c: *Integrate work*, is covered by and detailed in use cases 3.2.c-e that will be treated below. Use case 3.1.f: *Create awareness*, is outside the scope of this paper – it is usually part of the support supplied by the version control tool and is not specific to merge support. Use cases 3.2.a: *Architecture model development* and 3.2.b: *Design model development* are also left out here, because their primary purpose was to show the need for a compare operation and the varying number of people working in parallel – in this paper, we focus on the design setup.

3.1 Put Model under Version Control

Description and motivation: The version control system is the primary source of groupware support for a team. Furthermore, we would be interested in recording the history of evolution of our model.

Analysis: Traditionally when we put a project under version control, we have to select the configuration items (CI), which are the artefacts that we want to version. Usually version control systems handle files as CIs, so we need to supply the system with a set of files that make up the model. One extreme would be to have the whole model in one single file, another extreme to have each single model element in a file of its own.

Requirements: We will need the modelling language to have a mechanism for splitting up a model so it can be placed in several files, and we will need the version control system to support flexible units of versioning:

- *flexible unit of versioning (UV).* The UV is used by the version control system for concurrency detection. The finer the UV, the better the version control system can decide if parallel changes touch the same or different parts of the model. However, the finer the UV, the more fractioned the model will appear to the developers and the more work they will have in managing the version control. It is important for the developers to have flexibility for the UV, so they can tailor it to their specific needs.
- *modularization mechanisms.* The model language must have a mechanism for physically splitting up a model in smaller parts. If that is not the case, everyone will be working on the same artefact and all parallel changes will create a concurrency conflict triggering a merge situation for the artefact.

3.2 Investigate History

Description and motivation: When we have the historical evolution of a model preserved in the version control system, we would like to investigate that history to discover what changed between two specific versions. More generally, we would like to know what is the difference between any two versions of an artefact whether they are in the repository or in the workspace.

Analysis: We use the version control system to keep track of the versions we create of an artefact and that are committed to the repository. This will give us an overall picture of the evolution of an artefact. In case we want to know the details, we need an operation that given two versions from the repository can tell us exactly how they differ. Such an operation can also be used to tell the difference between a particular version in the repository and the version we have in our workspace. In all cases we will have a 3-way diff as there will always be a common ancestor – also to the workspace version as it has been checked out from the repository. For such a diff to be of practical use, it should present the differences in a way that makes sense to the user.

Requirements: We will need a diff operation, attention to presentational issues, a work process that focus on logical tasks, and flexibility in the unit of comparison:

- *diff operation*. Because we work in a context where we have the same type of model, we do not need a compare operation that can tell the differences between different types of models. The diff operation should be detached from the version control system to allow us more flexibility in selecting tools. Since we are not working on text files, the diff operation should be tailored to the type of model that is addressed.
- *presentational issues*. In order not to create information overflow, only important differences should be shown. For our context we do not consider layout changes to be significant. However, a good filtering mechanism will allow the user to define what he wants to see at any given moment.
- *work process that commits logical tasks*. Once the tool has shown the differences between two versions, we have to make sense of the details. To try to recreate the logical intention behind a number of detailed changes. This task is greatly helped if the work process prescribes that only complete tasks are committed and if each commit has a short log text associated with it.
- *flexible unit of comparison (UC)*. Just as for the presentational issues, we need flexibility in the unit of what is compared. In the textual case we do not want to be told that a file has changed; we want to know what line was changed and sometimes even what changed on that line. Likewise in the model case. Flexibility in the UC will allow us to tailor the diff operation to give us information at the level of detail that we are interested in at the moment.

3.3 Model Update without Merge

Description and motivation: When parallel development has happened we want to synchronize the work at some point. In the case where work has not been done on the same artefacts, we do not need to carry out a merge but can simply take the sum of changes to be the result.

Analysis: The normal way of working of a version control system is that when we want to commit our changes, it first carries out a concurrency check. If something new has arrived in the repository since we last updated our workspace there is a physical conflict on some of the artefact, and we will need to update our workspace version to avoid getting the "simultaneous update" problem [4]. However, if the artefacts that we changed have not changed in the repository, we can do a commit and add a new version. However, this is not always enough to ensure that we will have consistent configurations in the repository as there may be logical conflicts that are not detected by this mechanism.

Requirements: We will need a transaction mechanism that takes into account logical consistency:

- *strict long transactions*. The long transaction model [12] works as described in the analysis above and thus opens up for inconsistencies. However, the strict version of long transactions does the concurrency check at the logical level where we perform the commit. If anything has changed in the repository since we last updated our workspace we are not current anymore and must update – even if changes in the repository only regards artefacts that we have not changed in our workspace. Strict long transactions do not detect inconsistencies, but force us to update and create a new "configuration" in our workspace instead of directly in the repository. This means that we have the possibility to check for inconsistencies in the updated configuration before we finally commit it to the repository. For strict long transactions to be practical, we should be able to commit – and thus carry out concurrency checks – at other levels than the top level. Otherwise we will always be forced to do an update even when changes in the repository regard completely unrelated parts of the system.
- *flexible unit of versioning (UV)*. This will allow the developer to decide the granularity of concurrency detection. In the textual case the UV is always the file, but the developer decides what to put into the file. If that is not the case for models, then we would need the UV to have more flexibility.

3.4 Model Update with Automated Merge

Description and motivation: When work has been carried out in parallel on the same artefact(s), there will have to be performed a merge of the changes as part of the model update. In the simple case, the merge tool will be able to automatically resolve the changes and produce a successful merge result.

Analysis: The issues of concurrency detection were dealt with in the previous use case 3.3, so in this use case there is actually a physical conflict at the level of unit of versioning for at least one artefact. To be able to automatically resolve the conflicting changes we need to go more into details. We look at the internal structure of the unit of versioning to see if there are conflicting changes at the level of the unit of comparison. If not, we will have the same situation as for use case 3.3, but at the level of a single artefact and not of a whole configuration – this includes both the capability of producing a merge result, and the possibility of this result being logically inconsistent.

Requirements: We need to be aware of the semantics of the merge operator and we need flexible unit of comparison to allow better conflict resolution:

- *flexible unit of comparison (UC).* The granularity of the UC decides the level at which we can do conflict resolution. The finer the granularity, the better and more precise we can distinguish differences and decide on how to automatically resolve the merge. If the level of granularity is a class, then changes to different methods by different people will create an irresolvable merge conflict. Likewise, if "action code" is the unit of comparison then any modification to the "action code" will flag the whole "action code" as changed. It would be more helpful if "action code" had a UC at the level of a line of text, as we could then distinguish exactly what lines were changed and have better possibilities for resolving parallel changes to the "action code". However, if the level of granularity becomes too fine, then we can suffer performance penalties – and "incorrect" semantic behaviour at the level of the unit of versioning as discussed below.
- *semantics of merge operator.* Now that we – or rather the automated merge – actually change the internals of our model, it is important that it is clear in which way these changes are done. In the traditional text merge tools the semantics of the merge operator is very simple. If a line of text is changed in one of the alternatives, then it is also changed in the result. For model merge tools the situation will be much more complex. In many cases there will be more than one possibility and only explicit semantics of the model merge operator will make it clear for the user what happens. Furthermore, the text merge tool only guarantees to produce a "correct result" according to its own semantics – which is "lines of text" – even though the real semantics of the contents of the merged artefact is often quite different. From this perspective, it is perfectly reasonable for the merge tool to produce a result in the case where the declaration and use of an identifier has been removed in one alternative and a new use of that identifier added to the other alternative. It is obvious that what is correct semantics for the text merge tool will not be correct semantics for the Java compiler. It is not clear whether it will be possible – or practical – to avoid such a mismatch in semantics for model merge.

3.5 Model Update with Merge Conflict

Description and motivation: When work has been carried out in parallel on the same artefact, there will have to be performed a merge of the changes as part of the model update. In the complex case, the merge tool will not be able to automatically resolve the changes and will announce a merge conflict.

Analysis: From the analysis of use case 3.4 above, it is clear that we have the same needs for clear and explicitly defined semantics in this case. Likewise, the granularity of the unit of comparison is equally important for the possibility or impossibility to automatically resolve merge conflicts. The only difference to the above use case 3.4 is that in case both alternatives have changed the same unit of comparison, it will not be possible for the merge tool to choose which alternative to use – a merge conflict will have happened and the user will have to manually resolve it.

Requirements: We will need clear semantics, flexible unit of comparison, and definition of how to present conflicts:

- *flexible unit of comparison (UC)*. Identical to use case 3.4 above, so we refer to that discussion.
- *semantics of merge operator*. When we deal with the simple semantics of the text merge operator, it is clear that parallel changes to the same UC (line of text) will have to create a conflict. However, for model merge the case might not be that simple. However, in the model case there is much more information available than just "some text has changed" and the UCs might not always be of the same type. So it might in some cases be possible to define a reasonable merge result – or a preference to one alternative over the other – even when both alternatives have been changed.
- *presentational issues*. We need to deal with the presentation of merge conflicts at two levels. First, the presentation of the conflict has to be in such a way that it is clear to the user what the conflict consists of. As stated above, the richer semantics of the model merge operator should make it possible to provide that information. Second, the representation of the conflict has to be in such a way that the merged result can be loaded and modified in a model editor. This means that the underlying representation of the model will have to be able to handle and represent conflict markers. In text merge such conflict markers are not a problem for the editor, as they are text too – and standardization of the conflict markers have even made it possible to present conflicts in graphical editors.

3.6 Verify and Validate Merge Result

Description and motivation: Once we have produced an automated merge result, we would like to verify and validate its correctness.

Analysis: It will have become evident from the discussions in use cases 3.3, 3.4 and 3.5 above, that it will be virtually impossible to guarantee always 100% correct merge results. In text merge, that is a well-known fact and it is common practice to always check the result by doing a "build-and-smoke" test after an announced successful merge. Because that test is relatively fast and easy to do for the textual domain, users tend to have a preference for a high recall at the cost of a lower precision in the merge results. When discussing verification and validation of merge results, it is important to notice that also in the case of use case 3.3 above, there is actually performed a merge. The merge is not done at the level of the unit of comparison as in use cases 3.4 and 3.5, but at the level of unit of versioning.

Requirements: We should be able to verify the syntax and semantics and to validate the model logic:

- *verification of "syntax and semantics"*. In text merge this is a simple compilation of the program. If our model merge operator is not able to guarantee that the result always respects the syntax and semantics of the model language, we need to do a similar compilation for models too.

- *validation of "program logic"*. For text merge it is common practice to have a small suite of test cases that will catch the most blatant mistakes. It is much faster than complete testing and experience has shown that in most cases it is sufficient for finding merges that mistakably are announced as successful merges. A similar process should be adapted for model merge.

4 Discussion

In this chapter, we will discuss in more detail the requirements that we have identified in the preceding chapter. For ease, we have grouped the requirements into three related themes – semantics of model merge, division of responsibility and presentational issues – that are discussed for possible consequences of the requirements and for what should be taken into consideration when implementing them.

4.1 Semantics of Model Merge

This is in our opinion the most important and also controversial aspect of model merge. The semantics of text merge are really simple, if a line of text has changed it has changed. If the same line of text has changed in both alternatives, there is a conflict. There have been attempts at more fine-grained unit of comparison by looking at the syntax and semantics of the contents. However, lines are still what rules for text merge in practice.

For models the situation is not that simple. It is indeed possible to exploit the underlying textual representation of the model and use a textual merge tool. However, even minor changes to the layout of a model can have big consequences for the order in which things are stored, which will cause insurmountable problems for a textual merge tool. So we see no way around using the implicit structures dictated by the model language for a model merge tool. Furthermore, such an approach will also benefit from the possibility of defining a "richer" semantics, since we will have several different "types" of units of versioning and not just one (lines of text) as in textual merge. There have been early attempts to define such "rich" semantics for merge of structures [3] and [22], that revealed several cases where the desired merge result was open for discussion. The work of [8] is a first step towards model merge semantics, though they are more focused on the algebraic properties and compare and union operators.

That defining model merge semantics is not that easy can be seen from figure 1. One developer restricts the multiplicity of the class' relation to "0..2", while the other developer in parallel restricts it to "1..10". Now what should be the merged result of this: "1..2" (the most restrictive), "0..10" (the least restrictive) – or something third? In our opinion, the developer should never be left guessing, so in case the merge is automatically resolved, the result should never be a surprise – otherwise a merge conflict should be flagged. A recent tool evaluation [18] revealed other "unpleasant" surprises. One setup was that in both alternatives a new class with the same name as the existing class was added and the two alternatives were merged. One tool decided that the names were the same and therefore merged the two classes into one. The other tool decided that the two classes were different and kept both classes in the merge result. One can argue for the correctness of both approaches. In the first case, the merge tool made its decision based on the "similarity" of the two classes whereas the second tool made its decision based on the different UUIDs of the two classes (ignoring that they had the same name). This shows that in some cases model merge semantics are very open for interpretation. Therefore it is very important that the tool vendors make these semantics very explicit – and that the users continue to meticulously read the manuals until common standard semantics are agreed upon.

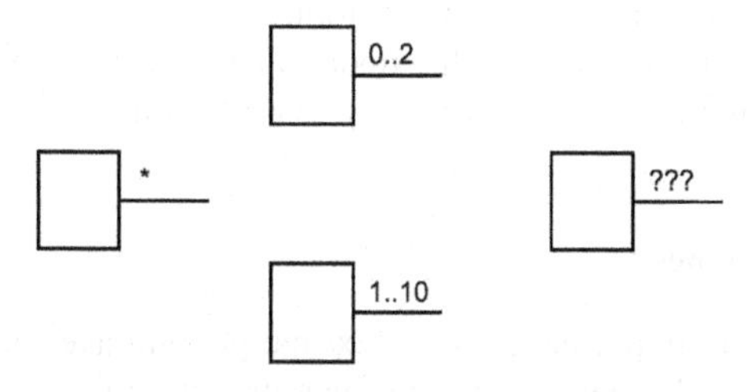

Fig. 1. Simple model merge dilemma

4.2 Division of Responsibility

The merge tool in itself is only a part of the groupware support for collaboration. In the great picture of support for the parallel work of a team we need more than just the physical merge of two artefacts – and we need to decide which tool should take care of which tasks. For parallel work there are two tasks: the concurrency detection and the conflict detection and resolution.

Concurrency detection is the discovery that parallel work has happened. That can be carried out in many different ways, but usually it is the responsibility of the version control tool to do that. It keeps track of the addition of new versions to the repository and should know the status of the files in the user's workspace. Based on that information it is easy to decide whether parallel work has been performed or not. There are different strategies for when to consider parallel work to have happened. The most "relaxed" is to look at each single file and decide on a file-to-file basis. That is, however, a very unsafe strategy as changes to different files in the same commit are usually related. Most common is therefore the long transaction strategy [12] where a concurrency conflict is announced – and the commit aborted – if not all single changes can be committed. Concurrency detection is tightly connected to the unit of versioning. The more fine-grained it is, the easier it is to decide if parallel work has happened on the same artefact.

Conflict detection, on the other hand, is the discovery of an unsuccessful merge of work that has been carried out in parallel on the same artefact (unit of versioning). And conflict resolution is when the outcome of the merge is successful. Conflict detection and resolution is usually the responsibility of the merge tool. As input is gets the two alternatives and their common ancestor from which it tries to create a merge. Conflict detection and resolution is tightly connected to the unit of comparison. The more fine-grained it is, the easier it is to distinguish if the same "thing" has changed in both alternatives, in which case there is a real conflict that might be difficult for the merge tool to automatically resolve. However, the richer set of units of versioning in model merge might provide more information that could allow automated merges even in these cases of apparent conflict, as discussed above.

Both unit of versioning and unit of comparison are very dependent on the nature of what is being versioned and merged. In the traditional textual case, unit of versioning is a file and unit of comparison is a line of text. For models we will have to use the file as unit of versioning if we use traditional version control tools, but depending on the modularization mechanisms of the model language, we can have more or less flexibility in what we are allowed to put into a single file. For the unit of comparison, we are bound by the decision of the merge tool, which in turn will be highly influenced by the syntax and semantics of the model language. A supportive model merge tool should have as fine-grained unit of comparison and as rich and well-defined semantics as possible.

4.3 Presentational Issues

Presentational issues are important also for text merge, but takes on even more importance for model merge. We have to present merges (and diffs) and in particular conflicts to the user in a way that he can understand the nature of the conflict (or change) and such that irrelevant details are left out. We also need to consider how the presence of merge conflicts should be represented in the model itself.

Even in the simple case of text merge, we often have presentational issues. Merge tools are not very good at handling these and users have to aware of that and behave in a way to avoid getting conflicts that are grounded in "irrelevant" layout. A typical example is the indentation of programs that is a frequent cause of "stupid" merge conflicts until people agree on a common setup of their editor. For model merge we would like the tool to be able to ignore layout changes, as they are not our primary focus and can obscure more important changes. This does not mean that a model merge tool should always ignore layout changes, as they may indeed be important too. Just that because it is virtually impossible to avoid layout changes when working with models (as opposed to text), the merge tool has be more supportive and allow us the flexibility to ignore – or consider – layout changes in the merge.

The standard behaviour of text merge tools is to work in batch mode. The tool tries to produce merge results for all files that have to be merged and leaves conflict markers in the files where it does not manage to resolve the merge conflicts. This works well for text, as we are able to open, read and understand the resulting files in our text editor. However, that is not the case for model merge. If we would leave conflict markers in the resulting merged model, we would not able to load it into our model editor – and we would be pretty stuck. Therefore, current model merge tools work in interactive mode and ask the user to manually resolve all the conflicts one by one before the result is created. For some cases that may be a good way of working, but if we would like to leave some flexibility to the user, we should allow for the batch mode as well. This can be done if we include conflict representation into the metamodel, such that models with conflict markers become valid models for the editor. We should also be aware that, since model editors are based on the syntax of the modelling language, they cannot cope with syntactically incorrect merge results in general, so extreme care has to be taken in constructing the merge result.

5 Conclusion

The experience at Ericsson AB from using models – and in particular UML– for model-centric development has been predominantly positive. The technology is mature and we get less complexity and good performance when using models. However, the support from engineering tools is not yet mature. In particular support for collaboration like merge and diff tools.

Based on a recent tool evaluation [18], we can conclude that model merge tools have improved since our initial evaluation and that of [5]. In this paper, we have identified and discussed a number of requirements for making them even better. At the present state it looks like there is too much diversity in principles and mindset for different model merge tools. Such diversity does not exist for text merge tools – and the fact that the principles are most often implicit makes the problem even bigger. However, we see that as a natural thing at this early, immature state and hope that "state of the practice" will now start to converge.

From our analysis and discussion of merge and diff problems a number of requirements emerged that can be dealt with on the long, medium and short term by various actors:

- long term: research issues and challenges
  - semantics of model merge
  - meta-model conflict representation
  - modularization mechanisms
- medium term: research to tool transfer possibilities
  - semantics of model merge
  - presentational issues
- short term: MDD process best practices
  - use a strict long transaction model
  - merge often to avoid irresolvable conflicts
  - verify and validate each merge result
  - educate users in the model merge tool semantics since it is so much more complex and not as "uniform" as for text merge

References

1. Alanen, M., Porres, I.: Difference and Union of Models. In: Stevens, P., Whittle, J., Booch, G. (eds.) UML 2003. LNCS, vol. 2863, pp. 2–17. Springer, Heidelberg (2003)
2. Alanen, M., Porres, I.: Basic Operations Over Models Containing Subset and Union Properties. In: Nierstrasz, O., Whittle, J., Harel, D., Reggio, G. (eds.) MoDELS 2006. LNCS, vol. 4199, pp. 469–483. Springer, Heidelberg (2006)
3. Asklund, U.: Identifying Conflicts During Structural Merge. In: Proceedings of NWPER 1994, Nordic Workshop on Programming Environment Research, Lund, Sweden, June 1-3 (1994)
4. Babich, W.A.: Software Configuration Management – Coordination for Team Productivity. Addison-Wesley, Reading (1986)
5. Barrett, S., Chalin, P., Butler, G.: Model Merging Falls Short of Software Engineering Needs. In: [16]

6. Bendix, L., Emanuelsson, P.: Diff and Merge Support for Model Based Development. In: [9]
7. Bendix, L., Emanuelsson, P.: Collaborative Work with Software Models – Industrial Experience and Requirements. In: Proceedings of the Second International Conference on Model Based Systems Engineering – MBSE 2009, Haifa, Israel, March 2-6 (2009)
8. Brunet, G., Chechik, M., Easterbrook, S., Nejati, S., Niu, N., Sabetzadeh, M.: A Manifesto for Model Merging. In: Proceedings of the International Workshop on Global Integrated Model Management, Shanghai, China, May 22 (2006)
9. Proceedings of the International Workshop on Comparison and Versioning of Software Models, Leipzig, Germany, May 17 (2008)
10. Proceedings of the International Workshop on Comparison and Versioning of Software Models, Vancouver, Canada, May 17 (2009)
11. Ellis, C.A., Gibbs, S.J., Rein, G.L.: Groupware – Some Issues and Experiences. Communications of the ACM (January 1991)
12. Feiler, P.H.: Configuration Management Models in Commercial Environments, Technical Report SEI-91-TR-7, Software Engineering Institute (March 1991)
13. Girschick, M.: Difference Detection and Visualization in UML Class Diagrams, Technical Report TUD-CS-2006-5, TU Darmstadt (August 2006)
14. Mehra, A., Grundy, J., Hosking, J.: A Generic Approach to Supporting Diagram Differencing and Merging for Collaborative Design. In: Proceedings of the 20th International Conference on Automated Software Engineering, Long Beach, California, November 7-11 (2005)
15. Proceedings of the Workshop on Model-Driven Software Evolution, Amsterdam, The Netherlands, March 20 (2007)
16. Proceedings of the Second Workshop on Model-Driven Software Evolution, Athens, Greece, April 1 (2008)
17. Nguyen, T.N., Thao, C., Munson, E.V.: On Product Versioning for Hypertexts. In: Proceedings of the 12th International Workshop on Software Configuration Management, Lisbon, Portugal, September 5-6 (2005)
18. Nåls, A., Auvinen, J.: Model Merge Study, internal Ericsson Technical Report (April 2009)
19. Oliveira, H., Murta, L., Werner, C.: Odyssey-VCS: a Flexible Version Control System for UML Model Elements. In: Proceedings of the 12th International Workshop on Software Configuration Management, Lisbon, Portugal, September 5-6 (2005)
20. Selonen, P.: A Review of UML Model Comparison Approaches. In: Proceedings of Nordic Workshop on Model Driven Engineering, Ronneby, Sweden, August 27-29 (2007)
21. Störrle, H.: A formal approach to the cross-language version management of models. In: Proceedings of Nordic Workshop on Model Driven Engineering, Ronneby, Sweden, August 27-29 (2007)
22. Westfechtel, B.: Structure-Oriented Merging of Revisions of Software Documents. In: Proceedings of the 3rd International workshop on Software Configuration Management, Trondheim, Norway, June 12-14 (1991)
23. Xing, Z., Stroulia, E.: UMLDiff: An Algorithm for Object-Oriented Design Differencing. In: Proceedings of the 20th International Conference on Automated Software Engineering, Long Beach, California, November 7-11 (2005)
24. Zito, A., Diskin, Z., Dingel, J.: Package Merge in UML 2: Practice vs. Theory? In: Proceedings of the 9th International Conference on Model Driven Engineering Languages and Systems, Genova, Italy, October 1-6 (2006)

Evaluating the Impact of UML Modeling on Software Quality: An Industrial Case Study*

Ariadi Nugroho and Michel R.V. Chaudron

LIACS – Leiden University, Niels Bohrweg 1, 2333 CA Leiden, The Netherlands
anugroho@liacs.nl, chaudron@liacs.nl
http://www.liacs.nl/~anugroho, http://www.liacs.nl/~chaudron

Abstract. The contribution of formal modeling approaches in software development has always been a subject of debates. The proponents of model-driven development argue that big upfront designs although require substantial investment will payoff later in the implementation phase in terms of increased productivity and quality. On the other hand, software engineers who are not very keen on modeling perceive the activity as simply a waste of time and money without any real contribution to the final software product. Considering present advancement of model-based software development in software industry, we are challenged to investigate the real contribution of modeling in software development. Therefore, in this paper we report on an empirical investigation on the impact of UML modeling on the quality of software system. In particular, we focus on defect density as a measure of software quality. Based on a significant industrial case study, we have found that the use of UML modeling potentially reduces defect density in software system.

Keywords: UML, Complexity, Coupling, Defect Density, Case Study.

1 Introduction

One of the most valued aspects of software models is that they provide means to design solutions to the problem domain that needs to be addressed by software systems. By modeling a system in a systematic manner we are assured that the system has gone through a technical analysis process that ensures the system is going to be developed in the right manner. Modeling also ensures that design decisions captured in the software models are well documented, thus minimizing loss of information and misinterpretation in communicating the decisions taken during development.

Another benefit of having software models is that it facilitates communication amongst team members. Obviously, this is true only if the developers have a common knowledge and sufficient experience with the modeling language. However, the role of modeling to facilitate communication might be most prominent in the contexts where the development team is not located in a single location

* Empirical results category paper.

A. Schürr and B. Selic (Eds.): MODELS 2009, LNCS 5795, pp. 181–195, 2009.

(distributed software development)—not to mention if the team is composed of people from different cultural background.

Despite the widely assumed benefits, the real benefits of modeling in industrial projects are not always clear. For example, it is not clear whether the use of modeling in real projects increases the quality of the final software product. If so, in what circumstances does modeling help? In order to address these questions more research needs to be done to evaluate the real benefits of modeling in industrial settings.

Taking the above concerns into consideration, in this paper we evaluate the impact of using UML modeling in a real software project. More specifically, we investigate the effect of UML modeling on the defect density (defects per source lines of code) of software modules (i.e., Java classes). The result of this study shows that the use of UML modeling is influential to reduce the introduction of defects during software development.

The rest of the paper is organized as follows. In section two we discuss some related works. In section 3, the design of this study will be discussed. Section 4 discusses the case study and the results of the analyses. In section 5, we further discuss the results and limitations of this study. Finally, in section 6 we outline some conclusions and future works.

2 Related Works

To the best of our knowledge, there has not been any research that investigates the use of UML modeling and its relation to the quality of the final implementation. Plenty of works, however, have been focused on investigating the impact of using certain styles, rigor, and UML diagram types on model comprehension and software maintenance.

Many studies that investigate the impact of modeling styles on model comprehension have been looking at the use of stereotypes. The work of Staron et al. for instance, suggests that UML stereotypes with graphical representation improve model comprehensibility [1]. Ricca et al. also found that stereotypes have a positive impact on diagram comprehension [2]. However, this finding was particularly true for inexperienced subjects—the impact was not statistically significant for experienced subjects. Genero et al. studied the influence of using stereotypes in UML sequence diagrams on comprehension [3]. While this study revealed no significant impact, it suggested that the use of stereotypes in sequence diagrams was favored to facilitate comprehension. Another study was conducted by Cruz-Lemus et al. to evaluate the effect of composite states on the understandability of state-chart diagrams [4]. The authors stated that the use of composite states, which allows the grouping of related states, improves *understandability efficiency* when reading state-chart diagrams. Nevertheless, subjects' experience with state-chart diagrams was considered as a prerequisite to gain the improved understandability.

A previous study that looked into the formality of UML models and its relation with model quality and comprehensibility is from Briand et al. [5]. In their experimental study, Briand et al. investigated the impact of using OCL (object constraint language) in UML models on defect detection, comprehension, and impact analysis of changes. Although the overall benefits of using OCL on the aforementioned activities are significant, they have found that the benefits for the individual activities are modest.

Other studies investigated the effect of using different UML diagram types (e.g., sequence and collaboration diagrams) on model comprehension. The work of Otero and Dolado for instance, looked into three UML diagrams types, namely sequence, collaboration, and state diagrams, and evaluated the semantic comprehension of the diagrams when used for different application domains [6]. A similar study comes from the work of Glezer et al. They evaluated the comprehensibility of sequence and collaboration diagrams, and finally concluded that collaboration diagrams are easier to comprehend than sequence diagrams in real-time systems [7]. Another study conducted by Torchiano [8] investigated the effect of object diagrams on system comprehensibility. In two of the four systems used in the experiment, the use of object diagrams to complement class diagrams was found to have significant effects on the comprehensibility of the systems.

A previous work that is closely related to this study is reported in [9]. In the paper the authors evaluate the impact of UML documentation on software maintenance. The results show that for complex tasks and after certain learning process, the availability of UML documentation may result in significant improvements in terms of functional correctness of changes and the design quality of the changes.

Different from the aforementioned previous works, in this paper we analyze whether the use of modeling, represented using UML, has any effect on the quality of the final implementation—measured in *defect density*. This paper is inline with our previous work that investigates the relation between level of detail (LoD) in UML models and the quality of the final implementation [10]. Nevertheless, in this paper we emphasize more on the impact of using (or not using) UML modeling on the quality of the final system.

3 Design of Study

3.1 Objective

This study aims to evaluate the impact of using UML modeling to model software modules (i.e., represented as Java classes) on the quality of the associated implementation. Therefore, the objective of this study according to the GQM template [11] can be described as follows:

Analyze the use of UML modeling
for the purpose of investigating its impact
with respect to defect density of Java classes
from the perspective of the researcher
in the context of an industrial Java system

3.2 Measured Variables and Hypothesis Formulation

The independent variable (predictor) in this study is the use of UML modeling. The use of modeling was defined as the presence or availability of UML diagram(s) that describe a given implementation class. Hence, the unit of analysis in this study is software modules, which was represented as Java classes (note that we use the term module and class interchangeably). The use of UML modeling is measured in a nominal scale with two categories: *Modeled Classes(MC)* and *Not Modeled Classes (NMC).* Two UML diagram types were considered, namely class diagram and sequence diagram. As such, the modeled classes can be of the following categories: modeled in class diagrams only and modeled in class- and sequence diagrams (as instances/objects of classes).

The dependent variable in this study is the quality of the final implementation, which was measured in defect density. Defect density of an implementation class was determined by the number of defects found in that class (defect-count) divided by the class size (in kilo SLoC). Defect-count, on the other hand, was measured from the number of times a class was modified to solve distinct defects. Hence, if a class was modified five times to solve the same defect, it would have been considered as having *only* one defect-count.

In addition to the independent and dependent variables, we selected two significant factors that might confound the main factor of this study, namely code complexity—measured using the McCabe's cyclomatic complexity metric (MCC) [12] and coupling between objects (CBO) [13]. MCC and CBO are well-known for their significant relations to class fault-proneness [14] [15]. Considering their strong influence on the defect density, in this study we considered MCC and CBO metrics as co-factors and control their effects on defect density. Having controlled these significant factors, we expect to see the true effect of using UML modeling on the defect density of software modules.

As discussed previously, the focus of this paper is to investigate whether there is a significant difference in defect density between software modules that are modeled using UML and modules that are not modeled. This question is based on the following observations. First, modeled components are generally well thought of and better designed. Second, modeled components are generally well described and well documented. Finally, all else being equal, modeled components should be easier to implement than the not modeled ones. Having these assumptions in mind, it is interesting to investigate whether such benefits materialize in terms of improved implementation correctness. To answer this research question, in this study we attempt to test the following hypothesis:

Null hypothesis ($\mathbf{H}_{null}$)
There is no significant difference in defect density between implementation classes that are modeled using UML and those that are not modeled.

Alternative hypothesis ($\mathbf{H}_{alt}$)
The use of UML significantly reduces defect density of implementation classes.

Note that we formulated the alternative hypothesis as a one-sided hypothesis because we have a specific assumption about the direction of cause-effect relationship between the use of UML modeling and defect density.

3.3 Data Collection and Preprocessing

Software project that we selected for the case study should meet two main conditions. First, the projects must use UML modeling to certain extent. Further, the UML models should be used for guiding the implementation and were modeled in machine-readable forms (e.g., utilizing UML CASE tools). We also required the UML CASE tools to have an XMI export facility, which will allow us to export the models to the measurement tool. Second, the project must utilize a bug tracking system with which it is possible to trace back source files that were modified to solve defects. Having selected the projects to be studied, we performed data collection to obtain data of UML models, source code, defect registration, and change sets (source files modified to solve defects). The collected UML data and source code were the latest version of project data that could be found in the CVS (concurrent versions system) repository.

To obtain data about UML classes and other metrics, the UML models first had to be exported from the UML CASE tools into an XMI format. Using a tool called SDMetrics [16], the XMI file was read and model information, such as classes and other structural diagrams, could then be easily extracted. However, due to a limitation from the UML CASE tool, sequence diagram information could not be exported to XMI. Therefore, we had to manually inspect every sequence diagram to register instances/objects of classes that were modeled in sequence diagrams.

The processing of source code was mainly aimed at calculating code metrics from the implementation classes. In this study we were mainly interested in the size, coupling, and complexity metrics. These code metrics were calculated using an open source tool called CCCC (C and C++ Code Counter), which in fact is also able to calculate metrics from Java files.

Processing defect data mainly involves two steps. The first step was to obtain registered defects from the ClearQuest repository and store them in the analysis database. The second step was to obtain change sets, which was performed automatically using a Perl script that recovers change sets associated with every defect. Because change sets were registered in a ClearQuest textual format and they contain other information, text parsing was performed to mine data of the modified files (note that only Java files were taken into account). Further, defect-count of each Java file was determined based on the frequency it was corrected to solve distinct defects. Java files that were modified to solve defects are hereafter referred to as *faulty classes*.

We employ a relational database to store the above data. This database can be accessed via a web interface to enable remote collaboration for data collection and analysis. Once the data of defects, UML classes, implementation classes, and faulty classes were stored in the analysis database, we could query various information, which include: 1) implementation classes that were modeled, and the diagrams in which they were modeled; 2) implementation classes that were not modeled; 3) code metrics of the implementation classes; 4) defect density of the implementation classes—if they were found to be faulty.

3.4 Analysis Methods

As the main objective of this study was to investigate the difference of defect density amongst faulty classes that were grouped based on the use of UML modeling, in the analysis we used statistical techniques to compare mean difference between groups. To this aim, we intended using ANCOVA (Analysis of Covariance) test [17] because it would allow us to control the effects of covariates on the outcome variable. However, as we later found out that our data set violated the assumptions of normality, we finally decided to use Mann-Whitney test [18] as the main statistical test. Nevertheless, ANCOVA test would still be used for the sake of result validation.

Because we could not use ANCOVA as the main statistical test, we needed to perform a pairwise sampling to account for the effect of the covariates. In section 4.3 we discuss the pairwise sampling in further detail.

In this study we have a specific assumption about direction of the hypothesis—that is, we hypothesize that the use of UML modeling will reduce the defect density of classes in the implementation. Consequently, testing of the mean difference between groups will be performed as one-tailed test. Further, in the analyses and hypothesis testing we considered significance level at 0.05 level ($p \leq 0.05$) to indicate a true significance.

Please also note that the case study used in this paper is the same project used in our previous study [10]. In this respect, we need to outline the main differences in the analysis approach. First, unlike the earlier study in which we analyzed only faulty classes, in this study we analyze both faulty and non-faulty classes. Second, in this paper we use all defects registered during testing. This approach is different from our previous study in which we systematically selected defects based on certain criteria. Finally, in the previous study we analyzed only classes that were modeled using UML, while in this study we also take into account classes that were not modeled. Obviously, these differences exist because current paper aims to answer a different research question. Nevertheless, we consider it important to distinguish differences in the analysis of the case study.

4 Case Study

4.1 Project Context

The system under study was an integrated healthcare system for psychiatrists in the Netherlands, hereafter referred to as IPS (not a real name). It was built as a web service using Java technology. In the IPS project, the RUP (Rational Unified Process) methodology was used, and this project involved off shoring to India. The modeling of the system was done in the Netherlands, while approximately 60 percent of the implementation and testing activities were done in India. For creating the UML models, the project used Rational XDE, and for the version control system and bug tracking system, the project used Rational ClearCase and Rational ClearQuest respectively.

In the IPS project, the UML model was used as an implementation guide. Thus, the models were created before writing the implementation code. The UML model was created by the designers and was later implemented by the developers in India and the Netherlands. When this study was conducted, the IPS project was already finished. The system was used by the client for sometime, but was later abandoned because of business economical reasons. Project summary is provided in Table 1.

Table 1. Project Summary

Projects	# of staffs	Duration	Off-shored	Status	Model Size	SLoC
IPS	25 people	2.3 years	India	finished	104 use cases 266 design classes 34 class diagrams 341 seq. diagrams	152,017

In addition to the UML models, textual specifications were also used to guide the implementation of the system. These specifications are textual and are mainly in the form of detailed use case descriptions. From our observation, most functional requirements generally have corresponding detailed use case descriptions. Additionally, a software architecture document that provides a high level description of the system is available. Hence, regardless of whether certain parts were modeled or not modeled using UML, there exists some textual specifications that describe how the system should be implemented.

4.2 Descriptive Statistics

The core part of the IPS system (excluding framework classes) consisted of 812 Java classes. Table 2 shows the descriptive statistics of defect density, coupling, complexity, and size of all classes across groups. One notable trend that we can see in Table 2 is that MC classes generally have higher complexity, coupling, and size than NMC classes. However, we can also see in the table (the mean value) that there is only a slight difference of defect density between the two class groups. Statistical tests confirm that except for defect density, the differences in

Table 2. Descriptive statistics of all Java classes

Measures	Not Modeled (NMC)				Modeled (MC)			
	N	Median	Mean	St. Dev	N	Median	Mean	St. Dev
Defect Density	638	0.000	0.016	0.032	174	0.000	0.012	0.029
Coupling	638	6.000	7.123	6.303	174	11.000	13.459	11.359
Complexity	638	1.000	11.747	72.034	174	10.500	26.770	45.932
Size (KSLoC)	638	0.039	0.103	0.290	174	0.179	0.312	0.689

complexity, coupling, and size between MC and NMC classes were statistically significant.

It is interesting to note that MC classes that are generally higher in terms of complexity, size, and coupling are in fact having a quite similar defect density as NMC classes. This is particularly true if we consider previous studies that report positive correlations between complexity, coupling, size and module fault-proneness (see for example in [19], [14], [15]). The results in Table 2 raise a question whether modeled classes, which are notoriously more complex, have lower defect density because they were modeled using UML, or because defects in larger and complex classes are more difficult (hidden) to find [20]. This discussion essentially shows that several factors might influence defect density, and thus it is important to identify them and control their effects in order to evaluate the true effect of UML modeling on defect density.

4.3 Controlling for the Confounding Factors

In this study we considered class coupling and complexity as the main confounding factor because both metrics have been considered influential to class fault-proneness. Ideally, we would use ANCOVA test to analyze the main effect of a treatment when several confounding factors are accounted for. With this analysis we could control the variance of the confounding factors, hence providing us with a pure effect of the main treatment if there is one. However, because the defect density data set violated the assumption of normal data distribution and transforming the data did not fix the normality problem, we could not rely on ANCOVA for the main statistical test.

An alternative way to do the analysis is to perform a pairwise sampling in which we selected classes of comparable complexity and coupling, and subsequently used a parametric test, i.e., Mann-Whitney, as the primary test to compare the defect density between groups. However, selecting classes that are comparable in terms of complexity and coupling would have left us with too few data points for a meaningful statistical test. Therefore, we decided to perform the pairwise sampling based on coupling, and the effect of complexity would subsequently be assessed using ANCOVA test.

To obtain classes of comparable coupling, we performed a pairwise sampling by systematically selecting classes from both NMC and MC classes that have coupling values from 8 up to 10. This range of coupling values was selected mainly because 1) the range is reasonably small; and 2) within this coupling range we obtained the best proportion of NMC and MC groups (note that we aimed to obtain balanced groups when possible). This pairwise sampling has reduced the amount of classes from 812 to 113 Java classes, of which 68 and 45 belong to NMC and MC groups respectively. These 113 classes had a standard deviation value of 0.8, which means coupling values of these classes are very close to the mean value (+/- 0.8). This result suggests that we have controlled the variance of class coupling to a minimum level.

Table 3. Descriptive statistics of the randomly sampled Java classes

Measures	Not Modeled (NMC)				Modeled (MC)			
	N	Median	Mean	St. Dev	N	Median	Mean	St. Dev
Defect Density	59	0.002	0.011	0.019	37	0.000	0.003	0.010
Coupling	59	9.000	9.000	0.809	37	10.000	9.270	0.902
Complexity	59	23.000	41.440	47.656	37	30.000	35.297	36.153
Size (KSLoC)	59	0.180	0.267	0.233	37	0.230	0.251	0.184

4.4 Testing the Hypothesis

The main question we wanted to answer was whether the use of UML help reduces defect density of software modules in the implementation. In section 4.3 we have discussed how we performed a pairwise sampling based on class coupling to control its effect on defect density. Therefore, in this section we discuss the main hypothesis testing based on the sampled data set.

To mitigate bias during the pairwise sampling, we further performed a random sampling on the sampled data set, in which we randomly selected 80 percent of the 113 Java classes for the analysis. Having done the random sampling we obtained 96 classes, of which 59 and 37 were NMC and MC classes respectively. Table 3 shows the descriptive statistics of these classes. If we look at the mean values in the table, we can see that after coupling was accounted for, NMC classes remained having a higher defect density than MC classes.

Figure 1 shows two box-plots that compare defect density between groups. The box-plots show a similar result presented in Table 3—that is, defect density of NMC group is higher than that of MC group. We subsequently performed a statistical test to assess whether the difference in defect density between NMC and MC groups was statistically significant.

Table 4 and 5 provide the results of Mann-Whitney test. We used this parametric test because the data set (i.e., defect density variable) violated the assumption of normal data distribution and data transformation could not solve the problem. For the sake of completeness we also provide the results for coupling, complexity, and size measures.

Table 4. Mann-Whitney test - Ranks

Variables	Groups	N	Mean Rank	Sum of Ranks
Defect Density	NMC	59	53.95	3183.00
	MC	37	39.81	1473.00
Coupling	NMC	59	45.11	2661.50
	MC	37	53.91	1994.50
Complexity	NMC	59	48.49	2861.00
	MC	37	48.51	1795.00
KSLoC	NMC	59	47.65	2811.50
	MC	37	49.85	1844.50

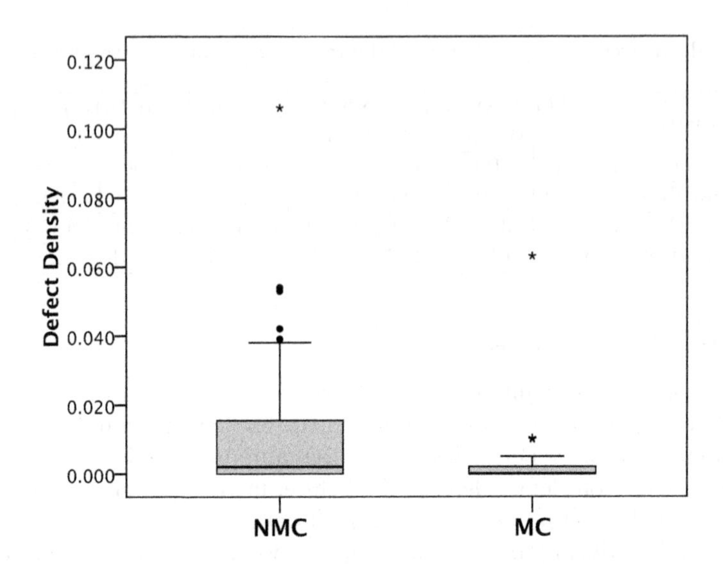

Fig. 1. Box-plots of defect density in NMC and MC classes

Table 5. Mann-Whitney test - Main results

	Defect Density	**Coupling**	**Complexity**	**KSLoC**
Mann-Whitney U	770.000	891.500	1091.000	1041.500
Wilcoxon W	1473.000	2661.500	2861.000	2811.500
Z	-2.704	-1.607	-.004	-.376
Asymp. Significance	**.003***	.108	.997	.707

(*) indicates significance at 0.01 level (1-tailed)

In Table 4, we can see that the mean rank of defect density for NMC classes are higher than that of MC classes. As Mann-Whitney test relies on ranking scores from lowest to highest, the group with the lowest mean rank (i.e., MC) is the one that contains the largest amount of lower defect density. Likewise, the group with the highest mean rank (i.e., NMC) is the group that contains the largest amount of higher defect density. Hence, the results show that classes that were not modeled tend to have higher defect density than the modeled classes.

Table 5 provides the actual Mann-Whitney tests. The most important part of the table is the significance value of the tests. We can see from the table that the difference in defect density was significant at 0.01 level ($p = 0.003$; 1-tailed). Note that none of the other measures were significantly different between NMC and MC groups. Having obtained these results, we can conclude that, on average, classes that were modeled using UML have significantly lower defect density than those that were not modeled. Therefore, we could reject the null hypothesis (H_{null}), and confirm the alternative hypothesis (H_{alt}): the use of UML modeling significantly reduces defect density of classes in the implementation.

Table 6. Results of ANCOVA

Source	Sum of Squares	df	Mean Square	F	Significance
UML Modeling	1.869E-03	1	1.869E-03	6.825	**.010**
Coupling	7.562E-08	1	7.562E-08	.000	.987
Complexity	1.430E-03	1	1.430E-03	5.224	**.025**
Error	2.519E-02	92	2.738E-04		

In addition to the Mann-Whitney test, we performed ANCOVA test to verify if the results are consistent. Performing ANCOVA test regardless of the violation of normality assumption was justified because ANCOVA is quite robust to violation of normality assumption [17]. In the ANCOVA test, we included class coupling and complexity as covariates. Class size was not included because it shares the same size factor as defect density. The results of the ANCOVA test is provided in Table 6.

The most important point to note from Table 6 is that the effect of using UML modeling remains significant ($p \leq 0.05$) even though coupling and complexity have been included as covariates in the analysis. This result basically means that the means of defect density between the groups, i.e., NMC and MC, were significantly different after controlling the effect of class coupling and complexity. Further, we see that complexity was a significant covariate, which is not surprising since we did not control its variance in the data set. Another thing to note is the value of sum of squares, which represents the amount of variation in defect density that is accounted for by the independent variable and the covariates. We can see in table that the independent variable (i.e., the use of UML modeling) has the highest sum of squares value; hence, it explains the variability of defect density better than the covariates.

It should be clear from the above discussion that the results of the ANCOVA test were consistent with the results of the Mann-Whitney test—that is, the use of UML modeling significantly explains the variability of class defect density. Although the ANCOVA test was performed on a data set that violates the assumption of normal data distribution, we should consider the results of the ANCOVA test as a complement to the results of the main statistical test. Overall, this result further strengthens the evidence about the effect of UML modeling on the defect density of software modules.

5 Discussion

In the previous section, we analyzed defect density in Java classes with regard to the use of UML modeling. From the case study, we obtained results that show modeled classes, on average, have a lower defect density that those that were not modeled. Statistical test confirms that the difference in defect density was statistically significant. We also need to underline the fact that we have accounted for class coupling and complexity as confounding factors, which are renown for their strong relations to class fault-proneness. Having controlled their effects, we were assured that the result of the analysis reveals a true effect of using UML modeling on defect density.

To understand why classes that were not modeled have significantly higher defect density, we first need to consider the nature of these classes. Experience has shown that designers generally choose classes that are important and complex to be modeled. Hence, it is quite natural to assume that classes that were not modeled generally are trivial classes or pertain to straightforward concepts. Nevertheless, this assumption is not always true. In the context of this study for example, by simply looking at the complexity metric, we could easily observe that some classes that were not modeled actually have a very high complexity and coupling. In fact, the one class with the highest complexity is a class that was not modeled. Hence, it is very likely that some classes that were not modeled are in fact classes that are not trivial and should have been modeled. Because these significant classes might involved in complex operations in the system, the absence of specifications that describe their behaviors might have led to incorrect implementation.

The implication of the results of this study on research in the area of model-driven software development is two-fold. First, the result of this study should encourage more research on how to improve the quality of models, for example by investigating methods and techniques for a practical quality assurance of software models. More specifically, we need to investigate which attributes of software models are most influential to the quality of software systems (note that the attributes should also embrace model's behavioral aspects because they might correlate better with defects in software). Additionally, the methods with which the model attributes are maintained and evaluated should also be investigated. Ideally, the methods should take into account their practicality and applicability in industry. The second implication is related to the trade-off of using modeling in software development. For instance, it should be investigated to what extent the quality improvement achieved by introducing modeling was not sacrificing other aspects such as productivity.

We also underline the implications of this study for software development in practice. First, the result of this study should encourage both project managers and software engineers to evaluate how UML is used in their projects. While we are aware of the fact that not all system parts needs be modeled, the decisions to model or not model system parts should be based on informed decisions. For example, components' complexity and criticality have been considered by developers as good candidates for more extensive modeling [21]. Second, based on the results of this study we also emphasize the needs for good quality models, which comprise syntactical and semantical aspects of models. To achieve this quality goal, practical model quality assurance activities such as design reviews and the use of modeling convention should be considered to be incorporated in the software development process (see the discussion in [22]). These quality assurance activities should help accentuate the impact of modeling on the final software quality.

It should be noted, however, that this study has been primarily concerned with whether classes being modeled or not modeled. We did not take into account how the modeled classes were actually modeled, for instance in terms of level of detail, completeness, and well-formedness. We really think that by taking into account quality aspects of UML models, we can learn much more about the relation between UML modeling and the quality of software.

5.1 Threats to Validity

In this section, we discuss validity threats of this study. These threats to validity will be presented in their order of importance [11]: internal validity, external validity, construct validity, and conclusion validity.

The main threat to the internal validity of this study concerns our ability to control influences from other factors beyond what have been accounted for in this study. Therefore, more advanced research design is required to address other confounding factors, such as requirement quality, team composition, and team experience.

External validity threats concerns limitations to generalize the results of a study to a broader industrial practice. We could not make a strong claim that the results of this study would be generalizable to other projects because every project is unique. Most importantly, the way UML models are used in a project will be very influential to how they might affect the quality of the final implementation. Nevertheless, we believe that the results of this study is generalizable to projects in which the UML models are used to guide the implementation (hence, posses a sufficient level of quality) and the developers, on the other hand, strictly conform to the models.

With respect to the threats of construct validity, we underline the effect of programming style on the defect density measure. For example, two supposedly similar classes (in terms of role and responsibility) might be written in different ways. Developers who have the style of verbose programming tend to produce more lines of code than those who are more effective in writing code. Thus, with the average defect-count being fairly equal, classes written by verbose developers will have lower defect density than those written by efficient developers. Nevertheless, careful analysis of class sizes between the modeled and not modeled classes shows no indication that verbose programming has distorted the defect density measure.

Threats to conclusion validity relate to the ability to draw a correct conclusion from a study. In this study we have addressed factors that might have threaten the conclusion validity of this study through a careful design of the approach and a rigorous procedure in the data analyses.

6 Conclusions and Future Works

In this paper we empirically investigate the impact of UML modeling on the quality of software. The main question this paper aims to answer is whether the use of UML can help improve the quality of the final software product. Using empirical data from an industrial Java system, we carefully evaluate the impact of using UML on the defect density of Java classes. After controlling for the effects of class coupling and complexity, we have found that the use of UML modeling remains a significant predictor that explains the variability of defect density in the implementation. More specifically, Java classes that were modeled using UML are found to have significantly lower defect density than those that were not modeled. This result indicates the potential benefits of UML modeling for improving the quality of software.

We realize that this study is still in the early step towards fully understanding the benefits of modeling in software development. Therefore, more research is needed to further investigate the benefits of modeling. To this aim, we are planning to replicate the same study using different industrial projects. Further, we also underline the importance of identifying and assessing other factors that might have significant influence on defect density, such as developers' experience. Assessing confounding factors will not only help us observe the pure effects of modeling, but also it might give us more insights about the circumstances under which modeling is effective to achieve better quality of software. Furthermore, we should consider conducting this type of study in experimental settings, which will allow us to control the effects of confounding factors better.

Acknowledgments

This work was accomplished under the FINESSE (des7015) project supported by the STW (Stichting Technische Wetenschappen), the Netherlands. We thank Logica (www.logica.com) and the project members of the IPS project for the discussions and support in providing the project data.

References

1. Staron, M., Kuzniarz, L., Wohlin, C.: Empirical assessment of using stereotypes to improve comprehension of UML models: a set of experiments. J. Syst. Softw. 79(5), 727–742 (2006)
2. Ricca, F., Di Penta, M., Torchiano, M., Tonella, P., Ceccato, M.: The role of experience and ability in comprehension tasks supported by UML stereotypes. In: ICSE 2007: Proceedings of the 29th international conference on Software Engineering, Washington, DC, USA, pp. 375–384. IEEE Computer Society, Los Alamitos (2007)
3. Genero, M., Cruz-Lemus, J.A., Caivano, D., Abrahao, S., Insfran, E., Carsí, J.A.: Assessing the influence of stereotypes on the comprehension of UML sequence diagrams: A controlled experiment. In: Czarnecki, K., Ober, I., Bruel, J.-M., Uhl, A., Völter, M. (eds.) MODELS 2008. LNCS, vol. 5301, pp. 280–294. Springer, Heidelberg (2008)
4. Cruz-Lemus, J., Genero, M., Morasca, S., Piattini, M.: Assessing the the understandability of UML statechart diagrams with composite states - a familiy of empirical studies. Empirical Software Engineering (to appear, 2009)

5. Briand, L.C., Labiche, Y., Penta, M.D., Yan-Bondoc, H.D.: An experimental investigation of formality in UML-based development. IEEE Transactions on Software Engineering 31(10), 833–849 (2005)
6. Otero, M.C., Dolado, J.: Evaluation of the comprehension of the dynamic modeling in UML. Information and Software Technology 46(1), 35–53 (2004)
7. Glezer, C., Last, M., Nachmany, E., Shoval, P.: Quality and comprehension of UML interaction diagrams-an experimental comparison. Information and Software Technology 47(10), 675–692 (2005)
8. Torchiano, M.: Empirical assessment of UML static object diagrams. In: International Workshop on Program Comprehension, pp. 226–230 (2004)
9. Arisholm, E., Briand, L.C., Hove, S.E., Labiche, Y.: The impact of UML documentation on software maintenance: An experimental evaluation. IEEE Transactions on Software Engineering 32(6), 365–381 (2006)
10. Nugroho, A., Flaton, B., Chaudron, M.R.V.: Empirical analysis of the relation between level of detail in UML models and defect density. In: Czarnecki, K., Ober, I., Bruel, J.-M., Uhl, A., Völter, M. (eds.) MODELS 2008. LNCS, vol. 5301, pp. 600–614. Springer, Heidelberg (2008)
11. Wohlin, C., Runeson, P., Höst, M., Ohlsson, M.C., Regnell, B., Wesslén, A.: Experimentation in software engineering: an introduction. Kluwer Academic Publishers, Norwell (2000)
12. McCabe, T.J.: A complexity measure. IEEE Trans. Softw. Eng. 2(4), 308–320 (1976)
13. Chidamber, S.R., Kemerer, C.F.: A metrics suite for object oriented design. IEEE Trans. Softw. Eng. 20(6), 476–493 (1994)
14. Subramanyam, R., Krishnan, M.S.: Empirical analysis of ck metrics for object-oriented design complexity: Implications for software defects. IEEE Trans. Softw. Eng. 29(4), 297–310 (2003)
15. Khoshgoftaar, T.M., Allen, E.B.: Ordering fault-prone software modules. Software Quality Control 11(1), 19–37 (2003)
16. SDMetrics: The UML design quality metrics tool, http://www.sdmetrics.com
17. Rutherford, A.: Introducing ANOVA and ANCOVA: a GLM approach. Sage, Thousand Oaks (2001)
18. Mann, H.B., Whitney, D.R.: On a test of whether one of two random variables is stochastically larger than the other. The Annals of Mathematical Statistics 18(1), 50–60 (1947)
19. Koru, A.G., Liu, H.: An investigation of the effect of module size on defect prediction using static measures. SIGSOFT Softw. Eng. Notes 30(4), 1–5 (2005)
20. Fenton, N.E., Neil, M.: A critique of software defect prediction models. IEEE Trans. Softw. Eng. 25(5), 675–689 (1999)
21. Nugroho, A., Chaudron, M.R.V.: A survey into the rigor of UML use and its perceived impact on quality and productivity. In: ESEM 2008: Proceedings of the Second ACM-IEEE international symposium on Empirical software engineering and measurement, pp. 90–99. ACM, New York (2008)
22. Nugroho, A., Chaudron, M.R.V.: Managing the quality of UML models in practice. In: Rech, J., Bunse, C. (eds.) Model-Driven Software Development: Integrating Quality Assurance. Information Science Reference, pp. 1–36. IGI Publishing, Hershey (2008)

Concern Visibility in Base Station Development – An Empirical Investigation*

Lars Pareto[1], Peter Eriksson[2], and Staffan Ehnebom[2]

[1] Chalmers | University of Gothenburg, Sweden
pareto@chalmers.se
[2] Ericsson AB, Sweden
{peter.r.eriksson,staffan.ehnebom}@ericsson.com

Abstract. Contemporary model driven development tools only partially support the abstractions occurring in complex embedded systems development. The paper presents an interpretive case study in which the concerns held by 7 engineers in a large product developing organization were compared to the concerns supported by the modeling tool in use. The paper's main finding is an empirically grounded catalogue of concerns, categorized with respect to visibility in models and other artefacts in use. In the studied case, 26% of the concerns were visible in the models, whereas 38% were visible elsewhere and 36% not visible at all. The catalogue has been presented to several stakeholders in the unit studied, with positive feedback: particularly appreciated were the notion of concern visibility as indicator of degree of implementation of model driven development, and that concerns have traceable connections to experiences of the unit's engineers.

Keywords: Model driven development (MDD), aspect oriented modeling (AOM), software architecture, viewpoints, concerns, base stations, telecommunication systems, embedded systems.

1 Introduction

A key objective in model driven development (MDD) is to support work at a high level of abstraction—one that is close to the problem domain and distant from the realization domain. In some areas, this objective has been met, e.g., in embedded systems development, statecharts based tools (such as Rhapsody, Rational Rose Realtime, and Bridgepoint) has led to significant abstraction in requirements-, architecture-, implementation-, and testing-work.

However, the success is partial. Contemporary MDD tools primarily raise the level of abstraction in definitions of reactive behaviour and process hierarchies. Other kinds of behaviour (e.g., algorithmic behaviour, data handling, platform interaction, scheduling control) and structure (e.g., deployments, data structures, and configurations) and non-functional aspects of the software (e.g., performance, persistence, resilience, security) are not significantly abstracted by these tools.

* Empirical results category paper.

A. Schürr and B. Selic (Eds.): MODELS 2009, LNCS 5795, pp. 196–210, 2009.

In large organizations this partial support for abstraction is a problem. When unsupported abstractions are handled by traditional means, i.e., text documents with informal diagrams and manual coding, two parallel modes of development occur—one for the model, one for the remainder. This has far-reaching consequences to software processes, tooling strategies, quality management, project management, and in the end the cost-effectiveness of MDD. Incidentally, experiences with large scale MDD within Ericsson's business unit Networks, are that MDD does not significantly reduce the overall software development costs compared to well executed document based, code centric development [1].

The overall purpose of the research presented in this paper is to *identify abstractions used in the development of complex embedded systems that lack effective support in contemporary MDD tools.* By abstractions we mean diagrams, mental views, and other knowledge representations used to understand a system from some viewpoint. By complex embedded systems we mean large, special purpose, real-time, multiple processor, computer systems part of larger, technical systems; by MDD tools, we mean statecharts- and UML-based tools, for formal modelling and code generation; by contemporary, we mean that tools are being applied in industry for large scale development; by lack of effective support, we mean that formal modeling of the abstraction is neither supported by the tool itself, nor by a plug-in, or that the support is not good enough, too difficult, or simply too costly to use in practice. (By formal modeling, we mean modeling in a language with syntax and semantics.)

Our overall approach is a three step, iterative process, based on IEEE 1471 [2]: identification of *stakeholders* (present and potential users of the modelling tools), identification of stakeholder *concerns* (interests which pertain to the embedded systems development), and assessment of *concern visibility* (whether or not the concerns are visible in models). By comparing the concerns held by the stakeholders, with those realizable by their modeling tools, we identify abstractions lacking effective support.

Our strategy of inquiry is case study research [3]. By investigating the use of abstractions in their real-life contexts, and by analytical reasoning, we construct evidence that certain abstractions lack effective support in contemporary MDD tools. Our case is a division within Ericsson responsible for a base station product line; it is a mature user of MDD (>10 years of application), it uses models in all stages of software development (analysis, design, implementation, testing), and has experiences from all tools listed above and many of their predecessors and successors.

The question investigated in this paper is as follows: *which of the division's concerns are visible in its models*? Our findings, based on interpretation of interviews with 7 engineers, and document analysis, are that out of 149 identified concerns, 39 of the concerns (26%) are visible in the models, whereas 57 concerns (38%) are visible elsewhere and 53 concerns (36%) not visible at all.

The paper is organized as follows: we describe our research design, and summarize our data collection and analysis (Section 2); we describe the concerns and their visibility in catalogue form (Section 3); we discuss causes of the observed partial concern visibility (Section 4); the paper ends with discussions of threats to validity (Section 5), related work (Section 6), our conclusions (Section 7), and future work (Section 8).

2 Research Design

Selection of the case was based on Ericsson's strategies (which involve increasing the efficiency of software development by better utilization of MDD), the studied divisions maturity of MDD (which is one of the highest within Ericsson), and the researchers access to the studied division's site (which is available through a site-dedicated software research program).

Our investigation had five phases: an interview phase, a model sampling phase, an analysis phase, an assessment phase, and a validation phase. The *interview phase* involved informant selection, individual, semi-structured interviews, and transcription, with the purpose of building an analyzable knowledge base reflecting the experiences, needs and abstractions perceived by the informants. The *model sampling phase* involved taking representative screenshots from the formal model, and collection of informal documents. *The analysis phase* involved open coding and inductive categorization of written sources along the lines of grounded theory [4], with the purpose of identifying non-standard, and project specific abstractions and concerns. The *assessment phase* involved searching for the found abstractions and concerns within the model samples, with the purpose of assessing the visibility of each concern. The *validation phase* involved interviews and workshops, in which the concerns were discussed. Phases were partly interleaved, but on the large whole sequential.

2.1 Our Case

The context of our case is Ericsson's business unit Networks, which develops a range of base stations and other telecommunication infrastructure components for an international market. Our case is a division within this unit responsible for one base station product line. The division has a matrix organization in which, roughly, verticals are responsible for knowledge related to a specific product line, and horizontals responsible for delivering and maintaining specific products.

In the studied division, software models are used for requirements and design work, along the lines of RUP (with project specific diagrams types), and for implementation work, using several MDD tools. Models are also used for design, implementation and description of hardware, some of which is developed by the division itself (in the form of special purpose boards), other of which is developed by a separate division (in the form of general purpose cabinets with accompanying software libraries).

Formal requirement-, design-, and implementation models are integrated in a *system model*, which also integrates artefacts on other forms such as informal diagrams, text documents, spreadsheets, and text-based formal specifications. The hardware models are not integrated in the system model; rather, the system model includes descriptive models of hardware aspects relevant for software design. The system model is developed in-house, with due attention to the division's many processes (e.g., design-, development-, testing-, maintenance-, and project management processes) and communications with other divisions involved in the product development.

In summary, the division's models are situated in an intricate web of maintenance, reuse, and evolution of requirements, design, and implementation artefacts, partly based on UML, partly on other formats, realised by several MDD tools, and with loose connections to underlying, shared, evolving hardware.

Despite the challenges of operating in such a context, modelling works well: product releases are timely; response times for defect reports and change requests are decreasing; time-to-market for new features has decreased. Although MDD has not reduced the development costs to the degree hoped for, there is faith in the approach and a presumption that the evolution of MDD tools, better adaptation of tools to address stakeholder concerns, and increased automation, will eventually give MDD a significant economical advantage over code centric development.

2.2 Informants and Interviews

Due to restrictions in access to sites and informants, we settled for a small sample of representative informants. Informants included producers and consumers of the modeling infrastructure in six roles (chief architect, system designer, software designer, system tester, software tester, project manager) from three sites. Ten informants were selected; all had more than 5 years of experience of base station development, some more than 25.

Interviews were semi-structured, lasted 1h each (2h in one case), and revolved around questions related to how well the diagrams of the present system model supported daily tasks, the completeness of diagrams with respect to perceived needs, and possible evolutions of the system model to accommodate for higher degrees of simulation, transformation, and consistency checking. Five of these interviews were transcribed and analyzed; the remainder influenced our interpretation of the transcribed interviews, and confirmed phenomena found, but were not analyzed per se.

In addition, notes from 1h project meeting with four architects, transcripts from a 6h workshop with a senior software designer and a senior software architect (both authors of this paper), and a document defining and explaining all system model concepts were added as data sources.

In the end, the interview phase resulted in the following: 16h of recordings, 7h of which were transcribed; 43 000 words of transcripts; 30 accompanying drawings and screenshots taking during the interviews; 1 complementary written source.

2.3 Model Sampling

To build a knowledge base of presently supported views, we traversed the system model, node by node, taking screenshots of representative diagrams in use; we collected all informal documents reachable from the system model, and extracted distinct diagram kinds from these. (We refrained from sampling the many implementation models as, according to several senior architects and designers, the views in these subsume those in the system model.)

The model samples amount to 217 screenshots from the formal models, and 1440 pages of informal documents describing base station architecture and design.

2.4 Analysis of Interviews

Data sources were coded in search for phenomena related to modeling. Codes were partitioned into the following categories: the *perspectives* of the developed system, the system model's *rationale*, and *characteristics;* the *fitness for purpose* of the system model. Codes were further partitioned into subcategories. Identical or similar codes within each subcategory were merged.

All codes were revisited in search for concerns. Those directly expressing concerns (in the sense of IEEE 1471) were labelled as such. For codes indirectly expressing concerns, the underlying data sources were re-visited: if these supported the concern, then it was introduced as an explicit such.

Identified concerns were partitioned into subcategories. When applicable, naming of these followed Kruchten [5]; in other cases, evocative names were introduced. Conceptually overlapping concerns within each subcategory were either merged or articulated. Some concerns exhibited family-member relationships, which lead to a distinction between *generic* and *concrete* concerns.

The interview analysis phase resulted in 10 generic, and 139 concrete concerns, organized into a 49 node category tree. (See Section 3.1.).

2.5 Assessment of Concern Visibility

Each concern found was classified as to whether it was *visible in the formal system model, visible in the informal documentation, visible in code,* or *not visible anywhere.* To support reasoning about effective support, concerns visible in informal documentations were further classified as being visible in *informal text*, in an *informal diagram,* or in a *table*.

Browsing of model samples and text searches (with the support of automated indexing) were used to assess the visibilities. Classification was conservative: a concern was classified as visible only if it was clearly recognizable in the artefact in case, i.e., the formal system model, etc. The outcome of the concern visibility assessment is presented in Section 3.3.

2.6 Validation

Validation was done in three steps: we verified that the concerns were reasonably comprehensible for Ericsson staff by discussing them in two workshops involving the authors and two Ericsson managers; we interviewed an independent Ericsson colleague, asking for general feedback on our analysis; we organized a workshop open to all informants, in which validation was one activity.

In the validation activity, informants were asked to comment on our interpretations. The codes and their underlying quotations were distributed; informants worked in pairs to review the codes of 1-2 categories during 1.5h; informants met during another hour to discuss their remarks.

In the end, 10 informants participated in the validation workshop, contributing some 20 critical remarks on our analysis results. (See Section 3.4.).

3 Concerns Catalogue

Our concerns catalogue consists of a taxonomy, a population of the taxonomy with empirically grounded concerns, and an assessment of the visibility of concerns in the system model studied.

3.1 Taxonomy

Our taxonomy is given in Table 1: the six top level categories (logical-, concurrency-, development-, physical-, organizational-, and viewpoint specific concerns) are based on Kruchten's taxonomy for architectural views. (To avoid ambiguity, following Rozanski and Woods [6], we use the term "concurrency" rather than Kruchten's term "process".) Subcategories are partly aligned with those of Kruchten's taxonomy. Some categories (static logical structure, interfaces and protocols, and aspect specific concerns) are richly populated, yet cohesive, which motivates a three-level categorization.

Table 1. Concern categories and subcategories

Logical concerns
  Static logical structure
    Overview
    Precision
    Decompositions
    Design quality
  Control flow
  Services
  Data
  Interfaces and protocols
    System boundary
    Interface abstraction
    Protocol abstraction
    Protocol realization
    Protocol viewpoints
    Interaction patterns
	Development concerns
	  Modules
	  Namespace
	  Configuration
	  Automation
	  Linkage
	
	Physical concerns
	  Static physical structure
	  Configuration
	  H/W relationships
	  H/W S/W relationships
	  Deployment
	
	Organizational concerns
	  Project
	  Product
	  Quality

Concurrency concerns
  Signal paths
  Availability
  Performance
  Capacity
  Scheduling and Distribution
	Viewpoint specific concerns
	  Aspect specific
	    Logging & Tracing
	    Understanding
	    Monitoring
	    Error detection & Correction
	    Verifiability
	    Evolution
	  Mode and phase specific
	  System domain specific

The number of concerns in each top-level category is given in Fig. 1:

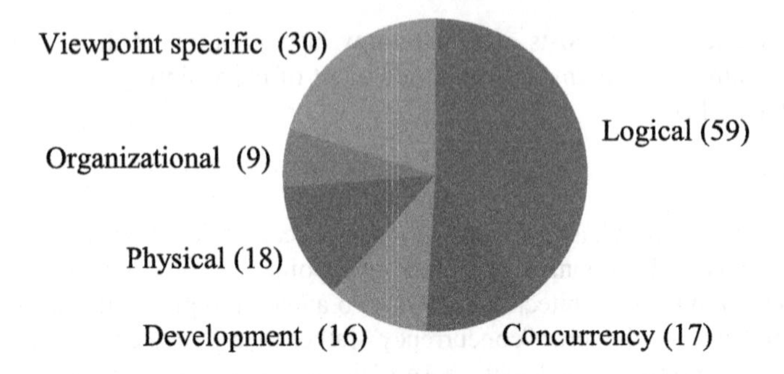

Fig. 1. The number of concerns in each top-level category

3.2 The Concerns

We have strived to make concern names brief and self explanatory by short evocative sentences expressed with established software engineering terminology. Although this approach leads to ambiguity, we have found this to be tolerable in practical work: when ambiguity is encountered, a visit to the data sources usually suffices to resolve

Table 2. Logical concerns

Logical Concerns	
Overview - overviews (g) - capability anatomy - functional areas - architectural whole - service anatomy - navigating the model from a side perspective - which tiers we should have	**Data** - persistence (g) - data identities - data parameters - data persistence - what data is static - dynamic view of data - class and capsule instantiation - locality (of reference)
Precision - clean and precise visualization of require-ments and behaviour	**System boundary** - actors and use cases - usage scenarios - external triggers
Decompositions - layering decomposition(g) - tiers(g) - application decomposition - functional part decomposition - capability realization anatomy - program execution handling decomposition - layer-to-layer decomposition - system/subsystem decomposition - capsule / sub-capsule decomposition - capability decomposition - platform oriented decomposition - interface decomposition - product structure decomposition	**Interface abstraction** - signal grouping and bundling - allocation independent client-server interaction
	Protocol abstraction - structural protocols - peer to peer signalling - protocol stack layering (à la OSI) - protocol abstraction (three signals at one level becoming one signal at a higher level)
	Protocol realization - layer-to-layer signalling - actual parameters (=data) sent in signals - formal parameters in signals - white-box (1st level) interaction - interaction between "Things" (functional parts)

Table 2. (*continued*)

Design quality - coupling and cohesion among service realizations and capability realizations	
Control flow - basic and alternate flows - logical control flow (in sequence diagrams) - call graph - activities and control flow (cf. activity diagrams)	**Protocol viewpoints** - allocation protocols - functional protocols - service realization (in terms of functional parts) - software interfaces - interaction flows between boards - use case realization (in terms of classes and objects)
Services - system services - capabilities - logical resources - relevant capabilities only	**Interaction patterns** - communication principles
Concurrency Concerns	
Signal paths - communication paths (declared) - SAP/SPP communication paths - interaction "holes" (using abstract ports) - capsule interface inheritance - communication over abstract ports	**Capacity** - memory capacity - memory utilization - (processor) load - bandwidth
Availability - downtime	**Scheduling and Distribution** - capsules onto threads - distribution - process priorities - scheduling
Performance - performance - response - queuing theoretic qualities (processor load, intensities, response times)	
Development Concerns	
Modules - load-module relationships	**Automation** - what parts are automatically checked - what parts are transformed
Namespace - document names (carrying essential concepts) - naming conventions - hardware identities	**Linkage** - traceability (g) (of what originates from what) - how manipulation of MO affects FRO:s and things below. - how project internal artefacts relate to system model - where, in white box, a certain requirement is realized - traceability in sequence diagrams (through tags) - what functional parts originate in
Configuration - DB configuration - MPU configuration - Cable configuration - AU configuration	

Table 2. *(continued)*

Physical Concerns	
Static physical structure - boards - virtual boards - board interfaces - how a board works **Configuration** - hardware variants **H/W relationships** - relationships between boards (g) - physical dependencies between boards - board connections (wiring) **H/W S/W relationships** - relationship between hardware-interfaces and software interfaces (g)	**Deployment** - deployment(g) - data deployment (relationship between data and their storage) - process deployment (relationships between Processes, Threads, and CPU:s) - signal flow onto card deployment - function onto code deployment - function onto platform deployment - code onto part deployment - link deployment (internal on physical) - functional deployment (logical- onto physic cal components)
Organizational Concerns	
Project - responsibility - deliverables - planning - division of work - baselines	**Product** - product structure (hardware+ load modules, PRIM) **Quality** - approval status - test coverage - design rule exemption
Viewpoint Specific Concerns	
Logging & Tracing - log(g) - trace(g) - hardware fault logging - error logging - system level logging **Understanding** - descriptive texts (in models)	**Mode and phase specific** - start-up - connection establishment - upgrade - software update - fault management (recovery) - hardware restart - (board) loading
Monitoring - observability **Error Detection and Correction** - fault handling **Verifiability** - verifiability **Evolution** - differences w.r.t. earlier versions (in CR:s)	**System domain specific** - power - climate - baseband use - traffic - redundancy - resource handling - understanding domain - resource object management domain - transaction handling - hardware - synchronization - test-system infrastructure - system understanding

it. To give an impression of the coverage of the concerns found, we include the names of all concerns identified: Table 2 lists the 149 concerns, and their categorization. In the table, families of concrete concerns are annotated with a *g* (as in generic), e.g., tiers(g) which entails the protocol stack layers among others.

3.3 Concern Visibility

The visibility of our identified concerns is shown in Fig. 2:

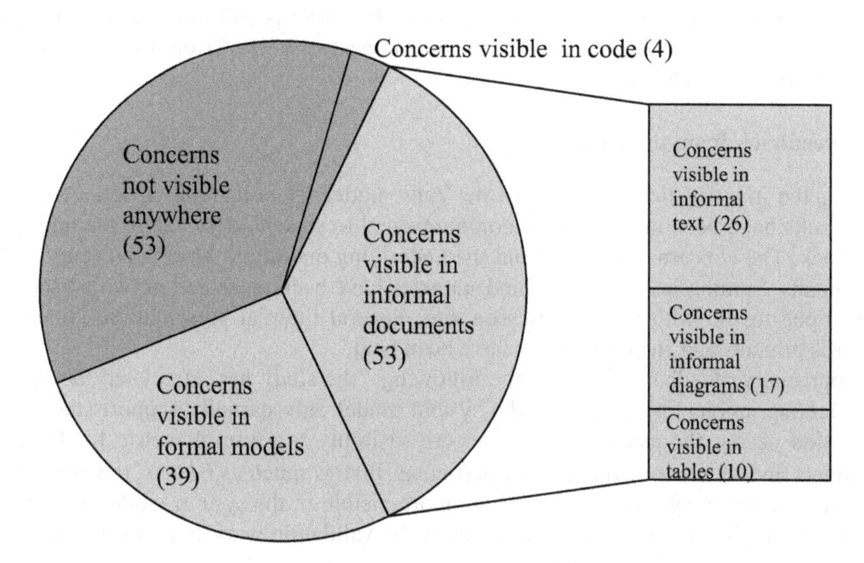

Fig. 2. Visibility of concerns

As this diagram clearly shows, 64% of the identified concerns are documented, either formally or informally. About 40% of the documented concerns are present in formal models (in a dialect of UML), whereas the remainder are present in informal documents and code.

The degrees to which concerns are visible in formal models, in each category of concern, are given by Fig. 3:

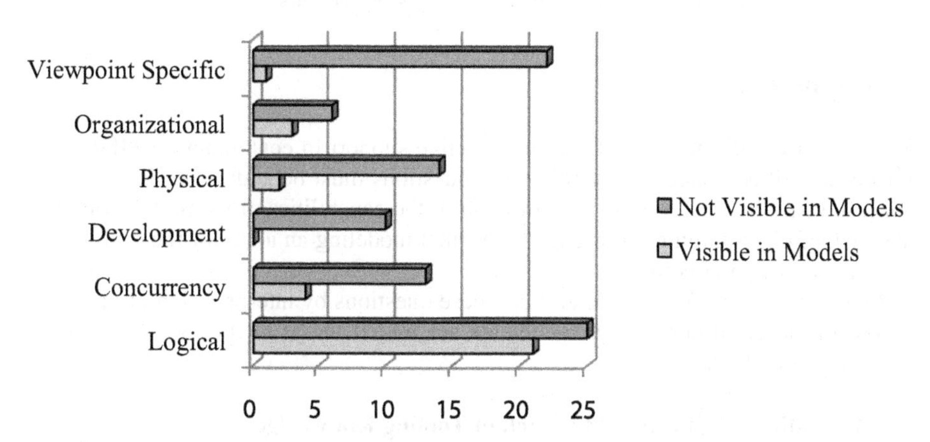

Fig. 3. Visibility of concerns in formal models for each concern category

Notice (in Fig. 3) that the concerns not visible in the formal models are dominant, in each concern category. The biggest differences are found among the viewpoint specific concerns where only 1 out of 23 (4%) of the concerns are modelled, and in the development concerns where none out of 10 concerns (0%) are modelled. The smallest difference is found among the logical concerns where 21 out of 46 (46%) of the concerns are modelled.

3.4 Feedback from the Unit

During the investigation, in Spirit of de Vens model for collaborative research [7], our results have been incrementally communicated to stakeholders within the unit for feedback. The concerns catalogue and the underlying quotations have been sent to all informants. Summaries of findings and statistics have been presented in two presentations open to the whole local Ericsson site. Several internal presentations directed towards project- and steering groups have been held.

Appreciative feedback included the following: the study has articulated the common feeling among engineers that the system model only partially supports their information needs; the assessment of concern visibility is a useful metric for higher managers and technology boards—in particular, that as much as 64% of the concerns in such a complex system as a base station are visible in the system model, is something that the division should be proud of; in the validation workshop, most concerns were recognized as valid and important.

Critique involved the following: that the notion of a concern is not precise and difficult to comprehend; that some of the concerns (20) were vague or ambiguous or overlapping or difficult to comprehend or placed in the wrong category; that the analyst's reasoning, that links concerns to the underlying quotations, were sometimes difficult to follow; that our concern catalogue was only based on the experiences of 7 out of approximately 300 users, and thereby incomplete; that project leaders and line managers were not found among our informants. In particular, the organizational concerns were regarded as overly generic, and likely to expand to larger sets of concrete concerns, with project- and line-managers as informants.

4 Discussions

To make any inferences about lack of effective support in contemporary MDD tools for our identified concerns, the following questions must be addressed. Is the partial concern visibility due to lack of knowledge of the capabilities of the tool in use? Is it due lack of diagramming knowledge? Is formal modeling an ideal for the division? Is it regarded as cost effective?

In the following sections, we address these questions by interpretation of our interviews. In these, all descriptive statements are rooted in the interviews, whereas the inferences are of our construct.

4.1 Partiality Is Not Caused by Lack of Tooling Knowledge

In the division studied, there is sufficient knowledge for a saturated utilization of the MDD tool used for system modeling. The tool has been used for implementation modeling for more than ten years. Over the last six years, a dedicated team of architects have extended the tool to also support system modeling: supported by consultants, the team has enriched the tool's basic capabilities with plug-ins for traceability, reviewing, versioning, requirement model integration, consistency checking, and other features; it has defined and implemented more than 30 project specific architectural views; it has defined meta-models for many of these.

Further, the team has developed a design methodology based on the tool's capabilities, and extended these to obtain "a whole solution" for the division's needs.

The team also has good connections to the modeling research community, as the following quotation shows

> "We had a lot of ideas about resolving these circular dependencies by adding extensions to the Href-Vref constructions, and asked a member of the UML2 committee, who forwarded the question to another member, who pointed us to a few academic papers that looked into this."

Given that the division has long experience from extending the tool to support system modeling, and good connections within the modeling research community, we can conclude that the partial concern visibility is not due to lack of tooling knowledge.

4.2 Partiality Is Not Caused by Lack of Diagramming Knowledge

As Fig. 2 shows, 17 concerns are represented in informal diagrams. A follow-up analysis of these diagrams revealed a rich and (reasonably) consistent use of modeling notations rooted in hardware modeling notations, operating system theory, queuing theory, and telecommunication standards.

We found many of the informal diagrams to be overlays of diagrams at different levels of abstractions, or from different domains, e.g., one diagram shows how logical channels are realized by underlying physical and virtual boards and brokers between these.

Given the richness of modeling notations present in the informal documentation, we can conclude that the partiality in concern visibility is not caused by lack of ideas of what diagrams would be useful.

4.3 Partiality Is Not Caused by Distrust in Formal Modeling

That formal modeling is an ideal of the division is clear from internal documents advocating MDD and its model based cousins, e.g., "Information at your fingertips" and "One source of information" are recurring slogans. Improvement initiatives in this direction, at several levels within the division, also witness to the ideal.

Given this ideal, we can conclude that partiality is not caused by distrust in formal modeling.

4.4 Partiality Is Partly Caused by Poor Cost Effectiveness of Modeling

In practice, what is visible and not visible in the system model depends on design trade-offs, with respect to costs and benefits of the supporting view: the development and maintenances costs of the tool support for the view, the development and maintenances costs for the view itself, the view's contribution to reduced development costs, improved time to market, and improved product quality. As stated by one informant:

> "One just has to face that, during the journey, there has been numerous things that we intended to do, but that we dropped, because they were too complicated, or did not add anything. [...] The purpose of the system model has never been to support very abstract and fluffy modeling. Its purpose is to get the next product out on the market as quickly as possible. [...] We never intended the design model to be a help for beginners getting into the system."

These, and several other statements in the same spirit show that, even though formal modeling is an ideal, it is also two-edge sword—easily doing more harm than good to a project. Thus cost effectiveness of formal modeling compared to informal diagramming (and compared to no modeling) is a clear cause of partiality in the studied case.

4.5 Partiality Is Partly Caused by the Relative Strengths of Formal and Informal Modeling

Follow-up discussions on the partiality with informants and other users of the system revealed that the formal modeling and informal diagramming had complementary merits: formal models excel at describing accurate and precise information, whereas informal diagrams excel at giving overviews and initial understanding.

A comparison of the formal models with the informal diagrams, revealed the reasons: informal diagrams were characterized by rich sets of objects and relations, elaborate renderings of these, multiple-view diagrams, and overlays; the formal models, at the other hand were (with the exceptions of sequence diagrams and statecharts) class-association oriented, and made no use of suggestive notations and combined views.

The difference in expressiveness between informal- and formal diagrams, partly explains why as much as (30%) of the concerns visible in diagrams were found in informal diagrams only.

5 Threats to Validity

Our research design is sensitive to following sources of errors, many of which are intrinsic to interpretive, case study research: (e_1) sampling is restricted to 7 users, and does not include project- and line-managers, so the concerns catalogue is hardly complete; (e_2) comparison of concerns with the model is based on a sampling of the model, thus we may have missed concerns embedded in other diagrams; (e_3) the concerns are influenced by the informants daily work, and deeper concerns may have been overlooked; (e_4) the concern identification is influenced the analysts conceptions; (e_5) sampling and interpretation may be consciously or unconsciously biased to researcher concerns; (e_6) validation may not reveal and correct all misinterpretations and misclassifications made by the analysts.

The following precautions have been taken to reduce the effect of these sources: for e_1 we have chosen informants with long experience in modelling of base stations in several roles; for e_2, we have sampled by a depth-first walkthrough of all formal diagrams, and all informal documents referenced from the model; for e_3, we have used open questioning from many perspectives to reveal areas of concerns beyond daily use; for $e_{4\text{-}5}$, we have engaged stakeholders in the theory building process, used a qualitative data analysis tool that supports traceability of concerns to underlying data sources, presented results to the unit for feedback, and taken feedback into account; to handle e_6 , we have used three complementary kinds of validation: engagement in theory building, individual interview, and a workshop.

6 Related Work

Practice based catalogues of abstractions are recurrent in software architecture research, e.g., Zachman's Information Systems Architecture Framework [8], Clements et al.'s Viewtype and Styles catalogue [9], Rozanski and Wood's viewpoint and perspectives catalogue [6]. Although these, and other catalogues we are aware of, identify many abstractions relevant to large scale embedded systems development, they do not relate the abstractions to their effective support by contemporary MDD tools.

7 Summary and Conclusions

We have investigated the use of a contemporary MDD tool in one division of Ericsson—a large, mature user of MDD. The question investigated is *which of the division's concerns are visible in their models.* We have identified 149 concerns, and found 39 of these to be visible in their formal models; we found that functional concerns have a reasonable degree of support (about 50%), whereas viewpoint specific, concurrency-, organizational-, physical-, and development concerns have weak support.

To explain the observed partiality, we have investigated five phenomena with obvious causal relationship to concern visibility: *lack of tooling knowledge*, *lack of diagramming knowledge*, *distrust in formal modeling*, *cost effectiveness of modeling*, and *relative merits of representations.* Our investigation shows that, among these factors, in the studied case, poor cost effectiveness of modeling for certain concerns and weaknesses of formal modeling notations compared to informal ones, are the strongest causes of partiality in this case.

All in all, we have some evidence that the MDD tool used by the division and other tools of its generation (which have similar capabilities), are only a half-way hut in model driven development of base stations: they allow some abstractions to be expressed, but give little support for others. Devoted extension and utilization of the tools improve the situation, but in practice, tools are more or less confined to built-in diagram types which only partially support the concerns in need for support. To fully realize the vision of MDD, domain specific modeling notations must be easier to define and maintain; better rendering capabilities, and better support for combined views are also needed.

Newer generation of MDD and MDA tools address some of these issues, but it is yet to be seen to which degree they support concerns in base station development.

8 Future Work

Continuations of this research would be to investigate the benefits of effective support for the identified non-visible and informally modelled concerns, to further investigate the relative strengths of formal and informal modeling, and to explore mixed formality diagramming, in which formal and informal elements are combined to support work at higher levels of abstractions, while maintaining consistency to lower level formal models, without the overhead that domain specific formal modeling brings.

Acknowledgments. This work has been supported by Ericsson Software Research through Ericsson's Software Architecture and Quality Centre (SAQC). TietoEnator AB and Ericsson AB provided access to informants, and engaged in the validation.

References

1. Zachrisson, P.: Managing Model Based Projects, Ericsson Internal Presentation, Ericsson AB (2007)
2. International Organization for Standardization: ISO/IEC 42010 — Systems and Software Engineering — Recommended Practice for Architectural Description of Software-Intensive Systems, International Standard, ISO (2007)
3. Yin, R.K.: Case Study Research: Design and Methods. Sage Publications, Thousand Oaks (2003)
4. Strauss, A.L., Corbin, J.M.: Basics of Qualitative Research: Techniques and Procedures for Developing Grounded Theory. Sage Publications, Thousand Oaks (1998)
5. Kruchten, P.: Architectural Blueprints — The "4+1" View Model of Software Architecture. IEEE Software 12(6), 42–50 (1995)
6. Rozanski, N., Woods, E.: Software Systems Architecture: Working with Stakeholders Using Viewpoints and Perspectives. Addison-Wesley, Upper Saddle River (2005)
7. van de Ven, A.H.: Engaged Scholarship: a Guide for Organizational and Social Research. Oxford University Press, New York (2007)
8. Zachman, J.A.: A Framework for Information Systems Architecture. IBM Systems Journal 26(3), 276–292 (1987)
9. Clements, P., Bachmann, F., Bass, L., Garlan, D., Ivers, J., Little, R., Nord, R., Stafford, J.: Documenting Software Architectures: Views and Beyond. Addison-Wesley, Reading (2003)

Influencing Factors in Model-Based Testing with UML State Machines: Report on an Industrial Cooperation*

Stephan Weißleder

Fraunhofer-Institut für Rechnerarchitektur und Softwaretechnik FIRST,
Kekuléstraße 7, 12489 Berlin, Germany
stephan.weissleder@first.fraunhofer.de
http://www.first.fraunhofer.de

Abstract. Automatic model-based test generation is influenced by many factors such as the test generation algorithm, the structure of the used test model, and the applied coverage criteria. In this paper, we report on an industrial cooperation for model-based testing: We used a UML state machine to generate test suites, the original system under test was not provided, and we conducted mutation analysis on artificial implementations. The focus of this report is on tuning the influencing factors of the test generation and showing their impact on the generated test suites. This report raises further questions, e.g. about the role of test model transformations for coverage criteria satisfaction.

Keywords: Model-Based Testing, State Machines, Coverage Criteria, Mutation Analysis, Industrial Cooperation.

1 Introduction

Testing is very important to validate system behavior. Functional model-based testing is focussed on comparing behavioral test models to the system under test (SUT): For this, test cases are generated from test models and executed with the SUT at source code level. A test case consists of a sequence of input stimuli and expected outputs. The input stimuli are fed into the SUT. The test case detects a fault if actual and expected output of the SUT differ. Test quality can be measured e.g. with coverage criteria. This paper is focussed on using a state machine of the Unified Modeling Language 2.1 (UML) [1] for automatic test suite generation. The used test generation approach is focussed on satisfying coverage criteria that are applied to the state machine.

In this paper, we report on a cooperation with a German rail engineering company. Test suites in the company are usually created manually. The objective of this cooperation was to investigate the use of model-based testing before adopting it as a new testing technique. Our task was to automatically generate unit tests based on a given UML state machine. For reasons of nondisclosure

* Empirical results category paper.

A. Schürr and B. Selic (Eds.): MODELS 2009, LNCS 5795, pp. 211–225, 2009.

the SUT was not provided. Instead, we manually created artificial implementations of the test model to conduct mutation analysis on them as a means to measure the fault detection ability of the generated test suite. This mutation analysis showed that the application of existing coverage criteria on the given state machine often did not result in a satisfying fault detection ability of the test suite. As a consequence, we tuned several influencing factors of the model-based test generation process to improve the results of mutation analysis: We transformed the test model, adapted test goals [2] of the applied coverage criteria, and combined coverage criteria. We also used the cooperation as a test for our prototype implementation ParTeG (Partition Test Generator) [3] under realistic conditions.

The paper is structured as follows. Section 2 covers the related work. Section 3 contains the preliminaries of this paper. In Section 4, we report on the cooperation and all the steps to improve the fault detection ability of the generated test suites. Section 5 contains conclusion, discussion, and future work.

2 Related Work

Model-based testing is often used as a black-box testing technique and is, therefore, of high interest for companies that want to source out testing activities and protect their business secrets at the same time. There are many books that provide surveys of conventional testing [4,5,6] and model-based testing [7,8]. Modeling languages like the UML [1] have been used to create test models. For instance, Abdurazik and Offutt [9] automatically generate test cases from state machines. Sokenou [10] combines state machines with sequence diagrams to improve the path selection in state machines. More corresponding work can be found in [11,12,13]. The focus of this paper is on UML state machines. In contrast to the cited work, we also consider state machine transformations.

Coverage criteria are heuristic means of test suite quality measurement and they can be applied e.g. to source code or test models [8, page 109]. Different kinds of coverage criteria have been investigated (e.g. focussed on data flow, control flow, or boundary value analysis). For instance, Lämmel and Harm [14] define a generic framework to characterize test cases. Briand et al. [15] consider coverage criteria for data flow. Kosmatov et al. [16] define boundary-based coverage criteria. In [17], we consider the combination of different kinds of coverage criteria, like control flow-based coverage criteria [18] and boundary-based coverage criteria [16]. Many test generation approaches are focussed on satisfying coverage criteria. This also holds for the tool that is used for the presented cooperation (ParTeG): A coverage criterion is transformed into a set of test model-specific test goals [2]. For each test goal, a test case is generated.

State machine transformations influence the fault detection ability of the generated test suite. For instance, Friske and Schlingloff instrument conditions of the state machine's transitions in order to satisfy All-Transition-Pairs [12]. Ranville [19] proposes a way to satisfy modified condition / decision coverage (MC/DC) [18] by traversing all transitions on a changed test model. Rajan et al. [20] examine the impact of the model's and the program's structure on the satisfaction of MC/DC. Transformations can even be used to make coverage criteria interchangeable [21]. This report is also focussed on test model transformations for test generation. In contrast, however, we do not focus on satisfying coverage criteria by applying model transformations but focus on increasing the test suite's fault detection ability independent of a certain coverage criterion.

In the presented report, we used mutation analysis to measure the fault detection ability of the generated test suites. Many mutation operators have already been declared for software [22,23] and for specifications [24]. As the result of several case studies [25,26,27], mutation analysis is a good predictor for the test suite's fault detection ability of real faults.

3 Preliminaries

In this section, we present the preliminaries of the cooperation report: We introduce the applied coverage criteria, the artificial SUTs, the notions of efficiency and redundancy for the SUT and test models, and mutation analysis.

3.1 The Applied Coverage Criteria

In the industrial cooperation, we applied the coverage criteria 1) transition coverage (TC), 2) masking MC/DC, and 3) multiple condition coverage (MCC).

1) Transition coverage (TC) requires to traverse all transitions of a state machine. It is considered the minimal coverage criterion to satisfy [8, page 120].

2) Modified condition / decision coverage (MC/DC) [18] is a condition-based coverage criterion that is focussed on the isolated impact of each atomic expression on the whole condition value. For this, the value of the condition must be shown to change if the atomic expression is changed and all other expression values are fixed [8, page 114]. There are several forms of MC/DC [28]. Masking MC/DC [29] allows to change other expressions than the investigated one if the additional changes do not influence the result of the condition value.

3) Multiple condition coverage (MCC) [8, page 114] is the strongest condition-based coverage criterion: Applied to the same test model, the satisfaction of MCC implies the satisfaction of MC/DC. MCC is satisfied iff for each condition all value assignments of the corresponding truth table are applied.

3.2 Efficiency and Redundancy for Artificial SUTs and Test Models

Our aim was to convince our client of the advantages of model-based testing. Thus, we wanted to maximize the generated test suite's fault detection ability for the company's SUT. Since this SUT was not provided, we created and used artificial SUTs, instead: (1) a small SUT with almost no redundancy - we call it the *efficient* SUT - and (2) a cumbersome SUT with a lot of copied source code and redundant function definitions - we call it the *redundant* SUT. The two SUTs are two extreme implementations regarding source code efficiency. Figure 1

```
if(eventIs('ev1')) {
  if(inState('B') ||
    inState('C') ||
    inState('D')) {
    if(a < b) {
      setState('E');
}}}
```

(a) Efficient condition definition.

```
if(eventIs('ev1')) {
  if(inState('B') && a < b) {
    setState('E'); }
  if(inState('C') && a < b) {
    setState('E'); }
  if(inState('D') && a < b) {
    setState('E'); }}
```

(b) Redundant condition definition.

Fig. 1. Examples for efficient and redundant SUT source code

contains a small example. Both SUTs are manually implemented in Java and show the same behavior as the test model. Since the redundant SUT contains more similar code snippets than the efficient SUT and each snippet can contain a fault, there are more possible places for faults in the redundant SUT and, thus, they are also assumed to be harder to detect than faults in the efficient SUT. We were aware that the company's SUT can be totally different to our artificial SUTs and we do not state that our approach is the best one. However, in the described situation we had no access to the company's SUT and considered the use of artificial SUTs a good solution. Using these artificial SUTs gives us at least an indication for the possible extreme performances of the generated test suites.

Likewise, we also call test models *efficient* or *redundant*: for instance, a hierarchical state machine is often more efficient than a flattened one because it needs less model elements to describe the same behavior (see Figure 2). The provided test model of the cooperation contains almost no redundancy. The used tool ParTeG [3] partly supports the insertion of redundancy such as flattening state machines, which allowed us to automatically generate redundant test models from efficient ones. During the cooperation, we considered two scenarios most interesting: (1) The test suite is generated from the efficient test model and executed on the efficient SUT. (2) The test suite is generated from the redundant test model and executed on the redundant SUT. Additionally, we also applied the test suite derived from the efficient test model on the redundant SUT and the test suite derived from the redundant test model on the efficient SUT in Section 4.7.

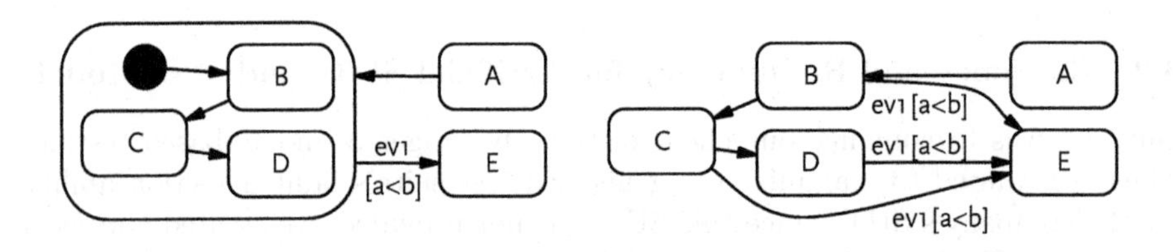

Fig. 2. Hierarchical and flat state machine

3.3 Mutation Analysis

In mutation analysis, fault-injecting mutation operators are applied to a correct SUT, which results in a set of mutated/faulty SUTs (so-called *mutants*). The number of detected (*killed*) mutants divided by the number of detectable mutants is called the *mutation score* of the test suite.

The correlation between the test suite's mutation score and its fault detection ability of real faults in real projects has been evaluated with case studies, e.g. in [25,26,27]. The results are that faults created by proper mutation operators are much closer to real faults than manually created faults, which are inserted by malicious testers. Thus, for a proper set of mutation operators, the mutation score is assumed to correlate with the test suite's fault detection ability.

For creating mutants, we applied the set of sufficient mutation operators identified by Offutt et al. [22]. We also applied the missing condition operator [24], which is considered to represent a frequently occurring fault, and the target state operator, which changes the SUT's equivalent of a transition's target vertex.

Since the focus of mutation operators is on syntactic changes, the concrete SUT is of high importance. Different SUTs can have the same behavior but different structures. Thus, in general, good mutation scores on artificial SUTs are no guarantee for good mutation scores on the company's SUT.

4 Report on the Industrial Cooperation

This section contains our report on the industrial cooperation with a German rail engineering company. A UML state machine was provided to automatically generate unit tests from. This state machine depicts the abstract communication behavior of modules within a train control system and comprised about 35 states and 70 transitions. The state machine is deterministic. It contains two parallel regions and composite states with a hierarchy depth of 4. Transitions are all triggered by call events. All generated tests are functional tests without time information. The test oracle was contained in the state machine (e.g. as state invariants) and the corresponding oracle code was also generated automatically.

For reasons of nondisclosure, the company's SUT was not provided. Instead, we got just the UML state machine to generate test suites from. We used our tool ParTeG [3] for automatic test generation. The tool is focussed on satisfying coverage criteria by searching transition paths from the initial node to model elements to cover [13]. After generating a test suite, we measured its fault detection ability with mutation analysis and manually identified all undetectable mutants. Furthermore, we investigated the reasons for detectable but undetected mutants, came up with solutions to detect them, and repeated the test suite generation. We applied the coverage criteria TC, masking MC/DC, and MCC to the test model. In the following, we describe all adaptations of the test generation process and present their impact on the generated test suites' fault detection abilities. Figure 3 shows an anonymised part of the provided state machine that contains only model elements for the aspects that were adapted during the cooperation. All following figures depict parts of Figure 3.

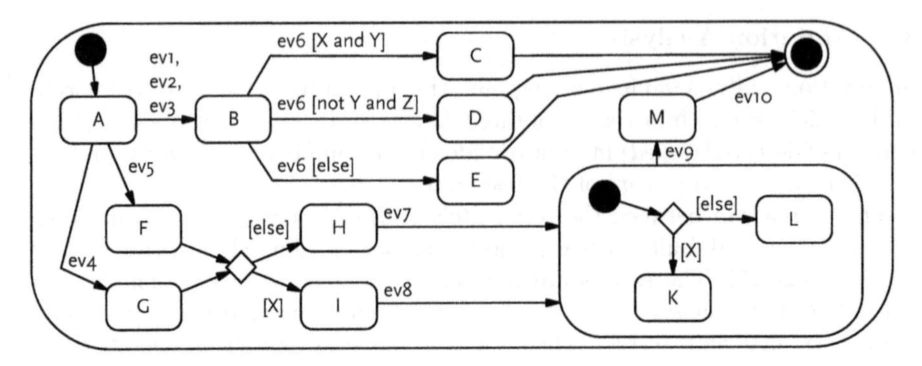

Fig. 3. Anonymised part of the provided state machine

4.1 Starting Point

This section contains a description of the cooperation's starting point. Table 1 shows the results of mutation analysis for the efficient and the redundant SUT with test suites generated from the efficient respectively redundant test model (TM). All following tables contain numbers in brackets about the absolute impact of the described adaptation on the *test suite size* as the number of test cases and on the *mutation score* as the percentage of killed mutants.

Table 1. Results of initial mutation analysis

Coverage Criterion	Efficient TM/SUT		Redundant TM/SUT	
	Test Suite Size	Mutation Score	Test Suite Size	Mutation Score
TC	33	185/255	117	610/872
masking MC/DC	46	212/255	197	790/872
MCC	54	217/255	257	810/872

4.2 Transition Trigger Distribution

Some transitions of the provided UML state machine are triggered by multiple events (e.g. from state A to state B). None of the applied coverage criteria is focussed on events but the SUT can contain separate source code snippets for each transition trigger. Thus, the satisfaction of any of the used coverage criteria does not necessarily result in the detection of a fault in each corresponding implementation branch. In theory, testing all (even the non-triggering) events for all transitions can be covered with sneak path analysis. This analysis, however, is very costly and we know of no supporting test tool [30].

We considered two solutions: the implementation of a better test generator and the transformation of the test model. For users of a model-based testing tool, the improvement of the test generator is next to impossible. Even if the tool vendor is willing to conduct the necessary implementations, this change would probably be costly. Transforming the test model, however, seemed to be easy: The transformation consists of creating several copies of the corresponding

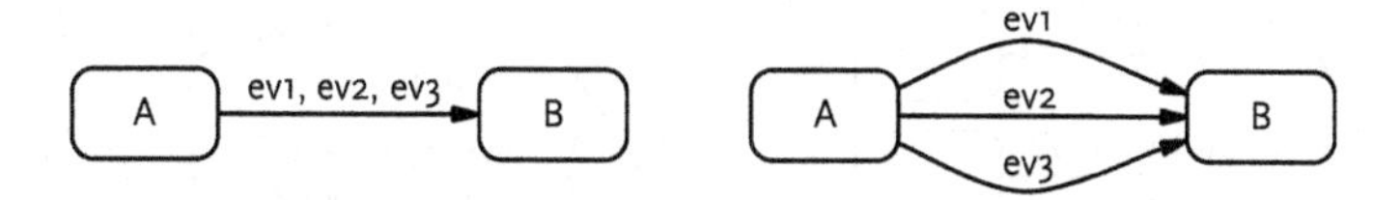

Fig. 4. Splitting transitions according to triggering events

transitions, each of which is triggered by exactly one of the original transition's events. Figure 4 shows the original and the transformed test model.

We implemented this solution in ParTeG and repeated the test suite generation. The results of the subsequent mutation analysis are presented in Table 2. The numbers in brackets describe the change caused by this test model transformation. The presented adaptation has a positive impact for the redundant TM/SUT and as good as no impact on the efficient TM/SUT. Since the SUT's redundancy is unknown, however, we consider this transformation valuable.

Table 2. Mutation analysis after limiting triggers per transition to 1

Coverage Criterion	Efficient TM/SUT		Redundant TM/SUT	
	Test Suite Size	Mutation Score	Test Suite Size	Mutation Score
TC	36 (+3)	185/255 (+0)	134 (+17)	627/872 (+17)
masking MC/DC	49 (+3)	212/255 (+0)	214 (+17)	807/872 (+17)
MCC	57 (+3)	217/255 (+0)	274 (+17)	827/872 (+17)

4.3 Dynamic Test Goal Adaptation

This section describes problems resulting from incomplete guard conditions and how we solved them by adapting the test goals derived from the selected coverage criterion and the test model.

Definition 1 (Influencing Expression Set). *Each guard condition of a transition is composed of a set of atomic expressions. For each state s of a state machine, we call the union of all atomic expressions of s's outgoing transitions' guards* s's influencing expression set.

Figure 5(a) shows a part of Figure 3. The state B of the state machine has three outgoing transitions. Its influencing expression set is $\{X, Y, Z\}$. The guards are mutually exclusive. Nevertheless, no guard references all elements of B's influencing expression set. We call such guard conditions *incomplete*. The following issue arises: One test goal for the satisfaction of MCC for *[X and Y]* is the satisfaction of the condition *[X and (not Y)]* when *ev6* is triggered in state B. For this condition, there are several possible resulting target states (D and E) – depending on the value of Z. As a consequence, the test oracle for the generated test case cannot deduce if a certain transition is traversed just from the satisfaction of *[X and (not Y)]*. Thus, we have almost no means to check the correct behavior of the SUT for such scenarios.

A possible solution seems to be the extension of the existing guard conditions with the missing elements of B's influencing expression set (see Figure 5(b)).

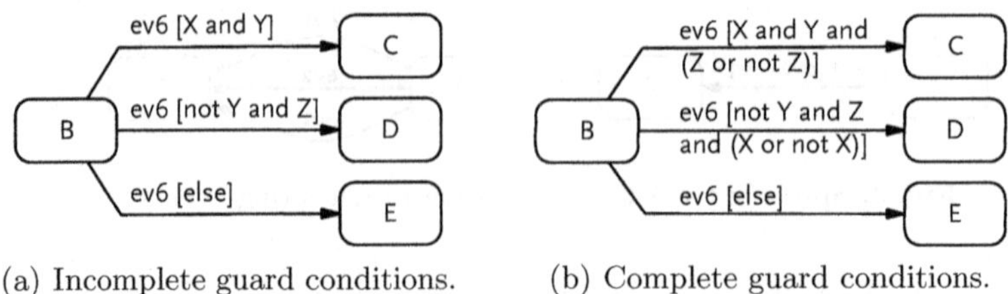

(a) Incomplete guard conditions. (b) Complete guard conditions.

Fig. 5. Add missing elements of B's influencing expression set

Table 3. Mutation analysis with additional dynamic test goal adaptation

Coverage Criterion	Efficient TM/SUT		Redundant TM/SUT	
	Test Suite Size	Mutation Score	Test Suite Size	Mutation Score
TC	34 (-2)	189/255 (+4)	131 (-3)	634/872 (+7)
masking MC/DC	50 (+1)	226/255 (+14)	215 (+1)	820/872 (+13)
MCC	57 (+0)	229/255 (+12)	274 (+0)	842/872 (+15)

Although this test model transformation solves the described problem, it creates a new one: The effect of condition-based coverage criteria depends on the structure of conditions [20]. Test model transformations change the structure of conditions and, thus, also influence the effect of the applied coverage criteria (possibly to a disadvantage).

We consider the dynamic adaptation of test goals the best solution. That means that ParTeG checks for each test goal if there are several target states. In this case, the conditions to satisfy the test goal are extended so that they satisfy the original test goal and missing elements of the influencing expression set are added. In our example, one test goal requires the satisfaction of *[X and (not Y)]*, which has two possible target states. The adapted test goal requires the satisfaction of *[X and (not Y) and Z]* or *[X and (not Y) and (not Z)]*. For each of these conditions, there is only one resulting target state. As a consequence, the oracle of each test case can predict the expected target state for each event trigger and the corresponding test case is able to detect more mutants. We implemented this dynamic test goal adaptation in ParTeG and generated the test suites again. Table 3 shows the results of the subsequent mutation analysis.

4.4 Choice Pseudostate Splitting

The state machine in Figure 3 contains transitions t_{no} that are not triggered explicitly. A problem occurs if a vertex has several incoming transitions and several outgoing transitions of type t_{no} with guard conditions. The satisfaction of a condition-based coverage criterion such as MC/DC or MCC is focussed on value assignments for guard conditions. It is not influenced by traversed transition paths. As a consequence, the value assignments can be distributed over several paths containing transitions t_{no}. Figure 6(a) shows a corresponding part of the state machine. The outgoing transitions of the choice pseudostate are not explicitly triggered by events. Each condition-based coverage criterion is

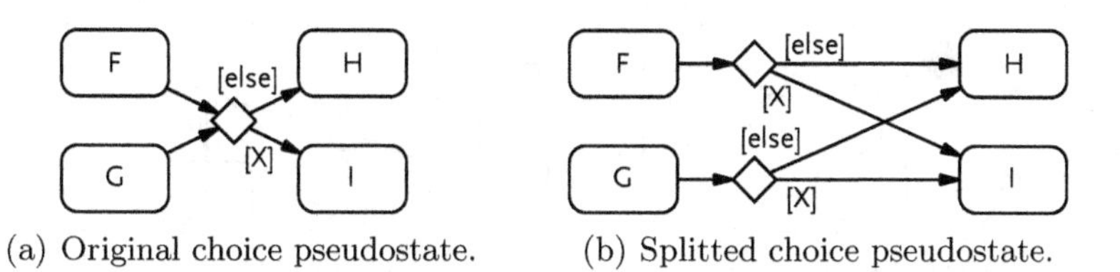

(a) Original choice pseudostate. (b) Splitted choice pseudostate.

Fig. 6. Split the choice pseudostate according to its incoming transitions

already satisfied, e.g. if the guard *[X]* is satisfied on a path including the state F and if *[else]* is satisfied on a path including the state G. Consequently, *[X]* may not be satisfied for paths including state G and *[else]* may not be satisfied for paths including state F. All corresponding mutants will remain unkilled.

The application of transition sequence-based coverage criteria [8, page 118] is no solution because they neglect guard values. We know of no coverage criterion that is focussed on transition sequences and on the value assignment of guards' atomic conditions at the same time. Our solution comprises a test model transformation – each choice pseudostate is split up according to its incoming transitions: Each new choice pseudostate has only one incoming transition but all outgoing transitions of the original choice pseudostate (see Figure 6(b)). As a consequence of this transformation, the satisfaction of condition-based coverage criteria implies that each guard condition on outgoing transitions of choice pseudostates has to be covered for each source state (F and G in the example). We implemented this test model transformation and rerun the test generation. Table 4 shows the results of the subsequent mutation analysis.

Table 4. Results of mutation analysis with splitted choice pseudostates

Coverage Criterion	Efficient TM/SUT		Redundant TM/SUT	
	Test Suite Size	Mutation Score	Test Suite Size	Mutation Score
TC	47 (+13)	209/255 (+20)	144 (+13)	660/872 (+26)
masking MC/DC	61 (+11)	239/255 (+13)	226 (+11)	840/872 (+20)
MCC	68 (+11)	241/255 (+12)	285 (+11)	860/872 (+18)

4.5 Composite States Transformation

Several choice pseudostates of the test model are contained in composite states and directly connected to the composite state's initial state (see Figure 7(a)). Since there is only one incoming transition for such choice pseudostates, all compound transitions from outside the composite state are united in the initial state and the previous test model transformation had no effect. For this case, we had to split incoming compound transitions [1, page 568] instead of splitting incoming transitions: We transform the initial state into an entry point of the composite state and connect it to all incoming transitions of the composite state (see Figure 7(b)). After that, the entry point is duplicated so that there is only one incoming transition for each entry point (see Figure 7(c)) and each entry point is connected to exactly one outer state (H and I). Furthermore, the choice

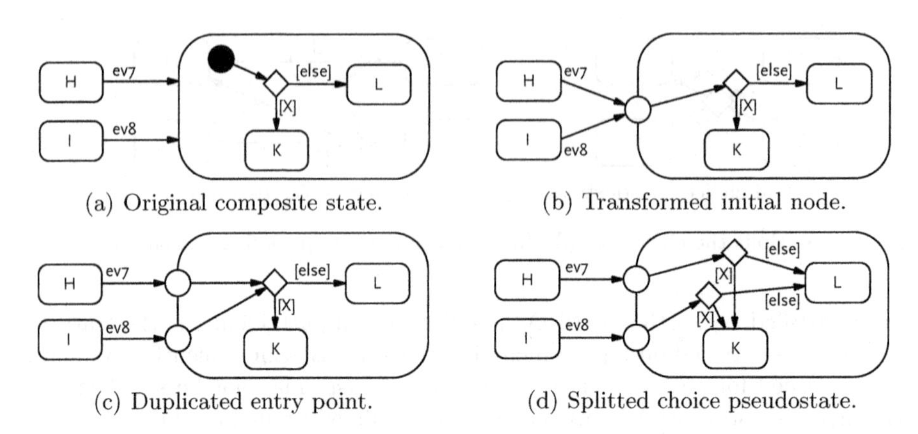

(a) Original composite state.

(b) Transformed initial node.

(c) Duplicated entry point.

(d) Splitted choice pseudostate.

Fig. 7. Transform composite states

Table 5. Mutation analysis with additionally transformed composite states

Coverage Criterion	Efficient TM/SUT		Redundant TM/SUT	
	Test Suite Size	Mutation Score	Test Suite Size	Mutation Score
TC	51 (+4)	213/255 (+4)	148 (+4)	661/872 (+1)
masking MC/DC	65 (+4)	242/255 (+3)	229 (+3)	843/872 (+3)
MCC	72 (+4)	244/255 (+3)	288 (+3)	863/872 (+3)

pseudostate has now several incoming transitions and the transformation of Section 4.4 results in several choice pseudostates (see Figure 7(d)). As a consequence of this adaptation, the guard conditions of choice pseudostates are also tested across boundaries of composite states for each start state of compound transitions. We implemented this model transformation in ParTeG and regenerated the test suite. Table 5 shows the results of the subsequent mutation analysis.

4.6 Coverage Criteria Combination

Mutation analysis showed that the generated test suites did not kill all detectable mutants. A closer look at the remaining mutants revealed that they are caused by small changes of boundary values in conditions with (in-)equations and variables of linear ordered types. For instance, if the correct SUT contained a condition $[x > 5]$, then the unkilled mutants could contain $[x > 4]$ or $[x \geq 5]$, instead. To detect such mutants, boundary value analysis had to be included in the test suite generation. Our tool ParTeG was created to deal with boundary value analysis. Boundary coverage criteria like Multi-Dimensional (MD) [16] are combined with control flow-based coverage criteria: For each abstract test case generated to satisfy one of the three introduced coverage criteria, the concrete input values are selected according to the boundary coverage criterion MD (cp. [17]). These combined coverage criteria are denoted with a preceding MD. We regenerated the test suites for all three considered coverage criteria combinations. The subsequent mutation analysis showed that the test suites that satisfy MDMCC (combination

Table 6. Mutation analysis with additionally combined coverage criteria

Combined Coverage Criterion	Efficient TM/SUT		Redundant TM/SUT	
	Test Suite Size	Mutation Score	Test Suite Size	Mutation Score
MDTC	102 (+51)	222/255 (+9)	296 (+148)	672/872 (+11)
masking MDMC/DC	128 (+63)	251/255 (+9)	456 (+227)	852/872 (+9)
MDMCC	140 (+68)	255/255 (+11)	572 (+284)	872/872 (+9)

of MD and MCC) on the efficient respectively redundant test model killed all mutants of the corresponding SUT (see Table 6).

4.7 Impact of the SUT

In the previous sections, we presented the results of running test suites derived from the efficient state machine on the efficient SUT and of running test suites derived from the redundant state machine on the redundant SUT. The results for both scenarios are comparable. In both cases, however, we assumed that the SUT and the test model have a similar degree of redundancy. Since the implementation details of the company's SUT are unknown, we also investigated the impact of the SUT redundancy on the fault detection ability of the test suite. For reasons of conciseness, we present the mutation analysis results just once for all the adaptations presented from Section 4.2 to 4.6.

Table 7 shows the results of the mutation analysis for the combination of efficient test model and redundant SUT as well as the results for the combination of redundant test model and efficient SUT: If the test model is efficient but the SUT is redundant, then the fault detection ability of the generated test suite is very low. None of the used coverage criteria killed at least one third of all detectable mutants! The results of the mutation analysis for the test suites derived from the redundant state machine applied to the efficient SUT are also not optimal: The test suite generated from the efficient state machine using MDMCC already killed all detectable mutants and no improvement of the fault detection ability is possible. Instead, the test suite size increased: the number of test cases is more than quadrupled for MDMCC.

Table 7. Combinations of efficient and redundant test models and SUT

Combined Coverage Criterion	Efficient TM/Redundant SUT		Redundant TM/Efficient SUT	
	Test Suite Size	Mutation Score	Test Suite Size	Mutation Score
MDTC	102	240/872	296	226/255
masking MDMC/DC	128	285/872	456	251/255
MDMCC	140	289/872	572	255/255

During the presented test generation process, the company's SUT was unknown to us. After delivering the test suites, however, we got feed-back about the number of failed test cases (see Table 8) and a short analysis of the reasons. Following that analysis, the test suite generated from the efficient test model detected one fault that caused four test cases to fail and the test suite generated from the redundant test model detected two faults that caused thirty-two test

Table 8. Failed tests and detected faults on the company's SUT

Combined Coverage Criterion	Efficient Test Model		Redundant Test Model	
	Failed Tests	Detected Faults	Failed Tests	Detected Faults
MDMCC	4/140	1	32/572	2

cases to fail. In random testing, this result might not surprise. Big test suites are likely to detect more faults than small test suites. Here, however, the test suites are generated from the same behavioral information using the same coverage criteria. Thus, the test model redundancy has an important impact: The test suite for the redundant test model does contain more test cases that detect a fault but also detects a higher absolute number of faults. This substantiates the importance of the described adaptations in realistic scenarios as well as the importance of considering different levels of test model redundancy.

5 Conclusion, Discussion and Future Work

Conclusion. In this paper, we reported on an industrial cooperation with a German rail engineering company. We described the initial situation and all the occurred relevant challenges of model-based black-box testing. We presented a solution for each occurred challenge. The application of all solutions resulted in the detection of all detectable mutants. We measured the fault detection ability of the generated test suites with mutation analysis on artificial SUTs and also got feed-back about the execution of the final test suites on the company's SUT. The goal of the presented cooperation was to investigate model-based testing before adopting it as a new testing technique. We were able to convince our client of the benefits of model-based testing: The quality of the generated test suites was comparable to manually created test suites and model-based testing requires considerably lower maintenance effort than manual test creation.

The contribution of this paper is the presented procedure for model-based testing in an industrial scenario with a hidden SUT. The main benefit of this procedure is the increased fault detection ability for automatically generated test suites. Novel elements of this report are the application of artificial SUTs, the purposeful transformation of test models, the adaptation of test goals, and the combination of coverage criteria in an industrial application.

Discussion. Most of the presented results can also be reached by improving the used test generator. In most cases, however, the tester has no influence on the used (commercial) test generator and the presented test model transformations are the only way to increase the generated test suite's fault detection ability.

Beyond, the result of this report is not a recommendation to create redundant test models as a new kind of "modeling paradigm". Such models would be hard to maintain. Instead, we recommend to create and maintain efficient test models, to transform copies of them automatically, and to use these transformed copies for automatic model-based test generation. Test models have to be adapted if the SUT is changed. Since test models are in general easier to understand than source code and test suites are generated automatically, we consider the corresponding effort lower than the effort for adapting manually created test suites.

We were skeptical about applying artificial SUTs for mutation analysis. There is no guarantee that a good mutation score on artificial SUTs implies a good mutation score for the company's SUT. Reasons can be that some information is missing in the test model. In our case, however, this technique was quite successful. As shown in Section 4.7, the artificial SUTs were necessary to improve the fault detection ability of test suites generated from redundant test models. Furthermore, the presented influencing factors were only investigated for artifical SUTs and it is questionable if their application also leads to the detection of all mutants in the company's SUT. However, the presented report shows that the adaptations do have a positive impact on the fault detection ability of the generated test suites.

We presented the incremental effect of the adaptations, i.e. the results of each adaptation already included the results of all previous adaptations. This is especially obvious for the adaptations in Sections 4.4 and 4.5, for which the second one is only intended to improve the effect of the first one. An isolated investigation of all adaptations would be interesting. This report just presents our experiences during the cooperation.

Furthermore, the combination of coverage criteria resulted in doubling the test suite size. Several case studies (e.g., in [26]) estimate an exponential growth of the test suite size with respect to the mutation score. These case studies also point out the importance of satisfying the last 10-20% of the (mutant) coverage.

Future Work. We consider the presented test model transformations very important. There are approaches to use them to increase the test suite's fault detection ability [12,20] and we reported on a few more. To our knowledge, however, there is no broad comparison of coverage criteria satisfaction and test model transformation. We assume that many coverage criteria can be satisfied by satisfying a possibly weaker coverage criterion on a transformed test model [21]. This would be a great support for commercial model-based test generators that are only able to satisfy a limited set of coverage criteria. As presented in Section 4.4, it is also possible to combine condition-based and transition-based coverage criteria beyond the sole union of the corresponding test suites. In the future, we plan to investigate the impact of test model transformations on coverage criteria satisfaction. We also plan to investigate the combination of different coverage criteria.

Furthermore, we used a technique to dynamically adapt test goals in Section 4.3. As presented in [2], the adaptation of test goals is an interesting research topic. It would be interesting to also categorize possible test goal adaptations and identify their impact on the test generation process.

Acknowledgements. This work was supported by grants from the DFG (German Research Foundation, research training group METRIK).

References

1. Object Management Group: Unified Modeling Language (UML), version 2.1 (2007)
2. Fraser, G., Wotawa, F.: Ordering coverage goals in model checker based testing. In: ICSTW 2008: Proceedings of the 2008 IEEE ICST Workshop, vol. 0, pp. 31–40 (2008)
3. Weißleder, S.: ParTeG (Partition Test Generator), `http://parteg.sourceforge.net`
4. Ammann, P., Offutt, J.: Introduction to Software Testing. Cambridge University Press, New York (2008)
5. Binder, R.V.: Testing object-oriented systems: models, patterns, and tools. Addison-Wesley Longman Publishing Co., Inc. (1999)
6. Myers, G.J.: Art of Software Testing. John Wiley & Sons, Inc., New York (1979)
7. Broy, M., Jonsson, B., Katoen, J.P.: Model-Based Testing of Reactive Systems: Advanced Lectures. LNCS, vol. 3472. Springer, Heidelberg (2005)
8. Utting, M., Legeard, B.: Practical Model-Based Testing: A Tools Approach. Morgan Kaufmann Publishers Inc., San Francisco (2006)
9. Offutt, J., Abdurazik, A.: Generating tests from UML specifications. In: France, R.B., Rumpe, B. (eds.) UML 1999. LNCS, vol. 1723, pp. 416–429. Springer, Heidelberg (1999)
10. Sokenou, D.: Generating Test Sequences from UML Sequence Diagrams and State Diagrams. In: INFORMATIK 2006, pp. 236–240 (2006)
11. Abdurazik, A., Offutt, J.: Using UML collaboration diagrams for static checking and test generation. In: Evans, A., Kent, S., Selic, B. (eds.) UML 2000. LNCS, vol. 1939, pp. 383–395. Springer, Heidelberg (2000)
12. Friske, M., Schlingloff, B.H.: Improving Test Coverage for UML State Machines Using Transition Instrumentation. In: Saglietti, F., Oster, N. (eds.) SAFECOMP 2007. LNCS, vol. 4680, pp. 301–314. Springer, Heidelberg (2007)
13. Weißleder, S., Schlingloff, B.H.: Deriving Input Partitions from UML Models for Automatic Test Generation. In: Giese, H. (ed.) MODELS 2008. LNCS, vol. 5002, pp. 151–163. Springer, Heidelberg (2008)
14. Lämmel, R., Harm, J.: Test case characterisation by regular path expressions. In: Brinksma, E., Tretmans, J. (eds.) Proc. Formal Approaches to Testing of Software (FATES 2001). Notes Series NS-01-4, BRICS, pp. 109–124 (2001)
15. Briand, L.C., Labiche, Y., Lin, Q.: Improving statechart testing criteria using data flow information. In: ISSRE 2005, pp. 95–104 (2005)
16. Kosmatov, N., Legeard, B., Peureux, F., Utting, M.: Boundary Coverage Criteria for Test Generation from Formal Models. In: ISSRE 2004, pp. 139–150. IEEE, Los Alamitos (2004)
17. Weißleder, S., Schlingloff, B.-H.: Quality of Automatically Generated Test Cases based on OCL Expressions. In: ICST, pp. 517–520. IEEE Computer Society, Los Alamitos (2008)
18. Chilenski, J.J., Miller, S.P.: Applicability of Modified Condition/Decision Coverage to Software Testing. Software Engineering Journal (1994)
19. Ranville, S.: MCDC Test Vectors From Matlab Models – Automatically. In: Embedded Systems Conference, San Francisco, USA (2003)
20. Rajan, A., Whalen, M.W., Heimdahl, M.P.E.: The effect of program and model structure on mc/dc test adequacy coverage. In: ICSE 2008, pp. 161–170. ACM, New York (2008)

21. Weißleder, S.: Semantic-Preserving Test Model Transformations for Interchangeable Coverage Criteria. In: MBEES 2009: Model-Based Development of Embedded Systems (April 2009)
22. Offutt, A.J., Lee, A., Rothermel, G., Untch, R.H., Zapf, C.: An experimental determination of sufficient mutant operators. ACM Transactions on Software Engineering and Methodology, 99–118 (1996)
23. Offutt, A.J., Lee, S.D.: An empirical evaluation of weak mutation. IEEE Transactions on Software Engineering 20(5), 337–344 (1994)
24. Black, P.E., Okun, V., Yesha, Y.: Mutation Operators for Specifications. In: ASE 2000: Proceedings of the 15th IEEE international conference on Automated software engineering, Washington, DC, USA, p. 81. IEEE Computer Society, Los Alamitos (2000)
25. Andrews, J.H., Briand, L.C., Labiche, Y.: Is mutation an appropriate tool for testing experiments? In: ICSE 2005, pp. 402–411. ACM, New York (2005)
26. Andrews, J.H., Briand, L.C., Labiche, Y., Namin, A.S.: Using Mutation Analysis for Assessing and Comparing Testing Coverage Criteria. IEEE Transactions on Software Engineering 32, 608–624 (2006)
27. Paradkar, A.: Case studies on fault detection effectiveness of model based test generation techniques. In: A-MOST 2005, pp. 1–7. ACM Press, New York (2005)
28. Chilenski, J.J.: MCDC Forms (Unique-Cause, Masking) versus Error Sensitivity, a white paper submitted to NASA Langley Research Center under contract NAS1-20341 (January 2001)
29. Certification Authorities Software Team: Position Paper-6: Rationale for Accepting Masking MC/DC in Certification Projects (2001)
30. Budnik, C.J., Subramanyan, R., Vieira, M.: Peer-to-peer comparison of model-based test tools. In: GI Jahrestagung (1). LNI, vol. 133, pp. 223–226. GI (2008)

Towards Composite Model Transformations Using Distributed Graph Transformation Concepts

Stefan Jurack and Gabriele Taentzer

Philipps-Universität Marburg, Germany
{sjurack,taentzer}@mathematik.uni-marburg.de

Abstract. Model-based development of highly complex software systems leads to large models. Storing them in repositories offers the possibility to work with these models in a distributed environment. However, they are not modularized and thus, do not especially support distributed development. An alternative is to consider composite models such that several teams can work largely independently. In this paper, we consider a general approach to composite models and their transformation based on graph transformation concepts. To illustrate this approach, we present a concrete setting for composite models based on the Eclipse Modeling Framework (EMF). EMF models can be distributed over several sites. While remote references can express import relations, export and import interfaces are not explicitly defined. In our approach, we sketch composite models with explicit and implicit interfaces using concepts of distributed graph transformation and outline different kinds of composite model transformations.

Keywords: Distributed modeling, graph transformation, Eclipse.

1 Introduction

Model-based software development has an increasing importance in software engineering. Models are ideal means for abstraction and support developers in mastering the increasing complexity of software systems. Highly complex software systems are usually developed by several teams working in a distributed setting. The question arises how model-based development can be performed by several distributed teams. An obvious idea is to set up a central repository for models which can be used by all teams. This solution is straight forward to implement. However, this solution is not always adequate: Considering for example open source development, software components are developed by independent teams. Thus, a central model repository would not suit well to this separation of concerns.

An alternative is a set of component models which are interconnected, i.e. composite models. To allow for independent component model development as much as possible, each component model should have explicit import and export interfaces. The import interfaces specify all required model parts, while the export interfaces describe model elements provided to the environment, i.e. to models of other teams.

Model-based and especially model-driven development heavily rely on model transformations. After having defined composite models, we also need transformation concepts for composite models. In this paper, we consider a general setting for composite

A. Schürr and B. Selic (Eds.): MODELS 2009, LNCS 5795, pp. 226–240, 2009.

model transformations and do not focus on transformation languages. On this basis, we discuss different kinds of composite transformations and formulate a consistency property for a restricted form of composite model transformations. All main concepts presented are formally defined to lay a basis for a precise approach to composite model transformation. This approach is based on the theory of algebraic graph transformation [1].

New concepts are motivated at two different development scenarios for component-oriented software systems: model-based development of business components and model-driven development of graphical editors. The second scenario is based on modeling concepts of the Eclipse Modeling Framework (EMF) [2]. EMF has evolved to one of the standard technologies for defining modeling languages. It provides a modeling and code generation framework for Eclipse applications based on structured data models. The modeling approach is similar to that of MOF, actually EMF supports Essential MOF (EMOF) as part of the OMG MOF 2.0 specification.

There are several approaches to manipulate EMF models by model transformations, e.g. ATL [3], Tefkat [4], EMF Tiger [5]. Since the focus of this paper is on general structuring concepts for models and model transformations, we do not consider transformation approaches in detail, but just as partial mappings between models.

This paper is structured as follows: Section 2 presents two example scenarios for composite model development. The second one is used to illustrate all main concepts of composite models and model transformations presented in Sections 3 and 4. Thereafter, we discuss related work and conclude our work.

2 Example Scenarios for the Development of Composite Software Models

In this section, we present two example scenarios for composite model development by distributed teams which differ considerably. The first scenario describes model-based development of a component-oriented business application, while the second scenario presents model-driven development of graphical editors.

2.1 Developing Composite Models for Component-Oriented Business Applications

Highly complex software systems are usually designed as component-oriented systems. Main functionality is structured in several components with clear interfaces. Reflecting this high-level design decision in composite models, the model-based development of business components by separate teams is supported. As long as all interfaces are stable, each team can work on its model, independently of other teams. However, it is quite natural that interfaces change over time. In that case, the distributed development can run into conflicts. For example, considering a software solution for ordering and delivering products, we might have components such as ordering, marketing and customer management, billing, and delivery. Each component has local data and data to be shared using interfaces. Moreover, each component offers a number of services such as adding, deleting, updating and searching customers offered by the customer management. While customer data manipulation is designed to be local to the customer management, searching is considered to be exported to other components. Furthermore, all detail information about customers are not considered for export, but just their names and some information on their classification (e.g. business or private customer). If for example, the export of customer data is to be extended by address information, the distributed development teams have to communicate with each other to clarify this situation. In contrast, private data is changed internally in the customer management component model.

2.2 Composite Models for Graphical Editor Development

Assume a domain modeler who cares about mapping the application domain to a data model as well as to services. Additionally, there are editor designers who develop domain-specific editors showing the domain model in one or more different views. The editor development shall be model-driven using the Graphical Modeling Framework (GMF) [6]. Similarly, the domain model might be a source for model-driven development used to generate a data base and data access objects. To support decoupling of domain model and editor development to some extent, we use a composite model which contains the domain model and the editor model as two components which are interconnected by interfaces. This means that the domain model may be extended and new model elements may be exported or editors may be changed as long as their import interfaces are not extended. We use this scenario to further illustrate our concepts for composite models and model transformations.

3 Composite Models Based on Distributed Graph Concepts

Modular concepts for software models are of increasing interest to the modeling community. The state-of-the-art concept to structure EMF models are physical distribution in separate files. They can be interconnected by remote references, i.e. references to remote model elements. This means that composite EMF models are supported and realized by uniform resource identifiers which allow to identify remote model elements. The lookup of remote model elements is realized by proxy model elements which resolve remote references. This mechanism realizes composite models with implicit interfaces. Remote references implicitly define an import interface. Additionally, all model elements are automatically exported, i.e. export interfaces are also defined implicitly. At the moment, there are no concepts for EMF models to declare import and export interfaces explicitly.

In this section, we want to consider composite models with different kinds of interconnections. One approach are component models with explicit import and export interfaces. To connect component models, import interfaces have to be served by export interfaces. This approach supports the explicit statement of all requirements in import interfaces and furthermore, allows to distinguish between public model elements, visible in exports, and private model elements. The explicit declaration of interfaces allows to define component models independently of each other and to connect them later, if their corresponding interfaces fit together.

The abstract syntax of software models can be considered as object structures which are formally defined by typed graphs with attributes and containment conditions. (See

[7].) Since we concentrate on the component aspect of models here, we do not consider attributes and containments throughout this paper. However, these aspects are orthogonal and can be added in a straight forward way.

In the following, we formally define distributed graphs in a general setting. Based on this definition, different kinds of composite models are discussed thereafter. Graphs consist of nodes and edges, i.e. edges are elements with their own identifiers. They relate nodes by source and target functions.

Definition 1 (Graph). *A graph $G = (G_N, G_E, s_G, t_G)$ consists of a set G_N of nodes, a set G_E of edges, as well as source and target functions $s_G, t_G : G_E \to G_N$.*

Definition 2 (Partial Graph Morphism). *Given two graphs G, H, a pair of partial functions (f_N, f_E) with $f_N : G_N \to H_N$ and $f_E : G_E \to H_E$ forms a partial graph morphism $f : G \to H$, short graph morphism, if it has the following properties:*

- $\forall e \in dom(f_E) : f_N \circ s_G(e) = s_H \circ f_E(e), with\ s_G(e) \in dom(f_N)$
- $\forall e \in dom(f_E) : f_N \circ t_G(e) = t_H \circ f_E(e), with\ t_G(e) \in dom(f_N)$

If f_N and f_E are both total, f is called total *graph morphism.*

All graphs and graph morphisms form a category, called $\mathcal{P}GRAPH$. This means that partial morphisms can be composed and for each graph there is an identity morphism. Similarly, all graphs and total graph morphisms as defined above form a category, called $GRAPH$. (For more information concerning these categories, see [8,1].) We use this fact to define the composition concepts presented throughout this paper.

Next, we recall type graphs to distinguish type and instance levels in our formal setting. Since we concentrate on composition concepts and want to keep the formalization as simple as possible within this paper, we do not consider subtypes here.

Definition 3 (Typed Graph). *Given a graph TG, called type graph, and a graph G. Graph G is typed over TG, if there is a total graph morphism $type\colon G \to TG$.*

Please note that the abstract syntax of software models can be formalized by typed graphs. (See e.g. [7] for a formalization of EMF models.) Composite models are not especially considered in that approach, but could be encoded in graphs. However, for an explicit consideration of composition concepts for models, it is better to separate the composition structure from object structures. In the following, we define distributed graphs which use graph concepts on two different abstraction levels: the network level and the object level. The network level describes the composition structure, while the object level specifies the object structures in each part as well as their interrelations.

Definition 4 (Distributed Graph). *Given a graph G, called network graph, a distributed graph over G is defined by functor $\hat{G} : G \to \mathcal{P}GRAPH$*[1].

[1] Graph G can induce a small category which contains all identical arrows on nodes and for each pair of arrows $i \xrightarrow{a} j$ and $j \xrightarrow{b} k$ in G an arrow $i \xrightarrow{c} k$. Functors are mappings between categories. See [9] for more details.

The network graph of a distributed graph defines its distribution structure. Each network node i is related to a graph $\hat{G}(i)$, called *local graph*, which describes a local object structure, while each network edge $e : i \rightarrow j$ is refined by a partial graph morphism $\hat{G}(e)\colon \hat{G}(i) \rightarrow \hat{G}(j)$, called *local graph morphism*. These morphisms can formalize relations between object structures.

In general, network graphs can specify arbitrary networks of models. In the following, we discuss two particular kinds of composite models.

Component models with shared interfaces are described by bipartite network graphs. Network nodes are either body nodes or interface nodes. Network edges always go from interface to body nodes. This kind of structure describes components which share objects in common interfaces. Thus, network edges are inclusions.

Networks of component models can be described by different kinds of composite models. We distinguish components with implicit interface definitions from those with explicit ones. See examples for distributed graphs with implicit and explicit interfaces in Fig. 1. Interface inclusion are indicated by arrow label $\subseteq$. Partial morphisms are depicted by arrows with a circle in the middle.

$$\hat{G}(i_A) \longrightarrow \hat{G}(i_B) \;\Big|\; \hat{G}(i_{BodA}) \xleftarrow{\supseteq} \hat{G}(i_{ImpA}) \longrightarrow \hat{G}(i_{ExpB}) \xrightarrow{\subseteq} \hat{G}(i_{BodB})$$

Fig. 1. Distributed graphs specifying components with implicit (left) and explicit (right) interfaces

A component with implicit interfaces can be described by just one local graph. The import of object nodes from other components is specified by a partial graph morphism. Such import relations can also be made explicit by explicitly showing the domains[2] of partial import morphisms. For example, the current version of EMF models can be considered to be of this kind. Remote references import model elements of other EMF models. (See the following examples for more details.)

A component model with explicit interfaces consists of a body model, a set of export interfaces, and a set of import interfaces all being parts of the body. Thus, all graph morphisms between export or import graphs on the one hand and body graphs on the other hand are intended to be inclusions, i.e. special total graph morphisms. Connecting two or more components, each import graph has to be connected to an export graph. This connection is defined by a partial graph morphism. If this graph morphism is really partial, i.e. not total, it describes an import which is not fully served by the export connected. Thus for component models with explicit interfaces, a network structure with total morphisms only is considered to describe a consistent composite model.

Considering network structures of component models with explicit interfaces, we can characterize the three different kinds of component parts described above by the following network properties:

- Body nodes are network nodes $G_{Bod} \subseteq G_N$ which are not source of any network edge in G_E.

[2] The domain of definition wrt. a partial graph morphism is meant here.

- Export nodes are network nodes $G_{Exp} \subseteq G_N$ where each export node is source of exactly one network edge with its target being a body part. I.e. for all $i \in G_{Exp}$ there is an edge $e \in G_E$ with $s_G(e) = i$ and $t_G(e) \in G_{Bod}$. Moreover, $\hat{G}(e)$ is a total graph morphism, namely an inclusion.
- Import nodes are network nodes $G_{Imp} \subseteq G_N$ where each import node is source of two or more network edges: The target of one network edge is a body part, i.e. for all $i \in G_{Imp}$ there is a network edge $e_B \in G_E$ with $s_G(e_B) = i$ and $t_G(e_B) \in G_{Bod}$. $\hat{G}(e_B)$ is a total graph morphism. All other network edges $e_k \in G_E$ with $k \in K$[3] have the import node as source, i.e. $s_G(e_k) = i$, and an export node as target, i.e. $t_G(e_k) \in G_{Exp}$. Each $\hat{G}(e_k)$ may be non-total.

The definition of distributed graphs is very general. It allows relations between graphs to be really partial. While partiality of relations in simple composite models with implicit interfaces is the normal case, real partiality can express some kind of inconsistency within component structures where each import interface is connected to exactly one export interface. In that case, network edges from import to export nodes being refined by non-total graph morphisms express that corresponding imports are not completely served.

Example 1. Fig. 2 shows the network structure of an example composite model on the left-hand side and the corresponding distributed graph on the right-hand side as defined in Def. 4. The network structure contains three components each consisting of a body part as well as export and/or import interfaces each. While body parts are represented by solid boxes, interfaces are depicted by dotted boxes.

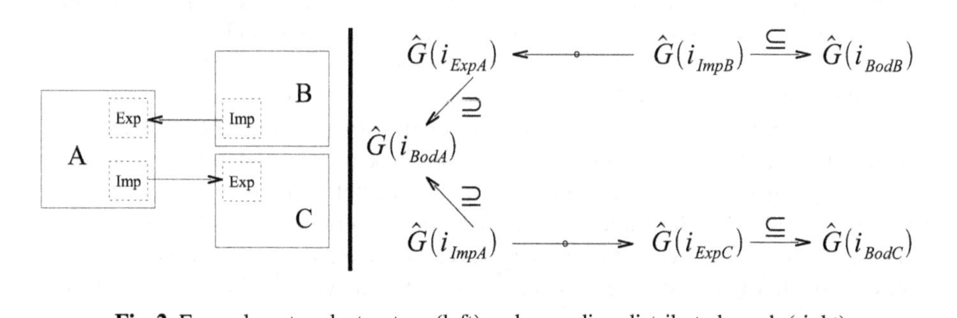

Fig. 2. Example network structure (left) and according distributed graph (right)

Definition 5 (Partial Distributed Graph Morphism). *A* partial distributed graph morphism, *short* distributed graph morphism, *between two distributed graphs $\hat{G}$ and $\hat{H}$ with network graphs G and H, is a pair $\hat{f} = (f, m)$ where*

- *$f: G \to H$ is a graph morphism and*
- *m is a family of graph morphisms $\{\hat{f}(n) | n \in G_N\}$ such that*
  - *for all nodes i in G_N : $\hat{f}(i): \hat{G}(i) \to \hat{H}(i)$ is a partial graph morphism and*

[3] K is a set of indices.

- *for all edges* $e : i \to j$ *in* G_E : $\hat{f}(j) \circ \hat{G}(e)(x) = \hat{H}(\hat{f}(e)) \circ \hat{f}(i)(x)$ *for all* $x \in dom(\hat{f}(j) \circ \hat{G}(e)) \cap dom(\hat{H}(\hat{f}(e)) \circ \hat{f}(i)(x))$ *(see the illustration in Fig. 3).*

If f *and* $\hat{f}(i)$ *for all* $i \in G_N$ *are total graph morphisms,* $\hat{f}$ *is also called* total.

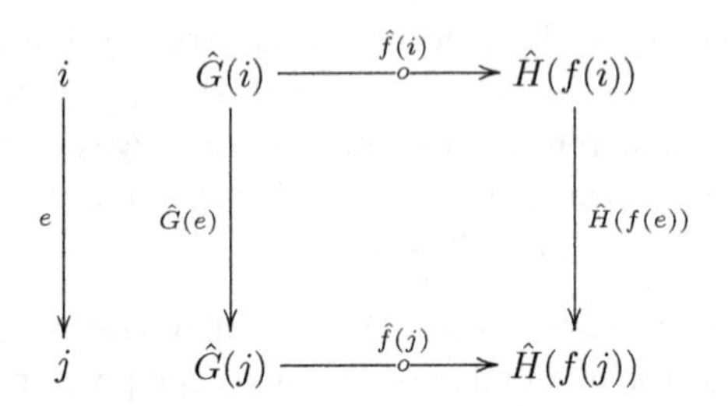

Fig. 3. Illustration of partial distributed graph morphism

Definition 6 (Typed Distributed Graph). *Given a distributed graph* $\hat{TG}$*, called distributed type graph, and a distributed graph* $\hat{G}$*. Graph* $\hat{G}$ *is typed over* $\hat{TG}$ *if there is a total distributed graph morphism* $\hat{type}: \hat{G} \to \hat{TG}$*.*

Example 2. In the following, we illustrate typed composite models by the editor development scenario introduced in Section 2.2. The domain model is based on EMF and the editor model uses GMF which in turn is an EMF model itself. We illustrate component models with explicit interfaces.

Fig. 4 shows a network structure for a typed composite model. At the top row, component model *Ecore* with an export interface and component model *gmfmap* with an import interface are shown. *Ecore* is the meta-model of EMF and used for domain modeling. Meta-model *gmfmap* is one of several meta-models of GMF each targeting different editor aspects. For clarity we stick to *gmfmap* only. While *Ecore* and *gmfmap* meta-models form body models on the type level, *website* and *pageeditor* are instances of them. In the following examples we show both, type models and instances, as trees. However, the underlying abstract syntax is graph-like. Note that the interface definition on the type level limits the definition of exports and imports in the instance level.

Fig. 5 shows the refinement of the type level, i.e. refinement of network nodes and edges. On the left-hand side, meta-model *Ecore* is shown by concentrating on its classes

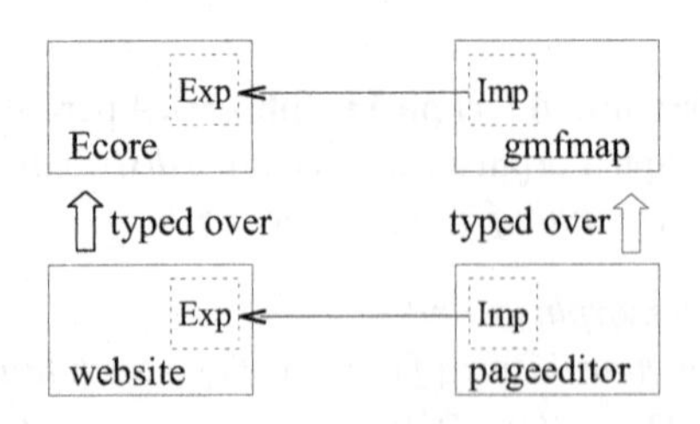

Fig. 4. Example network structure on type and instance levels (cf. detailed presentation of composite models Fig. 5 and Fig. 7)

and inheritance structure. On the right-hand side, classes and inheritance structure of meta-model *gmfmap* are shown. Arrows from right to left visualize references to remote classes where target elements are part of the import interface of *gmfmap*. Fig. 6 shows a more detailed view on remote references. In this case, class *MappingEntry* refers to class *EClass* residing in a different model i.e. *EClass* is part of the import interface of component model *gmfmap* and has to occur in the export interface of component model *Ecore* as well. Since we consider any *Ecore* meta-model element as exported per se in this example, the import of *gmfmap* can be completely mapped to the export of *Ecore*[4].

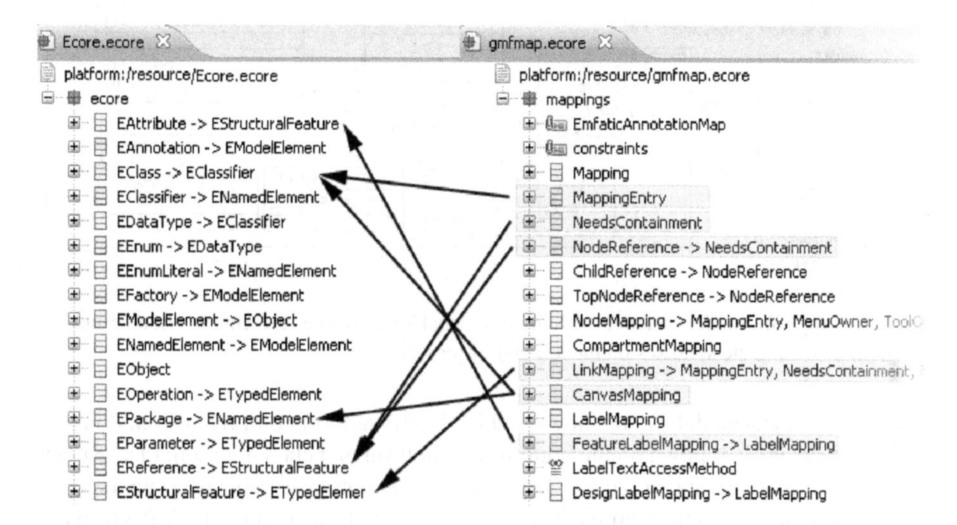

Fig. 5. Condensed view on meta-models *Ecore* and *gmfmap* with arrows showing remote references to imported classes

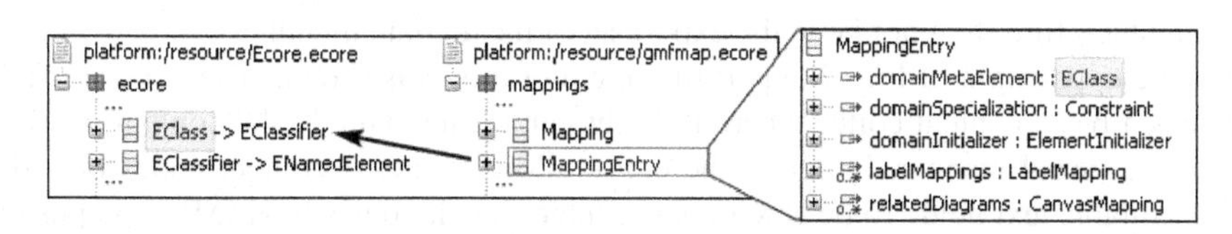

Fig. 6. Detailed view on import relation of meta-model *gmfmap*

Now we consider composite model instances of both meta-models as depicted in Fig. 7. This example shows a domain model for web sites and an editor model for a simple page editor, again in a tree-based view. The names of instance component models also indicate their typing, e.g. *pageeditor.gmfmap* is typed by *gmfmap.ecore*. As for meta-models, arrow targets indicate the import interface.

On the left-hand side, each entry below package *websiteModel* is an instance of *EClass* containing instances of *EAttribute* for its attributes and instances of *EReference*

[4] Please note that a small arrow behind a classes expresses an inheritance relationship. If a parent is exported, its children are exported consequently.

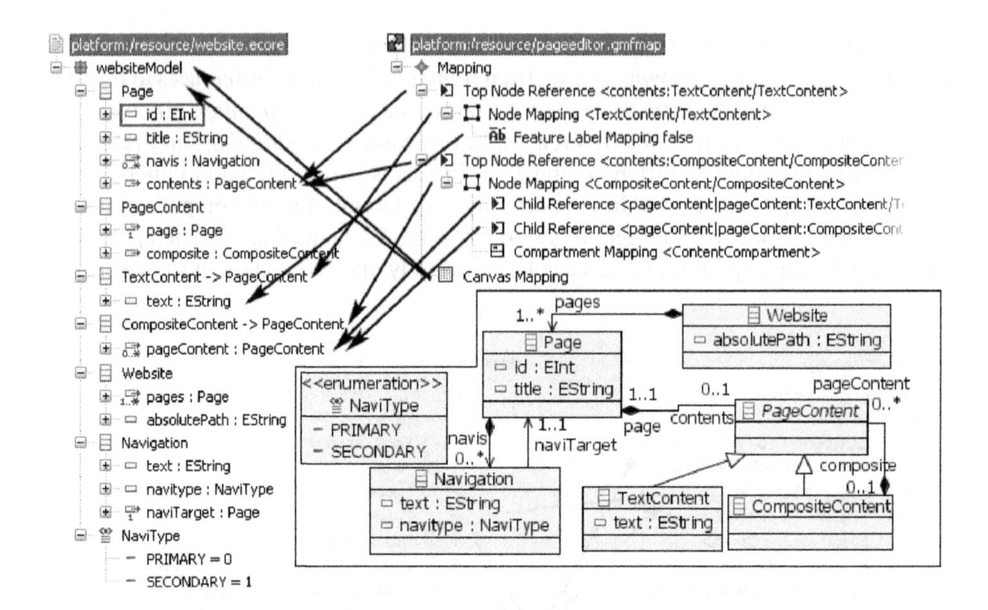

Fig. 7. A composite model instance with arrows visualizing remote references, instance model *website* in two concrete syntaxes on the left and lower right

for links (cf. meta-model *Ecore* shown in Fig. 5). To support comprehension, domain model *website* is also shown on the bottom right in form of a class diagram. Please note that both views, tree view and class diagram, show two kinds of concrete syntaxes. A web site may have several web pages each equipped with textual content. Pages may also have primary and secondary navigation links to other pages. All domain model elements except attribute *Page.id* are exported which is indicated by its red frame. In our model-driven environment, this attribute is relevant for internal generation processes only and therefore shall not be in the export set of the domain model.

On the upper right of Fig. 7, a part of the editor model is shown. The editor model specifies a basic content editor where the user can create and edit the content of web pages in a visual manner. In detail, the editor allows to insert content nodes providing an editable text field. To be able to nest contents analogously to HTML, composite content nodes are provided. New contents may be positioned within such a node. For that purpose two *Top Node Reference* entries (and their sub-entries) are listed in the *gmfmap* model, each one introducing a node type container in the editor. Accordingly, each entry is related to an (exported) element of the domain model. For example, the uppermost *Top Node Reference* represents the container for textual nodes. Therefore, it relates to reference *Page.contents*, the container for textual content in the domain model. Subentry *Node Mapping* is related to class *TextContent* and represents textual content nodes. Moreover, attribute *TextContent.text* is the target of a *Feature Label Mapping*. This entry represents the label of a textual content node containing concrete text. Analogously, a *Top Node Reference* and a *Node Mapping* are defined in correspondence with domain element *CompositeContent*. In addition *Child References* and *Compartment Mapping* are responsible for enabling nested nodes. Since all reference targets in component model *pageeditor* are in the export interface of component model *website*, this composite model is consistent.

4 Basic Concepts of Composite Model Transformations

Now we go one step further and consider transformations on composite models. Independent of any concrete model transformation approach, we can consider composite transformations as partial mappings of composite models. They can describe the major effects of model transformations which can be the creation, deletion or update of model elements and their references. Formally, such model mappings can be defined by partial graph morphisms. Creation of model elements and their references leads to non-surjective morphisms, while deletion of model parts leads to non-total morphisms.

In this paper, we consider basic transformation concepts only. Nevertheless, these concepts allow us to distinguish already four important classes of composite transformations: internal transformations, component transformations, synchronized transformations, and reconfigurations. Moreover, we can distinguish consistent component transformations from inconsistent ones.

Definition 7 (Distributed Graph Transformation). *Given a distributed type graph* $\hat{TG}$ *and two distributed graphs* $\hat{G}$ *and* $\hat{H}$ *typed over* $\hat{TG}$ *by* $\hat{t}_G$ *and* $\hat{t}_H$*, a distributed (graph) transformation is a partial distributed graph morphism* $\hat{tr}: \hat{G} \to \hat{H}$ *such that* $\hat{t}_H \circ \hat{tr} = \hat{t}_G$*. It implicitly defines a network transformation* $tr: G \to H$ *of network graph* G *to* H*.*

We can distinguish different kinds of distributed graph transformations which are presented in the following. Examples for each kind of transformation are given thereafter.

Internal model transformations are defined by transformations of single local graphs. The network transformation *tr* is an identical one, i.e. the network structure does not change. Interfaces, either implicitly or explicitly given, are not changed.

Example 3. On the left-hand side, Fig. 8 shows a *gmfmap* editor model before transformation; the right-hand side shows it afterwards. In this scenario, the editor model is enriched with additional properties which require class *TextContent* and its attribute *TextContent.text* leading to a default attribute value "Enter new text here..." for text nodes in the editor. As the required domain model elements are already contained in the import set (cf. Fig. 7), this transformation has no impact on any interface.

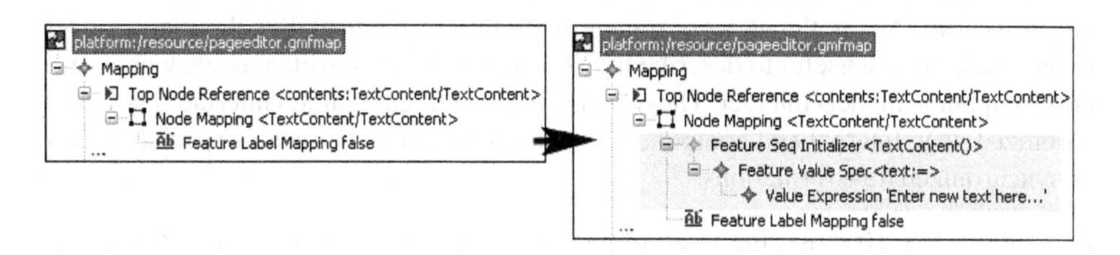

Fig. 8. Adding new editor properties to component model *pageeditor*

Component model transformations are concerned with manipulations of single components in composite structures. Again network structures are not changed, i.e. network transformation tr is identical. Moreover, there may be transformations $\hat{tr}(i_B)\colon \hat{G}(i_B) \to \hat{H}(i_B)$ for network nodes $i_B \in G_{Bod}$ as well as transformations of adjacent interfaces. In general, component transformations can yield inconsistent composite models. However, we can consider a restricted form of component transformations yielding consistent models only. Body and interfaces may be transformed such that synchronizations with other components are not necessary. This means that export interfaces may be extended and import interfaces may be restricted only. Formally, we can require

- for all $i_E \in G_{Exp}$ with $e \in G_E$ and $s(e) = i_E$ and $t(e) = i_B$: $\hat{tr}(e)$ to be total and $\hat{G}(i_E) \subseteq dom(\hat{tr}(i_B))$ and
- for all $i_I \in G_{Imp}$ with $e \in G_E$ and $s(e) = i_I$ and $t(e) = i_B$: $\hat{tr}(e)$ to be surjective and $dom(\hat{tr}(i_I)) \subseteq dom(\hat{tr}(i_B))$.

Later on, we argue that this kind of restricted component transformations yields consistent results only.

Example 4. Figure 9 shows a component transformation of the domain model. Class *ImageContent* is created inheriting from class *PageContent*. Elements of this kind shall be editable, too. Therefore, it has to be included into the export interface of model component $website$. Since the export interface is extended only, the resulting composite model is a consistent one.

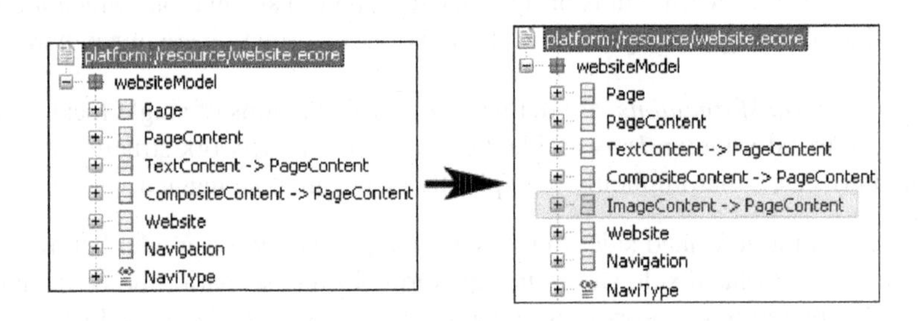

Fig. 9. Creation of a new class in domain model $website$

Synchronized model transformations are defined by several local transformations which run in parallel. Again, the network transformation tr is identical. Synchronized model transformations are useful to describe transformations of composite models where several component models interact. They are needed to change common interfaces in a synchronized way. Internal and component transformations can be seen as special classes of synchronized transformations.

Example 5. Fig. 10 shows the result of an example synchronized transformation. Considering the composite model depicted in Fig. 7, the creation of a new domain model element *ImageContent* as shown in the previous example has to lead to an adaptation of the related page editor. Again, the import mapping is illustrated by arrows from right to left. Note that arrows shown in Fig. 7 remain unaffected and therefore are left out in favor of readability. Three new entries are inserted into the editor model. A new *Top Node Reference* and its subentry directly relate to the domain model element *ImageContent* and its containment within *Page*. The new *Child Reference* entry deals with the fact that image contents may also be contained within a composite content. Therefore, it refers to the containment reference of *CompositeContent* in the domain model. Please note that both extensions, the domain model extension and the editor model extension, may also take place consecutively, first extending the domain model and then adapting the GMF model.

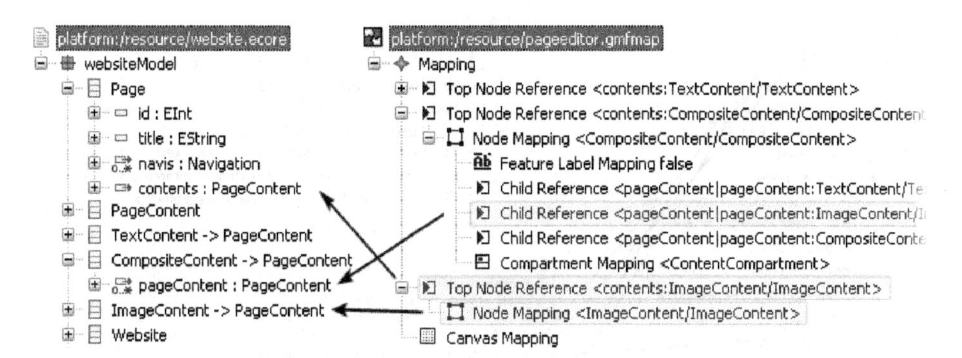

Fig. 10. Result of a synchronized transformation which extends domain model *website* as well as its page editor

Model reconfigurations. In contrast to the previous kinds of composite model transformations, model reconfigurations may change the network structure. Model reconfigurations can require certain modifications of adjacent models to adapt them to the changed network structure. Thus, there can be any synchronized model transformations on preserved network nodes. It is obvious that synchronized model transformations form a subset of reconfigurations.

Formally, model reconfigurations are defined by distributed graph transformations where network transformation tr may be non-identical morphisms here. A new network node may be inserted with an initial local graph, a new network edge with an initial graph morphism. Vice versa, a network node may be deleted together with its local graph. Moreover, (adjacent) network edges are deleted with their refining graph morphisms.

Example 6 (Reconfigurations). Considering again the composite model in Fig. 7, a reconfiguration may be performed as shown in Fig. 11 with the resulting new network structure in the right. The original model components are kept unchanged in our case. A new component model is created specifying a new editor specialized for the navigation system of a website. It provides a new body part with an import interface using the export of the domain model component. The new navigation editor model as shown in the resulting composite model (cf. Fig. 12) shows a *Top Node Reference* element referring to class *Page*, analogously to the page editor model (cf. explanations in

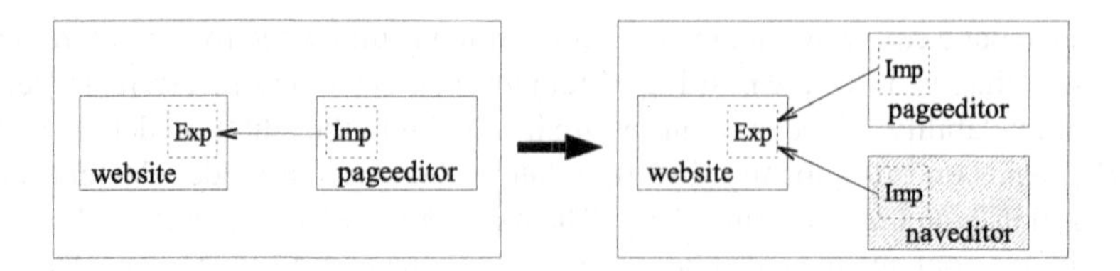

Fig. 11. Network structure transformation within example reconfiguration (cf. Example 6)

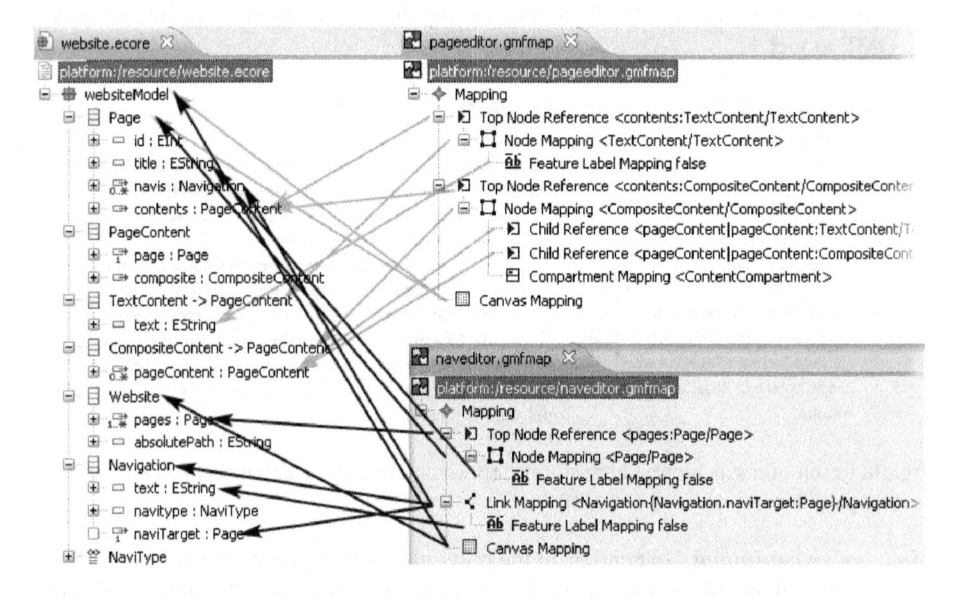

Fig. 12. Result of an example reconfiguration creating a new editor for domain model *website* (cf. Example 6)

Example 2). Its *Feature Label Mapping* refers to *Page.title* to show the title of a page. Furthermore, an entry *Link Mapping* with a *Feature Label Mapping* can be found representing a navigation link from one page to another. Corresponding domain elements are class *Navigation* and its attributes.

Component transformations are intended to run for each component independently. Thus, we conjecture that performing a restricted component transformation on a consistent distributed graph yields a consistent graph again. Since export graphs may be extended only and their corresponding body graphs have to cover export extensions, the morphisms between body and export as well as export and remote import interface graphs remain consistent. Import interfaces may be restricted only, since import interface transformations have to be surjective. The restricted interfaces have to be covered by the corresponding body graph transformations. Thus, the morphisms between body and import as well as import and remote export interface graphs remain consistent. Synchronized transformations and reconfigurations are not consistent in general, but also have to be restricted accordingly.

5 Related Work

There are software solutions for software modeling in distributed settings such as EMF CDO [10] and Poseidon for UML [11]. CDO provides one central or multiple model repositories to store EMF models. These repositories are managed by central servers. This solution is adequate as long as all developers shall have access to all models. However, there might be situations where a restricted access to models is required. For example, in open source developments, several teams develop their components independently of each other. ([12] provides an overview on repository technologies in general.)

In [13], an approach to distributed graphs and graph transformations is presented which allows the distribution of graph parts, but does not support explicit interfaces. In this sense, the distribution concepts of this approach and of EMF models are quite similar. Distributed graph transformations may concern various local graphs, but are not allowed to change remote graph parts. This distributed graph transformation model is used for code generation based on PROGRES. In [14], Mezei et.al. present distributed model transformations based on graph transformation concepts. Model transformations are not distributed logically, but in the sense that they are performed in a distributed way in order to increase efficiency. Hence, transformations are distributed automatically. Again, interfaces are handled implicitly. View-oriented modeling has already been specified by distributed graph transformation in [15]. However, the setting in this paper is more general. Last but not least, there are several approaches to modular graph transformation, e.g. distributed graph transformation units [16] where transformation units are encapsulated in transformation modules. In contrast to our approach, transformation modules encapsulate functionality only and no structures.

6 Conclusion

This paper presents a general approach to composite model transformations based on distributed graph transformation concepts. Several kinds of composite structures are discussed and mostly illustrated at distributed editor development with EMF and GMF. A composite model transformation is considered as partial mapping of a composite model and consists of a set of component transformations. Since we do not follow a specific transformation approach, component transformations are allowed to be performed by various approaches. Composite model transformation concentrates on some kind of "synchronization points", i.e. time points when all component transformations have finished. Starting at some composite model, several component transformations may take place in parallel. At certain time points, we can observe the composite model as a whole and can check its consistency. Composite models are consistent if all components are interrelated well.

Next we plan to define composite models with specific network structures as well as composite model transformations performing specific activities. A very interesting network structure is the component structure with explicit interfaces. Moreover, we like to substantiate scenarios for distributed development. Especially, we are interested in precisely defining transformations of composite EMF models consisting of components with explicit interface definitions.

References

1. Ehrig, H., Ehrig, K., Prange, U., Taentzer, G.: Fundamentals of Algebraic Graph Transformation. Springer, Heidelberg (2006)
2. EMF: Eclipse Modeling Framework, http://www.eclipse.com/emf
3. Jouault, F., Kurtev, I.: Transforming Models with ATL. In: Bruel, J.-M. (ed.) MoDELS 2005. LNCS, vol. 3844, pp. 128–138. Springer, Heidelberg (2006)
4. Lawley, M., Steel, J.: Practical Declarative Model Transformation With Tefkat. In: Bruel, J.-M. (ed.) MoDELS 2005. LNCS, vol. 3844, pp. 139–150. Springer, Heidelberg (2006)
5. Biermann, E., Ehrig, K., Köhler, C., Kuhns, G., Taentzer, G., Weiss, E.: Graphical Definition of Rule-Based Transformation in the Eclipse Modeling Framework. In: Nierstrasz, O., Whittle, J., Harel, D., Reggio, G. (eds.) MoDELS 2006. LNCS, vol. 4199, pp. 425–439. Springer, Heidelberg (2006)
6. GMF: Graphical Modeling Framework, http://www.eclipse.com/gmf
7. Biermann, E., Ermel, C., Taentzer, G.: Precise Semantics of EMF Model Transformations by Graph Transformation. In: Czarnecki, K., Ober, I., Bruel, J.-M., Uhl, A., Völter, M. (eds.) MoDELS 2008. LNCS, vol. 5301, pp. 53–67. Springer, Heidelberg (2008)
8. Löwe, M.: Extended Algebraic Graph Transformations. PhD thesis, Technical University of Berlin (1990); Short version in Theoretical Computer Science (109), 181–224
9. Taentzer, G.: Distributed Graphs and Graph Transformation. Applied Categorical Structures 7(4) (1999)
10. CDO: Eclipse Modeling Framework, http://wiki.eclipse.org/?title=CDO
11. Sturm, T.: Mannschaftssport - UML-Modellierung in verteilten Teams. ObjektSpektrum (4) (2004)
12. Bernstein, P., Dayal, U.: An Overview of Repository Technology. In: Bocca, J., Jarke, M., Zaniolo, C. (eds.) Proceedings of the 20th VLDB Conference, Santiago, Chile. Morgan Kaufmann, San Francisco (1994)
13. Ranger, U., Lüstraeten, M.: Search Trees for Distributed Graph Transformation Systems. Electronic Communication of the EASST 4 (2006)
14. Mezei, G., Juhasz, S., Levendovsky, T.: A distribution technique for graph rewriting and model transformation systems. In: Burkhart, H. (ed.) Proc. of the IASTED Int. Conference on Parallel and Distributed Computing Networks. IASTED/ACTA Press (2007)
15. Goedicke, M., Meyer, T., Taentzer, G.: ViewPoint-oriented Software Development by Distributed Graph Transformation: Towards a Basis for Living with Inconsistencies. In: Proc. 4th IEEE Int. Symposium on Requirements Engineering (RE 1999), University of Limerick, Ireland, June 7-11. IEEE Computer Society, Los Alamitos (1999)
16. Knirsch, P., Kuske, S.: Distributed Graph Transformation Units. In: Corradini, A., Ehrig, H., Kreowski, H.-J., Rozenberg, G. (eds.) ICGT 2002. LNCS, vol. 2505, Springer, Heidelberg (2002)

On-the-Fly Construction, Correctness and Completeness of Model Transformations Based on Triple Graph Grammars

Hartmut Ehrig, Claudia Ermel, Frank Hermann, and Ulrike Prange

Institut für Softwaretechnik und Theoretische Informatik
Technische Universität Berlin, Germany
{ehrig,lieske,frank,uprange}@cs.tu-berlin.de

Abstract. Triple graph grammars (TGGs) are a formal and intuitive concept for the specification of model transformations. Their main advantage is an automatic derivation of operational rules for bidirectional model transformations, which simplifies specification and enhances usability as well as consistency.

In this paper we continue previous work on the formal definition of model transformations based on triple graph rules with negative application conditions (NACs). The new notion of partial source consistency enables us to construct consistent model transformations on-the-fly instead of analyzing consistency of completed model transformations.

We show the crucial properties termination, correctness and completeness (including NAC-consistency) for the model transformations resulting from our construction. Moreover, we define parallel independence for model transformation steps which allows us to perform partial-order reduction in order to improve efficiency. The results are applicable to several relevant model transformations and in particular to our example transformation from class diagrams to database models.

Keywords: Model transformation, triple graph grammars, correctness.

1 Introduction

Model transformations based on triple graph grammars (TGGs) have been introduced by Schürr in [1]. TGGs are grammars that generate languages of graph triples, consisting of a source graph G^S and a target graph G^T, together with a correspondence graph G^C "between" them. From a TGG, operational rules can be derived which define various model integration tasks, such as consistency checking, consistency recovery and bidirectional model transformation. Since 1994, several extensions of the original TGG definitions have been published [2,3,4], and various kinds of applications have been presented [5,6,7].

For source-to-target model transformation, so-called *forward* transformation, we derive rules which take the source graph as input and produce a corresponding target graph. Major properties expected to be fulfilled for model transformations are termination, correctness and completeness.

A. Schürr and B. Selic (Eds.): MODELS 2009, LNCS 5795, pp. 241–255, 2009.

In a previous series of papers we focused on the formal definition of TGGs and the analysis of model transformation properties: in [8], we showed how to analyze bi-directional model transformations based on TGGs with respect to information preservation, which is based on a decomposition and composition result for triple graph grammar sequences. Moreover, completeness and correctness of model transformations have been studied on this basis in [9]. In [10], the formal results were extended to TGGs with negative application conditions (NACs), a key concept for many model transformations (see [2]). In contrast to the presented algorithm in [2] we use the concept of source consistency, where the the transformation is controlled by a parsing of the source model, and we introduced NAC consistency as an extension. In this way we could extend several important results to the case of TGGs with NACs. Model transformations based on triple rules with NACs were also analyzed in [11] for a restricted class of triple rules with distinct kernel elements. For this restricted class of triple graph grammars local confluence and termination can be analyzed and thus, model transformations can be checked for functional behavior.

As shown in [12] and [10] the notion of *source consistency* ensures correctness and completeness of model transformations based on triple graph grammars with and without NACs. However, source consistency does not directly guide the construction of the model transformation, because it has to be checked for the complete forward sequence. This means that possible forward sequences have to be constructed until one is found to be source consistent. Additionally, termination of this search is not guaranteed in general.

It is the main contribution of this paper to introduce a construction technique for correct and complete model transformation sequences *on-the-fly*, i.e. correctness and completeness properties of a model transformation need not to be analyzed after completion, but are ensured by construction. In our construction, we check source consistency while creating the forward sequences and define suitable conditions for termination. Thus, re-computations of model transformations may be avoided. Moreover, we present a characterization of parallel independence of forward transformation steps and use this notion for an optimization of efficiency based on partial order reduction [13]. Summing up, the paper provides the basis for efficient implementations of model transformation tools that ensure termination, correctness and completeness.

The paper is structured as follows: Sec. 2 reviews the definition of triple graph grammars with NACs from [10]. In Sec. 3 we introduce an *on-the-fly* construction of source consistent forward transformation sequences, generalizing the notion of source consistency to *partial* source consistency. The on-the-fly construction is analyzed in Sec. 4 regarding correctness and completeness of the model transformations, and termination of the construction. Moreover, parallel independence of forward transformation steps is defined and used to find switch equivalent model transformation sequences by performing an optimization based on partial order reduction. Sec. 5 discusses related work, and Sec. 6 concludes the paper. Our technical report [14] contains full definitions for Sec. 2 and full proofs for the presented results in Secs. 3 and 4.

2 Review of Triple Graph Grammars with NACs

Triple graph grammars [1] are a well known approach for bidirectional model transformations. Models are defined as pairs of source and target graphs, which are connected via a correspondence graph together with its embeddings into these graphs. In [3], Königs and Schürr formalize the basic concepts of triple graph grammars in a set-theoretical way, which is generalized and extended by Ehrig et al. in [8] to typed, attributed graphs. In this section, we briefly review triple graph grammars with negative application conditions (NACs) [2,10].

A triple graph $G = (G^S \xleftarrow{s_G} G^C \xrightarrow{t_G} G^T)$ consists of three graphs G^S, G^C, and G^T, called source, correspondence, and target graphs, together with two graph morphisms $s_G : G^C \to G^S$ and $t_G : G^C \to G^T$. A triple graph morphism $m = (m^S, m^C, m^T) : G \to H$ consists of three graph morphisms $m^S : G^S \to H^S$, $m^C : G^C \to H^C$ and $m^T : G^T \to H^T$ such that $m^S \circ s_G = s_H \circ m^C$ and $m^T \circ t_G = t_H \circ m^C$. A typed triple graph G is typed over a triple graph TG by a triple graph morphism $type_G : G \to TG$.

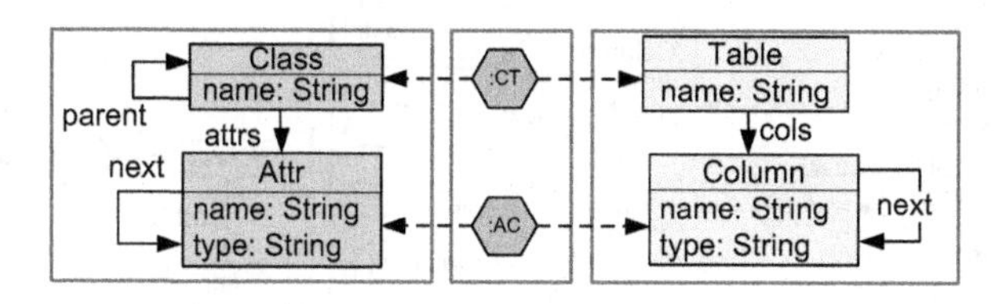

Fig. 1. Triple Type Graph for *CD2RDBM*

Example 1. Fig. 1 shows the type graph TG of the triple graph grammar GG for our example model transformation from class diagrams to database models. The source component of TG defines the structure of class diagrams while in its target component the structure of relational database models is specified. Classes correspond to tables and attributes to columns. Throughout the example, originating from [2] and [8], elements are arranged left, center, and right according to the component types source, correspondence and target. Morphisms starting at a correspondence part are given by dashed arrows. Note that the case study is equipped with attribution, which is based on the concept of E-graphs [15].

Triple rules synchronously build up source and target graphs as well as their correspondence graphs, i.e. they are non-deleting. A triple rule tr is an injective

$$\begin{array}{ccccccc} L = (L^S & \xleftarrow{s_L} & L^C & \xrightarrow{t_L} & L^T) & & L \xhookrightarrow{tr} R \\ tr\downarrow \quad tr^S\downarrow & & tr^C\downarrow & & tr^T\downarrow & & m\downarrow \quad (PO) \quad \downarrow n \\ R = (R^S & \xleftarrow[s_R]{} & R^C & \xrightarrow[t_R]{} & R^T) & & G \xhookrightarrow[t]{} H \end{array}$$

triple graph morphism $tr = (tr^S, tr^C, tr^T) : L \to R$ and w.l.o.g. we assume tr to be an inclusion. Given a triple rule $tr : L \to R$, an injective $m : L \to G$, a triple graph transformation step (TGT-step) $G \xRightarrow{tr,m,n} H$ from G to a triple graph H is given by a pushout of triple graphs with comatch $n : R \to H$ and transformation inclusion $t : G \hookrightarrow H$. A sequence of triple graph transformation steps is called triple (graph) transformation sequence, short: TGT-sequence. Furthermore, a triple graph grammar $TGG = (S, TG, TR)$ consists of a triple start graph S, triple type graph TG and a set TR of triple rules.

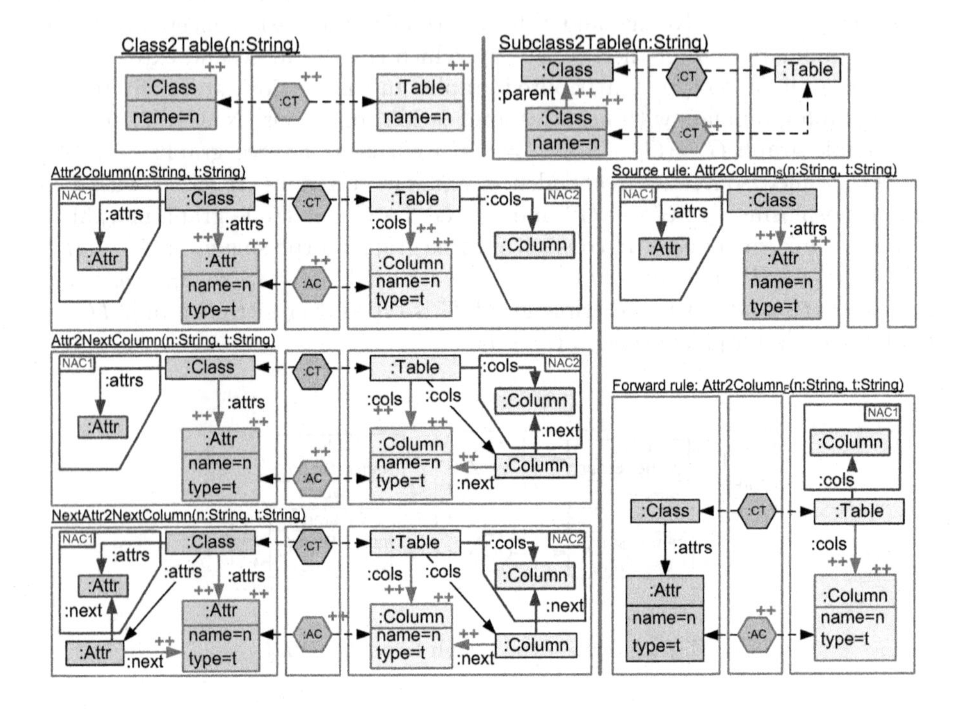

Fig. 2. Rules for the Model Tranformation *Class2Table*

Example 2 (Triple Rules). The top line of Fig. 2 shows two triple rules in short notation. Left and right hand side of a rule are depicted in one triple graph. Elements, which are created by the rule, are labeled with green "++" and marked by green line coloring. Rule "*Class2Table*" synchronously creates a class in a class diagram with its corresponding table in the relational database. Accordingly, subclasses are connected to the tables of its super classes. The further rules contain NACs which we introduce next.

The extension of the results of this paper to the case with attributes is straight forward, because all results can be shown in the framework of weak adhesive HLR categories [15]. According to [10] we present negative application conditions for triple rules. In most case studies of model transformations source-target NACs are sufficient and we regard them as the standard case.

Definition 1 (Negative Application Conditions). *Given a triple rule $tr = (L \rightarrow R)$, a general negative application condition (NAC) (N, n) consists of a* *triple graph* N *and an injective triple graph morphism* $n : L \rightarrow N$. *A NAC with* $n = (n^S, id_{L_C}, id_{L_T})$ *is called* source NAC *and a NAC with* $n = (id_{L_S}, id_{L_C}, n^T)$ *is called* target NAC. *This means that source-target NACs, i.e. either source or target NACs, prohibit the existence of certain structures either in the source or in the target part only.*

A match $m : L \rightarrow G$ *is NAC consistent if there is no injective* $q : N \rightarrow G$ *such that* $q \circ n = m$. *A triple transformation* $G \overset{*}{\Rrightarrow} H$ *is NAC consistent if all matches are NAC consistent.*

$$\begin{array}{ccc}
\begin{array}{c}
(L^S \longleftarrow \varnothing \longrightarrow \varnothing) \\
tr^S \downarrow \quad\quad \downarrow \quad\quad \downarrow \\
(R^S \longleftarrow \varnothing \longrightarrow \varnothing) \\
\text{source rule } tr_S
\end{array}
&
\begin{array}{c}
(\varnothing \longleftarrow \varnothing \longrightarrow L_T) \\
\downarrow \quad\quad \downarrow \quad\quad \downarrow tr^T \\
(\varnothing \longleftarrow \varnothing \longrightarrow R_T) \\
\text{target rule } tr_T
\end{array}
&
\begin{array}{c}
(R^S \xleftarrow{tr^S \circ s_L} L^C \xrightarrow{t_L} L^T) \\
id \downarrow \quad\quad tr^C \downarrow \quad\quad \downarrow tr^T \\
(R^S \xleftarrow{s_R} R^C \xrightarrow{t_R} R^T) \\
\text{forward rule } tr_F
\end{array}
\end{array}$$

Operational rules for model transformations are automatically derived from the set of triple rules *TR*. From each rule *tr* of *TR* we derive a forward rule tr_F for forward transformation sequences and a source rule tr_S for the construction resp. parsing of a model of the source language. Analogously, we derive a target rule tr_T for models of the target language and backward rules tr_B, which are not presented explicitly. Furthermore, tr_S contains all source NACs of *tr* and tr_F as well as tr_T contain all target NACs of *tr*. TR_S, TR_T and TR_F denote the sets of all source, target resp. forward rules derived from *TR*.

A set of triple rules *TR* with NACs and start graph $\varnothing$ generates a visual language *VL* of integrated models, i.e. models with elements in the source, target and correspondence component. Source language VL_S and target language VL_T are derived by projection to the triple components, i.e. $VL_S = proj_S(VL)$ and $VL_T = proj_T(VL)$. The set VL_{S0} of models that can be generated resp. parsed by the set of all source rules TR_S is possibly larger than VL_S and we have $VL_S \subseteq VL_{S0} = \{G_S \mid \varnothing \Rightarrow^* (G_S \leftarrow \varnothing \rightarrow \varnothing) \textit{ via } TR_S\}$. Analogously, we have $VL_T \subseteq VL_{T0} = \{G_T \mid \varnothing \Rightarrow^* (G_T \leftarrow \varnothing \rightarrow \varnothing) \textit{ via } TR_T\}$.

Example 3 (Triple Rules with NACs). Examples for triple rules with NACs and derived rules are given in Fig. 2. NACs are indicated by red frames with labels “NAC” and they control the construction of attribute lists in the source part and corresponding column lists in the target part. The first attribute of a class is either created by the rule “Attr2Column” or by “Attr2NextColumn” while rule “NextAttr2NextColumn” extends an existing list of attributes. Lists of columns are initialized by rule “Attr2Column” only, because there is no inheritance structure in data base tables, and they are extended by the other two rules. The source rule tr_S and forward rule tr_F of $tr =$“Attr2Column” are shown in the right part of Fig. 2, where tr_S contains the source NAC (NAC1) and tr_F the target NAC (NAC2) of *tr*. Forward transformations using the derived rules according to Section 3 process the attribute lists in the natural order, i.e. starting with the root element of a list.

As introduced in [8,10] we are now able to define model transformations based on source consistent forward transformations $G_0 \Rightarrow^* G_n$ via $(tr_{1,F}, \ldots, tr_{n,F})$, short $G_0 \xrightarrow{tr_F^*} G_n$. Source consistency of $G_0 \xrightarrow{tr_F^*} G_n$ means that there is a source sequence $\varnothing \xrightarrow{tr_S^*} G_0$ such that the sequence $\varnothing \xrightarrow{tr_S^*} G_0 \xrightarrow{tr_F^*} G_n$ is match consistent, i.e. the S-component of each match $m_{i,F}$ of $tr_{i,F}(i = 1..n)$ is uniquely determined by the comatch $n_{i,S}$ of $tr_{i,S}$, where $tr_{i,S}$ and $tr_{i,F}$ are source and forward rules of the same triple rules tr_i. Altogether the forward sequence $G_0 \xrightarrow{tr_F^*} G_n$ is controlled by the corresponding source sequence $\varnothing \xrightarrow{tr_S^*} G_0$, which is unique in the case of match consistency.

Definition 2 (Model Transformation based on Forward Rules). *A model transformation sequence* $(G_S, G_0 \xrightarrow{tr_F^*} G_n, G_T)$ *consists of a source graph* G_S*, a target graph* G_T*, and a NAC- as well as source consistent forward* TGT*-sequence* $G_0 \xrightarrow{tr_F^*} G_n$ *with* $G_S = proj_S(G_0)$ *and* $G_T = proj_T(G_n)$*.*

A model transformation $MT : VL_{S0} \Rrightarrow VL_{T0}$ *is defined by all model transformation sequences* $(G_S, G_0 \xrightarrow{tr_F^*} G_n, G_T)$ *with* $G_S \in VL_{S0}$ *and* $G_T \in VL_{T0}$*.*

Finally, let us note that we have shown in [8,10] that each TGT-sequence $G_0 \xrightarrow{tr^*} G_n$ with NACs can be decomposed into a match consistent TGT-sequence $\varnothing \xrightarrow{tr_S^*} G_0 \xrightarrow{tr_F^*} G_n$ with NACs and vice versa, which is the basis for correctness and completeness of model transformations in Sec. 4.

3 On-the-Fly Construction of Model Transformations

In order to construct a model transformation sequence $(G_S, G_0 \xrightarrow{tr_F^*} G_n, G_T)$ according to Def. 2 from a given G_S there have been two alternatives up to now [8,10]: Either we construct a parsing sequence $\varnothing \xrightarrow{tr_S^*} G_0$ first and then try to extend it to a match consistent sequence $\varnothing \xrightarrow{tr_S^*} G_0 \xrightarrow{tr_F^*} G_n$, or we construct directly a forward sequence $G_0 \xrightarrow{tr_F^*} G_n$ and check afterwards, whether it is source consistent. This means that many candidates of forward transformation sequences may have to be constructed before a source consistent one is found.

We present an on-the-fly check of source consistency using the new notion of partial source consistency. The construction proceeds stepwise and constructs partial source consistent forward sequences. For each step the possible matches of model transformation rules are filtered, such that sequences that will not lead to a source consistent one are rejected as soon as possible. Simultaneously, the corresponding source sequences of the forward sequences are constructed on-the-fly leading to complete source sequences for the complete forward sequences. Intuitively, this can be seen as an on-the-fly parsing of the source model.

Partial source consistency of a forward sequence, which is necessary for a complete model transformation, requires a corresponding source sequence such that both sequences are partially match consistent. This means that the matches of the forward sequence are controlled by an automatic parsing of the source model, given by inverting the source sequence. We incrementally extend partially source consistent sequences and can derive complete source consistent sequences ensuring that all elements of the source model are translated exactly once.

Definition 3 (Partial Match and Source Consistency). *Let TR be a set of triple rules with source and target NACs and let TR_F be the derived set of forward rules with target NACs. A NAC-consistent sequence*

$$\varnothing = G_{00} \xrightarrow{tr_S^*} G_{n0} \overset{g_n}{\hookrightarrow} G_0 \xrightarrow{tr_F^*} G_n$$

defined by pushout diagrams (1) and (3) for $i = 1 \ldots n$ with $G_0^C = \varnothing$, $G_0^T = \varnothing$ and inclusion $g_n : G_{n0} \hookrightarrow G_0$ is called partially match consistent, *if diagram (2) commutes for all i, which means that the source component of the forward match $m_{i,F}$ is determined by the comatch $n_{i,S}$ of the corresponding step of the source sequence with $g_i = g_n \circ t_{n,S} \ldots t_{i-1,S}$.*

$$\begin{array}{ccccccc}
L_{i,S} & \xhookrightarrow{tr_{i,S}} & R_{i,S} & \hookrightarrow & L_{i,F} & \xhookrightarrow{tr_{i,F}} & R_{i,F} \\
{\scriptstyle m_{i,S}}\downarrow & (1) & \downarrow{\scriptstyle n_{i,S}} & (2) & {\scriptstyle m_{i,F}}\downarrow & (3) & \downarrow{\scriptstyle n_{i,F}} \\
G_{i-1,0} & \xhookrightarrow[t_{i,S}]{} & G_{i,0} \xhookrightarrow[g_i]{} G_0 & \hookrightarrow & G_{i-1} & \xhookrightarrow[t_{i,F}]{} & G_i
\end{array}$$

A NAC-consistent forward sequence $G_0 \xrightarrow{tr_F^*} G_n$ is partially source consistent, if there is a source sequence $\varnothing = G_{00} \xrightarrow{tr_S^*} G_{n0}$ with inclusion $G_{n0} \overset{g_n}{\hookrightarrow} G_0$ such that $G_{00} \xrightarrow{tr_S^*} G_{n0} \overset{g_n}{\hookrightarrow} G_0 \xrightarrow{tr_F^*} G_n$ is partially match consistent.

Remark 1

1. If $g_n = id_{G_0}$, partial match consistency coincides with match consistency.
2. For $n = 0$ the partially match consistent sequence is given by $g_0 : G_{00} \hookrightarrow G_0$.

Example 4 (Partial Match and Source Consistency). Let us consider a sequence starting with triple graph G_0 (depicted in the center of Fig. 3) which represents a class diagram consisting of one class with two linked attributes. G_0 will be mapped to a corresponding table with two linked columns. Note that for this example, we assume the triple rules shown in Fig. 2, but first without NACs.

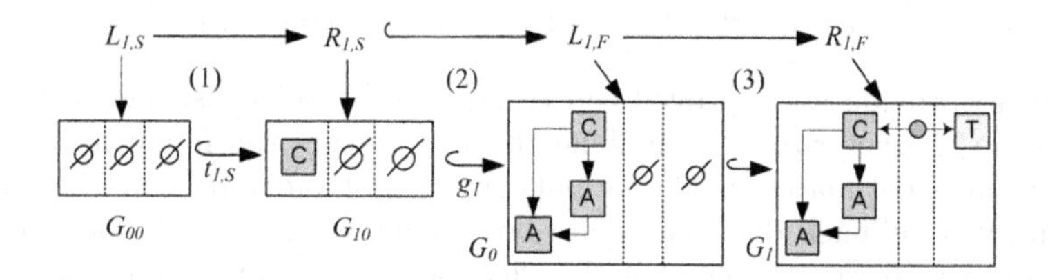

Fig. 3. Step 1 of the partially match-consistent sequence

In the first step ($i = 1$), shown in Fig. 3, we apply rule $tr_{1,S} = Class2Table_S$ to the empty start graph G_{00} yielding the source graph G_{10} which contains one class. Obviously, G_{10} is included in G_0. Hence, diagram (2) commutes for step 1. The corresponding forward rule $tr_{1,F} = Class2Table_F$ is applied to G_0 and maps the class node to a table node, resulting in G_1. For step $i = 2$ (not depicted), we apply the source rule $tr_{2,S} = Attr2Column_S$ to graph G_{10} which adds an attribute and links it to the class. The result graph is G_{20}. Again, G_{20} is included in G_0, which is included in G_1. The corresponding forward rule $tr_{2,F} = Attr2Column_F$ is applied to G_1, resulting in G_2, where the upper attribute of the class now is mapped to a column of the table.

In the third step ($i = 3$), shown in Fig. 4, we apply the same source rule once more, i.e. $tr_{3,S} = Attr2Column_S$, and add a second attribute to G_{20}, resulting in source graph G_{30}. This graph is included in G_0, which in turn is included in G_2. Diagram (2) commutes for step 3. The application of the corresponding forward rule $tr_{3,F} = Attr2Column_F$ at the co-match of $tr_{3,S}$ yields G_3, where now also the second attribute is mapped to a column of the table.

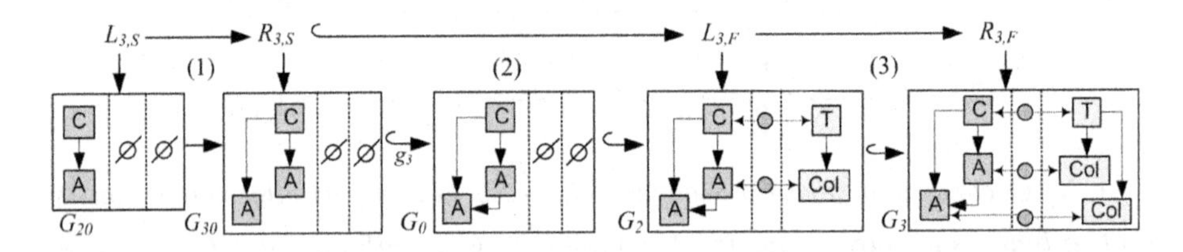

Fig. 4. Step 3 of the partially match-consistent sequence

Since for each considered step, diagram (2) of Def. 3 commutes, we conclude that sequence $\emptyset = G_{00} \stackrel{tr_{1,S}}{\Longrightarrow} G_{10} \stackrel{tr_{2,S}}{\Longrightarrow} G_{20} \stackrel{tr_{3,S}}{\Longrightarrow} G_{30} \stackrel{g_n}{\hookrightarrow} G_0 \stackrel{tr_{1,F}}{\Longrightarrow} G_1 \stackrel{tr_{2,F}}{\Longrightarrow} G_2 \stackrel{tr_{3,F}}{\Longrightarrow} G_3$ is partially match consistent. Hence, the forward sequence $G_0 \stackrel{tr_{1,F}}{\Longrightarrow} G_1 \stackrel{tr_{2,F}}{\Longrightarrow} G_2 \stackrel{tr_{3,F}}{\Longrightarrow} G_3$ is partially source consistent. Note that the forward sequence, although being partially source consistent, cannot be extended to a complete source consistent sequence. The reason is that after the third step, we do not find a new partially source consistent match for some $tr_{4,F}$. We will analyze in Ex. 6 what went wrong and how NACs in triple rules can help to improve the construction of valid source consistent sequences.

In order to provide an improved construction of source consistent forward sequences we characterize valid matches by introducing the following notion of forward consistent matches. The formal condition of a forward consistent match is given by a pullback diagram where both matches satisfy the corresponding NACs. Intuitively, it specifies that the effective elements of the forward rule are matched for the first time in the forward sequence (see Interpretation 1 below).

Definition 4 (Forward Consistent Match). *Given a partially match consistent sequence* $\varnothing = G_{00} \stackrel{tr_S^*}{\Longrightarrow} G_{n-1,0} \stackrel{g_n}{\hookrightarrow} G_0 \stackrel{tr_F^*}{\Longrightarrow} G_{n-1}$ *then a match* $m_{n,F} : L_{n,F} \to G_{n-1}$ *for* $tr_{n,F} : L_{n,F} \to R_{n,F}$ *is called* forward consistent *if there is a source match* $m_{n,S}$ *such that diagram* (1) *is a pullback and the matches* $m_{n,F}$ *and* $m_{n,S}$ *satisfy the corresponding target and source NACs, respectively.*

$$\begin{array}{ccccc} L_{n,S} & \hookrightarrow & R_{n,S} & \hookrightarrow & L_{n,F} \\ {\scriptstyle m_{n,S}}\downarrow & & (1) & & \downarrow{\scriptstyle m_{n,F}} \\ G_{n-1,0} & \underset{g_{n-1}}{\hookrightarrow} & G_0 & \hookrightarrow & G_{n-1} \end{array}$$

Interpretation 1. The pullback property of (1) means that the intersection of the match $m_{n,F}(L_{n,F})$ and the source graph $G_{n-1,0}$ constructed so far is equal to $m_{n,F}(L_{n,S})$, the match restricted to $L_{n,S}$, i.e. we have

$$(2) : m_{n,F}(L_{n,F}) \cap G_{n-1,0} = m_{n,F}(L_{n,F}).$$

This condition can be checked easily and $m_{n,S} : L_{n,S} \to G_{n-1,0}$ is uniquely defined by restriction of $m_{n,F} : L_{n,F} \to G_{n-1}$. Furthermore, as a direct consequence of (2) we have

$$(3) : m_{n,F}(L_{n,F} \setminus L_{n,S}) \cap G_{n-1,0} = \varnothing.$$

On the one hand, the source elements of $L_{n,F} \setminus L_{n,S}$ - called effective elements - are the elements to be transformed by the next step of the forward transformation sequence. On the other hand, $G_{n-1,0}$ contains all elements that were matched by the preceding forward steps, because matches of the forward sequence coincide on the source part with comatches of the source sequence. Hence, condition (3) means that the effective elements were not matched before, i.e. they do not belong to $G_{n-1,0}$.

Example 5 (Forward Consistent Match). In the partial match consistent sequence from Ex. 4, all forward rule matches are forward consistent. Consider for example the situation in step 3, shown in Fig. 5, where all mappings have been indicated explicitly by equal numbers. We can see that $L_{3,F} \cap G_{20} = L_{3,S}$, which implies that Diagram (1) from Def. 4 is a pullback. Analogously, the matches from forward rules in steps 1 and 2 are also forward consistent.

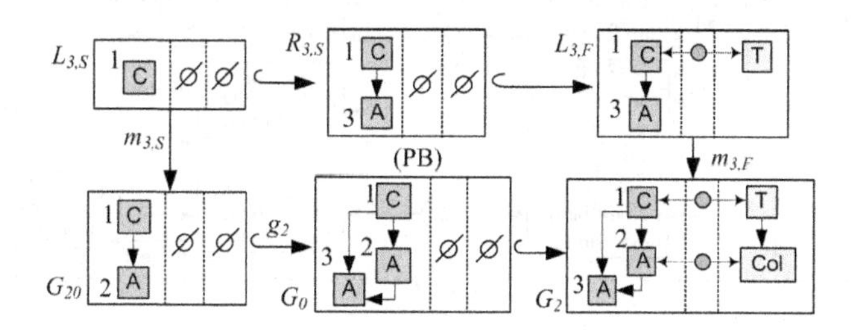

Fig. 5. Forward consistent match from step 3

In the following improved construction of model transformations, we check the matches to be forward consistent. This allows us to filter the available matches to those which can lead to correct model transformations while those matches that cannot lead to correct model transformations are rejected.

Theorem 1 (On-the-Fly Construction of Model Transformations). *Given a triple graph G_0 with $G_0^C = G_0^T = \varnothing$, execute the following steps:*

1. *Start with $G_{00} = \varnothing$ and $g_0 : G_{00} \hookrightarrow G_0$.*
2. *For $n > 0$ and an already computed partially source consistent sequence $s = \langle G_0 \xRightarrow{tr_F^*} G_{n-1} \rangle$ with $\varnothing = G_{00} \xRightarrow{tr_S^*} G_{n-1,0}$ and embedding g_{n-1} :*

$G_{n-1,0} \hookrightarrow G_0$ find a (not yet considered) forward consistent match for some $tr_{n,F}$ leading to a partially source consistent sequence $G_0 \xRightarrow{tr_F^*} G_{n-1} \xRightarrow{tr_{n,F}} G_n$ with $G_{00} \xRightarrow{tr_S^*} G_{n-1,0} \xRightarrow{tr_{n,S}} G_{n0}$ and embedding $g_n : G_{n0} \hookrightarrow G_0$. If there is no such match, s cannot be extended to a source consistent sequence. Repeat until $g_n = id_{G_0}$ or no new forward consistent matches can be found.

3. *If the procedure terminates with $g_n = id_{G_0}$, then $G_0 \xRightarrow{tr_F^*} G_n$ is source consistent leading to a model transformation sequence $(G_S, G_0 \xRightarrow{tr_F^*} G_n, G_T)$ with G_S and G_T being the source and target models of G_0 and G_n.*

The on-the-fly construction does not restrict the choice of a suitable n, $tr_{n,F}$, and match in Step 2. Hence, different search algorithms are possible, e.g.

- *Depth First:* If we increase n after every iteration, and only decrease n by 1 if no more new forward consistent matches can be found, a depth-first search is performed.
- *Breadth First:* If we increase n only after all forward consistent matches for n are considered, the construction performs a breadth-first search.

Depending on the type of the model transformation, other search strategies may be reasonable. In Sec. 4, we show how to make the construction more efficient by analyzing independent transformations.

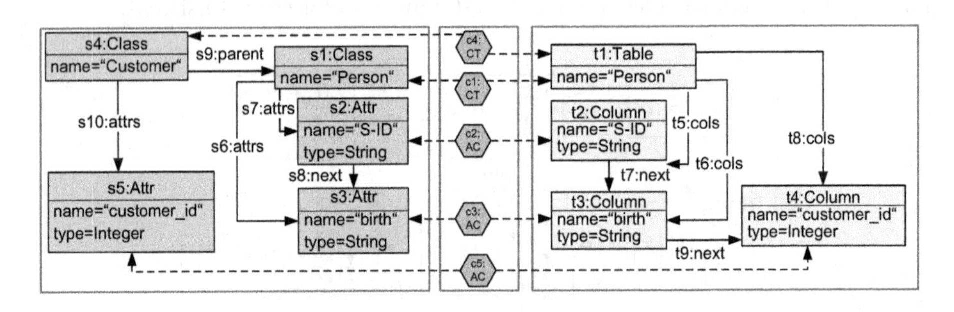

Fig. 6. G_5 of Forward Sequence

Example 6 (On-the-Fly Construction). Let us assume we have found already the partial match consistent sequence from Ex. 4 by depth-first search. All forward rule matches found so far are forward consistent. But after the third rule application step ($i = 3$), we do not find a new partial source consistent match for some $tr_{4,F}$. We cannot extend the sequence to a source consistent one, because there is no triple rule for inserting a *next* link between two existing attributes. The mistake we made was to use the wrong rule $Attr2Columns_S$ for the insertion of the second attribute. If we had used rule $NextAttr2NextColumns_S$ instead, we would have constructed a sequence which could be extended to a source consistent sequence. If a sequence cannot be extended to a source-consistent one, we have two choices: either, we have to try to apply a different rule in a previous step, or we restrict the applicability of our triple rules, e.g. by adding negative application conditions. Here, we can use the NACs in Fig. 2, which ensure that only one attribute-adding rule is applicable in each step. An example for a source-consistent sequence, constructed by partially source consistent sequences according to Thm. 1, is the model transformation $(G_S = G_{0,S}, G_0 \xrightarrow{tr_F^*} G_5, G_T = G_{5,T})$, where G_5 (shown in Fig. 6) is generated by the forward sequence $G_0 \xrightarrow{Class2Table} G_1 \xrightarrow{Attr2Col} G_2 \xrightarrow{Subclass2Table} G_3 \xrightarrow{NextAttr2NextCol} G_4 \xrightarrow{Attr2NextCol} G_5$, and G_0 is generated by the corresponding source sequence $\varnothing \xrightarrow{tr_S^*} G_0$. All elements in Fig. 6 are labeled with numbers. The following table specifies the matches and the created objects for each transformation step. Note that we cannot accidentally apply the rule $Class2Table_F$ at subclasses, because in this case the transformation will not become source consistent - the edge of the type "parent" will be missing.

	Source Sequence Elements		Forward Sequence Elements	
Step	Matched	Created	Matched	Created
1		s1	s1	c1,t1
2	s1	s2,s7	s1,s2,s7,c1,t1	c2,t2,t5
3	s1	s4,s9	s1,c1,t1,s4,s9	c4
4	s1,s2,s7	s3,s8	s1-s3,s6-s8,c1,t1,t2,t5	c3,t3,t6,t7
5	s4	s5,s10	s4,s5,s10,c4,t1,t3,t6	c5,t4,t8,t9

4 Analysis and Improvement of the Construction

In this section, we analyze the on-the-fly construction in Thm. 1 regarding correctness, completeness, and termination of the model transformations and show how to improve efficiency by parallel independence, which allows partial order reduction.

The on-the-fly construction is correct, which means that if it terminates both the source and target models of the resulting model transformations are valid models of the source and target languages, respectively. Moreover, it is also complete, which means that for any source model the procedure can find a model transformation sequence leading to a corresponding target model.

Theorem 2 (Correctness and Completeness)

- Correctness: *If the on-the-fly construction terminates with $g_n = id_{G_0}$, then the resulting model transformation $(G_S, G_0 \xrightarrow{tr_F^*} G_n, G_T)$ is correct, i.e. $G_S \in VL_S$ and $G_T \in VL_T$.*
- Completeness: *For each $G_S \in VL_S$ there exists $G_T \in VL_T$ with a model transformation $(G_S, G_0 \xrightarrow{tr_F^*} G_n, G_T)$, which can be obtained by the on-the-fly construction.*

Remark 2. Dually, for each $G_T \in VL_T$ there exists $G_S \in VL_S$ where the corresponding model transformation can be obtained dually by partially target consistent sequences.

In general, the termination of the on-the-fly construction cannot be guaranteed. But for the case that all source rules create new elements also the termination of the on-the-fly construction is ensured.

Theorem 3 (Termination). *The on-the-fly construction of a triple graph G_0 with $G_0^C = G_0^T = \varnothing$ terminates if all source rules $tr_{i,S}$ are creating, i.e. $R_{i,S} \setminus L_{i,S} \neq \varnothing$.*

Example 7 (Termination). The on-the-fly construction of triple graph G_5 in Ex. 6 terminates because all of the used source rules in the source sequence are creating, which can be seen in the left column of the table.

In the following, we describe how to improve efficiency by analyzing parallel independence of extensions. Two partially match consistent sequences which differ only in the last rule application are parallel independent if the last rule applications are parallel independent both for the source and forward sequence, and, in addition, if the embeddings into the given graph G_0 are compatible.

Definition 5 (Parallel Independence of Partially Match Consistent Extensions). *Two partially match consistent sequences*

$$\varnothing = G_{00} \xRightarrow{tr_S^*} G_{n0} \xRightarrow{tr_{1,S}} G_{n+1,0} \xhookrightarrow{g_{n+1}} G_0 \xRightarrow{tr_F^*} G_n \xRightarrow{tr_{1,F}} G_{n+1} \text{ and}$$
$$\varnothing = G_{00} \xRightarrow{tr_S^*} G_{n0} \xRightarrow{tr_{2,S}} G'_{n+1,0} \xhookrightarrow{g'_{n+1}} G_0 \xRightarrow{tr_F^*} G_n \xRightarrow{tr_{2,F}} G'_{n+1}$$

are parallel independent *if $G_{n0} \xRightarrow{tr_{1,S}} G_{n+1,0}$ and $G_{n0} \xRightarrow{tr_{2,S}} G'_{n+1,0}$ as well as $G_n \xRightarrow{tr_{1,F}} G_{n+1}$ and $G_n \xRightarrow{tr_{2,F}} G'_{n+1}$ are parallel independent leading to the diagram (1_S) and (1_F), and diagram (2) is a pullback.*

$$\begin{array}{ccc} G_{n0} & \xRightarrow{tr_{1,S}} & G_{n+1,0} \\ {\scriptstyle tr_{2,S}}\Downarrow & (1_S) & \Downarrow{\scriptstyle tr_{2,S}} \\ G'_{n+1,0} & \xRightarrow[tr_{1,S}]{} & G_{n+2,0} \end{array} \quad \begin{array}{ccc} G_n & \xRightarrow{tr_{1,F}} & G_{n+1} \\ {\scriptstyle tr_{2,F}}\Downarrow & (1_F) & \Downarrow{\scriptstyle tr_{2,F}} \\ G'_{n+1} & \xRightarrow[tr_{1,F}]{} & G_{n+2} \end{array} \quad \begin{array}{ccc} G_{n0} & \xhookrightarrow{t_{1,S}} & G_{n+1,0} \\ {\scriptstyle t_{2,S}}\downarrow & (2) & \downarrow{\scriptstyle g_{n+1}} \\ G'_{n+1,0} & \xhookrightarrow[g'_{n+1}]{} & G_0 \end{array}$$

In the case of parallel independence of the extensions, both extensions can be extended both in the source and forward sequences leading to two longer partially match consistent sequences which are switch-equivalent.

Theorem 4 (Partial Match Consistency with Parallel Independence). *If $\varnothing = G_{00} \xRightarrow{tr_S^*} G_{n0} \xRightarrow{tr_{1,S}} G_{n+1,0} \xhookrightarrow{g_{n+1}} G_0 \xRightarrow{tr_F^*} G_n \xRightarrow{tr_{1,F}} G_{n+1}$ and $\varnothing = G_{00} \xRightarrow{tr_S^*} G_{n0} \xRightarrow{tr_{2,S}} G'_{n+1,0} \xhookrightarrow{g'_{n+1}} G_0 \xRightarrow{tr_F^*} G_n \xRightarrow{tr_{2,F}} G'_{n+1}$ are* parallel independent *then the following upper and lower sequences are partially match consistent and called* switch equivalent.

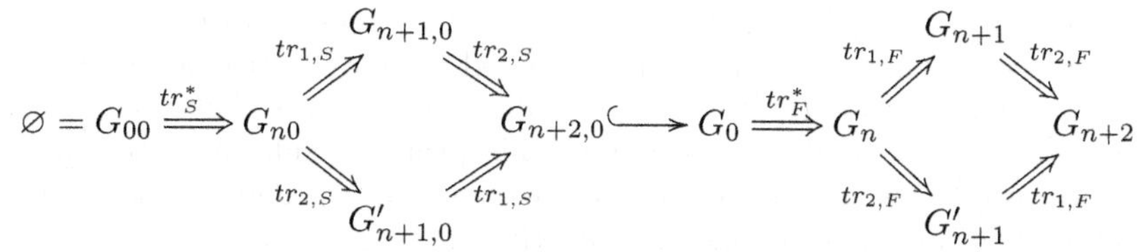

$$\varnothing = G_{00} \overset{tr_S^*}{\Longrightarrow} G_{n0} \; \substack{\overset{tr_{1,S}}{\nearrow} G_{n+1,0} \overset{tr_{2,S}}{\searrow} \\ \underset{tr_{2,S}}{\searrow} G'_{n+1,0} \underset{tr_{1,S}}{\nearrow}} \; G_{n+2,0} \hookrightarrow G_0 \overset{tr_F^*}{\Longrightarrow} G_n \; \substack{\overset{tr_{1,F}}{\nearrow} G_{n+1} \overset{tr_{2,F}}{\searrow} \\ \underset{tr_{2,F}}{\searrow} G'_{n+1} \underset{tr_{1,F}}{\nearrow}} \; G_{n+2}$$

Example 8 (Parallel Independence). Consider the sequence of rule applications in Ex. 6. Here, we may switch step 2 and step 3 without changing the result G_5 since the sequences $\varnothing = G_{00} \xrightarrow{Class2Table_S} G_{10} \xrightarrow{Attribute2Column_S} G_{2,0} \xhookrightarrow{g_2} G_0 \xrightarrow{Class2Table_F} G_1 \xrightarrow{Attribute2Column_F} G_2$ and $\varnothing = G_{00} \xrightarrow{Class2Table_S} G'_{10} \xrightarrow{Subclass2Table_S} G'_{2,0} \xhookrightarrow{g'_2} G_0 \xrightarrow{Class2Table_F} G_1 \xrightarrow{Subclass2Table_F} G'_2$ are parallel independent.

We can analyze parallel independence on-the-fly for the forward steps which are applicable to the current intermediate triple graph. Based on the induced partial order of dependencies between the forward steps we can apply several techniques of partial order reduction in order to improve efficiency. This means that we can neglect remaining switch-equivalent sequences, if one of them has been constructed. This improves efficiency of corresponding depth-first and breadth-first algorithms. For an overview of various approaches concerning partial order reduction see [13], where also benchmarks show that these techniques can dramatically reduce complexity.

5 Related Work and Evaluation of Our Approach

Since 1994, several extensions of the original TGG definitions have been published [2,3,4], and various kinds of applications have been presented [5,6,7]. For an extensive overview see [2]. A new extension of TGGs towards declarative, pattern-based model transformation is presented in [16], where triple rules are derived from triple graph constraints.

Furthermore, Kindler and Wagner [7] discuss that several applications of model transformations based on TGGs require an efficient strategy for finding a correct transformation sequence because of the non-deterministic character of the matching of forward rules. A new strategy for controlling the construction of a model transformation was given in [2], where elements of the source model are distinguished for each step of the model transformation whether they were translated so far. In this paper we have formalized this separation by specifying which elements were matched so far and we call the new matched elements in an intermediate model transformation step effective elements (see Def. 4).

As stated in Sec. 1 this paper extends concepts and results of our previous papers [8,11,9,10]. In the following we explain how our approach complies with the design principles of the "Grand Research Challenge of the Triple Graph Grammar Community", which was formulated by Schürr et al. in [2]:

1. *Correctness:* Model transformations shall be correct in the way that whenever the algorithm translates a source model G_S into a target model G_T then

there has to be a triple graph $G = (G_S \leftarrow G_C \rightarrow G_T) \in VL$. This property is shown in Thm. 2 for an algorithm based on our construction in Thm. 1.
2. *Completeness and Termination:* Completeness means that the algorithm translates each model $G_S \in VL_S$. This property subsumes Termination. Both properties are ensured for our construction by Thm. 2 and Thm. 3 if triple rules are creating on the source part.
3. *Efficiency:* Model transformations shall have polynomial space and time complexity with exponent k the maximal number of elements of a rule. Our construction does not guarantee this requirement in general. But note that the algorithm in [2] only meets this condition because it avoids backtracking by aborting a translation when the chosen sequence of model transformation steps does not lead to a target model, even if there may be a possible sequence. Therefore, completeness is not achieved in [2]. By Thm. 4 we are able to perform partial order reduction, which has shown to provide massive power for the reduction of complexity (see e.g. [13]).
4. *Expressiveness:* Features that are urgently needed for solving practical problems like NACs and attribute conditions shall be captured. Both, NACs and attributes are handled by our approach. It remains open, whether our restriction to source-target NACs rules out some interesting practical applications.

6 Conclusion and Future Work

In this paper we have given a new formal construction of model transformations based on triple graph grammars including crucial properties like NAC-consistency, correctness, completeness and a sufficient condition for termination. In contrast to previous formal constructions in [1,8,10] the new construction avoids a parsing of the source graph beforehand or afterwards, but allows to construct simultaneously NAC-consistent forward and source transformation sequences leading to an on-the-fly construction of model transformations. Moreover, we have shown correctness and completeness of this on-the-fly construction and termination for triple rules with non-identical source part. Currently, these constructions are being implemented by us based on Mathematica libraries [17].

Finally, we studied parallel independence of model transformation steps, which allows us to perform partial-order reduction in order to improve efficiency of the construction. We have not analyzed local confluence in this paper, which - together with termination - leads to functional behaviour of the model transformation. We are confident that our concept of parallel independence can be extended to study critical pairs and local confluence for model transformation sequences based on existing approaches for graph transformation systems [15] including tool support by AGG [18]. Furthermore, additional correctness criteria shall be developed for the case that source and target languages VL_S and VL_T are defined independently of the triple graph language VL generated by the TGG.

References

1. Schürr, A.: Specification of Graph Translators with Triple Graph Grammars. In: Mayr, E.W., Schmidt, G., Tinhofer, G. (eds.) WG 1994. LNCS, vol. 903, pp. 151–163. Springer, Heidelberg (1995)

2. Schürr, A., Klar, F.: 15 Years of Triple Graph Grammars. In: Ehrig, H., Heckel, R., Rozenberg, G., Taentzer, G. (eds.) ICGT 2008. LNCS, vol. 5214, pp. 411–425. Springer, Heidelberg (2008)
3. Königs, A., Schürr, A.: Tool Integration with Triple Graph Grammars - A Survey. ENTCS 148, 113–150 (2006)
4. Guerra, E., de Lara, J.: Attributed Typed Triple Graph Transformation with Inheritance in the Double Pushout Approach. Technical Report UC3M-TR-CS-2006-00, Universidad Carlos III, Madrid (2006)
5. Taentzer, G., Ehrig, K., Guerra, E., de Lara, J., Lengyel, L., Levendovsky, T., Prange, U., Varro, D., Varro-Gyapay, S.: Model Transformation by Graph Transformation: A Comparative Study. In: Proc. WMTP 2005 (2005)
6. Guerra, E., de Lara, J.: Model View Management with Triple Graph Grammars. In: Corradini, A., Ehrig, H., Montanari, U., Ribeiro, L., Rozenberg, G. (eds.) ICGT 2006. LNCS, vol. 4178, pp. 351–366. Springer, Heidelberg (2006)
7. Kindler, E., Wagner, R.: Triple Graph Grammars: Concepts, Extensions, Implementations, and Application Scenarios. Technical Report TR-ri-07-284, Universität Paderborn (2007)
8. Ehrig, H., Ehrig, K., Ermel, C., Hermann, F., Taentzer, G.: Information Preserving Bidirectional Model Transformations. In: Dwyer, M.B., Lopes, A. (eds.) FASE 2007. LNCS, vol. 4422, pp. 72–86. Springer, Heidelberg (2007)
9. Ehrig, H., Ermel, C., Hermann, F.: On the Relationship of Model Transformations Based on Triple and Plain Graph Grammars. In: Karsai, G., Taentzer, G. (eds.) Proc. of GraMoT 2008. ACM, New York (2008)
10. Ehrig, H., Hermann, F., Sartorius, C.: Completeness and Correctness of Model Transformations based on Triple Graph Grammars with Negative Application Conditions. Electronic Communications of the EASST 18 (to appear, 2009)
11. Ehrig, H., Prange, U.: Formal Analysis of Model Transformations Based on Triple Graph Rules with Kernels. In: Ehrig, H., Heckel, R., Rozenberg, G., Taentzer, G. (eds.) ICGT 2008. LNCS, vol. 5214, pp. 178–193. Springer, Heidelberg (2008)
12. Ehrig, H., Ehrig, K., Hermann, F.: From Model Transformation to Model Integration based on the Algebraic Approach to Triple Graph Grammars. Electronic Communications of the EASST 10, 1–14 (2008)
13. Godefroid, P.: Partial-Order Methods for the Verification of Concurrent Systems. LNCS, vol. 1032. Springer, Heidelberg (1996)
14. Ehrig, H., Ermel, C., Hermann, F., Prange, U.: On-the-Fly Construction, Correctness and Completeness of Model Transformations based on Triple Graph Grammars: Long Version. Technical Report 2009-11, TU Berlin (2009), `http://www.eecs.tu-berlin.de/menue/forschung/forschungsberichte/`
15. Ehrig, H., et al.: Fundamentals of Algebraic Graph Transformation. EATCS Monographs. Springer, Heidelberg (2006)
16. de Lara, J., Guerra, E.: Pattern-based model-to-model transformation. In: Ehrig, H., Heckel, R., Rozenberg, G., Taentzer, G. (eds.) ICGT 2008. LNCS, vol. 5214, pp. 426–441. Springer, Heidelberg (2008)
17. Brandt, C., Hermann, F., Engel, T.: Security and Consistency of IT and Business Models at Credit Suisse realized by Graph Constraints, Transformation and Integration using Algebraic Graph Theory. In: Proc. of EMMSAD 2009. LNBIP, vol. 29, pp. 339–352. Springer, Heidelberg (2009)
18. TFS-group, TU Berlin: AGG (2009), `http://tfs.cs.tu-berlin.de/agg`

Formal Support for QVT-Relations with Coloured Petri Nets

Juan de Lara[1] and Esther Guerra[2]

[1] Universidad Autónoma de Madrid, Spain
jdelara@uam.es
[2] Universidad Carlos III de Madrid, Spain
eguerra@inf.uc3m.es

Abstract. QVT is the OMG standard language for specifying model-to-model transformations in MDA. Even though it plays a crucial role in model driven development, there are scarce tools supporting the execution of its sublanguage QVT-Relations, and none for its analysis or verification. In order to alleviate this situation, this paper provides a formal semantics for QVT-Relations through its compilation into Coloured Petri nets, enabling the execution and validation of QVT specifications. The theory of Petri nets provides useful techniques to analyse transformations (e.g. reachability, model-checking, boundedness and invariants) and to determine their confluence and termination given a starting model. We also report on using CPNTools for the execution, debugging, and analysis of transformations, and on a tool chain to transform QVT-Relations specifications into the input format of CPNTools.

1 Introduction

Model-to-model transformation consists in translating a model from a source to a target language. This process is at the core of Model-Driven Engineering (MDE), where models are used to generate code, test, document and verify the applications to be built. Among the existing model-to-model transformation languages, QVT [15] stands out for being the transformation standard proposed by the OMG in the framework of the Model-Driven Architecture (MDA). QVT has a hybrid declarative/imperative nature. The declarative part provides a user-friendly, high-level language called *Relations* (QVT-R) whose semantics is given by its compilation into a lower-level language called *Core* (QVT-C). In its turn, the imperative part provides a language called *Operational mappings* (QVT-O).

Despite the popularity of the QVT standard, few tools support the execution of QVT-R [12,13], and even less its verification or validation. This fact hinders its use in industry, where the complexity of models and transformations makes essential the development of tools and techniques for transformation analysis, which can be only built on the basis of a formal semantics for the transformation language. At present, QVT-R is given a semantics in terms of QVT-C, whose semantics is in its turn semi-formally defined. Thus, the MDE community would benefit from a clean, formal semantics for QVT-R enabling the analysis of transformations and serving as a reference for tool builders.

A. Schürr and B. Selic (Eds.): MODELS 2009, LNCS 5795, pp. 256–270, 2009.

In this sense, Coloured Petri nets (CP-nets or CPNs in short) [8,9] is a formalism for modelling, simulation and analysis of systems in which concurrency, communication and synchronization are salient features. They extend normal Petri nets with data types, allowing tokens to carry data. CPNs have developed a rich body of theoretical results that permit analysing dynamic properties of the systems, like boundedness (number of tokens a net may have), invariants, transition persistence (i.e. conflicts) or reachability [8]. Many of these properties rely on the occurrence graph, a representation of the state space that can be model checked and used to determine termination and confluence of a transformation relative to a starting model. The CP-nets community has developed a number of tools – CPNTools [9] being the best known one – with a level of maturity that makes them usable for industrial projects.

In the present work, we profit from the theory and tools developed for this formalism by providing a formal semantics for QVT-R in terms of CPNs. This opens the door to interesting analysis possibilities, and builds a bridge between the MDE and the Petri nets communities. On the practical side, we leverage CPNTools for the execution and analysis of QVT transformations, overcoming the lack of support for QVT-R. The explicit and visual nature of CPN models allows debugging and validating the transformation execution graphically, while their executable semantics may serve as a reference implementation for tool builders. A prototype tool chain, based on the QVT-R parser of MediniQVT [12] and the code generation facilities of JET, provides automatic translation of QVT-R specifications, meta-models and models into the input format of CPNTools, allowing the execution, debugging, verification and validation of transformations.

Paper organization. Sections 2 and 3 introduce QVT-R and CPNs. Section 4 shows the compilation from QVT-R into CPNs. Section 5 presents our supporting architecture. Section 6 illustrates the use of CPNs for verification and validation of transformations. Section 7 compares with related research and Section 8 ends with the conclusions and lines for future work.

2 QVT-Relations

QVT-R is the highest-level of abstraction language of the QVT OMG standard [15]. It has a declarative nature and a dual graphical and textual syntax. In this language, a model-to-model transformation is made of relations with two or more domains (usually two). Domains are described by patterns similar to object diagrams. When a domain is marked as *enforced*, the models to which it is applied may be modified in order to satisfy the relation; whereas if it is *checkonly*, they are just inspected to check for disagreements.

Relations may contain *when* and *where* clauses. The former express conditions under which the relation needs to hold. They usually refer to other relations, to which they pass a number of parameters that appear as variables in the current relation. *Where* clauses may call other relations, similar to function calls in traditional programming. In addition, relations may be *top* or *non-top* level. The execution of a transformation requires that all its top-level relations hold, whereas the non-top level ones only need to hold when invoked from the *where* section of other relations.

QVT-R uses the check-before-enforce (CBE) semantics [15]. Thus, before creating new objects, it is checked whether existing ones satisfying the constraints of the relation can be reused. Transformations may declare *keys* as unique identifiers for objects. These are used by the CBE semantics to decide whether to create a new object. The semantics of QVT-R is given by its compilation into QVT-C, relying on the synthesis of tracing mechanisms.

For illustrative purposes, we provide a simple transformation from a tiny subset of UML class diagrams into relational database schemas. The example is a simplification of the one given in the QVT standard [15]. The meta-models for the source and target languages are shown in Fig. 1.

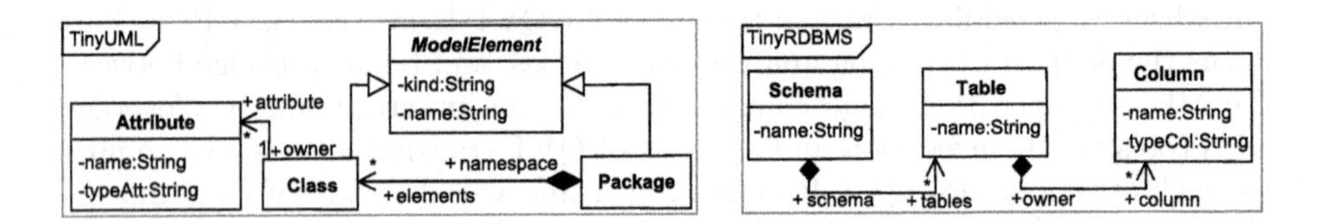

Fig. 1. The source and target meta-models

The QVT-R transformation is shown next. It defines three relations, two of them being top-level, and an auxiliary function. All relations enforce the RDBMS domain. The first one checks that for each persistent package in a UML model, there is a schema with same name (given by the pn String variable). The second one states that for each persistent class there must be a table with same name. The *when* section specifies that this relation has to hold only if relation *PackageToSchema* holds for the package and schema to which the class and table belong. The *where* clause asks the *AttributeToColumn* relation to hold for the class, table and an empty prefix. Finally, the last relation requires that for each attribute of a class there is a column with a name made of the received prefix plus the class name. The type of the column is calculated by the auxiliary function *PrimitiveTypeToSqlType*.

```
transformation umlToRdbms(uml:TinyUML, rdbms:TinyRDBMS) {
 top relation PackageToSchema { // maps each package to a schema
   pn: String;
   checkonly domain uml p:Package {name=pn, kind='persistent'};
   enforce domain rdbms s:Schema {name=pn};
 }
 top relation ClassToTable { // maps each persistent class to a table
   cn, prefix: String;
   checkonly domain uml c:Class {namespace=p:Package {},
                                  kind='persistent', name=cn};
   enforce domain rdbms t:Table {schema=s:Schema {}, name=cn};
   when { PackageToSchema(p, s); }
```

```
  where { prefix=''; AttributeToColumn(c, t, prefix); }
}
relation AttributeToColumn { // maps an attribute to a column
  an, pn, cn, sqltype: String;
  checkonly domain uml c:Class {attribute=a:Attribute {name=an, typeAtt=pn}};
  enforce domain rdbms t:Table {column=cl:Column {name=cn, typeCol=sqltype}};
  primitive domain prefix:String;
  where { cn = if (prefix = '') then an else prefix+'_'+an endif;
          sqltype = PrimitiveTypeToSqlType(pn); }
}
query PrimitiveTypeToSqlType(primitiveType:String):String {
  if (primitiveType='INTEGER') then 'NUMBER'
  else if (primitiveType='BOOLEAN') then 'BOOLEAN' else 'VARCHAR' endif
  endif;}
}
```

3 Coloured Petri Nets

CPNs is a popular formalism for describing concurrent systems, which is both state and action oriented. Here we give a brief introduction, see [8,9] for more details. A CPN model can be seen as a bipartite graph made of two kinds of nodes: *places* and *transitions*. The former represent the states of the net and are depicted as ovals with the name inside. Transitions model actions and are depicted as labelled rectangles. Places can be connected to transitions, and transitions to places, by means of *arcs*. As an example, Fig. 2 shows to the left a CPN with three places and one transition (exported from CPNTools). The net actually models the relation *PackageToSchema* of the example transformation.

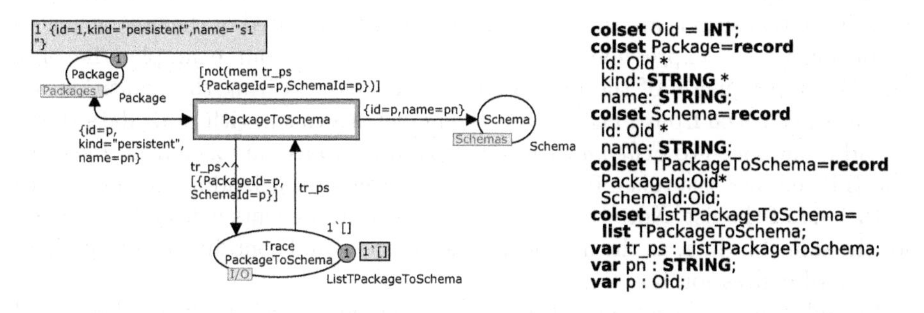

Fig. 2. Example CPN model: net (left) and colour set declarations (right)

Each place has a data type defining the kind of data it can contain, whose name is usually depicted next to the place. Data types (called *colour sets*) are declared in a language based on Standard ML, called CPN-ML [9]. The language allows declaring simple colour sets – like unit, booleans, integers, strings and enumerated – and compound ones, like products, records, lists, unions and subsets. The declarations for the example appear to the right of Fig. 2.

The state of a CPN is called its *marking*, and consists of a number of tokens located in the places. Each token contains data according to the colour set of the place where it is located. Places contain multi-sets of tokens. For the example, the *Package* and the *TracePackageToSchema* places contain one token each. The former is a record with value `{id=1, kind="persistent", name="s1"}`, while the latter is the empty list `[]`. The number of tokens in a place is indicated in a circle near the place, whereas the cardinality of each token in a multi-set is shown explicitly before the element value (e.g. `1'[]`).

Transitions are the dynamic elements in the net. An incoming arc to a transition indicates that the transition, if fired, will remove tokens from the connected places. Similarly, an outgoing place from a transition indicates that firing the transition will put tokens into the place. The tokens to be added or removed are given by the *arc expressions*. Transitions have a guard, shown between brackets, which is a boolean expression made of variables typed on the colour sets. The guard in the example checks the membership of a record in the `tr_ps` list.

A *binding* of one transition is an assignment of values to the variables in the incoming arcs and the guard. A transition is *enabled* if there is a valid binding for it, i.e. if the incoming places have enough tokens to bind the variables appearing in the incoming arcs, the variables in the guard are bound, and the expression evaluates to true. In the example, transition *PackageToSchema* is enabled (and hence highlighted) because the arc from *Package* demands one token with value "persistent" in the field `kind` (which exists), while the guard demands a token containing a list without any record whose two fields are equal to `p`. Hence, the transition is enabled with the binding $b_1 = \langle p = 1, pn = \text{"s1"}, tr\_ps = [] \rangle$.

An enabled *step* is a finite, non-empty multi-set of bindings enabling certain transitions. An enabled step can *occur*, changing the marking of the enabled transitions by the multi-set. In this way, the tokens needed to bind the incoming arcs of the transitions are removed, while tokens are created in the output places according to the expressions of the outgoing arcs. In our example, the only enabled step is made of the binding b_1 shown before. Firing the transition: (i) removes one token from *Package*, but then creates a token with same data there; (ii) adds one token to *Schema* with same `name` and `id` as the token from *Package*; and (iii) removes the token from the trace, but puts it back adding a new record at the end of the list. Note that firing the transition prevents it from firing again for the same binding, as the list in the trace place would contain a record making the guard expression false.

In addition to execution, CPNs have developed a rich body of theoretical results enabling analysis. Some of them are based on the occurrence graph, which contains which is a graph representation of the reachable markings [8]. Section 6 will use some CPN analysis techniques to verify QVT-R transformations.

CPNTools offers additional hierarchical and modular modelling capabilities. A large net can be divided into *pages* that can be connected by means of *Fusion Places* and *Substitution Transitions*. The latter are transitions that stand for a whole page of the net structure. For example, the net in Fig. 2 is represented as a single transition in Fig. 6, where we only show the *interface* places (marked *In*, *Out*, or *I/O* in the subnets). A fusion place is a place that has been equated with one or more other places, so that the fused places act as a single place with a single marking. We say that all these places belong to the same *Fusion Set*. For example, the place *Package* in Fig. 2 is the same as the place *Package* in Fig. 3, and both belong to the fusion set "Packages". Thus, these two mechanisms allow the modelling in different levels of abstraction (with the substitution transitions) and using multiple views (with the pages and fusion places).

4 Compiling QVT-Relations into CPNs

In this section we describe the compilation of QVT-R specifications into CPNs. We use the modular capabilities of CPNTools to create: two pages with places to store the objects of the source and target models; one page for each relation in the transformation; and a high-level view of the transformation with one substitution transition for each relation (linked to the corresponding page) and places depicting the *when* and *where* dependencies between relations.

4.1 Compiling the Meta-models and the Initial Model

The first step is to compile the source and target meta-models into colour sets declarations. For this purpose, we calculate the transitive closure of the inheritance relations in the meta-models so as to copy the attributes and relations from parent to children classes. Then a *record* is generated for each class and association in the meta-models. The record declares one field for each attribute in the class, plus an additional field *id* to store a unique object identifier. In case of an association, the record contains the identifier of the classes in each association end, as well as the attributes in case of an associative class.

As an example, the declarations for classes *Package* and *Schema* were shown in Fig. 2. As we will see in next subsections, further definitions will be added to store the traces of the relations, and parameter passing.

Next, we create one place for each created record, and populate it with tokens representing the model to be transformed. These tokens hold the values of each object attribute. We split the places of the source and target meta-models in two different pages to enhance readability. Each place is assigned a fusion set so that it can be referenced from other pages. Fig. 3 depicts a TinyUML model to be transformed, and the corresponding generated places and initial marking. The model contains two classes with equal name (since the meta-model allows this), having one attribute each with equal name.

4.2 Compiling the Relations

Next, we compile the relations. We restrict to the case with one domain enforced and the other checkonly, and neglect CBE semantics and keys for the moment.

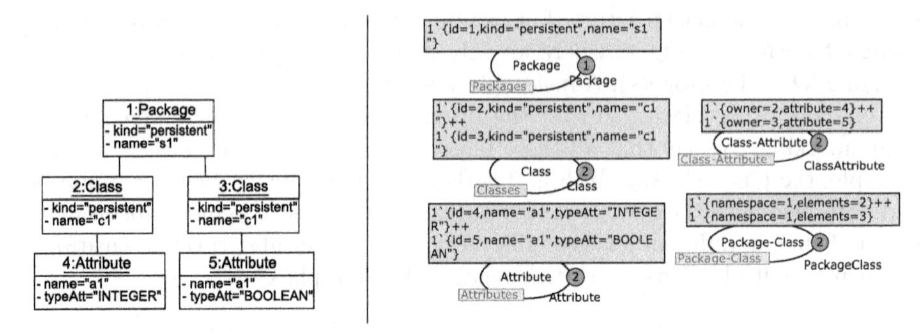

Fig. 3. Source model (left). Generated places and initial marking (right).

For each relation, we create a transition with its name in a different page. For each element in the relations domain, we create a place in the fusion set corresponding to the type of the element. If the domain is checkonly, the place is connected to the transition with a self-loop, whereas if it is enforced, the transition is connected to the place. The arc inscriptions contain variables with same name as in the QVT relation, binding the different fields of the record. In checkonly domains we make the following simplification: if the attributes of an object are not accessed, and the object is connected to another through a link `l`, then we do not test if the object is present, but just that there is a link `l`.

Finally, for each relation we generate a colour set for its trace which contains the identifiers of all objects appearing in the relation. This conforms to the standard semantics of the compilation of QVT-R into QVT-C [15]. Moreover, for each relation, we create one place with type equal to the list of traces of the relation. The transition inspects this place in order to check that the identifiers of the objects in the relation are not in the list. This avoids enforcing a relation more than once for the same binding. When the transition fires, the list of traces is added a new element with the processed objects. Later, we will also use the trace for the translation of the *when* clause.

Fig. 2 showed the transition generated for relation *PackageToSchema*. The trace place contains one token with the empty list. The read arc takes such list, the guard checks that a record with the identifiers of the involved objects is not present, and the write arc adds the record to the list when the transition fires. For simplicity, the created schema object is given the same identifier as the package, but in our implementation an ML function calculates unique identifiers.

4.3 Compiling the Where and When Clauses

After generating one transition per relation, we process the *when* and *where* clauses. The latter usually includes calls to other relations using as parameters bound objects of the current relation. For this reason, we create a colour set with fields corresponding to the parameters, and create a place with that type in a new fusion set. We add an arc from the transition to the place that writes one token with the given parameter values when the transition fires. Another place in the same fusion set is added to the page of the called relation, together with self-loop arcs.

As an example, Fig. 4 shows the transition generated for relation *ClassToTable*. The *ParamAttrCol* place is used to pass the three parameters to the relation *AttributeToColumn*. The marking shows the situation after firing the transition once, which creates a table with name `c1`. The transition remains enabled because there is a class which has not been processed, so its firing creates a new table also with name `c1`. As this does not conform to the CBE semantics, we will describe the needed modifications to the net in Section 4.5.

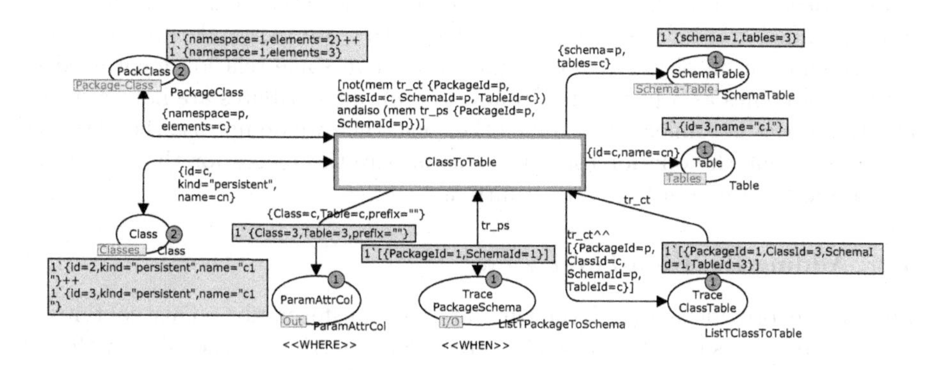

Fig. 4. Generated transition from relation *ClassToTable*

The transition for relation *AttributeToColumn* is shown in Fig. 5, where the parameters are received from place *ParamAttrCol*. The parameters are not deleted from the place as, in general, a relation may need to be enforced more than once. Should a relation be called with different parameter sets (e.g. 2 parameters instead of 3), we will have to replicate the transition for each set.

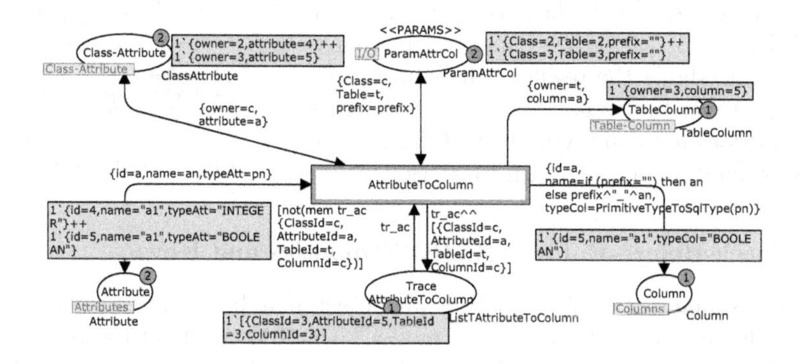

Fig. 5. Generated transition from relation *AttributeToColumn*

The *when* clause is handled by querying the trace places. In particular, for each relation r_w appearing in the *when* clause of a relation r, a self-loop arc reading a token from the trace place of r_w is attached to the transition of r. Then, a guard is added to the transition of r demanding the read token to have a record with the values given by the actual parameters. Moreover, all arcs adding tokens to a place of an enforced domain which corresponds to an element passed as parameter are deleted. As an example, the transition generated from *ClassToTable* in Fig. 4 reads the list of traces from place *TracePackageSchema*, and the guard checks that the list contains a record indicating that the package and the schema have already been processed. Moreover, the place corresponding to the schema is not added tokens as the schema is a parameter in the *when* clause. In fact, with our simplified way of assigning object identifiers, we can make the following optimization: if an object is bound (i.e. present in some relation mentioned in a *when*, or comes as a parameter from a *where*), its attributes are not accessed, and the object is connected to some other one; then we do not use the place for the object, but the one for the link. This is why the places for the schema in Fig. 4 and the table in Fig. 5 are omitted.

4.4 Adding the High-Level View

Finally, we provide a high-level view of the transformation. This contains a substitution transition for each QVT relation, referring to the page with the relation details as described in previous sections. The view also shows the places for the *when* and *where* clauses, so as to depict the execution flow and parameter passing between relations, allowing the identification of dependencies.

Fig. 6 shows the high-level view for the example. The top-level relations are shown with thicker border. Even though *ClassToTable* is top-level, it depends on *PackageToSchema* as the latter is referenced in the *when* clause of the former. Relation *AttributeToColumn* is not top-level, and can only be executed when it receives a token with the parameters produced by relation *ClassToTable*. Note how the comments in the QVT transformation are visualized in the net. The marking shows the result of the transformation, where two tables have been created. Since the result does not comply with the CBE semantics, we solve this problem in next section.

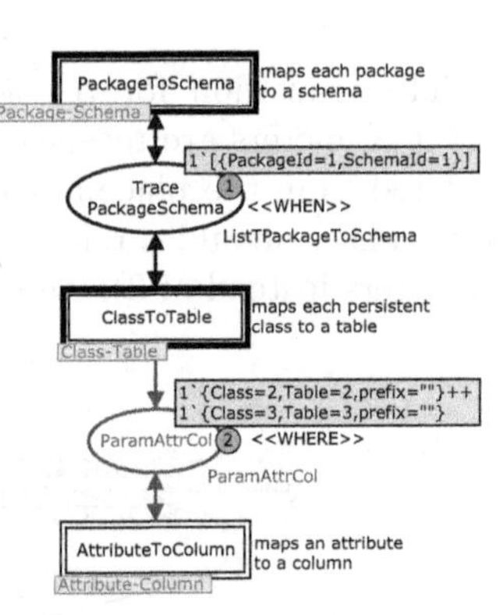

Fig. 6. High-level view

4.5 Check-Before-Enforce (CBE) Semantics and Keys

The CBE semantics ensures that, if an object matching the constraints in a relation already exists in an enforced model, such object will not be created. The *keys* define when two objects are considered equal. The presented compilation has not taken this semantics into account. Even though traces avoided enforcing a relation more than once for the same objects, we always created objects in the enforced domain instead of reusing them. Next we consider such semantics.

The idea is to generate several transitions for each relation. All transitions are mutually exclusive (at most one can fire at any given step), and each try to reuse increasingly bigger parts of the enforced domain. Hence, we build a partial order of graphs, the bottom element being the relation parameters (i.e. no reuse), and the top one the graph equal to the enforced domain (i.e. maximal reuse). The keys specify which attributes of an object need to be compared in order to decide whether an object already exists.

The generated transitions should check if some objects are not present. Negative tests are problematic in CPNs, as the normal arcs test the existence of tokens, not their absence. As inhibitor arcs are not supported by CPNs, we use tokens containing lists of records instead of records. Hence, each place in the enforced domain contains exactly one token, with a list of the objects present in the model. In this way, testing if an object is not present amounts to ensuring that the corresponding record is not in the list.

Fig. 7 shows the two transitions generated from *PackageToSchema*. The left one creates a new schema if it is not found on the list `sch` taken from place *AllSchemas*, actually checked by the function `existsSchema` in the transition guard. The right one is executed if the schema exists and reuses the schema.

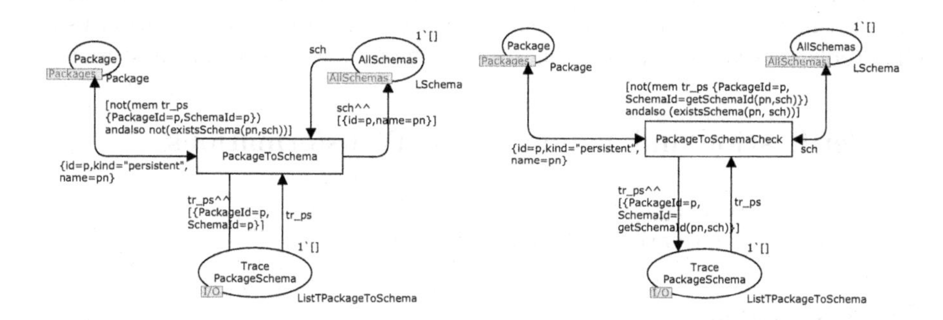

Fig. 7. Two transitions generated from *PackageToSchema* due to CBE

The left of Fig. 8 shows the high-level view of the transformation with all transitions generated by the CBE semantics. The key for the table was its name and schema, and for the column its name and table. The marking shows some of the traces after executing the net, where only one table and one column are created, in conformance with the CBE semantics. The created model can be inspected in the page corresponding to the target meta-model.

5 Supporting Architecture

We have implemented a prototype to transform QVT-R specifications into the input format of CPNTools, for the moment without considering CBE semantics.

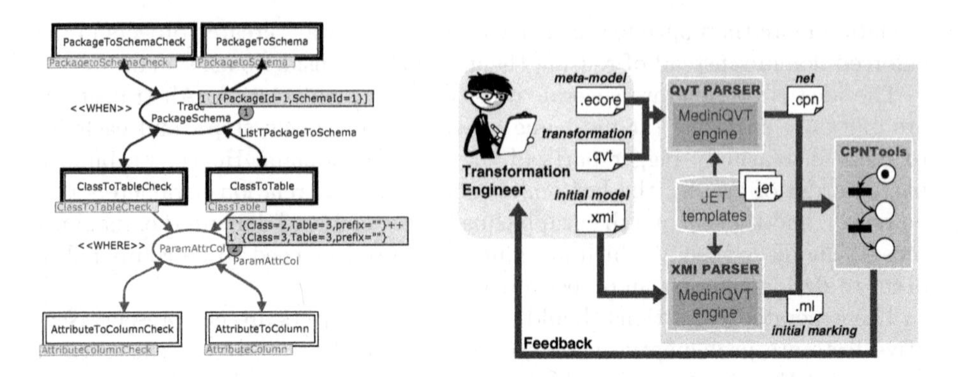

Fig. 8. High-level view with CBE semantics (left). Architecture of the solution (right).

The right of Fig. 8 shows its architecture. The engineer specifies the transformation using the textual format of QVT-R, and the source and target meta-models in *ecore*. We have built a code generator that parses these files using the MediniQVT parser [12], and then generates the input file to CPNTools through JET templates [10]. We also have developed another generator that, from an *xmi* model, generates a marking in a separate file that is read by the CPN model. In this way, no recompilation of the whole transformation is needed for different starting models. Then, the designer can execute the transformation using CPNTools, as well as to analyse it to find defects as we show in next section.

6 Verification and Validation of Transformations

This section presents some verification and validation techniques that are possible once the transformation is expressed in CPNs.

6.1 Verification

Many verification techniques for CPNs are based on the computation of the *occurrence graph* [8], a graph-based representation of the space of possible markings. Fig. 9 shows the graph for the example, considering CBE semantics and taking the starting model of Fig. 3. The graph shows the labels of two arrows, depicting the executed transition and part of the binding. To the right, the figure shows the TinyRDBMS models corresponding to nodes 13 and 14 of the graph.

Confluence. A transformation is confluent if it yields a unique result for every possible starting model. We can investigate confluence by inspecting the terminal nodes of the occurrence graph. As we use lists, having more than one terminal node does not imply non-confluence: the lists may contain equal elements but ordered differently. Also, we obtain two different terminal nodes for models with the same structure, but different object identifiers. Our example however is non-confluent. The transformation creates one table (as both classes have equal name) with one column. Processing the BOOLEAN attribute first creates a BOOLEAN column (nodes 16 and 13 in the graph), whereas processing the INTEGER first creates a NUMBER column (nodes 15 and 14). This is so because the key for attributes only considers their name and class but not its type. Considering also the column type solves this problem. Note however that CPNs only allows investigating confluence on individual starting models.

Another source of non-confluence is attribute computation using queries on enforced domains. For example, if the column name is computed as `cn=if (owner.column->size()=1) then '_'+ an else an`; we have non-determinism. This is so because the first column to be processed would be added a prefix `'_'`, and this choice can be non-deterministic. Furthermore, if the table is added several columns, actually adding the prefix for the first column is wrong. Since QVT-R is declarative, the expression `cn=...` is to be interpreted as an invariant. However it may yield a different result when evaluated during the transformation than *at the end* of the transformation. Hence, if there are two columns no attribute should be added the prefix. Thus, "constructive" operational mechanisms would run into troubles. In our approach, we forbid attribute computations using queries on enforced domains.

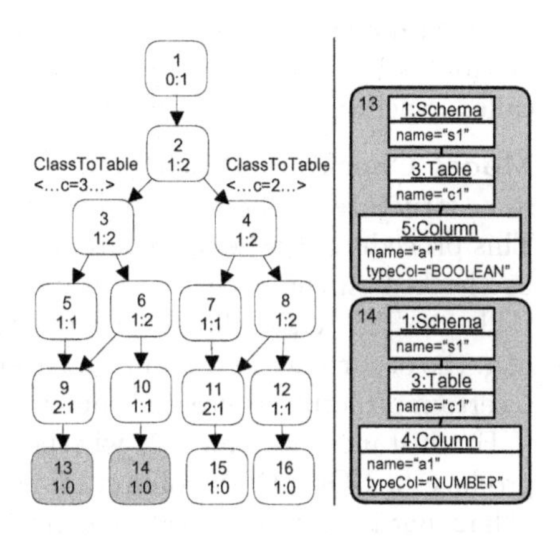

Fig. 9. Occurrence graph

Termination. This is undecidable for graph and term rewriting systems [4]. QVT-R transformations can be non-terminating due to e.g. a recursive relation which creates new elements, and passes them to the next step in the recursion in the *where* section. If the occurrence graph is finite and has no cycles, then the transformation always terminates for the given starting model. Our example transformation is terminating for the given initial model.

Relation Conflicts. Transition *persistence* allows discovering conflicts between relations. A transition is persistent if firing it does not disable other enabled transitions, and *weakly* persistent if it may disable itself at a different binding. Hence, if a transition is not persistent, it has conflicts and may lead to a non-confluent transformation. A conflict in QVT-R may arise if the execution of some relation depends on a query on an enforced domain, or if a relation A can be executed if some other B has not (by placing "*not* $B(\ldots)$;" in A's *when* section). In most cases all relations should be non-conflicting, leading to weakly persistent transitions in the CPN model. In the example, all transitions are weakly persistent as none disable others but may disable themselves. Persistence can be efficiently checked using the occurrence graph, and a sufficient condition for persistence exists by statically checking the underlying uncoloured net [14].

Boundedness and Invariants. A net is bounded if the number of tokens of all places remains bounded in all possible executions. This is automated by CPNTools and is useful to identify sources of non-termination as well as the maximum number of objects of a certain type that can be created. Invariants are expressions on the marking that remain true in all reachable states. In a QVT-R transformation we find two types of invariants: the preservation of elements in checkonly domains, and maybe the non-creation of some type of element in enforced domains. Thus, we can check whether for a TinyUML model without attributes it is an invariant that no column is generated. These invariants are called synchronization invariants [5] and can be automatically computed.

Model Checking. Reachability analysis can be used to investigate whether some structure can be produced in the enforced domain, given an initial marking. This procedure can be automated, as CPNTools allows expressing properties to be checked on the occurrence graph by means of a CTL-like logic called ASK-CTL [3]. This logic allows formulating queries about states and state changes (e.g. the occurrence of certain transitions). This search is useful to check whether a certain structure is created sometimes or always in each possible result.

For instance, we can ask whether transforming our example model always produces a BOOLEAN column by using the command `eval_node INV(POS(NF ("Has Bool Column", hasColumn))) InitNode`, which returns false as we may obtain a NUMBER column instead. In the previous command, `InitNode` is the initial marking, `hasColumn` is a user-defined function that checks whether a given marking contains a boolean column, `POS(A)` demands property A to be eventually satisfied, and `INV(A)` demands A to be satisfied in all possible paths. Checking whether sometimes such column is obtained is done through command `eval_node POS(NF("Has Bool Column", hasColumn)) InitNode`, which returns true. Other interesting properties include whether we always or sometimes obtain the same number of columns as attributes (false in both cases), the same number of tables as classes (false), the same number of schemas as packages (true) or whether a certain relation is always or sometimes executed.

6.2 Validation with CPNTools

In order to validate a transformation, we can use CPNTools to perform run-to-completion execution, as well as a step-by-step visual simulation for debugging. Similar to breakpoints in programming environments, one can set *monitors* establishing conditions (e.g. the marking exceeds a certain size, a transition occurs a certain number of times or a place becomes empty) under which some action is performed (e.g. pause the execution or write to a file). They can also be used to encode the OCL constraints of the target language, in order to check if they are violated. The multi-view and hierarchical features permit visualizing the execution flow in the high-level page, and checking the created elements in the page corresponding to the meta-models.

Simulation and verification can be combined using the occurrence graph, as it can be created incrementally, and visually inspected. Each node can show the marking, and it is possible to set the net in the state of a given node.

7 Related Work

There are previous attempts to formalize QVT, such as the one in [7] for QVT-C. Regarding QVT-R, in [1,11] the authors formalize it by using rewriting logic and Maude; however there is no comment about CBE semantics and no discussion on termination or confluence. In [6] the author uses OCL for representing the static semantics, and Alloy for the dynamics. Although Alloy permits execution and analysis, no discussion on analysis is given. That approach is similar to our previous work in [2], where we translated QVT-R into OCL and used a constraint solver for execution and analysis. In that case, the kind of possible analyses is different, as they are based on "model finding". For example, we tested whether a transformation is satisfiable, or whether a source model produces a valid target model (i.e. conformant to the meta-models and their integrity constraints). In our approach with CPNs, the validity of the target model has to be checked by loading and validating the model in the modelling tool, or by setting CPN monitors. However, CPNs allow the visual step-by-step execution and debugging of the transformation, which is not possible with constraint solvers. Other approaches like [16] use CPNs for transformations, but they have their own language, not QVT, and do not provide analysis techniques.

On the other hand, there are few tools for QVT-R. We can mention MediniQVT [12] and ModelMorf [13], but none of them provide analysis capabilities. Thus, we can see our work as a "low-cost" implementation of a QVT-R engine allowing both execution and analysis.

8 Conclusions and Future Work

In this paper we have presented an approach for the execution, verification and validation of QVT-R transformations through their compilation into CPNs. The approach supports when and where clauses and CBE semantics. We have shown how to use the occurrence graph to check termination and confluence, how to analyse relation conflicts by transition persistence, and how to determine whether certain structures are created in enforced domains using model checking, invariants and boundedness analysis. Finally, we have demonstrated that CPN-Tools can be used for execution, verification and validation of transformations; and presented a tool that automates the code generation for it.

One limitation of our proposal is the full support for OCL, which would require a complex compilation into ML. Up to now we support a small subset enough to translate the auxiliary query of the example. Complex queries involving negation would require using tokens with lists also in checkonly domains. We are currently improving our tool chain and defining back-annotation mechanisms so that the user does not realise that the execution is based on CPNs, e.g. by translating the final marking into XMI. It would be also interesting to develop a high-level language to specify the properties to be model-checked. The use of CPNs opens the door to other useful techniques, such optimizing the CPN [5] and translating such optimizations into QVT, or the verification of properties independently of the marking. We also plan to complement our analysis techniques with the automatic generation of initial markings for the nets.

Acknowledgments. Work supported by the Spanish Ministry of Science and Innovation, projects METEORIC (TIN2008-02081) and MODUWEB (TIN2006-09678).

References

1. Boronat, A., Carsí, J.A., Ramos, I.: Algebraic specification of a model transformation engine. In: Baresi, L., Heckel, R. (eds.) FASE 2006. LNCS, vol. 3922, pp. 262–277. Springer, Heidelberg (2006)
2. Cabot, J., Clarisó, R., Guerra, E., de Lara, J.: An invariant-based method for the analysis of declarative model-to-model transformations. In: Czarnecki, K., Ober, I., Bruel, J.-M., Uhl, A., Völter, M. (eds.) MODELS 2008. LNCS, vol. 5301, pp. 37–52. Springer, Heidelberg (2008)
3. Cheng, A., Christensen, S., Mortensen, K.H.: Model checking coloured petri nets exploiting strongly connected components. In: WODES, pp. 169–177 (1996)
4. Ehrig, H., Ehrig, K., Prange, U., Taentzer, G.: Fundamentals of algebraic graph transformation. Springer, Heidelberg (2006)
5. Evangelista, S., Haddad, S., Pradat, J.-F.: Syntactical colored petri nets reductions. In: Peled, D.A., Tsay, Y.-K. (eds.) ATVA 2005. LNCS, vol. 3707, pp. 202–216. Springer, Heidelberg (2005)
6. García, M.: Formalization of QVT-Relations: OCL-based static semantics and Alloy-based validation. In: MDSD today, pp. 21–30. Shaker Verlag (2008)
7. Greenyer, J.: A study of model transformation technologies: Reconciling TGGs with QVT. Master's thesis, University of Paderborn (2006)
8. Jensen, K.: Coloured Petri nets basic concepts, analysis methods and practical use (Monographs in theoretical computer science). Springer, Heidelberg (1997)
9. Jensen, K., Kristensen, L.M., Wells, L.: Coloured petri nets and CPN tools for modelling and validation of concurrent systems. STTT 9(3-4), 213–254 (2007), `http://wiki.daimi.au.dk/cpntools`
10. JET (2009), `http://www.eclipse.org/modeling/m2t/?project=jet`
11. Lucas, F.J., Álvarez, J.A.T.: Model transformations powered by rewriting logic. In: CAiSE Forum. CEUR Proc., vol. 344, pp. 41–44 (2008)
12. MediniQVT (2009), `http://projects.ikv.de/qvt/`
13. ModelMorf (2009), `http://www.tcs-trddc.com/ModelMorf/index.htm`
14. Ohta, A., Tsuji, K.: On some analysis properties of colored petri net using underlying net. In: MWSCAS 2004, vol. 3, pp. 395–398. IEEE, Los Alamitos (2004)
15. QVT (2005), `http://www.omg.org/docs/ptc/05-11-01.pdf`
16. Strommer, M., Wimmer, M.: A framework for model transformation by-example: Concepts and tool support. In: TOOLS. LNBIP, vol. 11, pp. 372–391. Springer, Heidelberg (1974)

An Example Is Worth a Thousand Words: Composite Operation Modeling By-Example*

Petra Brosch[1,**], Philip Langer[2], Martina Seidl[1], Konrad Wieland[1], Manuel Wimmer[1], Gerti Kappel[1], Werner Retschitzegger[3], and Wieland Schwinger[2]

[1] Business Informatics Group, Vienna University of Technology, Austria
lastname@big.tuwien.ac.at
[2] Department of Telecooperation, Johannes Kepler University Linz, Austria
firstname.lastname@jku.ac.at
[3] Information System Group, Johannes Kepler University Linz, Austria
werner@ifs.uni-linz.ac.at

Abstract. Predefined composite operations are handy for efficient modeling, e.g., for the automatic execution of refactorings, and for the introduction of patterns in existing models. Some modeling environments provide an initial set of basic refactoring operations, but hardly offer any extension points for the user. Even if extension points exist, the introduction of new composite operations requires programming skills and deep knowledge of the respective metamodel.

In this paper, we introduce a method for specifying composite operations within the user's modeling language and environment of choice. The user models the composite operation by-example, which enables the semi-automatic derivation of a generic composite operation specification. This specification may be used in various modeling scenarios, like model refactoring and model versioning. We implemented the approach in the Operation Recorder and performed an evaluation by defining multiple complex refactorings for UML diagrams.

Keywords: Refactoring, composite operation, by-example approach.

1 Introduction

Since modeling is hardly done in terms of single atomic operations but by performing a sequence of operations to reach a desired goal, a well established approach for specifying and communicating a recurrent sequence of operations is to give it a name and define a pattern, as is done, e.g., by Gamma et al. [1] and Fowler et al. [2]. In order to define patterns not only for human interaction, but also in a machine readable and executable format, composite operations may be described as model transformations.

* This work has been partly funded by the Austrian Federal Ministry of Transport, Innovation and Technology (BMVIT) and FFG under grant FIT-IT-819584.

** Funding for this research was provided by the fFORTE WIT - Women in Technology Program of the Vienna University of Technology, and the Austrian Federal Ministry of Science and Research.

A. Schürr and B. Selic (Eds.): MODELS 2009, LNCS 5795, pp. 271–285, 2009.

So far, the implementation of such model transformations has mainly been accomplished by experts, because they require extensive programming effort and deep knowledge of APIs of modeling environments, metamodels, and dedicated transformation languages. The contribution of this paper is to overcome this pitfall. To open the specification of patterns and refactorings to modelers, we present the Operation Recorder, a front-end for the user-friendly modeling of composite operations by-example.

The Operation Recorder enables the specification of composite operations by modeling concrete examples at the model layer, i.e., the same layer the pattern definition is applied. It allows the user to work within her preferred modeling language and editor of choice, without leaving the familiar environment. The examples consist of the initial model, the revised model, and the differences between them. These differences of the two models are then generalized by the Operation Recorder and may be applied to arbitrary models containing a pattern matching the initial model. In the research project AMOR [3], we use the Operation Recorder in two orthogonal modeling settings, namely for refactoring and versioning.

Refactoring. Predefined refactoring operations as known from IDEs like Eclipse[1] find their way into modeling environments. Since it is not possible to provide all refactorings out-of-the-box—this is especially the case if domain-specific modeling languages (DSMLs) are employed—the modeling editor should offer extension points for editing and adding user-defined refactorings [4]. The Operation Recorder is used as a user-friendly front-end for specifying user-defined composite operations.

Versioning. The state-based recognition of multiple atomic operations as one refactoring may also improve model versioning [5]. Since refactorings often have global effects in the overall model, subsuming a set of atomic changes to only one change makes it easier to read version histories and to understand model evolution. In the case of optimistic versioning, where parallel editing of model artifacts is allowed, the recognition of refactorings improves automatic merge as discussed in [6]. Even if an automatic merge cannot be performed, manual conflict resolution is accelerated by providing a more readable conflict report. A comprehensive model versioning environment is part of our future research.

The paper is organized as follows. Starting with a motivating example in Section 2 we outline the process of composite operation modeling by-example in Section 3. Section 4 provides a detailed account of the implementation of the Operation Recorder and Section 5 summarizes the evaluation results for complex refactorings of UML diagrams. Section 6 discusses related work and we conclude with an outlook on our future work in Section 7.

2 Motivating Example

To emphasize our motivation for developing the Operation Recorder, we discuss the refactoring "Introduce Composite State" for UML statecharts. The concrete

[1] http://www.eclipse.org/

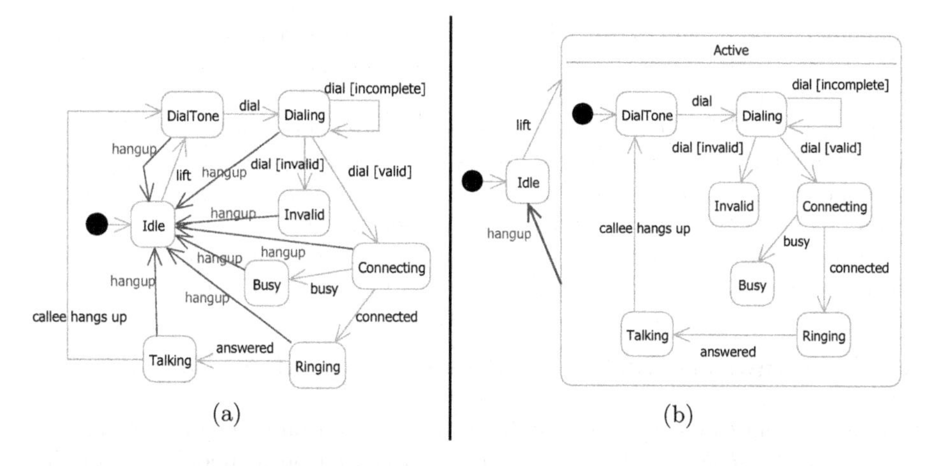

Fig. 1. (a) Initial Phone Statechart. (b) Refactored Phone Statechart. [7]

example illustrating the possible states and transitions of a phone conversation was taken from Sunyé et al. [7] (cf. Figure 1).

Whenever a hangup event occurs in the unrefactored model shown in Figure 1(a), the phone moves to the state *Idle*. The multitude of similar transitions, which are pointing to the state *Idle* and which are triggerd by the same event, suggests the application of the refactoring pattern "Introduce Composite State", i.e., introducing a composite state and folding the hangup transitions to one single transition as depicted in Figure 1(b). The modification consists of the following changes:

1. A composite state named *Active* is created.
2. All states except *Idle* are moved into *Active*.
3. The outgoing hangup transitions of these states are folded into one single transition which leaves the composite state *Active*.
4. The transition *lift* is split to an incoming transition of *Active* and to the initial pseudostate of *Active*.

In most modeling tools, the general specification of such a composite operation is only possible by an implementation in a textual programming language, which demands dedicated programming skills. Based on our experience when developing the "Introduce Composite State" refactoring in Java, the solution comprises nearly 100 lines of code implementing the pure refactoring logic, not counting preconditions on the applicability of the refactoring pattern and code realizing a front-end for the application of the refactoring pattern by the user.

Another alternative to specify composite operations is the use of dedicated model transformation languages. This enables the development of composite operations in a more compact form, since single operations may be described, e.g., by declarative transformation rules. However, specifying a set of transformation rules and their interactions is currently supported by only a few transformation engines, and requires a deep understanding of the transformation process. Furthermore, model transformation approaches are rarely included in current modeling environments. Thus, tool adapters are required to use these technologies and the users have to switch to a new environment, which again calls for dedicated knowledge.

Modelers, as the potential users of the composite operation specification facilities are familiar with the notation, semantics, and pragmatics of the modeling languages they use in daily activities. They are not experts, however, in programming languages, transformation techniques, or APIs.

With the Operation Recorder we aim at providing a tool, which makes the specification of composite operations practical to every modeler.

3 By-Example Operation Specification at a Glance

Composite operations may be described by a set of atomic operations, namely, *create*, *update*, *delete*, and *move* which are executed on a model in a specific modeling scenario, i.e., adhering to specific preconditions [8]. Furthermore, to enable the detection of occurrences of the specified composite operation in generic change scripts, we need to include also postconditions to the composite operation specification.

A straightforward way to realize composite operation specification by-example is to record each user interaction within the modeling environment as proposed in [9] for programming languages. However, this would demand an intervention in the modeling environment, and due to the multitude of modeling environments, we refrain from this possibility. Instead, we apply a state-based comparison to determine the executed operations after building up the initial model and the final model. This allows the use of any editor without depending on editor-specific modification recording. To overcome the imprecision of heuristic state-based approaches, a unique ID is automatically assigned to each model element before the user performes the changes. Moreover, the Operation Recorder is designed in such a way to be independent from any specific modeling language, as long as it is based on Ecore [10] or the metamodel may be mapped to Ecore.

Following our design rationale, we propose a two-phase by-example operation specification process as shown in Figure 2. In the following, we discuss this two-phase specification process step-by-step.

Phase 1: Modeling. In a first step, the user models the initial situation in her familiar modeling environment, i.e., the model required in order to apply the composite operation. The output of this step is called the *initial model*. In a second step, each element of the *initial model* is automatically annotated with an ID, and a so-called *working model*, i.e., a copy of the *initial model* for demonstrating the composite operation by applying changes, is created. The IDs preserve the relationship of the original elements in the initial model and the changed elements in the *revised model*. The IDs allow a precise detection of all atomic changes, i.e., also element moves. Consequently, the generated match between the initial model and the revised model is sound and complete. In the third step, the user performs the complete composite operation on the working model, again in her familiar modeling environment by applying all necessary

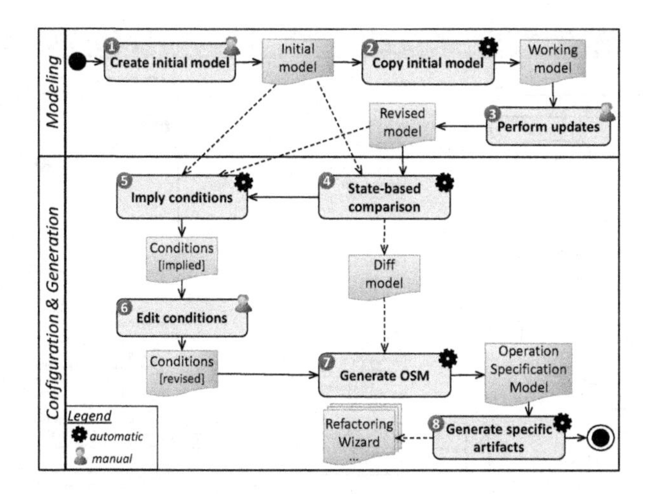

Fig. 2. By-Example Operation Specification Process

atomic operations. The output of this step is the revised model, which is together with the initial model the input for the second phase of the operation specification process.

Phase 2: Configuration & Generation. Due to the unique identifiers of the model elements, the atomic operations of the composite operation may be determined automatically in Step 4 using a state-based comparison. The results are saved in the *diff model*. Subsequently, an initial version of *pre-* and *postconditions* of the composite operation is inferred in Step 5 by analyzing the initial model and the revised model, respectively. Usually, the automatically generated conditions from the example are too strong and do not express the intended pre- and postconditions of the composite operation completely. They only act as a basis for accelerating the operation specification process and have to be refined by the user in Step 6. In particular, parts of the conditions may be activated and deactivated within a dedicated environment with one mouse click. Generated conditions may be modified by the user and additional conditions may be added. After the configuration of the conditions, the *Operation Specification Model* (OSM) is generated in Step 7, which consists of the diff model and the revised pre- and postconditions. Finally, from the OSM, specific artifacts may be generated in Step 8 such as refactoring wizards which allow the automatic execution of refactorings. Another use case of the OSM would be to directly act as a template for change scripts in order to find applications of composite operations between different model versions.

4 By-Example Operation Recorder in Action

In the previous section we illustrated the operation specification process from a generic point of view. In the following, we define the refactoring "Introduce Composite State" from Section 2 showing the operation specification process

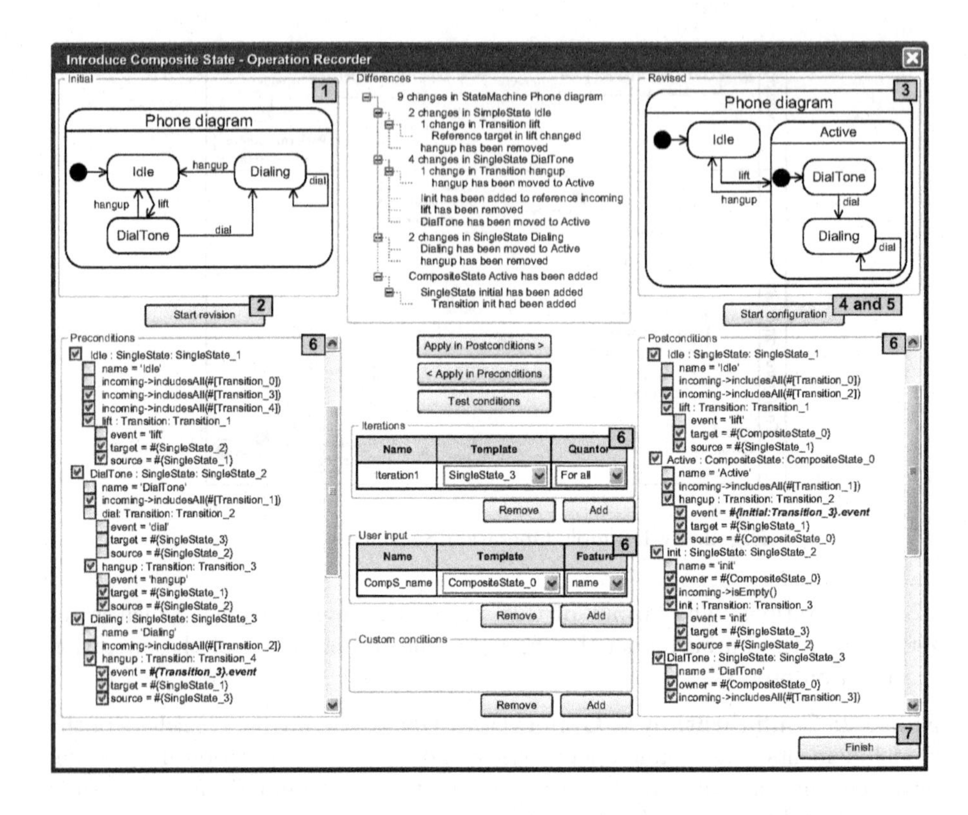

Fig. 3. Front-End of the Operation Recorder

from the user's point of view. The specification process is supported by the Operation Recorder using the front-end depicted in Figure 3 which is simplified for illustration purposes. For details on the implementation of the productive front-end we refer to [11].

Step 1: Create initial model. The modeler starts with modeling the initial situation in the upper left area labeled *Initial* (cf. Figure 3). For this task, the modeler may apply any editor of her choice, since the Operation Recorder is independent of editor-specific operation tracking, using a solely state-based comparison. The Operation Recorder allows to load any GMF[2]-based graphical editor for direct editing the example or Ecore XMI-serialized files which have been created in any other editor. In this step every model element, which is necessary to show the composite operation, has to be introduced. It is not necessary to draw every state of the diagram shown in Figure 1(a). Therefore, in the *Initial* area only those states are depicted, which will later on be modified differently. The first of those is the state *Idle*, which will remain outside the composite state we will add later. Second, the state *DialTone*, which will be moved to the newly added composite state acting as first state and finally the state *Dialing*, which

[2] http://www.eclipse.org/modeling/gmf/

only will be moved to the composite state loosing its transition to *Idle*. There is no need to model the state *Connecting* shown in Figure 1(a), since it is equally modified like *Dialing*. For these equally handled states the Operation Recorder provides techniques to define iterations in the later configuration phase.

Step 2: Copy initial model. When the modeler finishes the initial model she confirms it by pushing the button *Start editing*. This initiates the automatic copy process which adds a unique ID to every model element of the initial model before the working copy is created.

Step 3: Perform updates. After the ID-annotated working copy is created, it is displayed in the upper right area of the front-end, named *Revised*. Now, the modeler performs each operation of the composite operation on the revised model. In our example, the modeler has to add a composite state named *Active*, move the single states *DialTone* and *Dialing* into it, introduce a new initial state in *Active*, connect it with *DialTone* and change or remove the other transitions. As soon as the composite operation is completely executed, the modeler finalizes the modeling phase by pushing the *Start configuration* button.

Step 4: Execute state-based comparison. In this step, the comparison between the initial model and the revised model is done to automatically identify the previously executed changes. Internally, the comparison is realized on top of EMF Compare[3]. When the comparison is completed, the detected differences show up in the upper center area named *Differences*. For a precise definition of the composite operation it is important that the modeler performs only those operations which directly represent the composite operation.

Step 5: Imply conditions. Next, the Operation Recorder automatically implies the preconditions from the initial model and the postconditions from the revised model. The generation process for the pre- and the postconditions is similar. For each model element in the respective model, a so-called *template* is created. A template describes the role, a model element plays in the specific composite operation. When executing or detecting a defined composite operation, concrete model elements are evaluated against and subsequently bound to these templates. In the front-end the pre- and postconditions are illustrated on the lower left and lower right area, respectively. Each template contains conditions displayed beside the template names. Each automatically generated condition constrains the value of a specific feature. In our example, the area *Preconditions* shows three different templates in the first level for the model elements *Idle*, *DialTone*, and *Dialing* and their respective preconditions. These templates have a user-changeable symbolic name, e.g., *SingleState_1*, and are arranged in a tree to indicate their containment relationships. Templates may also be used as a variable in condition bodies to generically express a reference to other model elements or their values. We use the syntax `#{Transition_3}.event` to access the *event* property of the first element matching the template *Transition_3*. To reference *all* matching elements in a condition's body, the syntax `#[Template_name]`

[3] http://www.eclipse.org/modeling/emft/?project=compare

is used. The scope of a template is either the initial model or the revised model. It is still possible to access the template of the opposite model in the conditions using the prefixes `initial:` and `revised:`, respectively.

Step 6: Edit conditions. Usually, the conditions automatically generated in the previous step are too strong and do not express the intended pre- and post-conditions of the composite operation perfectly. They only act as a kickstart accelerating the operation specification process and have to be manually refined in this step. The Operation Recorder allows to adapt the generated conditions in three different ways.

First, the modeler may *relax* or *enforce* conditions. This is simply done by activating or deactivating the checkboxes beside the respective templates or conditions. If a template is relaxed all contained conditions are deactivated. By default, conditions constraining *string* features and `null`-values are deactivated, as in our experience they are not relevant in most of the cases. In the running example, four templates and three conditions in the preconditions as well as three templates and two conditions in the postcondition have to be relaxed additionally to the by-default deactivated conditions. For instance, the templates representing the initial state as well as the template representing the reflexive transition *dial* in state *Dialing* are not relevant in the preconditions and have to be relaxed properly. The same is true for the condition `incoming->includesAll(#{Transition_0})` in template *Idle* as it is not necessary that this state has the incoming transition matching *Transition_0*.

Second, the modeler may *modify* conditions by directly editing them. For our example it is necessary to specify that a state which is moved into the composite state has to own the event which is folded as an outgoing transition (in our example *hangup*). For this reason, the condition in the preconditions and the postconditions highlighted in bold font are modified to express this constraint.

Finally, users may adapt the composite operation specification by *augmentation*, e.g., introducing custom conditions, defining iterations, and annotating necessary user input for setting parameters of the composite operations. In our example, the modeler has to introduce one iteration for the template *SingleState_3*. This iteration specifies that the two operations executed on this template have to be repeated *for all* its matching model elements. In other words, for defining this iteration, all model elements containing the transition to be folded are moved to the composite state. Further, the modeler introduces a user input facility for the property *name* of template *CompositeState_0* to indicate a value which has to be set by the user of the refactoring. Obviously, iterations may only be specified for templates from the initial model and user input for features of templates from the revised model. To ensure the syntactic and semantic correctness of all conditions, the modeler may test all conditions against the initial or revised model by pushing the *Test conditions* button. A failing condition indicates a wrongly specified constraint, because the conditions have to match at least the example models.

Step 7: Generate OSM. To finalize the operation specification, the modeler pushes the *Finish* button. This initiates the generation of the OSM. This

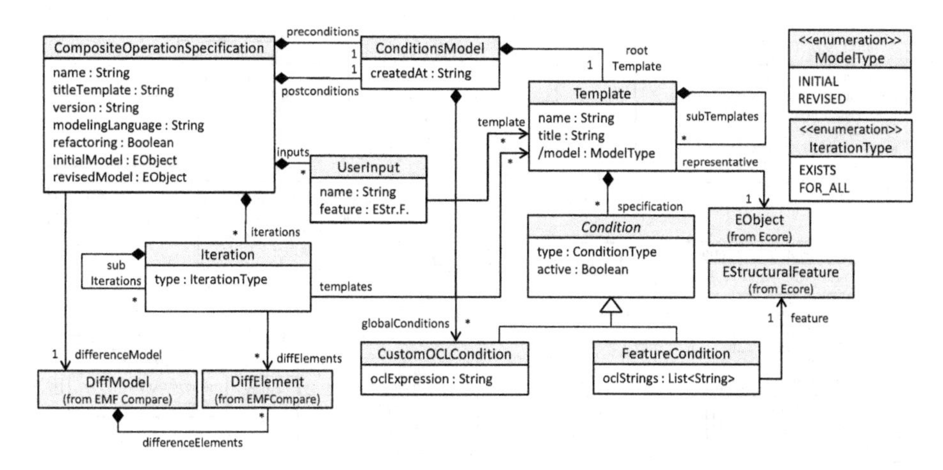

Fig. 4. Operation Specification Metamodel

model contains all necessary information for further usage like its detection of occurrences in generic difference models or its execution in various specific models. Operation specifications conform to the metamodel depicted in Figure 4. The class `CompositeOperationSpecification` contains general information about the operation like the name, a description as well as the initial and revised model, the pre- and postconditions, the iterations, and the differences. For the initial and the revised model kept in the attributes `initialModel` and `revisedModel`, the class `CompositeOperationSpecification` holds a reference to `ConditionsModel` which consists of a root `Template` representing the previously mentioned root object of the initial or revised model's conditions. Each template may have a number of subtemplates corresponding to the containment hierarchy of the elements in the initial or revised model. The specific model element in the initial or revised model is referenced in `representative`. Furthermore, a `Template` is specified by a list of custom conditions and feature conditions. `FeatureConditions` constrain the value of a specific feature and are generated automatically in Step 5.

Figure 5 illustrates an excerpt of the object diagram representing the OSM for the previously described statechart example. This diagram highlights some aspects, like the introduced iteration, the template hierarchy and its references to the concrete model elements as well as an instance of a `FeatureCondition` for the feature *name*. All of these components have their counterpart in the front-end already presented in Figure 3.

Step 8: Generate specific artifacts. The last step of the process is the generation of specific artifacts from the OSM for using it outside the Operation Recorder. To execute the refactoring specification depicted in Figure 3, the user has to choose which single state remains outside the composite state and which single state should be transformed to the starting node within the composite state. This is done by simply binding the respective single states to the templates *SingleState_1* and *SingleState_2*. To keep this process user-friendly, users

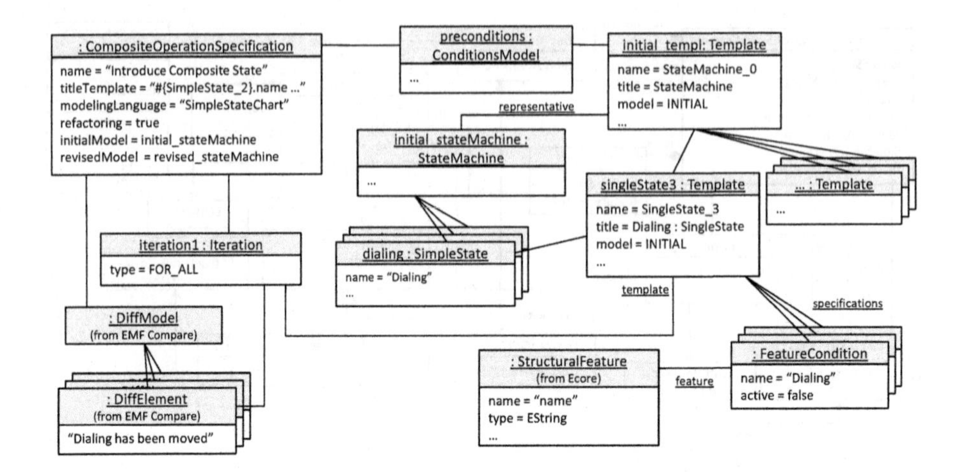

Fig. 5. Excerpt of the Operation Specification Model for the Running Example

Listing 1. Generated OCL Code

```
1 ...
2 attr singleState_1      : SingleState = ... /* selected by user */
3 attr transition_3       : Transition = ... /* selected by user */
4 ...
5 self.includesAll(self.outgoingTransition->select(
6     event = transition_3.event and target = singleState_1
7     and source = self))
```

Listing 2. Generated Refactoring Code

```
1  method introduceCompositeState(String cs_name,
2          Transition transition_3, SingleState singleState_1){
3      ...
4      //Create composite state
5      CompositeState cs = new CompositeState(cs_name);
6      ...
7
8      //Shift States into composite state
9      Iterator iter = states.select(s|cond(s)).iterator();
10     while (iter.hasNext()){
11         State state = iter.hasNext();
12         cs.ownedStates().add(state);
13         state.outgoing().remove(state.outgoing.select(t|
14             t.event = transition_3.event and
15             t.target = singleState_1);
16         ...
17     }
18
19     ... //Create additional elements and link them properly
20 }
```

do not have to bind model elements based on template names directly. Instead, users are referred to the example initial model and have to assign concrete elements to the elements of this example. Then, the direct binding to the templates is induced automatically. Based on this binding the concrete transition element matching *Transition_3* is evaluated. As an example for a generated artifact, in Listing 1 the OCL code evaluating all model elements the iteration has to be applied to (i.e., elements matching the template *SingleState_3*) is illustrated. The code implementing the iteration itself is shown in Listing 2.

5 Evaluation

For evaluating the effort necessary to define new composite operations with the Operation Recorder we performed a case study with the objective to specify five refactorings for the UML class diagram and two refactorings for the UML state diagram (cf. Table 1). Those well-known refactorings were adapted—if necessary—for the application on models as those refactorings are mostly defined for the application on code. The complexity of the refactorings varies from simple, e.g., "Move Attribute", to complex, e.g., "Introduce Composite State". Due to space limitations, we kindly refer to our project page for a detailed description [11].

The values shown in Table 1 reflect the effort for the user to specify the refactorings. The *#Template* column refers to the number of templates derived from the initial model and for the revised model, respectively, in order to establish the pre- and postconditions. The *#Conditions/#Selected* column contains the total number of pre- and postconditions as well as the number of initially selected conditions. These numbers are strongly related to the size of the metamodel employed for the editor. In our experiments, we used specialized UML editors which allowed us to focus on efficiently testing the refactorings. For example, if we had used the full UML2 editor for "Move Attribute" we would have obtained again four templates, but more than 100 conditions. To increase readability, we plan to integrate general condition filters in the Operation Recorder as well as to provide extension points for metamodel specific condition filters, which allow to hide unused metamodel feature conditions.

The column *#Diffs* shows the number of differences between the initial model and the revised model. The concrete value depends on the way a refactoring is modeled. We asked two modelers to specify the "Introduce Composite State" refactoring starting from the same initial model. Although their revised models contained the same elements, the one performed nine changes whereas the other needed 14 changes. The first reused the existing elements of the model and modified them accordingly, whereas the other deleted them and introduced new elements.

The configuration effort is reflected by the remaining columns of Table 1. The *#Relax/#Enforce* column describes how many conditions have to be (un)selected manually by the user. *#Modifications* refers to the number of edits which have to be performed and the last column shows the number of introduced iterations. In

Table 1. Refactorings: Move Attribute (mvAtt), Convert to Singleton (convSing), Encapsulate Variable (encVar), Replace Data Value with Object (repDV), Extract Superclass (extSC), Introduce Composite State (intCS), Merge States (merge)

Refactoring	#Templates		#Conditions/ #Selected		#Diffs	#Relax / #Enforce		#Modifications		#Iterations
	Pre	Post	Pre	Post		Pre	Post	Pre	Post	
mvAtt	4	4	13/3	13/3	1	3/0	3/1	0	1	0
convSing	3	4	8/2	11/4	2	2/2	2/2	1	1	0
encVar	3	7	8/3	16/8	4	3/0	2/4	0	3	0
repDV	3	5	8/3	16/6	4	3/0	2/2	0	1	0
extSC	5	5	16/4	18/6	6	0/2	0/0	1	2	1
intCS	11	13	41/27	48/32	9	7/0	5/0	1	1	1
merge	10	8	36/22	29/17	6	6/0	4/0	2	0	1

general, our case study showed, that the configuration effort mostly consists of relaxing conditions which is done with some clicks. The few condition modifications are typically needed to refer to properties of other templates and therefore are easily accomplished. Even for more complicated refactorings like, e.g., "Extract Superclass", only a few configuration steps are necessary.

Overall, the Operation Recorder approach allowed a very intuitive specification of the refactorings where the tasks which have to be performed by a human user are straightforward. In future, we plan to perform a more extensive evaluation with a wide range of modelers with different levels of modeling experiences.

6 Related Work

In this section, we give an overview of work related to our by-example operation specification approach organized in the categories *composite operations for models*, *user-friendly model transformation*, and *model transformation by-example*.

Composite operations for models. Most existing approaches for defining composite operations focus solely on model refactorings. One of the first investigations in this area was done by Sunyé et al. [7] who define a set of UML refactorings on the conceptual level by expressing pre- and postconditions in OCL. Boger et al. [12] present a refactoring browser for UML supporting the automatic execution of pre-defined UML refactorings within a UML modeling tool. While these two approaches only focus on pre-defined refactorings, approaches by Porres [13], Zhang et al. [8], Kolovos et al. [14], and Verbaere et al. [15] allow the introduction of user-defined refactorings in dedicated textual programming languages. A similar idea is followed by Mens [16] and Biermann et al. [17] who use graph transformations to describe the refactorings within the abstract syntax of the modeling languages. The application of this formalism comes with the additional benefit of formal analysis possibilities of dependencies between different refactorings. In any case, the definition of new refactorings requires intense knowledge of the modeling language's metamodel, of special APIs to process the models, and finally of a dedicated programming language. In other words, very specific expertise is demanded.

The Operation Recorder yields an orthogonal extension of existing approaches by providing a front-end to the modeler for defining the refactorings by modeling examples. The otherwise manually created refactoring descriptions are automatically generated from which representations in any language or formalism like graph transformation may be derived. Then it is possible to apply formal methods for analyzing the dependencies between refactorings as proposed by Mens.

User-friendly model transformation. Defining model transformation rules by using the abstract syntax of graphical modeling languages comes on the one hand with the benefit of generic applicability. On the other hand the creation of such transformation rules is often complicated and their readability is much lower compared to working with the concrete syntax as has been reported in several papers [18,19,20,21]. As a solution, the usage of the concrete syntax for the definition of transformation rules has been proposed like in AToM^3 [19]. More recently, Baar and Whittle [18] discuss requirements and challenge how to define transformation rules in concrete syntax within current modeling environments. A specific approach of describing transformation rules for web application models is presented by Lechner [22]. In the field of aspect-oriented modeling, transformations are also required for weaving aspect models into base models. Whittle et al. [23] describe aspect composition specifications for UML models by using their concrete syntax. Summarizing, all these approaches significantly contribute to the field of user-friendly development of transformations.

Model transformation by-example. Strommer and Wimmer [20] as well as Varró [21] go one step further by defining transformations purely by-example, i.e., instead of developing transformation rules, an example input model and the corresponding output model are given. From these example pairs, the general transformation rules are derived by a reasoning component. Currently, the focus lies on model-to-model transformations between different languages, e.g., class diagrams to relational models. In-place transformations required for composite operations such as refactorings have not been considered by these approaches.

With the Operation Recorder we fill the gap between composite operation definition approaches and model transformation by-example approaches. Although the need for introducing refactorings by the user of modeling tools as well as the need for describing transformations in a more user-friendly way have been frequently reported, to the best of our knowledge, the Operation Recorder is the first attempt to tackle the by-example definition of model transformations representing composite operations such as refactorings. The only comparable work we are aware of is [9] which allows to define composite operations by-example for program code using the Squeak Smalltalk IDE [24]. Although their general idea is similar to ours, three fundamental design differences exist, namely the Operation Recorder operates on models, is independent from any specific modeling language, and may be employed for any modeling environment.

7 Conclusions and Future Work

In this paper we introduced a tool for defining composite operations, such as refactorings, for software models in a user-friendly way. Modeling using the modeling language and environment of choice underlines this ease of use. Our by-example approach prevents modelers from acquiring deep knowledge about the metamodel and dedicated model transformation languages. The results of our evaluation emphasize the usability of our Operation Recorder because of minimizing the user's effort when defining such complex operations. We will integrate and use the Operation Recorder as component in a model versioning system. From this, we expect a reduction of merge conflicts and an improvement of conflict resolution.

In future work, we plan to enable the reuse of already defined refactorings for composing more complex refactorings. Preconditions of refactorings sometimes may include negative application conditions. For this reason, we will integrate the possibility of modeling forbidden model elements to match for non-existence of elements within preconditions. In a further step, translating operation specification models to graph transformations allows critical pairs analysis and, thus, the detection of conflicts between refactorings. Finally, we would like to extend the operation specification model by adding smells—indicating problematic model fragments [25]—that may be solved using the defined refactorings.

References

1. Gamma, E., Helm, R., Johnson, R., Vlissides, J.: Design Patterns: Elements of Reusable Object-oriented Software. Addison-Wesley Professional, Reading (1995)
2. Fowler, M., Beck, K., Brant, J., Opdyke, W., Roberts, D.: Refactoring: Improving the Design of Existing Code. Addison-Wesley, Reading (1999)
3. Altmanninger, K., Kappel, G., Kusel, A., Retschitzegger, W., Seidl, M., Schwinger, W., Wimmer, M.: AMOR - Towards Adaptable Model Versioning. In: 1st Int. Workshop on Model Co-Evolution and Consistency Management, MCCM 2008 @ MoDELS 2008 (2008)
4. Mens, T., Tourwé, T.: A Survey of Software Refactoring. IEEE Trans. Softw. Eng. 30(2), 126–139 (2004)
5. Brosch, P., Langer, P., Seidl, M., Wimmer, M.: Towards End-User Adaptable Model Versioning: The By-Example Operation Recorder. In: Int. Workshop on Comparison and Versioning of Software Models, MCVS 2009 @ ICSE 2009, pp. 55–60. IEEE, Los Alamitos (2009)
6. Dig, D., Nguyen, T.N., Manzoor, K., Johnson, R.: MolhadoRef: A Refactoring-aware Software Configuration Management Tool. In: 21st Conf. on Object-Oriented Programming Systems, Languages, and Applications, OOPSLA 2006, pp. 732–733. ACM, New York (2006)
7. Sunyé, G., Pollet, D., Le Traon, Y., Jézéquel, J.M.: Refactoring UML Models. In: Gogolla, M., Kobryn, C. (eds.) UML 2001. LNCS, vol. 2185, pp. 134–148. Springer, Heidelberg (2001)
8. Zhang, J., Lin, Y., Gray, J.: Generic and Domain-Specific Model Refactoring using a Model Transformation Engine. In: Model-driven Software Development—Research and Practice in Software Engineering, pp. 199–217. Springer, Heidelberg (2005)

9. Robbes, R., Lanza, M.: Example-Based Program Transformation. In: Czarnecki, K., Ober, I., Bruel, J.-M., Uhl, A., Völter, M. (eds.) MODELS 2008. LNCS, vol. 5301, pp. 174–188. Springer, Heidelberg (2008)
10. Budinsky, F., Steinberg, D., Merks, E., Ellersick, R., Grose, T.J.: Eclipse Modeling Framework (The Eclipse Series). Addison-Wesley, Reading (2003)
11. AMOR Project Website (July 2009), http://www.modelversioning.org
12. Boger, M., Sturm, T., Fragemann, P.: Refactoring Browser for UML. In: Aksit, M., Mezini, M., Unland, R. (eds.) NODe 2002. LNCS, vol. 2591, pp. 366–377. Springer, Heidelberg (2003)
13. Porres, I.: Rule-based Update Transformations and their Application to Model Refactorings. Software and System Modeling 4(4), 368–385 (2005)
14. Kolovos, D.S., Paige, R.F., Polack, F., Rose, L.M.: Update Transformations in the Small with the Epsilon Wizard Language. Journal of Object Technology 6(9), 53–69 (2007)
15. Verbaere, M., Ettinger, R., de Moor, O.: JunGL: A Scripting Language for Refactoring. In: 28th Int. Conf. on Software Engineering, ICSE 2006, pp. 172–181. ACM, New York (2006)
16. Mens, T.: On the Use of Graph Transformations for Model Refactoring. In: Lämmel, R., Saraiva, J., Visser, J. (eds.) GTTSE 2005. LNCS, vol. 4143, pp. 219–257. Springer, Heidelberg (2006)
17. Biermann, E., Ehrig, K., Köhler, C., Kuhns, G., Taentzer, G., Weiss, E.: Graphical Definition of In-Place Transformations in the Eclipse Modeling Framework. In: Nierstrasz, O., Whittle, J., Harel, D., Reggio, G. (eds.) MoDELS 2006. LNCS, vol. 4199, pp. 425–439. Springer, Heidelberg (2006)
18. Baar, T., Whittle, J.: On the Usage of Concrete Syntax in Model Transformation Rules. In: Virbitskaite, I., Voronkov, A. (eds.) PSI 2006. LNCS, vol. 4378, pp. 84–97. Springer, Heidelberg (2007)
19. de Lara, J., Vangheluwe, H.: AToM^3: A Tool for Multi-formalism and Meta-modelling. In: Kutsche, R.-D., Weber, H. (eds.) FASE 2002. LNCS, vol. 2306, pp. 174–188. Springer, Heidelberg (2002)
20. Strommer, M., Wimmer, M.: A Framework for Model Transformation By-Example: Concepts and Tool Support. In: Objects, Components, Models and Patterns, TOOLS 2008. LNBIP, vol. 11, pp. 372–391. Springer, Heidelberg (2008)
21. Varró, D.: Model Transformation by Example. In: Nierstrasz, O., Whittle, J., Harel, D., Reggio, G. (eds.) MoDELS 2006. LNCS, vol. 4199, pp. 410–424. Springer, Heidelberg (2006)
22. Lechner, S.: Web-scheme Transformers By-Example. PhD thesis, Johannes Kepler University Linz (2004)
23. Whittle, J., Moreira, A., Araújo, J., Jayaraman, P.K., Elkhodary, A.M., Rabbi, R.: An Expressive Aspect Composition Language for UML State Diagrams. In: Engels, G., Opdyke, B., Schmidt, D.C., Weil, F. (eds.) MODELS 2007. LNCS, vol. 4735, pp. 514–528. Springer, Heidelberg (2007)
24. Black, A., Ducasse, S., Nierstrasz, O., Pollet, D., Cassou, D., Denker, M.: Squeak by Example. Square Bracket Associates (2007)
25. Gorp, P.V., Stenten, H., Mens, T., Demeyer, S.: Towards Automating Source-Consistent UML Refactorings. In: Stevens, P., Whittle, J., Booch, G. (eds.) UML 2003. LNCS, vol. 2863, pp. 144–158. Springer, Heidelberg (2003)

Refactoring-Safe Modeling of Aspect-Oriented Scenarios

Gunter Mussbacher[1], Daniel Amyot[1], and Jon Whittle[2]

[1] SITE, University of Ottawa, 800 King Edward, Ottawa, ON, K1N 6N5, Canada
{gunterm,damyot}@site.uottawa.ca
[2] Dept. of Computing, InfoLab21, Lancaster University, Bailrigg, Lancaster, LA1 4YW, UK
whittle@comp.lancs.ac.uk

Abstract. Aspects use pointcut expressions to specify patterns that are matched against a base model, hence defining the base locations to which aspects are applied. The fragile pointcut problem is well-known in aspect-oriented modeling, as small changes in the base may lead to non-matching patterns. Consequently, aspects are not applied as desired. This is especially problematic for refactoring. Even though the meaning of the model has not changed, pointcut expressions may no longer match. We present an aspect-oriented modeling technique for scenarios that is refactoring-safe. The scenarios are modeled with Aspect-oriented Use Case Maps (AoUCM), an extension of the recent ITU standard User Requirements Notation. AoUCM takes the semantics of the modeling notation into account, thus ensuring pointcut expressions still match even after, for example, refactoring a single use case map into several hierarchical maps. Furthermore, AoUCM allows the composed model to be viewed without having to resolve complex layout issues. The general principles of our approach are also applicable to other aspect-oriented modeling notations.

Keywords: Aspects-oriented Modeling, User Requirements Notation, Aspect-oriented Use Case Maps.

1 Introduction

Aspect-oriented Modeling (AOM) [6] has attracted considerable attention in the modeling world over the last few years. One problem faced by AOM is the fragile pointcut problem [4, 11, 13] – the patterns that describe where in the base model an aspect is applied are often very susceptible to rather small changes in the base model (i.e., a small change is enough for the pattern to no longer match and the aspect not being applied as desired). This paper presents an approach that addresses this problem for a specific set of changes, i.e., refactoring operations which do not change the meaning of the model but only its syntactic representation. A modeler should rightly expect that such operations do not affect the specification and impact of an aspect.

This research is carried out in the context of the recent ITU standard User Requirements Notation (URN) [8], a modeling language for requirements engineering and high-level design that incorporates goal-oriented and scenario-based models in one framework. The Aspect-oriented User Requirements Notation (AoURN) is an effort that seeks to evolve URN into a complete aspect-oriented modeling environment for requirements engineering activities. We apply our approach to AoURN's

A. Schürr and B. Selic (Eds.): MODELS 2009, LNCS 5795, pp. 286–300, 2009.

scenario notation Aspect-oriented Use Case Maps (AoUCM). A prerequisite of this research is a clear semantic definition of UCM [8, 15]. While we use AoUCM to demonstrate our approach, its general principles are not just applicable to AoUCM but may be applied to other aspect-oriented modeling notations.

In the remainder of this paper, section 2 gives a brief overview of Use Case Maps (UCM) and Aspect-oriented Use Case Maps (AoUCM) including the current matching and composition approach. Section 3 first enumerates semantic equivalences of AoUCM models and common refactoring operations and then introduces the improved matching and composition algorithm based on semantics. The section concludes with an example of how to apply our technique to another modeling notation, namely UML sequence diagrams. Section 4 discusses related work, and finally, section 5 concludes the paper and identifies future work.

2 Overview of Aspect-Oriented Use Case Maps (AoUCM)

2.1 Use Case Maps

The User Requirements Notation (URN) [1, 8] supports the elicitation, analysis, specification, and validation of requirements. URN captures early requirements in a modeling framework containing two complementary sub-languages called Goal-oriented Requirement Language (GRL – for goal-oriented modeling) and Use Case Maps (UCMs – for scenario-based modeling). GRL models are used to describe and reason about non-functional requirements (NFRs), quality attributes, and the intentions of system stakeholders, whereas UCM models are used for operational requirements, functional requirements, and performance and architectural reasoning. While GRL identifies at a very high level of abstraction possible solutions to be considered for the proposed system, UCM models describe these solutions in more detail. In summary, URN has concepts for the specification of stakeholders, goals, non-functional requirements, rationales, behaviour, actors, scenarios, and structuring.

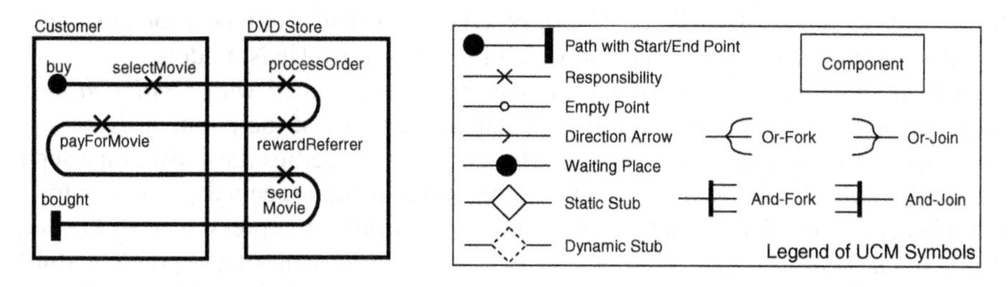

Fig. 1. The Buy Movie Use Case of a Simple Online DVD Store System

A UCM model consists of a path that begins at a *start point* (●) and ends with an *end point* (▌). A path may contain *responsibilities* (✕), identifying the steps in a scenario, and notational symbols for alternative (—<) and concurrent (—|=) branches. Path elements may be assigned to a *component* (□). *Stubs* are containers for sub-models called *plug-in maps*. Drilling into a stub leads to a submap that provides more details, thus allowing for hierarchical structuring of UCM models. A *binding* between the stub and elements on the plug-in map precisely defines how the scenario continues from the parent map to the submap and back to the parent map. A static stub (◇) may have only one plug-in map, while dynamic stubs (◇) may have several.

The most comprehensive URN tool available to date is the Eclipse plug-in jUCMNav [10]. Some support for aspect-oriented modeling is already available for jUCMNav. Further AO functionality is being prototyped and will be added to the tool in the near future. For more details about URN, visit the URN Virtual Library [21].

2.2 Aspect-Oriented Use Case Maps

The Aspect-oriented User Requirements Notation (AoURN) [16, 17, 18, 19] extends the User Requirements Notation (URN) with aspect-oriented concepts, allowing modelers to better encapsulate crosscutting concerns which are hard or impossible to encapsulate with URN models alone. AoURN adds aspect concepts to URN's sub-languages, leading to and integrating Aspect-oriented GRL (AoGRL) and Aspect-oriented UCMs (AoUCM). The three major aspect-oriented concepts that have to be added to URN are concerns, composition rules, and pointcut expressions. Note that the term aspect refers to a crosscutting concern, while the term concern encompasses both crosscutting and non-crosscutting concerns.

A *concern* is a new unit of encapsulation that captures everything related to a particular idea, feature, quality, etc. AoURN treats concerns as first-class modeling elements, regardless of whether they are crosscutting or not. Typical concerns in the context of URN are stakeholders' intentions, NFRs, and use cases. AoURN groups all relevant properties of a concern such as goals, behavior, and structure, as well as pointcut expressions needed to apply new goal and scenario elements to a URN model or to modify existing elements in the URN model.

Pointcut expressions are patterns that are specified by an aspect and matched in the URN model (often referred to as the base model). If a match is found, the aspect is applied at the matched location in the base model. The *composition rule* defines how an aspect transforms the matched location. AoURN uses standard URN diagrams to describe pointcut expressions and composition rules (i.e., AoURN is only limited by the expressive power of URN itself as opposed to a particular composition language). AoURN's aspect composition technique can fully transform URN models.

UCM pointcut expressions define the pattern to be matched with a *pointcut map*. Grey start and end points on the pointcut map are not part of the pointcut expression but rather denote its beginning and end. The aspectual properties are shown on a separate *aspect map*, allowing the pointcut expression and the aspectual properties to be individually reused. The aspect map is linked to the pointcut expression with the help of a *pointcut stub* (◇) (i.e., the pointcut map is a plug-in map of the pointcut stub). The causal relationship of the pointcut stub and the aspectual properties visually defines the composition rule for the aspect, indicating how the aspect is inserted in the base model (e.g., before, after, optionally, in parallel, interleaved, or anything else that can be expressed with UCM). The *replacement pointcut stub* (◆) is a special kind of pointcut stub, indicating that the aspect is replacing the matched base elements.

For example, Fig. 2 shows a simple Logging concern. The pointcut map matches against any responsibility of the DVD store (the wildcard * means any name). Hence, the pointcut expression matches each of the three responsibilities in the DVD store in

Fig. 1. The aspect map defines that a log is created after the loggable action occurred (i.e., the causal relationship of the pointcut stub and the aspectual property – the responsibility log in this case – states that log happens after the pointcut stub which means after the matched base elements).

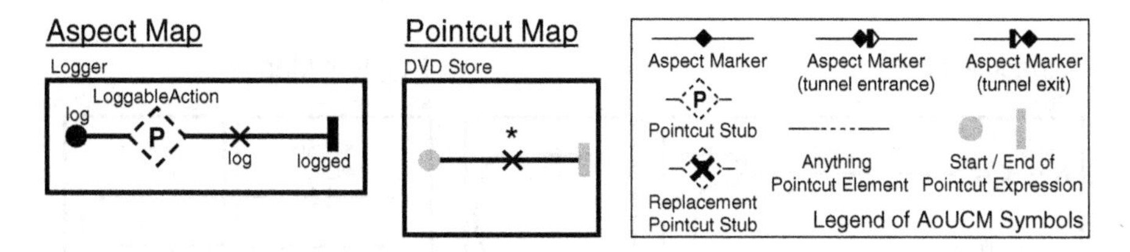

Fig. 2. Aspect Map and Pointcut Map for the Logging Concern

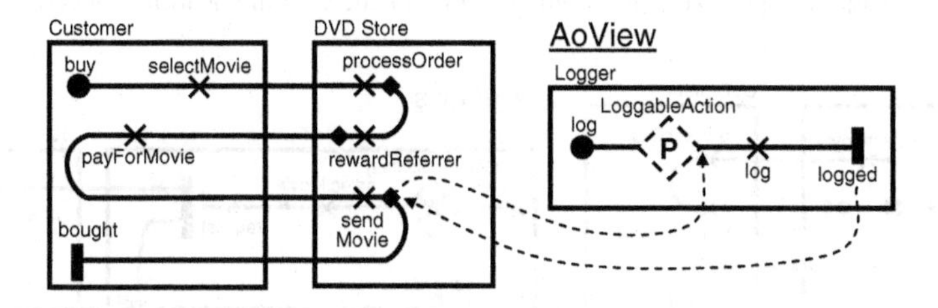

Fig. 3. Aspect Markers and Their Corresponding AoView for the Logging Concern

The three aspect markers (◆) in Fig. 3 indicate the affected base locations in the UCM model from Fig. 1. If the aspect adds elements before or after the base location matched by the pointcut expression, the aspect marker is added before or after the base location, respectively. An aspect marker is a kind of stub that links the base model with a submap, i.e., the aspect map. The AoView highlights the portion of the aspect map that is inserted. The aspect markers and the AoView effectively construct the composed model using the layout information provided by the modeler when the aspect was defined. When an aspect marker is reached in the Buy Movie scenario, the scenario continues with the aspectual behavior as highlighted in the AoView (i.e., right after the pointcut stub). When the end point is reached in the AoView, the scenario returns to the same aspect marker and continues with the Buy Movie scenario.

The purpose of the Communication concern in Fig. 4 is to define in more detail the interaction between the customer and the online DVD store. The pointcut map therefore matches against all interactions between the Customer and the DVD Store components that are started by any responsibility in Customer and followed immediately by an arbitrary sequence of elements in the DVD Store before the path crosses back into Customer. The *anything pointcut element* (.....) therefore ensures that the pointcut expression matches against selectMovie, processOrder, and rewardReferrer as well as payForMovie and sendMovie in Fig. 1.

Furthermore, *variables* ($initiateRequest, $performRequest, $Requester, and $Replier) are defined in the pointcut expression to allow matched elements to be reused in the aspect map. The replacement pointcut stub on the aspect map in Fig. 1

indicates that the matched elements are replaced with the aspectual properties described on the aspect map. The aspect map, however, reinserts the matched elements with the help of the variables. The aspect map also adds explicit request and reply responsibilities as well as a waiting place, specifying that the customer has to wait for the response of the DVD store.

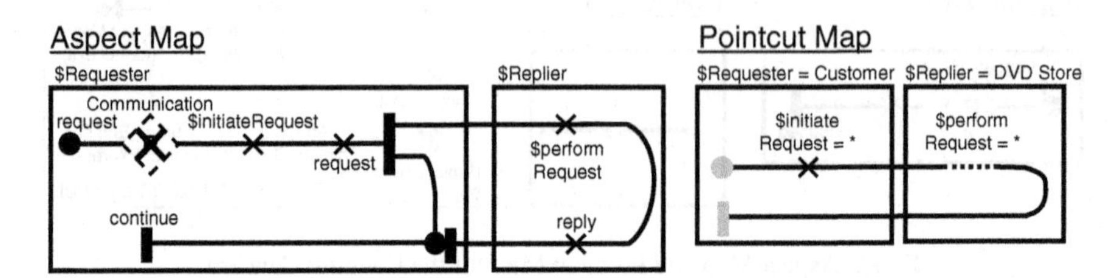

Fig. 4. Aspect Map and Pointcut Map for the Communication Concern

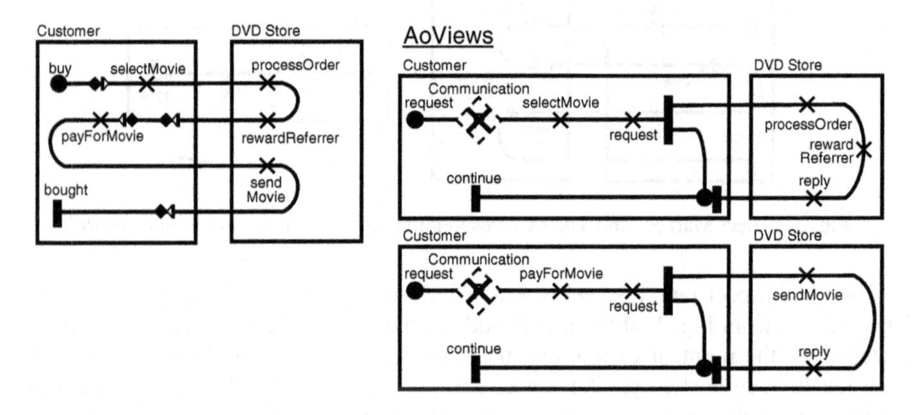

Fig. 5. Aspect Markers and Their Corresponding AoViews for the Communication Concern

In the base model in Fig. 5, a replacement is indicated by two special aspect markers. The *tunnel entrance aspect marker* (◆▷) is added before the matched elements and the *tunnel exit aspect marker* (◁◆) is added after the matched elements. In this case, two pairs of the tunnel aspect markers are added to the base model, because the pointcut expression is matched twice. The *AoViews* in Fig. 5 highlight the portion of the aspect map that is inserted. When the first tunnel entrance aspect marker is reached during the Buy Movie scenario, the scenario continues with the aspectual behavior on the aspect map (right after the pointcut stub) as shown in the top AoView. When the aspect map's end point is reached, the scenario continues with the first tunnel exit aspect marker, thus skipping the replaced base elements. The inserted portion for the second pair of tunnel aspect markers is shown in the bottom AoView.

Note how the variables in the aspect map have been replaced by the actual matched elements in the AoViews (i.e., $initiateRequest is replaced by selectMovie or by payForMovie; $performRequest is replaced by processOrder and rewardReferrer or by sendMovie; $Requester is replaced by Customer; and $Replier by DVD Store).

Furthermore, if the actual matched elements are complicated because a complex sequence was matched by the anything pointcut element, it may not be possible to add the matched elements directly to the aspect map. In this case, a static stub is added to the AoView and linked to the matched elements. This still allows layout information to be reused from the models defined by the requirements engineers.

The general approach of AoUCM's *matching algorithm* is to scan the base model and a pointcut expression in parallel. Starting with the first element of the pointcut expression, the matching algorithm tries to find a matching element in the base model. If a match is found, the algorithm moves on to the next element of the pointcut expression and tries to match it with the base element following the first matched base element. This continues until ideally the complete pointcut expression has been matched. For elements that may have more than one following element, all permutations are taken into consideration. For more details on the matching algorithm, the reader is referred to [17]. In summary, the matching algorithm uses the following criteria to decide whether a path node in the pointcut expression matches a path node in the base model. This list is the most up-to-date and includes all additions due to new capabilities of AoUCM that postdate the publication of [17]:

- The types and names of the path nodes must match.
- The node connection to the following path node (regular or timeout branch) and the direction of the path must match.
- The anything pointcut element may be matched to any sequence of path nodes and path node connections in the base model.
- The names of conditions must match, if the path nodes are start points, waiting places, timers, or OR-forks. If the pointcut expression does not specify conditions, any condition may be matched.
- The component hierarchy of the path nodes must be compatible.
- The location of the path nodes in their components must match (either first, last, or any location in the component).
- The metadata of the pointcut element must be a subset of the metadata of the base element (metadata are annotations in the form of name/value pairs that may be added to any URN model element).

3 Refactoring of AoUCM Models

The problem addressed in this section is how to ensure refactoring-safe AoUCM models. Refactoring-safe means that if the AoUCM model is refactored, then a pointcut expression that matches the initial model will also match the refactored model. Similarly, a pointcut expression that does not match the initial model will still not match the refactored model. As a refactoring operation transforms one model into a semantically equivalent model, the improved matching algorithm presented in section 3.2 somehow has to take into account the semantic equivalences discussed in section 3.1.

However, even if the matching algorithm is able to guarantee refactoring-safe AoUCM models, the composed model also needs to be automatically constructed to help the modeler understand the overall behaviour and assess the impact of aspects on the model. Finding the right layout for the composed model is a difficult problem for most aspect-oriented modeling notations. The layout must be intuitive to the modeler.

The AoUCM notation with its paths bound to components has proven to be difficult to layout automatically. jUCMNav's auto-layout mechanism [10] only works for rather simple models. This problem is compounded by the fact that the enhanced matching algorithm based on semantics now allows for pointcut expressions to be matched across map boundaries, e.g., the first part of a single pointcut expression may match one map while the remaining part of the pointcut expression may match another map that is connected to the first as discussed in section 3.2. The composition technique also described in section 3.2 addresses this problem because it does not require auto-layouting. Furthermore, the general principles of this technique may be applied to other aspect-oriented modeling notations and section 3.6 demonstrates this using UML sequence diagrams.

3.1 Semantic Equivalences in AoUCM Models

The following semantic equivalences can be found in the AoUCM notation. They also apply to traditional UCM models as defined in the URN standard [8]. Fig. 6.a shows the first and most straightforward equivalence type involving direction arrows (>), empty points (O), and connected end and start points (|●). These elements are simply ignored by the current matching algorithm.

The second type of equivalence involves hierarchical structuring with static, dynamic, or synchronizing stubs. The latter is defined in the recent standard as a dynamic stub whose plug-in maps are synchronized, requiring them to finish before traversal can continue past the stub. Flattened models that are equivalent to all three types of stubs are defined in the standard and are shown in Fig. 6.b. The flattened model of a synchronizing stub is not shown as it is very similar to the one of a standard dynamic stub. If the dynamic stub in Fig. 6.b were a synchronizing stub, then the OR-join o1 would be an AND-join instead. That is the only difference in the flattened model. The current matching algorithm also simply ignores static stubs and the start and end points of their plug-in maps. While this is mentioned in [17], the specific implications for the matching and composition mechanisms have not yet been presented. In any case, this approach is too simplistic as will be discussed further below. Furthermore, dynamic stubs are not addressed at all by the current algorithm.

Fig. 6.c illustrates the third and last type of semantic equivalences in UCM and AoUCM models, covering loop unrolling. This paper, however, focuses on the second type as the first is trivial and the last has been discussed in detail in [12]. While the findings of [12] could be incorporated into the AoUCM approach, we focus on hierarchical structuring because a) to the best of our knowledge this has not yet been addressed in literature, b) it introduces additional challenges, particularly regarding how to layout the composed model, and c) it is a much more common refactoring operation in AoUCM models than loop unrolling based on our decade of experience in creating and maintaining UCM and AoUCM models.

The particular refactoring operations that are to be supported for AoUCM models therefore are extracting a plug-in map, inlining a plug-in map (the reverse of the first), as well as the adding/deleting of direction arrows, empty points, and connected end and start points. These types of operations are applicable to most modeling notations as most notations provide some form of hierarchical structuring that can benefit from extracting/inlining as well as many notations have purely syntactical elements that do not change the meaning of the model but are visual aids for the modeler.

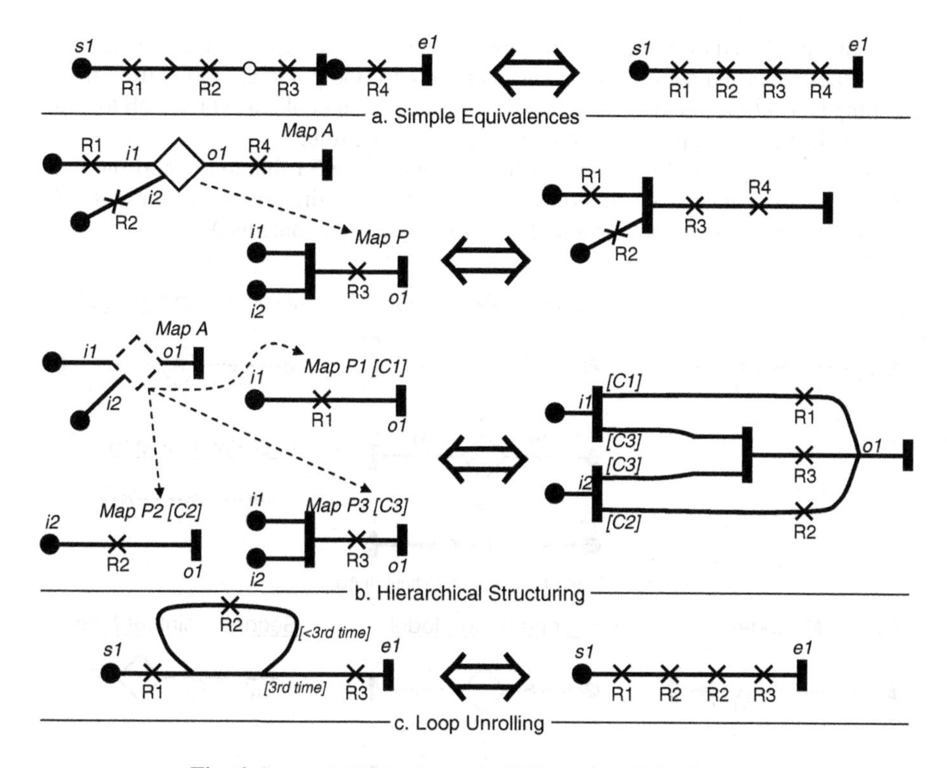

Fig. 6. Semantic Equivalences in UCM and AoUCM Models

3.2 Improved Matching and Composition Algorithms Based on Semantics

A first intuition is to use only the flattened model as the basis for the matching algorithm, thereby reducing each UCM model to its normalized form. In this case, pointcut expressions cannot match against stubs since flattened models do not contain stubs. However, there is no good reason to exclude stubs from pointcut expressions since a modeler may want to match stubs explicitly. Therefore, the improved matching algorithm distinguishes between model elements that can always be ignored (i.e., direction arrows, empty points, connected end and start points) and model elements that potentially can be ignored depending on the context (i.e., stubs and the start and end points on their plug-in maps).

For example, Fig. 7 depicts two equivalent UCM models with five responsibilities each (R1 to R5). The first UCM model consists of only one map whereas the second is split up over three maps. Three of the five responsibilities are matched by the first pointcut expression in Fig. 7.a. The aspect map adds two responsibilities A1 and A2 before and after the matched elements, respectively. Hence, aspect markers are added before R1 and after R3. The second pointcut expression in Fig. 7.b contains two responsibilities and a stub. In this case, the aspect markers are added before R1 and after the stub on the second-level map. The UCM model without stubs is not matched even though it is semantically equivalent to the UCM model with stubs, because the modeler's decision to require a stub in the matched pointcut expression takes precedence over matching based on semantics. If, however, the modeler adds a plug-in map to the stub in the second pointcut map, the normal form for the pointcut map is used by the matching algorithm as in this case, it is deemed that the modeler used the stub to structure a model hierarchically and not to explicitly match a stub.

For both examples in Fig. 7, the aspect markers before R1 link to the portion of the aspect map that contains A1, thus inserting it. Similarly, the aspect markers after R3 and after the stub link to the portion of the aspect map that contains A2.

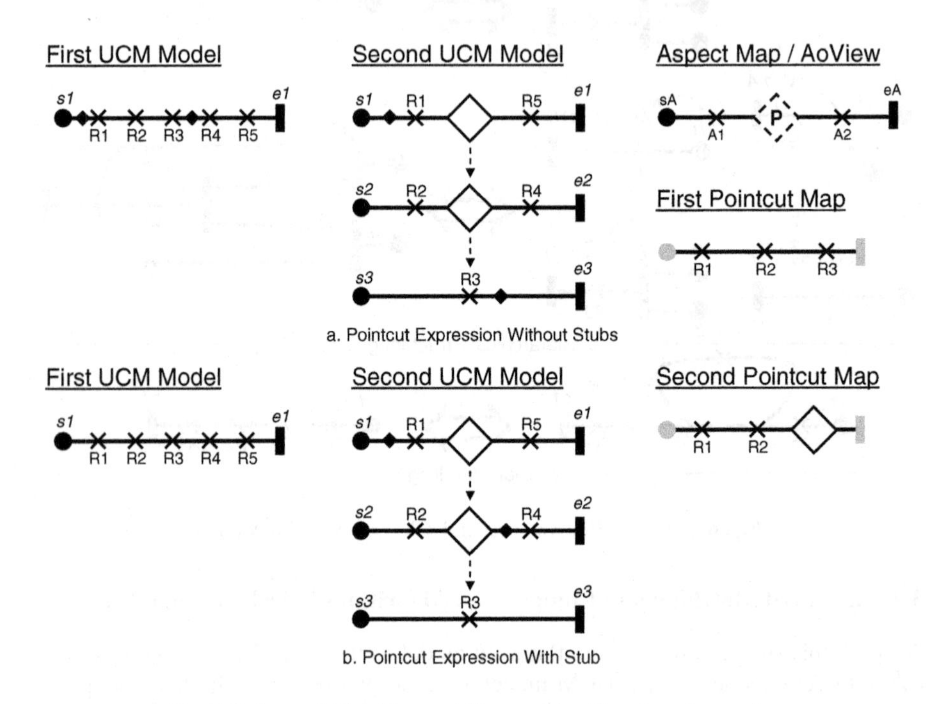

Fig. 7. Enhanced Matching and Composition Based on Semantics

Assume that the matching algorithm has already matched responsibility R1 in the second UCM model against the first responsibility in both pointcut expressions. The next element in the UCM model is a static stub, i.e. an element that may potentially be ignored. Both pointcut expressions, however, expect another responsibility. Therefore, the matching algorithm ignores the stub and its start point on the second-level map. It then continues with R2 and finds a match. At this point, the first pointcut expression expects a third responsibility whereas the second pointcut expression expects a stub. For the first pointcut expression, the matching algorithm ignores the stub on the second-level map and the start point on its plug-in map and matches the third responsibility. For the second pointcut expression, the stub is not ignored and matched against the pointcut expression.

Note that if the pointcut expression contains a named start/end point that needs to be matched, then the start/end points of plug-in maps are taken into account similarly to stubs being taken into account if they appear in the pointcut expression.

In summary, the matching algorithm takes the semantic equivalence for static stubs into account. If the stub in the UCM model is a dynamic stub, then the matching algorithm also ignores the stub but expects instead an AND-fork before continuing with the matching of elements on the plug-in map. An AND-fork is expected because the AND-fork is defined by the semantic equivalence (see Fig. 6.b). Furthermore, the matching algorithm expects an OR-join before continuing past the stub; again because it is so defined by the semantic equivalence.

3.3 Shared Plug-In Maps

There is, however, a problem with the approach presented in section 3.2 if a plug-in map is shared by several stubs. For example in Fig. 8, another map exists in the second UCM model that does not have the R1 responsibility but the XYZ responsibility instead. The plug-in maps, however, are reused. The pointcut expression does not match the hierarchy of maps that includes the map with XYZ but still matches the one with the map with R1. If the traversal of the UCM model arrives at the bottom-level map from the map with XYZ, the scenario must not continue via the aspect marker to the aspect map. The matching algorithm ensures that this is the case by encoding the required hierarchy context as a condition for the aspect marker (stubs have conditions that are checked before a plug-in map is chosen and, as mentioned earlier, an aspect marker is a type of stub). The condition for the aspect marker on the bottom-level map is as follows:

_context = stubID_on_map_with_R1 && stubID_on_mid_level_map

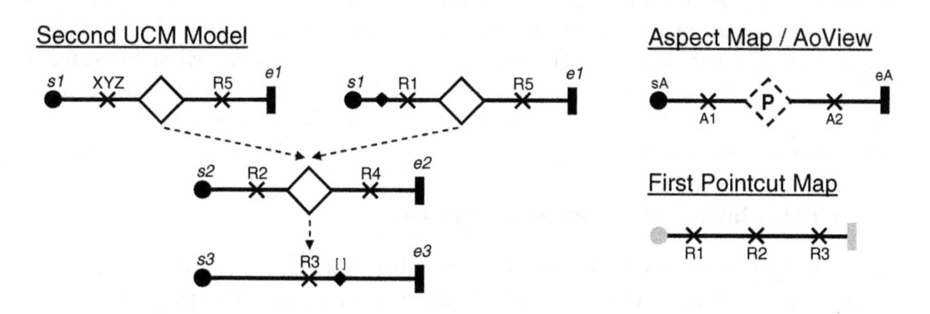

Fig. 8. Shared Plug-in Maps

The variable *_context* is a new variable provided by the UCM path traversal mechanism that allows access to the current stack of visited maps during the traversal. The current stack of visited maps must match the condition of the aspect marker for the traversal to continue on to the aspect map. In all other cases, the aspect marker is ignored and the traversal continues past the aspect marker. This possibility is indicated by brackets above the aspect marker (brackets are used in UCM for conditions).

3.4 Replacement Pointcut Stubs

Another problem appears when a replacement pointcut stub is used instead of a regular pointcut stub. In this case, the location of the aspect markers are exactly the same but the UCM path traversal mechanism loses important contextual information during the traversal of the UCM model. Fig. 9 illustrates what happens if a replacement pointcut stub is used. When the tunnel entrance aspect marker is reached in the UCM model, the traversal continues with the aspect. On the aspect map, A1 and A2 are traversed. Since the end point eA is connected to the tunnel exit aspect marker, the traversal continues with the bottom-level map. When its end point e3 is reached, the scenario should continue with the mid-level map because R4 used to be after R3 in the original model. However, the traversal mechanism is not aware of the mid-level map at this point, because it never reached the stub after R1.

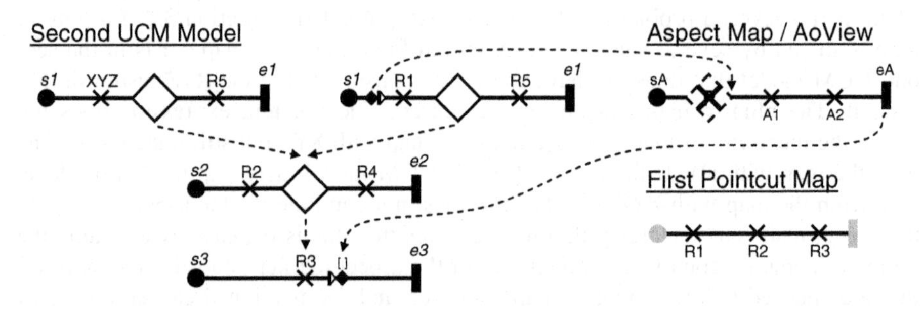

Fig. 9. Replacement Pointcut Stub

The matching algorithm, however, is aware of the hierarchy since the match spans all involved map levels. Therefore, the lost hierarchy information needs to be retained for the tunnel exit aspect marker by the matching algorithm. This is achieved by annotating the aspect marker with metadata. The name of the metadata is aspect, while the value is "context stubID_on_map_with_R1 stubID_on_mid_level_map". With this context information, the traversal mechanism adjusts the stack of visited maps – adding the mid-level map to it – and is then able to continue traversing the UCM model as required.

3.5 Multiple Matches of a Pointcut Expression

Finally, the last ambiguity that needs to be resolved for the improved matching and composition algorithm is related to multiple matches of a pointcut expression. If multiple matches exist, then the end point of the aspect map will be bound to many aspect markers. This is not a problem for simple before and after composition rules, because the scenario continues with the same aspect marker once the aspectual behaviour is finished. More complex replacement or interleaving composition rules, however, may not continue with the same aspect marker as shown in Fig. 10. When the traversal has reached the aspect map from the aspect marker of the map with responsibility R7, it is not clear which plug-in binding of end point eA to use. Therefore, the composition mechanism groups all tunnel entrance and tunnel exit aspect markers related to one match of the pointcut map. This is achieved by again adding metadata to each aspect marker. The name of the aspect marker is again aspect, while the value is "group <someID>". The UCM path traversal mechanism is then able to choose the correct plug-in binding of the end point eA by matching the group numbers of the tunnel entrance and tunnel exit markers.

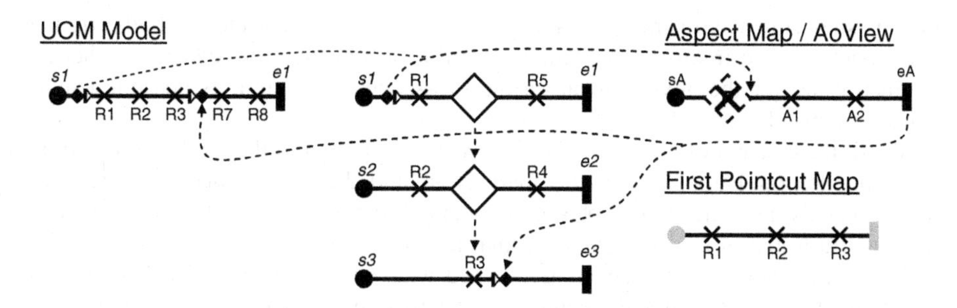

Fig. 10. Multiple Matches for a Pointcut Map

In summary, the improved matching algorithm now differentiates between three types of path nodes. Type I path nodes are matched as is and most path nodes fall into this category. Type II path nodes are always ignored, i.e., direction arrows, empty points, and connected end and start points. Type III path nodes are possibly ignored. Stubs and the start and end points of their plug-in maps fall into this category. If a direct match is not possible, the algorithm attempts to match type III path nodes based on semantic equivalences to their flattened representation.

The improved composition algorithm, on the other hand, supplements with the help of metadata all aspect markers with sufficient information to identify required and lost map traversal hierarchies and the groups to which aspect markers belong. All of this is possible without having to create a new layout for the composed model because the addition of aspect markers is the only change required for composition. Large scale changes to the original models created by the requirements engineer are not required. Hence, these models can be used, ensuring that requirements engineers can continue working with familiar base and aspect models even if the models are composed.

The improved matching and composition algorithm is important for AoUCM as it also allows AoUCM models to be matched more consistently even if aspects have already been applied. If aspects are applied, then aspect markers will appear in the AoUCM model. Since an aspect marker is a type of stub, it can now also be matched on a semantic level. At this point, aspect markers are interpreted as static stubs. In the future, however, they may have a slightly different semantic interpretation due to concern precedence rules. The approach presented in this section is extensible in that a flattened representation always can define a new semantic equivalence which can then be incorporated into the matching and composition algorithm with minor adjustments to the algorithm.

3.6 Applying the General Principles of Our Approach to Sequence Diagrams

In order to apply the general principles of our approach to another modeling notation, the following steps have to be followed. First, type II and III model elements need to be identified. For example, comments may be considered as type II elements for sequence diagrams (SDs). Type III elements, on the other hand, may be interaction uses (essentially references to sub-sequence diagrams).

Second, semantic equivalences for each type III element need to be defined. In the case of SDs, the semantic equivalence of a sequence diagram with an interaction use plus its sub-sequence diagram is a single sequence diagram that merges both original ones together. The improved matching algorithm would therefore consider either an interaction use or the next element on the sub-sequence diagram as possible candidates for a match.

Third, the concept of aspect markers needs to be applied to the modeling notation. Two options exist here. Either aspect markers are added as a new concept to the notation or an existing concept may be used or adapted. In the case of SDs, states could be used as illustrated in Fig. 11. The aspectual notation used for Fig. 11 is MATA [22]. In MATA, elements in the aspect stereotyped with <<create>> are added by the aspect to the base model while elements stereotyped with <<delete>> are to be matched in the base model and then removed from the base model when the aspect is applied.

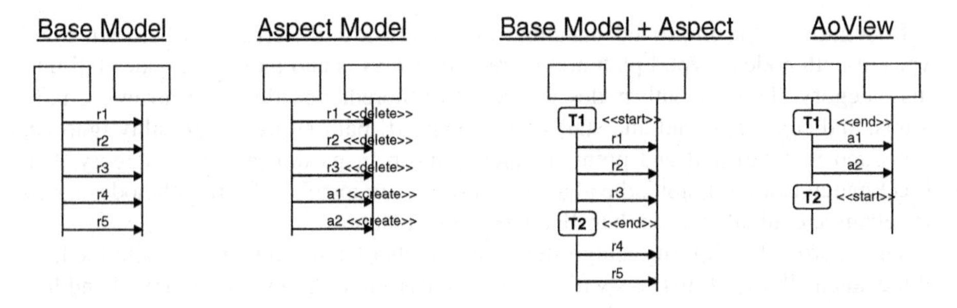

Fig. 11. "Aspect markers" in UML Sequence Diagrams

The states with the stereotypes <<start>> and <<end>> essentially encode the plug-in binding of the aspect markers in the AoUCM notation, connecting the base behavior with the aspectual behavior even if the match spans several hierarchical levels of SDs (not shown here due to space constraints). Additional tagged values (not shown in the figure) provide information on lost and required hierarchies as well as the groupings of the "aspect markers" for SDs as explained in section 3.2.

4 Related Work

While many aspect-oriented modeling techniques exist for requirements engineering such as use cases [2, 9], viewpoints [20], problem frames [14], and UML models [7, 22], none to the best of our knowledge addresses semantic equivalences in their matching and composition mechanisms with the exception of the following work in semantic-based aspect weaving. Chitchyan *et al.* [5] use natural language processing to take into account English semantics when composing textual requirements documents. For aspect-oriented modeling, Klein *et al.* [12] weave UML sequence diagrams by matching semantically equivalent but syntactically different sequences. Klein *et al.* give a thorough explanation on how to deal with loops but do not address the problems related to hierarchical structuring and replacements discussed in section 3.2. Furthermore, this work does not address complex layout issues that may have to be resolved when the woven end result is presented to the modeler. In the context of aspect-oriented programming, Bergmans [3] discusses the use of semantic annotations for composition filters.

5 Conclusion

We have presented an enhanced, semantics-based matching and composition algorithm for aspect-oriented scenario models. Our approach ensures that refactoring operations for which semantic equivalences were defined can be performed without a risk of breaking the aspects' pointcut expressions. Our approach is extensible as new refactoring operations may be added by defining their semantic equivalences and making small incremental adaptations to the existing algorithm. With this approach, aspect markers are also interpreted as model elements to which semantics-based matching may be applied, leading to a more consistent and powerful treatment of AoUCM models to which aspects have already been applied.

The composition mechanism makes use of the layout information provided naturally by the modelers themselves at the time the base and aspect models are defined. This allows the composed model to be presented in a familiar way to the modelers without having to resolve complex layout issues. The general principles of our work are also applicable to other aspect-oriented modeling notations as illustrated by aspect-oriented UML sequence diagrams expressed with the MATA notation. In future work, we plan to apply our approach to further AOM notations and to investigate empirically how intuitive the matching and composition algorithm and the usage of aspect markers is to requirements engineers, especially when base elements spanning multiple maps are replaced by an aspect.

Acknowledgments. This research was supported by NSERC Canada, through its programs of Discovery Grants and Postgraduate Scholarships.

References

1. Amyot, D., Mussbacher, G.: Development of Telecommunications Standards and Services with the User Requirements Notation. In: Workshop on ITU System Design Languages (2008), `http://www.itu.int/dms_pub/itu-t/oth/06/18/T06180000010012PDFE.pdf`
2. Araújo, J., Moreira, A.: An Aspectual Use Case Driven Approach. In: Pimentel, E., Brisaboa, N.R., Gómez, J. (eds.) VIII Jornadas de Ingeniería de Software y Bases de Datos (JISBD 2003), pp. 463–468. Alicante (2003)
3. Bergmans, L.M.J.: Towards Detection of Semantic Conflicts between Crosscutting Concerns. In: Workshop on Analysis of Aspect-Oriented Software (2003), `http://www.comp.lancs.ac.uk/~chitchya/AAOS2003/Assets/bergmans1.pdf`
4. Braem, M., Gybels, K., Kellens, A., Vanderperren, W.: Inducing Evolution-Robust Pointcuts. In: Duchien, L., D'Hondt, M., Mens, T. (eds.) Second International ERCIM Workshop on Software Evolution (EVOL 2006), pp. 17–22. Lille (2006)
5. Chitchyan, R., Rashid, A., Rayson, P., Waters, R.: Semantics-Based Composition for Aspect-Oriented Requirements Engineering. In: 6th International Conference on Aspect Oriented Software Development (AOSD), pp. 36–48. ACM, New York (2007)

6. Chitchyan, R., et al.: Survey of Analysis and Design Approaches, http://www.aosd-europe.net/deliverables/d11.pdf
7. Clarke, S., Baniassad, E.: Aspect-Oriented Analysis and Design: The Theme Approach. Addison-Wesley, Reading (2005)
8. ITU: Recommendation Z.151 (11/08): User Requirements Notation (URN) – Language definition, http://www.itu.int/rec/T-REC-Z.151/en
9. Jacobson, I., Ng, P.-W.: Aspect-Oriented Software Development with Use Cases. Addison-Wesley, Reading (2005)
10. jUCMNav website, University of Ottawa, http://softwareengineering.ca/jucmnav
11. Kellens, A., Gybels, K., Brichau, J., Mens, K.: A Model-Driven Pointcut Language for More Robust Pointcuts. In: Workshop on Software Engineering Properties of Languages for Aspect Technology (2006), http://aosd.net/workshops/splat/2006/papers/kellens.pdf
12. Klein, J., Hélouët, L., Jézéquel, J.M.: Semantic-based Weaving of Scenarios. In: 5th International Conference on Aspect Oriented Software Development (AOSD), pp. 27–38. ACM, New York (2006)
13. Koppen, C., Stoerzer, M.: Pcdiff: Attacking the Fragile Pointcut Problem. In: European Interactive Workshop on Aspects in Software (EIWAS 2004), Berlin, Germany (2004)
14. Lencastre, M., Araújo, J., Moreira, A., Castro, J.: Towards Aspectual Problem Frames: an Example. Expert Systems Journal 25(1), 74–86 (2008)
15. Mussbacher, G., Amyot, D.: Assessing the Applicability of Use Case Maps for Business Process and Workflow Description. In: 2008 International MCeTech Conference on eTechnologies (MCeTech), pp. 219–222. IEEE Computer Society, Washington (2008)
16. Mussbacher, G., Amyot, D.: Extending the User Requirements Notation with Aspect-oriented Concepts. In: Bilgic, A., Gotzhein, R., Reed, R. (eds.) SDL Forum Conference 2009. LNCS, vol. 5719, pp. 119–137. Springer, Heidelberg (2009)
17. Mussbacher, G., Amyot, D., Weiss, M.: Visualizing Early Aspects with Use Case Maps. In: Rashid, A., Aksit, M. (eds.) Transactions on AOSD III. LNCS, vol. 4620, pp. 105–143. Springer, Heidelberg (2007)
18. Mussbacher, G.: Aspect-Oriented User Requirements Notation: Aspects in Goal and Scenario Models. In: Giese, H. (ed.) MoDELS 2007. LNCS, vol. 5002, pp. 305–316. Springer, Heidelberg (2008)
19. Pourshahid, A., Mussbacher, G., Amyot, D., Weiss, M.: An Aspect-Oriented Framework for Business Process Improvement. In: Babin, G., Kropf, P., Weiss, M. (eds.) 4th International MCeTech Conference on eTechnologies (MCeTech 2009). LNBIP, vol. 26, pp. 290–305. Springer, Heidelberg (2009)
20. Rashid, A., Moreira, A., Araújo, J.: Modularisation and Composition of Aspectual Requirements. In: 2nd International Conference on Aspect Oriented Software Development (AOSD), pp. 11–20. ACM, New York (2003)
21. URN Virtual Library, http://www.usecasemaps.org/pub
22. Whittle, J., Jayaraman, P., Elkhodary, A., Moreira, A., Araújo, J.: MATA: A Unified Approach for Composing UML Aspect Models based on Graph Transformation. In: Transactions on Aspect-Oriented Software Development. LNCS. Springer, Heidelberg (to be published)

Model-Based Testing Using LSCs and S2A[*,**]

Shahar Maoz[1], Jani Metsä[2,***], and Mika Katara[2]

[1] The Weizmann Institute of Science, Rehovot, Israel
[2] Tampere University of Technology, Department of Software Systems, Tampere, Finland

Abstract. We report on our preliminary experience in using high-level visual scenario-based models for tests specification, test generation, and aspect-based test execution, in the context of an industrial application. To specify scenario-based tests, we used a UML2-compliant variant of live sequence charts (LSC). To automatically generate testing code from the models, we used a modified version of the S2A Compiler, outputting AspectC++ code. Finally, to examine the results of the tests, we used the Tracer, a prototype tool for model-based trace visualization and exploration. Our experience reveals the advantages of integrating models into industrial settings, specifically for model-based test specification and aspect-based execution: generating aspect code from visual models enables exploiting the expressive power of aspects for testing without manual coding and without knowledge of their rather complex syntax and semantics. We further discuss technological and other barriers for the future successful integration of our initial work in industrial context.

1 Introduction

Model-based test techniques may provide benefits over conventional script-based test automation solutions in terms of productivity and test coverage. Still, at least two major challenges hinder the adaption of such testing approaches. First, difficult deployment and suboptimal use of technology due to testers lack of specialized modeling skills. Second, the use of technology that limits the high-level testing of the system under test (SUT) to interface testing, where inputs are passed as parameters and the output is observed only from the return values.

In this work we introduce a novel approach to model-based testing where models based on *high-level visual scenarios* are compiled automatically into *test aspects*. This aims at partly addressing the above challenges, using a visual language to make test specifications more accessible to engineers while taking advantage of aspect-oriented technology in order to access the SUT internals.

Specifically, to visually specify testing scenarios we use a UML2-compliant variant of Damm and Harel's *live sequence charts* (LSCs) [1,2]. LSCs is a visual formalism

---

[*] Empirical results category paper.

[**] The first author would like to acknowledge partial funding from an Advanced Research Grant from the European Research Council (ERC) under the European Community's 7th Framework Programme (FP7/2007-2013). The other authors acknowledge partial funding from the Academy of Finland (grant number 121012).

[***] Part of this author's work was done while he was with Nokia Corp., Devices R&D.

A. Schürr and B. Selic (Eds.): MODELS 2009, LNCS 5795, pp. 301–306, 2009.

that extends classical sequence diagrams partial order semantics mainly by adding universal and existential hot/cold modalities, allowing a visual and intuitive specification of scenario-based liveness and safety properties. To execute the tests, we automatically translate the diagrams into test *scenario aspects* using a modified version of the *S2A compiler* [3]. After weaving with the SUT code, the generated aspects follow the execution of the tests specified in the diagrams and report on their run time progress and results using *scenario-based traces* [4], which are visualized and explored in a prototype tool called the *Tracer* [5].

Aspects have been used for testing before (see, e.g., [6]). Our approach to using generated scenario aspects for test execution has a number of advantages. First, test definition is done visually, using popular standard diagrams, within a commercial tool, and does not involve code writing. Second, the diagrams are automatically translated into test scenario aspects, which are woven into the code of the SUT, taking advantage of aspect technology in order to access the SUT internals without explicitly changing the original code. Third, the results of the tests are not limited to Boolean pass/fail output but instead provide rich information on traces of execution, exactly at the level of abstraction defined by the scenarios used for testing.

We report on a preliminary case study where we tried out our approach on an industrial system: a C++ application, running on Symbian OS, inside a Nokia smartphone. The case study has been carried out by the second listed author while he was at Nokia Corp., Devices R&D. We present the study results, and further discuss technological and other barriers for the future successful integration of our work in the industrial context.

This short paper focuses only on the introduction of the tool chain and on the initial case study evaluation. An extended version that includes background material, example diagrams and code snippets from the case study, additional technical details on the aspect code generation, a discussion of related work etc., is available as a tech. report[1].

2 Overview of the Tool Chain and Case Study

Defining the Scenarios. First, the test designer draws LSCs (that is, UML2-compliant modal sequence diagrams) using IBM RSA [7] (extended with the *modal* profile defined in [2]). The profile extension allows the engineer to set hot and cold modes to methods and conditions, as required by LSCs. In general, any UML2-compliant editor that supports profiles could be used to draw the LSCs. A number of LSCs are drawn, divided between several use cases for better manageability.

Some of the scenarios monitor for forbidden behaviors. If they occur, a violation is recorded. Note that the modeled scenarios combine monitoring with execution; they do not only listen for relevant events to monitor the progress of the tests. Rather, some methods are designated with the *execution mode*. When such a method is enabled in one chart and not violating in any other chart, the generated code, described next, executes

[1] Maoz, S., Metsä, J., Katara, M.: Model-Based Test Specification and Execution Using Live Sequence Charts and the S2A Compiler: an Industrial Experience. Technical Report 4, Tampere University of Technology, Department of Software Systems (2009)
http://practise.cs.tut.fi/publications.php?project=amoeba-testing

this method using generated inter-type declarations. Typically, a scenario includes a mix of monitoring and executing methods, to follow a test and advance it, alternately.

In our case study, we created test scenarios based on three test objectives: (1) generic monitoring, (2) monitoring for regression testing, and (3) simple new tests. The generic monitoring scenarios verify that the SUT actually behaves as designed to, e.g., that certain method calls are indeed followed by certain behavior. For regression testing, we created scenarios that had revealed certain problems in the older versions of the SUT. Finally, we created new test scenarios that after certain sequence of events exercise the target system with additional method calls. These scenarios were very simple, since we wanted to be able to notice other problems related to adopting the technique in the target platform. In total we had 32 different test scenarios. After modeling, the LSCs are compiled to generate executable test code.

Generating and Executing Testing Scenarios. The engineer runs the S2A compiler [3], (optionally) from within RSA, to generate AspectC++ scenario aspects. In addition to the LSCs, S2A reads a properties file that has properties such as the path for the target folder where the generated code should be written to, a list of files that need to be 'included' in the generated code, etc.

S2A translates LSCs, given in their UML2-compliant variant using the *modal* profile of [2], into AspectJ code. It implements the compilation scheme presented by Maoz and Harel in [8] and supports scenario-based execution following the play-out operational semantics of LSC [9]. Roughly, each sequence diagram is translated into a *scenario aspect*, which simulates an automaton whose states correspond to the scenario cuts; enabled events are represented by transitions that are triggered by pointcuts, and corresponding advice is responsible for advancing the automaton to the next cut state. The compiler comes with a runtime component (not generated), which includes code that is common to all scenario aspects, utility methods and super classes, making the generated aspect code more specific and readable. To use S2A with our industrial SUT, which is written in C++, we have designed and implemented a version of S2A that outputs AspectC++ [10] rather than AspectJ code.

The generated AspectC++ code is then copied onto the SUT environment. In our case, a mobile phone running Symbian OS and several applications written in C++. The generated aspect code is woven to the SUT code prior to compilation and linking, thus producing SUT instrumented with the generated test harness. The tests are performed according to the test plan exercising the SUT based on test cases defining test data and control. In our case study we used the test plan and related test cases defined for the SUT for release testing purposes.

Tracing and Trace Visualization and Exploration. S2A's runtime component supports scenario-based monitoring, that is, the generation of *model-based execution traces* [4] (specifically, *scenario-based traces*) from programs instrumented with S2A's generated aspects. In our context, the generated model-based traces provide information about the executed tests progress and completion states. These are viewed and explored using the Tracer (see [5,11]), a trace visualization and exploration tool, providing the engineer effective means to explore the test results.

3 Evaluation

Lessons learned include both technical issues and other issues that are more social or cultural. We present the strengths and weaknesses we have identified and list recommendations for future successful adaption of our work in the industrial context.

No need to know aspects. One clear strength of our approach to model-based testing and tool chain is that test scenario definition is done at a rather high-level of abstraction; while it takes advantage of aspects ability to access the SUT internals, it does so without requiring the engineer to know aspects and their complex semantics. This seems a potentially positive adaption factor, since a good command of aspect-oriented programming is not common in testing organizations (and in the industry in general). Moreover, the fact that the aspect code is automatically generated from the models guarantees certain quality in the code executing the tests.

End-to-end visualization. Another positive adaption factor is the end-to-end visual nature of our model-based testing tool chain. Visualization is known as a way to address complexity and to make tasks more accessible to engineers. Again, test developers need neither write nor even understand the generated (aspect) code.

Access to a model of the SUT. Based on our experiments, it is easy to create monitoring scenarios using LSCs. In case the class names and methods are known, it is easy to draw a scenario describing a sequence of method calls that should happen. However, it is mandatory to have a proper model of the SUT available, e.g., a class diagram, and to understand the model elements and their relationships to the scenario. Since test designers often tend to be unaware of the system internals, the true potential of the aspects may remain unused. Good knowledge of the SUT model, in terms of the classes and their relationships, is thus a necessary requirement for test developers. If such model is partly available, as in our case, some tests could be developed simply by copying sequence diagrams from the model's documentation and extending them with hot/cold modes etc. If this is not available it is difficult to draw useful LSCs.

Knowing the modeling language. Good knowledge of the modeling language itself, LSCs in our case, is another necessary requirement for test developers. While sequence diagrams in general and LSCs in particular are quite intuitive to draw and to understand, when combined with additional features such as symbolic instances, and when put against a real system with a complex structure, intuition alone does not suffice. When the test developer knows the SUT well but is not an expert in the modeling language, as in our case, some tests simply do not happen or result in unexpected behavior, as the generated aspects code does not match the developer's intention. One way to address this is to divide the work between a modeler and a tests engineer; the modeler would develop *scenario templates*, while the tests engineer would instantiate these with classes and methods specific to the SUT. Our experience shows that this could work in practice; many of our test scenarios were actually defined by taking a valid test scenario and just making changes in lifeline references and method signatures.

The modeling language expressive power and semantics. We used LSCs' semantics of symbolic lifelines, with a polymorphic interpretation. Thus, lifelines are labeled with class names, and any instance of the class may advance the related automaton. Although this allows defining powerful scenarios, it does not allow capturing issues related to certain specific instance of the class (when exploring the produced traces, it is possible to identify the instances. Thus we consider this issue as partly resolved). In addition, not all original test cases could be modeled using scenarios; some required more complex support for data and control. A different, considerable disadvantage, is the inability to create scenarios that explicitly cover behavior across separate threads or processes. The current semantics and implementation generates aspect code that can only be thread specific. This is a true limiting factor in many settings.

Single IDE support. We did not have a single integrated development environment (IDE) that could be used throughout the tool chain. Modeling was done in IBM RSA; S2A is written in Java but its AspectC++ output is weaved to and compiled with the SUT; resulting execution traces are viewed with the Tracer, outside the SUT. The lack of a single IDE resulted in technical problems and process overhead; for example, if the generated code does not compile with the SUT, it is difficult to know where to look for the problem. We acknowledge that this hinders industrial adoption; a solution needs to be developed to combine the different pieces into a single integrated environment.

4 Conclusion

The contribution of our work is twofold. First, the introduction of a new tool chain for model-based testing, presenting an end-to-end visual testing approach, from visual specifications to generated tests and from test execution to model-based trace generation for test result analysis. The new tool chain includes a modified version of the S2A compiler, generating AspectC++ scenario aspects. Second, the empirical evaluation of the presented tool chain, examined against an industrial system, yielding a discussion of technological and other advantages of and barriers to its future integration, from a practical perspective.

References

1. Damm, W., Harel, D.: LSCs: Breathing Life into Message Sequence Charts. J. on Formal Methods in System Design 19(1), 45–80 (2001)
2. Harel, D., Maoz, S.: Assert and Negate Revisited: Modal Semantics for UML Sequence Diagrams. Software and Systems Modeling (SoSyM) 7(2), 237–252 (2008)
3. Harel, D., Kleinbort, A., Maoz, S.: S2A: A Compiler for Multi-Modal UML Sequence Diagrams. In: Dwyer, M.B., Lopes, A. (eds.) FASE 2007. LNCS, vol. 4422, pp. 121–124. Springer, Heidelberg (2007)
4. Maoz, S.: Model-Based Traces. In: Chaudron, M.R.V. (ed.) Workshops and Symposia at MODELS 2008. LNCS, vol. 5421, pp. 109–119. Springer, Heidelberg (2009)
5. Maoz, S., Kleinbort, A., Harel, D.: Towards Trace Visualization and Exploration for Reactive Systems. In: VL/HCC 2007, pp. 153–156. IEEE Computer Society, Los Alamitos (2007)
6. Xu, G., Yang, Z., Huang, H., Chen, Q., Chen, L., Xu, F.: JAOUT: Automated Generation of Aspect-Oriented Unit Test. In: APSEC 2004, pp. 374–381. IEEE Computer Society, Los Alamitos (2004)

7. IBM Rational: IBM Rational Software Architect homepage, http://www-01.ibm.com/software/awdtools/swarchitect/websphere (Cited March 2009)
8. Maoz, S., Harel, D.: From Multi-Modal Scenarios to Code: Compiling LSCs into AspectJ. In: SIGSOFT FSE 2006, pp. 219–230. ACM, New York (2006)
9. Harel, D., Marelly, R.: Come, Let's Play: Scenario-Based Programming Using LSCs and the Play-Engine. Springer, Heidelberg (2003)
10. AspectC++ team: AspectC++ home page, http://www.aspectc.org/
11. Maoz, S.: Tracer website, http://www.wisdom.weizmann.ac.il/~maozs/tracer/

Model Driven Development of Graphical User Interfaces for Enterprise Business Applications – Experience, Lessons Learnt and a Way Forward*

Rahul Mohan and Vinay Kulkarni

Tata Research Development & Design Centre, 54, Hadapsar Industrial Estate, Hadapsar, Pune, India
{rahul.mohan,vinay.vkulkarni}@tcs.com

Abstract. We discuss our experience in applying model-driven techniques to build Graphical User Interfaces (GUI) of large enterprise business applications. Our approach involves capturing various user interface patterns in the form of platform independent parameterized templates and instantiating them with relevant application data, serving as the template arguments. Models thus instantiated are translated to platform specific GUI implementation artifacts by a set of template-specific code generators. We describe this approach in detail and share our experiences and the lessons learnt from using the approach in developing large database-centric business applications for the past fourteen years. Our ongoing work to address some of the limitations of this approach, especially on variability management of GUI in software product lines, is also presented in brief.

Keywords: Modeling, Graphical User Interfaces, Meta Modeling, Code Generation.

1 Introduction

Our foray into model driven development began fourteen years ago, when our organization decided to develop a banking product that was to be capable of being delivered on multiple technology platforms, and easily keeping pace with the technological advances. The product team approached the R&D team for coming up with an approach to achieve these qualities along with a requirement of making the average developer productive for building the product's functional capabilities without being concerned about the technological aspects. A specification-driven approach was suggested [1], wherein specifications abstract out low-level platform details that can be filled in later through code generation. The implementation code of a typical business application can be broadly classified into business logic and code for solution architecture that addresses concerns such as design strategies, architecture and technology platform. The implementation is characterized by a number of recurring code patterns pertaining to data access, distributed architecture, presentation, transaction-processing and so on.

* Empirical results category paper.

A. Schürr and B. Selic (Eds.): MODELS 2009, LNCS 5795, pp. 307–321, 2009.

Based on this observation, we devised an approach wherein models are used to capture these patterns, and a set of high-level model-aware languages are used for specifying business logic, complex data access queries, GUI event handling etc. We developed a set of tools to transform these models and high-level specifications to platform-specific implementations having the desired engineering properties [2]. Later, when UML [3] started gaining good traction within the industry we started aligning to it by using the UML metamodel with some specific extensions to model various aspects of our interest.

Section 2 presents a brief critical analysis of Graphical User Interfaces, isolates the various concerns in specifying GUIs in the form of retargetable specifications, and describes how our model driven development approach addresses some of these concerns. Section 3 describes our experience with this approach in terms of the various desirable characteristics of a typical model driven approach. Section 4 describes the lessons learnt from these experiences. Section 5 discusses the ongoing work inspired from the lessons we learnt. Section 6 briefly examines a few prominent approaches in model driven development of GUIs and positions our approach against them. Section 7 summarizes what we were able to achieve and what remains as open problems.

2 Our Model Driven Development Approach for GUI Development

Online functionality of business applications is typically implemented using a layered architecture consisting of presentation layer, business logic layer, and data access layer. We defined a metamodel for each layer by extending the UML metamodel. A unified metamodel, of which the layer-specific metamodel is a *view*, was then defined to ensure consistency between the three layers in specification as well as in implementation [2]. A simple projection sufficed as a view, for the kind of applications that interested us. The focus of this paper is only the presentation layer and its integration with the business logic layer.

The Presentation layer deals with the following four principal concerns: (i) the *presentation* concern specifying how the user interface is visually presented to the user (ii) the *user interaction* concern specifying user interaction capabilities of the interface (iii) the *event-reactional* concern capturing the behavior of a user interface in response to user actions and (iv) the *data-flow* concern specifying data flows within the user interface and with the business layer. The presentation and user interaction concerns are typically implemented by *widgets* which are basic GUI components with predefined presentation and user interaction capabilities. User interfaces are built by putting together many such widgets. The event-reactional concerns are specified using *event handlers*, which are executable reactions to the events raised by widgets. Data flow is realized by binding of these widgets to business layer messages.

The fundamental unit of development, deployment and user interaction in a database centric GUI is a *screen*. Most of the GUI platforms handle screens in the form of *windows*. Windows are special container widgets that identify a user interaction task, representing a business task or a part thereof. A navigation model connects these windows with one another forming a user interaction process, which can be thought of as a user view of an overarching business process. Specifying the presentation layer for an enterprise business application therefore narrows down to – identifying the windows, defining the window as a composition of widgets, defining the navigation model, defining the binding between the widgets and the business layer messages, and finally, defining the event handlers to specify the behavior of a window in response to each particular event possible.

In order to specify windows using widgets, we defined a *widget type library* which is a collection of *widget types* for a particular platform. Widget types are parameterized templates that can be instantiated with appropriate application models to get widgets, which can then be used to define windows. Widget types define their own presentation, user interaction capabilities and a set of events that they can raise. Presentation can be in the form of *textbox*, *tree*, *grid*, and so on, while user interaction capabilities can be like typing in a value, selecting a value from a list of values, and dragging a slider using mouse etc. The set of events that they can raise correspond with each of their user interaction capabilities. For example, *Click Event*, *Node-Expand Event*, and *Row-Select Event* etc. are events that correspond to clicking action, node expansion action and row selection action on a widget. The presentation, user interaction capabilities, and events supported by a widget type are seen to vary from one GUI technology platform to another. However, specification of GUIs for enterprise business applications needs a higher level of abstraction than what is offered by the widget type library of a platform. A good example is the defunct widget model for Grids in HTML which does not support events like *Row-Select*, *Column Sort* etc. Therefore, to be practically usable, a widget type library should be defined with widget types having capabilities that can be *simulated* on the target platform, rather than depending only on what is available on the target platform. For example, data pagination is a standard capability available on Grid Widgets in all database-centric business applications.

Consequently, widget libraries differ across platforms in all the three aspects mentioned earlier, namely, presentation, user interaction, and the events raised. This presents a fundamental problem in applying model driven techniques to the development of user interfaces - the specification has to refer to a technology platform specific widget library and at the same time be retargetable to various technology platforms. However, we decided not to attempt for a truly platform independent solution for the following two pragmatic reasons: (i) A truly platform independent GUI specification would offer only those capabilities that are common across the various target platforms and therefore would prevent the GUI developers from exploiting the capabilities of the underlying platform to the maximum extent to deliver rich user interfaces and (ii) Even though the lifespan of the targeted banking product was expected to be beyond a decade we knew that our focus would be on data intensive GUIs on a limited set of technology platforms. Retargetability can be achieved, even though technically restricted to platforms of similar capabilities, by using appropriate platform specific code generators for each widget type in the widget type library. Template-based code generation with different templates for different technology platforms sufficed as most of the code for GUI implementations is for the presentation , which is static after defined for a project. A widget is defined to be an instance of a widget type through a special *instance-of* association. As widget types are parameterized templates, each widget type defines its formal parameters, called *ParamType*s, and each widget specifies its actual parameters, called *Params. Params* are bound to the corresponding *ParamTypes* using the same *instance-of* associations to complete widget instantiation. The parameters for instantiating widget types can be of different kinds depending on the application architecture. In our case, the kinds of parameters we defined were – *OperationParamType* and *OperationParam*, *WindowParamType* and *WindowParam*, and *UIClassParamType and UIClassParam*. Each kind of *Param* can be mapped to only its corresponding *ParamType*. Further, an *OperationParam* can be bound only to an operation, a *WindowParam* can be bound only to a window and a *UIClassParam* can be bound only to a *UIClass*. A *UIClass* is a projection over message objects related to a screen. Elements of the UIClass are called *UIAttributes* which are displayed as fields on the screen using form widgets like textbox, drop-down box etc. and they define field level properties like *mandatory, read-only, visible etc. UIClasses* essentially form the data content of all screens. Fig. 1 shows this metamodel.

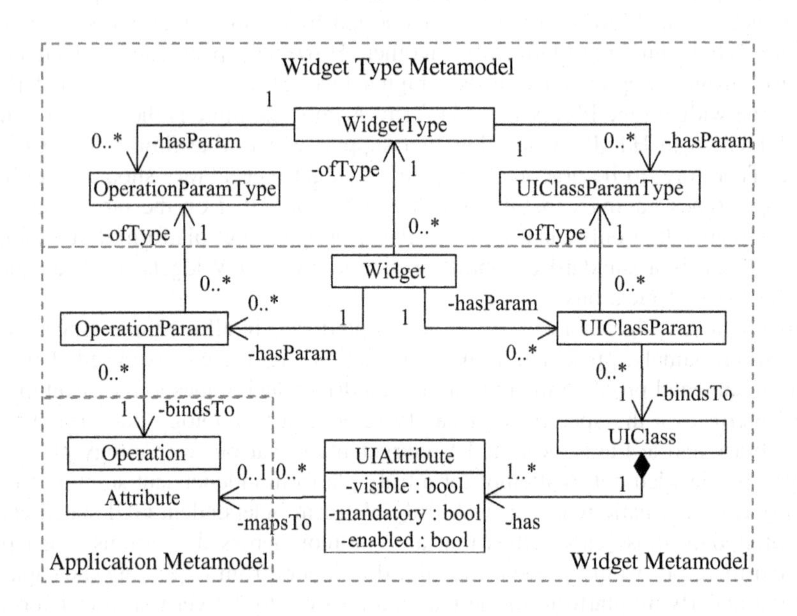

Fig. 1. Metamodel for defining and instantiating widgets

The widget type library is defined by instantiating the widget types with the correct number of parameters. These widget types are instantiated by the application developers to define the widgets that constitute the application screen. An example of this user model is shown in Fig. 2.

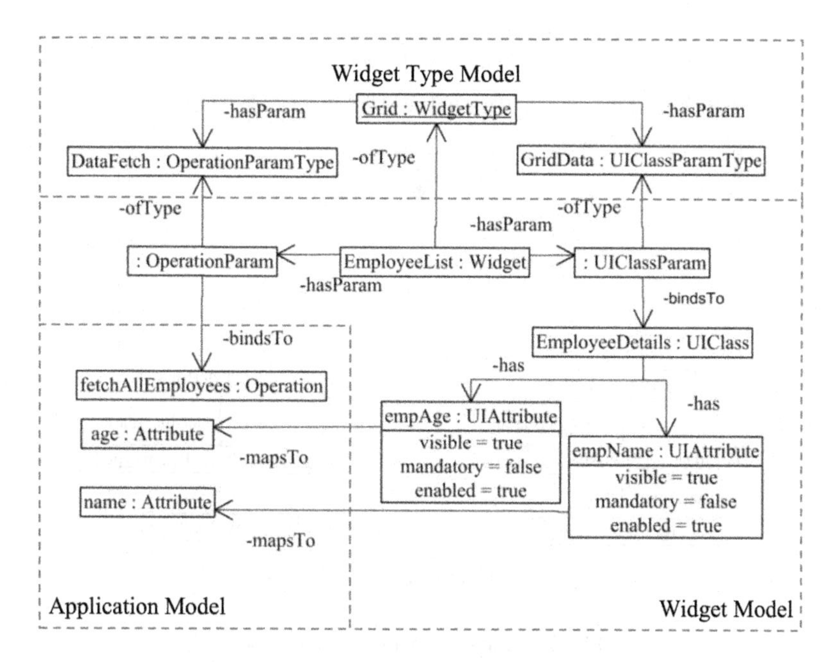

Fig. 2. A GUI Application Model Example

Larger patterns spanning multiple widgets are often found in GUI design. Since these are patterns, they can also be captured as widget types or as window types with its own formal parameter list. However, as these patterns are actually partially instantiated composition of other widgets, these higher level types can be specified as a composition of widgets with partially instantiated parameters, called *ParameterLinks*. As most of the formal parameters for the composite are actually handled by its constituents, our composition technique maps the composite's formal parameters to the formal parameters of the constituents using these *ParameterLink* objects. Using this approach, we could define commonly occurring window level patterns in the form of *Window types.* For example, a *Search-List* window type captures the data search pattern in an application which allows the user to specify parameters to a pre-defined search operation and invokes the operation. The result of this search gets displayed in a list pane. It is composed of a *form* widget type for entering search criteria and a *grid* widget type for displaying the search results. Fig. 3 shows the composition technique for defining a Search-List Window Type.

The composite type has parameters for *Search Criteria* and *Search Results*, both of type *UIClassParamType*. It also has a parameter, of type *OperationParamType*, for mapping the search operation (not shown in the figure for the sake of clarity). This window type is instantiated by defining a window with a type association to the window type. An instance of this window-type defines *UIClassParam* instances as arguments to the *SearchCriteriaParamType* and *SearchResultParamType* and an *OperationParam* application service as argument to the *SearchOperationParamType*. These parameters are internally passed to the constituents through the *ParameterLinks* to instantiate the window.

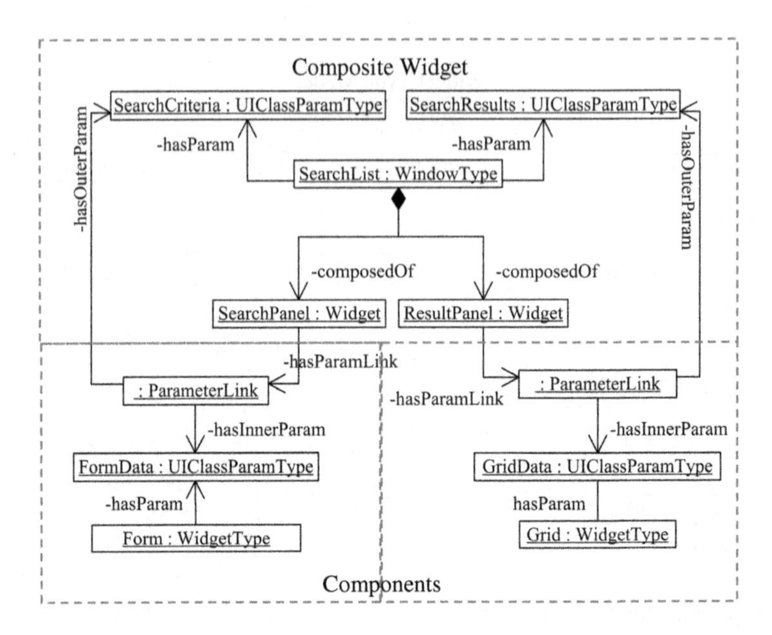

Fig. 3. Creating composite widget types

In addition to the structural aspect, window types typically capture some behavioral patterns as well. Considering the complexity involved in modeling behavior, we decided to embed the behavioural code as template text in the code generation templates for the window types. This behavioral part however introduces some constraints on the parameters. For example, a service mapped to the search service parameter of a search-list window type needs to have a signature that can work with the window behavior – i.e. pagination related parameters, returning a list of data and so on. We enforced these constraints through a set of constraint scripts written in our own model aware language.

For specifying the event handler implementation, we decided to use the language provided by the underlying platform itself. As different presentation platforms have different event processing capabilities, a generic event language would have been a least common denominator of these capabilities. Application developers felt that this would prevent them from exploiting the richness offered by a presentation platform.

3 Experience

Over the last 14 years, this approach has been used to deliver a product line (around 1000 screens), several large applications (>100 person years effort each and more than 100 screens each) and a few small to medium sized projects (5-10 person years effort each with 30-40 screens each). Using this approach we can generate the entire code for fully functional screens, such as screen layout, default event handling, screen navigation, and opening of a child screen with requisite data from its parent screen, from the model. Table 1 shows the percentage of delivery quality screens we could generate completely using our tool across various projects.

Table 1. Productivity Metrics across Various Projects

Project		Core Banking Product	Clearing and Settlement System	Commissions System	Payment and Loyalty Card System
Size (No of Screens)		>1000	580	54	200
Coverage (% of screens generated)		97	97	100	95
Effort / Screen (Person Days)	Avg.	3	3	1	2
	Hi	7	6	4	4
Technologies		Power Builder[15], Struts[13], ASP.Net[16]	JSP, Servlets, Struts	Struts	JSP, Servlets

Our observations regarding the various desirable properties from a model driven approach are discussed in the rest of this section.

Productivity: Specification driven approach by itself was found to increase overall productivity [1]. Table 1 shows the average developer productivity figures across some applications for windows with average complexity and for highly complex windows. This data shows that the average developer productivity using our tool is better than the corresponding industrial average values by a factor of 2 to 3. Capturing the frequently occurring patterns and their reuse further improved productivity, but our approach of capturing the patterns as new types in the Widget Type library model and instantiating it hindered efficient reuse due to three reasons – (i) GUI patterns across different applications were always found to be different though the variations were typically minor. This results in a large, unmanageable number of types being defined with only slight variations among them. (ii) Defining a type is invariably accompanied by writing a code generator for the new type, making the process of capturing and reusing patterns a complex programming task. This complexity was a principal deterrent in enthusiastic user acceptance even though GUI patterns do get identified naturally in every large development project. Also, programming is required for creating composite types as a composite type usually has its own code contribution in addition to what its constituents offer, and (iii) creating complex types requires knowledge of the type metamodel. This skill requirement further discouraged development teams from defining the types in the development phase.

Quality: GUI development, especially for web applications, is usually more prone to errors than the rest of the system because of the number of specification languages involved. Our approach eliminated these errors completely since the entire code, except for the event-handler implementation code, is generated. Architectural and design choices could therefore be encoded in the code generators thus guaranteeing application-wide uniformity and compliance in the implementation. However, as the event-handler coding was manual and used the language offered by the platform, we could neither enforce quality of the event codes nor automatically check for violations to the architectural and design principles.

Table 2. Template Fitment across Projects

Project	Template Fitment	
	Window Types	Type Fitment (% of screens)
Core Banking Product	Search List Type	40
	Form Type	36
	Form + Grid + Form	18
	Form + Editable Grid	6
Clearing and Settlement System	Search List Type	54
	Form Type	26
	Form + Grid + Form	9
	Form + Form + Button Panel + Editable Grid	4
	Form + Button Panel + Multi-select Grid	4
	Form + Button Panel + Editable Grid	3
Commissions System	Search List Type	16
	Form Type	12
	Form + 2 Grids	15
	Form + Form + Grid	57

Consistency: It was observed that three to four different window types could cover more than 80 percent of the application screens in most cases as shown in the type coverage data in Table 2. More than 50 percent of the screens in most business applications are of the same type - usually Search List Type. Defining these window types and employing template based code generation ensures consistency in the look and feel as well as in usability patterns throughout the application. By associating default widgets to domain data types, consistency in the widget types used for the each data type could also be ensured across screens in a developer independent manner, for instance, *date* is always displayed using *calendar* control. Template based code generation also ensured consistency in error reporting and displaying validation messages.

Ease of Testing: Independent and isolated testing of the presentation layer freed GUI developers and testers from waiting for the business layer to be available. Layout of the screens, navigation, user interaction, service invocation and copying of data between screens could thus be tested much early in the development lifecycle, using test data supplied in a text file wherever required. Since the GUI was modeled with binding to the business layer specifications and tested independently with stubs for services, integration with an implementation of the business layer specifications was found to be completely error-free, as expected. However, for really large applications, this approach for testing was often found to be extremely difficult to perform because of complex relationships between services and complex data dependencies, making simulation hard.

Change Management: Traceability across the layers was easily possible because of the unified metamodel we used. For instance, changes in the data type of a database column could be easily traced across the layers up to the fields on the screens. We developed an impact analysis tool that could report impact of changes at any layer of the application using a pattern directed model traversal. Making a change in the screen content and re-generating the screen takes only a couple of minutes. Presentation changes across the entire application could be made available in the implementation in one shot by re-generating code using modified templates. This allowed comments from the usability review team to be incorporated in the application throughout the development phase without impacting the functionality. Layout changes were not possible as it was auto generated by an algorithm in the code generation process. We solved this to an extent by externalizing the generated layout information in XML files for the later editing by developers. Subsequent code generation simply preserves the edited layout in the application screens. A better solution which allows the layout to be modified at any stage of development and shows the updated screen with the new layout within seconds is definitely required going ahead.

Retargetability: Usage of this approach has greatly helped retarget the application over many GUI platforms over the years, right from PowerBuilder [15] to ASP.Net [16] Windows Forms, Java Swing [17], Java Server Pages, and recently to Apache Struts [13] with Ajax and to JSF [14]. Retargeting GUI specifications to newer platforms is not limited to a re-translation, but enhancements in the specification were always found to be necessary to make effective use of the newer capabilities offered by new platforms. Combined with the fact that presentation technologies evolve much faster than the rest of the application layer technologies, this translates to a substantial investment in the evolution of an application; more so for software products. Our approach tried to tackle this need by enhancing the existing type library for the new target platform, writing new code generation templates, updating the model to utilize the new capabilities added, and re-writing the event handlers for the new platform. However, the metamodel itself often requires minor enhancements in addition to these steps thus complicating the retargeting process. Platform specific event handler code was also another source of concern. We feel the need for a platform independent event coding mechanism which can use the capabilities of the underlying platforms to the maximum extent. Another solution could be to reduce the event codes itself by providing a richer metamodel and constraints language to establish cross-field constraints. This richer metamodel is discussed later in the paper.

Reuse: We were able to reuse the same windows at multiple places by introducing a concept of window mode. A window can be opened in multiple modes like view mode, delete mode, authorize mode, approve mode and so on. The window would behave differently based on the mode and some of the fields would be enabled or disabled based on the mode. Reuse of parts of window was not found to be feasible since there would always be some context specific variations in its appearance and behavior. However, reuse of window parts at a specification level is possible where some parts of a window model - an address form panel, could be taken and copied to other places to kick-start the development of new windows. Such model fragments could be saved in a repository for long term reuse as well.

Ease of use: The absence of a WYSIWYG user interface for the GUI modeler was a prominent drawback in our implementation. Our dialogue based modeling tool posed a steep learning curve. Absence of an explicit navigation model is another drawback because of which developers are not able to see a window in its context. Developers often felt a lack of control over layout of the screen since the layout was visible only after code generation. The cycle time in introducing layout as well as other modifications, and seeing them reflect in the window was around one to two minutes. This needs to be reduced to the order of seconds. An incremental code generation mechanism that generates only the relevant parts of the code for a modification could be a solution.

Customizability: Look and feel customizations in GUI code generators are found to be much more frequent than the customizations for architectural and design changes. We found it not possible to completely separate the look and feel aspect from the other aspects in code generation since a lot of the generated scripts depend on the page structure. These customizations present a significant activity at the beginning of the development phase. Customizability of the code generation templates is restricted in our approach by the complexity of the dual metamodel – a metamodel to specify the windows, widgets, UIClasses etc, and another metamodel to specify the types which are then connected using instance-of associations. Poor separation of concerns in the templates also hindered customizability. Further, customizing the code generators requires knowledge of both the metamodels and our template language which was proprietary and did not support any mechanism like inheritance for code reuse.

Extensibility: Extensibility of the application is a major problem in software product line development. The product line team wound up maintaining separate copies of the application models for each customer, on which they do the customizations. Reconciling these branches to the main product line is an extremely cumbersome and laborious exercise, and hence is postponed for as long as possible. Extensibility of the specification capabilities itself were possible by extending the type model, but most of the extensions also required extending the application models. The code generators also needed to be modified either way. Extensibility was limited because of the difficulty in extending the dual metamodels, and in extending the code generators due to poor customizability as discussed earlier.

Acceptance of the approach: Technical architects, particularly those who are developing large applications and managing software product lines, find this approach very attractive and are benefitting from this. Architects for small to medium sized applications, however, are discouraged by the learning curve introduced by our implementation and by the difficulty in customizing the code generators, especially because the shelf life for those customizations are short. Developers tend to dislike our specification driven approach due to the following perspectives – (i) Learning a 'proprietary' technology or specification language, such as ours, does not contribute to the résumés of the developers (ii) The tools shield them from the technology platforms that they want to learn (iii) The modification turnaround time in the order of a few minutes makes the development process slow (iv)Developers often feel constrained by the specification language - that it is preventing them from writing the code they want. These are usually deviations from the design patterns enforced by the architect.

4 Lessons Learnt

On an average, 50 percent of screens in any database-centric business application can be generated from two window types – Form Type and Search List Type, which we provided out of the box. Another 40 percent of the windows can be generated by defining 2-4 project specific window types. Our approach lacked any mechanism for the developers to define these window types. Hence, these windows were developed as composite windows whose components are instantiated from the supplied widget type library. Providing a mechanism by which the developers themselves can define the window types and use them as new patterns get identified would improve productivity substantially – the biggest stumbling block in realizing this mechanism is the complexity of our metamodel. Nevertheless, there would always be some windows that do not fit into any window type, which accounts for the rest 10 percent. These would have to be developed as composite windows, provided that the widget type library is rich enough. Our experience shows that there would still be around 3 percent of the windows that either need to be developed outside and integrated or need to be generated and then modified outside the tool. Ease of integration with externally developed windows and with externally developed window components would help in such scenarios.

Separating the content model and type model is a good technique, but realizing the type model at the same level as the content model and typifying the content using a binding association with the types makes the metamodel very complex. Complexity in the metamodel reflects heavily on the code generators and also on the modeling tool thus affecting the overall productivity and customizability. Specification of the types as a metamodel to the GUI models would simplify the whole approach. A mechanism to modify the metamodel also should be part of the solution.

Since we had our reasons not to capture the GUI specifications as platform independent models, aligning to UML and realizing our metamodels as extensions to the UML metamodel did us little help. A custom metamodel described using MOF [4]would be a better proposition for us and would greatly help us in building configurability and extensibility around our modeling tool.

A truly platform independent specification of GUIs is difficult to achieve without compromising on the efficient use of platform capabilities. However, the platform specificity of the GUI models can be reduced to the level of a *class of platforms* and GUIs, rather than being fully platform independent for all classes of GUIs. We find this limited platform independence practical. Consequently, re-targeting such a GUI model will involve enhancements to the metamodel as well as applying transformations on the source model. Moving towards MOF described models would make this easier with the help of QVT [5].

Template based code generation is natural for generating the view layer code but the controller layer code seems better generated using procedural code generation. Re-writing our code generators, currently written using our proprietary template language, with a standardized template language, such as MOF2Text [6], would increase the acceptance of our approach and thereby increase willingness from the tool users to make the changes themselves. A code generation language that supports code reuse and isolation of concerns is critical for organizing the code generators and making them customizable. Aspectual decomposition of the code generators need to be evaluated for isolating the cross cutting concerns like validation, data conversion, logging, and error handling.

A WYSIWYG user interface for the screen modeler can reduce the turnaround time for minor modifications, especially in layout. Automatic layout generation is required but only for generating a default layout.

A very large number of screens in any database-centric business applications are of Create/Retrieve/Update/Delete (CRUD) type. A mechanism to create such screens rapidly from the data model can kick-start the GUI development with a lot of default content to work on.

A richer specification language can reduce the amount of event handler codes being written and improves the retargetability.

Explicit modeling of navigation would help the developers to see the windows they model in context and would greatly help in aligning to the related business process.

Socio-cultural concerns related to acceptance by tool users (developers) can be mitigated to a good extent by adopting industry wide standards like MOF, MOF2Text and QVT which would add to their resumes. Small to medium projects can benefit from a specification driven approach by reducing the learning curve (WYSIWYG interface for the modeler, for example) and improving customizability and turn-around time for code generation.

5 Ongoing Work

We could simplify the code generators by specifying the widget type model as a metamodel for the GUI models. Specifying these code generators using MOF2Text further improved their customizability. With MOF2Text, developers find it very easy to move the externally verified HTML fragments to template body facilitating rapid customization of code generators. Going a step ahead, we were able to define a metameta-model for GUI that, we feel, can be used to define the type models for a class of platforms and for a class of GUIs. Such an approach demonstrates the following benefits – (i) GUI models can be retargeted by defining the widget type library for the new platform and transforming the source model as an instance of the target metamodel using our QVT implementation which takes a mapping specification as input (ii) We can build an adaptive visual modeling tool that can operate on an evolving widget type library without requiring code modification, thus improving the tool extensibility and customizability.

The approach presented in this paper follows the conventional application development paradigm where *window-flows* realize the overarching implicit business process flow. Business process modeling and business process driven applications are gaining good traction in the industry. We are developing a specification and tool for GUI development using this paradigm, where the major part of the navigation flow will be controlled by the business process, instead of the UI controller. A key challenge in this area is supporting multi-channel interaction for business processes over multiple devices.

Our partnership with the banking product continues even today and has presented newer problems for us to work on. The product itself eventually evolved into a product line with multiple customer specific implementations for each product – essentially, a product line of product lines. Each product and each customer specific implementation inherits a lot from its parent, but has some variations. Implementing these variations on copies of the specifications quickly results in an irreconcilably large number of specification copies. We are attempting to solve this product line variability management problem by treating customizations as configurations which use available configuration options, and extensions which deals with building new options to existing configurations or as pure addition to the specifications. Our solution attempts to capture these variations using an extensibility and configurability metamodel.

In addition to the generative approach discussed in this paper, we are also exploring a hosted model of operation wherein an adaptive, multi-tenant GUI implementation can be deployed to deliver tenant-specific GUI content. The implementation would be driven by meta-data generated from the tenant specific specifications. This would require exposing the specification tool itself as a service as part of the platform. We feel that the growing number of PaaS [7] (Platform as a Service) providers would greatly benefit from this work.

6 State of Art

Numerous techniques for model driven development of GUIs have been suggested [12], but very few had the required maturity for usage in large enterprise business applications. AndroMDA [8] proposes a UML Profile [9] for annotating activity diagrams with GUI information to indicate the activities requiring screens, the widgets to be used for message elements etc. The code generator translates this model to a skeleton code which needs to be enhanced by the developer. Its approach of using Tiles [10] to separate the user written code and generated code is not practical for large application development. Further, the specification language is too sparse to express the complexities of today's business application screens. WebML [11] is a web application modeling language that specifies the composition and navigation of web application by defining views over the Entity Relationship Model of the application. The hypertext model is then augmented with a presentation model. All three models are used for code generation. This approach works well for data intensive small to medium web applications where generation of Search and Create/Modify/Delete (CRUD) screens alone gives good productivity advantage. Applicability of this technique for large enterprise applications is very limited as the screens are typically more complex than CRUD screens. Most of these approaches focus on a functional specification of GUIs using high level abstractions and filling in the details by a developer. In contrast, our approach proposes a presentation centric approach to specify the GUI *parallel* to the business or data layer development process. The independently developed presentation layer can be tested and bound to any business layer - be it Services, Business Processes or ER Models - without any programming. We feel that this approach is better because it allows modification in the design of the presentation layer and produces a demonstrable high-fidelity prototype quite early in the development phase.

7 Summary

We presented our experiences in applying model-driven techniques for GUI development for over 14 years in several large enterprise business applications. We described the approach in detail and showed how it resulted in substantially improved productivity. Our approach resulted in improved quality with application-wide uniformity and consistency in the implementation as the entire presentation layer code, except for event handlers, was generated with architectural and design choices encoded in the code generators. Our approach of defining a unified metamodel, of which the GUI specific metamodel is a view, ensured consistency between all the layers in specification as well as in implementation and resulted in better traceability and change management across the layers. We also highlighted the areas where the approach had a scope for improvement, namely, retargetability, customizability, extensibility, ease of use, and ease of testing. We discussed these limitations and the lessons learnt from the experience in detail. We concluded with a brief description of our ongoing work which tries to overcome these limitations. Availability of a key set of MDD standards like MOF, MOF2Text, and QVT, we believe, will help in realization of the ongoing work.

References

1. Kulkarni, V., Reddy, S.: A Model-Driven Approach for Developing Business Applications – Experience, Lessons Learnt and a Way Forward. In: Proceedings of the 1st conference on India software engineering conference, pp. 21–28. ACM, New York (2008), http://doi.acm.org/10.1145/1342211.1342220
2. Kulkarni, V., Venkatesh, R., Reddy, S.: Generating enterprise applications from models. In: Bruel, J.-M., Bellahsène, Z. (eds.) OOIS 2002. LNCS, vol. 2426, pp. 270–279. Springer, Heidelberg (2002)
3. UML 2.0 Infrastructure – Final Adopted Specification (December 2003), http://www.omg.org/uml/
4. Meta Object Facility, http://www.omg.org/cgi-bin/doc?ptc/2004-10-15/
5. MOF Query / View / Transformations, http://www.omg.org/docs/ptc/05-11-01.pdf
6. MOF Models to Text Transformations, http://www.omg.org/spec/MOFM2T/1.0/
7. Platform as a Service, http://www.forrester.com/Research/Document/Excerpt/0,7211,47335,00.html
8. AndroMDA, An Open Source MDA Generator, http://galaxy.andromda.org/

9. AndroMDA BPM4Struts Cartridge UML Profile for GUI Modeling, http://galaxy.andromda.org/docs-3.2/andromda-bpm4struts-cartridge/profile.html
10. Apache Tiles, An Open Source Template Framework, http://tiles.apache.org/framework/index.html
11. Web Modeling Language, http://www.webml.org/
12. Shauerhuber, A., Schwinger, W., Retschitzegger, W., Wimmer, M., Kappelet, G.: A survey on Web Modeling Approaches for Ubiquitous Web Applications. International Journal of Web Information Systems 4, 234–305 (2008)
13. http://struts.apache.org/1.3.10/index.html
14. http://java.sun.com/javaee/javaserverfaces/
15. http://www.sybase.com/products/modelingdevelopment/powerbuilder
16. http://www.asp.net/
17. http://java.sun.com/docs/books/tutorial/uiswing/

Business Process Models as a Showcase for Syntax-Based Assistance in Diagram Editors

Steffen Mazanek and Mark Minas

Universität der Bundeswehr München, Germany
{steffen.mazanek,mark.minas}@unibw.de

Abstract. Recently, a generic approach for syntax-based user assistance in diagram editors has been proposed that requires the syntax of the visual language to be defined by a graph grammar. The present paper describes how this approach can be applied to the language of business process models (BPMs), which is widely used nowadays. The resulting BPM editor provides the following assistance features: combination or completion of BPM fragments, generation of BPM examples, an extensive set of correctness-preserving editing operations for BPMs, and auto-link, i.e., the automatic connection of activities by sequence flow.

Furthermore, this paper contains a discussion of the scalability and scope of the used approach. This also comprises a characterization of the languages where it can be put to a good use.

Keywords: Diagram editor, syntax-based assistance, graph parsing.

1 Introduction

These days, meta-tools are widely used for the development of diagram editors. That way, an editor can be developed with virtually no programming effort. Just an abstract language specification, e.g., based on a metamodel or a kind of grammar, has to be provided from which the complete editor is generated. Well-known examples of meta-tools are MetaEdit+ [1] and GMF [2]. Beyond these there are several research tools like AToM^3 [3], Pounamu [4], or DiaGen [5].

State-of-the-art meta-tools provide a lot of assistance for the *editor developer*. For instance, the appearance of diagram components and the syntax of the language mostly can be specified in a visual way. In contrast, the generated editors often do not provide a lot of assistance for their *actual users* (such as help with incorrect diagrams). This observation motivates the development of generic approaches to user assistance in diagram editors. An important requirement for the adoption of such an approach surely is that minimal additional programming or specification effort should be imposed on the editor developer. Rather the already existing specification should be pushed to its limit.

Recently, such an approach has been proposed and integrated into DiaGen [6,7]. Furthermore, the different assistance features enabled by this approach have been described, i.e., auto-completion (deduce missing diagram components), diagram correction (combine diagram fragments) and example generation [7],

A. Schürr and B. Selic (Eds.): MODELS 2009, LNCS 5795, pp. 322–336, 2009.

correctness-preserving editing operations [8], and diagram contraction resp. autolink [9] — Sect. 3 provides concrete examples of all those. However, up to now this approach only has been applied to toy examples such as the archaic Nassi-Shneiderman diagrams or the equally simple Flowcharts. Although the results have been promising, a real world example is required to foster further adoption of the approach. Therefore, this paper discusses in detail how the approach can be applied to business process models (BPMs), which are certainly a highly relevant language today, and what has been achieved in doing so.

The paper is structured as follows: First, the language BPM is briefly introduced (Sect. 2). For the sake of motivation, this paper continues with the presentation of the actual outcome, i.e., the assistance features of the generated BPM editor (Sect. 3). Only then it is explained how the language had to be modeled in order to apply the approach (Sect. 4). Along the way the approach itself is recapitulated to make this paper self-contained (Sect. 5). Moreover, a basic understanding of the approach is also required in order to understand its scope, which is discussed in Sect. 6. This section contains some performance data as well. Finally, related work is reviewed (Sect. 7) and the paper is concluded.

2 Business Process Models

BPMs are mostly used to represent the processes (i.e., workflows) within an enterprise. In recent years a standardized visual notation, the Business Process Modeling Notation BPMN [10], has been developed, which is readily understandable by different kinds of business users with different levels of expertise. In this paper a subset of BPMN is considered that is outlined by example next.

Fig. 1 shows a typical sales process: A customer orders a product from a company, which ships it if available. The diagram consists of two pools (large rectangles), "Customer" and "Sales Department", which act as containers for the actual processes. The upper pool contains a start event (simple circle), an activity (rounded rectangle), an intermediate receive event (two nested circles),

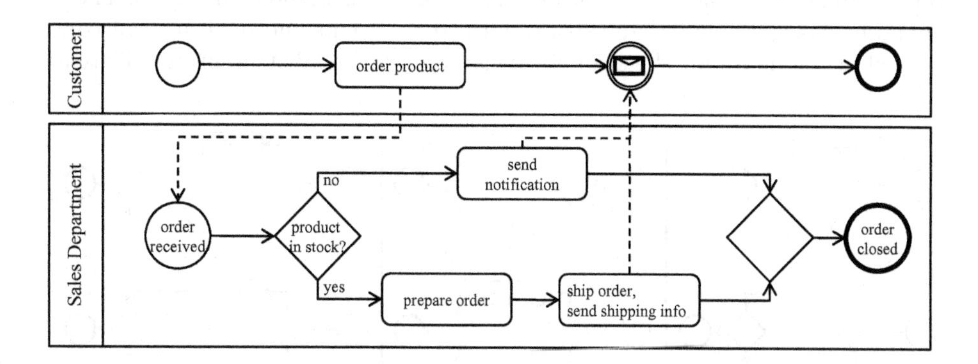

Fig. 1. Example BPM

and an end event (thick circle), which are connected by arrows representing the sequence flow. The other pool contains, among others, two gateways (diamonds), which are used to split and join the sequence flow. Finally, messages (dashed arrows) can be sent in the course of an activity.

In the following only well-structured BPMs are considered, i.e., it is required that splits and joins are properly nested such that each split has a corresponding join. This restriction is supposed to improve the quality of process models [11] similar to structured programming, which improves the quality of program code.

3 Resulting Assistance

Next, the assistance features are described that are provided by the generated BPM editor. It has to be stressed again that the realization of all these features has required virtually no extra programming effort.

Auto-completion: Incomplete BPMs usually occur as intermediate diagrams during modeling. But they might also result from a lack of knowledge of a beginner user. The developed editor can generate suggestions on how to complete such diagrams [7]. Actually, it computes all possible completions up to a user-defined size. Fig. 2 shows three examples how given incomplete BPM diagrams can be completed. For the first one, the smallest possible completion consists of a gateway and three arrows. The second one can be completed by adding a fresh activity with a default text and linking it properly. Finally, the two BPM fragments given at the right-hand side can be combined into a well-structured process just by introducing two arrows. Regarding the user interface, auto-completion is supported by a dialog that allows the user to browse and preview all possible completions for his diagram.

Example generation: An important special case of completion is the empty diagram, completions of which can be used to enumerate the language. Given the number of diagram components (arrows are not counted), all possible BPMs of this size without messages (cf. Sect. 6) can be generated. The user can browse this set to get valuable insight into the language. This is shown in Fig. 3. There are no BPMs of size less than three (intermediate events and pools are not considered in the figure for the sake of conciseness). Since all structurally different

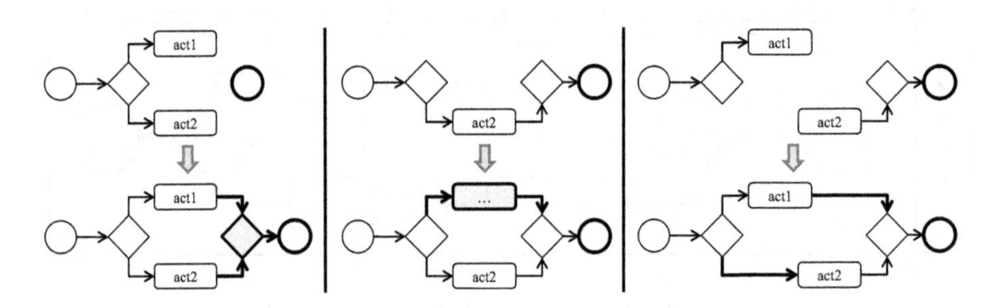

Fig. 2. Auto-completion of BPMs

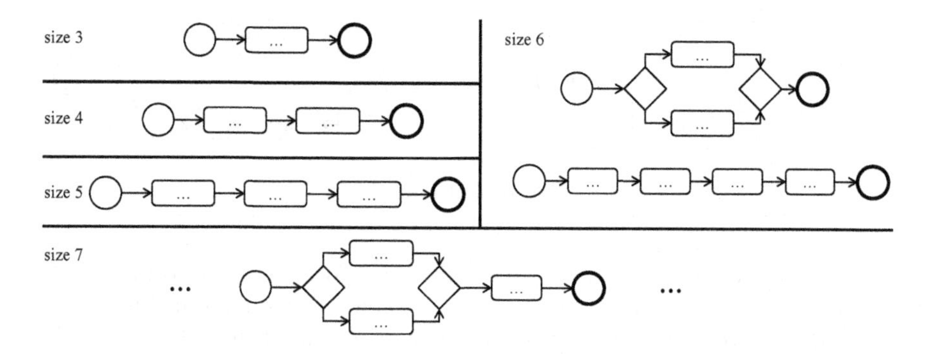

Fig. 3. Generation of BPM examples

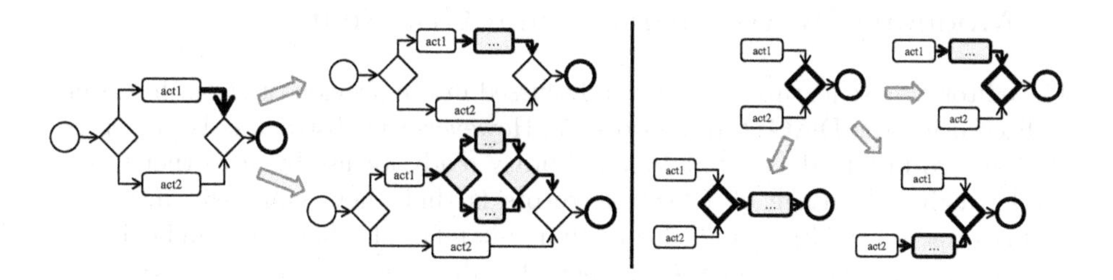

Fig. 4. Generation of correctness-preserving editing operations

examples are generated, their number grows exponentially with the size parameter. Still it is useful to have a look at some of them, in particular because an example can be selected to be the starting point of further editing.

Editing operations: In addition, powerful correctness-preserving editing operations can be generated [8]. Some example operations are shown in Fig. 4. In the diagram at the left-hand side, the thick arrow has been selected by the user to determine the context for the operations he is interested in. The highlighted components are introduced by the particular operation. The figure also shows that it is sometimes meaningful to allow operations to introduce more than one new component. Otherwise, a gateway could not be inserted into a correct BPM. On the right-hand side the operations provided in the context of a gateway are shown (only a fragment of a correct BPM is shown though). Besides operations that add components, there also is an intelligent remove operation. Therewith, one or several selected components can be removed and the remaining diagram is reconnected automatically (if possible), cf. Fig. 5.

Fig. 5. Intelligent remove

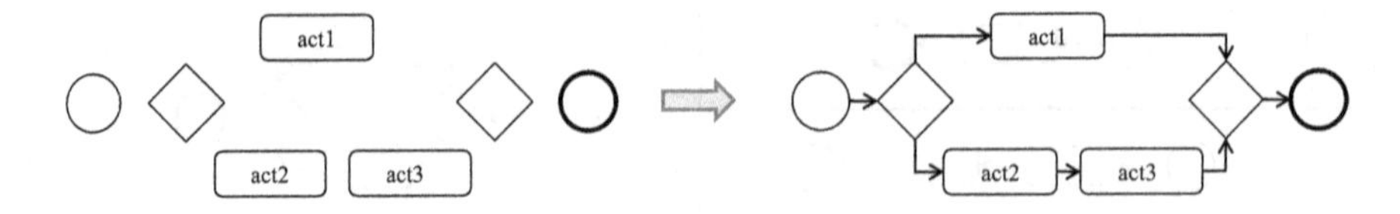

Fig. 6. Auto-link

Auto-link: Finally, inspired by [12], the editor provides auto-link to further improve the user's editing performance. This is shown by example in Fig. 6. The missing arrows are derived from the spatial arrangement of the activities, which is mostly preserved. The realization of auto-link is explained in detail in [9].

4 Modeling BPMs with a Graph Grammar

The editor, whose features have been discussed in the previous section, has been realized using the DiaGen framework [5]. However, the abstract assistance part of [6] is also provided as a stand-alone library ready for use by any other tool.[1]

The main advantage of DiaGen editors is that they seamlessly integrate syntax-directed and free-hand editing. In free-hand mode, diagrams can be drawn without any restrictions in the manner of a drawing tool. Thereby, feedback about the syntactical correctness of the diagram is consistently provided by an analysis module. On the other hand, syntax-directed editing operations can be defined by the editor developer to simplify frequent editing tasks of the users. With the newly developed user assistance described in the previous section further guidance is provided. So, for the sake of editing freedom the editor still does not prevent the user from drawing an incorrect diagram. But on request it offers powerful syntactical assistance helping him to end with a correct one.

DiaGen editors use hypergraphs as a diagram model and hypergraph grammars to define the syntax of the language. Furthermore, all editors generated with DiaGen follow the same general editing process. This process consists of several steps as shown in Fig. 7. Those are informally described next.

With the *drawing tool*, the editor user can create, delete, arrange and modify the diagram components as defined in the editor specification. Components usually have some layout attributes, e.g., the position and size of an activity. Additionally, a set of properties like the label of an activity or the type of an intermediate event can be defined, which can be manipulated via a special dialog.

The first processing step, the *modeler*, creates the Spatial Relationship Graph (SRG) from these components. Therefore, it first creates component hyperedges for each diagram component and nodes for each of their attachment areas. An attachment area is a determined part of a diagram component that can interact with other diagram components. Afterwards, the modeler checks for each pair of attachment areas whether they are related as defined in the specification. For instance, an arrow end and an event are *at*-related if both attachment areas

[1] `http://www.steffen-mazanek.de/graphcompl/`

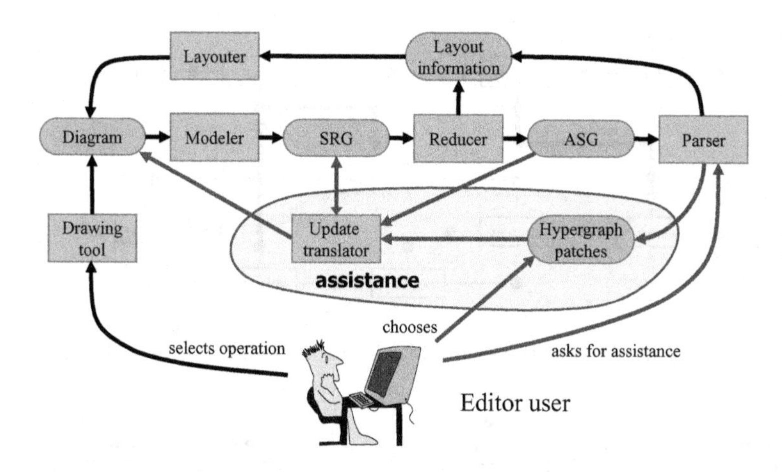

Fig. 7. Editing process of DiaGen editors

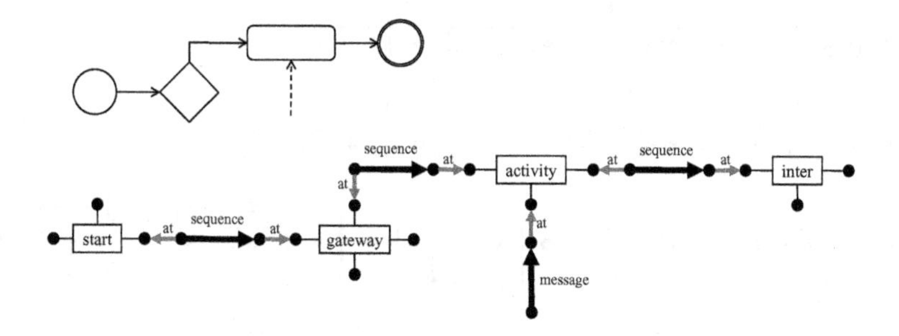

Fig. 8. BPM fragment and its SRG

overlap. As another example, a pool p_1 is *below* another pool p_2 if $p_1.y > p_2.y + p_2.h$. For each relationship detected, the modeler adds a corresponding relationship edge between the two attachment nodes involved. This graphical scanning step is crucial for free-hand editing.

In Fig. 8, a BPM fragment and its SRG are shown. The hyperedges are represented as rectangular boxes and the nodes as black dots. If a hyperedge and a node are incident, they are connected by a line.[2] Binary hyperedges (such as all relation edges, the sequence arrows, and the messages) are simply represented as arrows. Activities and intermediate events have three attachment areas: two for incoming resp. outgoing sequence flow, one for messages. Gateways have four attachment areas (namely their corners), and start events have three (one for the corresponding pool, one for messages, and one for outgoing sequence flow).

As one can already see, the SRG becomes quite large. DiaGen editors therefore do not analyze the SRG directly, but simplify it first according to the specification (similar to lexical analysis in compilers). This step is performed by the

[2] Each line represents a particular role (like "incoming sequence flow"). However, instead of using labels the graphical arrangement implicitly determines the roles.

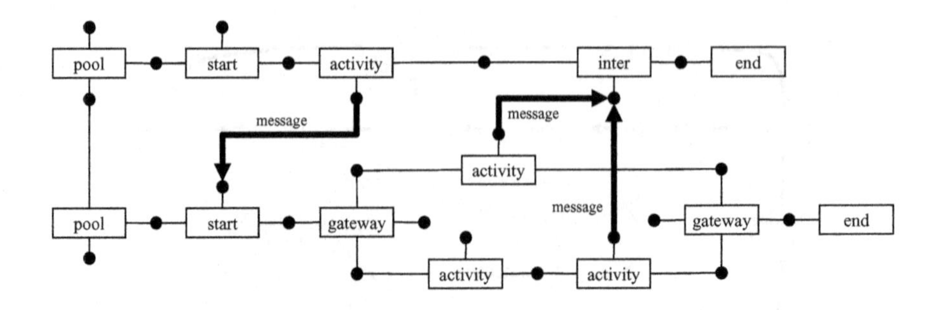

Fig. 9. ASG of the example sales process shown in Fig. 1

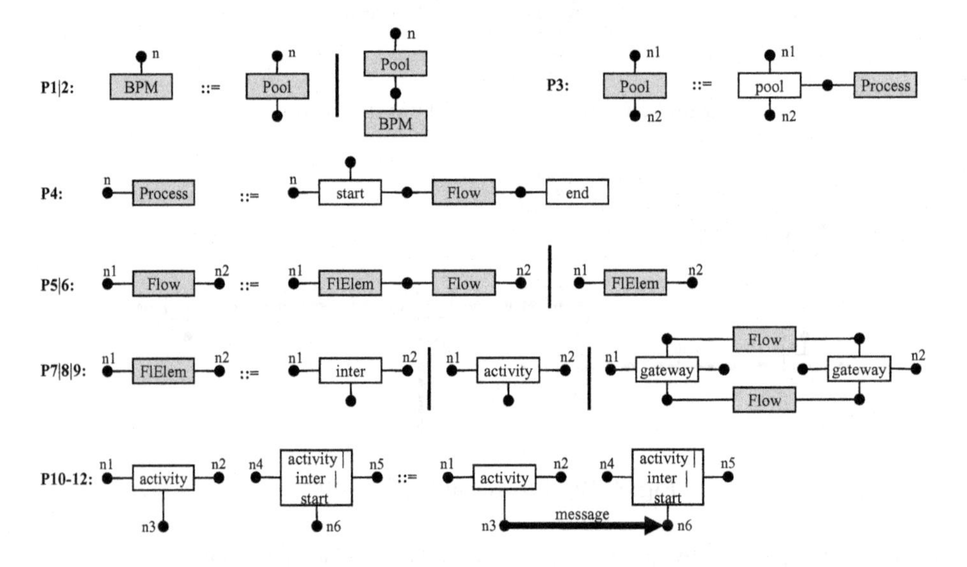

Fig. 10. Hypergraph grammar for BPMs

reducer, which creates the so-called Abstract Syntax Graph (ASG). In case of BPM there is a close correspondence between SRG and ASG. In the ASG, nodes of the SRG that are connected by a relationship edge are merged. Furthermore, the arrows for sequence flow do not occur in the ASG anymore. Rather the nodes connected by such an arrow are also merged. Fig. 9 shows the complete ASG of the example sales process. This ASG now directly represents the structure of the diagram and, thus, can be syntactically analyzed by the *parser*.

In DiaGen, hypergraph grammars are used for language definition. They generalize the idea of Chomsky grammars for strings as used by standard compiler generators. Each hypergraph grammar consists of two finite sets of terminal and nonterminal hyperedge labels and a starting hypergraph that contains only a single nonterminal hyperedge. Syntax is described by a set of productions. The hypergraph language generated by the grammar is defined by the set of terminally labeled hypergraphs that can be derived from the starting hypergraph.

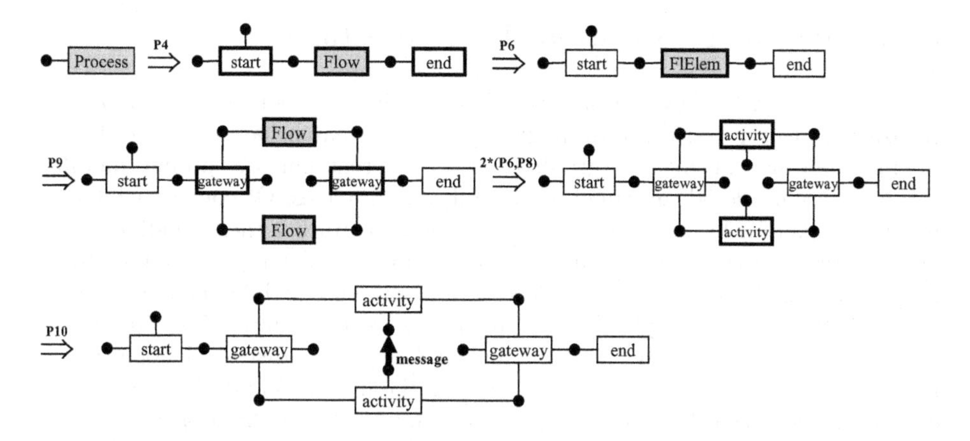

Fig. 11. Example derivation

Fig. 10 shows the productions of the hypergraph grammar G_{BPM} whose language is just the set of all ASGs of structured BPMs. For conciseness, productions $L ::= R_1, L ::= R_2, \ldots$ with the same left-hand side are drawn as $L ::= R_1|R_2|\ldots$ The types *pool*, *start*, *end*, *inter*, *activity*, *gateway* and *message* are terminal hyperedge labels being used in ASGs. The set of nonterminal labels consists of *BPM*, *Pool*, *Process*, *Flow* and *FlElem*. The starting hypergraph consists of just a single *BPM* edge with an incident node. Most of the required productions are context-free, i.e., their left-hand side consists of just a single nonterminally labeled hyperedge together with the appropriate number of nodes. There are only three non-context-free productions, P10-P12, that embed a *message* between two activities or an activity and a start resp. intermediate event.

The application of a context-free production removes an occurrence e of the hyperedge on the left-hand side of the production from the host graph and replaces it by the hypergraph H_r on the right-hand side. Matching node labels of both sides of a production determine how H_r has to fit in after removing e. Context-free hypergraph grammars are described in detail in [13]. Fig. 11 shows an example derivation starting from *Process*. Only for the last step, the introduction of a *message*, an embedding production has to be applied. The grammar G_{BPM} is *unambiguous*, so that there is a unique derivation tree (which can be constructed by the parser in an efficient way) for the context-free part of every hypergraph of the language.

The final processing step of a DiaGen editor is the *layouter*, which computes a layout for the diagram. The developed BPM editor relies on an incremental constraint-based layout, where the constraints are gathered, among others, from the derivation information resulting from the parser.

As already mentioned, DiaGen also allows the developer to explicitly specify editing operations. Hypergraph transformation rules are used to this end (see [5] for further information). The application of such an operation is performed by a so-called *transformer* component (omitted in Fig. 7).

5 Hypergraph Patches for User Assistance

In previous work [7], *hypergraph patches* have been proposed as a means for the realization of user assistance in diagram editors. A patch basically describes a modification of a given hypergraph H. Two different kinds of atomic modifications are considered: merging nodes and adding edges. Of course, arbitrary modifications of a hypergraph are not very helpful. Rather those modifications are required that transform H into a valid member of the language defined by a given grammar G. Such patches indeed can be computed while parsing [6].

Consider the hypergraph H given in Fig. 12 as an example. For simplicity, assume that *Process* is the start symbol of G_{BPM}, i.e., disregard pools for a moment. H then can be corrected by merging the nodes n5 and n6. However, it can also be corrected by inserting an *activity* hyperedge at the proper position. Note that there might be an infinite number of correcting patches. Actually, an arbitrary number of activities or intermediate events could be inserted between the *activity* and the *end* hyperedge in H. So the size of desired patches (i.e., the number of additional hyperedges) has to be restricted.[3]

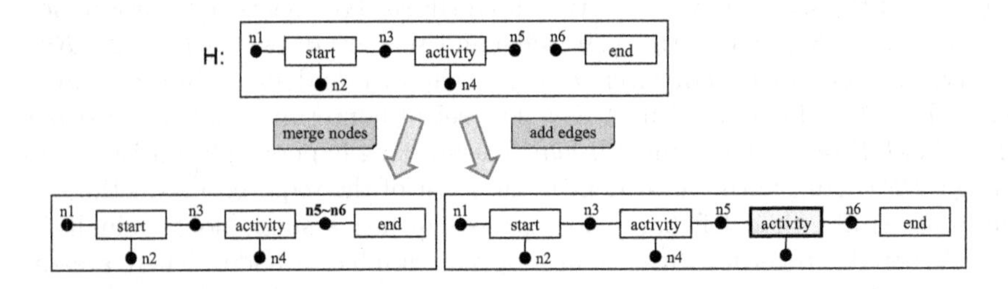

Fig. 12. Hypergraph patches in the context of BPM

Fig. 7 also shows how patches can be integrated into the DiaGen editing process: On user's request the parser is triggered with the desired size of patches as a parameter. It computes all possible correcting hypergraph patches of this size. From those the user has to choose. Next, the selected patch is applied and embedded into the SRG using a language-specific *update translator*. The editor then calls the reducer and parser again. Finally, the layouter arranges the new components within the diagram and adapts existing components if necessary.

The update translator for BPMs can be implemented quite straightforwardly. For instance, if n5 and n6 in Fig. 12 are to be merged, this is translated to embedding a sequence arrow (and some relations) between the activity and the end event. As another example, imagine n1 had to be merged with an attachment node of a particular *pool* edge. Then a spatial relationship edge *inside* has to

[3] The deletion of edges and the splitting of nodes has not been considered, because existing diagram components and "relevant" spatial relations of the user's diagram should be respected (except for intelligent remove). Also, patches are not allowed to introduce nonterminal edges, because those do not have a visual representation.

be inserted between the corresponding nodes in the SRG. After reduction and parsing, the layouter moves the corresponding sub-process inside of the pool.

Patches are also useful if the given diagram is correct already. For instance, the operations introduced in [8] even require the input diagram to be correct. Additionally, the user has to select a context in order to access possible operations. The key idea has been to separate those edges on the ASG level that correspond to the user's selection from the non-selected part. Roughly speaking, the ASG is artificially broken into pieces and repaired again with certain, relevant patches that constitute meaningful operations.

6 Discussion

It is important to stress that the described patches are solely computed from the grammar. Semantics is not at all considered. Therefore, an activity (or any other diagram component) inserted as assistance only carries a default label.

Generally, the possible assistance is heavily affected by the way a language is modeled. For instance, with the grammar shown in Fig. 10 only the start event is connected to the containing pool on the abstract syntax level. Therefore, an unconnected activity could even be moved to another pool for the sake of correction. One could have also modeled the language in a way such that each activity is connected to the pool it is surrounded by. This would prevent the movement of activities to other pools.

Another important issue is how to deal with the different gateway types that are possible in BPMN, cf. [10]. At the moment, the type (parallel, exclusive, etc.) can be adjusted in a property dialog, but it only affects the visual appearance of the gateway component. However, a branching can easily be prevented from being joined by a different type of gateway: It is sufficient to add another terminal symbol *par_gateway* and another production equal to P9, but with *par_gateway* edges instead of *gateway*. The grammar could also be extended to support more than two parallel branches or other kinds of structured concepts such as loops. However, with loops it has to be accepted that mostly there will not be a unique solution for auto-link anymore.

Note that based on G_{BPM} example generation yields a very large number of results (at least if used straight away). The problem is that activities and intermediate events can be used interchangeably according to the syntax of the language. So, in order to get an example with n activities, a lot of (i.e., $2^n - 1$) further examples will be generated with intermediate events instead of certain activities. Therefore, the editor developer can list such (somehow redundant) edge types so that the parser does not create those edges for the sake of completion. Of course, intermediate events drawn by the user are still perfectly accepted.

6.1 Who Benefits?

An empirical user study has not been conducted yet. At the moment, interviews with language experts (i.e., business modelers) are being planned to find out whether the provided functions are perceived as useful. Also it has to be studied whether users can learn new languages more easily once having learnt these features. However, some benefits of the provided assistance can already be discussed in an abstract way. Remarkably, both the users and the developer benefit.

Beginner users can quickly explore the visual language at hand by looking at example diagrams. That way, they do not need to know anything about grammars, which makes the editor more accessible. After having gained some insight in the particular language, they can start drawing diagrams. In case of modeling errors they can rely on the provided assistance.

Advanced users benefit from auto-link, which avoids the tedious work of drawing connections, and the generated editing operations, which provide a lot of flexibility and speed up editing.

The *editor developer* does not need to specify (certain) editing operations by hand anymore, which is a tedious and error-prone task. Rather diagram-specific editing operations are automatically computed from the grammar at runtime. Moreover, prototyping and testing of editors is simplified, because the generated examples can be used to quickly validate the specification.

6.2 Scope of the Approach

There is a severe general restriction of the approach: Only languages that are mostly context-free can benefit from its application. So, for the computation of patches, embedding productions are not considered. In case of BPMs this means that messages, which can be embedded between arbitrary activities, are not part of the computed patches. Existing messages drawn by the user are tolerated by the parser, of course. If only well-structured BPMs have to be covered, all other productions are context-free (cf. Fig. 10), so that the approach is still applicable. Arbitrary sequence flow, however, cannot be supported.

But why not consider embedding productions for the sake of completion? There is a simple intuition behind this restriction: The more restricted a language is, the more powerful the possible assistance can be. If everything is allowed, no corrections are required at all. Since messages can be inserted between arbitrary activities, just too many solutions would exist (n^2 for n activities). Those cannot be browsed easily anymore. A completely different user interface (e.g., drawing connectors by using special handles) would be required to make effective use of this information. Therefore, the parser does not create messages (and other kinds of embedded edges) as part of patches.

Another reason why languages such as class diagrams can hardly be supported is that graphs of this language usually consist of a lot of different connected components. However, heavily disconnected graphs can be derived from a grammar in a lot of different ways, i.e., the language is inherently ambiguous. Therefore, one and the same completion would be returned as a result very often. Even worse, for disconnected graphs parsing is known to be inefficient. To overcome this issue, DiaGen provides so-called set-productions that can be used if the order in which components are derived does not matter. But those are not supported (yet) for completion.

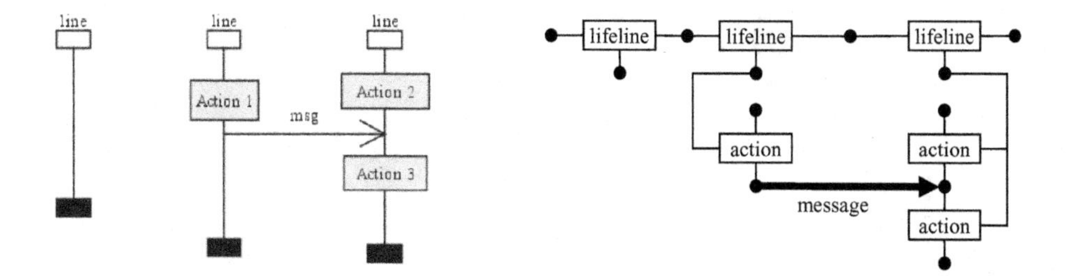

Fig. 13. Modeling MSCs: example diagram and corresponding ASG

However, several practical languages already can be modeled in a way that avoids these issues. For instance, an editor for Message Sequence Charts (MSCs) with user assistance has also been specified already. Lifelines thereby have to be arranged in the ASG in a particular order, i.e., from left to right.[4] Messages, again, are just embedded. Fig. 13 shows an MSC and its ASG to clarify this issue. Modeling MSCs that way allows for plenty of user assistance: Examples (without messages) can be generated, isolated actions can be moved onto lifelines, editing operations can be used to insert an action between existing actions and so on.

6.3 Performance

Performance has always been a problem of the approach (or, more precisely, its realization). However, recently a substantial improvement factor has been achieved with respect to performance, so that the patch-computing parser is now ready for practice. On the one hand, the algorithm itself has been improved by using more intelligent data structures. On the other hand, support for multi-threading has been added. Indeed, the filling of layers by the parser as described in [6] can be parallelized in a straightforward way (one thread per production).

Fig. 14 provides some performance data gathered on a standard Notebook (Intel Core2 Duo with 2GHz each, 2GB RAM). As input BPMs with several pools have been used that contain a process at a time consisting of a start event, an activity, and an end event. Every input graph contains exactly one error that can be repaired by merging two nodes. The x-axis determines the size of the input graph, i.e., the total number of edges. Data for different patch sizes (number of additional edges to be added by the parser) has been collected. With zero edges just the two separated nodes are merged. If several edges are to be introduced the only result is the introduction of this number of activities between the separated nodes. Performance naturally drops if too many edges are to be introduced. However, it can be seen that for most small and medium-sized diagrams assistance can be computed in less than a second.

Future performance improvements are possible by introducing better support for modularization. For instance, in BPM better performance could be achieved, if the pools with their respective contents would be treated independently.

[4] The same approach has also been used for modeling the pools in BPMs.

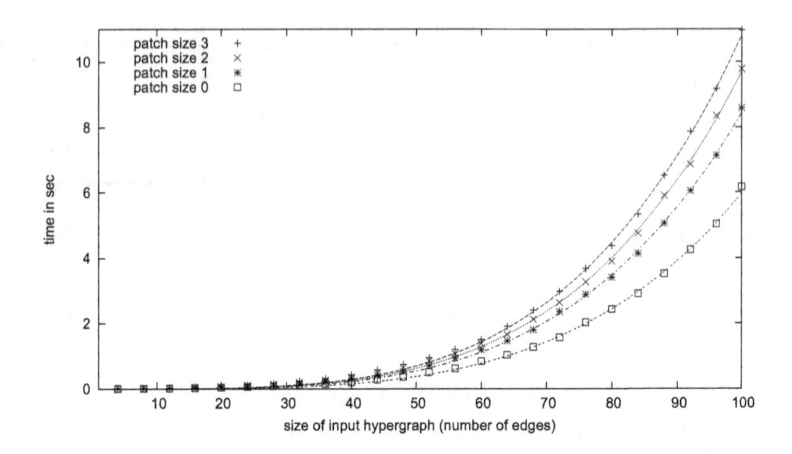

Fig. 14. Performance measurements when computing patches of different sizes

7 Related Work

Text editors: In the context of text editors, approaches for the combination of different editing modes have a long tradition. A widely known system is the Synthesizer Generator [14], which allows the generation of editors that support both structure and text editing. However, following this approach the editor developer has to decide which syntactic construct is to be edited in which mode. The Syned system [15] overcomes this limitation by seamlessly integrating both editing modes, so that the users can edit as they like and not as the developer thought they would like. However, this approach cannot directly be transferred to diagram editors, because in diagrams there is no obvious concrete representation of nonterminal symbols in general. Moreover, for a novice user it is probably easier to only deal with fully expanded diagrams (and still have syntax-directed operations at hand). Regarding error recovery, modern textual IDEs, be they generated or hand-crafted, certainly provide sophisticated user support [16].

Meta-tools: GMF [2] editors provide connector handles (drag connections out of a node) and action toolbars (fill compartments of a node, e.g., adding an attribute to a class). MetaEdit+ [1] provides different kinds of static assistance [17]. So, it automatically creates a language help based on the data entered by the language developer. It also supports the creation of so-called tutorial projects. The tool AToM^3 has been extended to support model completion [18]. Constraint logic programming is exploited to this end (as in SmartEMF [19], GEMS [20], or the check engine of [21]). Ehrig et al. suggest the generation of instance models of a particular metamodel by means of a graph grammar [22].

BPM tools: Koschmider et al. have proposed ideas for user assistance in BPM tools. In a recent approach [23] relevant process fragments are recommended based on a repository of semantically annotated processes. Such repository-based approaches have the advantage that best practices in modeling can be promoted.

Indeed, a syntactically correct process resulting from our assistance might still violate particular modeling guidelines or comprise semantical problems such as deadlocks. In [12] a pattern-based approach for BPM editing has been proposed and implemented for the IBM WebSphere Business Modeler. Also the autolink feature has been described already in [12]. Finally, it has to be admitted that special-purpose approaches usually are more efficient. Language-specific optimizations often can be incorporated into the parser. For instance, in [24] an efficient parser for workflow graphs has been proposed that runs in linear time.

8 Conclusion

In this paper a BPM editor with user assistance has been presented as a showcase for the previously introduced *generic* approach to syntax-based user assistance in diagram editors. With virtually no programming effort powerful assistance features have been realized most special-purpose modeling tools not even provide. Those features help both in learning and dealing with BPMs. Moreover, thanks to the underlying formal approach (hypergraph grammars and hypergraph transformation) the provided assistance satisfies several desirable properties, e.g., the preservation of correctness. Since the editor is generated from an abstract specification it can be extended or adapted easily. A screencast of this editor in action is provided at `http://www.unibw.de/inf2/DiaGen/assistance/bpm`. There, the editor is also available for download as an executable Java archive.

In future, an incremental version of the used parser has to be developed. This would have two benefits: First, the performance can be further improved. And second, it would be possible to provide assistance in a more pervasive way, i.e., suggestions could be given while editing and not only on user's request. Finally, a comparative user study has to be performed.

Acknowledgment. We thank Jana Koehler for fruitful discussions and the anonymous referees for their insightful remarks.

References

1. Kelly, S., Tolvanen, J.P.: Domain-Specific Modeling: Enabling Full Code Generation. Wiley-IEEE Computer Society (2008)
2. Gronback, R.C.: Eclipse Modeling Project: A Domain-Specific Language (DSL) Toolkit. Addison-Wesley Longman, Amsterdam (2009)
3. de Lara, J., Vangheluwe, H., Alfonseca, M.: Meta-modelling and graph grammars for multi-paradigm modelling in AToM^3. Softw. and Syst. Modeling, 193–209 (2004)
4. Zhu, N., Grundy, J., Hosking, J., Liu, N., Cao, S., Mehra, A.: Pounamu: A meta-tool for exploratory domain-specific visual language tool development. Systems and Software 80(8), 1390–1407 (2007)
5. Minas, M.: Concepts and realization of a diagram editor generator based on hypergraph transformation. Science of Computer Programming 44(2), 157–180 (2002)
6. Mazanek, S., Maier, S., Minas, M.: An algorithm for hypergraph completion according to hyperedge replacement grammars. In: Ehrig, H., Heckel, R., Rozenberg, G., Taentzer, G. (eds.) ICGT 2008. LNCS, vol. 5214, pp. 39–53. Springer, Heidelberg (2008)

7. Mazanek, S., Maier, S., Minas, M.: Auto-completion for diagram editors based on graph grammars. In: Proc. of the 2008 IEEE Symposium on Visual Languages and Human-Centric Computing, pp. 242–245. IEEE, Los Alamitos (2008)
8. Mazanek, S., Minas, M.: Generating correctness-preserving editing operations for diagram editors. In: Proc. of the 8th Int. Workshop on Graph Transformation and Visual Modeling Techniques. Electronic Communications of the EASST, vol. 18. European Association of Software Science and Technology (2009)
9. Mazanek, S., Minas, M.: Contraction of unconnected diagrams using least cost parsing. In: Proc. of the 8th Int. Workshop on Graph Transformation and Visual Modeling Techniques. Electronic Communications of the EASST, vol. 18. European Association of Software Science and Technology (2009)
10. Object Management Group: Business Process Modeling Notation, BPMN (2009), `http://www.omg.org/docs/formal/09-01-03.pdf`
11. Gruhn, V., Laue, R.: What business process modelers can learn from programmers. Science of Computer Programming 65(1), 4–13 (2007)
12. Gschwind, T., Koehler, J., Wong, J.: Applying patterns during business process modeling. In: Dumas, M., Reichert, M., Shan, M.-C. (eds.) BPM 2008. LNCS, vol. 5240, pp. 4–19. Springer, Heidelberg (2008)
13. Drewes, F., Habel, A., Kreowski, H.J.: Hyperedge replacement graph grammars. In: Rozenberg, G. (ed.) Handbook of Graph Grammars and Computing by Graph Transformation. Foundations, vol. I, pp. 95–162. World Scientific, Singapore (1997)
14. Reps, T.W., Teitelbaum, T.: The Synthesizer Generator: A System for Constructing Language-Based Editors. Springer, Heidelberg (1989)
15. Horgan, J.R., Moore, D.J.: Techniques for improving language-based editors. SIGSOFT Softw. Eng. Notes 9(3), 7–14 (1984)
16. Nilsson-Nyman, E., Ekman, T., Hedin, G.: Practical scope recovery using bridge parsing. In: Gašević, D., Lämmel, R., Van Wyk, E. (eds.) SLE 2008. LNCS, vol. 5452, pp. 95–113. Springer, Heidelberg (2009)
17. Tolvanen, J.P.: How to support language users? (2008), `http://www.metacase.com/blogs/jpt/blogView?entry=3405240161` (accessed July-09-2009)
18. Sen, S., Baudry, B., Vangheluwe, H.: Domain-specific model editors with model completion. In: Giese, H. (ed.) MODELS 2008. LNCS, vol. 5002, pp. 259–270. Springer, Heidelberg (2008)
19. Hessellund, A., Czarnecki, K., Wasowski, A.: Guided development with multiple domain-specific languages. In: Engels, G., Opdyke, B., Schmidt, D.C., Weil, F. (eds.) MODELS 2007. LNCS, vol. 4735, pp. 46–60. Springer, Heidelberg (2007)
20. White, J., Schmidt, D.C., Nechypurenko, A., Wuchner, E.: Model intelligence: an approach to modeling guidance. UPGRADE 9(2), 22–28 (2008)
21. Blanc, X., Mounier, I., Mougenot, A., Mens, T.: Detecting model inconsistency through operation-based model construction. In: Proc. of the 30th Int. Conference on Software Engineering, pp. 511–520. ACM, New York (2008)
22. Ehrig, K., Küster, J.M., Taentzer, G.: Generating instance models from meta models. Software and Systems Modeling (2008)
23. Hornung, T., Koschmider, A., Lausen, G.: Recommendation based process modeling support: Method and user experience. In: Li, Q., Spaccapietra, S., Yu, E., Olivé, A. (eds.) ER 2008. LNCS, vol. 5231, pp. 265–278. Springer, Heidelberg (2008)
24. Vanhatalo, J., Völzer, H., Koehler, J.: The refined process structure tree. In: Dumas, M., Reichert, M., Shan, M.-C. (eds.) BPM 2008. LNCS, vol. 5240, pp. 100–115. Springer, Heidelberg (2008)

Rule-Enhanced Business Process Modeling Language for Service Choreographies

Milan Milanović[1], Dragan Gašević[2], Gerd Wagner[3], and Marek Hatala[4]

[1] University of Belgrade, Serbia
[2] Athabasca University, Canada
[3] Brandenburg Technical University at Cottbus, Germany
[4] Simon Fraser University, Canada
milan@milanovic.org, dgasevic@acm.org,
G.Wagner@tu-cottbus.de, mhatala@sfu.ca

Abstract. To address problem of modeling service choreographies, the paper tackles the following challenges of the state of the art in choreography modeling: *i)* choreography models are not well-connected with the underlying business vocabulary models. *ii)* there is limited support for decoupling parts of business logic from complete choreography models. This reduces dynamic changes of choreographies; *iii)* choreography models contain redundant elements of shared business logic, which might lead to an inconsistent implementation and incompatible behavior. Our proposal – rBPMN – is an extension of a business process modeling language with rule and choreography modeling support. rBPMN is defined by weaving the metamodels of the Business Process Modeling Notation (BPMN) and REWERSE Rule Markup Language (R2ML).

Keywords: BPMN, R2ML, rules, processes, metamodels, MDE.

1 Introduction

Responding to the increasing demands for developing advanced solutions to the integration of business processes in collaborative information systems, service-oriented architectures (SOAs) emerged as a promising approach. Considering the present state in the area of SOA, we can witness a need for the development of new software engineering approaches suitable for this development context. Being grounded on proven principles of business process modeling, service engineers have prevalently based their approaches on languages such as BPMN [4]. Such languages offer a suitable way for requirements elicitation from stakeholders, which can (semi-)automatically be bound to the existing services and transformed onto the executable service compositions (i.e., languages such as BPEL). In the service composition task, we generally have two main approaches [7]: i) service orchestration – composition of service from the perspective of one of the participants. Orchestrations are typically modeled w.r.t. control flows, while workflow patterns are used as best practices and evaluation framework for comparison of orchestration languages; ii) service choreographies – composition of services from a global perspective where service interaction is the primary focus. In this paper, we exactly focus on the problem of modeling choreographies in order to address challenges from we give in the abstract.

A. Schürr and B. Selic (Eds.): MODELS 2009, LNCS 5795, pp. 337–341, 2009.

2 Background

2.1 BPMN Language: Graphical Concrete Syntax and Metamodel

BPMN represents an OMG adopted specification [1] whose intent is to model business processes. Business process models are expressed in business process diagrams. Each business process diagram consists of a set of modeling elements. BPMN includes three types of flow objects which defines behavior: Events, Activities and Gateways. *Events* can be partitioned into three types, based on their position in the business process: start events are used to trigger processes; intermediate events can delay processes, or they can occur during processes [4] [7]; and end events signal the termination of processes. A BPMN *activity* can be atomic or non-atomic (represented by a rectangle). BPMN supports three types of activities: Process, Sub-Process and Task. *Gateways* are used for guiding, splitting and merging control flow.

The key element of the definition of the BPMN language is a metamodel. Although BPMN is an OMG standard, there is presently no standard metamodel for BPMN. We choose a BPMN metamodel proposal given in [4], because it uses an explicit BPMN terminology; and its mapping relations to BPEL are clearer than in the case of other proposals.

2.2 Business Rules: REWERSE I1 Rule Markup Language

REWERSE I1 Rule Markup Language (R2ML) is a general rule language [5]. R2ML is completely built by using model-driven engineering principles, which means that the R2ML language definition consists of the three main parts: i) metamodel – an abstract syntax in the Meta-Object Facility (MOF) language; ii) textual concrete syntax – an XML based syntax that facilitates rule interchange; and iii) graphical concrete syntax – a graphical notation suitable for modeling rules in a style similar to software modeling languages. In fact, its graphical syntax is defined as an extension of UML and named UML-based Rule Modeling Language (URML) [6]. There are different categories of business rules such as [7] integrity, derivation, reaction, and production. R2ML defines all of these four types of rules and provides modeling concepts for defining vocabularies. All R2ML rule definitions (e.g., ReactionRule) are inherited from the Rule class. Each type of rule is defined over the R2ML vocabulary, where elements of the vocabulary are used in logical formulas (e.g., LogicalFormula – with no fee variables) through the use of Atoms and Terms.

3 rBPMN Metamodel: Rule and Choreography Modeling

The rBPMN metamodel is defined by importing the elements from the BPMN and R2ML metamodels. In Fig. 1, we show extension to the Process package of the rBPMN metamodel. *RuleGateway* is an element, which we added in the Process package of the BPMN metamodel and which actually relates to R2ML *Rule*s. In this way, we enabled that R2ML *Rule* can be placed into a process as a *Gateway*, but in the same time not to break the R2ML *Rule* syntax and semantics. We should note here that one rule gateway could have one or more rules attached to it. This is quite important, as in some cases, we need to first derive or constrain some part of the business logic, before being able to perform some other rules such as reaction or production. In Fig. 1, we can see that *RuleGateway* as a *Gateway* can be connected by using *SequenceFlow* with other *FlowElements* such as *Tasks*, *Events* and *Gateways*. This enables us to use rules in different places in rBPMN process models. Additionally, we added a *RuleCondition* concept, which is used to show rule condition directly attached to the *RuleGateway* in a business process diagram.

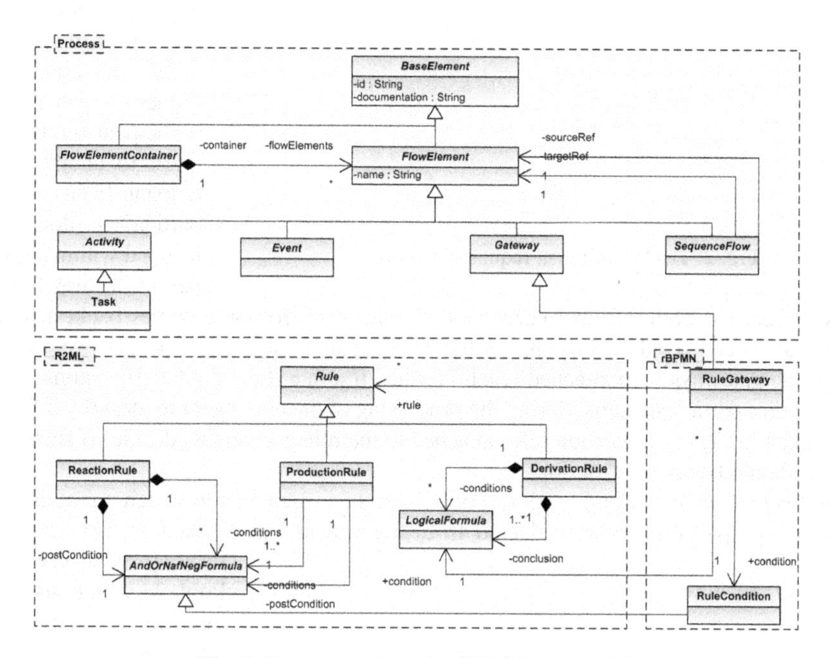

Fig. 1. Process package in rBPMN metamodel

We can have a rule as a valid element in a business process, but we should also have a way to connect underlying data models to business rules. In rBPMN, we use R2ML Vocabulary as an underlying data model, so that any BPMN message can be represented with an R2ML concepts. The *StructureDefinition* element is used to specify a *Message* structure.

As the standard BPMN cannot capture several choreography aspects, as recognized in [3]. In order to fully support these patterns we need to integrate several aspects into rBPMN. Those aspects are as follows: Multiplicity of Participants, References and Correlation information.

4 Service Interaction Patterns: A Contingent Requests Example

There are two approaches to modeling of choreographies: interaction models and interconnected interface behavior models (interconnection models) [2]. Interaction models are built up of basic interaction, while interconnected interface behavior models define control flows of each participant a choreography. As rBPMN can be used

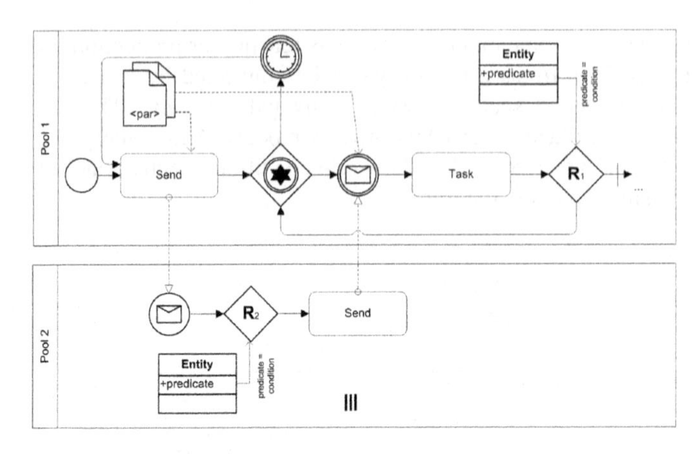

Fig. 2. The "Contingent requests" pattern

for both modeling approaches, we here show an example of Contingent requests pattern [9] expressed in rBPMN only as interaction model, because lack of space.

In the contingent requests pattern, a participant sends a request to another participant. If this second participant does not respond within a given period of time, the request is sent to another (third) participant. Again, if no response comes back, a fourth participant is contacted, and so on. For the decision about delayed responses, we propose using rule gateways with attached reaction rules. If a late (time-outdated) response from some earlier participant came during the processing of the contingent request (by a Pool 2 participant in Fig. 2), a reaction rules attached to the rule gateway R_1 decides if such a response should be accepted or not.

In this pattern, the "Send" task in Pool 1 selects participants to which a request will be sent. The participants are selected from the attached participant set (<par>). The message is received by Pool 2, which uses its own logic represented with the rule gateway R_2 to decide whether to respond or not. Pool 1 waits for some amount of time for a message from Pool 2 and when such a message arrives in, Pool 1 invokes its "Task", which is followed by a rule gateway R_1 to determine if this process will end or it will return to the event-based gateway to wait for new messages. If the message from Pool 2 is not received in a given amount of time, the intermediate timer event occurs and the sequence flow is returned to the start (the "Send" task).

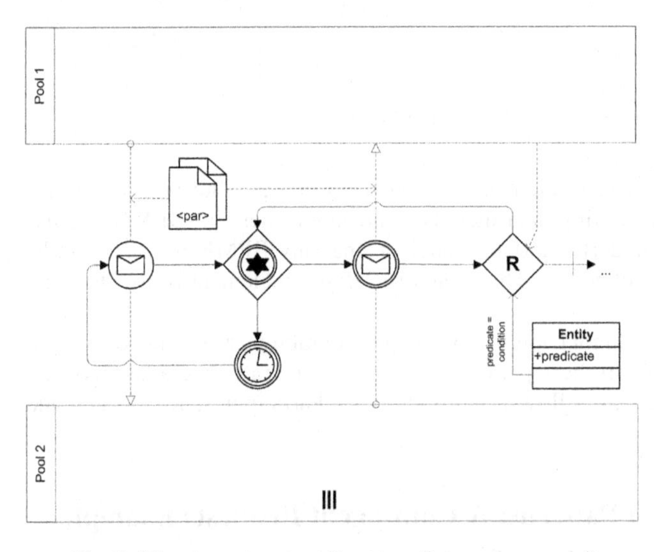

Fig. 3. "Contingent requests" pattern (interaction model)

The contingent requests pattern as an interaction model in rBPMN is shown in Fig. 3. In this model, we have a message that is sent on the start of the process from Pool 1 to one of the participants of the Pool 2 type, by using a reference to that participant from the participant set (<par>). Then, response messages are expected from Pool 2 in a given amount of time. When the message arrives from Pool 2, the rule gateway is used to determine whether the process will end or it will be back to wait for another message.

Another important implication of our model is that for each reaction rule in R2ML, we can also generate its implementation in a concrete rule-based language. In our experiments, we provide full definition several languages (e.g., Drools or Jess) by simulating semantics of reaction rules on production rule engines. We call such rules "how-to-use" rules, as they specify conditions under which a service can be used.

5 Conclusion and Future Work

To the best of our knowledge, the presented work is the first modeling language that integrates business rules with a process-oriented language for modeling service choreographies. Our evaluation demonstrated that the proposed rule and choreography modeling support resulted in the improvement of modeling of service-interaction patterns comparing to other relevant languages. Another important contribution of our work is that the metamodel-based systematic integration of rules in choreography model is also advances the state of the art in the integration of rules into business process modeling. Given that our rule language of choice (R2ML) can define business rules and message types over business vocabularies, our models have two key benefits: process models and business vocabularies are integrated (i.e., type safety is improved); and we can make use of the transformations of R2ML into executable rule engines.

References

1. Eijndhoven, T., Iacob, M.E., Ponisio, M.L.: Achieving Business Process Flexibility with Business Rules. In: Proceedings of the 12th international IEEE EDOC Conf., pp. 95–104 (2008)
2. Decker, G., Puhlmann, F.: Extending BPMN for Modeling Complex Choreographies. In: Proceedings of the OTM Confederated International Conferences, pp. 24–40 (2007)
3. OMG, BPMN 1.0: OMG final adopted specification (2006), `http://www.omg.org/cgi-bin/doc?dtc/2006-02-01`
4. OMG, Business Process Model and Notation (BPMN) Specification 2.0, initial submission, `http://www.omg.org/cgi-bin/doc?bmi/08-02-06`
5. REWERSE Rule Markup Language, `http://oxygen.informatik.tu-cottbus.de/rewerse-i1/?q=node/6`
6. UML-based Rule Modeling Language, `http://oxygen.informatik.tu-cottbus.de/rewerse-i1/?q=node/7`
7. Wagner, G., Giurca, A., Lukichev, S.: A Usable Interchange Format for Rich Syntax Rules Integrating OCL, RuleML and SWRL. In: Proceedings of Reasoning on the Web, Edinburgh, Scotland (2006)
8. Weske, M.: Business Process Management. Springer, Heidelberg (2007)
9. Barros, A., Dumas, M., ter Hofstede, A.: Service Interaction Patterns: Towards a Reference Framework for Service-based Business Process Interconnection, TR FIT-TR-2005-02, QUT, Australia (2005)

Change-Driven Model Transformations*

Derivation and Processing of Change Histories

István Ráth[1], Gergely Varró[2], and Dániel Varró[1]

[1] Budapest University of Technology and Economics,
Department of Measurement and Information Systems
{rath,varro}@mit.bme.hu

[2] Department of Computer Science and Information Theory,
H-1117 Magyar tudósok krt. 2, Budapest, Hungary
gervarro@cs.bme.hu

Abstract. Nowadays, evolving models are prime artefacts of model-driven software engineering. In tool integration scenarios, a multitude of tools and modeling languages are used where complex model transformations need to incrementally synchronize various models residing within different external tools. In the paper, we investigate a novel class of transformations, that are directly triggered by model changes. First, model changes in the source model are recorded incrementally by a *change history model*. Then a model-to-model transformation is carried out to generate a change model for the target language. Finally, the target change history model is processed (at any time) to incrementally update the target model itself. Moreover, our technique also allows incremental updates in an external model where only the model manipulation interface is under our control (but not the model itself). Our approach is implemented within the VIATRA2 framework, and it builds on live transformations and incremental pattern matching.

Keywords: Incremental model transformation, change models, change-driven transformations.

1 Introduction

Model transformations play a key role in model-driven software engineering by providing embedded design intelligence for automated code generation, model refactoring, model analysis or reverse engineering purposes.

Most traditional model transformation frameworks support *batch transformations* where the execution of a transformation is initiated (on-demand) by a systems designer. As an alternate solution (proposed recently in [1, 2]), *live transformations* (or active transformations) run in the background as daemons, and continuously react to changes in the underlying models. In this respect, a transformation can be executed automatically as soon as a transaction on the model has completed. Up to now, the design and execution of batch transformations and live transformations were completely separated, i.e. the same transformation problem had to be formulated completely differently.

* This work was partially supported by EU projects SENSORIA (IST-3-016004) and SecureChange (ICT-FET-231101).

A. Schürr and B. Selic (Eds.): MODELS 2009, LNCS 5795, pp. 342–356, 2009.

In the paper, we bridge this conceptual gap by introducing change-driven model transformations. More specifically, we first define the concept of a *change history model* to serves as a history-aware log of elementary model changes, which record causal dependency / timeliness between such changes. We show how change history models can be derived incrementally by live transformations during model editing. Then we describe how change history models can be used to incrementally update a model asynchronously (at any desired time) by propagating changes using batch transformations.

The use of change history models in model-to-model transformation scenarios has far-reaching consequences as incremental model transformations can be constructed with minimal knowledge about the current structure of the target model. For instance, transformations can still be implemented when only identifiers and a model manipulation interface are known, but the rest of the actual target model is non-materialized (i.e. does not exist as an in-memory model within the transformation framework). As a result, our concepts can be easily applied in the context of runtime models as well as incremental model-to-code transformation problems (where the latter will actually serve as the running example of the paper).

The rest of the paper is structured as follows. In Section 2, a motivating case study is introduced as a running example for our paper. The main concepts of change-driven transformations and change history models are introduced in Section 3. Section 4 details the main steps of the approach on the running example. Finally, Section 5 summarizes related work and Section 6 concludes our paper.

2 Motivating Scenario

Our motivating scenario is based on an actual tool integration environment developed for the SENSORIA and MOGENTES EU research projects. Here high-level workflow models (with control and data flow links, artefact management and role-based access control) are used to define complex development processes which are executed automatically by the JBoss jBPM workflow engine, in a distributed environment consisting of Eclipse client workstations and Rational Jazz tool servers. The process workflows are designed in a domain-specific language, which is automatically mapped to an annotated version of the jPDL execution language of the workflow engine. jPDL is an XML-based language, which is converted to an XML-DOM representation once the process has been deployed to the workflow engine.

A major design goal was to allow the process designer to edit the process model and make changes without the need for re-deployment. To achieve this, we implemented an *asynchronous incremental code synchronizing model transformation*. This means that (i) while the user is editing the source process model, the changes made are recorded. Then (ii) these changes can be mapped incrementally to the target jPDL XML model without re-generating it from scratch. Additionally, (iii) the changes can be applied directly on the deployed XML-DOM representation through jBPM's process manipulation DOM programming interface, but, (iv) in order to allow the changes to be applied to the remote workflow server, the actual XML-DOM manipulation is executed on a remote host asynchronously to the operations of the process designer.

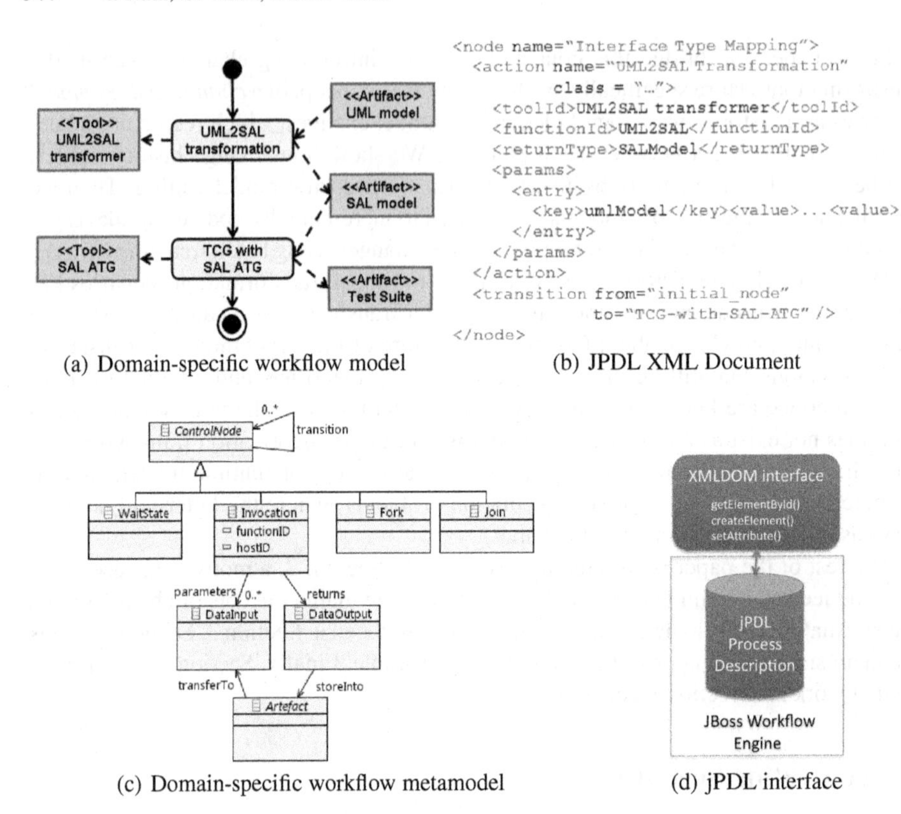

(a) Domain-specific workflow model (b) JPDL XML Document

(c) Domain-specific workflow metamodel (d) jPDL interface

Fig. 1. Model representations in the motivating scenario

Example. A simple tool integration workflow model is given in Fig. 1(a) together with its jPDL XML representation (in Fig. 1(b)). Moreover, a metamodel of the source language is given in Fig. 1(c). In case of the target language, an interface is provided to manipulate XML documents (see Fig. 1(d)).

Metamodeling background. Since the actual tool integration framework is built upon the model repository and transformation support of the VIATRA2 framework [3], we also use it for the current paper for demonstration purposes. However, all metamodels will be presented as a traditional EMF metamodel to stress that all the main concepts presented could be transferred to other modeling environments as well.

VIATRA2 uses the VPM [4] metamodeling approach for its model repository, which uses two basic elements: entities and relations. An *entity* represents a basic concept of a (modeling) domain, while a *relation* represents the relationships between other model elements. Furthermore, entities may also have an associated value which is a string that contains application-specific data.

Model elements are arranged into a strict containment hierarchy, which constitutes the VPM model space. Within a container entity, each model element has a unique local name, but each model element also has a globally unique identifier which is called a fully qualified name (FQNs are constructed by hierarchical composition of local names, e.g. "workflow.model.node0").

There are two special relationships between model elements: the *supertypeOf* (inheritance, generalization) relation represents binary superclass-subclass relationships (like the UML generalization concept), while the *instanceOf* relation represents type-instance relationships (between meta-levels). By using an explicit *instanceOf* relationship, metamodels and models can be stored in the same model space in a compact way.

3 Change History Models in Incremental Model Synchronization

In the current paper, we investigate a model synchronization scenario where the goal is to *asynchronously* propagate changes in the source model M_A to the target model M_B. This means, that changes in the source model are not mapped on-the-fly to the target model, but the synchronization may take place at any time. However, it is important to stress that the synchronization is still *incremental*, i.e. the target model is not re-generated from scratch, but updated according to the changes in the source model.

Moreover, our target scenario also requires that M_B is not materialized in the model transformation framework, but accessed and manipulated directly through an external interface IF of its native environment. This is a significant difference to traditional model transformation environments, where the system relies on model import and export facilities to connect to modeling and model processing tools in the toolchain.

To create asynchronous incremental transformations, we extend traditional transformations (which take models as inputs and produce models as output) by *change-driven transformations* which take model manipulation operations as inputs and/or produce model manipulation operations as output. By this approach, our mappings may be executed without the need of materializing source and target models directly in the transformation system, and may also be executed asynchronously in time.

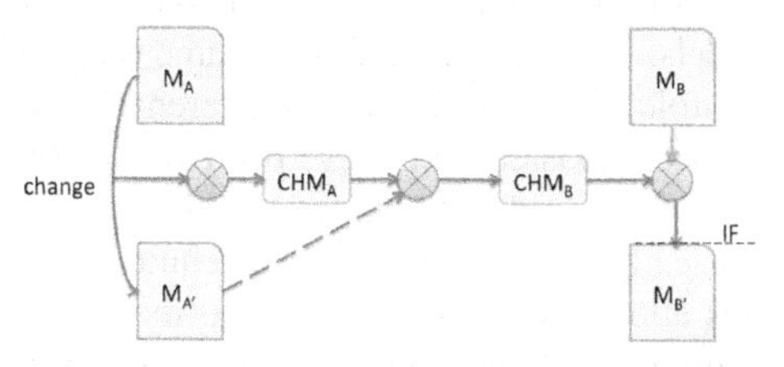

Fig. 2. Model synchronization driven by CHMs

As we still rely on model transformation technology, operations on models need to be represented in the model space by special trace models which encode the changes of models as model manipulation sequences. We call these models *change history models* (CHMs in short). These models are generated automatically on-the-fly as the source model changes (see CHM_A in the left part of Fig. 2) using *live transformations* [2]. Live transformations are triggered by event-driven condition-action rules whenever a change is performed in the model space, and create an appropriate change history model fragment (connected to those parts of the model which were affected by the change).

The actual model transformation between the two languages is then carried out by generating a change history model CHM_B for the target language as a separate transformation (see middle part of Fig. 2, and also note that traceability information between CHM_A and CHM_B can recorded as inter-model links).

As change history models represent a trace of model evolution, they may be automatically applied to models (see right part of Fig. 2). More precisely, we combine a snapshot of the model M_B (representing the initial state) and a change history model CHM_B (representing a sequence of operations applicable starting from the initial state) to create the final snapshot M'_B. In other words, the change history model CHM_B represents an "operational difference" between M'_B and M_B, with the order of operations preserved as they were actually performed on M_B.

3.1 Change History Models

Change history models are conceptually derived from the model manipulation operations defined on the host language. These operations may be generic (i.e. corresponding to graph-level concepts such as "create node", "create edge", "change attribute value"), or domain-specific (corresponding to complex operations such as "remove subprocess", "split activity sequence"). In this paper, we discuss the generic solution in detail, however, we also show how our approach can be extended to domain-specific languages.

Change history metamodel. The generic change history metamodel for VPM host models is shown in Fig. 3. CHM fragments are derived from the abstract *Operation* class, which can be optionally tagged with a Timestamp attribute for time-based tracing of, e.g. user editing actions. Operations are connected to each other by relations of type *next*, which enables the representation of operation sequences (transactions).

It is important to stress that CHMs do not directly reference their corresponding host models, but use fully qualified name (or unique ID) references. The reason for this is two-fold: (i) by using indirect references, CHMs may point to model elements that are no longer existent (e.g. have been deleted by a consecutive operation), and (ii) CHMs are not required to be materialized in the same model space as the host model (symmetrically, host models are not required to be materialized when processing CHMs). This allows decoupling the actual models from the transformation engine which is a requirement for non-invasive scenarios where target models are indirectly manipulated through an interface.

By our approach, change history metamodel elements are either *EntityOperation*s or *RelationOperation*s. Entity operations use the *parentFQN* reference to define the containment hierarchy context in which the target entity is located *before* the operation represented by the CHM fragment was executed. Analogously, relation operations use *srcFQN* and *trgFQN* to define source and target endpoints of the target relation element (prior to execution). Note that we omitted inheritance edges from *EntityOperation* and *RelationOperation* in Fig. 3 for the sake of clarity.

All CHM elements correspond to elementary operations in the VPM model space, in the following categories:

- *creation* (shown on the far left): *CreateEntity* and *CreateRelation* represent operations when an entity or relation has been created (an entity in a given container, a relation between a source and target model element). Both CHM fragments carry information on the *type* (*typeFQN*) of the target element.
- *deletions* (shown on the near left): *DeleteEntity* and *DeleteRelation* correspond to deletions of entities and relations.

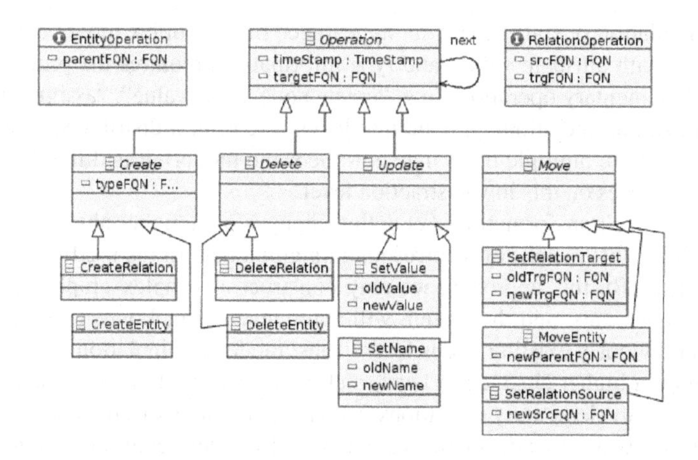

Fig. 3. Generic change history metamodel

- *updates* (shown on the near right): *SetValue* indicates an operation where the *value* field of an entity is overwritten; similarly, *SetName* represents an update in the local name of the target (in this case, as always, *targetFQN* points to the original FQN of the target model element, so this CHM fragment needs to be used carefully).
- *moves* (shown on the far right): *MoveEntity* corresponds to the reparenting of an entity in the VPM containment hierarchy. *SetRelationTarget* and *SetRelationSource* represent retargeting and resourcing operations.

4 Change-Driven Transformations

In this section, we demonstrate the concept and application of change-driven transformations (see Fig. 2) using change history models by the elaboration of the motivating scenario described in Section 2. First, we demonstrate (in Section 4.1) how CHMs can be derived automatically by recording model manipulations using live transformations. We introduce both generic (metamodel-independent) and domain-specific (metamodel-dependent) techniques to achieve this. Then we discuss (in Section 4.2) how model transformations can be designed between two CHMs of different languages. Finally, we describe (in Section 4.3) how CHMs can be asynchronously processed to incrementally update a model resided in a model repository or within a third-party tool accessed via an external interface.

4.1 Automatic Generation of CHMs by Live Transformations

First, we demonstrate the automatic generation of change history models for recording modification operations carried out on the host model. Model changes may be observed using various approaches, e.g. by model notification mechanisms such as the EMF notification API, where the model persistence framework provides callback functions for elementary model changes. This approach is limited to recording only basic model manipulation operations, i.e. an appearance of a complex model element (e.g. a graph node with attribute values and type information) requires the processing of a *sequence* of elementary operations (e.g. "create node", "set value", "assign type", etc). If the modification operations may be interleaving (e.g. in a distributed transactional environment, where multiple users may edit the same model), it is difficult to process operation sequences on this low abstraction level.

In contrast, live transformations [2] define changes on a higher abstraction level as a new match (or lost match) of a corresponding graph pattern (as used in graph transformations [5]). By this approach, we may construct a complex graph pattern from elementary constraints, and the system will automatically track when a new match is found (or a previously existing one is lost) – thus, model manipulation operations may be detected on a higher abstraction level, making it possible to assign change history models not only to elementary operations, but also to domain-specific ones.

More precisely, live transformations are defined by event-condition-action triples:

- an *event* is defined with respect to a graph pattern, and may correspond to an appearance of a newly found match, or a disappearance of a previously existing one.
- *conditions* are evaluated on the transaction of elementary operations which resulted in the triggering of the event. They correspond to elementary operations affecting elements of the subgraph identified by the event's (newly found or deleted) match.
- *actions* are model manipulation operations to be carried out on the model.

Basic patterns. Fig. 4 shows three basic graph patterns and their VIATRA2 transformation language representations. Pattern `entity_in_parent` encompasses a containment substructure where an entity E is matched in a given parent entity *Parent*. A new match for this pattern occurs when any entity is created in the host model (when a new match is detected, concrete references as substitutions for pattern variables $E, Parent$ are passed to the transformation engine). Similarly, pattern `relation_source_target` corresponds to a relation R with its source S and target T elements, while pattern `modelelement_type` references any model element with its type. These patterns correspond to basic notions of the VPM (typed graph nodes and edges), and may be combined to create precondition patterns for event-driven transformation rules.

Generic derivation rules. On the left, Fig. 5 shows a sample CHM generation rule for tracking the creation of model elements. A triggered graph transformation rule is defined for a composite disjunctive pattern, which combines cases of new appearances of entities and relations into a single event. Condition clauses (`when(create(E))`, `when(create(R))`) are used to distinguish between the cases where an entity or a relation was created. Finally, action sequences (encompassed into `seq{}` rules after the when-clauses) are used to instruct the VIATRA2 engine to instantiate the change history metamodel, create a *CreateEntity* or *CreateRelation* model element and set their references to the newly created host model entity/relation.

The right side of Fig. 5 shows an example execution sequence of this rule. The sequence starts with a model consisting only of a top-level container node *w*0 of type *Workflow*. In Step 2, the user creates a new *Invocation* node *i*0 inside *w*0. Note that on the VPM level, the creation of *i*0 actually consists of three operations: (1) create entity, (2) set entity type to *Invocation*, (3) move entity to its container. However, the

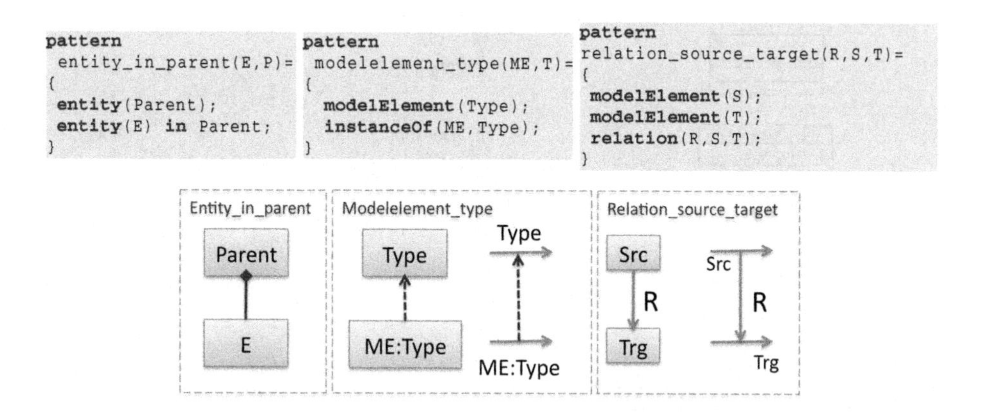

```
pattern
 entity_in_parent(E,P)=
{
 entity(Parent);
 entity(E) in Parent;
}
```

```
pattern
 modelelement_type(ME,T)=
{
 modelElement(Type);
 instanceOf(ME,Type);
}
```

```
pattern
relation_source_target(R,S,T)=
{
 modelElement(S);
 modelElement(T);
 relation(R,S,T);
}
```


Fig. 4. Patterns for identifying relevant model manipulation events

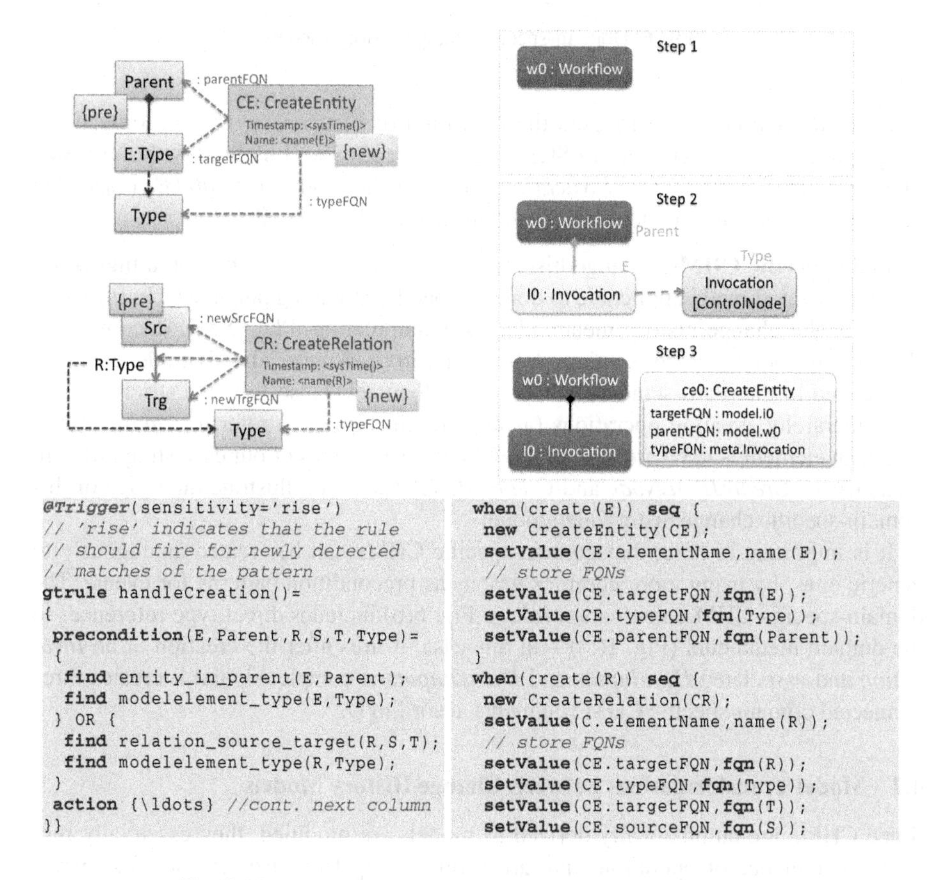


```
@Trigger(sensitivity='rise')
// 'rise' indicates that the rule
// should fire for newly detected
// matches of the pattern
gtrule handleCreation()=
{
 precondition(E,Parent,R,S,T,Type)=
 {
  find entity_in_parent(E,Parent);
  find modelelement_type(E,Type);
 } OR {
  find relation_source_target(R,S,T);
  find modelelement_type(R,Type);
 }
 action {\ldots} //cont. next column
}}
```

```
when(create(E)) seq {
 new CreateEntity(CE);
 setValue(CE.elementName,name(E));
 // store FQNs
 setValue(CE.targetFQN,fqn(E));
 setValue(CE.typeFQN,fqn(Type));
 setValue(CE.parentFQN,fqn(Parent));
}
when(create(R)) seq {
 new CreateRelation(CR);
 setValue(C.elementName,name(R));
 // store FQNs
 setValue(CE.targetFQN,fqn(R));
 setValue(CE.typeFQN,fqn(Type));
 setValue(CE.targetFQN,fqn(T));
 setValue(CE.sourceFQN,fqn(S));
```

Fig. 5. Live transformation rule for automatic CHM generation

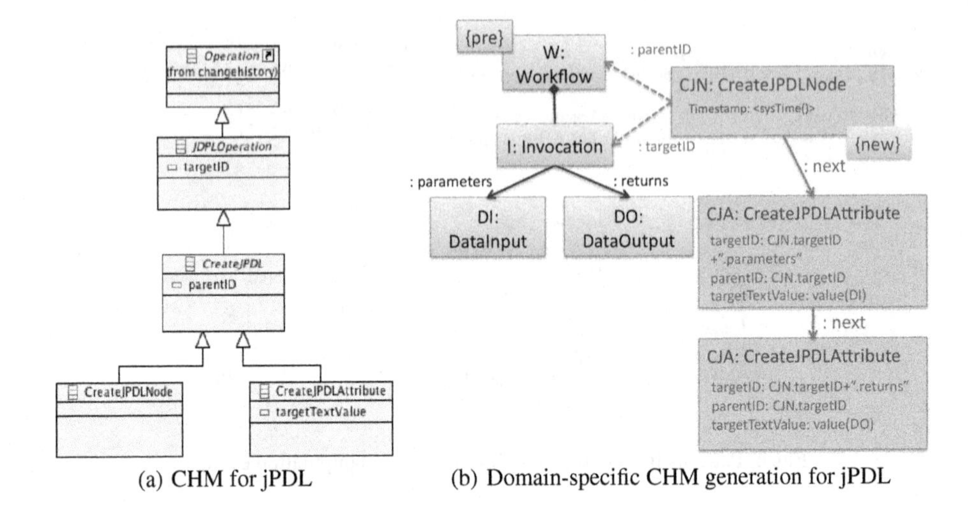

(a) CHM for jPDL (b) Domain-specific CHM generation for jPDL

Fig. 6. Domain-specific change history models

live transformation engine triggers the execution of `handleCreation()` only if the subgraph $w0 - i0$ is complete. In Step 3, `handleCreation()` is fired with the match $\{Parent = w0, E = i0, Type = Invocation\}$, and – as the condition $create(E)$ is satisfied in this case – the appropriate *CreateEntity* instance *ce*0 is created.

Domain-specific CHMs. Change history models can also be defined on a higher abstraction level, directly applicable to domain-specific modeling languages. In Fig. 6(a), a part of the change history metamodel for manipulating jPDL XML documents is shown. This metamodel uses unique *ID*s to refer to (non-materialized) model elements (as defined in the jPDL standard); since jPDL documents also follow a strict containment hierarchy, creation operations (as depicted in Fig. 6(a)) refer to a *parentID* in which an element is to be created. In the follow-up examples of our case study, we will make use of *CreateJPDLNode* and *CreateJPDLAttribute* to illustrate the usage of this domain-specific change history metamodel.

It is important to note, that domain-specific CHMs can be created analogously to generic ones, by using more complex graphs as precondition patterns for events. The domain-specific CHM construction rule in Fig. 6(b) includes direct type references to the domain metamodel (Fig. 1(c)) – in this case, it fires after the creation of an *Invocation* and associated *DataInput*s and *DataOutput*s is completed, and it creates three connected domain-specific CHM fragments accordingly.

4.2 Model Transformations between Change History Models

Since CHMs are automatically derived as models are modified, they essentially represent a sequence of operations that are valid starting from a given model snapshot (Fig. 2). As such, they may be used to drive mapping transformations between two modeling languages: such a change-driven transformation takes CHMs of the source model and maps them to CHMs of the target model.

This is a crucially different approach with respect to traditional model transformations in the sense that the mapping takes place between *model manipulation operations* rather than models, which makes non-invasive transformations possible (where the models are not required to be materialized in the transformation system).

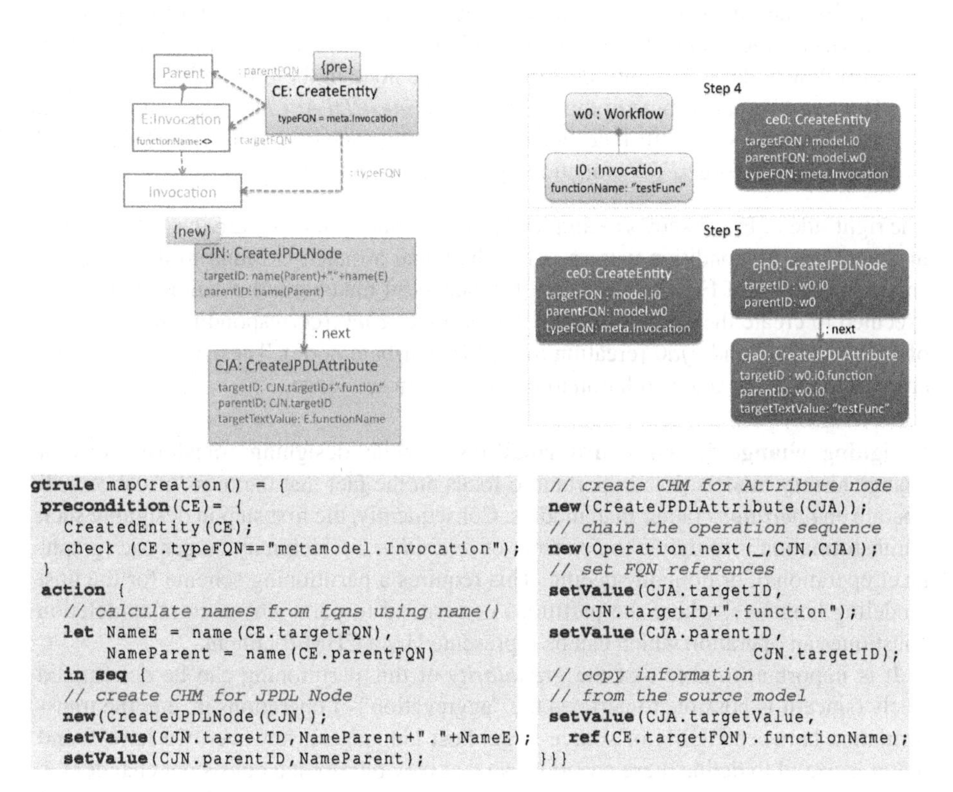

Fig. 7. Transformation of change history models

Fig. 7 shows an example transformation rule where the creation of an *Invocation* in the domain-specific workflow language is mapped to the creation of a corresponding jPDL Node and its attribute. In this case, a batch graph transformation rule is used, however, this transformation may also be formulated as a live transformation. The rule looks for a *CreateEntity* element referencing a node of type *Invocation*, and maps it to the domain-specific CHMs of the jPDL language. As *Invocations* are represented by jPDL Nodes with an attribute node, the target CHM will consist of two "create"-type elements, chained together by the *Operation.next* relation.

The core idea of creating CHM transformations is the appropriate manipulation of reference values pointing to their respective host models (as CHMs only carry information on the type of the operation, the contextual information is stored in their references). In this example, we make use of the fact that both source and target models have a strict containment hierarchy (all elements have *parent*s), which is used to map corresponding elements to each other:

- Based on *parentFQN* in the source model, we calculate the target parent's ID *parentID* as *name(CE.parentFQN)*.
- Similarly, the target jPDL node's ID *targetID* is calculated as the concatenation of *parentID* and *name(CE.targetFQN)* to place the target node under the target parent.
- Finally, the attribute *functionName* designates a particular function on a remote interface which is invoked when the workflow engine is interpreting an *Invocation* workflow node. It is represented by a separate node in the jPDL XML-DOM tree. The *targetValue* attribute of the additional *CreateJPDLAttribute* element is derived from the appropriate attribute value of *Invocation* node in source model (as denoted by the *ref(CE.targetFQN)* function in the sample code).

The right side of Fig. 7 shows a sample execution result of the `mapCreate()` rule. First, in Step 4, the precondition pattern is matched, and a match is found to the subgraph created in Step 3 of Fig. 5. Following the successful matching, the action sequence is executed to create the domain-specific CHM nodes $cjn0$ (corresponding to a creation of a jPDL Node) and $cja0$ (creation of a jPDL attribute node). These CHM nodes are chained together by a *next* relation to be executed in sequence.

Designing change-driven transformations. When designing transformations of change history models, it is important to focus on the fact that the transformation will operate on *operations* rather than models. Consequently, the first step in designing such a transformation is to define the concept of *operation* – which may be generic (graph-level operations), or domain-specific. This requires a partitioning scheme for the host modeling language, where the partitions correspond to parts whose creation/deletion constitutes an operation which can be represented by a CHM fragment.

It is important to note that the *granularity* of this partitioning can be determined freely (since it is possible to perform the "aggregation" of operations in, e.g. the transformation between CHMs of source-target host languages); however, we have found that it is useful to define these partitions so that they represent a consistent change (i.e. the results of valid modification steps between two consistent states of the host model).

4.3 Processing Change History Models

On the macro level, change history models are represented as chains of parametrized elementary model manipulation operations. As such, they can be processed linearly, progressing along the chain until the final element is reached (thus modeling the execution of a transaction). The consumption of a CHM element is an interpretative step with the following actions performed in the context defined by the CHM's references:

- *creation*: the target entity/relation is created with the correct type assignment; entities are created in the container designated by the parent's fully qualified name (`parentFQN`), relations are created between source and target elements referenced by `sourceFQN` and `targetFQN`, respectively.
- *moves*: for *MoveEntity*, the target entity is moved to the container designated by `newParentFQN`; for *SetRelationSource*, the source end of the target relation is redirected according to `newSourceFQN`.

- *updates*: *SetName* and *SetValue* are mapped to updates in the name and value attributes. *SetRelationTarget* is handled similarly to *SetRelationSource*.
- *deletions*: *DeleteEntity* and *DeleteRelation* are interpreted as deletions of their targets (`targetFQN`).

Applying CHMs to non-materialized models. As Fig. 2 shows, we apply CHMs to manipulate non-materialized models through an interface. The speciality of this scenario is that instead of working on directly accessible in-memory models, the transformation engine calls interface functions which only allow basic queries (based on ids) and elementary manipulation operations. In this case, CHMs are very useful since they allow *incremental* updates, as they encode directly applicable operation sequences.

Case study technical details. For the jPDL models of the motivating scenario, we mapped the XML-DOM process model manipulation programming interface to VIATRA2's *native function* API, which enables the system to invoke arbirary Java code from the transformation program. The following native functions are used:

- *getElementById(ID)*: retrieves a jPDL element identified by its unique ID.
- *createElement(parentRef,targetID)*: creates a new jPDL DOM element as a child of its parent (identified by *parentRef*), with a given unique ID (*targetID*).
- *addElement(elementRef,DocID)*: adds the element *elementRef* to the jPDL DOM identified by *DocID*.
- *setContents(elementRef,text)*: sets the textual content of the given DOM element (*elementRef*) to *text*.

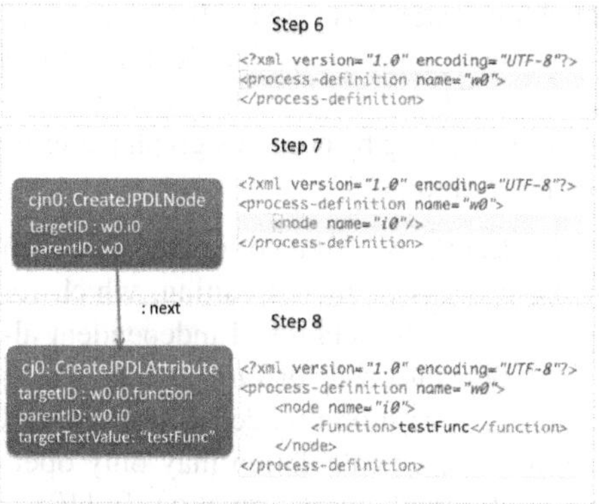

Step 6

```
<?xml version="1.0" encoding="UTF-8"?>
<process-definition name="w0">
</process-definition>
```

Step 7

```
<?xml version="1.0" encoding="UTF-8"?>
<process-definition name="w0">
    <node name="i0"/>
</process-definition>
```

Step 8

```
<?xml version="1.0" encoding="UTF-8"?>
<process-definition name="w0">
    <node name="i0">
        <function>testFunc</function>
    </node>
</process-definition>
```

cjn0: CreateJPDLNode
targetID : w0.i0
parentID: w0

: next

cj0: CreateJPDLAttribute
targetID : w0.i0.function
parentID: w0.i0
targetTextValue: "testFunc"

```
gtrule newCompoundJDPLNode(JPDL_DOM) = {
 precondition(CJN,CJA) = {
  CreateJPDLNode(CJN);
  CreateJPDLAttribute(CJA);
  Operation.next(_,CJN,CJA);
 }
 action {
   \ldots // See contents below
 }
}
```

```
// create JPDL Node -- Step 7
let TargetNode = createElement(getElementById(CJN.parentID),CJN.targetID),
    Result0 = addElement(TargetNode, JPDL_DOM) in
      println("Debug created JPDL Node:"+Result0);
// create JPDL Attribute -- Step 8
let TargetAttrNode = createElement(getElementById(CJA.parentID),CJA.targetID),
    Result1 = setContent(TargetAttrNode,ref(CJN.targetFQN).functionName),
    Result2 = addElement(TargetAttrNode,JPDL_DOM) in
      println("Debug created JPDL Attribute:"+Result2);
```

Fig. 8. Applying CHMs through the jPDL XML-DOM API

Example transformation rule. In this final case study example, we define an application rule based on domain-specific CHMs for the jPDL XML-DOM model (Fig. 6(a)). Fig. 8 shows the `newCompoundJPDLNode()` rule, which is used to interpret a subsequence of CHM chains for the jPDL domain. More precisely, this rule's precondition matches the pair of *CreateJPDLNode* and *CreateJPDLAttribute* CHM fragments which correspond to the addition of a new "compound" jPDL node (with a specified function invocation attribute). The rule uses native functions `createElement`, `addElement` to instantiate new jPDL XML elements directly in the deployed process model on the workflow server; `setContent` is used to overwrite the attribute node's textual content.

The left side of Fig. 8 shows the final three steps of our running example. In Step 6, the initial state of the deployed workflow model, the process definition corresponding to *Workflow* *w*0 is still empty. During the rule's execution, first, the jPDL Node *i*0 is created (Step 7), and then in Step 8, the attribute node is added with the appropriate textual content. (Debug calls are used to write debugging output to the VIATRA2 console.)

The entire algorithm which applies CHMs follows the linear sequence of operations along the relations with type *Operation.next*; the first operation in a transaction can be determined by looking for a CHM fragment without an incoming *Operation.next* edge.

5 Related Work

Now an overview is given on various approaches showing similarity to our proposal.

Event-driven techniques. Event-driven techniques, which are the technological basis of live model transformations, have been used in many fields. In relational database management systems (RDBMS), even the concept of triggers [6] can be considered as simple operations whose execution is initiated by events. Later, event-condition-action (ECA) rules [7] were introduced for active database systems as a generalization of triggers, and the same idea was adopted in rule engines [8] as well. The specification of live model transformations is conceptually similar to ECA rules (see Section 4.1). However, ECA-based approaches lack the support for triggering by complex graph patterns, which is an essential scenario in model-driven development.

Calculation of model differences. Calculating differences (deltas) of models has been widely studied due to its important role in the process of model editing, which requires undo and redo operations to be supported. In [9], metamodel independent algorithms are proposed for calculating directed (backward and forward) deltas, which can later be merged with initial model to produce the resulting model. Unfortunately, the algorithms proposed by [9] for difference and merge calculation may only operate on a single model, and they are not specified by model transformation. In [10], a metamodel independent approach is presented for visualizing backward and forward directed deltas between consecutive versions of models. Differences (i.e., change history models) have a model-based representation (similarly to [11]), and calculations are driven by (higher order) transformations in both [10] and our approach. However, in contrast to [10] to [11], our current proposal operates in an exogeneous transformation context to propagate change descriptions from source to target models.

Incremental synchronization for exogeneous model transformations. Incremental synchronization approaches already exist in model-to-model transformation context (e.g. [12]). One representative direction is to use triple graph grammars [13] for maintaining the consistency of source and target models in a rule-based manner. The proposal of [14] relies on various heuristics of the correspondence structure. Dependencies between correspondence nodes are stored explicitly, which drives the incremental engine to undo an applied transformation rule in case of inconsistencies. Other triple graph grammar approaches for model synchronization (e.g. [15]) do not address incrementality. Triple graph grammar techniques are also used in [16] for tool integration based on UML models. The aim of the approach is to provide support for change synchronization between various languages in several development phases. Based on an integration algorithm, the system merges changed models on user request. Although it is not a live transformation approach, it could benefit from being implemented as such. The approach of [17] shows the largest similarity to our proposal as both (i) focus on change propagation in the context of model-to-model transformation, (ii) describe changes in a model-based and metamodel independent way, and (iii) use rule-driven algorithms for propagating changes of source models to the target side. In the proposal of [17] target model must be materialized and they can also be manually modified, which results in a complex merge operation to be performed to get the derived model. In contrast, our algorithms can be used on non-materialized target models, and the derived models are computed automatically on the target side.

6 Conclusion and Future Work

In the paper, we discussed how model synchronization can be carried out using change-driven model transformations, which rely upon the history of model changes. We presented an approach to automatically (and generically) derive change history models by recording changes in a (source) model using live transformations. Then a change history model of the target language is derived by a second (problem-specific) model transformation. Finally, the target change history model can automatically drive the incremental update of the target model itself even in such a case when only an external model manipulation interface is available for the target model. Our approach was exemplified using an incremental code generation case study.

As future work, we plan to investigate how to derive aggregated and history independent change delta models (like in [10]) automatically as union of change history models. Additionally, we also plan to work on elaborating the design methodologies of change-driven transformations, and intend to investigate the correctness and consistency checking of change-driven transformations (with respect to a batch transformation reference). Furthermore, we aim at using change history models for model merging.

References

1. Hearnden, D., Lawley, M., Raymond, K.: Incremental model transformation for the evolution of model-driven systems. In: Nierstrasz, O., Whittle, J., Harel, D., Reggio, G. (eds.) MoDELS 2006. LNCS, vol. 4199, pp. 321–335. Springer, Heidelberg (2006)
2. Ráth, I., Bergmann, G., Ökrös, A., Varró, D.: Live model transformations driven by incremental pattern matching. In: Vallecillo, A., Gray, J., Pierantonio, A. (eds.) ICMT 2008. LNCS, vol. 5063, pp. 107–121. Springer, Heidelberg (2008)

3. Varró, D., Balogh, A.: The Model Transformation Language of the VIATRA2 Framework. Science of Computer Programming 68(3), 214–234 (2007)
4. Varró, D., Pataricza, A.: VPM: A visual, precise and multilevel metamodeling framework for describing mathematical domains and UML. Software and Systems Modeling 2(3), 187–210
5. Ehrig, H., Montanari, U., Kreowski, H.J., Rozenberg, G. (eds.): Handbook on Graph Grammars and Computing by Graph Transformation. Concurrency and Distribution, vol. 3. World Scientific, Singapore (1999)
6. Garcia-Molina, H., Ullman, J.D., Widom, J.: Database Systems: The Complete Book. Prentice Hall, Englewood Cliffs (2001)
7. Dittrich, K.R., Gatziu, S., Geppert, A.: The active database management system manifesto: A rulebase of ADBMS features. In: Sellis, T.K. (ed.) RIDS 1995. LNCS, vol. 985, pp. 1–17. Springer, Heidelberg (1995)
8. Seiriö, M., Berndtsson, M.: Design and implementation of an ECA rule markup language. In: Adi, A., Stoutenburg, S., Tabet, S. (eds.) RuleML 2005. LNCS, vol. 3791, pp. 98–112. Springer, Heidelberg (2005)
9. Alanen, M., Porres, I.: Difference and union of models. In: Stevens, P., Whittle, J., Booch, G. (eds.) UML 2003. LNCS, vol. 2863, pp. 2–17. Springer, Heidelberg (2003)
10. Cicchetti, A., Di Ruscio, D., Pierantonio, A.: A metamodel independent approach to difference representation. Journal of Object Technology 6(9), 165–185 (2007)
11. Gruschko, B., Kolovos, D.S., Paige, R.F.: Towards synchronizing models with evolving metamodels. In: Proc. Int. Workshop on Model-Driven Software Evolution held with the ECSMR (2007)
12. Xiong, Y., Liu, D., Hu, Z., Zhao, H., Takeichi, M., Mei, H.: Towards automatic model synchronization from model transformations. In: ASE 2007: Proceedings of the twenty-second IEEE/ACM international conference on Automated software engineering, pp. 164–173 (2007)
13. Schürr, A.: Specification of graph translators with triple graph grammars. Technical report, RWTH Aachen, Fachgruppe Informatik, Germany (1994)
14. Giese, H., Wagner, R.: Incremental model synchronization with triple graph grammars. In: Nierstrasz, O., Whittle, J., Harel, D., Reggio, G. (eds.) MoDELS 2006. LNCS, vol. 4199, pp. 543–557. Springer, Heidelberg (2006)
15. Klar, F., Königs, A., Schürr, A.: Model transformation in the large. In: ESEC-FSE 2007: Proceedings of European Software Engineering Conference, pp. 285–294. ACM, New York (2007)
16. Becker, S.M., Haase, T., Westfechtel, B.: Model-based a-posteriori integration of engineering tools for incremental development processes. Software and Systems Modeling 4(2), 123–140 (2005)
17. Jimenez, A.M.: Change propagation in the MDA: A model merging approach. Master's thesis, The University of Queensland (June 2005)

An Incremental Algorithm for High-Performance Runtime Model Consistency*

Christopher Wolfe[1], T.C. Nicholas Graham[1], and W. Greg Phillips[2]

[1] School of Computing, Queen's University, Kingston, Ontario, Canada
{wolfe,graham}@cs.queensu.ca
[2] Department of Electrical and Computer Engineering,
Royal Military College of Canada, Kingston, Ontario, Canada
greg.phillips@rmc.ca

Abstract. We present a novel technique for applying two-level runtime models to distributed systems. Our approach uses graph rewriting rules to transform a high-level source model into one of many possible target models. When either model is changed at runtime, the transformation is incrementally updated. We describe the theory underlying our approach, and show restrictions sufficient for a simple and efficient implementation.

We demonstrate this implementation in *Fiia.Net*, our model-based toolkit for developing adaptive groupware. Developers using *Fiia.Net* control components and connections through a high-level conceptual runtime model. Meanwhile, the toolkit transparently maintains the underlying distributed system, and propagates failures back into the conceptual model. This approach provides high stability, and performance that is sufficiently fast for interactive applications.

Keywords: Adaptive groupware, runtime models, incremental model transformation.

1 Introduction

Recent years have seen a proliferation of computing devices, ranging from smart telephones and PDAs, to netbooks and tablet PCs. When connected over a network, these devices enable new styles of communication and collaboration in mobile settings. Applications include meetings at a distance [1], tele-health [2] and online games [3]. Such applications, which we term adaptive groupware, are fundamentally distributed systems which undergo significant runtime adaptation: as users move between tasks, roles, devices and locations; and as network conditions and connections change. Adaptive groupware systems are difficult to build, because they must provide intuitive user interfaces while maintaining high performance in the face of varying user demands and partial failure.

Model-based techniques have great potential for aiding the development of adaptive groupware. High-level conceptual models [4,5,6,7] can describe the

* We gratefully acknowledge the funding of the Natural Science and Engineering Research Council of Canada and the NECTAR CSCW research network.

A. Schürr and B. Selic (Eds.): MODELS 2009, LNCS 5795, pp. 357–371, 2009.

system's structure, abstracting low-level issues like data sharing and caching policies, concurrency control algorithms, and network protocols. Distribution models can help reason about architecture trade-offs [8] or configure an implementation [9].

To address the challenges of adaptive groupware, we have developed a model-based system which supports runtime adaptation in both conceptual and distribution models:

- The runtime system automatically refines the conceptual model into a distribution model. This mechanism allows many possible implementations of each conceptual model.
- Developers specify high-level changes as runtime adaptations to the conceptual model (e.g., a user changes device, or new data is shared between users). The runtime system propagates these adaptations through refinement to the distribution model.
- The underlying distributed system is reconfigured following the distribution model, and reports failures as distribution adaptations (e.g., a smartphone's battery dies, or a network becomes unavailable). Following failure, the runtime system restores the models to a consistent state, allowing the application to detect and manage failures via the conceptual model.

This approach requires us to maintain consistency between the two models at runtime. Existing model transformation techniques, outlined in Sec. 2, do not support bidirectionality, limit the flexibility of the transformation, or are too slow for use in a running groupware system.

Underpinning our solution is a novel algorithm for maintaining bidirectional model consistency. Using this algorithm, refinement from a conceptual model to a distribution model is specified using unordered graph rewriting rules. Both models are maintained at runtime. Arbitrary changes in the conceptual model and removals from the distribution model are rapidly propagated through the transformation. The algorithm performs adaptations incrementally, and with minimal change to the models.

Our algorithm is possible because we forbid additions to the distribution model. In our application, direct changes to the distribution level result from partial failure, so are always expressed as removals. This restriction avoids the need to reverse-engineer newly-added distribution model elements, so permits extremely general rules and high performance. Our algorithm does not otherwise depend on the behavior of distributed systems, and is independent of our particular metamodels and rewriting rules.

We have used this algorithm in the *Fiia.Net* groupware development toolkit [10]. *Fiia.Net* has been used to develop a range of applications, distributed across desktop PCs, smartphones, and tabletop computers. Significant examples include a game sketching tool [11] and a furniture layout application [10].

This paper is organized as follows. After reviewing related work, we describe the framework underlying our algorithm, building from abstract examples to the underlying theory and pseudocode. Finally, we provide a short evaluation of the algorithm as implemented in *Fiia.Net*.

2 Related Work

Model transformations are often applied to link two-level models of software architecture, as popularized by the OMG MDA [12] initiative. As software evolves, designers and developers make changes to both levels. Incremental bidirectional transformations allow these changes to be propagated through to the opposite model [13]. Unlike our runtime approach, however, these traditional techniques focus on static design and source code.

Most model transformations represent models as graphs. Triple Graph Grammars (TGGs) [14] are a common basis for incremental bidirectional transformations (e.g. [15,16]).TGGs are difficult to apply to graphs which have dissimilar structure [16], primarily because TGG rules map directly from source to target models without performing intermediate steps. This presents problems for our application to distributed systems: high-level behaviors are typically built from lower-level behaviors, and our rules naturally follow this structure using intermediate elements and non-determinism.

Other approaches for bidirectional model transformation impose a wide variety of restrictions [17]. QVT [18] defines two user languages: QVT Relational is similar to TGGs [19], and similarly does not support intermediate steps. QVT Operational, meanwhile, is an imperative language that would require hand-coded inverse rules to support bidirectionality. This relational versus operational split is typical of the remaining literature.

The Atlas Transformation Language (ATL) is a notable exception. It is an imperative model rewriting system, which has been extended to support conceptual adaptations and distribution removals [20]. The ATL-based technique does not preserve partial transformations, so is not stable in the presence of non-determinism.

Without supporting bidirectionality, Hearnden at al. [21] present a technique for incrementally updating a model transformation. Their formulation is similar to ours, but based on maintaining the tree of possible derivations in a logic language.

Model transformations are also used in the area of distributed systems to specify adaptation between different configurations [22,9]. These systems support high level specification of changes in a single-level model. We believe that similar techniques will be useful extensions to the *Fiia.Net* conceptual model API.

To the best of our knowledge, none of these systems satisfy our joint requirements of speed, generality, stability and limited bidirectionality.

3 Framework

The core of our approach is the use of two runtime models representing snapshots of the conceptual and distribution-level configuration of the distributed interactive system. These models are related via a *refinement* model transformation, while *adaptations* result in runtime changes to these models.

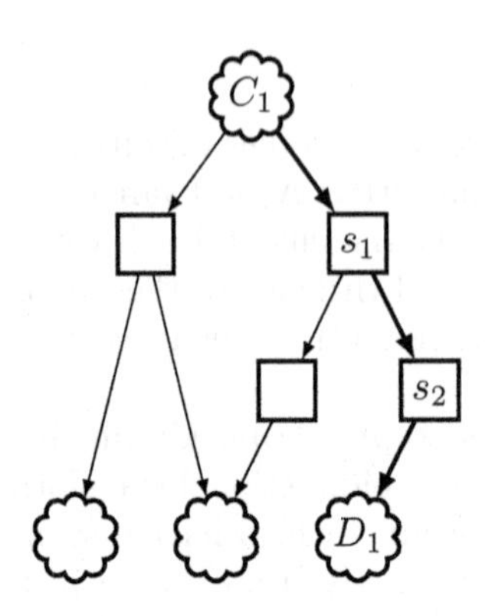

Fig. 1. One refinement in a tree of possibilities

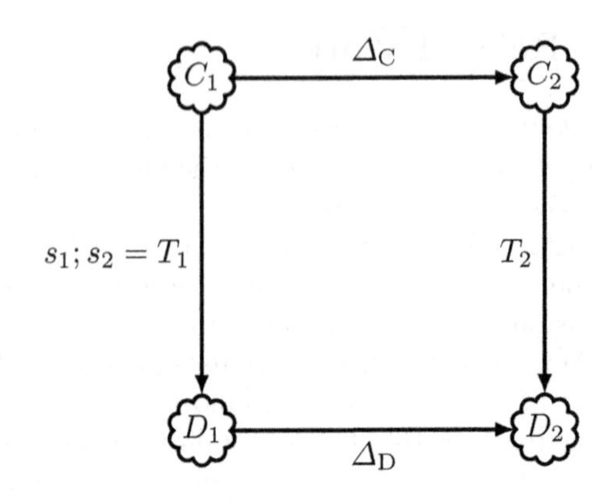

Fig. 2. Commuting of refinements over adaptations

The high-level *conceptual* model is exposed to applications via reflection, events, and an editing API. Applications call into the API to specify runtime adaptations, and use events and reflection to gauge the effects of partial failure.

The low-level *distribution* model describes the underlying distributed system. It is modified automatically through refinement, as a result of conceptual adaptations. Partial failures are first reported as distribution adaptations, and then propagated up through the refinement to the developer's conceptual view.

Figure 1 shows the relationship between the models. A conceptual model C_1 corresponds to a distribution model D_1 through a sequence of transformation steps (such as s_1, s_2). Many different sequences of steps are possible, often leading to different distribution models. Figure 2 combines the steps into a single transformation T_1. The transformation steps are generated by non-deterministic application of a set of refinement rules.

At runtime, either model may be modified, as shown in Fig. 2. If a modification Δ_C is applied to C_1, the resulting conceptual model C_2 may not correspond with D_1. The runtime system must find a new transformation T_2 and distribution model D_2 which are compatible with C_2. Likewise, if a modification Δ_D is applied to D_1, the runtime system must find T_2 and a new conceptual model C_2.

The fact that updates are applied to both models excludes many transformation techniques. As we shall see in the following sections, limiting distribution adaptations to deletion allows our algorithm to support both general rules and fast, incremental updates. In summary, the main features of our approach are:

- Unordered graph rewriting rules are used to refine from conceptual to distribution models.
- Arbitrary changes may be applied to the conceptual model.
- Removals may be applied to the distribution model.
- Updates are applied stably, and at speeds suitable for interactive systems.

In the next sections, we expand on our algorithm and the underlying theory. We first describe how the model transformation is recorded into a trace of steps. From there, we show how the trace and distribution are updated following changes in the conceptual model. Finally, we expand the algorithm to deal with removals from the distribution model.

4 Refinement and Trace

Refining the conceptual model into a distribution requires a very general refinement algorithm. There are multiple implementations of each conceptual mode, so the refinement must deal with non-determinism. Choosing the implementation of many patterns involves a set of nested choices, so the rules are most naturally written using *intermediate elements*, which appear in neither conceptual nor distribution model. Furthermore, adaptation must be permitted at either level. To the best of our knowledge, this combination is not addressed by existing techniques. Our algorithm solves a significant subset of this problem by supporting arbitrary adaptations at the conceptual level and removals at the distribution level. This section defines how we perform refinements and establish a trace. This information is then used to perform conceptual (Sect. 5) and distribution (Sect. 6) adaptations.

The relationship between conceptual and distribution models is specified via a set of graph rewriting rules. These rules are applied in arbitrary order until no more rules match, and their effects are recorded in a *trace*. This process is outlined in Alg. 1. As in other unordered graph rewrite systems, the rules can be very general: they need not be bidirectional, and can include non-determinism, intermediate elements, and multiplicities.

Rather than limit the behavior of individual rules, we enact adaptations by manipulating the trace. This section describes our formalization of the graphs, rules and trace.

The conceptual and distribution models are stored as graphs, each represented as a set of directed edges. Edges have a source vertex, a target vertex, and a label. Vertices are implicit, existing only as unique identifiers associated with

$g \leftarrow$ the graph to refine;

while any rules match g **do**
    $r \leftarrow$ any matching rule;

    append step s to trace **where:**
        s.consumes = edges consumed by the rule;
        s.requires = edges required by the rule, but not modified;
        s.produces = edges produced by the rule;

    $g \leftarrow g - s$.consumes; `/* Delete edges */`
    $g \leftarrow g \cup s$.produces; `/* Add edges */`
end

the resulting distribution graph $\leftarrow g$;

Alg. 1. refine: apply rewriting rules to a graph

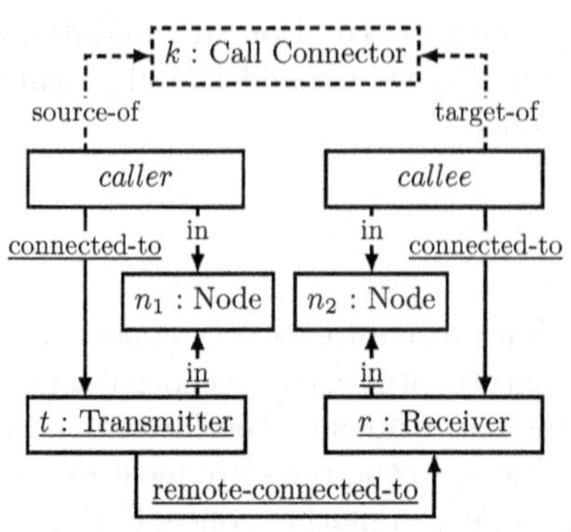

(a) Rule definition. Dashed elements are consumed, while underlined ones are produced.

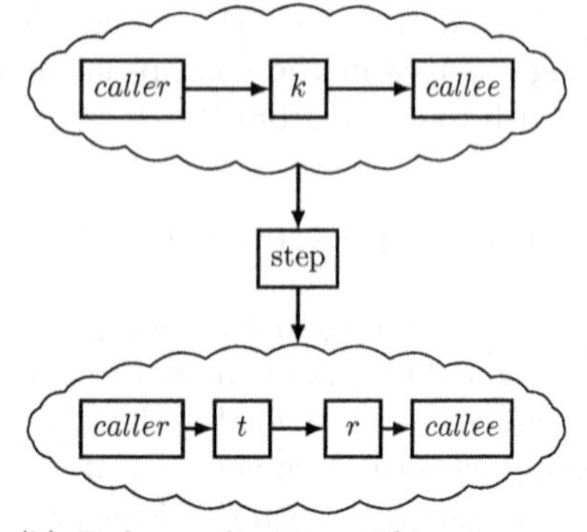

(b) Rule application. This step replaces k with a network RPC link via t and r.

Fig. 3. Example *Fiia.Net* rule: Implement a synchronous call connector as an RPC link

an edge. All modifications to a model or intermediate graph can therefore be expressed via the removal and addition of edges.

Rewriting rules are represented as three sets of edges, plus subrules and executable code for advanced features. The three sets of edges describe most of the rule's behavior, so are where we focus this discussion. Each set describes a sub-graph, with the following meanings:

consumes: must exist for the rule to match, will be deleted;
requires: must exist for the rule to match, will not be modified;
produces: must not exist for the rule to match, will be added.

These sets describe both the prerequisites of a rule, and its effects when applied. This design is similar to many others, including the well-known double-pushout approach [23]. We now present an example of a *Fiia.Net* rule, and continue with the details of the trace.

In *Fiia.Net*, the conceptual model specifies a component-oriented distributed system. Components interact via explicit connectors, which express patterns of communication. For example, a *synchronization connector* between two components establishes them as copies of the same shared data, while a *stream* connector conveys realtime data such as sound or video. There are many possible ways to implement these connectors, expressed via a choice of refinement rules.

A much simpler connector is the *call connector*, which enables blocking method calls. In *Fiia.Net*'s rule set, a call connector can be implemented as a local pointer or remote procedure call (RPC). The remote procedure call can be direct, cached, or routed via a server.

The *Fiia.Net* rule for rewriting a call connector into a direct RPC is sketched in Fig. 3(a). This rule deletes a call connector (k) between two endpoints (*caller* and *callee*) on different physical nodes (n_1 and n_2). It replaces the call connector

```
t ← the trace to apply;
g ← the original graph;
for each s in t do
    /* Ensure the preconditions are met.                                        */
    if s.consumes ⊈ g ∨ s.requires ⊈ g ∨ s.produces ∩ g ≠ ∅ then
        raise the graph and trace are incompatible;
    end
    g ← g − s.consumes;                              /* Removed consumed edges. */
    g ← g ∪ s.produces;                                  /* Add produced edges. */
end
the resulting graph ← g;
```

Alg. 2. apply: apply a trace to a graph

with a network RPC link (t to r), as shown in Fig. 3(b). Call connectors appear in the *Fiia.Net* conceptual model, and are produced by many other rules. Even the *caller* and *callee* are often the product of earlier rules.

Matching a rule against a target graph consists of finding an *embedding*. An embedding is a mapping from a rule's precondition vertices (those consumed or required) to vertices in the target. As in other systems, the mapping must be injective, and applying it to the rule must produce a subgraph of the target. Vertices in the rule are either variables (e.g. k and *caller*), which could map to any one of many graph vertices, or exact values (e.g. "Call Connector")[1].

If an embedding exists, the rule can be applied to the target graph. Rule application consists of deleting consumed edges and adding produced edges. Produced variables which do not appear in the embedding (e.g. t and r) are mapped to unique new vertices.

Each trace step records the effect and dependencies of a single rule application, i.e., the sets of edges consumed, required, and produced. The trace of a refinement is a sequence of trace steps recording all its rule applications.

A trace can sometimes be applied to graphs other than its original conceptual model. This process is shown in Alg. 2. If the graph is missing edges consumed or required by the trace, the **apply** will fail. In this case, the graph and trace are *incompatible*.

The rules are applied in an unordered fashion. When multiple rules match, or multiple embeddings are possible, one is chosen arbitrarily[2]. The transformation continues applying rules until none match. This approach requires that the rule set be terminating and complete: all sequences of rule applications must be finite, and the final graph must be a distribution model.

[1] We express negative and repeated patterns as subrules. Matching a negative pattern prevents the containing rule from matching. Repeated patterns match zero or more times, and contribute to steps produced from their containing rule.

[2] A steering algorithm can be attached to the rule refinery in order to guide these non-deterministic choices based on application-specific criteria, e.g. to minimize latency between components.

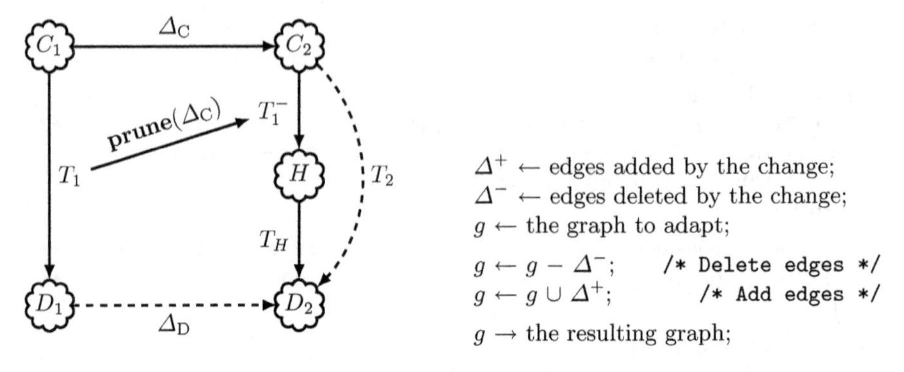

Fig. 4. Steps used in performing a conceptual adaptation

Alg. 3. adapt: apply a change to a graph

In the next sections, we build from these properties to the complete theory of our algorithm.

5 Conceptual Adaptations

Conceptual adaptations typically represent local changes within a larger model. Because the changes reconfigure a live system, they need to be propagated through the refinement quickly and incrementally. Existing techniques for such incremental updates greatly restrict the space of supported rules. Our algorithm solves this problem for unordered rewrite rules. This section describes how we apply conceptual adaptations to an existing refinement, using the explicit trace defined in Sec. 4.

Conceptual adaptations are defined using the graph representation of the conceptual model. An adaptation is a set of edges which are removed from the graph, and a set of edges which are added. Figure 4 shows the operations used to resolve a conceptual adaptation. From initial models C_1 and D_1, corresponding via trace T_1, and a conceptual adaptation Δ_C, our algorithm proceeds as follows:

1. Using Δ_C, **adapt** C_1 to C_2 (Alg. 3).
2. Using Δ_C, **prune** T_1 to a partial refinement of C_2, producing T_1^- (Alg. 4).
3. **apply** T_1^- to C_2, producing H (Alg. 2).
4. **refine** H, producing a trace T_H and model D_2 (Alg. 1).
5. Concatenate the steps of T_1^- and T_H, producing a new trace T_2.

The **prune** operation converts T_1 into a trace which represents a partial refinement of C_2. It does this by discarding steps which would not have been generated by a **refine** of C_2. Determining which steps to discard depends on the consumes, requires, and produces sets saved in each step. We now give an example of this pruning, and then present the complete algorithm.

Consider the abstract initial state shown in Fig. 5(a). Edges e_a and e_b exist in the conceptual model C_1. The first refinement step (s_1) consumes e_b and

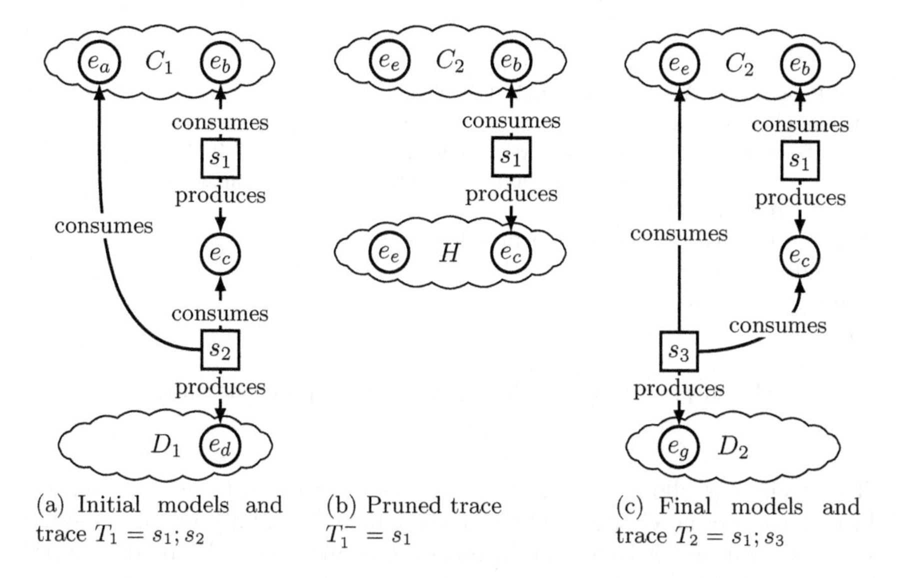

(a) Initial models and trace $T_1 = s_1; s_2$

(b) Pruned trace $T_1^- = s_1$

(c) Final models and trace $T_2 = s_1; s_3$

Fig. 5. Example conceptual adaptation $\Delta_C = \{$ **del:** e_a, **add:** e_e $\}$

produces e_c. After the first step, the intermediate model consists of e_a and e_c. The second step (s_2) consumes both e_a and e_c, producing e_d. After the second step, no more rules match, so the distribution model consists of only e_d.

Now suppose that we apply a conceptual adaptation Δ_C that removes e_a and adds the new e_e. This causes the trace to be pruned to the T_1^- shown in Fig. 5(b). T_1^- is the same at T_1, except that steps that no longer apply in C_2 have been removed. Specifically, s_2 consumes e_a, so must be discarded. With the loss of s_2, e_d is no longer available. As neither e_c nor e_e are consumed in the trace, they appear in the intermediate model H.

Applying rewriting rules to H and concatenating the traces yields the T_2 shown in Fig. 5(c). s_1 remains unchanged from the initial state, but s_2 has been replaced by s_3.

The operational definition of **prune** is show in Alg. 4. It performs the dependency search outlined above based on the ordering of steps in the trace. Each step is defined from a graph rewrite operation in the transformation. As a result, all edges consumed or required by a step s_i in T_1 must appear in C_1, or be produced by a previous step (s_p where $p < i$). The iteration will always consider s_p before s_i, so can show dependency using a simple set intersection check.

For simplicity, this definition ignores negative and repeated patterns. In the complete algorithm, these are handled during the iteration. Negative patterns are checked against an intermediate graph when Alg. 4 considers the step compatible. Repeated patterns may expand or contract the step if their number of matches has changed. Both cases add to the complexity of the operation, but their use in *Fiia.Net* does not significantly impact runtime speed.

```
t ← T₁;
r ← edges removed by Δ_C;
/* Propagate Δ_C down through the trace.                          */
for each s in t do
    if removed ∩ s.consumes ≠ ∅ or removed ∩ s.requires ≠ ∅ then
        /* A prerequisite is unavailable, so delete this step.    */
        delete s from t;
        removed ← removed ∪ s.produces;
    end
end
T₁⁻ ← t;
```

Alg. 4. prune: update the trace for a conceptual adaptation

This technique allows us to quickly update an existing transformation with arbitrary conceptual changes. The resulting trace T_2 will always correspond to a possible sequence of rule applications on C_2, and so can be used in further adaptations. Unlike other approaches to live model transformation, our approach maintains general graph rewriting semantics throughout.

6 Distribution Adaptations

Partial failures in distributed systems are notoriously hard to resolve. A two-level runtime model provides a natural way of capturing this behavior: failures are removals in the distribution model, and are propagated back to the conceptual model. This allows the developer to work exclusively with the conceptual model, rather than delving into implementation details to diagnose and repair problems.

Our requirement for general rewriting rules excludes existing techniques for bidirectional adaptation. Restricting distribution adaptations to removals allows us to apply them quickly and incrementally. We are not aware of any other algorithm for unordered rewrite rules that offers this capability. This section defines how we handle distribution adaptations, building on operations defined earlier.

Like conceptual adaptations, distribution adaptations are specified as graph edits; however, they are restricted to removals. Figure 6 shows the operations used to resolve a distribution-level adaptation. Initial models C_1 and D_1 correspond via trace T_1. The distribution adaptation Δ_D produces a new distribution D_i from D_1. The unrestricted rule set implies that D_i might not correspond to any conceptual model. Our algorithm resolves this conflict by removing additional distribution edges to restore consistency (Δ_{D2}). This whole operation is performed as follows:

1. **findSourceDelta** with Δ_D and T_1 to generate Δ_C (Alg. 5).
2. Using Δ_C, **adapt** C_1 to C_2 (Alg. 3).
3. Using Δ_C, **prune** T_1 to its parts compatible with C_2, producing T_1^- (Alg. 4).

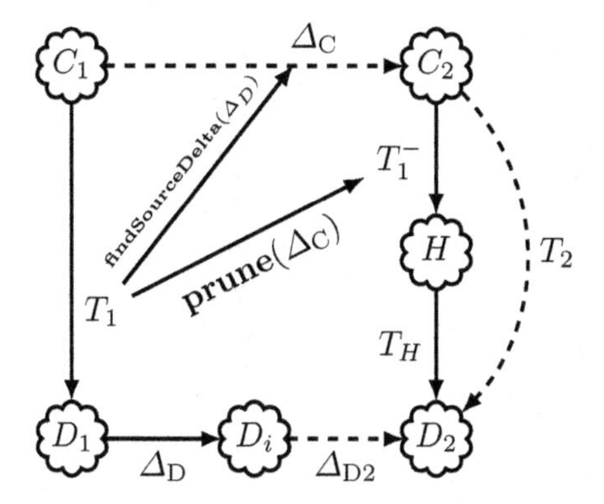

Fig. 6. Steps used in performing a distribution adaptation

4. **apply** T_1^- to C_2, producing H (Alg. 2).
5. **refine** H, producing a trace T_H and model D_2 (Alg. 1).
6. Concatenate the steps of T_1^- and T_H, producing a new trace T_2.

The **findSourceDelta** operation finds conceptual removals Δ_C sufficient to cause Δ_D. The derived Δ_C is then applied like a normal conceptual update, following the algorithm described in Sect. 5. This conceptual update often removes more distribution elements than Δ_D, causing the additional Δ_{D2}.

Consider the abstract example shown in Fig. 7(a). We apply a distribution update Δ_D which removes e_d. The task of **findSourceDelta** is then to identify the conceptual edges which led to e_d, so they can be removed. e_d was produced by s_2, which, in turn, consumes e_a. As a result, Δ_C will remove e_a.

Applying **prune** with $\Delta_C = \{$ **del:** $e_a \}$ produces the T_1^- trace shown in Fig. 7(b). Without e_a, pruning discards both s_2 and s_3. This leaves only e_c, no longer consumed by s_3, to appear in the intermediate model H.

To refine H to a valid distribution model, we rely on the earlier property of completeness. The trace T_1^- describes a sequence of rule applications from the conceptual model C_2 to H. In our example, e_c happens to be an intermediate element, which can not appear in the distribution model. For the completeness property to hold, applying the refinement rules must eventually refine H into a distribution model. In this example, s_4 is sufficient, and yields the final T_2 shown in Fig. 7(c).

The operational definition of **findSourceDelta** is shown in Alg. 5. It performs the inference described above by walking backward through the trace. As for **prune**, all edges consumed by a step must appear in C_1 or be produced by a previous step. This iteration always considers the consume before the produce, so can accumulate the banned edges in "removed".

This technique quickly updates an existing transformation to apply distribution removals. Our approach is particularly unique, because it does not require bidirectional rules. Indeed, the transformation used in our *Fiia.Net* system is neither bijective nor surjective, and is massively non-deterministic.

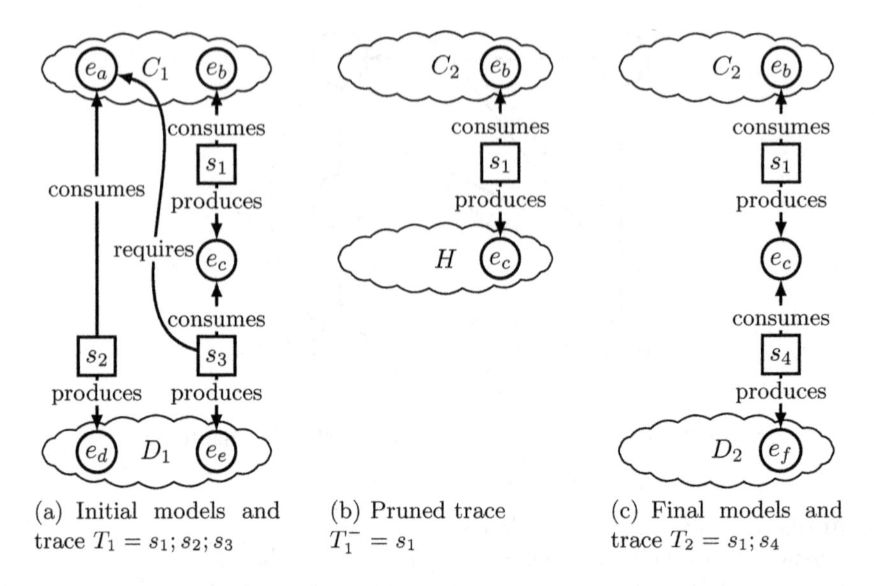

(a) Initial models and trace $T_1 = s_1; s_2; s_3$

(b) Pruned trace $T_1^- = s_1$

(c) Final models and trace $T_2 = s_1; s_4$

Fig. 7. Example distribution adaptation $\Delta_D = \{$ **del:** $e_d \}$

```
T ← T1;
Δ⁻ ← edges removed by ΔD;
/* Propagate ΔD up to the conceptual model.                        */
for each s in reverse T do
    /* Check whether this step is compatible with the change.      */
    if Δ⁻ ∩ s.produces ≠ ∅ or Δ⁻ ∩ s.requires ≠ ∅ then
        delete s from T;           /* Discard the incompatible step. */
        /* Discarding this step means more edges should not exist.  */
        Δ⁻ ← Δ⁻ ∪ s.consumes;
    end
end
ΔC ← { del: Δ⁻ ∩ ΔC } ;        /* Compute the conceptual adaptation. */
```

Alg. 5. findSourceDelta: find a sufficient conceptual removal for a distribution removal

7 Experience

The algorithm presented in this paper is used by our *Fiia.Net* toolkit. *Fiia.Net* represents a distributed interactive system using a high-level conceptual model which is visible to the application, and a low-level distribution model which configures the actual implementation [10]. An application enacts adaptations by modifying the conceptual model, while the underlying implementation removes any failed elements from the distribution model. Our algorithm efficiently propagates both types of updates through the transformation. *Fiia.Net*'s rule set consists of

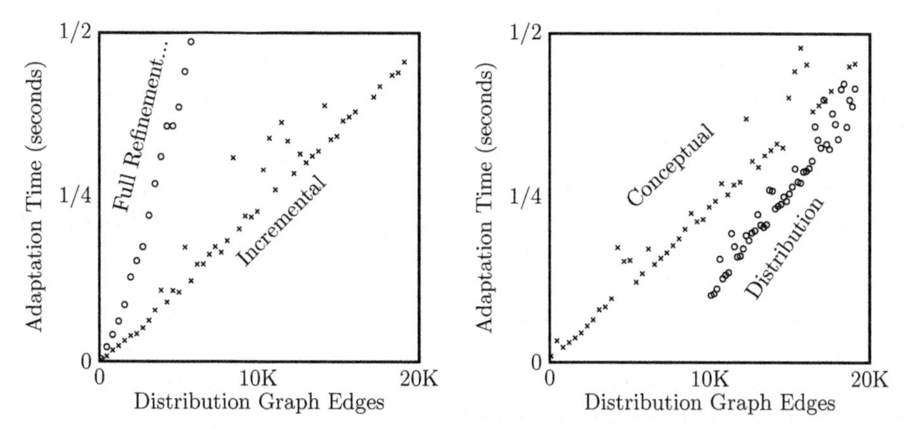

(a) Conceptual adaptations to add game entities.

(b) Conceptual and distribution adaptations to remove game entities.

Fig. 8. Adaptation times for varying model sizes

34 graph rewrite rules, each of which is simple, but which in combination express a rich set of possible implementations for each conceptual model.

We have used *Fiia.Net* to implement several applications within our lab. These include a shared presentation program; a multimodal furniture layout [10] involving participants using an electronic tabletop surface, a standard PC, and a smartphone; a textual chat application; and a collaborative game prototyping tool [11]. These examples have shown the effectiveness of the two-level model for groupware, and the practicality of using *Fiia.Net* toolkit for rapid application development.

To evaluate the performance impact of our model transformation algorithm, we have recorded the time it requires for various adaptations based on the Raptor game prototyping tool [11]. Raptor allows designers to add and control in-game entities while a tester plays. Each in-game entity is a single *Fiia.Net* component. Adding, removing, and connecting entities causes Raptor to make changes in the conceptual model. Similarly, partial failures will cause changes to the distribution model.

Figure 8(a) compares the incremental algorithm, described in this paper, to a straight-forward full refinement. In both cases, the experiment gradually introduces 1000 new entities into a game world via conceptual adaptations. All transformation is performed in one thread, on an Acer Aspire 5110 (AMD TL-50 1.6GHz with 2GB RAM, running Windows XP and Microsoft .Net 3.5). The size of the trace and models grows linearly with the number of entities. At 1000 entities, it reaches 8022 steps, with 16054 and 19076 edges in the conceptual and distribution graphs, respectively. Applying a full refinement after each adaptation rapidly becomes too expensive for interactive applications, peaking at nearly 4 seconds. Our incremental algorithm performs much better, remaining below 500 ms. This gap appears because **prune** preserves almost all of the previous steps, so the ensuing **refine** requires few graph searches.

Figure 8(b) shows the same system, removing entities from the game world via conceptual and distribution adaptations. Applying the adaptations in the conceptual model behaves similarly to the incremental additions. The distribution adaptations are slightly different, because removing components from the distribution model indicates their failure. To ease application recovery, *Fiia.Net* preserves some information about connections to failed components. This behavior is responsible for both the slightly higher performance of, and the 10076 distribution edges remaining after the distribution case. Again, performance is adequate for interactive use.

Our current graph rewriting engine is relatively crude. It stores all intermediate models as untyped graphs, and dynamically matches rules using recursive search. In spite of these shortcuts, our current implementation works well with a few thousand components and connections.

While our approach is motivated by the difficulties of developing distributed systems, the algorithm is independent of *Fiia.Net*'s models and rules.

8 Conclusion

In this paper, we have presented an efficient algorithm for maintaining consistency in two-level runtime models. This allows systems like *Fiia.Net* to maintain all the flexibility of model-driven architecture, in a highly-adaptive and fault-tolerant runtime.

Because our algorithm is built on graph rewriting and tracing, it should also permit many optimizations and heuristics that we have not explored. We believe that this approach will prove useful for similar two-level runtime models, whether specialized for groupware or other fields.

References

1. Graham, T.C.N., Kazman, R., Walmsley, C.: Agility and experimentation: Practical techniques for resolving architectural tradeoffs. In: ICSE, pp. 519–528. IEEE Computer Society, Los Alamitos (2007)
2. Pinelle, D., Dyck, J., Gutwin, C.: Aligning work practices and mobile technologies: Groupware design for loosely coupled mobile groups. In: Chittaro, L. (ed.) Mobile HCI 2003. LNCS, vol. 2795, pp. 177–192. Springer, Heidelberg (2003)
3. Achterbosch, L., Pierce, R., Simmons, G.: Massively multiplayer online role-playing games: the past, present, and future. Computers in Entertainment 5(4) (2007)
4. Graham, T., Urnes, T.: Linguistic support for the evolutionary design of software architectures. In: ICSE 18, pp. 418–427. IEEE Computer Society, Los Alamitos (1996)
5. Calvary, G., Coutaz, J., Nigay, L.: From single-user architectural design to PAC*: A generic software architecture model for CSCW. In: CHI 1997, pp. 242–249. ACM Press, New York (1997)
6. Hill, R., Brinck, T., Rohall, S., Patterson, J., Wilner, W.: The Rendezvous language and architecture for constructing multi-user applications. ACM TOCHI 1(2), 81–125 (1994)

7. Laurillau, Y., Nigay, L.: Clover architecture for groupware. In: CSCW 2002, pp. 236–245. ACM Press, New York (2002)
8. Graham, T., Phillips, W., Wolfe, C.: Quality analysis of distribution architectures for synchronous groupware. In: CollaborateCom (2006)
9. Morin, B., Fleurey, F., Bencomo, N., Jézéquel, J.-M., Solberg, A., Dehlen, V., Blair, G.S.: An aspect-oriented and model-driven approach for managing dynamic variability. In: Czarnecki, K., Ober, I., Bruel, J.-M., Uhl, A., Völter, M. (eds.) MoDELS 2008. LNCS, vol. 5301, pp. 782–796. Springer, Heidelberg (2008)
10. Wolfe, C., Graham, T.N., Phillips, W.G., Roy, B.: Fiia: User-centered development of adaptive groupware systems. In: EICS, pp. 275–284. ACM Press, New York (2009)
11. Wolfe, C., Smith, J.D., Phillips, W.G., Graham, T.C.N.: Fiia: A model-based approach to engineering collaborative augmented reality. In: Dubois, E., Nigay, L., Gray, P. (eds.) The Engineering of Mixed Reality Systems. Springer, Heidelberg (to appear, 2009)
12. OMG: MDA guide version 1.0.1. Technical Report omg/03-06-01, OMG (2003)
13. Kurtev, I.: State of the art of QVT: A model transformation language standard. In: Schürr, A., Nagl, M., Zündorf, A. (eds.) AGTIVE 2007. LNCS, vol. 5088, pp. 377–393. Springer, Heidelberg (2008)
14. Schürr, A.: Specification of graph translators with triple graph grammars. In: Mayr, E.W., Schmidt, G., Tinhofer, G. (eds.) WG 1994. LNCS, vol. 903, pp. 151–163. Springer, Heidelberg (1995)
15. Giese, H., Wagner, R.: Incremental model synchronization with triple graph grammars. In: Nierstrasz, O., Whittle, J., Harel, D., Reggio, G. (eds.) MoDELS 2006. LNCS, vol. 4199, pp. 543–557. Springer, Heidelberg (2006)
16. Kindler, E., Wagner, R.: Triple Graph Grammars: Concepts, extensions, implementations, and application scenarios. Technical Report tr-ri-07-284, Department of Computer Science, University of Paderborn (June 2007)
17. Stevens, P.: A landscape of bidirectional model transformations. In: Lämmel, R., Visser, J., Saraiva, J. (eds.) Generative and Transformational Techniques in Software Engineering II. LNCS, vol. 5235, pp. 408–424. Springer, Heidelberg (2008)
18. OMG: Meta object facility (MOF) 2.0 query/view/transformation specification. Technical Report formal/2008-04-03, OMG (2008)
19. Greenyer, J., Kindler, E.: Reconciling TGGs with QVT. In: Engels, G., Opdyke, B., Schmidt, D.C., Weil, F. (eds.) MoDELS 2007. LNCS, vol. 4735, pp. 16–30. Springer, Heidelberg (2007)
20. Xiong, Y., Liu, D., Hu, Z., Zhao, H., Takeichi, M., Mei, H.: Towards automatic model synchronization from model transformations. In: Stirewalt, R.E.K., Egyed, A., Fischer, B. (eds.) ASE, pp. 164–173. ACM, New York (2007)
21. Hearnden, D., Lawley, M., Raymond, K.: Incremental model transformation for the evolution of model-driven systems. In: Nierstrasz, O., Whittle, J., Harel, D., Reggio, G. (eds.) MoDELS 2006. LNCS, vol. 4199, pp. 321–335. Springer, Heidelberg (2006)
22. Bencomo, N., Grace, P., Flores, C., Hughes, D., Blair, G.S.: Genie: supporting the model driven development of reflective, component-based adaptive systems. In: Robby (ed.) ICSE, pp. 811–814. ACM, New York (2008)
23. Corradini, A., Montanari, U., Rossi, F., Ehrig, H., Heckel, R., Löwe, M.: Algebraic approaches to graph transformation - Part I: Basic concepts and double pushout approach. In: Rozenberg, G. (ed.) Handbook of Graph Grammars, pp. 163–246. World Scientific, Singapore (1997)

Traceability-Based Change Awareness

Jonas Helming, Maximilian Koegel, Helmut Naughton,
Joern David, and Aleksandar Shterev

Technical University Munich, Department for Computer Science,
Chair for Applied Software Engineering,
85748 Garching, Munich
{helming,koegel,naughton,david,shterevg}@in.tum.de

Abstract. Many tools in software engineering projects support the visualization and collaborative modification of custom sets of artifacts. This includes tools for requirements engineering, UML tools for design, project management tools, developer tools and many more. A key factor for success in software engineering projects is the collective understanding of changes applied to these artifacts. To support this, there are several strategies to automatically notify project participants about relevant changes. Known strategies are limited to a fixed set of artifacts and/or make no use of traceability information to supply change notifications. This paper proposes a change notification approach based on traceability in a unified model and building upon operation-based change tracking. The unified model explicitly combines system specification models and project management models into one fully traceable model. To show the benefit of our approach we compare it to related approaches in a case study.

Keywords: Change awareness, traceability, unified model, operation-based, notification.

1 Introduction and Related Work

A common technique to handle the complexity in software development projects is the use of different models. On the one hand, models such as requirement models and detailed specifications are used to describe the system under construction on different levels of abstraction. We call this the *system model*. On the other hand, there is the *project model* [7] containing tasks lists, schedules, or the organizational structure. All these do not describe the system, but the project itself. In the course of a software project, all models constantly evolve over time. A change in one model often triggers a change in another. For example, a change in the functional requirements most likely affects the work break down structure.

Change awareness is the ability to keep up with changes that were made to development documents and artifacts. It is difficult to achieve this without computer assistance, especially for complex systems [10]. As a consequence, most tools, which store software engineering models, offer some degree of support for change awareness. To notify project participants only about changes relevant to them, change notification strategies are required. Existing approaches provide notification strategies based on either the system and project model (e.g. [3], [5], [11], [13], [15]), based on source code (e.g. [1], [12]) or even both (e.g. [4], [9]). Unfortunately, the effects of changes

A. Schürr and B. Selic (Eds.): MODELS 2009, LNCS 5795, pp. 372–376, 2009.

crossing the boundaries between the system model and the project model have been studied a lot less. A comparison done by Storey et. al. [14] showed that none of the 12 tools included in the study made significant use of project documentation (e.g. requirements, tests, design or architecture).

This paper proposes a novel change notification approach to notify project participants about such relevant changes based on traceability. The approach was implemented and evaluated based on a CASE-Tool called UNICASE [3]. UNICASE provides a unified model, which explicitly combines the system model and the project model into one model stored in one repository. The underlying unified model enables model-based notifications: As even the user is part of the unified model, notifications can be generated based on the context-rich and highly traceable model. For example, a user can be notified about direct or indirect changes on artifacts he is currently working on. To show the benefit of our approach, we compare it to related approaches in a case study.

2 Traceability-Based Change Notification

Our suggested change awareness approach uses links between system model and project model to determine which notifications are relevant for project participants. For example if a project participant is working on a task, which refers to a functional requirement, he might be interested in any change pertaining to this functional requirement. Furthermore he also might be interested in changes related to the detailing use case of the requirement as well as changes in requirements that refine the requirement he is working on. The proposed change notification strategy would trace these links and notify the user about changes on all mentioned model elements.
In the example (see Figure 1), a change of the functional requirement by *UserA* would lead to a notification of *UserB*, because he or she is working on a task related to the functional requirement. Starting from the task the change notification strategy follows a trace of length one. Therefore we will call this type of change notification trace-based change notification of length one.

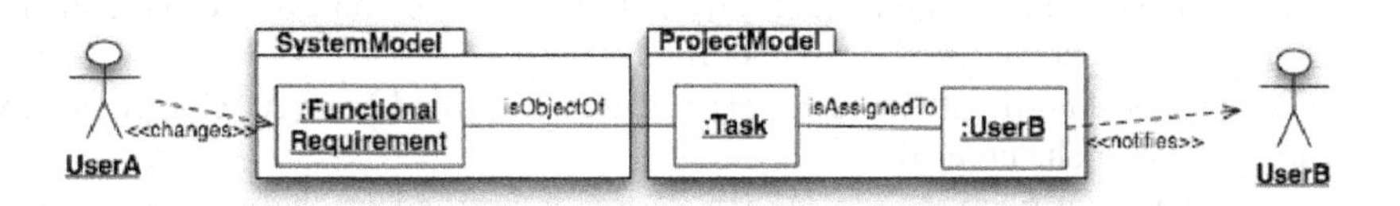

Fig. 1. Notification workflow (custom UML diagram)

The exclusive use of trace-based notifications of length one would ignore the fact that there are dependencies inside the system model, which require change propagation. If there was a detailing use case for the functional requirement in the previous example, *UserB* should be also notified about changes on that use case. UNICASE provides a concept called *opening link taxonomy* [6], which determines which links require such change propagation. The opening link taxonomy allows us to find all model elements that are influencing a given model element in a way that the model element in question cannot be entirely completed without completing these. In other words, the opening links allow us to calculate the transitive closure on model elements a user is working on.

This leads to trace-based change notifications of length two or more. We will compare different lengths later in the evaluation in chapter 3.

In an application context the notifications are generated whenever the user receives changes from the central repository to synchronize the local model instance. The changes in UNICASE are represented as so-called operations [8]. An operation describes one atomic change on a model such as assigning a task to user. Using operation-based change tracking to generate notifications results in two major benefits: performance and time-order preservation. The changes do not have to be calculated and are in the order in which they occurred in time [15]. This means the notifications can be generated efficiently and are ordered by the time at which they occurred. From the list of given operations a set of notifications is derived and presented to the user in a list oriented view.

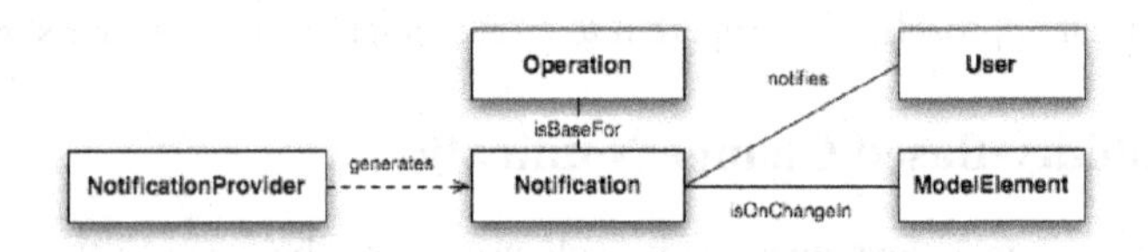

Fig. 2. TraceNotificationProvider (UML class diagram)

A *NotificationProvider* generates notifications based on a certain strategy (see figure 2). Each *Notification* is targeted at a specific *User*, describes a change on a certain *ModelElement* and was derived from a given *Operation.*

3 Evaluation

To evaluate our approach we conducted a case study in which users manually rated change notifications according to their personal relevance. To allow for comparison with other approaches, we implemented the most common automatic approaches for providing change notifications:

- Modifier-based notifications (e.g. [5]): A user is notified on every change in any artifact he or she has previously modified.
- Creator-based notifications (e.g. [23]): A user is notified on every change on any artifacts he or she created.
- Assignment notifications (e.g. [25]): A user is notified on the assignment of a task and on any subsequent change to an assigned task.

We did not include notification strategies that rely on manual selection of the artifacts the user wants to be notified about, since they are not comparable with automatic approaches and have a different objective. The data for our case study was collected in a project named DOLLI2 (Distributed Online Logistics and Location Infrastructure) at a major European airport. More than 20 developers worked on the project for about five months. All modeling was performed in UNICASE resulting in a comprehensive project model that consisted of about 1000 model elements and a history of more than 600 versions. Using the traceability-based notification provider as well as the three other notification providers, we generated notifications for the DOLLI2 project data post mortem. To evaluate the quality of the notifications generated by the different providers, we interviewed 5 project participants on 12 of their notifications randomly selected for each provider. Figure 3 shows an overview of the statistics of the number of notifications and their percentage for the different users and for the different providers.

		Trace	Assignment	Creator	Modifier	All
User A	#	27	66	195	11,025	11,313
	%	0.24	0.58	1.72	97.45	100.00
User B	#	150	162	218	10,871	11,401
	%	1.32	1.42	1.91	95.35	100.00
User C	#	8	114	508	9,084	9,714
	%	0.08	1.17	5.23	93.51	100.00
User D	#	60	96	306	10,505	10,967
	%	0.55	0.88	2.79	95.79	100.00
User E	#	41	128	506	8,286	8,961
	%	0.46	1.43	5.65	92.47	100.00
All	#	1,249	2,123	9,832	333,391	346,595
	%	0.36	0.61	2.84	96.19	100.00

Fig. 3. Notification Overview Statistics Table

Out of the three notification providers we implemented for comparison, we expected the assignment provider to be rated highest based on the assumption, that everybody should be notified about changes in his or her directly assigned tasks. Further, we expected the creator provider to be rated second best, as the creation of an artifact usually implies some kind of ownership. As the modifier-based provider also includes creator-based notification, but generates a significantly higher number of notifications, it was expected to be rated third.

The table shows that the trace provider generates relatively few notifications, whereas other providers generate up to 1000 times more notifications for the same data. In a practical appliance the number of change notifications provided should be as low as feasible in order not to overwhelm the notified users. As the traceability-based notification provider generates a low number of total notifications, but also produces notifications not covered by other providers (because of the traces between system and project model), we claim it is useful if it is rated better than at least one of the existing notification providers. Our hypothesis was that the TaskTrace provider would result in a significantly higher rating than the Modifier provider, since we measured the mean ratings as $m_{Modifier} = 2.53$ and $m_{TaskTrace} = 3.19$ based on $n_1=60$ and $n_2=47$ items in each category, respectively. The negative correlation $\varrho(L,R)=-0.127$ (Pearson) between the trace length L and the rating R showed a tendency of shorter trace lengths causing higher ratings. Therefore, we only used those ratings that concerned notifications with a trace length of less or equal than two (resulting in 47 instead of 60 items). We used the non-parametric Kolmogorov-Smirnov test to analyze the difference in the user rating. To perform this kind of test, two (discrete) empirical distribution functions F and F' – one for the Modifier rating and one for the TaskTrace rating – had to be computed from the data sample. The supremum of the differences of the distribution functions $d_n=\sup_x |F_n(x) - F_n'(x)|$ for $n:=n_2=47$ was $d_{47}=0.2341 > c(\alpha=5\%; n) = 1.36 / n^{1/2} = 0.198$, which means that the maximum of the distances exceeds the acceptable constant $c(\alpha=5\%; n)$ corresponding to the 5% level. Thus the null-hypothesis has to be rejected on the 5% level of significance.

Summing up this statistical result, we showed that our traceability-based notification provider performs better than the modifier-based notification provider. Regarding the significantly lower number of created notifications, we claim our traceability-based notification provider to be useful in practical appliance.

References

1. Biehl, J.T., Czerwinski, M., Smith, G., Robertson, G.G.: FASTDash: a visual dashboard for fostering awareness in software teams. In: Proceedings of the SIGCHI conference on Human factors in computing systems, pp. 1313–1322. ACM, New York (2007)
2. Bruegge, B., Creighton, O., Helming, J., Kögel, M.: Unicase - an Ecosystem for Unified Software Engineering Research Tools. In: Third IEEE International Conference on Global Software Engineering, ICGSE 2007 (2008)
3. Carroll, J.M., Neale, D.C., Isenhour, P.L., Rosson, M.B., McCrickard, D.S.: Notification and awareness: synchronizing task-oriented collaborative activity. International Journal of Human-Computer Studies 58(5), 605–632 (2003)
4. Cheng, L., Hupfer, S., Ross, S., Patterson, J.: Jazzing up Eclipse with collaborative tools. In: Proceedings of the 2003 OOPSLA workshop on eclipse technology eXchange, pp. 45–49. ACM, New York (2003)
5. De Lucia, A., Fasano, F., Oliveto, R., Tortora, G.: Enhancing an artefact management system with traceability recovery features. In: Proceedings of 20th IEEE International Conference on Software Maintenance, 2004, pp. 306–315 (2004)
6. Helming, J.: Integrating Software Lifecycle Models into a uniform Software Engineering Model. In: Software Engineering Conference - Workshop Proceedings, Gesellschaft für Informatik, pp. 157–164 (2008)
7. Helming, J., Koegel, M., Naughton, H.: Towards Traceability from Project Management to System Models. In: ICSE 2009, 5th International Workshop on Traceability in Emerging Forms of Software Engineering Vancouver, British Columbia, Canada (2009)
8. Koegel, M.: Towards Software Configuration Management for Unified Models. In: ICSE 2009, CVSM 2009: Proceedings of the CVSM workshop, pp. 19–24. ACM, New York (2009)
9. LaToza, T.D., Venolia, G., DeLine, R.: Maintaining mental models: a study of developer work habits. In: Proceedings of the 28th international conference on Software engineering, pp. 492–501. ACM, New York (2006)
10. Luqi: A graph model for software evolution. IEEE Transactions on Software Engineering 16(8), 917–927 (1990)
11. Papadopoulou, S., Norrie, M.: How a structured document model can support awareness in collaborative authoring. In: International Conference on Collaborative Computing: Networking, Applications and Worksharing, 2007. CollaborateCom 2007, pp. 117–126 (2007)
12. Sarma, A., Noroozi, Z., van der Hoek, A.: Palantir: raising awareness among configuration management workspaces. In: Proceedings of 25th International Conference on Software Engineering, 2003, pp. 444–454 (2003)
13. Sinha, V., Sengupta, B., Chandra, S.: Enabling Collaboration in Distributed Requirements Management. IEEE Softw. 23(5), 52–61 (2006)
14. Storey, M.D., Čubranić, D., German, D.: On the use of visualization to support awareness of human activities in software development: a survey and a framework. In: Proceedings of the ACM symposium on Software visualization, pp. 193–202. ACM, New York (2005)
15. Tam, J., Greenberg, S.: A framework for asynchronous change awareness in collaborative documents and workspaces. Int. J. Hum.-Comput. Stud. 64(7), 583–598 (2006)
16. Koegel, M.: Operation-based conflict detection and resolution. In: ICSE 2009, CVSM 2009: Proceedings of the CVSM workshop. ACM, New York (2009)

Interaction Design and Model-Driven Development

Larry L. Constantine

University of Madeira, Portugal
LConstantine@uma.pt

Abstract. Throughout the evolution of software development and software engineering methods, human interaction and the interfaces that support it have been too often ignored or treated as secondary concerns. Most modern modeling languages and methods - UML and the unified process most definitely among them - have been devised with a highly focused concern for representing procedures, information, and software structures. The needs of interaction design and designers have been addressed, if at all, in afterthought. Instead of well-conceived notations and techniques, interaction designers have been given awkward adaptations of models conceived for completely different and largely incompatible purposes. Instead of placing users and use at the center of developmental and methodological focus, the dominant modeling languages and methods have relegated them to the periphery. Despite noble calls for rapprochement and valiant attempts to build bridges, the gap between software engineering on the one side and human-computer interaction on the other remains stubbornly deep and wide, filled with misunderstanding and devoid of meaningful integration.

Model-driven development, the latest in a long series of well-intentioned initiatives tracing all the way back to the first so-called auto-coders, is an approach that, like its antecedents, promises to eliminate or radically reduce the need for manual coding by automatically generating software from higher-level descriptions and models. Unfortunately, model-driven development may be on track to perpetuate many of the problems and shortcomings of its forerunners. This presentation will critically examine the place of users, usability, and user interfaces in modern model-based software development methods. It will argue that the user interfaces of software intended for human use are more than mere surface projections of underlying process and information models and that interaction design is more than mere spit-and-polish added onto that surface. It will consider both the promises and the problems in current thinking and will propose specific solutions and new directions grounded in models and techniques tailored to the core issues of interaction design but which are also well integrated with established software engineering models. Outstanding problems and work-in-progress will also be reported.

A. Schürr and B. Selic (Eds.): MODELS 2009, LNCS 5795, p. 377, 2009.

Towards Test-Driven Semantics Specification

Christian Soltenborn and Gregor Engels

Institut für Informatik, Universität Paderborn,
33098 Paderborn, Germany
{christian,engels}@uni-paderborn.de

Abstract. Behavioral models are getting more and more important within the software development cycle. To get the most use out of them, their behavior should be defined formally. As a result, many approaches exist which aim at specifying formal semantics for behavioral languages (e.g., Dynamic Meta Modeling (DMM), Semantic Anchoring). Most of these approaches give rise to a formal semantics which can e.g. be used to check the quality of a particular language instance, for instance using model checking techniques.

However, if the semantics specification itself contains errors, it is more or less useless, since one cannot rely on the analysis results. Therefore, the language engineer must make sure that the semantics he develops is of the highest quality possible. To help the language engineer to achieve that goal, we propose a test-driven semantics specification process: the semantics of the language under consideration is first informally demonstrated using example models, which will then be used as test cases during the actual semantics specification process. In this paper, we present this approach using the already mentioned specification language DMM.

Keywords: Semantics specification, testing, model checking.

1 Introduction

In today's world of software engineering, behavioral models play an increasingly important role within the software development process. Just a couple of years ago, models were mainly used for documentation purposes: for instance, a UML Activity served as an easily understandable sketch of some process, but was not supposed to be used e.g. for code generation or direct execution. One consequence of this usage of behavioral diagrams was that an informal description of a language's semantics was considered appropriate (the UML specification [1] probably is the most prominent example here).

However, this approach of describing a language's semantics has severe drawbacks: an informal semantics description will in almost all cases leave room for interpretations, therefore leading to models having an ambiguous semantics. This does not only hamper the usage of models as a base for discussion (e.g. when groups with different skills are working together), but also does not allow for an automatic analysis of a complex model's behavior. As an example, analyzing

A. Schürr and B. Selic (Eds.): MODELS 2009, LNCS 5795, pp. 378–392, 2009.

a Petri net or UML Activity for *soundness* [2,3] only becomes possible because both languages are equipped with a formal semantics[1].

As a result, quite some approaches for specifying formal semantics have been proposed (e.g. [4,5,6,7], more on this in Sect. 5). However, all these approaches focus on delivering a semantics which can then be used for model analysis as described above, but they do not consider the quality of the semantics specification itself. This is surprising, since a semantics specification is only useful if it is correct in some sense – otherwise, one cannot rely on the analysis results.

Given a formal specification, the first and obvious idea is to define a notion of correctness by means of requirements the specification shall fulfill, and then to *prove* that this is indeed the case. Unfortunately, the experiences from software development seem to imply that proving the correctness of a reasonable complex system is often just not feasible; therefore, the most important technique in software quality assurance is *testing*.

In this paper, we propose a pragmatic approach to help creating high-quality semantics, which is inspired by the well-known approach of *Test-Driven Development* [8]. This is motivated by the fact that a semantics specification basically follows the Input-Process-Output (IPO) model, where a certain model can be seen as the input, and the semantics of that model is the output (e.g., represented as a transition system).

Figure 1 shows our approach and its relation to the testing of software systems. In the latter case, a test case consists of some input for the software system and the system's expected result. The test succeeds if the actual output of the system is equal to the expected result.

In contrast to that, we want to test a semantics specification. Therefore, a test consists of an example model ad its expected behavior. From that model and the semantics specification, a transition system can be computed which represents the model's behavior. The test succeeds if the actual behavior conforms to the expected behavior. There is only one requirement on the semantics specification technique used: the behavior of a model must be represented as a transition system which can be model checked for certain *execution events*, i.e., events occuring when a model is executed.

In the following, we will consider two scenarios while discussing our approach: the *UML scenario* and the *DSL scenario*. The former has already been introduced above: a language is given which is already equipped with an informal semantics which has to be formalized. Consequently, the goal must be to create a formal semantics specification which is as close to the informal one as possible.

The second scenario occurs when defining a *Domain Specific Language* (DSL). This type of language—only usable within a certain, usually narrow domain—has become increasingly important in the last years, partly due to the fact that the task of defining a language (including abstract and concrete syntax) is now supported by sophisticated tooling (e.g., the Eclipse foundation's *Graphical Modeling Framework* or Microsoft's *DSL Tools* [9,10]). The main difference to the

[1] Note that in the case of UML Activities, there is no commonly accepted formal semantics yet.

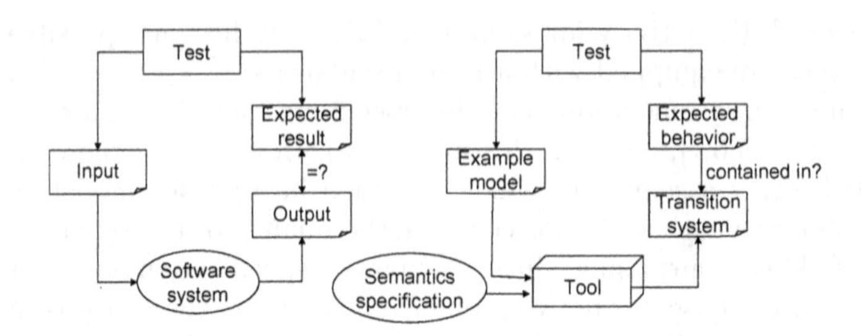

Fig. 1. Comparison of testing of software systems (left) and semantics specifications (right); the test subject is depicted as an oval

UML scenario is the lack of an informal description of the DSL's semantics; the semantics specification has to be created from scratch, usually together with a documentation targeting the users of the DSL.

In a nutshell, our approach works as follows: In a first step, a set of example models will be created which demonstrate the constructs the language under consideration consists of. Additionally, the expected semantics of each example will be identified and fixed in terms of *traces of execution events.* In the second step, the actual semantics specification is performed and tested continously, using a formalization of the traces identified in step 1.

The result is a semantics specification which realizes the expected behavior of the example models. Additionally, the language engineer has a set of examples at hand which can be used e.g. for documentation purposes within the DSL scenario.

In the following, we will explain our approach of test-driven semantics specification in detail. We will use the semantics of UML Activities as the running example, and we will construct a semantics specification using the already mentioned DMM technique. While doing this, we will lay out differences between the two scenarios where appropriate.

Structure of paper: The following section will briefly introduce the DMM specification technique, using UML Activities as the language whose semantics is to be formalized. Section 3 will show how to systematically create example models, and how to describe the expected behavior of those models in terms of traces of execution events. Section 4 will then show how to derive test cases from the example models and the associated traces, and how to use these test cases to ensure that the semantics specification indeed works as expected. Section 5 will investigate related work, and Sect. 6 will conclude and give an outlook on work to be performed in the future.

2 Dynamic Meta Modeling

We have argued in Sect. 1 that the lack of a formal semantics seriously hampers the usability of a language. There is one drawback of most formalisms, though:

they can only be used by experts of that formalism. For instance, the π calculus is a powerful formalism for semantics specification, but the average language user can not be expected to understand a π calculus specification, let alone use it to specify the semantics of a language.

DMM aims at delivering semantics specifications which indeed can be understood by such users. It does that by providing a visual language for semantics specification. Additionally, a DMM specification is based on the metamodel of the according language, allowing users who are familiar with that metamodel to easily read a DMM specification.

In a nutshell, a DMM specification is created by first extending the language's metamodel with concepts needed to express states of execution; the enhanced metamodel is called *runtime metamodel*. Then, the behavior is defined by creating operational rules which modify instances of that runtime metamodel. An overview of DMM is provided as Fig. 2.

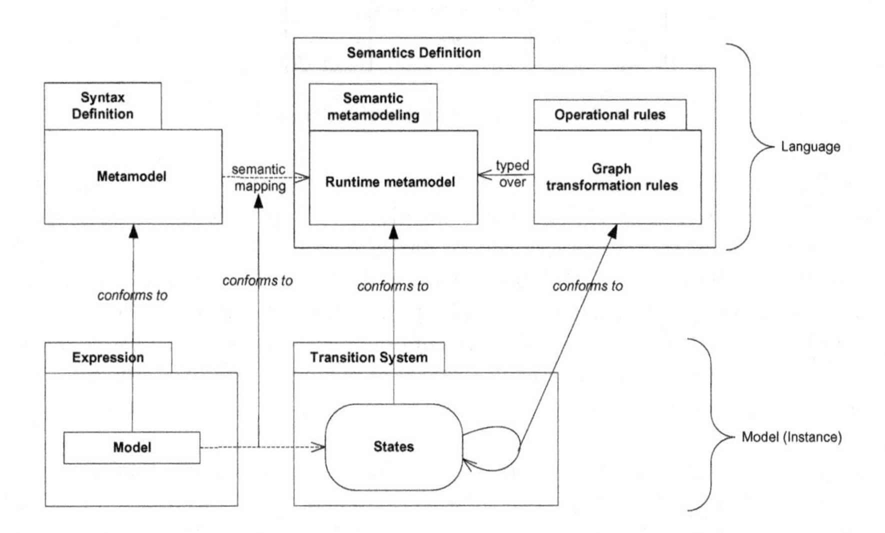

Fig. 2. Overview of the DMM approach

Let us investigate the semantics specification of UML Activities: the metamodel provided by the OMG only contains static information, i.e., it describes the set of valid UML Activities. The language's dynamic semantics is specified using natural language: for instance, the UML specification document states that "the semantics of Activities is based on token flow". However, the language's metamodel does not contain the concept of token.

Therefore, the runtime metamodel adds that concept: A class `Token` is introduced such that instances of that class are associated to the language elements they are located at (e.g., `Actions`). Therefore, an instance of the runtime metamodel describes a state of execution of an Activity by having `Token` objects sitting at particular elements.

Now, the operational rules come into play; a (simplified) DMM rule is depicted as Fig. 3. Its semantics is as follows: The rule can be applied if all incoming ActivityEdges of an Action carry at least one token. If this is the case, the rule is applied: all tokens are deleted from the incoming edges, and a new token is created on the Action, corresponding to the fact that the Action has started execution.

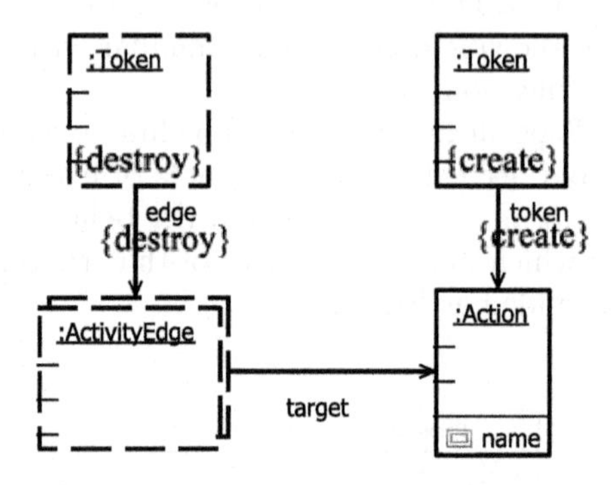

Fig. 3. DMM rule action.start(action.name)

The underlying formalism of DMM are *graph transformations*. Using the GROOVE toolset [11], DMM specifications give rise to transition systems which describe the complete behavior of the according models. The start state of such a transition system is a model (in our case, a UML Activity). Now, every rule of the DMM specification is checked for applicability; if a rule can be applied, the application will lead to a new (and different) state (where e.g. the location of tokens has changed); the resulting transition is labeled with the applied rule. For every newly derived state, the process starts over again until no new states are found.

A transition system computed in that way can then be analyzed using model checking techniques. The properties to be verified need to be formulated over the applications of rules. For instance, if we want to know if a certain Action can ever be executed, we need to check if the transition system contains a transition which is labeled with the rule corresponding to the Action's execution.

There is only one generic rule implementing the semantics of Actions. Therefore, DMM rules can be parameterized; in our example, the rule's parameter is the name of the Action the rule is working on. Consequently, if we want to know if the Action with name "A" is ever executed, we have to check whether the transition system representing the model's behavior contains a transition labeled action.start("A").

3 Creating Example Models

Defining formal semantics for a language is not an easy task. Typically, working with a formalism is more difficult than working with a standard programming language like Java, partly due to the fact that for the latter, there is very sophisticated tool support, which is not the case for the formalism used (DMM is no exception here, although we believe that DMM is more intuitive than most other formalisms; however, the tool support does not (yet) meet standards set by e.g. Java IDEs).

This is only part of the problem, though: especially in the UML scenario, one obviously has to figure out the exact meaning of the language constructs before their behavior can be formalized. This is where example models come into play: if they are chosen appropriately, they can serve as a good base for discussion of the meaning of the example's language elements.

But what means "appropriate" in this case? The example models should

- concentrate only on a few language elements and their meanings,
- all together cover all elements of the language under consideration, and
- give rise to a finite transition system.

Section 4 shows how the last requirement is needed to reuse an example model as a test case. In this section, we will describe how to systematically create appropriate example models, and we will show how to precisely but informally describe their meanings. The steps described within this section are shown in Fig. 4.

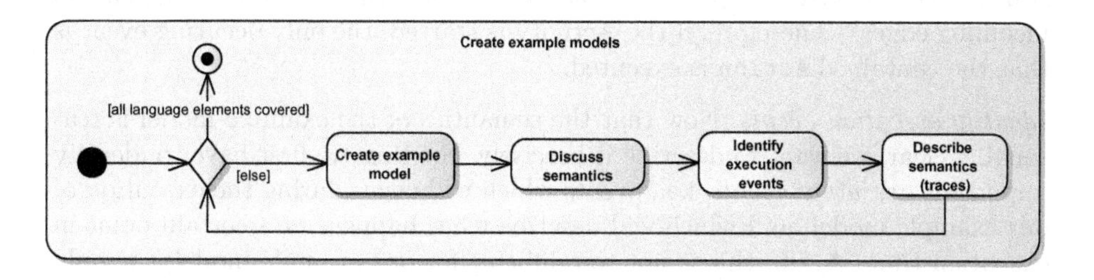

Fig. 4. Create example models

The starting point is the abstract syntax of the language under consideration. It defines all language elements and their relations with each other. In the case of the UML, the abstract syntax is given as a metamodel, but other descriptions could be used here, e.g. some kind of grammar. Based on the abstract syntax, the example models should be created step by step, systematically going from the most basic to more complex language constructs[2].

3.1 A Very Simple Example

Create example model: The very first step is the creation of an example model which should be as simple as possible. Let us investigate this in the case of UML

[2] The example models can of course be created using the language's concrete syntax.

Activities. The UML metamodel is structured into packages which depend on each other, and which indeed start with the most fundamental language elements (contained in the package `FundamentalActivities`) up to the sophisticated language elements contained in package `ExtraStructuredActivities`. Obviously, this is helpful for our task of systematically creating example models.

In fact, the package `FundamentalActivities` only allows to create Activities containing `Actions` which can be grouped using `ActivityGroups`[3]. Therefore, the first example model we create only contains one `Action`; it is depicted as Fig. 5.

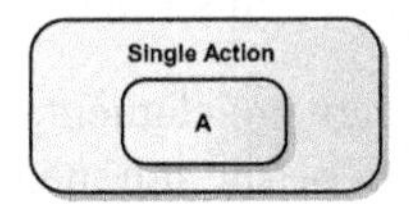

Fig. 5. Example Activity "Action" containing only one `Action` having name "A"

Discuss semantics: The next step will be to figure out the supposed behavior of our newly created example. For our simple Activity containing only one `Action`, this is not very difficult: the UML specification states that "when an activity starts, a control token is placed at each action or structured node that has no incoming edges". Therefore, if the Activity is started, the only occuring event is that the contained `Action` is executed.

Identify execution events: Now that the semantics of the example model is reasonably clear, we want to describe it precisely. For this, we first have to identify important *execution events*, i.e., events which will occur during the execution of our example model, and which will describe what happens at a certain point in execution time. Again, this is not too difficult for our example model: the only event is that the contained `Action` is executed. We therefore define an execution event ActionExecutes. Since we will later refer to more than one `Action`, we parameterize that execution event with the `Action`'s name.

Describe semantics: The last step of treating the current example model is to actually describe the model's semantics. We do that in terms of *traces of execution events*: Here, a trace is just a possible sequence of events as identified above. Our example model only has one possible trace, which we can describe as

ActionExecutes("A")

Obviously, the example presented is very simple, but it serves well to demonstrate the overall approach. The next step would now be to proceed to more complex examples, taking the package structure of the UML metamodel into account. It turns out that the concept of `ActivityEdges` is introduced in package

[3] Note that according to the UML specification, `ActivityGroups` "have no inherent semantics" and are therefore not used in our examples.

BasicActivities, together with concepts like InitialNode (which produces a token when the Activity starts) and ActivityFinalNode (which consumes tokens). Therefore, the next example model will consist of a sequence of two Actions, connected by an ActivityEdge, with an according trace consisting of the execution of the two Actions in the according order. We skip that example model and proceed to a more complex one in the next section.

3.2 A More Complex Example

Let us now turn to a (slightly) more complex example model, which is depicted as Fig. 6. Its purpose is to demonstrate the semantics of the DecisionNode and MergeNode.

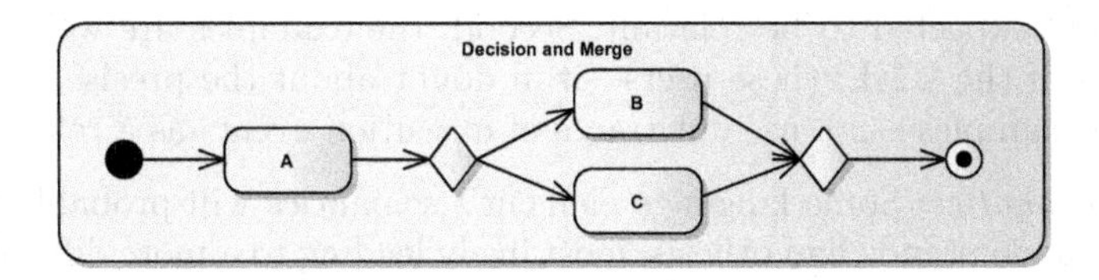

Fig. 6. Example Activity containing a simple DecisionNode/MergeNode structure

This example is interesting because of the fact that it allows for more than one possible execution: a token flowing through the Activity will—as soon as it has passed Action "A"—be routed either to Action "B" *or* to Action "C". Therefore, we will describe the model's behavior by two traces of execution events:

ActionExecutes("A") ActionExecutes("B")

and

ActionExecutes("A") ActionExecutes("C")

We decided to reduce the semantics of Activities to the possible orders of execution of Actions, since the Actions are the places where the actual work will be performed. However, it would also be possible to use more fine-grained traces like InitialNode() ActionExecutes("A") DecisionNode() ActionExecutes("B") MergeNode() ActivityFinalNode().

In fact, some execution events (e.g., when a token traverses an edge) might become important only when investigating more complex examples at a later stage. If this is the case, an additional event can (and should) of course be used to describe the complex model's behavior. Note that this does not render the traces of the simpler examples useless: if such an execution event does occur in a simpler model, too, but has not been used to describe that model's behavior, it is not important for that behavior; otherwise, it would have been added to the traces of the simpler model when its behavior was investigated. In other words: there is no need to refine the traces of a simple model at a later stage.

3.3 Guidelines for Creating Example Models

We have seen how to systematically create example models, and how to precisely but informally describe their behavior. Before we continue with the actual semantics specification and derivation of test cases from the examples, we will outline a few more guidelines for the creation of the examples.

Existing Examples: In the UML scenario, the starting point for semantics specification is the existing but informal specification provided by the OMG. That specification already contains many example models, which should be reused for two reasons: first, these models have been developed by the UML creators and are therefore expected to be relevant. Second, the examples are well-known to other users of the UML; these users—if in doubt about the precise meaning of one of the examples—can use our traces of execution events as a reference.

Difficult Semantics: Some language element's semantics will probably be more difficult to understand than other's, most likely leading to a more difficult to implement semantics specification (leading to a higher probability of introducing flaws into the semantics specification). Such elements will probably be identified when discussing their precise meaning. In this case, more example models containing these elements should be created, and each of these examples should concentrate on one or more of the identified difficulties.

Language creation: In the DSL scenario, a new language has to be created from scratch, having certain target users in mind (e.g., business analysts). Creation of the new language should involve these users, and the easiest way to do this is through the discussion of example models, including their precise meanings. In other words: the example models should be created in parallel with the actual language. The examples can later be reused for documentation of the new language.

4 Creating the Semantics Specification and Deriving Test Cases

We have already argued in Sect. 3 that formal semantics specification is a difficult task. Therefore, we have described how to first gain an understanding of the semantics to be created by investigating example models, and by precisely describing the example's behavior by means of traces of execution events. In this section, we will perform the actual semantics specification, and we will test that specification using the example models and their behavior. As formalism, we will use DMM as briefly introduced in Sect. 2. The overall process is depicted as Fig. 7.

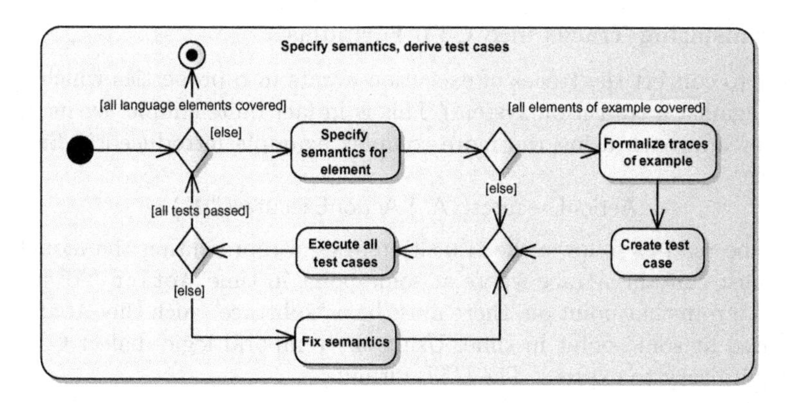

Fig. 7. Specify semantics, create test cases from example models

4.1 Creating the Semantics Specification

Recall from Sect. 2 that DMM uses operational rules to describe behavior: a DMM rule has a precondition and a postcondition, formulated in terms of typed graphs. If a state fulfills the precondition (i.e., if the precondition's graph can be found within the current state graph), the rule will be applied, leading to a new state which fulfills the postcondition (i.e., the precondition's graph will be replaced by the postcondition's graph within the current state, leading to a new state).

This means that in principle, one ore more DMM rules have to be defined for each language construct. Naturally, one starts with defining DMM rules for the more simple language constructs and adds rules for more complex constructs step by step. Now, the idea is that as soon as all language constructs a particular example model consists of are covered, that example is executable, and its execution should result in a behavior similar to the one identified when creating the example (and described by traces of execution events).

In other words: the example model and the current state of the semantics specification should give rise to a transition system, and that transition system should contain the traces of execution events (and only those traces). This puts a requirement on the DMM specification we are creating: in Sect. 2, we have seen that the transition systems produced by a DMM specification and a model can be model checked against CTL expressions about the application of DMM rules. Since we want to check the transition systems for traces of execution events, we must make sure that for each such event, a corresponding DMM rule exists.

Note that this is not a restriction, but a benefit of our approach: one of the goals of creating a formal semantics specification is to check the behavioral quality of models, i.e., to check whether certain behavioral properties hold for the model under consideration. These properties need to be expressed in terms of execution events. To put it another way: our approach makes sure that the resulting semantics specification indeed allows for the verification of such properties.

4.2 Translating Traces into CTL Formulas

But how to convert the traces of execution events into properties which can be checked against a transition system? This is in fact quite simple; let us demonstrate our approach using the more complex example introduced in Sect. 3.2. The trace

ActionExecutes("A") ActionExecutes("B")

can also be read as follows: the transition system representing the model's behavior must contain a trace where at some point in time, `Action` "A" must be executed. From that point on, there must be a "subtrace" such that `Action` "B" is executed at some point in time. Using the temporal logic dialect CTL [12], this is quite easy to express: The CTL formula

$$\mathbf{EF}(r)$$

expresses the fact that there must **E**xist a path such that **F**inally[4], property r holds. Since we model check against the application of DMM rules, r will be a such a rule (and reveals information about the state the rule is applied to: it must be the case that the precondition of r holds for that state).

Now, our DMM specification will contain a rule action.start(action.name), corresponding to the execution event ActionExecutes(name) as described earlier. Therefore, the trace shown above can be translated into the following CTL formula, which can then be checked against the transition system:

$$p_1 := \mathbf{EF}(\mathsf{action.start("A")} \land \mathbf{EF}(\mathsf{action.start("B")}))$$

Checking that the CTL formula is true with respect to our transition system ensures that it indeed contains the trace as desired. There is one remaining problem, though: Up to now, we only know that there are traces such that `Actions` "A" and "B" are executed, but we do not know what happens before "A", between "A" and "B", and after "B".

To make our CTL formula more precise with respect to that problem, we have to dive deeper into CTL: we have to make use of the **U**ntil operator, the ne**X**t operator, and the **A**ll quantifier. To explain the new formula, we first define some helper constructs.

First, to be able to use a more compact representation, we will write action.start("A") as a_A (a_B, a_C accordingly). Now, let $R = \{a_A, a_B, a_C\}$ be the set of all rules corresponding to execution events relevant for the model under consideration. Finally, we define the predicate $\hat{R}$ as $\bigwedge_{r \in R}(\neg r)$.

We will now construct the formula step by step. The first part looks as follows:

$$P_1 := \mathbf{E}(\hat{R}\,\mathbf{U}\,X_A)$$

The intuition is that we want to find the first occurrence of rule a_A on some path; therefore, we require that none of the rules contained in R occurs **U**ntil a_A occurs (which will be part of X_A). The definition of X_A reads as

$$X_A := a_A \land \mathbf{EX}\,\mathbf{E}(\hat{R}\,\mathbf{U} X_B)$$

[4] "Finally" must be understood as "at some point in time" here.

This is the most important part of the formula to construct. The idea is that since we have found the first occurrence of a_A, we want to make sure eventually in the future X_B will hold, and before that, now other rules out of R will occur. Note that the **EX** is needed since we have to look at the next state, because in the current state, a_A holds, so $\hat{R}$ can never be true. Now for X_B:

$$X_B := a_B \wedge \mathbf{AX}\,\mathbf{AG}(\hat{R})$$

This formula completes our definition of P_1. It expresses the fact that after a_B has occurred, no other rule from R will ever occur again on all paths.

All together, P_1 expresses exactly the desired property of our transition system: it is true iff the transition system contains a trace such that a_A and a_B occur in the desired order, and there are no other occurrences of rules from R at other places. Additionally, it is easy to see that the above construction can be extended to traces of arbitrary length by using several expressions similar to X_A, where a_A is replaced by the rule to be checked, and by nesting them as above.

4.3 Creating Test Cases

In the last section, we have seen how to translate a trace of execution events into a CTL formula, which can then be model checked against the transition system. It is now straight-forward to create a test case from a model and a set of such traces.

First, all the traces belonging to the example model under consideration have to be translated into CTL formulas as explained above. In the case of our more complex UML Activity, this will result in two CTL formulas P_1 and P_2 (we have seen P_1 in the last section). Then, a model checker can be used to verify if all these properties hold. If this is the case, we know that the expected behavior is contained within the transition system; this means that our semantics specification so far produces the behavior as desired. Otherwise, we know which trace of execution events is not contained in the resulting behavior, and we can use that information to fix the semantics specification.

It remains to show whether this is the only behavior produced by our semantics specification: there might be other traces which do not fulfill P_1 or P_2, i.e., some undesired behavior is going on. Therefore, we check one more property which ensures that the transition system indeed only contains the desired behavior:

$$\mathbf{AF}(P_1 \vee P_2)$$

The above formula holds iff for all traces through the transition system, either P_1 or P_2 hold. Its verification will fail if the transition system contains undesired behavior. In this case, the model checker will provide a counter example, i.e., a trace which does not belong to the expected ones. That counter example can then be used to fix the semantics specification.

4.4 Automatic Execution of Test Cases

To support the creation of DMM semantics specifications, we have implemented a Java framework which enables the automatic execution of test cases as described above. For this, we have used JUnit, which provides convenient ways to execute our test cases, including a GUI showing which tests passed or failed for which reasons. An execution of a test case works as follows:

First, the example model under consideration is translated into a GROOVE graph, which serves as the start state for the transition system to be computed. Next, the traces of execution events are translated into CTL formulas as described in Sect. 4.2; the traces themselves are (for now) contained in a simple text file. Then, the generation of the transition system is started, using the current state of the DMM specification to be built. Finally, the CTL formulas are verified one by one; if a verification fails, the according JUnit test will fail, providing a message which points at the trace not being contained in the transition system.

4.5 Generalizing the Approach

We have proposed in Sect. 1 that our approach can be used for every semantics specification which gives rise to transition systems on which the occurrence of execution events can be model checked. In Sect. 4.2, we have seen how this works for DMM specifications, where the execution events correspond to DMM rules whose application can indeed be model checked.

It is now straight-forward to generalize our approach to other semantics specification techniques: for each execution event e, a property p has to be defined such that if p holds for a state s, that state corresponds to the occurrence of the according event e. The property p can then be used within the CTL formulas, just as we did with the corresponding DMM rule. The construction of the CTL formulas as well as the execution of the test cases does not change.

5 Related Work

The existing work related to our approach of test-driven semantics specification can mainly be grouped into two categories: related test approaches and language engineering. For the former, a comparable approach is the so-called *scenario-based testing*. Xuandong et.al. [13] use UML Sequence diagrams to validate Java programs for safety consistency (sequences of method calls which must not occur during execution) and mandatory consistency (sequences of methods calls which have to occur). The main difference to our approach is that scenario-based testing focuses on testing a concrete object-oriented system, i.e., the communication between some objects, whereas we are testing semantics specifications describing the behavior of a complete language.

In the area of language engineering, several approaches for defining DSLs exist. For instance, MetaCase provides MetaEdit [14], Microsoft provides the DSL

Tools as part of MS Visual Studio [15], and the Eclipse foundation provides the Graphical ModelingFramework [9]; all these approaches aim at an easy creation of visual languages. openArchitectureWare [16] provides a set of tools which allow for the easy creation of textual languages, including powerful editor support.

To our knowledge, all the above approaches focus on defining a DSL's behavioral semantics by providing support for code generation, but they do not provide a means to systematically create high-quality code generators; the generation is pretty much done ad-hoc.

The same holds for other semantics specification techniques which can be used in language engineering, e.g., the π calculus [17], Structural Operational Semantics [6], and others – we are not aware of a comparable test-driven process which helps to create high-quality semantics specifications.

6 Conclusion

In this paper, we have shown a test-driven semantics specification process which helps the language engineer to create high-quality semantics specifications. Our process is divided into two phases: in the first phase, the semantics of the language under consideration is discussed using example models, and the supposed behavior is described precisely as traces of execution events.

The actual semantics specification is performed in the second phase, where the example models serve as test cases: the traces of execution events are formalized using CTL and then model checked against the transition systems resulting from the example models and the language's semantics specification.

Test-driven software development has a positive impact on the quality of software systems in several ways: for instance, when implementing new features, resulting regressions can be identified by executing tests of the old code; there is also some evidence that the test-driven approach leads to cleaner interfaces and helps the developer to focus on the functionality to be implemented; last, but not least, the developer has confidence that the resulting code at least works for the existing test cases [8].

We believe that our approach transfers these benefits of test-driven software development into the world of semantics specifications, resulting in specifications of higher quality. Additionally, in the DSL scenario, the resulting test cases can be used not only for testing, but also for discussions with the customer and for documentation purposes.

The description of a model's behavior as traces of execution events has one drawback, though: such traces might be quite redundant. For instance, consider the UML Activity shown as Fig. 6: if `Action` "A" would be replaced by a sequence of 10 `Actions`, the resulting traces would be much longer, and they would only differ in the very last `Action` execution. Therefore, we plan to investigate more compact representations of the example model's behavior.

Acknowledgements. We want to thank our colleagues Jan-Christopher Bals and Björn Metzler for many helpful discussions.

References

1. Object Management Group: OMG Unified Modeling Language (OMG UML) – Superstructure, Version 2.2. (February 2009), http://www.omg.org/docs/formal/09-02-02.pdf
2. van der Aalst, W.: Verification of Workflow Nets. In: Azéma, P., Balbo, G. (eds.) ICATPN 1997. LNCS, vol. 1248, pp. 407–426. Springer, Heidelberg (1997)
3. Engels, G., Soltenborn, C., Wehrheim, H.: Analysis of UML Activities using Dynamic Meta Modeling. In: Bosangue, M.M., Johnsen, E.B. (eds.) FMOODS 2007. LNCS, vol. 4468, pp. 76–90. Springer, Heidelberg (2007)
4. Hausmann, J.H.: Dynamic Meta Modeling. PhD thesis, University of Paderborn (2005)
5. Zhang, K.B., Orgun, M.A., Zhang, K.: Visual Language Semantics Specification in the VisPro System. In: Jin, J.S., Eades, P., Feng, D.D., Yan, H. (eds.) Selected papers from the 2002 Pan-Sydney workshop on Visualisation (VIP 2002). ACM International Conference Proceeding Series, vol. 161, pp. 121–127. Australian Computer Society, Inc., Darlinghurst (2003)
6. Plotkin, G.D.: A Structural Approach to Operational Semantics. J. Log. Algebr. Program. 60–61, 17–139 (2004)
7. Hemingway, G., Su, H., Chen, K., Koo, T.J.: A semantic anchoring infrastructure for the design of embedded systems. In: COMPSAC (1), pp. 287–294. IEEE Computer Society, Los Alamitos (2007)
8. Beck, K.: Test-Driven Development by Example. Addison-Wesley Longman, Amsterdam (2002)
9. Eclipse Foundation: Graphical Modeling Framework (2009), http://www.eclipse.org/modeling/gmf/ (accessed 5-5-2009)
10. Microsoft: DSL Tools (2009), http://msdn.microsoft.com/en-us/library/bb126235.aspx (accessed 5-5-2009)
11. Rensink, A.: The GROOVE Simulator: A Tool for State Space Generation. In: Pfaltz, J.L., Nagl, M., Böhlen, B. (eds.) AGTIVE 2003. LNCS, vol. 3062, pp. 479–485. Springer, Heidelberg (2004)
12. Clarke, E.M., Emerson, E.A., Sistla, A.P.: Automatic Verification of Finite-State Concurrent Systems using Temporal Logic Specifications. ACM Trans. Program. Lang. Syst. 8(2), 244–263 (1986)
13. Xuandong, L., Linzhang, W., Xiaokang, Q., Bin, L., Jiesong, Y., Jianhua, Z., Guoliang, Z.: Runtime Verification of Java Programs for Scenario-Based Specifications. In: Pinho, L.M., Harbour, M.G. (eds.) Ada-Europe 2006. LNCS, vol. 2006, pp. 94–105. Springer, Heidelberg (2006)
14. Smolander, K., Lyytinen, K., Tahvanainen, V.P., Marttiin, P.: MetaEdit: a Flexible Graphical Environment for Methodology Modelling. In: Andersen, R., Solvberg, A., Bubenko Jr., J.A. (eds.) CAiSE 1991. LNCS, vol. 498, pp. 168–193. Springer, Heidelberg (1991)
15. Cook, S., Jones, G., Kent, S., Wills, A.: Domain-Specific Development with Visual Studio DSL Tools. Addison-Wesley Professional, Reading (2007)
16. Haase, A., Völter, M., Efftinge, S., Kolb, B.: Introduction to openArchitectureWare 4.1.2. MDD Tool Implementers Forum (Part of the TOOLS 2007 conference, Zürich) (2007)
17. Milner, R., Parrow, J., Walker, D.: A Calculus of Mobile Processes, I. Information and Computation 100(1), 1–40 (1992)

Scalable Semantic Annotation Using Lattice-Based Ontologies*

Man-Kit Leung[1], Thomas Mandl[2], Edward A. Lee[1],
Elizabeth Latronico[2], Charles Shelton[2], Stavros Tripakis[1], and Ben Lickly[1]

[1] UC Berkeley, Berkeley CA 94720, USA
{mankit,eal,stavros,blickly}@eecs.berkeley.edu
[2] Bosch Research LLC, Pittsburgh, PA 15212 USA
thomas.mandl@at, elizabeth.latronico@us, charles.shelton@us.bosch.com

Abstract. Including semantic information in models helps to expose modeling errors early in the design process, engage a designer in a deeper understanding of the model, and standardize concepts and terminology across a development team. It is impractical, however, for model builders to manually annotate every modeling element with semantic properties. This paper demonstrates a correct, scalable and automated method to infer semantic properties using lattice-based ontologies, given relatively few manual annotations. Semantic concepts and their relationships are formalized as a lattice, and relationships within and between components are expressed as a set of constraints and acceptance criteria relative to the lattice. Our inference engine automatically infers properties wherever they are not explicitly specified. Our implementation leverages the infrastructure in the Ptolemy II type system to get efficient and scalable inference and consistency checking. We demonstrate the approach on a non-trivial Ptolemy II model of an adaptive cruise control system.

1 Introduction

Model-integrated development for embedded systems [1,2] commonly uses actor-oriented software component models [3,4]. In such models, software components (called actors) execute concurrently and communicate by sending messages via interconnected ports. Examples that support such designs include Simulink, from MathWorks, LabVIEW, from National Instruments, SystemC, component and activity diagrams in SysML and UML 2 [5,6,7], and a number of research tools such as ModHel'X [8], TDL [9], HetSC [10], ForSyDe [11], Metropolis [12], and

* This work was supported in part by the Center for Hybrid and Embedded Software Systems (CHESS) at UC Berkeley, which receives support from the National Science Foundation (NSF awards #0720882 (CSR-EHS: PRET) and #0720841 (CSR-CPS)), the U. S. Army Research Office (ARO #W911NF-07-2-0019), the U. S. Air Force Office of Scientific Research (MURI #FA9550-06-0312), the Air Force Research Lab (AFRL), the State of California Micro Program, and the following companies: Agilent, Bosch, Lockheed-Martin, National Instruments, Thales, and Toyota.

A. Schürr and B. Selic (Eds.): MODELS 2009, LNCS 5795, pp. 393–407, 2009.

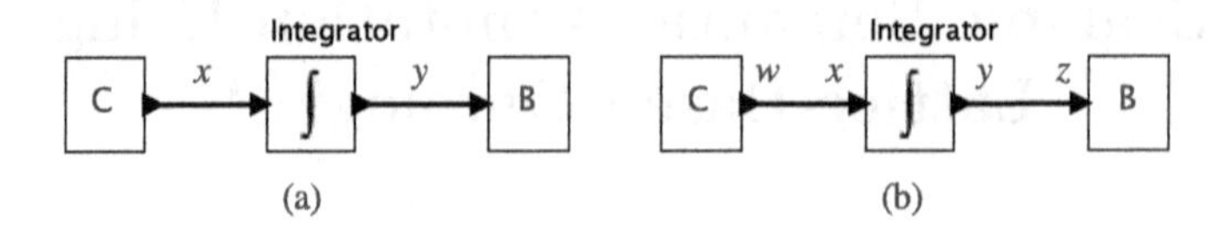

Fig. 1. Models using an Integrator, where (a) labels connections and (b) labels ports

Ptolemy II [13]. The techniques of this paper can also be extended for equational models such as Modelica [14].

The goal of this paper is to improve model engineering techniques by providing semantic annotations. Semantic annotations help in several ways. First, if we can check consistency across such annotations, then they expose modeling errors early in the design process. This is similar to the benefits provided by a good type system. Second, they engage a designer in a deeper understanding of the model. Third, they help standardize semantic information across a development team. This can help prevent misunderstandings. Annotations can be provided manually by the designer or inferred by a tool. A model may have multiple sets of annotations, each specific to a particular use case domain.

To illustrate the key idea, consider a simple modeling component commonly used in a language such as Simulink for control system design, an Integrator. Such a component might be represented graphically as shown in Figure 1. The inputs and outputs of this component are represented as ports, depicted as small black triangles, with the input port pointing in to the component and the output port pointing out. These ports mediate communication between components. Components are composed by interconnecting their ports, and our goal is to ensure that such composition is consistent with the designer's intent.

The Integrator component has some particular properties that constrain its use. First, its input and output ports receive and send continuous-time signals, approximated in a software system by samples. Second, the samples will have data type double. Third, if the input represents the speed of a vehicle, then the output represents the position of the vehicle from some starting point; if the input represents acceleration, then the output represents speed. Fourth, the output value may vary over time even if the input does not.

A conventional type system can check for correct usage with respect to the second property, the data type of the ports. Such a type system can check for incompatible connections, and also infer types that may be implied by the constraints of the components. A behavioral type system can check for correct usage with respect to the first property, the structure of the signals communicated between components [15]. The purpose of this paper is to give a configurable and extensible mechanism for performing checks and inference with respect to properties like the third and fourth.

We refer to the third and fourth properties as **semantic types**, or more informally as **properties**. Properties in a model will typically be rather domain specific. The fact that a model operates on signals representing "speed" and "acceleration" is a consequence of the application domain for which the model is built. Thus, unlike type systems, in our case it is essential for the model builders to be able to construct their own domain-specific **property system**. Our goal is to provide a framework for doing that without requiring that application designers understand the nuances of type theories.

An even more essential goal is that our system be sound, correct, and scalable. This will be our primary goal. Making it easy to construct and use such a property system is a secondary goal, equally important to the success of the technique, but useless without the primary goal. To accomplish the primary goal, we build on the theory of Hindley-Milner type systems [16], the efficient inference algorithm of Rehof and Mogensen [17], the implementation of this algorithm in Ptolemy II [18], and the application of similar mathematical foundations to formal concept analysis [19].

The paper is organized as follows: we introduce first the concept lattice data structure and review some of its useful properties. Section 3 then gives an overview of the mathematical foundation of our property system as a fixed point of a monotonic function. Section 4 shows how the monotonic function can be defined implicitly by a set of composable constraints associated with model components. We then give an in-depth application in Section 5, an adaptive cruise control model. Finally, we briefly describe the software architecture of our implementation in Section 6 and discuss related work in Section 7.

2 Concept Lattice

In a Hindley-Milner type system, data types are elements of a complete lattice, an example of which is illustrated in Figure 2. In that diagram, each node represents a data type, and the arrows between them represent an ordering relation. In type systems this relation can be interpreted as an "is a" relation or as a "lossless convertability" relation. For example, an Int can be converted losslessly to a Long or a Double, but a Long cannot be converted to a Double nor vice versa.

A **complete lattice** is a set P and a binary relation $\leq$ satisfying certain properties. Specifically, the relation is a **partial order relation**, meaning it is **reflexive** ($\forall\ p \in P, p \leq p$), **antisymmetric** ($\forall\ p_1, p_2 \in P, p_1 \leq p_2$ and $p_2 \leq p_1 \Rightarrow p_1 = p_2$), and **transitive** ($\forall\ p_1, p_2, p_3 \in P, p_1 \leq p_2$ and $p_2 \leq p_3 \Rightarrow p_1 \leq p_3$). A lattice also requires that any two elements $p_1, p_2 \in P$ have a unique least upper bound (called the **join** and written $p_1 \vee p_2$) and a greatest lower bound (called the **meet** and written $p_1 \wedge p_2$). To be a complete lattice we further require that every subset of P has a join and a meet in P. Every complete lattice has a top element and a bottom element. The top element is typically written as $\top$ and the bottom element $\bot$. A concept lattice is a complete lattice.

3 Property Systems

A **property system** consists of a **concept lattice**, a collection of constraints associated with modeling components, and a collection of acceptance criteria. The type lattice of Figure 2 is an example of a concept lattice, as are figures 3

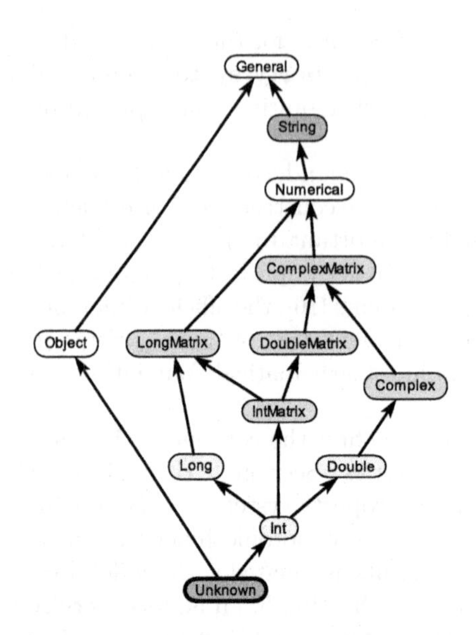

Fig. 2. A type lattice modeling a simplified version of the Ptolemy II type system

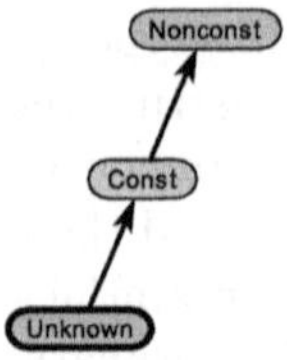

Nonconst
Const
Unknown

Fig. 3. A property lattice modeling signal dynamics

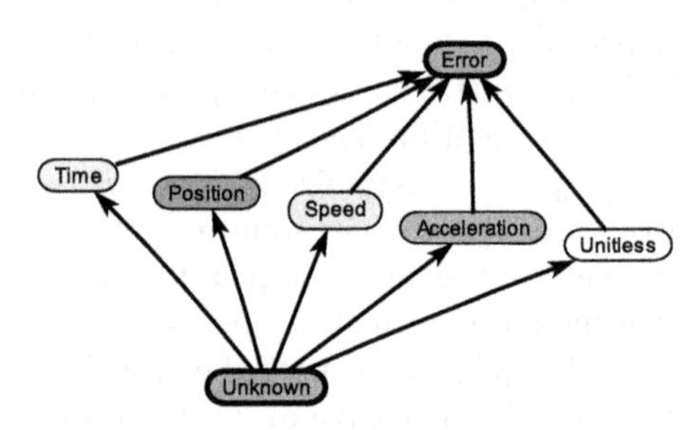

Fig. 4. A lattice ontology for dimensions Time, Position, Speed, Acceleration, and Unitless (dimensionless)

and 4. We will illustrate how to use the *dimension* concept lattice (Figure 4) to check for correct usage of an Integrator component as discussed above.

Consider a very simple model with three components as shown in Figure 1(a). Component C provides samples of a continuous-time signal to the integrator, which performs numerical integration and provides samples of a continuous signal to component B. Suppose that we associate the input x of the Integrator with a concept p_x in the concept lattice L. We say that the input of the Integrator "has property" p_x. We wish to catch errors, where, for example, component C sends position information to the Integrator, and component B expects speed information. This is incorrect because position is the integral of speed, not the other way around. We can construct a property system that systematically identifies such errors.

The concept lattice for this property system is shown in Figure 4. To complete the property system, we need to encode the constraints imposed by the integrator. To do this, we leverage mathematical properties of a complete lattice.

Suppose we have a model that has n model elements with properties. In Figure 1(a), we have two such elements, x and y, and their properties are $(p_x, p_y) \in L^2$, where L is the concept lattice of Figure 4. A property system for this model defines a **monotonic function** $F\colon L^2 \to L^2$ mapping pairs of properties to pairs of properties. Monotonic means that

$$(p_x, p_y) \leq (p'_x, p'_y) \Rightarrow F(p_x, p_y) \leq F(p'_x, p'_y).$$

A **fixed point** of such a function is a pair (p_1, p_2) where $(p_1, p_2) = F(p_1, p_2)$. The theory of lattices tells us that any such function has a unique least fixed point that can be found iteratively as follows

$$(p_1, p_2) = \lim_{n \to \infty} F^n(\bot, \bot). \tag{1}$$

We define the **inferred properties** of a model to be this least fixed point. The least fixed point associates with each model element a property in the lattice, which is the inferred property for that model element. If the lattice is finite, the above induction terminates in a finite number of steps.

Even for the simple Integrator example above, defining the function F is rather tedious (we explain below that it can be defined implicitly in an elegant and modular way). To reflect the constraints of the integrator, the function is

$$F(p_x, p_y) = \begin{cases} (\top, \top) & \text{if } p_x = \top \text{ or } p_y = \top \\ (p_x \vee A, p_y \vee S) & \text{else if } p_x = A \text{ or } p_y = S \\ (p_x \vee S, p_y \vee P) & \text{else if } p_x = S \text{ or } p_y = P \\ (p_x \vee U, p_y \vee T) & \text{else if } p_x = U \text{ or } p_y = T \\ (p_x \vee p_y, p_x \vee p_y) & \text{otherwise} \end{cases} \tag{2}$$

where $L = \{\bot, T, P, S, A, U, \top\}$ are the elements of the lattice in Figure 4.

The least fixed point of this function is $(p_x, p_y) = (\bot, \bot)$, found in one step by (1), which we interpret to mean that we do not have enough information to draw conclusions about the properties associated with x and y.

Suppose that component B is known to read data at its input that is interpreted as Speed. Then the function F simplifies to

$$F(p_x, p_y) = \begin{cases} (\top, \top) & \text{if } p_x = \top \text{ or } p_y = \top \\ (p_x \vee A, S) & \text{otherwise.} \end{cases}$$

In this case, the least fixed point is $(p_x, p_y) = (A, S)$. The fact that x has property Acceleration is inferred.

Suppose further that component C is known to provide data at its output that is interpreted as Position. We can encode that fact together with the previous assumptions with the function:

$$F(p_x, p_y) = (\top, \top)$$

which has least fixed point $(p_x, p_y) = (\top, \top)$, which we can interpret as a modeling error. Of course, we don't want model builders to directly give the function F. We will show below how it is inferred from constraints on the components.

We are closer to being able to formally define a property system. A **property system** for n modeling elements is a concept lattice P, a monotonic function $F\colon P^n \to P^n$, and a collection of **acceptance criteria** that define whether the least fixed point yields an acceptable set of properties. We next show how the monotonic function F can be implicitly defined in a modular way by giving constraints associated with the components.

4 Property Constraints and Acceptance Criteria

Rehof and Mogensen [17] give a modular and compositional way to implicitly define a class of monotonic functions F on a lattice and an efficient algorithm for finding the least fixed point of this function. The algorithm has been shown to be scalable to very large number of constraints, and is widely used in type systems, including that of Ptolemy II, which we leverage. Specifically, for a fixed concept lattice L, this algorithm has a computational upper bound that scales linearly with the number of inequality constraints, which is proportional to the number of model components, or the model size.

First, assume model element x (such as a port) has property $p_x \in L$, and model element y has property $p_y \in L$. For any two such properties $p_x, p_y \in L$, define an **inequality constraint** to be an inequality of the form

$$p_x \leq p_y. \tag{3}$$

Such an inequality constrains the property value of Y to be higher than or equal to the property value of X, according to the ordering in the lattice. An arbitrary collection of inequality constraints implicitly defines a monotonic function $F\colon L^n \to L^n$ that yields the least $(p_1, \cdots, p_n)$ that satisfies the inequality constraints for modeling elements 1 through n. Of course, two inequality constraints can be combined to form an **equality constraint**,

$$p_x \leq p_y \text{ and } p_y \leq p_x \Rightarrow p_x = p_y \tag{4}$$

because the order relation is antisymmetric.

In Figure 1(a), we implicitly assumed an equality constraint for the output of C and the input of the Integrator. We could equally well have assumed that each port was a distinct model element, as shown in Figure 1(b), and imposed inequality constraints $p_w \leq p_x$ and $p_y \leq p_z$. These constraints are implied by each connection between ports. Our tool permits either interpretation for the port connections, equality or inequality constraints.

Rehof and Mogensen also permit constraints that we call **monotonic function constraints**, which have the form

$$f(p_1, \cdots, p_n) \leq p_x \tag{5}$$

where $p_1, \cdots, p_n$ and p_x represent the properties of arbitrary model elements, and $f\colon P^n \to P$ is a monotonic function whose definition as a function of the property variables $p_1, \cdots, p_n$ is part of the definition of the constraint. Notice that this function does not have the same structure as the function F above. Its domain and range are not necessarily the same, so it need not have a fixed point. An example of such a monotonic function is a **constant function**, for example

$$f_s(p_1, \cdots, p_n) = S$$

where S represents Speed. Hence, to express that component B in Figure 1(b) assumes its input is Speed, we simply assert the constraint

$$f_s(p_1, \cdots, p_n) \leq p_z \ ,$$

which of course just means

$$S \leq p_z \; . \tag{6}$$

However, this does not quite assert that $p_z = S$. Indeed, that assertion would require an inequality different from (5) that is not permitted by Rehof and Mogensen's algorithm. Hence, to complete the specification, we can specify **acceptance criteria** of the form

$$p_i \leq l \tag{7}$$

where $l \in L$ is a particular constant and p_i is a variable representing the property held by the ith model element. For example, we can give the acceptance criterion

$$p_z \leq S \; , \tag{8}$$

which when combined with (6), means $p_z = S$, or z is Speed. We can also declare an acceptance criterion that for each model element i with property p_i,

$$p_i < \top \; , \tag{9}$$

which means that $\top$ is not an acceptable answer for any property.

Acceptance criteria do not become part of the definition of the monotonic function F, and hence have no effect on the determination of the least fixed point. Once the least fixed point is found, the acceptance criteria are checked. If any one of them is violated, then we can conclude that there is no fixed point that satisfies all the constraints and acceptance criteria. We declare this situation to be a modeling error.

Constraints of the Integrator include one given in the form of (5) as

$$f_I(p_z) \leq p_x \quad \text{where} \quad f_I(p_z) = \begin{cases} \bot & \text{if } p_z = \bot \\ S & \text{if } p_z = P \\ A & \text{if } p_z = S \\ U & \text{if } p_z = T \\ \top & \text{otherwise} \end{cases} \tag{10}$$

This constraint is a property of the Integrator and is used together with other constraints to implicitly define the monotonic function F. The constraint (10) is more intuitive than (2) because it directly describes constraints of the Integrator component, and more modular because it only describes a constraint of the Integrator. The complete constraints for the Integrator is shown in Table 1.

To see how this works in Figure 1(b), suppose we assume constraints (6) and (10). Together, these imply that $A \leq p_x$. Our inference engine finds the least fixed point to be $p_w = p_x = A$ and $p_y = p_z = S$. This solution meets the acceptance criterion in (8). We leave it as an exercise for the reader to determine that if instead of (6) we require $A \leq p_z$, then the least fixed point is $p_w = p_x = p_y = p_z = \top$, which fails to meet acceptance criterion (9). This would be a modeling error because the output of the Integrator cannot represent Acceleration in our ontology.

In summary, a **property system** is a concept lattice, a set of constraints in the form of (3) or (5), and a set of acceptance criteria in the form of (7). The constraints come from component definitions, an interpretation for connections between components, and annotations made on the model by the model builder.

5 Adaptive Cruise Control Example

We now give a detailed example showing how this mechanism can be used in practical models. Consider an adaptive cruise control system that detects slower vehicles in front of a following vehicle and adjusts the speed of the following vehicle accordingly. Adaptive cruise control requires some form of inter-vehicle coordination, which can be implemented with a radar transmitter/receiver in the following vehicle [20]. The system must tolerate faults in coordination, such as sensor misalignment or erroneous power supply voltage for radar transceivers.

A model of such a system is shown in Figure 5 (inspired by Ptolemy II demo created by Jie Liu). In that (oversimplified) example, a leading car transmits via some channel a packet that consists of a time stamp and its current acceleration, speed, and position. A following car will use that information to adjust its speed, but only if it trusts the information it is receiving. To determine whether it trusts that information, it checks the information against a simple model of the leading car. Specifically, if a packet indicates a certain position and speed at a particular time, then when it gets a new packet, it performs a simple sanity check to see whether the new position makes sense, given the previous position and speed. If it does, then it trusts the packet.

The model composes submodels, and our task will be to show that our ontology framework can detect errors in such composition, and thus help ensure correctness of the model. Our framework can also help transform or optimize models by enabling transformations that are based on semantic annotations.

The component on the far left of Figure 5 is a model of a driver, the internals of which are not shown. The driver submodel feeds data to a car model (labeled Leading Car Model), the internals of which are shown in Figure 6. This models

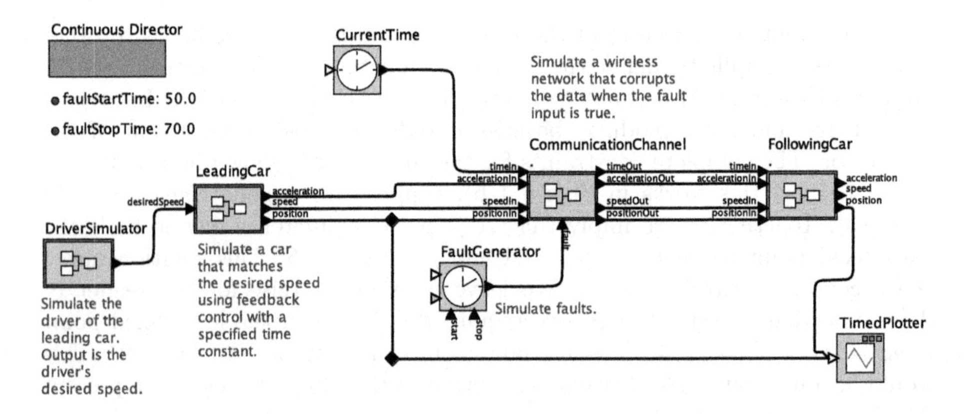

Fig. 5. Top level of an actor-oriented model of an adaptive cruise control system

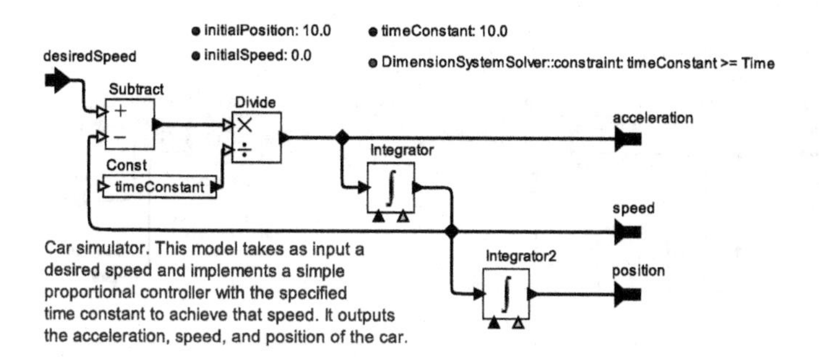

Fig. 6. A model of a car that accepts a desired speed and matches it using a feedback control loop. This model has three parameters, the initial position, the initial speed, and the time constant of the control loop.

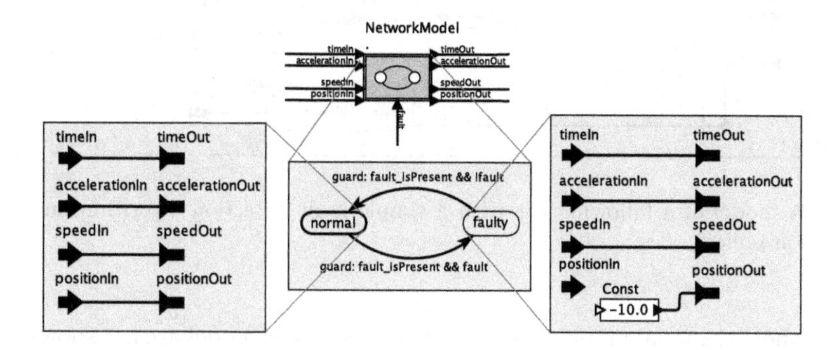

Fig. 7. A model of a wireless network that passes inputs to outputs unchanged in normal operation, but replaces an input with an arbitrary constant upon faults

the dynamics of the leading car. Specifically, given an input desired speed, it accelerates to achieve that speed using a control loop with a specified time constant. It uses an Integrator component to convert acceleration to speed, and another Integrator to convert speed to position. The output is the acceleration, speed, and position as a function of time. These data are then sampled and transmitted over a wireless network, as shown in the middle of Figure 5.

Given a suitable ontology, our framework can infer that if the input to the Leading Car Model is a Speed, then its outputs are Acceleration, Speed, and Position, respectively. Moreover, our ontology system can be used to check that the Following Car model uses the position as a Position, not as a Speed, and vice versa. Many possible design errors can be caught by such models.

The wireless network submodel is shown in Figure 7. This is a **modal model** with two modes of operation, normal and faulty. In the normal mode, inputs are passed directly to the outputs. In the faulty mode, one of the inputs is replaced with an arbitrary constant (-10 in this simple example).

The model of the following car is shown in Figure 8, where a Fault Detector component performs the above mentioned sanity check, and uses the result to

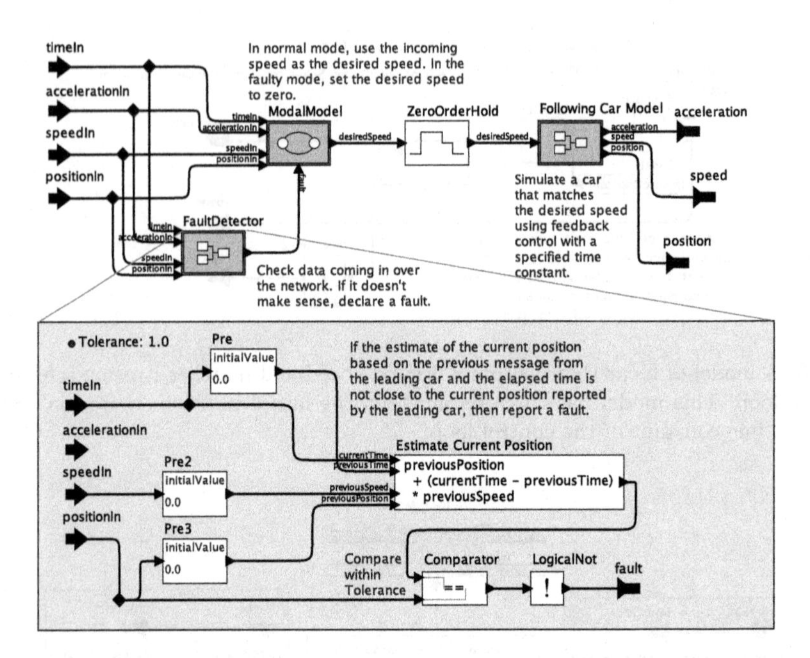

Fig. 8. A model of a following car with a simple fault detection algorithm and fault adaptation policy

control another modal model. The details of this modal model are not shown, but like that of Figure 7, it has two modes, normal and faulty. In the normal mode, its output is equal to the input speed, and in the faulty mode its output is zero. Thus, the policy of this particular cruise control algorithm is for the following car to stop if it does not trust the data coming from the leading car, thus returning control to the driver. The output of the modal model is a desired speed, which is converted to a continuous-time signal by the ZeroOrderHold component, which then feeds it into another car model like that shown in Figure 6, which simulates the dynamics of the following car.

To perform property inference and checking for the adaptive cruise control example, we need a collection of constraints for components in the model, an illustrative subset of which are shown in Table 1. These constraints form part of a property system that can be reused in a variety of models. In addition, we added constraints and acceptance criteria that are specific to this model. Once these are specified, we can run our property inference tool on the model. A portion of the result of such a run is shown in Figure 9, where the inferred properties of ports and parameters are highlighted by the tool in a color matching that of the concept lattice elements in Figure 4. The inferred properties are also shown in text next to each port.

In Figure 9, there is exactly one constraint specified by the model builder, which is that the *timeConstraint* parameter has a property greater than or equal to Time. The input to this model resolves to Speed because we have specified

Table 1. Some of the constraints for components used in the Cruise Control example

Component	Elements	Constraints	Where
CurrentTime	output y	$T \leq p_y$ $p_y \leq T$	
Add/Subtract	plus x, minus y, output z	$p_y \vee p_z \leq p_x$ $p_x \vee p_z \leq p_y$ $p_x \vee p_y \leq p_z$	
Integrator	input x, initialState y, output z	$f_I(p_z) \leq p_x$ $f_O(p_x) \leq p_z$ $p_y \leq p_z$ $p_z \leq p_y$	$f_I(p_z) = \begin{cases} \bot & \text{if } p_z = \bot \\ S & \text{if } p_z = P \\ A & \text{if } p_z = S \\ U & \text{if } p_z = T \\ \top & \text{otherwise} \end{cases}$ $f_O(p_x) = \begin{cases} \bot & \text{if } p_x = \bot \\ P & \text{if } p_x = S \\ S & \text{if } p_x = A \\ T & \text{if } p_x = U \\ \top & \text{otherwise} \end{cases}$
Divide	multiply x, divide y, output z	$f_D(p_x, p_y) \leq p_z$	$f_D(p_x, p_y) = \begin{cases} \bot & \text{if } p_x = \bot \text{ or } p_y = \bot \\ A & \text{if } p_x = S \text{ and } p_y = T \\ S & \text{if } p_x = P \text{ and } p_y = T \\ T & \text{if } p_x = P \text{ and } p_y = S \\ T & \text{if } p_x = S \text{ and } p_y = A \\ U & \text{if } p_x = p_y \\ p_x & \text{if } p_y = U \\ \top & \text{otherwise} \end{cases}$
Scale	input x, factor y, output z	$f_S(p_x, p_y) \leq p_z$	$f_S(p_x, p_y) = \begin{cases} \bot & \text{if } p_x = \bot \text{ or } p_y = \bot \\ S & \text{if } p_x = A \text{ and } p_y = T, \text{ or } \\ & \quad p_x = S \text{ and } p_y = U \\ P & \text{if } p_x = S \text{ and } p_y = T, \text{ or } \\ & \quad p_x = P \text{ and } p_y = U \\ p_y & \text{if } p_x = U \\ p_x & \text{if } p_y = U \\ \top & \text{otherwise} \end{cases}$

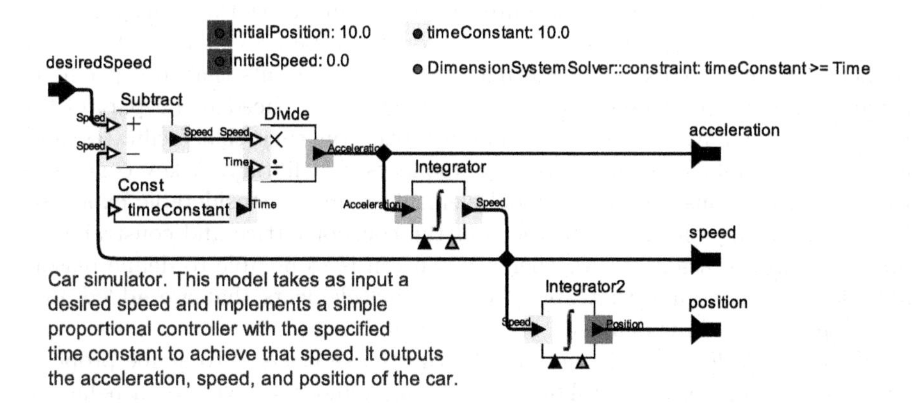

Fig. 9. Car model of figure 6 with properties resolved

similar constraints upstream in the driver model (not shown). Everything else resolves to Time, Acceleration, Speed, or Position as a consequence of the component constraints in Table 1 and the constraints implied by connections between components. Such a visual display of the inferred properties makes it easy to identify inconsistencies in the model, if there are any. Our model has none.

A property system is domain specific. We can construct multiple property systems, and even use them within the same model. Another example of a concept lattice is given in Figure 3. We interpret the property Const, when associated with a port, to mean that the value of data on that port is constant throughout the execution of the model. The property Nonconst means that the value may change during execution. We have applied this property system to analyzing the same cruise control example, and find that it successfully identifies portions of the model where messages between components have a constant value. This can be used to optimize the model automatically, or, more interestingly, to manage multiple models that represent product families. Specifically, variants of a model may result in different parts of the model being constant due to different parameterizations, which enables optimization of particular variants of the model without losing the generality of the master product family model.

6 Software Architecture

Our tool is an extension of the Ptolemy II type system that enables the definition of a concept lattice and the specification of constraints and acceptance criteria. The lowest level of the tool is a set of Java base classes for defining the lattice, constraints, and acceptance criteria. We have provided as well a set of model elements that can be incorporated with a Ptolemy II model that associate all of these objects with the model. Thus, a model designer can browse from a library of preconfigured property systems, and choose to use those that are useful.

Defining a property system requires a fair amount of work. A property system can be specific to a particular model, or it can be provided in a library of property systems for use with multiple models. Constraints that are specific to a particular model element, like the Integrator above, need to be part of the property system. We have developed an **adapter pattern** that facilitates associating constraints with preexisting components in a library. A key concern is that specifying constraints for model elements requires considerable expertise. We are exploring visual specifications of the concept lattice and constraints in order to improve usability. Another key concern is to be able to define reasonable default constraints that apply to modeling elements that are added after the property system is defined.

We provide a few generic mechanisms that make it easier to define property systems for complex models. For example, many models have modal behavior, as illustrated in Figure 7. A modal model is a finite state machine (FSM) where each state may contain refinement models. The public interface (e.g. ports and parameters) of the modal model is shared across its refinement models. Each refinement defines the behavior of the modal model component when it is in that mode. A reasonable default strategy is that the constraints of the modal model should be the conjunction of the constraints of the refinements. While our framework permits overriding this default, most model builders will likely find it to be exactly what they want. An interesting extension would be to combine property analysis with model checking to get less conservative analysis.

Another generic mechanism we provide concerns arithmetic expressions. Figure 8, for example, contains a component labeled " Estimate Current Position," which is an instance of the Ptolemy II Expression actor, whose behavior is given by the expression shown in its icon. The constraints of Table 1 apply equally well to nodes of the abstract syntax tree (AST) of such expressions as to actors that add, subtract, multiply, or divide signal values. Hence, property inference and checking works automatically across such expressions. Again, we provide reasonable defaults for setting up the constraints, but the framework supports fine-grained customization to allow easy experimentation.

7 Assessment and Related Work

Much work in formal concept analysis attempts to extract an ontology from a set of object instances. It is more concerned with concept mining or clustering. Our property analysis, on the other hand, infers concept values for model objects based on a given ontology specification. Our focus, therefore, is on facilitating correct modeling by providing better model engineering tools that, like type systems, expose errors early in the design process and facilitate transformation.

Our work can also be viewed as providing a mechanism for incremental or partial construction of a metamodel. A traditional metamodel is more complete than our property systems need to be. A simple property system can be associated with a complex model and incrementally elaborated as the model evolves.

Our property systems are comparable to ontology modeling supported by OWL-protègè and EMF. These tools provide a flexible set of primitives to model complex ontologies. Like them, our lattice ontology description is based on the principle of modeling concepts and relationships. OWL leverages description logic for specifying relationship between classes of concepts. EMF specializes in a subset of relationships borrowed from UML to provide useful features such as model querying and model-to-text support. Our lattice ontology can be viewed as a specialization that restricts ontologies to a lattice structure and constraints to those compatible with efficient inference and checking. Our objectives are also similar to [21], but our lattice foundation ensures unique inference results, supports cyclic dependencies, and scales to large models.

There are a number of obvious extensions to this work. For example, our property system with the lattice in Figure 4 stops short of checking units, although limited forms of such checks are known to be possible [22]. Our ontology includes concepts like "speed," but not "meters per second" or "miles per hour." An open question is the extent to which our lattice ontology approach can be extended to include units. Most unit analysis systems we are aware of check for consistent use of units at run time, not at compile time. We are aware of three exceptions: a static unit system in Ptolemy II created by Roland Johnson [unpublished], the SIunits library [23], which uses C++ templates, and SCADE [24]. Brown's approach in [23] relies on the type checking of C++. However, the C++ type system in general does not conform with our lattice structure (witness multiple inheritance), so such an approach may not yield unique solutions.

Schlick, et al. in [24] point out that unit checkers face a fundamental problem with "ambiguous units" like work and torque, both of which are Newton-meters. They suggest introducing "radial meters" to disambiguate the two, suggesting that associating more general ontology information with units is useful. Their mention of multiple disjoint uses of dimensionless numbers also reinforces this need for more general ontology information.

Another interesting obvious extension is to support infinite concept lattices. The Ptolemy II type system already does this, in order to support composite types such as arrays and records. Inference in such systems is known to become undecidable in general (witness dependent types), but practical heuristics lead to very usable inference algorithms, at least for type systems. One key question is whether such heuristics would work for domain-specific property systems. It is also challenging to find or invent mechanisms for model builders to define infinite lattices easily and specify constraints over them.

8 Conclusions

We have described a strategy for annotating models with semantic information and automatically performing inference and consistency checking. Our mechanism is scalable and customizable, and thus provides a foundation for research in domain-specific model ontologies and model engineering. Its mathematical foundation ensures that inference results are unique. A model builder can specify just a few semantic annotations, and the implications of these annotations throughout the model are automatically inferred. This will expose modeling errors early, will help designers to better understand their models, and help design teams to agree on interfaces between subsystems, on design concepts, and on terminology.

References

1. Karsai, G., Sztipanovits, J., Ledeczi, A., Bapty, T.: Model-integrated development of embedded software. Proceedings of the IEEE 91(1), 145–164 (2003)
2. Jantsch, A.: Modeling Embedded Systems and SoCs - Concurrency and Time in Models of Computation. Morgan Kaufmann, San Francisco (2003)
3. Lee, E.A.: Model-driven development - from object-oriented design to actor-oriented design. In: Workshop on Software Engineering for Embedded Systems: From Requirements to Implementation (The Monterey Workshop), Chicago (2003)
4. Lee, E.A., Neuendorffer, S., Wirthlin, M.J.: Actor-oriented design of embedded hardware and software systems. Journal of Circuits, Systems, and Computers 12(3), 231–260 (2003)
5. Bock, C.: SysML and UML 2 support for activity modeling. Syst. Eng. 9(2), 160–186 (2006)
6. Rumbaugh, J.: The unified modeling language reference manual, 2nd edn. Journal of Object Technology 3(10), 193–195 (2004)

7. OMG: System modeling language specification v1.1. Technical report, Object Management Group (2008)
8. Hardebolle, C., Boulanger, F.: Modhel'x: A component-oriented approach to multiformalism modeling. In: MODELS 2007 Workshop on Multi- Paradigm Modeling, Nashville, Tennessee, USA. Elsevier Science B.V (2007)
9. Pree, W., Templ, J.: Modeling with the timing definition language (tdl). In: Broy, M., Krüger, I.H., Meisinger, M. (eds.) ASWSD 2006. LNCS, vol. 4922, pp. 133–144. Springer, Heidelberg (2008)
10. Herrera, F., Villar, E.: A framework for embedded system specification under different models of computation in SystemC. In: Design Automation Conference (DAC), San Francisco. ACM Press, New York (2006)
11. Sander, I., Jantsch, A.: System modeling and transformational design refinement in ForSyDe. IEEE Transactions on Computer-Aided Design of Circuits and Systems 23(1), 17–32 (2004)
12. Goessler, G., Sangiovanni-Vincentelli, A.: Compositional modeling in Metropolis. In: Sangiovanni-Vincentelli, A., Sifakis, J. (eds.) EMSOFT 2002. LNCS, vol. 2491, pp. 93–107. Springer, Heidelberg (2002)
13. Eker, J., Janneck, J.W., Lee, E.A., Liu, J., Liu, X., Ludvig, J., Neuendorffer, S., Sachs, S., Xiong, Y.: Taming heterogeneity—the Ptolemy approach. Proceedings of the IEEE 91(2), 127–144 (2003)
14. Fritzson, P.: Principles of Object-Oriented Modeling and Simulation with Modelica 2.1. Wiley, Chichester (2003)
15. Lee, E.A., Xiong, Y.: A behavioral type system and its application in Ptolemy II. Formal Aspects of Computing Journal 16(3), 210–237 (2004)
16. Milner, R.: A theory of type polymorphism in programming. Journal of Computer and System Sciences 17, 348–375 (1978)
17. Rehof, J., Mogensen, T.A.: Tractable constraints in finite semilattices. In: Cousot, R., Schmidt, D.A. (eds.) SAS 1996. LNCS, vol. 1145, pp. 285–300. Springer, Heidelberg (1996)
18. Xiong, Y.: An extensible type system for component-based design. Ph.D. Thesis Technical Memorandum UCB/ERL M02/13, University of California, Berkeley, CA 94720 (May 1, 2002)
19. Ganter, B., Wille, R.: Formal Concept Analysis: Mathematical Foundations. Springer, Berlin (1998); Translated by C. Franzke
20. Bauer, H.: ACC Adaptive Cruise Control. Robert Bosch GmbH (2003)
21. Bowers, S., Ludäscher, B.: A calculus for propagating semantic annotations through scientific workflow queries. In: Grust, T., Höpfner, H., Illarramendi, A., Jablonski, S., Mesiti, M., Müller, S., Patranjan, P.-L., Sattler, K.-U., Spiliopoulou, M., Wijsen, J. (eds.) EDBT 2006. LNCS, vol. 4254, pp. 712–723. Springer, Heidelberg (2006)
22. Hayes, I.J., Mahony, B.P.: Using units of measurement in formal specifications. Formal Aspects of Computing Journal 7, 329–347 (1995)
23. Brown, W.E.: Applied template meta-programming in SIunits: the library of unit-based computation. In: Workshop on C++ Template Programming, Tampa Bay, FL, USA (2001)
24. Schlick, R., Herzner, W., Sergent, T.L.: Checking SCADE models for correct usage of physical units. In: Górski, J. (ed.) SAFECOMP 2006. LNCS, vol. 4166, pp. 358–371. Springer, Heidelberg (2006)

OntoDSL: An Ontology-Based Framework for Domain-Specific Languages

Tobias Walter[1,2], Fernando Silva Parreiras[1], and Steffen Staab[1]

[1] ISWeb — Information Systems and Semantic Web,
Institute for Computer Science, University of Koblenz-Landau
Universitaetsstrasse 1, Koblenz 56070, Germany
{walter,parreiras,staab}@uni-koblenz.de
[2] Institute for Software Technology, University of Koblenz-Landau
Universitätsstrasse 1, Koblenz 56070, Germany

Abstract. Domain-specific languages (DSLs) are high-level and should provide abstractions and notations for better understanding and easier modeling of applications of a special domain. Current shortcomings of DSLs include learning curve and formal semantics. This paper reports on a novel approach that allows the use of ontologies to describe DSLs. The formal semantics of OWL together with reasoning services allow for addressing constraint definition, progressive evaluation, suggestions, and debugging. The approach integrates existing metamodels, concrete syntaxes and a query language. A scenario in which domain models for network devices are created illustrates the development environment.

Keywords: Domain-Specific Languages, Technical Space, Ontologies, Reasoning Services.

1 Introduction

Domain-specific languages (DSLs) are used to model and develop systems of application domains. Such languages are high-level and should provide abstractions and notations for better understanding and easier modeling of applications of a special domain. A variety of different domain-specific languages and fragments of their models are used to develop one large software system. Each domain-specific language focuses on different problem domains and as far as possible on automatic code generation [1].

There is an agreement about the challenges faced by current DSL approaches [2]: *(challenge (1))* tooling (debuggers, testing engines), *(challenge (2))* interoperability with other languages, *(challenge (3))* formal semantics, *(challenge (4))* learning curve and *(challenge (5))* domain analysis.

Addressing these challenges is crucial for the success adoption of DSLs. For example, improving tooling enhances user experience. The interoperability between different languages plays an important role, because more than one language has to be combined in the modeling of systems. Finally, formal semantics is the basis for interoperability and formal domain analysis.

A. Schürr and B. Selic (Eds.): MODELS 2009, LNCS 5795, pp. 408–422, 2009.

Issues like interoperability and formal semantics motivated the development of ontology languages. Formal semantics precisely describes the meaning of models, such that they do not remain open to different interpretations by different persons (or machines). For example, Description Logics formalize the W3C standard Web Ontology Language (OWL) [3] and provides a language for ontologies. Indeed, OWL, together with automated reasoning services, provides a powerful solution for formally describing domain concepts in an extensible way, allowing for precise specification of the semantics of domain concepts.

Taking into account that some of the main challenges of DSLs were motivation for developing OWL, the following two questions arise naturally: which characteristics of ontology technologies may help in addressing current DSL challenges? What are the building blocks of a solution for applying ontology technologies in DSLs?

Recent works have explored ontologies to address some DSL challenges. Tairas et al. [4] apply ontologies in the early stages of domain analysis to identify domain concepts (*challenge (5)*). Guizzard et al. [5] propose the usage of an upper ontology to design and evaluate domain concepts (*challenge (3)*) whereas Bräuer and Lochmann[6] propose an upper ontology for describing interoperability among DSLs (*challenge (2)*). Nevertheless, the application of ontology languages and ontology technologies to address the remaining *challenges (1) and (4)* as well as a comprehensive integration is an open issue.

We present *OntoDSL*, an ontology-based framework for DSLs that allows for defining DSLs enriched by formal class descriptions. It allows DSL users to check the consistency of DSLs models and helps to verify and debug DSL models by using reasoning explanation. Moreover, novice DSL users may rely on reasoning services to suggest domain concepts according to the definition of the domain-specific language.

1.1 Advantages

The pragmatic advantages of the ontology-based *OntoDSL* framework are primarily the guidance of DSL designers and DSL users during the modeling process, the support of incomplete knowledge of concepts a DSL provides and the possibility of debugging domain models. Furthermore, *OntoDSL* provides DSL users with suggestions during building domain models and progressive evaluation of domain constraints. To get these and more advantages, *OntoDSL* provides automated reasoning services that can be practically used by DSL designers and DSL users.

The correctness of the domain-specific language in development is important for DSL designers. Thus, they want to *check the consistency* of the developed language, or they might exploit information about *concept satisfiability*, checking if it is possible for a concept in the metamodel to have any instances.

If DSL users want to verify whether all restrictions and constraints imposed by the DSL metamodel are observed, they can use a reasoning service to *check the consistency* of domain models. It is important for a domain model, that its elements have the most specific type. Thus, DSL users should be able to select a model element and call by pressing a button a reasoning service for *dynamic classification*. Dynamic classification allows for dynamically determining the classes which model objects belongs to, based on object descriptions. Later this might be useful, for example, to generate the most specific and complete source code from it. Further, it might be interesting for DSL users to retrieve existing model elements of a model repository by describing the concept in different possible ways. Here, *OntoDSL* can support the reuse of elements with retrieval services.

1.2 Methodology

To help DSL designers to define languages compatible with the aforementioned services, we create a new technical space (M3 metametamodel). The framework with its own technical space is arranged according to the OMG's layered architecture depicted in Figure 1 and the roles of DSL user and DSL designer are assigned to the different layers they are responsible for. The metametamodel consists of the KM3 metamodel, the OWL2 metamodel and the OCL metamodel (cf. section 4.2). KM3 is used to define the general structure of the language, OWL2 is used to define its semantics, OCL is used to define operations for calling the reasoning services.

To support the aforementioned reasoning services, we propose OWL to define constraints and formal semantics of DSLs. OWL is formalized by Description Logics, which provides the reasoning simultaneously on the M1-layer (model) and M2-layer (metamodel). In order of possible ontology reasoning, the DSL metamodel and domain model are transformed into a Description Logics knowledge base (TBox and ABox).

In order to reduce the learning effort, *OntoDSL* allows for using the familiar Java-like KM3 syntax to a very large extent. If DSL designers recognize that it is not expressive enough they can benefit from an easy to implement OWL natural style syntax to define semantics, constraints and restrictions (cf. section 4.3).

DSL users should not be confronted with the ontology technology. They only have to call operations that automatically invoke the reasoning services. Only DSL designers have contact with OWL, to define constraints and restrictions on the DSL metamodel.

In the scope of this paper, a DSL framework is a model-driven underlying structure to support the DSL development process and usage. Section 4 gives more details about the *OntoDSL* framework.

We organize the remaining sections as follows: Section 2 describes the running example used through the paper and analyzes the DSL challenges to be addressed with ontology technologies. Section 3 describes the state-of-the-art in domain-specific languages with ontology technologies and discusses the usage of Description Logics to formally describe domain models. The *OntoDSL* framework is described in section 4 by presenting its metametamodel, its implementation and an example of using it. We revisit the running example in section 5 and analyze related work in section 6. Section 7 finishes the paper.

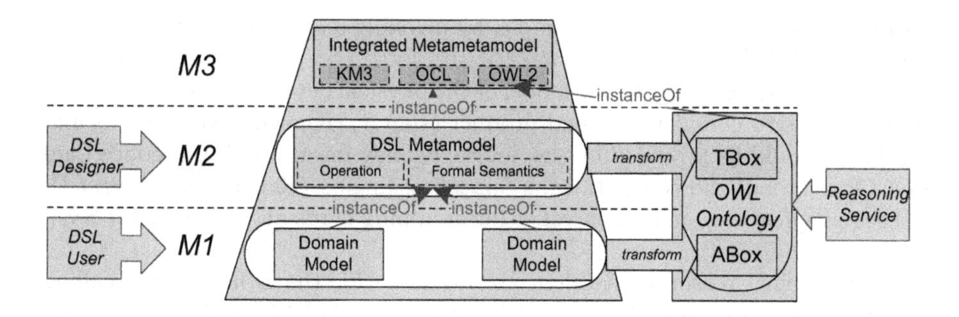

Fig. 1. DSL Designer and DSL User in the OMG' four-layered architecture

2 Running Example

Comarch[1], one of the industrial partners in the *MOST project*[2] has provides the running example used in this paper. It is a suitable simplification of the user scenario being conducted within the MOST project.

Comarch is specialized in designing, implementing and integrating IT solutions and services. For software development, Comarch uses model-driven methods where different kinds of domain-specific languages are deployed during the modeling process.

Comarch uses a domain-specific language defined using MOF (metametamodel at M3-layer) to model physical network devices. Using such a language, Comarch DSL designers design a DSL to define device structures (e.g. all devices from the Cisco 7600 family) at the M2-layer. Here, the goal of DSL designers is to formally define the logical structures of devices and restrictions over these structures (which leads to the below listed *requirement (1)*).

DSL users use DSLs defined by DSL designers to write DSL models that model concrete physical devices (M1-layer). A framework that instructs and guides DSL users during this process is desirable. For example, the consistency of DSL models should be verified, domain concepts should be suggested to DSL users, incomplete parts in the models should be detected and redundancies should be removed [7].

Let us elaborate the following example: The general physical structure of a Device consists of a Bay which has a number of Shelfs. A Shelf contains Slots into which Cards can be plugged. Logically, a Shelf with its possible Slots and Cards is stored as a Configuration.

Figure 2 depicts the development of a DSL model of physical devices by a given DSL user. Firstly (*step 1*), the DSL user starts with an instance of the general concept Device. A device requires at least one configuration. Thus he plugs in a Configuration element into the device.

In *step 2*, the DSL user adds exactly three slots to the device model. At this point, the DSL user wants to verify whether the configuration satisfies the DSL

[1] `http://www.comarch.com/`

[2] `http://www.most-project.eu/`

restrictions, which is done, for example, by invoking a query against the current physical device model (*requirement (2)*).

After adding three slots to the model of the physical device, the DSL user plugs in some cards to complete the end product (*step 3*). Knowing which cards and interfaces should be provided by the device, he may insert an SPA Interface Card for 1-Gbps broadband connections, a Supervisor Engine 720 card for different IP and security features and a controller for swapping cards at runtime (Hot Swap Controller).

At this point, reasoning services are available for the DSL user by calling operations that are provided by model elements in his DSL model. The calling of operations in our *OntoDSL* is realized by right-clicking on model elements, opening a context menu. This menu provides a list of the reasoning services that can be directly executed in the context of the model element.

The DSL defines the knowledge of which special types of cards are provided by a Configuration. Having further the information that its instance is connected with three slots, the refinement of the Configuration type of the instance by the more specific type Configuration7603 is recommended to the DSL user (*requirement (3)*) as result of activating the reasoning service. Moreover, the DSL user is informed how this suggestion takes place and about restrictions related to such a configuration. Here, debugging support is required (*requirement (4)*).

Since it has been inferred that the device has the Configuration7603, in *step 4*, the available reasoning service for the Device element infers that the device is one of type Cisco7603. The necessary and sufficient condition to be a Cisco7603 are verified and achieved by reasoning services.

Steps *2a and 2b* shows a second path in the scenario of modeling a physical device where debugging comes into play. After creating elements for a device, a configuration and slots, the DSL user plugs into one slot a HotSwappableOSM card and into the remaining slots two SPAInterface cards (*step 2a*). Here, the DSL user can invoke the debugging functionality provided by *OntoDSL*. It explains that each configuration must have a slot in which a SuperVisor720 card is plugged in. *OntoDSL* advises the type change of one of the SPAInterface elements to SuperVisor720 (*requirement (4)*). Having a correct configuration, the DSL user can continue with *steps 3 and 4* as described above.

2.1 Requirements

Although the list of requirements for a DSL framework may be extensive, we concentrate on those requirements derived from the running example and from the challenges mentioned in section 1, mainly on *challenges 1 and 4*. The requirements are classified by two actors: DSL designer and DSL user. At first we present the ones for the DSL designer:

1. *Constraint Definition* (*challenge (3)*). The DSL development environment should allow defining constraints over the DSL metamodel. DSL designers have to define formal semantics of the DSL in development to describe constraints and restrictions the DSL models have to fulfill.

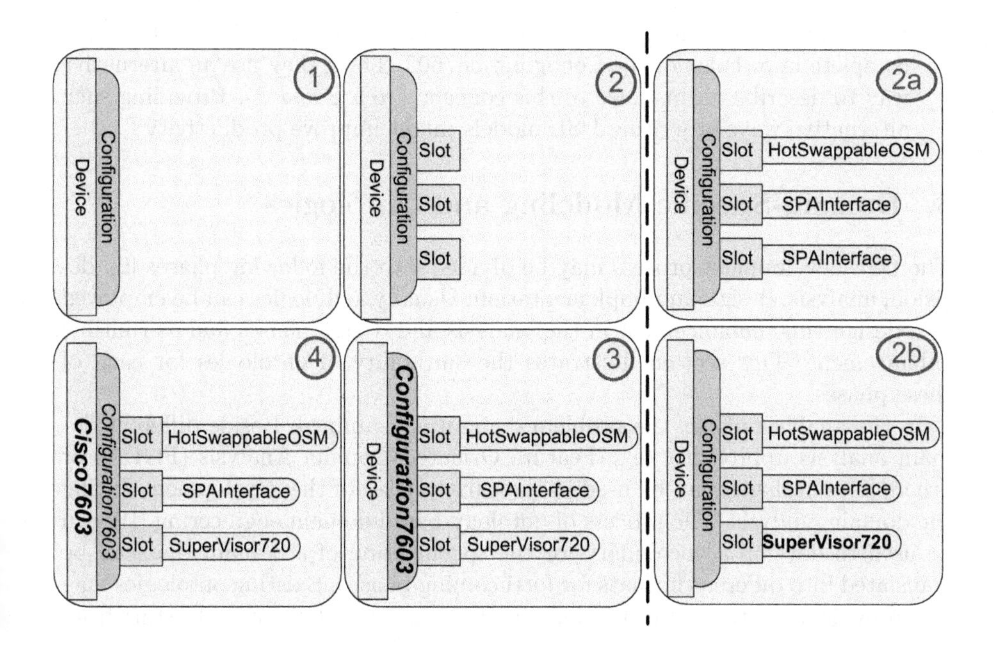

Fig. 2. Modeling a physical device in four steps (M1 layer)

The following requirements we assign to the DSL user:

2. *Progressive verification* (*challenges (1), (4)*). Even with an incomplete model, the DSL development environment must provide means by verifying constraints. For example during the modeling phase in *step 2a* the DSL user wants to debug his domain model in the aforementioned scenario, where the inconsistency occurs after adding the two SPAInterface cards.
3. *Suggestions of suitable domain concepts to be used* (*challenge (4)*). The DSL development framework should be able to dynamically classify the elements of the DSL model according to class descriptions in the DSL metamodel. DSL users normally start the modeling with general concepts, e.g. with Device or Configuration in the aforementioned scenario. The framework suggests the refinement of elements to the most suitable ones, e.g. to Configuration7603 or Cisco7603 (*step 3, 4*). Further, such classifications together with explanation help novice DSL users to understand how to use the DSL.
4. *Debugging (reasoning explanation)* (*challenges (1), (4)*). Debugging is a requirement for the success of the DSL [8]. DSL users want to debug their domain models to find errors inside them and to get an explanation how to correct the model. They want to have information about consequences of applying given domain constructs. In the scenario, DSL users want to know that they have to replace an SPAInterface card with a Supervisor720 card (*step 2b*).
5. *Different ways of describing constructs (syntactic sugar)* (*challenge (4)*). DSL users are not always familiar with all specific concepts a DSL provides.

In the aforementioned scenario, for example, DSL users do not have the complete knowledge of the Configuration7603. Thus, they use an alternative way to describe an instance of this concept (*step 2 and 3*). Providing such alternative ways of writing DSL models might improve productivity.

3 Domain-Specific Modeling and Ontologies

The DSL development process may be divided into the following phases [9]: decision, analysis, design and implementation. Usually, ontologies can be employed as a design time enhancement in the analysis and design phases and as runtime enhancement. This section illustrates the suitability of ontologies for each of these phases.

In the analysis phase, the problem domain is examined. Beside different domain analysis approaches (e.g. Feature Oriented Domain Analysis (FODA) or others [9]) ontologies can be used in the early phases of the development during the domain analysis. The process of ontology-based domain engineering [10] can be used to develop a vocabulary for the specification of a domain that can be translated into different formats for forthcoming phases. Existing ontologies may also provide a starting point for domain analysis without the need to start from scratch.

In the design phase, the domain model produced in the analysis phase is used to define the metamodel of the DSL. MOF-like metametamodels usually describe the metamodels. The semantics of MOF-based metamodels is limited compared to the ones of ontologies, i.e., ontology languages are more expressive than MOF-like technical spaces and provide a better support for reasoning than MOF-based languages [11].

In the implementation phase, interpretation and compilation of the DSL are addressed. Here, DSL compilers or interpreters may implement calls to reasoner APIs to enable services like reasoning explanation, instance checking, consistency checking and query answering.

To sum up, ontologies may be applied during different phases of the DSL development process. Ontology-based approaches lead to formal domain-specific models that may be exploited for a variety of services, from consistency checking [12] to semi-automatic engineering and to explanations [13].

3.1 Ontologies as Conceptual Models

Among ontology languages, we highlight the W3C standard OWL. OWL actually stands for a family of languages with increasing expressiveness. OWL2, the emerging new version of OWL, is more expressive and still allows for sound and complete calculi that are decidable as well as pragmatically efficient.

The capability to describe classes in many different ways and to handle incomplete knowledge distinguishes OWL from class-based modeling languages like UML class diagrams, MOF and Ecore. These OWL features increase the expressiveness of the metamodeling language, making OWL a suitable language to formally define DSL metamodels.

We use the running example to illustrate these features. In the following list, we describe the knowledge base of the running example. The class Supervisor720 is a subclass of SupervisorCard (eq. 1). The class Card is a complete generalization of HotSwappableOSM, SPAInterfaceProcessor and SupervisorCard (eq. 2).

$$Supervisor720 \sqsubseteq SupervisorCard \quad (1)$$

$$Card \equiv HotSwappableOSM \sqcup SPAInterfaceProcessor \sqcup SupervisorCard \quad (2)$$

$$Configuration \sqsubseteq \exists \geq 1 hasSlot.Slot \sqcap \exists hasSlot.(\exists hasCard.SupervisorCard) \quad (3)$$

$$Configuration7603 \equiv \exists = 3 hasSlot.Slot \sqcap \exists hasSlot.(\exists hasCard.(HotSwappableOSM \sqcup SPAInterfaceProcessor)) \quad (4)$$

$$Cisco7603 \equiv \exists hasConfiguration.Configuration7603 \quad (5)$$

$$Configuration \sqcap Slot \sqsubseteq \bot \quad (6)$$

Addressing Constraint Definition. OWL allows for describing logical restrictions over classes. For example, the class Configuration requires at least one Slot and a Slot in which a SupervisorCard is inserted (eq. 3). Moreover, class descriptions may be declared as equivalent (eq. 2, 4, 5), e.g., the class Configuration7603 is equivalent to an anonymous class that has exactly 3 Slots, one of them with either a HotSwappableOSM or SPAInterfaceProcessor inserted (eq. 4). It means that individuals of the class Configuration7603 belong to the anonymous class and *vice versa.*

Addressing Progressive Verification. The logical restrictions above can be verified progressively. For example, supposing that a DSL user adds an instance of the class Configuration7603. The reasoner infers that this instance has exactly 3 slots. If there are less than 3 slots in the model, the reasoner will throw an inconsistency. As soon as the DSL user adds 3 slots, the model becomes consistent again. Although the DSL user did not associate the 3 slots with the Configuration7603, the reasoner infers that there is a relation. When the DSL user associates the 3 slots with another instance of the class Configuration, the reasoner points the inconsistency again.

Addressing Debugging. Reasoning services may be combined with non-standard reasoning services to provide reasoning explanation. The goal is to identify minimal and sufficient sets of axioms that explain relationships between domain elements, i.e., to identify justifications [13].

Addressing Syntactic Sugar. By declaring two classes as equivalent, DSL designers give DSL users the possibility of modeling a concept in two different ways. In our example, DSL users have different ways of creating instances of the concept Cisco7603 (eq. 5): by declaring it directly or by creating an Device with one Configuration7603. As illustrated, OWL provides various means for expressing classes: enumeration of individuals, property restrictions (eq. 3), intersections of classes (eq. 6), unions of class descriptions (eq. 2), complements of a class description or combinations of any of those means.

Open vs. Closed World Assumption. While the underlying semantics of UML-based class modeling adopts the closed world assumption, OWL adopts open world assumption by default. However, research in the field of combining description logics and logic programming [14] provides solutions to support OWL reasoning with closed world assumption. Different strategies have been explored like adopting an epistemic operator [15], already supported by the tableau-based OWL reasoner Pellet [16,17]. Thus, it allows us to avoid the semantic clash in merging the two languages.

In this section, we have seen that Description Logics can attend as conceptual models for describing domain-specific languages. However, our intention is not to demand DSL designers to develop DSLs directly and completely as ontologies. Instead, we have an ontology-based domain-specific language framework which provides a seamless and integrated development of formal semantics within the language definition itself using some natural to use and simple to learn ontology languages, which can be used in combination with other, more familiar concrete syntaxes.

4 An Ontology-Based Framework for DSLs

In this section, we introduce our ontology-based domain-specific language framework – *OntoDSL*. After presenting the general idea of our approach in section 4.1, we concentrate on the implementation of the new technical space in section 4.2. We integrate the KM3 metametamodel, a simplified subset of MOF, with the OWL2 metamodel and additionally with the OCL metamodel at the M3 layer. Thus, we can provide a new technical space which allows implementing DSL metamodels with formal semantics, conditions and queries. Finally, we give an example of defining a new metamodel in *OntoDSL* concrete syntax in section 4.3.

4.1 Overall Approach

As already mentioned in ection 1.2, figure 1 depicts the layered architecture and provides an overview of all roles and models considered in the running example. Now we consider more technical details of the framework.

At the M3 layer, we first have a seamless integration of the MOF based metametamodel KM3, the OWL metamodel and the OCL metamodel. Having the integrated metametamodel at the M3-layer (the new technical space), DSL designers can define domain-specific languages using KM3, OWL and OCL constructs in seamless manner. They describe the static structure of DSL metamodels (e.g. using KM3 constructs), formal semantics (e.g. using OWL constructs) or operations (e.g. using OCL constructs).

DSL users may then use the developed DSL with additional benefits. Results are domain models (M1-layer). Having formal semantics of the DSL, consistency checking is available. Furthermore, the execution of operations in the context of a model element is available. These operations call reasoning services which work on ontologies constituted from the DSL metamodel and the domain models DSL users have created.

4.2 Implementation

In this subsection we consider the implementation of *OntoDSL*. We mainly focus on how we build the abstract syntax of the new technical space and how we developed the concrete syntax. Both, the abstract syntax, represented as metamodel and the textual concrete syntax can be downloaded from our project website `http://ontodsl.semanticsoftware.eu`

Abstract Syntax. The core of our technical space (our M3 metametamodel) consists of KM3 [18], OCL [19] and OWL2 [20]. We use our metamodel integration approach presented in [21] and [22] to combine the different metamodels. The result is the integrated metametamodel at the M3 layer which describes the abstract syntax of our technical space.

The *OntoDSL* metamodel provides all classes of the KM3 metametamodel, the OCL and OWL metamodel. It contains different adapter classes to integrate, for example, *OWL class* with *KM3 class*, *OWL Object Property* with *KM3 reference attribute* or *OWL Data Property* with *KM3 simple attribute*. Thus, we build a bridge between the different languages. Furthermore, we define that classes can contain operations. A new operation class in the integrated metametamodel is associated to classes for OCL operation definitions of the OCL metamodel.

Overall, with the new abstract syntax we describe all aspects DSL designers can use to define metamodels. To provide reasoning based on domain metamodels and models we implemented several transformations, e.g. using ATL [23], that translate the metamodels and models to pure OWL ontologies. We use the Pellet reasoner [16] to provide OWL reasoning services.

Concrete Syntax. Listing 1 in the section below gives an example of using the concrete syntax to define a metamodel.

The concrete syntax of *OntoDSL* is based on KM3. The motivation is that DSL designers should use the Java-like KM3 syntax as much as they can. To take benefit from OWL or OCL, they should be able to annotate elements of their DSL metamodel in a textual manner. Hence, we extend the grammar of the KM3 concrete syntax by new non-terminals which are defined in grammars of a textual OWL2 concrete syntax or of a textual OCL concrete syntax.

For example, we are able to annotate KM3 classes with OWL class axioms, KM3 reference attributes with OWL Object Property axioms or implement OCL operations within KM3 classes. We have developed our own *OWL 2 natural style syntax* which is an adaptation of the OWL Manchester Syntax [24] to get a natural controlled language for coding OWL2 ontologies. As OCL concrete syntax we take the one from [19].

Overall, we have a grammar which consists of rules to produce KM3 statements in combination with textual OWL annotations and embedded OCL operation definitions.

We solve the mapping between abstract and concrete syntax by using the Eclipse component TCS [25] for textual concrete syntax specification of DSLs.

4.3 Example in Concrete Syntax

In Listing 1, we see an excerpt of an M2 metamodel that is created by a DSL designer using the new integrated metametamodel. Using the KM3 syntax, he defines that a Device has Configurations, a Cisco7603 is a specialization of Device, each Configuration has Slots and in each Slot one to many cards can be plugged in.

Furthermore, the DSL designer defines some formal semantics using the OWL natural style concrete syntax, which is integrated with the existing KM3 syntax. In Listing 1, he states that every Cisco7603 device has at least one Configuration7603. A Configuration is a Configuration7603 if and only if it has exactly three slots in which either a HotSwappableOSM card or a SPAinterfaceProcessors card is plugged in.

At the end of Listing 1, we see the definition of the class Thing, which is in OWL the superclass of all classes. Here, using OCL syntax, we define a new operation getSpecificSubClasses(). Because of inheritance from the superclass Thing, this operation can be executed in the context of all classes. Having an operation called getSpecificSubClasses(), the DSL designer can support the DSL user with suggestions of suitable domain concepts. In this case, the DSL user has to call the operation in the context of a model element and gets as feedback the suggestion to refine the type of the current model element (*requirement (3)*).

Listing 1. Example of defining an M2 metamodel

```
1  class Device {
2    reference hasConfiguration [1-*]: Configuration;
3  }
4
5  class Cisco7603 extends Device, equivalentWith restrictionOn
       hasConfiguration with min 1 Configuration7603 {
6  }
7
8  class Configuration extends IntersectionOf(restrictionOn hasSlot with
        min 1 Slot, restrictionOn hasSlot with some restrictionOn
       hasCard with some SuperVisor720){
9    reference hasSlot [1-*]: Slot;
10 }
11
12 class Configuration7603 extends Configuration, equivalentWith
       IntersectionOf(restrictionOn hasSlot with exactly 3 Slot,
       restrictionOn hasSlot with some restrictionOn hasCard with some
       UnionOf(HotSwappableOSM, SPAinterfaceProcessor) {
13 }
14
15 class Slot {
16   reference hasCard [1-*]: Card;
17 }
18
19 class Thing {
20   query getSpecificSubClasses (): Set(Thing)
21   = self.owlAllTypes()
22 }
```

5 Analysis of the Approach

In this section, we establish the viability of our approach by a proof of concept evaluation. We analyze the approach with respect to the requirements of section 2.1.

To address formal semantics and constraints (*requirement (1)*), we integrated the EMOF based metametamodel KM3 and its concrete syntax with OWL, allowing for a formal and logical representation of the solution domain. Thus, DSL designers count on an expressive language that allows for modeling logical constraints over DSL metamodels (*requirement (1)*). Reasoners check the consistency of metamodels and constraints and debugging services clarify the inferences (*requirement (4)*).

Formal semantics enable the usage of reasoning services to help DSL users to find appropriate constructs based on DSL models (*requirement (3)*). For example, DSL users may get suggestions of devices to be used in their DSL models based on the configuration of the device.

The expressiveness of OWL enables DSL designers to define classes and properties as equivalent. DSL designers may use this functionality to provide DSL users with different means for declaring objects (*requirement (5)*). For example, a DSL user may describe a Cisco 7603 device in two different ways: by creating an instance of class Device with a configuration with three slots and a supervisor card in one slot; or by directly creating an instance of class Cisco7603.

The nature of the logical restrictions allowed by OWL enables progressive evaluation of DSL model consistency (*requirement (2)*). For example, a DSL user may drag a new configuration into a DSL model with already two supervisor cards. A configuration requires at least one supervisor card. Even though it is not asserted that any of the supervisor cards are part of the new configuration, the reasoner assumes that at least one of the cards is related with this configuration.

DSL users call OCL-like queries defined by DSL designers within the DSL metamodel to query objects in DSL models (*requirement (3)*). These queries are the interface between DSL users and reasoning services. For example, a DSL user may use a reasoning service which is implemented as query defined in the DSL metamodel and queries all classes that describe an object in the DSL model.

While solutions provided by DSL development environments for teaching DSL users are usually limited to help files and creation of the example models, we have an interactive assisted solution by suggesting concepts and explaining inferences (*requirement (3)*). Nevertheless, addressing the aforementioned requirements lead us to new challenges as well as it demands to consider trade-offs between expressiveness and completeness/soundness, expressiveness and user complexity.

6 Related Work

In the following, we group related approaches into two categories: approaches with formal semantics and approaches for model-based domain-specific language development.

Among approaches with formal semantics, one can use languages like F-Logic or Alloy to formally describe models. In [26], a transformation of UML+OCL to Alloy is proposed to exploit analysis capabilities of the Alloy Analyzer [27]. In [28], a reasoning environment for OWL is presented, where the OWL ontology is transformed to Alloy. Both approaches show how Alloy can be adopted for consistency checking of UML models or OWL ontologies. F-Logic is a further prominent rule language that combines logical formulas with object oriented and frame-based description features. Different works (e.g. [29,30]) have explored the usage of F-Logic to describe configurations of devices or the semantics of MOF models.

The integration in the cases cited above is achieved by transforming MOF models into a knowledge representation language (Alloy or F-logic). Thus, the expressiveness available for DSL designers is limited to MOF/OCL. Our approach extends these approaches by enabling DSL designers to specify class descriptions *à la* OWL together with MOF/OCL, increasing expressiveness.

Examples of model-based DSL development environments are MetaEdit+ [31], XMF (eXecutable modelling framework) [32], Generic Modeling Environment (GME) [33] and ATLAS Model Management Architecture (AMMA) [34]. These approaches are aligned with the OMG four-layer metamodel architecture and provide support to OCL-like languages (like in XMF GME and AMMA) for specifying queries and constraints. Our approach adds value on them by providing a logic-based approach to define formal semantics of DSLs. The logic-based approach allows us to provide functionalities based on Description Logics constructs like equivalence, class descriptions to DSL users. Concretely, it allows us to support guidance and suggestions to DSL users.

7 Conclusion

In this paper, we presented an approach how to address major challenges in the field of domain-specific languages with OWL ontologies and automated reasoning. The new technical space integrates EMOF and OWL at the M3-layer and enables applications of reasoning to help DSL designers and DSL users through the development and usage of DSLs. DSL designers profit by formal representations, an expressive language and constraint analysis. DSL users profit by progressive verification, debugging support and assisted programming. The approach has been used and tested in the telecommunication domain under EU STReP MOST. Future work into this direction would investigate ways of extending concrete syntaxes to support the flexibility of OWL.

Acknowledgement. We like to thank Krzysztof Miksa from Comarch for providing the use cases. Further, we like to thank Prof. Dr. Juergen Ebert for comments and improvement remarks. This work is supported by CAPES Brazil and EU STReP-216691 MOST.

References

1. Kelly, S., Tolvanen, J.: Domain-Specific Modeling. John Wiley & Sons, Chichester (2007)
2. Gray, J., Fisher, K., Consel, C., Karsai, G., Mernik, M., Tolvanen, J.P.: Panel - DSLs: the good, the bad, and the ugly. In: OOPSLA Companion 2008. ACM, New York (2008)
3. McGuinness, D.L., van Harmelen, F.: OWL Web Ontology Language overview (February 2004), `http://www.w3.org/TR/2004/REC-owl-features-20040210/`
4. Tairas, R., Mernik, M., Gray, J.: Using ontologies in the domain analysis of domain-specific languages. In: Proceedings of the 1st International Workshop on Transforming and Weaving Ontologies in Model Driven Engineering 2008. CEUR Workshop Proceedings., CEUR-WS.org, vol. 395 (2008)
5. Guizzardi, G., Pires, L.F., van Sinderen, M.: Ontology-based evaluation and design of domain-specific visual modeling languages. In: Proceedings of the 14th International Conference on Information Systems Development. Springer, Heidelberg (2005)
6. Brauer, M., Lochmann, H.: An Ontology for Software Models and Its Practical Implications for Semantic Web Reasoning. In: Bechhofer, S., Hauswirth, M., Hoffmann, J., Koubarakis, M. (eds.) ESWC 2008. LNCS, vol. 5021, pp. 34–48. Springer, Heidelberg (2008)
7. Miksa, K., Kasztelnik, M.: Definition of the case study requirements. Deliverable ICT216691/CMR/WP5-D1/D/PU/b1, Comarch (2008) (MOST Project)
8. Gilmore, D.J.: Expert programming knowledge: a strategic approach. In: Psychology of Programming. Academic Press, London
9. Mernik, M., Sloane, A.: When and how to develop domain-specific languages. ACM Computing Surveys (CSUR) 37(4), 316–344 (2005)
10. de Almeida Falbo, R., Guizzardi, G., Duarte, K.: An ontological approach to domain engineering. In: Proc. of SEKE 2002, pp. 351–358. ACM Press, New York (2002)
11. Happel, H.J., Seedorf, S.: Applications of ontologies in software engineering. In: Proc. 2nd International Workshop on Semantic Web Enabled Software Engineering (SWESE 2006), Athens, USA, November 6 (2006)
12. Van Der Straeten, R., Mens, T., Simmonds, J., Jonckers, V.: Using Description Logic to Maintain Consistency between UML Models. In: Stevens, P., Whittle, J., Booch, G. (eds.) UML 2003. LNCS, vol. 2863, pp. 326–340. Springer, Heidelberg (2003)
13. Schlobach, S., Cornet, R.: Non-standard reasoning services for the debugging of description logic terminologies. In: IJCAI International Joint Conference on Artificial Intelligence, pp. 355–362. Morgan Kaufmann, San Francisco (2003)
14. Motik, B., Horrocks, I., Rosati, R., Sattler, U.: Can owl and logic programming live together happily ever after? In: Cruz, I., Decker, S., Allemang, D., Preist, C., Schwabe, D., Mika, P., Uschold, M., Aroyo, L.M. (eds.) ISWC 2006. LNCS, vol. 4273, pp. 501–514. Springer, Heidelberg (2006)
15. Donini, F.M., Nardi, D., Rosati, R.: Description logics of minimal knowledge and negation as failure. ACM Trans. Comput. Logic 3(2), 177–225 (2002)
16. Parsia, B., Sirin, E.: Pellet: An OWL DL Reasoner. In: Proc. of the 2004 International Workshop on Description Logics (DL 2004). CEUR Workshop Proceedings, vol. 104 (2004)

17. Katz, Y., Parsia, B.: Towards a Nonmonotonic Extension to OWL. In: Proceedings of the OWLED 2005, Galway, Ireland, November 11-12. CEUR Workshop Proceedings, vol. 188 (2005)
18. Jouault, F., Bezivin, J.: KM3: A DSL for Metamodel Specification. In: Gorrieri, R., Wehrheim, H. (eds.) FMOODS 2006. LNCS, vol. 4037, pp. 171–185. Springer, Heidelberg (2006)
19. OMG: Object Constraint Language Specification, version 2.0. Object Modeling Group (June 2005)
20. Motik, B., Patel-Schneider, P.F., Horrocks, I.: OWL 2 Web Ontology Language: Structural Specification and Functional-Style Syntax (April 2009), `http://www.w3.org/TR/2009/WD-owl2-syntax-20090421/`
21. Silva Parreiras, F., Staab, S., Winter, A.: TwoUse: Integrating UML models and OWL ontologies. Technical Report 16/2007, University of Koblenz-Landau, `http://isweb.uni-koblenz.de/Projects/twouse/tr162007.pdf`
22. Parreiras, F.S., Walter, T.: Report on the combined metamodel. Deliverable ICT216691/UoKL/WP1-D1.1/D/PU/a1, University of Koblenz-Landau (2008) (MOST Project)
23. Jouault, F., Kurtev, I.: Transforming Models with ATL. In: Bruel, J.-M. (ed.) MoDELS 2005. LNCS, vol. 3844, pp. 128–138. Springer, Heidelberg (2006)
24. Horridge, M., Patel-Schneider, P.: Manchester syntax for OWL 1.1. In: International Workshop OWL: Experiences and Directions, OWLED 2008 (2008)
25. Jouault, F., Bézivin, J., Kurtev, I.: TCS: a DSL for the specification of textual concrete syntaxes in model engineering. In: Proceedings of the GPCE 2006, pp. 249–254. ACM Press, New York (2006)
26. Anastasakis, K., Bordbar, B., Georg, G., Ray, I.: UML2Alloy: A challenging model transformation. In: Engels, G., Opdyke, B., Schmidt, D.C., Weil, F. (eds.) MoDELS 2007. LNCS, vol. 4735, pp. 436–450. Springer, Heidelberg (2007)
27. Jackson, D.: Software Abstractions: logic, language, and analysis. The MIT Press, Cambridge (2006)
28. Wang, H., Dong, J., Sun, J., Sun, J.: Reasoning support for Semantic Web ontology family languages using Alloy. Multiagent and Grid Systems 2(4), 455–471 (2006)
29. Sure, Y., Angele, J., Staab, S.: OntoEdit: Guiding ontology development by methodology and inferencing. LNCS, pp. 1205–1222. Springer, Heidelberg
30. Gerber, A., Lawley, M., Raymond, K., Steel, J., Wood, A.: Transformation: The missing link of MDA. LNCS, pp. 90–105. Springer, Heidelberg (2002)
31. Kelly, S., Lyytinen, K., Rossi, M.: MetaEdit+: A Fully Configurable Multi-User and Multi-Tool CASE and CAME Environment, pp. 1–21. Springer, Heidelberg (1996)
32. Clark, T., Sammut, P., Willans, J.: Applied Metamodelling: a Foundation for Language Driven Development, 2nd edn. Ceteva (2008)
33. Ledeczi, A., Maroti, M., Bakay, A., Karsai, G., Garrett, J., Thomason, C., Nordstrom, G., Sprinkle, J., Volgyesi, P.: The Generic Modeling Environment. In: Proceedings of the IEEE Workshop on Intelligent Signal Processing (WISP 2001). IEEE, Los Alamitos (2001)
34. Bézivin, J., Jouault, F., Kurtev, I., Valduriez, P.: Model-Based DSL Frameworks. In: OOPSLA, pp. 22–26. ACM, New York (2006)

Domain-Specific Languages in Practice: A User Study on the Success Factors*

Felienne Hermans, Martin Pinzger, and Arie van Deursen

Delft University of Technology
{f.f.j.hermans,arie.vandeursen,m.pinzger}@tudelft.nl

Abstract. In this paper we present an empirical study on the use of a domain-specific language(DSL) in industry. This DSL encapsulates the details of services that communicate using Windows Communication Foundation (WCF). From definitions of the data contracts between clients and servers, WCF/C# code for service plumbing is generated. We conducted a survey amongst developers that use this DSL while developing applications for customers. The DSL has been used in about 30 projects all around the world.

We describe the known success factors of the use of DSLs, such as improved maintainability and ease of re-use, and assert how well this DSL scores on all of them. The analysis of the results of this case study also shows which conditions should be fulfilled in order to increase the chances of success in using a DSL in a real life case.

1 Introduction

Domain-specific languages(DSLs) are languages tailored to a specific application domain [1]. DSLs have been described in literature for several decades. They often appear under different guises, such as special purpose [2], application-oriented [3], specialized [4] or task-specific [5] programming languages. An overview of widespread DSLs can be found in [1]. Most authors agree that the use of domain-specific languages has significant benefits, amongst which reduced time-to-market [6] and increased maintainability [7,8].

However, very little research has been done to the use of DSLs in industry. Are DSLs really as helpful as we think when used within large companies? And if they are, what makes them?

In order to answer this, empirical studies of actual DSL usage are required. In this paper, we report on such a study. It involves the DSL called ACA.NET that is used to create web services that communicate using Windows Communication Foundation (WCF). ACA.NET has been used in over 30 projects all around the world.

In this paper we investigate factors that contribute to the success of this DSL. We conducted a study among 18 users of ACA.NET, by means of a systematic survey, investigating issues such as usability, reliability, and learnability. With the results of this study, we seek to answer the following research question

– What are the main factors contributing to the success of a DSLf?

* Empirical results category paper.

A. Schürr and B. Selic (Eds.): MODELS 2009, LNCS 5795, pp. 423–437, 2009.

The remainder of this paper is structured as follows. In Section 2 we summarize related work with focus on papers describing known success factors of DSLs. Section 3 introduces ACA.NET, the studied DSL, to the reader. Section 4 presents DSL success factors, the questionnaire and the experimental set-up. The results of the survey can be found in Section 5. In Section 6 the research question is answered, both for ACA.NET as well as for domain-specific languages in general. A summary of our contributions and an outlook towards future work can be found in Section 7.

2 Related Work

Several papers discuss advantages and disadvantages of the use of DSLs. For instance, van Deursen and Klint [8] observes that DSLs can substantially ease the *maintenance* , however it also indicates that the cost of extending a DSL for unanticipated changes can be substantial. Kieburtz *et al.* describes that DSLs can increase *flexibility*, *productivity* and *reliability* [9]. *Reusability* is also mentioned as an advantage of the use of DSLs, for instance by Ladd and Ramming [10] and Krueger [11]. The latter furthermore points out that a DSL can reduce the effort to create a system from a specification. From Bell [12] and Spinellis and Guruprasad [13] we learn that DSLs can *ease design and implementation* of a system, by reducing the distance between problem and program.

Spinellis [14] describes *reliability* as an advantage; because of the small domain and limited possibilities of a DSL, correctness of generators or interpreters can be easily verified. However, he also discusses disadvantages, such as training costs for users of the DSL and the lack of knowledge of how to fit the use of a DSL into standard software development processes [14]. Finally, Mernik *et al* [1] mentions that a DSL can also be used as a *domain-specific notation*. This way, existing jargon can be formalized.

Most of these papers primarily provide anecdotal evidence for the benefits claimed, often based on a handful of usage scenarios for the language in question. While this provides useful information, more confidence can be gained from rigorous empirical studies. Unfortunately, we only found a few of such studies in the literature. Batory *et al* [7] describes a case study where a DSL is used for simulations. They report improved *extensibility* and *maintainability*. Kieburtz *et al.* [9] describes a series of experiments comparing code generation using a DSL to code generation via templates. Herndon and Benzins [6] reports on improvements, amongst which *reduced time-to-market* and *improved maintainability* due to the use of DSLs. Unfortunately they lack to report how they come to their observations. Furthermore, their *Kodiyak* language has been used in only four cases. Both Weiss [15] and Bhanot *et al.* [16] report on a productivity increase of 500%, but is is not made explicit how these numbers were obtained.

Empirical work in the area of model-driven engineering in general is somewhat more common. For example, Baker *et al.* [17] describes a large case study, in which source code and test cases were generated from models. It presents numbers on *increased productivity*, *quality* and *maintainability*. White *et al.* [18] also describes a case study in which code is generated. Their paper reports on reduced effort on development and improved quality, but they only describe the results of one case. We have found one account where a questionnaire was used to study the ideal situations for model-driven development [19]. This questionnaire, however, addressed model-driven engineering in general, rather than the specific merits of the domain-specific notation used in a software project. To the best of our knowledge, no user study like ours has been performed before.

3 About ACA.NET

ACA.NET,[1] Avanade Connected Architectures for .NET, is a visual DSL developed by Avanade.[2] It is used to build web services that communicate via Windows Communication Foundation.[3] Developers from Avanade noticed that for many projects in which a service oriented application had to be created, the same simple, but time consuming tasks had to be repeated for each project. Typical tasks include creating classes for service contracts, data contracts, writing service configuration, writing endpoint definitions and creating service clients. Because these tasks appeared very similar for each project, Avanade decided to create an abstraction for these tasks.

With ACA.NET a large part of the development of service oriented applications can be automated. ACA.NET enables the user to draw a model of a service oriented application on the Visual Studio-integrated design surface. This model consists of server and client objects and the data contracts between them. From this model, a large part of the C#-code is generated. Only the business logic that describes the behavior of the service has to be implemented by hand, which can be done through C# partial classes.

ACA.NET is built with Microsoft DSL Tools [20]. The code generation is implemented using Microsoft's Text Template Transformation Toolkit (T4) that is part of the DSL Tools suite.

4 Experimental Design

To measure the success of ACA.NET we conducted a survey amongst ACA.NET developers. The survey was set up according to the guidelines of Pfleeger and Kitchenham [21]. Their guidelines propose to start by setting the survey objective. The objective of our study is to provide an answer to the following ACA.NET specific research question

- What are the main factors contributing to the success of ACA.NET?

4.1 DSL Success Factors

To reason about the success of ACA.NET, we identified a number of success factors of DSLs. We obtained these factors from the related work in the field which has been presented in the Section 2. We aimed at making this list of factors specific to the use of DSLs. Thus general success factors, such as commitment from higher management or the availability of skilled staff were not taken into consideration, as they are not directly affected by the use of a DSL.

---

1 See `http://www.avanade.com/delivery/acanet/`

2 Avanade is a joint venture between Accenture and Microsoft. See `www.avanade.com`

3 See `http://en.wikipedia.org/wiki/Windows_Communication_Foundation`

The resulting factors under consideration are:

Reliability (I) [14,9]**:** With a DSL, large parts of the development process can be automated, leading to fewer errors.

Usability (U) [12,13]**:** Tools and methods supporting the DSL should be easy and convenient to use.

Productivity (C) [6]**:** The DSL helps developers to model domain concepts that otherwise are time-consuming to implement. The corresponding source code is generated automatically. This lowers development costs and shortens time-to-market.

Learnability (L) [14]**:** Developers have to learn an extra language, which takes time and effort. Furthermore, as the domain changes the DSL has to evolve and developers need to stay up-to-date.

Expressiveness (E) [1]**:** Using a DSL, domain specific features can be implemented compactly, however, the language is specific to that domain and limits the possible scenarios that can be expressed.

Reusability (R) [10,11]**:** With a DSL, reuse is possible at model level, making it easier to reuse partial or even entire solutions, rather than pieces of source code.

With the reliability we mention we do not mean the number of bugs per line of code or other objective measures. We did not use that kind of measures for a few distinct reasons. Firstly, these measurements were not available for all of the projects in which ACA.NET was used. Secondly, since large parts of the code are generated, the amount of lines of code is not comparable to projects without ACA.NET. We believe the *perceived* reliability we use is a good measure, because developers often have a good feeling for improved quality of the software. They know whether the number of bugs is reasonable with respect to both the complexity and the size of the project. The same goes for the productivity. Since we did not have project data like lines of code or hours spent on it, we asked the developers to estimate it. We believe developers have a good idea on how much time they spent on their projects.

4.2 Questionnaire to Measure DSL Success Factors

Every question in the questionnaire relates to one or more of these factors of a DSL, because to cite [21] *it's essential that the survey questions relate directly to the survey objectives.* In the following we review the success factors and describe the questions that we use to measure them. Every success factor is covered by at least one Likert question, so it is possible to measure it. Open questions are added to the questionnaire to obtain more insight into the results. Table 1 provides an overview of the questionnaire. A pdf version of the questionnaire can be downloaded from `http://www.st.ewi.tudelft.nl/~hermans/`

The questionnaire consists of three parts. The first part, questions Q1 and Q2, concerns the background of the subject. The second part, questions Q4–Q10, contains the questions related to *one* specific ACA.NET project. For all subjects we investigated the set of projects for which they were listed as contact person. The third part of the survey, questions Q11–Q20, comprises questions on ACA.NET in general. In this part, we limited the answer-space to two five-point Likert scales to facilitate the measurement

Table 1. Overview of the questionnaire used for the ACA.NET survey

ID	Question	Factor
Background Questions		
Q1	How many years have you worked as a professional software developer?	L
Q2	How much experience do you have with ACA.NET	L
Project specific questions		
Q3	Was this a new ACA.NET project or built on an existing version?	R
Q4	If you start a new ACA.NET project, how do you proceed?	R
Q5	Did the ACA.NET user interface help you modeling?	U
Q6	Did you use other tools for modeling in this project, next to the ACA.NET interface?	U
Q7	Can you estimate the percentage of time that would be spent on the following tasks if ACA.NET was not used for this project?	C
Q8	Can you estimate the percentage of time that you actually spent on the following tasks?	C
Q9	Estimate the percentage of code that was generated	C
Q10	How many lines of code did this project consist of?	C
General ACA.NET questions		
Q11	How many days did it take you to get to know ACA.NET?	L
Q12	How many hours a month does it take you to stay up to date on ACA.NET?	L
Q13	Did you ever consider to use ACA.NET but decided against?	U
Q14	In case you answered Yes to the previous question, please indicate why.	U,E
Q15	Indicate your agreement with	
Q15a	The code is more readable	I
Q15b	Fewer errors occur	I
Q15c	The product complies better with the customers requirements	I
Q16a	ACA.NET makes designing easier	U
Q16b	ACA.NET makes implementing easier	U
Q16c	ACA.NET is powerful	U,E
Q17	Did you ever deny a customer a feature because you knew you would not be able to implement it using ACA.NET?	E
Q18	Did you ever have to write extra code (other than custom code for business logic) to implement features?	E
Q19	Indicate your agreement with	
Q19a	ACA.NET is difficult to use	U
Q19b	ACA.NET restricts my freedom as programmer	E
Q19c	ACA.NET doesn't have all features I need	E
Q20a	I look into the generated code in order to be able to understand the underlying models	E
Q20b	I look into the generated code in order to be able to be able to write custom code	E

of the various success factors. The first one ranges from strongly disagree, disagree, neutral, agree, to strongly agree. The second Likert scale ranges from very often, often, sometimes, seldom, to never.

Reliability of ACA.NET solutions (I). The first success factor we consider is reliability. Because parts of the development process are automated, software constructed using a DSL is expected to be less error prone. To measure the reliability of ACA.NET we ask the subjects whether they think that the use of ACA.NET increases the quality of the delivered code in the following ways: the code is more readable (Q15a), fewer bugs occur (Q15b), and the product complies better with the customer requirements (Q15c). The possible answers to each question are defined by a five point Likert scale. We expect that DSLs help to communicate requirements better to the customer and developers. Furthermore, ACA.NET code is assumed to be more readable and easier to understand. Both aspects are expected to lead to fewer bugs in ACA.NET web services. We want to stress again that we measure *perceived* reliability, meaning we measure how users feel about the increased reliability.

Usability of ACA.NET (U). Another factor is ease of using the DSL and the tools that support it. We included several questions dedicated to the usability of the ACA.NET toolkit for developing web services. For instance, does the ACA.NET user interface help in modeling web-services (Q5) and were other tools used in the project (Q6). We asked whether subjects decided against the use of ACA.NET (Q13) in any project, and, if yes, reasons why they did so (Q14). Descriptions of reasons could be provided in free-text. We also added questions to assess whether ACA.NET eases designing (Q16a) and implementing web services (Q16b), and summarizing, whether ACA.NET is a powerful DSL (Q16c). Question Q19a is used to obtain the level of agreement on the statement that ACA.NET is difficult to use.

Productivity of ACA.NET (C). With the use of ACA.NET, developers can focus on the business logic while other web-service related source code is generated by ACA.NET. Therefore time spent on tasks related to web-services is assumed to be shorter and development costs are assumed to be lower. For measuring the effect of ACA.NET on productivity, we formed a set of questions related to the experiences with the selected project. For instance, we ask each subject to estimate the percentage of time that would have been spent on the following tasks if ACA.NET was *not* used: write data contracts, write service configuration, and write business logic (Q7). Next, we ask the subjects to estimate the percentage of time they spent on actually: design contracts, generate the source code, and write the business logic with ACA.NET for the selected project (question Q8). In addition, we ask the subjects to estimate the percentage of source code that has been generated with ACA.NET (Q9).

Learnability of ACA.NET (L). The time invested in actually learning and staying up-to-date represents another success factor for DSLs. For measuring the learnability of ACA.NET we first ask the subjects for their level of experience in terms of years worked as professional software developer (Q1) and in terms of years worked with ACA.NET (Q2). Later on in the questionnaire we ask for the detailed effort numbers. In particular, we were interested in the number of days invested in learning ACA.NET (Q11) and the number of hours invested in staying up-to-date on ACA.NET (Q12).

Expressiveness of ACA.NET DSL (E). To measure the expressiveness of ACA.NET we asked the subjects how often they had to deny a customer a feature, because it could not have been implemented with ACA.NET (Q17) and how often they had to write extra code to implement a feature (Q18). Answers to both questions are given by a five-point Likert scale. Furthermore we investigated whether respondents feel that ACA.NET restricts their freedom (Q19b) and whether ACA.NET provides all the features needed to develop web services (Q19c). The answers to the latter two questions are also given with a five-point Likert scale.

To obtain a deeper insight into the expressiveness of ACA.NET we added questions Q20a and Q20b. We ask whether developers look into the source code to understand the models defined with ACA.NET (Q20a). Question Q20b assesses whether developers use the generated source code instead of the models to add custom code. Frequent use of the generated code indicates the model does not express all properties of the domain.

Reusability of ACA.NET models (R). As with traditional software engineering, one goal of a DSL is to reuse existing solutions. We addressed the reusability of ACA.NET models in question Q3. We ask the subjects whether they reuse models of existing projects. For instance, when they start a new project do they start from existing assets or from scratch.

4.3 Survey Set-Up

We conducted our survey online, in a Sharepoint environment, making it cost-effective and also appropriate, because our target group is used to this kind of surveys. We choose a self-control study [21], comparing user experience with and without the use of ACA.NET. The fact that the subjects are not able to see each others results makes the survey more resilient to bias. The fact that the survey is cost-effective, appropriate and resilient to bias, makes it *efficient* according to Pfleeger and Kitchenham [21]. Furthermore, automation reduces the contact between subjects and researchers, giving the researchers less opportunity to bias responders.

In total we invited 48 people to participate in this survey. Of 21 subjects we knew for sure they used ACA.NET and of 27 people we thought they might have experience with it. 28 people responded, of which 10 indicated they did not use ACA.NET, or their experience was too limited to answer the questions. We got 18 meaningful results, giving our survey an effective response rate of 38%. Since our target population is small, we did not use any form of sampling.

Together with the invitation for the survey, developers received an email explaining them the purpose of the survey; helping to improve the tool set they work with everyday. We expect this to be a good motivation for them to participate, especially since there has been no opportunity to give official feedback, other than bug reports on ACA.NET.

By testing the survey, we estimated the time needed to fill out the questionnaire at about 60 minutes, which is appropriate for a self-administered survey on a subject important to responders. As recommended by Pfleeger and Kitchenham [21], we added a neutral option to all Likert-scaled [22] questions.

We believe there is little risk of researcher bias, because the researchers are not part of the users or designers of ACA.NET. When creating this survey, we ensured that subjects got the possibility to reflect on both, the positive and the negative aspects of ACA.NET.

5 Results

In this section we present the results of the survey, grouped by success factor.

5.1 Reliability (I)

Developers clearly believe that the use of ACA.NET increases the quality of the delivered code, since 40% of the respondents agree with, and 50% strongly agree with Question 15b as shown in Figure 1. As one of the respondents put it: *"The application becomes less error prone since lots of tasks are automated"*. Note that only one respondent disagrees with this statement.

5.2 Usability (U)

Over 75% of the developers indicate that ACA.NET aids them in modeling by giving them a good overview of the whole connected system of servers and clients (Figure 2). The reasons indicated by the respondents include that *"using ACA.NET gives us a better overview at higher abstraction"*, and that *"the DSL design surface helps to model the services even before business logic has been designed"*. Furthermore, the ACA.NET tools were considered easy to use (*"ACA.NET provides an easy to use interface that can be taught to others very quickly."*). Note that none of the respondents agrees to the statement that ACA.NET is difficult to use (Question 19a) as shown in Figure 3.

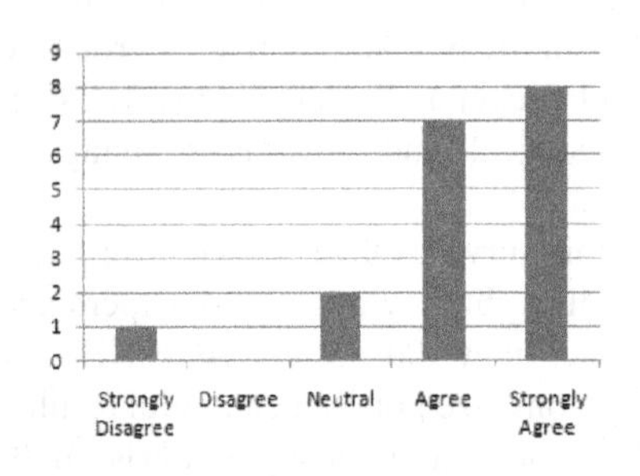

Fig. 1. Question 15b. Agreement with the statement that "fewer errors occur"

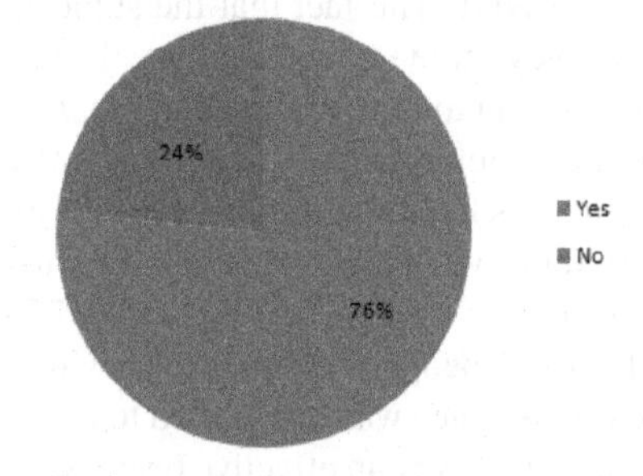

Fig. 2. Question 5. Did the ACA.NET user interface help you in modeling?

5.3 Productivity (C)

Based on the results of the survey, we can conclude that the use of ACA.NET indeed increases productivity. One of the respondents says: *"ACA.NET speeds up the implementation of trivial tasks"*. From the answers to Question 7 and Question 8 we can conclude that time spent on actually coding the services is reduced from 46% to only 18%, as shown in Figure 6. The shift in focus to the more important business logic is also underlined by a subject who responded: *"We don't think too much about Windows Communication Foundation services or the Data Access Layer anymore as we are able to concentrate on the business requirements."*

Time is not the only measure for increased productivity: we also take the amount of generated code into account. The respondents estimate that on average 40% of the code is generated, distributed as shown in Figure 4.

According to the answers on Question 16a and Question 16b, developers also feel that ACA.NET eases the design and implementation phases (Figure 5), which is likely to result in less time spent on these tasks.

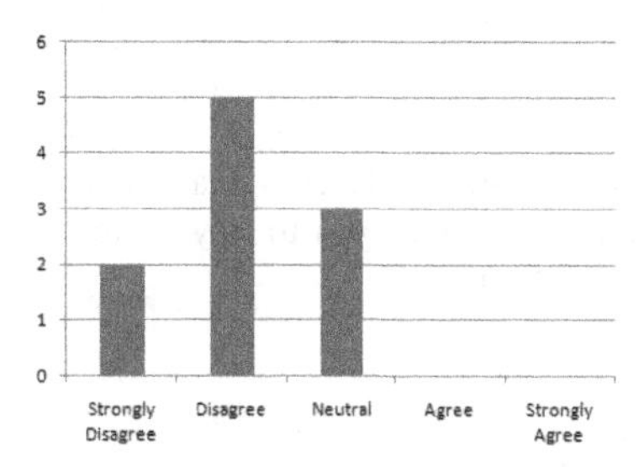

Fig. 3. Question 19a. ACA.NET is difficult to use

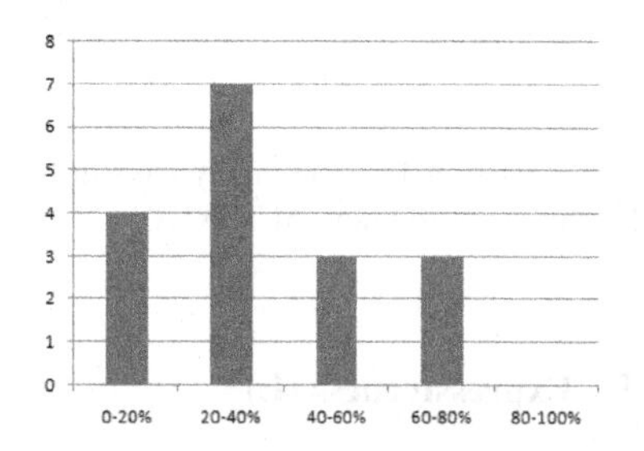

Fig. 4. Question 9. Estimate the percentage of code that was generated

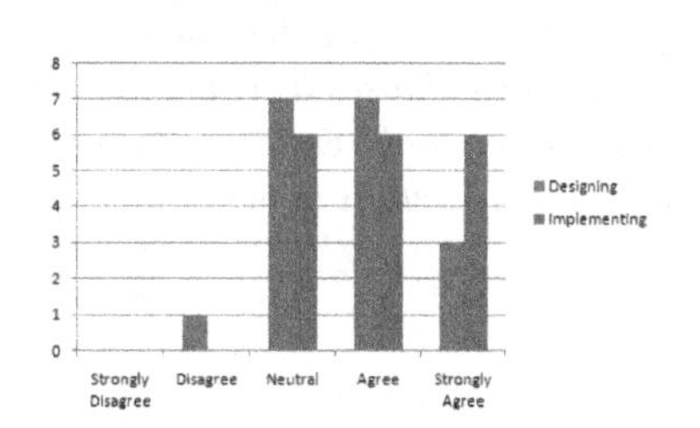

Fig. 5. Question 16. ACA.NET makes designing and implementing easier

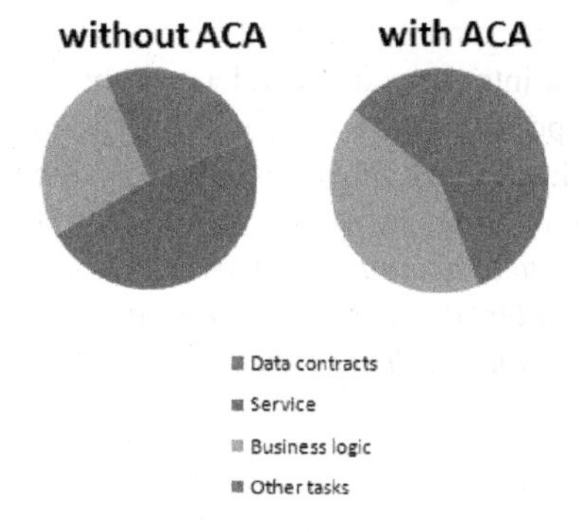

Fig. 6. Question 7 and 8. Please estimate the percentage of time you spent on typical development tasks

5.4 Learnability (L)

The respondents indicate that it took them quite some time to learn the basics of ACA.NET, as shown in Figure 7. Most respondents were able to learn ACA.NET within one week, while the maximum time mentioned was 15 days. Apart from learning ACA.NET, it also takes time to stay up to date, as shown in Figure 8.

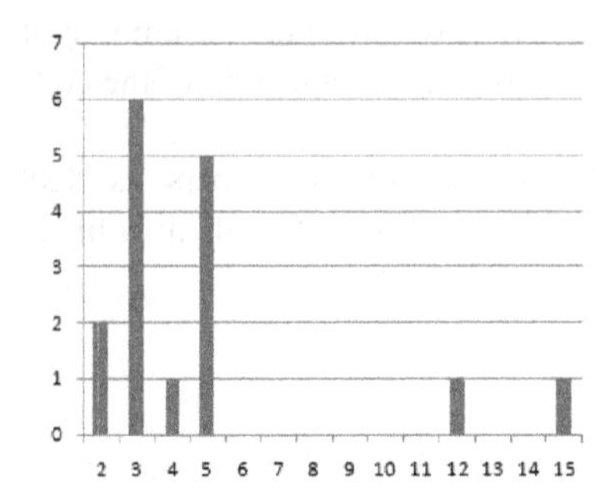

Fig. 7. Question 11. How many days did it take you to get to know ACA.NET?

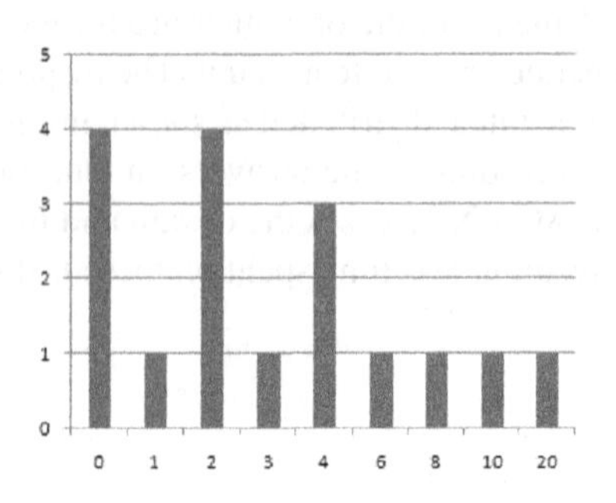

Fig. 8. Questions 12. How many hours a month does it take you to stay up to date on ACA.NET?

5.5 Expressiveness (E)

The developers turn out to be satisfied with the expressive power of ACA.NET: 60% of them agrees that ACA.NET is powerful (Figure 9). Furthermore, we see that the limited scope is not considered a problem; only few developers indicate their freedom is restricted (Figure 10). There are however some developers that indicate they miss features (Question 19c, Figure 10).

The model is a good representation of the code, since developers do not have to look into the code to understand or complete their own code (see Figure 11). However, respondents mention that it is very hard to evolve the models along with the code, which indicates lack of expressiveness. *"When the models get more complicated, such as for the web factory where you can set a lot of properties, the model loses its value - its not practical to maintain or set a lot of properties using the visual tool."* and *"For the more complex, it was to time-consuming to maintain the graphical details between updates, and you lost the overview."*

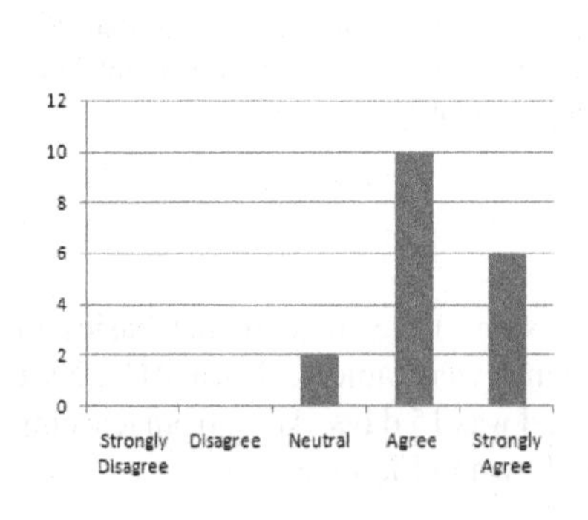

Fig. 9. Question 16c. Is ACA.NET powerful?

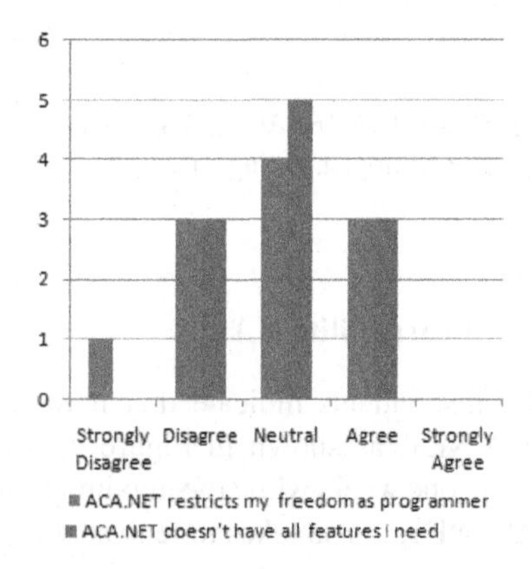

Fig. 10. Question 19. Is ACA.NET restrictive / feature-incomplete?

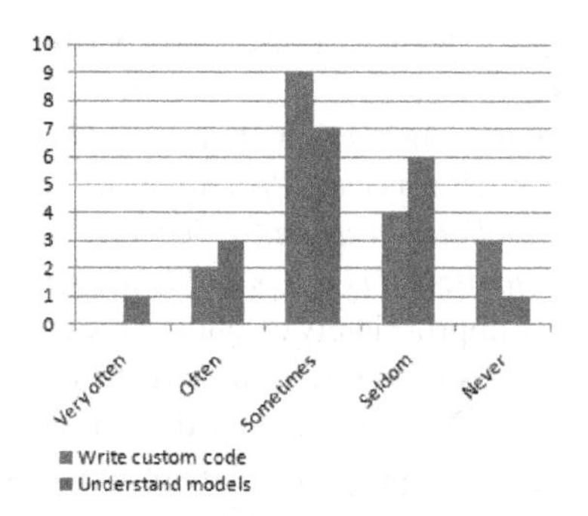

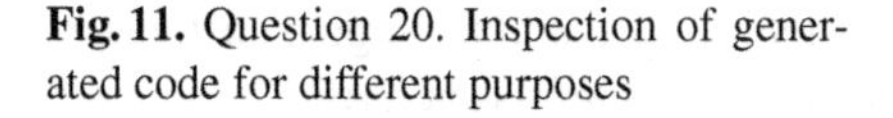

Fig. 11. Question 20. Inspection of generated code for different purposes

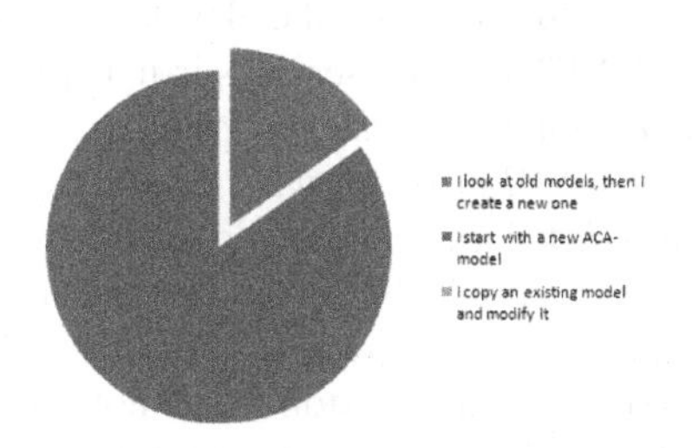

Fig. 12. Question 3. If you start with a new ACA-project, how do you proceed?

5.6 Reusability (R)

A somewhat surprising result is that *reuse* hardly contributes to the success of ACA.NET. The answers to Question 3, Figure 12, tell us ACA.NET models are never reused. Even conceptual designs are hardly ever reused, in only 10% of the cases. One possible explanation is that the current ACA.NET implementation does not directly support exporting or importing models. In particular, respondents indicated that they would like to be able to import parts of earlier models, to reuse standard architectures for services across projects, and to compose services from multiple earlier defined models. As one responder said: *"ACA.NET could be improved by providing import mechanisms which allow the importation of other ACA-files into the model."*

6 Discussion

6.1 Lessons Learned Concerning ACA.NET

Based on our study we can draw several lessons concerning ACA.NET. First, the developers indicate ACA.NET helped in increasing productivity by reducing time spent on programming services. Because project managers at Avanade indicate that programming a web service accounts for a large part of the development process, we conclude that ACA.NET also lowers time-to-market. The results also show that ACA.NET helped in increasing reliability, the vast majority of developers agree that the use of ACA.NET helps to avoid faults.

Underlying success factors were usability of the language and tool set (which was rated as positive), the learnability of the language (several days initial learning, and several hours per month to stay up to date), and the expressiveness of the language which was focused specifically towards the web services domain (and which was rated as powerful). Much to our surprise, reuse of models did not contribute to the success of ACA.NET.

Conducting the study also resulted in several suggestions for improving the ACA.NET language and tool set. A first observation is that adding the possibility to import or export partial models would make it possible to actually reuse (parts of) models, adding even more benefits to the use of ACA.NET.

Second, some of the developers observed that the abstraction that is made in ACA.NET for web services is not specific to .NET/WCF services: *"ACA.NET is very good for modeling the service layer of an enterprise application structure, but only code for the .NET based services can be generated. Unfortunately it is not possible to generate code for Java or SAP platform based services."* By appropriately extending the code generators, ACA.NET could be used to integrate services from different platforms.

Furthermore, several respondents indicated that ACA.NET was not used as often as possible, because customers do not want to make use of or be dependent on proprietary software. To cite one of the respondents: *"Customers don't use ACA.NET in quite some cases since it's an Avanade specific tool."* A way out of this could be to give customers access to the source code of the underlying code generation infrastructure.

Last but not least, several of the developers would have liked access themselves to the generator and underlying meta-models, as this would enable them to build in customer-specific features in an easier way. This actually calls for proper extension points and hooks in the language, and suggests that the level of expressiveness of the language could be further improved.

6.2 Beyond the Case at Hand

An interesting question is which general lessons we can learn from the case at hand.

First of all, the case provides further evidence that the use of a domain-specific language can reduce time-to-market and can improve system reliability. The evidence, in this case, not just comes from the creators of the language, but from the people who are actually using the language to deliver working software to their customers.

Second, the case suggests that reuse is not a critical success factor. Reuse is a notoriously hard problem, involving the identification, adaptation, and integration of existing parts. For many application domains, light-weight, copy-paste based forms of reuse may be enough, having the additional benefit of full flexibility.

Another lesson we can draw from the study is that the questionnaire itself is a useful instrument for, e.g., identifying opportunities for improving the language. In fact, we would recommend engineers involved in the design of a new domain-specific language to compose a questionnaire as part of their design effort. This questionnaire, for which ours can form a starting point, can then be used in a later stage to evaluate whether the language has met its design goals.

6.3 Threats to Validity

Content Validity. One of the threats to *content validity* when conducting an (online) survey is the fact that respondents could be influenced by other replies [21]. Therefore we made sure that it was not possible for respondents to view each others results. Furthermore, responses came from different divisions of Avanade, making it less likely that responders spoke to each other about the survey.

Another threat to content validity is the fact that respondents have to estimate the percentage of generated code and time spent on different tasks. This is the case because corresponding data were not collected during the development process. Developers could be imprecise in their memory. Because all results show similar numbers, we believe the results are sufficiently reliable.

The survey was pre-tested on a focus group, consisting of domain experts — the developers that created ACA.NET — and members of the target population. The survey questions were also reviewed by university staff with experience in empirical research. Their feedback helped in further assuring content validity.

Internal Validity. The calculations used to manipulate the data were all very simple, and constitute no threat to internal validity.

An issue of concern could be that the respondents have a commercial interest in putting up a bright picture, thus giving answers that are too positive. While we cannot exclude this possibility, we do not believe this is the case. We explicitly announced the questionnaire as an opportunity to suggest improvements for ACA.NET, encouraging them to be as critical as possible.

Survey Reliability. In order to ensure repeatability of the experiment, the full questionnaire including answer options and descriptions is available online.[4] Unfortunately we were not able to make Avanade's answers available too, for reasons of confidentiality.

External Validity. Some of the issues concerning external validity were discussed in Section 6.2, where we addressed the implications of our study beyond ACA.NET. Furthermore, we have no reason to believe that our results are specific to the *web services* domain. One characteristic of this domain, however, is that it is a "horizontal" domain, applicable in many different settings, and aimed at developers as language users. This has clearly had some influence on our questionnaire, which is tailored towards developers.

Another issue may be that the results were obtained in a *commercial* setting: we have no reason to believe that they would be different for, e.g., open source projects.

7 Conclusions

The goal of the present paper is to obtain a deeper understanding of the factors affecting the success of a domain-specific language in practice. To that end, we have analyzed experiences of developers that made use of the ACA.NET DSL in over 30 projects around the world.

The key contributions of this paper are as follows:

- The identification of a number of DSL success factors;
- A questionnaire that can be used to assess these factors in concrete DSL projects.
- The ACA.NET empirical study, in which we use the proposed questionnaire to evaluate success factors in the use of ACA.NET.

[4] See `http://www.st.ewi.tudelft.nl/~hermans/`

The outcomes of the study indicate that in the given case study the DSL helped to improve reliability, and to increase productivity. Furthermore, conducting the survey resulted in a number of suggestions for improving the DSL under study, such as increasing the level of reuse.

We see several areas for future work. One direction is to conduct a similar survey in a DSL from a less technical (horizontal) domain, but from a vertical, highly specialized DSL. The challenge here will be to find such a DSL in industry and the corresponding industrial partner that is willing to collaborate in such a survey. A second direction is to compare the results we obtained from interviewing with "hard" data obtained from, e.g., measurements on code or the software repository used. One of the challenges here will be the availability of accurate data on, e.g., reliability of projects conducted with the DSL under study.

Acknowledgements. We owe our gratitude to all responders that took the time to fill out our survey. Special thanks go out to Gerben van Loon and Steffen Vorein, for reviewing the questionnaire itself extensively.

References

1. Mernik, M., Heering, J., Sloane, A.: When and how to develop domain-specific languages. ACM Computing Surveys 37(4), 316–344 (2005)
2. Wexelblat, R.L. (ed.): History of programming languages I. ACM, New York (1981)
3. Sammet, J.E.: Programming languages: history and future. Communications of the ACM 15(7), 601–610 (1972)
4. Bergin Jr., T.J., Gibson Jr., R.G. (eds.): History of programming languages—II. ACM, New York (1996)
5. Nardi, B.A.: A small matter of programming: perspectives on end user computing. MIT Press, Cambridge (1993)
6. Herndon, R., Berzins, V.: The realizable benefits of a language prototyping language. IEEE Transactions on Software Engineering 14, 803–809 (1988)
7. Batory, D., Johnson, C., MacDonald, B., von Heede, D.: Achieving extensibility through product-lines and domain-specific languages: A case study. In: Frakes, W.B. (ed.) ICSR 2000. LNCS, vol. 1844, pp. 117–136. Springer, Heidelberg (2000)
8. van Deursen, A., Klint, P.: Little languages: little maintenance. Journal of Software Maintenance 10(2), 75–92 (1998)
9. Kieburtz, R., McKinney, L., Bell, J., Hook, J., Kotov, A., Lewis, J., Oliva, D., Sheard, T., Smith, I., Walton, L.: A software engineering experiment in software component generation. In: International Conference on Software Engineering (ICSE 1996), pp. 542–552. IEEE Computer Society, Los Alamitos (1996)
10. Christopher, D.L., Ramming, J.: Two application languages in software production. In: USENIX Symposium on Very High Level Languages Proceedings, pp. 169–187. USENIX (1994)
11. Krueger, C.W.: Software reuse. ACM Computing Surveys 24(2), 131–183 (1992)
12. Bell, J., Bellegarde, F., Hook, J., Kieburts, R.: Software design for reliability and reuse: a proof-of-concept demonstration. In: Proceedings Conference on TRI-Ada, pp. 396–404. ACM Press, New York (1994)
13. Spinellis, D., Guruprasad, V.: Lightweight languages as software engineering tools. In: Proceedings of the Conference on Domain-Specific Languages (DSL 1997), pp. 67–76. USENIX (1997)

14. Spinellis, D.: Notable design patterns for domain-specific languages. Journal of Systems and Software 56, 91–99 (2001)
15. Weiss, D.: Creating domain-specific languages: the fast process. In: First ACM-SIGPLAN Workshop on Domain-specific Languages: DSL 1997, University of Illinois, Technical Reports (1997)
16. Bhanot, V., Paniscotti, D., Roman, A., Trask, B.: Using domain-specific modeling to develop software defined radio components and applications. In: Proceedings of the 5th OOPSLA Workshop on Domain-Specific Modeling (DSM 2005), Computer Science and Information System Reports, Technical Reports (2005)
17. Baker, P., Loh, S., Weil, F.: Model-driven engineering in a large industrial context – motorola case study. In: Briand, L.C., Williams, C. (eds.) MoDELS 2005. LNCS, vol. 3713, pp. 476–491. Springer, Heidelberg (2005)
18. White, J., Schmidt, D.C., Gokhale, A.: Simplifying autonomic enterprise java bean applications via model-driven development: A case study. In: Briand, L.C., Williams, C. (eds.) MoDELS 2005. LNCS, vol. 3713, pp. 601–615. Springer, Heidelberg (2005)
19. Staron, M.: Adopting model driven software development in industry: A case study at two companies. In: Nierstrasz, O., Whittle, J., Harel, D., Reggio, G. (eds.) MoDELS 2006. LNCS, vol. 4199, pp. 57–72. Springer, Heidelberg (2006)
20. Cook, S., Jones, G., Kent, S., Wills, A.C.: Domain-Specific Development with Visual Studio DSL Tools. Microsoft.NET Development Series. Addison-Wesley, Reading (2007)
21. Pfleeger, S., Kitchenham, B.: Principles of survey research. ACM SIGSOFT Software Engineering Notes 26, 16–18 (2001)
22. Likert, R.: A technique for the measurement of attitudes. Archives of Psychology 22(140) (1932)

Evaluating Context Descriptions and Property Definition Patterns for Software Formal Validation*

Philippe Dhaussy[1], Pierre-Yves Pillain[1], Stephen Creff[1], Amine Raji[1], Yves Le Traon[2], and Benoit Baudry[3]

[1] UEB, Laboratoire LISyC, ENSIETA, BREST, F-29806 cedex 9
{dhaussy,pillaipi,creffst,rajiam}@ensieta.fr
[2] Université du Luxembourg, Campus Kirchberg
yves.letraon@uni.lu
[3] Equipe Triskell, IRISA, RENNES, F-35042
bbaudry@irisa.fr

Abstract. A well known challenge in the formal methods domain is to improve their integration with practical engineering methods. In the context of embedded systems, model checking requires first to model the system to be validated, then to formalize the properties to be satisfied, and finally to describe the behavior of the environment. This last point which we name as the proof context is often neglected. It could, however, be of great importance in order to reduce the complexity of the proof. The question is then how to formalize such a proof context. We experiment a language, named CDL (Context Description Language), for describing a system environment using actors and sequence diagrams, together with the properties to be checked. The properties are specified with textual patterns and attached to specific regions in the context. Our contribution is a report on several industrial embedded system applications.

Keywords: Formal methods, context description, property patterns, observers, timed automata, model checking.

1 Introduction

In the field of embedded systems, software architectures must be designed to ensure increasingly critical functions subjected to strong reliability and real time constraints. Due to these constraints, embedded software architectures often have to go through certification which requires a rigorous design process based on tight rules. However, due to the increasing complexity of systems, there is no guarantee that such a design process leads to error free systems. Formal methods offer rigorous and powerful solutions for helping embedded system designers analyze, validate, or transform systems in a provable sound way. For that purpose, behavior checking methods have been explored for several years by many research teams [2, 8], but also by major companies.

* Empirical results category paper.

A. Schürr and B. Selic (Eds.): MODELS 2009, LNCS 5795, pp. 438–452, 2009.

Nevertheless, integration of formal methods in the engineering process is still too weak comparatively to the huge need for reliability in critical systems. This contradiction partly finds its causes in the actual difficulty to handle theoretical concepts within an industrial framework. Besides, formal verification techniques suffer from the combinatorial explosion induced by the internal complexity of the software to be verified. This is particularly recurrent when dealing with real-time embedded systems, interacting with a large number of actors. Additionally, formally checking properties on system models requires the expression of these properties in the form of temporal logic formula such as LTL [18] or CTL [16]. While these languages have a high expressiveness they are not easily readable and easy to handle by the engineers in industrial projects. To overcome this problem, some approaches [5, 12, 10] propose to formulate temporal properties using textual definition patterns.

One way to circumvent the problem of combinatorial explosion consists of specifying/restricting the system environment behavior or the context in which the system will be used. The system is then tightly synchronized with its environment. This context corresponds to well-defined operational phases, such as, for example, initialization, reconfiguration, degraded modes, etc. Moreover, properties are often related to specific use cases of the system. So, it is not necessary to verify them over all the environment scenarios. To the best of our knowledge, no approach currently provides such feature dedicated to an industrial use. In the case of an environment composed of several parallel actors, describing the environmental context can be a difficult task. To address these problems, we proposed [21, 22] the Context Description Language (CDL). This DSL allows specifying the context with scenarios and temporal properties using property patterns. Moreover, CDL provides the ability to link each expressed property to a limited scope of the system behavior.

In this paper, we provide a two years experience feedback on applying our formal verification approach on several aeronautic and military case studies. This paper presents the approach and discusses the results on an exercise in bringing engineers to use a formal method. First, we show that specifying more precisely the context in which the system will be used can reduce the problem of state explosion. Second, we show how to formalize, with CDL, specifications of an execution context, how to formalize properties and how to attach these properties to specific regions in this context.

For better understanding, this approach is illustrated with one industrial case study: the software part of an anti-aircraft system (S_CP[1]), shown Fig.1. It controls the internal modes of the system, its physical devices (radars, sensors, actuators...) and their actions in response to incoming signals from the environment. Due to page limitation, only one requirement (Listing 1) and one sequence diagram are considered to illustrate our approach along the paper.

The paper is organized as follows: Section 2 sets the scope of our work in current formal verification practices and presents related work. Section 3 describes our DSL for contexts and properties specification. Section 4 presents the proposed methodology used for the experiments, as well as the framework supporting it. In section 5 we give selected results on several industrial case studies. Finally, section 6 discusses our approach and future work and concludes.

---

[1] For confidential reasons, company and system names are not mentioned in this paper.

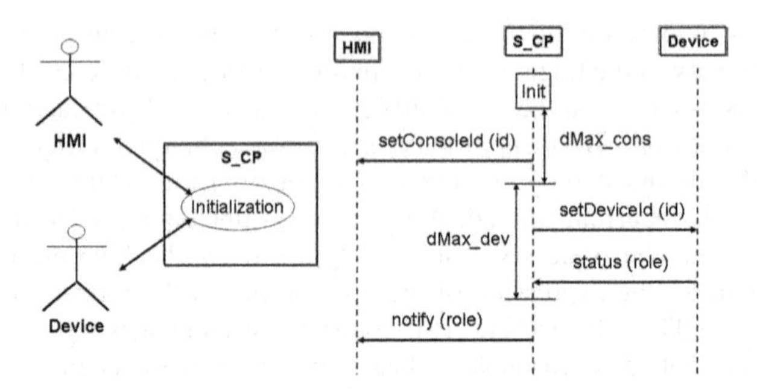

Fig. 1. S_CP system: partial use case and sequence diagram describing the behavior of the system during the initialization phase

> **Requirement:** "During initialization procedure, the S_CP shall associate a generic device identifier to one or several roles in the system (Device), before dMax_dev time units. It shall also associate an identifier to each console (HMI), before dMax_cons time units. The S_CP shall send a notifyRole message for each connected generic device, to each connected console. Initialization procedure shall end successfully, when the S_CP has set all the generic device identifiers and all console identifiers and all notifyRole messages have been sent."
> **End Requirement**

Listing 1. Initialization requirement for the S_CP system

2 Context and Related Work

These days, embedded software systems integrate more and more advanced features, such as complex data structures, recursion, multithreading. These features pose challenging theoretical and practical problems to developers of automatic analysis and verification methods. Despite the increased level of automation, users of finite-state verification tools are still constrained to specify the system requirements in their specification language, which is most of the time informal. This fact is more challenging than it appears because of the difficulty to write logic formula correctly without some expertise in the idioms of the specification languages. While temporal logic based languages allow a great expressivity for the properties, these languages are not adapted to practically describe most of the requirements expressed in industrial analysis documents. First, a requirement can refer to many events related to the execution of the model or environment (cf. Listing 1). Then, it depends on an execution history that has to be taken into account when checking it. As a result, the logical formulas are of great complexity and become difficult to read and to handle by engineers. It is thus necessary to facilitate the requirement expression with adequate languages: abstracting some details in the property description, at a price of reducing the expressivity. This conclusion has been done by many authors a long time ago and some [5, 12, 10] proposed to formulate the properties using definition patterns. Patterns are textual templates that capture common temporal properties and that can be instantiated in a specific context to express application-specific properties.

Specification patterns [5, 10] have been proposed to assist engineers in expressing system requirements directly in a formal specification language, such as linear-time temporal logic (LTL). These patterns represent commonly occurring types of real-time properties found in several requirement documents for appliances and automotive embedded systems applications.

In addition to the ease of writing real time properties, the patterns proposed by Dwyer [5] and Cheng [10] have been defined to deal with high-level specifications. Providing high-quality requirements is important since they serve as a baseline between multiple teams working on the model under study (MUS[2]). Besides, Hassine et al. [17] suggest an abstract high level pattern-based approach to the description of property specifications based on Use Case Maps (UCM). They propose to build property pattern systems that consider architectural aspects. Smith et al. developed *Propel* [12], in which they extended the specification patterns of Dwyer et al. [5] to address important aspects about properties. They extend the patterns with options that can be used explicitly on these patterns.

In this paper, we reuse the categories of Dwyer's patterns and extend them to deal with more specific temporal properties which appear when high-level specifications are refined. Furthermore, in several industrial projects, intended requirements are not associated to the entire lifecycle of software, but only to specific steps in its lifecycle. In the system specification documents, requirements are often expressed in a context of the system execution. For that reason, in addition to the use of property patterns, we propose to link formalized properties to a specific execution context and thus to limit the scope of the property. Hassine et al.[17] consider applying patterns to architectural aspects; we focus on applying them to specific functional contexts, which refer to system use cases. The benefit is to explicitly specify the conditions under which is its meaningful to check the validity of a given property. So, according to this feature, properties will be checked only in a specific execution context. Consequently, the number of states over which the property is checked considerably decreases. In this paper, we address the problem of applying property patterns in industrial practices and provide concrete statistical results.

3 Context Description Language

In our approach, CDL aims at formalizing the context with scenarios and temporal properties using property patterns. This DSML[3] is based on UML 2. A CDL model describes, on the one hand, the context using activity and sequence diagrams and, on the other hand, the properties to be checked using property patterns. The originality of CDL is its ability to link each expressed property to a context diagram, i.e. a limited scope of the system behavior. For formal validation, CDL associates a formal semantics to UML models, described as a set of traces [7, 13, 22]. The language is designed and tooled to offer a simple and usable context description framework.

The syntax of the CDL language is specified in multiple and complementary ways. One is the metamodel (e.g. the domain ontology) enhanced with OCL constraints. The

[2] In this paper, MUS denotes the component model specified by the industrial in languages such as UML 2, AADL [19], SDL [4], etc.

[3] Domain Specific Modeling Language.

metamodel is an ECore model (EMF). It is annotated with OCL invariants to enforce its semantics. A diagrammatical concrete syntax is created for the context description and a textual syntax for the property expression. The following paragraphs outline: (i) the proof context formalization, (ii) the property expressions.

In [11], we proposed a context description language using UML 2 diagrams (cf. Fig.2 for case study illustration). It is inspired by Use Case Charts of [13]. We extend this language to allow several entities (as Device and HMI in Fig.1 and Fig.2) to compose the proof context. Those entities are running in parallel. CDL is hierarchically constructed in three levels: Level-1 is a set of use case diagrams which describes hierarchical activity diagrams. Either alternative between several executions (alternative/merge) or a parallelization of several executions (fork/join) is available. Level-2 is a set of scenario diagrams organized by alternatives. Each scenario is fully described at Level-3 by UML 2 sequence diagrams. These diagrams are composed of two lifelines, one for the proof context and another for the MUS. Delayable interaction event occurrences are specified on these lifelines. Counters limit the iterations of diagram executions. It ensures the generation of finite context automata, as described in [11]. Transitions at Level-1 and Level-2 are enabled according to the values of some un-timed guards or timed guards. As mentioned in the introduction, the approach links the context description (Level-1 or Level-2) to the specification of the properties (as P1 and P2 in Fig.2) to be checked by stereotyped links property/scope. A property can have several scopes and several properties can refer a single diagram. Semantics of Level-1 and Level-2 is described in terms of traces, inspired by [7]. Level-1 and Level-2 are based on the semantics of the scenarios and expressed by construction rules of sets of traces built using *seq*, *alt* and *par* operators (*par* only for Level-1). At Level-3, the semantics of a scenario is expressed by a set of traces as described in [7] and in accordance with the semantics of UML 2 sequence diagrams. A scenario trace is an ordered events sequence which describes a history of the interactions between the context and the model. A scenario with several interactions is described by a set of traces.

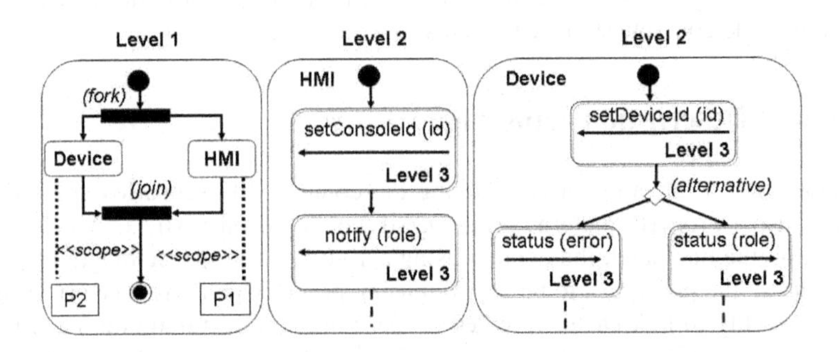

Fig. 2. S_CP case study: partial representation of the context. Initial Use cases and Sequence diagrams (cf. Fig.1) are transformed and completed to create the context model. All context scenarios are represented, combined with parallel and alternative operators, in terms of CDL.

For the property specification, we use a pattern-based approach and integrate property patterns description in the CDL language (we refer the reader to [22] for details). Patterns [5] are classified in basic families, which take into account the timed aspects of the properties to be specified. The patterns identified allow properties of answer (*Response*), the necessity one (*Precedence*), of absence (*Absence*), of existence (*Existence*) to be expressed. The properties refer to detectable events like transmissions or receptions of signals, actions, and model state changes. These basic forms are enriched by options (*Pre-arity*, *Post-arity*, *Immediacy*, *Precedence*, *Nullity*, *Repeatability*) using annotations [10]. The property must be taken into account during all the model execution, before, after or between occurrences of events. Patterns have the possibility of expressing guards on the occurrences of events expressed in the properties [22]. Guards refer to variables declared in the context model. This mechanism adds precision to the property/scope reference introduced in the previous section. Another extension of the patterns is the possibility of handling sets of events, ordered or not ordered similar to the proposal of [9]. The operators *AN* and *ALL* respectively specify if an event or all the events, ordered (*Ordered*) or not (*Combined*), of an event set are concerned with the property. Illustrating with our case study, Fig.3 depicts one bounded liveness property (P1) obtained from the *R1* requirement decomposition as explained in section 4:

> ***R1:*** *During initialization procedure, the S_CP shall associate an identifier to NC console (HMI), before dMax_cons time units.*

R1 is linked to the communication sequence between the S_CP and consoles (HMI). According to the sequence diagram of Fig.1, the association to other devices has no effect on *R1*.

```
Property P1 ;
   exactly one occurence of  S_CP_hasReachState_Init
   eventually leads-to [0..dMax_cons]
   ALL Ordered
        exactly one occurence of  sendSetConsoleIdToHMI1
        exactly one occurence of  sendSetConsoleIdToHMI2
   end
   S_CP_hasReachState_Init  may never occurs
   one of sendSetConsoleIdToHMI1  cannot occur before  S_CP_hasReachState_Init
   one of sendSetConsoleIdToHMI2  cannot occur before  S_CP_hasReachState_Init
   repeatibility : true
```

Fig. 3. S_CP case study: A response pattern from R1 requirement

In the illustrated case study, the number of consoles (*HMI*) considered is two (*NC*=2). R1 specifies an observation of event occurrences. *S_CP_hasReachState_Init* refers a state change in a MUS process. *sendSetConsoleIdToHMI1* and *sendSetConsoleIdToHMI2* refer to the ones described in the CDL model (Fig.2). As mentioned in section 4, our OBP toolset transforms each property into an observer automaton [6], including a *reject* node. With observers, the properties we can handle are of safety and bounded liveness type. The accessibility analysis consists of checking if there is a *reject* state reached by a property observer. This *reject* node is reached after detecting event "*S_CP_hasReachState_Init*" if the sequence "*sendSetConsoleIdToHMI1*" and "*sendSetConsoleIdToHMI2*" is not produced in that order before *dMax_cons* time units. Conversely, the *reject* node is not reached either if event "*S_CP_hasReachState_Init*" is never received, or if the sequence of the two events above is correctly produced (in the right order and with the right delay). Consequently, such a property can be verified by using reachability analysis implemented in a formal model checker.

4 Methodology and OBP Toolset

Our proposed specification and analysis process is based on checking a set of requirements on the system interacting with its environment. To perform such checking, we suppose that the set of properties can be formalized into a logic form, that the environment interactions are also formally modeled as well as the possibility to simulate the MUS in order to use a formal verification tool. With this hypothesis, the process is decomposed into the following steps:

– *Context Description* (Fig.4.a): The environment interactions are formally modeled with CDL activities diagrams (as illustrated Fig.2). This activity produces a set of CDL context diagrams.
– *Property Specification* (Fig.4.b): The set of properties are formalized with property patterns (as illustrated Listing 1). This activity produces a set of CDL pattern-based properties.

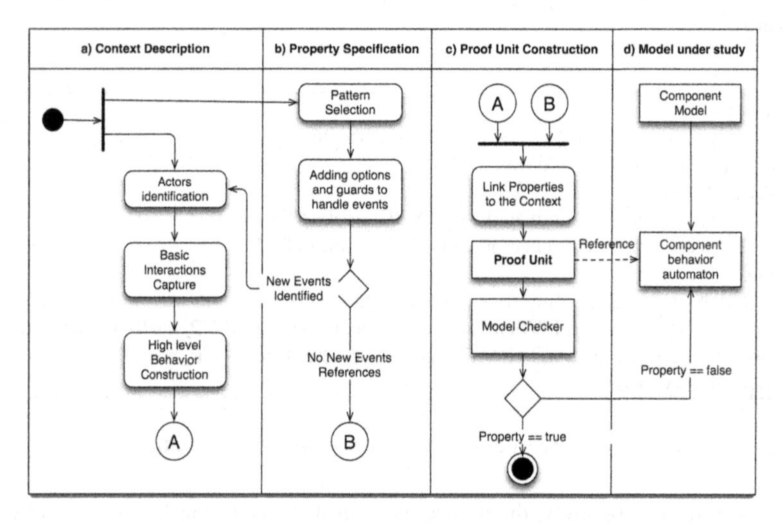

Fig. 4. Activity diagram overviewing our specification and analysis process

– *Proof Unit Construction* (Fig.4.c): We proposed in [20] the *Proof Unit* (PU) concept, which gathers all required data to perform proof activities, i.e. a reference to the model to be checked (MUS), the context models and the properties (CDL model) to be verified. The set of constructed PUs represents the set of requirements to be checked on the MUS to prove it is correct (cf. Fig.5).

– *Model Under Study* (Fig.4.d): It has to be simulated in order to use a formal verification tool. For this, OBP produces set of error observers. The observers perform dynamic diagnosis and play the role of probes to locate the cause of an error. When a fault is located, it is necessary to modify the model and create or modify requirement

The prerequisite of the methodology is the organization of the industrial specifications into two sets: (i) the design models that represent the MUS structure and behavior; (ii) the requirements that design models have to fulfill. This organization is necessary to extract useful information about the context execution for a given requirement (conditions under which a requirement has to be fulfilled). Indeed, in industrial requirement documents, this contextual information is very often implicit or disseminated in several documents and long discussions with engineers are usually needed to precisely understand the different contexts for the system and capture them in a model. Considering our case study, the given requirement (Listing 1) can be decomposed and reordered into four sub-requirements, stated as follow:

R1: *During initialization procedure, the S_CP shall associate an identifier to NC console (IHM), before dMax_cons time units.*

R2: *After, the S_CP shall associate a generic device identifier to NE roles in the system (Device), before dMax_dev time units.*

R3: *Each device returns a statusRole message to S_CP before dMax_ack time units.*

R4: *The S_CP shall send an notifyRole message for each connected generic device, to each connected console. Initialization procedure shall end successfully, when the S_CP has set all the generic device identifiers and all console identifiers and all notifyRole messages have been sent.*

After this decomposition, the user can specify more easily these requirements with definition property patterns.

We use the CDL language to represent the context, using actors and sequence diagrams, and all the requirements. The constructed CDL models reference elements of the MUS (events, variables). Elements of CDL models and MUS are at the same abstraction level. Moreover, we extract a formal specification describing the MUS's behavior. This description is generally represented as a timed automaton so that it can be executed by a simulator after model transformations. Property patterns capture, with a textual format, types of properties translated from the requirement documents.

It is obvious that providing all these verification proof units is not a trivial activity. It takes a great part of time and effort within a project. Besides, verification efforts made to check whether an implementation meets the requirements have to be capitalized. This capitalization captures the business logic to be used to redo the proof if the requirements and thus the implementation evolve over the development lifecycle. The definition of a general formal framework for the proof unit concept is out of the scope of this paper and left for future work.

To carry out our experiments, we implemented the *Observer Based Prover* (OBP[4]) tool onto the Eclipse platform through plug-ins. OBP takes as input the MUS behavior model and CDL models. OBP is an implementation of a CDL language translation

[4] OBP is available (version 2.0) under EPL license at : http://gforge.enseeiht.fr/projects/obp

in terms of formal languages, i.e. IF2 [2] or FIACRE [15] language. IF2 is based on timed automata [1] extended to the asynchronous communicating process context. Work is in progress to finalize the translation into FIACRE language and thus take benefits from the TINA [14] model checker. The essence of a translational approach to semantics is to move to a technological space that has a precise semantics [3] and tools. As depicted in Fig.5, OBP leverages existing academic simulators and model checkers, as TINA, IFx [2] or CADP [8].

To handle the gap between CDL meta-model and the final DSLs (e.g. IF2 or FIACRE) the translation has several stages. We defined an ad-hoc domain-specified transformation language in terms of ECore metamodel and define a Model to Model transformation chain. From CDL context diagrams, OBP tool generates a set context path automata which represent the set of the environment runs. OBP generates all the possible paths. Each path represents one possible interaction between model and context. The OBP tool generates, with a similar model transformation technique, the observer automata from the properties. Each generated context path is transformed into an IF2 automaton which is composed with the MUS and the generated observer automata by the IFx simulator. To validate the component model, it is necessary to compose each path with the model and the observers. Each property must be verified for all paths. The accessibility analysis is carried out on the result of the composition between a path, a set of observers and the MUS. If there is a *reject* state reached of a property observer for one of paths, then the property is considered as false.

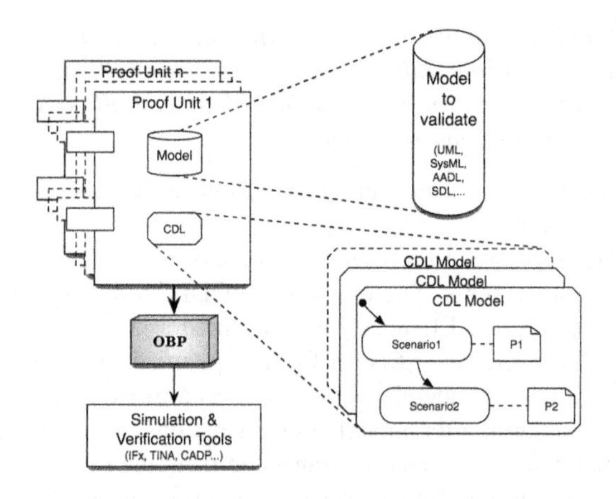

Fig. 5. Proof Units transformation with OBP

At present time, the input MUS of OBP (Fig.5) are imported currently with IF2 format. To import models with standard format as UML 2, AADL [19] or SDL [4], it is necessary to implement adequate translators as studied in projects such as TopCased[5] or Omega[6]. The model driven developed tool OBP set out in this paragraph was used in several case studies which are summed up in the experiment following section.

[5] http://www.topcased.org
[6] http://www-omega.imag.fr

5 Experiments and Results

Our approach was applied to several embedded systems applications in avionic or electronic industrial domain. These experiments are carried out with our french industrial partners. This section reports on six case studies (CS_1 to CS_6). Four of the software components come from an industrial A and two from a B. For each industrial component, the industrial partner provided requirement documents (use cases, requirements in natural language) and the component executable model. Component executable models are described with UML, completed by ADA or JAVA programs, or with SDL language. The number of requirements in Table 1 evaluates the complexity of the component. To validate these models, we follow the methodology described in section 4. So, we describe the following phases: property specification, context description and proof unit construction.

Table 1. Industrial case study classification

	CS_1	CS_2	CS_3	CS_4	CS_5[7]	CS_6
Modeling language	SDL	SDL	SDL	SDL	UML2	UML2
Number of code lines	4 000	15 000	30 000	15 000	38 000[8]	25 000[9]
Number of requirements	49	94	136	85	188	151

5.1 Property Specification

Requirements are inputs of our approach. Here, the work consists in transforming natural language requirements into temporal properties. To create the CDL models with patterns-based properties, we analyzed the software engineering documents of the proposed case studies. We transformed textual requirements. We focused on requirements which can be translated into observer automata. Firstly, we note that most of requirements had to be rewritten into a set of several properties (as shown in the S_CP case study along the paper). Secondly, model requirements of different abstraction levels are mixed. We extracted requirement sets corresponding to the model abstraction level. Finally, we observe that most of the textual requirements are ambiguous. We had to rewrite them consequently to discussion with industrial partners.

Table 2 shows the number of properties which are translated from requirements. We consider three categories of requirements. *Provable* requirements correspond to requirements which can be captured with our approach and can be translated into observers. The proof technique can be applied on a given context without combinatorial explosion. *Non computable* requirements are requirements which can be interpreted by a pattern but cannot be translated into an observer. For example, liveness properties cannot be translated because they are unbounded. Observers capture only bounded liveness properties. From the interpretation, we could generate another temporal logic formula, which could feed a model checker as TINA. *Non provable*

[7] CS_5 corresponds to the S_CP case study described partially in section 2.
[8] The UML model is implemented by 38 000 lines ADA program.
[9] The UML model is implemented by 25 000 lines JAVA program.

Table 2. Table highlighting the number of expressible properties in 6 industrial case studies

	CS_1	CS_2	CS_3	CS_4	CS_5	CS_6	Average
Provable properties	38/49 (78%)	73/94 (78%)	72/136 (53%)	49/85 (58%)	155/188 (82%)	41/151 (27%)	428/703 (61%)
Non-computable properties	0/49 (0%)	2/94 (2%)	24/136 (18%)	2/85 (2%)	18/188 (10%)	48/151 (32%)	94/703 (13%)
Non-provable properties	11/49 (22%)	19/94 (20%)	40/136 (29%)	34/85 (40%)	15/188 (8%)	62/151 (41%)	181/703 (26%)

requirements are requirements which cannot be interpreted at all with our patterns. It is the case when a property refers to undetectable events for the observer, such as the absence of a signal.

For the CS_5, we note that the percentage (82%) of provable properties is very high. One reason is that the most of 188 requirements was written with a good property pattern matching. For the CS_6, we note that the percentage (27%) is very low. It was very difficult to re-write the requirements from specification documentation. We should have spent much time to interpret requirements with our industrial partner to formalize them with our patterns.

5.2 Context Description

After property definition, we had to link each property to environment scenarios. Here, the work consisted in transforming use cases into context with our CDL language. One or several CDL contexts have been created according to the complexity of behavior contexts and to the environment actor number. Table 3 shows the number of paths obtained for different CDL models for the case study CS_1. This number depends on alternative and parallel operators, actors, interactions used in the CDL model. We linked a set of properties related to a specific phase or scenarios at each CDL model. We note that the verification time can be long (for example, 20 minutes for CDL_4 and CS_1) because the compilation time for state graphs IFx generation for each context path. In the future work, we focus on path reduction and evaluating how paths can be equivalent with respect to a particular property.

Table 3. Table highlighting the number of CDL and paths generated for CS_1

	CDL_1	CDL_2	CDL_3	CDL_4	CDL_5
Number of actors	1	3	3	5	3
Number of path	3	128	82	612	96
Time of verification (sec)	6	256	164	1224	192

5.3 Proof Unit Exploitation

In the case studies, for each CDL model, one proof unit is created. A proof unit enables to organize a set of observers and one context. For each path generated by OBP, one accessibility graph is generated and represents the set of all possible model executions.

A property is not verified by the tool if a "*reject*" observer automata state exists. For this, OBP produces set of error observers. During simulation execution, combinatorial explosion may appear. We do not resolve this point, but we propose this partial solution. It is necessary to create specific contexts in order to restrict the behaviors of the model. The solution is to initialize the system in specific configurations and to create specific CDL models which restrict scenario spaces with counters, actors, message parameters. So, partial verification is made on restricted scenario spaces.

6 Discussion and Conclusion

CDL is a prototype language to formalize contexts and properties. But CDL concepts can be implemented in another language. For example, context diagrams are easily described using UML 2. CDL permits us to check our methodology. In future work, CDL can be viewed as an intermediate language. Today, the results obtained using the currently implemented CDL language and OBP are very encouraging. For each case study, it was possible to build proof units which take CDL models as input and which generate sets of paths.

6.1 Approach Benefits

CDL contributes to overcome the combinatorial explosion by allowing partial verification on restricted scenarios specified by the context automata. CDL permits to formalize contexts and non ambiguous properties. Property can be linked to whole or specific contexts. During experiments, we noted that some requirements were often described in the available documentation in an incomplete way. The collaboration with engineers responsible for developing this documentation has motivated them to consider a more formal approach to express their requirements, which is certainly a positive improvement. In some case study, 70% textual requirements can be rewritten more easily with pattern property. So, CDL permits a better formal verification appropriation by industrial partners.

Contexts and properties are verification data. The set of proof units gather all these data to perform proof activities and validate models. These data have to be "capitalized" if the implementation evolves over the development lifecycle. Proof units formalize proof contexts. It thus appears essential to study a framework to describe and formalize proof contexts as MDA components jointly describing the requirements to be checked and environment behaviors in which the model is plunged at the time of simulations and the formal analysis.

6.2 Using the CDL Language

In case studies, context diagrams were built, on the one hand, from scenarios described in the design documents and, on the other hand, from the sentences of requirement documents. Two major difficulties are raised. The first one is the lack of complete and coherent description of the environment's behavior. Use cases describing interactions between the MUS (S_CP for instance) and its environment are often incomplete. For instance, data concerning interaction modes may be implicit. CDL diagrams development thus required discussions with experts who have designed the models under study in order to explicit all context assumptions.

The problem comes from the difficulty to formalize system requirements into formal properties. These requirements are expressed in several documents of different (possibly low) levels. Furthermore, they are written in a textual form and many of them can have several interpretations. Others implicitly refer to an applicable configuration, operational phase or history without defining it. Such information, necessary for verification, can only be deduced by manually analyzing design and requirements documents and by interviewing expert engineers.

The use of CDL as a framework for formal and explicit context and requirement definition can overcome these two difficulties: it uses a specification style very close to UML and thus readable by engineers. In all case studies, the feedback from industrial collaborators indicates that CDL models enhance communication between developers with different levels of experience and backgrounds. Additionally, CDL models enable developers, guided by behavior CDL diagrams, to structure and formalize the environment description of their systems and their requirements.

Furthermore, constraints from CDL can guide developers to construct formal properties to check against their models. As a result, developers can formalize system requirements. Using CDL, they have a means to rigorously check whether requirements are captured appropriately in the models using simulation and model checking techniques. Nevertheless, property patterns will continue to evolve as we receive feedback from academia and industry about possible improvements.

6.3 Property Proofs

In the case studies, about forty significant requirements have been formally verified. These requirements were written by using the property language presented section 3, and then was translated automatically into IF2 observer automata. About 13% (non-computable) of the requirements (cf Table 2) required manual translation. They did not match the safety and bounded response time translation pattern,. The 61% (provable) are translated and afterwards verified automatically. For the others 26%, the requirements have to be discussed with the industrial partners to improve their use. Following that approach, we found, in two case studies (CS_1 and CS_5), an execution that didn't meet the requirements. Each case study corresponds to an operational embedded system. The classical simulation techniques could not permit to find these errors.

6.4 Future Work

One element highlight, working on embedded software case studies with industrial partners, is the need of formal verification expertise capitalization. Given our experience in formal checking for validation activities, it seems important to structure the approach and the data handled during the proof. For that purpose, we identified MDA components, called *proof units*, referencing all the data, models, meta-models, etc. necessary to the verification. The definition of such MDA components can take part in a better methodological framework, and afterwards a better integration of validation techniques in model development processes. Indeed, *proof units* themselves are handled as models, and are managed like a product resulting from the specification activities. As a conceptual framework, they allow the activity and the knowledge to be capitalized by gathering the necessary data to the proof. Consequently, the development process must include a step of environmental specification making it possible to generate sets of bounded behaviors in a complete way. This assumption is not formally justified in this article but is based on the essential idea that the designer can correctly develop a software system only if he knows the constraints of use. This must be provided formally by the process analysis of the designed software architecture, using a framework of development process. Although the CDL approach has been shown scalable on several industrial case studies, the approach suffer from a lack of methodology. The handling of contexts, and then the formalization of CDL diagrams, must be done carefully in order to avoid the combinatorial explosion when generating linear context path to be composed with the observer automata. The definition of such a methodology will be addressed by the next step of this work.

One essential point, dealing with model transformations, is the feedback obtained in the formal target technical space into the source one. We take advantages of model driven techniques and transformation traces in tooling to have validation feedbacks on source models. Current and future works are dealing with increasing diagnosis feedbacks to different users, including requirement managers and component model designers.

In addition, work is still in progress at CDL level. It focuses on path reduction, evaluating how paths can be equivalent with respect to a particular property. This optimization aims at reducing the combinatorial explosion, allowing treating larger and larger applications. Otherwise, experiments shown that part of the requirements found in industrial specification documents were not translatable into property patterns proposed by the approach. Several directions are followed to face the problem, one is to extend actual patterns, and another is to create other patterns. Implementation of experimental extended patterns is in progress.

Acknowledgments. This work results from collaboration between the authors and other members of the Ensieta team. We thank Leilde V. for his contribution in the OBP development and Aizier B. for his experiments and results.

References

1. Alur, R., Dill, D.: A Theory of Timed Automata. Theoretical computer Science 126(2), 183–235 (2004)
2. Bozga, M., Graf, S., Mounier, L.: IF2: A validation environment for component-based real-time systems. In: Brinksma, E., Larsen, K.G. (eds.) CAV 2002. LNCS, vol. 2404, p. 343. Springer, Heidelberg (2002)
3. Clarke, T., Evans, A., Sammut, P., Willians, J.: Applied Meamodeling: A foundation for Language Driven Development. Technical report, version 0.1, Xactium (2004)
4. ITU-T. Recommendations Z-100. Specification and Description Language (SDL) (1994)
5. Dwyer, M.B., Avrunin, G.S., Corbett, J.C.: Patterns in property specifications for finite-state verification. In: Proc. of the 21st Int. Conf. on Software Engineering, pp. 411–420. IEEE Computer Society Press, Los Alamitos (1999)
6. Halbwachs, N., Lagnier, F., Raymond, P.: Synchronous observers and the verification of reactive systems. In: 3rd int. Conf. on Algebraic Methodology and Software Technology, AMAST 1993 (1993)

7. Haugen, O., Husa, K.E., Runde, R.K., Stolen, K.: Stairs: Towards formal design with sequence diagrams. Journal of Software and System Modeling (2005)
8. Fernandez, J.-C., et al.: CADP: A Protocol Validation and Verification Toolbox. In: Alur, R., Henzinger, T.A. (eds.) CAV 1996. LNCS, vol. 1102. Springer, Heidelberg (1996)
9. Janssen, W., Mateescu, R., Mauw, S., Fennema, P., Stappen, P.: Model Checking for Managers. In: Dams, D.R., Gerth, R., Leue, S., Massink, M. (eds.) SPIN 1999. LNCS, vol. 1680, pp. 92–107. Springer, Heidelberg (1999)
10. Konrad, S., Cheng, B.: Real-Time Specification Patterns. In: Proc. of the 27th Int. Conf. on Software Engineering (ICSE 2005), St Louis, MO, USA (2005)
11. Roger, J.C.: Exploitation de contextes et d'observateurs pour la vérification formelle de modèles, Phd report, Univ. of Rennes I (2006)
12. Smith, R., Avrunin, G.S., Clarke, L., Osterweil, L.: Propel: An Approach Supporting Property Elucidation. In: Proc. of the 24th Int. Conf. on Software Engineering, pp. 11–21. ACM Press, New York (2002)
13. Whittle J.: Specifying precise use cases with use case charts. In MoDELS 2006, Satellite Events, pp. 290–301 (2005)
14. Berthomieu, B., Vernadat, F.: Time Petri nets analysis with TINA. In: 3rd Int. Conf. on the Quantitative Evaluation of Systems (QEST 2006), Riverside, USA, pp. 123–124 (2006)
15. Berthomieu, B., Bodeveix, J., Filali, M., Garavel, H., Lang, F., Peres, F., Saad, R., Stoecker, J., Vernadat, F.: The Syntax and Semantics of FIACRE, Version 1.0 alpha. Technical report projet ANR05RNTL03101 OpenEmbeDD (2007)
16. Clarke, E.M., Emerson, E.A., Sistla, A.P.: Automatic verification of finite-state concurrent systems using temporal logic specifications. ACM Trans. Program. Lang. Syst. 2, 244–263 (1986)
17. Hassine, J., Rilling, J., Dssouli, R.: Use Case Maps as a property specification language. Software System Model 8, 205–220 (2009)
18. Manna, Z., Pnueli, A.: The temporal logic of reactive and concurrent systems. Springer, New York (1992)
19. Feiler, P., Gluch, D.P., Hudak, J.J.: The Architecture Analysis and Design Language (AADL): An introduction.Technical report, Society of Automotive Engineers, SAE (2006)
20. Dhaussy, P., Boniol, F.: Mise en œuvre de composants MDA pour la validation formelle de modèles de systèmes d'information embarqués, pp. 133–157. RSTI (2007)
21. Dhaussy P., Auvray J., De Belloy S., Boniol F., Landel E.: Using context descriptions and property definition patterns for software formal verification, Workshop Modevva 2008 (hosted by ICST 2008), Lillehammer, Norway (2008)
22. Dhaussy, P., Creff, S., Pillain, P.Y., Leilde, V.: CDL language specification (Context Description Language). Technical report version N° DTN/2009/8, ENSIETA (2009)

Anatomy of a Visual Domain-Specific Language Project in an Industrial Context*

Christoph Wienands and Michael Golm

Siemens Corporate Research, 755 College Rd East, Princeton, NJ 08540, USA
{Christoph.Wienands,Michael.Golm}@Siemens.com

Abstract. Domain-specific languages (DSL) are specialized modeling languages targeting a narrow domain. In this paper, we present the results of a research project on visual DSLs set in an industrial context, using the domain of elevator controllers. After domain analysis and inception of new, abstract modeling concepts a language prototype was developed, considering aspects such as usability, combination of visual and textual DSLs, and performance of generated code. We describe the challenges encountered during the project, such as defining a user-friendly concrete syntax or tool limitations, and analyze them in retrospective. The paper concludes with several metrics to support the findings.

Keywords: Domain-specific language, visual, textual, code generation.

1 Introduction

Domain-specific languages (DSL) are specialized modeling languages that target narrow domains and provide organized abstraction over concepts in those domains. DSLs allow for managing complexity through abstraction, involving domain experts and developing software more efficiently than with general purpose programming and modeling languages (e.g. UML). Models based on such DSLs are typically used as input for code generation (model to text, or M2T) and model-to-model (M2M) transformations, therefore elevating models from pure documentation to first-class citizens of software development. Visual DSLs, as opposed to textual DSLs, are advantageous for modeling graphs and complex hierarchies. The richness of a truly visual representation can further improve the modeling experience and efficiency, and increase model expressiveness.

However, the development of visual DSLs and their introduction into an organization is typically a labor-intensive task, even with today's available DSL workbenches. Contributing factors can be limited experience of DSL authors, difficulties to find appropriate and usable visual representations, complexity of implementing them, customizing the tool chain, etc.

The goal of this research project was to develop a visual DSL set in an industrial context from inception to a finished product to gain more experience with model-driven development, identify pitfalls, verify previous assumptions and findings, collect metrics and evaluate the results. We chose the domain of elevators for several

* Empirical results category paper.

A. Schürr and B. Selic (Eds.): MODELS 2009, LNCS 5795, pp. 453–467, 2009.

reasons. 1) Elevator controllers represent the application domain of embedded control systems which are very relevant to Siemens, 2) the domain is relatively small but non-trivial and can be comprehended in an acceptable amount of time, and 3) a software elevator simulator can be developed with relative ease to eliminate the need for expensive hardware.

In this paper, we will first give a short introduction to the elevator controller domain, our elevator simulator and the general architecture of the DSL. After that, relevant challenges and findings during the development of the DSL will be presented. The paper will end with an evaluation of gathered metrics to better substantiate some of the findings.

2 Elevator Controllers as Research Subject for DSLs

Elevator controllers control the movement of one or more elevator, which are grouped together in elevator banks. High-level aspects of controlling an elevator bank consist of opening/closing doors, accelerating/decelerating elevator car and reacting to floor and car calls (buttons pressed on the floors outside respectively inside the car). The first two aspects can be solved for each elevator individually but responding to floor and car calls requires synchronization between elevators.

Serving floor calls involves the concept of 'committed direction'. The committed direction is the direction an elevator car will travel after the next stop and is not necessarily the same as the current traveling direction. Fig. 1, a screenshot from our elevator simulator, shows passengers waiting on the 1st, 3rd, and 5th floor wanting to travel up, down and down respectively. The committed direction is shown by the arrow inside the elevator. Under normal circumstances, passengers will only enter an elevator car whose committed direction is the same as their desired travel direction.

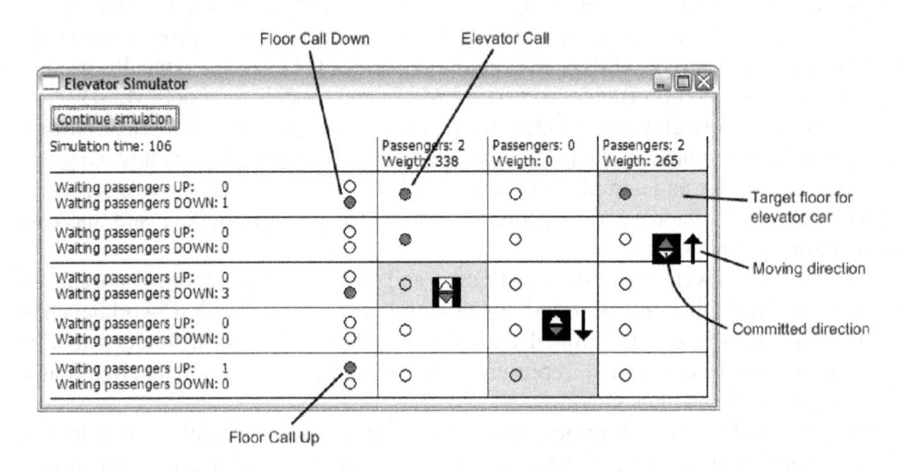

Fig. 1. Elevator simulator showing concepts of moving and committed direction

The main sources of complexity in elevator controllers are the optimized assignment of floor calls to individual controllers, the coordination of moving and committed direction, and opening doors. Beyond a regular operating mode, elevators typically support several maintenance and emergency modes, or special operating modes such as the 'Sabbath' mode (elevator automatically stops at each floor and continuously travels up and down a building).

According to [9], in regular operating mode elevators and passengers need to follow these rules: (1) Car calls always take precedence over floor calls, (2) an elevator must not reverse its direction of travel with passengers in the car, (3) an elevator must stop at a passenger's destination floor, (4) passengers wishing to travel in one direction must not enter an elevator car committed to travel in the opposite direction, and (5) an elevator must not open its doors at a floor where no passengers wish to enter or leave the car.

For the purposes of this research project, an elevator simulator was developed that allows for plugging in different elevator controller implementations, which will be generated from visual models. Controllers are invoked periodically by the simulator and can query the simulator for the current elevator and building status. Controllers can send elevator cars to target floors, set their committed direction and request that doors be opened. The low-level, but security-relevant functionality of controlling the movement of elevator cars (acceleration and deceleration) and door operation (delaying and closing) of doors is built into the simulator. Furthermore, the elevator generates random traffic patterns in a building by using a set of configuration parameters, such arrival and exit rate.

3 DSL Tooling Architecture

This section describes the applied technologies and the resulting architecture of the elevator controller DSL. The most influential choice was to use the Graphical Modeling Framework (GMF) as workbench for the visual part of the DSL, which we found the most powerful of royalty free tools during an evaluation of workbenches for visual DSLs. GMF is part of the Eclipse Modeling Project initiative [1]. Table 1 explains the purpose of each applied technology.

Table 1. Applied technologies

Technology	**Description**
Graphical Modeling Framework (GMF)	Eclipse-based workbench for visual DSLs
Eclipse Modeling Framework (EMF)	Underlying (meta) model library
Graphical Editing Framework (GEF)	Underlying library for editors
Java Emitter Templates (JET)	Code generation, model-to-text
openArchitectureWare Xtext	Parser for mini scripting language
openArchitectureWare Xpand	Code generation for scripting language

Fig. 2 shows the complete DSL tool chain. 1) A JET template processes an elevator controller model, during which 2) condition and action scripts (explained below) are passed on to an Xtext parser and 3) Xpand generator template. 4) The target platform-specific output is returned to the JET template, which 5) combines both the output from the model transformation and the script output in the generated controller. 6) The controller is then compiled and can be loaded by the elevator simulator.

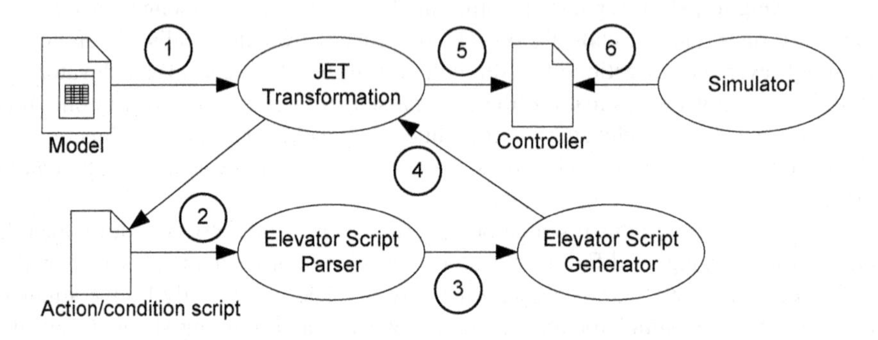

Fig. 2. Tool chain from model to execution in simulator

4 Domain Engineering

The power of domain-specific languages comes from the abstractions incorporated in the modeling concepts. These abstractions make modeling more intuitive and efficient than manually writing code for a target platform. Typically in DSL projects, these abstractions can be elicited from domain experts, technical literature, or by analyzing existing software.

In absence of elevator controller specialists, analysis of literature and of several software elevator simulators did not reveal any high level abstractions that could be used in a visual modeling language. Therefore, we incepted three abstract modeling concepts: State machine, call lists and call list projections. For a better understanding, we provide an actual screenshot of a model in Fig. 3.

4.1 Choice of Diagram Type – State Machine

The diagram type of a visual DSL is a combination of visual, representational elements and some of its semantics. Analysis of existing DSLs (e.g. as described in [2]) yielded frequently used diagram types, which are presented in Table 2. Some DSLs are actually a mix of two or more types, or have other visual enhancements, but one diagram type typically dominates and determines the character of a DSL. It is no coincidence that the general purpose modeling language UML contains entity relationship, state and activity diagrams. Other UML diagram types such as use case or sequence diagrams are rarely encountered in DSLs because they lack the precision of those other diagram types [8], making them less suited for model transformations and code generation.

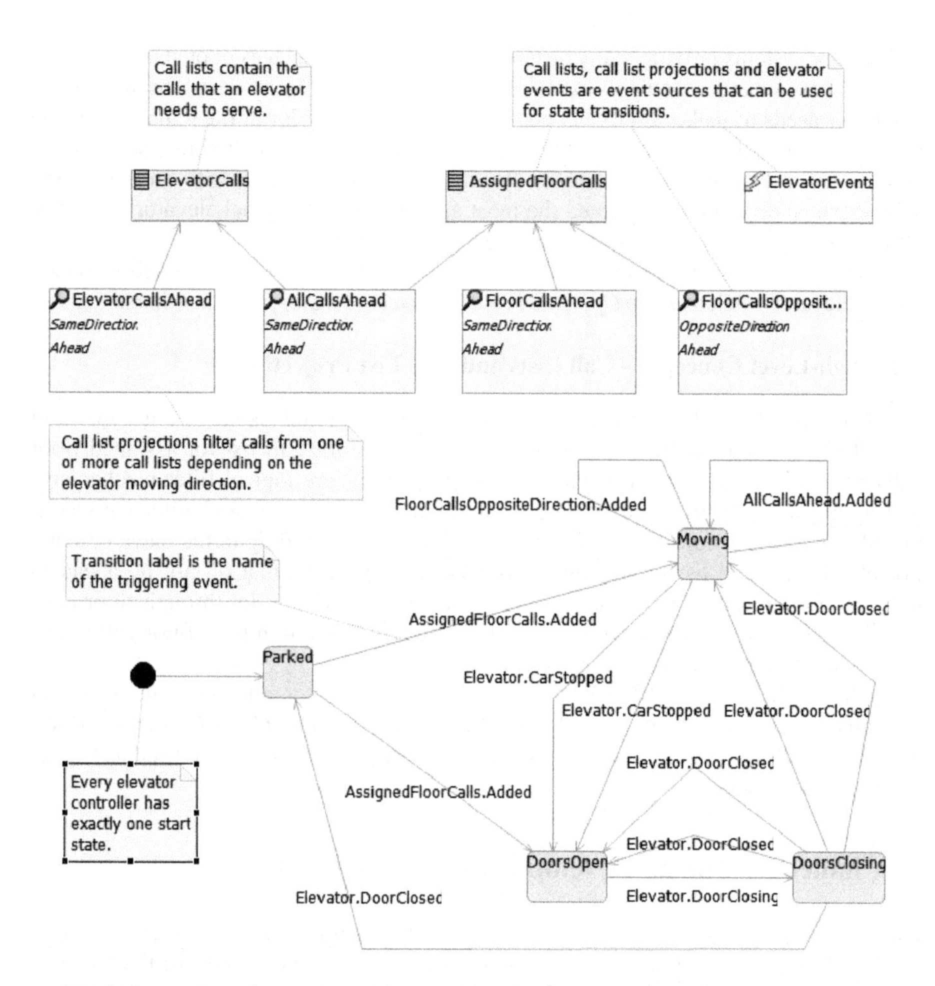

Fig. 3. Screenshot of a regular mode controller (29 lines of TSL script code not shown)

Table 2. Frequently used diagram types of visual DSLs

Style	Description
Entity relationship diagram	Static structures consisting of related elements. Especially well-suited for cyclical graphs but also to hierarchical trees limited in size.
Tree diagram	Strictly hierarchical structures.
Activity diagram	Sequential workflows, with actions, decisions, loops
State diagram	States connected by transitions, which are guarded by conditions and triggered by events.
User interface editor	Editor for graphical user interfaces, XAML for Windows Presentation Foundation, etc.

Elevator systems provide many different types of events, such as door status changes, floor or speed changes, and pressed or released call buttons. Many decisions an elevator controller needs to make strictly depend on the status of the elevator, e.g. buttons inside the car are pressed so the elevator first needs to drop of passengers before responding to buttons pressed on the outside floors. Therefore, a state diagram with an underlying state machine concept was deemed the most appropriate for a visual elevator controller DSL. This was further confirmed through whiteboard exercises.

Transitions in a state machine require trigger events. Several events are provided by the elevator, such as *DoorOpened*, *FloorChanged, CarStopped* and others.

4.2 High-Level Concepts – Call Lists and Call List Projections

A call list is a logical construct, a dynamic list that contains calls (of any type) and sorts them ordered by floor. Every elevator will have one call list for assigned floor calls and one for its own car calls. Call list projections are logical filter mechanisms that aggregate calls from one or more input call lists, and sort and filter calls contained in the lists according to some static settings *and* according to the elevator state. For example, a call list projection might filter out any calls that do not lie ahead in moving direction of an elevator car, or another one might only let through floor calls pointing the opposite direction as the elevator moving direction (e.g. floor call pointing down when elevator is moving upwards).

Both call lists and call list projections are event sources and make more events available beyond the events provided by the elevator, namely *CallAdded* and *CallRemoved*. Therefore, events from call lists and call list projections can be used as trigger events for transitions.

5 Challenges during Development of Visual DSL

During the development of the DSL and the code generator, we encountered several hurdles. Many of the challenges were caused by a steep learning curve of the underlying technologies, especially of GMF and the technologies it is based upon, EMF and GEF. Because GMF ties together these independently developed technologies, DSL authors need to be proficient in each one of those. The last section in this paper is dedicated to metrics, which will go into more detail about ramp-up efforts. The remainder of this section will cover challenges that are more generally applicable to DSL development and less dependent on technology choices.

5.1 Defining and Implementing an Efficient Concrete Syntax

Structural features for concrete syntaxes include containment shapes (elements visibly containing other elements), explosion and decomposition (two forms of diagram partitioning into subdiagrams). In [5], the author identifies three key challenges to designing modeling languages: (1) The need to simultaneously support different levels of precision, (2) the need to represent multiple different but mutually consistent views of certain model elements, and (3) the graph-like nature of most modeling languages. Solving these challenges often requires using structural language features appropriately.

Our experience from working with several visual DSL workbenches showed that not all DSL workbenches support the same set of structural features and that there are great differences in ease of use of those workbenches. Table 3 gives a brief overview of capabilities of three well-known DSL workbenches: GMF, Microsoft DSL Tools [14], and MetaCase's MetaEdit+ [15].

Table 3. Support for structural concrete syntax features in DSL workbenches

Structural Feature	GMF v3.4.1	MS DSL Tools '08	MetaEdit+ v4.5
Containment shapes	Yes, free or ordered layout	Yes, list layout	Yes, free layout
Explosion (subdiag. same type)	Yes	No	Yes
Decomposition (subdiag. other type)	Yes, but requires much manual work	No	Yes
Multi-element connectors	No	No	Yes

During the conception phase of the elevator controller DSL, several prototypes for concrete syntaxes were evaluated on a whiteboard. The most favored concrete syntax candidate used decomposition, where a double click on a certain element type in a diagram would open up a subdiagram of a different diagram type. Unfortunately, support for decomposition is still very weak in GMF and requires an elaborate work-around [6]. Because of limited resources, a simplified concrete syntax that combines two modeling aspects in one diagram type was chosen.

GMF posed some further challenges during the creation of the concrete syntax. GMF provides a lot of flexibility for mapping an ecore metamodel to a concrete syntax, or even multiple concrete syntaxes. The example in Fig. 4 shows how a connector in concrete syntax might be derived from an association, or from an explicit association class using containment and association.

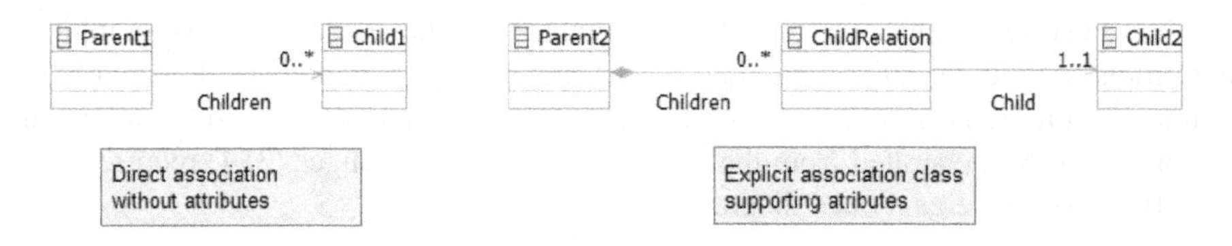

Fig. 4. Two metamodel association concepts mapped to a connector in concrete syntax

In GMF, the mapping model binds together three independent (and independently edited) artifacts: The domain model, the graphical definition model, and the tooling definition. The mapping model provides a large and flexible set of options how metamodel elements, graphical definitions and tooling definitions can be combined.

The trade-off for such flexibility is the inherent complexity. Despite basic support through derivation wizards, it is difficult to identify the correct settings for advanced features in a concrete syntax and most of the time we had to develop features incrementally in minimal steps with immediate testing.

In comparison, other DSL workbenches are more restrictive how a particular metamodel can be mapped to a concrete syntax and the metamodel to a large degree already determines what the concrete syntax will look like. For example, in MS DSL Tools, the concrete syntax is defined in the same diagram as the metamodel. While this facilitates the creation of a DSL in general, the downside is that DSL authors will more likely be influenced to adapt the metamodel to the concrete syntax capabilities of the DSL workbench.

5.2 Customization of DSL and DSL Editor

Unlike textual concrete syntaxes, visual concrete syntaxes provide a much richer feature set that can be used to design a usable, efficient, intuitive modeling language. Basic feature include nodes (rectangles, circles, icons, etc.), edges (lines, arrows), regions (complex shapes made up of primitives), decorators (icons, labels, etc.) [7]. Many DSLs require customization of visual elements and behavioral adaptation (e.g. conditional display of decorators). Features for concrete syntax customization provided by DSL workbenches are complementary to the structural features described earlier.

The number and complexity of built-in customization features greatly depends on the DSL workbench. Products such as GMF and Microsoft DSL Tools do not include as many or as complex features because DSL authors can implement them manually using the underlying open and documented frameworks. Workbenches without such open frameworks, like MetaEdit+, therefore provide more customization possibilities that are readily accessible from graphical editors, without the need for programmatic extensions and manual customizations.

In the case of the elevator controller DSL, these customizations included (1) read-only attributes derived from attribute values of referenced objects, (2) propagating attribute and reference change notifications, (3) initializing model graphs with element instances, (4) pre-populating diagrams, (5) and context menus.

Most customizations required changes outside of the model artifacts graphical definition, tooling definition, mapping model, and had to be implemented manually in a time-consuming fashion. For example, changes (1, 2) required code modifications in the object model generated from the metamodel, whereas changes (3, 4) require code modifications to the generated diagram editor.

6 Transition Scripting Language

Transitions in the modeled state machine require guard conditions and actions. Early on it was determined that it would be very difficult to model these visually, but rather that a textual representation was more appropriate. During the first project iteration, conditions and actions were merely Java code that was passed through by the code generator unchanged into the generated elevator controller.

The goal of a later iteration was to not only generate Java-based elevator controllers but also to target a native C platform by implementing a second code generator. Native C platforms are much more common for embedded devices and metrics for code generation results would become more meaningful. This in turn caused problems because the scripts stored inside transitions were Java platform-specific and could not easily and reliably be transformed into valid C code.

This challenge prompted the introduction of a mini textual scripting language specialized for transition conditions and actions. The transition scripting language (TSL) is therefore a small textual DSL used inside the larger visual elevator controller DSL. A newly introduced Xtext-based parser component parses TSL scripts into abstract syntax trees, from which a platform-specific Xpand-based generator template will generate the appropriate output.

The introduction of a textual DSL raises the following concern: If users of the visual DSL, who are thought to not necessarily be programmers, have to develop textual scripts, where is the advantage of having a visual DSL in the first place and would writing these scripts be too challenging? The next section will address these concerns.

6.1 Simplicity of Transition Scripting Language

The TSL was purposely designed to have a minimal syntax and a minimal API. Table 4 demonstrates several expressions and statements from actual controller models. The scripting language's syntax is very similar to other scripting languages and features objects, properties, enumerations, static methods, integer constants and basic Boolean operators. However, the concepts offered by the scripting language are reduced to the absolute minimum required to build elevator controllers (e.g. no variables, no type declarations, namespaces, limited operators, no assignments, etc.). Therefore, mastering such a minimal scripting language and the available API will require significantly less effort than learning a more complex language like Java or C#.

Table 4. Examples of scripts for transition conditions and actions

Conditions (expressions)	`AssignedFloorCalls.Size != 0 || ElevatorCalls.Size != 0`
	`CallsAhead.Size != 0 && ElevatorDirection == Direction.Up`
	`Elevator.Floor == Building.FloorCount - 1`
Actions (statements)	`SetElevatorTarget(CallsAhead.First);`
	`SetElevatorCommittedDirection(Direction.Up);`

TSL has a very simple C-like grammar, and an excerpt is shown in the listing below. Xtext uses EBNF-style grammars but is not 100% compliant with ISO standard 14977 [4]. Production rules in Xtext parsers are contained in the grammar itself, which makes editing the grammar and defining the parse tree very easy.

```
Statement: ex=PrimaryExpr ";";

PrimaryExpr: niex=NonInfixExpr (iex+=InfixExpr)*;

InfixExpr: op=InfixOp ex=NonInfixExpr;

NonInfixExpr: ID | INT | ParenthesizedExpr |
  PropertyAccessExpr | InvocationExpr | UnaryExpr;

UnaryExpr: op=PrefixOp ex=PrimaryExpr;

ParenthesizedExpr: "(" ex=PrimaryExpr ")";

PropertyAccessExpr: obj=ID "." prop=ID;

InvocationExpr: method=ID "(" (args=ArgumentList)? ")";

ArgumentList: ex+=PrimaryExpr ("," ex+=PrimaryExpr)*;

InfixOp: "||" | "&&" | "==" | "!=" | "<" | ">" |
  "<=" | ">=" | "+" | "-" | "*" | "/" | "%";

PrefixOp: "!" | "-";
```

6.2 Use of Textual DSLs Inside Other Visual DSLs

Combining modeling languages has been described many times [12 and 13], whether visual DSLs, textual DSLs or a combination thereof. Nevertheless, the argument, that using a textual DSL within a greater visual DSL would invalidate the concept of having a visual DSL in the first place, prompted us to find and empirically study other products that incorporate both visual and textual DSLs in a similar fashion as the elevator controller DSL. Two of them we document here.

UML Class Diagrams. The textual Object Constraint Language (OCL) is used to describe constraints on class diagrams that otherwise cannot be expressed through the capabilities of the class diagram notation. For example, OCL is used in several GMF-related graphical editors to define integrity checks and automatically derived values in domain models.

Siemens SIMATIC STEP 7. The SIMATIC STEP 7 automation platform allows for creating control software for programmable logic controllers. STEP 7 in fact provides several DSLs, out of which three are used for developing programs: Ladder logic diagrams, function block diagrams, and statement lists (textual). These languages are defined by IEC 61131 [10].

While the combination of visual and textual DSLs in STEP 7 is not exactly the same scenario as with the elevator DSL, we believe that it still serves as a good example where different types of DSLs are used to achieve the higher efficiency by allowing users to choose and model in the most appropriate language.

7 Optimization of Code Generator for Native C Platform

A commonly heard argument against using domain-specific modeling is that software generated from models is not as performant or requires more resources than manually written and optimized software. Indeed, the code generator developed during the first iteration of the elevator controller DSL targeted the Java platform and a custom developed domain framework, which supported the generated code.

The domain framework for the Java platform provided software components that directly mapped to the abstract concepts used in the high-level modeling language, such as a dynamic event registration and invocation mechanism, dynamic call lists and projections, a rich object model and more. While the development of the domain framework and the code generator were straightforward, the result principally was ill-suited for embedded platforms, which typically require frugal use of resources: Memory consumption of dynamic array lists is not easily predictable, call-by-name method invocations are slower than statically linked invocations, and object models consume more memory than basic structures such as arrays.

One goal of the elevator controller DSL project was to examine the potential for optimization of generated code. Therefore in a later iteration, an optimized domain framework based on a native C platform and a code generator targeting this domain framework were developed. The remainder of this section describes the applied optimization techniques.

7.1 Avoiding Dynamic Memory Allocation

The first optimization during the implementation of the C domain framework (which to some degree was a port of the Java domain framework to C) was to avoid, where possible, dynamic memory allocations and to move all remaining allocations into the initialization code. As a result, the memory footprint of the elevator controller remains constant at runtime.

7.1.1 Static Linking of Event Chains

The Java domain framework provided a dynamic event registration and invocation mechanism. Because elevator controllers do not require reconfiguration at runtime, the event mechanism could completely be replaced with statically linked method invocations generated by the code generator. Generated empty event handlers and invocations thereof are of no concern because they will be detected and pruned in a later step by the C compiler.

7.1.2 Optimized Queries for Call List Projections

The filter algorithm for call list projections is fairly complex because of the many independent input variables. Static, configuration-time input variables are projection direction (same direction, opposite direction), projection coverage (ahead, behind, all), and maximum elevator acceleration/deceleration. Runtime input variables are elevator position, elevator moving direction, elevator speed, and door status.

To simplify and optimize filter queries, the C code generator generates filter expressions specific to each call list projection element by eliminating checks for configuration-time input variables and hardcoding their logic instead.

7.2 Minimal Status Update

As it is common practice for components in embedded systems, the generated elevator controller will query the elevator simulator during its invocation cycle and update its internal status. The simulator provides many information types such elevator speed, weight, position, button and door status. However, depending on the modeled elevator controller, not all of these information types are needed as a less sophisticated elevator controller might not take car weight (~number of persons in car) into consideration.

Therefore, as a further optimization the C code generator applies a static code analysis step to transition scripts to identify what information types are truly required, and eliminates memory allocations and query/update operations for those that are not.

Obviously, the above described optimizations are not necessarily applicable to other domains and target platforms. Additionally, as we will document in the next section about project metrics, the amount of effort spent on optimizing a code generator was significantly higher than writing a single implementation manually. However, this optimization process shall serve as an example that it is possible to optimize code generators such that they create output with similar attributes as manually written code.

8 Metrics

This section presents the metrics that were collected during and after the elevator DSL project. Table 5 shows the effort spent on the creation of the DSL tool chain. Prominent is the large ramp-up effort to learn the GMF, Xtext and Xpand technologies.

After completion of the DSL, we performed an experiment where a domain expert (one of the authors) and a novice to the elevator domain (still an expert developer) would build elevator controllers for the regular operating mode. First, controllers were built using the elevator controller DSL, then manually from scratch. The results shown in Table 6 suggest that even novices will significantly gain efficiency when developing elevator controllers.

Table 5. Effort spent during creation of Elevator Controller DSL

Work item	**Effort (days)**
Domain frameworks	3.0 (Java) + 2.5 (C) = 5.5
GMF ramp-up	4.5
Xtext/Xpand ramp-up	4.0
Visual DSL editor	2.5
Elevator script DSL	3.0
Code generation	3.0 (JET) + 2.5 (Xpand) = 5.5
Total	**25.0**

Table 6. Effort for creation of a elevator controller by domain expert vs. domain novice

Development method	Effort expert (hours)	Effort novice (hours)
Using Elevator DSL (therefore works on both target platforms)	1.0	5.0
Manually developed against C domain framework	1.5	-
Manually developed for C platform (no domain framework)	4.0	8.0+ (out of time, believed to be at least 12h until complete)

The last metrics are dedicated to measuring the efficiency of the generated code. The static analysis results in Table 7 compare lines of code for generated controllers with manually implemented controllers (excluding JNI and other overhead). If we subtract the effect of intentional code duplication for optimization, we observe a two-fold increase in code size. However, the relative difference in binary size is considerably smaller, due to runtime library overhead.

Table 7. Efficiency of generated code

Metric	DSL-based controller	Manually dev. controller
Static analysis		
LOC	791 domain framework + 462 generated controller =1253 total	508 controller
Binary size	56kB	40kB
Implementation effort	4 call list projections, 5 states, 13 transitions and 29 lines of TSL script (conditions, actions)	508 lines of C code
Runtime analysis		
Avg. instructions/cycle	184	223

To judge the runtime behavior of generated code vs. manually written code, both controller versions were annotated with performance counter code. Both code bases were manually reviewed to ascertain that the injected code would not favor either version. Then, three simulations with identical settings were executed for each controller and the results averaged. The runtime analysis results in Table 7 came indeed as a little surprise: The generated code required 17% less instructions per invocation cycle than the manually developed controller. Further investigation showed that the manual controller, which we thought was built fairly optimal though not using an explicit state machine concept, needs to execute more filter and search routines than the generated controller, which is built on a true state machine and therefore optimally reduces the number of conditions that need to be checked.

9 Further Research and Need for Improvements

Having completed the elevator controller DSL, we see room for improvements and further research. In the current version, TSL scripts are edited in a regular textbox, which means that users have no auto-completion support and syntax errors are not reported until model validation in a later step. Xtext technology allows for generation of auto-complete capable editors, which would have to be integrated with the visual editor. This measure would greatly increase the usability of the embedded scripting language and immediately reduce syntax errors.

A critical point is the disconnect between controller models at design-time and their behavior at execution time. The underlying domain frameworks print out tracing information to the console, which is currently the only way to debug race conditions in controller state machines. According to [3], model level debugging is still a very young field with little tool support. MetaEdit+ supports a model-level tracing mechanism but no true step-by-step debugging on the model level. We believe that advancements in this field are crucial for the broader adoption and warrant further research.

Finally, having worked with other DSL workbenches before, the efforts for GMF ramp-up and editor customization seem very high. A future case study could port the elevator controller DSL to other visual DSL workbenches, such as MS DSL Tools or MetaCase's MetaEdit+, to compare learning curve, customization support and integration of an embedded scripting language between tools.

10 Summary

In this paper we presented the development of a DSL for elevator controllers set in an industrial context. GMF, JET and openArchitectureWare Xtext/Xpand were used to build the DSL tool chain.

A thorough domain analysis yielded important abstract concepts not found in existing elevator controller implementations: State machines as underlying diagram type, and call lists and call list projections as event sources. Among the challenges during development were a steep learning curve, mapping the metamodel to a concrete syntax, and customization of DSL and DSL editor.

The evaluation of our elevator controller case study supports previous findings that model-driven development and domain-specific languages increase productivity. For development effort, we measured efficiency gains up to 75%, which partly depend on the previous domain knowledge of the user. With small additional effort, we introduced support for a second target platform through a platform-specific code generator.

During the evaluation of code generation efficiency, the runtime behavior of generated code actually was slightly better than that of manually developed code. We believe the determining factors were a justifiable investment into the underlying domain framework and the optimizations implemented in the code generator.

Acknowledgements. We would like to thank our colleague Brad Wehrwein for patiently testing our elevator controller DSL, and developing multiple elevator controllers.

We would also like to thank Chris Voice, whose Elevator Challenge simulator [11] provided much inspiration for our own elevator simulator.

References

1. Eclipse Modeling Project, http://www.eclipse.org/modeling/
2. Kelly, S., Tolvanen, J.: Domain-Specific Modeling. Wiley, Hoboken (2008)
3. Uhl, A.: Model-Driven Development in the Enterprise. IEEE Software 25(1) (2008)
4. ISO 14977, http://www.iso.org/iso/iso_catalogue/catalogue_tc/catalogue_detail.htm?csnumber=26153
5. Selic, B.: A Systematic Approach to Domain-Specific Language Design Using UML. In: Proceedings of the 10th IEEE International Symposium on Object and Component-Oriented Real-Time Distributed Computing (2007)
6. The Eclipse Foundation (GMF cookbook): Diagram Partitioning, http://wiki.eclipse.org/Diagram_Partitioning
7. Mezei, G., Lengyel, L., Levendovszky, T., Charaf, H.: A Model Transformation for Automated Concrete Syntax Definitions of Metamodeled Visual Languages. In: Proceedings of the Second International Workshop on Graph and Model Transformation
8. Fowler, M.: UML Distilled: A Brief Guide to the Standard Object Modeling Language, 3rd edn. Addison-Wesley, Reading (2003)
9. Barney, G., Santos, S.: Elevator Traffic Analysis, Design and Control. IEEE, London (1985)
10. PLCopen, http://www.plcopen.org
11. Elevator Challenge, http://www.elevatorchallenge.com/
12. Fowler, M.: Language Workbenches: The Killer-App for Domain Specific Languages, http://martinfowler.com/articles/languageWorkbench.html
13. Short, K., Greenfield, J.: Software Factories: Assembling Applications with Patterns, Models, Frameworks, and Tools. Wiley, Indianapolis (2004)
14. Microsoft DSL Tools, http://msdn.microsoft.com/en-us/library/bb126235.aspx
15. MetaCase MetaEdit+, http://www.metacase.com/

A Goal-Based Modeling Approach to Develop Requirements of an Adaptive System with Environmental Uncertainty*

Betty H.C. Cheng[1], Pete Sawyer[2], Nelly Bencomo[2], and Jon Whittle[2]

[1] Department of Computer Science and Engineering, Michigan State University, East Lansing, Michigan 48824, USA

[2] Computing Department, InfoLab21, Lancaster University, LA1 4WA, United Kingdom

chengb@cse.msu.edu, {sawyer,nelly,whittle}@comp.lancs.ac.uk

Abstract. Dynamically adaptive systems (DASs) are intended to monitor the execution environment and then dynamically adapt their behavior in response to changing environmental conditions. The uncertainty of the execution environment is a major motivation for dynamic adaptation; it is impossible to know at development time all of the possible combinations of environmental conditions that will be encountered. To date, the work performed in requirements engineering for a DAS includes requirements monitoring and reasoning about the correctness of adaptations, where the DAS requirements are assumed to exist. This paper introduces a goal-based modeling approach to develop the requirements for a DAS, while explicitly factoring uncertainty into the process and resulting requirements. We introduce a variation of threat modeling to identify sources of uncertainty and demonstrate how the RELAX specification language can be used to specify more flexible requirements within a goal model to handle the uncertainty.

Keywords: Requirements engineering, goal models, uncertainty, dynamically adaptive systems.

1 Introduction

Dynamically adaptive systems (DASs) are systems designed to continuously monitor their environment and then adapt their behavior in response to changing environmental conditions. DASs tend to be *cyberphysical systems*, where the physical environment is tightly intertwined with the computing-based system. Example domains where DASs are necessary include power grid management systems, telecommunication systems, and ubiquitous systems. For these systems,

* This work has been supported in part by NSF grants CCF-0541131, CNS-0551622, CCF-0750787, CNS-0751155, IIP-0700329, and CCF-0820220, Army Research Office grant W911NF-08-1-0495, Ford Motor Company, and a grant from Michigan State University's Quality Fund.

A. Schürr and B. Selic (Eds.): MODELS 2009, LNCS 5795, pp. 468–483, 2009.

the software may need to be reconfigured at run time (e.g., software uploaded or removed) in order to handle new environmental conditions.

Specifying the requirements for DASs is a challenging task because of the inherent uncertainty associated with an unknown environment. This paper presents an approach in which goals [1] are used to systematically model the requirements of a DAS. In particular, we use a variation of threat modeling (see, e.g., [2]) to uncover places in the model where the requirements need to be updated to support adaptation. In this case, threats correspond to changes in the environment that may require the software to dynamically adapt at run time in order to maintain high-level goals. This process results in a goal-based requirements model that explicitly captures where adaptations are needed, documents the level of flexibility supported during adaptation, and takes into account enviromental uncertainty.

This paper builds directly on our previous work. Previously, we observed that a DAS is conceptually a collection of *target systems*, each of which handles a different combination of environmental conditions [3]. As such, we can model the requirements of individual target systems and the adaptive logic that transitions between the configurations as separate concerns. The LOREM process [4] describes how to use this strategy to develop goal models to represent the individual target systems and the adaptive logic. However, LOREM does not support requirements engineers in identifying the requirements for these target systems. Recently, we introduced the RELAX language, a textual language for dealing with uncertainty in DAS requirements that allows requirements to be temporarily relaxed if necessary to support adaptation [5]. This flexibility is required, for example, if non-critical requirements must be partially neglected in order to satisfy short-term critical requirements. RELAX, however, was not integrated with modeling approaches used in the requirements engineering community.

This paper, therefore, makes three main contributions. Firstly, it gives a process for identifying requirements for target DAS systems that can then be modeled using a process such as LOREM. Secondly, it integrates our previous work on RELAX with goal modeling. Finally, the paper presents a novel application of threat modeling to systematically explore environmental uncertainty factors that may impact the requirements of a DAS.

We illustrate our approach by applying it to Ambient Assisted Living (AAL), an adaptive system providing assistance to elderly or handicapped persons in their homes. The remainder of the paper is organized as follows. Section 2 introduces AAL as our running example and presents our approach, including the stepwise process for creating the goal and uncertainty models. Section 3 describes the details of applying the approach to the AAL system. Section 4 discusses related work. Finally, in Section 5, we present conclusions and discuss future work.

2 Modeling Approach

A key characteristic of a DAS is that there may be numerous approaches to realizing its high-level objectives, where a specific set of run-time environmental conditions will dictate which particular realization is appropriate at a particular point in time. In order to support this type of variation, this paper uses goal modeling to describe requirements of a DAS, since goal-based modeling offers a means to identify and visualize different alternatives for satisfying the overall objectives of a system [1,6]. The alternatives may be due to different tradeoffs between non-functional goals (e.g., performance, reliability, etc.); and, in the case of DASs, different goal paths may be due to uncertainty factors in the environment. As such, goal-based modeling offers a means to explicitly capture the rationale for how and why goals and requirements are decomposed (as represented by alternate paths of goal refinements). Furthermore, requirements identified through goal modeling can be used as the basis for model-driven engineering (MDE) [1,7,3]. The rationale for a particular path of goal refinement can be captured in a goal model and may be used as constraints and/or guidance during the MDE process [3].

2.1 Running Application

To validate our approach, we conducted a case study provided by Fraunhofer IESE in the form of an existing concept document describing a smart home for assisted living. The concept document was written previously and independently of this research. We present an excerpt of the document here to serve as a running example for introducing our approach.[1]

Mary is a widow. She is 65 years old, overweight and has high blood pressure and cholesterol levels. Mary gets a new intelligent fridge. It comes with 4 temperature and 2 humidity sensors and is able to read, store, and communicate RFID information on food packages. The fridge communicates with the ambient assisted living (AAL) system in the house and integrates itself. In particular, it detects the presence of spoiled food and discovers and receives a diet plan to be monitored based on what food items Mary is consuming.

An important part of Mary's diet is to ensure minimum liquid intake. The intelligent fridge partially contributes to it. To improve the accuracy, special sensor-enabled cups are used: some have sensors that beep when fluid intake is necessary and have a level to monitor the fluid consumed; others additionally have a gyro detecting spillage. They seamlessly coordinate in order to estimate the amount of liquid taken: the latter informs the former about spillages so that it can update the water level. However, Mary sometimes uses the cup to water flowers. Sensors in the faucets and in the toilet also provide a means to monitor this measurement.

Advanced smart homes, such as Mary's AAL, rely on adaptivity to work properly. For example, the sensor-enabled cups may fail or Mary may forget to drink, but since maintaining Mary's hydration levels is a life-critical feature, the AAL should be able to respond by achieving this requirement in some other way.

2.2 Overview of Approach

Our approach follows the principles of the model-based approach described by Zhang and Cheng [3] which considers a DAS to comprise numerous target

[1] See www.iese.fraunhofer.de/fhg/iese/projects/med_projects/aal-lab/index.jsp

systems, each of which supports behavior for a different set of environmental conditions (posed by the environmental uncertainty). At run time, the DAS transitions from one target system to another, depending on the environmental conditions. While the earlier work emphasized design-phase models, this paper focuses on the identification of the goals and requirements for each of the target systems.

Scope of Uncertainty. Before we start the goal derivation process, we identify the top-level goal for the system; this goal should state the overall objective for a system, while not being prescriptive for how to realize the objective. And we also create a conceptual domain model (as a UML class diagram) that identifies the key physical elements of the system and their relationships (e.g., sensors, user interfaces); see Figure 1. It also includes actors that may be human (e.g. Person) or software-controlled (e.g. iCup, an intelligent cup with sensors). These elements identify the environmental conditions and the uncertainty that must be handled by the system. In essence, the domain model serves to scope the uncertainty for the system; that is, elements in the domain model are either the sources of uncertainty or they are used to monitor environment conditions that pose uncertainty. (In general, it is not practical nor useful to model every element in the environment, particularly, if they play little or no role in the functionality of the system.)

Target System Modeling. From the top-level goal, we develop a goal lattice using a process of goal refinement, where the first level of subgoals are termed *high-level goals*, representing the key services to be provided by the system. This refinement process is informed by the conceptual domain model and any problem descriptions, use-cases or other sources of information elicited about the problem to be tackled by the system under development (herein referred to as system). We use KAOS, a goal-oriented requirements engineering language [1]; one influencing factor for using KAOS is its support for threat modeling. In KAOS, goals describe required properties of a system that are satisfied by different agents such as software components or humans in the system's environment. Goal refinement in KAOS stops when responsibility for a goal's satisfaction can be assigned to a single agent. KAOS defines such a goal as a *requirement* if satisfied by a software agent or an *expectation* if satisfied by a human agent. Requirements and expectations form leaves of the goal lattice. It should be noted that the KAOS definition of requirement is specific to KAOS but, for consistency sake, we shall use the KAOS convention in the remainder of this paper.

Figure 2 gives a goal model for the AAL system, where the top-level goal is to keep Mary healthy (i.e., Maintain[Health]). The right leaning parallelograms represent goals, while the left leaning parallelograms represent KAOS *obstacles* that act to confound goal satisfaction. Considering the goals first, requirements and expectations are denoted as goals with embolded outlining. The hollow circles represent goal refinement junctures, where multiple edges represent AND goals (all subgoals must be satisfied in order to satisfy a parent goal). Goals can also be OR-ed, denoted by multiple arrows directly attached to a parent goal;

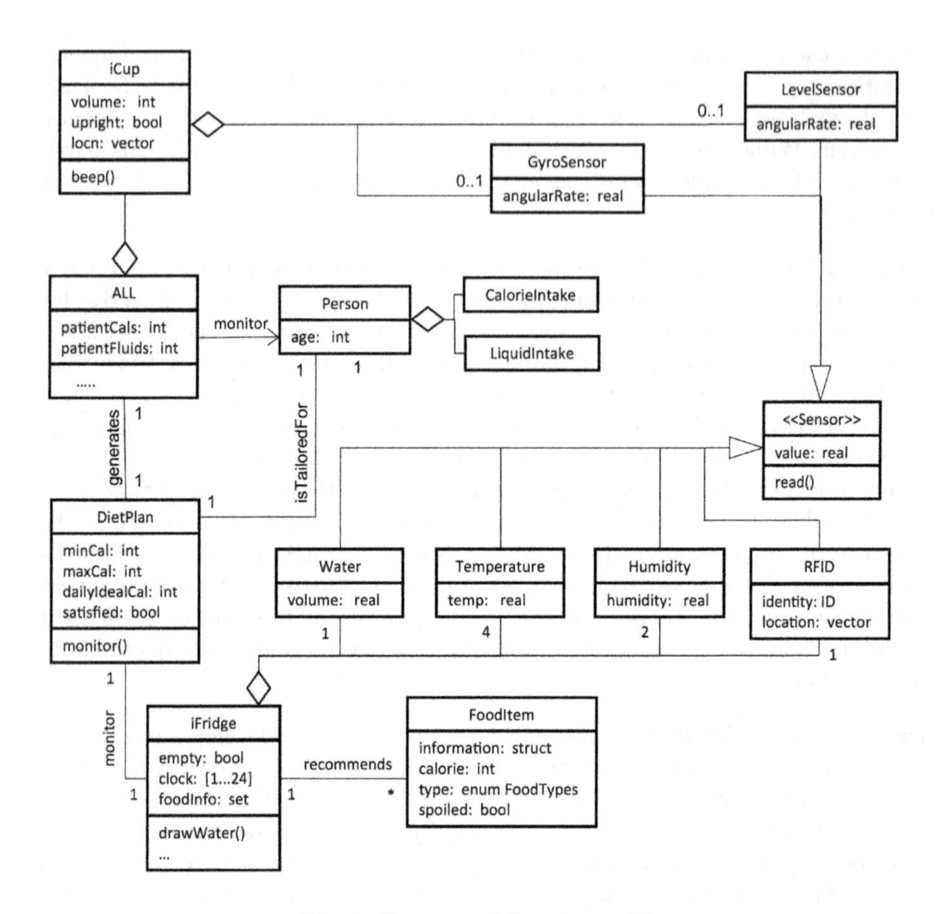

Fig. 1. Conceptual domain model

an example appears in Figure 5. Goals can be elaborated to provide a number of attributes including a definition. The dashed box attached to the Maintain[Health] goal shows its definition formulated as a conventional SHALL statement.[2] Finally, agents are represented by hexagons. The network of goal-related elements form a *goal lattice*.

Identifying Uncertainty. We use a combination of bottom-up and top-down strategies to identify uncertainty. We start by assessing the goal lattice in a bottom-up fashion, looking for sources of uncertainty (i.e., elements in the domain model) that might affect the satisfaction of the goals. When looking for mitigation strategies for dealing with the uncertainty, new (high-level) goals may be introduced that may, in turn, uncover other sources of uncertainty (thus corresponding to top-down uncertainty discovery).

[2] *SHALL* statements are commonly used to specify requirements, indicating a contractual relationship between the customer and the developer as to what functionality should be included in the system.

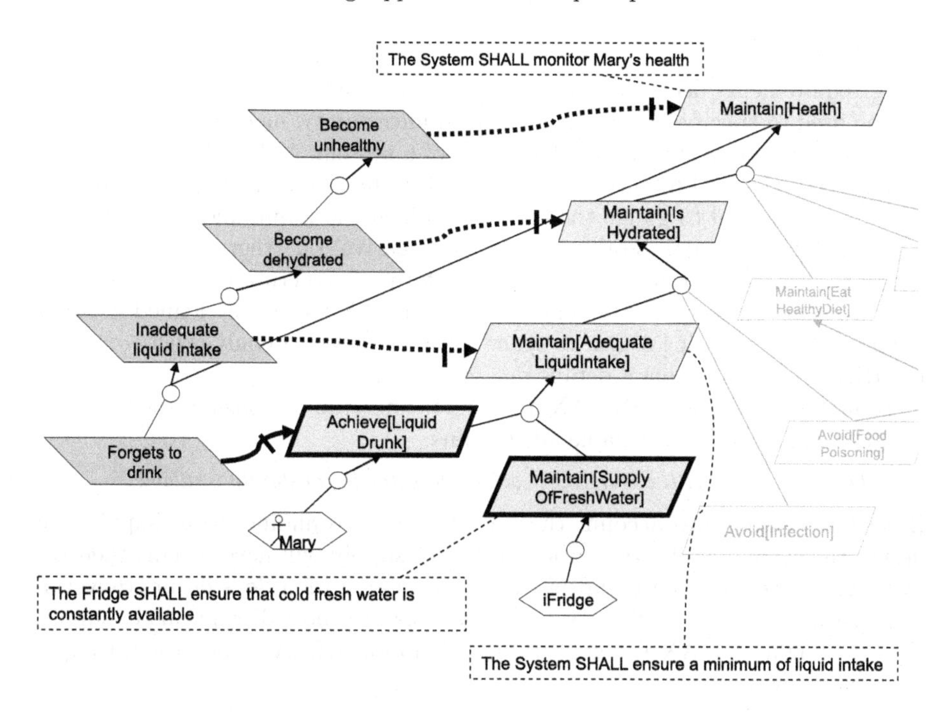

Fig. 2. Initial refinement of goals to keep Mary hydrated

Previously, threat modeling has been used to identify threats that might exploit (security) vulnerabilities of system assets [8,9]. In this current work, we introduce a variation of threat modeling to identify uncertainty. More specifically, in the case of DASs, the "threats" are the various environmental conditions (or the impact of environmental conditions) that pose uncertainty at development time and thus may warrant dynamic adaptation at run time to ensure acceptable behavior. The obstacles in Figure 2 represent uncertainty factors impacting the goals which, like the goals, form a lattice, termed *uncertainty lattice*, in which obstacles can be AND-ed and OR-ed to combine their effects and propagate uncertainty upwards towards the top-level goal. The lower uncertainty nodes represent the sources of uncertainty. The barred arrows indicate the goals that they affect. The upper uncertainty nodes and the barred, broken arrows that lead from them represent the impact of the uncertainty.

Mitigating Uncertainty. The impact of the uncertainty is assessed to determine what type of mitigation, if any, is needed. Three possible tactics can be used to mitigate the offending uncertainty factors, with each requiring different levels of effort to realize. For a goal affected by uncertainty, the least costly mitigation tactic is to define new behavior in the form of a further subgoal to handle the condition; this step equates to adding incremental functionality to a target system. If the subgoal refinement is not sufficient to mitigate the uncertainty, but partial satisfaction of the goal is tolerable, then we attempt to add flexibility to the goal to account for the uncertainty. For this tactic, we use the RELAX specification language [5] to add flexibility to the goal specification by specifying requirements declaratively, rather than by enumeration. Briefly, RELAX can be used to specify several dimensions of uncertainty, including duration and frequency of system states; possible states of a system; and configurations for a system. A RELAXed requirement also specifies the elements of the domain that must be monitored to gauge the extent to which the requirement is being satisfied and their impacts (both positive and negative) on other requirements [5]. While the RELAX specifications are in the form of structured natural language with Boolean expressions, the semantics for RELAX have been defined in terms of temporal fuzzy logic [5]. Due to space constraints, we can only briefly overview the RELAX language here; details may be found in [5].

To illustrate the use of RELAX to mitigate uncertainty, consider the following goal that may not be satisfiable all the time.

"The System SHALL ensure that cold fresh water is constantly available."

If we fail to take into account the uncertainty surrounding water supply and design the system as if interruptions in water supply will never occur, then the system may be too brittle and fail when an interruption does occur. However, if the recipient of the system's services can tolerate short disruptions in supply, then we might RELAX the goal using a temporal RELAX operator (in upper case) as follows:

"The System SHALL ensure that cold fresh water is AS CLOSE AS POSSIBLE to constantly available."

The RELAXed goals can be realized by implementations that have built-in flexibility (e.g., through parameter definitions or alternate branches of functionality). Note that goals for which partial satisfaction is not tolerable are considered to be *invariants* – must always be satisfied even during adaptation.

If the adverse impact of the uncertainty cannot be mitigated by formulating new subgoals or by RELAX-ation, then we have to consider the given goal as *failed.* As such, we need to create a new high-level goal that captures the objective of correcting the failure. This uncertainty-mitigation tactic is the most costly since the new high-level goal and its subsequent refinement correspond to the goal lattice for a new target system. Examples of each uncertainty-mitigation tactic are described in Section 3.

Not shown in the text or the figures above are two key non-functional requirements that guided the goal refinement process: the solutions offered by the AAL should, as far as practicable, be *non-invasive* and of *low cost.* Since the focus of this paper is on detecting and modeling uncertainty in the context of DASs, we only consider the non-functional requirements implicitly in this discussion. In the LOREM work [4], we described how to use goal modeling of non-functional requirements (e.g., performance, battery usage) as the sole basis for dynamic adaptation, where the different combinations of environmental conditions were explicitly enumerated. In contrast, this paper describes a technique for identifying the environmental conditions warranting dynamic adaptation (e.g., sensor failure, violation of safety conditions).

2.3 Process Overview

The analysis steps described above can be applied systematically using the following stepwise process: Figure 3 gives the data flow diagram for the process. Processes, data flows, and data stores are represented by ovals, arrows, and parallel lines, respectively.

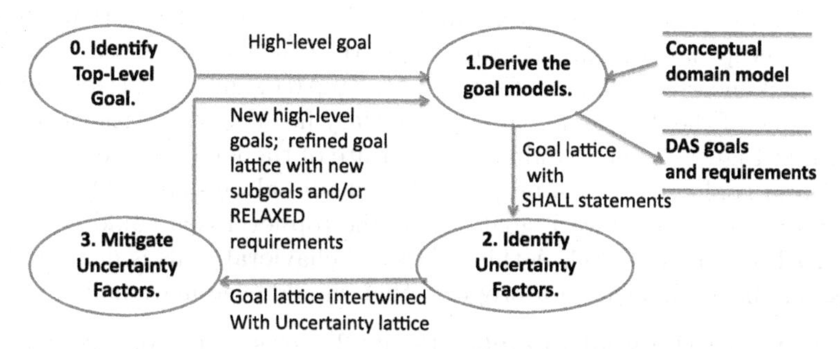

Fig. 3. Process for Goal-Based Modeling of Adaptive Systems

Step 0: Identify Top-level goal and Environment: Identify the top-level goal for system. Create a conceptual domain model that identifies the observable environmental elements relevant to the system; these elements are potential sources of uncertainty for the system.

Step 1: Derive the goal models: Perform goal refinement until we derive leaf requirements/expectations and their respective agents.

Step 2: Identify Uncertainty Factors: Starting from the leaf requirements/ expectations identify the uncertainty factors that might prevent their satisfaction. These uncertainty factors represent environmental conditions that potentially affect the behavior of the system. The uncertainty and/or the impact of the uncertainty factors may propagate up the goal lattice if not adequately mitigated.

Step 3: Mitigate Uncertainty Factors:
Below are the mitigation tactics, presented in order of increasing cost (i.e. effort to realize).

i. No refinement: If the uncertainty factors do not prevent satisfaction of the goals, then do not modify the respective goal.

ii. Add low-level subgoals: If the uncertainty can be mitigated by introducing new low-level goals, then refine with new subgoals.

iii. RELAX goals: If the uncertainty prevents high-level goals from being completely satisfied but we can accept their partial satisfaction, then RELAX the highest level goal impacted by the corresponding uncertainty.

iv. Add high-level goal: If the effect of uncertainty on a high-level goal is unacceptably severe (i.e., environmental conditions have changed significantly beyond previous expectations), then identify a new (high-level) goal to mitigate the uncertainty. This new goal represents a new target system and the closer to the top-level goal it is, the greater the implied cost of implementation. Steps 1 - 3 must be applied to the new portion of the goal lattice for refinement.

3 Application of Goal Modeling for the AAL System

This section describes the results of applying our modeling approach to the AAL system. Due to space constraints, we can only present excerpted goal models of each of the types of uncertainty mitigation.

Step 0: Identify Top-level goal and Environment. Recall that Figure 1 gives the conceptual domain model for the AAL, which serves to scope the environment and uncertainty factors for the AAL. Step 0 of our analysis identified the top-level goal of the AAL house as keeping Mary healthy (i.e., Maintain[Health]), as shown in Figure 2. The 'Maintain' predicate of the label denotes the goal as a behavioral goal specifying a property that should always hold. The inverse of a 'Maintain' goal is an 'Avoid' goal. Hence the top-level goal could be denoted by the goal Avoid[BadHealth]. A third class of behavioral goals is denoted by an 'Achieve' predicate, indicating a property that should eventually hold.

Step 1: Derive the goal models. Figure 2 shows Step 1 of our process to refine the top-level goal as a lattice of subgoals. We elide all but one branch of the lattice to illustrate the refinement of the goals concerned with ensuring that liquid intake is sufficient. The branch has been refined to a single expectation that Mary drinks and a single requirement that the iFridge supplies cold drinking water. These are AND-ed to indicate that both need to be satisfied in order to satisfy the goal of maintaining adequate liquid intake.

Step 2: Identify Uncertainty Factors. Following identification of the goals, Step 2 analyses the extent to which they are satisfiable by developing the uncertainty model using KAOS obstacles. The key uncertainty factor in Figure 2 is represented by the obstacle Forgets to drink. It is uncertain whether Mary will drink enough liquid; she could forget to drink and the effect of this would mean that she gets too little liquid, becomes dehydrated, and ultimately, unhealthy.

Step 3(ii): Mitigate Uncertainty Factors. Completion of the uncertainty model triggers Step 3 whose purpose is to evaluate the uncertainty factors and decide whether to try to mitigate them. Assuming that the uncertainty is sufficiently serious that some mitigation is needed, we start by attempting to apply 3(ii), adding a new subgoal to mitigate the obstacle. Uncertainty about whether Mary will drink enough, which is represented by the Forgets to drink obstacle in Figure 4, has been mitigated by adding a new goal Achieve[ReminderToDrinkIssued], highlighted by the block arrow 3(ii). This new goal is AND-ed with the expectation that Mary drinks and the requirement that the iFridge supplies cold drinking water. In other words, we can reduce the likelihood of Mary forgetting to drink by giving her a reminder by exploiting the iCups' capability to beep; this new goal mitigates the obstacle Forgets to drink, denoted by a solid bold arrow from goal to obstacle. An implication of the new goal, however, is that we need to estimate how much Mary drinks over time and issue reminders if her liquid intake falls below some ideal level. Hence, identification of the Achieve[ReminderToDrinkIssued] goal triggers a repeat of Step 1 to refine it down to the level of requirements, followed by Step 2 to build an uncertainty model for these new requirements.

This mitigation tactic is illustrated in Figure 4; the goal lattice is extended with the goal Achieve[RemindertoDrinkIssued] and its refinements, and the corresponding uncertainty lattice is extended with the nodes Doesn't act on prompt and Calculated liquid intake shortfall inaccurate, along with their respective refinements. The extended goal lattice also includes a domain *assumption*, denoted by the trapezoid labelled Most drinking vessels are iCups, which we use here to record an assumption upon which the correctness of our analysis depends; that Mary will drink most of her water from iCups.

Step 3(iii): Mitigate Uncertainty by RELAXation. Performance of Step 3 on the new goals and uncertainty factors is interesting because it reveals that the uncertainty can be mitigated but not be entirely eliminated. In this case, the mitigation tactic is to add flexibility that accounts for the uncertainty directly into the goal specification, assuming that the goal is not an invariant. Hence,

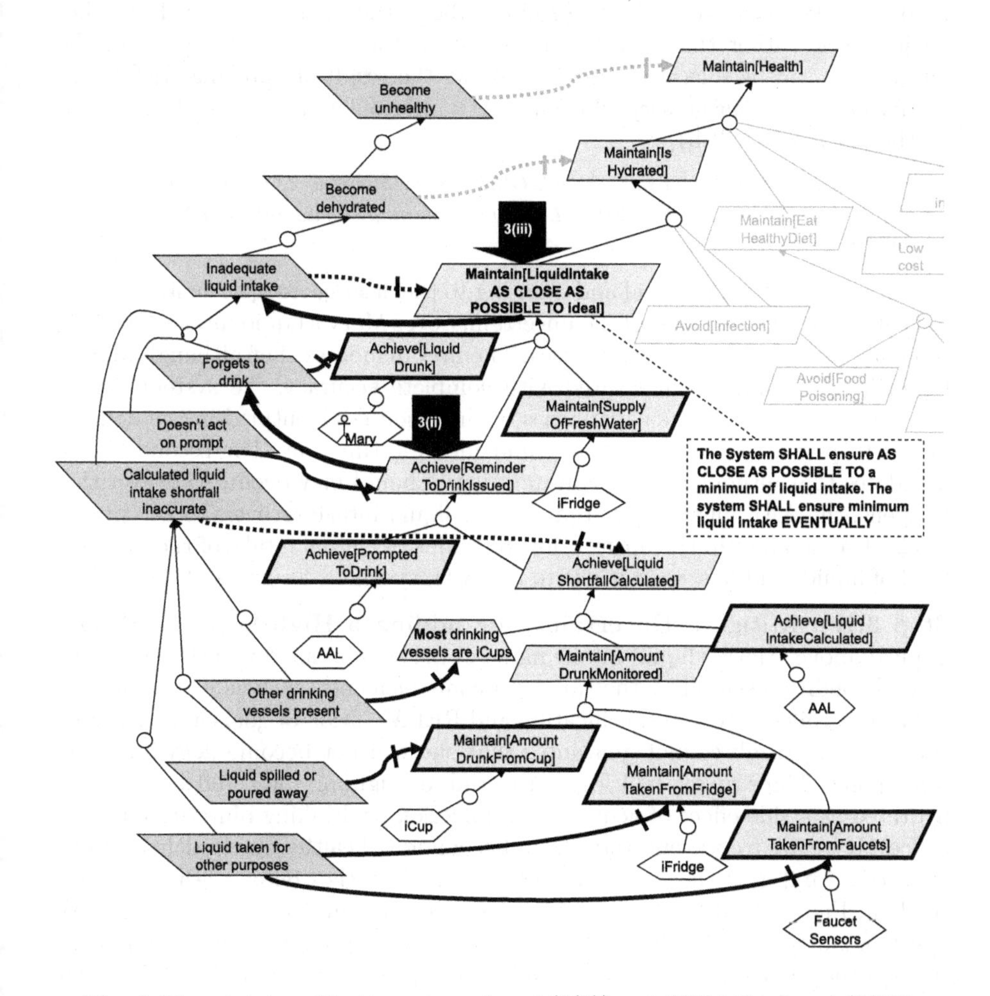

Fig. 4. Uncertainty mitigation: new subgoal (3(ii)) and RELAX subgoal (3(iii))

for example, the amount of liquid being taken from an iCup can be sensed, but it cannot be guaranteed that the liquid taken is being consumed by Mary. Mary might be using it to water her potted plants or simply spilling it. As a consequence, the Maintain[AdequateLiquidIntake] goal from Figure 2 cannot be guaranteed to be satisfiable under all circumstances. This uncertainty poses a problem; there does not appear to be a technological solution that can guarantee to accurately measure Mary's liquid intake, or one that will guarantee that Mary will act on reminders that she should drink. On the other hand, a temporary shortfall in the ideal liquid consumption may:

- Be normal - the temperature may be low, causing Mary to lose less liquid through perspiration;
- Be recouped later - it may lead to a mild headache (which may in turn prompt Mary to drink) rather than immediate organ failure;

Step 3 reveals that there is uncertainty about the environment (Mary's behavior), yet, rather than calling into question the viability of the AAL, the uncertainty can be tolerated. Figure 4 shows the result of applying RELAX to Maintain[AdequateLiquidIntake], which has been reformulated as the goal (indicated by the block arrow 3(iii))

> *The System SHALL ensure AS CLOSE AS POSSIBLE TO a minimum of liquid intake. The system SHALL ensure minimum liquid intake EVENTUALLY.*

The arc leading from the goal and pointing to the Inadequate liquid intake obstacle indicates partial mitigation of the uncertainty over Mary's liquid intake. The goal is a composite comprising two clauses. The first mandates that although Mary's liquid intake cannot be measured with complete accuracy, the system should be designed to exploit the capabilities of the resources identified in the domain model to provide a best effort at liquid intake estimation. The second clause mandates that although under-consumption of liquid may occur, whenever this happens, the AAL must ensure that Mary's liquid intake recovers to acceptable levels at some point in the future. How to achieve eventual intake of the minimal level of liquid, and how soon is left to the AAL system's designers to determine.

Step 3(iv): Mitigate Uncertainty by adding a High-Level Goal. As implied above, Mary's liquid intake may fall below minimal levels (i.e., environmental condition sensed by the various domain elements, such as iCups, sensors in faucets, toilets, etc.) so specification and RELAX-ation of goals aimed at getting Mary to drink cannot guarantee that she will not become dehydrated at some point. Mary might still forget to drink enough, or she could become dehydrated as a side-effect of acquiring an infection or drinking diuretics (such as coffee). If we are to prevent Mary from becoming unhealthy due to dehydration, we need to mitigate the uncertainty represented by the Become dehydrated obstacle in Figure 4. Mitigation of this uncertainty requires recourse to the most costly of our tactics, which is represented as Step 3(iv) of our process. Step 3(iv) triggers the search for a new high-level goal, a peer goal to our RELAXed goal to maintain Mary's liquid intake, concerned with *rehydrating* Mary.

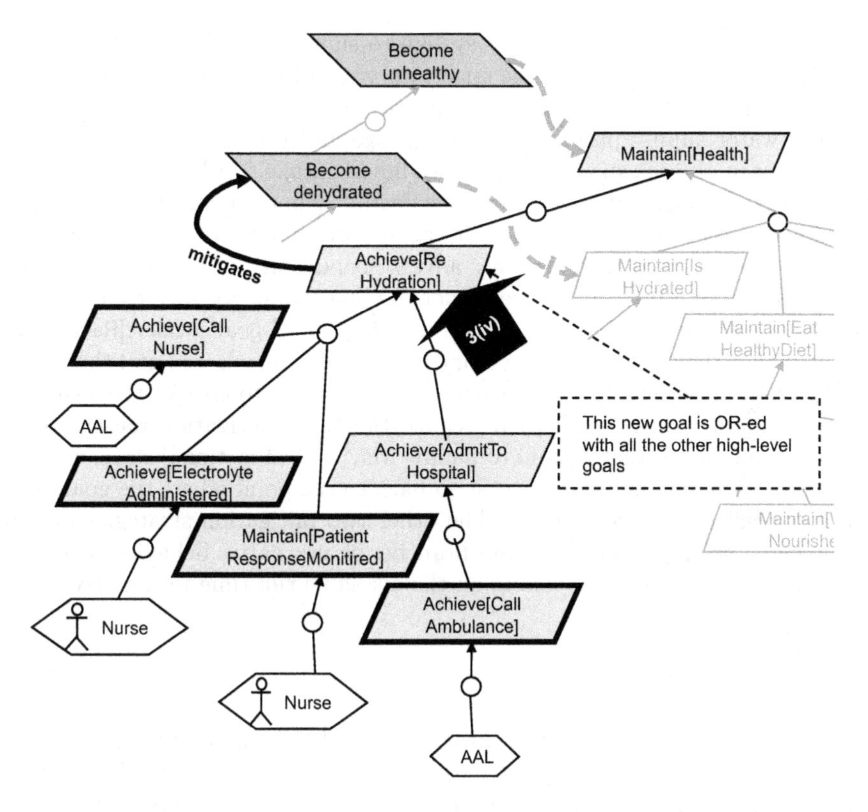

Fig. 5. Uncertainty mitigation with new high-level goal for new target system

This mitigation approach is shown as the goal Achieve[ReHydration], indicated by the block arrow 3(iv) in Figure 5. Rehydrating Mary represents a radical change in the system behavior; that is, we have identified a new target system. Instead of merely getting her to drink enough, we now need to cope with the emergency situation of getting her rehydrated before organ damage occurs. So urgent is this condition, that the new goal is OR-ed with the other high-level goals. In other words, the AAL suspends its goal of maintaining a healthy diet along with all the other goals that need to be satisfied if Mary is to lead a normal life, and diverts resources into getting her rehydrated. This high-level goal represents a new target system, specified by refining the Achieve[ReHydration] goal and, of course, applying uncertainty modeling to ensure this new goal's refined sub-lattice is robust too. The arc leading from the new goal Achieve[ReHydration] to the obstacle Become dehydrated indicates the mitigation of the associated uncertainty.

Discussion. In summary, this example illustrated three different mitigation strategies for handling uncertainty in the environment. At the end of this process for addressing the Maintain[IsHydrated] goal, we included functionality in the requirements for the original target system to support a reminder to drink feature in the iCups to account for the uncertainty with Mary's behavior. In order to make the target system more flexible with respect to the uncertainty associated with the water supply provided by the iFridge and take into account the lack of accuracy in the sensors measuring the liquid intake, we RELAXed the goal Maintain[AdequateLiquidIntake] to introduce flexibility in the quantity of liquid consumed and the time frame in which it can be consumed. Finally, to handle the uncertainty associated with severely adverse conditions with Mary (either her unwillingness to respond to the reminders or illness) and/or adverse conditions with the water supply, we introduced a new high-level goal Achieve[Rehydration] to account for the situation where Mary has become dehydrated and the system must provide new behavior (via a new target system) to correct the situation. Dynamic adaptation is required to realize the third mitigation tactic since it requires a different target system to handle Mary's dysfunctional state, with the objective of bringing her and the system back to the point where the goal Maintain[IsHydrated] is satisfiable again. The other two mitigation strategies may be implemented statically with different branches of alternative behavior or realized by run-time adaptation, depending on the available run-time technology.

4 Related Work

The increasing demand for self-adaptation has led to a surge of interest in software engineering for self-adaptive systems – see [10] for a recently compiled summary. Most of this work has been in the design of software architectures that enable flexible adaptations [11]. In general, such architectures share common characteristics that enable them to monitor and respond to environmental changes. Much less work has been carried out on how to explicitly incorporate the inherent uncertainty associated with adaptive systems into existing modeling languages. UML profiles exist that provide stereotypes for marking model elements that are in some way uncertain – e.g., an uncertainty profile [12] for capturing uncertainty in process modeling and fuzzy UML [13] for representing imperfect information in databases. Uchitel *et al.* [14] have also dealt with uncertainty using partial labelled transition systems (PLTS) to model aspects of the system behaviour that are unknown and remain undefined.

Limited work has also been performed in modeling and monitoring requirements for adaptive systems. Goal-based modeling notations, such as i* [15] and KAOS [1], have been applied to the specification of requirements of self-adaptive systems. Specifically, goal-based models are well suited to exploring alternative requirements and it is natural to use goal models to represent alternative behaviors that are possible when the environment changes [4,16,17,6]. Furthermore, goal models can effectively be used to specify the requirements for transition between adaptive behaviours [4,18]. With these approaches, however, the modeler must explicitly enumerate all possible alternative behaviours. In contrast, RELAX [5] supports a declarative approach for specifying requirements for a DAS, thus accounting for more flexibility in the system behavior.

Run-time monitoring of requirements dynamically assesses the conformance of run-time behaviour to the specified requirements [19]. This capability is a crucial enabler for self-adaptive systems as non-conformance to requirements may trigger an adaptation. Requirements monitoring approaches often rely on *ad-hoc* run-time representations of the requirements [20]. A more promising approach is to monitor goal models at run time as described in [21], where failed goals are diagnosed and fixed at run time using AI theories of diagnosis. More generally, in the context of self-adaptive systems, it may only be possible to *partially* satisfy run-time goals – that is, goal satisfaction is not a "yes" or "no" decision. Adaptation decisions, therefore, may have to be made probabilistically. Letier and van Lamsweerde [22] have proposed a technique to quantify degrees of satisfaction in goal models but the work has not yet been applied to adaptive systems.

5 Conclusions and Future Work

Goals are objectives or statements of intent that the system should accomplish. For the case of adaptive systems, different environmental uncertainty factors may put at risk the accomplishment of such goals. In this paper, we have presented a goal-based modeling approach to specify the requirements of a DAS, where environmental uncertainty associated with the goal specifications are explicitly integrated. The approach offers a systematic use of a range of tactics for adaptation to deal with uncertainty on a rising scale of costs. The tactics include adding low-level goals (the least costly approach), RELAXing requirements to express bounded uncertainty to accomplish a partial but still suitable satisfaction of the goals, and the identification of a new (high-level) goal to mitigate the uncertainty that leads to the identification of a new target system.

The general objective of goal modeling is to refine goals so that the set of subgoals that satisfy their parent goal is necessary and sufficient. One key lesson from reasoning with uncertainty is that, where uncertainty exists, the most we can hope for is that the subgoals are necessary. They will never be sufficient. Uncertainty must be handled, therefore, by assigning responsibility to a human agent or by introducing some intelligent or adaptive behavior into the software.

Several avenues for future research are possible. Estimation of the risk posed by uncertainty is implicit in the application of our process; i.e., our work requires risk to be inferred from the goal and uncertainty models. Further work is required towards systematic techniques to quantify the risk as a complement to threat modelling, understanding what we can RELAX (i.e. what is variant vs. what is invariant), and the extent to which we can RELAX requirements. We speculate that risk could be made explicit by quantifying it in the manner of attack trees [2]. The systematic approach for identifying target systems makes it possible to extend existing MDE-based approaches to DAS development (e.g., [3,23]) to start at a higher-level of abstraction. That is, with the results from this work, we can start with a conceptual domain model of a DAS and systematically progress from goals and requirements to their designs and implementation.

References

1. van Lamsweerde, A.: Requirements Engineering: From System Goals to UML Models to Software Specifications. John Wiley & Sons, Chichester (2009)
2. Schneier, B.: Attack Trees - Modeling security threats. Dr. Dobb's Journal (1999)
3. Zhang, J., Cheng, B.H.C.: Model-based development of dynamically adaptive software. In: ICSE 2006: Proc. of the 28th Int. Conf. on Software engineering, pp. 371–380 (2006)
4. Goldsby, H., Sawyer, P., Bencomo, N., Hughes, D., Cheng, B.H.C.: Goal-based modeling of dynamically adaptive system requirements. In: 15th IEEE Int. Conf. on the Engineering of Computer Based Systems, ECBS (2008)
5. Whittle, J., Sawyer, P., Bencomo, N., Cheng, B.H.C., Bruel, J.M.: Relax: Incorporating uncertainty into the specification of self-adaptive systems. In: Proc. of IEEE Int. Requirements Engineering Conf., RE 2009 (to appear, 2009)
6. Yijun, Y., Lapouchnian, A., Liaskos, S., Mylopoulos, J., Leite, J.: From Goals to High-Variability Software Design. In: An, A., Matwin, S., Raś, Z.W., Ślęzak, D. (eds.) Foundations of Intelligent Systems. LNCS (LNAI), vol. 4994, pp. 1–16. Springer, Heidelberg (2008)
7. Mylopoulos, J., Chung, L., Yu, E.: From object-oriented to goal-oriented requirements analysis. Commun. ACM 42(1), 31–37 (1999)
8. Mead, N.: Identifying Security Requirements using the SQUARE Method. In: Integrating Security and Software Engineering: Advances and Future Visions, pp. 44–69. Idea Group, USA (2006)
9. den Braber, F., Dimitrakos, T., Gran, B.A., Lund, M.S., Stölen, K., Aagedal, J.O.: The coras methodology: model-based risk assessment using uml and up. In: UML and the unified process, pp. 332–357. IGI Publishing, Hershey (2003)
10. Cheng, B.H.C., et al.: 08031 – software engineering for self-adaptive systems: A research road map. In: Cheng, B.H.C., de Lemos, R., Giese, H., Inverardi, P., Magee, J. (eds.) Software Engineering for Self-Adaptive Systems. Number 08031 in Dagstuhl Seminar Proceedings (2008)
11. Kramer, J., Magee, J.: Self-managed systems: an architectural challenge. In: Briand, L.C., Wolf, A.L. (eds.) FOSE, pp. 259–268 (2007)
12. Jing, X., Pinel, P., Pi, L., Aranega, V., Baron, C.: Modeling uncertain and imprecise information in process modeling with UML. In: COMAD, Computer Society of India, pp. 237–240 (2008)
13. Ma, Z.M., Yan, L.: Fuzzy XML data modeling with the UML and relational data models. Data Knowl. Eng. 63(3), 972–996 (2007)
14. Uchitel, S., Kramer, J., Magee, J.: Behaviour model elaboration using partial labelled transition systems. In: ESEC/FSE-11, pp. 19–27 (2003)
15. Yu, E.S.K.: Towards modeling and reasoning support for early-phase requirements engineering. In: Proc. of 3rd IEEE Int. Symp. on Requirements Engineering, RE 1997 (1997)
16. Lapouchnian, A., Liaskos, S., Mylopoulos, J., Yu, Y.: Towards requirements-driven autonomic systems design. In: Workshop on the Design and Evolution of Autonomic Application Software, DEAS 2005 (2005)
17. Lapouchnian, A., Yu, Y., Liaskos, S., Mylopoulos, J.: Requirements-driven design of autonomic application software. In: Proc. of CASCON 2006 (2006)
18. Morandini, M., Penserini, L., Perini, A.: Modelling self-adaptivity: A goal-oriented approach. In: SASO 2008: Proc. of 2008 Second IEEE Int. Conf. on Self-Adaptive and Self-Organizing Systems, pp. 469–470 (2008)

19. Fickas, S., Feather, M.: Requirements monitoring in dynamic environments. In: 2nd IEEE Int. Symp. on Requirements Engineering, RE 1995 (1995)
20. Dingwall-Smith, A., Finkelstein, A.: Checking complex compositions of web services against policy constraints. In: MSVVEIS, pp. 94–103. INSTICC Press (2007)
21. Wang, Y., McIlraith, S.A., Yu, Y., Mylopoulos, J.: An automated approach to monitoring and diagnosing requirements. In: ASE, pp. 293–302. ACM, New York (2007)
22. Letier, E., van Lamsweerde, A.: Reasoning about partial goal satisfaction for requirements and design engineering. In: Proc. of 12th ACM SIGSOFT Int. Symp. on Foundations of Software Engineering, pp. 53–62 (2004)
23. Morin, B., Fleurey, F., Bencomo, N., Jézéquel, J.M., Solberg, A., Dehlen, V., Blair, G.: An aspect-oriented and model-driven approach for managing dynamic variability. In: Czarnecki, K., Ober, I., Bruel, J.-M., Uhl, A., Völter, M. (eds.) MODELS 2008. LNCS, vol. 5301, pp. 782–796. Springer, Heidelberg (2008)

A Use Case Modeling Approach to Facilitate the Transition towards Analysis Models: Concepts and Empirical Evaluation

Tao Yue[1], Lionel C. Briand[2], and Yvan Labiche[1]

[1] Carleton University, Software Quality Engineering Lab,
1125 Colonel By Drive Ottawa, ON K1S 5B6, Canada
{tyue,labiche}@sce.carleton.ca
[2] Simula Research Laboratory & University of Oslo,
P.O. Box 134, Lysaker, Norway
briand@simula.no

Abstract. Use case modeling (UCM) is commonly applied to document requirements. Use case specifications (UCSs) are usually structured, unrestricted textual documents complying with a certain template. However, because they remain essentially textual, ambiguities are inevitable. In this paper, we propose a new UCM approach, which is composed of a set of well-defined restriction rules and a new template. The goal is to reduce ambiguity and facilitate automated analysis, though the later point is not addressed in this paper. We also report on a controlled experiment which evaluates our approach in terms of its ease of application and the quality of the analysis models derived by trained individuals. Results show that the restriction rules are overall easy to apply and that our approach results in significant improvements over UCM using a standard template and no restrictions in UCSs, in terms of the correctness of derived class diagrams and the understandability of UCSs.

Keywords: Use Case, Use Case Modeling, Use Case Template, Restriction Rules, Analysis Model, Controlled Experiment.

1 Introduction

Use case modeling (UCM), including use case diagrams and use case textual specifications, is commonly applied to structure and document requirements [6, 8, 11]. Use Case Specifications (UCS) are usually textual documents complying with a use case template that, though helping read and review use cases, inevitably contains ambiguities. In this paper, we propose a set of restriction rules and a new template, which are based in part on the results of a thorough literature review [25]. The goal is to restrict the way users can document UCSs in order to reduce ambiguity and facilitate automated analysis to derive initial analysis models, which in the Unified Modeling Language (UML) [15] are minimally composed of class and interaction diagrams, and possibly other types of diagrams and constraints. We denote our UCM approach as RUCM, which stands for Restricted Use Case Modeling.

The restriction rules and the use case template we specify should be applied during the requirements elicitation phase of use case-driven software development (e.g., [4])

A. Schürr and B. Selic (Eds.): MODELS 2009, LNCS 5795, pp. 484–498, 2009.

in order to produce, to the extent possible, precise and unambiguous use case models. A use case diagram in UML [15] is used to represent relationships among actors and use cases described by UCSs. The restriction rules are applied to restrict the way users can write UCSs; the use case template is a means to structure UCSs. With a use case model documented by applying RUCM, initial analysis models of higher quality can hopefully be derived with greater ease. This step is usually manually performed by system analysts but the derivation of an initial analysis model could potentially be automated. This paper, however, does not address automation but focuses on describing RUCM and assessing empirically its limitations and benefits.

More precisely, by means of experimentation, we aim at assessing whether our restriction rules are easy to apply while developing use case models and whether the overall approach helps the designer generate higher quality analysis models. Our experiment, involving fully trained, senior undergraduate students, shows that RUCM results into higher quality class diagrams and that restriction rules are perceived overall to be easily applicable.

The rest of the paper is organized as follows. The related work is reported in Section 2. In Section 3, we discuss RUCM: the use case template and the restriction rules. The experimental evaluation of these rules and the use case template is presented in Section 4 (experiment planning), Section 5 (experiment results and analysis), and Section 6 (threats to validity). We conclude in Section 7.

2 Related Work

Various use case templates (e.g., [5, 9, 11-13]) have been suggested in the literature to satisfy different application contexts and purposes. These templates share common fields such as: use case name, brief overall description, precondition, postcondition, basic flow, and alternative flows. In addition to capturing requirements, use cases can also facilitate the automated derivation of initial analysis models – one of our goals. The systematic review [25] we conducted to examine works that transform textual requirements into analysis models reveals that six approaches require use cases. Their proposed templates (e.g., [7, 10, 14, 20]) are similar to conventional ones but with some variations to facilitate the process of automatically deriving analysis models.

The use case template we propose in this paper (Section 3.1) integrates elements from many related works. It contains fields similar to those encountered in conventional templates but also seeks to better specify the structure of the flow of events. The ultimate motivation is to reduce ambiguity when models are derived manually but also support the automated generation of analysis models. Given our goals, we made the following decisions: (1) We included fields commonly encountered in most templates; (2) Some of the fields (e.g., scope) proposed in the literature to capture requirements were excluded since they do not help deriving analysis models; (3) We excluded the fields (e.g., the three-column steps modeling style proposed in [7]) that, on the one hand may increase the precision of UCSs but, on the other hand require that the designer provide much more information that in the end we do not need for our purpose. In other words, we believe that the additional precision does not warrant the additional cost, and that these fields do not bring clear advantages with respect to our objectives; (4) Six interactions types (five from [5], one we newly propose) are suggested to describe action steps in flows of events; (5) Differing from most of existing use case templates that suggest having one postcondition for one use case, our template enforces that each flow of events (both basic flow and alternative flows) of a UCS contains its own postcondition.

In [25], we summarize and classify the restriction rules applied in [19-21, 23], which propose transformations from requirements to analysis models. Some guidelines on writing UCSs are also provided in various sources (e.g., [1, 3, 5]), based on practitioners' experience and to reduce ambiguities in UCSs or to facilitate the process of (automatically) deriving analysis models from them. In this paper, we propose a total of 26 restriction rules on the use of natural language to document UCSs that complies with our use case template. None of the related works we looked at relies on a set of rules as complete as the one we suggest. We reused some of the existing rules, excluded others, recommended new ones, and classified all the rules. Additionally, we explicitly describe why each of our restriction rules is needed either to reduce ambiguities or facilitate the process of (automatically) deriving analysis models, a crucial piece of information that is often omitted in the literature. We also indicate how and where to apply (Section 3.2) each of our restriction rules, another piece of information often left out by most papers on the topic. Several rules we newly propose in this work are based on our experience with several natural language parsers (e.g., [22]) and are proposed because sentences with certain structures cannot be correctly parsed. These rules can also help reduce ambiguity of UCSs and therefore help to manually derive analysis models from them. Furthermore, as opposed to many related works, our restriction rules are integrated with our use case template together as a comprehensive solution for UCM: several of our restriction rules refer to some of the features of our use case template (Section 3.1).

Some empirical studies (e.g., [1, 2, 17]) evaluated the impact of applying restriction rules on the quality of UCSs in terms of, for example, their completeness, structuredness and understandability. Results showed that using restriction rules led to more complete and better structured UCSs. These experiments evaluated restriction rules as a whole only, whereas we evaluate our restriction rules both individually and as a whole. By doing so, we can tell which rule(s) are difficult to apply and therefore require extra focus during training. It is also worth noticing that previous works assess the quality of UCSs against some quality criteria (e.g., understandability, structuredness, completeness), rather than test the ability of individuals to extract relevant information from UCSs to derive analysis models. In this paper, we report on a controlled experiment which evaluates the impact of our restriction rules and use case template both on the understandability of UCSs and the quality of analysis models generated from them in terms of correctness, completeness, and redundancy.

3 Use Case Modeling Approach (RUCM)

3.1 Use Case Template

Our use case template has eleven first-level fields (1st column in Table 1). The last four fields are decomposed into second-level fields (2nd column in the last four rows). The last column of each row explains the corresponding field(s). There is no need to further discuss the first seven fields since they are straightforward and commonly encountered in many templates. Below we focus the discussion on the *Basic Flow* and *Alternative Flows* fields.

A basic flow describes a main successful path. It often does not include any condition or branching [13]. It is recommended to describe separately the conditions and branching in alternative flows. A basic flow is composed of a sequence of steps and a postcondition. Each UCS can only have one basic flow. *Alternative flows* describe all the other scenarios or branches, both success and failure. An alternative flow always depends on a condition occurring in a specific step in a flow of reference, referred to as *reference flow*, and that reference flow is either the basic flow or an alternative flow itself. The branching condition is specified in the reference flow by following restriction rules (R20 and R22—Section 3.2). We refer to steps specifying such conditions as *condition steps* and the other steps as *action steps*. Similarly to the basic flow, an alternative flow is composed of a sequence of numbered steps. The action steps can be one of the following five interactions (which are reused from [5] except for the fifth): 1) Primary actor → system: the primary actor sends a request and data to the system; 2) System → system: the system validates a request and data; 3) System → system: the system alters its internal state (e.g., recording or modifying something); 4) System → primary actor: the system replies to the primary actor with a result; 5) System → secondary actor: the system sends requests to a secondary actor. All steps are numbered sequentially. This implies that each step is completed before the next one is started. If there is a need to express conditions, iterations, or concurrency, then specific keywords, specified as restriction rules should be applied.

We classify alternative flows into three types: specific, global, and bounded alternative flows. This classification is adapted from [3]. A *specific alternative flow* is an alternative flow that refers to a specific step in the reference flow. A *bounded alternative flow* is a flow that refers to more than one step in the reference flow–consecutive steps or not. A *global alternative flow* (called *general alternative flow* in [3]) is an alternative flow that refers to any step in the reference flow. Distinguishing different types of alternative flows makes interactions between the reference flow and its alternative flows much clearer. For specific and bounded alternative flows, a RFS (Reference Flow Step) section, specified as rule R19, is used to specify one or more (reference flow) step numbers. Whether and where the flow merges back to the reference flow or terminates the use case must be specified as the last step of the alternative flow. Similarly to the branching condition, merging and termination are specified by following restriction rules (R24 and R25—Section 3.2). By doing so, we can avoid potential ambiguity in UCSs caused by unclear specification of interactions between the basic flow and its corresponding alternative flows. Each alternative flow must have a postcondition (enforced by restriction rule R26—Section 3.2).

It is usual to provide a postcondition describing a constraint that must be true when a use case terminates. If the use case contains alternative flows, then the postcondition of the use case should describe not only what must be true when the basic flow terminates but also what must be true when each alternative flow terminates. The branching condition to each alternative flow is then necessarily part of the postcondition (to distinguish the different possible results). In such a case, the postcondition becomes complex and the branching condition for each alternative flow is redundantly described (both in the steps of flows and the postcondition), which therefore increases the risk of ambiguity in UCSs. Our template enforces that each flow of events (both basic flow and alternative flows) of a UCS contains its own postcondition and therefore avoids such ambiguity.

Table 1. Use case template

Use Case Name	The name of the use case. It usually starts with a verb.	
Brief Description	Summarizes the use case in a short paragraph.	
Precondition	What should be true before the use case is executed.	
Primary Actor	The actor which initiates the use case.	
Secondary Actors	Other actors the system relies on to accomplish the services of the use case.	
Dependency	Include and extend relationships to other use cases.	
Generalization	Generalization relationships to other use cases.	
Basic Flow	Specifies the main successful path, also called "happy path".	
	Steps (numbered)	Flow of events.
	Postcondition	What should be true after the basic flow executes.
Specific Alternative Flows	Applies to one specific step of the reference flow.	
	RFS	A reference flow step number where flow branches from.
	Steps (numbered)	Flow of events.
	Postcondition	What should be true after the alternative flow executes.
Global Alternative Flows	Applies to all the steps of the reference flow.	
	Steps (numbered)	Flow of events.
	Postcondition	What should be true after the alternative flow executes.
Bounded Alternative Flows	Applies to more than one step of the reference flow, but not all of them.	
	RFS	A list of reference flow steps where flow branches from.
	Steps (numbered)	Flow of events.
	Postcondition	What should be true after the alternative flow executes.

3.2 Restriction Rules

The restriction rules are classified into two groups: restrictions on the use of natural language, and restrictions enforcing the use of specific keywords for specifying control structures. The first group of restrictions is further divided into two categories according to their location of application (see below). Each restriction rule is assigned a unique number.

Restriction rules R1-R16 in Table 2 constrain the use of natural language: the table explains why they are needed to reduce ambiguity. Rules R1-R7 apply only to action steps; they do not apply to condition steps, preconditions or postconditions. Rules R8-R16 apply to all sentences in a UCS: action steps, condition steps, preconditions, postconditions, and sentences in the brief description. Rules R8-R11 and R16 aim to reduce ambiguity of UCSs; the remaining rules (R12-R15) can help reduce ambiguity and also facilitate automated generation of analysis models. Recall that, as we discussed in Section 1, facilitating automated derivation of initial analysis models from UCSs is also one of our goals, though this is not discussed in this paper. These two sets of restrictions are thought to be good practice for writing clear and concise UCSs (e.g., [3, 5, 18]) except for R13 and R15. We add these two rules because we observed that negative adverbs, negative adjectives, and participle phrases are very difficult to parse by natural language parsers. R9 requires using words consistently to document UCSs. A common approach to do so is to use a domain model and glossary (e.g., [13], [4]) as a basis to write UCSs.

Table 2. Restrictions (R1-R16)

#	Description	Explanation
R1	The subject of a sentence in basic and alternative flows should be the system or an actor.	Enforce describing flows of events correctly. These rules conform to our use case template (the five interactions).
R2	Describe the flow of events sequentially.	
R3	Actor-to-actor interactions are not allowed.	
R4	Describe one action per sentence. (Avoid compound predicates.)	Otherwise it is hard to decide the sequence of multiple actions in a sentence.
R5	Use present tense only.	Enforce describing what the system does, rather than what it will do or what it has done.
R6	Use active voice rather than passive voice.	Enforce explicitly showing the subject and/or object(s) of a sentence.
R7	Clearly describe the interaction between the system and actors without omitting its sender and receiver.	
R8	Use declarative sentences only. "Is the system idle?" is a non-declarative sentence.	Commonly required for writing UCSs.
R9	Use words in a consistent way.	Keep one term to describe one thing.
R10	Don't use modal verbs (e.g., *might*)	Modal verbs and adverbs usually indicate uncertainty; therefore metrics should be used if possible.
R11	Avoid adverbs (e.g., *very*).	
R12	Use simple sentences only. A simple sentence must contain only one subject and one predicate.	Reduce ambiguity and facilitate automated NL parsing.
R13	Don't use negative adverb and adjective (e.g., *hardly, never*), but it is allowed to use *not* or *no*.	
R14	Don't use pronouns (e.g. *he, this*).	
R15	Don't use participle phrases as adverbial modifier. For example, the italic-font part of the sentence "ATM is idle, *displaying a Welcome message*", is a participle phrase.	
R16	Use "the system" to refer to the system under design consistently.	Keep one term to describe the system; therefore reduce ambiguity.

The remaining ten restriction rules (R17-R26) constrain the use of control structures, except R26 that specifies that each basic flow and alternative flow should have its own postcondition. R17 and R18 specify keywords to describe use case dependencies include and extend. Sentences containing the keywords INCLUDE USE CASE and EXTENDED BY USE CASE are referred to as dependency sentences. R19 specifies keyword RFS, which is used in a specific (or bounded) alternative flow to refer to a step number (or a set of step numbers) of a reference flow that this alternative flow branches from. Rules R20-R23 specify the keywords used to specify conditional logic sentences (IF-THEN-ELSE-ELSEIF-ENDIF), concurrency sentences (MEANWHILE), condition checking sentences (VALIDATES THAT), and iteration sentences (DO-UNTIL), respectively. Keyword VALIDATES THAT (R22) specifies that a condition is evaluated by the system and must be true to proceed to the next step. This rule also requires that an alternative flow describing what happens when the validation fails (the condition does not hold) be described. Rules R24 and R25 specify that an alternative flow ends with a step using either keyword ABORT or keyword RESUME STEP, thereby clearly specifying whether the flow returns back to the reference flow and where (using keyword RESUME STEP followed by a returning step number) or terminates (using keyword ABORT).

R17-R21 and R23 have been proposed in the literature and we reused them with some variation. R22, R24 and R25 are newly proposed in this work for the purpose of making the whole set of restrictions as complete as possible so that flows of events and interactions between the basic flow and the alternatives can be clearly and concisely specified. Applying these rules helps reducing ambiguity in UCSs, and also facilitates automated NL processing (e.g., correctly parse sentences with our specified keywords) and the generation of analysis models, especially sequence diagrams.

The detailed description of all the 26 restriction rules and an example of applying RUCM are provided in [26].

4 Experiment Planning

In this section, we follow the experiment reporting template proposed in [24]. All aspects of the experiment we conducted to assess our use case template and restriction rules are described and justified.

4.1 Experiment Definition

We are interested in the applicability of the restriction rules, combined with the use case template we propose. We refer to a use case model with UCSs that follow our restriction rules and template as a *restricted* use case model. We are also interested in the impact of a restricted use case model on the quality of analysis models that are manually derived from it, for instance by following standard guidelines for building analysis models (e.g., [4]). Indeed, if the restriction rules actually reduce ambiguity, then such models should exhibit higher quality. The experiment objectives are: characterizing each restriction rule with respect to their applicability (Goal 1), and evaluating the restriction rules and the template with respect to their impact on quality of derived analysis models (Goal 2). The evaluation of Goal 1 is a necessary prerequisite to the investigation of Goal 2 in order to ensure that the restriction rules can be applied at a reasonable level of correctness. If the result of the experiment for Goal 1 shows that the restriction rules are applicable, then reliable use case models can be produced and we can go further to evaluate whether these restriction rules have an impact on the quality of manually generated analysis models (class and sequence diagrams in our experiment). In this paper, we focus on the experiment for Goal 2. Due to space limitation, the detailed discussion of the experiment for Goal 1 is omitted but is however provided in [26] for reference. Most noticeably, results for Goal 1 indicate that our 26 restriction rules are easy to apply [26].

4.2 Context Selection and Subjects

The context of the experiment is a 4th Software Engineering course at Carleton University, Ottawa, Canada. The subjects selected were the 34 students registered in this course. The students were all trained in UML-based, object-oriented software development over the three years prior to the experiment and had therefore received substantial training. Additionally, a lecture was given to them regarding the restriction rules and the use case template before the experiment. One assignment was also designed for the students to practice the restriction rules and the template. The results of the assignment were used to group the students into two blocks and therefore ensure better homogeneity across the two groups involved in the experiment. The experiment plan had been reviewed and received clearance through the Carleton University's Research Ethics Committee.

4.3 Hypotheses Formulation

The experiment for Goal 2 has one independent variable *Method*, with two treatments: *UCM_R* and *UCM_UR*, respectively denoting the use or not of the restriction rules, and two dependent variables *CD* and *QC*, respectively denoting the quality of analysis class diagrams and the correctness of responses to a comprehension questionnaire. We therefore can formulate the following null hypotheses (H_0) to be tested for each dependent variable of the experiment for Goal 2: there is no significant improvement in terms of CD and QC when using restricted use case models. The alternative hypotheses (H_a) is then one-tailed and stated as: restricted use case models result in high quality analysis models or high correctness of responses to the comprehension questionnaire when compared to unrestricted use case models.

4.4 Experiment Design

As stated previously, an assignment was designed to train the students to apply our restriction rules and use case template. Individual feedback was given to each student and a solution to the assignment was also provided before the experiment was conducted. Based on the grades of the assignment preceding the experiment, we defined the following three blocks: grades B to A+, grades B- to F, and absent (ABS). The students were then divided into two groups: A and B. Each of the two groups was then randomly assigned students from the three blocks in nearly identical proportions.

The students were asked to perform two tasks over two laboratories (3 hours each). In Lab 1 (Task 1), the students in group A were asked to produce UCSs of the Video Store (VS) system by applying the restriction rules and the use case template, whereas the students in group B did the same task on the Car Part Dealer (CPD) system. This first task was designed to address Goal 1: recall that this is omitted from this paper due to space limitation (the interested reader is referred to [26]). In Lab 2 (Task 2), which is dedicated to Goal 2, we further divided the students of group A into groups A1 and A2, so that the students in A1 derive class and sequence diagrams from a restricted use case model for the CPD system, while the students in A2 do the same from the unrestricted use case model following a standard template [4] of the same system. A discussion on the differences between the standard template and our template is provided in [26]. The same strategy was followed for group B but using the VS system instead. These two sub-groupings follow the same blocking strategy as the one used to group the students for Task 1 into groups A and B. Note that we use different systems for the two labs for each group of students in order to avoid learning effects that would otherwise constitute a threat to validity. For example, group A uses the VS system in Lab 1 but the CPD system in Lab 2. In total, 26 data points were obtained for Task 1 and Task 2 (14 data points for treatment UCM_R and 12 for treatment UCM_UR) respectively; however only 23 data points (14 for treatment UCM_R and 9 for treatment UCM_UR) were used for analyzing Task 2. Three data points were excluded from the analysis in order to avoid constituting a threat to validity: one student missed the lab for Task 2 and had to perform the task at home, another spent 3 hours 40 mins on Task 2, and the other produced a very incomplete result (no class diagram were derived).

4.5 Instrumentation

The instruments of an experiment are classified into three types: experiment objects, guidelines, and measurement instruments [24]. In this section we discuss our experiment instruments for Task 2 by conforming to this classification.

Experiment objects. The CPD and VS systems come in two versions for this part of the experiment: they contain the same use case diagram but have different UCSs (with or without restrictions). Both sets of UCSs—one with our restrictions and template, one with a standard template—were created by the first author of this paper. Both use case model versions were carefully reviewed by the authors to ensure that they contained equivalent information. Notice that the students were equally trained to understand our use case template and the standard template.

Experiment guidelines. A lab description was provided to the students at the beginning of each lab, describing the list of documents provided, the task of the lab, and the submission guidelines. The students belonging to different groups were monitored to ensure they would not access each other's documents during the entire lab duration. With a use case model as input documents, the students were asked to design a class diagram. We made it clear in the lab description that the students should, based on the use case description, assign meaningful names for each class, attribute, and operation, and apply the traditional *Entity/Boundary/Control* stereotype classification for each class. The students were also asked to complete a comprehension questionnaire during the lab, which was designed to evaluate how well they were able to understand the flow of events of each UCS. The students were also asked to derive sequence diagrams for two selected use cases; however most of the students were not able to derive these diagrams due to time constraints, which were therefore not analyzed.

Measurement instruments. A comprehension questionnaire was designed for each system to quickly evaluate, in a repeatable and objective way, the extent to which students understood the main body (flows of events) of each UCS. The standard guidelines proposed in [16] were followed to create the questionnaires. To avoid introducing any bias, we ensured comprehension questions were answerable by the students using both the restricted or unrestricted use case models. The complete questionnaires for the two systems are discussed in [26].

4.6 Evaluation Measurement and Data Collection

There are two dependent variables for Goal 2, for which data must be collected in Task 2: the quality of class diagrams (abbreviated as CD) and the correctness of responses to the comprehension questionnaires (abbreviated as QC).

Variable CD. The quality of an analysis class diagram is evaluated from three aspects: *Correctness*, *Completeness*, and *Redundancy*. We used reference class diagrams, designed by the authors, as the basis to evaluate class diagrams designed by the students. Data are collected from the reference class diagrams (i.e., number of classes, associations and generalizations), and data are also collected from the class diagrams of each student (e.g., number of missing classes, missing attributes of a class, incorrect associations, and redundant classes). All these data are then used to compute the measures of *Completeness*, *Correctness* and *Redundancy* of a student class diagram. The completeness of a class diagram is inversely related to the numbers of missing classes, associations and generalizations, which are considered to be three important element types in a class diagram; the correctness of a class diagram is determined by the correctness of matching classes (computed as the average, over the complete class diagram, of the class measures of *Completeness* and *Correctness*) and associations; the redundancy of a class diagram is computed as the ratio of redundant classes over all the classes of a student's class diagram. The completeness of a class is related to whether its stereotype is missed and whether there are missing attributes and operations; the correctness of a class is determined by whether the class is correctly named, stereotyped and specified as abstract, and whether a single logical concept is represented and a cohesive set of responsibilities is assigned to the class. The detailed description of the measures and calculation formulas is provided in [26] due to space limitations.

For each reference class of the reference class diagram of a case study system, we look for a class with the same name as the reference class in a student class diagram. If such a class is found, then this matching class is evaluated according to the quality measures for a class; otherwise, we keep looking in the student class diagram for a design equivalent[1] to the reference class. If no such equivalent design exists in the student class diagram, then we identify the reference class as missing and therefore the student diagram as incomplete. When all the reference classes in the reference class diagram have been looked at, there are three outputs: 1) a set of matching classes are identified and evaluated by using the quality measures for a class; 2) a set of equivalent designs are identified but not measured because either a subjective measurement or a large number of specific measures would be required to measure them. Besides, not many such equivalent designs have been found and not measuring them does not really impact the measurement of CD; and 3) a set of reference classes, missing in the student class diagram (i.e., not matching classes or equivalent design), are listed. A procedure similar to this identification of matching class, missing class, and equivalent class designs is also applied to identify matching/missing attributes, operations, associations, and generalizations.

Variable QC. Data about the correctness of responses to the questions of the comprehension questionnaires of Task 2 are used to evaluate the understandability of UCSs, which is normalized between 0 and 1:

For the CPD system: $QC_{\_CPD} = number\ of\ correct\ responses\ /\ 15$
For the VS system: $QC_{\_VS} = number\ of\ correct\ responses\ /\ 25$

where the denominators are the total numbers of questions in each system questionnaire.

[1] An equivalent design may contain one or more model elements, which could be attributes, multiple classes connected by associations, etc. It is difficult to determine such an equivalent design and it would probably easier to prove the equivalence of sequence diagrams since such information is already included in UCSs.

5 Experiment Results and Analysis

In this section, we present the results from the controlled experiment described in the previous section. Though the two systems used for the experiment might lead to different results, the number of observations does not allow us to perform a separate analysis for each of them. We, however, counter-balance their possible effect by ensuring a similar proportion of observations coming from each system, for each of the tasks. Recall that Goal 1 is to evaluate whether RUCM (the use case template and the restriction rules) is easy to apply while developing use case models. Each restriction rule is evaluated in terms of its understandability, applicability, restrictiveness, and error rate. Though we do not report these results in detail here, they indicate that our 26 restriction rules are easy to apply and with appropriate tool support and focused training on the rules receiving higher error rates, error rates can be expected to decrease, as detailed in [26]. Based on these results, we are therefore confident that trained engineers are capable to properly apply our restriction rules and template and obtain UCSs from which to derive analysis models. In the rest of the section, we report the experiment results for Goal 2 (Task 2).

As we have discussed in Section 4.3, Goal 2 involves one independent variable (*Method*) with two treatments, *UCM_R* and *UCM_UR*, respectively denoting the use or not of restriction rules, and two dependent variables *CD* and *QC*, respectively denoting the quality of analysis class diagrams and the correctness of responses from a comprehension questionnaire. In this section, we report on one-tailed *t*-test results using the factor *Method*.

Table 3. Descriptive statistics of all measures

	Completeness		Correctness		Redundancy		QC	
Methods	**Mean**	**Size**	**Mean**	**Size**	**Mean**	**Size**	**Mean**	**Size**
UCM_R	0.260	14	0.882	14	0.093	14	0.913	12
UCM_UR	0.178	9	0.807	9	0.141	9	0.527	8
All Methods	0.219	23	0.845	23	0.117	23	0.72	20

The descriptive statistics of all measures are presented in Table 3. As shown in this table, all means for *Completeness* are below 0.3. This means that less than 30% of required class diagram elements (e.g., classes, associations, and generalizations) were derived from UCSs by the students. This is likely due to time constraints of the experiment. All means for *Redundancy* are below 0.15, which indicates that student-derived class diagrams have very low redundancy[2]. This can also be explained by time constraints during the experiment: the students were not able to completely design class diagrams (low *Completeness*) and there was therefore less opportunity to define redundant classes. *Correctness* evaluates each matching class and association[3] in the students' class diagrams; therefore time constraints have no impact on the results of this measure. This statement is also supported by the data shown in Table 3: All *Correctness* means are

[2] Only redundant classes are used to measure *Redundancy* of class diagrams.

[3] Missing classes and associations are taken care of by *Completeness* and redundant classes are measured by *Redundancy*.

above 0.8, which means a 80% *Correctness* in the matching classes and associations of the students' class diagrams. The QC (Questionnaire) mean of treatment UCM_R is over 90%, which means that time constraints had little impact on QC results: the students had enough time to correctly answer over 90% of the questions. The students with treatment UCM_UR only correctly answered 52.7% of the questions during the same period of time. The significant difference between the two treatments is what we expected (i.e., restrictions helped), which is analyzed next.

Table 4 presents a summary of the statistical *t*-test results for dependent variables CD and QC. Regarding CD, the students with treatment UCM_R performed slightly better in terms of *Completeness* and *Redundancy* than otherwise, but the difference is not statistically significant, due perhaps to time constraints of the experiment (both of the two measures received low mean values as shown in Table 3) and the small size of our sample. However, there is a statistically significant difference regarding *Correctness*: the students with treatment UCM_R produced significantly higher quality class diagrams than the students with treatment UCM_UR. Regarding QC, the *t*-test result also shows a significant difference between the two treatments in the expected direction, thus indicating an increased understanding due to restriction rules and the template. The magnitude of the difference is also very large: 38.7% (Table 4). Non-parametric tests were also performed. The results are not very different from the *t*-test results and are therefore not presented in this paper.

Table 4. *t*-test – CD and QC

Measures	**Mean difference (UCM_R – UCM_UR)**	**DF**	**t-value**	**p-value**
Completeness	0.082	17	1.552	0.0695
Correctness	0.074	17	**2.348**	**0.0155**
Redundancy	-0.048	12	-0.792	0.2218
QC	0.387	8	**5.189**	**<0.0004**

As stated previously, statistically significant differences are obtained in terms of both *Correctness* and QC (differences of 0.074 and 0.387, respectively—Table 4). The difference in size between the effect on *Correctness* and QC can also be explained. As discussed in Section 3.2, R1-R7 put restrictions on the use of natural language but can only be applied to action steps; R8-R16 also put restrictions on the use of natural language but can be applied to both action steps and condition steps; R17-R25 are rules on the use of control structures specified as keywords. By looking at those rules, it appears that R1-R7 and R17-R25 primarily put restrictions on documenting flows within steps (sentences) or flows of steps in UCSs, while R8-R16 are more related to the vocabulary being used in all the sentences of a UCS. Therefore we believe that R8-R16 impacted the quality of derived class diagrams (CD) to a larger extent than the other rules. On the other hand, we believe that rules R1-R7 and R17-R25 had a greater impact on the result of comprehension questionnaires (QC) than R8-R16, since questionnaires evaluated the extent to which students understood the flows of events of each UCS. Then because a much larger number of restriction rules have an impact on QC than CD, the mean differences between the two treatments in terms of CD *Correctness* and QC are likely to reflect that difference of impact: the mean difference in QC is much larger than the mean difference in CD *Correctness*. This intuition could perhaps be confirmed by studying the quality of interaction diagrams generated by students: since they relate more to flow than vocabulary we would expect their quality to be higher. However, recall that due to time constraints, our students did not have time to produce interaction diagrams.

6 Threats to Validity

Two main threats to external validity are relevant to our experiment, and are typical of what can be found when running controlled experiments in artificial settings and within time constraints: 1) Are the subjects representative of software professionals? 2) Is the experiment material representative of industrial practice?

Regarding issue 1), recall that in Task 1 the students designed use case models by applying RUCM. This task is usually performed by requirements engineers during the requirements elicitation phase of a typical software development lifecycle. Given the state of practice in most of the software industry, whether for students or professional requirements engineers, it is likely to require training. The students of our experiment are 4th year software and computer engineering students who had received training in use case modeling in previous courses. In addition, they were given a 90 minute lecture and an assignment specifically focusing on how to apply the restriction rules and template. In our context, the main difference between students and professional requirements engineers, is that the latter could have more experience on designing use case models, and thus we assume that they would probably apply more effectively RUCM than students given the same amount of training. Thus, professional requirements engineers would be able to further benefit from RUCM, and thus provide a more positive opinion on the rules' applicability. As for Task 2, the students derived analysis models from both the restricted and unrestricted use case models. This task is usually performed by system analysts in industry. Again, our 4th year software and computer engineering students had received extensive training on software modeling with the UML, through several courses, and this is more than what we have observed in most software development environments.

As for issue 2) above, the scale of the systems is not likely to have a significant impact on the results of the experiment for Task 1. Indeed, this task does not require an overall understanding of the systems as the use case diagrams of the two systems were provided to the students as part of the experiment material. The students were only asked to write some UCSs by applying the restriction rules and the use case template. Due to time constraints (two three-hour laboratories), it was anyway not feasible to consider larger scale systems (with more UCSs) for Task 2.

Construct validity is related to our measurement instruments: the two comprehension questionnaires used respectively for the two tasks. The questions of the comprehension questionnaire for Task 2 are designed to be answerable from the use case models with or without restrictions, therefore introducing no bias for any of the treatments. Three students presented problems related to internal validity. One of them missed the lab for Task 2 and had to perform the task at home; another spent 3 hours 40 mins on Task 2; the other produced a very incomplete result (no class diagram was derived). These three data points were excluded from the analysis.

7 Conclusion

Use case modeling (UCM) is one of the most common practices for capturing functional requirements. However, use case specifications (UCSs) are essentially textual documents and therefore ambiguity is inevitably introduced. To facilitate the transition towards analysis models, whether manual or automated, the UCSs are expected to be the least ambiguous possible. In this paper, we propose a UCM approach, denoted Restricted UCM (RUCM), which is composed of 26 well-defined restriction rules and a use case template, to restrict the way users can document UCSs. The objective is both to reduce ambiguity and also facilitate the (automated) transition towards analysis models.

A controlled experiment was conducted, in the context of a 4th year Software Engineering course, to evaluate whether RUCM is easy to apply while developing use case models and whether it helps obtain higher quality analysis models. Each restriction rule was evaluated in terms of its understandability, applicability, restrictiveness, and error rate. Though not presented in full details here, the experiment results indicate that our 26 restriction rules are easy to apply and can therefore help obtain UCSs that are a reliable source from which to derive analysis models. This was a prerequisite to the investigation reported in this paper.

The second part of the controlled experiment, presented in detail here, was to evaluate whether RUCM helps derive higher quality analysis models, by comparing it to a common UCM approach that does not put restrictions on natural language. The quality of analysis class diagrams is evaluated in terms of their correctness, completeness, and redundancy. The results show that RUCM leads to significant improvements regarding the correctness of derived class diagrams, but not their completeness and redundancy. We believe this is likely due to the time constraints of the experiment; the students were not even close to complete the class diagrams and there was therefore less opportunity to define redundant classes. Furthermore, RUCM resulted in a large improvement in term of the students' comprehension of the use case model as measured by a carefully designed questionnaire.

Based on our knowledge, this study represents the first controlled experiment that evaluates the applicability of restriction rules used to document UCSs, both individually and as a whole, and that also evaluates the impact of these rules and our proposed use case template on the quality of generated analysis class diagrams. The measures we have defined to characterize restriction rules and evaluate the quality of analysis class diagrams can be reused for similar experiments in the future.

During the second part of the experiment, the students were also asked to derive sequence diagrams for two use cases. However, most of the students were not able to do so due to time constraints. Evaluating the impact of RUCM on the quality of analysis sequence diagrams would be relevant future work. In addition, we also plan to replicate the experiment to see whether significant differences between two treatments can be identified in terms of completeness and redundancy of generated analysis class diagrams if more time is given to participants of the experiment.

References

1. Achour, C.B., Rolland, C., Maiden, N.A.M., Souveyet, C.: Guiding use case authoring: Results of an empirical study. In: 4th IEEE International Symposium on Requirements Engineering, pp. 36–43. IEEE Computer Society, Los Alamitos (1999)

2. Anda, B., Sjoberg, D., Jorgensen, M.: Quality and understandability of use case models. In: Knudsen, J.L. (ed.) ECOOP 2001. LNCS, vol. 2072, pp. 402–428. Springer, Heidelberg (2001)
3. Bittner, K., Spence, I.: Use Case Modeling. Addison-Wesley, Boston (2002)
4. Bruegge, B., Dutoit, A.H.: Object-Oriented Software Engineering Using UML, Patterns, and Java, 2nd edn. Prentice Hall, Upper Saddle River (2003)
5. Cockburn, A.: Writing effective use cases. Addison-Wesley, Boston (2001)
6. Dobing, B., Parsons, J.: How UML is used. J. CACM 49, 109–113 (2006)
7. Insfrán, E., Pastor, O., Wieringa, R.: Requirements Engineering-Based Conceptual Modelling. J. Requir. Eng. 7, 61–72 (2002)
8. Jacobson, I.: Use cases - yesterday, today, and tomorrow. J. SoSyM. 3, 210–220 (2004)
9. Jacobson, I., Christerson, M., Jonsson, P., Overgaard, G.: Object-oriented software engineering: a use case driven approach. Addison-Wesley, New York (1992)
10. Kof, L.: Text Analysis for Requirements Engineering. Thesis, Institut für Informatik, Technische Universität München (2005)
11. Kruchten, P.: The Rational Unified Process: An Introduction. Addison-Wesley, Boston (2003)
12. Kulak, D., Guiney, E.: Use cases: requirements in context. Addison-Wesley, Boston (2000)
13. Larman, C.: Applying UML and Patterns: an introduction to object-oriented analysis and design, 3rd edn. Prentice-Hall, Upper Saddle River (2004)
14. Liu, D.: Automating Transition from Use Cases to Class Model. Thesis, University of Calgary, Department of Electrical and Computer Engineering (2003)
15. UML 2.0 Superstructure Specification (2009), `http://www.omg.org/spec/UML/2.2/`
16. Oppenheim, A.N.: Questionnaire design, interviewing, and attitude measurement. Pinter (1992)
17. Phalp, K.T., Vincent, J., Cox, K.: Improving the quality of use case descriptions: empirical assessment of writing guidelines. J. SQJ 15, 383–399 (2007)
18. Schneider, G., Winters, J.P.: Applying use cases: a practical guide. Addison-Wesley, Boston (1998)
19. Śmiałek, M., Bojarski, J., Nowakowski, W., Ambroziewicz, A., Straszak, T.: Complementary Use Case Scenario Representations Based on Domain Vocabularies. In: Engels, G., Opdyke, B., Schmidt, D.C., Weil, F. (eds.) MODELS 2007. LNCS, vol. 4735, pp. 544–558. Springer, Heidelberg (2007)
20. Somé, S.S.: Supporting use case based requirements engineering. J. IST 48, 43–58 (2006)
21. Subramaniam, K., Liu, D., Far, B.H., Eberlein, A.: UCDA: Use Case Driven Development Assistant Tool for Class Model Generation. In: 16th International Conference on Software Engineering and Knowledge (2004)
22. The Stanford Parser version 1.6, `http://nlp.stanford.edu/software/lex-parser.shtml`
23. Wahono, R.S., Far, B.H.: A framework for object identification and refinement process in object-oriented analysis and design. In: 1st International Conference on Cognitive Informatics, pp. 351–360. IEEE Computer Society, Washington (2002)
24. Wohlin, C., Runeson, P., Höst, M., Ohlsson, M.C., Regnell, B., Wesslén, A.: Experimentation in Software Engineering: An Introduction. Springer, Heidelberg (2000)
25. Yue, T., Briand, L.C., Labiche, Y.: A Systematic Review of Transformation Methodologies between User Requirements and Analysis Models. Technical Report SCE-09-03, Carleton University (2009)
26. Yue, T., Briand, L.C., Labiche, Y.: A Use Case Modeling Approach to Facilitate the Transition Towards Analysis Models: Concepts and Empirical Evaluation. Technical Report SCE-09-05 (Version 2), Carleton University (2009)

Polymorphic Scenario-Based Specification Models: Semantics and Applications*

Shahar Maoz

Department of Computer Science and Applied Mathematics,
The Weizmann Institute of Science, Rehovot, Israel
shahar.maoz@weizmann.ac.il

Abstract. We present *polymorphic scenarios*, a generalization of a UML2-compliant variant of Damm and Harel's live sequence charts (LSC) in the context of object-orientation. Polymorphic scenarios are visualized using (modal) sequence diagrams where lifelines may represent classes and interfaces rather than concrete objects. Their semantics takes advantage of inheritance and interface realization to allow the specification of most expressive, succinct, and reusable universal and existential inter-object scenarios for object-oriented system models. We motivate the use of polymorphic scenarios, formally define their trace-based semantics, and present their application for scenario-based testing and execution, as implemented in the S2A compiler developed in our group.

1 Introduction

Scenario-based modeling, where interactions between system objects are specified using variants of sequence diagrams, has been adapted to the UML2 standard and has attracted much research efforts in recent years (see, e.g., [1,2,3]). Specifically, we are interested in a UML2-compliant variant of Damm and Harel's live sequence charts (LSC) [4,5], which extends classical sequence diagrams with universal/existential and must/may modalities.

Polymorphism – the ability of a type T_1 to appear and be used like another type T_2 – is a fundamental characteristics of object-oriented design, enabling important features such as modularity and reuse. While UML class diagrams syntax includes constructs that support a polymorphic interpretation, such as inheritance and interface realization relations, a polymorphic interpretation for UML inter-object behavioral diagrams, such as sequence diagrams, seems to be missing. This limits the applicability of these diagrams to object-oriented system models.

* This research was supported by The John von Neumann Minerva Center for the Development of Reactive Systems at the Weizmann Institute of Science. In addition, part of this research has been funded by an Advanced Research Grant from the European Research Council (ERC) under the European Community's 7th Framework Programme (FP7/2007-2013).

A. Schürr and B. Selic (Eds.): MODELS 2009, LNCS 5795, pp. 499–513, 2009.

In this paper we address this limitation by presenting *polymorphic scenarios*, as a generalization of sequence diagrams in the context of object-oriented system models. In polymorphic scenarios, sequence diagram lifelines may represent classes or interfaces rather than specific objects. Semantically, they thus apply to all objects directly or indirectly instantiated from the represented classes, or all objects realizing the represented interfaces in the model.

Combined with the expressive power of LSC, the polymorphic extension results in a powerful modeling language. A polymorphic scenario-based specification made of a set of universal and existential scenarios is a succinct specification that entails a rather strong notion of *behavioral sub-typing*: liveness and safety properties of a super class's interaction with its environment hold for all objects directly or indirectly instantiated from it in the model. Thus, *inter-object behavior common to all objects derived directly or indirectly from a certain type, can be formally specified at the most abstract level where it is applicable, instead of being repeated for each class (or worse, for each object).*

The polymorphic extension is independent of other semantic concerns related to sequence diagrams, e.g., the existential vs. universal interpretations, the use of negative scenarios, strict vs. weak sequencing, synchronous vs. asynchronous messages etc., supported by UML2 interactions. Similar to the lifeline composition extension of [6], the focus of the polymorphic extension is on the relations between the lifelines that appear in the interaction and the objects in the system.

The main technical contribution of our work is in defining a semantics for a polymorphic extension of the UML2-compliant variant of LSC. Specifically, we give a trace-based semantics that generalizes the definitions given in [5] from the concrete to the polymorphic case. Technically, this is done by adding to the automata defined in [5] a dynamic (ad-hoc, late) binding mechanism supporting classical object-oriented polymorphism. Moreover, following LSC, the semantics is defined not only for single diagrams, but also for *scenario-based specifications*, which include several, possibly inter-dependent interactions. When realized in a system model, the polymorphic interpretation may result in different concrete interpretations based on the inter-dependencies in the specification model.

The polymorphic interpretation has far reaching consequences on the use of scenario-based models throughout the development cycle. Specifically, we discuss its application to scenario-based testing and execution. An implementation of scenario-based testing and execution supporting the polymorphic semantics has been carried out in *S2A* [7], a compiler that translates UML2-compliant LSCs into AspectJ code. See Sec. 4.

Finally, our work on polymorphic scenarios extends and generalizes the notion of symbolic lifelines presented for LSC in [8]. We are not aware of any other work that explicitly and formally considers a polymorphic interpretation for sequence diagrams. See Sec. 5 for a discussion of related work.

The paper is organized as follows. Sec. 2 presents a motivating example, demonstrating the advantages and unique features of the polymorphic interpretation. Sec. 3 formally defines the syntax and semantics of polymorphic scenario-based specifications. A discussion of applications, specifically, polymorphic model-based testing and execution and their implementation, appears in Sec. 4. Sec. 5 discusses related work, and Sec. 6 concludes and suggests future research directions.

2 Motivating Example

We start off with a motivating example. The example is intentionally small and simple, to help us focus on the specific issue of interest.

Consider a model of an alarm system, made of an alarm controller, some sensors, and a buzzer. We consider a single simple use case where the alarm controller activates a sensor, the sensor notifies the controller when it senses a movement, and the alarm controller starts the buzzer. More formally, see the class diagram shown in Fig. 1, which includes the class `CBuzzer`, an abstract class `CAlarm` and its two sub classes `CStdAlarm` and `CAdvAlarm`, two classes `CDoorSensor` and `CFireSensor` realizing the `ISensor` interface, and a class `CSimpleLogger` realizing the interface `ILogger`. One difference between the standard alarm controller and the advanced one is that the latter maintains a log of alarm notifications, using a class realizing the `ILogger` interface.

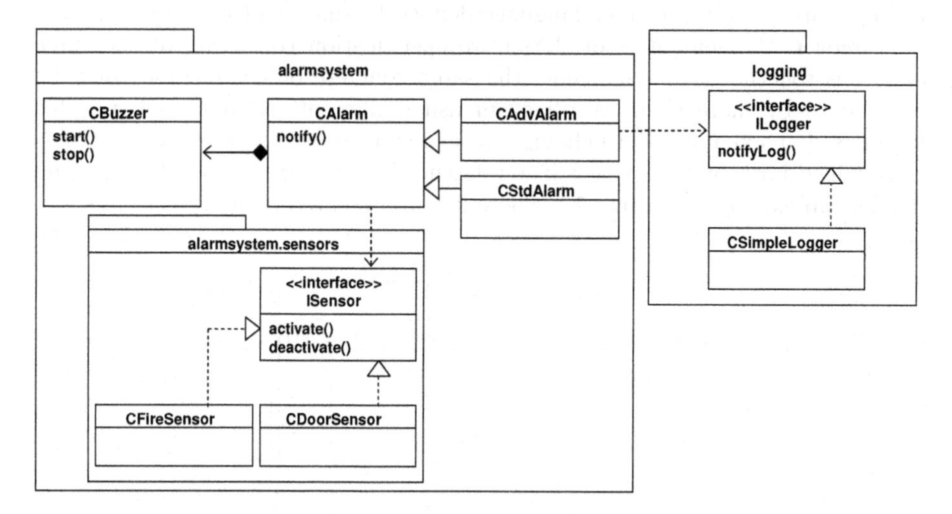

Fig. 1. The class diagram of the alarm system model

Consider the following semi-formal behavioral specification:

R1: Whenever an alarm controller (an object of type `CAlarm`) sends the message `activate` to a sensor (realizing the `ISensor` interface), and the sensor some time later sends the message `notify` to the alarm controller, the controller must eventually send the message `start` to a buzzer.

R2: Whenever a sensor sends the `notify` message to an advanced alarm controller (an object of type `CAdvAlarm`), the advanced alarm controller must eventually send the message `notifyLog` to a logger (implementing the `ILogger` interface).

R3: The following sequence of events must be possible: an alarm controller sends the message `activate` to a sensor, the sensor sometime later sends the message `notify` to the alarm controller, and the alarm controller sends the message `activate` to the sensor (again).

The above specification is formalized in Fig. 2, which includes two universal diagrams `D1` and `D2` and an existential diagram `D3`. First, recall the universal/existential modality of LSC. Roughly, the universal diagrams specify a temporal invariant that must hold on all system runs, and from every point in a run; whenever the cold (dashed, blue) messages happen in the specified order, eventually the hot (solid, red) messages must happen in the specified order. The existential diagram specifies an example trace that must hold (that is, must happen in the specified order) in at least one point of some system run.

Second, and more importantly in the context of this paper, the sequence diagrams shown in this example have a *polymorphic interpretation*. That is, their semantics, when given as a set of system-model event traces (or 'runs'), includes events occurring on all objects derived from the referenced classes or realizing the referenced interfaces. For example, the traces `tr1` and `tr2` shown in Fig. 3 are both in the trace-language defined by diagram `D1` shown in Fig. 2.

Moreover, the semantics of the entire specification consisting of the three diagrams together is polymorphic: the same concrete object instance may be referred to by more than one diagram using different (ad hoc) polymorphic bindings. For example, the behavior of an instance of the class `CAdvAlarm` is constrained both by `D1` – where it is referenced as its super class `CAlarm` using implicit up-casting – and by `D2` – where it is represented by its direct class.

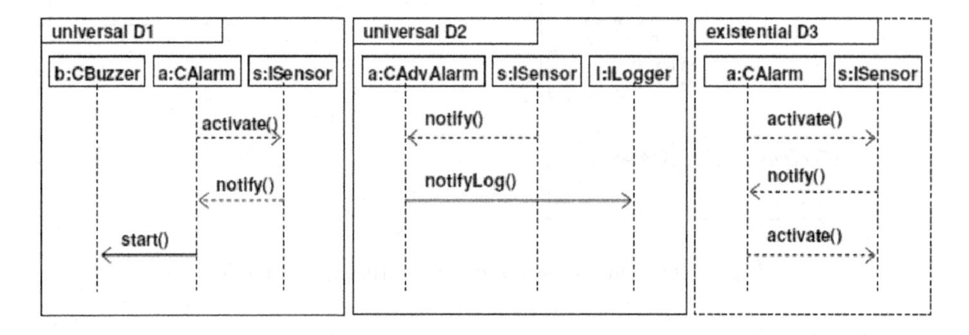

Fig. 2. A scenario-based specification model for the alarm system. Cold messages are drawn using dashed lines, hot messages are drawn using solid lines (see [4,5]).

Note how the polymorphic interpretation allows us to create *succinct* specifications; *inter-object behavior common to all objects derived directly or indirectly from a certain type is specified at the most abstract level where it is applicable*, instead of being repeated for each class (or worse, for each object). The resulting specifications may thus also be *reusable* and applicable to other systems, e.g.,

```
tr1: <cstdalarm,activate,fs1><cstdalarm,activate,ds1><fs1,notify,cstdalarm>
<cstdalarm,start,cbuzzer><cstdalarm,activate,ds1>...

tr2: <cadvalarm,activate,fs3><cadvalarm,activate,ds1><fs3,notify,cadvalarm>
<cadvalarm,notifyLog,simplelogger><cadvalarm,start,cbuzzer>...
```

Fig. 3. Two excerpts from traces of the alarm system. Events are represented as triplets of the form ⟨caller object id, message signature, receiver object id⟩.

where we may have different realizations of some of the same interfaces. For example, if another type of sensor is added to the system, say a `CFloodSensor`, the scenario-based specification model need not change.

The example demonstrates the significant consequences the polymorphic interpretation may have on the use of scenario-based models throughout the development lifecycle. Requirements can be formally specified in a succinct way, at the highest level of abstraction where they are applicable. Scenario-based tests may be succinctly defined and capture polymorphic behaviors. We return to these applications and to the alarm system example in Sec. 4.

The next section provides the required formal definitions for the syntax and semantics of polymorphic scenario-based specifications.

3 Polymorphic Scenarios

We now give trace-based semantics for polymorphic scenarios. For simplicity we limit the presentation to synchronous messages. We assume the reader is familiar with well-known basic notions in the context of classical sequence diagrams such as the partial order on events induced by a diagram and the notion of a cut, and thus concentrate on the features unique to the polymorphic extension. We use the terms interaction and scenario interchangeably.

A polymorphic interaction, represented by a sequence diagram, is made of a set of *lifelines*, each of which represents a class or an interface in a system-model. Trace-based semantics for a scenario-based specification is given by constructing an automaton for each diagram in the specification and relating the language accepted by the automaton to inter-object event traces of the system-model. We adopt the *modal* profile defined in [5] and the distinction of LSC between existential and universal diagrams (see [4,5]).

The following generalizes the formal definitions given in [5] from concrete to polymorphic scenarios. We start off with formal definitions of the system-model and the syntax of polymorphic scenarios. We then give the semantics of universal and existential polymorphic scenarios, first informally and then formally. Finally, we relate a polymorphic scenario-based specification to a system-model. For simplicity, we consider here only *Messages*. Adding other constructs available for UML2 interactions such as *StateInvariants* (LSC conditions) and *InteractionFragments* with *InteractionOperators* such as *alt* and *loop*, does not change the essence of the construction. We assume strict sequencing only.

3.1 The Basics

System-Model. We consider a *system-model* $Sys = \langle O, Ty, type, \leq_{Ty} \rangle$, which includes a (possibly infinite) set of objects $O = \{o_1, o_2, \ldots\}$, a partially ordered set of types $Ty = \{ty_1, ty_2, \ldots, ty_m\}$, and a mapping from each object in O to its type $type : O \longrightarrow Ty$. The mapping $type$ derives an $instanceof$ Boolean function $instanceof : (O \times Ty) \longrightarrow \{true, false\}$ such that $instanceof(o, ty) = true$ iff $type(o) \leq_{Ty} ty$.

A type $ty \in Ty$ has a finite set of method signatures $m(ty) = \{m_1, m_2, \ldots, m_s\}$. The subtyping partial order $\leq_{Ty}$ over Ty implies signatures set inclusion: $\forall ty_1, ty_2 \in Ty, ty_1 \leq_{Ty} ty_2$ implies $m(ty_2) \subseteq m(ty_1)$. We allow multiple inheritance with a disjoint signatures restriction: $\forall ty_1, ty_2, ty_3 \in Ty$, if $ty_1 \leq_{Ty} ty_2$ and $ty_1 \leq_{Ty} ty_3$ and $ty_2 \not\leq_{Ty} ty_3$ and $ty_3 \not\leq_{Ty} ty_2$ then $m(ty_2) \cap m(ty_3) = \emptyset$. Note that we ignore the difference between class and interface types as it has no semantic significance in the trace-based semantics we present.

A *system-model event* e is a tuple $\langle o_{src}, m, o_{trg} \rangle$ where $o_{src}, o_{trg} \in O$ and $m \in m(type(o_{trg}))$, carrying the intuitive meaning of object o_{src} calling method m of object o_{trg} (we allow $o_{src} = o_{trg}$). A *system-model trace* is an infinite sequence of events $e_1, e_2, e_3, \ldots$.

Polymorphic Scenario. A *(modal) polymorphic scenario* is a tuple $D = \langle mode, L, ltype, LPME, eventMode \rangle$ where:

- $mode \in \{existential, universal\}$ is the mode of the scenario;
- $L = \{l_1, l_2, \ldots, l_k\}$ is a finite set of lifelines; each lifeline l_i includes an ordered set of r_i event occurrence specifications (denoting message sent or received) on this lifeline: $\forall i, 1 \leq i \leq k, l_i = \{l_i^1, l_i^2, \ldots, l_i^{r_i}\}$;
- $ltype : L \longrightarrow Ty$ is a mapping from each lifeline to a type;
- $LPME$ is a set of lifeline-polymorphic-message-event triplets $\langle l_{src}^p, m, l_{trg}^q \rangle$ where l_{src}^p is a send message event occurrence specification on the source lifeline, l_{trg}^q is a receive message event occurrence specification on the target lifeline, and $m \in m(ltype(l_{trg}))$ is the signature of the message;
- and $eventMode : LPME \longrightarrow \{cold, hot\}$ is a mapping giving a temperature to each message triplet in D (in existential diagrams we consider cold messages only).

The set of lifelines L and the mapping $ltype$ define the set of possible bindings $Bind(L) \subseteq (O \cup \{\bot\})^k$ such that $\langle o_1, o_2, \ldots, o_k \rangle \in Bind(L)$ iff $\forall i, 1 \leq i \leq k, o_i = \bot \vee instanceof(o_i, ltype(l_i))$. A given binding $\langle o_1, o_2, \ldots, o_k \rangle \in Bind(L)$ defines a trivial projected function $bind : L \longrightarrow (O \cup \{\bot\})$ from a lifeline to its bound object: $\forall i, 1 \leq i \leq k, bind(l_i) = o_i$.

For a lifeline-polymorphic-message-event triplet $lpme = \langle l_{src}^p, m, l_{trg}^q \rangle \in LPME$ we use $src(lmpe)$, $m(lpme)$, $trg(lpme)$ to denote its source lifeline, message signature, and target lifeline, resp. Based on $LPME$ we define the set of polymorphic-message-events in D: $PME = \{\langle ty_{src}, m, ty_{trg} \rangle | \exists lpme \in LPME \text{ s.t. } ty_{src} = ltype(src(lpme)) \wedge ty_{trg} = ltype(trg(lpme)) \wedge m = m(lmpe)\}$. PME abstracts away lifeline locations and identities, but keeps their types. We use PME in the definition of the semantics below. Note that the same triplet $\langle ty_{src}, m, ty_{trg} \rangle \in PME$ may correspond to more than one message event occurrence in $LPME$ over identical lifelines in different locations or over different pairs of lifelines.

The Semantics of a Polymorphic Scenario. The semantics of a polymorphic scenario D is given using an automaton A_D; the trace-language of a scenario is the language accepted by its automaton $L(A_D)$. The construction of the automaton A_D is based on an *unwinding structure* S (see, e.g., [9]). Intuitively, this structure is made of states representing cuts and includes paths for all possible linearizations of the partial order between events defined by the diagram; that is, where event occurrences on each lifeline are ordered from top to bottom, and message send event precedes the same message receive event.[1] For simplicity in this paper we treat message send and receive as a single event. We consider only well-formed diagrams, that is, that indeed induce a partial-order (see [10]).

The unwinding structure is made of a set of cut-states S (with a designated minimal cut-state $s_{min} \in S$), and a partial (transition) function $R : S \times LPME \longrightarrow S$.

The set of *enabled*-lifeline-polymorphic-message-event-occurrences in a cut $s \in S$ is defined by $EnLPME(s) = \{e \in LPME | \exists s' \in S : R(s,e) = s'\}$. The set of *enabled*-polymorphic-message-events in a cut s is defined by $EnPME(s) = \{\langle ty_{src}, m, ty_{trg} \rangle \in PME | \exists e \in EnLPME(s) : m(e) = m \wedge ty_{src} = ltype(source(e)) \wedge ty_{trg} = ltype(target(e))\}$.

The mapping $eventMode : LPME \longrightarrow \{cold, hot\}$ of the diagram is extended in the unwinding structure S to cut-states as follows: $mode : S \longrightarrow \{cold, hot\}$ is defined s.t. $mode(s) = hot$ if $\exists e : e \in EnLPME(s) \wedge eventMode(e) = hot$; otherwise $mode(s) = cold$. That is, a cut is hot iff at least one of its enabled message event occurrences is hot. The intended semantics of a hot cut is that of an unstable state; when the scenario is in a hot cut, there is at least one message that must eventually occur in order for the scenario to be satisfied (see [5]).

Note that while the 'alphabet' for messages appearing in a polymorphic scenario D is the 'abstract' type-level events alphabet $\Sigma_{abs} \subseteq Ty \times M \times Ty$ such that $\Sigma_{abs} = \{\langle ty_1, m, ty_2 \rangle | ty_1, ty_2 \in Ty \wedge m \in m(ty_2)\}$, the alphabet Σ for the automata defined below is the 'concrete' object-level message events alphabet $\Sigma \subseteq O \times M \times O$ such that $\Sigma = \{\langle o_1, m, o_2 \rangle | o_1, o_2 \in O \wedge m \in m(type(o_2))\}$. We define the set of concrete object-level message events in Σ that may be unified with polymorphic message events in PME as follows: $CPME = \{\langle o_{src}, m, o_{trg} \rangle | \langle o_{src}, m, o_{trg} \rangle \in \Sigma \wedge \exists \langle ty_{src}, m, ty_{trg} \rangle \in PME \text{ s.t. } instanceof(o_{src}, ty_{src}) \wedge instanceof(o_{trg}, ty_{trg})\}$.

The intended semantics for a universal polymorphic scenario is that of a temporal invariant that holds on all system-model traces and from any point on those traces. Thus, the semantics of a universal polymorphic scenario is given using an alternating automaton (see below). Roughly, for each run of the automaton,

[1] This structure is common to most variants of sequence diagrams presented in the literature; we thus assume the reader is familiar with it and concentrate on the issues unique to the polymorphic extension we present here.

instantiated following the occurrence of a minimal event in the partial-order induced by the diagram, the automaton checks whether the message of this event is enabled or violating with regard to the current cut. If it is enabled, it checks for a binding: if there are free (yet unbound) lifelines that can bind to the event's concrete source and target object (or there are lifelines that are already bound to the event's source or target), it binds the free lifeline(s) and advances the cut-state accordingly. Otherwise, it ignores the event. If the message in this event is violating, that is, it appears in the diagram but is not currently enabled, the automaton checks for binding too: if there are lifelines that are already bound to the event's source and target, the event is indeed violating and the violation is handled according to the current cut-state mode: if the cut is hot, it is a hot violation, and the run moves to a rejecting sink state. If the cut is cold, it is a cold violation, and the run moves to an accepting sink state. If the automaton reaches the maximal cut-state it moves to its accepting sink too.

The intended semantics of an existential polymorphic scenario is that of an example; there must be at least one possible system-model run where the scenario 'happens' at least once. Thus, the semantics of an existential polymorphic scenario is given using a nondeterministic automaton whose first state needs to 'guess' when does an accepting sequence begin. A similar mechanism to the one described above for binding of enabled events is used in the existential case.

The above intended semantics and informal automata constructions are formalized in the definitions of the two automata given in the following subsections.

3.2 Universal Polymorphic Scenarios: Formally

The semantics of universal polymorphic scenarios is given using an alternating automaton; the trace-language of a diagram is the language accepted by its automaton. Recall that in an alternating automaton the transition function is defined as $\delta : Q \times \Sigma \longrightarrow B^+(Q)$ where $B^+(Q)$ is the set of positive Boolean formulas over Q (see, e.g., [11]). Given a universal diagram D we construct an alternating Büchi automaton $A_D = \langle \Sigma \cup \epsilon, Q, q_{in}, \delta, \alpha \rangle$, where

- $\Sigma = \{\langle o_1, m, o_2 \rangle | o_1, o_2 \in O \wedge m \in m(type(o_2))\}$;
- $Q = S \times Bind(L) \cup \{q_{rej}, q_{acc}\}$ is a set of states (we use $cut(q)$ to denote the cut-state s of a state $q = \langle s, \langle o_1, \ldots, o_k \rangle \rangle$);
- $q_{in} = \langle s_{min}, \langle \{\perp\}^k \rangle \rangle$ is the initial state;
- $\alpha = \{\langle s, \langle o_1, \ldots, o_k \rangle \rangle | mode(s) = cold\} \cup \{q_{acc}\}$ is the accepting condition (that is, all cold states and q_{acc} are accepting);
- and $\delta : Q \times \Sigma \longrightarrow B^+(Q)$ is a transition function defined as follows:

- Σ labeled self transitions on q_{acc} and q_{rej}:

  $\forall cme \in \Sigma : \delta(q_{acc}, cme) = q_{acc}, \delta(q_{rej}, cme) = q_{rej}$
- $\Sigma \setminus CPME$ labeled self transitions on all cut-states:

  $\forall q \in Q \setminus \{q_{rej}, q_{acc}\}, \forall cme \in \Sigma \setminus CPME : \delta(q, cme) = q$

– Handling message events in $CPME$:

$\forall q = \langle s, \langle o_1, \ldots, o_k \rangle \rangle \in Q \setminus \{q_{in}, q_{rej}, q_{acc}\}, \forall cme \in CPME$:

- (the source and target objects of cme are already bound)
  for l^i_{src}, l^j_{trg} s.t. $source(cme) = bind(l_{src}) \wedge target(cme) = bind(l_{trg}) \wedge \langle l^i_{src}, m(cme), l^j_{trg} \rangle \in EnLPME(cut(q))$:
  $\delta(q, cme) = \langle R(cut(q), e), \langle o_1, \ldots, o_k \rangle \rangle$ where $e = \langle l^i_{src}, m(cme), l^j_{trg} \rangle$;

  for l^i_{src}, l^j_{trg} s.t. $source(cme) = bind(l_{src}) \wedge target(cme) = bind(l_{trg}) \wedge \langle l^i_{src}, m(cme), l^j_{trg} \rangle \notin EnLPME(cut(q))$:
  - if $mode(cut(q)) = cold$ then $\delta(q, cme) = q_{acc}$,
  - if $mode(cut(q)) = hot$ then $\delta(q, cme) = q_{rej}$;
- (otherwise, the source object of cme is already bound and the target can bind to a free lifeline)
  for l^i_{src} s.t. $source(cme) = bind(l_{src})$
  for all l^j_{trg} s.t. $instanceof(target(cme), ltype(l_{trg})) \wedge bind(l_{trg}) = \perp \wedge \langle l^i_{src}, m(cme), l^j_{trg} \rangle \in EnLPME(cut(q))$:
  $\delta(q, cme) = \bigwedge_{l^j_{trg}} \langle R(cut(q), e), \langle \overline{o}_1, \ldots, \overline{o}_{l_{trg}}, \ldots, \overline{o}_k \rangle \rangle$
  where $e = \langle l^i_{src}, m(cme), l^j_{trg} \rangle \wedge \overline{o}_{l_{trg}} = target(cme) \wedge \forall h \neq l_{trg} : \overline{o}_h = o_h$;
- (otherwise, symmetrically, the target object of cme is already bound and the source can bind to a free lifeline)
  Same as above only replace $source(cme)$ and $target(cme)$, l_{trg} and l_{src}.
- (otherwise, the source and the target objects of cme are not yet bound but each can bind to a free lifeline)
  for all l^i_{src}, l^j_{trg} s.t. $bind(l_{src}) = \perp \wedge bind(l_{trg}) = \perp \wedge$
  $instanceof(target(cme),$
  $ltype(l_{trg})) \wedge instanceof(source(cme), ltype(l_{src})) \wedge \langle l^i_{src}, m(cme), l^j_{trg} \rangle \in EnLPME(cut(q))$:

  $\delta(q, cme) = \bigwedge_{l^i_{src}, l^j_{trg}} \langle R(cut(q), e), \langle \overline{o}_1, \ldots, \overline{o}_{l_{src}}, \ldots, \overline{o}_{l_{trg}}, \ldots, \overline{o}_k \rangle \rangle$

  where $e = \langle l^i_{src}, m(cme), l^j_{trg} \rangle \wedge \overline{o}_{l_{src}} = source(cme) \wedge \overline{o}_{l_{trg}} = target(cme) \wedge \forall h \neq l_{trg}, l_{src} : \overline{o}_h = o_h$;
- (otherwise, cme is ignored)
  $\delta(q, cme) = q$;

and for the initial state $q_{in} = \langle s_{min}, \langle \{\perp\}^k \rangle \rangle$, $\forall cme \in CPME$:

$\delta(q_{in}, cme) = q_{in} \wedge \bigwedge_{l^i_{src}, l^j_{trg}} \langle R(s_{min}, e), \langle \overline{o}_1, \ldots, \overline{o}_{l_{src}}, \ldots, \overline{o}_{l_{trg}}, \ldots, \overline{o}_k \rangle \rangle$
for all l^i_{src}, l^j_{trg} s.t.
$instanceof(target(cme), ltype(l_{trg})) \wedge instanceof(source(cme), ltype(l_{src})) \wedge \langle l^i_{src}, m(cme), l^j_{trg} \rangle \in EnLPME(cut(q_{in}))$

where $e = \langle l^i_{src}, m(cme), l^j_{trg} \rangle \wedge \overline{o}_{l_{trg}} = target(cme) \wedge \overline{o}_{l_{src}} = source(cme) \wedge \forall h \neq l_{src}, l_{trg} : \overline{o}_h = o_h$.

Below we add some important remarks about the construction above.

Remark 1 (multiple copies). The automaton construction induces two types of 'multiple scenario copies'. First, multiple copies of the same scenario where lifelines bind to different concrete objects. These are 'instantiated' whenever the automaton reads a minimal event that has a new binding. Second, multiple copies of the same scenario where lifelines bind to the same objects. These are 'instantiated' whenever the automaton reads a minimal event that has an existing binding that is also currently enabled in another copy. Both 'instantiations' are formalized in the universal 'and' transition defined on the initial state. In the existential case defined in the next subsection no 'multiple copies' are induced.

Remark 2 (multiple binding choices). When two or more lifelines in a single diagram represent the same type (or different types related by $\leq_{Ty}$), two or more transitions for a single event but with different bindings may be enabled at some state. In the construction above this case is represented by the 'and' choices over source and target lifeline selection (recall that the automaton is alternating, hence allowing both 'and' and 'or' transitions). Formally, this means that for the trace to be accepted, all possible transitions resulting from the different binding choices must be extended to an accepting trace. That said, one may consider the above to be too strong a requirement, and instead suggest a non-deterministic 'or' selection between binding choices (in the above construction this means replacing $\bigwedge$ with $\bigvee$, except for the 'and' transition on the initial state).

For lack of space in this proceedings, we can neither give an explicit example for the multiple binding choices problem nor evaluate the two different semantic possibilities. We hope to present this in a future paper.

Remark 3 (combining static and dynamic binding). The above automaton construction is a conservative generalization of the non-symbolic case, where lifelines are statically bound to concrete objects. To handle non-symbolic lifelines, use an initial state q_{in} where lifelines are already bound (that is, where not all lifelines are bound to $\perp$). Note that this supports the definition of scenarios where some lifelines are statically bound while others are dynamically bound. We consider this to be a useful feature of our work.

Remark 4 (single binding constraint). Note that our construction ensures that no two lifelines bind to the same object (in a single 'instance' of the scenario). That is, although we allow (as we should allow) two lifelines in the same scenario to represent the same type (or two related types), the construction of the transition function δ ensures they will never bind to the same concrete object in a single path in the automaton runs tree.

3.3 Existential Polymorphic Scenarios: Formally

The semantics of existential polymorphic scenarios is given using a non-deterministic automaton; the trace-language of the diagram is the language accepted by the automaton.

Given an existential diagram, we construct a non-deterministic Büchi automaton $A = \langle \Sigma, Q, q_{in}, \delta, \alpha \rangle$, where

- $\Sigma = \{\langle o_1, m, o_2 \rangle | o_1, o_2 \in O \wedge m \in m(type(o_2))\}$;
- $Q = S \times Bind(L) \cup \{q_{rej}\}$ is a finite set of states (we use $cut(q)$ to denote the cut-state s of a state $q = \langle s, \langle o_1, \ldots, o_k \rangle \rangle$);
- $q_{in} = \langle s_{min}, \langle \{\bot\}^k \rangle \rangle$ is the initial state;
- $\alpha = \{q \in Q : cut(q) = s_{max}\}$ is the accepting condition;
- and $\delta : Q \times \Sigma \longrightarrow 2^Q$ is defined as follows:

- Σ labeled self transitions on q_{max} and q_{rej}:

  $\forall cme \in \Sigma : \delta(q_{max}, cme) = \{q_{max}\}, \delta(q_{rej}, cme) = \{q_{rej}\}$;
- $\Sigma \setminus CPME$ labeled self transitions on all cut-states:

  $\forall q \in Q \setminus \{q_{rej}\}, \forall cme \in \Sigma \setminus CPME : \delta(q, cme) = \{q\}$;
- Handling message events from $CPME$:
  Same as in the universal case, only replace the conjunction $\bigwedge$ with set union $\bigcup$ and have bounded $\langle l^i_{src}, m(cme), l^j_{trg} \rangle \notin EnLPME(cut(q))$ leading to $\{q_{rej}\}$. On the initial state q_{in} replace the conjunction $\wedge$ with set union.

Remark 5 (existential acceptance). According to the construction above, a single possible completion of an existential scenario, at whatever level of abstraction in the type hierarchy, is enough for trace acceptance. We could have suggested other, different, semantics, following different notions of *polymorphic coverage*: all combinations at all derived levels (which may be too strong), all derived objects at least once (very strong requirement but may be useful), or all types at least once (that is, one object per type has to participate). We leave the formal definitions of these and the evaluation of their usefulness for future work.

3.4 Relating a Polymorphic Specification to a System-Model

Recall that the *trace-language* of a polymorphic scenario D is the word language $L(D)$ accepted by its automaton. Following LSC, a *specification* is a set $Spec = Ex \cup Un$, where Ex and Un are sets of existential and universal diagrams, resp. (see [4,5]). We denote the runs of a system-model Sys by L_{Sys}. We say that a system-model Sys *satisfies* a specification $Spec = Ex \cup Un$ iff

- $\forall D \in Un, \forall r \in L_{Sys} : r \in L(D)$
- $\forall D \in Ex, \exists r \in L_{Sys} : r \in L(D)$

4 Applications

4.1 Polymorphic Scenario-Based Testing

A common use of sequence diagrams in model-driven development is for testing purposes. That is, one may specify testing scenarios using sequence diagrams.

Taking advantage of the polymorphic extension, testing scenarios can be defined at a rather high level of abstraction, i.e., at the interface or abstract classes level, and thus be applicable to, and reused across, all concrete system models realizing the generic behavior.

As an example, recall the alarm system described in Sec. 2. One may use diagram `D1` as a test case, activating a sensor, generating a notification, and waiting for the alarm object to call the buzzer. The test is specified at the `ISensor` interface and `CAlarm` abstract class level; its definition need not change when applied to different system model implementations of the alarm system, e.g., with different sensors or an instance of a new class derived from `CAlarm`.

An implementation of polymorphic scenario-based testing, following the semantics presented in this paper, has been carried out in the context of Java within the *S2A compiler* [7]. S2A (for Scenarios to Aspects) is a compiler that translates (universal) LSCs, given in their UML2-compliant variant using the modal profile, into AspectJ code [12], and thus provides full code generation of reactive behavior from visual declarative scenario-based specifications. S2A implements a compilation scheme presented in [13]. Roughly, each sequence diagram is translated into a *scenario aspect*, implemented in AspectJ, which simulates an automaton whose states correspond to the scenario cuts; transitions are triggered by AspectJ pointcuts, and corresponding advice is responsible for advancing the automaton to the next cut state.

Most important in the context of this paper, though, is that S2A supports polymorphic scenarios. Taking advantage of AspectJ and Java semantics, the generated code is able to monitor the activation and progress of all realizations of the polymorphic UML2-compliant LSCs as they come to life during an execution of a reference Java program. This includes the instantiation of multiple copies of each scenario aspect and the implementation of the late binding and unification mechanism of the trace-based semantics formally defined in the previous section. That is, the generated aspect advice code is responsible not only for advancing the automaton to the next cut state but also for checking and handling late binding and 'new automata' instantiation.

We have created a Java implementation of a simple simulation of an alarm system following the design shown in Sec. 2. We used the diagrams shown in Fig. 2 as input for S2A and generated scenario aspects for them. Thus, when executing the (automatically instrumented) system, we were able to view how the polymorphic semantics is realized. For example, multiple instances of scenario `D1` were created, each with a binding to a different sensor. Then, when one sensor notified the alarm, only the corresponding scenario instance, where the notifying sensor was bound, advanced to its next cut state.

Next, we modified the implementation: replaced the `CStdAlarm` with a `CAdvAlarm` and added another sensor. Then, we were able to reuse exactly the same test case specifications for the modified system. Moreover, now we could also observe how diagram `D2` is realized; after activation and notification, the alarm object was bound as a `CAdvAlarm` to an instance of diagram `D2`, and at the same time as a `CAlarm` to all instances of diagram `D1`, resulting in a truly polymorphic setting. These observations were made visible using *scenario-based traces*, see [14].

S2A supports not only method calls but also conditions (defined using UML2 `StateInvariants`), `alt` and `loop` interaction fragments, and exact, symbolic, and opaque method parameters. It also supports combined static and dynamic lifeline binding (see Rem. 3). However, S2A does not support 'and' or 'or' multiple binding choices (see Rem. 2); in S2A, binding non-determinism is solved ad-hoc by arbitrarily choosing an available binding if one exists.

4.2 Polymorphic Scenario-Based Execution (Play-Out)

S2A supports not only polymorphic scenario-based monitoring and testing but also execution (play-out). Play-out, originally defined and implemented in the Play-Engine tool [15], is an operational (executable) semantics for LSC, that is, a method to simulate or execute an LSC specification. Recalling the details of play-out and describing an operational (play-out) semantics for polymorphic scenarios is outside the scope of this paper. However, for readers familiar with play-out, we briefly present the following issues.

A key part of play-out semantics concerns the strategy for choosing the next method to execute. The original (so called naïve) play-out arbitrarily chooses one enabled method that is not violating in any chart and executes it. In a polymorphic settings, however, this becomes more complicated: the 'same' method may be simultaneously enabled (or violating) in different scenarios at different levels of the type hierarchy (or even within a single scenario, see Rem. 2 about multiple binding choices). Also, in some cases, a method may be enabled for execution (not just monitoring) while one of (or both of) its lifelines are not yet bound. These problems need to be addressed when defining an operational play-out semantics for polymorphic scenarios. Note that the smart play-out mechanism defined in [16] does not support LSCs with symbolic instances.

The code generated by S2A supports play-out in a polymorphic settings (see the section on the coordinator and the strategy in [13]). However, some of the complicated cases mentioned above, e.g., where the 'same' method is simultaneously enabled for execution (or violating) in different scenarios at different levels of the type hierarchy, are not fully addressed. The complete definitions of play-out semantics for the polymorphic case and their implementation in S2A is beyond the scope of this paper.

5 Related Work

Our work extends and generalizes the notion of symbolic lifelines originally presented for LSC in [8] and implemented in the Play-Engine [15]. There, an extension of play-out is defined for LSCs with symbolic lifelines, such that a lifeline representing a type may apply to any object of this type. A generalization to support class hierarchies and interfaces in the context of object-orientation is not defined. Moreover, a trace-based semantics is not given. Thus, also, some of the issues discussed above in subsection 4.2 do not appear in this previous work.

[17] presents a UML-based technique for pattern specification, including interaction pattern specifications (IPSs), where lifelines are labeled with role names. Conformance rules are defined between a pattern and its concretization. However, a polymorphic interpretation is not explicitly and formally considered.

[18] considers MSCs with symbolic lifelines; symbolic execution semantics is defined, allowing to validate models capturing interactions between unbounded number of objects. The semantics presented in [18] is different than LSC semantics. Also, unlike in our work, object-oriented hierarchies are not considered.

STAIRS [1] is an approach for the compositional development of UML interactions. It defines a trace-based three-valued semantics and a number of refinement mechanisms. To the best of our knowledge, STAIRS does not consider polymorphism. Extending STAIRS to support polymorphism seems possible.

We are aware of a number of research efforts towards a semantics for UML2 interactions (see, e.g., [19,20,2]). It seems that none of these considers the relationship between interactions and a polymorphic object-oriented system-model.

6 Conclusion and Future Work

The main contribution of this paper is in extending sequence diagrams with symbolic lifelines to support object-oriented inheritance and interface realization, and providing the extension with formal trace-based semantics. The work extends the expressive power of UML interactions in the context of object-oriented modeling, and presents its application to scenario-based testing and execution.

[8] suggests a distinction between existential and universal bindings for symbolic lifelines, and a notion of a lifeline's binding rule (which appears also, albeit differently, in the UML2 standard). We did not consider these in the present work. Our binding semantics for polymorphic lifelines may be viewed as 'existential binding'. A 'universal binding' would have resulted in the ability to specify 'broadcasting'. Binding rules allow to limit lifeline bindings beyond the constraint defined by its type. Adding these features or a variant thereof to the polymorphic scenarios presented in this paper is a possible future work direction.

Finally, we consider additional applications for polymorphic scenario-based specifications. Specifically, these include the extension of recent work in the area of model-checking sequence diagrams (e.g., [21]) and synthesis from sequence diagrams (e.g., [22,23,3]) to support a polymorphic semantics.

Acknowledgements. I would like to thank Yoram Atir, David Harel, Amir Kantor, Assaf Marron, Itai Segall, and the anonymous reviewers for comments on a draft of this paper.

References

1. Haugen, Ø., Husa, K.E., Runde, R.K., Stølen, K.: STAIRS Towards Formal Design with Sequence Diagrams. Software and Systems Modeling (SoSyM) 4(4), 355–367 (2005)

2. Krüger, I.: Capturing Overlapping, Triggered, and Preemptive Collaborations Using MSCs. In: Pezzé, M. (ed.) FASE 2003. LNCS, vol. 2621, pp. 387–402. Springer, Heidelberg (2003)
3. Whittle, J., Kwan, R., Saboo, J.: From Scenarios to Code: An Air Traffic Control Case Study. Software and Systems Modeling 4(1), 71–93 (2005)
4. Damm, W., Harel, D.: LSCs: Breathing Life into Message Sequence Charts. J. on Formal Methods in System Design 19(1), 45–80 (2001)
5. Harel, D., Maoz, S.: Assert and Negate Revisited: Modal Semantics for UML Sequence Diagrams. Software and Systems Modeling (SoSyM) 7(2), 237–252 (2008)
6. Atir, Y., Harel, D., Kleinbort, A., Maoz, S.: Object Composition in Scenario-Based Programming. In: Fiadeiro, J.L., Inverardi, P. (eds.) FASE 2008. LNCS, vol. 4961, pp. 301–316. Springer, Heidelberg (2008)
7. Harel, D., Kleinbort, A., Maoz, S.: S2A: A Compiler for Multi-Modal UML Sequence Diagrams. In: Dwyer, M.B., Lopes, A. (eds.) FASE 2007. LNCS, vol. 4422, pp. 121–124. Springer, Heidelberg (2007)
8. Marelly, R., Harel, D., Kugler, H.: Multiple Instances and Symbolic Variables in Executable Sequence Charts. In: OOPSLA 2002, pp. 83–100 (2002)
9. Klose, J., Wittke, H.: An Automata Based Interpretation of Live Sequence Charts. In: Margaria, T., Yi, W. (eds.) TACAS 2001. LNCS, vol. 2031, pp. 512–527. Springer, Heidelberg (2001)
10. Westphal, B., Toben, T.: The Good, the Bad and the Ugly: Well-Formedness of LSCs. In: Baresi, L., Heckel, R. (eds.) FASE 2006. LNCS, vol. 3922, pp. 230–246. Springer, Heidelberg (2006)
11. Kupferman, O., Vardi, M.Y.: Weak Alternating Automata Are Not That Weak. ACM Trans. Comput. Log. 2(3), 408–429 (2001)
12. AspectJ., `http://www.eclipse.org/aspectj/`
13. Maoz, S., Harel, D.: From Multi-Modal Scenarios to Code: Compiling LSCs into AspectJ. In: SIGSOFT FSE 2006, pp. 219–230. ACM, New York (2006)
14. Maoz, S.: Model-Based Traces. In: Chaudron, M.R.V. (ed.) Workshops and Symposia at MODELS 2008. LNCS, vol. 5421, pp. 109–119. Springer, Heidelberg (2009)
15. Harel, D., Marelly, R.: Come, Let's Play: Scenario-Based Programming Using LSCs and the Play-Engine. Springer, Heidelberg (2003)
16. Harel, D., Kugler, H., Marelly, R., Pnueli, A.: Smart Play-out of Behavioral Requirements. In: Aagaard, M.D., O'Leary, J.W. (eds.) FMCAD 2002. LNCS, vol. 2517, pp. 378–398. Springer, Heidelberg (2002)
17. France, R.B., Kim, D.K., Ghosh, S., Song, E.: A UML-Based Pattern Specification Technique. IEEE Trans. Software Eng. 30(3), 193–206 (2004)
18. Roychoudhury, A., Goel, A., Sengupta, B.: Symbolic Message Sequence Charts. In: ESEC-FSE 2007, pp. 275–284. ACM, New York (2007)
19. Cengarle, M.V.: System Model for UML – The Interactions Case. In: MMOSS. Dagstuhl Seminar Proc., vol. 06351 (2006)
20. Knapp, A.: A Formal Semantics for UML Interactions. In: France, R.B., Rumpe, B. (eds.) UML 1999. LNCS, vol. 1723, pp. 116–130. Springer, Heidelberg (1999)
21. Knapp, A., Wuttke, J.: Model Checking of UML 2.0 Interactions. In: Kühne, T. (ed.) MoDELS 2006. LNCS, vol. 4364, pp. 42–51. Springer, Heidelberg (2007)
22. Harel, D., Kugler, H.: Synthesizing State-Based Object Systems from LSC Specifications. Int. J. of Foundations of Computer Science 13(1), 5–51 (2002)
23. Krüger, I., Grosu, R., Scholz, P., Broy, M.: From MSCs to Statecharts. In: DIPES. IFIP Conf. Proc., vol. 155, pp. 61–72. Kluwer, Dordrecht (1998)

Aspect Model Unweaving*

Jacques Klein[1], Jörg Kienzle[2], Brice Morin[3], and Jean-Marc Jézéquel[3]

[1] Centre de Recherche Public Gabriel Lippmann
klein@lippmann.lu
[2] School of Computer Science, McGill University
Joerg.Kienzle@mcgill.ca
[3] INRIA, Centre Rennes - Bretagne Atlantique / IRISA, Université Rennes1
Brice.Morin@inria.fr, jezequel@irisa.fr

Abstract. Since software systems need to be continuously available, their ability to evolve at runtime is a key issue. The emergence of models@runtime, combined with Aspect-Oriented Modeling techniques, is a promising approach to tame the complexity of adaptive systems. However, with no support for aspect unweaving, these approaches are not agile enough in an adaptive system context. In case of small modifications, the adapted model has to be generated by again weaving all the aspects, even those unchanged. This paper shows how aspects can be unwoven, based on a precise traceability metamodel dedicated to aspect model weaving. We analyze traceability models, which describe how aspects were woven into a base, to determine the extent to which an aspect has affected the woven model in order to determine how it can be unwoven. Aspect unweaving is finally performed by applying inverse operations of a sub-sequence of the weaving operations in opposite order.

1 Introduction

Since software systems need to be continuously available, their ability to evolve at runtime is a key issue. A very promising approach is to implement such systems as Dynamically Adaptive Systems (DAS), including self-adaptation and dynamic evolution facilities. Modern execution platforms like Fractal [1], OpenCOM [2] or OSGi [3] propose low-level APIs to reconfigure (add/remove/update components, add/remove bindings, etc) a system at runtime. However, with no higher level support, reconfiguration rapidly becomes a daunting and error-prone task to specify, validate, implement and understand. Indeed, implementing a reconfiguration script consists in identifying the components and bindings involved in the reconfiguration, and writing the whole sequence of atomic actions in a correct order. It is really difficult to validate the effect of such a script before actually executing it, detect dependencies or interactions between different scripts, etc.

Recently, some approaches [4,5] use Model-Driven Engineering (MDE) and Aspect-Oriented Modeling (AOM) techniques at runtime (*models@runtime* [6])

* This work was partially funded by the SPLIT project (FNR and CNRS funding) and the DiVA project(EU FP7 STREP, contract 215412, http://www.ict-diva.eu/).

A. Schürr and B. Selic (Eds.): MODELS 2009, LNCS 5795, pp. 514–530, 2009.

to tame the complexity of DAS. Keeping a model synchronized with the running system offers a high-level support for reasoning about the system [4] before actual adaptation. The first step of the dynamic adaptation process consists in selecting, according to the context, the most adapted architectural model. Then, after validation of the model, the running system is automatically adapted by analyzing the selected model. This prevents the designer from writing low-level platform-specific reconfiguration scripts by hand.

However, AOM approaches and tools [7,8,9,10,11] were formerly designed to operate at design-time, where performance (especially time) issues are not so critical. The key problem of current AOM weavers is that in case of small modifications, the adapted model has to be generated by again weaving all the aspects, even those unchanged. In other words, if the configuration is currently composed of n aspects, and if one of them should be "unwoven" (because of a change in the context), we have to restart from a core base model (containing the mandatory elements) and weave the $n-1$ unchanged aspects. More precisely, this means that we should detect the join points of the $n-1$ aspects, matching their associated pointcut model, and weave these aspects. The weaving process itself is efficient: it simply consists in adding or removing some model element and setting attributes and references. However, the join point detection step is more complex: for example, it can rely on graph theory to match sub-graphs in a graph, or rely on Prolog (logic programming) back-end [12] to execute queries on a fact base. In the second case, this requires to transform back and forth the base model, its metamodel (fact) and the pointcut (query) into Prolog artifacts, before actually executing the query. With no real support for aspect unweaving, AOM is not agile enough in an adaptive system context.

This paper shows how aspects can be unwoven, based on a precise traceability metamodel dedicated to aspect model weaving. We analyze traceability models, which describe how aspects were woven into a base, to determine the extent to which an aspect has affected the woven model in order to determine how it can be unwoven. Aspect unweaving is finally performed by applying inverse operations of a sub-sequence of the weaving operations in opposite order.

The remainder of the paper is organized as follows. Section 2 presents an overview of the existing approaches used in this paper. Section 3 introduces essential definitions on the unweaving of aspect models. Section 4 describs a traceability metamodel for aspect model weaving, and shows how a traceability model can be exploited. The main section of this paper is Section 5 which details our unweaving method. Finally, Section 6 presents related work and Section 7 concludes this paper.

2 Background

This section presents first GeKo [13], a generic aspect model weaver, and then an operation-based model construction approach. The objective of this paper is to present how we combined GeKo with this approach to support the unweaving of aspect models.

2.1 GeKo: A Generic Aspect Model Weaver

GeKo [13] is a generic aspect-oriented model composition and weaving approach easily adaptable to any metamodel with no need to modify the domain metamodel or to generate domain specific frameworks. It keeps a graphical representation of the weaving between an aspect model and the base model. It is a tool-supported approach with a clear semantics of the different operators used to define the weaving. The formalization of GeKo allows clearly identifying the sets of removed, added and altered elements.

In this sub-section, we introduce GeKo through an example of class diagram weaving, but GeKo can be used to weave other models such as state diagrams, sequence diagrams, feature diagrams, etc...

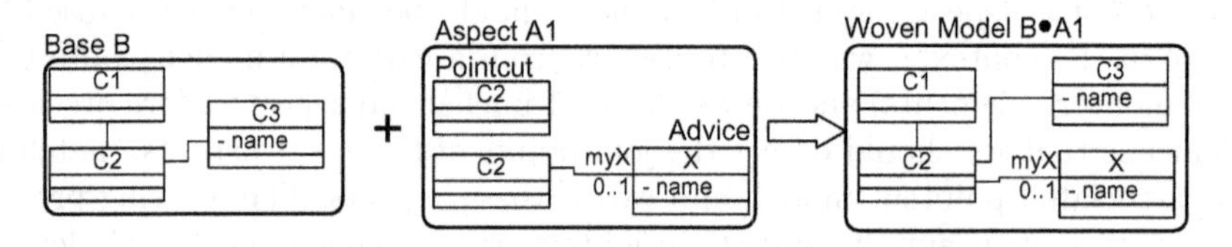

Fig. 1. Example of Class Diagram Weaving with GeKo

Fig. 1 shows an example of weaving with GeKo. The result of the weaving of the advice class diagram into the base class diagram is shown in the *Woven Model* of Fig. 1. The weaving process is two-phased. The first step consists in the detection of the match points corresponding to the *Pointcut* diagram. This detection step uses a Prolog-based pattern matching engine which yields a mapping from the pointcut model to the base model for each detected join point. In Fig. 1, the detection yields a mapping from the class $C2$ of the *Pointcut* model to the class $C2$ of the *Base* model. The second step consists in the composition of the advice model with the base model at the level of the match points previously detected (for each match point the advice model is composed). The composition is based on the definition of a mapping between the pointcut and the base model (automatically obtained from the detection step), and a mapping between the pointcut and the advice model (specified by the user). These mappings are defined over the concrete syntax of models by linking model elements. These links are fully generic and do not use any domain-specific knowledge, so that we can define mappings for any domain metamodel. These mappings allow the identification of several sub-sets of objects in the base and advice models characterizing the objects of *base* which have to be kept, to be removed and to be replaced with those of *advice*. Note that in the remainder of the paper, when the mapping between the pointcut and the advice model is obvious, we will omit to specify it.

2.2 Operation-Based Model Construction

In [14], the authors proposed to use a sequence of model construction operations to check consistency rules. In our paper, we present an approach which allows the generation the sequence of construction operation corresponding to the weaving of a sequence of aspects $A_1, A_2, \ldots, A_n$ in a base model B. Consequently, similar to [14], we can use the generated sequence of operations to check consistency rules, but in this paper, we will rather use the operation-based approach to efficiently unweave an aspect from a woven model.

More specifically, in [14] the authors propose to represent models by sequences of elementary construction operations, rather than by the set of model elements they contain. They propose four elementary operations inspired from the *MOF* reflective API [15] : 1) *create(me,mc)* corresponds to the creation of a model element instance *me* of the meta-class *mc*; 2) *delete(me)* corresponds to the deletion of the model element instance *me*; 3) *setProperty(me,p, Values)* corresponds to the assignment of a set of *Values* to the property *p* of the model element *me*; 4) *setReference(me,r,References)* corresponds to the assignment of *References* to the reference *r* of the model element *me*.

3 Unweaving Definitions

Let *mp* be a match point corresponding to pointcut of an aspect A_i and a base model B, i.e., *mp* is a place in B where the pattern defined by the pointcut model in A_i matches. The weaving of A_i in B at the level of *mp* can be defined by a sequence of construction operations:

$$weave(A_i, mp) = \sigma^i_{mp,1} \bullet \sigma^i_{mp,2} \bullet \ldots \bullet \sigma^i_{mp,k}$$

Fig. 1 shows a weaving example with class diagrams. Since there is only one match point *mp* at which the pointcut of A_1 matches, the sequence of construction operation to implement the weaving of A_1 is:

$$\begin{aligned}&weave(A_1, mp) = create(X, EClass) \bullet setProperty(X, name, \{X\}) \bullet \\ &create(nameAtt, EAttribute) \bullet setProperty(nameAtt, name, \{\text{“}name\text{''}\}) \bullet \\ &setReference(X, EAttribute, \{nameAtt\}) \bullet create(ref, EReference) \bullet \\ &setProperty(ref, name, \{\text{“}myX\text{''}\}) \bullet setProperty(ref, EType, \{X\}) \bullet \\ &setReference(C2, EReference, \{ref\})\end{aligned}$$

If A_i matches B h times, the weaving of the aspect A_i into B can be defined by the sequence of construction operations:

$$\begin{aligned}weave(A_i) &= weave(A_i, mp_1) \bullet weave(A_i, mp_2) \bullet \ldots \bullet weave(A_i, mp_h) \\ &= \sigma^i_{mp_1,1} \bullet \ldots \bullet \sigma^i_{mp_1,k} \bullet \sigma^i_{mp_2,1} \bullet \ldots \bullet \sigma^i_{mp_2,k} \bullet \ldots \bullet \sigma^i_{mp_h,1} \bullet \ldots \bullet \sigma^i_{mp_h,k}\end{aligned}$$

The weaving of a sequence of aspects $A_1, A_2, \ldots, A_n$ is defined by:

$$weave(A_1, A_2, \ldots, A_n) = weave(A_1) \bullet weave(A_2) \bullet \ldots \bullet weave(A_n)$$

Undoing a weave operation

For an aspect A_i and a match point *mp*, we define the *undo* operation $undo(A_i, mp)$ as the execution, in opposite order, of the sequence of *inverse* construction operations of the construction operations of $weave(A_i, mp)$. More formally:

$$undo(A_i, mp) = undo(\sigma^i_{mp,1} \bullet \sigma^i_{mp,2} \bullet ... \bullet \sigma^i_{mp,k})$$
$$= inverse(\sigma^i_{mp,k}) \bullet inverse(\sigma^i_{mp,k-1}) \bullet ... \bullet inverse(\sigma^i_{mp,1})$$

where the corresponding *inverse* operation of an operation is detailed in Table 1.

Table 1. Corresponding *inverse* operations

$\sigma_{mp,j}$	$inverse(\sigma_{mp,j})$
$create(me, mc)$	$delete(me)$
$delete(me)$	$create(me, mc)$ (in practice, mc is easily obtained from the sequence of construction operations)
$setProperty\ (me, p, value)$	if $\exists setProperty(me, p, value') \in weave(A_{k,k<i})$ then $setProperty(me, p, value')$ else $setProperty(me, p, \emptyset)$
$setReference\ (me, r, ref)$	if $\exists setReference(me, r, ref') \in weave(A_{k,k<i})$ then $setReference(me, r, ref')$, else $setReference(me, r, \emptyset)$

If we note $mp_k, k \in \{1, \ldots, h\}$ the match points corresponding to the weaving of an aspect A_i in a base B, we can extend the notion of *undo* to all the match points by:

$$undo(A_i) = undo(A_i, mp_h) \bullet undo(A_i, mp_{h-1}) \bullet \ldots \bullet undo(A_i, mp_1)$$

Unweaving

Let $A_1, A_2, ..., A_n$ be a sequence of aspects that have been woven into a base model B to result in a woven model BW. Unweaving of an aspect A_i from BW should result in a model that is equivalent to the model obtained by starting again with the base model B and weaving all aspects into B again in the same order, but omitting A_i. More formally, $\forall i \in \{1, ..., n\}$,

$$unweaving(A_i) = \begin{cases} weave(A_2, A_3, ..., A_n) & i = 1 \\ weave(A_1, A_2, ..., A_{i-1}, A_{i+1}, ..., A_n) & 1 < i < n \\ weave(A_1, A_2, ..., A_{n-1}) & i = n \end{cases}$$

4 Aspect Traceability Metamodel

4.1 Traceability Metamodel for GeKo

Weaving in GeKo is asymmetric, i.e., the weaving process is performed by applying a set of operations on a *base model*[1]. During the model weaving process, to compose an advice model with a base model, GeKo can: (1) *Remove* a model element from the base model; (2) *Add* a model element to the base model. The added model element is defined in the aspect's advice model; (3) *Replace* a model element of the base model by a model element of the aspect's advice model. This *replace* operation can be considered as a sequence of *remove* and *add* operations (remove the

[1] Since aspects can be applied to other aspects, the GeKo base model can, of course, be any model, even an advice model of some other aspect.

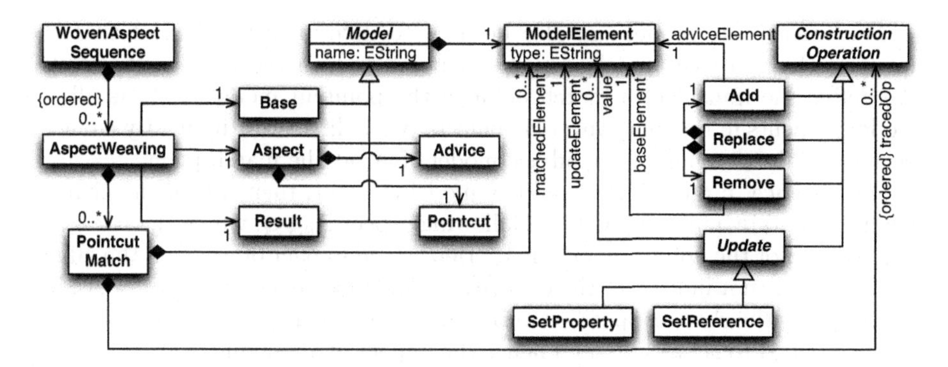

Fig. 2. Traceability Metamodel

replaced element and add the element which replaces it); (4) *Update* the *properties* of a base model element (e.g. change the name of a model element); (5) *Update* the *references* that a base model element has towards other model elements.

We propose to keep a trace of the application of these operations as the weaving takes place. For this, we defined the traceability metamodel for aspect model weaving presented in Fig. 2. The *WovenAspectSequence* class is the root class of the metamodel presented in Fig. 2. It contains a sequence of *AspectWeaving*. An *AspectWeaving* references a *Base*, a *Result* and an *Aspect* model. An *Aspect* model is composed of a *Pointcut* and an *Advice* model. All these models are defined by a list of *ModelElements*. The *AspectWeaving* class is also associated with a list of *PointcutMatches*. Each *PointcutMatch* stores the list of base model elements that were used to obtain this particular match when matching the pointcut of the aspect model to the base model. Each of the referenced base model elements is essential, i.e., if only one were omitted, the pointcut model would not match the base anymore. Finally, the class *PointcutMatch* also stores the effects of the weaving of the advice model of the aspect at this particular match point. *PointcutMatch* is associated with a sequence of *ConstructionOperations*. There are five types of possible operations corresponding to the five GeKo operations: *Replace*, *Remove*, *Add*, *UpdateReference*, *UpdateProperty*.

4.2 Using the Traceability Model

Once a sequence of aspects $A_1, A_2, \ldots, A_n$ is woven with a base model B to produce a woven model BW, the information stored in the traceability model contains the complete trace of operations that transformed B into BW. To re-execute the weaving, it suffices to start with B, and execute the associated sequence of elementary construction operations, which can be easily obtained by concatenating the sequence of *tracedOp* for each aspect weaving and for each associated match point. This sequence of construction operations is used in the algorithms presented in the next section.[2]

[2] Note that the construction operations defined in the traceability metamodel are implemented using the MOF primitives presented in subsection 2.2.

The traceability model can also be used to determine the *impact* that the weaving of an advice model at a match point had on the final woven model. We define the impact of a match point of the pointcut model in A_i as all the model elements in the final woven model that were directly or indirectly changed because of the weaving of the advice model of A_i at the match point.

For instance, if an aspect A_i adds a model element, then this model element might be used in a match point of a following aspect $A_{k,k>i}$, which again triggers the weaving of the advice model of A_k. Hence, the impact of weaving the advice model of A_i is not limited to the changes specified in the advice model of A_i, but also includes the changes specified in the advice model of A_k. The same reasoning can be applied to A_k as well, and hence the impact of a weaving of A_i at a match point can potentially include changes in all advice models of aspects $A_{k,k>i}$.

To determine the impact of a pointcut match, not only *Add* operations have to be considered. $SetReference$ and $SetProperty$ operations can also result in the creation of a match point of subsequent aspects $A_{k,k>i}$. For instance, the $SetProperty$ operation can be used by an aspect A_1 to change the value of the *balance* field of an object to 200. A following aspect A_2 might declare a pointcut which matches for all objects that have a *balance* attribute with a value ≥ 100. In this case, the impact of A_1 should only include the changes specified in the advice model of A_2 if the previous value of *balance*, i.e., the value that *balance* had *before* weaving A_1, was < 100. The detailed algorithm that calculates the impact of a match point *mp* of an aspect A_i is shown in Alg. 1.

Algorithm 1. *Impact*(A_i, mp)

Input: the aspect A_i, the match point *mp*, the traceability model corresponding to the weaving of the aspects $A_1, A_2, \ldots, A_n$ in a base model B
Output: the set of pairs (A_k, mp') where the match point mp' of the aspect $A_{k,k>i}$ is impacted by the weaving of A_i at the match point *mp*

```
k ← i + 1
while k ≤ n do
    foreach operation σ ∈ weave(A_i, mp) do
        foreach match point mp' of A_k do
            if σ == add(elt, eltType) and elt is shared with mp' then
                impact ← impact ∪ (A_k, mp')
            end
            if σ == setReference(elt, ref, {eltList}) and elt and ref are shared
            with mp' and the previous set of values for the reference ref is not
            included in the set of values for the reference ref of elt of the
            pointcut of A_k then
                impact ← impact ∪ (A_k, mp')
            end
        end
    end
    k ← k + 1
end
```

5 Using the Traceability Model for Unweaving of Aspects

This section presents the core contribution of our paper. It shows how the tracing information gathered during the model weaving (see section 4) can be used to unweave aspects from a woven model in an efficient way.

Let $A_1, A_2, ..., A_n$ be a sequence of aspects woven into a base model B resulting in a woven model BW. As presented in the definitions section, unweaving an aspect from BW is equivalent to re-weaving all aspects $A_1...A_n$ into B except for A_i. Re-weaving is, however, very inefficient. Not only does the tool have to re-execute all construction operations defined by the $n-1$ advice models of the aspects $A_{j,j \neq i}$, but it also has to re-execute the pattern matching algorithm that searches for match points based on the patterns defined in the $n-1$ pointcut models.

The technique presented in this paper allows a tool to unweave an aspect A_i from BW without having to re-weave all the aspects $A_{j,j \neq i}$ into B. Depending on the nature of the relation between the aspect A_i and the aspects $A_{k,k>i}$ that were woven into the base model after A_i, unweaving A_i is more or less complicated. In the following discussion, we distinguish 3 different cases. At this point, the reader is reminded that our solution is based on the use of the generic weaver called GeKo, which performs aspect weaving using the operations 1) *add* model element, 2) *remove* of a model element, 3) *replace* model element (which can be seen as a remove followed by an add), 4) *set property*, and 5) *set reference.*

5.1 Case 1, Independent Aspects

Informal description: In the most advantageous case, A_i is independent of the aspects $A_{k,k>i}$ that were woven after A_i to obtain BW. This situation occurs when A_i neither introduced model elements which were used in a match point of one of the aspects $A_{k,k>i}$, nor removed model elements which could have formed a match point for a $A_{k,k>i}$, nor changed any properties or references that were used or could have been used in a match point of one of the aspects $A_{k,k>i}$.

Fig. 3 shows an example illustrating this case. The example presents the weaving of an aspect A_2 into the model obtained after the weaving of the aspect A_1 already presented in Fig. 1. The resulting model is $B \bullet A_1 \bullet A_2$. In this example, A_1 is independent from A_2, because the model elements introduced (the class X) and the changes to model elements (adding of the reference to $C2$) are not part of the match point of A_2 (which matches on the class $C1$). Also, A_1 does not remove any model elements from B.

Unweaving of Independent Aspects: Unweaving of aspect A_i simply consists in undoing the weave operation, i.e., in applying, for each match point, the inverse construction operations in opposite order of the construction sequence defined by $weave(A_i, jp)$. More formally:

If match point mp of A_i is independent of $A_{k,k>i}$:$unweave(A_i, mp) = undo(A_i, mp)$
$\Rightarrow$ If A_i independent of $A_{k,k>i}$: $unweave(A_i) = undo(A_i) = \forall mp_{A_i} : undo(A_i, mp)$.

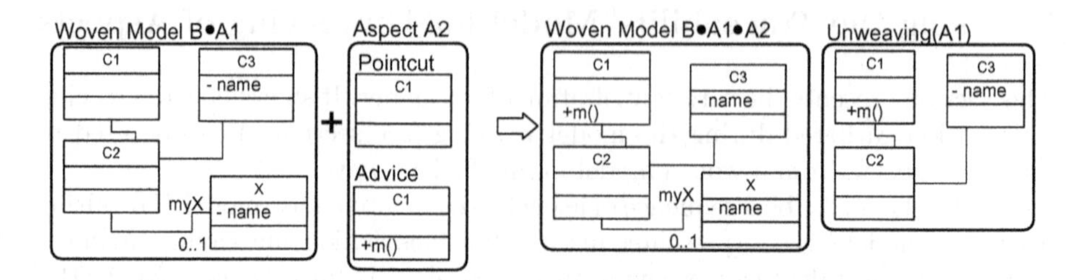

Fig. 3. Weaving of A_2 and Unweaving of A_1 (previously presented in Fig. 1)

Therefore, in Fig. 3, the unweaving of A_1 consists in applying $undo(A_1)$, i.e., applying inverse operations in opposite order of the construction sequence $weave(A_1)$.

$unweave(A_1) = undo(A_1) = setReference(C2, EReference, \emptyset) \bullet setProperty(ref, EType, \emptyset) \bullet setProperty(ref, name, \emptyset) \bullet delete(ref) \bullet setReference(X, EAttribute, \emptyset) \bullet setProperty(nameAtt, name, \emptyset) \bullet delete(nameAtt, \emptyset) \bullet setProperty(X, name, \emptyset) \bullet delete(X)$

5.2 Case 2, General Aspects

Informal description: In the worst case, when the weaving of an aspect A_i removes or changes model elements in the base model, it is possible that these elements could have been used to form a match point of an aspect $A_{k,k>i}$. As a result, the unweaving of the aspect A_i could introduce completely new match points for the following aspects $A_{k,k>i}$. In this case, the unweaving of A_i cannot be done by simply applying a sequence of undo operations. Unfortunately, the pattern matching operation that detects match points corresponding to the pointcut models in the aspects $A_{k,k>i}$ has to be launched again.

Fig. 4 shows an example of Final State Machine (FSM) weaving illustrating this case. The example presents the successive weaving of the aspect A_1 and A_2 into the base model B. The resulting model is $B \bullet A_1 \bullet A_2$. The weaving of aspect A_1 consists in replacing the state c by a state e and by removing the state a. The weaving of aspect A_2 consists in replacing the state a by a state b with a loop transition. After the weaving of A_1, A_2 matches only once, but without A_1, the pointcut of A_2 would also match against the first a state that was removed when A_1 was woven. This example shows that the only solution to unweave A_1 is first to unweave A_2, then to unweave A_1 and finally to weave A_2 again.

Unweaving General Aspect A_i: To unweave a general aspect A_i the idea is to first compute index $j > i$ such that A_i is not general for the aspects $A_{h,i \leq h<j}$. The second step consists in unweaving of the aspects $A_{k,k \geq j}$ in the opposite order of the sequence of weaving, i.e., A_n first, then A_{n-1}, ..., A_j. For these unweavings, since the aspect unwoven is always the last aspect that had been woven, the unweaving operation corresponds to the *undo* operation. The next step is to unweave A_i. The final step consists in weaving of the aspects $A_{k,k \geq j}$ in the same order as the initial sequence of weaving.

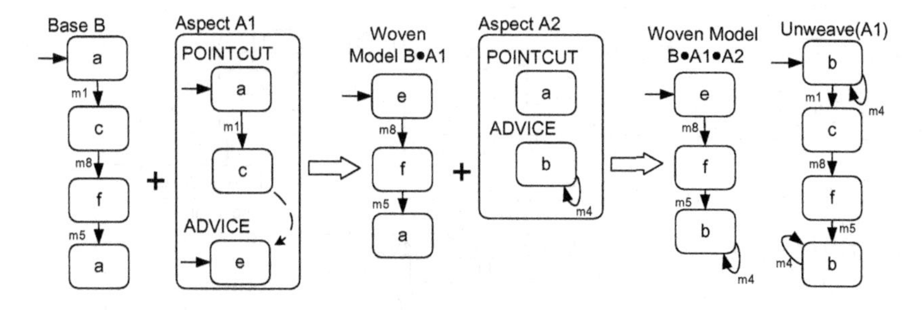

Fig. 4. Weaving of A_1 and A_2 into B, and Result of the Unweaving of A_1

Depending on the value of i and j, it might be faster to start from scratch, i.e., start with B and re-execute the weave operations of the aspects $A_1 \ldots A_{i-1}$ stored in the traceability model rather than to unweave aspects $A_j \ldots A_n$ and A_i. The cut off values of i and j at which it is better to re-weave than to unweave depends heavily on the number of match points of each aspect, and the number of construction operations needed to implement the weaving of each match point. If the length of the sequence of construction operations for weaving aspects $A_1 \ldots A_{i-1}$ is smaller than the length of the sequence of operations for weaving $A_i, A_j \ldots A_n$, then re-weaving is more efficient than unweaving.

5.3 Case 3: Additive Aspects

Informal description: Some aspects A_i are not general, i.e., they did not remove or alter elements which could have been used in a match point of a following aspect $A_{k,k>i}$, but are also not independent, because they added or changed model elements which were later on used in a match point of at least one of the $A_{k,k>i}$. We call these *additive* aspects.

Fig. 5 presents an example of this case. A_1 introduces a message $m4$ from $O2$ to $O3$ after an exchange of messages $m1, m2$ between $O1$ and $O2$. A_2 introduces an message $m5$ after any message $m4$. If we consider the sequence of weaving $A_1 \bullet A_2$ as shown in Fig. 5, A_1 is clearly an additive aspect. The message $m4$ introduced by A_1 is matched by the pointcut model of aspect A_2 and hence creates a match point. Also, A_1 does not remove any model elements.

Unweaving of Additive Aspects: In the case of an additive aspect A_i, the unweaving of the aspect does not simply consist in undoing the weave operation of A_i as for the case of independent aspects, because some elements added by the weaving of A_i have been used to form match points of aspects $A_{k,k>i}$, and hence resulted in further changes to the model. Therefore, the unweaving operation has to also undo the weaving of all advice of aspects $A_{k,k>i}$ that were woven because of a pointcut match that contained elements that A_i added or changed.

Let us consider the example of Fig. 5. To unweave the aspect A_1, we have to remove both the operations directly related to the weaving of A_1 (i.e., the introduction of a message $m4$) and the operations related to the match point

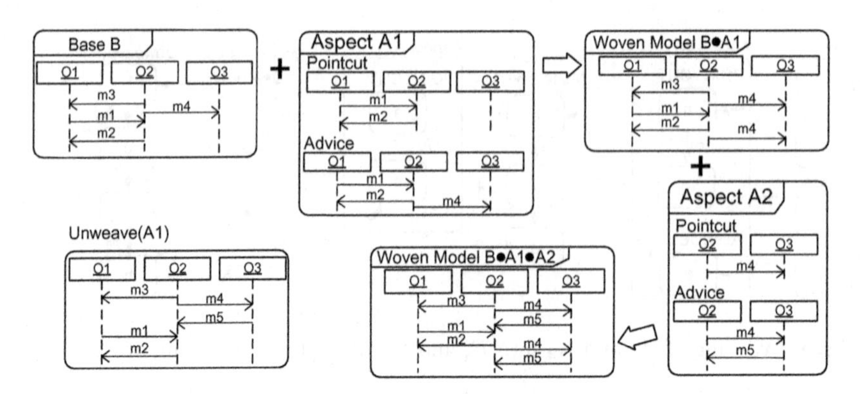

Fig. 5. Weaving of A_1 and A_2 into B, and Result of the Unweaving of A_1

of A_2 formed by elements introduced by A_1. In Fig. 5, the pointcut model of A_2 matched twice in the model $B \bullet A_1$, once on each message $m4$. However, only the second match is due to A_1, and therefore only the second introduction of a new message $m5$ has to be undone.

More formally, to unweave an aspect A_i, we apply the algorithm described in Alg. 2 for all the match points of A_i. It describes that, to unweave an additive aspect A_i, we have to also recursively unweave the *impacted* match points of aspects $A_{k,k>i}$. These impacted match points can, of course, be of any type, i.e., independent, additive, or general.

5.4 Classification of Aspects

This section presents how our tool classifies a match point of an aspect into one of the 3 cases described above, followed by the complete algorithm of classification.

Conditions for Detecting General Aspects: To determine if mp of A_i is *general*, we must check if A_i modified or removed model elements that could have created a match point for one of the pointcuts of one of the following aspects $A_{k,k>i}$. Note that when the advice model in A_i *removes* an element which corresponds to an element of a match point of an aspect $A_{k,k>i}$, mp is immediately classified as general. However, as specified in Algorithm 3, additional conditions have to be respected in the case where A_i only modifies (with $setReference$ or $setProperty$) an element which corresponds to an element of a pointcut of an aspect $A_{k,k>i}$. For instance, when A_i modifies the reference of an element elt, this modification cannot remove a match point if elt was previously added by A_i.

Condition for Detecting Additive Aspects: To determine if mp of A_i is *additive*, we check if A_i is not general and if A_i adds and modifies any model elements which are used to form a match point of a following aspect $A_{k,k>i}$. Note that when A_i *adds* an element used to form a match point mp' of an aspect $A_{k,k>i}$, mp' cannot be a match point of A_k anymore when A_i is unwoven. However, when A_i modifies an element that used to form a match point mp' of an aspect $A_{k,k>i}$

Algorithm 2. $additiveUnweave(A_i, mp, A_{k,1 \leq k \leq n})$

Input: the aspect A_i, the additive match point mp to unweave, the traceability model corresponding to the weaving of the sequence of aspects $A_1, A_2, \ldots, A_n$ in a base model B. The sequence $A_{k,1 \leq k \leq n}$ is such as there is no genral match point mp' of an aspect A_j impacted by A_i or recursively by a match point of an aspect impacted by A_j

Output: the sequence of unweaving operations σ

```
σ ← undo(A_i)
Let impact be the set of model elements added or modified by the advice model
of A_i when applied to mp (see Alg. 1)
j ← i + 1
while j ≤ n do
    foreach match point mp' of the aspect A_j do
        Let me be the set of model elements associated with the match point mp'
        if me ∩ impact ≠ ∅ then
            σ ← unweave(A_j, mp') • σ
        end
    end
    j ← j + 1
end
```

(with $setReference$ or $setProperty$), mp' can still be a match point even after A_i is unwoven. This is the case if the *previous* value of the property or reference being modified also resulted in the creation of the same match point.

Condition for Detecting Independence: mp of A_i is *independent*, if mp is neither general nor additive.

More formally, to classify the match point of an aspect A_i with respect to the following aspects $A_{k,k>i}$, we apply Alg. 3. Note that for space reasons, Alg. 3 does not show how to handle the $setProperty$ operation, but the conditions are exactly the same as for the $setReference$ operation. To extend this classification for a mach point of A_i to the aspect A_i itself, we use the following rules: 1) A_i is general if for all match points of A_i, at least one match point is general; 2) A_i is additive if A_i is not general and at least one match point of A_i is additive; 3) A_i is independent if A_i is neither general nor additive.

5.5 Complete Unweaving Algorithm

To unweave A_i, the first step consists in the determination of the lowest index $j \geq i$ of an aspect that contains a *general* match point mp that needs to be unwoven because of the unweaving of A_i. In other words, j is the index of the first aspect A_j in the sequence of aspects whose match point mp cannot be unwoven by applying a sequence of undo operations.

This is done by the $lowestGeneralIndex$ algorithm presented in Alg. 4. This index is then used in the general unweaving algorithm presented in Alg. 5. The first foreach loop unweaves the general aspects. The *lowestGeneralIndex* allows us to ensure that for all unweaving operations in the second foreach loop (even

---

Algorithm 3. *classify*(A_i, mp)

Input: the aspect A_i, the match point mp, the traceability model corresponding to the weaving of the sequence of aspects $A_1, \ldots, A_n$ in a base model B

Output: Classification of the application of the advice model of A_i at the match point mp and the aspects $A_{k,k>i}$

if $i = i$ **then**
  mp is independent
else
  if *∃delete(elt) ∈ weave(A_i, mp) such as elt corresponds to a model element of a pointcut of $A_{k,k>i}$ OR ∃setReference(elt, ref, {eltList}) ∈ weave(A_i, mp) such that elt is shared with a match point of $A_{k,k>i}$ and elt is an element not added by A_i and the previous set of values for the reference ref is not included in the set eltList* **then**
    mp is general
  else
    if *∃add(elt, eltType) ∈ weave(A_i, mp) such as elt is shared with a match point of $A_{k,k>i}$ OR ∃setReference(elt, ref, {eltList}) ∈ weave(A_i, mp) such as elt and ref are shared with a match point of $A_{k,k>i}$ and the previous set of values for the reference ref is not included in the set of values for the reference ref of elt of the match point of A_k* **then**
      mp is additive
    else
      mp is independent
    end
  end
end

Algorithm 4. *lowestGeneralIndex*(A_i)

Input: the aspect A_i, the traceability model corresponding to the weaving of the sequence of aspects $A_1, \ldots, A_n$ in a base model B

Output: the *lowest index of a general aspect impacted by* A_i

Let j be the smallest index $> i$ such that A_i is not general for the sequence of aspects $A_{h,i \leq h<j}$
lowestGeneralIndex $\leftarrow j$
foreach *couple* (A_h, mp') *impacted by the match points of* A_i **do**
  if *∃l such that $h < l < j$ and the match point mp' of A_h is general for a match point of A_l* **then**
    lowestGeneralIndex $\leftarrow l$
  end
end

---

for the operations recursively called), the match point mp is either independent or additive, but never general. As a result, the unweaving operation consists in either the undo operation or the operation described in Alg. 2. Finally, the last for loop executes the necessary re-weaving, if any.

Algorithm 5. *unweave*(A_i)

Input: the aspect A_i, the traceability model corresponding to the weaving of the sequence of aspects $A_1, A_2, \ldots, A_n$ in a base model B

```
j ← lowestGeneralIndex(A_i)
for k = n...j do
| apply undo(A_k)
end
foreach match point mp of the aspect A_i do
|  if classify(A_i,mp) = independent then
|  | apply undo(A_i, mp)
|  else
|  | additiveUnweave(A_i, mp, A_{k,1≤k≤j−1})
|  end
end
for k = j...n do
| weave(A_k)
end
```

6 Related Work

Although the method described in this paper is applied in the context of the GeKo aspect model weaver, the same ideas can easily be generalized to other model weavers (such as [9,16,17,18]), once an appropriate traceability model is constructed.

In [17], the authors present an interesting way to modify models before and after their composition, by means of the use of a language of directives. This support is not automatised, but in our approach, the directive language could be used to apply the generated unweaving sequence of elementary operations.

To the best of our knowledge and belief, no Aspect-Oriented Modeling approach provides support for aspect model unweaving. At the platform level, however, some approaches provide support for weaving and unweaving.

FAC (Fractal Aspect Component) [19] is an open-source aspect-oriented extension to the Fractal component model [1]. It combines Component-Based Software Development (CBSD) and Aspect-Oriented Programming (AOP) by integrating CBSD notions into AOP, and vice-versa. FAC introduces new aspect-oriented structures into the Fractal platform: Aspect Component (AC), Aspect Domain (AD) and Aspect Binding (AB). An Aspect Component is a regular component that encapsulates a crosscutting concern providing advice pieces of code as services. An Aspect Binding is a binding that links an AC to other components. Finally, an AC and all the aspectized components bound via ABs constitute an Aspect Domain (AD). Note that FAC leverages the notion of shared components provided by Fractal to allow components to be contained in several ADs. Basically, weaving an aspect component consists in creating the composite component corresponding to the AD, containing the components of the aspect itself as well as the components impacted by the aspect (still contained by their former container), and introducing bindings. Unweaving the aspect consists in removing all these previously introduced elements. However, no real description of the unweaving process is provided, especially when an aspect depends on other aspects.

Very similar to FAC is AOpenCOM [20], which provides aspect-oriented construction for the OpenCOM component model [2]. Again, very few details are provided about the unweaving process.

CaesarJ [21] extends Java with aspect-oriented constructs. It combines AspectJ-like constructions (pointcut/advice) with advanced modularization and composition techniques such as virtual classes and mixins. Aspects can dynamically be deployed or undeployed on all the join points currently identified in the JVM matching the pointcut. Similarly to above mentionned approaches, no detail is given on the unweaving strategy, especially when aspects are interacting.

In this paper, we have proposed clear and formalized unweaving strategies at the model level, independently from any metamodel. Depending on how an aspect interacts with the other, we precisely determine the way the aspect should be unwoven. With the emergence of the notion of *models@runtime*, it becomes important to optimize approaches and tools usually used at design-time. In previous work [4], we use AOM and MDE in order to manage complex dynamic software product lines at runtime. Each dynamic feature of the system is represented as an aspect model [22] (an architecture fragment), which is selected depending on the context. When the context changes, new aspects can be selected while others are discarded. Working at the model level provides a better basis for reasoning, validation, and automation [4,5]. However, without support for unweaving, we had to systematically restart from a core base model and weave again all the aspects, which is very inefficient.

7 Conclusion

In this paper we have presented a method to efficiently unweave an aspect A_i from a sequence of aspects $A_1 \dots A_n$ woven into a base model B. Our method is based on the use of a traceability model recording construction operations at weave-time. The traceability model allows the determination of the relation between A_i and the following aspects. According to this relation, which is either *independent*, *additive* or *general*, the unweaving is more or less complicated. If no general relationship is detected, unweaving can be performed by directly applying a set of undo operations to the woven model.

Although the method described in this paper is applied in the context of the GeKo aspect model weaver, we believe the same ideas can easily be applied in other tools, once an appropriate traceability model is constructed.

In the future, we plan to apply and evaluate the performance of our unweaving method in the context of dynamic, adaptive systems.

References

1. Bruneton, E., Coupaye, T., Leclercq, M., Quéma, V., Stefani, J.: The FRACTAL Component Model and its Support in Java. Software Practice and Experience 36(11-12), 1257–1284 (2006)

2. Blair, G., Coulson, G., Ueyama, J., Lee, K., Joolia, A.: Opencom v2: A component model for building systems software. In: IASTED Software Engineering and Applications, USA (2004)
3. The OSGi Alliance: OSGi Service Platform Core Specification, Release 4.1 (May 2007), http://www.osgi.org/Specifications/
4. Morin, B., Barais, O., Nain, G., Jézéquel, J.M.: Taming Dynamically Adaptive Systems with Models and Aspects. In: ICSE 2009, Vancouver, Canada (May 2009)
5. Morin, B., Fleurey, F., Bencomo, N., Jézéquel, J.M., Solberg, A., Dehlen, V., Blair, G.: An Aspect-Oriented and Model-Driven Approach for Managing DynamicVariability. In: ACM/IEEE MoDELS 2008, Toulouse, France (October 2008)
6. Bencomo, N., Blair, G., France, R.: Proceedings of the international workshops on models@run.time (2006-2008)
7. Clarke, S., Baniassad, E.: Aspect-Oriented Analysis and Design: The Theme Approach. Addison Wesley, Reading (2005)
8. Whittle, J., Jayaraman, P.: Mata: A tool for aspect-oriented modeling based on graph transformation. In: AOM at Models 2007 (2007)
9. Groher, I., Voelter, M.: Xweave: Models and aspects in concert. In: AOM Workshop 2007 at AOSD, March 12 (2007)
10. Kienzle, J., Abed, W.A., Klein, J.: Aspect-oriented multi-view modeling. In: ACM (ed.) AOSD 2009, Charlotteville, Virginia, USA, March 2009, pp. 87–98 (2009)
11. Klein, J., Hélouet, L., Jézéquel, J.-M.: Semantic-based weaving of scenarios. In: AOSD 2006, Bonn, Germany, pp. 27–38. ACM Press, New York (2006)
12. Ramos, R., Barais, O., Jézéquel, J.M.: Matching Model Snippets. In: Engels, G., Opdyke, B., Schmidt, D.C., Weil, F. (eds.) MODELS 2007. LNCS, vol. 4735, pp. 121–135. Springer, Heidelberg (2007)
13. Morin, B., Klein, J., Barais, O., Jezequel, J.M.: A generic weaver for supporting product lines. In: Early Aspects Workshop at ICSE, Leipzig, Germany (May 2008)
14. Blanc, X., Mounier, I., Mougenot, A., Mens, T.: Detecting model inconsistency through operation-based model construction. In: ICSE 2008, Leipzig, Germany, pp. 511–520. ACM/IEEE (2008)
15. OMG: Mof core specification , v2.0. OMG Document number formal/2006-01-01 (2006)
16. Whittle, J., Jayaraman, P.: MATA: A Tool for Aspect-Oriented Modeling based on Graph Transformation. In: AOM@MoDELS 2007: 11th International Workshop on Aspect-Oriented Modeling, Nashville, TN, USA (October 2007)
17. Reddy, R., Ghosh, S., France, R.B., Straw, G., Bieman, J.M., Song, E., Georg, G.: Directives for composing aspect-oriented design class models. In: Rashid, A., Aksit, M. (eds.) Transactions on Aspect-Oriented Software Development I. LNCS, vol. 3880, pp. 75–105. Springer, Heidelberg (2006)
18. Sanchez, P., Fuentes, L., Stein, D., Hanenberg, S., Unland, R.: Aspect-oriented model weaving beyond model composition and model transformation. In: Czarnecki, K., Ober, I., Bruel, J.-M., Uhl, A., Völter, M. (eds.) MODELS 2008. LNCS, vol. 5301, pp. 766–781. Springer, Heidelberg (2008)
19. Pessemier, N., Seinturier, L., Coupaye, T., Duchien, L.: A Model for Developing Component-based and Aspect-oriented Systems. In: Löwe, W., Südholt, M. (eds.) SC 2006. LNCS, vol. 4089, pp. 259–274. Springer, Heidelberg (2006)

20. Surajbali, B., Coulson, G., Greenwood, P., Grace, P.: Augmenting reflective middleware with an aspect orientation support layer. In: Proceedings of the 6th Workshop on Adaptive and Reflective Middleware, ARM 2007 (2007)
21. Aracic, I., Gasiunas, V., Mezini, M., Ostermann, K.: An Overview of CaesarJ. In: Rashid, A., Aksit, M. (eds.) Transactions on Aspect-Oriented Software Development I. LNCS, vol. 3880, pp. 135–173. Springer, Heidelberg (2006)
22. Perrouin, G., Klein, J., Guelfi, N., Jézéquel, J.-M.: Reconciling Automation and Flexibility in Product Derivation. In: 12th International Software Product Line Conference, Limerick, Ireland, pp. 339–348. IEEE Computer Society, Los Alamitos (2008)

Model Composition Contracts

Jon Oldevik[1,2,3], Massimiliano Menarini[1], and Ingolf Krüger[1]

[1] Univ. of California San Diego, Dep. of Computer Science and Engineering, La Jolla, USA
[2] Department of Informatics, University of Oslo, Norway
[3] SINTEF Information and Communication Technology, Oslo, Norway
jonold@ifi.uio.no, mmenarini@ucsd.edu, ikrueger@ucsd.edu

Abstract. The state-of-the-art in aspect-oriented programming and modeling provides flexible querying and composition mechanisms that allow virtually unrestricted modifications to base code or models using static or dynamic weaving. There is, however, a lack of support for specifying and controlling the permitted effects of compositions with respect to the base models involved. We present model composition contracts, which govern access to the base models via aspects; in essence, the contracts control how aspect compositions may or may not access and change the models, or the underlying code reflected by models. The composition contracts define constraints in terms of pre- and post-conditions restricting the eligibility for composition. We argue that composition contracts improve reliability of model composition in software engineering, and evaluate their effects on model designs and implementations using a case study. We support the approach with a prototype tool for specifying and checking contracts.

Keywords: Model composition, design by contract, aspect-oriented development.

1 Introduction

Aspect-oriented techniques for programming and modeling languages [1,2] provide flexible ways of separating and recomposing cross-cutting concerns. In many approaches, there is a clear separation of the base model and the aspects applied to it. There is a *unidirectional* relation between aspects and base models; base models are unaware of, or oblivious to, the existence of aspects. AspectJ [3] is an example of such an approach. Obliviousness is a major discussion topic in the aspect-oriented community [4]. While we do not argue against obliviousness, we acknowledge that it can harm the evolution of the base model. In fact, aspects can break the interfaces and assumptions the creator of the base model relies on. Therefore, we propose to extend model composition by associating composition contracts with the base model.

In aspect-oriented systems with oblivious composition, the base model has no control over what happens to its structure or behavior. For example, in AspectJ, an aspect may intercept any private method and override its behavior. This breaks the encapsulation assumptions of the base code programmer. To obtain a working program, the creator of the aspect must know the base code, and make sure that the base code business logic will still work correctly when the aspect is applied. Unfortunately, this is not possible, in general, if the base code is modified after the aspect has been created.

A. Schürr and B. Selic (Eds.): MODELS 2009, LNCS 5795, pp. 531–545, 2009.

To support a more controlled model composition paradigm where models are shielded from unintended changes, we propose *Model Composition Contracts*. In this approach, a contract-like mechanism controls *what* compositions (such as the weaving-in of aspects) are allowed to do. This resembles the *Design by Contract* (DbC) methodology, where assertions are used to specify contracts between suppliers and consumers of services in terms of obligations (preconditions) and guarantees (post-conditions). DbC was originally defined as part of the Eiffel language [5], and provides more precise specifications that improve system reliability and robustness.

Inspired by DbC, we propose to associate *contracts* with base models. Contracts constrain the effects of aspect composition on models, by specifying which elements of the base model an aspect can access; hence, they act as an extended interface for the base model. They constrain the changes that can be made not only by restricting access, but also by enforcing invariants on the composite model. Our contract specification approach uses Object Constraint Language (OCL) for constraint specification, and is generally applicable to any Meta Object Facility (MOF)-based language; in this paper, however, we narrow the focus to scenario descriptions. This allows us to tackle a problem highly relevant in practice: modeling the key interaction patterns of complex software systems, while factoring out cross-cutting interactions aspects, such as message type transformation, encryption, or failure management. The resulting interaction models are more concise, and display a clear relationship between desired base behavior and allowed modifications via aspects. We posit that this increases the overall readability, quality, and utility of the resulting models.

The interaction specifications we use as a case study in this paper come from the *Common Component Modeling Example (CoCoME)* [6]. CoCoME displays many of the complexities of enterprise systems; specifically, it has interesting interaction patterns for product exchange among multiple distributed, interdependent department stores. We will use the interaction pattern for trading of stocked items when one store runs low on a particular product as an example of a base model. Furthermore, CoCoME also allows us to represent realistic examples of cross-cutting aspects. We will use message parameter type transformation (to adapt among different product representations between stores), and message encryption among stores and between stores and banks as examples of interaction aspects to be composed with the base model. Specifically, we will define contracts that will *allow* message parameter type transformation, and *disallow* message encryption to show how contracts limit aspects' accesses to base models.

We support our composition contract approach with a prototype tool for *specifying* and *checking* contracts associated with base models. Fig. 1 shows the high-level activities implemented by the contract checking tool. The tool checks the composition contract specified by the author of the base model against an *assumption contract* we derive from the aspect. The assumption contract summarizes what the aspect "plans to do" to the base code. The composition contract summarizes what any aspect *is allowed* to do to the base code. The tool's *pre-check* analyzes the assumption contract exported from the aspect against the base model contract to determine contract violations. If the first pre-check (1) result is uncertain (this can happen if the OCL queries in the contract are too complex to evaluate by the pre-check), a second pre-check (2) executes and compares the results from the queries in the contract with those from the assumption

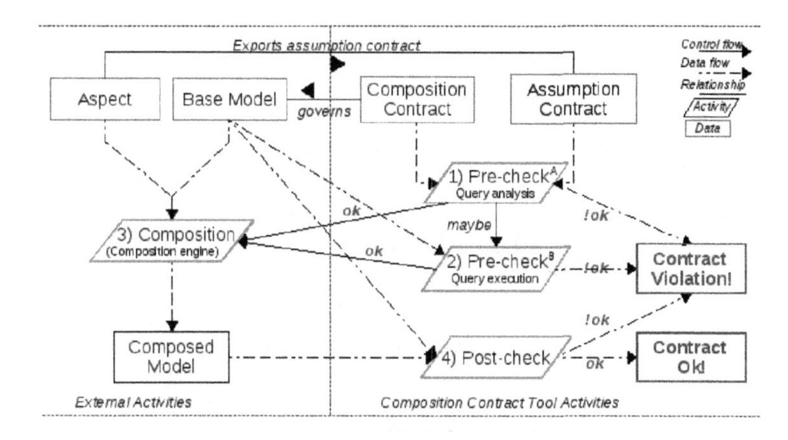

Fig. 1. Contract Prototype Process Overview

contract. If the aspect passes the pre-check, the composition can commence. After composition (3), a post-check (4) is performed to check the contract post-conditions on the composite model. If the contract is violated, the composition is undone.

Outline. The paper is organized as follows: in Section 2, we introduce our case study and show how concerns may violate policies governing our system. Then, in Section 3, we describe the concepts in our composition contract approach and how contracts are specified and checked. Section 4 evaluates the approach and Section 5 discusses benefits and trade-offs of our approach. We present the related work in Section 6, and conclude in Section 7.

2 Motivating Case Study – CoCoME

The Common Component Modeling Example - CoCoME - is a distributed software system that supports an enterprise with different points of sale. It manages products ordering from suppliers, product exchanges between stores, along with sales to customers. It was introduced as a common modeling example for a Dagstuhl seminar [6]. For this seminar, we modeled CoCoME as a service-oriented architecture with a focus on interaction models that define the interplay among all the services/features of the overall enterprise. Specifically, we used UML sequence diagrams to specify interactions among the various services. Each lifeline in the sequence diagrams represents a *role* that is mapped to a service in the implemented system; the system was realized using an *enterprise service bus* infrastructure (ESB), *Mule* [7].

The system contains cross-cutting behaviors we want to describe as separate concerns. These are specified using sequence diagrams that show how the respective aspect affects other interaction patterns in the system when they are composed. We wanted to control how these behaviors are allowed to modify our system by allowing modification by composition (imposed by aspects), but restricting the kind of changes that can occur. Why? Composition contracts will allow teams of engineers with interdependent

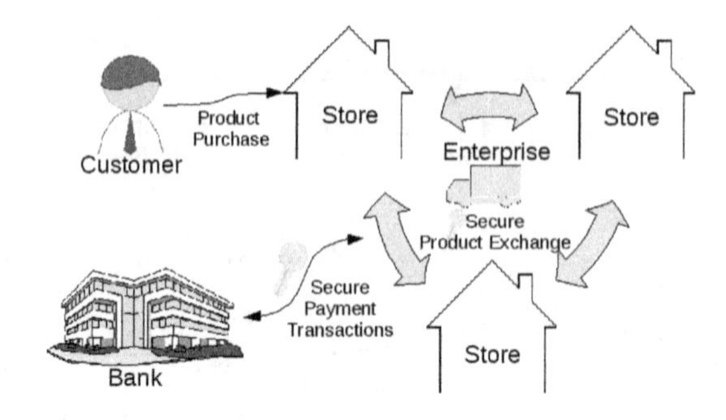

Fig. 2. The CoCoME Trading System Overview

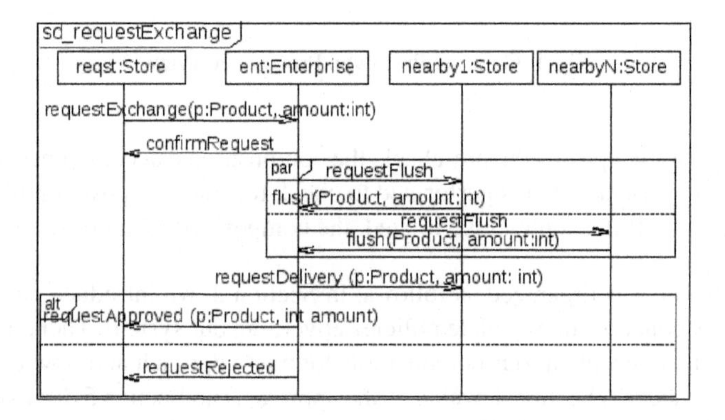

Fig. 3. Product Exchange Scenario in the CoCoME Case Study

development tasks to work together without violating system constraints. This will reduce potential errors in the composition process, making the development process more efficient, and, in the end, increasing the robustness of systems.

In the CoCoME system, *Stores* collaborate as an enterprise to exchange products from one store to another when stock is low in one of the stores (Fig. 2). Purchases from stores may result in payment transactions with the *bank*. The domain requires the product exchange and bank payment transactions to be secured by encryption. However, the infrastructure cannot be allowed to see plain-text messages, so encryption must be introduced at the endpoints rather than by the infrastructure.

The sequence diagram in Fig. 3 shows how a store requests a product exchange from another nearby store in the collaboration, by interacting with the *enterprise* role. The *enterprise* sends a *flush request* for the products to all nearby stores in parallel and receives results back. If the products requested can be delivered by a nearby store, the enterprise requests delivery. Finally, it sends a response back to the requesting store.

In the context of this case study, several concerns are identified and described separately. One is a *message filtering* concern, where messages between the *store* and *enterprise* roles are intercepted and their content filtered to meet context-specific requirements. Another is a security concern regarding communication between stores in an enterprise – it is handled by encrypting the communication. Note that both of these are realistic concerns that, today, are increasingly handled by aspect-oriented *runtime* environments such as dependency-injection and Enterprise Service Bus (ESB) technologies. However, the communication protocol between stores is subject to change over time, and thus aspect definition and composition are brittle unless special provisions are made. Here, we show how composition contracts can reduce this brittleness.

Message Filtering. When stores communicate with the enterprise for requesting product exchange, the product information required at different stores may vary. An interceptor is provided for filtering/modifying relevant messages between the roles. In our case, the interceptor should intercept certain messages and change their content arguments to match the requirements for the different stores.

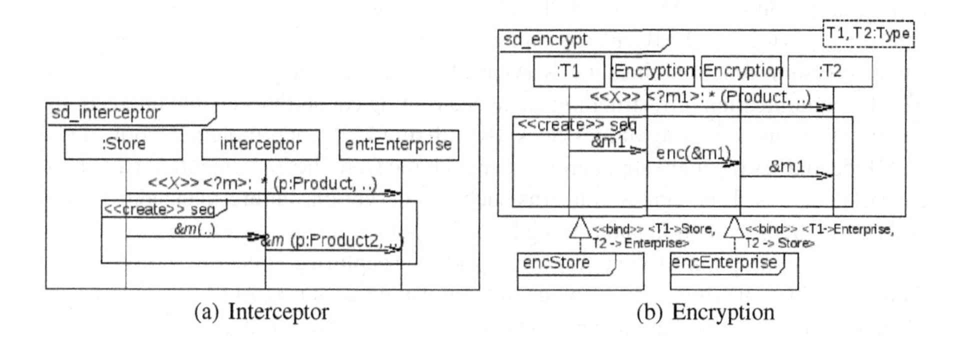

(a) Interceptor (b) Encryption

Fig. 4. Message Filtering and Encryption Concerns

To illustrate our examples for base code and composition contracts, we use a notation adapted from [8]; this notation allows us to specify interaction aspects by specifying "queries", yielding modeling items to which an aspect will be applied. The query part of the aspect is defined by messages specified as regular expressions, as in AspectJ. To simplify query specification, we use identifiers that can be assigned a query by using the `<?id>` notation before the query search criteria. The identifier can then be referenced other places in the sequence diagram to refer back to the matching modeling element(s). An `<<X>>` stereotype signifies deletion of matches. References to identifiers are specified using the '&' symbol followed by the identifier name. The advice part of the sequence diagram aspect is placed within a combined fragment with a `<<create>>` stereotype.

The interceptor is described as an aspect by using sequence diagram notation. The aspect (pointcut) queries for messages going from roles of *type Store* to an *Enterprise* role that pass *Product* as an argument. It replaces its findings with copies of this message going via the interceptor. The *interceptor* forwards the message to the *enterprise*, but modifies the *argument* by sending an object of a different type *(Product2 vs Product).*

Encryption. Encryption is required for communication between stores in an enterprise and between the enterprise and the bank. Here, our focus is on the exchange between stores. The aspect in Fig. 4(b) specifies that any message sending product information between a store and an enterprise role should be routed through encryption roles. The notation is the same as for Fig. 4(a). In addition, standard template mechanisms are used to templatize the aspect. Two concrete aspect instances are described, covering communication going to *and* from the enterprise. As mentioned earlier, however, the infrastucture cannot be allowed to access plain-text message contents, and to prevent this, the composition contract requires that encryption/decryption is taken care of by the endpoints rather than the infrastructure. Therefore, the aspect will violate the contract policy, which prevents introduction of encryption.

The Implementation Code. We can now discuss how the terminology we just introduced is relevant for our CoCoME case study. We implemented the CoCoME system using an enterprise service bus (ESB) infrastructure, the Mule ESB [7]. ESBs support decomposition of system functionalities into services. Services are composed using a message-based communication infrastructure; advanced routing capabilities enable interception, modification, and rerouting of messages. By utilizing Mule, our implementation of CoCoME decouples the main application business logic from the implementation of cross-cutting concerns. It delegates concerns such as encryption, failure management, and auditing to the interception and routing layer of Mule.

From a coding point of view, we use aspects for capturing concerns and separating them into aspect modules. We implement them using the Spring AOP framework. The aspects are implemented as state machines, which are derived from sequence diagrams that model the interactions we want to advise. When the state machine reaches a state matching a pointcut, the advice prescribed by the aspect is executed. Our code is then the implementation of a sequence diagram aspect, which is applied to the normal application message flow without cross-cutting concerns. The implementation of the aspect generation is based on the work on mapping MSC semantics to state machines in [9]. The details of the mapping from sequence diagram aspect to implementation are given in [10].

Contracts for aspect composition play a key role in systems such as our CoCoME implementation. In fact, since ESBs empower developers to arbitrarily change the message flow of a service interaction, unmanaged changes to the basic services of the application can jeopardize the functionality of the whole program. This is especially true in the context of service oriented architectures (SOAs). In fact, SOAs aim at decoupling service definitions from implementations. Service instances are expected to be replaceable by other implementations of the same service during the lifetime of the application. Contracts help in defining a clear interface against which aspects can be applied. This interface is separated from all the interfaces of the services that compose the system. Thus, contracts give system architects an opportunity to impose restrictions on which details of the service integration are accessible to cross-cutting concerns implementations. Contracts enable the creation of architectures that are open to future modifications and still can utilize the power of ESBs.

3 Specifying and Checking Composition Contracts

We extend model-based aspect composition by introducing *composition contracts*. Such contracts extend the definition of base models and specify which parts of the base model can be queried and modified by a composition/aspect using constraints. A contract is, therefore, an interface of the base model that governs its accessibility via compositions/aspects. A contract shields the base models features from unwanted external modifications. We use OCL with extensions to specify access constraints.

We use the term *query* to denote *pointcuts* that access model join points, and the term *modifier* to denote *advice* that modifies a model in the context of a query. We call the mechanism that performs composition of an aspect a *composition system*. A join point is any element, or set of elements, that can be queried within the (domain) model at hand. For instance, if our modeling language is UML sequence diagrams (as in this paper), our join points can be interaction fragments, messages, and lifelines. The actual set of join points is determined by the composition system; for example, if our composition system is AspectJ, the join points are all observable calls or executions. In our context, we also consider static features to be join points, for example, the attributes declared for a class. A *contract-aware* composition system checks and adheres to base model composition contracts.

The *contract checking process* has two phases: (1) the pre-composition checking, which compares the access required by a composition model (aspect) with the access provided by the base model contract, and (2) the post-composition checking, which compares a resulting composition with contract post-conditions. Any violation of the contract found during pre-composition checking should result in prevention or abortion of the composition process. Any post-condition violations should result in a rollback of the composition. If the contract is respected in both phases, the composed model should be kept.

3.1 Composition Contracts Concepts

A composition contract is defined by a meta-model, which is populated with elements that refer to and constrain elements in a base model. The full details of the meta-model go beyond the scope of this paper; instead, we describe the essential concepts in a composition contract, as illustrated in Fig. 5.

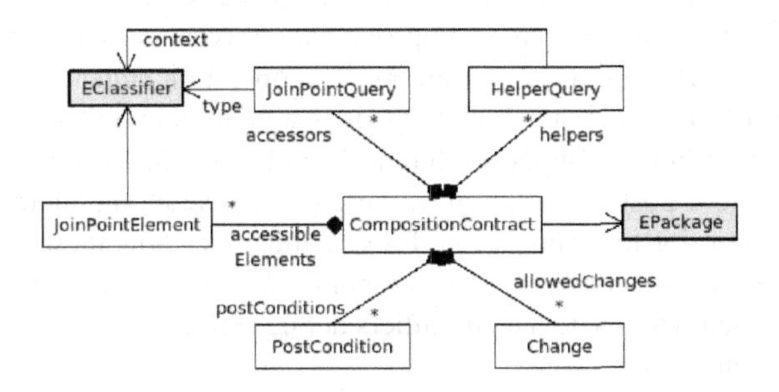

Fig. 5. Contract Concepts

A *CompositionContract* references the base model to which it applies. The *accessibleElements* define the type of elements a composition may access by linking to base model elements. *JoinPointQueries* define accessors for the base model with OCL constraints related to base model types. These may for instance express that *'only messages that are public can be queried'*. The set of join point queries represent a *'query interface'* offered by the base model, which restricts the eligibility of queries to access the base model. The *allowedChanges* are used to specify legal modifications (changes) in the context of allowed queries. They define which features an aspect is allowed to perform changes on, and the nature of those changes. Types of modifiers are *'introduction'*, *'removal'*, and *'modification'*, which allow introduction of elements for a feature, removal of elements for a feature, and any change to a feature, respectively. For example, a composition may only be allowed to modify the *'arguments'* feature of queried messages. Contract post-conditions specify invariant constraints on the composition result using OCL. A post-condition may, for instance, specify that *'all messages that were in the original base model should be present in the composition.'*. Finally, helper queries allow the definition of named OCL queries that can be used within other OCL expressions, within join point queries, and post-conditions.

3.2 Textual Contract Language

A contract is an instance of the meta-model conceptualized by Fig. 5, which can be expressed in terms of textual syntax or populated in graphical editors. We have defined a textual syntax, which provides a declarative way of defining the contract. Prog. 1 illustrates a simple contract associated with a UML Interaction (sequence diagram).

This contract allows querying messages of interactions where the sender role type is 'Store', the receiver role type is 'Enterprise', and the message name matches any string (using Java-style regular expressions - '.*'). The *modifiers* allow arguments of queried messages to be modified (i.e., arguments can be added, removed, or modified). They also allow lifelines to be *introduced* to interactions. The *helper queries sendRole* and *receiveRole* return the sending and receiving lifelines associated with a message, and the *type()* returns the type name associated with a lifeline. The first *post-condition* specifies that the number of fragments (events) on a lifeline must be preserved by a composition. The second one specifies that *encryption* cannot be introduced by a composition, in accordance with the infrastructure policy.

All constraints in a contract are specified using Object Constraint Language (OCL). We have defined OCL extensions to improve expressiveness of matching in queries and to support *pre-values* in post-conditions. The operation *matches('')* is introduced to support regular expression matching for strings within join point queries. The operation *preval()* is introduced to support references to object values prior to a composition in post-conditions. A post-condition may, therefore, constrain the model state relative to the model state prior to composition. Prog. 1 illustrates how these additional OCL operations are used. The constraints in join point queries, post-conditions, and helper queries are specified with OCL. The modifiers define feature constraints by referencing features of its context type.

Prog. 1. Contract Example

```
context uml="http://www.eclipse.org/uml2/2.1.0/UML";
contract InteractionContractCoCoME {
  elements Interaction, Lifeline, Message;
  accessor Message[*] msgs : self.sendRole().type().matches('Store')
        and self.receiveRole().type()='Enterprise' and
        self.name.matches('.*');
  accessor Interaction[*] interactions: true;
  modification msgs::validMod2() {feature argument;}
  introduction interactions::newlifelines() {feature lifeline;}
  query Message::sendRole() : self.sendEvent.oclAsType(Message
        OccurrenceSpecification).covered->asOrderedSet()->first();
  query Message::receiveRole() : self.receiveEvent.oclAsType(
         MessageOccurrenceSpecification).covered->asOrderedSet()->first();
  query String Lifeline::type() : self.represents.type.name;
  /**** Post-cond: each lifeline should have the same number of fragments ****/
  context Lifeline post: self.preval() <> null implies self.coveredBy->size()
    = self.preval().oclAsType(Lifeline).coveredBy->size();
  /**** Post-cond: Encryption cannot be introduced ****/
  context Lifeline post: self.type()='Encryption' implies self.preval() <> null;
}
```

3.3 Checking and Enforcing Contracts

The purpose of a composition contract is to make composition less prone to semantic errors and to prevent illegal modifications to occur. As mentioned, the contract must be checked in two separate steps, pre- and post-composition checking.

The constraints on element access, join point queries, and modifications can all be checked *before* a composition takes place. This puts certain requirements on the composition system itself, which must be *contract-enabled*. By this, we mean that it must be able to either (1) export the set of queries and modifiers defined by a composition specification (i.e., aspect), or (2) itself be able to read associated base model contracts *and comply to them*. In the following, we assume scenario (1). We call an exported set of queries and modifiers the *assumption contract*. It is represented in the same language as the contract itself, but only specifies the *actual join point queries* and *modifiers* imposed by the aspect. An assumption contract corresponding to the SD aspect from Fig. 4(a) is shown in Prog. 2.

Prog. 2. The Assumption Contract Exported from the Interception Aspect

```
context uml="http://www.eclipse.org/uml2/2.1.0/UML";
contract SdAspectJoinPoints {
  elements Interaction, Lifeline, Message;
  accessor Message[*] messages : self.sendRole()type().name='Store' and
     self.receiveRole().type().name='Enterprise' and
     self.name='.*' and self.hasArgType('Product');
  accessor Interaction[*] interaction: true;
  modification messages::msgmods() {feature argument}
  introduction interaction::intmods() {feature lifeline, messages;}
  query Message::hasArgType(s String) : self.argument->exists(iv2:
     ValueSpecification | iv2.oclIsTypeOf(InstanceValue) and iv2.oclAsType(
     InstanceValue).instance.classifier->exists(c|c.name=s);
}
```

We currently check the assumption contract in two separate activities. The first performs a partial analysis of the expression tree and attempts to determine whether the *assumption contract expressions* are valid *sub expressions* of the *contract*, meaning that the queries should always return subsets of the contract query values. This analysis is, however, limited to expressions without complex operators such as iterators, existence, or type checking. Property references (in OCL, *PropertyCallExp*) are compared by syntactic equality. Operations such as '=' are evaluated by checking equality of each operand. Logical operators *(and, or, not)* are checked by analyzing their operands and evaluating the coherence with the contract expressions. For example, the expression α *or* β in the assumption contract is *not* valid for the contract query α *or* γ, for $\gamma \neq \beta$, while the expression α *and* β *is* valid. Binary Decision Diagrams (BDD) [11] could have been used to represent and compare these expressions; the BDD of the assumption contract should *never* yield a boolean true/1 value result where the contract yields a false/0 value. We have, however, not studied the mapping and solving of OCL expressions by SAT solvers here; this problem has been addressed by others (e.g., in [12]).

The analysis can determine contract adherence if the queries in the contract specification are *not* using complex OCL operations. If this is not case, the analysis returns with an uncertainty value (*maybe*). The assumption contract can then be checked by a second activity, *query execution*. The queries associated with the assumption contract are evaluated on the base model and compared with a base model evaluation. To comply, the object set in evaluation resulting from the assumption contract queries should be a subset of those from the contract evaluation. If it is not a subset, the contract is violated. If it is a subset, the assumption contract is valid for this particular base model; it may, however, not be generally valid for other base models.

If the pre-composition checking is successful and the contract is not violated, the composition process can commence. The contract may express post-conditions that constrain the *result* of the composition. These constraints are like ordinary OCL invariants for the base model, with the exception of using *preval()* to reference base model state *prior to* composition. This again puts requirements on the composition system; it must produce a trace map between elements of the newly composed model to the original base model. These links are used to evaluate OCL expressions containing the *preval()* operation. The contract in Prog. 1 shows an example of a post-condition. If post-composition checking fails, the composition-system should rollback the composition performed on the base model, and let the base model return to its original state.

3.4 Contract Example for the CoCoME Case Study

Prog. 3 shows a contract related to the message filtering concern. (This contract also contains the queries, modifiers, and post-conditions from Prog. 1, but these are omitted here for brevity, as are the details of some of the queries.) The example illustrates queries related to the types of object arguments being passed in sequence diagrams. In addition to Prog. 1, there is one post-condition: all messages to/from lifelines in the composition must be refinements of messages to/from the corresponding (preval) base model lifeline. Refinement in this context is defined by the contract as equality of message names and type compatibility of instance value arguments being sent in messages.

Prog. 3. CoCoME Contract Allowing Only Argument Refinement and new Lifelines in Sequence Diagrams

```
context uml="http://www.eclipse.org/uml2/2.1.0/UML";
contract MessageDataRefinementPolicy {
  query Message::refinementOf (m2 Message) : (self.name=m2.name) and (m2.argument
    ->isEmpty() and self.argument->isEmpty()) or (m2.argument->notEmpty() implies
    m2.argument->forAll(iv:ValueSpecification | iv.oclIsTypeOf(InstanceValue)
    implies self.argument->exists(iv2:ValueSpecification | iv2.oclIsTypeOf(
    InstanceValue) and iv2.oclAsType(InstanceValue).refinementOf(
    iv.oclAsType(InstanceValue)))));
  query InstanceValue::refinementOf (iv2 InstanceValue) : ..................
  query InstanceSpecification::refinementOf (is InstanceSpecification) : ....
  query Class::refinementOfClass (cl Class) : ............................
  context Message post: let m:Message=self, life:Lifeline=self.receiveRole() in
    life.preval() <> null implies life.preval().oclAsType(Lifeline).
    coveredBy->exists(prefrag:InteractionFragment | prefrag.oclIsKindOf(
    MessageOccurrenceSpecification) and m.refinementOf(prefrag.oclAsType(
    MessageOccurrenceSpecification).message));
}
```

As this contract addresses quite complex relationships of the UML model, the constraints become elaborate. Hence, good tool support, and knowledge of OCL and the domain meta-model are important to provide efficient support for contract specifiers. The same, however, is true for general OCL constraint authoring. The contract in Prog. 3 will invalidate any composition that modifies a message argument to an illegal type. In this example, we use the instance values in the message argument as basis for defining message refinement. An aspect that tries to modify a message with missing or incompatible instance values will not be accepted by the composition checker.

4 Evaluation

Implementation. We have implemented a prototype to support our composition contract approach. It provides an editor and parser for the contract language. The parser generates an EMF (Eclipse Modeling Framework) model instance of the contract. Standard OCL support is provided by the EMF OCL and Query frameworks, which we have extended to support the *regexp matching* and the *preval* operations. Contract helper queries are added to the OCL environment during contract parsing, and can therefore be used by the join point queries and post-conditions.

The prototype implements the contract checking process as illustrated in Fig. 1. Both query analysis and query execution testing have been implemented and tested against the case study models. The post checking implementation checks invariants for the composed model. This process relies on element trace links from the composed model to the original base model being provided in order to implement the *preval* operation. We have currently tested our tool on UML Sequence Diagram Aspects, where trace links are set up between lifelines in the composition and the base model. The approach, however, is general, and can be used for contract specification and checking for all EMF-based modeling languages. Important examples of such languages are UML and extensions obtained by means of new profiles.

Applying Contracts. A contract may reduce potential errors in the composition process and increase system consistency. This may apply both to the system model *and* the system implementation. In our ESB implementation of the CoCoME system, the model-level contracts have a direct relation to the system through the mapping of the aspects. The contracts could, therefore, potentially also be reflected in the implemented system (e.g., for providing run-time checking of contract constraints). This is, however, subject to future investigations.

In the case of composition at the model level, the contract pre-conditions specify assumptions on the part of the aspects, which is analyzed by the *pre-checking* activity. We evaluated our approach using the aspect examples shown in Fig. 4. Each of these represents an assumption contract, one of which was shown in Prog. 2. The checking of these contracts proceeds as follows:

- The assumption contract for the interceptor (Prog. 2) is accepted by the contract pre-checking.
- For the encryption concern(s), there will be two assumption contracts – one for each binding of the templates. One of these is not accepted by the contract checking, since its queries for message sender and receiver are *not* matched by the contract.

The contract post-conditions in our example were tested using our tool on the compositions resulting from applying our aspects on the *productExchange* and other interactions in the case study. Any composition that adds messages to lifelines from the original base model will break the contract if they are not refinements of a corresponding base model message. A slightly modified interceptor aspect that modifies instance value message arguments to non-compatible (non-refinement) values, will violate the contract post-condition. The encryption aspect violates the post-condition, as it introduces an illegal Lifeline (Encryption) in the interaction.

5 Discussion

The contracts we have introduced specify which parts of the base model are exposed for composition with aspects. In particular, contracts restrict the changes that aspects can perform on base model elements. A complementary approach would be to enable the definition of contracts for aspects. Aspect contracts would define which elements a base model must expose and the type of changes an aspect can impose on such elements. This would be equivalent to the assumption contract, which can be derived from an aspect.

The contract post-conditions specify invariants for the composed model. We are currently exploring the extension of contracts with invariants also for the base models. This will make the interface toward the base models even clearer, since it provides guarantees with respect to base model properties. This can simplify the creation of contracts, since we can rely on compliance with the invariants when specifying queries. For the base modeler, defining invariants is a natural activity, whereas reasoning about accessibility of meta-model elements may be more challenging. Moreover, invariants can potentially improve the base model quality; even without being composed with an aspect, the base model should comply with its invariants. On the other hand, the weaving process becomes more challenging because the weaver must prove that applying an aspect will not break the invariants. However, they may, similar to post-conditions, be evaluated after the composition has been done. Decidability and complexity analysis of verifying such invariants *prior* to composition are left as future work.

Our approach extends the standard aspect weaving process with two additional steps. First, before applying an aspect, our contract checker verifies that the pointcut does not select any join point forbidden by the contract. Then, it verifies that all advices modify the model only according to the contract rules. In case one of those two conditions is not fulfilled: the weaving process fails, the aspect is not applied, and the base model is not modified. Letting the weaving process fail, however, is not the only reasonable solution. We could choose at least two other approaches. First, we could try to apply the aspect only partially. To this end, we can include in the pointcut selection only the join points that are visible according to the contract. This approach would extend the applicability of aspects, but it would reduce the guarantees they can provide. Second, we could eliminate from the system the base models whose contracts are violated by some aspect. This second approach is a good candidate for federated systems, where aspects define system policies. In this scenario, when a base model contract conflicts with an aspect, the service it defines is not able to cope with the infrastructure requirements; therefore, it cannot be run.

OCL is a general constraint language, and constraints may become complex to write and understand. The complexity of the meta-model is an important contributing factor to this complexity. Simpler meta-models can help simplify contracts. In the case of UML sequence diagrams, this can be done by creating a simplified sequence diagram meta-model and an automated mapping to this meta-model. The contract may then be authored against the simplified meta-model. The downside is the added workload of creating the simplified meta-model *and* the transformation to that meta-model. The upside is simplified contract authoring. As a proof of concept, we rewrote our contract example for a highly simplified interaction meta-model. It saved about 40 percent in terms of contract length (number of characters). This, of course, is not a statement about the comprehension complexity of the resulting contract per se.

The contracts control the eligibility for composition, thus protecting the base model from undesired changes. The contracts do not, however, prevent aspects from interfering with each other. The aspects in our example will interfere with each other, since they query and modify overlapping parts of the base model. By comparing the assumption contracts, we may be able to detect these interferences and take them into account when applying the aspects, or consider a redesign of the aspects. However, the composition contracts currently do not address this problem explicitly.

6 Related Work

Composition contracts for aspects provide means for controlling how join points of base models are exposed to aspects. The same issue has been tackled by Griswold et. al., in the context of programming-level aspects, using crosscutting programming interfaces (XPIs) [13]. XPIs provide a way of insulating aspects from implementation details *and* exposing only the desired behaviors. This approach enables specifying invariants, and supports checking and reporting any violation. While XPIs are defined using AspectJ, the same approach can support other technologies as well. One drawback of XPIs is that they may require redesigning the base model. Moreover, they rely on object-oriented interfaces, which are not directly applicable to our modeling context. Our approach is inspired by this work; we define an interface (the contract) that limits the access to the internals of a base model as well. However, we take advantage of meta-models to define contracts that are not dependent on a specific modeling language. Contracts can, therefore, base their rules on elements coming from different models, even those expressed using different modeling languages. For example, we can base a contract for a sequence diagram on deployment information defined in a deployment model.

In [14], Ossher describes a hiding mechanism that requires a base program to explicitly *confirm* or *deny* pointcuts that aspects can use in advising it. In addition, the decision can be based on organizational roles and responsibilities (e.g., any aspect defined by a particular organization is *confirmed*). The concept of confirmed roles and organizations, currently not supported by our contracts, could be a useful extension in a future version of our language. In our context, to implement this feature we must relate organizational models to implementation models. Dantas and Walker [15] define *harmless advices* aspects that do not influence the final result produced by the base program. In our context, given that base models can be defined in multiple languages, identifying harmless advices is not easy. To support multiple modeling languages, we define contracts based on a meta-model common to the different languages. Unfortunately, such meta-models do not encode enough execution information to define what "harmless" means. Klaeren et. al. [16] define an aspect composition and validation mechanism based on assertions. Their composition approach uses a *knowledge base* of valid aspect configurations to specify, for each class, which aspects are valid. In particular, it supports specifying valid configurations of several aspects. A similar knowledge base could complement our finer-grained approach, where we do not consider interactions of multiple aspects.

7 Summary and Conclusion

We have described an approach for specifying, checking, and enforcing model composition contracts. Composition contracts constrain both the *pointcuts* and *advices* that can be applied to a base model. Constraints are defined using an extended Object Constraint Language supporting *quantification* and *pre-value* references in post-conditions. We showed by examples from our case study how authoring of contracts and the details of the contract checking process work, specifically for behaviors described by sequence diagrams. We developed a prototype supporting specification and checking of contracts for general EMF models.

Future work will address further the mapping of the contracts to implementation level and how to validate the contracts at the code-level. Also, improvements to our tools to support more expressive contracts (e.g., by allowing base model invariants also offer excellent opportunities for further research). Increasing the usability of contract specifications by looking at increased integration with modeling environments and graphical notations will enhance the utility of the overall approach for practical applications even further.

Acknowledgments

This work has been done in the context of the SWAT project (Semantics-preserving Weaving - Advancing the Technology), funded by the Norwegian Research Council (project number 167172/V30). Our work was also supported by NSF grant CCF-07027 91, as well as by funds from the California Institute for Telecommunications and Information Technology (Calit2). We thank Barry Demchak for his insightful comments on this manuscript.

References

1. Kiczales, G., Lamping, J., Mendhekar, A., Maeda, C., Lopes, C., Loingtier, J.M., Irwin, J.: Aspect-Oriented Programming. In: Aksit, M., Matsuoka, S. (eds.) ECOOP 1997. LNCS, vol. 1241, pp. 220–242. Springer, Heidelberg (1997)
2. Clarke, S., Walker, R.J.: Composition Patterns: An Approach to Designing Reusable Aspects. In: International Conference of Software Engineering (ICSE), pp. 5–14. IEEE Computer Society, Los Alamitos (2001)
3. Kiczales, G., Hilsdale, E., Hugunin, J., Kersten, M., Palm, J., Griswold, W.G.: An Overview of AspectJ. In: Knudsen, J.L. (ed.) ECOOP 2001. LNCS, vol. 2072, pp. 327–353. Springer, Heidelberg (2001)
4. Filman, R., Friedman, D.: Aspect-Oriented Programming is Quantification and Obliviousnessm. In: Workshop on Advanced Separation of Concerns, OOPSLA 2000. Technical Report 01.12, RIACS (2001)
5. Meyer, B.: Applying "Design by Contract". IEEE Computer 25(10), 40–51 (1992)
6. Demchak, B., Ermagan, V., Farcas, E., Huang, T., Krüger, I., Menarini, M.: A Rich Services Approach to CoCoME. In: Rausch, A., Reussner, R., Mirandola, R., Plasil, F. (eds.) The Common Component Modeling Example. LNCS, vol. 5153, pp. 85–115. Springer, Heidelberg (2008)
7. mulesource.org: Mule - Open Source ESB (2009), `http://www.mulesource.org`
8. Oldevik, J., Haugen, O.: From Sequence Diagrams to Java-Stairs Aspects. In: Proc. of the 8th ACM Int. Conf. on Aspect-Oriented Software Development, pp. 99–110 (2009)
9. Krüger, I.H.: Distributed System Design with Message Sequence Charts. PhD thesis, Technischen Universität München (2000)
10. Krüger, I.H., Meisinger, M., Menarini, M.: Runtime Verification of Interactions: From MSCs to Aspects. In: Sokolsky, O., Taşıran, S. (eds.) RV 2007. LNCS, vol. 4839, pp. 63–74. Springer, Heidelberg (2007)
11. Akers, S.B.: Binary Decision Diagrams. IEEE Trans. of Comp. 27(6), 509–516 (1978)
12. Czarnecki, K., Pietroszek, K.: Verifying Feature-based Model Templates Against Wellformedness OCL Constraints. In: Proceedings of the 5th International Conference on Generative Programming and Component Engineering (GPCE 2006), pp. 211–220 (2006)
13. Griswold, W.G., Sullivan, K., Song, Y., Shonle, M., Tewari, N., Cai, Y., Rajan, H.: Modular Software Design with Crosscutting Interfaces. IEEE Software 23(1), 51–60 (2006)
14. Ossher, H.: Confirmed Join Points. In: AOSD Workshop on Software Engineering Properties of Languages and Aspect Technologies, SPLAT (2006)
15. Dantas, D.S., Walker, D.: Harmless Advice. In: 33rd ACM SIGPLAN-SIGACT Symposium on Principles of Programming Languages (POPL 2006), New York, USA, pp. 383–396 (2006)
16. Klaeren, H., Pulvermueller, E., Rashid, A., Speck, A.: Aspect Composition Applying the Design by Contract Principle. In: GCSE 2000: Proceedings of the Second International Symposium on Generative and Component-Based Software Engineering, London, UK, pp. 57–69. Springer, Heidelberg (2001)

Abstracting Complex Languages through Transformation and Composition*

Jendrik Johannes[1], Steffen Zschaler[2], Miguel A. Fernández[3], Antonio Castillo[3], Dimitrios S. Kolovos[4], and Richard F. Paige[4]

[1] Technische Universität Dresden
jendrik.johannes@tu-dresden.de
[2] Computing Department, Lancaster University
szschaler@acm.org
[3] Telefónica Research & Development
mafg@tid.es, acastillo@polar.es
[4] Department of Computer Science, University of York
{dkolovos,paige}@cs.york.ac.uk

Abstract. Domain-specific languages (DSLs) can simplify the development of complex software systems by providing domain-specific abstractions. However, the complexity of some domains has led to a number of DSLs that are themselves complex, limiting the original benefits of using DSLs. We show how to develop DSLs as abstractions of other DSLs by transfering translational approaches for textual DSLs into the domain of modelling languages. We argue that existing model transformation languages are at too low a level of abstraction for succinctly expressing transformations between abstract and concrete DSLs. Patterns identified in such model transformations can be used to raise the level of abstraction. We show how we can allow part of the transformation to be expressed using the concrete syntax of the concrete DSL.

1 Introduction

Domain-specific languages (DSLs) [1] are used to reduce the complexity arising when developing software systems using general-purpose languages (GPLs). A DSL contains a relatively small number of constructs that are immediately identifiable to domain experts and allow modellers to construct concise models capturing the design of the system at an appropriate level of abstraction. While DSLs typically start off with a small number of constructs, they tend to grow over time: as they are used, new concepts, features and relationships are identified and are subsequently added to the DSL—making it more flexible within a wider domain. This flexibility introduces accidental complexity as modellers need to make decisions about using each feature. This can eventually compromise the very aims for which the DSL was built: domain focus and conciseness.

* This research has been co-funded by the European Commission within the FP6 projects MODELPLEX (contract no. 34081) and AMPLE (contract no. 33710).

A. Schürr and B. Selic (Eds.): MODELS 2009, LNCS 5795, pp. 546–550, 2009.

However, the additional concepts and features have been added for specific purposes and cannot be simply dismissed; the complexity of the DSL is intentional. One example of such a complex DSL is the Common Information Model (CIM) [2] DSL for network configuration. While CIM is a DSL, its size in terms of the number of concepts and features it contains has progressively become comparable to that of a GPL such as the UML. Many of the internal details of devices in a network configuration, however, are quite irrelevant when we try to model and understand the configuration as a whole. Still, these details are very much relevant when the configuration is to be implemented or manipulated.

This paper is about how we can efficiently develop layers of DSLs; that is, new DSLs that provide abstractions of the concepts in existing DSLs. Such abstractions also may help to obtain models with desirable properties, e.g., models that can be more easily navigated for transformation purposes. The abstractions can also support ensuring the correctness of the models by construction instead of relying solely on post-construction verification, by allowing only particular combinations of model elements to be used.

The main contribution of this paper is the presentation of a generic translational approach for abstract DSLs, based on the identification of patterns in model transformations. The approach works for all situations where each concept in the abstract DSL can be translated into a partial model in a concrete DSL. Complete models in an abstract DSL are then translated into compositions of partial models in the concrete DSL. The approach has been implemented prototypically using existing model transformation and composition technologies. Due to space restrictions, we cannot give more than a general overview. Readers interested in a more detailed discussion are referred to [3].

An obvious solution to the problem of building layers of DSLs is to design a more *abstract* DSL using a standard modelling framework (e.g. EMF) and then to use a model-to-model (M2M) transformation language such as QVT, ATL or ETL to transform models expressed in the *abstract* DSL, into models that conform to the *concrete* DSL. The main advantage of this approach is that it is based on robust and well-understood technologies. Nevertheless, having written several such abstract DSLs and transformations we have also identified several shortcomings. First, the produced transformations are very much alike and demonstrate several recurring patterns which need to be implemented from scratch every time. Moreover, as single elements in models expressed in the *abstract* DSL typically correspond to fragments consisting of several elements in the target models that conform to the *concrete* DSL, constructing such fragments needs to be done programmatically in the context of the M2M transformation—which we have found to be counter-intuitive and error-prone.

If creating an abstract DSL from a more concrete one was a one-off, building new tool support for automating it would most likely be unreasonable. From our experience in providing tool-support for DSLs for industrial partners in the ModelPlex EU project, this appears to be a recurring pattern. To address the aforementioned shortcomings in a systematic way, a mechanism is needed which allows developers to abstract from the commonalities of these concrete-to-abstract DSL mappings and specify the mapping logic in a high level declarative formalism that provides first-class support for recurring patterns.

2 Language Mapping Patterns

We have identified the following recurring patterns in the relationship between abstract DSL model elements and concrete DSL model elements:

1. *Element Mapping.* This pattern embodies the fundamental form of abstraction in our scenario: the representation of a recurrent configuration of concrete DSL model elements by a single model element in the abstract DSL.
2. *Element Mapping with Variability.* This pattern maps an abstract DSL model element to a network of model elements of the concrete DSL. The model elements in the network and their connections are selected based on the value(s) of one or more attributes of the abstract DSL model element.
3. *Attribute Mapping.* This pattern maps the value of an attribute of an abstract DSL model element to the value(s) of one or more attributes of concrete DSL model element(s). This mapping pattern is essential because, unlike the two patterns discussed above, it allows concrete data values to be passed from the abstract DSL model into the concrete DSL model.
4. *Link Mapping.* This pattern maps a link between two abstract DSL model elements to one or more links between concrete DSL model elements. This pattern is essential to translate relationships between elements in an abstract DSL model into relationships in a concrete DSL model.

To make transformations easier to understand and write, it would be useful to make explicit the use of each mapping pattern. That is, rather than manually writing the complete transformation, one could, for example, annotate the abstract DSL metamodel with appropriate mapping patterns and generate the transformation from these annotations in an automated manner. Generating the transformation has the added benefit that each pattern can be implemented consistently wherever it is instantiated.

By modelling the concrete-DSML configurations as separate model fragments and referencing these fragments from the pattern annotations, we can further improve our specifications. This avoids cluttered specifications, allows the use of concrete-DSML editors for defining large parts of the transformation, and can remove scattering and tangling from the transformation specification [3].

3 Implementation

Here, we present a prototypical implementation of our approach, based on the Reuseware Composition Framework [4] as well as the Epsilon Transformation Language (ETL) [5] and the Epsilon Generation Language (EGL) [6]. Figure 1 gives an overview of the prototype and the process of using it. Most of the steps presented are automatic, artefacts that need to be provided to the prototype have been highlighted in grey in the figure. There are two phases to using the

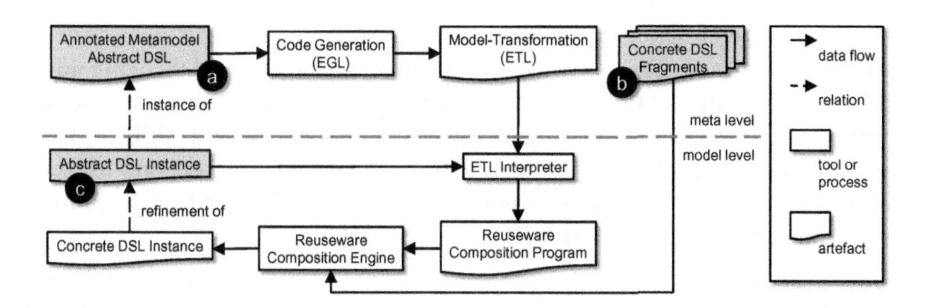

Fig. 1. Overview of the architecture of our prototypical implementation

prototype: The first phase (named 'meta level' in Fig. 1) comprises the design of the abstract DSL, while the second phase (named 'model level' in Fig. 1) starts when the abstract DSL is used.

To define a new abstract DSL, language designers need to provide two artefacts: 1) a metamodel of the abstract DSL (labelled 'a' in Fig. 1), annotated to define the transformation to the concrete DSL, and 2) a set of partial models (labelled 'b' in Fig. 1) that will be mapped to by this model transformation. Partial models are represented in our prototype through the notion of 'Model Fragments' defined in Reuseware. Among other things, developers can assign a *Unique Fragment Identifier (UFI)* to each model fragment. Reuseware then provides an API to obtain a model fragment by its UFI. These UFIs can be used in the metamodel annotations to uniquely refer to a fragment to map to.

From an annotated metamodel, our prototype then generates a model transformation program in ETL. The code generator that creates this model transformation is written in EGL and contains the definitions of the four patterns identified in Sect. 2. The generated ETL model transformation expects an instance of the abstract DSL metamodel and transforms this into a composition of the appropriate model fragments.

Reuseware provides a so-called *composition interface* for each fragment. This interface contains two types of named points: *reference points* and *variation points*. The former allow to extract a partial model from a complete model, while the latter define points in a partial model that can be modified from the outside. The actual inner structure of the fragment is hidden behind its composition interface: which model elements a certain point maps to and whether it maps to one or more model elements is completely transparent to the user of the fragment. Names of points can be used for reference, e.g., from other patterns.

Fragments are composed by replacing a variation point in one fragment with the contents of a reference point in another fragment (i.e., with a partial model). Reuseware will ensure that such compositions always result in syntactically correct models. Compositions of fragments are expressed in *composition programs*. In addition to composition links, a composition program may also include *settings* through which attributes of elements of a model fragments can be set directly (by providing a primitive value rather than other model fragments). The model transformation generated by our prototype (cf. Fig. 1) produces a composition program for each instance of the abstract DSL metamodel.

Once these preparations have been completed, we can begin using our new abstract DSL. Editors for creating instances of the abstract DSL can, for example, be built using EuGENia [7], which uses an approach similarly based on annotations of the metamodel to generate graphical editors for DSLs. Once an instance of the abstract DSL is created (labelled 'c' in Fig. 1), our prototype transforms it into a Reuseware composition program, which is then executed to produce the corresponding model in the concrete DSL.

4 Conclusions

We have presented a translational approach for defining abstract languages based on more concrete languages. In contrast to an approach where a single monolithic model transformation is constructed from scratch, our approach provides the following benefits:

1. *Simplified construction of abstract languages:* details of the metamodel of the concrete DSML are encapsulated in annotations for the mapping patterns.
2. *Vertical separation of concerns in the model transformation.* The approach separates two concerns in the model transformation: 1) which configurations of concrete-language model elements represent a specific abstract-language model element, and 2) the mapping pattern to use when translating abstract-language model elements into concrete-language model elements.
3. *Use of concrete language tooling for the definition of concrete language configurations.* The approach allows the concrete-language model to be composed from partial template models, each of which can be created and manipulated using standard concrete-language tooling without any need to refer back to the concrete-language metamodel.

References

1. van Deursen, A., Klint, P., Visser, J.: Domain-specific languages: an annotated bibliography. SIGPLAN Not. 35(6), 26–36 (2000)
2. Distributed Management Task Force Inc. (DMTF): Common Information Model Standards (2008), `http://www.dmtf.org/standards/cim/` (Last visited 28/10/2008)
3. Johannes, J., Zschaler, S., Fernández, M.A., Castillo, A., Kolovos, D.S., Paige, R.F.: Abstracting complex languages through transformation and composition. Technical Report TUD-FI09-08 July 2009, Technische Universität Dresden (2009)
4. Heidenreich, F., Henriksson, J., Johannes, J., Zschaler, S.: On language-independent model modularisation. In: Katz, S., et al. (eds.) Transactions on AOSD VI. LNCS, vol. 5560, pp. 39–82. Springer, Heidelberg (2009)
5. Kolovos, D.S., Paige, R.F., Polack, F.A.: The Epsilon Transformation Language. In: Vallecillo, A., Gray, J., Pierantonio, A. (eds.) ICMT 2008. LNCS, vol. 5063, pp. 46–60. Springer, Heidelberg (2008)
6. Rose, L.M., Paige, R.F., Kolovos, D.S., Polack, F.A.C.: The Epsilon Generation Language (EGL). In: Schieferdecker, I., Hartman, A. (eds.) ECMDA-FA 2008. LNCS, vol. 5095, pp. 1–16. Springer, Heidelberg (2008)
7. Kolovos, D.S., Rose, L.M., Paige, R.F., Polack, F.A.C.: Raising the Level of Abstraction in the Development of GMF-based Graphical Model Editors. In: Proc. 3rd MISE Workshop of ICSE (2009)

An Approach for Evolving Transformation Chains*

Andrés Yie[1,2], Rubby Casallas[1], Dennis Wagelaar[2], and Dirk Deridder[2]

[1] Grupo de Construcción de Software, Universidad de los Andes, Colombia
{a-yie,rcasalla}@uniandes.edu.co

[2] Software Languages Lab, Vrije Universiteit Brussel, Belgium
{ayiegarz,dennis.wagelaar,dirk.deridder}@vub.ac.be

Abstract. A transformation chain (*TC*) generates applications from high-level models that are defined in terms of problem domain concepts. The result is a low-level model that is rooted in the solution domain. The evolution of a TC is a complex and expensive endeavor since there are intricate dependencies between all its constituent parts. More specific, an evolution problem arises when we need to add an unanticipated concern (e.g., security) that does not fit the expressiveness of the high-level metamodel, because such an addition forces us to adapt existing assets (i.e., metamodels, models, and transformations). We present a solution that adds a new concern model to the TC, in an independent way.

Keywords: Model Driven Engineering, Model transformation, Model composition.

1 Introduction

Model-Driven Engineering (*MDE*) implementations promote the use of models expressed in terms of problem domain concepts (e.g. Bank Account, Insurance Claim) as the prime artifact to develop software. These models, to which we refer as high-level models, are used as input for a transformation chain (*TC*). A TC is a sequence of transformation steps that converts the high-level model, which is rooted in the problem domain, into a low-level model, which is rooted in the solution domain. In addition to the translation from problem domain concepts to solution domain concepts (e.g., mapping a Business Entity onto a Java Class), the TC adds implementation details in every transformation step.

For high-level models, the metamodels are rooted in the problem domain. These metamodels define the abstract syntax of a domain-specific modeling language (*DSML*) that is suitable to be used by domain experts [1]. For the low-level models, the metamodels are rooted in the solution domain. These metamodels are typically closer to the definition of general-purpose languages (*GPLs*).

The particular problem we address is the addition of a new concern (e.g., security, monitoring, etc.) that was not anticipated in the existing MDE implementation. No real problem arises if the new concern can be cleanly expressed

* This research was performed in the context of the Caramelos project (VLIR), the VariBru project (ISRIB), and the MoVES project (IAP, Belgian Science Policy).

A. Schürr and B. Selic (Eds.): MODELS 2009, LNCS 5795, pp. 551–555, 2009.

using the existing high-level metamodel. However, if this is not the case, then a number of problems arise when trying to extend the existing high-level metamodel with new concepts (e.g., the notion of security in a business domain metamodel): 1) the existing metamodel will be polluted with concepts that do not belong to its main problem domain, 2) including all the new elements in the core application model produces a single monolithic model which is detrimental to the overall maintainability, and 3) the new concepts will impact the TC by imposing intricate changes (adding, updating or deleting TC elements) to its existing implementation, which increases the complexity and the number of dependencies within the TC. These problems make it hard to evolve an existing MDE implementation and to maintain applications.

To overcome these problems we propose a strategy that consists of specifying the new concern in a separate high-level model. This leaves the original model unaltered and oblivious of the added concern. The concern-specific model can thus be specified using concepts close to its domain which is expressed in a separate meta-model. Therefore, we have two high-level models that conform to two different metamodels. Consequently, to obtain the final application, it is necessary to compose both models. If we perform a high-level composition, then we face a *heterogeneous composition* because both models conform to two different metamodels (e.g., composition of a business entity from the business domain and a secured resource from the security domain). A heterogeneous composition is a complex task and requires a particular composition mechanism for every added concern. Therefore, we chose to align the high-level models using a *Correspondence Model* (CM) [2], which explicitly describes the relationships among the elements of different models. We use these correspondence relationships to identify the elements to compose.

We have developed a mechanism to automatically derive the CM through the various steps in the TC. The actual composition is postponed until the lowest level. At this level, every model conforms to the same metamodel (e,g,. Java metamodel), or to metamodels that are extensions of this metamodel. Having models that conform to the same low-level metamodel and a low-level CM relating these models allows us to perform a *homogeneous composition* (e.g., composition of two Classes). This reduces the complexity of the composition and it gives the means to use a single composition mechanism for multiple concerns. In our case study, we use a model composition strategy based on the *UML Package Merge* [3] mechanism that composes the low-level models into a single model that conforms to the existing low-level platform metamodel.

2 Approach Overview

The overall approach is to add a new TC next to the existing MDE implementation that takes a high-level concern-specific model as input and produces a low-level concern model as output. We align the new high-level model with the original one by using a *Correspondence Model* (CM), which needs to be propagated through the TC. The main challenge is to define a mechanism to automatically derive the new correspondence relationships, having in mind that the TC increments the complexity of the models by adding elements at each step. Once we reach the lowest level, the models conform to the same existing metamodel (e,g,. Java metamodel), or conform to an extension of it. Therefore, both TCs produce two complementary low-level models that can be composed using a common composition mechanism.

To derive a low-level CM it is necessary to trace back the elements of the low-level models and to check if they come from pairs of related elements in the high-level. With a trace model (TM) [4] we determine the elements in both low-level models that come from a couple of related elements in the high-level. For instance, an Attribute in the business model is transformed into an Attribute, a GetterMethod and a SetterMethod in the low-level model. In the security model a ResourceAttribute with a ReadPermission is transformed in a private Attribute and an annotated ReadMethod in the low-level security model. Therefore, it is necessary to trace back all these low-level elements and verify that the high-level source element (Attribute) from which they originate, is related with a correspondence relationship to the high-level concern-specific element (ResourceAttribute).

Once the elements in the low-level models that have a pair of correspondent elements as sources are determined, we have to relate these elements by identifying the correct match for each one. For instance, a GetterMethod (in the low-level application model) can be related to a ReadMethod (in the low-level security model) but not to a WriteMethod. To avoid, erroneous correspondences, the modeler has to specify some constraints. A constraint is a relationship between two metaclasses that defines if the correspondence link between the concepts that conform to them can be established or not. In our solution this set of constraints is called a Derivation Model (DM).

Figure 1 presents the general schema of our approach. The original TC is in the left (MM_{bus}, M_{bus}, MM_{java}, M_{java}, T_1)[1]. The new concern (e.g., security) TC is presented in the right (MM_{sec}, M_{sec}, $MM_{sec-java}$, $M_{sec-java}$, T_2). $CM_{high-level}$ is the high-level correspondence model that aligns the two high-level models. TM_A and TM_S are the trace models that relate the high-level models with the low-level models. The DM relates the low-level metamodels with constrains between their metaclasses. The DM is used to generate the transformation T_3, that uses the trace models and the $CM_{high-level}$ to generate the $CM_{low-level}$. Finally, the low-level models are composed and transformed into code by the original model-to-text transformation (G_1).

3 Derivation of Correspondence Model and Composition

The key element in our approach is the derivation of the low-level CM in order to perform an homogeneous composition which we will briefly detail below.

We align the two high-level models using the $CM_{high-level}$ which relates the elements to be composed. For example, the business model (M_{bus}) contains the

[1] MM = Metamodel, M = Model, T = Transformation chain.

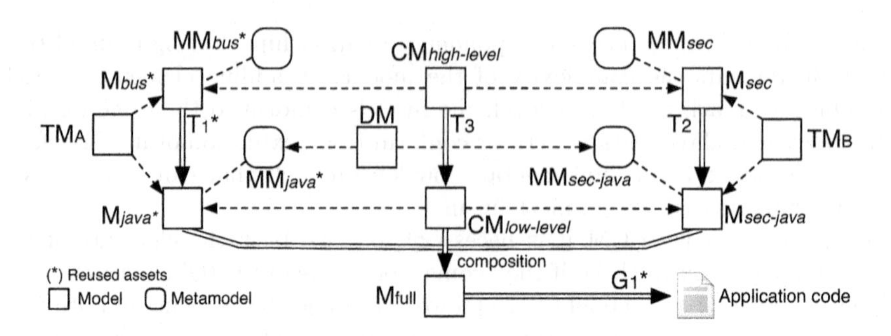

Fig. 1. General Schema

Attribute *dueDate* and the security model (M_{sec}) contains the Resource *date* that needs to be protected. These two elements are related by a correspondence relationship in $CM_{high-level}$. The modeler creates these correspondence links because he knows the meaning of the relationships between elements.

Low-level correspondence relationships are derived automatically by the transformation (T_3). For instance, two elements a' and b', from M_{java} and $M_{sec-java}$ models respectively, will have a correspondence relationship if: 1) There is a CM relationship at the higher level between a and b, where a' was produced from a by T_1, and b' was produced from b by T_2. 2) The metaclasses ma' and mb' where a' conforms to ma' and b' conforms to mb', allow for a correspondence relationship between their instances. Intuitively, the first condition establishes that elements a' and b' trace back to a pair of elements that have a high-level correspondence relationship between them. The second condition means that the metaclasses ma' and mb' are the same metaclass or extensions of the same one. Therefore, it is permitted to define correspondence links between their instances and finally to compose them. If both conditions are satisfied for an element a' and b', T_3 will produce a correspondence link between a' and b'.

In order to fulfill the first condition, we need *traceability*. For instance, when T_1 is applied to the Attribute *dueDate*, it is transformed into the Attribute *dueDate*, the GetterMethod *getDueDate* and the SetterMethod *setDueDate*. To make this information available to T_3, we generate trace links between target elements and source elements. The same happens in the T_2 side, T_3 needs to know if the ReadMethod traces back to a related Resource. Once T_1 and T_2 are executed, two tracing models are generated (TM_A and TM_S); with these links, T_3 can find the elements in both lower-level models that trace back to the pair of related elements in both higher-level models.

To fulfill the second condition, the modeler has to define a Derivation Model (DM) to make explicit if the instances of two metaclasses can be related by a correspondence link. Furthermore, the modeler has to decide constraints stating if a couple of metaclasses can be composed. We have defined different types of constraints in the Derivation Metamodel. These types are: *Inheritable constraint* (to allow submetaclasss), *Final constraint* (to reject submetaclasses), *Incompatible constraint* (to explicitly reject two metaclasses), and *Composition constraint* (to allow composites). Due to space restrictions the details of the semantics of these constraints are out of the scope of this paper.

To generate the CM Transformation (T_3), the DM is processed by a High Order Transformation (HOT). This HOT analyzes the constraints in the DM and generates the CM transformation T_3. Therefore, it is not necessary to develop a new transformation for every pair of metamodels. The developer only requires defining the constraints between them.

The final step is the composition of both low-level models, which uses the generated $CM_{low-level}$. This CM model has the information of *what* will be composed. For instance, Classes in the application low-level model M_{java} will be composed with the annotated Classes in the security low-level model $M_{sec-java}$, the Attributes in M_{java} with the private Attributes in $M_{sec-java}$, and the Methods in M_{java} with the annotated methods in $M_{sec-java}$. By using the correspondence links every pair of elements to be composed is identified. We use a mechanism based on the *UML Package Merge* [3] to preform the composition.

4 Conclusions

Our approach facilitates the modeling of multiple concerns in separated models each one close to the problem domain. The different concern models are aligned using a CM, which explicitly capture the overlapping and dependencies among their elements. Our approach offers an automatic derivation mechanism to maintain both models aligned from the high-level until the lowest level through the TC. This is one factor that differentiates our approach from others approaches where the correspondence relationships are only defined as an input, but not maintained during the TC. As a result of delaying the composition to the lowest level, where all the models conform to the same metamodel, it is possible to perform a homogeneous composition using a single composition mechanism.

Summarizing, our approach offers several advantages: 1) it facilitates the modeling of multiple concerns in separated models and close to the problem domain, 2) it offers an automatic derivation mechanism to identify the elements to compose in the low-level models based on relationships defined in the high-level, 3) it eases the use of a single composition mechanism at low-level of abstraction, 4) it reuses the existing assets (metamodels, models and transformations).

References

1. Tolvanen, J.P., Kelly, S.: Defining domain-specific modeling languages to automate product derivation: Collected experiences. Software Product Lines, 198–209 (2005)
2. Bézivin, J., Bouzitouna, S., Del Fabro, M., Gervais, M.P., Jouault, F., Kolovos, D., Kurtev, I., Paige, R.F.: A canonical scheme for model composition. In: ECMDA-FA, pp. 346–360 (2006)
3. Dingel, J., Diskin, Z., Zito, A.: Understanding and improving UML package merge. Software and Systems Modeling 7(4), 443–467 (2008)
4. Aizenbud-Reshef, N., Nolan, B.T., Rubin, J., Shaham-Gafni, Y.: Model traceability. IBM Systems Journal 45(3), 515–526 (2006)

Deterministic UML Models for Interconnected Activities and State Machines

Zamira Daw and Marcus Vetter

Department of Embedded Systems,
Hochschule Mannheim – University of Applied Sciences,
D-68163 Mannheim, Germany
{z.daw,m.vetter}@hs-mannheim.de

Abstract. The interconnection between UML activities and state machines enables the comprehensible modeling of systems based on data flows and events. In this paper, we propose a novel approach to guarantee a deterministic behavior for models in which activity and state diagrams work together. At first, deterministic models are ensured independently within both diagrams by using our UML profile for Deterministic Models for signal processing embedded systems (DMOSES). The relationship between executions of the model elements is analyzed according to interconnections of the activity and state diagrams described in the UML standard. To avoid nondeterministic models, we define the execution behavior of cooperating activities and state machines. The interconnection of both diagrams and their corresponding behavior are illustrated in an embedded system example that uses parallel processing for data as well as for events. Our approach simplifies the development of deterministic embedded systems by code generation from UML models.

Keywords: Activity, state machine, deterministic behavior.

1 Introduction

The need for systems with high performance results in an increased utilization of parallel processing (e.g. multi-core and multi-threading). Development of embedded systems has become more complicated due to the guaranteeing of deterministic behavior within parallel processing systems. Modeling techniques support the development of embedded systems at a higher abstraction level. The Unified Modeling Language (UML) [1] is the most widely used modeling language in this area. Therefore, many efforts are undertaken to generate code from UML models. However, the UML semantics in some diagrams is not completely defined. This makes a consistent generation code difficult. Furthermore, uncertainty in the modeling semantics of embedded systems with parallel processing leads to unpredictable behavior.

Flow processing and event-driven systems are usually present in embedded systems. Those can be modeled in UML by using activity and state machine diagrams. Hence, interconnecting both diagrams provides precise models for

A. Schürr and B. Selic (Eds.): MODELS 2009, LNCS 5795, pp. 556–570, 2009.

embedded systems. However, the execution behavior of interconnected activities and state machines is not precisely defined in the UML standard.

Several UML tools can generate code from UML models. Nevertheless, not all diagram types are supported for code generation, e.g. not many tools can handle the activity diagram in that aspect. Furthermore, the interconnection of activities and state machines is not at all taken into account.

In this paper, we introduce the UML profile DMOSES for *Deterministic MOdels of Signal Processing Embedded Systems.* This profile ensures deterministic behavioral models independently of the hardware structure. Modeling of parallel processing is especially considered within activity and state machine diagrams to avoid uncertain execution order. The semantics of concurrent state machines (CSM) are extended avoiding nondeterministic results if they are not completely independent. Information about the execution is added within the diagrams by using DMOSES stereotypes. This guarantees a deterministic behavior of the generated code. We show different forms to interconnect activities and states machines as defined in the UML standard. Furthermore, the relationship between the execution of the interconnected elements is analyzed for ensuring the deterministic behavior of the whole system.

The remainder of this work is organized as follows: in the next section we present related work. Section 3 introduces the DMOSES profile for behavioral diagrams. Deterministic behavior of interconnected activities and state machines is explained in section 4. The paper concludes with a summary and an outlook.

2 Related Work

Embedded systems development has been supported by using UML models. Several UML profiles are developed to model embedded systems more accurately. The UML/SPT profile (*UML for Schedulability, Performance and Time*) [2] [3], adopted by the OMG in 2002, centers on the analysis of schedulability. The profile *TURTLE* (*Timed UML and RT-LOTOS Environment*) [4] [5] is a UML profile for the modeling of real-time systems which is not standardized by the OMG. This profile extends the UML classes and activities for the structural and behavioral modeling of real-time systems. Furthermore, time units can be modeled with TURTLE. The profile MARTE (*Modeling and Analysis of Real Time and Embedded Systems*) [6] was standardized by the OMG in 2007. This profile supports the modeling of software and hardware platforms, and is also focused on the analysis of scheduling and performance.

Our approach focuses on the UML diagrams: *activity* and *state machine.* System behavior can be modeled by using these diagrams. The semantics precision of UML *activities* has been improved in the UML 2.0. Nevertheless, their semantics are still lacking. [7] analyzes the semantics in relation to the Petri-Nets and proposes some features for the activity diagrams, namely exceptions, traverse-to-completion, and streaming. [8] confronts practical problems with the *activities* semantics and suggests possible solutions. This lack of the semantics led OMG to develop the *Semantics of a Foundational Subset for Executable UML Models* (fUML) [9] [10] that offers a precise definition of the execution semantics.

The semantics of *state machines* in UML are quite robust. However, the semantics of concurrent state machine (CSM) are not precise enough to allow a coherent execution. The behavior and advantage of CSMs is describe by [11] [12] [13] [14].

In this paper, we present a UML profile, DMOSES, for modeling of embedded systems. This area is also the focus of the profiles mentioned above. However, our profile centers on the description of executable models that ensure a deterministic system behavior. Furthermore, we increase the possibilities of the UML standard to interconnect *activities* and *state machines*. Interconnections completely defined for the description of asystem more precise and comprehensible. Our approach expands the UML semantics to describe the functionality of CSMs, guaranteeing stable models.

3 Deterministic Behavioral UML Models by Using the DMOSES Profile

Due to increased parallel processing in embedded systems, it is becoming more difficult to ensure systems with a deterministic behavior. Nondeterministic parallel processing leads to an unstable system. Therefore, its behavior can not be predicted. For example, the same input can produce different results, even with varying propagation time. Our approach guarantees a deterministic behavior at the model level by using the DMOSES profile. Furthermore, the development of deterministic embedded system can be simplified and improved through code generation based on DMOSES models. In this section, we describe the DMOSES profile that ensures a deterministic behavior within activity and state machine diagrams.

3.1 DMOSES Profile

The UML offers the possibility to be adapted to a specific domain by profiling. Our DMOSES profile is a UML profile for *deterministic models of signal processing embedded systems*. The main goal of the DMOSES profile is to extend the UML semantics to guarantee deterministic behavior of embedded systems models independent of the hardware platform. DMOSES *models* have additional information about the model execution. This information provides a precise description of the system behavior. The profile is divided into two subprofiles: *Hardware Management* and *Deterministic Behavior*.

Usually, multiple resources are used simultaneously due to the need for systems with high performance. The *Hardware Management* package supports the relationship between hardware structure and the behavioral models (Figure 1). DMOSES activities and state machines are assigned to a specific execution unit within the behavioral diagrams by using stereotypes defined in this sub profile. The platform related to the stereotype *resource* corresponds to a resource which is described within the deployment diagram. Furthermore the *Hardware Management* package extends the deployment diagram for a complete modeling of

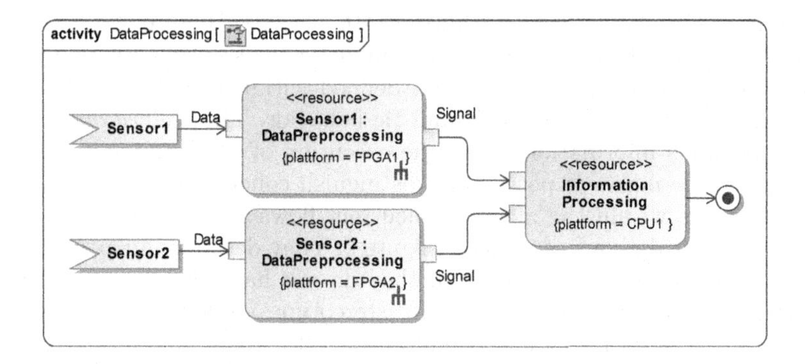

Fig. 1. Assignation of execution unit within an activity

the processing units. The information about the execution unit related to the model functionality can be used to analyze synchronization and parallelism in the model.

The *Deterministic Behavior* package extends the UML activities and state machines to avoid nondeterministic models. The extended behavioral diagrams are named DMOSES activity and DMOSES state machine. By using stereotypes of this package, deterministic behavior is ensured specially for parallel processing. Elements of this profile add information about the execution within the both behavioral diagrams.

3.2 Behavior of DMOSES Activities

DMOSES activities guarantee deterministic behavior at the model level. Parallel processing can be unstable if it is not completely described. Concurrency within a UML activity diagram can be modeled through non-related flows or by the use of determinate model elements as shown in figure 2. The most common element to model concurrent flows is the *ForkNode* (Figure 2(b)). The UML standard specifies concurrent flows when they are not related within the model. In that account, concurrent flows can be modeled by using multiple *InitialNodes*

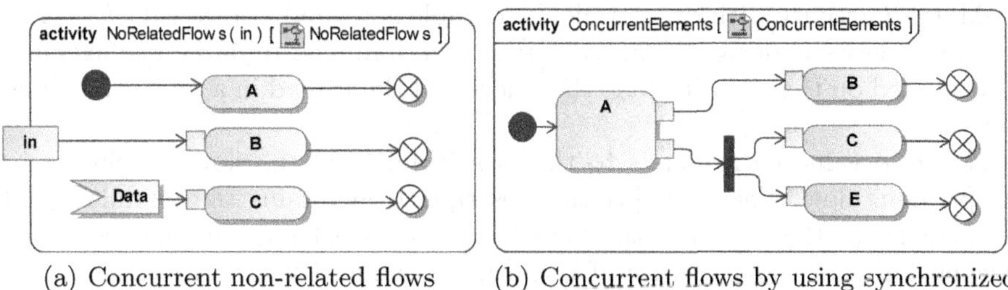

(a) Concurrent non-related flows

(b) Concurrent flows by using synchronized model elements

Fig. 2. Models of concurrency in UML

and *ActivityParameterNodes* within a UML activity (Figure 2(a)). Multiple outgoing flows of a UML action can also model concurrency. Although, the execution order of model elements is not defined within the model. The lack of this information causes a nondeterministic behavior. The *Deterministic behavior* package adds information about the execution of *DMOSES activities.* The stereotype *async* makes it possible to distinguish concurrent flows and parallel executable flows within the model. Concurrent flows are modeled by using the element mentioned above as shown in figure 2. They describe independent flows which will be executed sequentially if they do not have the stereotype, *async.* A *DMOSES activities edge* with *async* stereotype models a concurrent flow that will be executed in parallel (simultaneously) if there are enough resources (Figure 3). In this way, hardware resources can be managed. For example, the creation of threads in a multitasking system can be controlled by the use of the *async* stereotype. By using this stereotype, developers can define which flows with independent functionality must be executed simultaneously or sequentially. Furthermore, this method allows that the same model can be used for a different amount of resources without additional effort. The model behavior, thus, will not change.

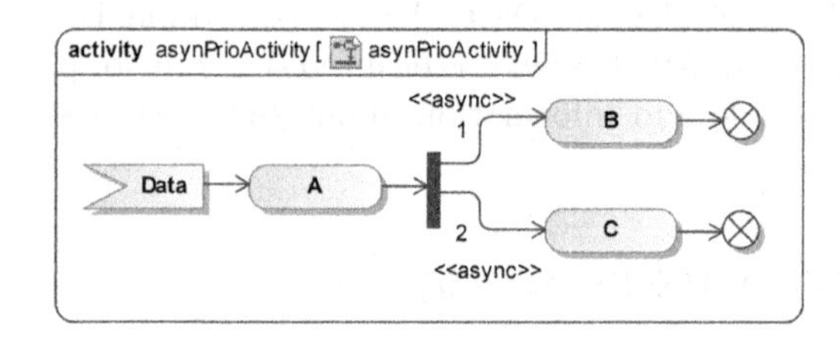

Fig. 3. Prioritization of parallel executable flows with in a DMOSES activity

Uncertainty in the execution order of concurrent flows causes nondeterministic behaviors. For this reason, the execution order is defined within DMOSES activities by using prioritization of *ActivitiesEdges* as shown in figure 3. The execution order of model elements is based on the incoming flows priority. In this way, the user can define the execution order at the model level. Figure 3 depicts a DMOSES activity with two parallel executable flows and prioritized *edges.* The priority of flows is derived from *edge* prioritization. The resource management is also based on this priority (e.g. the priority of the thread in a multi-threading system).

The *edge* value corresponds to the local priority of the flow in relation to the previous flow. The local priority description maintains the modularity of the models. In this manner, the model element is behaving in the same way independently of the structure of the whole system. The priority distribution through the DMOSES activity must be specified to ensure an exact behavioral modeling. Some elements of the UML activity diagram can increase or reduce the number of flows. Only for these model elements, the handling of flow priority must be defined. Elements that can split flows are the same that can model concurrent flows mentioned as above. The DMOSES activity *PrioDistActivity* models flow splitting by using two *ForkNodes* (Figure 4). Priorities 1 and 2 are assigned to the parallel executable flows of the DMOSES actions B and C respectively. After the second *ForkNode*, the flow of the action C is split in two parallel executable flows that also have defined local priorities. If the action B is still executing, the global execution priorities 2 and 3 are assigned to the actions E and D, respectively, the action B has first priority with respect to the all flows derived from the flow of the action C. If the first *ForkNode* would not have any *async-edge* the action C and its following actions can be only executed after the action B is completely executed.

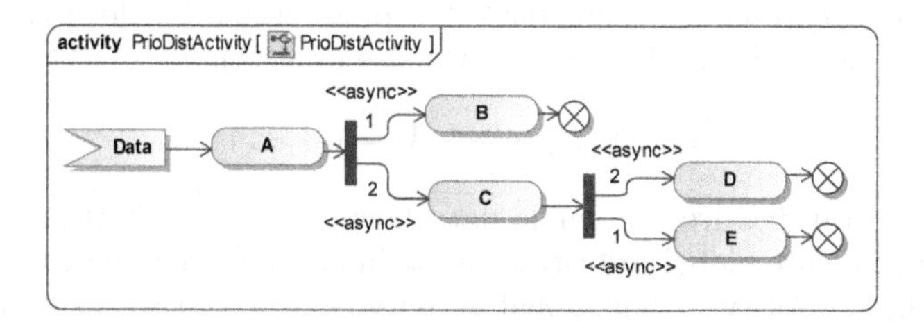

Fig. 4. Edge prioritization for parallel executable flows in DMOSES

Figure 5(a) and 5(b) show three model elements that can join multiple incoming edges. The *merge node* offers all tokens on incoming edges to the outgoing edge. There is no synchronization of flows or joining of tokens. The execution priority of the action C depends on the flow priority of the incoming token (Figure 5(a)). For instance, the actions A and B are executed simultaneously, but if the execution of A is shorter than B, the flow of action C will have the local priority 1.

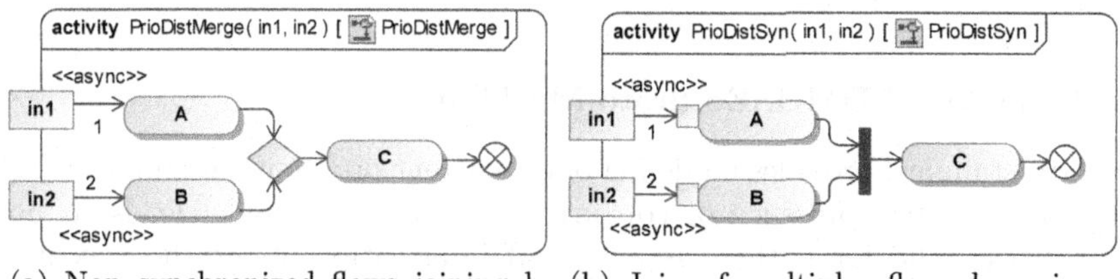

(a) Non synchronized flows joining by using Priority a *merge node*

(b) Join of multiples flows by using a DMOSES action

Fig. 5. Priority distribution for elements that join flows

UML action as well as UML *joinNode* synchronize the incoming edges. Per default, the highest priority of the incoming edges is assigned as the priority reference. The priority of the outgoing flows is based on this reference (e.g. the outgoing flow with the priority 1 receives the highest priority of all incoming flows). In this way, the execution priority of the model element can be changed in every place within a DMOSES activity. The flow prioritization allows the user to add information about the model execution while ensuring deterministic system behavior.

Unambiguous execution order guarantees deterministic system behavior. This is defined on the model level using local priorities for the activity edges and orthogonal regions within the state machine (next section). Figure 6 shows a directed graph of branches from data flow in a DMOSES system. The first hierarchy level contains only one vertex which is the root of the entire system which is abstract and thus not implemented. The second level is descibed for flows off *Inital Node*, *Activity Parameter Node* and *Send Action Node* within an activity. A graph vertex represents a single data flow of an activity. A local and a global priority are assigned for each vertex by the use of a 2-tuple.

$$G = (V, E) \ where \ V = (P_l, P_g) \tag{1}$$

Edges depict branches from a single data flow. The graph is transversed in a preorder to calculate global priorities taking in account that the left child node has the highest priority 1. The global activity edge priorities ensure an unique execution order.

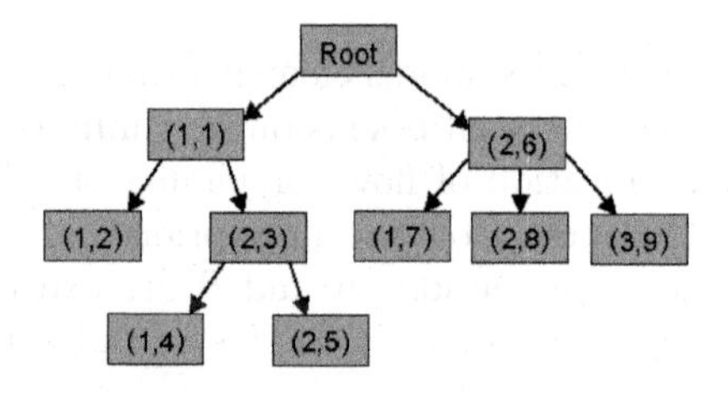

Fig. 6. Graph of data flow branches with local and global priorities

3.3 Behavior of DMOSES State Machine

The UML standard provides modeling of concurrent processing within the UML state machine. The presence of concurrency within the model leads to non-deterministic behavior if there is a lack of information about the execution. To avoid unstable system models, the DMOSES profile extends the UML state machine. Concurrent states can be modeled by using orthogonal regions within a *composite state*. Figure 7 depicts a *composite state* with two orthogonal regions. The *composite state*, State1, can be in two states simultaneously due to the orthogonal regions. A UML state can own three behaviors that can be described for UML activities. Their execution order is linked with the following labels: *entry*, *do* and *exit*. These labels define when the behaviors must be executed in relation to the activation of the state.

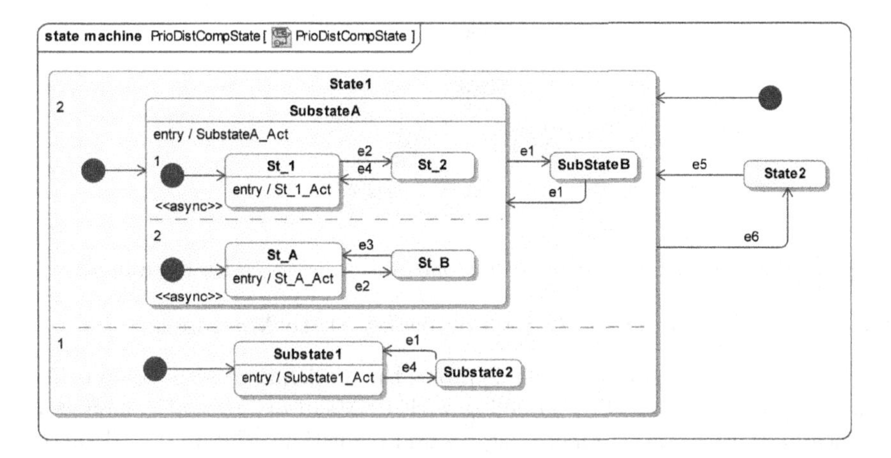

Fig. 7. DMOSES state machine with concurrent states by the use of orthogonal regions

The DMOSES profile offers in its *Deterministic behavior* package a group of stereotypes to define the execution order within the DMOSES state Machine. The information about the model execution is related to the orthogonal regions by using stereotypes. These stereotypes are also used within the DMOSES activity diagram. The transition execution is linked with the region properties. The stereotype *async* within orthogonal regions models that behaviors corresponding to states (e.g. *do* behavior) will be executed simultaneously (Figure 7). Nevertheless, the stereotype cannot force a simultaneous execution if there are not enough resources available. If there is only one resource or the stereotype *async* is not included, the triggered transitions and states behaviors are executed sequentially. The execution order of the transition is determined for the region priority to avoid uncertain conditions. Figure 7 illustrates a DMOSES state machine with prioritized regions. A non-deterministic behavior can already occur at the entrance of the *composite state*, State1, due the execution order of the behavior not being defined. The regions priorities define the execution order between the *entry* behaviors of the DMOSES states *SubState1* and *SubStateA*. Region priority is a local value that is only valid within the *composite state.*

The priority distribution in the DMOSES state machine must be specified. This distribution also take into consideration model elements that change the number of flows defined within the DMOSES activities. Within a *state diagram*, this situation occurs when a state contains multiple regions. Every orthogonal region is represented for a vertex within the prioritiy graph. An edge is depicted when a state contains orthogonal regions. Figure 8 shows the graph of the state machine on figure 7. This figure shows a rectangle with a subgraph. The subgraph represents an asynchronous area. This area is asynchronous executed in relation to the entire system.

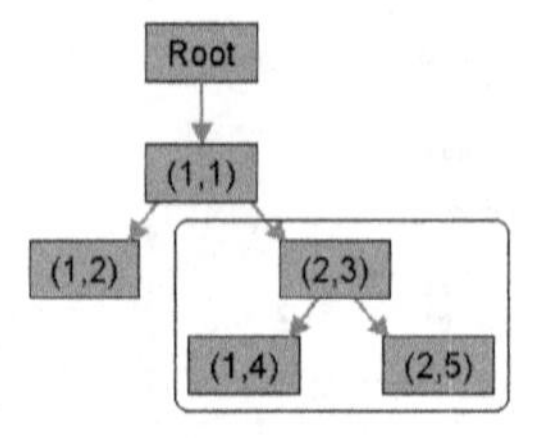

Fig. 8. Priority distribution of *PrioDistCompState* (Figure 7) described in a graph

3.4 Deterministic DMOSES Concurrent State Machines

Concurrent state machines (CSM) facilitate the modeling of orthogonal or independent state machines. The modeling with CSMs of orthogonal behaviors can drastically decrease the number of states and transitions. Figure 9(a) depicts an example of one state machine. The state machine *ExaStateMachine* has 9 states and 22 transitions. In this diagram, the orthogonality between the states can be identified. The state machine, *ExaStateMachine*, can be transformed into two concurrent state machines as shown in figure 9(b). The final number of states is reduced to 6 as well as the number of transitions to 8.

The UML standard defines the assumption *run-to-completion* to process an event occurrence. *Run-to-completion* processing means that an event occurrence can only be processed if the previous is fully completed. The processing is concluded when all transitions are completed as well as the invocation of the corresponding activities. Multiple transitions can be triggered within one UML state machine if it has orthogonal regions. The firing order of these transitions is not determined in the UML standard. This causes the state machine to behave nondeterministically.

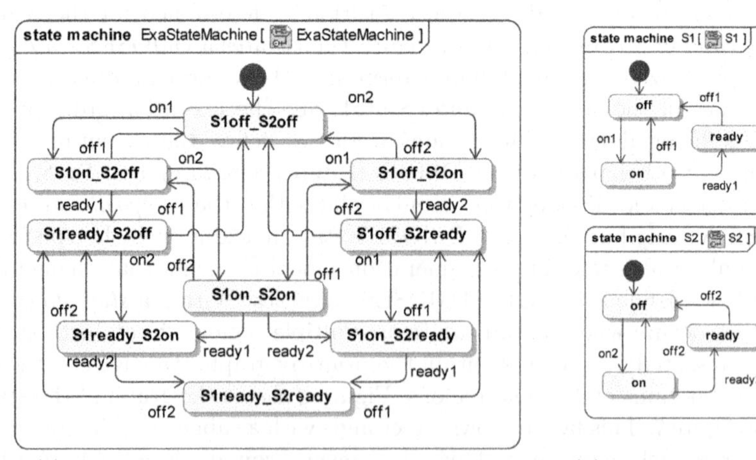

(a) One state machine with independent state

(b) Concurrent state machines

Fig. 9. Decrease of the model complexity by using concurrent states

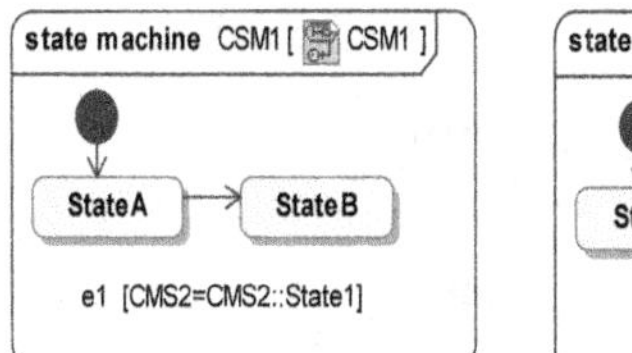

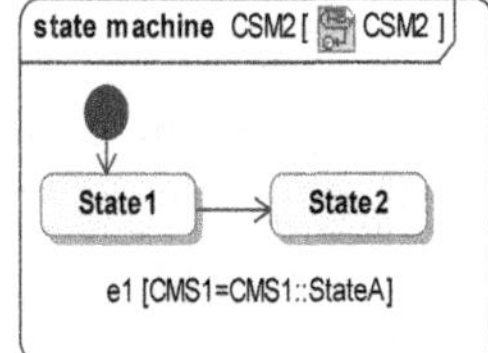

Fig. 10. Reciprocal state query of two concurrent state machines with the same transition trigger

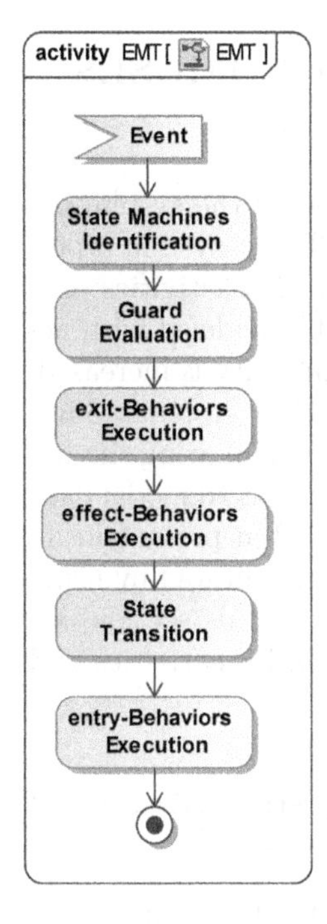

Fig. 11. Execution sequence for multiple transitions

In the CSMs, multiple transitions can be fired as well as within orthogonal regions. Furthermore, the CSMs can query each other. The multiple transitions and the reciprocal state queries lead to different results for each execution order of the individual transitions. Figure 10 depicts two CSMs that respond to the same event *e1*. Both transitions have guards that query the state of the other state machine. If the transition of the state machine, *CSM1*, is executed first then the result of the event is *StateB* and *State1*. But if the execution order is reversed then the resulting states are *StateA* and *State2*. Since the order in which the transitions fire is not defined in the UML standard, we propose to extend the *run-to-completion*, to guarantee a deterministic behavior of CSM. The activity, *ExecutionMultipleTrans*, of figure 11 illustrates the extended *run-to-completion* process for multiple transitions. When an event occurrence is detected the state machines involved are identified. Guards of the potential transitions are verified. Once all transitions to be executed are found, the corresponding *exit*-activities are invoked followed by the behaviors associated with the transition, named *effect*-behaviors. After this, the state change of all state machines is carried out and then the *entry*-activities are executed. The execution order ensures that the result of state queries to other state machines is independent of the transition execution order. It must be considered, that the query can also be made within some state behavior (e.g. *exit* behavior).

To guarantee a deterministic behavior of the CMSs, the execution order between the behaviors of the same type must be defined. Figure 12 shows how to define this order. This DMOSES state machine *PrioDistGCSM* has a stereotype named *globalStateMachine*. Region priorities within the *composite state* with this stereotype determine the relationship between the global concurrent state machines (GCSM). The execution order of the activities associated with a transition is derived from this relationship.

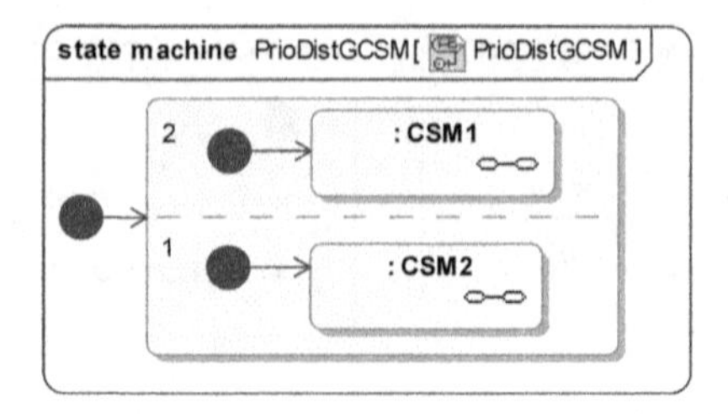

Fig. 12. Priority distribution for global concurrent state machines by using orthogonal regions

4 Deterministic Behavior for Interconnected DMOSES Activities and States

In our approach, activity and state diagrams are used to model the system behavior. Nevertheless, each diagram is focused to describe different system types. Systems based in data flow processing can be best modeled with activities (e.g. the signal processing area). Event-driven systems can also be modeled with activities diagrams. Therefore, the effort of modeling and complexity is increased. State diagrams are especially designed to describe this kind of systems. Since UML 2.0, activities and state diagram have become orthogonal allowing the use of both independently. We propose to interconnect both diagrams to model data flow processing as well as event-driven systems. Those are often present in an embedded system. The development of embedded systems is facilitated by using code generation from interconnected activities and states. In this section, we describe deterministic models based on interconnected DMOSES activities and state machines.

4.1 Interconnection Forms between Activities and States Described in the UML Standard

The UML standard provides different mechanisms to relate UML activities with states and vice versa. The behavior of model elements within a UML state machine can be described for UML activities. It can be associated to a UML state as well as to a transition. The invocation point of a UML activity depends on the activation of the corresponding element within the UML state diagram. For instance, the UML activity linked to a transition is executed when the transition is carried out. A UML state can have up to three UML activities. Each of these activities are related to the following labels: *entry*, *do* and *exit*. These labels define the execution point of the associated UML activities in relation to the activation of the UML state. Between the UML activity and the state, there is not any data transfer. The UML standard allows the invocation of behaviors from UML activity diagrams by using *InvocationActions*. *SendSignalAction* is an *InvocationAction* that creates a signal instance, and transmits it to the target object. This model element can be used to fire a UML state machine transition.

Figure 13(a) shows a *SendSignalAction* within the UML activity, *FireTrans*, that fires a transition of the UML state machine, *TriggerfromAct*, between the state *State1* and *State2*.

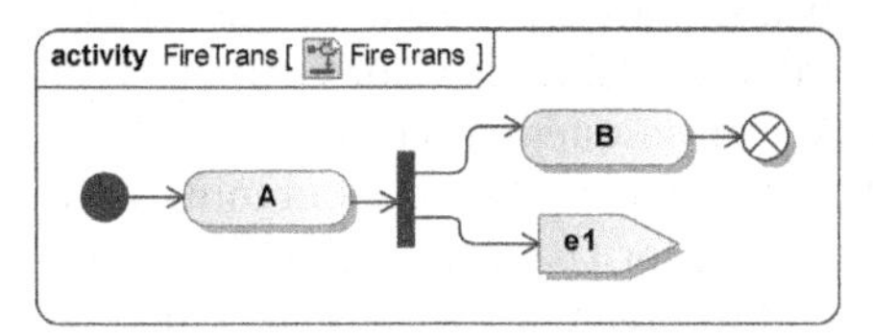

(a) Signal Sending to fire a transition within a state machine

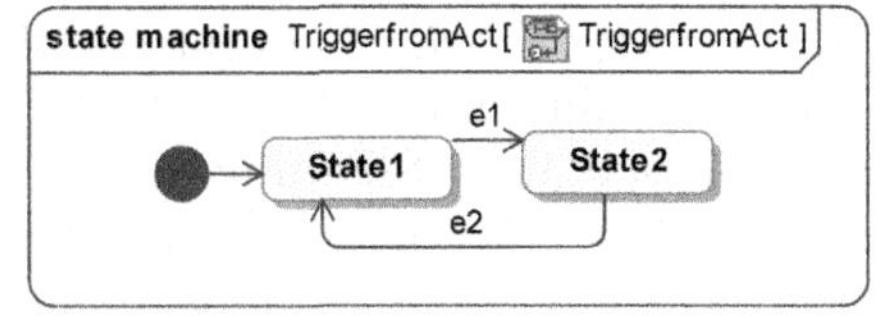

(b) State machine responds to an event sent within an activity

Fig. 13. Transition fired within an activity by the use of a *SendSignalAction*

4.2 Interconnection of DMOSES Models

The UML standard describes a possible interconnection between activities and states by using state behaviors (e.g. *exit* behavior). This kind of interconnection will be maintained for DMOSES model elements. Furthermore, we introduce additional relationships between both diagrams to facilitate modeling of embedded systems. For instance, the processing flow within a DMOSES activity changes depending on the state of a DMOSES state machine. This can be realized by using a *DecisionNode*. Guards of the *DecisionNode* outgoing flows can be related to the state of any DMOSES state machine. Within the DMOSES activity of figure 14, the action *B* is only executed if the state machine *SMA* is in the state *State1*. In this manner, different flows can be executed depending on the state of a state machine.

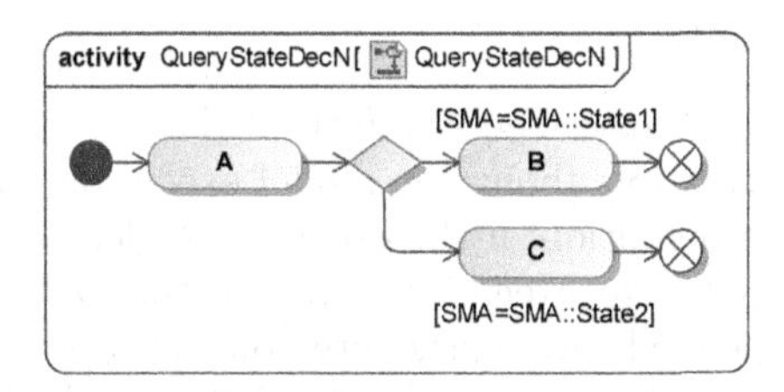

Fig. 14. Query of a state within a UML activity diagram

The behavior of a UML state machine can be modeled by using UML activities. The DMOSES profile enables activities and actions to have their own DMOSES state machine by the use of the stereotype, *stateAction* as shown in figure 15(a). With this relationship, the state of a DMOSES activity execution can be described as well as an Action. The information saved within a state machine can be used to change the processing flow within an activity. In this manner, errors or features in the outgoing data can also be modeled, and considered outside of the action or the activity. Figure 15(a) depicts the DMOSES activity, *ActivitySt*, that have the state machine *St_Act*. A transition of *St_Act* can be only fired within the *ActivitySt* (e.g. by using *SendSignalAction*). Furthermore, the state of *St_Act* determines which signal will be sent because of the *DesicionNode*. *ActivitySt* executes a different processing flow for each state of *St_Act*. In addition, the state of the activity can be queried within an external DMOSES activity as shown in figure 15(b). In this example, the outgoing data of the DMOSES action, *Action1*, is not processed for the next DMOSES action when the outgoing data is negative and the state machine of *Action1* is in the state, *State2*.

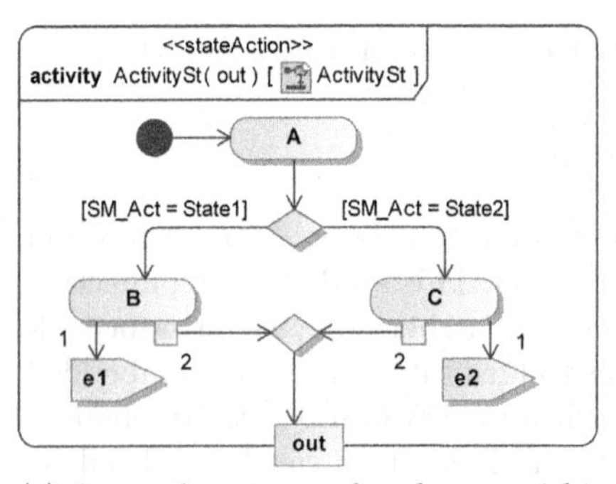

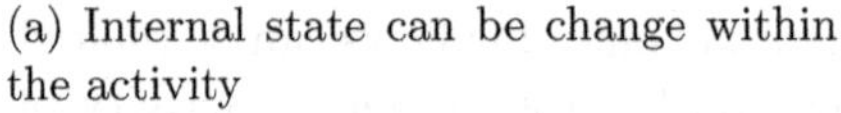

(a) Internal state can be change within the activity

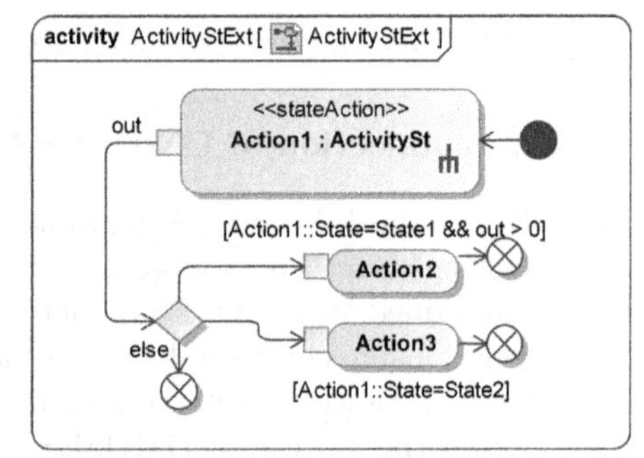

(b) External state queries of the state machine associated with an activity

Fig. 15. DMOSES activity having a state machine

4.3 Deterministic Behavior of the Interconnection between DMOSES Models

The DMOSES profile guarantees deterministic behavior for activities as well as states separately. Information about the model execution within the DMOSES elements allows for the definition of the execution order of the model elements. The relationship between the execution order of the DMOSES activities and State Machines is not defined. Hence, the interconnection of both model elements leads to an uncertain model behavior. Figure 16 shows a DMOSES activity that fires a transition a the state Machine with this event. The execution of this transition entails the invocation of the corresponding behaviors. The execution order of these behaviors must be related to the *PrioSendSig* to avoid nondeterministic behaviors. The execution priority of the state machine behaviors is associated to the flow priority of the *SendSignalAction* that triggers the transition.

The execution behavior of a DMOSES state machine can be executed in parallel by using the stereotype *async* for the *SendSignalAction* as shown in figure 16. In this manner, the user can decide the priority of a transition (e.g. a new thread with a high priority can be created to execute the transition in a multithreading-system). The transition can be executed in parallel by using *async* in the *edge* of the *SendSignalAction*-incoming. The priority of this flow is assigned to the transition while the following flow assumes a priority level lower (e.g. the flow of C). The action D is executed after the transition execution is completed due to the fact that the flow does not have any *async* stereotype. The same priority distribution is valid for DMOSES activities and actions that contain a DMOSES state machine.

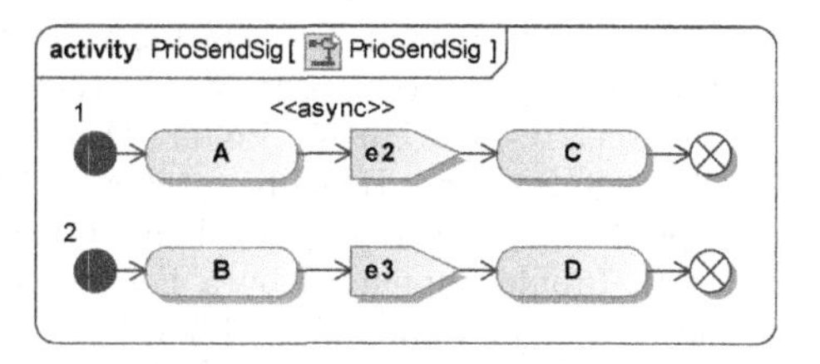

Fig. 16. Different forms to prioritize transitions of a state machine

5 Conclusions and Future Work

In this paper, we have presented a novel approach for interconnection between activities and state machines ensuring a deterministic behavior. We have shown how to describe deterministic models by using the DMOSES profile. Information about the execution is included within the model. This allows the user to manage the resource at the model level. Furthermore, we demonstrate that the concurrent state machines cause uncertain execution if any relationship between their executions is not defined within the model. A new semantics for DMOSES profile, is introduced to extend the interconnection between activities and state machines. To maintain a deterministic behavior of the entire model, we add some stereotypes to this profile package. Future work is to ensure the development of deterministic signal processing embedded systems. For this reason, we will develop a tool to support code generation from DMOSES models. The generated code is based on a framework that maintains a deterministic behavior in the implementation.

Acknowledgments

This research is supported by the European Union, European Regional Development Fund (ERDF) and the federal state of Baden-Wuerttemberg, Germany.

References

1. Object Management Group: UML Unified Modeling Language, Superstructure, V2.1.2
2. Gherbi, A., Khendek, F.: From UML/SPT models to schedulability analysis: a metamodel-based transformation. In: Proceedings of the Ninth IEEE International Symposium on Object and Component-Oriented Real-Time Distributed Computing, pp. 343–350. IEEE Computer Society, Los Alamitos (2006)

3. Shousha, M., Briand, L., Labiche, Y.: A UML/SPT Model Analysis Methodology for Concurrent Systems Based on Genetic Algorithms. In: Czarnecki, K., Ober, I., Bruel, J.-M., Uhl, A., Völter, M. (eds.) MODELS 2008. LNCS, vol. 5301, pp. 475–489. Springer, Heidelberg (2008)
4. Apvrille, L., Courtiat, J.-P., Lohr, C., Saqui-Sannes, P.: TURTLE: A Real-time UML Profile Supported by a Formal Validation toolkit. IEEE Transactions on Software Engineering,, 473–487 (2004)
5. Apvrille, L., Saqui-Sannes, P., Khendek, F.: TURTLE-P: A UML Profile for the Formal Validation of Critical and Distributed Systems. In: Software and Systems Modeling (SoSyM), pp. 449–466. Springer, Heidelberg (2006)
6. Object Management Group: UML Profile for MARTE (2007)
7. Störrle, H., Hausmann, J.-H.: Towards a Formal Semantics of UML 2.0 Activities. In: Proceedings German Software Engineering Conference. LNI, vol. P-64, pp. 117–128 (2005)
8. Schattkowsky, T., Forster, A.: On the Pitfalls of UML 2 Activity Modeling. In: Proc. International Workshop on Modeling in Software Engineering MISE 2007: ICSE Workshop 2007 (2007)
9. Object Management Group: Semantics of Foundational Subset for Executable UML Models. ptc/2008-11-03
10. Crane, M., Dingel, J.: Towards a Formal Account of a Foundational Subset for Executable UML Models. In: Czarnecki, K., Ober, I., Bruel, J.-M., Uhl, A., Völter, M. (eds.) MODELS 2008. LNCS, vol. 5301, pp. 675–689. Springer, Heidelberg (2008)
11. Nam, H.-L., Tai, H.-K., Sung, D.-C.: Construction of Global Finite State Machine for Testing Task Interactions written in Message Sequence Charts. In: The Fourteenth International Conference on Software Engineering and Knowledge Engineering (SEKE 2002), pp. 369–376 (2002)
12. Schäfer, T., Knapp, A., Merz, S.: Model Checking UML State Machines and Collaborations. Electronic Notes in Theoretical Computer Science, pp. 357–369. Elsevier, Amsterdam (2001)
13. Wiktor, B.-D.: Real Time Model Checking Using Timed Concurrent State Machines. International Journal of Computer Science & Applications, 1–12 (2007)
14. Gang, L., von Bochmann, G., Petrenko, A.: Test selection based on communicating nondeterministic finite-state machines using a generalized Wp-method. IEEE Transactions on Software Engineering, 149–162 (1994)

Automated Encapsulation of UML Activities for Incremental Development and Verification

Frank Alexander Kraemer and Peter Herrmann

Norwegian University of Science and Technology (NTNU),
Department of Telematics, N-7491 Trondheim, Norway
{kraemer,herrmann}@item.ntnu.no

Abstract. With their revision in the UML 2.x standard, activities have been extended with streaming parameters. This facilitates a reuse-oriented specification style, in which dedicated functions can be contributed by self-contained activities as building blocks: Using streaming parameters, activities can be composed together in a quite powerful manner, since streaming parameters may also pass information while activities are executing. However, to compose them correctly, we must know in which sequence an activity may emit or accept these streaming parameters. Therefore, we propose special UML state machines that specify the externally visible behavior of activities. Further, we develop an algorithm to construct these state machines automatically for an activity based on model checking. Using these behavioral contracts, activities can then be composed without looking at their internal details. Moreover, the contracts can be used during system verification to reduce the complexity of the analysis.

Keywords: System Composition, UML Activities, UML State Machines, UML Streaming Parameters, Model Reuse, Verification.

1 Introduction

UML activities can be used on several levels of decomposition for the specification of systems. On a high level, activities may cover coarse business processes and provide the big picture of a system's behavior. Activities are also equipped with the necessary concepts to express fine-grained logic on a more detailed level, close to an implementation in a programming language. These different levels of abstraction are not in conflict with each other, and can all be part of a consistent specification: By using *call behavior actions*, an activity may refer to subordinate activities, so that a complete system specification may be decomposed on numerous levels, from the high level focusing on the overall behavior, towards such a degree of detail that code can be generated from them.

When referred to via call behavior actions, activities may pass data and control flow between each other using input and output parameter nodes. With version 2.0 of the UML standard [1], activity parameter nodes were extended with the concept of *streaming* parameters. While non-streaming parameters may

A. Schürr and B. Selic (Eds.): MODELS 2009, LNCS 5795, pp. 571–585, 2009.

only accept tokens at the start or emit tokens at the termination of an activity, streaming parameters may pass tokens throughout the execution of an activity, in any order and frequency. This enables more elaborate dependencies between activities, so that related functionality can still be encapsulated within one activity, but a detailed synchronization between those activities is enabled by using streaming parameter nodes. This is a form of interleaving composition, and from the experience gained from our case studies introduced later we have seen that enabling this composition fosters the reuse of activities in the form of building blocks.

To effectively exploit the potential of interleaving compositions enabled by streaming parameter nodes, however, we need a description of the external behavior of an activity relevant for an enclosing context. This is a kind of interface, hiding the internal details of an activity. For this purpose, we complement activities with so-called *External State Machines* (ESMs) which are a variant of UML state machines. An ESM describes the order in which tokens can pass the various parameter nodes of an activity. This order has to be obeyed to guarantee a correct interplay between an activity and its environment. The concise notion of the external behavior of activities by ESM offers a number of advantages for the incremental development and verification of system specifications:

- Developers reusing an activity do not have to consider its internal details, but may rely on the description given by its ESM.
- The formal interface description described by an ESM can be used to verify that the activity is correctly embedded in a surrounding specification.
- ESMs support the incremental development of systems. In a bottom-up style, activities can be encapsulated by ESMs, facilitating their composition to more comprehensive models since details are hidden. In a top-down style, ESMs can be used to first sketch the external behavior of an activity, which can be subsequently implemented separately from a global model, just by considering its ESM.
- ESMs can be used to guard changes in models. The internals of an activity can be modified without affecting models referring to it if it still complies with its ESM, which can be verified automatically by tools.
- ESMs enable incremental verification. During a formal analysis of a system specification based on model checking, activities can be analyzed separately. This reduces the state space needed during the analysis significantly. Moreover, once an activity is verified, this verification does not have to be repeated when the activity is reused. The surrounding context only has to comply with its ESM.

As one realization of a model-driven development process using UML activities and ESMs, we have proposed the engineering method SPACE [2,3], depicted in Fig. 1. Systems are specified as hierarchies of activities encapsulated by ESMs. Those activities useful in several applications are stored together with their ESMs as self-contained building blocks in libraries for different domains. Currently, we have libraries for embedded sensor systems [4], trust management [5], and web service-based telecom services [6].

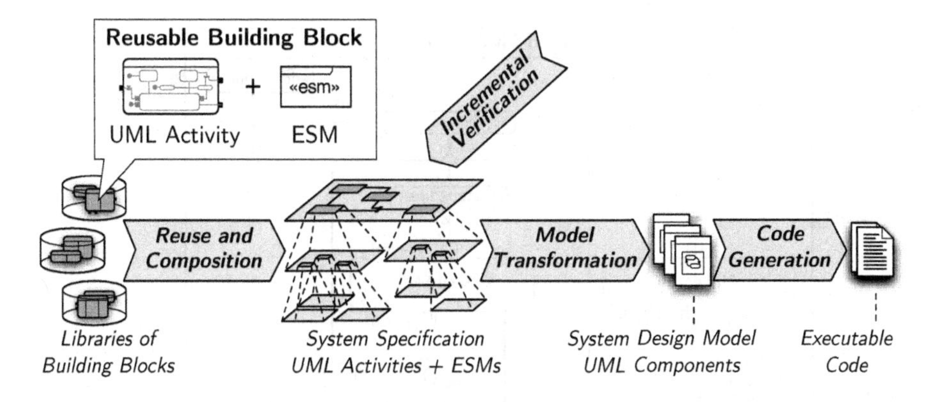

Fig. 1. Model-driven development method based on UML activities and ESMs

The method aims at a high degree of automation. With the tools described in [7,8], activities and their compositions can be checked automatically for numerous properties that should hold for any applications. This analysis is performed incrementally, i.e., on each activity separately and utilizes the reduction of state space as provided by the ESMs. To automatically implement the systems specified by activities, we developed and implemented a transformation algorithm that synthesizes UML state machines and composite structures [9,10]. From these state machines, we generate code for different execution platforms, for example for Java in different editions [11,12].

In this article we focus on the encapsulation of activities by ESMs, how this process can be automated, and present the impact on the development and verification from our case studies. In the following two sections, UML activities and ESMs are introduced. Thereafter, we discuss in Sect. 4 how ESMs can be utilized to perform incremental development. The contribution of the ESMs to reduce the complexity of model checking is pointed out in Sect. 5 while Sect. 6 introduces a tool to generate ESMs automatically from activities. We close with a discussion of related work and concluding remarks.

2 Activities and Streaming Parameter Nodes

Figure 2 shows an activity which sends SMS messages to mobile phone users. The surrounding system passes SMS messages to be sent out via streaming parameter node *send*. The actual sending happens via a web service call to a Parlay X server [13] within action *s*, which refers to a subordinate activity, taken from [6]. Since this invocation takes some time, SMS messages arriving in the meantime via *send* are stored in a buffer variable. In addition, the logic in Fig. 2 takes care of authentication and optional re-sending in case of errors. This activity is part of our library for telecom services provided by the PATS laboratory operated by Telenor [14], further described in [6].

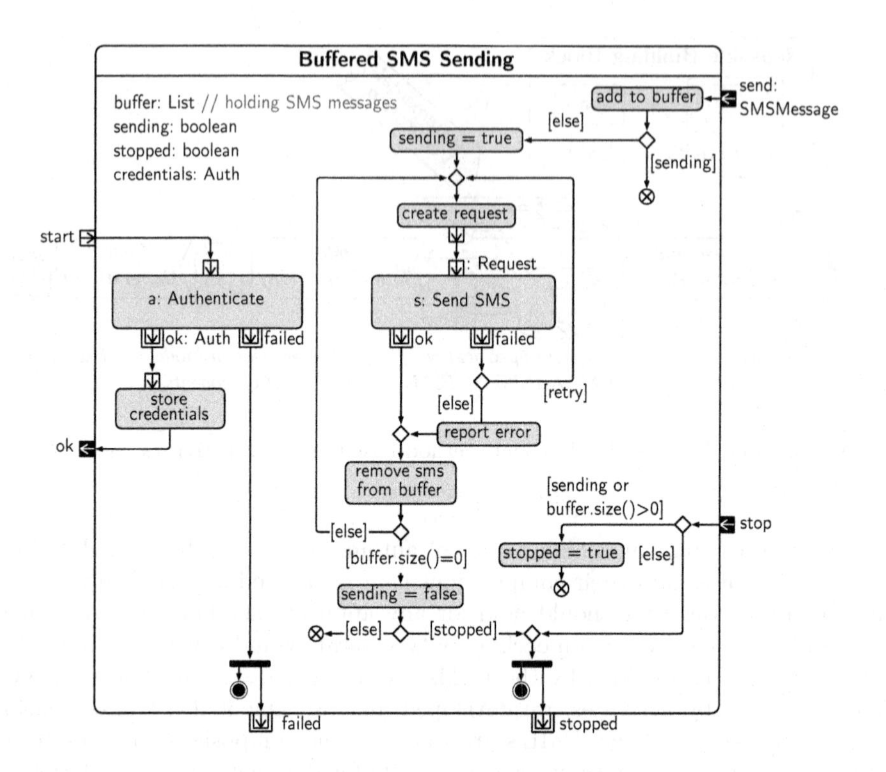

Fig. 2. Activity for Buffered SMS Sending

The activity is started via pin *start*, which invokes call behavior action *a: Authenticate* to retrieve authentication credentials from the Parlay-X server. If this inquiry fails via pin *failed* on *a*, activity *Buffered SMS Sending* terminates via *failed*. If the authentication is successful, the credentials are stored, and a token is emitted via *ok* to signal the surrounding system that SMS messages for sending are accepted from now on. These SMS messages arrive via parameter node *send*, and are added to the buffer. If the activity is currently in the process of sending another SMS, indicated via variable *sending*, the token flow ends. If it is not sending, the flow continues by setting flag *sending* and preparing a sending request, which combines the first SMS in the buffer with the authentication credentials. This request is used to start action *s*. If the sending of the SMS fails, a repetition is possible, depending on guard *retry*, which we do not detail further. If the sending of the SMS was successful or should not be repeated, the SMS is removed from the buffer. In case there are further messages in the list, sending continues with the next message.

To terminate the activity, the surrounding system sends a token via node *stopped*. If the activity is currently sending an SMS message, or the buffer is not yet emptied, only flag *stopped* is set, and the termination is deferred until the buffer is emptied. In the other case, the activity is stopped immediately and a token is emitted via *stopped*.

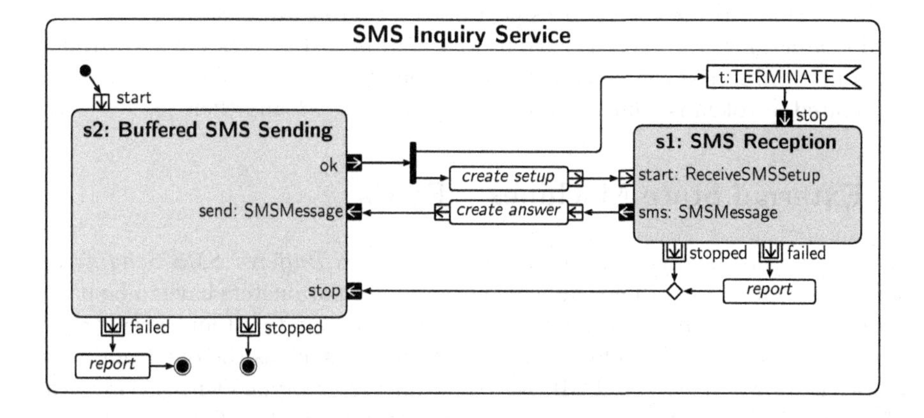

Fig. 3. Example system composing two building blocks *s1* and *s2*

The activity in Fig. 2 uses different types of parameter nodes. The input parameter (⊡) activates an activity and the output parameters (⊡) emit tokens once the activity has terminated. Since the output nodes *failed* and *stopped* are alternatives, they are assigned to different parameter sets, indicated by the additional box. The other parameters *ok*, *send* and *stop*, are *streaming* parameters, here shown as filled boxes (■). They can emit or accept tokens during the execution of an activity, i.e., while it is active.

Streaming parameter nodes enable an interleaving composition in which several call behavior actions may be active, modeling separate functionalities of a system, and may synchronize with each other every now and then. In the systems of our case studies introduced in Sect. 4.1, such interleaving compositions using streaming parameters occur very often. About 65% of all building blocks in our libraries use them.

The activity in Fig. 3 illustrates such an interleaving composition of two subordinate activities, referred to by call behavior actions *s1* and *s2*. The system realizes a simple SMS-based inquiry service, in which mobile phone users may request information such as a weather forecast by sending a certain keyword to a special number. To the right, call behavior action *s1* refers to an activity *SMS Reception* taken from our library. This activity can receive incoming SMS messages that are sent by mobile phone users to a certain number. Call behavior action *s2* refers to the activity for sending out SMS messages described above. With the activity nodes and edges surrounding them, these two building blocks are composed to obtain the complete system specification. When the system starts, a token is emitted by the initial node (•) and action *s2* starts the block for buffered SMS sending by contacting the corresponding web service. In case the startup fails, a token is emitted via *failed* of *s2* and the system is terminated. In case of success, a token is emitted via pin *ok*, which starts sub-activity *s1*. In addition, it places a token into accept signal action *t: TERMINATE*, which receives a token when the system should be terminated. Once users send in SMS messages, they are received by *s1* and a corresponding data object is emitted via pin *sms*. This SMS is then processed by operation *create answer*. For the keyword *weather*, for example, the current weather forecast is retrieved and wrapped into a new SMS message which is then sent out to the user. When the system is terminated, a token is emitted from *t*, stopping first *s1* and then *s2*.

3 External State Machines – ESMs

An engineer not involved in the design of activities *Buffered SMS Sending* and *SMS Reception* does not know in which exact order parameters have to be passed to or expected from the activity. To construct a sound system, however, this knowledge is necessary. To hide the internal details such as the one from Fig. 2, we use the ESMs. These are UML state machines, stereotyped with ≪esm≫, that refer with their transitions to the activity parameter nodes of the activity they describe. Parameter nodes are referred to as either *triggers* or *effects*, separated by a "/", depending on where a flow originates. The stereotypes and constraints are further detailed in our profile for service engineering [2].

Figure 4 shows the ESM for the buffered SMS sending activity of Fig. 2. It specifies that after the start of the activity via *start*, the activity is in a starting phase, which can result in the termination via *failed*. Since *start* is invoked from the outside, the label declares *start* as trigger, while */failed* points out that the termination is caused by the internals of the activity, perceived by the surrounding context as a spontaneous transition. If, however, the start is successful, *ok* emits a token, and the activity is in its active phase. Within this phase, the activity accepts SMS messages via *send*. To stop the activity, we may in this phase send a token through *stop*. If the block's internal buffer is empty and no SMS messages are left to send out, the stopping happens immediately, and a corresponding token is emitted via the output node *stopped*. This is specified by the transition labeled *stop/stopped*. If there are still SMS messages to send out, the eventual termination of the activity is delayed until all messages are processed, and output node *stopped* emits a token after phase *stopping*. Figure 5 shows the ESM of the SMS Reception activity.

Obviously, for a system to be sound, all activities must actually implement the behavior described by their ESMs, i.e., all ESMs must be true abstractions of their respective activities. For this reason, we defined the formal semantics of

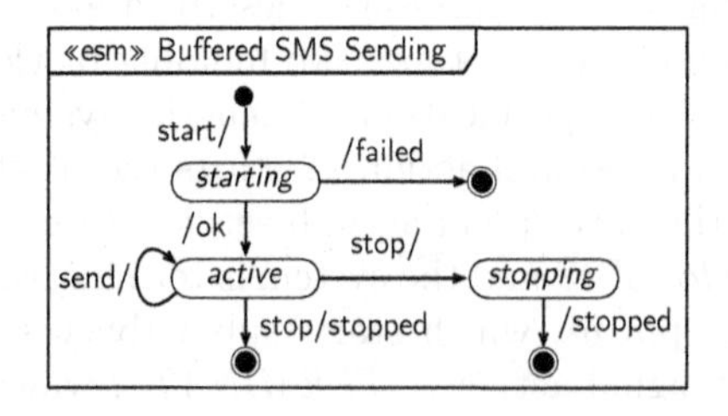

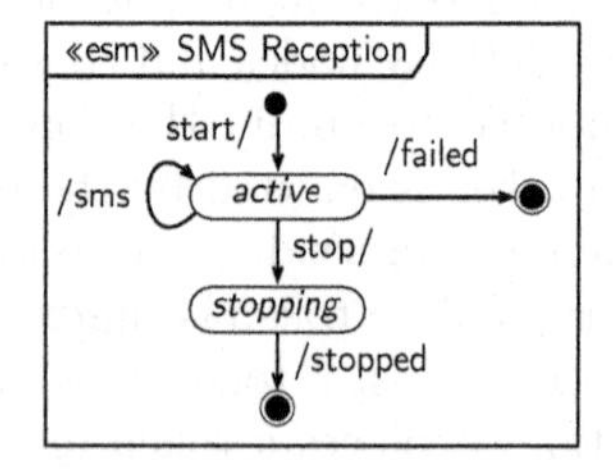

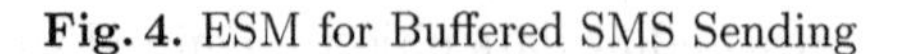

Fig. 4. ESM for Buffered SMS Sending

Fig. 5. ESM for SMS Reception

activities using the Temporal Logic of Actions (TLA, [15]), as introduced in [16]. Each activity corresponds to a temporal logic specification A_i, describing all its possible behaviors by a set of actions. An ESM is expressed by a specification E_i. Since an implementation relation in TLA corresponds to logical implication, for any building block i, $A_i \Rightarrow E_i$ must hold. This formula means that each action of an activity maps to a compatible action of the ESM, or the ESM is not involved in the action.

To ensure this sound relation between an activity and its ESM, our tools support two strategies, named *encapsulation* and *refinement*:

- **Encapsulation of existing Activities by an ESM.** Following this development strategy, an existing activity A_x solving a certain problem x is encapsulated by an ESM E_x, so that $A_x \Rightarrow E_x$ holds. In Sect. 6, we describe a tool to generate the ESM from a given activity.
- **Refinement of a given ESM by an Activity.** In this development strategy, a building block to contribute some function y is first described by its externally visible behavior E_y. Since A_y is more detailed than E_y, it can in general not be automatically derived from E_y and is a manual engineering step. However, the necessary refinement relation that must hold can be ensured by an automated verification based on model-checking. We have implemented this by our tools presented in [8,17,18].

We should note that users of our tools are not required to work with temporal formulas. Feedback about the consistency of a specification is given on the level of activities, as explained later. TLA is therefore merely used as a reasoning instrument to ensure that the method and tools are sound.

4 Incremental Development with ESMs

The encapsulation of activities in ESMs facilitates an incremental development style, in which systems can be specified activity by activity, with the ESMs as contracts separating the individual activities from each other. In particular, two styles are enabled by the previously introduced strategies of encapsulation and refinement:

- The strategy of *encapsulation* supports a bottom-up development style, depicted in Fig. 6, in which an ESM is generated for an activity A_x, which can be composed in an enclosing activity S_x together with other activities.
- Vice versa, the strategy of *refinement*, in which an ESM Ey is used to initially specify the abstracted behavior of an activity A_y, supports a top-down development style, illustrated in Fig. 7. Here a higher level specification S_y is developed first, and the subordinate activity A_y is in a first step only described by its ESM E_y. Later on, E_y can be implemented even by a developer unaware of S_y since its expected behavior is described by E_y.

Systems usually have several decomposition levels, with each level corresponding to an activity referred to by call behavior actions. Throughout the development

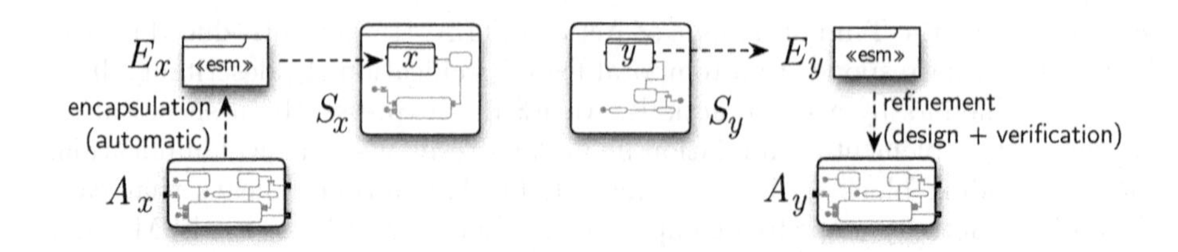

Fig. 6. Encapsulating an activity

Fig. 7. Refining an ESM

of a system, both styles may be combined: An activity developed bottom-up may at some level be composed with one that is to be developed top-down, and an initial top-down design of an application may be refined until a level is reached where existing activities can be used and encapsulated. If an activity is useful in a number of applications, it can be stored in a library and reused later in other systems.

4.1 Case Studies

To evaluate the impact of the presented specification technique with streaming parameters and ESMs, we conducted a number of case studies, covering several domains:

Web Services. For the orchestration of web services, we demonstrated in [6] how WSDL descriptions can be imported automatically as activities. Each web service operation can be invoked by corresponding streaming parameter nodes. The ESMs ensure that these operations are invoked in a sensible order only.

Embedded Systems. In [4] we composed a sensor network from reusable building blocks. A complete leader election protocol is contributed by one single activity, encapsulated by an ESM. The system was automatically implemented on Sun SPOTs for embedded Java [19].

Mobile Services. In [17] we developed a mobile, location-aware application, in which users solve tasks depending on their current location. This system is used within the FABULA project for mobile learning platforms [20]; the developed activities are also usable in other application areas.

Home Automation. Within the project ISIS (Infrastructure for Integrated Services), we develop solutions for the domain of home automation together with our project partner Telenor. In [7], we demonstrate the composition of a remote fire alarm, in which most parts are reused from libraries.

Trust Management. [5] presents a number of activities encapsulated by ESMs for the domain of trust management.

4.2 Libraries of Reusable Building Blocks

The ESMs act as behavioral interfaces [21] that can be used to separate the work of different developers. When a new activity is introduced providing some functionality, only its ESM needs to be known in order to use it correctly in an enclosing activity. This facilitates the provision of domain-specific libraries by experts. With the library for trust management [5], for instance, also non-experts in trust management can provide trust-based functions in systems. Due to the ESMs, the correct invocation of these activities is ensured, which guarantees that the trust-based functions are applied correctly.

To determine the degree of reuse enabled by the activities encapsulated by ESMs, we use the reuse proportion R described in [22]. This metric represents the proportion of reused code lines to overall code lines. For the application to UML models, we count the number n of nodes and edges in an activity instead. For a system specification consisting of many activities, each n is then either added to n_{reused} or $n_{specific}$, depending on if it is reused from a library or developed specifically for the application. The resulting reuse proportions R in percent for each system from our case studies is shown in Table 1. The numbers indicate that, in average, 71% of a system specification are contributed by reusable blocks from libraries.

Table 1. Reuse proportions R in percent

	n_{reused}	$n_{specific}$	R
Trusted Auction System [5]	228	76	**75%**
Telecom Web Service System [6]	334	89	**79%**
Treasure Hunt System [17]	131	73	**64%**
Mobile Alarm System [7]	145	70	**68%**
Embedded Sensor System [4]	144	75	**71%**

To use the words of Wills and D'Souza in [23], the reuse enabled by ESMs is a "good one," since it goes beyond simple copy-paste of specification fragments. This is also characterized as compositional *black-box* or *verbatim* reuse [24]. In Sect. 5 we will point out that the reuse holds also for verification purposes, i.e., an activity once verified does not have to be verified again when is is reused. This implies that a reuse proportion of 71% implies real gains in productivity.

The ESMs also serve as an effective guard for changes: Any activity may be modified arbitrarily without affecting the soundness of the system as long as it complies with its original ESM. From a practical point of view, this means we can update and improve the internal realization of a building block in a library without affecting applications using it. Illegal changes harming the ESM are detected by our automatic analysis tools.

5 Incremental Verification with ESMs

Due to the formal definition of the activity semantics based on temporal logic in [16], we can use the technique of model checking for the analysis of specifications. The examples in [8,17] demonstrate how this process can be performed automatically on UML activities in order to check numerous properties that should hold for any application, like the freedom of deadlocks or bounded communication queues. Problems identified are presented in the form of animations and annotations within the diagrams, as demonstrated in [7], so that engineers do not require a formal background to assure the quality of their models.

A well-known challenge of model checking is the problem of state explosion [25], i.e., that realistic systems often have so many reachable states that a complete analysis cannot be handled within acceptable time. By using ESMs, however, we can verify systems *incrementally*, since each activity is analyzed *separately*. When an activity is model checked, all its subordinate activities referred to by call behavior actions are represented by their respective ESMs. This reduces the number of states to be checked significantly, since the ESMs have usually much less states as they are more abstract than the activities they encapsulate. To achieve that, our model checker verifies two properties for each activity:

(i) The activity has always to comply with its own ESM, i.e., $A_x \Rightarrow E_x$ as mentioned in Sect. 3 holds.
(ii) An activity must always fulfill the ESMs of its subordinate activities.

Formally, a system S using activity A_x is described by $S \triangleq A_x \wedge N$, with N as the behavior of the surrounding context of A_x (see [16]). To prove a property I during the analysis, $P_A \triangleq S \Rightarrow \Box I$ must hold.[1] Using the ESMs instead, the model checker verifies the less complex proof $P_E \triangleq E_x \wedge N \Rightarrow \Box I$. Since $P_E \wedge (A_x \Rightarrow E_x) \Rightarrow P_A$ holds trivially and (i) holds, the replacement of the activities by their ESMs is formally correct. (See also [2].)

The degree of reduction of the size of the state space is discussed below. Further, when an activity is reused, the analysis effort spent will be reused as well. We assume that the designer of a building block only adds an activity to a library after it passed the analysis and does not contain any errors. Thus, other engineers may simply apply the building block without the need to check the correctness of it's internal behavior again. They only have to prove that the environment of the block complies with its ESM.

It is also beneficial for the human developers that the analysis is focused on one activity at a time: Once an erroneous situation is identified by the model checker, the underlying problem is typically easier to understand and solve when only a single activity has to be understood. This makes it also possible to study intricate synchronization problems isolation, as demonstrated in [8].

5.1 Scalability and Reduction of State Space

To make a point in case, we consider a simple example from the domain of Grid technology. These systems stand out for their high number of processes running in parallel. Here, each combination of the local process states forms a

[1] In temporal logic, $\Box$ is the "always" operator stating that a property holds in all states of a system description.

unique system state to be checked separately. Formally, if a system consists of p independent processes and each process may reach s different process states, the overall system contains up to s^p many different system states. If, however, we model each process by a separate activity, this will comprise only s different states. The ESMs of the activities typically contain only two or three states modeling whether the process is either *idle*, *active*, or *terminated*. Thus the overall system model encompassing p call behavior actions for each of the processes affords only two or three states since all processes can be started and terminated at once. Thus, if the sub-activities differ for each process, we have to check altogether only $p \cdot s + 3$ different states. In the case that all processes are identical and we can model them by the same activity, the effort is even reduced to $s + 3$ reachable states since this activity has to be verified only once. So, we can reduce exponential complexity with respect to the number of processes and polynomial complexity with regard to the number of process states to linear complexity.

Also for systems with less parallel behavior than the one sketched above, the reduction of states to be proven is still significant. For instance, the trusted auction system presented in [5] has in total 957 distinct reachable states when the global specification is explored, although it only models two communicating parties and has only three decomposition levels. When we use the ESMs, however, and analyze each activity of the system separately, the state spaces to explore have only a size of 38, 63, 5, 6, 54, and 50 states. Thus, even for such a relatively small system, we could reduce the maximum number of states to be checked in one single run from 957 to 63. The fact that four of these six blocks, including the largest one, were taken from our libraries and were already verified, reduced the effective effort even more.

6 Automatic Generation of ESMs from Activities

When designing an activity, the designer needs to make some assumptions about the environment. To describe these, the activity to encapsulate is placed within a minimal environment. In our editor, such an environment is part of a building block, since it is helpful to illustrate a building blocks usage. Figure 8 shows an environment for the buffered SMS sending: repeated SMS sending by the surrounding system is represented by a periodic timer, and the termination is triggered by a timer. Once the activity is instantiated in its context, the construction of the ESM is completely automated and consists of the following steps:

1. Following the semantics defined in [16], the discrete action steps of the activity within its minimal environment are generated using the tool described in [26]. The state space exploration starts then with the initial marking, in which all initial nodes hold one token. From this initial state, all reachable states are computed by executing all enabled activity steps. As a result, we obtain the state space graph G_x, with the reachable states as nodes and the executed activity steps as edges. The state space during this analysis is limited, since all call behavior actions within the activity to encapsulate are abstracted by their respective ESMs.

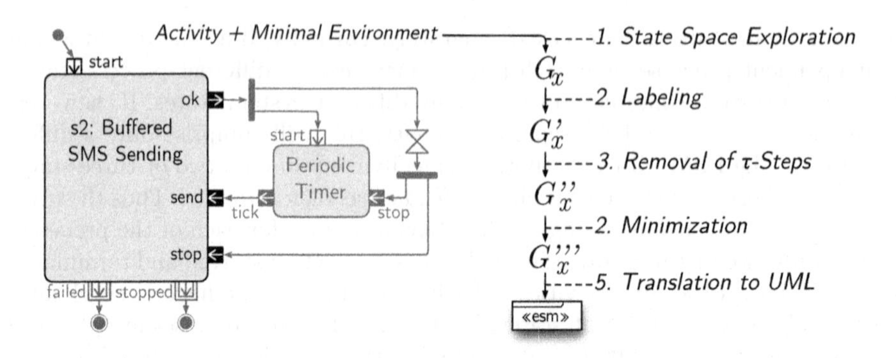

Fig. 8. Illustration of the steps for the automatic encapsulation

2. For each step in the state space, we analyze which parameter nodes of the activity to encapsulate are passed, and assign a corresponding label to the step. If no parameter node has been passed, the step is labelled with τ.
3. The τ-steps do not contribute to the visible behavior expressed by an ESM and therefore removed. For that, every pair of states that is connected by a τ-step is merged, and the τ-step is deleted.
4. After the removal of τ-steps, the resulting graph is minimized using the algorithm for state machine minimization described by Holzmann in [27].
5. From the resulting minimized graph, the UML representation in form of the ESM is constructed. The initial graph state is represented by an initial pseudo state. Each remaining graph state is represented by a UML state, resp. final state if the graph state has no outgoing steps.[2] For each graph step, an ESM transition referring to the corresponding activity parameter nodes is added.

We implemented the algorithm as an Eclipse plug-in, integrated with our modeling tool Arctis [7,28], using the UML repository of the Eclipse Modeling Project [29]. So far, we have used it on over 200 of our activities to encapsulate them by ESMs.

The implication relation between the ESM and the activity is ensured *by construction*, due to the layout of the algorithm. Formally, this can be verified by a refinement proof $A_x \Rightarrow E_x$ in temporal logic. The necessary refinement mapping (see [30]) can be obtained from the algorithm, by observing which states are merged during τ-step removal and minimization. For the Buffered SMS Sending example, we verified this refinement using the model checker TLC [31].

7 Related Work

There exists a number of language constructs to describe the visible behavior of components at distinct interaction points. ROOM [32], for instance, used protocols to define the ordering of signals transmitted by actors. The UML 2.x

[2] The algorithm assigns generic names to the states, which can be renamed in an optional, manual step.

standard proposes *protocol state machines* to define the allowed invocation sequences for operations on an object. Mencel [33] extends these descriptions by *port state machines*, to handle also nested calls and dependencies between required and provided interfaces. For the derivation of visible component behavior, Floch describes in [34] an algorithm that projects the observable behavior (i.e., the transmission of signals) of SDL processes towards specific gates. This work has been adapted in [35] for UML state machines. Our work, in contrast, handles the encapsulation of behavior on the level of activities; components and state machines are generated in an automated process, as described in [10]. The interfaces derived in [34] describe the transmission of signals *between* components. ESMs describe interfaces of activities that are composed *within* components, and do not imply signal transmissions. Rather, two activity flows connected via ESMs can be implemented by the same state machine transition.

Formally, the encapsulation of activities resembles the work of Kellomäkki and Mikkonen [36], who use the DisCo language [37] to capture specifications that are reusable solutions to problems. To reuse solutions in an application, they show that it suffices to integrate a more abstract template, and that properties proven for the solution are maintained when the template is applied. While this work is also based on temporal logic and uses refinement relations, it does not provide a mapping to UML as our work does.

8 Concluding Remarks

The streaming parameters of UML 2.x activities are a useful concept to enable the composition of systems from building blocks expressed by activities. From all building blocks involved in the case studies presented in Sect. 4.1, about two third make use of streaming parameters, so that activities may be composed in an interleaving manner. This enables that related functions may be offered as coherent, self-contained building blocks in the form of activities, but still can synchronize control and data flows with other parts of the system throughout their execution. To abstract from inner details and focus on the visible behavior at the streaming pins of an activity, we proposed the concept of ESMs, and described and implemented an algorithm to construct it. We have shown how this facilitates the provision of libraries, and how the compositional verification of systems is made possible by using ESMs as an abstraction mechanism. In addition, since, once consistent, a building block is encapsulated, an incremental development style is possible, in which systems can be designed, verified and composed *block by block*.

References

1. Object Management Group. Unified Modeling Language: Superstructure, version 2.0, formal/2005-07-05 (2005)
2. Kraemer, F.A.: Engineering Reactive Systems: A Compositional and Model-Driven Method Based on Collaborative Building Blocks. PhD thesis, Norwegian University of Science and Technology (2008)

3. Kraemer, F.A., Herrmann, P.: Service Specification by Composition of Collaborations — An Example. In: Proceedings of the 2006 WI-IAT Workshops (2006 IEEE/WIC/ACM International Conference on Web Intelligence and Intelligent Agent Technology), pp. 129–133. IEEE Computer Society, Los Alamitos (2006)
4. Kraemer, F.A., Slåtten, V., Herrmann, P.: Model-Driven Construction of Embedded Applications based on Reusable Building Blocks – An Example. In: Bilgic, A., Gotzhein, R., Reed, R. (eds.) SDL 2009. LNCS, vol. 5719, pp. 1–19. Springer, Heidelberg (2009)
5. Herrmann, P., Kraemer, F.A.: Design of Trusted Systems with Reusable Collaboration Models. In: Etalle, S., Marsh, S. (eds.) Trust Management. IFIP International Federation for Information Processing, vol. 238, pp. 317–332. Springer, Heidelberg (2007)
6. Kraemer, F.A., Samset, H., Bræk, R.: An Automated Method for Web Service Orchestration based on Reusable Building Blocks. In: Proceedings of the 7th International IEEE Conference on Web Services (ICWS), pp. 262–270. IEEE Computer Society, Los Alamitos (2009)
7. Kraemer, F.A., Bræk, R., Herrmann, P.: Compositional Service Engineering with Arctis. Telektronikk, vol. 1.2009 (2009)
8. Kraemer, F.A., Slåtten, V., Herrmann, P.: Engineering Support for UML Activities by Automated Model-Checking — An Example. In: Proceedings of the 4th International Workshop on Rapid Integration of Software Engineering Techniques, RISE (2007)
9. Kraemer, F.A., Bræk, R., Herrmann, P.: Synthesizing Components with Sessions from Collaboration-Oriented Service Specifications. In: Gaudin, E., Najm, E., Reed, R. (eds.) SDL 2007. LNCS, vol. 4745, pp. 166–185. Springer, Heidelberg (2007)
10. Kraemer, F.A., Herrmann, P.: Transforming Collaborative Service Specifications into Efficiently Executable State Machines. In: Ehring, K., Giese, H. (eds.) Proceedings of the 6th International Workshop on Graph Transformation and Visual Modeling Techniques (GT-VMT 2007). Electronic Communications of the EASST, vol. 7. EASST (2007)
11. Kraemer, F.A.: Rapid Service Development for Service Frame. Master's thesis, University of Stuttgart (2003)
12. Merha, B.T.: Code Generation for Executable State Machines on Embedded Java Devices. Project Thesis, Norwegian University of Science and Technology, Trondheim, Norway (2008)
13. Parlay Group. Parlay X Web Services Specification, Version 2.1 - Short Messaging, `http://www.parlay.org/en/specifications/pxws.asp`
14. PATS Lab Website, `http://www.pats.no`
15. Lamport, L.: Specifying Systems. Addison-Wesley, Reading (2002)
16. Kraemer, F.A., Herrmann, P.: Formalizing Collaboration-Oriented Service Specifications using Temporal Logic. In: Networking and Electronic Commerce Research Conference 2007 (NAEC 2007), pp. 194–220. ATSMA Inc. (2007)
17. Kraemer, F.A., Slåtten, V., Herrmann, P.: Tool Support for the Rapid Composition, Analysis and Implementation of Reactive Services. Journal of Systems and Software (to appear, 2009)
18. Slåtten, V.: Automatic Detection and Correction of Flaws in Service Specifications. Master's thesis, Norwegian University of Science and Technology (2008)
19. `http://www.sunspotworld.com`

20. Kathayat, S.B., Bræk, B.: Platform Support for Situated Collaborative Learning. In: Proceedings of the 2009 International Conference on Mobile, Hybrid, and Online Learning, Cancun, Mexico, pp. 53–60. IEEE Press, Los Alamitos (2009)
21. Beugnard, A., Jézéquel, J.-M., Noël, P., Watkins, D.: Making Components Contract Aware. IEEE Computer 32(7), 38–45 (1999)
22. Gaffney, J.E., Durek, T.A.: Software Reuse – Key to Enhanced Productivity: Some Quantitative Models. Information and Software Technology 31(5), 258–267 (1989)
23. D'Souza, D.F., Wills, A.C.: Objects, Components, and Frameworks with UML: the Catalysis Approach. Addison-Wesley, Reading (1999)
24. Frakes, W., Terry, C.: Software Reuse: Metrics and Models. ACM Computing Surveys 28(2), 415–435 (1996)
25. Clarke, E.M., Grumberg, O., Peled, D.A.: Model Checking. The MIT Press, Cambridge (1999)
26. Slåtten, V.: Model Checking Collaborative Service Specifications in TLA with TLC. Project Thesis, Norwegian University of Science and Technology, Trondheim, Norway (2007)
27. Holzmann, G.: Design and Validation of Computer Protocols. Prentice Hall Software Series. Prentice-Hall, Englewood Cliffs (1991)
28. Arctis Website, `http://arctis.item.ntnu.no`
29. Eclipse Modeling Project, `http://www.eclipse.org/modeling`
30. Abadi, M., Lamport, L.: The Existence of Refinement Mappings. Theoretical Computer Science 82(2), 253–284 (1991)
31. Yu, Y., Manolios, P., Lamport, L.: Model Checking TLA^+ Specifications. In: Pierre, L., Kropf, T. (eds.) CHARME 1999. LNCS, vol. 1703, pp. 54–66. Springer, Heidelberg (1999)
32. Selic, B., Gullekson, G., Ward, P.T.: Real-Time Object-Oriented Modeling. John Wiley & Sons, Inc., New York (1994)
33. Mencl, V.: Specifying Component Behavior with Port State Machines. Electronic Notes in Theoretical Computer Science 101, 129–153 (2004)
34. Floch, J.: Towards Plug-and-Play Services: Design and Validation using Roles. PhD thesis, Norwegian University of Science and Technology (2003)
35. SIMS Project Website, `http://www.ist-sims.org`
36. Kellomäki, P., Mikkonen, T.: Design Templates for Collective Behavior. In: Bertino, E. (ed.) ECOOP 2000. LNCS, vol. 1850, pp. 277–295. Springer, Heidelberg (2000)
37. Järvinen, H.-M., Kurki-Suonio, R., Sakkinen, M., Systä, K.: Object-Oriented Specification of Reactive Systems. In: Proceedings of the 12th International Conference on Software Engineering, pp. 63–71. IEEE Computer Society Press, Los Alamitos (1990)

Using UML Statecharts with Knowledge Logic Guards*

Doron Drusinsky** and Man-Tak Shing

Department of Computer Science,
Naval Postgraduate School,
Monterey, CA 93943, USA
{ddrusins,shing}@nps.edu

Abstract. This paper describes an extension of UML statecharts, called K-statechart, suitable for the formal specification, modeling, and runtime verification of system behavior that depends on knowledge and belief in distributed multi-agent systems. With K-statecharts, statechart transition guards allow the use of knowledge-logic formulae, a form of modal logic used for reasoning about multi-agent systems. We demonstrate the proposed formalism using an example of a multi-agent system that consists of three traffic-light controllers. We also describe a newly developed K-statechart code generator that is part of the StateRover Eclipse-IDE plug-in for statechart-based modeling and formal specification.

Keywords: K-statechart, knowledge-logic, adaptive behavior, formal specification, runtime verification.

1 Introduction

The new demand for autonomous agents to collaborate and produce intelligent behavior necessitates the specification and modeling of adaptive behavior based on human-like reasoning aspects such as knowledge and belief. However, most system and software engineers are unfamiliar with the text-based languages for specifying system behavior that depends on knowledge and belief, nor are these languages tied with common software engineering standards such as the UML.

Harel statecharts [1], currently part of the UML standard, are typically used for design analysis and implementation. In his recent book [2], the author suggested using deterministic and non-deterministic statecharts-assertions for formal requirement specification and run-time verification. This approach is currently in active use by the NASA IV&V Facility. Statecharts augment traditional state diagrams and as such contain states and transitions. A statechart transition

* The views and conclusions contained herein are those of the authors and should not be interpreted as necessarily representing the official policies or endorsements, either expressed or implied, of the U.S. Government. The U.S. Government is authorized to reproduce and distribute reprints for Government purposes notwithstanding any copyright annotations thereon.

** Also with Maya Software Inc. www.time-rover.com

A. Schürr and B. Selic (Eds.): MODELS 2009, LNCS 5795, pp. 586–590, 2009.

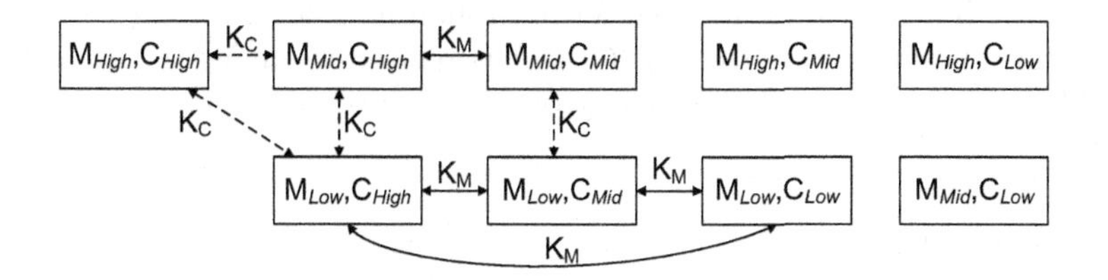

Fig. 1. A possible-worlds model example

is annotated with a triggering event, an optional condition guard, and an optional action, written as event[guard]/action [2]. A transition "A $\rightarrow_{event[guard]/action}$ B" fires when the event occurs and the guard formula evaluates to true while the statechart is visiting state A. Typically, the guard is written using standard propositional logic. This paper describes an extension to this notation that allows *knowledge-logic* guards.

Epistemic logic (knowledge logic) [3] is a form of modal logic that deals with knowledge and belief. Epistemic logic represents modalities using two primary modal operators: $\Box$ (interpreted as *knows*) and $\Diamond$ (interpreted as *has reason to believe*). A formula is evaluated given a Kripke structure $M = (S, \pi, K_1, \cdots, K_m)$, where S is set of states (or possible worlds), π is an assignment of truth values to the primitive propositions for each state $s \in S$, and K_i, $1 \geq i \geq m$, is a reflexive and transitive relation of agent i on S. $\Box_i P$ ($\Diamond_i P$) holds in system state s if and only if P holds true in all (some) states reachable from s using relation K_i. $\Box_i P$ in state s is read as: *agent i knows P when in state s*; $\Diamond_i P$ is read as: *agent i has reason to believe P when in state s*. The K_i relations represent the availability of information to agent i while in a given system state. For example, Figure 1 shows the possible-world model[1] of a system consisting of two agents M and C, one residing in Monterey and the other in Cupertino. Each agent has three states $\{Low, Mid, High\}$, representing temperatures *below 40 degrees*, *between 40 and 60 degrees*, and *above 60 degrees* in their corresponding cities. The edges $K_c(\langle M_x, C_{High}\rangle, \langle M_y, C_{High}\rangle)$, $x, y \in \{Low, Mid, High\}$, represent the fact that given the information at hand (above 60 degrees in Cupertino and the knowledge that temperatures in Cupertino are never lower than those in Monterey), the Cupertino agent cannot distinguish whether the temperature in Monterey is above 60, between 40 and 60, or below 40. Suppose now that the weather state combination on a particular day is $\langle M_{High}, C_{High}\rangle$. The Cupertino agent can then formally say he *has reason to believe* the weather in Monterey is 40-60. This is because some state that $\langle M_{High}, C_{High}\rangle$ is related to under the K_c relation (e.g. $\langle M_{Mid}, C_{High}\rangle$) satisfies the basic property: *weather in Monterey is between 40 and 60 degrees.* The Cupertino agent, however, cannot

[1] This model is symmetric, i.e., all relations are symmetric. However, this is not generally required. Furthermore, we omit the arrows representing the reflexive relations $K_c(\langle M_x, C_y\rangle, \langle M_x, C_y\rangle)$ and $K_m(\langle M_x, C_y\rangle, \langle M_x, C_y\rangle)$, $x, y \in \{Low, Mid, High\}$ to reduce the crowdedness of the figure.

formally say that he *knows* the weather in Monterey is 40 to 60 degrees. This is because not all states that $\langle M_{High}, C_{High} \rangle$ is related to under the K_c relation (e.g. $\langle M_{Low}, C_{High} \rangle$) satisfy the basic property: *weather in Monterey is 40 to 60 degrees.*

2 K-Statecharts

The syntax of K-statecharts is a straightforward hybrid of the syntax of statecharts with that of knowledge logic. In fact, the only syntactic difference between statecharts and K-statecharts is in the statechart transition guard. A K-statechart transition guard extends a statechart transition in that a guard condition may contain knowledge-logic Boolean formulae, as illustrated in Figure 2. As discussed in section 1, an integral part of knowledge logic is the definition of a possible-worlds model. We consider this relation to be defined as part of a dynamic data-model associated with the statechart. The semantics of K-statecharts are a straightforward hybrid of the semantics of the statecharts with that of knowledge logic, as follows. A K-statechart guard evaluates to true if its formula evaluates to true using the knowledge-logic semantics described earlier. Consider a system-of-systems (SoS) consisting of three Traffic-Light Controllers (TLCs) depicted in Figure 2, where the proposition *pedestrianIsAllowed* only holds in TLC-C's *Red* state. Note the guard condition ρ in the timeout transition from the *Red* state to the *Green* state in the statechart for TLC-A:

$$\rho\text{: } \textit{this.believes(get\_b().knows(get\_c().pedestrianIsAllowed()))}.$$

This reads as: TLC-A *has reason to believe* that TLC-B *knows* that TLC-C is now *allowing a pedestrian to cross the junction*, where the notion of belief is described below.

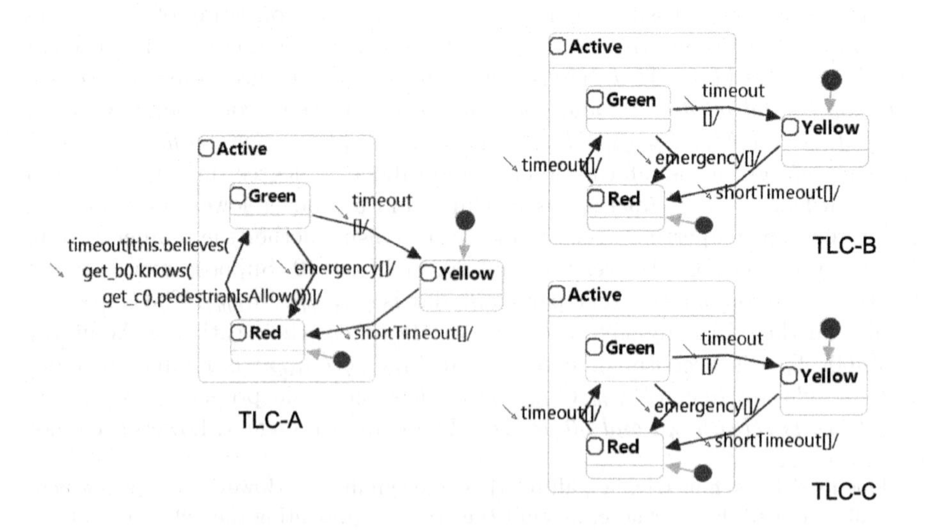

Fig. 2. The multi-agent TLC K-Statechart model

The source state of the associated transition (state *Red* of TLC-A) is the context for this formula, i.e., the condition ρ is evaluated when TLC-A is in its *Red* state. The evaluation of ρ depends on the visibility each TLC agent has into the present-state of the other TLC agents, defined using a possible-worlds model, as follows. First, let us consider the situation where visibility is perfect, i.e., each TLC can distinguish the present state of all other TLCs down to their lowest level of granularity. The formal possible-worlds visibility model consists of all possible 3-tuples $\langle a, b, c\rangle$, where a, (resp. b and c) can be one of TLC-A's (resp. TLC-B's and TLC-C's) 3 states. Having perfect visibility means there are no relation edges in the possible-worlds model. Assume that the TLC system is in the state-configuration $s = \langle Red, b, c\rangle$. Then TLC-A will consider b and c as the only possible state TLC-B and TLC-C can be in at the time. ρ evaluates the belief operator by examining all states K_{TLC-A} related to s (there is only one such state, namely $\langle Red, b, c\rangle$ itself) to see if some of those states satisfy the remaining part of the formula ρ, namely,

ψ: *TLC-B knows that TLC-C is now allowing a pedestrian to cross the junction*

When the system is in $\langle Red, b, c\rangle$, TLC-B is in state b; consequently, the evaluation of ψ is performed by evaluating whether TLC-B, when in state b, knows that TLC-C is now *allowing a pedestrian to cross the junction.* Again, because of perfect visibility, the only possible state of TLC-C is state c. Evaluation is now atomic, it returns the Boolean result of the evaluation of the *pedestrianIsAllowed* proposition (implemented as a Boolean method) in state c. Consequently, the ρ transition guard of Figure 2 succeeds if TLC-C's state c happens to be *Red*, and fails otherwise.

Now consider another situation where the possible-worlds model contains partial visibility, visibility that reflects the fact that TLC-B is designed to be synchronized with TLC-C, i.e., they are always in the same respective states. Here, the possible-worlds model contains no K_{TLC-B} edges connecting to or from a state $\langle a, b, c\rangle$ where $b \neq c$. With this model, TLC-A considers all states of TLC-B possible, no matter what state it is in, because TLC-A has no information regarding the present state of TLC-B. Consequently, as in the previous case, for ρ to satisfy that TLC-A *has reason to believe* ψ while in the *Red* state, ψ must be satisfied in one of the three states of TLC-B; one such candidate is TLC-B's *Red* state. When TLC-B is in the *Red* state, all K_{TLC-B} related state-configurations have TLC-C in its *Red* state, a state that satisfies the *pedestrianIsAllowed* proposition. Hence, the ρ transition guard in Figure 2 succeeds.

3 The StateRover K-Statechart Code Generator and Run-Time Model

The StateRover is an Eclipse plug-in that supports graphical editing, automatic code generation, and visual debug animation of statecharts [2]. It is used for model-driven development and for light-weight formal verification. It supports code generation for Java, C, and C++. The K-statechart code generator extends the existing StateRover Java code generator and generates Java source code. This code is exercised or invoked, by an external driver. When executing in a modeling or testing environment this driver is most often JUnit, the de-facto standard Java unit testing framework.

The driver issues statechart events by calling the respective statechart methods. For example, a JUnit driver invokes TLC-C's transition from state *Red* to state *Green* by calling *c.timeout()*; where *c* is the TLC-C object. The driver also sets the run-time possible-worlds model. This means that the multi-agent K-statechart model can be used with a dynamically changing possible-worlds model, thereby enabling computer-aided modeling of a multi-agent system in which information visibility changes over time. For example, listing 1 contains a JUnit driver that sets the run-time possible-worlds model and fires TLC events.

Listing 1. A JUnit test-case scenario driver for the multi-agent TLC example

```
// Fire events that move TLC-A, TLC-B, TLC-C to Red
a.shortTimeout(); b.shortTimeout(); c.shortTimeout();

// Set Yellow and Red states of TLC_B (the b object) to
// both be possible when TLC_A (the a object) is in Red
EquivalenceSet equiv = new EquivalenceSet();
equiv.add("Yellow"); equiv.add("Red");
a.knowledge.setEquivalence("Red", b, equiv);

// Set the Red state of TLC_C (the c object) to be possible
// when TLC_B (the b object) is in Red
EquivalenceSet equiv1 = new EquivalenceSet();
equiv1.add("Red");
b.knowledge.setEquivalence("Red", c, equiv1);

// Fire event to invoke transition with knowledge-logic guard:
a.timeout();
assertTrue(a.isState("Green"));
```

References

1. Harel, D.: Statecharts: A Visual Formalism for Complex Systems. Science of Computer Programming 8, 231–274 (1987)
2. Drusinsky, D.: Modeling and Verification Using UML Statecharts. Elsevier Publishing, Burlington (2006)
3. Rescher, N.: Epistemic Logic: A Survey Of the Logic Of Knowledge. University of Pittsburgh Press, Pittsburgh (2005)

A Modeling Language for Activity-Oriented Composition of Service-Oriented Software Systems

Naeem Esfahani, Sam Malek, João P. Sousa, Hassan Gomaa, and Daniel A. Menascé

Department of Computer Science,
George Mason University
{nesfaha2,smalek,jpsousa,hgomaa,menasce}@gmu.edu

Abstract. The proliferation of smart spaces and emergence of new standards, such as Web Services, have paved the way for a new breed of software systems. Often the complete functional and QoS requirements of such software systems are not known a priori at design-time, and even if they are, they may change at run-time. Unfortunately, the majority of existing software engineering techniques rely heavily on human reasoning and manual intervention, making them inapplicable for automatic composition of such software systems at run-time. Moreover, these approaches are primarily intended to be used by technically knowledgeable software engineers, as opposed to domain users. In this paper, we present *Service Activity Schemas (SAS)*, an activity-oriented language for modeling software system's functional and QoS requirements. SAS targets service-oriented software systems, and relies on an ontology to provide domain experts with modeling constructs that are intuitively understood. SAS forms the centerpiece of a framework intended for user-driven composition and adaptation of service-oriented software systems in a pervasive setting. We provide a detailed description of SAS in the context of a case study and formally specify its structural and dynamic properties.

Keywords: Requirements Modeling, Domain Specific Modeling Languages, Model Driven Development, Autonomic Computing, Pervasive Systems.

1 Introduction

Software systems are increasingly permeating a variety of domains, including medical, industrial automation, defense, and emergency response. The growth of service-oriented software systems and the emergence of new standards have made it possible to develop pervasive systems that were not even conceivable a few years ago.

In particular, the decoupling of service providers from consumers and the flexibility of dynamically discovering and binding to services have facilitated the development of software systems intended for execution in smart spaces. The proliferation of portable and embedded computing devices and the recent advances in wireless network connectivity have further made the service-oriented architecture (SOA) paradigm a viable option in such settings. Web Services [1] have also played a crucial role in enabling interoperability and alleviating integration challenges in pervasive settings.

Domain experts and end-users increasingly rely on such systems for their day to day activities. The software deployed in such settings needs to deal with the inherently

A. Schürr and B. Selic (Eds.): MODELS 2009, LNCS 5795, pp. 591–605, 2009.

dynamic and unpredictable nature of pervasive environments. Finally, the functional requirements of such software systems are often not completely known at design-time, and even if they were, they may change at run-time.

These characteristics have forced the designers of such systems to deal with two emerging and increasingly important classes of daunting challenges: (1) rapid composition of software systems at run-time based on the users' changing needs, and (2) autonomous adaptation of the software system at run-time to satisfy the system's functional and non-functional requirements. However, the majority of existing software engineering techniques for representing, analyzing, and composing software systems rely heavily on human reasoning and manual intervention, making them unwieldy for use in this setting. Moreover, these approaches are primarily intended to be used by technically knowledgeable software engineers, as opposed to domain experts that use such systems on a daily basis.

Motivated by the aforementioned challenges, we have developed a framework entitled *Self-Architecting Software Systems (SASSY)* [2]. SASSY enables autonomic composition and adaptation of service-oriented software system based on the domain users' requirements. To that end, domain users express their functional and Quality of Service (QoS) requirements in an intuitively understood visual modeling language. SASSY in turn automatically generates an architectural model that satisfies the system's requirements, and deploys it through discovery and coordination of available services. Moreover, SASSY continuously monitors the running system and, if necessary, adapts the architecture and running system to ensure the user's requirements are satisfied throughout the system's execution.

In this paper, we present *Service Activity Schemas (SAS)*, an activity-oriented language for modeling the user requirements in the SASSY framework. SAS allows for the representation of both functional and QoS requirements in terms of modeling constructs that are intuitively understood by domain experts. The SAS modeling notation relies on a domain ontology that clearly specifies the semantics of the domain entities and their interrelationships.

Unlike existing low-level service coordination languages (e.g., BPEL [3] semantic BPEL[4], JOpera [5]) and software modeling languages (e.g., UML [6], ADL [7]), the language is intended to be usable by domain experts. While SAS is motivated by business process modeling languages (e.g., BPMN [8]), it represents a departure from them as it codifies the system requirements in a manner that enables the automatic generation of executable pervasive SOA software systems.

We have developed an implementation of SAS as a Domain Specific Modeling Language (DSML) on top of the Generic Modeling Environment (GME) [9]. The static and dynamic characteristics of the language are formally specified using the GME meta-models and Z notation [10], respectively. Our experiences with applying the language and environment to pervasive SOA software systems have been very positive. In all cases, the language proved to be both usable and rich enough to accurately represent the domain expert's requirements. A subset of one of these systems for a fire emergency application is described throughout this paper.

The remainder of the paper is organized as follows. Section 2 introduces the SASSY framework and describes the role of SAS in the overall scheme. Section 3 presents the related work. Section 4 describes a case study, which is used to introduce the language in Section 5. Section 6 details the process of using the language for the composition of service-oriented software system. Sections 7 and 8 present the structural and dynamic semantics of SAS, respectively. Finally, the paper concludes with an outline of our future work.

2 The SASSY Framework

SASSY [2] is a model-driven framework for composing SOA software systems (see Fig. 1 for an overview). The domain expert specifies the functional and QoS requirements using the SAS language, which is the focus of this paper. With the help of a domain ontology, these requirements are translated into the system's base software architecture. The domain ontology provides the means for unambiguously distinguishing different concepts and elements, which as outlined further below facilitate discovery of services and resources in support of activities. We assume the domain ontology is created and maintained by a consortium of domain experts, who specify the various domain activities and concepts, including the properties of respective services that realize them.

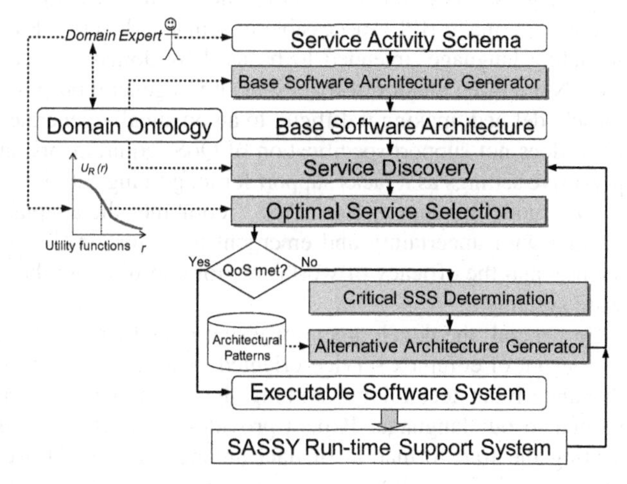

Fig. 1. An overview of SASSY framework

Examples of such ontology and directories provided by the US government for various domains can be found at [11].

After generating the base architecture, SASSY instantiates the architecture by discovering the required services and selecting the ones that maximize a global utility function that depends on the system's QoS requirements. SASSY generates alternative architectures by exploring and applying architectural patterns that increase the utility. For instance, in a situation where a service provider's availability causes the utility to be reduced, SASSY may employ a replication pattern to compose two services in a way that one can be used as a hot standby for the other.

At run-time, SASSY monitors the services and computes the value of the global utility function. When it is reduced by a given threshold, SASSY re-architects the system and adapts it accordingly. Similarly, SASSY re-architects the system when the domain experts change the system requirements, and thus evolves the system.

3 Related Work

There are fundamentally two schools of thought concerning the modeling of activities: one focuses on the modeling of human activities, the other focuses on the modeling of workflow of computational and/or business processes.

The first has its roots in psychology, going back to Leont'ev's modeling of craftsmen activities [12], which inspired design approaches in human-computer interaction based on the modeling of user activities (e.g., [13]). This approach recognizes that users carry out actions to achieve their goals, but that the specific actions and their ordering is adapted to the material conditions of execution, that is, it cannot be prescribed a priori: a concept called *situated* action.

In contrast, workflow modeling prescribes a concrete flow of actions to be followed. Recently, there has been considerable work on Business Process Execution Language (BPEL [3]), and Business Process Modeling Notation (BPMN [8]). BPEL is an executable business process language, serialized in XML, to support programming in the large (e.g., see [14] for an overview and formal semantics and [4] for application of ontology to make BPEL accessible in semantic level). BPMN [8] is a business process modeling language, intended to be used by domain experts in a variety of domains. BPMN has three major drawbacks: (1) it is a general purpose language and semantically loosely defined, making it difficult to automatically generate executable models from it; (2) it does not support specification of QoS requirements; and (3) it is not suitable for pervasive settings as it lacks support for long living activities.

Our modeling approach in SASSY combines the adaptability of situated action, for dealing with uncertainty and emergent behaviors in domains such as emergency response, and the efficacy of workflow, for coordinating the behaviors of complex software systems.

In general, the development of visual modeling languages and tools for supporting the design of complex service-oriented systems is lagging behind the development of the underlying technology. Among the existing works, JOpera [5] is most closely related to our language. JOpera provides a workflow modeling language for representing the transformation of data among services. However, unlike SAS, the language provided by JOpera is very low-level and not intended for use by domain experts. Moreover, JOpera does not provide support for modeling QoS requirements, long living activities, and distinguishing local activities from services.

Finally, UML [6,15] is a commonly used notation for the visual modeling of today's software systems. UML's diagrams provide a standard notation for representing the various structural and behavioral aspects of a system's software. Several approaches extend UML's notation via stereotypes [16,17]. However, using UML to visualize the requirements of a software system has several drawbacks: UML's diagrams are relatively static; they do not consider services as first-class modeling entities; do not provide native support for representing and visualizing the parameters that affect the system's QoS properties; and are not semantically constrained to enable automatic composition of SOA software. Moreover, UML is not aligned with SASSY objectives, as it is geared to software engineers, instead of domain experts.

4 Case Study

We use a software system, called *Fire Emergency Response System (FERS),* for describing the language and demonstrating its properties throughout this paper. FERS is developed internally and motivated by existing standards [11]. It targets SOA-enabled smart spaces and is intended for use by emergency response organizations to automatically detect, respond, and manage fire emergencies.

An FERS school is equipped with two types of sensors: smoke detectors and fire sprinklers. There may be many smoke detectors and fire sprinklers throughout a school. A sensor exposes a web service that provides operations for accessing its status and controlling it. For instance, a fire sprinkler service provides operations that allow other entities in the system to turn the sprinkler on/off. A school also exposes a service that provides profile information, such as the name of the school, location, number of students, and hours of operation.

An FERS fire station has a fire monitoring service (FMS) that keeps track of all the sensors in the schools. A fire station also has several fire engines. Once smoke is detected by the FMS, it uses the fire station's fire dispatch service to dispatch the closest smart fire engines to the scene. In order to determine the number of required fire engines that need to be dispatched, the dispatch service uses a heuristic based on the information (e.g., number of students, size of the school, and hours of operation) made available by the school's profile service and the number of smoke sensors that have detected smoke.

A fire engine constantly communicates its status and progress to the station's dispatch service. As soon as the fire has been extinguished, the system resets the smoke detectors, turns off the fire sprinklers, and orders the fire engines to return to base.

5 Language Overview

This section introduces the SAS language through a small subset of the FERS system. In Sections 7 and 8, we revisit the language constructs and precisely define their semantics.

Fig. 2 shows some of the modeling constructs available in the SAS language. *Events* are messages exchanged between two separate entities. *Gateways* manage the flow of control within an entity. Some of the supported gateways include *InclusiveGateway* (Conditional-Or), *ExclusiveGateway* (Switch), and *ParallelGateway* (Fork and And-Join).

The language distinguishes local *Activities* from *ServiceUsages*, i.e., activities performed by external entities (another organization). An underlying assumption in our work is that activities and service types are defined in a domain ontology, and commonly understood by domain experts. SAS also supports hierarchical composition through the notion of *Sub-SAS*. *Activities, Sub-SASs*, and *ServiceUsages* are represented by rectangles with round corners. A *Sub-SAS* is delineated with a plus sign, for bringing up the internal composition, and a *ServiceUsage* with a server icon. Communication with a service is via *Input* and *Output* events, while communication with a *Sub-SAS* is via *StartLink* and *EndLinks*.

An SAS model is a graph where nodes correspond to activities and services that are coordinated to realize some functionality. In fact, as detailed in Section 6, an SAS may realize the functionality of a service type defined in the ontology.

Fig. 2b shows an SAS model that realizes the dispatching service of FERS. When a *dispatch* message arrives, dispatching service calculates which fire engines should be assigned to the incident. The SAS is divided into two parallel sequences through a

ParallelGateway, which behaves as a fork/join. The first path queries the *School* service where the smoke detector is located to get an estimate of the number of people in the school. The second path uses the *createInc* interface of the *MissionManager* Sub-SAS to create a record for the incident.

When both the *incident* and *occupancy* messages have arrived, they are joined by a *ParallelGateway* into a single sequence. *assignFE* is a looping activity that uses this information to determine which fire engines (FE), if any, should be dispatched.

When the dispatching service receives a *normalcy* message, it uses the *cancelMis* interface of *MissionManager* to send a *callBack* message to command the fire engines to return to base. Throughout the mission each fire engine periodically reports its status to the dispatch service by sending a *report* message.

Fig. 2c shows the association of a QoS requirement with a path through the dispatching service SAS. A QoS requirement is specified via a *Service Sequence Scenario (SSS)*. In this case, the *response* SSS indicates that the *School* service should respond to a request made by the coordinator within a pre-specified time. Section 7 describes how such QoS requirements are specified as attributes of an SSS.

An SAS may be made available for reuse as a service, a Sub-SAS, or both. An SAS exposed as a service may be used by external organizations for constructing their own SASs. Similarly, a Sub-SAS allows for hierarchical composition of SASs, and enables reuse within the same organization. The details of SAS reuse are further discussed in Section 6.

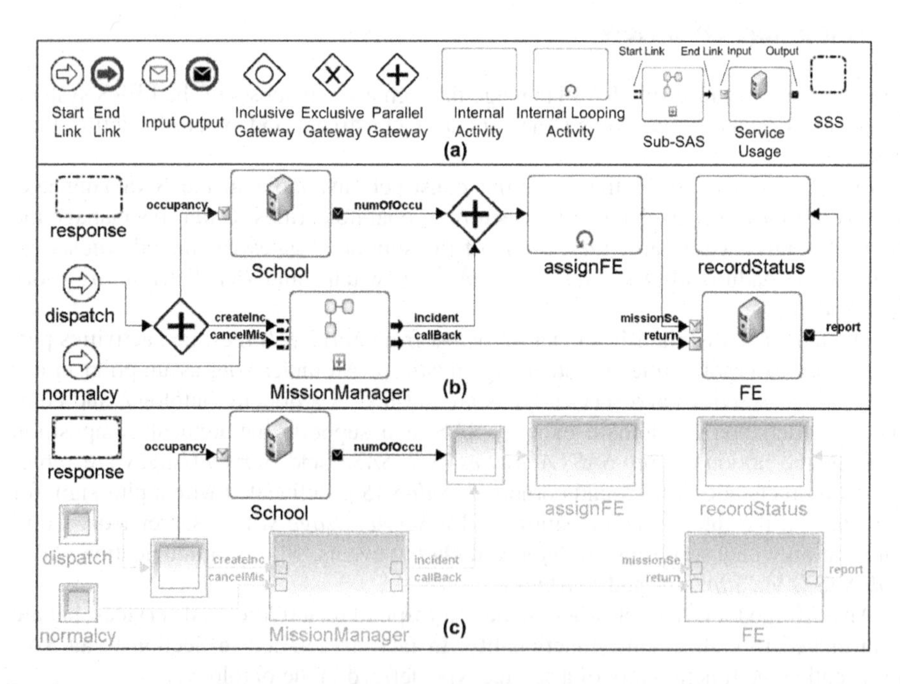

Fig. 2. SAS for dispatch service: a) language constructs, b) basic flow, and c) response SSS is selected

Note that since one of our objectives has been to make the SAS language usable by domain experts, the coordinator is implicitly defined. In other words, an SAS model represents the coordination between internal activities and external services. This differs from a software design perspective, where a coordinator component is explicitly delineated and separated from the rest of the system. Our approach is compatible with existing business process modeling languages (e.g., BPMN [8]) that are also intended for use by domain experts.

6 Building Service-Oriented Systems with SAS

In our work we assume each domain has either a standard body or an organization in charge of defining the domain ontology. For example, in the emergency response domain a government authority typically defines the corresponding ontology (e.g., [11]). SAS enables an organization to realize a service type defined in the ontology, and make it available for external use by registering it in a service directory (e.g., UDDI [18,19]). In this way each organization retains its autonomy. At the same time, the ontology enables interoperability and integration among the various organizations, and forms them into a coherent task force. We further elaborate on the details of this process below.

Defining a service type in the ontology consists of specifying (1) the service's interfaces, and (2) the service's interaction protocol. A service type's interfaces correspond to its input and output messages, similar to the information provided in a WSDL [18]. A service type's interaction protocol describes the relationship between the service's interfaces. It indicates the output messages and the order they are generated when the service receives a particular input.

For defining the interaction protocol a subset of the SAS constructs (i.e., *Input*, *Output*, *Gateway*, and *Flow*) is used. Fig. 3a shows the interaction protocol for the FE service (recall example of Fig. 2b). This interaction protocol specifies that a service of FE type receives *return* and *missionSend* messages and as result of that generates one or more *report* messages. The flow from the gateway to itself in Fig. 3a specifies that in response to one request message several *report* messages can be generated.

Organizations query the ontology for a service type's definition to determine how an instance of it can be used in their own SAS. An organization that intends to provide an instance of a service type creates a corresponding SAS as follows: replaces the *Inputs* and *Outputs* messages with *StartLink* and *EndLinks*, respectively; and provides an implementation for each of the service's interfaces that comply with its interaction protocol. The constructed SAS is then made available to other organizations by registering it in a service directory.

Fig. 3b illustrates the corresponding SAS for the interaction protocol of the FE service shown in Fig. 3a. As a result of the FE service receiving a return order, the fire engine goes back to its base station. The location of base station is a parameter in the *return* message that is delivered to *goToLocation* activity. While on its way back, the *goToLocation* activity periodically sends a *report* message, which as you may recall from recall Fig. 2b updates the fire station of the vehicle's current status.

When the FE service receives the *missionSend* message, the vehicle is directed to go to the fire scene, and as before continuously sends updates of its current status.

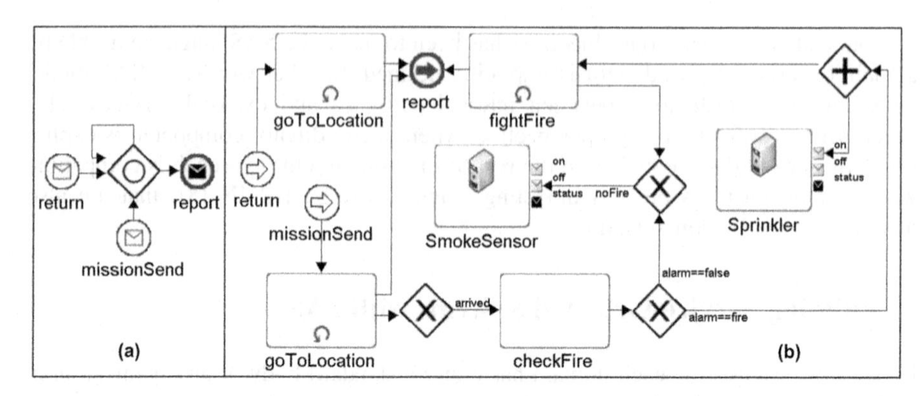

Fig. 3. Fire engine (FE) service: a) interaction protocol specification, and b) an SAS implementing the service specification

When the fire engine arrives, it checks whether there is a real fire or not. If it is a *false* alarm, the smoke sensors are turned off. Otherwise, the sprinklers are turned on, and the FE is directed to extinguish the fire. Meanwhile, the FE continuously sends *report* messages to update the fire station of its progress.

Note that activities such as *goToLocation*, *fightFire*, and *checkFire* may either be automatically enabled, or rely on a firefighter to manually check the existence of a fire and inform the system through a user interface. In other words, we model the humans through the user-interface (itself a service) they use for the interaction with the system. The domain experts are advised to be careful with the specification of QoS goals (*SSS*) involving such activities, since the ability to satisfy such QoS properties relies on the humans, whose behavior cannot be controlled by SASSY.

The SAS depicted in Fig. 3b is only one implementation of the FE service. Other organizations may provide their own implementation of FE using different SASs. The only restriction is that the SAS needs to adhere to the interface definition and the interaction protocol (i.e., Fig. 3a) described in the ontology. Note that our approach does not prevent organizations from providing an implementation of a service type using other more traditional techniques (e.g., programming languages, BPEL).

7 Structure of SAS

The linguistic structure of SAS is defined using the meta-model provided by the Generic Modeling Environment toolkit (GME) [9]. GME is a general purpose model-driven engineering environment that enables the development of domain-specific modeling languages. Just as formal grammars define the structure of valid sentences for textual languages, meta-models play a similar role for graphical languages. GME has the ability to interpret a given meta-model and automatically build a modeling environment that enforces the structural rules.

The meta-modeling language supported by GME is a stereotyped variant of UML, which we explain below, as needed.

Fig. 4 shows the meta-model for SAS divided into three parts, for readability: graph, service, and QoS. Starting with graph, an *SAS* model contains *Nodes*, *ServiceUsages*, and *Flows* between those. Nodes may be either *ActivityUsages* or *Gateways*, which in turn may be *Parallel*, *Inclusive*, or *Exclusive*. We elaborate on each of these below.

Furthermore, hierarchical decomposition is supported by allowing an *SAS* to contain other *SAS*s (i.e., a *Sub-SAS*). A parent *SAS* interacts through *StartLink* and *EndLink* nodes, which act respectively as input and output interfaces to a child *SAS*. Ultimately, a number of *SAS*s may be included in a hierarchical structure of folders containing the *Requirements* for a system.

With respect to the stereotypes that annotate this meta-model, GME defines *Model* which corresponds to a diagram, *Set* for defining subsets of objects within a diagram, *Atom* which has a graphical representation, and *Connection*, represented as a line between two atoms. Additionally, *Reference* provides a mechanism to describe several usages of a single definition. First class object (*FCO*) is a super type of the above used for organizing the meta-model, and has no associated graphical representation of its own, e.g., *SAS* is a *Model*, an *Exclusive* gateway is an *Atom*, and *Gateway* is an *FCO*.

A *Flow* represents a line between two *GenericNodes*: the source and destination of the flow. A *Flow* carries data from between two nodes. The *Condition* field of a *Flow* determines whether a particular data can traverse that *Flow*. The *Mapping* field of a *GenericNode* specifies the transformation of data as it enters and exits a node. This transformation describes which data is passed into the node, and which data is returned from the node. Since the transformation of data is a common feature of several SAS constructs (e.g., *Gateways*, *ActivityUsages*, *Links*), it is modeled as an attribute of *GenericNode*. *Gateways* play a key role in coordinating the behavior of an SAS, and are best explained in behavioral terms: see Section 8.

7.1 Services and Activities

ServiceUsage and *ActivityUsage* constitute the basic functional elements of an SAS. While an *activity* is carried out internally by the component, e.g., a call to a system library, a *service* is requested to another component, possibly across the network. A *LoopingActivityU* may repeat a number of times determined by the *Condition* field, before completion. An *Activity* may have a return value which can be specified using *Result*. The *Results* are added to the outgoing data.

Both *ActivityUsage* and *ServiceUsage* are stereotyped with *Reference*, which allows for referring to existing *Activity* and *Service* definitions. Such definitions exist in *ActivityDirectory* and *ServiceDirectory*, respectively, which are populated based on the information available in a domain ontology, and may be consulted by the domain experts while designing an SAS.

Fig. 4b shows the meta-model for services. A *ServiceDirectory* is a *Folder* containing multiple *Service* definitions. A *Service* is a *Model*, that is, it has an associated diagram containing *Input* and *Output* interface nodes. The role of the latter is similar to the role of the *StartLink* and *EndLink* interface nodes: to facilitate the interaction between other constructs in the *SAS* and the internals of the particular box (a service or sub-SAS, respectively). *Outputs* are responsible for returning the *Result* from the *Service*. The *Proxies* that annotate the meta-model are simply a mechanism provided by GME for referring to objects defined in other parts of the meta-model.

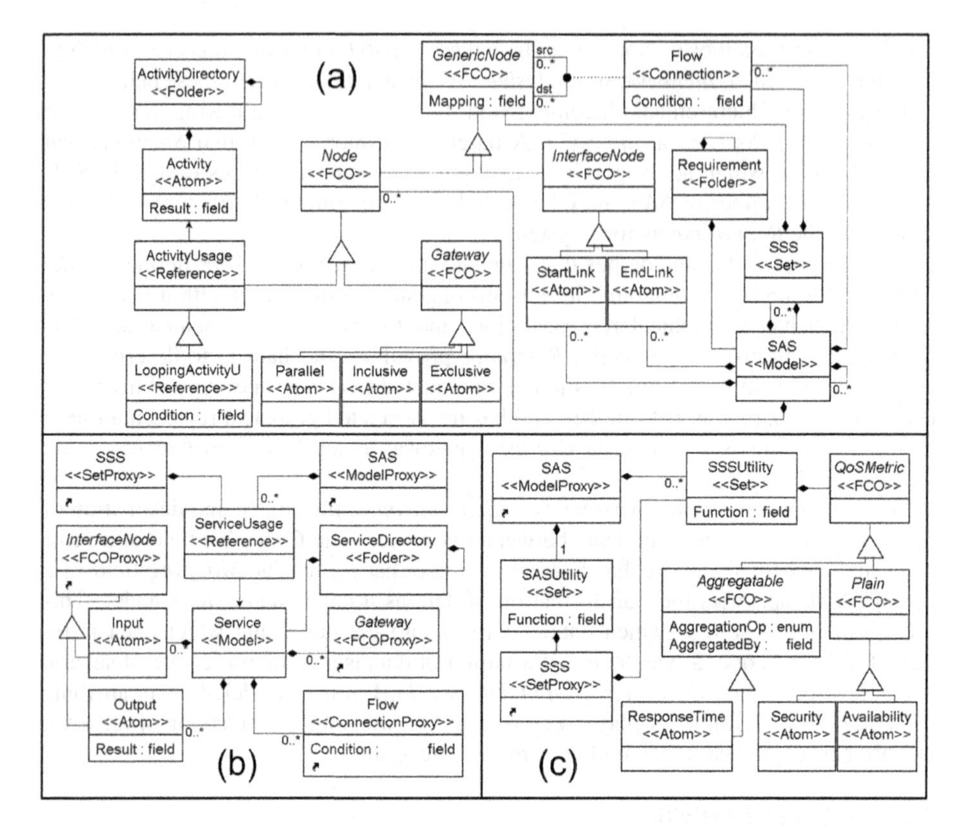

Fig. 4. Meta-model for SAS in three parts: a) graph, b) service, and c) QoS

7.2 Service Sequence Scenarios and QoS

Service Sequence Scenarios (SSS) are used to represent the user's QoS preferences. For that, each SSS defines a path through the SAS (recall Fig. 2c). In the meta-model, we represent an SSS path as a set of *GenericNode* and *Flow* constructs. Naturally, an SAS may contain several SSS sets, each modeling a separate QoS concern. Fig. 4c shows the internal structure of an *SSS*, which consists of *QoSMetric* and *SSSUtility* for defining the QoS and the user's preferences, respectively.

QoSMetric may be typed as *Plain* or *Aggregatable*. Values of *Plain* QoS cannot be aggregated into more complex measures, e.g., a measure of *Security* in a qualitative scale could be: *Low*, *Medium*, *High*. In contrast, the values of *Aggregatable* ones may be combined using aggregation operators, such as summation or mean, in the case of numbers. For example, a measure of throughput may be derived from measures of response time and parallel capacity. Fig. 4c shows *ResponseTime* as an *Aggregatable* measure, but the approach is not limited to a predetermined set of metrics.

An *SSSUtility* contains one or more *QoSMetric*s and provides a *Function*, which returns the utility associated with a given level of *QoSMetric*(s) for a user.

Finally, an SAS contains a global utility function, called *SASUtility*. It includes a set of SSS and is used to specify the users' preferences in resolving the trade-offs among multiple SSS constructs. Its *Function* field specifies the relationship between the contained SSS constructs, i.e., quantifies the impact of achieving QoS specified in the *SSSUtilities* on the value of the global utility (*SASUtility*).

8 Behavior of SAS

The model presented in this section complements the meta-model in section 7 by clarifying the behavior of the different kinds of *Node*s (Fig. 4). Similar to BPMN and Petri Nets [20], this model is based on the notion of execution *token*. Specifically, the purpose of the behavior model herein is to answer the question: if a token is presented as an input to a node, how does that node process the token?

By specifying the behavioral semantics of the nodes in SAS, this model offers a precise guideline for the automatic generation of implementation code (i.e., coordination logic) from SASs. We selected Z [10] as a convenient notation to express the behavior of SAS constructs. Z builds on set theory and offers constructs such as base sets, functions, schemas, and operations, which are explained by example, below.

Tokens and nodes are modeled as elements of base sets *Token* and *Node*, respectively. At the implementation level, tokens correspond to messages circulating in the system, possibly with a data payload, and nodes correspond to the functional elements that process those messages and decide what to do next. By modeling tokens as elements of a base set, they are individually distinguishable, but their internal structure is abstracted out. The same holds for nodes. The left side of the model below shows the definitions for these base sets, an enumeration, *Type*, and a schema, *SAS*:

$[Node, Token]$
$Type ::= In \mid Out \mid Start \mid End \mid ExclusiveGW \mid InclusiveGW \mid ParallelGW \mid Activity \mid LoopingActivity$

SAS
$Tokens : \mathbb{P}\ Token$

$Input: Node \times \mathbb{P}\ Token \rightarrow \mathbb{P}\ Token$
$Loop: Node \times \mathbb{P}\ Token \rightarrow \mathbb{P}\ Token$
$Merge: Node \times \mathbb{P}\ Token \rightarrow \mathbb{P}\ Token$
$Generate: Node \times \mathbb{P}\ Token \rightarrow \mathbb{P}\ Token$
$All: Node \times \mathbb{P}\ Token \rightarrow \mathbb{P}\ Token$
$Possible: Node \times \mathbb{P}\ Token \rightarrow \mathbb{P}\ Token$
$OnePoss: Node \times \mathbb{P}\ Token \rightarrow \mathbb{P}\ Token$

The *Type* enumeration captures the type of node as defined in section 7: activities, start and end links of Sub-SASs, etc. The set of tokens currently in circulation characterizes the execution state of an SAS. The schema *SAS* above holds the *Tokens* set as a state attribute. This set is modified by operations that capture the behavior of the different kinds of nodes. Consumed tokens are removed from *Tokens*, while the produced ones are added to it. To help specify the behavior of nodes, a number of functions are defined on the right side of the model excerpt above. These functions can be grouped into three categories: query, generate, and replication functions.

Input, *Loop*, and *Merge* query the availability of tokens at the input of nodes. These three functions take two arguments: a node of interest and the set of tokens currently in circulation in the SAS. Specifically, *Input* returns (a set containing) a token that is present at an input flow of the node, if such a token is available among the ones currently in circulation in the SAS (passed as the second argument). If not, *Input* returns the empty set. *Loop* returns (a set containing) a token, if the node is a *LoopingActivity* that currently holds a token, and if its associated looping condition remains true. *Merge* returns a set of tokens, one token taken from each of the inputs leading up to the node, provided each of the inputs has at least one token available. The *Generate* function abstracts out the transformations of the data payload of tokens that may occur within nodes. Specifically, given a node and a set of tokens at the node's input, *Generate* returns the token produced by the node.

All, *Possible*, and *OnePoss* are replication functions. They take a newly generated token and a node, and place copies of the token on the node's output flows.

Replication functions take into account the constraints on the flow of tokens, as represented by the *Condition* in the *Flow* object in Fig. 4a. Specifically, *Possible* places a token on each of the output flows where the associated condition holds, while *OnePossible* does the same for only one of the output flows, selected non- deterministically. For nodes that do not impose constraints on the output flows, such as the *ParallelGateway*, the *All* function places a new token on each output flow.

8.1 Services and Sub-SAS

The SAS initialization function and the specifications of *Input*, *Out*, and *Link* are:

SASInit

SAS'

$Tokens' = \emptyset$

InputNode

$\Delta SAS;\ n?: Node;\ t?: Type$

$t? = In \wedge Tokens' = Tokens \setminus Input(n?, Tokens)$

OutputNode

$\Delta SAS;\ n?: Node;\ t?: Type$

$t? = Out \wedge Tokens' = Tokens \cup Possible(n?, Generate(n?, \emptyset))$

LinkNode

$\Delta SAS;\ n?: Node;\ t?: Type;\ i: \mathbb{P}\ Token$

$(t? = Start \vee t? = End) \wedge i = Input(n?, Tokens)$

$Tokens' = (Tokens \cup Possible(n?, Generate(n?, i))) \setminus i$

SASInit specifies that initially there are no *Tokens* inside the SAS. A *Link* could be considered an interface of an SAS that connects its constructs to those outside of it. A *Link* passes a subset of the data on an arriving *Token* to the output *Token*. A *StartLink* does this on *Tokens* received from the outside of an SAS, while the *EndLink* does this on the *Tokens* leaving an SAS.

Note that a sub-SAS shares the same set of *Tokens* with the parent SASs. As you may recall from Section 6, an SAS may expose its interfaces as services, in which case the run-time environment (i.e., the coordination engine) provides the inputs to its *StartLinks* and collects the outputs at its *EndLinks*.

The *In* and *Out* are the interfaces of a *ServiceUsage* (see Fig. 4b), and hence they serve as destination and source of tokens, respectively. The run-time environment transfers the *Tokens* between the SAS and external services.

8.2 Gateways

Gateways synchronize activities by forking and joining several threads of activities. The *ParallelGateway* requires all the inputs to arrive (And-join) and activates all the output flows (fork) at the same time. When an input flow is activated, the *InclusiveGateway* (Conditional-Or) activates a subset of the output flow. For an outgoing flow to be activated, the condition specified on the flow must be satisfied. On the other hand, the *ExclusiveGateway* activates the first outgoing flow that has its condition satisfied. The outgoing sequence that is activated is selected non-deterministically. The join semantic for both the *InclusiveGateway* and *ExclusiveGateway* are the same.

The behavior of *ExclusiveGateway* and *InclusiveGateway*, which are the main constructs for enforcing conditions in forking and joining, are specified as follows:

ExclusiveNode

ΔSAS; $n?$: $Node$; $f?$: $Type$; i: $\mathbb{P}\ Token$

$f? = ExclusiveGW \wedge i = Input(n?, Tokens)$
$Tokens' = (Tokens \cup OnePoss(n?, Generate(n?, i))) \setminus i$

InclusiveNode

ΔSAS; $n?$: $Node$; $f?$: $Type$; i: $\mathbb{P}\ Token$

$f? = InclusiveGW \wedge i = Input(n?, Tokens)$
$Tokens' = (Tokens \cup Possible(n?, Generate(n?, i))) \setminus i$

The *ExclusiveGateway* consumes the available input and generates a token for one of the possible output flows. The *InclusiveGateway* does the same thing except it generates a token for all the output flows where the associated condition holds.

Finally, the behavior of the *ParallelGateway* is:

ParallelNode

ΔSAS; $n?$: $Node$; $f?$: $Type$; m: $\mathbb{P}\ Token$

$f? = ParallelGW \wedge m = Merge(n?, Tokens)$
$Tokens' = (Tokens \cup All(n?, Generate(n?, m))) \setminus m$

The *ParallelGateway* merges all of the input flows and produces tokens for all of the outgoing ones, regardless of the conditions specified on the outgoing flows. If one of the input tokens is not available, *ParallelGateway* does nothing (i.e., it does not consume or generate tokens).

8.3 Activities

The *Activity* operation captures the behavior of *ActivityUsage* nodes, and is very similar to the *Link* operation. The only difference is that the *Generate* function for *Activity* may add new data (i.e., result of the activity) to *Tokens*.

A *Looping* activity is an extension of a regular activity. It queries for an available token as follows: it first uses the *Loop* function to find any available tokens inside the *Looping* activity to consume, when there are no more tokens available in the activity, it uses the *Input* function to consume tokens from the inputs.

These concepts are specified as follows:

ActivityNode

ΔSAS; $n?$: $Node$; $t?$: $Type$; i: $\mathbb{P}$ $Token$

$t? = Activity \wedge i = Input(n?, Tokens)$
$Tokens' = (Tokens \cup Possible(n?, Generate(n?, i))) \setminus i$

LoopingNode

ΔSAS; $n?$: $Node$; $t?$: $Type$; i,l: $\mathbb{P}$ $Token$

$t? = LoopingActivity \wedge i = Input(n?, Tokens) \wedge l = Loop(n?, Tokens)$
$(l \neq \emptyset \wedge Tokens' = (Tokens \cup Possible(n?, Generate(n?, l))) \setminus l) \vee$
$(l = \emptyset \wedge Tokens' = (Tokens \cup Possible(n?, Generate(n?, i))) \setminus i)$

9 Conclusion

The emergence of SOA-enabled systems in pervasive settings calls for major advances in the software engineering methods currently employed. In this paper, we presented SAS, a novel visual modeling language intended to alleviate the existing shortcomings by automating the composition of such systems. SAS relies on a domain ontology to allow an expert specify the system's functional and QoS requirements using commonly understood terminology. The formal specifications of the structural and behavioral semantics of SAS provide a precise guideline for the automatic generation of a system's architectural model and executable code (i.e., coordination logic), respectively.

Unlike the existing software design languages (e.g., UML [6], ADLs [7]), SAS is intended for use by domain experts, as opposed to software engineers. To that end, the language is motivated by existing business process modeling languages (e.g., BPMN [8]), which are commonly used by domain experts. However, in contrast, SAS codifies the software requirements in a manner that enables the automatic composition of service-oriented systems.

SAS is part of an ongoing research effort on Self-Architecting Software Systems (SASSY) framework [2]. SAS models have been used in SASSY to successfully compose service-oriented system. Some of the ongoing research include, automatically finding the optimal architecture with respect to QoS objectives specified in SAS models, adaptation of a running system in response to environmental changes, and evolution of a system due to changes in the SAS models.

Acknowledgments. This work is partially supported by grant CCF-0820060 from the National Science Foundation.

References

1. W3C Web Services, http://www.w3.org/2002/ws/
2. Malek, S., Esfahani, N., Menascé, D.A., Sousa, J.P., Gomaa, H.: Self-Architecting Software Systems (SASSY) from QoS-Annotated Activity Models. In: ICSE 2009 workshop on Principles of Engineering Service Oriented Systems (PESOS 2009), Vancouver (2009)
3. OASIS WS-BPEL ver 2.0, http://docs.oasis-open.org/wsbpel/2.0/OS/wsbpel-v2.0-OS.html
4. Nitzsche, J., Wutke, D., Van Lessen, T.: An ontology for executable business processes. In: Proceedings of the Workshop on Semantic Business Process and Product Lifecycle Management (SBPM), Innsbruck (2007)
5. Pautasso, C., Heinis, T., Alonso, G.: JOpera: Autonomic Service Orchestration. IEEE Data Eng. Bull. 29, 32–39 (2006)
6. OMG UML ver 2.0, http://www.omg.org/spec/UML/2.0/
7. Medvidovic, N., Taylor, R.N.: A Classification and Comparison Framework for Software Architecture Description Languages. IEEE Trans. Softw. Eng. 26, 70–93 (2000)
8. OMG BPMN Spec. ver 1.1, http://www.omg.org/spec/BPMN/1.1/
9. Generic Modeling Environment, http://www.isis.vanderbilt.edu/Projects/gme/
10. Spivey, J.M.: The Z notation: a reference manual. Prentice-Hall, Inc., NJ (1989)
11. US Government Web Services and XML Data Sources, http://www.usgovxml.com/
12. Leont'ev, A.N., Hall, M.J.: Activity, consciousness, and personality. Prentice-Hall, Englewood Cliffs (1978)
13. Bdker, S.: Through the interface: A human activity approach to user interface design. L. Erlbaum Associates Inc., Hillsdale (1991)
14. Ouyang, C., et al.: Formal Semantics and Analysis of Control Flow in WS-BPEL. Science of Computer Programming 67, 162–198 (2007)
15. Fowler, M., Scott, K.: UML distilled: a brief guide to the standard object modeling language. Addison-Wesley Longman Publishing Co., Inc., Boston (2000)
16. Medvidovic, N., et al.: Modeling software architectures in the Unified Modeling Language. ACM Transactions on Software Engineering and Methodology 11, 2–57 (2002)
17. Greenfield, J.: UML Profile for EJB. Public Review Draft, JSR-000026 (2001)
18. Weerawarana, S., Curbera, F., Leymann, F., Storey, T., Ferguson, D.F.: Web Services Platform Architecture: SOAP, WSDL, WS-Policy, WS-Addressing, WS-BPEL, WS-Reliable Messaging and More. Prentice Hall PTR, Englewood Cliffs (2005)
19. Papazoglou, M.: Web Services: Principles and Technology. Pearson-Prentice Hall, London (2007)
20. Petri, C.A.: Kommunikation mit automaten, Auch im Handel als: Schriften d. Rheinisch-Westfalischen Instituts f. instrumentelle Mathematik an Universitat Bonn, Germany (1962)

A Domain Specific Modeling Language Supporting Specification, Simulation and Execution of Dynamic Adaptive Systems*

Franck Fleurey and Arnor Solberg

SINTEF, Oslo, Norway
{Franck.Fleurey,Arnor.Solberg}@sintef.no

Abstract. Constructing and executing distributed systems that can automatically adapt to the dynamic changes of the environment are highly complex tasks. Non-trivial challenges include provisioning of efficient design time and run time representations, system validation to ensure safe adaptation of interdependent components, and scalable solutions to cope with the possible combinatorial explosions of adaptive system artifacts such as configurations, variant dependencies and adaptation rules. These are all challenges where current approaches offer only partial solutions. Furthermore, in current approaches the adaptation logic is typically specified at the code level, tightly coupled with the main system functionality, making it hard to control and maintain. This paper presents a domain specific modeling language (DSML) allowing specification of the adaptation logic at the model level, and separation of the adaptation logic from the main system functionality. It supports model-checking and design-time simulation for early validation of adaptation policies. The model level specifications are used to generate the adaptation logic. The DSML also provides indirection mechanisms to cope with combinatorial explosions of adaptive system artifacts. The proposed approach has been implemented and validated through case studies.

1 Introduction

Context-aware software systems that can automatically adapt to changes in their environments play increasingly vital roles in society's infrastructures. The demand for Dynamic Adaptive Systems (DAS) appears in many domains, ranging from crisis management systems such as disaster or power management, to entertainment and business applications such as mobile interactive gaming, tourist guiding and business collaborations applications. However, constructing and executing DAS are complicated. A main challenge is to cope with the variability that can lead to explosion of several adaptive system artifacts. The set of possible configurations of an adaptive system is typically specified by identifying variation points, which represents points in the software where variability may occur. Having variability at each variation point

* This work was partially funded by the DiVA project (EU FP7 STREP, contract 215412). See http://www.ict-diva.eu/

A. Schürr and B. Selic (Eds.): MODELS 2009, LNCS 5795, pp. 606–621, 2009.

implies a combinatorial explosion of configurations and quadratic explosion of possible configuration transitions, which again can cause possible explosion of variant dependencies and adaptation rules. This makes it difficult to provide consistent adaptation rules and to convey optimized configurations for the particular context. To cope with DAS complexities proper modeling and validation techniques all along the development cycle are needed.

Current approaches rely on the direct use of language or platform mechanisms such as reflection, dynamic loading of code or architecture reconfigurations to build and execute DAS. Most modern languages and middleware platforms include these kinds of low-level mechanisms to support runtime adaptation. Using such techniques, the adaptation is captured in low-level platform specific scripts and tightly coupled with the application code. The development of these scripts typically comes very late in the development cycle, is particularly error-prone, and the resulting system is brittle to any change in the platform or in the application.

To overcome these problems, the state of the art has recently evolved to support variability and adaptation modeling, and also to make use of models at runtime to drive and monitor runtime adaptation [3][4][7][10][11]. Two main families of formalisms have been proposed in order to capture adaptation policies. The most common one is based on event-guard-action rules relating environment events to reconfiguration actions (e.g., [7][11]). These approaches benefit from using well-known policy definition formalisms, they can be implemented very efficiently and allow early simulation and verification. These approaches are very well suited for small to medium scale[1] context-aware systems (e.g., many embedded systems). However, they have scalability problems related to the management and validation of large sets of rules when context and variability spaces grow. To cope with the scalability issue, optimization based approaches have been proposed (e.g., [4][10]). These approaches do not explicitly capture the adaptation rules, instead they use utility functions to capture high level goals such as for example "optimizing the performance". The utility is evaluated at runtime for all possible configurations to choose the optimal one. These more abstract adaptation policy expressions solve the scalability problem related to specifying adaptation policies. However, the problem with these approaches is a costly runtime adaptation process since the system has to solve a complex optimization problem for every adaptation, and weaker support for early validation.

The contribution of this paper is an approach that combines the strength of rule-based and optimization-based techniques in order to offer a solution scalable to highly-adaptive systems while providing abstraction, efficiency and early verification and validation capabilities. The idea of the approach is to combine local adaptation rules and property-based adaptation goals. The approach provides a Domain Specific Modeling Language for capturing context information, system variability, constraints and adaptation policies. The DSML allow for design-time model-checking and simulation of the adaptation models. Moreover, platform specific adaptation logic can be generated form the models. The approach has been implemented in Eclipse and is

[1] To better qualify scalability here: *small-scale* implies that the complete set of possible configuration can be enumerated by the developer, *medium-scale* implies that the complete set can be processed by a computer, *large-scale* implies that the set of possible configuration is too large to be enumerated at all.

integrated in a complete model-driven approach for DAS development. The scalability of the approach is evaluated on two industrial case studies. Initial results show that the proposed formalism is able to cope with large-scale adaptive systems.

The paper is structured as follows: Section 2 presents an illustrative example. Section 3 presents the abstract syntax of the DSML and its application using the illustrative example. Section 4 details the semantics of the language and shows how early validation can be performed through model-checking and simulation. Section 5 briefly describes the implementation and usage of the proposed approach. Section 6 presents the results of four case studies. Section 7 compares the proposed formalism with existing techniques. And finally, Section 8 presents concluding remarks and future work.

2 Illustrative Example: A Semi-autonomous Exploration Robot

To illustrate our approach we use a simple example of a mapping robot. The system is a semi-autonomous exploration robot which builds a map of an unknown environment when in motion. The robot is connected to a central system which collects the topographic data and can give directions to the robot. The robot has 3 main modes: i) idle, ii) going to a specific location or iii) exploring autonomously. It is equipped with three different sensors which can be used alternatively for routing and for drawing the map: i) *Camera*, which provides the most detailed map, ii) *Infrared sensors*, which can work without light sources and use limited resources, *and iii) Ultrasonic sensors*, which consumes limited resources while providing good routing capabilities.

While being drawn, the map is either stored locally in the robot's memory with periodic transmissions or directly streamed to a server. To allow for transmissions as well as for receiving commands the robot is equipped with Bluetooth and GPRS networking capabilities. The robot can employ three different routing strategies: i) *local routing strategy* that uses the sensors to navigate, ii) *map routing strategy* that uses pre-knowledge of the terrain, and iii) *external routing strategy* that involves interactions with a central computer or an operator. Furthermore, to build the map when moving, the robot can either use a simple or detailed map drawing strategy.

Depending on its environment, i.e., on its mode, on the terrain conditions or on the resources available, the robot has to dynamically adapt in order to optimize the map building and to use appropriate sensors and algorithms.

3 Modeling Dynamic Variability and Adaptation

The role of the adaptation model is to formalize how and when a system should adapt. The adaptation model thus has to capture the variability in the system, the variability in the context of the system and rules to link changes in the context of the system with the configuration to be used. In the following we first present the abstract syntax of the proposed formalism and then an actual adaptation model for the mapping robot are build using a corresponding concrete syntax. An Eclipse based editor is implemented for specifying the adaptation models.

3.1 Overview of the DSML Abstract Syntax

Fig. 1 presents the main concepts of the abstract syntax of the proposed DSML for adaptation modeling. The proposed languages can be logically divided in three parts: it provides i) simple mechanisms to model the variability in the DAS, ii) simple mechanisms to model the context of the DAS and iii) an innovative combination of hard constraints and property optimization policies to model adaptation. We have chosen simple mechanisms to model variability and context to provide ease of use. Moreover, these mechanisms have been sufficient for modeling the current set of case studies (see section 5).

The system variability is modeled using *Dimension*, *Variant* and *VariantConstraint*s. A dimension typically corresponds to a variation point in the system and the variants correspond to the alternatives for this variation point. The multiplicity on the dimension (*upper* and *lower* properties of class *Dimension*) specifies how many of the variants can be included in order to build a valid configuration. Dimensions and variants can be easily represented as a feature diagram. Arbitrary dependency constraints between variants belonging to different dimensions can be expressed by attaching dependency constrains to the variants. The application of such constraints is elaborated further when describing the modeling of the robot example in the following subsections.

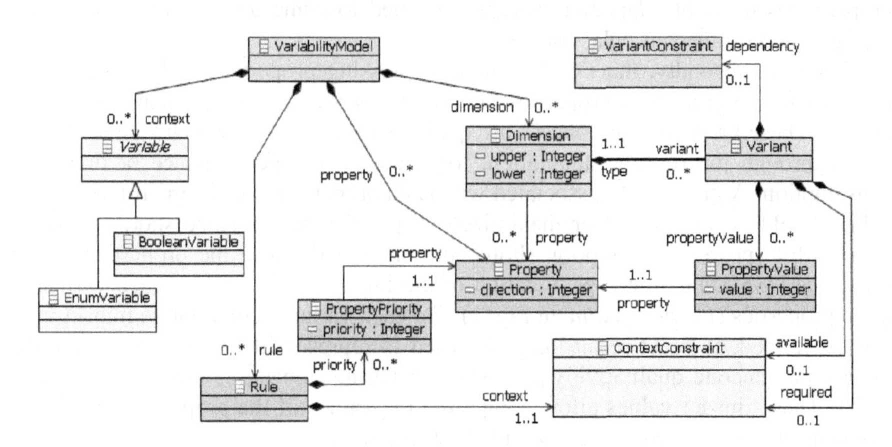

Fig. 1. Excerpt of the adaptation DSML abstract syntax

The context of the system is modeled using a set of variables (*Variable* and its subclasses on the diagram of Fig. 1). The objective of these context variables is to capture the elements of the environment which can implicate a system adaptation. To keep simplicity and remain at a high-level of abstraction, the proposed approach captures all the context information in either Boolean or Enumerated variables. If the configuration of a system depends on continuous value such as for example the amount of available memory, these will be abstracted into discrete ranges such as {LOW, MEDIUM, HIGH}. This kind of abstraction has the benefit of decoupling the adaptation model from the actual values and thresholds for a particular domain or application. Thus, the actual values might be unknown at design-time, and they may be adjusted at deployment time or even at runtime.

The most important part of the DSML is to support the specification of the adaptation logic, in essence, the relations between the context and the variability of the system. As discussed in the introduction, existing approaches are either based on event-guard-action rules or on global optimization of some utility function associated to the system configurations. The approach proposed in this paper is a combination of constraints and property optimization which intent to provide a scalable solution in order to handle large-scale adaptive systems, and at the same time enable early simulation and validation (detailed comparisons with existing approaches are presented in section 7).

To determine the adaptation logic the DSML enable firstly to specify constraints associated to variants. In Fig. 1 these constraints corresponds to the two compositions named *available* and *required* between *Variant* and *ContextConstraint*. These constraints are local to each variant and specify in which context the variant can (*available*) or must (*required*) be used. The constraint can be any first order logic expression combining context variables. Concrete examples are provided with the robot example in the next subsection. In practice, variant constraints allow reducing the set of configuration suitable for a particular context. However, in general constraints cannot point to the specific configuration which should be used. The idea of the proposed approach is to enable specification of adequate local hard constraints in order to break the combinatorial explosion of the potential number of configurations to be considered, then, a general property-based set of adaptation rules is specified to come up with the best suitable configuration for the particular context.

Therefore, secondly, the DSML enable expressing property-based rules. This includes associating a set of properties of concern for the adaptive system (*Property* in Fig. 1). These properties of concern are qualities of the system which should be optimized through the runtime adaptation, for example, the performance or the power consumption. A direction is associated with each property to determine if the property value should be minimized or maximized. Typically, performance should be maximized while power consumption should be minimized. Once the properties are defined, the DSML facilitate specification of the impact implicated by each variant on these properties (*PropertyValue* in Fig. 1). For each variant, a qualitative impact value can be defined. In practice an integer is used to represent the impact value but this integer just encode qualitative values such as {0: no impact, 1: low, 2: medium, 3: high}. These impact values allow comparing the values of the properties for alternative configuration in order to choose the best suited one.

Finally, the DSML support specification of priority rules (*Rule* and *PropertyPriority* in Fig. 1). These rules allow linking the context with the particular set of properties which should be optimized. Each rule is related to a context to determine in which context the rule applies and it specifies a set of property priorities for the particular context. Basically these rules allow specifying which properties should be optimized depending on the context. The main benefit of this approach is that the general adaptation policy is captured at a high-level of abstraction. An example of rule at this level might be "if the battery runs low, the power consumption should be prioritized over performances". By computing the specified impact each variant has with respect to the properties, these rules can be used to evaluate alternative configurations and to choose the most suited.

The next sub-section details how the proposed adaptation language is applied to the robot example. Then section 4 comes back to the details of the semantics of the language and presents how adaptation can be simulated.

3.2 Step by Step Modeling of the Mapping Robot

This section walks through the modeling of the adaptation logic of the mapping robot example to show an application of the DSML and elaborate further on its elements. We have implemented an Eclipse based editor to support the modeling.

Fig. 2 presents how the context of the mapping robot was modeled using the Eclipse based modeling editor. We have identified 5 context variables for the system. The Mode variable captures what the robot has been instructed to do. The robot has 3 main modes: IDLE, EXPLORE and GOTO. The two next variables "Light" and "Bluetooth Signal Available" specifies characteristics of the physical environment of the robot. Finally, the two last variables "Low Memory" and "Low Battery" specifies resources of the robot itself.

	Name	ID	Values
Enum	Mode	Mode	{IDLE, EXPLORE, GOTO}
Literal	IDLE	IDLE	-
Literal	EXPLORE	EXPLORE	-
Literal	GOTO	GOTO	-
Boolean	Light	LIGHT	-
Boolean	Blutooth Signal Available	BTSig	-
Boolean	Low Memory	LowMem	-
Boolean	Low Battery	LowBatt	-

Fig. 2. Model of the context of the robot

In general, the context variables can correspond to any stimuli of the system that should be taken into account for runtime adaptation. It includes user interactions, interaction with other systems or sub-systems as well as data coming from sensors. For example, in the case of the robot, the *LowMem* variable is used to determine whether the system is running out of memory. When modeling, the actual amount of memory the robot will have is not necessarily known. At runtime, probes have to be implanted in the system to compute the actual values of these variables and an actual threshold for *LowMem* need to be set.

	Name	ID	Lower	Upper	Dependency	Avalable	Required
Dimension	Routing	RTG	0	1	-	-	-
Variant	Local Routing	LR	-	-		Mode = GOTO	
Variant	Map Based Routing	MBR	-	-		not LowMem and Mode = GOTO	
Variant	External Routing	ER	-	-	GPRS or BT	Mode = GOTO	
Dimension	Networking	NET	0	1	-	-	-
Variant	Bluetooth	BT	-	-		BTSig	
Variant	GPRS	GPRS	-	-		not BTSig	
Dimension	Sensors	SEN	0	1	-	-	-
Variant	Camera	CS	-	-		LIGHT and not Mode = IDLE	
Variant	Infrared	IRS	-	-		not Mode = IDLE	
Variant	Ultrasonic	USS	-	-		not Mode = IDLE	
Dimension	Map Building Strategy	MBS	1	1	-	-	-
Variant	Simple Map	SM	-	-			
Variant	Detailed Map	DM	-	-	BUFFER or BT		
Dimension	Data Transmission	DATA	1	1	-	-	-
Variant	Streaming	STREAM	-	-	BT or GPRS		LowMem
Variant	Buffering	BUFFER	-	-		not LowMem	

Fig. 3. Model of the variability and constraints in the robot

Fig. 3 presents the variability of the mapping robot and the dependency and adaptation constraints. For example, the robot has 3 alternative routing strategies (see the *routing dimension* and its three *variants*). A maximum of one of these strategies (specified with the *lower* and *upper* multiplicity [0..1]) can be used for a particular configuration of the robot. The *External Routing* strategy involves requesting a central computer for a route, and then to follow the instructions. To be able to use *External Routing,* communication with the central computer is required either through a Bluetooth network or via GPRS. This hard constraint is modeled in the dependency column: The expression *GPRS or BT* expresses the fact that the variant can only be used together with the GPRS or Bluetooth variants. The *Available* and *Required* expressions correspond to contexts in which the variant respectively can or must be used. For example, it only makes sense to consider a routing strategy when the robot is in *GOTO* mode as it is the only mode which requires routing capabilities.

	Name	ID	Direction
Property	Power Consumption	PWR	0
Property	Network usage	NETUSE	0
Property	Map Detail	MAP	1
Property	Routing accuracy	ROUTE	1
Property	Data Latency		0

Fig. 4. Properties of concern of the robot

At this point, the context variables, variants and adaptation constraints have been modeled. Next we model the properties of concern. Fig. 4 presents the 5 properties of concern identified for the mapping robot. These properties correspond to functional or extra-functional properties of the system which should be optimized through adaptations. Each property has a name and ID and a direction. The direction specifies if the property value should be minimized (0) or maximized (1). For the robot the directions specify that we want to minimize *Power Consumption*, *Network Usage* and *Data Latency* and we want to maximize the *Routing accuracy* and the *Map Detail.*

	Power Consumption	Network usage	Map Detail	Routing accuracy	Data Latency
Routing (RTG)	true	false	false	true	false
Local Routing (LR)	Low	-	-	Medium	-
Map Based Routing (MBR)	High	-	-	Medium	-
External Routing (ER)	Medium	-	-	High	-
Networking (NET)	true	false	false	false	false
Bluetooth (BT)	High	-	-	-	-
GPRS (GPRS)	Medium	-	-	-	-
Sensors (SEN)	true	false	true	true	false
Camera (CS)	High	-	High	High	-
Infrared (IRS)	Low	-	Medium	Low	-
Ultrasonic (USS)	Low	-	Low	Medium	-
Map Building Strategy (MBS)	true	true	true	false	false
Simple Map (SM)	Low	Low	Low	-	-
Detailed Map (DM)	High	High	High	-	-
Data Transmission (DATA)	true	false	false	false	true
Streaming (STREAM)	High	-	-	-	Low
Buffering (BUFFER)	Low	-	-	-	High

Fig. 5. Impact of the variants on the properties of the robot

Fig. 5 shows the specification of the impact each variant has on the properties of concern. The rows of this table correspond to the dimensions and variants defined earlier and the columns corresponds to the properties of the system. For each dimension the value *true* specifies that this dimension has an impact on the corresponding property. In this case, for each variant a qualitative appreciation of its impact on the property has to be specified. In the example of the mapping robot only the values *Low*, *Medium* and *High* have been used. If we consider for example the *Routing* dimension, the model specifies that the routing strategy impacts the power consumption and the routing accuracy. For each routing strategy variant, values for this impact are provided: The *local routing* has low power consumption but only a medium routing accuracy while the *external routing* has medium power consumption but a high accuracy. This table is the base to make different trade-offs and to find the optimal configuration for the actual context.

Finally, Fig. 6 presents the adaptation rules specified for the mapping robot. These rules are *Priority Rules*: they capture what properties of the system matters depending on the context. For example rules 4 and 5 corresponds to the battery level. Rule *Battery is low* specifies that if the battery is low, optimizing the power consumption of the robot has a high priority. Conversely, rule 5 specifies that when the battery is ok, optimizing the power consumption is a secondary concern for the mapping Robot.

	Name	ID	Guard	Power Consumption	Network usage	Map Detail	Routing accuracy	Data Latency
Rule	IDLE Mode	NM	Mode = IDLE	High	High	Low	Low	N/A
Rule	Exploration mode	PM	Mode = EXPLORE	N/A	N/A	High	Low	Low
Rule	Go to mode	FM	Mode = GOTO	N/A	N/A	Low	High	Medium
Rule	Battery is Low	LB	LowBatt	High	N/A	N/A	N/A	N/A
Rule	Battery is OK	LB	not LowBatt	Low	N/A	N/A	N/A	N/A
Rule	BT available	BT	BTSig	N/A	Low	N/A	N/A	N/A
Rule	no BT	GP	not BTSig	N/A	High	N/A	N/A	N/A

Fig. 6. Adaptation rules of the robot

In this example the guard for every rule is a single context variable, however, the DSML allow arbitrary context expressions. If several rules match a given context simple strategies such as using the maximum value for each property are used to combine them.

4 Simulation and Validation of the Adaptation Model

The tables presented in the previous section present the complete adaptation model defined for the mapping robot. This section discusses the semantics of the adaptation model and describes the tools that were developed in order to simulate and verify it.

4.1 Semantics and Implementation of the Adaptation Model

Conceptually, the adaptation model is separated in two parts. On the one hand the context variables, the variants and the hard constraints and on the other hand the properties and priority rules. From a given context, processing the adaptation model

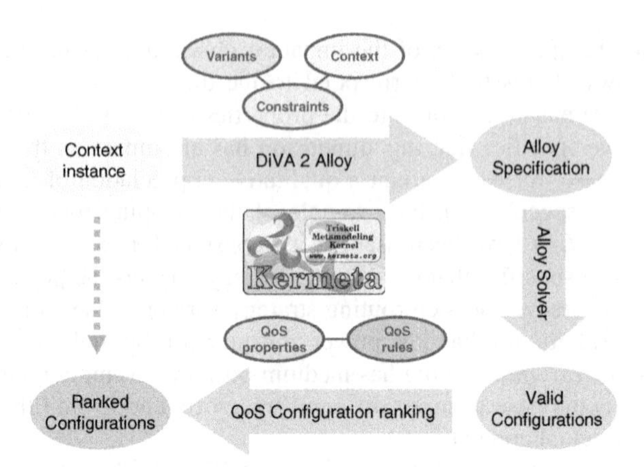

Fig. 7. Implementation of the adaptation simulator

has to yield the best suited configuration for the system in that context. In the proposed approach this is done in two steps:

1. The hard constraints are processed in order to enumerate candidate configurations for the system.
2. The priority rules are used to compute a score and rank the candidate configuration.

After the second step, the candidate configuration which has the best score is chosen and the system can be adapted.

To do early testing and validation an adaptation simulator is implemented. Fig. 7 presents an overview of the implementation of the adaptation simulator. The simulator starts with a set of values for the context variables and outputs a set of ranked configuration which can be used in that context. The first step is to solve the constraints to find valid configurations. This is done by deriving an Alloy specification from the adaptation meta-model and using constraint solving capability of the Alloy framework to output a set of valid configurations. The valid configurations can then be ranked according to their properties. The transformation to an Alloy specification and the computation of configuration scores are implemented within the Kermeta environment. The ranking of configurations is done in four steps:

1. Compute the values of each property for each configuration. The value of a property p for a configuration C is computed by summing the contributions of the variants it contains. If we denote p(C) the value of property p for configuration C, d_p the direction of property p and p(v) the impact of variant v on property p, then:

$$\forall C = \{v_1, \ldots, v_n\},\ p(C) = \sum_{i=1}^{n} (-1)^{d_p}\, p(v_i) \tag{1}$$

2. Compute the priority w associated to each property p. This is done by evaluating the guards of all adaptation rules and combining the priorities provided

by the rules R_{true} which guard is true. Let w(p) be the priority of property p and w(r, p) the priority of property p in rule r, w(p) is:

$$w(p) = \max_{r \in R_{true}}(w(r,p)) \tag{2}$$

3. Compute a score S for each configuration C. This is done by summing the values of all properties for each configuration using weight corresponding to property priorities. If we denote S(C) the score of configuration C:

$$S(C) = \sum_{p} K^{w(p)} p(C) \tag{3}$$

   Where K is a constant greater than 1 (fixed to 5 in our experiments). The constant K corresponds to a weigh associated to priorities. K=5 means that 5 contributions with a "Low" priority adds up to the same score as 1 contribution with a "Medium" priority.
4. Rank the configuration according to their scores S.

The ranking process involves summing property values and priorities, however, in the model these elements are defined as qualitative values (such as "Low", "Medium" and "High" in the robot example). For the simulation, simple strategies are applied to transform these qualitative values to integers:

- For the impact of variants the values can be {N/A, Very Low, Low, Medium, High, Very High} which is mapped to {0, 1, 2, 3, 4, 5}.
- For priorities the values can be {N/A, Low, Medium and High} and they are mapped to {0, 1, 2, 3}

We have kept the computation of the score very simple and based on integer arithmetic since so far our experiments do not seem to require more advanced computation. In the literature more advance mechanisms such as fuzzy-logic have been defined in order to handle qualitative values consistently. As future work we will investigate further if the proposed approach can benefit from such mechanisms.

4.2 Simulation of the Mapping Robot Adaptation Model

The meta-model based implementation of the DSML allows simulating the adaptation model. Provided with a set of values for the context variables, the simulator outputs the ranking of valid configurations together with their scores. The interface of the simulator is currently text based.

Fig. 8 shows the output of one simulation for the mapping robot. The first line correspond to the context of the system, it is the input of the simulation. The variables which do not appear (such as "Low Battery") have the value false. For this simulation, the robot is in exploration mode, Bluetooth signal is available, the memory is low and there is light in the area. Based on the hard constraints of the adaptation model, only 8 configurations are valid in this context. The scores of these configuration range from 36 to 182. Based on these score, the best configuration to use according to the adaptation model includes the following variants: Bluetooth network,

```
(BTSig LIGHT LowMem Mode=EXPLORE)
BT SM STREAM          (SCORE = 36)
BT DM STREAM          (SCORE = 82)
BT SM STREAM USS      (SCORE = 87)
BT IRS SM STREAM      (SCORE = 111)
BT DM STREAM USS      (SCORE = 133)
BT CS SM STREAM       (SCORE = 136)
BT DM IRS STREAM      (SCORE = 157)
BT CS DM STREAM       (SCORE = 182)
-> | Bluetooth | Camera | Detailed Map | Streaming |
```

Fig. 8. Simulation output for a single context

Camera sensor, detail mapping strategy and data streaming to the central computer. This intuitively corresponds to what we expected in such a context.

4.3 Validation of the Adaptation Model

Like any specification or implementation task, the specification of the adaptation model can be error-prone. Before assuming that an adaptation model is correct, it needs to be properly validated. Besides the fact that it provide separation of concern, the benefit of modeling the adaptation logic separately from the main system functionality is that this model can be validated before it is integrated with the rest of the application. Two types of validations can be carried out: the verification of invariant properties and the simulation of adaptation scenarios.

The verification of invariant properties allows validating the constraints defined in the adaptation model. The modeler can express invariants using both context variables and variants and check that these constraints hold in all reachable configurations of the system. If a constraint does not hold the constraint solver can enumerate the configuration which violates the invariant.

For the mapping robot we might for example express that GPRS network should never be used when Bluetooth could be used: ***Invariant:*** *not BTSig and GPRS.*

To check such invariants, they are translated to the Alloy specification and just like for the simulation, the Alloy constraint solver is applied and yields the potentially valid configurations which violate the invariant. In the case of the example no violation is found (which is quite trivial when looking at the availability constraints of the adaptation model).

Checking for properties is a good way of validating the constraints present in the adaptation model. For the verification of the impact with respect to the properties of concern and the adaptation rules, applying simulation on typical adaptation scenario is a complementary way of catching unexpected behaviors of the adaptation model. Because the total number of contexts for an adaptive application is huge (it grows exponentially with the number of context variables), in general complete simulations taking all context into consideration cannot be performed. However, the adaptation can be tested with representative context evolution scenarios. The way such representative scenarios can be chosen is out of the scope of the paper and part of our ongoing research based on software testing techniques.

Fig. 9 presents the simulation of an adaptation scenario for the mapping robot. Each step of the scenario corresponds to a change in the context of the system.

(BTSig LIGHT Mode=IDLE) → | Buffering | Simple Map |
1) Robot is switched to goto mode
(BTSig LIGHT Mode=GOTO) → | **Bluetooth** | **Camera** | External Routing | Simple Map | Streaming |
2) The robot is in the dark
(BTSig Mode=GOTO) → | **Bluetooth** | External Routing | Simple Map | Streaming | **Ultrasonic** |
3) Robot is switched to exploration mode
(BTSig Mode=EXPLORE) → | Buffering | Detailed Map | **Infrared** |
4) The internal available memory runs low
(BTSig LowMem Mode=EXPLORE) → | **Bluetooth** | Detailed Map | **Infrared** | Streaming |
5) The Bluetooth signal is lost
(LowMem Mode=EXPLORE) → | **GPRS** | **Infrared** | Simple Map | Streaming |
6) The robot gets to a lighten area
(LIGHT LowMem Mode=EXPLORE) → | **Camera** | **GPRS** | Simple Map | Streaming |
7) The Bluetooth signal comes back
(BTSig LIGHT LowMem Mode=EXPLORE) → | **Bluetooth** | **Camera** | Detailed Map | Streaming |
8) The robot has some free memory
(BTSig LIGHT Mode=EXPLORE) → | Buffering | **Camera** | Detailed Map |
9) The robot is running out of batteries
(BTSig LIGHT LowBatt Mode=EXPLORE) → | Buffering | **Infrared** | Simple Map |
10) Robot is switched to goto mode
(BTSig LIGHT LowBatt Mode=GOTO) → | Buffering | Local Routing | Simple Map | **Ultrasonic** |
11) Robot is back to IDLE mode
(BTSig LIGHT LowBatt Mode=IDLE) → | Buffering | Simple Map |

Fig. 9. Simulation output for a simple context evolution scenario

5 Case Studies and Initial Results

A complete environment for the presented DSML to support both modeling and validation has been developed. This environment includes an editor, a simulator and validation tools. The environment has been built using the Eclipse-Modeling Framework (EMF) and the Kermeta platform for semantics and simulation support. The editor is a table-based editor which allows editing all the aspects of the adaptation model (see the screenshot figures in Section 3). The tools are developed as open-source and are available from the DiVA project web page http://www.ict-diva.eu/.

In the context of the DiVA project, the adaptation DSML presented in this paper is introduced as the core of a platform for development and execution of adaptive systems. At runtime, the DiVA approach relies on AOM dynamic weaving techniques to adapt the running system. A detailed description of how MDE and AOM techniques are combined for that matter can be found in [2].

The usability and scalability of the proposed approach has been evaluated on a set of academic examples and on two industrial scenarios in the context of the DiVA project. The academic examples include the mapping robot presented in this paper and a flood prediction system developed at Lancaster University. The industrial cases are an airport crisis management system and a Customer Relationship Management (CRM) system.

Fig. 10 presents some characteristics of the adaptation models that have been modeled using the DSML environment presented in this paper for the four case studies. For each adaptation model we have counted the number of elements which have to be modeled and computed the number of actual contexts and configurations the system has to consider. The number of context implies all possible combinations of values for the context variables. The number of configurations corresponds to all valid combination of variants according to the multiplicities defined on the variability dimensions. The results show that comparing the academic examples and the industrial scenarios, there is an explosion of the number of possible contexts and configurations (e.g., 884736 contexts and 1474560 configurations for the airport crisis management system). However, there is no explosion in terms of the size of the adaptation model, the factor is only between 2 or 3 for the number of context variables, variants and constraints. The differences in terms of the number of properties and rules are minor. More case studies are need to draw any definitive conclusions, but the current results indicate that the proposed approach do scale to handle realistic sized industrial cases.

	# Variables	# Context	# Variants	# Config.	# Const.	# Prop.	# Rules
Maping Robot	5	**48**	12	**192**	13	5	7
Flood Prediction	5	**48**	9	**112**	9	3	5
Airport Crisis	18	**884736**	27	**1474560**	33	8	8
CRM	15	**98304**	20	**92160**	25	4	7

Fig. 10. Characteristics of the adaptation model for four case studies

The second element that needed to be validated is the ability of the simulator and model checking capability to scale properly. Early results indicate that acceptable simulation times can be achieved. For example, in the case of the CRM system, simulating the adaptation model for a particular context only takes a few seconds. This simulation includes the transformation to an Alloy specification, the resolution of constraints, the evaluation of properties priorities and the computation of configuration scores. Overall, the approach seems to be well suited for the applications which were considered. We are currently in the process of applying the approach to other domains such as a real-time video processing application and to even larger industrial scenarios. The initial results of these are promising, however, they are not yet fully completed.

6 Related Work

There are several recent state of the art reviews in the area of adaptive application modeling and execution, e.g., [1][16][17]. [1] focuses especially on surveying adaptive system construction and execution approaches that are based on model-driven engineering techniques and aspect-oriented techniques, [16] focuses on surveying middleware based self adaptation approaches and related model based approaches supporting adaptive system design, [17] focuses especially on surveying adaptation in a distributed service oriented environment. While general approaches for adaptive system development and execution are contextually relevant for the work presented in this paper, we narrow the scope in this related work section and compare our work with existing techniques for expression of adaptation policies. This is appropriate since the presented DSML is not a complete environment for adaptive system construction and execution, instead our DSML could be an alternative for modeling the adaptation logic in these broader scoped approaches. In general there are two families of approaches that have been defined for capturing adaptation policies: i) approaches based on explicit event-condition-action (ECA) rules and ii) approaches based on the definition of utility functions to be optimized. The two-level formalism proposed in this paper has been built in an attempt to combine the strengths of these two approaches with respect to efficiency, scalability and verification capabilities.

Most existing approaches are based on using an ECA type of rules to formalize adaptation policies [7][11][14]. For example, in [14] the adaptation rules are triggered by context events and express system reconfigurations. In [7] the rules use guards and the actions details how the reconfiguration should be performed at the platform level. The approach presented in [11] uses event-condition-action rules and has a specific focus on conflict resolution and negotiation between interacting adaptive systems. An overview of these techniques can be found in [13].

The main strengths of ECA approaches are twofold; i) the readability and elegance of each individual rules, and ii) the efficiency with which the rules can be processed. At runtime, rules are matched and applied to adapt the system configuration. On the other hand, the main limitations of these techniques are related to scalability and validation. Managing a large set of interacting adaptation rules rapidly becomes difficult. Validation becomes a major issue: how to ensure that the set of rules will yield the best possible configuration for every possible context of the application.

To overcome the validation problem, [15] proposes to capture adaptation policies early in the development cycle using temporal logic. The proposed formalism is an extended version of linear temporal logic which includes adaptation specific operators. Formal validation and verification technique associated with this approach are detailed in [6]. In [5] the authors proposes to represent the adaptation policy under the form of a state-transition system in which the states correspond to the system configurations and the transitions correspond to the adaptations between these configurations. This technique makes adaptation policies easy to understand but can only be applied to systems with a very limited number of configurations and possible adaptations. In [3] an equivalent state-transition model is derived through design-time simulation of condition-action rules. The state-transition model is used for validation and verification purposes. The approach is easier to use but still requires the enumeration of all possible configurations and adaptations of the system which limits its applicability for large systems.

The second family of techniques consists in viewing adaptation as an optimization problem. The adaptation policies are expressed as high-level goals to achieve and at runtime the configuration of the system is optimized with respect to these goals [4][10][11]. The proposed approach uses parameterization and compositional adaptation. Each component type describes the properties it needs and the properties it offers, while their implementations are responsible for describing how these properties are computed. Moreover, each component implementation has to describe a utility function. These utility functions describe whether a given component implementation is useful in a particular context.

The main benefit of optimization-based approaches is the abstraction they provide through properties in order to allow to expressing much simpler adaptation rules. In addition, utility functions are an efficient way to determine how well suited a configuration is, depending on the context. However, specifying these functions may not be easy for designers and may require several iterations in order to adjust. Also, while the approach does not explicitly describe all the possible configurations of the system a priori, the runtime reasoning has to calculate utility values for all of them, thus encountering scalability and efficiency issues.

The approach proposed in this paper is a compromise between rule-based approaches like [3] and optimization-based approaches like [4] which enable for design-time validation techniques such as defined in [6]. This makes the proposed approach a good trade-off for large-scale dynamic adaptive system by mastering the combinatorial explosion of the number of contexts and configurations.

7 Conclusion and Future Work

In this paper we proposed a modeling language and associated tools for capturing and validating runtime adaptation early in the development cycle. The proposed approach allows expressing high-level adaptation rules based on properties of the adaptive system. Simulation and model-checking capabilities have been implemented to allow for the validation of the adaptation model. The approach has been validated on several academic case studies and two industrial scenarios.

The proposed approach has four main benefits. Firstly, it copes with the explosion of the number of contexts and configuration by using property-based policies. The case studies show that the number of element in the adaptation model only grows linearly when the number of contexts and configuration grow exponentially. Secondly, it allows for early verification and validation. The proposed approach allows statically simulating runtime adaptation at design-time in order to model-check properties on it or to test it on context evolution scenarios. Thirdly, it permits the automated generation of the adaptation logic. To implement the adaptation the adaptation is processed directly by a generic runtime adaptation framework in order to drive the architecture adaptations in the running system. And fourthly, it provides separate specification of the adaptation logic at the model level, abstracting complexity and avoiding adaptation logic and system logic tangling.

Based on additional studies, future work will include refining how the variants and context variables are modeled. We will investigate the possibility of using well defined formalisms such as feature diagrams to better organize variants. For the context modeling, we will investigate the introduction of some structuring mechanism (such as classes for instance). Both these evolutions might have an impact on the adaptation meta-model but will not change the two-stage philosophy of the approach. We will also investigate alternative simulation semantics. For instance, the computation of configurations scores could rely on fuzzy-logic instead of integer arithmetic.

References

[1] Deliverable D3.1: Survey and evaluation of approaches for runtime variability management, part of FP7 project DiVA, EU FP7 STREP, contract 215412 (2008)

[2] Morin, B., Fleurey, F., Bencomo, N., Jézéquel, J.-M., Solberg, A., Dehlen, V., Blair, G.: An aspect-oriented and model-driven approach for managing dynamic variability. In: Czarnecki, K., Ober, I., Bruel, J.-M., Uhl, A., Völter, M. (eds.) MODELS 2008. LNCS, vol. 5301, pp. 782–796. Springer, Heidelberg (2008)

[3] Fleurey, F., Dehlen, V., Bencomo, N., Morin, B., Jézéquel, J.M.: Modeling and Validating Dynamic Adaptation. In: The Models@run.time at MODELS 2008, Toulouse, France (2008)

[4] Floch, J., Hallsteinsen, S., Stav, E., Eliassen, F., Lund, K., Gjorven, E.: Using architecture models for runtime adaptability. Software IEEE 23(2), 62–70 (2006)
[5] Bencomo, N., Grace, P., Flores, C., Hughes, D., Blair, G.: Genie: Supporting the model driven development of reflective, component-based adaptive systems. In: ICSE 2008 - Formal Research Demonstrations Track (2008)
[6] Zhang, J., Cheng, B.H.C.: Model-based Development of Dynamically Adaptive Software. In: Proceedings of the ICSE 2006 Conference, New York, NY, USA, pp. 371–380 (2006)
[7] David, P., Ledoux, T.: Safe Dynamic Reconfigurations of Fractal Architectures with FScript. In: Proceeding of Fractal CBSE Workshop, ECOOP 2006, Nantes, France (2006)
[8] Pessemier, N., Seinturier, L., Coupaye, T., Duchien, L.: A Safe Aspect-Oriented Programming Support for Component-Oriented Programming. In: WCOP 2006@ECOOP, vol. 2006–11 of Technical Report, Nantes, France. Karlsruhe University (2006)
[9] Soria, C.C., Pérez, J., Cars, J.A.: Dynamic Adaptation of Aspect-Oriented Components. In: Schmidt, H.W., Crnković, I., Heineman, G.T., Stafford, J.A. (eds.) CBSE 2007. LNCS, vol. 4608, pp. 49–65. Springer, Heidelberg (2007)
[10] Hallsteinsen, S., Stav, E., Solberg, A., Floch, J.: Using product line techniques to build adaptive systems. In: Proceedings of SPLC 2006, Washington, DC, USA, pp. 141–150 (2006)
[11] Kephart, J.O., Das, R.: Achieving Self-Management via Utility Functions. IEEE Internet Computing 11(1), 40–48 (2007)
[12] Capra, L., Emmerich, W., Mascolo, C.: CARISMA: Context-Aware Reflective mIddleware System for Mobile Applications. IEEE TSE 29(10), 929–945 (2003)
[13] Keeney, J., Cahill, V., Haahr, M.: Techniques for Dynamic Adaptation of Mobile Services. In: The Handbook of Mobile Middleware, Auerbach, ISBN: 0849338336
[14] Keeney, J., Cahill, V.: Chisel: A Policy-Driven, Context-Aware, Dynamic Adaptation Framework. In: Proceedings of Policy 2003, Lake Como, Italy, pp. 3–14. IEEE, Los Alamitos (1933)
[15] Zhang, J., Cheng, B.H.: Specifying adaptation semantics. In: Proceedings of the, Workshop on Architecting Dependable Systems. WADS 2005, St. Louis, Missouri, May 17, pp. 1–7. ACM, New York (2005)
[16] Romain Rouvoy Deliverable D1.1 Requirements of mechanisms and planning algorithms for self-adaptation. MUISIC, FP6 Integrated project, Contract no 035166 (October 2007), http://www.ist-music.eu/MUSIC/results/music-deliverables
[17] ALIVE Deliverable D2.1State of the Art. ALIVE project FP7 project number FP7-215890, http://www.ist-alive.eu/

Executable Domain Specific Language for Message-Based System Integration

Michael Shtelma, Mario Cartsburg, and Nikola Milanovic

Technische Universität Berlin
{mshtelma,mcartsbg,nmilanov}@cs.tu-berlin.de

Abstract. Heterogeneous IT-systems rarely rely on a common data format and structure, so in order to integrate them, the corresponding data/message transformations must be developed. Transformations may also be required by the business logic. We present a platform-independent approach for message transformation specification, in form of a system integration DSL, and discuss approaches for making it executable.

Keywords: System integration, domain specific language, model execution.

1 Introduction

Enterprise application integration tasks usually include message transformation step, which can be caused either by the business logic requirements or data incompatibility. Transformations can be implemented using general purpose programming languages, but in this case the business logic vanishes in different cross-cutting concerns and therefore can be understood only by qualified software developers, not by domain experts; reuse is also limited. Transformations can also be implemented using workflow executable languages (e.g., BPEL) which can arguably be better understood by domain experts, but these languages suffer from the lack of expressiveness and standard features offered by programming languages, such as collections or library support. In this paper we introduce a novel workflow modeling and transformation solution, including the DSL for system integration modeling, expression support and model execution environment.

2 Related Work

Workflows and message transformations can be defined using modeling languages such as BPMN [1], using CWM metamodel [2] as well as schema matching approaches [3]. Their support for specifying behavior of message transformations is limited. Service oriented architecture (SOA) approaches support message oriented middleware concepts for system integration, but almost all approaches are based on XML transformations, and expressions are specified using platform-specific programming languages. Executable workflow languages, such as BPEL,

A. Schürr and B. Selic (Eds.): MODELS 2009, LNCS 5795, pp. 622–626, 2009.

support direct transformation execution, but most workflow execution servers have custom language extensions, which are not compatible with each other.

OMG proposes EAI profile [4], included in several UML modeling tools. Model elements based on this and similar profiles often have no pre-defined relations and property requirements (tag definitions) which leaves model structure and element descriptions completely to the user. [5] proposes an object-oriented workflow modeling language which is limited to modeling Web applications.

Executable models are included in concepts such as executable UML or the UML virtual machine [6]. In [7] transformation from UML activities to executable code in the TAAL programming language is proposed. [8] and [9] make transformation to BPEL, while [10] defines execution semantics for specific UML actions. These and similar proposals employ proprietary operational semantics, only textual action semantics languages are offered and dependency on UML make them overloaded with technical concepts from the OO analysis.

3 Domain Specific Language for System Integration

In this section we describe developed DSL for EAI pattern-based connector and expression modeling. We introduce the abstract language syntax as well as three concrete syntaxes: graphical syntax for connector modeling and graphical and textual syntax for expression specification which can be used interchangeably.

3.1 Abstract Syntax

Packages *structure*, *types* and *message* contain the static structure description of used libraries, in particular class structure, type system and supported message types. We will not discuss them further here. Instead we focus on packages *connector* and *expression* which form DSL abstract syntax. The *connector* package contains elements of message processing components (EAI patterns), application endpoints and message routing logic. The *expression* package contains elements for expression modeling. Message processors have references to corresponding message transformation expressions, which define their behavior.

The connector package (Figure 1 right) specifies the upper abstraction level for connector design and references expression package for behavior specification of message processors. Using messages and message processors to abstract connectors seems to be the most generic and accepted approach, and it enables service-oriented connector realization. There are two types of connector components: application endpoints and message processors. Application endpoints generate and consume messages by wrapping system interfaces, and message processors manipulate messages. Components send or receive messages of the specific message type via ports. Messages are transported by message channels which have a message channel type and a message exchange pattern.

The following predefined library elements are included in DSL: message processor types (Aggregator, Content Enricher, Filter, Content-based Router, Splitter, Timer and Transformer), message channel types (Point-to-Point and

Publish-Subscribe) and message exchange patterns (Out-Only , Robust Out-Only, Out-In and Out-Optional-In).

The expression package (Figure 1 left) specifies expressions which define behavior of message processors. Expressions can be modeled with arbitrary function/operation calls, support for the high-order function calls and lambda expressions. The expression flow metamodel is built using abstract notions, which allows us to define actual types of the activities in runtime. *Activity* metaclass represents the actual function or operation call, determined by the corresponding *ActivityType*. The *Pin* metaclass shows a formal parameter value that is passed to a function call. The value is determined using *ActivityEdge* metaclass, which shows directed flow from one *Pin* to another. The expression metamodel allows definition of domain specific semantics and custom operations and functions.

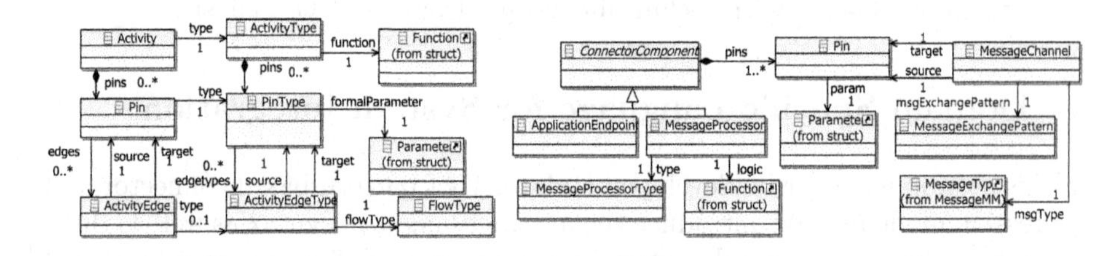

Fig. 1. Connector and expression metamodels (excerpt)

3.2 Concrete Syntax

Figure 2 shows an instance of the *connector* package, realized using our graphical syntax. Application endpoints and message processors are parts of the integration flow and can generate/consume/transform event and data messages. Message types are specified as properties and are not visualized in the process flow. They are assigned to ports of application endpoints and message processors to specify data schema requirements of connector component interfaces.

Supported activity types of the *expression* package (graphical and textual syntax) are given in Table 1. Note that presented DSL is a functional language, and it enables system integrators to create Lambda-expressions and high-order functions. Support of functional concepts allows to offer rich set of collection processing possibilities, such as filtering, sorting or mapping. As additional possibility we introduce collection flow that acts as 'for' operator. Finally, the conditional activity allows to implement branching of message flow.

4 Model Execution

We defined the following requirements for the model runtime environment: complete and directly executable connector component generation; connector deployment process should be straightforward and accomplished by domain experts without technical assistance; if business requirements change, domain experts

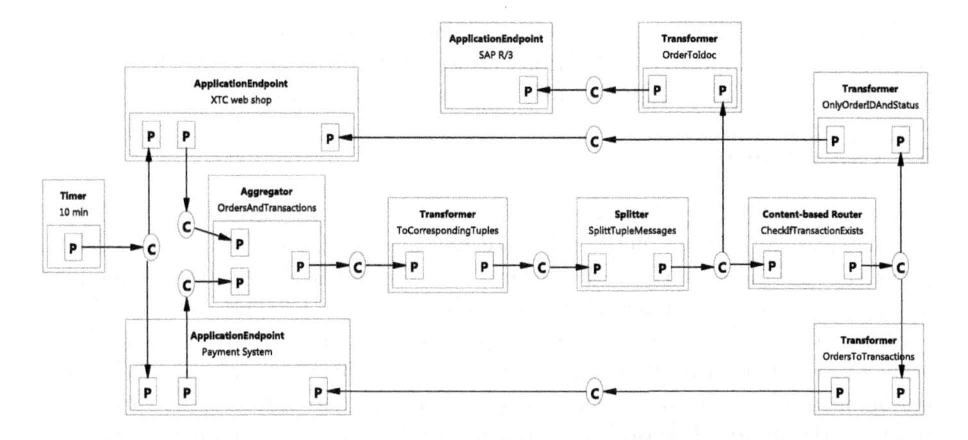

Fig. 2. Example of the connector package instance

Table 1. Activity Types in the DSL Graphical Concrete Syntax

Activity Type Name	Graphical Notation	Textual Concrete Syntax
Function/Operation Call	Operation/Function Call	getOrders()
Property Accessors	Property Accessor	getOrders().first().name
Variable/Parameter	Parameter	Order order=getOrders().first();
Lambda Expression		o|o.name.startsWith("Michael")
Pin		NA
High-Order Function Call	High-Order Function Call	getOrders().select(o|o.name.startsWith("Michael"))
For/Iterator	for	List<Item> l = for(o : orders) returning new Item(o);
Conditional Operator	- +	if(expression) { doSmth();} else { doSmthElse();}
Message Flow		NA
Conditional Flow		NA
Collection Flow		getOrders()->items.sum();

should be able to reconfigure running connector alone and perform redeployment process without technical assistance.

The executable connector application generation process can be represented as the following chain of automated transformation, generation, compilation and deployment steps. The connector model is transformed to BPEL process skeleton by instantiating the BPEL schema using xTend transformation language. The expression model is transformed to Java Abstract Syntax Tree (AST), which is implemented using Eclipse JDT. Then Java code is generated by the AST implementation library. Afterwards, the code is compiled, built and packaged and BPEL process skeleton is completed with calls to compiled Java components containing expressions. Fully generated BPEL process and Java bytecode are packaged into Composite Application Service Assembly (CASA) which is directly deployed to the Sun GlassFish ESB as an executable component.

5 Conclusion

We presented design and implementation of the system integration DSL, where message transformation, dictated by interface incompatibility and business logic, plays the crucial role. Up to now, such transformations have been embedded in the workflow logic using XML-based languages or specified using platform-specific languages, which leads to the low visibility, reusability and maintainability of the transformation logic. Industrial practice showed that hidden and undocumented transformation logic is a constant source of errors, frustration and costly workarounds. The proposed solution enables modeling of custom message transformations, including complex expressions.

Nevertheless, open issues remain related to the use of legacy code, APIs, message formats, and cross-cutting concerns (security, logging, transactions). We intend to resolve some of them by adding more modeling and runtime facilities, such as platform specific workflow models that wrap target platform API.

References

1. White, S.A., et al.: Business process modeling notation specification. Object Management Group (2006), http://www.bpmn.org
2. Object Management Group: Common Warehouse Metamodel (2003), http://www.omg.org/cgi-bin/doc?formal/03-03-02
3. Rahm, E., Bernstein, P.A.: A survey of approaches to automatic schema matching. VLDB Journal 10(4), 334–350 (2001)
4. Object Management Group: UML Profile and Interchange Models for Enterprise Application Integration (EAI) Specification (2004)
5. Hemel, Z., Verhaaf, R., Visser, E.: Webworkflow: An object-oriented workflow modeling language for web applications. In: Czarnecki, K., Ober, I., Bruel, J.-M., Uhl, A., Völter, M. (eds.) MODELS 2008. LNCS, vol. 5301, pp. 113–127. Springer, Heidelberg (2008)
6. Crane, M.L., Dingel, J.: Towards a uml virtual machine: implementing an interpreter for uml 2 actions and activities. In: Proceedings of CASCON, pp. 96–110 (2008)
7. Engels, G., Kleppe, A., Rensink, A., Semenyak, M., Soltenborn, C., Wehrheim, H.: From uml activities to taal - towards behaviour-preserving model transformations. In: Schieferdecker, I., Hartman, A. (eds.) ECMDA-FA 2008. LNCS, vol. 5095, pp. 94–109. Springer, Heidelberg (2008)
8. Bordbar, B., Howells, G., Evans, M., Staikopoulos, A.: Model transformation from owl-s to bpel via sitra. In: Akehurst, D.H., Vogel, R., Paige, R.F. (eds.) ECMDA-FA. LNCS, vol. 4530, pp. 43–58. Springer, Heidelberg (2007)
9. Yu, X., Zhang, Y., Zhang, T., Wang, L., Zhao, J., Zheng, G., Li, X.: Towards a model driven approach to automatic bpel generation. In: Akehurst, D.H., Vogel, R., Paige, R.F. (eds.) ECMDA-FA. LNCS, vol. 4530, pp. 204–218. Springer, Heidelberg (2007)
10. Crane, M.L., Dingel, J.: Towards a formal account of a foundational subset for executable uml models. In: Czarnecki, K., Ober, I., Bruel, J.-M., Uhl, A., Völter, M. (eds.) MODELS 2008. LNCS, vol. 5301, pp. 675–689. Springer, Heidelberg (2008)

Architectural Mining: The Other Side of the MDD

Grady Booch

IBM Thomas J. Watson Research Center
gbooch@us.ibm.com

Abstract. A back-of-the-envelope calculation suggests that - very, very conservatively - the world produces well over 33 billion lines of new or modified code every year. Curiously, the moment that code springs into being and is made manifest in a running system, it become legacy. The relentless accretion of code over months, years, even decades quickly turns every successful new project into a brownfield one. Although software has no mass, it does have weight, weight that can ossify any system by creating intertia to change and deadly creeping complexity. It requires energy to make such a system simple, and to intentionally apply that energy requires that one be able to reason about, understand, and visualize the system as built.

Considerable research and labor has been invested in model-driven development for the purposes of transforming models into running systems, and while these efforts have yielded some useful results they have not led to the revolution that some expected. Similarly, considerable work has been undertaken in static and dynamic analysis and design pattern discovery, and while they too have yielded some useful results, these efforts have been rather scattered. Still, we believe that there is much more that can be done. One of the explicit goals we made in the early years of the UML was that it be a language for reasoning about a system, and so in this presentation, we'll reexamine that early goal. In particular, we'll look at efforts to consider the other side of MDD, the mining of the architecture of an as-built system from its source code and its execution.

A. Schürr and B. Selic (Eds.): MODELS 2009, LNCS 5795, p. 627, 2009.

Generic Model Refactorings*

Naouel Moha, Vincent Mahé, Olivier Barais, and Jean-Marc Jézéquel

INRIA Rennes – Bretagne Atlantique/IRISA, Université Rennes 1,
Triskell Team, Campus de Beaulieu, 35042 Rennes Cedex, France
{moha,vmahe,barais,jezequel}@irisa.fr

Abstract. Many modeling languages share some common concepts and principles. For example, Java, MOF, and UML share some aspects of the concepts of classes, methods, attributes, and inheritance. However, model transformations such as refactorings specified for a given language cannot be readily reused for another language because their related metamodels may be structurally different. Our aim is to enable a flexible reuse of model transformations across various metamodels. Thus, in this paper, we present an approach allowing the specification of generic model transformations, in particular refactorings, so that they can be applied to different metamodels. Our approach relies on two mechanisms: (1) an adaptation based mainly on the weaving of aspects; (2) the notion of model typing, an extension of object typing in the model-oriented context. We validated our approach by performing some experiments that consisted of specifying three well known refactorings (Encapsulate Field, Move Method, and Pull Up Method) and applying each of them onto three different metamodels (Java, MOF, and UML).

Keywords: Adaptation, Aspect Weaving, Genericity, Model Typing, Refactoring.

1 Introduction

Software reuse has been largely investigated in the last two decades by the software engineering community [3,23]. Basili *et al.* [2] have demonstrated the benefits of software reuse on the productivity and quality in object-oriented systems. In the domain of Model-Driven Engineering (MDE), which is often based on object-oriented metamodels, few works have been devoted to model-driven reuse [5]. For example, many modeling languages share some common concepts and principles: Java, MOF, and UML share some aspects of the concepts of classes, methods, attributes, and inheritance. However, a given model transformation such as the refactoring Pull Up Method specified for the UML metamodel might not be reused, for instance, for the Java metamodel because these metamodels are structurally different. Thus, the specification of model transformations are highly dependent on specific metamodels. Our aim is to

* This work was realized in the context of the MOVIDA project, funded by the ANR (French National Research Agency) CONVENTION N 2008 SEGI 011.

A. Schürr and B. Selic (Eds.): MODELS 2009, LNCS 5795, pp. 628–643, 2009.

enable a flexible reuse of such model transformations across various metamodels to enhance productivity and quality in the model-driven development.

In this paper, we present an approach to specify model transformations in a generic way, so that they can be applied to different metamodels. Our approach relies on two mechanisms: (1) an adaptation based mainly on the weaving of aspects; (2) the notion of model typing [31], an extension of object typing in the model-oriented context. We choose to illustrate and demonstrate our approach on well known model transformations, namely refactorings [10]. A refactoring is a particular transformation performed on the structure of software to make it easier to understand and cheaper to modify without changing its observable behavior [10]. For example, the refactoring Pull Up Method consists of moving methods to the superclass if these methods have same signatures and/or results on subclasses [10]. We validated our approach by performing some experiments that consisted of specifying three well known refactorings (Encapsulate Field, Move Method, and Pull Up Method) and applying each of them onto three different metamodels (Java, MOF, and UML). The specification of refactorings has been performed with Kermeta, a meta-language for defining the structure and behavior of models [25].

This article is organized as follows. Section 2 provides an overview of our motivation. Section 3 introduces the executable metamodeling language, Kermeta, and highlights some of its new features including the notion of model typing. Section 4 presents our approach along with the Pull Up Method refactoring. Section 5 describes the experiments that we performed for the three refactorings (Encapsulate Field, Move Method, and Pull Up Method) on three different metamodels (Java, MOF, and UML). Section 6 surveys related work. Section 7 concludes and presents future work.

2 Motivation

Our motivation is to enable the specification of generic refactorings, so that they can be applied to different metamodels. In this section, we clearly state this motivation using the concrete example of the Pull Up Method refactoring on three different metamodels (Java, MOF, and UML).

2.1 The Pull Up Method Refactoring

The Pull Up Method refactoring consists of moving methods to the superclass when methods with identical signatures and/or results are located in sibling subclasses [10]. This refactoring aims to eliminate duplicate methods by centralizing common behavior in the superclass. A set of preconditions must be checked before applying the refactoring. For example, one of the preconditions to be checked consists of verifying that the method to be pulled up is not a constructor. Another precondition checks that the method does not override a method of the superclass with the same signature. A third precondition consists of verifying that methods in sibling subclasses have the same signatures and/or results.

The example of the Pull Up Method refactoring presented in [22] of a Local Area Network (LAN) application [15] and adapted in Figure 1 shows that the method `bill` located in the classes `PrintServer` and `Workstation` is pulled up to their superclass `Node`.

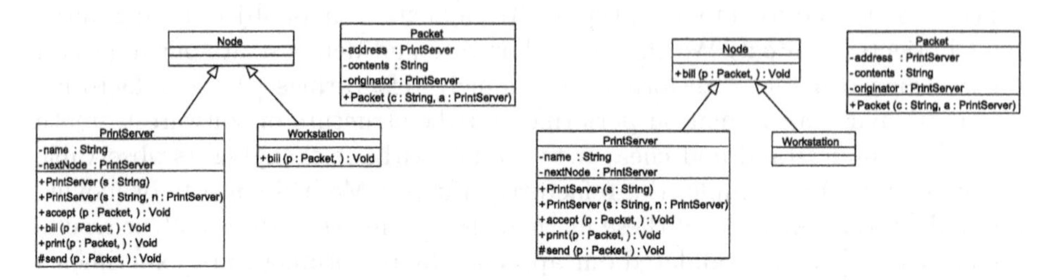

Fig. 1. Class Diagrams of the LAN Application Before and After the Pull Up Method Refactoring of the Method `bill`

2.2 Three Different Metamodels

We consider three different metamodels (Java, MOF, and UML), which support the definition of object-oriented structures (classes, methods, attributes, and inheritance). The Java metamodel described in [14] represents Java programs with some restrictions over the Java code. For example, inner classes, anonymous classes, and generic types are not modeled. As MOF metamodel, we consider the metamodel of Kermeta [25], which is an extension of MOF [27] with an imperative action language for specifying constraints and operational semantics of metamodels. The UML metamodel studied in this paper corresponds to the version 2.1.2 of the UML specification [29]. This Java metamodel is *one* possible representation of Java programs; there is no standard for such metamodel in contrast to UML and MOF metamodels.

We provide an excerpt of each of these metamodels in Figures 2, 3, and 4. These metamodels share some commonalities, such as the concepts of classes, methods, attributes, parameters, and inheritance (highlighted in grey in the figures). These concepts are necessary for the specification of refactorings, and in particular for the Pull Up Method refactoring. However, they are represented differently from one metamodel to another as detailed in the next paragraph.

2.3 Problems

We list here some of the problems encountered when trying to specify one common Pull Up Method refactoring for all three metamodels:

- **The metamodel elements** (such as classes, methods, attributes, and references) **may have different names.**

  For example, the concept of attribute is named `Property` in the MOF and UML metamodels whereas in the Java metamodel, it is named `Variable`.

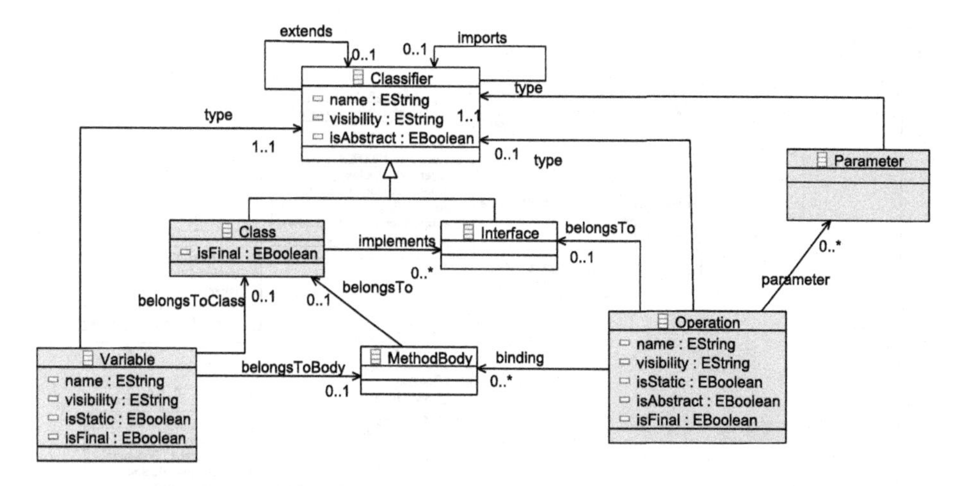

Fig. 2. Subset of the Java Metamodel

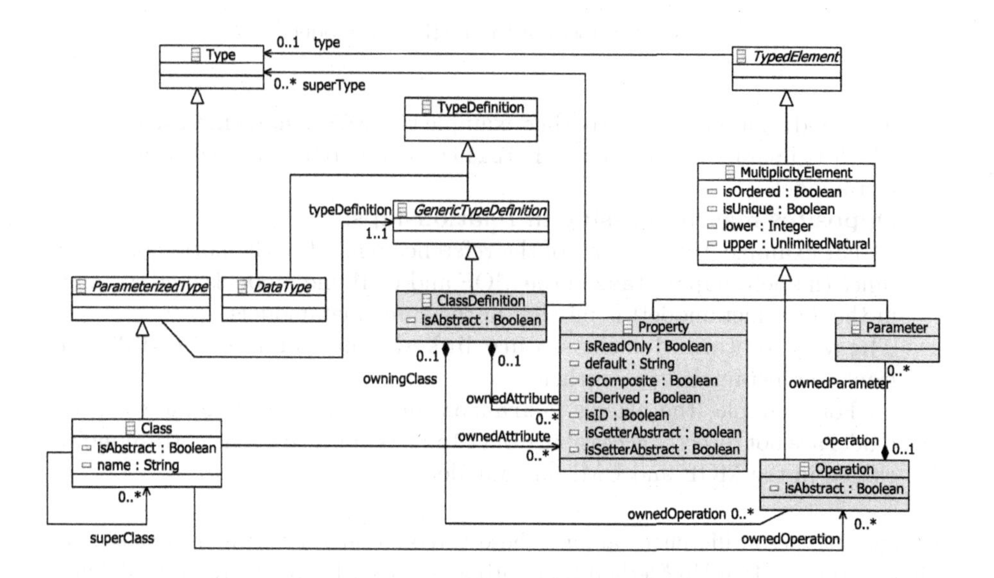

Fig. 3. Subset of the MOF Metamodel

- **The types of elements may be different.**

  For example, in the UML metamodel, the attribute `visibility` of `Operation` is an enumeration of type `VisibilityKind` whereas the same attribute in the Java metamodel is of type `String`.
- There may be **additional or missing elements** in a given metamodel compared to another.

  For example, `Class` in the UML metamodel and `ClassDefinition` in the MOF metamodel have several superclasses whereas `Class` in the Java

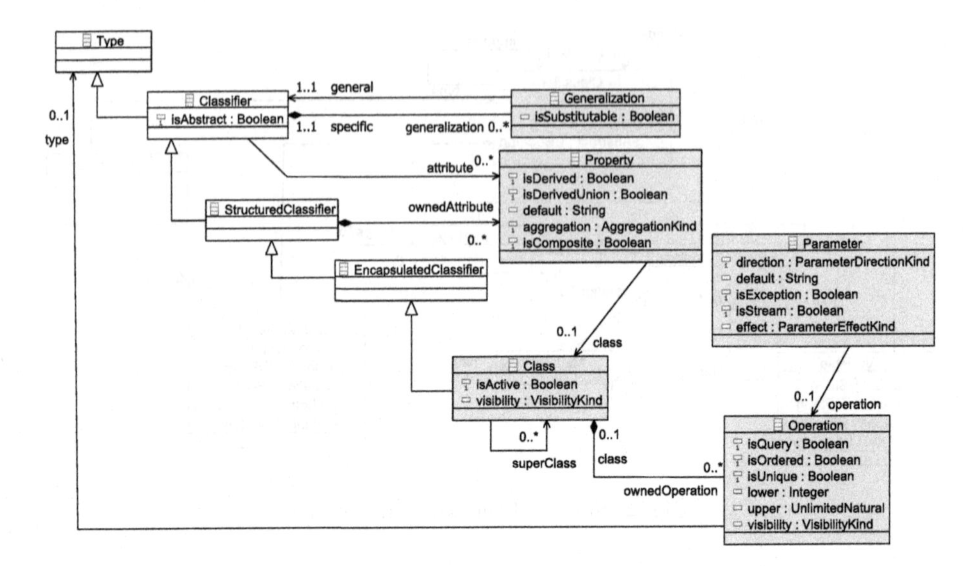

Fig. 4. Subset of the UML Metamodel

metamodel has only one. Another example is the `ClassDefinition` in MOF, which is missing an attribute `visibility` compared to the UML and Java metamodels.

- **Opposites may be missing in relationships.**

  For example, the opposite of the reference related to the notion of inheritance (namely, `superClass` in the MOF and UML metamodels, and `extends` in the Java metamodel) is missing in the three metamodels.
- **The way metamodel classes are linked together may be different** from one metamodel to another.

  For example, the classes `Operation` and `Variable` in the Java metamodel are not directly accessible from `Class` as opposed to the corresponding classes in the MOF and UML metamodels.

Because of these differences among these three metamodels, we are not able to directly reuse a Pull Up Method refactoring accross all three metamodels. Thus, we are forced to write three refactorings, one for each of the three metamodels. In Section 4, we present an approach that allows the specification of one common refactoring for these different metamodels.

3 Kermeta and Model Typing

We introduce here new features of the Kermeta language and the notion of model typing to ease the comprehension of our approach presented in Section 4.

3.1 New Features of Kermeta

In the current version of Kermeta, its action language provides new features for weaving aspects, adding derived properties, and specifying constraints such as invariants and pre-/post-conditions. Indeed, the first new feature of Kermeta is its ability to extend an existing metamodel with new structural elements (classes, operations, and properties) by weaving aspects (similar to inter-type declarations in AspectJ or open-classes [7]). This feature offers more flexibility to developers by enabling them to easily manipulate and reuse existing metamodels while separating concerns. The second new key feature is the possibility to add derived properties. A derived property is a property that is derived or computed through getter and setter accessors for simple types and `add` and `remove` methods for collection types. The derived property thus contains a body, as operations do, and can be accessed in read/write mode. Thanks to this feature, it is possible to figure out the value of a property based on the values of other properties belonging to the same class. The last new feature is the specification of pre- and post-conditions on operations and invariants on classes. These assertions can be directly expressed in Kermeta or imported from OCL (Object Constraint Language) files [28].

3.2 Model Typing

The last version of the Kermeta language integrates the notion of model typing [31], which corresponds to a simple extension to object-oriented typing in a model-oriented context. Model typing can be related to structural typing found in languages such as Scala. Indeed, a model typing is a strategy for typing models as collections of interconnected objects while preserving type conformance, used as a criterion of substitutability.

The notion of model type conformance (or substitutability) has been adapted and extended to model types based on Bruce's notion of type group matching [6]. The matching relation, denoted $<\#$, between two metamodels defines a function of the set of classes they contain according to the following definition:

> Metamodel *M'* matches another metamodel *M* (denoted $M' <\# M$) iff for each class *C* in *M*, there is one and only one corresponding class or subclass *C'* in *M'* such that every property *p* and operation *op* in *M.C* matches in *M'.C'* respectively with a property *p'* and an operation *op'* with parameters of the same type as in *M.C*.

This definition is adapted from [31] and improved here by relaxing two strong constraints. First, the constraint related to the name-dependent conformance on properties and operations was relaxing by enabling their renaming. The second constraint related to the strict structural conformance was relaxing by extending the matching to subclasses.

Let's illustrate model typing with two metamodels *M* and *M'* given in Figures 5 and 6. These two metamodels have model elements that have different names and the metamodel *M'* has additional elements compared to the metamodel *M*.

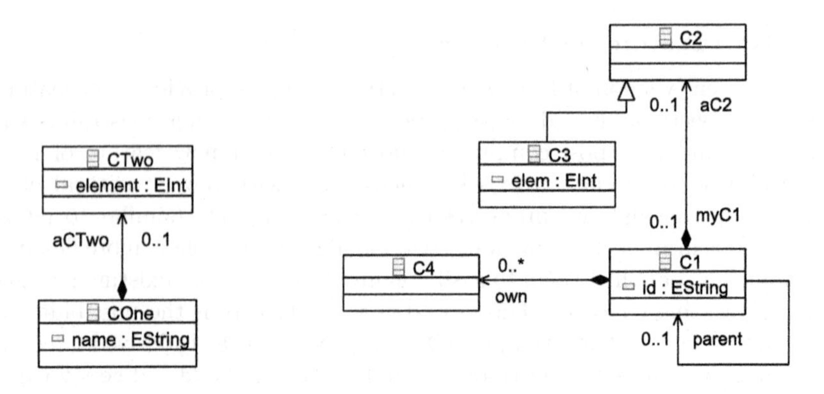

Fig. 5. Metamodel *M*

Fig. 6. Metamodel *M'*

C1 <# *COne* because for each property *COne.p* of type *D* (namely, *COne.name* and *COne.aCTwo*), there is a matching property *C1.q* of type *D'* (namely, *C1.id* and *C1.aC2*), such that *D'* <# *D*.

Thus, *C1* <# *COne* requires *D'* <# *D*, which is true because:

- *COne.name* and *C1.id* are both of type *String.*
- *COne.aCTwo* is of type *CTwo* and *C1.aC2* is of type *C2*, so *C1* <# *COne* requires *C2* <# *CTwo* or that a subclass of *C2* matches *CTwo*. Only *C3* <# *CTwo* is true because *CTwo.element* and *C3.elem* are both of type *String.*

Thus, matching between classes may depend on the matching of their related dependent classes. As a consequence, the dependencies involved when evaluating model type matching are heavily cyclical [30]. The interested reader can find in [30] the details of matching rules used for model types.

However, the model typing with the mechanisms of renaming and inheritance is not sufficient for matching metamodels that are structurally different. We show in the next section with our approach how we overcome this limitation of the model typing using aspect weaving.

4 Approach: Specification of Generic Refactorings

In this section, we present our approach for generic model refactoring. The four steps of the approach are illustrated in Figure 7. The first step consists of specifying a generic metamodel `GenericMT`[1], which corresponds to a metamodel that only contains elements required for applying refactorings. The second step consists of specifying refactorings based on the source metamodel `GenericMT` using a model transformation language such as Kermeta. The third step aims to adapt the target metamodels (Java, MOF, and UML) to the metamodel `GenericMT`.

[1] MT refers to Model Type.

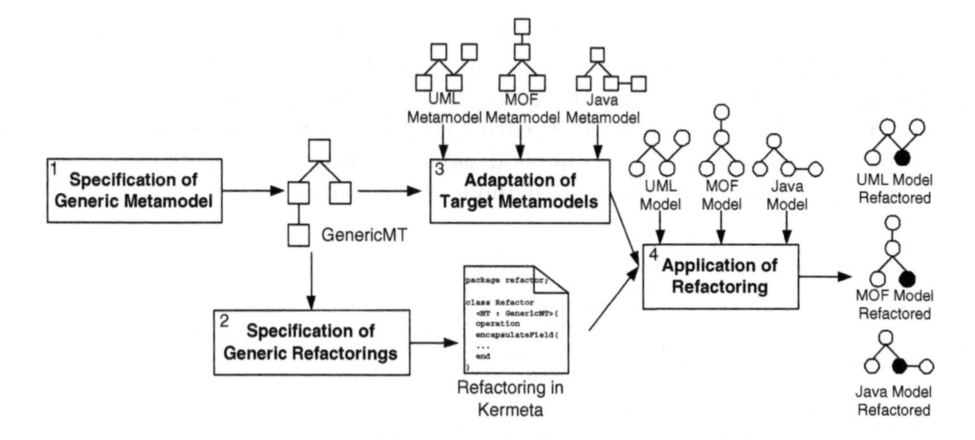

Fig. 7. Approach for the Specification of Generic Refactorings

In the last step, refactorings are directly applied to models of all target metamodels. We detail in the following each of these steps using the Pull Up Method refactoring as a running example.

Step 1: Specification of Generic Metamodel. Our approach consists first of specifying a lightweight metamodel that contains the minimum required classes, methods, and attributes for specifying refactorings. The generic metamodel, called `GenericMT` and given in Figure 8, has been designed to specify refactorings. `GenericMT` contains concepts common to most of object-oriented metamodels such as classes, methods, attributes, and parameters.

Step 2: Specification of Generic Refactorings. In the second step, refactorings are specified based on the generic metamodel `GenericMT`. Listing 1 gives

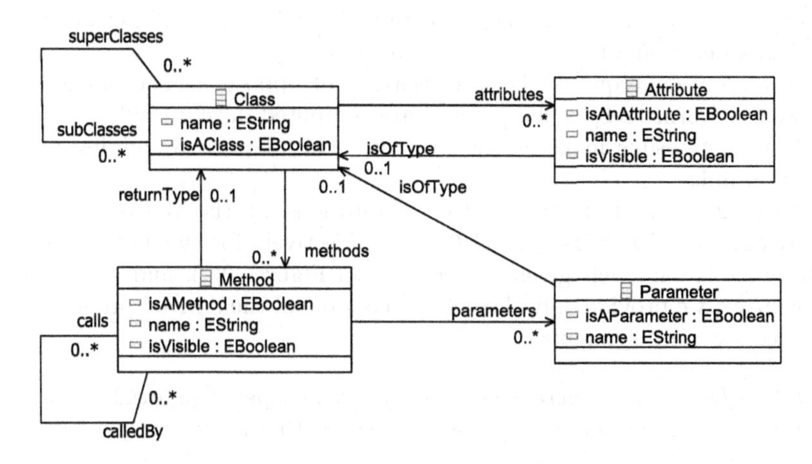

Fig. 8. Generic Metamodel `GenericMT`

a Kermeta code[2] excerpt of the class `Refactor`, which contains the operation `pullUpMethod`. This operation aims to pull up the method `meth` from the source class `source` to the target class `target`. This operation contains a precondition that checks if the sibling subclasses have methods with the same signatures. In the body of the operation, the method `meth` is added to the methods of the target class and removed from the methods of the source class.

```
package refactor;

class Refactor<MT : GenericMT> {

    operation pullUpMethod( source : MT::Class, target : MT::Class,
                            meth   : MT::Method) : Void

    // Preconditions
    pre sameSignatureInOtherSubclasses is do
        target.subClasses.forAll{ sub |
            sub.methods.exists{ op | haveSameSignature(meth, op) } }
    end

    // Operation body
    is do
        target.methods.add(meth)
        source.methods.remove(meth)
    end
}
```

Listing 1. Kermeta Code for the Pull Up Method Refactoring

Step 3: Adaptation of Target Metamodels. The third step aims to adapt the target metamodels to the generic metamodel `GenericMT` using the new Kermeta features for weaving aspects and adding derived properties. The adaptation consists of weaving, in the target metamodels, derived properties that match with those of the generic metamodel. This step of adaptation is necessary because the model typing is too restrictive for allowing a matching between metamodels that are structurally too different. Thus, this adaptation virtually modifies the structure of the target metamodel with additional elements, and uses the model typing to match the metamodels.

The adaptation requires also the weaving of opposites. The opposites are identified in Kermeta by a sharp ♯ and are computed during the loading of the model. The opposites make easier the writing of adapters by adding required navigation links.

Listings 2, 4, and 3 present the adaptations of the derived properties `superClasses` and `subClasses` of `Class` respectively for the Java, MOF, and UML target metamodels given respectively in Figures 2, 3, and 4. Because of lack of space, we provide only the getter accessors of the derived properties; the setter accessors are symmetric.

Adaptation for the Java metamodel. The derived property `superClasses` corresponds to a simple access to the property `extends` that is then wrapped in a Java

[2] The interested reader can refer to the Kermeta syntax in [16].

Class. However, for the derived property subClasses, the opposite inv_extends of the property extends was weaved by aspect on the class Classifier and used to get the set of subclasses.

```
package java;

require "Java.ecore"

aspect class Classifier {
    reference inv_extends : Classifier[0..*]#extends
    reference extends : Classifier[0..1]#inv_extends
}

aspect class Class {

    property superClasses : Class[0..1]#subClasses
        getter is do
            result:=self.extends
        end

    property subClasses : Class[0..*]#superClasses
        getter is do
            result := OrderedSet<java::Class>.new
            self.inv_extends.each{ subC | result.add(subC) }
        end
}
```

Listing 2. Kermeta Code for Adapting the Java Metamodel

Adaptation for the UML metamodel. In UML, the inheritance links are reified through the class Generalization. Thus, the derived property superClasses is computed by accessing to the class Generalization and the reference property general. As in Java and MOF, an opposite inv_general is specified to get the set of subclasses.

```
package uml;

require "http://www.eclipse.org/uml2/2.1.2/UML"

aspect class Classifier {
    reference inv_general : Generalization[0..*]#general
}

aspect class Class {

    property superClasses : Class[0..*]#subClasses
        getter is do
            result := OrderedSet<uml::Class>.new
            self.generalization.each{ g | result.add(g.general) }
        end

    property subClasses : Class[0..*]#superClasses
        getter is do
            result := OrderedSet<uml::Class>.new
            self.inv_general.each{ g | result.add(g.specific) }
        end
}
```

Listing 3. Kermeta Code for Adapting the UML Metamodel

```
package kermeta;

require kermeta

aspect class ParameterizedType {
 reference typeDefinition: GenericTypeDefinition[1..1]#
      inv_typeDefinition
}

aspect class GenericTypeDefinition {
 reference inv_typeDefinition: ParameterizedType[1..1]#typeDefinition
}

aspect class Type {
 reference inv_superType: ClassDefinition[0..*]#superType
}

aspect class ClassDefinition {

    reference superType : Type[0..*]#inv_superType

    property superClasses : ClassDefinition[0..*]#subClasses
        getter is do
            result := OrderedSet<ClassDefinition>.new
            self.superType.each{ c |
                var clazz : Class init Class.new
                clazz ?= c
                var clazzDef : ClassDefinition init ClassDefinition.new
                clazzDef ?= clazz.typeDefinition
                result.add(clazzDef) }
        end

    property subClasses : ClassDefinition[0..*]#superClasses
        getter is do
            result := OrderedSet<ClassDefinition>.new
            var clazz : Class
            clazz ?= self.inv_typeDefinition
            clazz.inv_superType.each{ superC | result.add(superC) }
        end
}
```

Listing 4. Kermeta Code for Adapting the MOF Metamodel

Adaptation for the MOF metamodel. Because of the distinction in the MOF between `Type` and `TypeDefinition` to handle the generic types, it is less straightforward to compute the derived properties `superClasses` and `subClasses`. Several opposites are required as shown in Listing 4.

Step 4: Application of Refactoring. The last step of our approach consists of applying the refactoring on the target metamodels as illustrated in Listing 5 for the UML metamodel. We reuse the example of the method `bill` in the LAN application. We can notice that the class `Refactor` takes as argument the UML metamodel, which thanks to the adaptation of Listing 3 is now a subtype of the expected supertype `GenericMT` as specified in Listing 1. The model typing guarantees the type conformance between the UML metamodel and the generic metamodel.

```
package refactor;

require "http://www.eclipse.org/uml2/2.1.2/UML"

class Main {
    operation main() : Void is do

        var rep : EMFRepository init EMFRepository.new

        var model : uml::Model
        model ?= rep.getResource("lan_application.uml").one

        var source : uml::Class init getClass("PrintServer")
        var target : uml::Class init getClass("Node")
        var meth   : uml::Operation init getOperation("bill")

        var refactor : refactor::Refactor<uml::UmlMM>
                           init refactor::Refactor<uml::UmlMM>.new

        refactor.pullUpMethod(source, target, meth)
    end
}
```

Listing 5. Kermeta Code for Applying the Pull Up Method Refactoring on the UML metamodel

5 Experiments and Discussion

We specified three well known refactorings (Encapsulate Field, Move Method, and Pull Up Method [10]) on models of the LAN application [15] conforming to three different metamodels (Java, MOF, and UML). We were able to successfully apply our approach on these metamodels although they were structurally different. We experimented also a fourth metamodel, which a subset is given in Figure 9. In this metamodel, the two classes (corresponding to `Class` and `Parameter` in the generic metamodel) are unified in a same class (`Type`). This case introduced an ambiguous matching with the generic metamodel since these classes are distinct in the latter. This special case illustrates a limitation of our approach that needs to be overcome and will be investigated in future work. Thus, the only prerequisite of our approach is that each element in the generic metamodel should correspond to a distinct element in the target metamodel. The approach is thus not very restrictive since the mechanism of adaptation enables to raise the inherent limitations of metamodels.

Our approach theoretically relies on the model typing and is feasible in practice thanks to the mechanism of adaptation. Writing adaptations can be more or less difficult depending on the developers' knowledge of the target metamodels. However, once the adaptation is done, the developers can reuse all model refactorings written for the generic metamodel. Conversely, if a developer specifies a new refactoring on the generic metamodel, it can readily be applied on all target metamodels if adaptations are provided.

Although we use a specific kind of model transformations, namely refactorings, for demonstrating the feasibility of our approach, this one can be applied to any other endogenous model transformation. In addition, our approach also fits well in the context of metamodel evolution. Indeed, all model transformations written

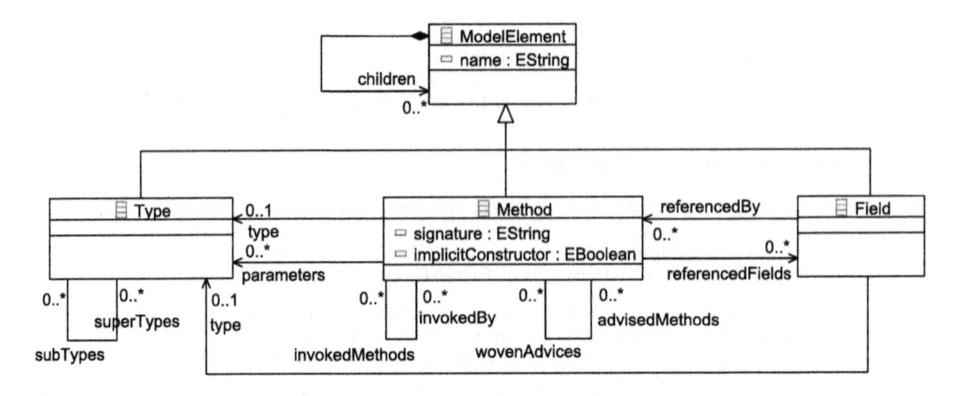

Fig. 9. Subset of the Fourth Metamodel

for an old version of a given metamodel (for example, UML 1.2) can be reused for a new version (for example, UML 2.0) once the adaptation is done. Moreover, the models do not need to be migrated from the old version to the new one. Finally, our approach (with the model typing, the mechanism of adaptation, and the generic metamodel) can be seen as a framework for specifying arbitrary model transformations for arbitrary metamodels.

6 Related Work

Genericity and reuse in MDE have not been sufficiently investigated as in object-oriented (OO) programming. However, we observe some efforts in the MDE community that are directly inherited from type-safe code reuse in OO programming and, in particular, from generic programming.

Generic programming is about making programs more adaptable by making them more general [11]. This style of programming allows writing programs that differ in their parameters, which may be either other programs, types and type constructors, class hierarchies, or even programming paradigms [11]. Aspects [17] and open-classes [7] are powerful generic programming techniques for adapting programs by augmenting their behavior in existing classes [12,18]. Similarly, in our approach, we use aspects to align target metamodels with the generic metamodel. Other languages that provide support for generic programming are Haskell and Scala [26]. The use of Haskell has been investigated [21] to specify refactorings based on high level graph algorithms that could be generic accross a variety of languages (XML, Pascal, Java), but its applicability does not seem to go beyond a proof of concept. Scala's implicit conversions [9] simulate the open-class mechanism in order to extend the behavior of existing libraries without actually changing them. Although Scala is not a *model-oriented* language, developers can build type-safe reusable model transformations on top of EMF thanks to its good integration with Java. However, it would require to write a significant amount of code and manage relationships among generic types.

In the MDE community, Blanc *et al.* proposed an architecture, called Model Bus, that allows the interoperability of a wide range of modeling services [4]. The term '*modeling service*' defines an operation having models as inputs and outputs such as model edition, model transformation, and code generation. Their architecture is based on a metamodel that ensures type compatibility checking by describing services as software components having precise input and output definitions. However, the type compatibility defined in this metamodel relies on a simple notion of model types as sets of metaclasses, but without any notion of model type substitutability. Other work [1,24] study the problem of generic model transformations using a mechanism of parameterization. However, these transformations do not apply to different metamodels but to a set of related models.

Modularity in graph transformation systems was also explored [13]. In this area, an interesting work was done by Engels *et al.* who presented a framework for classifying and defining relations between typed graph transformation systems [8]. This framework integrates a novel notion of substitution morphism that allows to define the semantic relation between the required and provided interfaces of modules in a flexible way.

From another perspective, our approach also relates to the Aspect Oriented Modeling (AOM) field [19], or more precisely to AO metamodeling. From the AOM perspective, our notion of model type can indeed be interpreted as a *pointcut* defining a (model) pattern to be matched in a specific metamodel (e.g. UML or Java). The definition of our generic refactorings then would play the role of *advices* to be woven into these metamodels through some kind of adaptation as available in SmartAdapters [20]. Thus from this perspective our paper could have been title "Weaving refactoring aspects into metamodels".

7 Conclusion

In this paper, we have presented an approach for generic model refactorings, that is refactorings that can be reused on structurally different metamodels. This approach relies on the model typing and a mechanism of adaptation based mainly on the weaving of aspects. We illustrated our approach on the Pull Up Method refactoring and validated it on three different refactorings (Encapsulate Field, Move Method, and Pull Up Method) for three different metamodels (Java, MOF, and UML) in a concrete application. We demonstrated that our approach ensures a flexible reuse of model transformations, in particular refactorings. This approach seems to be generalisable to other endogenous model transformations such as the computation of metrics, detection of patterns and inconsistencies. As future work, we plan to increase the repository of refactorings on other metamodels and experiment with other model transformations.

References

1. Amelunxen, C., Legros, E., Schurr, A.: Generic and reflective graph transformations for the checking and enforcement of modeling guidelines. In: Proceedings of the 2008 IEEE Symposium on Visual Languages and Human-Centric Computing (VLHCC 2008), Washington, DC, USA, pp. 211–218. IEEE Computer Society, Los Alamitos (2008)

2. Basili, V.R., Briand, L.C., Melo, W.L.: How reuse influences productivity in object-oriented systems. Communications of ACM 39(10), 104–116 (1996)
3. Biggerstaff, T.J., Perlis, A.J.: Software Reusability Volume I: Concepts and Models, vol. I. ACM Press, Addison-Wesley, Reading (1989)
4. Blanc, X., Gervais, M.-P., Sriplakich, P.: Model bus: Towards the interoperability of modelling tools. In: Aßmann, U., Aksit, M., Rensink, A. (eds.) MDAFA 2003. LNCS, vol. 3599, pp. 17–32. Springer, Heidelberg (2005)
5. Blanc, X., Ramalho, F., Robin, J.: Metamodel reuse with mof., pp. 661–675 (2005)
6. Bruce, K.B., Vanderwaart, J.: Semantics-driven language design: Statically type-safe virtual types in object-oriented languages. Electronic Notes in Theoretical Computer Science 20, 50–75 (1999)
7. Clifton, C., Leavens, G.T., Chambers, C., Millstein, T.D.: Multijava: Modular open classes and symmetric multiple dispatch for java. In: Proceedings of the 15th International Conference on Object-Oriented Programming, Systems, Languages, and Applications (OOPSLA), pp. 130–145 (2000)
8. Engels, G., Heckel, R., Cherchago, A.: Flexible interconnection of graph transformation modules. In: Kreowski, H.-J., Montanari, U., Orejas, F., Rozenberg, G., Taentzer, G. (eds.) Formal Methods in Software and Systems Modeling. LNCS, vol. 3393, pp. 38–63. Springer, Heidelberg (2005)
9. Odersky, M., et al.: An overview of the scala programming language. Technical Report IC/2004/64, EPFL Lausanne, Switzerland (2004)
10. Fowler, M.: Refactoring – Improving the Design of Existing Code, 1st edn. Addison-Wesley, Reading (1999)
11. Gibbons, J., Jeuring, J. (eds.): Generic Programming, IFIP TC2/WG2.1 Working Conference on Generic Programming, Dagstuhl, Germany, July 11-12. IFIP Conference Proceedings, vol. 243. Kluwer Academic Publishers, Dordrecht (2003), `http://www.comlab.ox.ac.uk/oucl/work/jeremy.gibbons/publications/wcgp-preface.pdf`
12. Hannemann, J., Kiczales, G.: Design pattern implementation in java and aspectj. SIGPLAN Not. 37(11), 161–173 (2002)
13. Heckel, R., Engels, G., Ehrig, H., Taentzer, G.: Classification and comparison of module concepts for graph transformation systems. In: Handbook of graph grammars and computing by graph transformation. Applications, languages, and tools, vol. 2, pp. 669–689. World Scientific, Singapore (1999)
14. Hoffman, B., Pérez, J., Mens, T.: A case study for program refactoring. In: GraBaTs (September 2008)
15. Janssens, D., Demeyer, S., Mens, T.: Case study: Simulation of a lan. Electronic Notes in Theoretical Computer Science 72(4) (2003)
16. Kermeta, `http://www.kermeta.org/`
17. Kiczales, G., Lamping, J., Mendhekar, A., Maeda, C., Lopes, C.V., Loingtier, J.-M., Irwin, J.: Aspect-oriented programming. In: Aksit, M., Matsuoka, S. (eds.) ECOOP 1997. LNCS, vol. 1241, pp. 220–242. Springer, Heidelberg (1997)
18. Kiczales, G., Mezini, M.: Aspect-oriented programming and modular reasoning. In: Proceedings of the 27th international conference on Software engineering (ICSE 2005), pp. 49–58. ACM, New York (2005)
19. Kienzle, J., Abed, W.A., Jacques, K.: Aspect-oriented multi-view modeling. In: AOSD 2009: Proceedings of the 8th ACM international conference on Aspect-oriented software development, pp. 87–98. ACM, New York (2009)

20. Lahire, P., Morin, B., Vanwormhoudt, G., Gaignard, A., Barais, O., Jézéquel, J.-M.: Introducing variability into aspect-oriented modeling approaches. In: Engels, G., Opdyke, B., Schmidt, D.C., Weil, F. (eds.) MODELS 2007. LNCS, vol. 4735, pp. 498–513. Springer, Heidelberg (2007)
21. Lämmel, R.: Towards Generic Refactoring. In: Proceedings of Third ACM SIGPLAN Workshop on Rule-Based Programming RULE 2002, Pittsburgh, USA, October 5, 14 pages. ACM Press, New York (2002)
22. Mens, T., Van Gorp, P.: A taxonomy of model transformation. Electronic Notes in Theoretical Computer Science 152, 125–142 (2006)
23. Mili, H., Mili, F., Mili, A.: Reusing software: Issues and research directions. IEEE Transactions of Software Engineering 21(6), 528–562 (1995)
24. Münch, M.: Generic Modelling with Graph Rewriting Systems. PhD thesis, RWTH Aachen, Berichte aus der Informatik (2003)
25. Muller, P.-A., Fleurey, F., Jézéquel, J.-M.: Weaving executability into object-oriented meta-languages. In: Briand, L.C., Williams, C. (eds.) MoDELS 2005. LNCS, vol. 3713, pp. 264–278. Springer, Heidelberg (2005)
26. Oliveira, B.C.D.S., Gibbons, J.: Scala for generic programmers. In: Hinze, R., Syme, D. (eds.) WGP 2008: Proceedings of the ACM SIGPLAN workshop on Generic programming, pp. 25–36. ACM, New York (2008)
27. OMG. Mof 2.0 core specification. Technical Report formal/06-01-01, OMG, April 2006. OMG Available Specification
28. OMG. The Object Constraint Language Specification 2.0, OMG Document: ad/03-01-07 (2007)
29. OMG. The uml 2.1.2 infrastructure specification. Technical Report formal/2007-11-04, OMG, April 2007. OMG Available Specification
30. Steel, J.: Typage de modèles. PhD thesis, Université de Rennes (April 1, 2007)
31. Steel, J., Jézéquel, J.-M.: On model typing. Journal of Software and Systems Modeling (SoSyM) 6(4), 401–414 (2007)

Constraining Type Parameters of UML 2 Templates with Substitutable Classifiers

Arnaud Cuccuru, Ansgar Radermacher, Sébastien Gérard, and François Terrier

CEA LIST, Boîte 94, Gif-sur-Yvette, F-91191, France
first_name.last_name@cea.fr

Abstract. Generic programming is a field of computer science which consists in defining abstract and reusable representations of efficient data structures and algorithms. In popular imperative languages, it is usually supported by a template-like notation, where generic elements are represented by templates exposing formal parameters. Defining such generic artifacts may require defining constraints on the actual types that can be provided in a particular substitution. UML 2 templates support two mechanisms for expressing such constraints. Unfortunately, the UML specification provides very few details on their usage. The purpose of our article is to provide such details with regard to one of these constraining mechanisms (namely, "substitutable constraining classifiers") as well as modeling patterns inspired by practices from generic programming.

1 Introduction

UML 2 templates [1] (chapter 17.5) are inspired by template-like mechanisms of popular programming languages such as C++ or Java. They provide support for the three fundamental notions of template-based design: templates (i.e., metaclass *TemplateableElement*), formal parameters (i.e., *TemplateSignature*, *TemplateParameter* and *ParameterableElement*) and bindings (i.e., *TemplateBinding* and *TemplateParameterSubstitution*). A template is a kind of abstract element whose definition is parameterized by other elements. Elements that are exposed as parameters of a template definition are called its formal parameters. A concrete element (usually called bound element) can then be instantiated by binding a template, i.e., specifying a substitution for each of its formal parameters.

Defining generic structures or algorithms typically requires making assumptions on the types exposed as formal parameters of a template, by defining constraints on the actual types that can be provided in a particular substitution. For this purpose, UML 2 templates provide a refinement of the metaclass TemplateParameter called ClassifierTemplateParameter (used for the exposure of classifiers) that can be associated with a set of constraining classifiers. An additional boolean property of ClassifierTemplateParameter, called *allowSubstitutable*, enables two potential interpretations of these constraining classifiers. In the case where it is false, the interpretation is object-oriented. It indeed implies that a valid actual type must have a direct or indirect generalization relationship with each of the constraining classifiers. This approach will not be discussed in

A. Schürr and B. Selic (Eds.): MODELS 2009, LNCS 5795, pp. 644–649, 2009.

this article (see [2] and [3] for details). In the case where it is true, the set of constraining classifiers simply specifies a kind of contract. Any actual classifier satisfying this contract is a valid substitution for the formal parameter, i.e., it is substitutable. Unfortunately, the UML specification provides very few details on the usage of this constraining mechanism. It is the purpose of this article to provide such details and guidelines.

We propose a simple pattern where contracts (i.e., substitutable constraining classifiers) are defined as template classifiers and used as namespaces containing any element useful for the definition of a generic behavior or structure. We show that it is then possible to explicitly specify how an actual classifier realizes the contract by combining Realization and TemplateBinding relationships. The details of our proposal are described in section 2. In section 3, we discuss related works from the generic programming community. Section 4 then concludes this article and sets guidelines for future research.

2 Substitutable Constraining Classifiers in Action

Using substitutable constraining classifiers is a very loose form of specifying type compatibility rules. The semantic relationship between an actual classifier and the constraining classifiers is in fact equivalent to a Realization relationship. In UML, a Realization relationship is a kind of assertion that a given classifier realizes another one. It needs to be augmented with information explicitly specifying how the realization of the specification is actually done. In order to illustrate how this information can be made more explicit, let us consider a generic activity called *accum*, that computes the sum of the elements contained in a collection.

This activity is generic from two standpoints: 1.) the type of the elements to be accumulated (which must support the operator "+") and 2.) the type of the collection containing the elements (which is required to be "iterable forward"). In the following subsections, we illustrate our proposal by focusing on the second standpoint. We first describe a template class *Iterator* with a formal type parameter C (i.e., the type of the collection) and its associated substitutable constraining classifier *IterableForward*. Then, we show how the substitutability of a given classifier (Vector in our example) with respect to the contract represented by IterableForward can be explicitly specified.

2.1 Specifying the Contract

Descriptions of the class Iterator and the constraining classifier IterableForward (which constrains parameter C) are shown in Fig. 1. On the left-hand side of the figure (i.e., template signature of Iterator), the standard keyword "contract" associated with the formal parameter C renders the fact that *allowSubstitutable* is true.

Our proposal consists in using the members of IterableForward (shown in the *nestedClassifier* and *ownedBehavior* compartment of the class) to capture the requirements that must be fulfilled by a given classifier to be considered as a valid substitution for parameter C. Literally, a classifier satisfies the contract

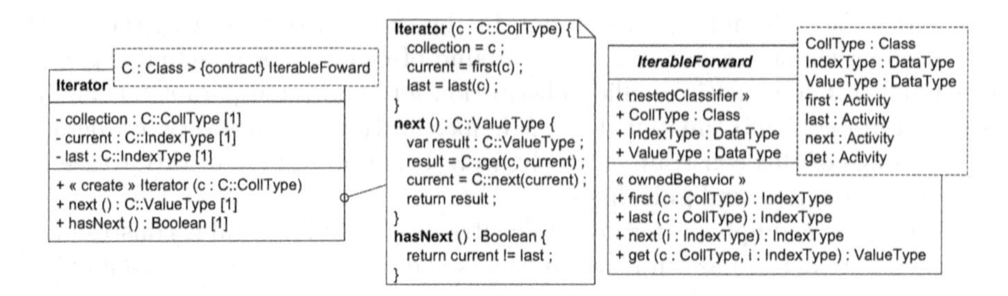

Fig. 1. Specification of Iterator and its constraining classifier IterableForward

represented by IterableForward if, from this classifier: 1.) It is possible to derive the type of the collection (*CollType*), the type of the element used as an index for accessing elements contained in the collection (*IndexType*) and the type of the elements it contains (*ValueType*) (In the C++ terminology, these types would be called "traits" [4] of IterableForward.) and 2.) It is possible to derive the activities that compute the index of the first element (*first*), the index of the last element (*last*), the index following a given index (*next*) and the value of the element at a given index (*get*).

Provided the definition of IterableForward, it is then possible to generically specify the class Iterator with respect to its formal parameter *C*. In the left-hand side of Fig. 1, we can see that the model of the class Iterator relies on explicit references to traits and activities of *C* (as illustrated by the usage of fully qualified names for each element) for typing its properties and implementing its operations. For a given actual classifier *S* provided as a substitution for parameter *C* (in a binding of the template Iterator), any reference to a member *M* of *C* will be substituted with an element derived from *S* (provided that *S* realizes IterableForward). Defining how a classifier *S* actually realizes IterableForward is the purpose of the following section.

2.2 Specifying the Substitutability

Let us show how a class *Vector* can be made a valid substitution for the parameter *C* of template Iterator. Determining how Vector realizes IterableForward (and each of its members) can be achieved by specifying a template binding relationship between Vector and IterableForward (along with a substitution for each of these members). This solution is illustrated in the left-hand side of Fig. 2.

We can see that the substitutions associated with the binding relationships state that: CollType will be played by Vector itself, IndexType by Integer and ValueType by T (which is itself exposed as a parameter of Vector). Similarly, a substitution is provided for each of the activities of Iterator. The actual activities (*first_vector*, *last_vector*, *next_vector* and *get_vector*) are signature compatible with those of IterableForward, except that the type of their parameters has been substituted with the actual types provided as substitutions for traits of IterableForward. Additionally, they encapsulate an implementation suited to

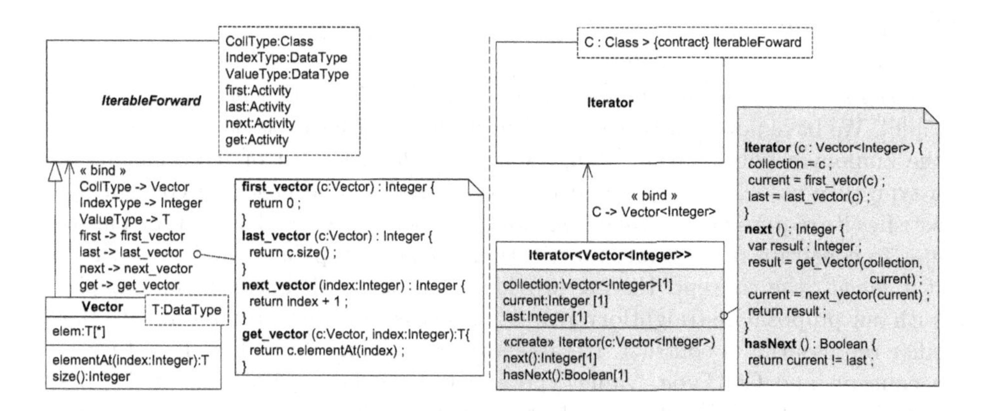

Fig. 2. Realization of the contract IterableForward and instanciation of Iterator

the specificities of Vector (e.g., activity *get_ vector* is described using operation *elementAt* of Vector).

In UML 2, defining a binding relationship between a bound element and a template normally implies a two steps generative process. It consists in replicating the template and then substituting any reference to formal parameters with actual elements provided in the binding. In the case of Vector, we clearly do not want this generative process to apply. The presence of the Realization relationship (appearing on the left side of the binding relationship in Fig. 2) captures this intention. The Realization relationship is just used as an assertion that Vector realizes IterableForward and the TemplateBinding relationship explicitly specifies how this realization is actually done without requiring any replication. This reasonable interpretation is the only extension we introduce in standard UML 2 templates. Regarding the template Iterator and its formal parameter C, the binding relationship between Vector and IterableForward provides sufficient information for determining the substitution to be operated if an instance of the template Vector (e.g., Vector<Integer>) is provided as a substitution for the formal parameter C. The result of the substitution is illustrated in the right-hand side of Fig. 2.

Applying the same principles, the activity *accum* can be specified with two formal parameters: *C:Class > {contract}IterableForward* and *T:DataType = C::ValueType > Addable<T>*. Just like for Iterator, parameter *C* represents a collection type. It is associated with IterableForward as a substitutable constraining classifier. The additional formal parameter *T* represents the elements contained in the collection. Its constraining classifier Addable<T> is not substitutable (it represents an abstract class owning an operation *add(T,T):T*). Note that *T* has a default substitution (in the UML2 metamodel, it corresponds to the property *default* of metaclass TemplateParameter). It means that for a given binding of activity *accum*, the only required substitution concerns parameter *C*. The substitution for parameter *T* will be automatically inferred from *C* (i.e., C::ValueType). The following section sets links between these proposals and the fundamental principles put into action in the field of generic programming.

3 Related Works

Concepts and *models* are the most fundamental notions of generic programming [5] [6]. We have not used these words until now in order to avoid confusion with the homonym notions from MDE. A *concept* defines a set of requirements on a type (like associated types and functions), and a type *models* a concept if it satisfies its requirements. A *concept* can be associated with a formal type parameter to constrain the possible substitutions. A given type is a valid substitution if it *models* the concept. Having provided these basic definitions, the mapping with our proposal is straightforward. A *concept* is captured with a template classifier representing a contract. IterableForward (illustrated in Fig. 1) is thereby a concept, and CollType, ValueType and IndexType are its associated types. Activities *first*, *last*, *next* and *get* are used to describe the signatures of functions that should be available for a given type to *model* the concept. The fact that a type (for example Vector of Fig. 2) *models* a concept is captured by the combined usage of Realization and TemplateBinding relationships.

Concerning works more directly related to UML 2 templates and the expression of constraints on type parameters, we have shown in previous publications [2] [3] how classifiers could be parameterized with policy classes by using non-substitutable constraining classifiers. Except these works, there are (to our knowledge) no other publications directly addressing the subject.

4 Conclusion

UML 2 provides support for template-based modeling, as well as dedicated mechanisms for expressing constraints on type parameters. Expressing such constraints is crucial when considering behavioral aspects. For that purpose, we have proposed modeling patterns related to the usage of substitutable constraining classifiers. Our middle-term goal is now to put these proposals in practice for the definition of a generic library similar to the STL of C++ (i.e., generic collection types and iterators). While we have explained that the mechanisms we have proposed directly map to fundamental notions of generic programming, it would not make sense to directly map the hierarchy of *concepts* (with their associated requirements) of the STL, as it is strongly influenced by the facilities of the language (i.e., pointers, increment and dereferencing operators, etc.). Further studies are therefore required to adapt this hierarchy, taking into account the specific properties of UML.

References

1. OMG: Unified Modeling Language: Superstructure version 2.2 (2008)
2. Cuccuru, A., Mraidha, C., Terrier, F., Gérard, S.: Templateable Metomodels for Semantic Variation Points. In: Akehurst, D.H., Vogel, R., Paige, R.F. (eds.) ECMDA-FA. LNCS, vol. 4530, pp. 68–82. Springer, Heidelberg (2007)

3. Cuccuru, A., Mraidha, C., Terrier, F., Gérard, S.: Enhancing UML Extensions with Operational Semantics. In: Engels, G., Opdyke, B., Schmidt, D.C., Weil, F. (eds.) MODELS 2007. LNCS, vol. 4735, pp. 271–285. Springer, Heidelberg (2007)
4. Myers, N.: A New and Useful Template Technique: "Traits". In: Lippman, S.B. (ed.) C++ Gems, pp. 451–457. SIGS Publications, Inc., New York (1996)
5. Austern, M.H.: Generic Programming and the STL. Addison-Wesley Pro., Reading (1999)
6. Gregor, D., Järvi, J., Siek, J., Stroustrup, B., Dos Reis, G., Lumsdaine, A.: Concepts: Linguistic Support for Generic Programming in C++. In: OOPSLA 2006, pp. 291–310. ACM, New York (2006)

Generating Assertion Code from OCL: A Transformational Approach Based on Similarities of Implementation Languages

Rodion Moiseev, Shinpei Hayashi, and Motoshi Saeki

Department of Computer Science, Tokyo Institute of Technology,
Ookayama 2–12–1–W8–83, Meguro-ku, Tokyo 152–8552, Japan
{rodion,hayashi,saeki}@se.cs.titech.ac.jp

Abstract. The Object Constraint Language (OCL) carries a platform independent characteristic allowing it to be decoupled from implementation details, and therefore it is widely applied in model transformations used by model-driven development techniques. However, OCL can be found tremendously useful in the implementation phase aiding assertion code generation and allowing system verification. Yet, taking full advantage of OCL without destroying its platform independence is a difficult task. This paper proposes an approach for generating assertion code from OCL constraints by using a model transformation technique to abstract language specific details away from OCL high-level concepts, showing wide applicability of model transformation techniques. We take advantage of structural similarities of implementation languages to describe a rewriting framework, which is used to easily and flexibly reformulate OCL constraints into any target language, making them executable on any platform. A tool is implemented to demonstrate the effectiveness of this approach.

Keywords: OCL, constraints, assertion code, programming languages.

1 Introduction

Model-centric methodologies for software development such as OMG's Model-Driven Architecture (MDA) [1] are becoming significant in academia and industry, and Unified Modeling Language (UML) and Object Constraint Language (OCL) [2] play an important role in these methodologies. For instance, UML class diagrams express the structural design of the system, where OCL specifies properties that must be satisfied at particular times in the system. Figure 1 illustrates how class diagrams and OCL descriptions could be used during development. The code skeleton is automatically generated from the class diagram, e.g., by using Eclipse UML, which is then used by developers to complete the implementation. The OCL specifications can then be used to generate code for checking the system at runtime, and/or unit test code. We will generally refer to it as *assertion code* hereafter. If we take Java as a possible implementation language, we should translate the OCL specification into Java-based assertion code. Similarly, for Python and Perl,

A. Schürr and B. Selic (Eds.): MODELS 2009, LNCS 5795, pp. 650–664, 2009.

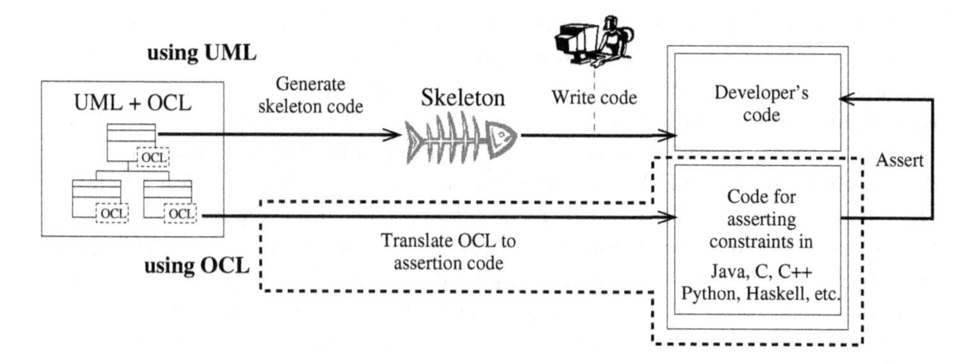

Fig. 1. UML and OCL usage overview

we need translators from OCL into Python and Perl respectively. It means that we should have an OCL translator for each programming language that can be an implementation language. However, a tremendous amount of effort is necessary to develop an OCL translator from scratch for each language.

We have established a possible usage of OCL that spans implementations in different languages, which imposes a need for existence of OCL translators for multiple languages within one design. In such cases using OCL is most desirable since OCL is independent of the implementation technology. However, as outlined in Fig. 1, currently available UML modelling tools, despite having the facility to input and perform code generation from UML, and for some of them provide the user with an interface to input OCL constraints, not many allow to take OCL to the implementation level (dotted section of Fig. 1). Also, looking at the current approaches (see Sect. 5) we can conclude that currently there exists no approach suitable for working with OCL constraints on the implementation level for multiple languages. Thus we should have a technique to develop an OCL translator for each programming language with least possible effort.

In this paper, we propose an approach to allow developers to make use of OCL from UML diagrams and to check developers' programmes written in any programming language of choice. This will be achieved by translating constraints in OCL into their equivalent assertion code in the target language (e.g., Java, C, C++, Python). Our OCL translator is based on model-driven techniques, especially model transformation. One of the advantages of model transformation is the ability to reuse transformation rules when developing similar application software, more concretely, transforming semantically similar models. Specifications of the OCL and implementation languages can be modelled as an abstract syntax tree (AST). The transformation rules between these two models can be used to achieve generation of assertion code that can be executed on the implementation language platform. Consider two different programming languages that could be possible targets for generating OCL assertions. If these two languages are similar, e.g., both of them are imperative programming languages, some of their transformation rules can be shared, so that we can reduce the efforts to design the transformation rules. Therefore we can mitigate the above problem mentioned in the last paragraph, i.e., larger efforts to develop an OCL translator for each programming language. In addition, we have applied a model transformation technique to a new area of language processing.

The approach focuses on making sure that most of the OCL translation can be done within one framework independent of the target implementation language. On the other hand, because of this lack of dependency, creating an OCL translator for an additional target language requires little understanding of OCL itself on behalf of the developer, which is important for cases when software designer (person working with OCL) and programmer (person working with implementation languages) are not the same person. The translation process is hierarchically managed which makes it easily modifiable and extendible. The approach was designed to make the following improvements upon existing approaches:

Extendibility:
- Lower efforts when creating OCL assertion code generators for languages with no OCL support.
- Minimise efforts when creating support for a new language that is an extension or a modification of an existing language.

Maintainability:
- Lower modification efforts by having semantically decoupled modules that make it easier to locate the modification target.
- Because of semantically hierarchical structure, modifications can be made at higher (more abstract) levels independently of concrete language implementations. This can be said to be equivalent to the paradigm of aspect-oriented programming [3], where a good example of useful modification include: logging, constraint checking, etc.

Understandability:
- OCL assertion code generators can be created with minimum understanding of OCL concepts.
- Working at more abstract levels alleviates understanding of concrete implementation details.

The contribution of the paper can be summarised as follows: 1) providing a technique to develop an OCL assertion code generator using model transformation with less efforts and 2) showing a new application area, i.e., language processors for model transformation. The evaluation in this paper shows that by using our approach we can develop OCL translators for four different programming languages with less transformation rules (hence, less effort), opposed to developing each translator separately.

The rest of this paper is organised as follows. In the next section, we describe our approach. Section 3 describes its architecture, pointing out how it realises the contributions we have claimed. In Sect. 4, we cover an evaluation experiment for our approach and summarise the results. Some related work is covered in Sect. 5, followed by conclusion in Sect. 6.

```
for apple in basket:
  if apple.colour == "red":
    ...
```

(a) Sample Python code.

```
for (Iterator i = basket.iterator();
        i.hasNext(); ) {
  Apple apple = (Apple) i.next();
  if (apple.getColour().equals("red")) {
    ...
```

(b) Sample Java code.

```
For Each apple In basket Do:
  If apple.colour Is "red" Then
    ...
```

(c) Pseudo-code of the same action.

Fig. 2. Language similarities extraction

2 Proposed Approach

Our approach comprises a framework that allows developers to easily and with minimum effort create a generator of OCL assertion code for any text-based language of choice by reusing the mappings to OCL from other languages' structural and semantic concepts.

In order to understand the main concept behind our approach, consider the sample code shown in Fig. 2. We have a sample Python code in Fig. 2(a) that checks each `apple` in a collection of apples, `basket`, to see whether it is of red colour. The above semantics are expressed in terms of a for-loop and an if-statement nested inside it. If you further consider a sample Java code in Fig. 2(b), you will find that even though syntactically it looks somewhat different, semantically and structure-wise it is nearly identical. First, the idea of a for-loop for iterating over the collection, and an if-statement for doing logical checks is the same as in the Python example. Also the if-statement is again nested inside the for-loop. These show that Python and Java programming languages resemble in their conceptual vocabulary and in structure, even though the detailed syntax is different.

In fact, we can make similar observations with most imperative programming languages, including Java, Python, Ruby, Perl, C++ and C#. Since all of these languages are based on the same *imperative* programming paradigm, they will contain for-loops, if-statements, sub-procedures, etc. regardless of whether they are strongly-typed, interpreted, run in a virtual machine or have some other unique quality. Because of this similarity, we can describe for-loops such as the one in Figs. 2(a) and 2(b), with a pseudo-language description which captures the semantics of the performed action, shown in Fig. 2(c). What we are trying to say is that, imperative languages all bear similarities in their semantics originally and therefore share a lot of common programming structures. Of course, other language types, like *functional* languages also all share common structures, since most of them were designed to solve the same problem.

If we can extract common language features from all languages that fall under a particular category, such as imperative languages, we could create, for example, an imperative pseudo-language that captured all of the common constructs available in imperative programming languages. Such imperative pseudo-language could be used to describe behaviour of OCL constructs in terms of *imperative*

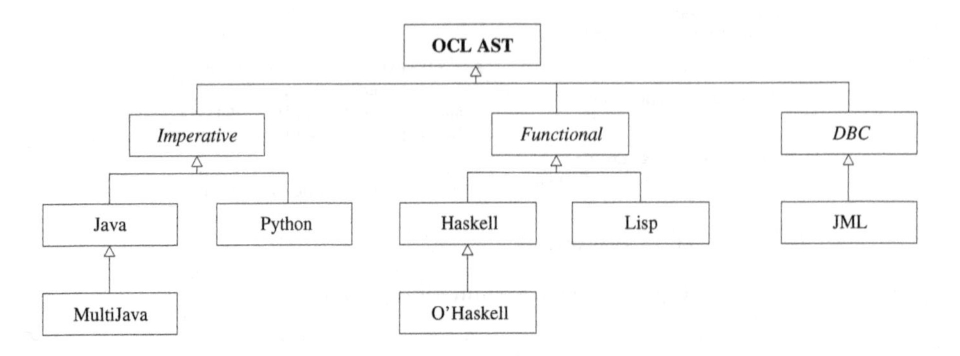

Fig. 3. Hierarchy of languages based on their structural similarities

constructs. By doing this, not only we can make the translation to the target imperative language easier, but also alleviate the need to completely comprehend every OCL expression. Based on this idea, in our approach we define a hierarchy, based on structural similarities of commonly available languages. Refer to Fig. 3 for an example of such hierarchy. Some languages can be further subdivided into sub-hierarchies to capture similarities that are more fine-grained, and thus more specific to particular imperative languages. An example of such languages would be Python and Java, which both have *for-each* loops. What such hierarchy allows us to do is to describe OCL concepts in terms of the intermediary pseudo-languages (e.g., imperative pseudo-language or functional pseudo-language) in one or more steps, therefore capturing the most conceptually difficult parts of OCL at a higher level of abstraction and thus making them more language independent. This means that at the lower, more concrete levels, the developer will only need to provide details specific to language syntax and grammar to complete the mapping.

3 Implementing Our Approach

In order to assess the feasibility of our approach we have implemented an OCL translation tool based on the language similarities. Our tool was implemented using the Maude System [4], a term rewriting system, which comprises powerful equational and rewriting logic capabilities, that would be useful for our multi-step translation.

3.1 Generation Process

As mentioned in the last section, we have two major steps of translation; 1) from OCL (precisely, an AST obtained by parsing an OCL description) to pseudo-code and 2) from pseudo-code to the target source code. The structure of pseudo-code depends on the class of the target languages. For example, we have a class of pseudo-code for imperative languages such as Java, C and Python, and have another class for functional programming languages such as Haskell and Lisp. We

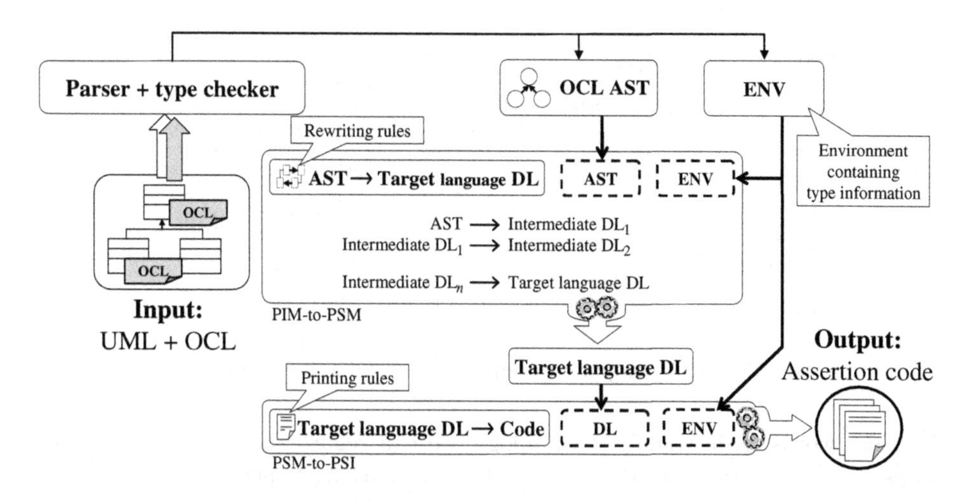

Fig. 4. Generation process

call this language of pseudo-code *Definition Language* (DL). The transformation then follows the hierarchy defined for the target language (see Fig. 3) starting at the top and proceeding to the leaf DL, performing translations for each intermediate step. The example in Fig. 2(c) is the pseudo-code written in Imperative DL. Figure 4 shows the overview of our process of generating an OCL assertion code from an arbitrary UML/OCL model, which consists of three main steps:

1. UML + OCL → OCL AST
   The initial input to our system is a UML diagram annotated with OCL constraints. We therefore require means of interpreting the UML diagram and parsing the OCL constraints beforehand. After parsing a syntactically correct OCL description, it is then converted into its AST representation. UML, e.g., a class diagram, is used in the background to form an *environment* containing the type information.
2. OCL AST → Target language DL
   The target language for OCL constraints being executed is selected, and the hierarchy is traversed starting from OCL AST definition step-by-step, until the final output in the DL of the target language (target language DL) is produced. The translation is defined as rewriting rules in Maude and executed by using these rewriting rules and the type information. The details of using the Maude will be mentioned later. This step is repeated until the target language DL, e.g., Python DL, is obtained.
3. Target language DL → Code
   Finally, the target language DL can be transformed into its equivalent executable code by applying a set of *printing rules*. We call this stage *printing*. The technique for this transformation is the same as the last step, i.e., we define the printing rules as rewriting rules in Maude.

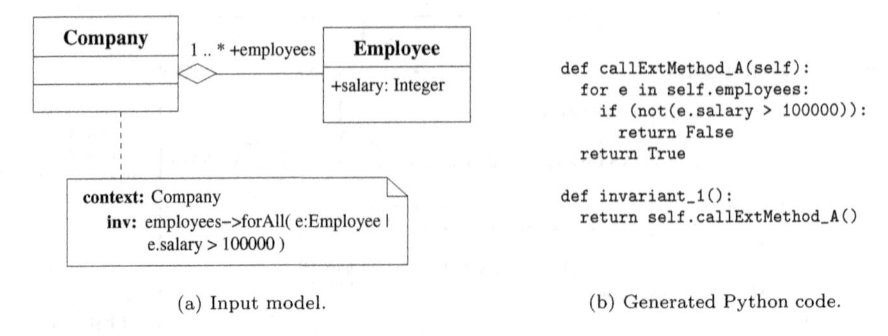

(a) Input model. (b) Generated Python code.

Fig. 5. A company example with an OCL invariant

In other words with MDD's terminology, we can regard the second and third steps as PIM-to-PSM and PSM-to-PSI transformations respectively.

Combined, these three steps represent a pluggable architecture, which could be inserted into an existing Integrated Development Environment (IDE) and used as a provider of assertion code bits fetched from the model specification. Such assertion code bits can be used in test cases or for run-time assertion.

For implementing the tool to automate the above generation process, as mentioned above, we have used the Maude language [4], which uses equational and rewriting logic. The language contains a functional-like data definition language used to define data structure and reduction rules, and a rewriting language used to describe rewriting rules between data structures. In our tool implementation, the data definition language was used to create each of the DL's, e.g., OCL AST (Fig. 6) or Imperative DL (Fig. 8), while the rewriting language was used for defining mappings between the different levels in the hierarchy, e.g., between OCL AST and Imperative DL (Fig. 7).

3.2 Example of Transformation Process

Suppose you were given a simple model of a company shown in Fig. 5(a). If there was a company requirement that all employees must earn over 100,000, in OCL it could be expressed as an invariant on the `Company` class as shown at the bottom of the figure. This OCL constraint consists of a `forAll` expression, which enforces all `Employee` objects contained in the `employees` collection to have the `salary` property set to a value greater than `100000`. Generated Python assertion code is shown in Fig. 5(b). The given OCL is transformed to the method `callExtMethod_A` and it is checked as the invariant via the function `invariant_1`.

As described in the architecture model in Fig. 4, the first step is to convert OCL expressions from the model into their AST representation. The OCL expression in our example can be expressed in the Maude language as shown in the bottom part of Fig. 6, showing an example of mapping from OCL to its AST. Note that at the top-level hierarchy we have the `iteratorExp`, applied to the `employees` collection, where the type of the iterator expression is `forAll`, shown

All employees in the company earn more than 100,000

```
employees->forAll( e : Employee | e.salary > 100000 )

iteratorExp
  (assocEndCallExp simpleName("self") . simpleName("employees"))
  -> simpleName("forAll") ( varDecl(simpleName("e"), pathName("Employee")) |
    operCallExp(
      attrCallExp simpleName("e") . simpleName("salary"),
      simpleName(">"),
      intLitExp("100000")
    )
  )
```

Fig. 6. AST representation of OCL constraint in Maude

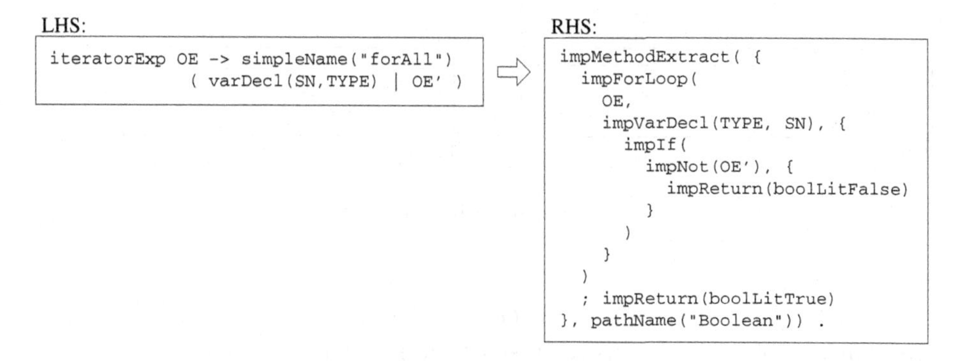

Fig. 7. A rewriting rule for OCL AST → Imperative DL

in lines 1, 2 and 3 of the OCL AST part respectively. Lower down the iterator and the sub-expression to be checked are declared.

At the second step of Fig. 4, we enter the OCL AST rewriting stage where by means of rewriting rules we transform the OCL AST into the DL for a concrete programming language. The intention of this step is to declare a transformation of the OCL concept into an abstract imperative code for its assertion. In our example, we declare a rewriting rule as shown in Fig. 7. At the top of the figure, the left-hand-side of the rule is declared to match all occurrences of `forAll` expressions, on arbitrary collection expressions `OE`. Other variable parts of the matching rule are expressed in capitals. To transform the matched expression into Imperative DL's one the right-hand-side states that it should be expressed as an external method call (`impMethodExtract`) of return type `Boolean` that loops (`impForLoop`) through the target collection `OE` and tests (`impIf`) whether the sub-expression `OE'` holds. If sub-expression is not satisfied, the method returns (`impReturn`) with the boolean value *false* (`boolLitFalse`). The prefix `imp` identifies that the following structure belongs to the Imperative DL, and thus expressions such as *for-loops*, *if-statements* and *return-statements* are marked with that prefix. One possible implementation of this abstraction in Python is shown in Fig. 5(b).

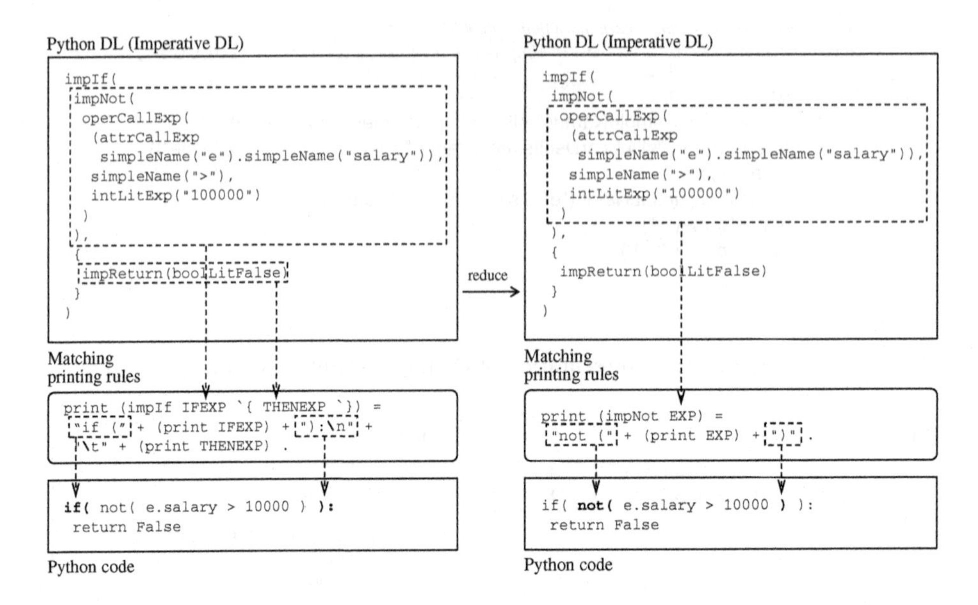

Fig. 8. Printing rules

By applying the above rule to the OCL AST in Fig. 6, we obtain the imperative definition of the OCL constraint, shown in the top part of Fig. 8, the external method call and the *for-loop* where omitted for clarity. In this transformation, the iterator expression `e.salary > 100000` is mapped to the variable `OE'`, and as a result, appears inside the `impIf(impNot(···))` statement in the third line of Fig. 8. The OCL constraint is now expressed in terms of the desired imperative language constructs.

To produce executable Python code from the Imperative DL it can first be transformed into Python DL in the same manner as the OCL AST was transformed into the Imperative DL. However, in our example, Imperative DL constructs are already semantically and structurally close enough to Python for it to be considered a valid Python DL. Therefore, we have obtained the most concrete definition language for Python and can apply printing rules to generate the actual executable code (see bottom part of Fig. 8).

Printing rules for the target language are matched and applied to the obtained DL top-down (Imperative DL in our case). An example of the printing process is depicted in Fig. 8. The printing rule for *if-block* `impIf` is matched to the DL, and its sub-expressions, *if-expression* and *then-expression* are matched to variables `IFEXP` and `THENEXP` respectively. The printing rule states that in Python syntax *if-block* starts with `"if ("`, followed by the *if-expression*, then the closing bracket, a colon and then an indented *then-expression*. This reduction process is then repeated for each sub-expression (`impNot` on the right hand side of Fig. 8), until the whole DL is translated into Python code. For each target language a *printing module* is declared, containing such printing rules for all syntactical concepts of the language. Common syntactical rules can be expressed at higher levels of the hierarchy, for instance, the `impIf` rule in Fig. 8 is declared at the *imperative* level and therefore need not be declared explicitly at the Python level. Applying Python printing rules makes an executable Python code that can be plugged into a class implementing the `Company` and used to check the original OCL invariant.

Note that for defining an OCL translator for a new language using our approach, it is generally enough to define a set (or modify an existing set) of printing rules to capture syntactical rules of that language, therefore understanding of OCL will not be required. Modifications to output assertion code on syntactical level will always be reflected though changes to the printing rules. On the other hand, modifying structure will be done by changing rewriting rules higher up in the hierarchy e.g., Imperative DL (Fig. 7). One could also, for example, easily inject a logging action for whenever a *for-all* evaluation is made by adding `log("message");` appropriately in the RHS of Fig. 7. This operation does not require direct understanding of how each concrete language implementation performs logging. If logging is not appropriate for some concrete language it can be omitted during next transformation or printing stage.

4 Experimental Evaluation

To evaluate our approach, we carried out an experiment. The aim of the experiment is to show that our approach gives us the ability to flexibly create OCL assertion code generators for any language, gaining savings in manual efforts required to implement each generator.

4.1 Procedure

For evaluation, we will implement four OCL translators for four different languages. Two languages from under the imperative languages hierarchy, Java and Python; and two from under the functional languages hierarchy, Haskell and O'Haskell. Then the efforts required to implement each one of those OCL translators will be measured and compared to an estimated effort required to create an OCL translator for the same language using a direct approach, i.e., the development from scratch. The direct approach assumes an implementation of OCL requiring minimum effort, realised by simply implementing a set of transformation rules that directly translate each OCL expression (see Table 1) into the target language, i.e., no printing rules and no intermediate definition languages are used. Finally, generated assertion code for each OCL translator will be checked to make sure they exhibit desired behaviour.

We first build an OCL translator for Python, using the direct approach, and use the resulting effort figure as a yardstick for estimating direct approach efforts for other languages. Secondly, we pre-build the Imperative and the Functional DLs, and then implement OCL translators for each one of the four languages by extending the Imperative or the Functional DLs as appropriate, and measure

Table 1. Evaluation targets

Logical Operators	Iterator Expressions		Collection Operations		
xor	iterate	select	includes	isEmpty	sum
implies	forAll	reject	excludes	notEmpty	size
	exists	any	includesAll	union	first
	isUnique	one	excludesAll	intersection	last
	collect	sortedBy	including	flatten	at
			excluding		

the efforts during each implementation. Lastly, the efforts that were required to create each OCL translator as an extension in our approach, are compared to the efforts for the direct approach.

To evaluate the effort at each step we need a comparable indicator that can be used to measure and compare these efforts. Translation of OCL concepts into concepts of other programming languages requires a description of their structural transformation, for each concept. Regardless of which approach one decides to undertake, to translate an OCL concept to the concept in the target language, one will have to specify a *transformation rule* that would provide for the translation of the concept. If one did not have to specify as many transformation rules to translate all of the OCL concepts into the target language, then it would be valid to claim that one did not spend as much effort on specifying the translation.

Based on this claim, we will be using the number of transformation rules as an indicator of the amount of effort spent on translating a fixed set of OCL concepts into the target language. However, the effort involved in creating a transformation rule also has to be taken into account, thus to provide a fairer view of complexity we need to consider the number of semantic units introduced into the system. The larger the number of semantic units, the more difficult it becomes to grasp all of the concepts used in a transformation rule, and thus we could say that the complexity of the system also becomes greater. Therefore, we will also count the number of additional semantic structures that had to be defined in order to provide for creation of these rules. Semantic units are specified as definitions in Maude.

In our approach, at the final stage of translation process we use printing rules to produce executable code. These rules are also one kind of transformation rules and are therefore taken into account as effort units as well. From the above discussion, we can summarise the following evaluation parameters to be used to evaluate the effort: 1) the number of rule definitions in the rewriting language (RR), 2) the number of declarations in the data definition language (S), and 3) the number of definitions in the printing module (PR) in Maude, for each generator. For evaluation the total of the above parameters will be compared with the number of rewriting rules required to create an OCL assertion code generator without the use of the intermediate definition languages i.e., the *direct* approach.

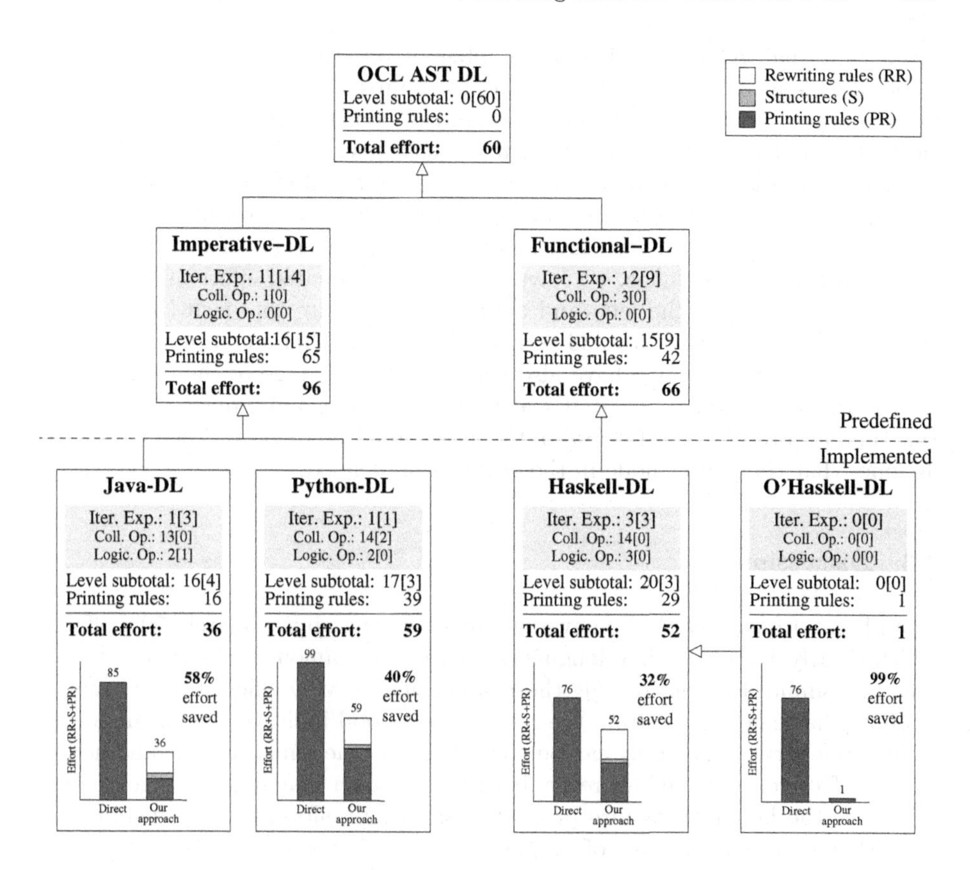

Fig. 9. Evaluation results

Note that the main feature of our approach is in the fact that creating an OCL assertion code generator for a new language only requires the developer to provide details specific to the language in its category. For example, creating a generator for Java would require to provide structural description and syntax for Java class cast expressions as they will be used in the *for-each* loops in Java but not necessarily in other imperative languages, such as Python. For this reason, the evaluation parameters described only need to be counted when creating the final node (the leaf) in our hierarchy, since we can assume that parent nodes are predefined.

The complete list of all implemented OCL features is given in Table 1. All features are subdivided into three main groups: *iterator expressions*, *collection operations* and *logical operations*.

4.2 Results

In order to clearly show the efforts saved using our approach compared to implementing directly, we have summarised our results in Fig. 9. The numbers are given in format *RR*[*S*] showing the number of rewriting rules and number of structures defined, subdivided according to groups in Table 1. In the example of Java, the numbers of rewriting rules and of structures for iterative expressions are 1 and 3 respectively. Note that O'Haskell is an extension of the Haskell language comprising several behavioural and syntactical changes. However, implementation of OCL assertion code generator only required a modification in one syntactical rule in the printing module (see bottom right of Fig. 9).

For each target language, we have shown the estimated effort of direct implementation (bar on the left) and actual effort by our approach (bar on the right). In the example of Java, 36 and 85 rules were written in our approach and direct one respectively. We have also shown the percentage of the effort saved in case when our approach is undertaken. In Java, we could reduce 49 (85 – 36) rules and as a result, 58% (49/85) of the effort could be reduced. Each bar-chart assumes that the parent node in the graph is predefined.

4.3 Discussion

From Fig. 9 we can see that on average we are saving approximately 50% effort, which clearly indicates that languages share a fair amount of structural and semantic similarities and reusing those similarities is very efficient. The savings in effort that can be seen from the results are a good indication that languages in the same structural family can be related also on the semantic level and hence can be effectively grouped for reuse. It was also shown that small changes in the syntax of the language require proportionally small efforts of implementation. Note that representativeness of evaluation results is not ideal as all evaluation procedures were carried out by the same person. For a fairer result evaluation with adding new languages by several persons should be considered.

Measuring effort involved in implementing an OCL translator in an unbiased manner was a very difficult task. In our effort evaluation strategy we have tried to cover most complexity aspects associated with implementation of OCL translators, by quantitatively measuring the number of rewriting rules, printing rules and semantic structures. However, implementation of some rewriting rules was more complex than others, and not because of their size, but because of their dependency on other rewriting rules (i.e., application of such rule must be followed by application of another rule). Even though we have tried to take into account the complexity of rewriting rules by counting the number of structures defined to support them, it was not always a complete indication of effort. On the other hand, some rewriting rules were very easy to specify, because they were simply representations of a concept in the target language, such as a *for-loop*, and were not directly related to OCL.

In addition, as can be seen from Fig. 9, most of the complex OCL iterator expressions (Iter. Exp.) could be rewritten using non-OCL concepts, in other words concepts from Imperative DL or Functional DL, which are independent of OCL. This underlines the fact that our approach alleviates the need to understand OCL completely.

5 Related Work

Currently available approaches for evaluating OCL constraints can be split into three main types: metamodel-based model validation, source code assertion and translating OCL to another Design-by-Contract (DBC) language.

Metamodel-based model validation. Checking for correctness of OCL constraints for a model using its meta-model description can be advantageous since such approach can take arbitrary data models as their input, and therefore in theory it is possible to validate absolutely any type of data. Some researches that use this approach include Kent OCL Tool [5], NAOMI [6], and ITP/OCL [7]. However, very few language platforms provide direct access to objects at run-time which would be necessary for validation.

Checking constraints on the implementation level. Source code assertion approaches usually use code instrumentation or aspect-oriented techniques to achieve code checking at run-time. However, all such approaches, including jContractor [8], Handshake [9], ocl2j [10], Jass [11], and iContract [12], are tailor-made for a specific programming language.

Translating OCL to JML. Another approach is to translate OCL to another OCL-like DBC language such as JML [13,14,15]. Hamie has proposed a set of mappings from OCL to JML [16] to which we have previously contributed with our own extensions [17]. However, the problem with such approaches is that there is currently no other DBC language that can be applied to any programming language.

6 Conclusion and Future Work

To conclude, we have first identified the possible reasons to why OCL finds it difficult to dissolve into industry, and proposed our approach to remedy this problem and also performed an experiment to confirm the claimed effort savings when using our approach. We showed how new OCL translators can be added without knowledge of OCL and how functionalities such as logging can be easily injected into OCL translator implementations.

Some OCL functionality was not covered, such as history expressions, OCL messages and the `allInstances` call, that we have not implemented and left for future work. We have also realised of certain limitations of our approach, such as difficulty in introducing DLs into the middle of the hierarchy because this would cause change to propagate to all nodes below and would be difficult to automate. Also, carrying out evaluation with several persons, on a greater variety of target languages, possibly including languages that share similarities in multiple language families will be considered for future work.

Confirming whether the generated assertion code exhibits consistency, accuracy and determinateness, as proposed by Gogollain et al. [18], is also important and will be considered for future work.

References

1. OMG: Model-Driven Architecture, http://www.omg.org/mda/
2. OMG: Object Constraint Language specification, version 2.0, http://www.omg.org/technology/documents/formal/ocl.htm
3. Kiczales, G., Irwin, J., Lamping, J., Loingtier, J.M., Lopes, C.V., Maeda, C., Mendhekar, A.: Aspect-oriented programming. In: Aksit, M., Matsuoka, S. (eds.) ECOOP 1997. LNCS, vol. 1241, pp. 220–242. Springer, Heidelberg (1997)
4. The Maude Team: The Maude System, http://maude.cs.uiuc.edu/
5. Akehurst, D.H., Patrascoiu, O.: OCL 2.0 – implementing the standard for multiple metamodels. Electronic Notes in Theoretical Computer Science 102, 21–41 (2004)
6. Chabarek, F.: Development of an OCL-parser for UML-extensions. Master's thesis, Technical University of Berlin (2004)
7. Clavel, M., Egea, M.: ITP/OCL: A rewriting-based validation tool for UML+OCL static class diagrams. In: Proc. 11th International Conference on Algebraic Methodology and Software Technology, pp. 368–373 (2006)
8. Karaorman, M., Hölzle, U., Bruno, J.L.: jContractor: A reflective Java library to support design by contract. In: Cointe, P. (ed.) Reflection 1999. LNCS, vol. 1616, pp. 175–196. Springer, Heidelberg (1999)
9. Duncan, A., Hölzle, U.: Adding contracts to Java with Handshake. Technical Report TRCS98-32, Department of Computer Science, University of California (1998)
10. Dzidek, W.J., Briand, L.C., Labiche, Y.: Lessons learned from developing a dynamic OCL constraint enforcement tool for Java. In: Bruel, J.-M. (ed.) MoDELS 2005. LNCS, vol. 3844, pp. 10–19. Springer, Heidelberg (2006)
11. Bartetzko, D., Fischer, C., Möller, M., Wehrheim, H.: Jass – Java with assertions. Electronic Notes in Theoretical Computer Science 55(2), 1–15 (2001)
12. Kramer, R.: iContract – the Java design by contract tool. In: Proc. Technology of Object-Oriented Languages and Systems, pp. 295–307 (1998)
13. Burdy, L., Cheon, Y., Cok, D., Ernst, M., Kiniry, J., Leavens, G.T., Leino, K.R.M., Poll, E.: An overview of JML tools and applications. International Journal on Software Tools for Technology Transfer 7(3), 212–232 (2005)
14. Cheon, Y., Leavens, G.T.: A runtime assertion checker for the Java Modeling Language (JML). In: Proc. International Conference on Software Engineering Research and Practice, pp. 322–328 (2002)
15. Leavens, G.T., Leino, K.R.M., Poll, E., Ruby, C., Jacobs, B.: JML: notations and tools supporting detailed design in Java. In: Companion Proc. 21st International Conference on Object-Oriented Programming Systems, Languages and Applications, pp. 105–106 (2000)
16. Hamie, A.: Translating the Object Constraint Language into the Java Modelling Language. In: Proc. 2004 ACM Symposium on Applied Computing, pp. 1531–1535 (2004)
17. Moiseev, R., Russo, A.: Implementing an OCL to JML translation tool. IEICE Technical Report 106(426) SS2006–58, 13–17 (2006)
18. Gogolla, M., Kuhlmann, M., Büttner, F.: Benchmark for OCL engine accuracy, determinateness, and efficiency. In: Czarnecki, K., Ober, I., Bruel, J.-M., Uhl, A., Völter, M. (eds.) MODELS 2008. LNCS, vol. 5301, pp. 446–459. Springer, Heidelberg (2008)

OCLLib, OCLUnit, OCLDoc: Pragmatic Extensions for the Object Constraint Language*

Joanna Chimiak-Opoka

Institute of Computer Science, University of Innsbruck, Austria
joanna.opoka@uibk.ac.at
http://qe-informatik.uibk.ac.at/

Abstract. The usage of the Unified Modeling Language in the industrial context becomes increasingly popular. There is an agreement in academia that the Object Constraint Language (OCL) is suitable for defining model constraints and queries. However, it has not yet been broadly adopted by practitioners because they find it difficult to define OCL expressions. Thus, simplification is desirable to increase the use of OCL in practice. We propose OCL libraries (**OCLLib**), which simplify the development of OCL expressions and enable a high reuse factor, are configurable, testable (**OCLUnit**) and documented (**OCLDoc**). In this paper we present the underlying concepts related to OCL library development we used in UML specific and domain specific projects conducted in academic and industrial contexts, respectively.

Keywords: Systematic development of OCL, OCL libraries, OCL testing, OCL documentation.

1 Introduction

The Unified Modeling Language (UML) is the well–supported, de–facto standard for object–oriented design and analysis of software systems used to design *large scale models*. The quality management of models can be supported by the use of constraints and queries expressed in the Object Constraint Language (OCL). The maturity of the OCL **syntax and semantics** caused its utilisation within other Object Management Group (OMG) standards and extension of its scope to any language based on Meta Object Facility (MOF). In our recent projects we have successfully used OCL for model assessment and found that OCL is *expressive* [1] and its interpretation is *fast* [2] enough for querying large scale models. In contrast to the syntax and semantics, the **pragmatics** of OCL needs further improvements. Despite the fact that the language became broadly supported by modelling tools [3], practitioners still find OCL specifications difficult to understand [4] and their development difficult, error–prone and time–consuming [5].

* The research herein is partially conducted within the competence network Softnet Austria (www.soft-net.at) and funded by the Austrian Federal Ministry of Economics (bm:wa), the province of Styria, the Steirische Wirtschaftsfoerderungsgesellschaft mbH. (SFG), and the city of Vienna in terms of the center for innovation and technology (ZIT).

A. Schürr and B. Selic (Eds.): MODELS 2009, LNCS 5795, pp. 665–669, 2009.

The twofold characteristic of OCL (it was designed to be used at the modelling level but has a textual notation closer to the programming level) causes that model designers may find it too formal and programmers too abstract. The positive consequence of OCL being similar to programming languages is the fact that some best practices known from the software development context can be used for development of OCL expressions.

Before we introduce our solution we want to discuss selected **challenges** related to development of OCL specifications. *(C1) Error–free OCL development* is hardly feasible. For the software development no error–detecting approach will ever be able to produce error–free software [6]. For large and complex OCL specifications the same problem is encountered, but it is possible to reduce the number of syntax and semantic errors. As the syntactical correctness is crucial it is already reflected at theoretical and technical levels, but not all issues related to the semantical correctness are solved. *(C2) Easy to understand OCL expressions.* Correct expressions (C1) should be understandable by developers and users [4]. In general, all techniques used in programming languages can be supportive for this challenge, e.g. usage of simple algorithms and data structures, meaningful names, following coding conventions, documentation, tracing and debugging. *(C3) Easy and efficient OCL development* is an idealistic and subjective view. The language itself can not be simplified but its complexity can be leveled by providing learning (C2) and development support. Experience knowledge should be stored and shared. If there are examples of correct OCL expressions (C1) available (which can be customized, or even better, only parametrised) then the development of OCL expressions should be easier and more efficient. For this challenge technical support plays a huge role. *(C4) Easy to evolve OCL expressions.* Similarly, as any piece of code OCL specifications are evolving [4]. There are two critical dangers: the meaning of some parts of the specification can be forgotten and as such hard to evolve or refactor to cover new requirements; and introducing new parts or updating existing ones can have undesired impact of other parts of a specification.

We propose to use the following established techniques: a *systematic development* including usage of libraries, testing and in–code documentation. In the remainder of the paper we present the extended development process (Section 2) and discuss our results and future work in the context of the aforementioned challenges (Section 3).

2 The Extended Development Process

In this section we present the idea of testable and documented libraries of OCL expressions and their usage. Depending its purpose, a library can consist of different components: definitions, constraints, queries, tests and their documentation. A collection of libraries and test models forms an OCL library project. Such a project can be used by another tool, e.g. constraints can be used in a modelling tool and queries can be used in a model analysis tool. An overview of the OCL library project **development and usage process** is illustrated in Fig. 1. The upper swimlane corresponds to the OCL library project **development** stage (Fig. 1). It starts with a specification of OCL *definitions* and *tests*. We denoted these activities as being parallel while different approaches can be used here. One can traditionally start with the definition specification or can follow the test driven approach [7] and define tests and *test models* first. This is up to the developer. As soon as definitions, tests and test models are defined the tests can be evaluated. If the tests return expected results (denoted as `[pass]` in the diagram), and in the meantime the *documentation* was created, one can start using the definitions. Otherwise (denoted as `[fail]`) the development process should be continued. As already mentioned, we consider different **usage** scenarios of OCL library project: tested and documented definitions can be used in other definitions, *constraints* or *queries*. In Fig. 1 we present the latter case. At this stage queries are designed and used in model querying on project models. The difference between test and project models is that for the former the expected results are known and test models should not change. If a test model changes then the corresponding tests should be updated to reflect these modifications. Due to the space limitations we give only an overview of the proposed extensions. More details can be found at `http://squam.info/ocleditor/`

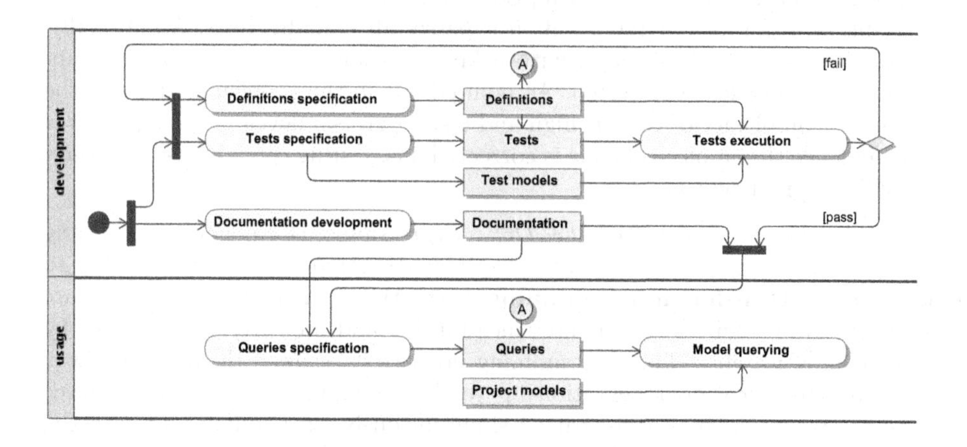

Fig. 1. The library development and usage process

OCLLib—Collection of OCL Expressions. The main goal of a **library** is to provide a set of useful and easily reusable OCL expressions (C3). If OCL expressions are split into small chunks, following the modularity and separation of concerns paradigms, then the probability of OCL expression reuse by parametrisation but without adaptation is high. Additionally, as OCL expressions depend on an underlying metamodel (MOF or MOF based) they have to be modularised into libraries specific to this metamodel, which specifies the scope of application of the library. Furthermore, modularisation based on particular parts of the metamodel can be considered, e.g. libraries specific to UML class diagrams or activity diagrams. To increase and configure reuse, import and visibility concepts are used. A library consists of definitions, constraints, queries and tests which are grouped into blocks, which may be documented. **Definition** and **constraints** are concepts adopted from the OCL/UML standard specifications. Definitions enable better modularisation and higher reuse: defined methods can be used in other libraries, whereas, defined attributes can be additionally used to configure (the parametrisation principle) a library. For example, a collection of metrics can be defined in a library and upper bounds for them in another one, then the metric library can import the configuration library. Both, definitions and constraints can be used by other tools. A **query** is an enhanced concept from the Query/Views/Transformations standard adding parts specific to model querying and as such can be used in model design and analysis tools.

OCLUnit—Testing of OCL Expressions. Validation (C1) is required before OCL definitions are used in other libraries or by other developers (C3). In programming practice testing plays a manifold role during the lifetime of a piece of code. Introducing testing to the OCL development practice addresses **all challenges** discussed in Section 1. Testing reduces bugs (C1) and moreover, bugs need only to be found once [8], if they are again introduced due to code changes (C4) they can be automatically detected with prior defined tests. Moreover, a piece of code is usable (C3) for anyone (else) only if it passes all available tests. Additionally, a test case is a simple scenario with a known result, and can be used to understand (C2) code being tested. As pointed out in the problem statement the perceived complexity of OCL is high and testing gives a developer a high degree of confidence that a piece of code is correct. Thus, testing can increase the usage of OCL by practitioners.

OCLDoc—Documentation of the OCL Expressions. Documentation of any software artefact is important for many reasons. Among others as a mean to **knowledge transfer and communication**. Moreover, high–quality software documentation reduces the maintenance burden and improves productivity by enhancing reusability. The programming practice [8] showed that the best way to keep a technical documentation up–to–date is to generate it out of source code comments, as it can be written simultaneously with coding and with the same tool by a programmer. Based on documentation OCL developers can easier search for similar expressions and reuse or refactor them, where are OCL users can make a proper choice of needed expressions.

3 Discussion and Conclusion

In this paper we analysed challenges for a pragmatic OCL development. We presented three extensions as a possible partial solution to these challenges. We successfully used the described development process in a number of didactic and research projects. The largest project, regarding the size of OCL libraries, was conducted during the previous semester and had didactic purposes and an evaluation aim. In a period of 2 weeks 10 students developed 50 libraries

(4.5kLOC excluding comments) to implement a set of UML metrics [9] in OCL. Even though students had low experience with OCL they found the assigned task easy. The largest project regarding the size of models, was conducted this year within an industrial context. The aim of the project was to document and improve a business process and IT infrastructure. In this project model queries were successfully used to improve the quality of process models (250 entity elements).

The solution we proposed address all challenges at the conceptual (introduced extensions) and at the implementation level (the tool). To address the challenges we currently implement tracing and debugging (C1–C2) and in the future we want to integrate concepts of patterns and to collect and evaluate guidelines for an efficient OCL library development (C3). Another open issues are impact analysis, regression testing and refactoring support (C4).

Acknowledgement. I want to express my gratitude to Barbara Weber and Berthold Agreiter for numerous discussions and their constructive feedback, and to Nicolas Rouquette and Dan Chiorean for their feedback and improvements ideas for our tool. Moreover, my gratefulness goes to all members of the OCL editor development team for their great cooperation in tool development and discussions on underlying concepts.

References

1. Chimiak-Opoka, J., Lenz, C.: Use of OCL in a model assessment framework: An experience report. Electronic Communications of the EASST 5 (2006)
2. Chimiak-Opoka, J., Felderer, M., Lenz, C., Lange, C.: Querying UML Models using OCL and Prolog: A Performance Study. In: Model Driven Engineering, Verification, and Validation, Lillehammer, Norway (April 2008); presented at MoDeVVa
3. Baar, T., et al.: Tool support for OCL and related formalisms - needs and trends. In: Bruel, J.-M. (ed.) MoDELS 2005. LNCS, vol. 3844, pp. 1–9. Springer, Heidelberg (2006)
4. Correa, A.L., et al.: An empirical study of the impact of ocl smells and refactorings on the understandability of ocl specifications. In: Engels, G., Opdyke, B., Schmidt, D.C., Weil, F. (eds.) MODELS 2007. LNCS, vol. 4735, pp. 76–90. Springer, Heidelberg (2007)
5. Ackermann, J.: Fallstudie zur spezifikation von fachkomponenten. In: Turowski, K. (ed.) 2. Workshop Modellierung und Spezifikation von Fachkomponenten, Bamberg, Deutschland, pp. 1–66 (2001) (in German)
6. Glass, R.L.: Two mistakes and error-free software: A confession. IEEE Softw. 25(4), 96 (2008)
7. Beck, K.: Test Driven Development: By Example. Addison-Wesley Longman Publishing Co., Inc., Boston (2002)
8. Hunt, A., Thomas, D.: The pragmatic programmer: from journeyman to master. Addison-Wesley Longman Publishing Co., Inc., Boston (1999)
9. Genero, M., Piattini, M., Calero, C.: A survey of metrics for uml class diagrams. Journal of Object Technology 4(9), 59–92 (2005)

Variability within Modeling Language Definitions

María Victoria Cengarle[1], Hans Grönniger[2], and Bernhard Rumpe[2]

[1] Software and Systems Engineering, Technische Universität München, Germany
[2] Lehrstuhl Software Engineering, RWTH Aachen, Germany

Abstract. We present a taxonomy of the variability mechanisms offered by modeling languages. The definition of a formal language encompasses a syntax and a semantic domain as well as the mapping that relates them, thus language variabilities are classified according to which of those three pillars they address. This work furthermore proposes a framework to explicitly document and manage the variation points and their corresponding variants of a variable modeling language. The framework enables the systematic study of various kinds of variabilities and their interdependencies. Moreover, it allows a methodical customization of a language, for example, to a given application domain. The taxonomy of variability is explicitly of interest for the UML to provide a more precise understanding of its variation points.

Keywords: Modeling languages, variability, formal semantics, UML.

1 Introduction

A complete definition of a formal modeling language consists of the description of its syntax and its semantics (meaning) [1]. It is widely accepted that a commonly agreed formal definition (especially semantics) of a language helps to avoid misunderstandings and lack of interoperability between tools.

In [2], we presented a tool-based approach to define textual modeling languages and to formalize their semantics in a flexible way using a theorem prover. While one of our main targets is the formalization of the Unified Modeling Language (UML 2) [3,4], the approach is more general and applies to any modeling language based on objects.

In this paper, we investigate how variability in a language definition can be formally specified. This work is inspired by the introduction of semantic variation points in UML where portions of the language have been deliberately incompletely specified. The benefits of systematically describing UML's variability have been noted early [5]. The treatment of semantic variation points in the UML, however, is rather disappointing. It was not systematically carried out, semantic variation points are dispersed across the documentation. Moreover, the standard fails to tag them completely: it suffices to look for underspecified semantic definitions in order to realize that there are far more semantic variation points than those explicitly labeled as such.

A. Schürr and B. Selic (Eds.): MODELS 2009, LNCS 5795, pp. 670–684, 2009.

Beyond UML, we are interested in a general treatment of variability in modeling languages which may be of semantic and also of syntactic nature. Hence, one goal of this work is to classify the kinds of variability that a modeling language may offer and their interdependencies. Additionally, we extend our approach from [2] and present a tool-based solution to define and configure variability within a language definition.

A systematic approach to variability should make it possible to explicitly state all (possibly implicit) assumptions and previously chosen variants. This allows a systematic customization of a language for a given application domain. Furthermore, tool builders can refer to particular variants in order to document design decisions. Variation points of modeling languages, unlike those of product lines, are not associated with a binding time [6]. That is, tool builders may delay the binding of a variation point to a variant and leave the decision to project managers. Moreover, these may even forward the disambiguation to modelers. As for UML, currently *implementors may provide [...] informal feature support statements [...] for less precisely defined dimensions such as presentation options and semantic variation points"* [3, Sect. 2.3]. We improve this situation by making precise the definition of the variability mechanisms offered by a language.

The rest of this paper is organized as follows. Sect. 2 describes the constituents of a modeling language definition. Sect. 3 presents our classification of variability in a language definition. Sect. 4 introduces our tool-supported solution using feature diagrams. The approach is illustrated with a simple example of UML-like class diagrams. Sect. 5 discusses related work and Sect. 6 draws conclusions and sketches future work.

2 Constituents of a Modeling Language Definition

As shown in Fig. 1, a complete definition of a modeling language consists of the following basic parts:

- the concrete syntax of the language, which may be a graphical or textual syntax or a combination of both,
- the abstract syntax to which the concrete syntax is mapped. For a textual syntax this may be given as abstract syntax trees. In case of graphical modeling, metamodels are typically used. Additionally, a set of well-formedness rules or context conditions are defined,
- some minimal abstract syntax that can be derived from the abstract syntax by expressing more complex constructs of the language by primitive ones. Thereby the number of constructs but not the expressive power of the language is reduced. This eases the definition of the semantics of the language. This step may not be required for some languages,
- a semantic domain, a domain well-known and understood, typically based on a well-defined mathematical theory, and
- the semantic mapping that relates elements of the (minimal) abstract syntax to elements of the semantic domain.

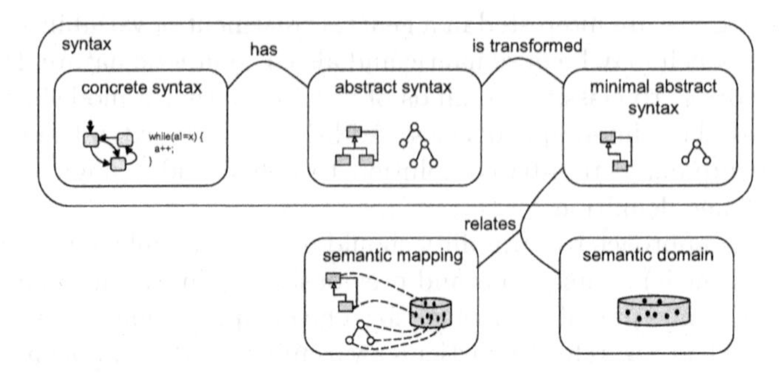

Fig. 1. Basic parts of a modeling language definition

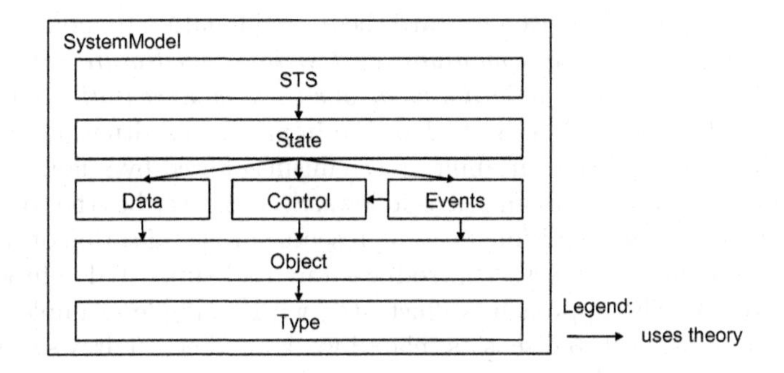

Fig. 2. Theories that constitute the system model

Characteristic for our approach to define the semantics of a modeling language is a set-valued or predicative semantic mapping of the form $sem(.) : \mathcal{L} \rightarrow \wp(\mathcal{S})$. The semantics of a model as an element of the (minimal) abstract syntax $m \in \mathcal{L}$ is therefore the set $sem(m)$ of elements in the semantic domain $\mathcal{S}$.

We defined a single semantic domain $\mathcal{S}$ used as a target for the semantic mapping of various kinds of object-oriented modeling languages [7]. This domain, called system model, captures and integrates all aspects of object-oriented systems using basic mathematical theories. It is rather detailed as it defines various structural, behavioral, and interaction aspects, and is built in a modular fashion as depicted in Fig. 2. Systems in the system model are state transition systems (theory STS). They operate on a global system state which is composed of object individual states (theory State). States constitute a data store for attribute values of objects (theory Data), a control store (theory Control) for active threads and computational states of methods, and an event store for unprocessed events (theory Events). States evolve dynamically. Static information (e.g., which classes, methods, etc., exist) is defined through underspecified universes containing abstract identifiers only. For example, `UTYPE` is the universe of type names (defined in theory Type). Classes are elements of the universe `UCLASS` (theory Object) and are only described by functions that yield information about their attributes or methods, i.e., they are not constructed from records. Thus, the definition of the system model is predicative and not constructive. For a complete picture of the system model features, the reader is referred to [7].

The system model as a single semantic domain and the set-valued semantic mapping enable a straightforward treatment of composition and refinement of possibly incomplete and underspecified models of various modeling languages [8]. For example, the integrated semantics of models $m_1, \ldots, m_n$ from possibly different languages $\mathcal{L}_1, \ldots, \mathcal{L}_n$ is given as $sem_{\mathcal{L}_1}(m_1) \cap \ldots \cap sem_{\mathcal{L}_n}(m_n)$. In the same way, $m' \in \mathcal{L}$ is a refinement of $m \in \mathcal{L}$, exactly if $sem(m') \subseteq sem(m)$.

3 Classification of Variability

In this section, we develop a classification of variability that a modeling language may offer. We do not restrict our attention to semantic variability (in UML terms, semantic variation points) but also consider syntactic variability.

In a very abstract view, the syntax of a formal language is defined by a set of words over some alphabet A, i.e., $\mathcal{L} \subseteq A^*$. *Syntactic variability* allows for defining more than one syntax, say $\mathcal{L}_1$ and $\mathcal{L}_2$, which normally contain many common words but are different. That is, there is at least one model (i.e., word) $m \in (\mathcal{L}_1 \cup \mathcal{L}_2) \backslash (\mathcal{L}_1 \cap \mathcal{L}_2)$ that is in one but not both languages. The semantics of a syntax $\mathcal{L}$ over some semantic domain $\mathcal{S}$ can be defined as $sem \subseteq \mathcal{L} \times \mathcal{S}$ (in a relational style). *Semantic variability* means more than one semantics, say sem_1 and sem_2, for a given syntax $\mathcal{L}$. These mappings may have different codomains $\mathcal{S}_1 \neq \mathcal{S}_2$ or not. As with the syntax, sem_1 and sem_2 are mostly the same but there is at least one model m and an element s for which $(m, s) \in (sem_1 \cup sem_2) \backslash (sem_1 \cap sem_2)$. So the meaning of the model differs according to which semantics is chosen.

There naturally may be languages containing both kinds of variability, and relationships between both exist. In the following, we concretize this abstract view by analyzing how variants and their interdependencies can be classified.

3.1 Syntactic Variability

Regarding concrete syntax (see Fig. 1), differences can be given by, e.g., alternative keywords such as "public" or "+" in case of modifiers, or the font size, line thickness, and color of some graphical element. In UML, these are called *presentation options* and can be classified as *presentation variability.* They improve the readability of models. Nevertheless, presentation options are so defined that the abstract syntax of models remains the same even if the options are changed.[1]

[1] This is an important assumption we make on presentation options, namely that they do *not* alter abstract syntax and hence the intended semantics of the presented model element. Font size, for instance, may have a meaning in cartography, where cities with bigger labels have more inhabitants. In the case of cartography, therefore, font size does matter and is not a presentation option.

We do not classify presentation options as syntactic variability since they do not make it possible to define different languages. Their effect exclusively concerns the concrete syntax. They must, nevertheless, be registered and documented.

The syntax of a language may allow the use of *stereotypes*. The term stereotype, borrowed from UML, is used here to designate a general principle of extending the syntax of a language. The concrete set of defined stereotypes (e.g., as part of a profile in case of UML) is classified as syntactic variability.

Another kind of syntactic variability also found in the syntax is given by so-called *language parameters*. Concerning for instance UML, the language of state machines defines transition systems whose transitions are triggered by a stimulus subject to a condition on the stimulus and/or the internal state of the object. The language in which conditions (or guards) are expressed is not specified. This constitutes a syntactic variability.

In the abstract syntax, *optional context conditions* may exist. Examples thereof, for instance for a particular code generator to operate, are the enforcement of types of attributes of a class to be defined, and the restriction to single inheritance only. Context conditions rule out certain models based on syntactic criteria. Only if the context conditions are met, the model is *well-formed* and it makes sense to give the model a semantics.

The syntax also may offer constructs that enhance readability and are semantically equivalent to other, usually more involved, expressions of the language. Such constructs are often referred to as "syntactic sugar" and may be safely omitted, since models of the language obtained by the use of those constructs can be replaced by equivalent models that do not use the *abbreviations*. We classify this as presentation variability. In particular, the language can be reduced to a minimal one, which not necessarily is unique. Note that a minimal language derived this way may still allow synonyms, i.e., syntactically different models m_1 and m_2 that denote the same semantics $sem(m_1) = sem(m_2)$.

Summarizing, we classify any variability as syntactic variability that still may be present in the minimal abstract syntax of a modeling language and hence interacts with the semantics. This variability originates from stereotypes, language parameters, and optional context conditions.

3.2 Semantic Variability

While UML only uses the term semantic variation point, we further subdivide semantic variability into *semantic mapping variability* and *semantic domain variability*; cf. Fig. 1. A helpful analogy might be to see the variability of the semantic mapping similar to configuration options of a code generator while variability of the semantic domain has its analogy with properties of an underlying run-time system or target platform.

Regarding semantic domain variability, the system model defined in [7] already contains explicit variability in form of extensions through optional definitions. In general, semantic domain variants may provide alternative realizations of functions, additional constraints to properties of existing definitions, or optional structures and definitions. Alternative realizations are, for example, different notions of type-safe method overriding. Additional constraints are, for example, the restriction to single inheritance only, or the requirement of certain predefined types like, e.g., "String."

Similarly, in the semantic mapping, the same mechanisms to introduce variants apply. Semantic mapping variability often manifests as alternative choices for specific mapping functions while the target domain remains the same. For instance, one mapping of super-classes of classes in a UML class diagram assumes multiple inheritance in the semantic domain, while an alternative mapping uses some delegation mechanism for a domain that may lack multiple inheritance. As this example shows, there are also various relationships between variants on the different levels which will be discussed in more detail in the following. As another example, consider the representation of states of a state machine in an implementation as, e.g., a simple enumeration or using the state pattern [9].

Note that semantic variability is transparent to the modeler. But it may be necessary to allow the modeler to select one or the other interpretation of a construct. We propose to model these interpretation choices as syntactic variability by providing corresponding stereotypes. For instance, consider the example of a semantic mapping for a class which states that only a single instance of that class may exist at run-time. One possibility would be to encode this syntactically as a stereotype "singleton" which can be used by the modeler and which is used by the semantic mapping to associate exactly this meaning to the given class.

Table 1 provides a comprehensive summary of our modeling language variability classification.

Table 1. Variability classification summary

presentation variability	variability not present in a minimal abstract syntax
presentation options	affect concrete syntax only
abbreviations	can be omitted without losing expressiveness
syntactic variability	variability affecting a minimal abstract syntax
stereotypes	syntactic encoding of semantic variability
language parameters	usable with different independent languages
context conditions	constrain the set of well-formed models
semantic variability	variability in the semantics
semantic domain variability	variability in the underlying target domain
semantic mapping variability	different choices for mapping functions

3.3 Interdependency and Consistency

Dependencies between variants exist. These are characterized with the help of examples. Consider the integration of multiple languages: One language might be parameter to another, e.g., a constraint or action language. Additionally, languages may be mainly orthogonal and used to describe different views of the same system such a class and state machine diagrams. In any of these cases, different assumption on the underlying domain may be made, i.e., different variants of the semantic domain may be assumed. Moreover, a language that is parameter to another is equipped with a semantics that has to fit the assumptions made by the parametric language.

Context conditions may influence the selection of a specific semantic mapping. For instance, if the context conditions for UML class diagrams guarantee that multiple inheritance is syntactically excluded, then one can safely select a semantic mapping that only handles single inheritance. Similarly, if a semantic domain only allows for single inheritance, then a delegate mechanism must be resorted to by the semantic mapping of UML class diagrams in case multiple inheritance is allowed syntactically.

From these examples we conclude that it is important to capture all possible variants and their interdependencies. We propose to model them using feature diagrams including constraints that state inclusion or exclusion between variants [10].[2] As a supplement, informal descriptions of the variabilities can be given to explain their raison d'être. The proposed approach is completely supported by tools and will be described in the next section.

Unfortunately, capturing variants as feature diagrams and constraints does not guarantee that a concrete configuration of variants that conforms to the given feature diagrams is consistent. Since we have many configuration options, we might have not captured all constraints to rule out inconsistent, unwanted, or simply uninteresting configurations. Especially when integrating multiple languages, there is a possible risk of contradicting mapping functions. One way to obtain a consistent set of theories is to actually prove consistency. That is, given two languages $\mathcal{L}_1$ and $\mathcal{L}_2$ with semantic mappings sem_1 and sem_2, to show

$$sem_1(m_1) \cap sem_2(m_2) \neq \emptyset$$

for some witnesses $m_1 \in \mathcal{L}_1$ and $m_2 \in \mathcal{L}_2$.

4 Definition and Configuration of Variability

We now describe the actual definition and configuration of variability in a modeling language with respect to the configurable semantic mapping and the likewise configurable semantic domain. Syntactic variability such as optional context conditions and language parameters can be handled similarly and are therefore omitted here. The presentation is accompanied by a simple running example.

The whole approach of defining a language and its variabilities is supported by two tools. The basic tool-based approach (neglecting variability) has been presented in [2] and is summarized below. It features a complete, formal, flexible, and machine-readable definition of modeling languages using the tools MontiCore and Isabelle/HOL.

[2] There is an inclusion relation between two or more variants if the choice of one makes it mandatory to choose the other(s). There is an exclusion relation between two or more variants if the choice of one forbids the choice of the other(s).

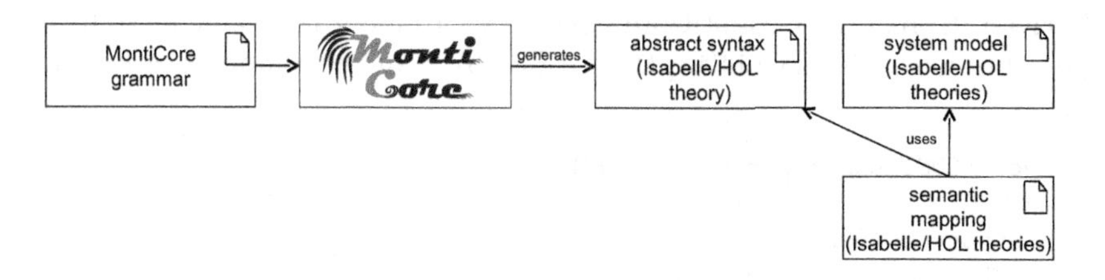

Fig. 3. Approach with tool support

4.1 Prerequisites

The basic approach is depicted in Fig. 3. MontiCore [11] is a framework for the textual definition of languages based on an extended context-free grammar format. We use MontiCore to define the concrete syntax of a language because it provides enhanced modularity concepts like language inheritance and embedding (not used in the simple running example, though). Sophisticated framework functionality allows, for example, an easy development of generators. Note that the general idea can similarly be implemented using, e.g., metamodeling.

To provide a semantics developer with maximum flexibility and also with some machine checking (e.g., type checking) as well as the potential for verification applications, we use the theorem prover Isabelle/HOL [12] for

- the formalization of the system model as a hierarchy of theories,
- the representation of the abstract syntax of the language as a deep embedding [13], and
- the actual semantic mapping that uses the generated abstract syntax and maps each language construct to predicates over systems of the formalized system model.

Concrete Syntax. The example grammar `CDSimp` in Fig. 4 defines UML-like class diagrams with classes that can have super-classes. MontiCore grammars

```
1  grammar CDSimp {
2    CDDefinition = "classdiagram" Name:IDENT "{" (CDClass)* "}";
3
4    CDClass =
5      "class" Name:IDENT ("extends" scl:IDENT ("," scl:IDENT)*)?";";
6  }
```

Fig. 4. MontiCore grammar of class diagrams

have terminal symbols enclosed in quotes (see, e.g., Fig. 4, line 2) and support Kleene closure (*) and option (?), among other constructs. The two rules of `CDSimp` use the built-in identifier rule `IDENT`. Nonterminals may be prefixed by descriptive names followed by a colon (like `IDENT`, l. 2). According to Fig. 4, a class diagram definition (l. 2) has a name and a set of classes. Classes (l. 4) have a name and a comma separated list of names that refer to super-classes.

Abstract Syntax. A MontiCore generator produces the Isabelle/HOL data type definition in theory CDSimpAS (see Fig. 5) from the grammar in Fig. 4.

```
1  theory CDSimpAS imports GeneralAS
2  begin
3  datatype CDClass =
4      CDClass IDENT "IDENT list"
5
6  datatype CDDefinition =
7      CDDefinition IDENT "CDClass list"
8  end
```

Fig. 5. Generated abstract syntax data type in Isabelle/HOL

Isabelle/HOL data types have a name (e.g., CDClass in Fig. 5, l. 3), a constructor (also CDClass, l. 4), and a list of arguments. Data type IDENT is defined in the imported, re-usable theory GeneralAS and iteration in a grammar is translated to the built-in data type list (e.g., l. 4). A complete account on the mapping of MontiCore grammars to Isabelle/HOL can be found in [2].

System Model. We have formalized the system model, introduced in Sect. 2, in Isabelle/HOL as a hierarchy of theories.

```
1  theory Object imports Type
2  begin
3  datatype iCLASS = Class "char list"
4
5  consts
6   UCLASS :: "SystemModel ⇒ iCLASS set"
7   sub :: "SystemModel ⇒ iCLASS ⇒ iCLASS ⇒ bool"
8
9  fun psubRefl :: "SystemModel ⇒ bool"
10  where "psubRefl sm = (∀ C ∈ UCLASS sm . sub sm C C)"
11 end
```

Fig. 6. Isabelle/HOL theory Object (excerpt)

Fig. 6 shows a small excerpt from the theory Object which introduces the universe of classes UCLASS (line 6) as a function that yields a set of class names (of type iCLASS). consts is Isabelle's way of declaring a constant without defining it. Additionally, a subclassing relation sub is declared. The boolean function definition psubRefl is a simple example of a predicate that must hold in all valid systems and requires reflexivity of the subclassing relation.

The top-level theory SystemModel-base (Fig. 7) imports all basic definitions and defines a predicate valid-base. In our abbreviated example, only theory Object is imported. The full theory would import all other theories from Fig. 2 and combine all predicates (like psubRefl) into valid-base, describing all properties of a valid system in the system model.

```
1  theory SystemModel-base imports Object
2  begin
3  fun valid-base :: "SystemModel ⇒ bool"
4   where "valid-base sm = (psubRefl sm ∧ ... )"
5  end
```

Fig. 7. Isabelle/HOL theory `SystemModel-base` (excerpt)

Semantic Mapping. The semantic mapping of our simplified class diagrams is likewise formalized in Isabelle/HOL. The theory in Fig. 8 imports the abstract syntax and the system model theory and defines the mapping. We only state the signatures of the mapping functions, which are built in a modular fashion along the abstract syntax. Note that the mapping functions for classes and class diagrams, `mCDClass` and `mCDDefinition`, are function definitions (using the keyword `fun`) while the mapping of super-classes of a class, `consts mSuperClasses`, again is just a function declaration whose body has not yet been defined.

```
1  theory CDSimpSem-base imports CDSimpAS SystemModel
2  begin
3  consts mSuperClasses :: "iCLASS ⇒ IDENT list ⇒ SystemModel ⇒ bool"
4
5  fun mCDClass :: "CDClass ⇒ SystemModel ⇒ bool"
6   where ...
7
8  fun mCDDefinition :: "CDDefinition ⇒ SystemModel set"
9   where ...
10 end
```

Fig. 8. Semantic mapping of the simplified class diagram in Isabelle/HOL

4.2 Definition of Variants

We start by introducing a variant for the system model. Fig. 9 contains a theory with an additional constraint for the transitive subclassing relation, restricting it to single inheritance. That is, for all classes `C1`, `C2`, `C3`, if `C1` is a sub class of `C2` and `C3`, then `C2` and `C3` have to be in a subclass relationship (or equal due to reflexivity of `sub`).

As explained before, we model variants of theories as feature diagrams like the one in Fig. 10[3]. Ignoring the check mark for a moment, the feature diagram therein states that `SingleInheritance` is an optional feature of the theory `Object`. Other variants may be associated with other theories as the other variation point `vType` indicates.

[3] In our tool suite, we use a textual version of feature diagrams and configuration files but we stick to the standard graphical form for the sake of clarity of the presentation.

```
1  theory SingleInheritance imports Object
2  begin
3  fun valid-SingleInheritance :: "SystemModel ⇒ bool"
4   where "valid-SingleInheritance sm = (∀ C1 C2 C3.
5       sub sm C1 C2 ∧ sub sm C1 C3 ⟶ (sub sm C2 C3 ∨ sub sm C3 C2))"
6  end
```

Fig. 9. Definition of an Isabelle/HOL predicate about single inheritance

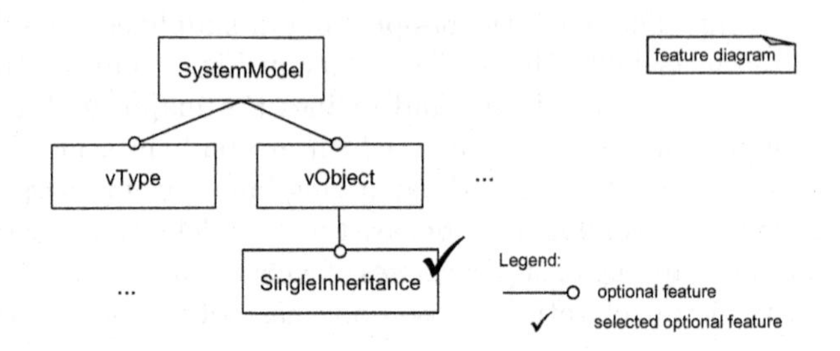

Fig. 10. Semantic domain feature diagram (fragment)

Additionally, the feature diagram for the variants of the semantic mapping can be found in Fig. 11. The class diagram semantics has two variants for the mapping of super-classes. The variant `mapSuperCDirect` carries an additional constraint which excludes the use of variant `SingleInheritance` for the system model. The actual implementation of the theories has been omitted.

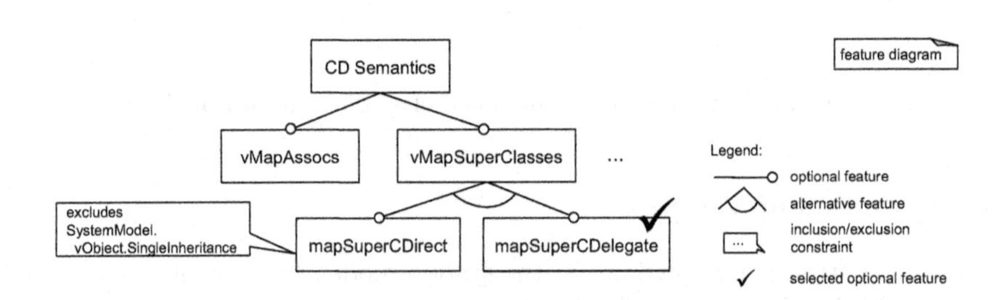

Fig. 11. Semantic mapping feature diagram (fragment)

4.3 Configuration

The configuration space of the simple class diagram language has been defined above with the help of feature diagrams. A concrete configuration for a system model is also given in Fig. 10, in which the single inheritance variant is selected as indicated by the check mark. As a configuration for the class diagram semantic mapping, we select variant `mapSuperCDelegate` (see Fig. 11); choosing the other variant would violate the exclusion constraint.

A generator written for MontiCore processes a set of configuration files (multiple configurations of, e.g., the system model may be defined). It first combines configuration files that refer to the same feature diagram. Then, it checks if the configurations conform to the feature diagrams and if the constraints have been observed. Afterwards, the configured theories for the system model and the semantic mapping are generated. In case of a system model configuration, the generated theory (see Fig. 12) combines all predicates (line 4) from the imported theories that constitute the configuration. This is done by name convention: The theory `SingleInheritance` has to provide a predicate called `valid-SingleInheritance`.

```
1  theory SystemModel imports SystemModel-base
2                                  "vObject/SingleInheritance"
3  begin
4  constdefs "valid sm == valid-base sm ∧ valid-SingleInheritance sm"
5  end
```

Fig. 12. Resulting generated system model theory in Isabelle/HOL

Fig. 13 shows the resulting (generated) class diagram semantic mapping. It simply combines the chosen theories using the Isabelle/HOL import mechanism. The loose end in Fig. 8, namely the declaration `mSuperClasses`, is automatically bound to the definition provided in theory `MapSuperCDelegate`.

```
1  theory CDSimpSem imports CDSimpSem-base
2                               "vMapSuperClasses/MapSuperCDelegate"
3  begin end
```

Fig. 13. Resulting generated class diagram semantics theory in Isabelle/HOL

Finally, the theory in Fig. 14 uses the generated semantic mapping theory. The generated system model theory was already used in Fig. 8 by the base version of the semantic mapping. Presenting a meaningful verification application is outside the scope of this paper, a simple verification example has been given in [2]. The scenario in Fig. 14, however, suffices to show, on the one hand, how variants in a language definition can be systematically handled using feature diagrams. On the other, it shows that the whole approach can be supported by tools. In this scenario, property `P` (Fig. 14, l. 3) ranges over all class diagrams and all systems. In [2], we also presented an additional generator that translates concrete textual models to instances of the generated abstract syntax data type. This makes it also possible to reason about properties of concrete models.

The instantiation of variants is done at the theory level. We could have made all variation points type parameters, similar to [14]. A configuration would then correspond to instantiating type parameters with concrete types. We refrained from doing so because the readability of the theories would have been drastically reduced and it would be no longer possible to leave variants underspecified.

```
1  theory myVerifyApp imports CDSimpSem
2  begin
3  lemma "∀ cd sm . mCDDefinition cd sm ∧ valid sm  ⟶ P cd sm"
4   ... done
5  end
```

Fig. 14. A possible verification scenario in Isabelle/HOL

5 Related Work

To the best of our knowledge, there is no previous work on a general classification of variability mechanisms offered by modeling languages. [15] also suggests feature models to express language variabilities. The focus is on syntactic variability and variable code generators, formal semantics is not addressed.

Regarding the presented tool support for formal language definitions, most related approaches do not consider variability. For example, a complete language definition (including syntax, typing rules, and operational semantics) can be expressed in Alloy [16], which has the advantage of immediate analyzability. Semantic anchoring [17] is another approach to define semantics with tool support. Operational semantics is given by generated abstract state machines.

Other works support semantic variability to a certain extent. Template semantics [18] can be used to define the behavioral semantics of state-based modeling notations. The execution semantics is based on parametric hierarchical transition systems whose behavior can be configured with the help of predefined template parameters. In [19], template semantics is employed to define the semantics of UML state machines. The semantics explicitly models the variability found in the UML standard. [20,21] describe semantically configurable Java code generation and analyzable models using template semantics. Template semantics provides a rich theory for state-based modeling notation variants but is restricted to behavioral semantics that furthermore fits the computational model. Templatable metamodels, introduced in [22,23], is a similar approach presented for metamodeling the abstract syntax and operational semantics of a domain specific modeling language. It uses the UML 2 profile and template mechanisms to define variation points at the metamodel level and to bind the introduced generic types to concrete types at the metamodeling or modeling level. Like template semantics, the approach is targeted towards behavioral semantics but its mechanisms are more compliant with the UML standard. Quite differently, [24] proposes an approach to model semantic variation points and implementation choices as class models in their own right. These are transformed together with a source UML model into a specific target UML model that reflects the chosen variants. The focus in this work is also behavioral semantics in that variants correspond to operations implemented in an action language. We are not aware of any other framework that supports defining and configuring syntactic and semantic variability in a formal language definition.

6 Conclusion

The contribution of this work is twofold. First, we presented a taxonomy of variability mechanisms that may be found in a modeling language definition. Variability may be of presentation, syntactic or semantic nature. Opposed to UML, which only talks about "semantic variation points" in general, we further classify semantic variability according to semantic domain and semantic mapping variability. Semantic domain variability can be thought of as variability in some run-time system modeling the underlying platform assumptions, while semantic mapping variability would correspond to configuration options in a generator targeting a previously chosen (i.e., configured) run-time system.

Second, we extended our framework for defining the syntax and semantics of an object-oriented modeling language by integrating the variability mechanisms that we have identified. The tool suite built on MontiCore and Isabelle/HOL uses feature diagrams with inclusion/exclusion constraints to model variants and their interdependencies in the syntax, semantic domain, and semantic mapping. Given a configuration of variants for possibly multiple modeling languages, the framework generates a set of theories representing the integrated language definitions. This set of theories can be used in several verification scenarios. Note that, while the framework is tailored towards object-oriented modeling languages, the taxonomy mentioned above applies to any kind of modeling language. Likewise, the framework could be used for semantic domains other than the system model.

Future work will be concerned with elaborating variability for concrete modeling languages; larger case studies will contribute to validate the proposal and, in particular, the tool support. The long term goal, regarding one of our main targets UML, is to provide a comprehensive feature model for UML variability which ultimately could replace the currently used informal definitions and feature support statements. Another line of work is verification within our framework. Theorem proving is challenging. The effect of variability in concrete verification scenarios is not very well discussed and may require substantial further research.

References

1. Harel, D., Rumpe, B.: Meaningful Modeling: What's the Semantics of "Semantics"? Computer 37(10), 64–72 (2004)
2. Grönniger, H., Ringert, J.O., Rumpe, B.: System Model-Based Definition of Modeling Language Semantics. In: Lee, D., Lopes, A., Poetzsch-Heffter, A. (eds.) FMOODS/FORTE 2009. LNCS, vol. 5522, pp. 152–166. Springer, Heidelberg (2009)
3. Object Management Group: Unified Modeling Language: Superstructure Version 2.1.2 (07-11-02) (2007), http://www.omg.org/docs/formal/07-11-02.pdf
4. Object Management Group: Unified Modeling Language: Infrastructure Version 2.1.2 (07-11-04) (2007), http://www.omg.org/docs/formal/07-11-04.pdf
5. Cook, S., Kleppe, A., Warmer, J., Mitchell, R., Rumpe, B., Wills, A.C.: Defining UML Family Members Using Prefaces. In: Proc. of TOOLS 1999, Washington, DC, USA, pp. 102–114. IEEE Computer Society, Los Alamitos (1999)

6. Deelstra, S., Sinnema, M., Nijhuis, J., Bosch, J.: COSVAM: A Technique for Assessing Software Variability in Software Product Families. In: Proc. of ICSM 2004, pp. 458–462. IEEE Computer Society, Los Alamitos (2004)
7. Broy, M., Cengarle, M.V., Grönniger, H., Rumpe, B.: Modular Description of a Comprehensive Semantics Model for the UML (Version 2.0). Informatik-Bericht 2008-06, Technische Universität Braunschweig (2008)
8. Rumpe, B.: Formale Methodik des Entwurfs verteilter objektorientierter Systeme. Doktorarbeit, Technische Universität München (1996)
9. Gamma, E., Helm, R., Johnson, R., Vlissides, J.: Design patterns: elements of reusable object-oriented software. Addison-Wesley Professional, Reading (1995)
10. Czarnecki, K., Eisenecker, U.W.: Generative Programming: Methods, Tools, and Applications. Addison-Wesley, Reading (2000)
11. Krahn, H., Rumpe, B., Völkel, S.: MontiCore: Modular Development of Textual Domain Specific Languages. In: Proceedings of Tools Europe (2008)
12. Nipkow, T., Paulson, L.C., Wenzel, M.: Isabelle/HOL - A Proof Assistant for Higher-Order Logic. Springer, Heidelberg (2002)
13. Wildmoser, M., Nipkow, T.: Certifying Machine Code Safety: Shallow versus Deep Embedding. In: Slind, K., Bunker, A., Gopalakrishnan, G.C. (eds.) TPHOLs 2004. LNCS, vol. 3223, pp. 305–320. Springer, Heidelberg (2004)
14. Shankar, S., Asa, S., Sipos, V., Xu, X.: Reasoning about real-time statecharts in the presence of semantic variations. In: Proc. of ASE 2005, pp. 243–252. ACM, New York (2005)
15. Völter, M.: A Family of Languages for Architecture Description. In: 8th OOPSLA Workshop on Domain-Specific Modeling (DSM 2008), University of Alabama at Birmingham (2008)
16. Kelsen, P., Ma, Q.: A Lightweight Approach for Defining the Formal Semantics of a Modeling Language. In: Czarnecki, K., Ober, I., Bruel, J.-M., Uhl, A., Völter, M. (eds.) MODELS 2008. LNCS, vol. 5301, pp. 690–704. Springer, Heidelberg (2008)
17. Chen, K., Sztipanovits, J., Abdelwahed, S., Jackson, E.K.: Semantic anchoring with model transformations. In: Hartman, A., Kreische, D. (eds.) ECMDA-FA 2005. LNCS, vol. 3748, pp. 115–129. Springer, Heidelberg (2005)
18. Niu, J., Atlee, J.M., Day, N.A.: Template Semantics for Model-Based Notations. IEEE Trans. Software Eng. 29(10), 866–882 (2003)
19. Taleghani, A., Atlee, J.M.: Semantic Variations Among UML StateMachines. In: Nierstrasz, O., Whittle, J., Harel, D., Reggio, G. (eds.) MoDELS 2006. LNCS, vol. 4199, pp. 245–259. Springer, Heidelberg (2006)
20. Prout, A., Atlee, J.M., Day, N.A., Shaker, P.: Semantically Configurable Code Generation. In: Czarnecki, K., Ober, I., Bruel, J.-M., Uhl, A., Völter, M. (eds.) MODELS 2008. LNCS, vol. 5301, pp. 705–720. Springer, Heidelberg (2008)
21. Atlee, J.M., Day, N.A., Niu, J., Kang, E., Lu, Y., Fung, D., Wong, L.: Metro: An Analysis Toolkit for Template Semantics. Technical Report CS-2006-34, David R. Cheriton School of Computer Science, University of Waterloo (2006)
22. Cuccuru, A., Mraidha, C., Terrier, F., Gérard, S.: Templatable Metamodels for Semantic Variation Points. In: Akehurst, D.H., Vogel, R., Paige, R.F. (eds.) ECMDA-FA. LNCS, vol. 4530, pp. 68–82. Springer, Heidelberg (2007)
23. Cuccuru, A., Mraidha, C., Terrier, F., Gérard, S.: Enhancing UML Extensions with Operational Semantics. In: Engels, G., Opdyke, B., Schmidt, D.C., Weil, F. (eds.) MODELS 2007. LNCS, vol. 4735, pp. 271–285. Springer, Heidelberg (2007)
24. Chauvel, F., Jézéquel, J.M.: Code Generation from UML Models with Semantic Variation Points. In: Briand, L.C., Williams, C. (eds.) MoDELS 2005. LNCS, vol. 3713, pp. 54–68. Springer, Heidelberg (2005)

Variability Modelling throughout the Product Line Lifecycle*

Christa Schwanninger[1], Iris Groher[2], Christoph Elsner[1], and Martin Lehofer[3]

[1] Siemens Corporate Technology Erlangen
[2] Johannes Kepler University Linz
[3] Siemens VAI Linz
{Christa.Schwanninger,Christoph.Elsner.ext,
Martin.Lehofer.ext}@siemens.com,
Iris.Groher@jku.at

Abstract. This paper summarizes our experience with introducing feature modelling into several product lines within Siemens. Feature models are used for solving various tasks in the product line lifecycle, starting with scoping the reusable asset base up to support for actual product configuration. Using feature models as primary artefacts for managing variability early in the lifecycle, we could improve the efficiency and transparency of scoping activities considerably and made the development efforts way easier to schedule. On the other end of the lifecycle, feature models lowered the engineering efforts in solution business in supporting product configuration and instantiation.

1 Introduction

Product line engineering [1, 2] denotes a collection of engineering techniques supporting the efficient reuse of a common set of core assets when developing similar products. There are three main measures to achieve this reuse: proper scoping of the domain and deriving platform scoping decisions from business considerations, managing variability, and building up a reuse culture. Siemens business groups have a lot of domain knowledge and many success stories to tell; nevertheless staying competitive requires constant improvement and a product line approach is very promising to decrease time-to-market for those business groups developing similar or successive products in the same domain.

Feature modelling [3] was introduced as part of the domain analysis and domain modelling phase to systematically describe the common and variable features shared among the products of a product line. We found that feature modelling supports several areas of product line engineering very well, especially *scoping* [4] and the *configuration and derivation* [5] of products from the reuse infrastructure, but also activities like project planning and tracking, testing and customer negotiations.

We introduced feature modelling as a concept together with appropriate tool support in several business groups within Siemens, mainly to support either scoping and project planning or (partly) automatic product configuration and derivation. In this

* Empirical results category paper.

A. Schürr and B. Selic (Eds.): MODELS 2009, LNCS 5795, pp. 685–689, 2009.

experience paper, we will describe the introduction processes in two business groups together with the improvements achieved, and the lessons learned.

2 Experiences with Feature Models for Scoping

The first group we report on comprises one platform unit developing reusable core assets and several application engineering units. This distribution of responsibility requires considerable effort to communicate the platform scope and support for transparent tracking of asset development. Application units add features to each product and want to know exactly what the platform will deliver when. Feature modelling supported all steps for setting up a product line approach described subsequently.

2.1 Structure the Requirements and Build Up a Domain Vocabulary

Why? The business group had structured their requirements mainly in use cases before. While this made the requirements easily understandable, it was hard to determine if they were complete and what the commonalities and variations were in the platform. Moreover, many of the 5000 requirements were not included in the use case descriptions because this was not really feasible for some parts of the overall domain, e.g. UI frameworks or frameworks for data management.

How? The feature model was built in a top-down and a bottom-up manner. Top down a couple of sub-domains were identified with two of them being workflow-driven. These workflows are kind of standardized, so they can easily be utilized to check for the complete coverage of these sub-domains. In a bottom-up approach the existing requirements, which partly used to be assigned to use cases, were grouped underneath the top-down features. The feature model thus lead to a rearrangement of existing requirements, giving the opportunity to identify missing areas and to make the whole requirements base easier to understand through hierarchical decomposition. Overall, the user visible features became top level features, while internal features either ended up in the lower level of the feature model or in separate, more technical sub-domain feature models. Consequently, we classified the feature nodes into different types with a different set of attributes depending on their characteristics. The feature modelling tooling [6] is integrated with the requirements management tooling. The requirements meta model resembles most of the feature modelling meta model. This allows for importing the feature models into the requirements management tool and adding additional information and traces there.

2.2 Use Feature Modelling for the Platform Scoping Negotiation Process

Why? The business group is split into a domain engineering and several application engineering units. Requirements for the reusable asset base are not mined from customer contracts, but come from application engineering. Negotiations about which functionality should be a commonality and should therefore be supported by the platform had traditionally high conflict potential. Every application unit tried to get as much of their specific functionality into the platform as possible because platform development was pre-funded by application units. The challenge was then to consistently de-scope from all the requirements that had no or only low reuse potential.

How? The use case structure of the requirements had made a commonality/variability analysis among all involved units very hard. With the feature model that consists of user visible features on the top level and getting more detailed with features that reflect functional specification decisions a good communication basis is set up for negotiation. The application engineering units are interested in this detailed information about platform internals because they partially extend the platform features with product specific features or variants. The feature model is used as central repository for feature negotiation. First of all it makes it a lot easier to identify commonalities among applications because it forms a common vocabulary. Second, information about the value of a feature for each customer (i.e. how important is this feature to support a product and estimations how often this product will be sold) together with cost estimations of the platform development unit are the basis for prioritizing features. The decisions on what should be part of the business group became more transparent, decreasing the conflict potential considerably.

2.3 Trace Features to the Architecture

Why? For safety reasons, collecting tracing data is an important issue when developing medical software. Before the feature model was created, single requirements were traced from market requirements down to design specifications. However, this is very work-intensive, error-prone, and inefficient to maintain and even not required by regulation organizations.

How? The detailed tracing is replaced by tracing of features, which are an order of magnitude less than requirements, to architectural entities. In parallel to feature models, an architectural entity model reflecting the static structure of the architecture is built. This model is hierarchical like the feature model, only with subsystems, components and classes as the elements of this hierarchy. Features trace into the architectural elements in a many-to-many relationship. From this model it is then possible to investigate the effect of requirements on single architectural building blocks either in design specifications attached to building blocks or in the code.

2.4 Support Project and Iteration Planning and Project Controlling with Feature Modelling

Why? After using the feature model for scoping, it is only consequent to use it for project planning and controlling as well. The development process is an agile, iterative one, therefore features are ideal items to be put into backlogs and be planned in iterations.

How? The features of the feature model are used as first class artefacts for project planning and controlling. They are augmented with attributes regarding the acceptance criteria for each feature, development status, and schedule. Therefore, the common vocabulary is not only present in product management and development but also in project planning and controlling. Furthermore, the linkage to the architecture models allows tracking the degree of completion of each feature. For iteration planning the features are further decomposed into iteration features that can be implemented in a single iteration. The iteration features are the smallest units for planning, but they are always seen in the context of their parent feature and are planned in a way that iteration features belonging to one feature are assigned to consecutive iteration steps.

2.5 The Feature Model as Product Derivation Support

Using the feature model for platform configuration and derivation is a long term goal. To achieve this it is not sufficient to establish links form features to architectural building blocks. All variations have to be linked to the concrete variation implementations in solution space, e.g. to configuration parameters or removable application code building blocks. A derivation infrastructure has to be developed that evaluates the links and configures the application, e.g., by setting the parameters or by omitting building blocks according to the feature selection.

3 Experience with Variability Modelling for Product Derivation

Siemens VAI is the world's leader in the domain of engineering and building plants for the iron, steel, and aluminium industry and uses variability modelling techniques for product derivation in its CC-L2 product line. The product line provides process automation to continuous casting plants in steel mills and consists of several applications on different technical platforms like C++, Java and .Net, at a total of about 2 MLoC. Modelling techniques are used heavily in the server core, which consists of more than 800 components. To the average customer, about 600 selected components are delivered and custom extensions to the product line are made.

With their academic partner, the Christian Doppler Laboratory for Automated Software Engineering they developed the DOPLER approach [5]. Based on detailed sales support documents and the problem space knowledge of product management, the features and the variability of the product line were mined and consolidated into a model. This model has extended product derivation capabilities, as the features are attached with questions in natural language. During application engineering, answering the questions in close cooperation with the customer leads to decisions triggering the feature selection and therefore to a concrete product configuration. The resulting models are used as domain-specific language (DSL) to resolve the problem space variability together with the customer based on concrete product requirements.

The solution space of the CC-L2 product line comprises a component-based architecture. Because of the clearly defined mapping between problem space and solution space variability it is possible to automatically select and configure the assets required to build the desired product.

In the last years, the product line approach helped Siemens VAI to deliver more than 150 projects on schedule and on budget. Before, they had serious problems with code changes causing problems during start-up of plants. They were able to significantly reduce project execution time and travel times. Through defining a PLE evolution and planning process, Siemens VAI was able to reduce their development efforts and increased the reuse of software components.

4 Lessons Learned and Conclusion

Important lessons learned while using feature models for scoping are:

- Early involvement of solution space knowledge: It is necessary to consider solution space knowledge early when identifying features and variants of a product line. In our examples products or systems were already built before the migration to product line engineering was started. The structure of existing systems helps to identify meaningful sub-domains. Linking features to existing solution space assets, or at least to architectural entities that are under design, helps to estimate cost early and keeps the whole effort grounded.
- Co-development of feature model: Development should be integrated early in building the feature model. There is considerable knowledge about past products or systems in development that helps to establish parts of the feature model with its variability quickly. The communication between product management and development furthermore leads to a common understanding of the requirements on the one hand and of the cost to implement those requirements, especially variability, on the other.
- Sub-domain division: Covering the whole problem domain with one feature model is too complex, if the goal is to model not only variability but to cover the whole system including all commonalities. Therefore, domains should be divided into sub-domains modelled in separate feature models.

At the other end of the life cycle feature models are very well suited to build DSLs for supporting automatic product derivation. The vast majority of variability in our domains is configurative variability. The hierarchical form of feature models makes them easy understandable by all stakeholders, not only the customer.

We did not do a project yet that combined feature modelling at both ends of the product line lifecycle. However, within the first described business group, we want to augment the feature model built for scoping to support product derivation.

References

1. Clements, P., Northrop, L.: Software Product Lines: Practices and Patterns. Addison-Wesley, Reading (2001)
2. Pohl, K., Böckle, G., van der Linden, F.: Software Product Line Engineering: Foundations, Principles, and Techniques. Springer, Heidelberg (2005)
3. Kang, K.C., et al.: Feature-oriented domain analysis (FODA) feasibility study. Technical Report CMU/SEI-90TR-21, Software Engineering Institute, Carnegie Mellon University, Pittsburgh, PA, USA (1990)
4. Schmid, K.: A comprehensive product line scoping approach and its validation. In: 24th International Conference on Software Engineering, pp. 593–603. ACM, New York (2002)
5. Rabiser, R., Gruenbacher, P., Dhungana, D.: Supporting Product Derivation by Adapting and Augmenting Variability Models. In: 11th International Software Product Line Conference, pp. 141–150. IEEE, Los Alamitos (2007)
6. pure systems GmbH. Variant Management with pure: variants. Technical Whitepaper (2006)

Weaving Variability into Domain Metamodels*

Brice Morin[1], Gilles Perrouin[2], Philippe Lahire[3], Olivier Barais[1,4], Gilles Vanwormhoudt[5], and Jean-Marc Jézéquel[1,4]

[1] INRIA, Centre Rennes – Bretagne Atlantique, Equipe Triskell, F-35042 Rennes Cedex
[2] University of Luxembourg, LASSY, L-1359 Luxembourg-Kirchberg, Luxembourg
[3] I3S Nice-Sophia Antipolis, Equipe Rainbow, F-06903 Sophia-Antipolis Cedex
[4] IRISA, Université de Rennes1, Equipe Triskell, F-35042 Rennes Cedex
[5] Institut Telecom / LIFL, Université de Lille 1, F-59655 Villeneuve d'Ascq Cedex

Abstract. Domain-Specific Modeling Languages (DSMLs) describe the concepts of a particular domain and their relationships, in a metamodel. From a given DSML, it is possible to describe a wide range of different models. These models often share a common base and vary on some parts. Current approaches tend to distinguish the variability language from the DSMLs themselves, implying greater learning curve for DSMLs stakeholders and a significant overhead in product line engineering of DSMLs. We propose to consider variability as an independent aspect to be woven into the DSML to introduce variability capabilities. In particular we detail how variability is woven and how to perform product line derivation. We validate our approach through the weaving of variability into two very different metamodels: Ecore and SmartAdapter, our Aspect-Oriented modeling weaver, thus adding flexibility in the weaving process itself. These results emphasize how new abilities of the language can be provided by this means.

1 Introduction

In an always more competitive environment, the ability for a company to rapidly propose new products or variations of existing products is the key to meet user requirements. However, proposing a wide range of different products is risky: products should be designed, validated, implemented rapidly, at a low cost. The Software Product Line [1] (SPL) community proposes techniques and tools in order to engineer families of related products. The main idea behind SPL is to capture the commonalities of the different products as well as the specificities (variability) of each particular product. In this paper, we focus on Model-Driven SPL [2] where the product line itself and the derived products are models. The models are derived using Model-Driven Engineering techniques, such as model transformation, model composition or aspect model weaving.

Several approaches exist to describe SPLs : *i)* to use a general-purpose metamodel like the UML [3] including the concepts allowing designers to describe

* This work was realized in the context of the MOVIDA and the FAROS projects, funded by the ANR (French National Research Agency).

A. Schürr and B. Selic (Eds.): MODELS 2009, LNCS 5795, pp. 690–705, 2009.

the variability of a model, *ii)* to build a metamodel without variability and then extend it in order to include the necessary variability. The first category allows the domain stakeholder to directly design a family of products thanks to the expressiveness provided by the metamodel. The second category allows designers to focus on the domain itself but not on its variability and then to update it in order to include the needed variability. The main drawback of this approach is that the variability should be included manually. For example, this is what we have done when we included variability into our aspect model weaver "SmartAdapters" [4], in order to be able to design more flexible and more reusable aspect models.

In this paper, we propose a reusable variability aspect, defined at the metamodel level, describing the variability concepts and their relationships independently from any domain metamodel. Using Aspect-Oriented Modeling [5] (AOM) techniques, this aspect can be woven into a given domain metamodel to include variability. More precisely, we use our aspect model weaver, SmartAdapters, to weave this variability aspect. This makes possible the integration of variability in a semi-automatic way into a wide range of domain metamodels.

We demonstrate our approach by introducing the variability *i)* into EMF, which is the *de-facto* standard integrated within Eclipse to define metamodels (similar to class diagrams) and *ii)* into SmartAdapters itself. However, our approach is generic and can be applied to any metamodel conforming to Ecore/EMOF, which includes the UML, to extend it with variability mechanisms. This demonstrates that decoupling the description of variability from the domain allows addressing, with a minimal additional effort, the two categories we mentioned.

This paper is organized as follows. In Section 2 we present a generic variability metamodel. In Section 3, we illustrate how we can introduce variability by hand into an excerpt of the EMF metamodel. In Section 4 we present our model weaver SmartAdapters and give an overview of the variability aspect associated to the variability metamodel presented in Section 2. Then we propose in Section 5 to apply the variability aspect to the SmartAdapters metamodel. Section 6 details how we can take advantage of SPL techniques in order to derive models with respect to variability woven at the metamodel level. Section 7 outlines some relevant research in the field and Section 8 wraps up with conclusions as well as discusses some interesting future perspectives.

2 Variability

In this section, we present a generic variability metamodel inspired from [2]. It relies upon formal studies of variability management in SPL [6,7] and in particular feature diagramming [8,9,10,11], which is a very popular notation in this community. Despite their wide acceptation, many variants have been proposed and there is no *de-facto* standard for feature diagrams. One interesting result of these formal studies is that it is possible to extract a pivot abstract syntax subsuming the expressiveness of these existing notations hence forming a universal basis independent of any peculiar notation. This abstract syntax is the source of our metamodel (see [2] for details).

Our generic variability metamodel (See Figure 1) is a customization of the feature metamodel [2] tailored to describe variability amongst Ecore concepts. In particular the notion of feature hierarchy, which is very specific to feature diagram, has been omitted because this hierarchy is imposed by the target metamodel (see Section 6). The main metaclass is *PointOfVariability* which provides the possibility to metamodel elements on which this class is woven to have variants. *PointOfVariability* has a concrete sub-class called *VariabilityOfElement* allowing a given domain concept to hold variability. Variability is described in terms of boolean operators that describe the kind of variability relationships applies to elements. *And* operator holds true iff all the elements to which it applies are chosen (mandatory elements). *Xor* denotes an alternative (only one element have to be chosen) and *Or* at least one. *Opt* denotes the optionality of presence. Finally $Vp(i, j)$ [7] will return true iff at least i and at most j elements are chosen. This operator can embed the semantics of all other operators [6] and could hence be the unique operator provided. However, "classic" operators are more practical and well-known; They are therefore left for usability matters.

In addition in this metamodel we make the distinction between *homogeneous* and *heterogenous* operators. Homogeneous operators are associated to *VariabilityOfElement* and apply only on element of the same type (EClass, etc.). Heterogeneous operators are associated to *PointOfVariability* and apply to elements of different types. The "choice" semantics is the same for homogenous and heterogeneous operators. However, we distinguish the hierarchy of operators associated to *homogeneousOperator* and *heterogenousOperator* because we support the idea that the domain expert should be able to add to its metamodel, only the expressiveness he needs. Thus he should be able to choose the suitable homogeneous as well as heterogeneous operators.

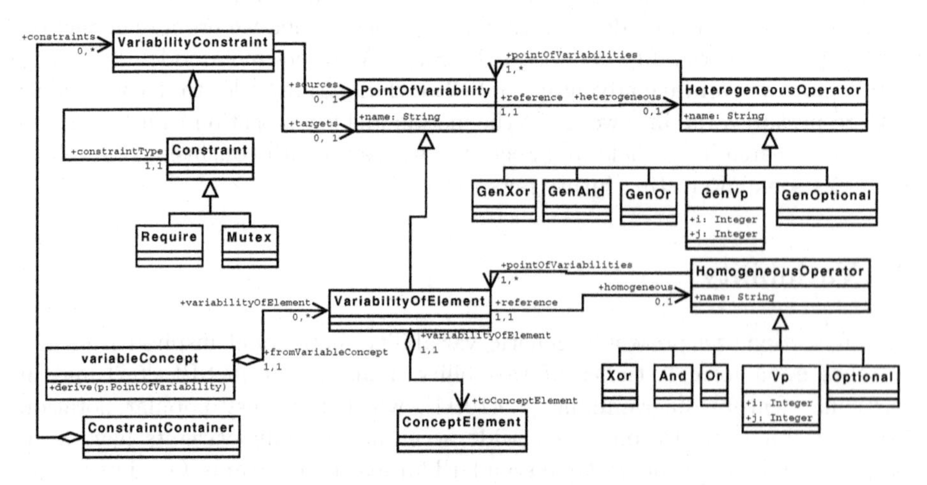

Fig. 1. The variability metamodel

Additionally, it is possible to define constraints between points of variability, whether there are targeted by the same operator or not. These constraints are of two types: *requires* which implies that the required element have also to be selected if the requiring element is selected, and *mutex* which excludes that both referred elements are present in the same selection. There exists other kinds of constraints [2,6,7] but as there mostly informal (expressed in natural language) we decided to let the designer include them manually after weaving.

3 Patterns for Introducing Variability

As noted by Haugen *et al.* [12], there are two categories of techniques to introduce variability into languages (represented as metamodels); *amalgamated* and *separated.* The first one proposes to augment the metamodel with variability constructs while the second one keeps them distinct and relates them via simple referencing. We chose the first kind of approach because we want to clearly express variability among elements [12] and enable conformance checking in a standard way.

For example in EMF, if it is required that *i)* some classes, operations, or attributes are optional, and *ii)* some model elements are part of the same variant, and *iii)* alternative and constraints may exist among variants, then this information cannot be attached into the EMF metamodel and have to be put in a feature diagram or in a DSL as proposed by Haugen et al.

In this paper, our aim is to describe models containing variability, based on the concepts defined in the domain metamodel. In order to do that, we construct on demand a new metamodel MM' that integrates concepts from product-lines described in Section 2 and the domain-specific concepts of the MM. The main idea is to introduce a new meta-class on each association to capture the fact that

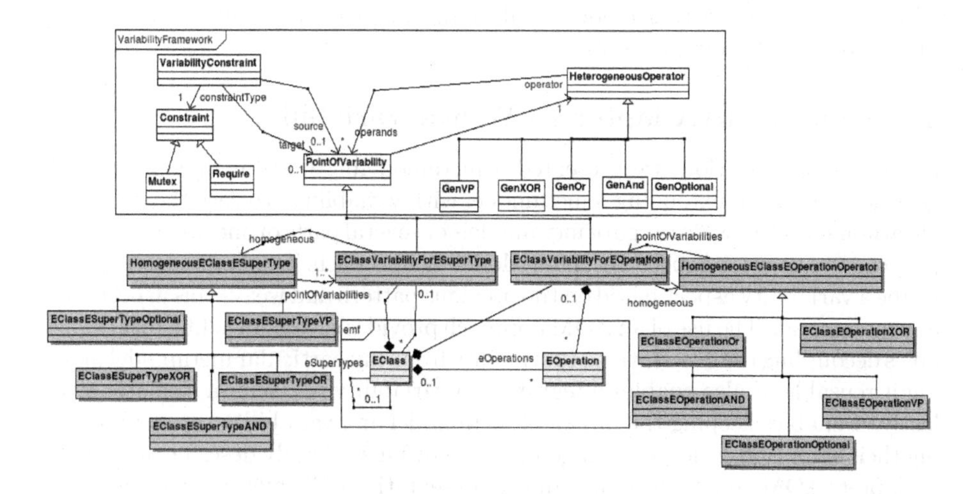

Fig. 2. EMF meta-model with Variability

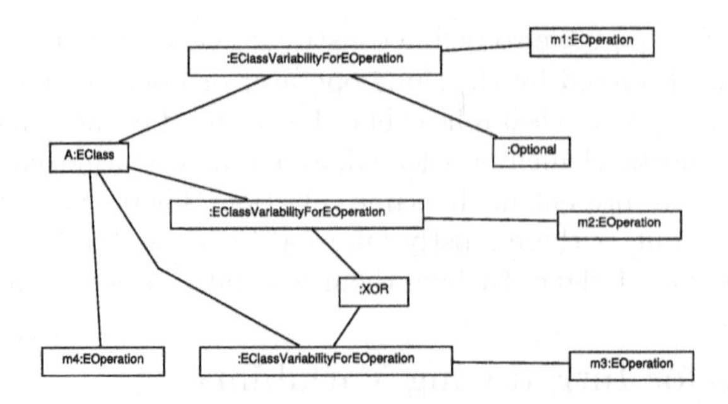

Fig. 3. EMF model with Variability

a model element can be a variant as illustrated in Figure 2 for an excerpt of the EMF metamodel. As an example, it allows to capture the fact that a method $m1$ in a class A is optional and two methods $m2$ and $m3$ are alternatives as described in Figure 3.

Implications of this approach are that the variability aspect can also be standardized, and that DSMLs (MM) can be designed without variability mechanisms. These mechanisms are woven on demand to create MM'.

We still want to keep the possibility to specify that a class A has a method $m4$ which is not a variable part of the model. Consequently, we do not remove existing associations, but extend the domain metamodel with new class-associations ($EClassVariabilityForEOperation$ and $EClassVariabilityForESuperType$ in Figure 2), which capture the variability.

The idea of the pattern to introduce variability is to match each association and create new meta-classes for creating the connection between MM and the variability aspect. This way, the former metamodel MM is simply extended. Since all the existing meta-classes and their properties (from MM) are kept in MM', all the pre-existing models conforming to MM can easily be converted into models conforming to MM'.

4 Using SmartAdapter to Weave Variability

In the previous section, we presented a metamodeling pattern that provides a generic solution for extending a metamodel with variability. To ease the inclusion of variability into a wide range of metamodels or several parts of one metamodel, we propose to adopt an Aspect-Oriented Modeling approach. The main idea is to describe a variability aspect based on the previous pattern and weave this aspect into any metamodel. The use of an AOM approach provides several benefits: first, it enables decoupling the description of variability from any particular metamodel making it reusable; it also enables integration of variability in a semi-automatic way; lastly, it enables keeping the design of metamodel and variability separate, making their evolution easier to manage.In the following we briefly describe our SmartAdapters AOM approach [4] including a presentation of its metamodel, where we will weave variability (Section 5). Then we present its use to describe the variability aspect and apply this aspect for introducing variability into Ecore.

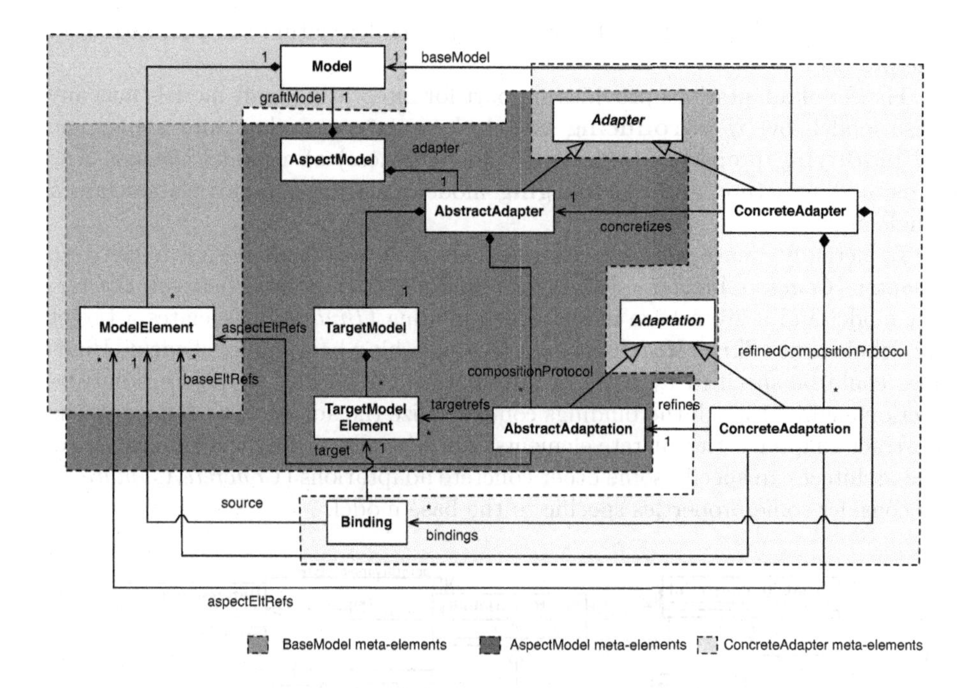

Fig. 4. The SmartAdapters metamodel

SmartAdapters is a generic AOM approach. It relies on four key concepts : aspect model, graft model, target model and adaptations. An aspect model consists of *i)* a graft model that encapsulates a given concern, and *ii)* an abstract adapter that describes *where* (target model) and *how* (adaptations) the aspect model will be woven into other base models.

The metamodel describing the concepts of SmartAdapters is shown at Figure 4. This metamodel is not tied to a specific domain metamodel and can be customized to weave aspects into different kinds of model (provided that aspect and base model rely on the same domain metamodel). Here, since we are interested to weave aspects into any metamodel, we assume the customization of SmartAdapter to MOF/Ecore metamodels.

The target model (*TargetModel*) is an abstract interface between the aspect model (*AspectModel*) and any base models (*Model*). It is a model fragment that identifies the hooks required on the base model. It contains roles (*TargetModelElement*) that may be substituted, at binding time, by base model elements and structural constraints that every binding (a set of elements substituting the roles) should respect.

An abstract adapter (*AbstractAdapter*) is the composition protocol of an aspect model: it guides and controls the composition of the aspect, independently from any base model. It contains Adaptations (*AbstractAdaptation*) which are composition operations describing how to weave the aspect model into the target model. In a composition protocol, the designer can refer to any role from the target model or model element from the graft model, within the adaptations of the protocol.

The set of adaptations provides support for integrating graft models into any base model, by: *i)* **introducing** model elements *e.g.* a class into a package, *ii)* **modifying** properties (attributes and references) of a model element *e.g.*, a method signature, and *iii)* **merging** model elements *e.g.* two classes into a single one.

To actually weave an aspect model, an architect must design a concrete adapter (*ConcreteAdapter*). It specifies bindings (join points) between the target model and a given base model. Each binding (*Binding*) associates a target model element (*TargetModelElement*) to a matching base model element. Bindings could be specified by hand or automatically identified by a join point detection engine [13]. All the bindings contextualize the adaptations defined in the abstract adapter with concrete elements. Additionally, during the binding stage, the architect can specify some other concrete adaptations (*ConcreteAdaptation*) to consider some properties specific to the base model.

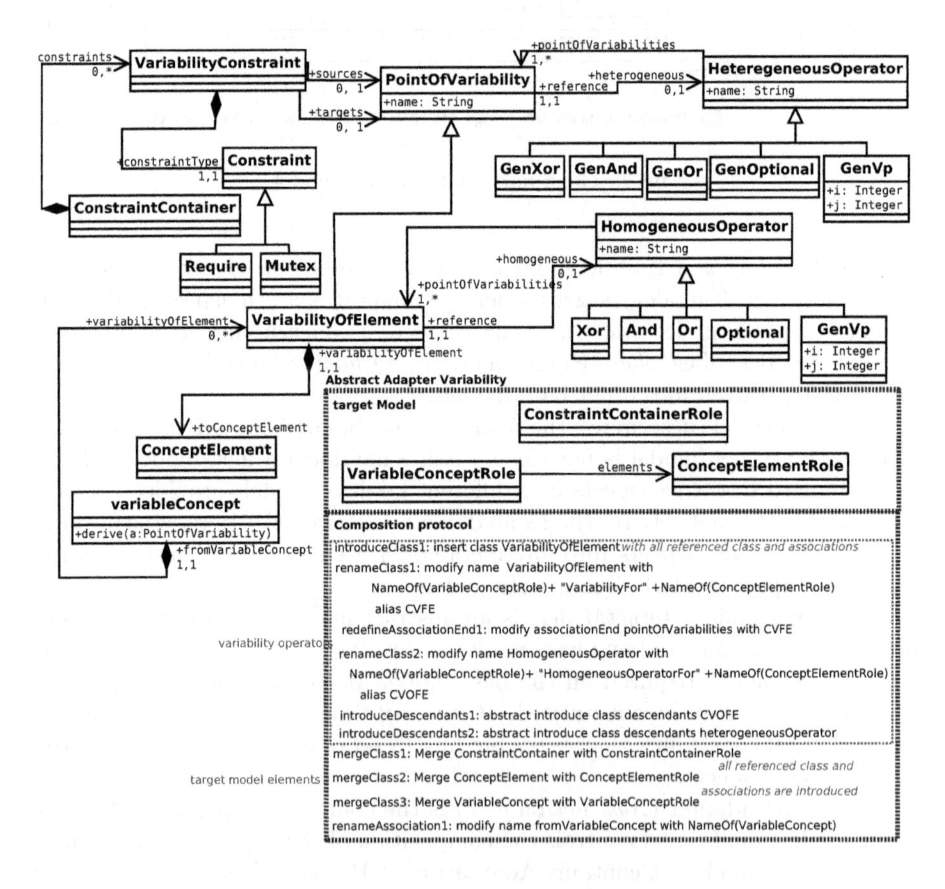

Fig. 5. The Variability Aspect including Composition Protocol

Figure 5 shows the variability aspect. Basically, the graft model of the aspect contains the concepts from the feature metamodel presented in Section 2 and those from the metamodeling pattern presented in Section 3.

The target model contains roles to specify that three classes and one relationship must be present in a base model to apply the aspect. *ConstraintContainerRole* identifies the class in a metamodel where constraints for controlling variability must be attached. *VariableConceptRole*, *ConceptElementrole* and *elements* relationship identify a couple of linked classes in a metamodel where variability must be introduced.

The basic principle of the composition protocol is to: *i*) keep unchanged the relationship between the two classes (*VariableConceptRole* and *ConceptElementrole*) of the target model (to allow defining mandatory element), and *ii*) create a new relationship between these two classes, controlled by a variability manager, in order to allow defining variable elements.

More precisely the composition protocol mainly contains adaptations for introducing model elements (*insert*) which allow to introduce a given element (e.g. class *VariabilityOfElement*) with implicitly all elements that it references. When an element already exists in the base model (for example when the aspect is applied two times on the same model), it is not added a second time.

Another important remarks deals with the use of renaming (*modify name*). One relationship (*fromVariableConcept*) and two classes (*variabilityOfElement* and *VariabilityOperator*) are renamed. Main advantages in present situation is that n applications of the aspect in the same base model will create n samples of the same relationship or metaclass.

Finally for each application of the aspect we may choose the expressiveness of the variability. We simply select the descendant classes of *VariabilityOperator* after its renaming (the renamed class is accessible with the *alias* CVOFE). The choice is made accordingly to the base model (at composition time), so that the adaptation is abstract and will be defined in a concrete adapter (*ConcreteAdapter*).We may choose the same approach for the different types of constraints. This would be particularly interesting if we propose a larger set of constraint types. In order to reduce the complexity of the schema we decided to provide all the types of constraints (*Require* and *Mutex*) for each application of the aspect. In order to provide a centralized access to all constraints in a given element of the base model, we declare this element in the target model.

In our composition protocol we also propose to merge each of the three elements mentioned in the target model with one element of the graft model. This way, base model elements bound to target model elements now include their respective functionalities (*e.g.* the class(es) bound to *VariableConceptRole* will include the *derive* method and the association-end *variabilityOfElement*).

Figure 6 shows the concrete adapter to apply the variability aspect to EMF and introduce the ability for an Ecore package to support variability for the Ecore classes. This concrete adapter achieves this ability by binding elements from the target model (resp. *VariableConceptRole*, *ConceptElementRole*, *elements* and *ConstraintContainerRole*) to elements of the Ecore metamodel (resp.

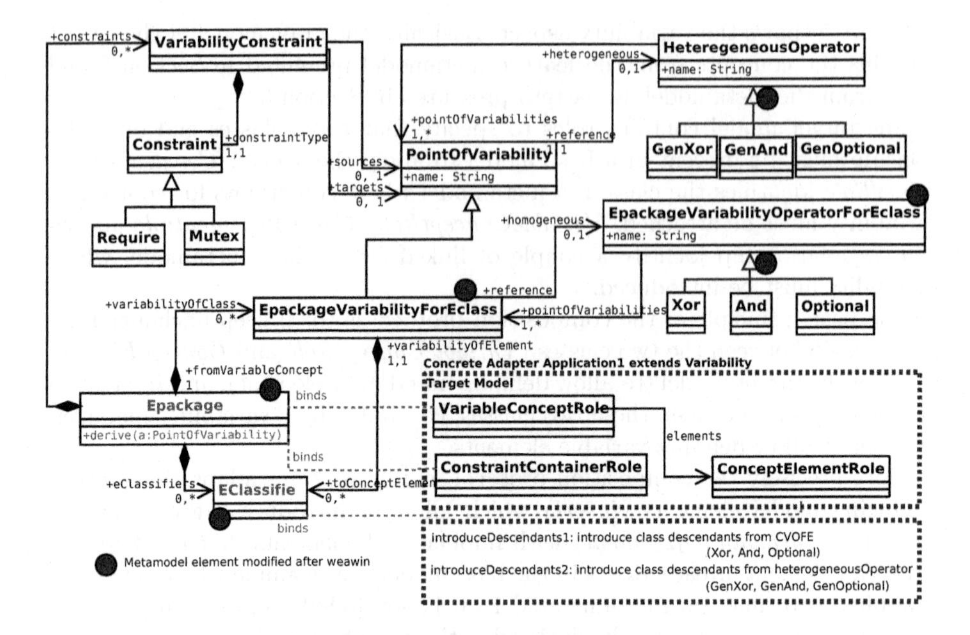

Fig. 6. The variability aspect

EPackage, *EClassifier*, *eClassifiers* and *EPackage*). As a result of these bindings, *EPackageVariableForEClass* and *EPackageVariabilityOperatorForEClass* classes are introduced with their dependent classes and relationships and *EPackage* is extended with a new relationship to *EPackageVariabilityForEClass* (see left part of the figure). Finally, the concrete adapter also contains redefined adaptations (*introduceDescendants1* and *introducedDescendants2*) to select the subset of operators that are appropriate for classes variability.

5 Introducing Variability into SmartAdapters

In [4], we pointed out that aspect reusability is limited in AOM approaches because an aspect model must match exactly the structure of base models and is always woven according to the same rules. To address this issue, we proposed to extend AOM approaches with matching variability and composition variability. This variability was introduced in an ad-hoc way. Supporting these two dimensions of variability in our SmartAdapter approach have been achieved by extending the notion of adapter with the following variability mechanisms:

- **Optional targets:** In order to specify that some elements from the target model may be present or not in the base model where we want to weave the aspect.
- **Alternative adaptations:** In order to specify that there exists several possible ways to compose the aspect. All the variants are exclusive *i.e.*, we can only choose exactly one variant per alternative.

- **Optional adaptations:** In order to specify that some adaptations of the composition protocol are not mandatory.
- **Constraints between targets and/or adaptations:** In order to specify that some variants are dependent or in mutual exclusion. With these constraints, we can ensure the consistency of the composition protocol, after derivation.

Using these mechanisms, a designer can build an aspect model that is adaptable to different contexts. Figure 7 illustrates an aspect model using these mechanisms to integrate the well-know observer pattern into a base model. The target model declares an option to deal with the presence or not of the association between classes playing *SubjectTargetClass* and *ObserverTargetClass*. The composition protocol includes two variants to integrate the classes and association of the pattern into a base model, either by merging or by inheritance.

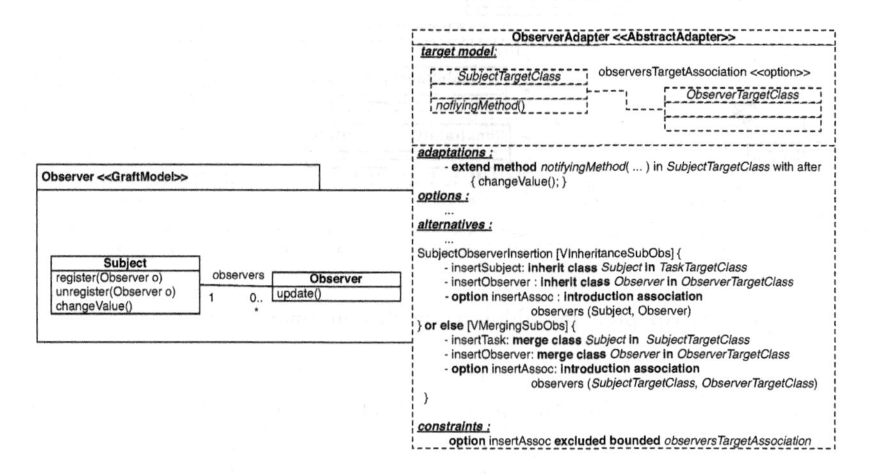

Fig. 7. Example of an aspect model with variability

All the mechanisms presented above can be added to our SmartAdapter approach by applying the previous variability aspect to its metamodel, using SmartAdapter itself. Figure 8 and 9 show the definition of two concrete adapters to achieve this operation. They specialize and complete the abstract adapter of the variability aspect described in Section 4.

The first concrete adapter (*SmartAdapter1*) handles the declaration of options and alternatives within a composition protocol. It binds elements from the target model (resp. *ConstraintContainerRole*, *VariableConceptRole*, *ConceptElementRole*, *elements*) to elements of the SmartAdapters metamodel (resp. *Model*, *AbstractAdapter*, *AbstractAdaptation*, *compositionProtocol*). This adapter causes the contextualization of adaptations from the variability aspect with the following results:

- the *VariabilityOfElement* class is inserted as a subclass of *PointOfVariability* and this new class is renamed *AAVariabilityForAAdaptation*. This class introduces variability capacities for the *AbstractAdapter* class.

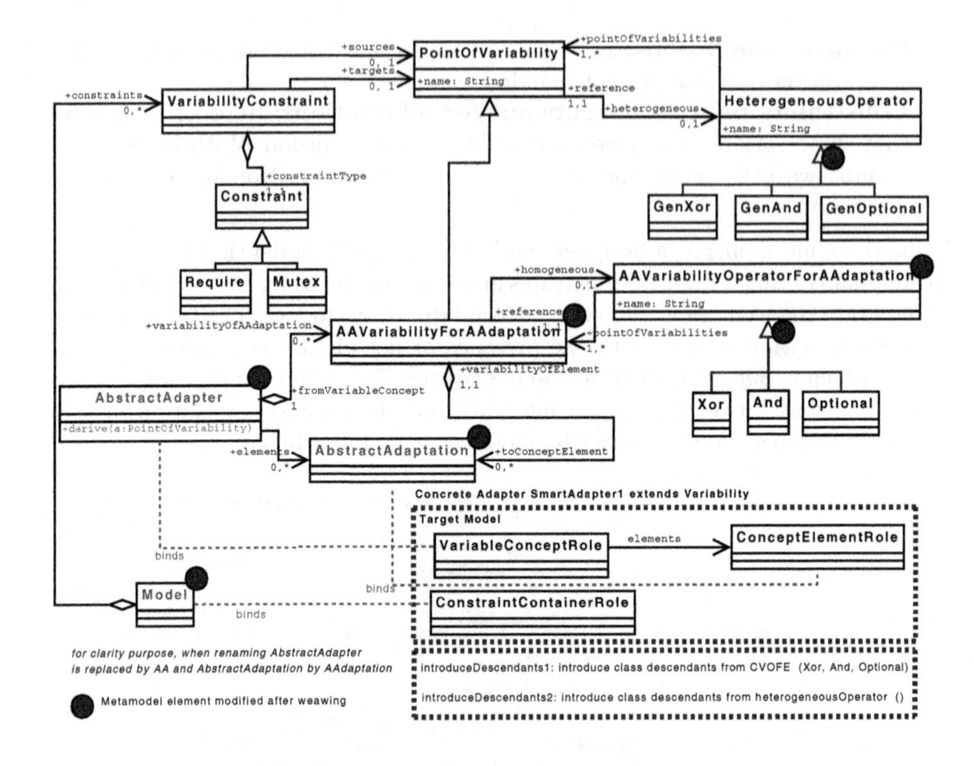

Fig. 8. Adapters for adding variability in SmartAdapters (1)

- the content of *VariableConcept* is merged into *AbstractAdapter* class. As a result of this merging, the *AbstractAdapter* is extended with the *derive* method and one aggregation relationship to hold *AAVariabilityForAdaptation* elements.
- the insertion of classes required for describing constraints and operators as well as their relationships.
- the insertion of *AAVariabilityOperatorForAAdaptation* as a superclass for the set of operators (Xor, And, Optional) defined for *AbstractAdapter*.

The second concrete adapter (*SmartAdapter2*) handles the optionality of target elements. It applies the variability aspect to metaclasses of the metamodel representing the target model and its content, by binding *VariableConceptRole* to *TargetModel*, *ConceptElementRole* to *TargetModelElement* and *elements* to *targetElts*. According to these bindings, the *TargetModel* class is extended with the content of the *VariableConceptRole* and with a new relationship to *TMVariabilityForTMElement* that defines the variability for *TargetModelElement*. The operator that can be used for this variability is defined by *TMVariabilityOperatorForTMElement* which is inserted as superclass of *Optional*. Note that classes for describing constraints and operators are only inserted once, even when the aspect is woven in several places.

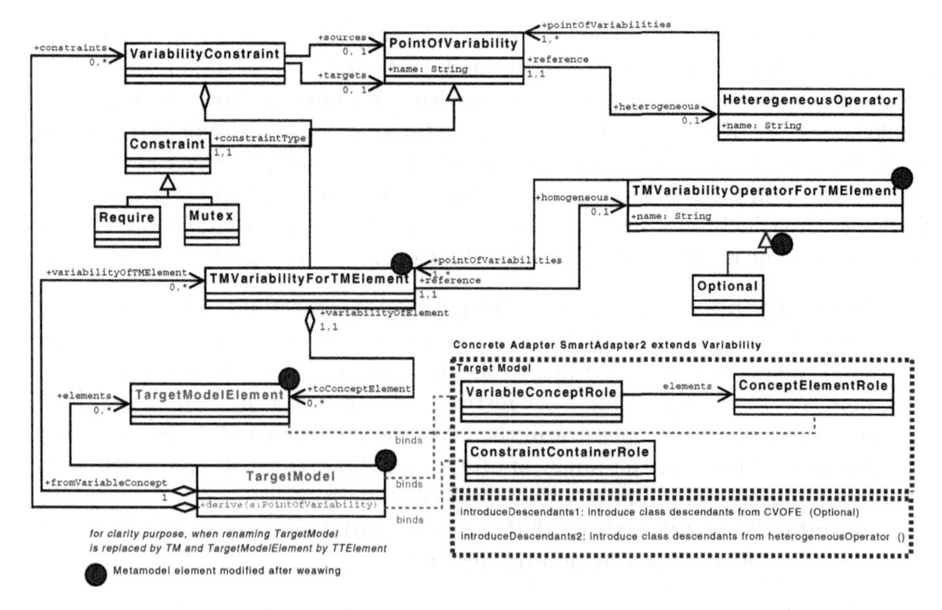

Fig. 9. Adapters for adding variability in SmartAdapters (2)

6 Towards Software Product Line

The previous sections explained how we can flexibly add variability concepts to a domain metamodel, like Ecore or SmartAdapters, in order to be able to easily design models containing variability. In this section, we describe how we derive products (models with no variability, conforming to the former metamodel) from a product line model (model with variability, conforming to the extended metamodel, where the variability aspect has been woven).

As mentioned in Section 2, one of the most practical techniques is *feature modeling* which aims at representing the common and variable *features*[1] (or concepts) of a product family. Feature modeling is not only relevant to requirement engineering but it can also be applied to design or code levels. Hence, every stakeholder can manipulate features "as is", independently of the kind of variability and the level of abstraction. Moreover, feature models (FMs) encourage to define a standard vocabulary for a domain language and are ideal abstractions that customers, experts, and developers can easily understand. FMs hierarchically structure domain concepts into multiple levels of increasing detail thus proposing a taxonomy. When decomposing a feature into sub-features, the subfeatures may be optional or mandatory or may form Alternative, Or, or And groups. FMs describe the variability and the commonality of features and represent a set of valid *configurations*. A valid configuration is obtained by selecting features while respecting the parent-child and an intuitive decomposition semantics. Feature models are represented as graph which have a tree-like structure as shown on Figure 10.

[1] According to [14] a feature is "an increment in product functionality".

In order to take advantage of existing feature-based modeling tools [15], derivation approaches [2,16] or formal analysis techniques [17,18,6], we offer to compute a feature diagram from a model with variability as shown in Section 3. To do so, we use Kermeta [19] which is a metamodelling environment dedicated to Ecore models manipulation. The initial step is to obtain the root feature which corresponds to the root package of the EMF model. Then we traverse the EMF model (which imposes its structure to the feature diagram) by navigating the containment relationships. For each relationship, there are two options:

- **Variability point:** If this relationship contains a variability point (instance of the woven $VariabilityOfElement$ metaclass), we create an operator of the right type (or,xor,vp) according to the operator associated to this variability point. We then retrieve all other instances of $VariabilityOfElement$ which are referenced by the operator in the EMF model. The sub-features are then obtained by forming the union of all $ConceptElement$ instances referenced by the collected $VariabilityOfElement$ instances.
- **"Standard" relationship:** If there is no variability point, we treat the referenced element as a mandatory feature.

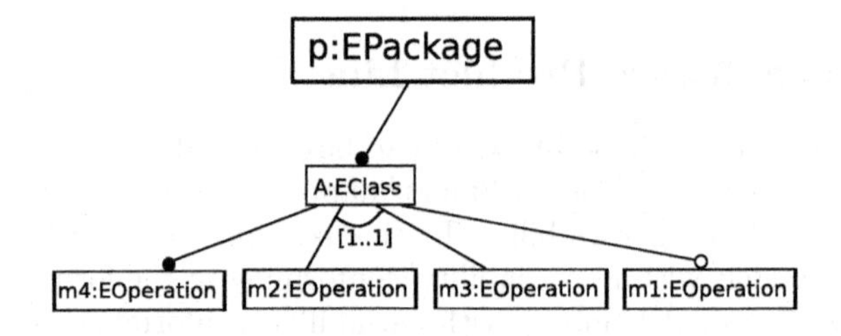

Fig. 10. Computed Feature Diagram for EMF Model with Variability

Figure 10 shows the feature diagram resulting from the application of the procedure on the EMF model shown Figure 3. Once the feature diagram is built, we can perform product derivation [20,2,16]. When a set of features is selected from the feature diagram, the last step consists in actually deriving the product model. For all the selected features, we call the derive operation associated to the model element (*e.g.* an instance of `EPackage` in Ecore metamodel or an instance of `AbstractAdapter` in SmartAdapters). This operation is implemented in Kermeta in a generic way, directly in the domain metamodel. It sets the former references with the model elements contained by the point of variability, which is removed. In a second pass, once all the points of variability have been derived, we remove all the remaining points of variability, corresponding to non-selected features. Finally, we can save the product model using the former domain metamodel. This derivation operator is built on top of the Kermeta Model-Development Kit (MDK)[2] for Feature Modeling [2]. We reuse some parts

[2] http://www.kermeta.org

of the Feature Diagram metamodel, some parts of its graphical editor and we have extended the static checker. The derivation process has been designed from scratch.

7 Related Work and Discussion

We do not address here the composition of models in general but the different approaches to introduce variability into metamodels and models.

Feature modeling is very much adapted to the description of the variability but the hierarchical approach does not provide the expressiveness that is needed and that may be provided by OO modeling approaches. This is the reason why some approaches like [2] use both UML and FMs for modeling a domain. Moreover on the contrary of our approach, the formalism used to describe the domain model contains already the expressiveness for the description of variability.

Other techniques like Ziadi *et al.* extend the UML metamodel in order to include features for modeling variability [20]. Those approaches work at the meta-meta level and extend an existing formalism in order to include variability modeling capabilities. The variability is included in various UML diagrams like class diagram or Sequence diagram. The capabilities introduced in those diagrams are very similar to the ones of our variability aspect which is applied here to class diagram but which could be applied also to other diagrams like sequence diagrams.

The software product line community recently investigated the use of variability techniques to assist the engineering of DSMLs. In [12] the authors propose a metamodel for describing variability which is independant from the models needing variability. In this respect the approach is similar to ours but there are several differences. First they do not aim to compose the two metamodels as we do; on the contrary the metamodel describes only possible substitutions. Second those substitutions are not defined according to the metamodel but to the models and these are the instances which are modified. They promote the idea that variability should not be defined at the metamodel level but at the model level.

In [21] Voelter presents an approach that addresses variability implementation, management and tracing by integrating model-driven and aspect-oriented software development. Features are separated in models and composed by aspect-oriented composition techniques on model level. This approach differs significantly from our approach: the variability is described at the model level with feature models which are transformed in AspectJ source code. They use AOSD as a techniques to compose variants, we use AOM to integrate the variability mechanisms in a domain metamodel.

8 Conclusion and Future Work

Building families of models related to the same domain is a key issue. It is widely addressed by the SPL community which propose the expressiveness needed by the description of the commonalities and the specificities of each model of the family (i.e. the variability of the family). Variability is a possible orthogonal concern of any domain metamodel and we propose an approach to compose this concern with domain metamodels. The effort of the domain model designer to introduce variability into its models must be reduced as much as possible. We propose to use the SmartAdapters approach which allows i) to minimize the information to be given at composition time and, ii) to guide and control the reuse of the variability aspect in various contexts. A first contribution of this paper is the specification of a variability aspect. We apply this aspect in two different contexts: EMF and SmartAdapters itself. A second contribution is the demonstration that AOM approaches could benefit from the concepts found in SPL without extending their underlying mechanisms, but using only the weaving techniques already present in AOM approaches. We use a version of SmartAdapter without variability (Figure 5) to weave the variability aspect into the SmartAdapter metamodel. We obtain the same expressiveness that the SmartAdapters version with manually introduced variability [4].

This validation of the approach for enhancing domain metamodel (DSMLs) with variability is a first step towards a better modularity in the metamodels. In the short term we aim to reuse this approach in order to introduce other features into DSML (e.g. model checking, editing facilities, etc.) making it more attractive but not more cumbersome especially when these facilities are not needed.

References

1. Pohl, K., Böckle, G., van der Linden, F.J.: Software Product Line Engineering: Foundations, Principles and Techniques. Springer, Secaucus (2005)
2. Perrouin, G., Klein, J., Guelfi, N., Jézéquel, J.M.: Reconciling automation and flexibility in product derivation. In: 12th International Software Product Line Conference (SPLC 2008), Limerick, Ireland, pp. 339–348. IEEE Computer Society, Los Alamitos (2008)
3. OMG: OMG Unified Modeling Language OMG UML, Superstructure Version 2.2. Technical Report formal/2007-02-03, Object Management Group (2007)
4. Lahire, P., Morin, B., Vanwormhoudt, G., Gaignard, A., Barais, O., Jézéquel, J.M.: Introducing variability into aspect-oriented modeling approaches. In: Engels, G., Opdyke, B., Schmidt, D.C., Weil, F. (eds.) MODELS 2007. LNCS, vol. 4735, pp. 498–513. Springer, Heidelberg (2007)
5. Gray, J., Sztipanovits, J., Schmidt, D.C., Bapty, T., Neema, S., Gokhale, A.: Two-level aspect weaving to support evolution in model-driven synthesis, pp. 681–709. Addison-Wesley, Reading (2005)
6. Schobbens, P.-Y., Heymans, P., Trigaux, J.-C., Bontemps, Y.: Feature Diagrams: A Survey and A Formal Semantics. In: RE, Minneapolis, Minnesota, USA (2006)
7. Schobbens, P.Y., Heymans, P., Trigaux, J.C., Bontemps, Y.: Generic semantics of feature diagrams. Computer Networks 51, 456–479 (2007)
8. Kang, K., Cohen, S., Hess, J., Novak, W., Peterson, S.: Feature-Oriented Domain Analysis (FODA) Feasibility Study. Technical Report CMU/SEI-90-TR-21, Software Engineering Institute (1990)
9. Czarnecki, K., Helsen, S., Eisenecker, U.: Formalizing Cardinality-based Feature Models and their Specialization. Software Process Improvement and Practice 10, 7–29 (2005)

10. Griss, M.L., Favaro, J., d' Alessandro, M.: Integrating Feature Modeling with the RSEB. In: ICSR, Washington, DC, USA (1998)
11. Kang, K.C., Kim, S., Lee, J., Kim, K., Shin, E., Huh, M.: FORM: A Feature-Oriented Reuse Method with Domain-Specific Reference Architectures. Ann. Softw. Eng. 5, 143–168 (1998)
12. Haugen, O., Moller-Pedersen, B., Oldevik, J., Olsen, G.K., Svendsen, A.: Adding standardized variability to domain specific languages. In: Software Product Line Conference, pp. 139–148 (2008)
13. Ramos, R., Barais, O., Jézéquel, J.M.: Matching model-snippets. In: Engels, G., Opdyke, B., Schmidt, D.C., Weil, F. (eds.) MODELS 2007. LNCS, vol. 4735, Springer, Heidelberg (2007)
14. Batory, D.S.: Feature models, grammars, and propositional formulas. In: Obbink, H., Pohl, K. (eds.) SPLC 2005. LNCS, vol. 3714, pp. 7–20. Springer, Heidelberg (2005)
15. PureSystems. Pure:: Variants Website (2006), `http://www.pure-systems.com/`
16. Czarnecki, K., Antkiewicz, M.: Mapping Features to Models: A Template Approach based on Superimposed Variants. In: Glück, R., Lowry, M. (eds.) GPCE 2005. LNCS, vol. 3676, pp. 422–437. Springer, Heidelberg (2005)
17. Benavides, D., Segura, S., Trinidad, P., Ruiz-Cortes, A.: FAMA: Tooling a framework for the automated analysis of feature models. In: Proceeding of the First International Workshop on Variability Modelling of Software-intensive Systems (VAMOS), pp. 129–134 (2007)
18. Metzger, A., Pohl, K., Heymans, P., Schobbens, P.-Y., Saval, G.: Disambiguating the documentation of variability in software product lines: A separation of concerns, formalization and automated analysis. In: IEEE Conference on Requirements Engineering, pp. 243–253. IEEE Computer Society, Los Alamitos (2007)
19. Muller, P.-A., Fleurey, F., Jézéquel, J.-M.: Weaving executability into object-oriented meta-languages. In: Briand, L.C., Williams, C. (eds.) MoDELS 2005. LNCS, vol. 3713, pp. 264–278. Springer, Heidelberg (2005)
20. Ziadi, T., Jézéquel, J.-M.: Product Line Engineering with the UML: Deriving Products. In: Families Research Book. Springer, Heidelberg (2006)
21. Voelter, M., Groher, I.: Product line implementation using aspect-oriented and model-driven software development. In: 11th International Software Product Line Conference, Kyoto, Japan, p. 10 (2007)

Automatic Domain Model Migration to Manage Metamodel Evolution

Anantha Narayanan, Tihamer Levendovszky, Daniel Balasubramanian, and Gabor Karsai

Vanderbilt University, Nashville TN 37235, USA
{ananth,tihamer,gabor,daniel}@isis.vanderbilt.edu

Abstract. Metamodel evolution is a significant problem in domain specific software development for several reasons. Domain-specific modeling languages (DSMLs) are likely to evolve much more frequently than programming languages and commonly used software formalisms, often resulting in a large number of valuable instance models that are no longer compliant with the metamodel. In this paper, we present the Model Change Language (MCL), aimed at satisfying these requirements.

1 The Model Change Language

The Model Change Language (MCL) defines a set of idioms and a composition approach for the specification of the migration rules that describe how the models compliant with the old metamodel should be migrated into models compliant with the new metamodel. The MCL also includes the UML class diagrams describing both the versions of the metamodel being evolved, and the migration rules may directly include classes and relations in these metamodels. MCL was defined using a MOF-compliant metamodel. For space reasons, we cannot show the entire metamodel, rather we introduce the language through examples. Note that MCL uses the metamodel of the base metamodeling language, and MCL diagrams model relationships between metamodel elements.

The basic pattern that describes a metamodel change, and the required model migration, consists of an LHS element from the old metamodel, an RHS element from the new metamodel, and a *MapsTo* relation between them (stating that the LHS type has "evolved" into the RHS type). The pattern may be extended by including other node types and edges into the migration rule. The node at the left of the *MapsTo* forms the context. The rest of the pattern is matched based on this context. Another special link, called the *WasMappedTo* link, in the pattern is used to match a node that was previously migrated, by an earlier migration rule. For the sake of flexibility, it is possible to specify additional mapping conditions or imperative commands along with the mapping. This basic pattern is extended based on various evolution criteria, as explained below. Figure 1 shows a simple migration rule with these rule elements. The main *MapsTo* portion is shown darkened, and the rest of the rule is grayed out for clarity.

The MCL rules can be used to specify most of the common metamodel evolution cases, and automate the migration of instance models necessitated by the evolution of the metamodel. The core syntax and semantics is rather simple.

A. Schürr and B. Selic (Eds.): MODELS 2009, LNCS 5795, pp. 706–711, 2009.

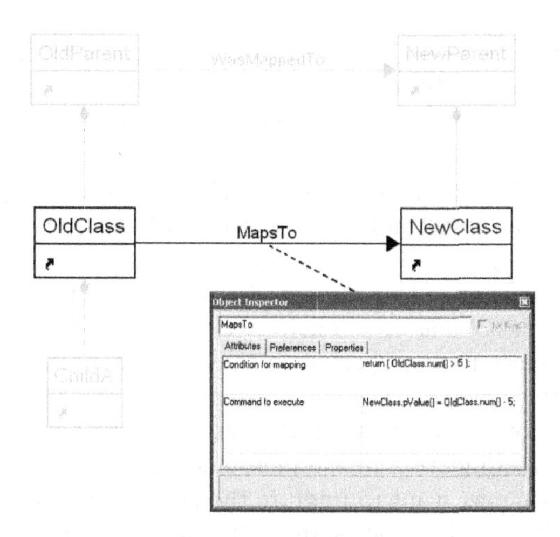

Fig. 1. MapsTo relation to specify mapping of classes

(a) Adding a new element (b) Deleting an element

Fig. 2. MCL rules for adding and deleting elements

A metamodel may be extended by adding a new concept into the language, such as a new class, a new association, or a new attribute. In most cases, old models are not affected by the new addition, and will continue to be conformant to the new language, except in certain cases. If the newly added element holds some model information some model information that was stored in a different element in the old version of the metamodel, the information must be appropriately preserved in the migrated models. In fact, this falls under the category of "modification" of representation, and is described further below.

If the newly added element plays a role in the well-formedness requirements, then the old models will no longer be well formed. The migration language must allow the migration of such models to make them well formed in the new metamodel. For instance, suppose that the domain designer adds a new model element called *Thread* within a *Component* - and adds a constraint that every *Component* must contain at least one *Thread*. The old models can then be migrated by creating a new *Thread* within each *Component*, as shown in Fig. 2(a). The LHS or 'old' portion of the MCL rule is shown in a greyed rectangle for clarity in this and all subsequent figures.

Another change to a metamodel may be the removal of an element. If a type is removed, and replaced by a different type, it implies a modification in the representation of existing information, and is handled further below. On certain occasions, elements may be removed completely, if that information is no longer relevant in the domain. In this case, their representations in the instance models must be removed. The removal of an element is specified by using a "NULL-Class" primitive in MCL, as shown in Fig. 2(b).

This implies that all instances of *ClassA* in the model are to be removed. Removal of an object may result in the loss of some other associations or contained objects.

The most common change to a metamodel is the modification of certain entities, such as the names of classes or their attributes. The basic *MapsTo* relation shown in Fig. 1 suffices to specify this change. The mapping of related objects is not affected by this rule. If other related items have also changed in the metamodel, their migration must be specified using additional rules.

Another type of modification in the metamodel is adding new sub-types to a class. In this case, we may want to migrate the class' instances to an instance of one of its sub-types. Fig. 3(a) shows an MCL rule that specifies this migration. The subtype to be instantiated may depend on certain conditions, such as the value of certain attributes in the instance (this is encoded within the migration rule using a Boolean condition for each possible mapping). The rule in Fig. 3(a) states that an instance of *srcClass* in the original model is replaced by an instance of *dstSubclass1* or *dstSubclass2* in the migrated model, or deleted altogether.

Local structural modifications are key issues in MCL. Some more complex evolution cases occur when changes in the metamodel require a change in the structure of the old models to make them conformant to the new metamodel. Consider a metamodel with a three level containment hierarchy, with a type *Class* contained in *Parent*, and *Parent* contained in *ParentParent*. Suppose that this metamodel is changed by moving *Class* to be directly contained under *ParentParent*. The intent of the migration may be to move all instances of *Class* up the hierarchy. The MCL rule to accomplish this is shown in Fig. 3(b) (the *WasMappedTo* link is used to identify a previously mapped parent instance).

Note that this rule only affects Class instances. The other entities remain as they are in the model. Any *Parent* instances within *ParentParent* remain unaffected. If *Class* contained other entities, they continue to remain within *Class*, unless modified by other MCL rules.

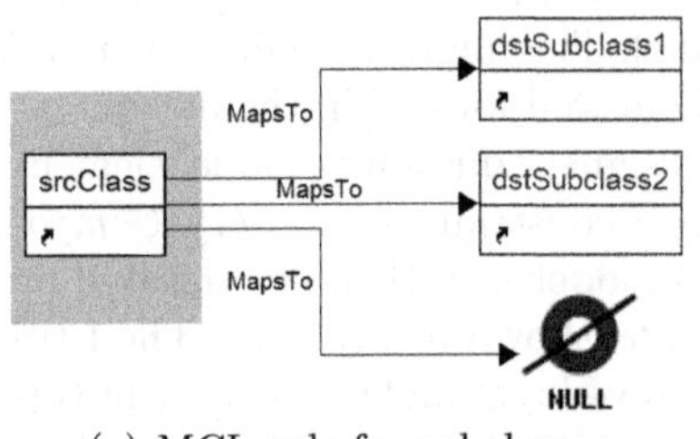

(a) MCL rule for subclasses

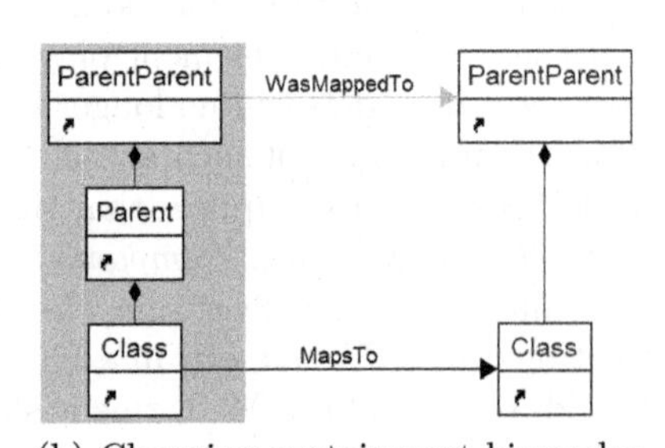

(b) Changing containment hierarchy

Fig. 3. MCL Rules

The execution of MCL rules has two main notions. (i) The rules are executed with depth first search. (ii) The execution of the rules that need previous results is delayed until those results have been available.

2 Related Work

Our work on model-migration has its origins in techniques for database schema evolution [1]. Drawing from experience in very large scale software evolution, [2] uses several examples to draw analogies between tradition programming language evolution and meta-model and model co-evolution. As opposed to providing a general transformation interface for the migrator[3], MCL provides a DSML as the specification language.

Using two industrial meta-models to analyze the types of common changes that occur during meta-model evolution, [4] gives a list of four major requirements that a model migration tool must fulfill in order to be considered effective. The first, reusing migration knowledge, is accomplished by the main MCL algorithm: meta-model independent changes are automatically deduced and migration code is automatically generated. Expressive, custom migrations are accomplished in MCL by (1) using the meta-models directly to describe the changes, and (2) allowing the user to write domain-specific code with a well-defined API. Our MCL tool also meets the last two requirements of [4]: MCL is modular in the sense that the specification of one migration rule does not affect other migration rules, and the history of the meta-model changes in persistent and available to migrate models at any point in time.

[5] performs model migration by first examining a difference model that records the evolution of the meta-model, and then producing ATL code that performs the model migration. Their tool uses the difference model to derive two model transformations in ATL. [5] does not specify exactly how the difference models are calculated, only that they can be obtained by using a tool such as EMFCompare or SiDiff. MCL, on the other hand, uses a difference model explicitly defined by the user, and uses its core algorithm to automatically deduce and resolve the breaking resolvable changes. Changes classified as breaking and unresolvable are also specified directly in the difference model, which makes dealing with unresolvable changes straightforward: the user defines a migration rule using a graphical notation that incorporates the two versions of the meta-model and uses a domain-specific C++ API for tasks such as querying and setting attribute values.

[6] describes the benefits of using a comparison algorithm for automatically detecting the changes between two versions of a meta-model. Rather than have the changes between meta-model versions defined explicitly by the user, they slightly modify the ChangeRecorder facility in the EMF tool set and use this to capture the changes as the user edits the meta-model. Their migration tool then generates a model migration in the Epsilon Transformation Language (ETL). In contrast to this, MCL allows the user to define complex migration rules with a straightforward graphical syntax, and then generates migration code to handle these rules and links it with the code produced by the main MCL algorithm.

[7] presents a language called COPE that allows a model migration to be decomposed into modular pieces. However, in [7], the meta-model changes must be specified programmatically, as opposed to MCL, in which the meta-model changes are defined using a straightforward graphical syntax.

Rather than manually changing meta-models, the work in [8] proposes the use of QVT relations for evolving meta-models and raises the issue of combining this with a method for co-adapting models. While this is an interesting idea, our MCL language uses an explicit change language to describe meta-model changes rather than model transformations.

3 Conclusions

The main contribution of MCL is a high-level visual language for describing metamodel evolution that is both powerful and easy to use for domain designers. It allows the domain designer to specify patterns that capture the intent of the metamodel evolution, as opposed to a mere syntactical difference. Our approach addresses the key requirements for a model evolution solution for DSMLs - we require only the specification of the changes to the metamodel, and automatically handle the portions that have not changed; we present a graphical language that can be used to specify complex relations between meta entities, and can be extended with imperative C++ conditions and commands for complex migration tasks; we use a visual language that closely relates to UML, the industrial scale language commonly used for specifying the metamodels, making the MCL easy to learn for domain designers.

Acknowledgment. This work was sponsored by DARPA, under its Software Producibility Program. The views and conclusions presented are those of the authors and should not be interpreted as representing official policies or endorsements of DARPA or the US government.

References

1. Banerjee, J., Kim, W., Kim, H.J., Korth, H.F.: Semantics and Implementation of Schema Evolution in Object-Oriented Databases. In: Proceedings of the Association for Computing Machinery Special Interest Group on Management of Data, pp. 311–322 (1987)
2. Favre, J.M.: Meta-models and Models Co-Evolution in the 3D Software Space. In: Proceedings of the International Workshop on Evolution of Large-scale Industrial Software Applications (ELISA) at ICSM (2003)
3. Sprinkle, J.: Metamodel Driven Model Migration. PhD thesis, Vanderbilt University, Nashville, TN 37203 (August 2003)
4. Herrmannsdoerfer, M., Benz, S., Jürgens, E.: Automatability of Coupled Evolution of Metamodels and Models in Practice. In: Czarnecki, K., Ober, I., Bruel, J.-M., Uhl, A., Völter, M. (eds.) MoDELS 2008. LNCS, vol. 5301, pp. 645–659. Springer, Heidelberg (2008)
5. Cicchetti, A., Ruscio, D.D., Eramo, R., Pierantonio, A.: Automating Co-evolution in Model-Driven Engineering. In: 12th International IEEE Enterprise Distributed Object Computing Conference, ECOC, pp. 222–231 (2008)

6. Gruschko, B., Kolovos, D.S., Paige, R.F.: Towards Synchronizing Models with Evolving Metamodels. In: Proceedings of the International Workshop on Model-Driven Software Evolution, MODSE (2007)
7. Herrmannsdoerfer, M., Benz, S., Juergens, E.: COPE: A Language for the Coupled Evolution of Metamodels and Models. In: MCCM Workshop at MoDELS (2009)
8. Wachsmuth, G.: Metamodel Adaptation and Model Co-adaptation. In: Ernst, E. (ed.) ECOOP 2007. LNCS, vol. 4609, pp. 600–624. Springer, Heidelberg (2007)

Model Transformation by Demonstration

Yu Sun[1], Jules White[2], and Jeff Gray[1]

[1] Dept. of Computer and Information Sciences, University of Alabama at Birmingham
{yusun,gray}@cis.uab.edu
[2] Institute for Software Integrated Systems, Vanderbilt University
jules@dre.vanderbilt.edu

Abstract. Model transformations provide a powerful capability to automate model refinements. However, the use of model transformation languages may present challenges to those who are unfamiliar with a specific transformation language. This paper presents an approach called model transformation by demonstration (MTBD), which allows an end-user to demonstrate the exact transformation desired by actually editing a source model and demonstrating the changes that evolve to a target model. An inference engine built into the underlying modeling tool records all editing operations and infers a transformation pattern, which can be reused in other models. The paper motivates the need for the approach and discusses the technical contributions of MTBD. A case study with several sample inferred transformations serves as a concrete example of the benefits of MTBD.

Keywords: Model transformation, Program inference, Refactoring.

1 Introduction

Model transformation is a core part of Domain-Specific Modeling (DSM) and plays an indispensible role in many applications of model engineering (e.g., code generation, model mapping and synchronization, model evolution, and reverse engineering [1]). The traditional way to implement model transformations is to use executable model transformation languages to specify the transformation rules and automate the transformation process [2]. However, the use of model transformation languages may present some challenges to users, particularly to those who are unfamiliar with a specific transformation language. Although declarative expressions are supported in most model transformation languages, the transformation rules are defined at the metamodel level, which requires a clear and deep understanding about the abstract syntax and semantic interrelationships between the source and target models. In some cases, certain domain concepts are hidden in the metamodel and difficult to unveil [3, 4]. These implicit concepts make writing transformation rules challenging. Moreover, a model transformation language may not be at the proper level of abstraction for an end-user and could result in a steep learning curve. One advantage of DSM is that by raising the level of abstraction, domain experts and non-programmers can become participants in software development. However, the difficulty of specifying metamodel-level rules and the associated learning curve may prevent domain experts from

A. Schürr and B. Selic (Eds.): MODELS 2009, LNCS 5795, pp. 712–726, 2009.

contributing to certain model transformation tasks from which they have much domain experience.

Model Transformation By Example (MTBE) is an innovative approach (first introduced in [5]) to address the challenges inherent from using model transformation languages. Instead of writing transformation rules manually, MTBE enables users to define a prototypical set of interrelated mappings between the source and target model instances, and then the metamodel-level transformation rules can be inferred and generated semi-automatically. In this context, users work directly at the model instance level and configure the mappings without knowing any details about the metamodel definition or the hidden concepts. With the semi-automatically generated rules, the simplicity of specifying model transformations is greatly improved.

The current state of MTBE research still has some limitations that may prevent it from being a widely used model transformation approach. The semi-automatic generation often leads to an iterative manual refinement of the generated rules; therefore, the model transformation designers may not be isolated completely from knowing the transformation languages and the metamodel definitions. In addition, the inference of transformation rules depends on the given sets of mapping examples. In order to get a complete and precise inference result, one or more representative examples must be available for users to setup the prototypical mappings, but seeding the process with such examples is not always an easy task in practice. Furthermore, current MTBE approaches focus on mapping the corresponding domain concepts between two different metamodels without handling complex attribute transformations. For instance, in practice, it is quite common to transform an attribute in the source model to another in the target model with some arithmetic or string operations, which is expressed by imperative transformation rules in some transformation languages. Unfortunately, these imperative expressions can only be added manually to the generated rules using current MTBE approaches.

To further simplify the model transformation process, we propose a new approach – Model Transformation By Demonstration (MTBD). Instead of the MTBE idea of inferring the rules from a prototypical set of mappings, users are asked to demonstrate how the model transformation should be done by directly editing (e.g., add, delete, connect, update) the model instance to simulate the model transformation process step by step. A recording and inference engine has been developed, as part of a prototype called MT-Scribe, to capture all user operations and infer a user's intention in a model transformation task. A transformation pattern is generated from the inference, specifying the precondition of the transformation and the sequence of operations needed to realize the transformation. This pattern can be reused by automatically matching the precondition in a new model instance and replaying the necessary operations to simulate the model transformation process.

We have successfully applied this approach to implement endogenous model transformations, where both the source and target models conform to the same metamodel. Our initial experience in using MTBD suggests improvement in the efficiency and simplicity of specifying model transformations. The current contributions of MTBD include the following:

- MTBD represents onc of the first attempts to simplify the specification of endogenous model transformations (in contrast to the exogenous focus of previous MTBE approaches), which offers improvement for automating model evolution activities (e.g., model refactoring, scaling, and aspect weaving).

- MTBD can be used to specify model transformations without the need to use a model transformation language. Furthermore, an end-user can describe a desired transformation task without detailed understanding of a specific metamodel.
- The current status of MT-Scribe includes: (1) a recording engine to completely capture all user operations and related context; (2) an algorithm to optimize the recorded operations, eliminating meaningless operations; (3) an algorithm to automatically match a transformation precondition in any model instance; (4) support to infer transformations with attribute operations; (5) a correctness checking and undo mechanism to guarantee the correctness of the transformation process; (6) fully automatic generation of a transformation pattern, without iterative manual refinement.

The rest of this paper is organized as follows. A motivating example is first given in Section 2. The paper demonstrates the concept of MTBD through two endogenous model transformation examples. Section 3 presents the overview and main steps of our approach, followed by an explanation of the technical implementation and algorithms through a running example in Section 4. An additional example is also given at the end of Section 4 to further illustrate the idea. Related transformation techniques are compared in Section 5, and Section 6 offers concluding remarks and summarizes future work.

2 MazeGame – A Motivating Example

This section introduces an endogenous transformation task in a simple modeling language called MazeGame. For the purpose of introducing MTBD, the MazeGame examples presented in this paper are simple transformation cases in a small domain. From the metamodel definition in Figure 1, a maze consists of rooms, which can be connected to each other. Each room can contain gold, a weapon or a monster with the `powerValue` attribute to specify the power. This modeling language is used to generate a textual game in Java, enabling players to type textual commands to move in the maze and collect all the gold without being killed by monsters. A model instance describes a specific maze configuration. Collecting weapons during game-play increases a player's power, which can be used to kill monsters. We constructed this metamodel in GEMS (Generic Eclipse Modeling System) [6]. A model instance is shown in Figure 2.

In the context of this domain, a transformation task can be specified as: for those rooms that contain gold and a weapon (the two unfolded rooms in Figure 2, Room2 and Room6), the transformation removes one gold piece, replaces the weapon with a monster, and sets the `powerValue` of the new monster to be half of the `powerValue` of the weapon being replaced. This transformation is used when the maze designer discovers that the number of monsters is far less than that of weapons, making the game too easy.

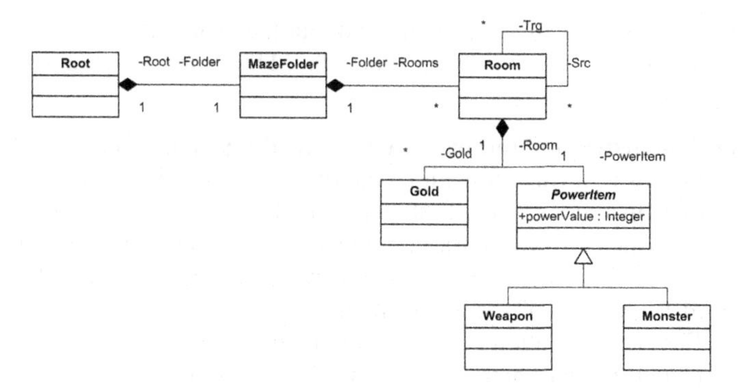

Fig. 1. The MazeGame metamodel

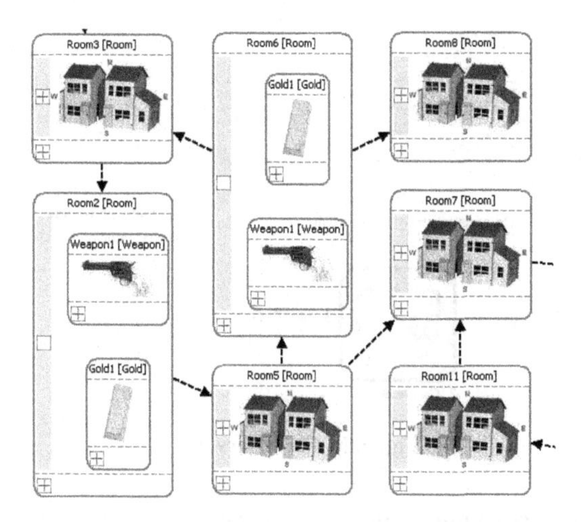

Fig. 2. Part of a MazeGame model instance

Some model transformation languages supporting endogenous transformation (e.g., ATL [7] and C-SAW [8]) can be used to complete this task by specifying the transformation rules. However, domain experts, or in this case, maze designers who have very little knowledge about computer science may find it challenging to learn a transformation language and understand the metamodel definition. To use MTBE, the appropriate source and target models are needed that fit the desired transformation task. Such examples may not be readily available and may require a large amount of time to create for large models. Also, the attribute modify operation (e.g., transforming the `powerValue` of the weapon) cannot be inferred and generated automatically by existing MTBE approaches.

3 Overview of MTBD

MTBD is motivated by the difficulties of learning new model transformation languages and understanding metamodel definitions, and the limitations of MTBE. By analyzing the recorded user operations, a transformation pattern can be inferred and then reused by automatic pattern matching without the availability of model transformation language support in a modeling tool. The MTBD process (Figure 3) consists of five main steps.

Step 1: User demonstration and operations recording. A user-recorded demonstration provides the base for transformation pattern analysis and inference, so accurately recording all user operations is the first step. The demonstration is given by directly editing a model instance (e.g., add a new model element or connection, modify the attribute of a model element) to simulate a transformation task. An event listener has been developed as part of MT-Scribe to monitor all the operations occurring in the model editor. For each operation that is captured, all the information about the operation is encapsulated into an object, similar to a Command pattern. Finally, the list of objects represents the sequence of operations needed to finish a transformation task.

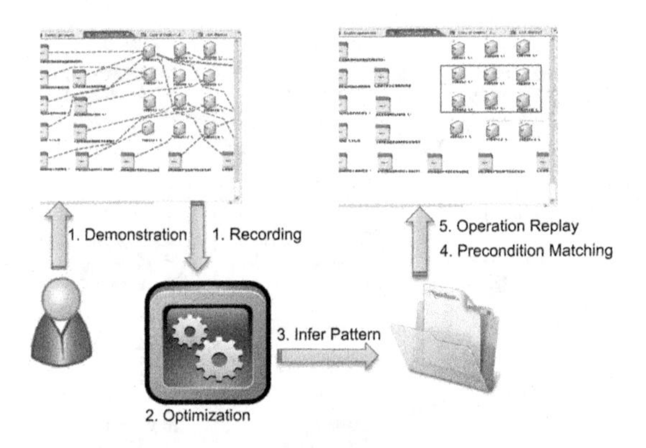

Fig. 3. MTBD overview

Step 2: Optimize recorded operations. The sequence of operations recorded directs how a transformation should be performed. However, not all operations are meaningful. For instance, without a careful design of the demonstration, it is possible that a user first adds a new element and modifies its attributes, and then deletes it in another operation; the result being that all the operations regarding this element actually did not take effect in the transformation process and therefore are meaningless. The presence of meaningless operations not only has the potential to make the inferred transformation preconditions inaccurate, but also exerts a negative influence on the efficiency of a transformation, especially when it executes on a large model instance. Thus, an optimization that eliminates all meaningless operations is automatically done after the recording.

Step 3: Infer the transformation pattern. Because our approach does not rely on a model transformation language, it is not necessary to generate specific transformation rules; instead, a general transformation pattern is inferred. This pattern describes the precondition of a transformation (i.e., where the transformation should be performed) and the actions of a transformation (i.e., how the transformation should be realized). By analyzing the recorded operations, the related meta-information of model elements and connections is extracted to construct the precondition, while the actions are specified by the operation sequence.

Step 4: Precondition matching. After a pattern is summarized, it can be reused and applied to any model instance from the same metamodel. By selecting a pattern from the repository, the MT-Scribe engine automatically traverses the model instance to search all locations that match the selected pattern. A notification is given if no matching locations are found. In MTBD, a matching location contains the necessary model elements and connections on which the recorded operations could be executed correctly.

Step 5: Replay operations and correctness checking. When a matching location is found, the recorded operations are replayed to transform the current model instance. The pattern matching step guarantees that operations can be executed with necessary operands. However, it does not ensure that executing them will not violate the metamodel. Therefore, each applied operation is logged and model instance correctness checking is performed after every operation execution. If a certain operation violates the metamodel definition, all executed operations are undone and the whole transformation replay is cancelled.

4 Technical Implementation and Algorithms Supporting MTBD

An Eclipse plug-in has been implemented in GEMS to realize the MTBD approach. To illustrate the usage and implementation of each step from Section 3, the process of inferring a user-demonstrated transformation is presented using the motivating example. A second MazeGame transformation is introduced to illustrate the idea further.

4.1 Demonstration of MTBD Using the MazeGame

GEMS provides an extension point to capture all events that occur during user interaction on a model instance. To infer a transformation pattern, the model editing operations performed by the user must be recorded. In GEMS, user operations can be classified into six categories. By filtering out unrelated events, all operations are recorded in sequence and stored as operation objects, with the necessary information encapsulated as listed in Table 1. The final list of operation objects serves as the fundamental knowledge base for the pattern inference and summary in later steps.

Table 1. Six types of recorded user operations

Operation Type	*Information Recorded*
Add an Element	Location of the parent element and its meta type The newly added element and its meta type
Remove an Element	Location of the element being removed and its meta type
Modify an Element	Location of the element being modified and its meta type The attribute name, the old value and the new value
Add a Connection	Location of the parent source and target elements and their meta types The newly added connection and its meta type
Remove a Connection	Location of the connection being modified and its meta type
Modify a Connection	Location of the connection being modified and its meta type The attribute name, the old value and the new value

To demonstrate the transformation in the motivating example from Section 2, a user must first find a room that contains a gold piece and a weapon. The four operations listed in Table 2 are performed during the user demonstration. The whole model changing process is shown in Figure 4. The remove and add operations in the first three steps are realized by the basic editing actions in the editor, and the fourth operation to modify the attribute is implemented by choosing the attribute from the attribute tree and specifying the arithmetic expression. When the `powerValue` of `weapon1` is chosen, its value (80) is displayed. A user may type " / 2" in the expression editor to identify the way that a numeric attribute is changed by a transformation. By clicking the evaluate button in the recording dialog, the final value for the attribute (40) is calculated and assigned to the current attribute being edited. As a result, the recording has defined this attribute operation as "`monster1.powerValue = weapon1.powerValue / 2`". In this way, constant values and formulas are typed directly, while referenced attributes are selected from the attribute tree. Attribute computation is therefore enabled in the user demonstration process using a real model instance, rather than at the metamodel level. This is currently impossible in most MTBE implementations.

Table 2. The sequence of operations demonstrated to realize motivating example

No.	*Operation*	*Information Recorded*
1	Remove Gold1	Location: Root1.MazeFolder1.Room2.Gold1 Meta type: Root.MazeFoler.Room.Gold
2	Remove Weapon1	Location: Root1.MazeFolder1.Room2.Weapon1 Meta type: Root.MazeFoler.Room.Weapon
3	Add a Monster	Location: Root1.MazeFolder1.Room2 Meta type: Root.MazeFoler.Room New element: Monster1 Meta Type: Monster
4	Modify Monster1	Location: Root1.MazeFolder1.Room2.Monster1 Meta type: Root.MazeFolder.Room.Monster Attribute: powerValue Old value: 0 New value: Weapon1 / 2

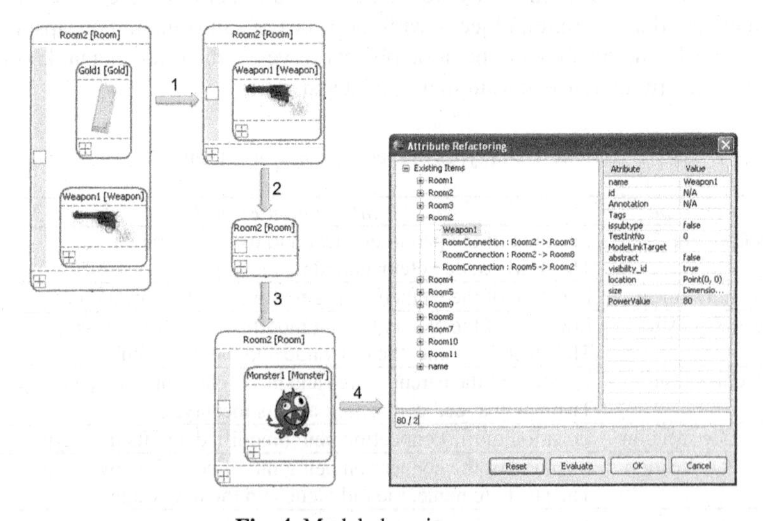

Fig. 4. Model changing process

Algorithm 1. Optimize Operation List

```
for each op in the input operation list
 switch (op.type)
   case ADD_ELEM:
     for each op_temp after the current op in the list
       if op_temp.type == REMOVE_ELEM and op_temp removes what op added
         then remove both op and op_temp from the list
     end for
   case MODIFY_ELEM:
     traverse the final model instance and search the element being modified
     if not found then remove op from the list
     if found then compare the attribute value with the value stored in op
       if different then remove op from the list
   case ADD_CONN:
     for each op_temp after the current op in the list
       if op_temp.type == REMOVE_CONN and op_temp removes what op added
         then remove both op and op_temp from the list
     end for
   case MODIFY_CONN:
     traverse the final model instance and search the connection being modified
     if not found then remove op from opList
     if found then compare its attribute value with the value stored in op
       if different then remove op from opList
end for
```

Given the final list of recorded operations and the final model instance after user demonstration, an optimization phase that removes meaningless operations is performed by analyzing each operation in the list of recorded operations. The optimization algorithm is given in Algorithm 1. Based on the optimized operation list, the transformation pattern is inferred. Because no transformation language is used in the inference, the result is called a transformation pattern rather than a transformation rule (Please note: we can also generate concrete transformation rules from the inferred pattern). A transformation pattern consists of a precondition and the transformation actions.

Table 3. Model object list in precondition

elem1.elem2.elem3.elem4
elem1.elem2.elem3.elem5
elem1.elem2.elem3 (elem6)
elem1.elem2.elem3.elem6

Table 4. Model objects type table

Model Object	Meta Type
elem1	Root
elem2	MazeFolder
elem3	Room
elem4	Gold
elem5	Weapon
elem6	Monster

Table 3 and Table 4 together specify the precondition of the example inferred from the operation list, i.e., all the rooms that contain a gold piece and a weapon. The inference is accomplished by extracting the meta information of the recorded operations and generalizing them. In Table 3, elem6 in parenthesis denotes a newly added element. Instead of the specific IDs in the recorded operations, generic names with a meta type mapping table are used to describe the precondition. This precondition guarantees that the operations could be executed correctly with sufficient operands. To implement more powerful transformations, more complex preconditions need to be enabled, which are mentioned in Section 6. Table 5 gives the actions as recorded operations with generic element names. The summarized transformation pattern is serialized and stored in a pattern repository.

Table 5. Transformation actions with generic element names

Remove elem4 from elem3
Remove elem5 from elem3
Add elem6 in elem3
Modify elem6: elem6.powerValue = elem5.powerValue / 2

To apply a reusable transformation to a model instance, a pattern is selected from the repository and applied to a portion of the model instance. The MTBD plug-in will traverse the model instance and find all locations that match the precondition in the pattern. The backtracking algorithm (Algorithm 2) is used in the matching process. To enable more flexible matching in the model instance, two matching modes are supported. The default mode traverses the whole model instance to search all locations that match the precondition. A customized mode assists users in selecting parts of the model instance to traverse. In either mode, the MTBD plug-in reports if no locations are matched on a specific model instance.

After a precondition is matched to a location in the model instance, the transformation operations will be replayed automatically in sequence to realize the transformation process. Because an operation is implemented by low-level APIs provided by GEMS, an operation might be executed without consideration by the model correctness checking mechanism in the model editor. The possible result is a metamodel violation (e.g., if an operation is to add a monster in a room, it can still be replayed in a room even if a monster already exists, but at most one monster is allowed to be in a room according to the metamodel). To ensure a correct transformation, the model correctness checking is done after replaying each operation by calling the GEMS model checking module. Each replay is also logged in a stack, so that if a violation occurs, the replayed operations can be undone and rolled back to restore the original model instance.

Algorithm 2. Precondition Matching

```
initialize a candidate object list of all the elements and connections in the selected model instance
for each entry e in the model object list
   for each obj in the candidate object list
      if obj matches e then assign obj to e and break
      if obj does not match e then continue
   end for
   if e is assigned and is the last entry in the list then matching succeeds
   if e has not been assign then backtrack the previous e and try again
   if no further backtracking is allowed then matching fails
end for
```

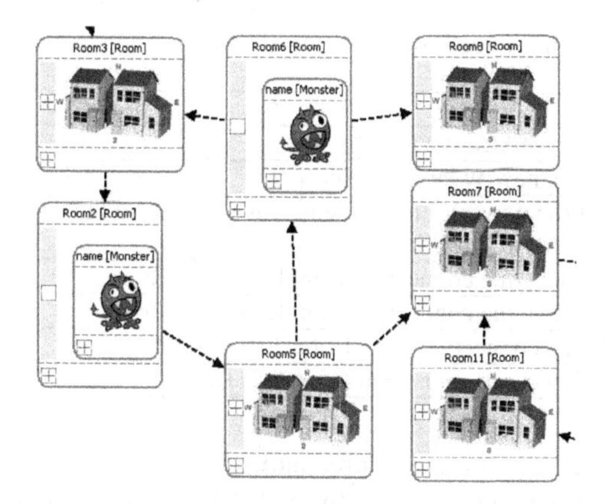

Fig. 5. Part of the model instance after the transformation

Figure 5 shows part of the model instance after applying the transformation pattern example in a MazeGame model instance. The gold piece is removed and the weapon is replaced with a monster whose `powerValue` is half as before. The whole process with more detailed information can be viewed as a video on the project website [22].

4.2 Another Transformation Example: Balancing Game Play

A perfect maze game has a balance of power between monsters and weapons, so winning a game should be neither too easy nor too hard. To make the motivating example more difficult to play, a weapon is replaced with a monster if it is in a room together with a gold piece, so that getting a piece of gold first requires killing a monster. In some other cases, the game may accidentally become too difficult. For example, sometimes monsters appear in a sequence of rooms and the consequence is that a player will encounter several monsters in a row. Figure 6 (left) shows a part of a maze where three rooms connected with each other all contain a monster. To balance the power, it is necessary to replace the monster in the third room with a weapon, and the `powerValue` of the weapon defined as the sum of the monsters in the first two rooms. In addition, to avoid encountering three monsters in a row, it is necessary to reconnect the rooms so that the first monster room connects to the third weapon room, which then connects to the second monster room, as shown in Figure 6 (right). Table 6 indicates the operations needed for this transformation.

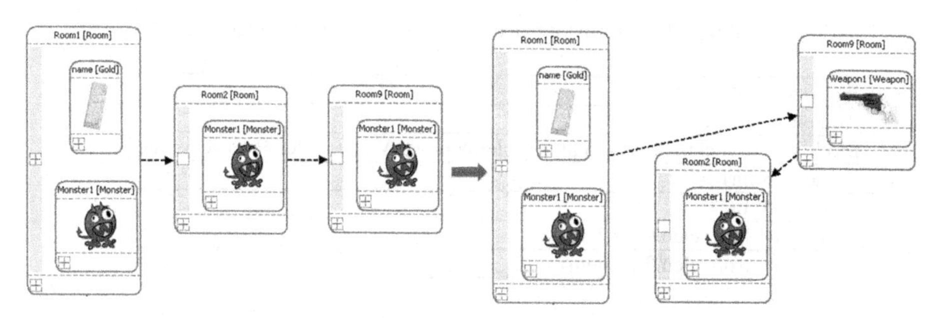

Fig. 6. Avoid encountering three monsters in a row

Table 6. The sequence of operations demonstrated to avoid three monsters in a row

No.	*Operation*
1	Remove Monster1 in Room 9
2	Add a new Weapon in Room 9
3	Set the powerValue of the new weapon to be the sum of two monsters in Room1 and Room2
4	Remove the connection from Room1 to Room2
5	Remove the connection from Room2 to Room9
6	Add a connection from Room1 to Room9
7	Add a connection from Room9 to Room2

The final generated transformation precondition is shown in Tables 7 and 8, representing all three rooms connected one-by-one with each containing a monster. The stored transformation actions are listed in Table 9. Even though this is a very simple case study, the transformation of `powerValue` in this example transformation cannot be accomplished by MTBE, which mainly focuses on direct concept mappings. Our MTBD approach provides an opportunity to define a computation used within a transformation.

Table 7. Model object list in precondition

elem1.elem2.elem3.elem4
elem1.elem2.elem3 (elem5)
elem1.elem2.elem6.elem8
elem1.elem2.elem7.elem9
elem1.elem2.conn1:elem6->elem7
elem1.elem2.conn2:elem7->elem3
elem1.elem2(conn3:elem6->elem3)
elem1.elem2(conn4:elem3->elem7)

Table 8. Model objects type table

Model Object	Meta Type
elem1	Root
elem2	MazeFolder
elem3	Room
elem4	Monster
elem5	Weapon
elem6	Room
elem7	Room
elem8	Monster
elem9	Monster
conn1	RoomConnection
conn2	RoomConnection
conn3	RoomConnection
conn4	RoomConnection

Table 9. Transformation actions with generic element names

Remove elem4 from elem3
Add elem5 in elem3
Modify elem5: elem5.powerValue = elem8.powerValue + elem9.powerValue
Remove conn1
Remove conn2
Add conn3 from elem6 to elem3
Add conn4 from elem3 to elem7

5 Related Work in Model Transformation Inference

MTBD aims to simplify implementation of model transformation tasks, following the similar direction of MTBE approaches. Balogh and Varró introduced MTBE by using inductive logic programming [9, 10]. The idea is to generate graph transformation rules from a set of user-defined mappings between the source and target model instances by applying an inductive logic engine. Similarly, Strommer and Wimmer implemented an Eclipse prototype to enable generation of ATL rules from the semantic mappings between domain models [11, 12]. Both approaches provide semi-automatic generation of model transformation rules, which need further refinement by a user. Because both approaches are based on semantic mappings, they are more appropriate in the context of exogenous model transformations between two different metamodels. However, the generation of rules to transform attributes is not well supported in most MTBE implementations.

MTBD and MTBE are actually extensions of the "by-example" concept. Query-by-example [13] provides a graphical query interface to enable users to use visual tables to specify example query elements and conditions. A similar idea to our approach is called programming-by-example [14, 15], which is used to infer new behaviors by demonstrating the actions on concrete examples. In addition, the "by-example" idea has also been applied to XML document transformation [16]. XML schema transformers can be derived from examples, which then generate XSLT code to transform XML documents.

Although our contribution focuses on model transformations, a similar work has been done to carry out program transformations by demonstration [17]. To perform a program transformation, users first manually change a concrete program example, and all the changes will be recorded by the monitoring plug-in. Then, the recorded changes will be generalized in a transformation. After editing and specifying the generated transformation, it can be applied to other source code locations. Although it also supports the specification of how variable values are computed, it is in a separate step with much manual editing involved. MTBD automates this step in the demonstration process and is focused on demonstrating changes on model instances, not source code.

6 Conclusion and Future Work

This paper introduces a new approach to simplify model transformation tasks, which does not rely on any model transformation language or the understanding of a specific metamodel. To avoid iterative user refinements after the generation process, we made the process fully automated by enabling users to demonstrate not only the transformation precondition, but also the transformation actions, including attribute computations. The generated transformation patterns are stored in a repository, which can be applied to any model instance in the same metamodel from which the transformation was recorded. A complete Eclipse plug-in for GEMS, called MT-Scribe, has been developed to implement the MTDB approach. The examples presented in this paper are simple transformation cases in a small domain, which are used to focus on the MTBD approach. The examples also illustrate the type of challenges that are encountered when using the direct mapping approach of most MTBE implementations. The current implementation can also carry out other complex transformations in practical domains, such as UML refactoring. More details and examples about MTBD, including video demonstrations, are available at [22]. The MTBD idea can be applied to improve many model evolution tasks, such as:

- **Model refactoring.** Like program refactoring, model refactoring improves the internal structure of a system model without changing its external behavior. The traditional approach is to use a model transformation engine with a refactoring language [18]. The current version of MTBD can be used to support model refactoring. MTBD allows end-users to build a set of reusable refactorings that are domain-specific.
- **Aspect-Oriented Modeling (AOM).** AOM addresses crosscutting concerns in models by separating each concern and weaving it within a base model. Aspects can be defined by using either a textual constraint language [19] or graphical modeling language [20]. MTBD can also be applied to automate AOM, with preconditions representing pointcuts and the transformation actions corresponding to advice.
- **Model scalability.** A model transformation engine can be used to scale model instances, such as the replicators implemented in [21]. Instead of specifying scaling rules, users can demonstrate the scaling process by using MTBD.

We believe that MTBD can also be used in exogenous model transformations. In a modeling environment where editing two model instances from two different domains are allowed, users can edit the source model and change it to the desirable target model. Then the transformation pattern or rules could be inferred from the editing operations, which is our future main focus.

In the current version of MT-Scribe, one limitation is that only the basic or the weakest precondition can be inferred. For instance, in the motivating example, the precondition is all the rooms that contain at least one gold piece and one weapon. However, it is impossible to further restrict it to only the rooms with more than two connections and the `powerValue` of the contained weapon is more than 100. This inflexibility of specifying preconditions exerts a negative influence on the power of MTBD. To enable more powerful precondition definitions, we will implement one more step to ask users to demonstrate the precondition as well. Users will be asked to select the model objects in the editor and setup the conditions that need to be satisfied.

Furthermore, the attribute operations currently supported are only basic arithmetic operations and string concatenation. However, more powerful operations and functions (e.g., `max()` and `min()`) are available in some model transformation languages. Hence, to make MTBD more practical, these additional attribute operations should be supported in the demonstration process.

Acknowledgement. This work was supported by NSF CAREER award CCF-0643725.

References

1. Czarnecki, K., Helsen, S.: Feature-based survey of model transformation approaches. IBM Systems Journal 45(3), 621–645 (2006)
2. Sendall, S., Kozaczynski, W.: Model transformation - The heart and soul of model-driven software development. IEEE Software, Special Issue on Model Driven Software Development 20(5), 42–45 (2003)
3. Wimmer, M., Strommer, M., Kargl, H., Kramler, G.: Towards model transformation generation by-example. In: Proceedings of the 40th Hawaii International Conference on Systems Science, Big Island, HI, January 2007, p. 285 (2007)
4. Kappel, G., Kapsammer, E., Kargl, H., Kramler, G., Reiter, T., Retschitzegger, W., Schwinger, W., Wimmer, M.: Lifting metamodels to ontologies - a step to the semantic integration of modeling languages. In: Proceedings of International Conference on Model Driven Engineering Languages and Systems, Genova, Italy, October 2006, pp. 528–542 (2006)
5. Varró, D.: Model transformation by example. In: Proceedings of Model Driven Engineering Languages and Systems, Genova, Italy, October 2006, pp. 410–424 (2006)
6. Generic Eclipse Modeling System (GEMS), `http://www.eclipse.org/gmt/gems/`
7. Jouault, F., Allilaire, F., Bézivin, J., Kurtev, I.: ATL: A model transformation tool. Science of Computer Programming 72(1/2), 31–39 (2008)
8. Gray, J., Lin, Y., Zhang, J.: Automating change evolution in model-driven engineering. IEEE Computer, Special Issue on Model-Driven Engineering 39(2), 51–58 (2006)
9. Balogh, Z., Varró, D.: Model transformation by example using inductive logic programming. In: Software and Systems Modeling. Springer, Heidelberg (2009)
10. Varró, D., Balogh, Z.: Automating model transformation by example using inductive logic programming. In: Proceedings of the 2007 ACM Symposium on Applied Computing, Seoul, Korea, March 2007, pp. 978–984 (2007)
11. Strommer, M., Wimmer, M.: A framework for model transformation by-example: Concepts and tool support. In: Proceedings of the 46th International Conference on Technology of Object-Oriented Languages and Systems, Zurich, Switzerland, July 2008, pp. 372–391 (2008)
12. Strommer, M., Murzek, M., Wimmer, M.: Applying model transformation by-example on business process modeling languages. In: Proceedings of Third International Workshop on Foundations and Practices of UML, Auckland, New Zealand, November 2007, pp. 116–125 (2007)
13. Zloof, M.: Query-By-Example: The invocation and definition of tables and terms. In: Proceedings of International Conference on Very Large Data Bases, Framingham, Massachusetts, 1975, pp. 1–24 (1975)
14. Cypher, A. (ed.): Watch what I do: Programming by demonstration. MIT Press, Cambridge (1993)
15. Lieberman, H.: Special issue on Programming by example. Communication of ACM 43(3), 72–114 (2000)
16. Lechner, S., Schrefl, M.: Defining web schema transformers by example. In: Mařík, V., Štěpánková, O., Retschitzegger, W. (eds.) DEXA 2003. LNCS, vol. 2736, pp. 46–56. Springer, Heidelberg (2003)
17. Robbes, R., Lanza, M.: Example-based program transformation. In: Proceedings of the 11th International Conference on Model Driven Engineering Languages and Systems, Toulouse, France, October 2008, pp. 174–188 (2008)

18. Zhang, J., Lin, Y., Gray, J.: Generic and domain-specific model refactoring using a model transformation engine. In: Model-driven Software Development, ch. 9, pp. 199–218. Springer, Heidelberg (2005)
19. Zhang, J., Cottenier, T., Berg, A., Gray, J.: Aspect composition in the Motorola aspect-oriented modeling weaver. Journal of Object Technology, Special Issue on Aspect-Oriented Modeling 6(7), 89–108 (2007)
20. Balasubramanian, K., Gokhale, A., Lin, Y., Zhang, J., Gray, J.: Weaving deployment aspects into domain-specific models. International Journal on Software Engineering and Knowledge Engineering, Special Issue on Aspect-Oriented Modeling 16(3), 403–424 (2006)
21. Gray, J., Lin, Y., Zhang, J., Nordstrom, S., Gokhale, A., Neema, S., Gokhale, S.: Replicators: Transformations to address model scalability. In: Proceedings of Model Driven Engineering Languages and Systems, Montego Bay, Jamaica, October 2005, pp. 295–308 (2005)
22. MTBD Project Page, `http://www.cis.uab.edu/softcom/mtbd`

Reviving QVT Relations: Model-Based Debugging Using Colored Petri Nets*

Manuel Wimmer[1], Angelika Kusel[2], Johannes Schoenboeck[1], Gerti Kappel[1], Werner Retschitzegger[3], and Wieland Schwinger[2]

[1] Vienna University of Technology, Austria
{wimmer,schoenboeck,kappel}@big.tuwien.ac.at
[2] Johannes Kepler University Linz, Austria
kusel@bioinf.jku.at, wieland.schwinger@jku.ac.at
[3] University of Vienna, Austria
werner.retschitzegger@univie.ac.at

Abstract. The standardized QVT Relations language, one cornerstone of Model-Driven Architecture (MDA), has not yet gained widespread use in practice, not least due to missing tool support in general and inadequate debugging support in particular. Transformation engines interpreting QVT Relations operate on a low level of abstraction, hide the operational semantics of a transformation and scatter metamodels, models, QVT code, and traces across different artifacts. We propose a model-based debugger representing QVT Relations on bases of TROPIC, a model transformation framework which utilizes a variant of Colored Petri Nets (CPNs) providing an explicit runtime model and a homogenous view on all artifacts of a transformation.

Keywords: QVT Relations, Debugging, Model Transformations, CPN.

1 Introduction

In the MDA paradigm, model transformation languages play a vital role, leading already to the standardization of the Query/View/Transformation (QVT) language [1]. Especially for declarative transformation languages, such as QVT Relations, appropriate debugging facilities are of outermost importance, as is also the case for declarative languages in general, since the missing operational semantics hampers observation, tracking and fixing of bugs [2]. Existing approaches for executing and debugging QVT Relations (e.g., mediniQVT[1]) are still in its infancy [3] and often provide only low-level debugging information such as logging messages or variable values, hide the execution order of transformation rules and scatter metamodels, models, rules and traces across different artifacts.

We propose a model-based debugger [4] representing QVT Relations on bases of TROPIC (Transformations on Petri Nets in Color) [5,6], a model transformation framework based on Colored Petri Nets (CPNs) [7], adapted to the needs of

* This work has been partly funded by the Austrian Science Fund (FWF) under grant P21374-N13.

[1] http://projects.ikv.de/qvt

A. Schürr and B. Selic (Eds.): MODELS 2009, LNCS 5795, pp. 727–732, 2009.

transformation designers [8]. With this, firstly, an explicit runtime model is provided, which can be easily exploited for debugging purposes, e.g., by using OCL queries, thus representing a white-box view on the transformation. Secondly, a homogenous view on all transformation artifacts is ensured by representing them in terms of the basic CPN concepts places, tokens and transitions.

The remainder of this paper is structured as follows. Section 2 introduces the basics of QVT Relations and TROPIC as well as of the translation in between. Section 3 introduces an interactive debugging environment offering several features for model-based debugging of transformations and finally, Section 4 provides an outlook on future work.

2 QVT Relations and TROPIC at a Glance

This section briefly illustrates the main language concepts of QVT Relations and TROPIC for describing transformation logic, details their main differences on the execution level and discusses the design rationale of the translation between the language concepts.

QVT Relations. Using QVT Relations, transformation logic between two different metamodels is specified as a set of relations that must hold for the transformation to be successful. Relations contain a set of so-called *DomainPatterns* used to match for existing source model elements in order to instantiate new target model elements or to modify existing ones. During execution of a transformation by an engine (cf. left part of Fig. 1) trace information is available in order to verify the transformation result, only, leaving the full operational semantics within in a black box.

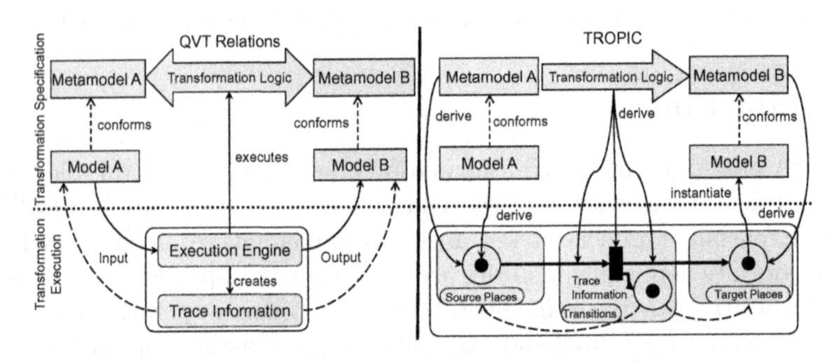

Fig. 1. Model Transformations in QVT Relations and TROPIC

TROPIC. TROPIC uses Colored Petri Net concepts [7], being mainly *places*, *tokens* and *transitions*, for the specification and execution of model transformations. In particular, places are derived from elements of metamodels, tokens from elements of models and transitions from the actual transformation logic (shown in the right part of Fig. 1). The existence of certain model elements allows transitions to fire and thus stream tokens to the target places representing instances of the target metamodel to be created and thereby establishing trace information in terms of tokens in additional places. TROPIC, thus, provides a white-box view on model transformation execution, i.e., the specification does not need to be translated into some low-level executable artifact, but can be executed right away. Therefore, no impedance mismatch between specification and execution occurs, allowing for enhanced debuggability of model transformations.

Translation between QVT Relations and TROPIC. The translation between the concepts of QVT Relations and TROPIC has been performed on basis of their metamodels. We assume a syntactically correct QVT Relations specification since only in this case we can guarantee a correct translation to TROPIC and the propagation of changes in the transformation logic represented by TROPIC back to QVT Relations. Whereas QVT Relations only references the metamodel files, TROPIC explicitly represents each element of the metamodels as first class concept in terms of places. Regarding models, QVT Relations provides no explicit representation mechanism, which is again in contrast to TROPIC, where each model element is explicitly represented by tokens residing in corresponding places. Finally, in the textual syntax of QVT Relations the correspondences between source elements and target elements as well as the interplay among different relations are hard to grasp. TROPIC on the other hand visualizes these correspondences as well as the interplay among the relations utilizing transitions consisting of a LHS representing the pre-conditions of a certain transformation, and a RHS depicting its post-condition by means of color patterns. For further details on this translation it is referred to [9].

3 Debugging Environment for QVT Relations

Our debugging environment is based on Eclipse and includes two editors, one that presents the QVT Relations in textual syntax (cf. Fig. 2a) and another one that shows the graphical representation thereof in TROPIC (cf. Fig. 2b). The TROPIC editor toolbar (cf. Fig. 2c) provides common debugging functionalities to figure out the operational semantics such as stepwise debugging by firing transitions including an undo/redo mechanism. Furthermore, functionalities are provided to save the generated target model, i.e., to switch from the token representation to a model representation, or to load a new source model into the debugging environment.

OCL for Debugging. The utilization of a dedicated runtime model allows to employ OCL for two different debugging purposes. Firstly, OCL can be used to define conditional breakpoints at different levels of granularity, e.g., if a certain token is streamed into a certain place, or if tokens occur in several different places. Secondly, OCL can be used to tackle the well-known debugging problem that programs execute forward in time whereas programmers must reason backwards in time to find the origin of a bug. For this, a dedicated debugging console based on the *Interactive OCL Console* of Eclipse (cf. Fig. 2d) is supported, providing several pre-defined debugging functions to explore and to understand the history of a transformation by determining and tracking paths of produced tokens (exemplarily shown in Table 1).

Table 1. OCL operations for debugging

Context	QCL Debugging Operation	Description
Place	`getMatchingTokens:Set(Token)`	tokens that match a transition
	`getMismatchedTokens:Set(Token)`	tokens not matching a transition
Token	`getCreator:Transition`	transition that created a token
Transition	`getInputTokens(Token):Set(Token)`	source tokens of a transition

Debugging Phases. In the following a possible usage scenario of our debugging environment is described according to the three debugging phases, observing facts, tracking origins and fixing bugs (cf. Fig. 2).

Observing Facts. Observing facts during a certain transformation execution can be done either by simulating the transformation and watch for unexpected behavior or by debugging the transformation step-by-step. In order to detect unexpected behavior automatically, the resulting target model can be compared to an expected target model to identify wrong or missing target tokens. If such faulty parts of the target model are detected, the owning target places as well as the transitions that produce tokens in these places are highlighted to ease finding the reasons for the errors (cf. indicated by exclamation marks in Fig. 2).

Tracking Origins. The origin of an error has to be discovered by reasoning backwards in time, questioning, e.g., why certain tokens have been created.

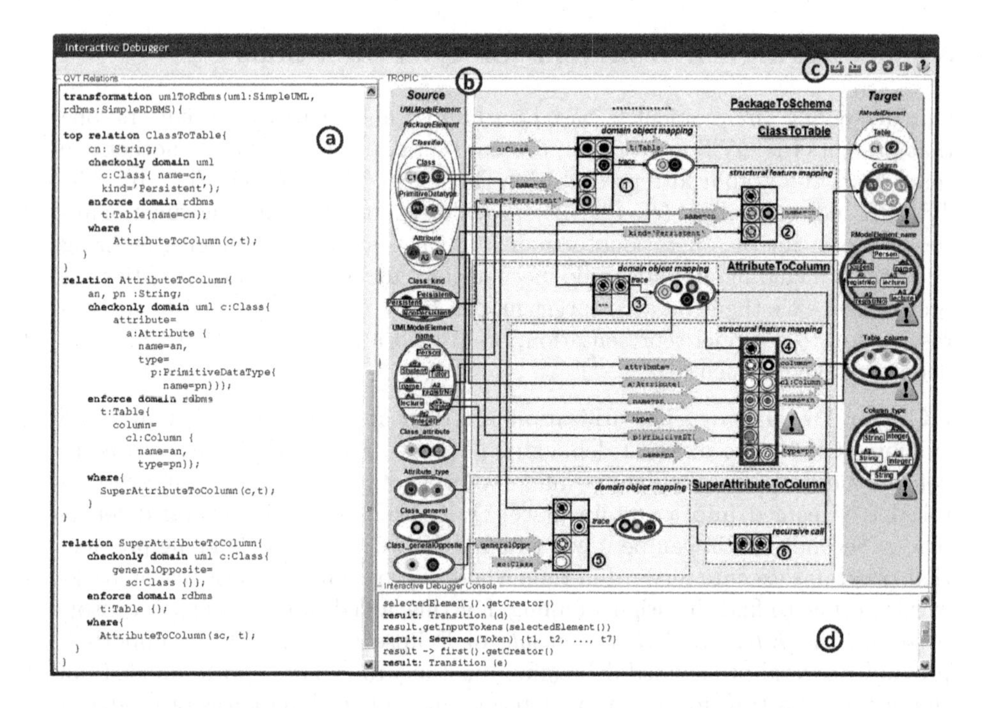

Fig. 2. Debugging Environment showing parts of the UML2Relational Example [1]

The graphical representation in Fig. 2 shows that the tokens in question have been created by transition 4, the source tokens responsible for creating exactly these tokens, however, are unknown. The paths of these produced tokens can be tracked back by means of our predefined OCL functions.

Fixing Bugs. After finding the origins of a bug, it is possible to adapt the transformation logic during debugging directly in TROPIC and propagate the changes back to QVT Relations.

4 Further Work

Several issues for future work remain open. As stated in [10], the QVT standard defines the operational semantics of QVT Relations twofold and only informally, firstly in natural language and secondly by a translation to QVT Core, being incompatible to each other. This situation led to different implementations of the operational semantics in different tools. Currently, our translation is based on the implementation of mediniQVT, but we are planning to investigate the implementations of different tools. Additionally, as TROPIC is based on a variant of CPNs we will explore if Petri Net properties such as persistence or liveness can be used to check for potential shortcomings in QVT Relations specifications.

References

1. Object Management Group: Meta Object Facility (MOF) 2.0 Query/View/ Transformation Specification (2007), `http://www.omg.org/docs/ptc/07-07-07.pdf`
2. Wadler, P.: Why no one uses functional languages. SIGPLAN Not. 33(8), 23–27 (1998)
3. Kurtev, I.: State of the Art of QVT: A Model Transformation Language Standard. In: Int. Workshop on Applications of Graph Transformation with Industrial Relevance (2007)
4. Kusel, A., Schwinger, W., Wimmer, M., Retschitzegger, W.: Common Pitfalls of Using QVT Relations - Graphical Debugging as Remedy. In: Int. Workshop on UML and AADL @ ICECCS 2009 (2009)
5. Reiter, T., Wimmer, M., Kargl, H.: Towards a runtime model based on colored Petri nets for the execution of model transformations. In: 3rd Workshop on Models and Aspects @ ECOOP 2007, Berlin (2007)
6. Wimmer, M., Kusel, A., Reiter, T., Retschitzegger, W., Schwinger, W., Kappel, G.: Lost in Translation? Transformation Nets to the Rescue!. In: 8th Int. Conf. on Information Systems Technology and its Applications (UNISCON 2009), Sydney (2009)
7. Jensen, K., Kristensen, L.M.: Coloured Petri Nets - Modeling and Validation of Concurrent Systems. Springer, Heidelberg (2009)

8. Wimmer, M., Kusel, A., Schoenboeck, J., Reiter, T., Retschitzegger, W., Schwinger, W.: Let's Play the Token Game – Model Transformations Powered by Transformation Nets. In: Proc. of Int. Workshop on Petri Nets and Software Engineering, Paris (2009)
9. Wimmer, M., Kusel, A., Schoenboeck, J., Kappel, G., Retschitzegger, W., Schwinger, W.: A Petri Net based Debugging Environment for QVT Relations. Technical report, Vienna University of Technology (2009)
10. Stevens, P.: A simple game-theoretic approach to checkonly QVT Relations. In: Paige, R.F. (ed.) ICMT 2009. LNCS, vol. 5563, pp. 165–180. Springer, Heidelberg (2009)

Incremental Development of Model Transformation Chains Using Automated Testing*

Jochen M. Küster, Thomas Gschwind, and Olaf Zimmermann

IBM Zurich Research Laboratory, Säumerstr. 4, 8803 Rüschlikon, Switzerland
{jku,thg,olz}@zurich.ibm.com

Abstract. Model transformations are a key technique in model-driven engineering. If several transformations are composed into a model transformation chain, an approach is needed that allows software engineers to incrementally improve the quality of the model transformation chain. In this paper, we propose incremental development of model transformation chains based on automated testing. We present four test design techniques and a test framework architecture for testing transformation chains and report on the validation of our approach when developing a transformation chain for model version management.

Keywords: Model transformation, automated testing.

1 Introduction

Model transformations are nowadays used in model-driven engineering for model refinement, model abstraction, and code generation. Model transformations can either be implemented directly in a programming languages (such as Java^{TM}) or using one of the available transformation languages that have been developed in recent years (e.g. [1,2,3]). For complex transformation problems, several model transformations can be composed into a model transformation chain [4] that enables reuse, distributed development and isolated testing of individual model transformations.

Systematic development of high-quality model transformations becomes an important issue for wide-spread adoption of solutions incorporating model transformations. To ensure high quality of model transformations, existing software engineering techniques for improving software quality [5], such as requirements analysis, modeling, automated testing and formal verification, can be applied over the development life cycle of model transformations. As model transformations are a relatively new paradigm in software engineering, existing techniques must be adapted and possibly extended to take into account characteristics of model transformations.

Existing work is primarily concerned with testing of model transformations (see [6] for an overview), where one key challenge is the construction of 'interesting' test cases that show the presence of defects. For black-box testing of model transformations, the meta model of the input language of the transformation can be used to systematically generate a large set of test cases [7,8,9]. For gray-box testing, also transformation rules can be taken into account [10]. With regards to model transformation chains, testing

* Empirical results category paper.

A. Schürr and B. Selic (Eds.): MODELS 2009, LNCS 5795, pp. 733–747, 2009.

each individual model transformation must be combined with testing of the model transformation chain, and suitable test design techniques must be devised.

For obtaining high-quality model transformations and model transformation chains, testing alone is not sufficient. In the software engineering community, it is well-accepted that software quality is also influenced by the development process. Nowadays, it is common practice to follow an iterative development process (e.g. the Rational Unified Process [11]) or even an agile development process [12]. Similarly, when developing a model transformation chain, several iterations are required and it must be ensured that the solution gradually improves.

To ensure incremental improvement of the quality of a transformation chain, several requirements must be addressed: Firstly, software engineers must be able to change their transformation internally without breaking the overall transformation chain. Secondly, when adding new functionality, existing functionality must be preserved, and thirdly, when fixing defects of a transformation chain, software engineers must be given a means to ensure that no additional defects are being introduced.

In this paper, we present an approach for incremental development of model transformation chains that is based on automated testing. To establish automated testing of a model transformation chain, we propose four test design techniques and describe an architecture for a fully automated test framework for a model transformation chain. Our approach enables the software engineer to improve the quality of the model transformation chain systematically when adding new functionality, fixing defects or changing a transformation of the overall chain: Automated testing techniques for the transformation chain are used to validate all changes, following the established principle of test-driven development. We validate our approach by developing a model transformation chain for version management for the IBM® WebSphere® Business Modeler [13].

The paper is structured as follows: We first provide background on version management of process models, which requires the development of a model transformation chain. In Section 3, we present an overview of our approach for incremental development and explain why it ensures gradual improvement of the model transformation under development. We discuss requirements for testing transformation chains in Section 4, present four test design techniques in Section 5, and explain an architecture for a test framework in Section 6. In Section 7 we report on applying the approach when developing a version management solution for process models. We conclude with a discussion of related work, conclusions and future work.

2 Case Study: Version Management of Business Process Models

In business-driven development [14], process models are developed in a team environment and iteratively refined. To support business-driven development, a version management approach for process models is needed that allows a modeler to detect and resolve differences between two process models V and V_1. At some point in time, the two versions need to be consolidated into a common version by inspecting all changes and applying selected changes.

Figure 1 a) shows a first version V of a process model from the insurance domain and a second version V_1 that has been derived from V. Both models are expressed in the

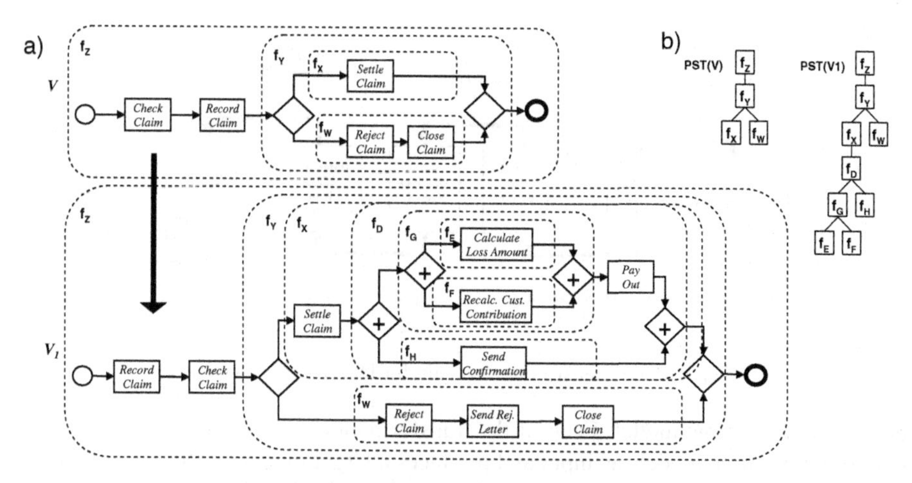

Fig. 1. Two process models and their Process Structure Trees

Business Process Modeling Notation (BPMN) [15]. In addition, Figure 1 a) also shows a decomposition of the process models into fragments (e.g. f_Z,..). These fragments can be arranged into a Process Structure Tree (PST) of a process model [16], as shown in Figure 1 b).

To realize process model version management, we can distinguish a difference detection phase and a difference resolution phase: In difference detection, a Difference Model containing all change operations (shown in Figure 2) must be computed and visualized such that the business user can inspect all changes. Then, in the difference resolution phase, the business user can apply selected change operations to construct a consolidated process model.

For difference detection if no change log is available [17], several model transformations are part of the solution, as illustrated in Figure 3: First, a concrete process model expressed in the language BPMN is transformed into a Process Graph by a *BPMN to Process Graph Transformation*. Then, given a Process Graph, a *PST Computation* creates the PST [16]. Two PSTs and a set of correspondences between BPMN models are used in the *Correspondence Computation* to establish a mapping between PSTs which we call the Joint Process Structure Tree [17].

Δ(V, V1):
a) MoveAction("Check Claim", -, -, -, -)
b) InsertFragment(f_D, -, -)
c) InsertAction("Pay Out", -, -)
d) InsertAction("Send Confirmation", -, -)
e) InsertFragment(f_I, -, -)
f) InsertAction("Calculate Loss Amount", -, -)
g) InsertAction("Recalc. Cust. Contribution", -, -)
h) InsertAction("Send Rej. Letter", -, -)

Fig. 2. Difference Model for example (textual form)

The Joint Process Structure Tree is then used in the *Difference Computation* to produce a Difference Model that represents the change operations between the first and second version of the input models, see Figure 2. The Difference Model containing the change operations is then further transformed. The *Dependency Computation* establishes dependencies between change operations [18]. Differences not applicable on the concrete BPMN model are filtered using a *Filtering* transformation. Finally, *Parameter Computation* establishes change operation parameters by selecting suitable predecessor

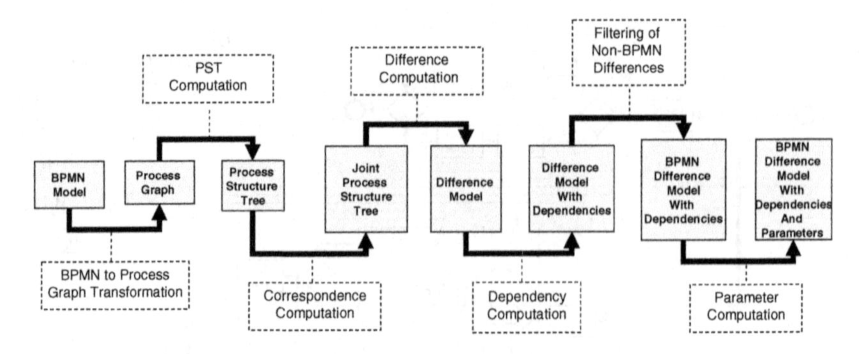

Fig. 3. Model transformation chain for Difference Detection

and successors in the model. Each of the transformations previously introduced takes one or more source models as input and produces a target model. Further details of the foundations of these transformations can be found in [17,18].

As the transformation chain for Difference Detection is complex and requires design and implementation of several model transformations, a development approach is needed that supports incremental development and improvement of the transformation chain.

3 Incremental Development of Model Transformation Chains

Existing software development processes such as the Rational Unified Process [11] are incremental and iterative. For model transformations, recent work by Siikarla et al. [19] argues that model transformations must also be developed in several iterations. With regards to a model transformation chain as the one above where input models are very diverse and several different individual transformations are assembled into a chain, an incremental and iterative approach is required to handle complexity and manage the development process.

In the following, we present our approach for incremental and iterative development of model transformations which focusses on design, implementation and testing activities of model transformation development. Figure 4 provides an overview of our approach:

- After requirements specification and analysis of the model transformation, development starts with the design and implementation of a first version of the model transformation. The details of the design and implementation activity depend on the transformation language and environment used, but the goal of this activity is in all cases a first running implementation of the transformation.
- An initial test case set is created for the model transformation. This initial test case set can be based on the design step of the model transformation by extracting design information and the required outcome of the transformation on a set of sample input models. Optionally, it can even be created before designing and implementing a first version of the transformation.
- The model transformation is tested using the test case set and possible defects may occur. These defects can be categorized according to their severity and then treated

in an improvement activity of the model transformation. These two activities (testing and improvement) are repeated until the model transformation passes all test cases. In the case of a model transformation chain, the model transformation causing the defect must be located and improved.
- Once a model transformation passes all test cases, several activities can be performed: The test case set can be extended by additional tests, new functionality can be designed and implemented if there are requirements that have not yet been addressed in previous iterations, or refactoring techniques can be applied to improve internal architecture and code quality. Each of these activities is followed by the two activities of running all test cases and removing any defects that may have surfaced.

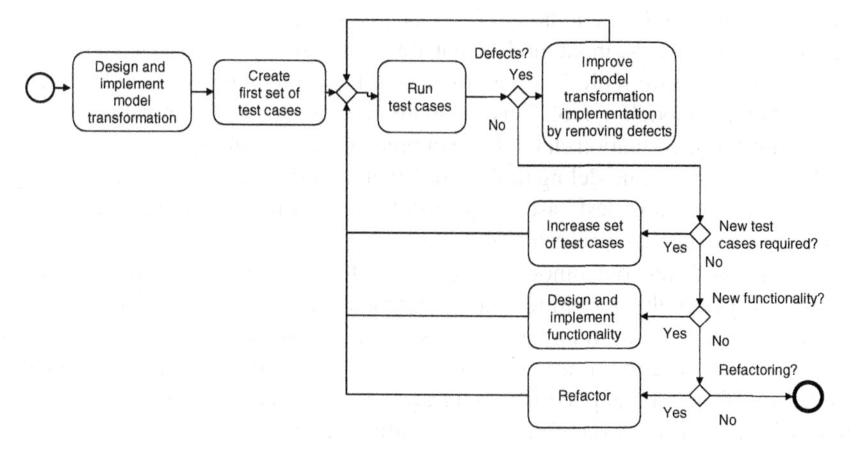

Fig. 4. Incremental development approach for model transformations

Currently, our approach does not include activities for requirements specification, analysis and detailed roles involved in the process. For these activities, we refer to the body of existing work on model transformation design (e.g. [20,21]).

When following the incremental approach, the model transformation will always pass all test cases in the test case set. As such, the quality of the model transformation will gradually increase over time if the activities (refactoring, increasing of test cases, adding functionality) are aimed at increasing the quality of the model transformation under development. For example, test cases must be carefully chosen to ensure necessary coverage of all input models for the transformation, and refactoring must be applied to improve the internal architecture of the transformation.

If the approach is applied to the development of a model transformation chain, then test design techniques must take into account the characteristics of a transformation chain. For example, test cases must be designed that encompass the entire transformation chain and are not restricted to an individual transformation, to establish an end-to-end testing of the transformation chain. With regards to established software testing, this corresponds to testing of individual components and system testing [22]. In the following section, we elaborate on the requirements for testing model transformation chains.

4 Requirements for Automated Testing of Model Transformation Chains

Testing of model transformations is difficult and a topic of ongoing research [6]. In the following, we discuss the background and derive requirements for testing model transformations that are part of a transformation chain and for testing the model transformation chain itself.

There are two main challenges in model transformation testing: the creation of a test collection consisting of sample input models for the transformation under test and the specification of test outcomes (test oracle) for the sample input models [6].

In general, sample input models can be created manually using the modeling environment or automatically using a model generation approach. With regards to automatic generation of input models, although first research results are available [8,9], the challenge of generating those input models that are meaningful remains. Manual creation of input models can be difficult if a transformation takes as input model a model that is not supported by the modeling tool. This is usually the case for model transformations applied within a transformation chain: For example, in our case the Process Structure Tree is not supported by the modeling tool itself. Whether test cases are created manually or automatically, the set of test cases must fulfill the meta model coverage requirement, again a topic of ongoing research [23].

With regards to test outcomes, we are confronted with another challenge. One approach is to specify the desired test case outcome for each test case manually. In practice, this can be done by running the transformation on the test case and inspecting the outcome. If it is correct, it is set as the desired test case outcome. With regards to a model transformation applied within a transformation chain, a missing visualization can make manual inspection of the outcome difficult.

For model transformation chains, in addition to testing each individual transformation the overall transformation chain must be tested. Additional challenges arise because when developing a model transformation chain, test design techniques applied to each individual transformation must be economical with regards to development resources and test case data produced.

As several model transformations are composed into a transformation chain, additional tests are needed in order to detect whether changes in an individual transformation affect the overall transformation. These tests are important to allow internal changes of a transformation, which are common in iterative development.

To summarize, there are several requirements for test design techniques of model transformation chains: The first is that test design techniques are required that allow the testing of the end-to-end model transformation chain. The second is that test design techniques are required that allow the detection of functional changes of individual transformations that are relevant to the overall transformation chain. The third is that test design techniques for individual transformations should be economical with regards to the amount of work needed to put them into place and the number of input models created. Another important requirement for the feasibility of the incremental approach is the ability to perform testing in a fully automatic manner.

5 Test Design Techniques for Automated Testing

In the following, we describe four test design techniques for model transformations that fulfill the requirements: integrity test of created model structures, inspected reference outcomes, invariant validation, and deviation testing.

Integrity test of created model structures aims at automatically inspecting the created model structures and determining whether they violate a correctness condition. This means that for this test design technique, the test oracle is obtained from the specification of the model structure or modeling language in which a model is created. One correctness condition consists of syntactic correctness of the created model structures or of a property that must always be fulfilled. Another type of a correctness condition consists of semantic correctness of the created model structures. A third type of correctness condition can sometimes also be derived from a transformation contract if such a means is applied in the design phase of the transformation. Correctness conditions can be encoded as conditions to be checked after running the transformation.

For the *PST Computation*, a straightforward integrity test of created model structures is obtained by checking that each fragment in the PST has a single entry and exit edge[1]. Another correctness condition for the produced PST is that each edge is either an entry or exit edge of a fragment or must connect two nodes within the same fragment. These two correctness conditions can be encoded as conditions and can then be checked on the result of the *PST Computation*.

For the *Parameter Computation*, an integrity test of created model structures can use as a correctness condition that after parameter computation a change operation must have computed parameters. In addition, computed parameters must also be meaningful. Such a simple semantic correctness condition can be validated for, e.g., the InsertAction change operation by ensuring that the parameters point to model elements in between which the action is to be inserted. Note that integrity tests of created model structures do not require the storing of additional test case data.

Inspected reference outcomes is a test design technique that produces a collection of inspected reference outcomes for the model transformation. These inspected reference outcomes can then be reused when testing a model transformation by automatically comparing the result of the current model transformation with the previously inspected result. If the two do not coincide, the test case fails. This technique involves model comparison which can be realized in a text-based form or by using model comparison techniques [24].

Because of the manual overhead involved in inspecting the outcome of a transformation for setting the reference outcome, the number of test cases for this approach is limited and cannot be as high as the test cases used, e.g., within the integrity test of created model structures. On the other hand, there has to be a certain number of test cases following this approach to ensure the quality of the transformations. Figure 5 shows an inspected reference outcome for the two process models introduced in Figure 1. It shows the resulting BPMN Difference Model (in textual form) with the parameters of those differences computed that are applicable.

---

[1] The idea of the process structure tree is to decompose a process model into these single-entry single-exit fragments [16]. The PST abstracts data flow edges of a process model into control flow edges.

```
MOVE (Check Claim,[Start Node,Record Claim],Record Claim,Decision)
INSERT (Parallel Fragment,Settle Claim,Merge)
INSERT (Send Rej. Letter,Reject Claim,Close Claim)
INSERT (Parallel Fragment,,)
INSERT (Pay Out,,)
INSERT (Send Confirmation,,)
INSERT (Calculate Loss Amount,,)
INSERT (Recalc. Cust. Contribution,,)
```

Fig. 5. Inspected reference outcome example

Invariant validation can be applied if the transformation is supposed to conform to certain invariants. These invariants first have to be identified and expressed and then encoded such that they can be checked after applying a transformation. Invariants can be formulated about newly created model structures or about modified model structures. Moreover, also constraints about the models may be used for invariant validation. Invariant validation has similarities to the integrity test of model structures because in both techniques the result of the transformation is automatically inspected based on a correctness condition. For the integrity test of created model structures, a correctness condition is needed that has to be derived from the modeling language. Invariant validation allows one to verify arbitrary invariants on the result of the transformation.

In our case, the *Correspondence Computation* is a transformation that establishes correspondences between the nodes of two PSTs. A straightforward invariant for this transformation is that after its application, correspondences should have been established for every PST node where the children nodes have correspondences. This invariant can be encoded and checked after applying the Correspondence Computation. Another example in which invariant validation can be used is the creation of the Difference Model and the *Dependency Computation*. Here, one invariant is that there are no cyclic dependencies. Again, this invariant can be encoded as a test and then checked.

Deviation testing is a test design technique that does not aim at testing complete correctness but that is usually inexpensive to establish. For deviation testing, one determines data that is to be computed on the outcome of a model transformation. This data is then automatically computed and stored each time the transformation is executed. If the transformation is called again, then a new data collection is computed and compared with the previous data collection. If the data collections are not equal, then a warning is generated. Deviation testing generates outcomes of test cases by successful executions of the system under test, i.e., as a test oracle an implementation is used that is considered to be correct. One strength of deviation testing is the detection of defects during refactoring or error removal of model transformations. In addition, we can use deviation testing for abstracting from irrelevant details of the outcome of a model transformation that are not relevant to successor transformations. Due to its characteristics, deviation testing should not be used in isolation, but must be combined with other test design techniques.

We have applied deviation testing for the *BPMN to Process Graph Transformation* and the *PST Computation*. The goal was to detect changes in the behavior of the two transformations that are relevant to subsequent transformations. Figure 6 shows a (simplified) meta model of the model generated from the *PST Computation* and illustrates how to derive appropriate deviation test data. In the example, the number of nodes, edges and fragments are chosen for the deviation test data because these are relevant for subsequent transformations (e.g. the *Difference Computation* detects differences based

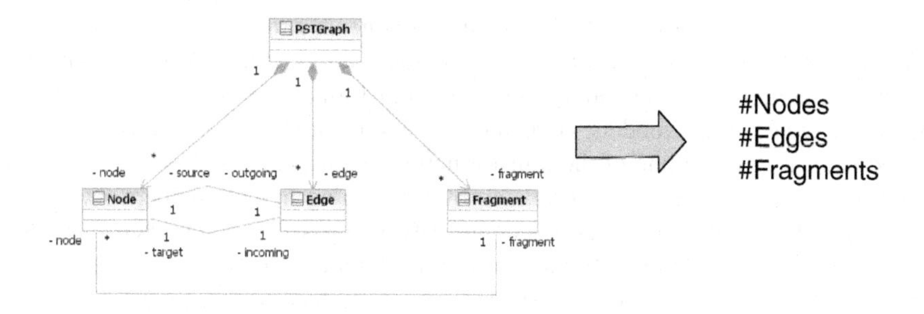

Fig. 6. Deriving deviation test data from a model

on the fragments). More fine-grained test data such as the number of associations can be integrated if they are important for subsequent transformations.

In addition to the techniques described above, we can also apply combinations of these techniques. For example, one can combine the deviation technique with the integrity test of created model structures to increase the reliability of the deviation technique. With regards to test automation, integrity tests of created model structures, invariant validation and deviation testing are fully automatic and can be applied on a large number of possibly also automatically created test models.

6 Architecture of a Test Framework

The test design techniques described above require the execution of test cases, the comparison of outcomes of transformations with reference outcomes, and the evaluation of invariants as well as other test data. Automatic execution of test cases is supported in existing test frameworks such as JUnit [25]. For testing model transformation chains using the test design techniques, additional support (such as model comparison) is needed. In this section, we propose a test framework, illustrated in Figure 7 for setting up such an automated test environment for model transformations.

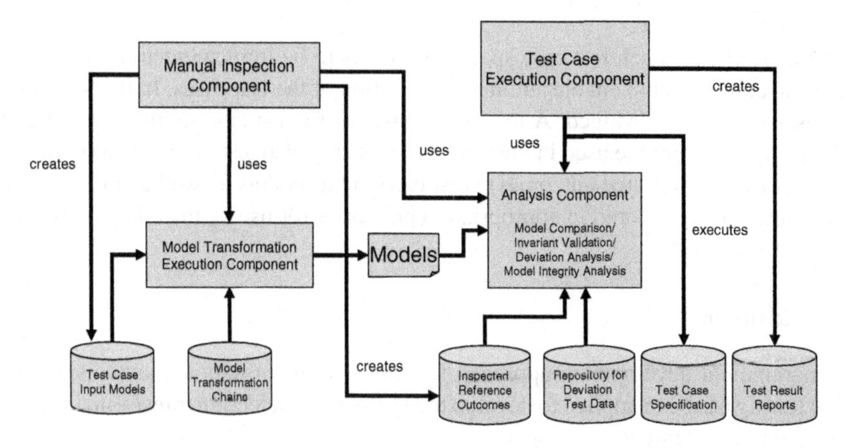

Fig. 7. Architecture of a test framework for automated testing of model transformation chains

The architecture consists of four main components and several repositories. The *Model Transformation Execution Component* takes a model transformation chain and a test case input model and applies the model transformations in the chain to the input models to create output models. Here, the model transformation chain can either be encoded in Java or using one of the transformation languages. The *Analysis Component* analyzes the result of the transformation by performing model comparison, invariant validation, deviation analysis, or model integrity analysis. This component enables automatic test result evaluation. It makes use of relevant data, depending on the test case (e.g. reference outcomes or deviation test data). Both the *Analysis Component* and the *Model Transformation Execution Component* are used by the *Manual Inspection Component* and the *Test Case Execution Component*. The latter automates the execution of a larger number of test cases and in addition interprets the result of the *Analysis Component* to produce an appropriate test result report. The *Manual Inspection Component* allows the software engineer to create test case input models as well as inspected reference outcomes. Usually, it is integrated into the development environment of the model transformation chain. The *Manual Inspection Component* can also be used to inspect the outcome of a particular test case.

In addition, the test framework contains a set of test cases in which each test case conforms to a test case specification obtained from applying a test design technique. For setting up a test framework based on this architecture, we propose the following procedure:

In the first step, the model transformations used in the transformation chain are enumerated, together with their source and target languages. Then, in the second step, for each model transformation, one (or more) test design techniques for obtaining test case specifications are chosen. Depending on the technique, the information required for the test case specification is completed: If an integrity test of created model structures is applied, then the correctness criterion has to be specified and the model elements have to be specified for which the correctness criterion should hold. In the case of inspected reference outcomes, the model that should be compared has to be identified and an approach for comparison (e.g. text-based or full model comparison) has to be chosen. For invariant validation, the invariant and the models that should satisfy it have to be identified. If deviation testing is applied in the test case specification, then the data collection needs to be determined.

In the third step, each test case specification has to be implemented in the test case execution component to enable automatic execution of the test cases. In the fourth step, test cases need to determined. A test case consists of a test case input model and, depending on the technique used in the test case, possibly also test output data (in the case of the inspected reference outcomes). Test case input models as well as inspected reference outcomes are stored in appropriate repositories for use by the other components in the test framework.

7 Evaluation

The incremental development approach for model transformation chains using automated testing has been applied to develop the Difference Detection transformation chain for version management.

As the IBM WebSphere Business Modeler is built on top of Eclipse, we were able to use the JUnit [25] functionality of Eclipse for the test case execution component and start the runtime environment of Eclipse with a prepopulated workspace that contains all test case input models. In our environment, all the transformations introduced are implemented in Java.

For the transformation chain for Difference Detection, we developed several test case specifications according to the test design techniques described previously. Figure 8 shows an overview of these test case specifications:

For the *PST Computation*, the *Dependency Computation* and the *Parameter Computation*, we applied an integrity test of created model structures. For the *Correspondence Computation*, we applied an invariant test.

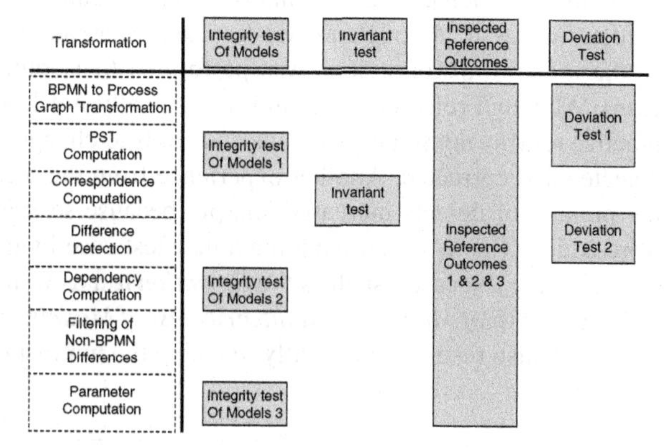

Fig. 8. Test case specifications applied to each transformation

We applied the inspected reference outcomes technique for the testing of the complete transformation chain, involving all transformations. To overcome the challenge of model comparison, we adopted a simple approach of saving models into text files which can then be easily compared using string comparison.

For the *BPMN to Process Graph Transformation*, the *PST Computation*, and the *Difference Computation*, we chose to apply a deviation test to detect changes.

Our test case input models consist of a first and a second version of a process model, together with the correspondences between the model elements in the two versions. These models are passed to the *BPMN to Process Graph Transformation*, which creates two Process Graphs for each of the process models. Subsequent transformations then use and create new models. As we do not use inspected reference outcomes for any of the intermediate transformations, we do not need to create a separate set of test case input models, but can use the ones created by the transformations. In addition to the test cases, we also designed and implemented a test report for each test case which provides a detailed overview of the test cases that passed and those that failed.

To ensure sufficient coverage of our tests case input models, we applied several techniques. First, we have to ensure that meta models of the source and the target language of the transformation chains are covered. As there are, to our knowledge, no tools available for measuring this, we manually designed test case input models without measuring meta model coverage precisely. Second, we have to ensure code coverage of the transformation code. Here, we applied code coverage analysis tools, such as [26], to identify deficits. In addition, we also used code inspection of selected core classes to identify deficits in coverage. We then manually added suitable test case input models to increase coverage.

The transformation chain for Difference Detection of process models was developed over a period of several months, using the incremental development process. Overall, we started with 80 test case input models for each of the test case specifications and gradually increased this to over 200 test case input models (to be used by all 7 test case specifications), giving rise to $200 * 7 = 1400$ test cases.

Figure 9 shows the number of test case input models and the relationship to defects over an extended period of time. It shows how the number of test case input models (and thereby the test cases) was incrementally increased and how after such an increase the number of defects was gradually reduced again. At several dates, the number of defects increased, although no new test cases were added. During that time, refactoring of the model transformations was performed that could also lead to failures of test cases: Although refactoring should theoretically not lead to a change of behavior, in practice refactoring sometimes fails and leads to change of behavior which needs to be detected and corrected. Another experience from the measurements is that sometimes the number of defects increased sharply because several new test case input models were added. This is because adding a new test case input model can lead to defects in several of the test cases, such as the *Deviation test* as well as the *Integrity test of Models 1*, *Integrity test of Models 2* and *Integrity test of Models 3*. As a consequence, fixing one defect can also result in drastically reducing the number of defects reported.

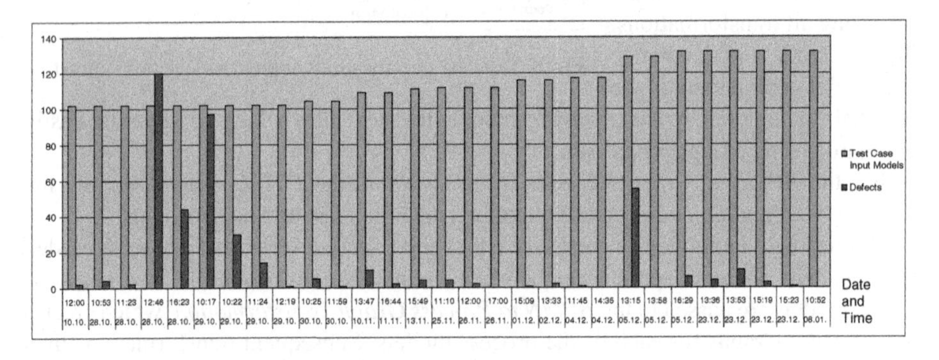

Fig. 9. Test case input models and defects over an extended period of time

In the following, we summarize the lessons learnt while developing the model transformation chain:

- Incremental development for model transformation chains is required in practice; iterative improvement of the transformations is the reality.
- Systematic quality improvement is not possible without automated testing.
- Code quality is an important issue when implementing model transformations in Java. As model transformation code can be complex, established software quality principles, such as readability and maintainability, become important issues.
- Versioning is required also for test cases. As the model transformation evolves over time, also the test case input models evolve and it is important to be able to associate them with the version of the model transformation.
- A major drawback is the lack of coverage analysis tools for test case input models.

- One has to choose the accuracy of the inspected sample outcomes carefully. Our textual comparison of test models could have been replaced with a model comparison. However, then this could lead to noise in the test case set, i.e., during refactoring deviations and failed test cases could occur that are not relevant to the outcome of the transformation.

8 Related Work

Concerning model transformation testing, recent work by Kolovos et al. [27] describes a unit testing framework for model management operations which is integrated into the Epsilon component for model management operations. The idea to use unit testing is similar to our idea of automating testing of model transformations; however, we provide detailed test design techniques for model transformation chains and evaluate their usage in an industrial context.

Fleurey et al. [7] describe an approach to generate test models for model transformations. They first calculate the effective meta model for the transformation and then determine a coverage criterion based on this effective meta model. The coverage criterion is used for generating test models. Following this approach, Mottu et al. [28] describe mutation analysis testing for model transformations using mutation operators. A mutation operator for model creation is to replace a creation of an object with a parent class. The mutation analysis can be used to ensure the quality of the test case set and has therefore a different focus than our work. Earlier work by Andrews et al. [29] presented several techniques for testing systems based on their UML design models. Among them, they propose test criteria for class diagrams such as the creation of class attributes from a representative attribute value set. These test criteria can be used as a basis for defining coverage of a model transformation and could also be applied in our scenario.

A development process for model transformations is described by Siikarla et al. [19]. They propose that first several example correspondence models are specified, then a transformational pattern is designed, which is then later implemented. In contrast to their approach, we focus on incremental development of transformation chains based on automated testing. Our test design techniques are not limited to our specific scenario because they can also be used if model transformations are defined using one of the transformation authoring environments such as ATL [2].

9 Conclusion

If several model transformations are composed into a model transformation chain, a development approach is needed that allows the quality of the model transformation chain to be improved incrementally, and simultaneously allows a developer to change an individual transformation without affecting the model transformation chain. In this paper, we have presented an approach for incremental development of model transformation chains that is based on automated testing. We first established requirements for automated testing of model transformation chains and then presented four test design techniques for testing model transformation chains. We have proposed a test framework architecture that can be used for incremental development of model transformation chains. Our techniques have been validated with the incremental development of a model transformation chain for version management of process models.

Future work will include the development of coverage criteria for transformation chains. Another direction of future work is concerned with the early phases of transformation chain development and with leveraging the specification of model transformations for test case generation.

Acknowledgements. We thank Jana Koehler for her valuable feedback on an earlier version of this paper and Christian Gerth for his work on the version management prototype.

References

1. Csertán, G., Huszerl, G., Majzik, I., Pap, Z., Pataricza, A., Varró, D.: VIATRA: Visual Automated Transformations for Formal Verification and Validation of UML Models. In: ASE 2002, September 2002, pp. 267–270 (2002)
2. Jouault, F., Allilaire, F., Bézivin, J., Kurtev, I.: ATL: A model transformation tool. Sci. Comput. Program. 72(1-2), 31–39 (2008)
3. Karsai, G., Agrawal, A., Shi, F., Sprinkle, J.: On the Use of Graph Transformation in the Formal Specification of Model Interpreters. Journal of Universal Computer Science 9(11), 1296–1321 (2003)
4. von Pilgrim, J., Vanhooff, B., Schulz-Gerlach, I., Berbers, Y.: Constructing and Visualizing Transformation Chains. In: Schieferdecker, I., Hartman, A. (eds.) ECMDA-FA 2008. LNCS, vol. 5095, pp. 17–32. Springer, Heidelberg (2008)
5. International Standards Organization (ISO): ISO/IEC 9126-1: 2001, Software Quality Attributes, Software Engineering – Product Quality, Part 1: Quality Model (January 2001)
6. Baudry, B., Dinh-Trong, T., Mottu, J.M., Simmonds, D., France, R., Ghosh, S., Fleurey, F., Traon, Y.L.: Model Transformation Testing Challenges. In: Proceedings of IMDT workshop in conjunction with ECMDA 2006, Bilbao, Spain (2006)
7. Fleurey, F., Steel, J., Baudry, B.: Model-Driven Engineering and Validation: Testing model transformations. In: Proceedings SIVOES-MoDeVa Workshop (November 2004)
8. Bunyakiati, P., Finkelstein, A., Rosenblum, D.S.: The certification of software tools with respect to software standards. In: IRI 2007, IEEE Systems, Man, and Cybernetics Society, pp. 724–729 (2007)
9. Ehrig, K., Küster, J.M., Taentzer, G.: Generating instance models from meta models. Software and Systems Modeling (to appear, 2009)
10. Stürmer, I., Conrad, M., Dörr, H., Pepper, P.: Systematic testing of model-based code generators. IEEE Trans. Software Eng. 33(9), 622–634 (2007)
11. Kruchten, P.: The Rational Unified Process: An Introduction. Addison-Wesley, Reading (1999)
12. Martin, R.: Agile Software Development: Principles, Patterns, and Practices. Prentice Hall, Englewood Cliffs (2002)
13. IBM Corporation: IBM WebSphere Business Modeler, `http://www.ibm.com/software/integration/wbimodeler/`
14. Koehler, J., Hauser, R., Küster, J., Ryndina, K., Vanhatalo, J., Wahler, M.: The Role of Visual Modeleling and Model Transformations in Business-Driven Development. In: Proceedings of the 5th International Workshop on Graph Transformations and Visual Modeling Techniques, pp. 1–12 (2006)

15. Object Management Group (OMG): Business Process Modeling Notation, V1.1 (January 2008)
16. Vanhatalo, J., Völzer, H., Leymann, F.: Faster and More Focused Control-Flow Analysis for Business Process Models Through SESE Decomposition. In: Krämer, B.J., Lin, K.-J., Narasimhan, P. (eds.) ICSOC 2007. LNCS, vol. 4749, pp. 43–55. Springer, Heidelberg (2007)
17. Küster, J.M., Gerth, C., Förster, A., Engels, G.: Detecting and Resolving Process Model Differences in the Absence of a Change Log. In: Dumas, M., Reichert, M., Shan, M.-C. (eds.) BPM 2008. LNCS, vol. 5240, pp. 244–260. Springer, Heidelberg (2008)
18. Küster, J.M., Gerth, C., Engels, G.: Dependent and Conflicting Change Operations of Process Models. In: Paige, R., Hartman, A., Rensink, A. (eds.) ECMDA-FA 2009. LNCS, vol. 5562, pp. 158–173. Springer, Heidelberg (2009)
19. Siikarla, M., Laitkorpi, M., Selonen, P., Systä, T.: Transformations Have to be Developed ReST Assured. In: Vallecillo, A., Gray, J., Pierantonio, A. (eds.) ICMT 2008. LNCS, vol. 5063, pp. 1–15. Springer, Heidelberg (2008)
20. Vanhooff, B., Baelen, S.V., Hovsepyan, A., Joosen, W., Berbers, Y.: Towards a Transformation Chain Modeling Language. In: Vassiliadis, S., Wong, S., Hämäläinen, T.D. (eds.) SAMOS 2006. LNCS, vol. 4017, pp. 39–48. Springer, Heidelberg (2006)
21. Küster, J.M., Ryndina, K., Hauser, R.: A Systematic Approach to Designing Model Transformations. Technical report, IBM Research, Research Report RZ 3621 (July 2005)
22. Binder, R.: Testing Object-Oriented System Models. Addison Wesley, Reading (1999)
23. Brottier, E., Fleurey, F., Steel, J., Baudry, B., Traon, Y.L.: Metamodel-based Test Generation for Model Transformations: an Algorithm and a Tool. In: ISSRE 2006, pp. 85–94. IEEE Computer Society, Los Alamitos (2006)
24. Kolovos, D.S., Paige, R., Polack, F.: Model Comparison: a Foundation for Model Composition and Model Transformation Testing. In: Proc. First International Workshop on Global Integrated Model Management 2006 (2006)
25. JUnit.org: Resources for Test-Driven Development, `http://www.junit.org/`
26. Harold, E.: Measure test coverage with Cobertura (2005), `http://www.ibm.com/developerworks/java/library/j-cobertura/`
27. Kolovos, D.S., Paige, R., Rose, L., Polack, F.: Unit Testing Model Management Operations. In: 5th Workshop on Model Driven Engineering Verification and Validation (MoDeVVa). IEEE, Los Alamitos (2008)
28. Mottu, J.M., Baudry, B., Traon, Y.L.: Mutation Analysis Testing for Model Transformation. In: Rensink, A., Warmer, J. (eds.) ECMDA-FA 2006. LNCS, vol. 4066, pp. 376–390. Springer, Heidelberg (2006)
29. Andrews, A., France, R.B., Ghosh, S., Craig, G.: Test adequacy criteria for UML design models. Softw. Test., Verif. Reliab. 13(2), 95–127 (2003)

Test-Driven Development of Model Transformations*

Pau Giner and Vicente Pelechano

Centro de Investigación en Métodos de Producción de Software
Universidad Politécnica de Valencia
Camino de Vera s/n, 46022 Valencia, Spain
{pginer,pele}@pros.upv.es

Abstract. Model transformations enable the automated development paradigm proposed by Model Driven Engineering. However, since the requirements for building a model transformation are usually expressed informally, requirements descriptions are difficult to keep updated and synchronized with their corresponding implementations. Therefore, human effort is usually required for validating model transformations. The present work defines a test-driven method for the development process of model-to-model transformations. This method is focused on the capture of requirements for transformations in such a way that guides the development and the documentation of model transformations. Requirements are expressed by means of test cases that can be automatically validated. The proposal has been applied to the MOSKitt open source CASE tool in an industrial scenario.

Keywords: Model-to-model transformations, test-driven development.

1 Introduction

Model-to-model transformations have a central role in Model Driven Engineering (MDE). Although many proposals exist for supporting the definition and execution of model transformations [1,2,3,4], there is a lack in the methodological support for capturing their requirements. Bézivin et al. indicate in [5] that in early project development phases it might be advisable to concentrate on transformation properties by expressing them in transformation models. The *transformation model* idea promotes the description of transformations from an abstract perspective regardless of its executability.

Model transformations are normally described in natural language[1]. From these informal descriptions, transformation developers define the mappings in a formal way. Once implemented, model transformations can be validated using several techniques [6,7,8,9]. However, the consistency between the description of the transformation and the current implementation requires manual effort for keeping them synchronized.

* This work has been developed with the support of MEC under the project SESAMO TIN2007-62894 and cofinanced by FEDER.

[1] See some examples at http://www.eclipse.org/m2m/atl/atlTransformations/

A. Schürr and B. Selic (Eds.): MODELS 2009, LNCS 5795, pp. 748–752, 2009.

The main contribution of this work is a methodological approach for the definition of transformation models that guides the development of the model transformation and automates the consistency check between specification and implementation. This is achieved following a test-driven approach [10]. The proposal has been applied to different model transformations included in the MOSKitt[2] modeling tools.

The remainder of the paper is structured as follows. Section 2 defines how requirements for a model transformation are captured. Section 3 indicates how requirements and implementation of model transformations can be kept consistent. Section 4 shows how the approach has been put into practice. Related work is presented in Section 5. Finally, Section 6 concludes the paper.

2 Capturing Requirements for Model Transformations

Our approach makes use of transformation examples as test-cases to guide the development of the corresponding transformation. Figure 1 shows a test case illustrating a particular requirement for the UML2DB transformation included in MOSKitt. The test case includes versioning and identification information, and the formal definition of some example input data and the corresponding expected result.

Num	Version	Intent	Mapping: UML2DB
1	1	A concrete class generates a table with the same name.	
Test data		Expected result	

Class "Class1"{
isAbstract: false
}
		Inclusion: Table "Class1"{
		columns: Column "PK_Class1"{
		}
		}
		Assertion: "Has primary key"
		self.getPrimaryKey().isDefined()
		Assertion: "PK is the key column"
		self.getPrimaryKey().members.first() =
		self.columns->any(c|c.name='PK_Class1')	

Fig. 1. Template for specifying test cases

Test data is defined using Human Usable Textual Notation (HUTN) [11]. HUTN is a specification by the OMG to define models in a textual form. HUTN is *generic*, as it can be applied to any MOF-based metamodel; it is *fully automated* since the generation of models from HUTN definitions requires no human intervention; and it has been designed to be *human-usable*. In the example of Fig. 1, a class named "Class1" is defined with its *isAbstract* attribute set to *false*.

The expected result is expressed by means of *result parts* and *assertions*. Each *result part* is formed by a model –specified using HUTN– and a comparison

[2] http://www.moskitt.org/

criterion. The comparison criteria can be *inclusion*, *exclusion* or *exact*. It represents the relation that the model part should have with respect to the result. In the example, the *inclusion* criteria is used to indicate that the obtained result must contain a *Table* named "Class1" with a *Column* named "PK_Class1".

For a more fine-grained control in the definition of the obtained result, Epsilon Validation Language (EVL) [12] is used. In Fig. 1, two EVL assertions are defined for checking that a primary key exists and that it corresponds to the column defined.

In addition, test cases can be used to produce end-user documentation by generating graphical representations of HUTN definitions. The MOSKitt documentation[3] follows this approach.

3 Keeping the Consistency

The test-driven development approach proposed in this work is a cyclic process –see Fig. 2. In each development cycle the implementation is extended to cover a new test case. For each of these increments the implementation is validated according to the specification and the documentation is created/updated. In this way, implementation and specification are continuously synchronized.

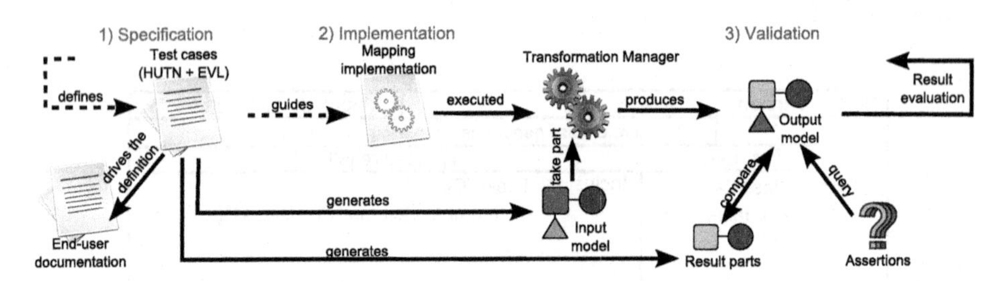

Fig. 2. Method overview

The validation stage is the key step for ensuring the consistency between implementation and specification. Different tools are coordinated for performing the validation. First, the test data specified in HUTN is processed to generate the *input model*. Then, the model transformation is applied to this model to obtain the *output model*. Finally, the obtained result is compared to the expected result. In order to perform the comparison model parts are converted into assertions, and the model is checked against each assertion.

An Eclipse plug-in has been developed to extend the JUnit capabilities in order to support the execution of model validations and model transformations programmatically. The JUnit plug-in coordinates the execution of the different plug-ins that support each part of the validation process. The edition and parsing of HUTN and EVL definitions is based on the Epsilon[4] project. The execution of the transformation is done using the Transformation Manager (TM) API

[3] http://www.moskitt.org/eng/manuales/

[4] http://www.eclipse.org/gmt/epsilon/

defined in MOSKitt. The TM provides a unified API for the execution of different transformation engines.

4 Applying the Proposal

First, the proposal was applied for the validation of an existing transformation between class diagrams and relational database models –namely UML2DB. Test cases were used for validation purposes. Then, we realized the potential of using test cases to guide the development of new functionality. So, a paradigm shift was then produced and from that moment, test cases were used for specifying the transformation requirements.

Test cases were defined following our proposal for guiding the implementation of a parameterized version of the UML2DB transformation. Taking the original test cases as a basis, new ones were defined to exemplify how the transformation was affected by the configuration model. In this way, new test cases were used to guide the implementation and to verify that the new requirements are fulfilled and backward compatibility was preserved.

5 Related Work

The transformation model idea is illustrated in [5] by using UML/MOF class diagram together with OCL constraints. Transformation models in that approach are defined at metamodel level while our approach captures the requirements for a model transformation by means of relevant examples based on HUTN. The benefits of using HUTN for the definition of models were described in [13].

Some of the method steps presented can be addressed in different ways. Techniques already exist for assessing the quality of test cases [14,15], for automating result comparison [16,8], and even for automating the development of the transformation from these test cases [17,18]. However, these aspects are not considered in the present work since we are focused on how the requirements for a transformation can be captured in such a way that enables the application of test-driven principles.

Several approaches [19,20] are focused on the generation of test cases from a given transformation implementation. These approaches assume that the transformation to be tested already exists. However our approach promotes the definition of test cases prior to the implementation of the transformation.

6 Conclusions

The present work introduces a method for a test-driven development of model-to-model transformations. The method is focused on describing transformation requirements in a way that is useful to developers and end-users. On the one hand, since the used notations allow test cases to be expressed by including only test-relevant data, the intent of the test can be easily determined –i.e., irrelevant attributes do not blur the specified requirement. On the other hand, maintainability is improved since (1) changes in the metamodel only impact on tests for which the affected information is relevant and (2) the notations used are formal-enough to allow automation in the validation.

References

1. OMG: MOF QVT Final Adopted Specification (June 2005)
2. Jouault, F., Kurtev, I.: Transforming models with atl (ISBN=0302-9743). In: Bruel, J.-M. (ed.) MoDELS 2005. LNCS, vol. 3844, pp. 128–138. Springer, Heidelberg (2006)
3. Lawley, M., Steel, J.: Practical declarative model transformation with tefkat. In: Bruel, J.-M. (ed.) MoDELS 2005. LNCS, vol. 3844, pp. 139–150. Springer, Heidelberg (2006)
4. Cuadrado, J.S., Molina, J.G.: Building domain-specific languages for model-driven development. IEEE Softw. 24(5), 48–55 (2007)
5. Bézivin, J., Büttner, F., Gogolla, M., Jouault, F., Kurtev, I., Lindow, A.: Model transformations? transformation models! In: Nierstrasz, O., Whittle, J., Harel, D., Reggio, G. (eds.) MoDELS 2006. LNCS, vol. 4199, pp. 440–453. Springer, Heidelberg (2006)
6. Fleurey, F., Steel, J., Baudry, B.: Validation in model-driven engineering: testing model transformations. In: Proc. of MODEVA 2004, pp. 29–40 (2004)
7. Küster, J.M.: Definition and validation of model transformations. Software and Systems Modeling 5(3), 233–259 (2006)
8. Lin, Y., Zhang, J., Gray, J.: A testing framework for model transformations. In: Model-Driven Software Development. Springer, Heidelberg (2005)
9. Steel, J., Lawley, M.: An MDA approach to testing the tarzan model transformation engine. In: Proc. of ISSRE 2004, St Malo, France (November 2004)
10. Beck, K.: Test Driven Development: By Example. Addison-Wesley Longman Publishing Co., Inc., Boston (2002)
11. OMG: Human-Usable Textual Notation Specification, Version 1.0 (August 2004)
12. Kolovos, D.S., Paige, R.F., Rose, L.M., Polack, F.A.: Epsilon, Department of Computer Science, The University of York (September 2008)
13. Rose, L.M., Paige, R.F., Kolovos, D.S., Polack, F.: Constructing models with the human-usable textual notation. In: Czarnecki, K., Ober, I., Bruel, J.-M., Uhl, A., Völter, M. (eds.) MODELS 2008. LNCS, vol. 5301, pp. 249–263. Springer, Heidelberg (2008)
14. Fleurey, F., Baudry, B., Muller, P.A., Traon, Y.L.: Qualifying input test data for model transformations. SoSyM 8(2), 185–203 (2009)
15. Küster, J.M., Abd-El-Razik, M.: Validation of model transformations - first experiences using a white box approach. In: MoDeVa 2006. Springer, Heidelberg (2006)
16. Polack, D., Paige, R., Rose, L., Polack, F.: Unit testing model management operations. In: ICSTW 2008, April 2008, pp. 97–104 (2008)
17. Varró, D.: Model transformation by example. In: Nierstrasz, O., Whittle, J., Harel, D., Reggio, G. (eds.) MoDELS 2006. LNCS, vol. 4199, pp. 410–424. Springer, Heidelberg (2006)
18. Varró, D., Balogh, Z.: Automating model transformation by example using inductive logic programming. In: SAC 2007, pp. 978–984. ACM, New York (2007)
19. Brottier, E., Fleurey, F., Steel, J., Baudry, B., Le Traon, Y.: Metamodel-based test generation for model transformations: an algorithm and a tool. In: ISSRE 2006, Washington, DC, USA, pp. 85–94. IEEE Computer Society, Los Alamitos (2006)
20. Darabos, A., Pataricza, A., Varró, D.: Towards testing the implementation of graph transformations. Electron. Notes Theor. Comput. Sci. 211, 75–85 (2008)

Educators' Symposium at MODELS 2009

Robert France[1] and Martin Gogolla[2]

[1] Computer Science Department, Colorado State University, USA
[2] Computer Science Department, University of Bremen, Germany

1 Context and Aim

The Educator's Symposium at the MODELS conference, the premier conference devoted to the topic of model-driven engineering of software-based systems, is intended as a forum in which educators and trainers can meet to discuss pedagogy, use of technology in the classroom, and share their experience pertaining to teaching modeling techniques and model-driven development.

Model-driven development approaches and technologies for software-based systems, in which development is centered round the manipulation of models, raise the level of abstraction and thus, improve our abilities to develop complex systems. A number of languages (e.g., UML, Alloy), approaches (e.g., OMG's MDA, MIC, Multi-Modeling), and tools (e.g., Fujaba, GME, USE, OCLE) have been proposed for the model-driven development (MDD) of software-based systems.

Putting the model-driven development vision into practice requires not only sophisticated modeling approaches and tools, but also considerable training and education effort. Practitioners in industry as well as education and training specialists need to understand the principles underlying MDD, and the strengths and limitations of current MDD tools and techniques. Such understanding is needed for proper selection and use of MDD technologies in industrial software development projects.

Industry is striving to improve their practice of software development by adopting MDD. The adoption, nevertheless, is determined by the availability of skilled software engineers who have been educated and trained in modeling and model-driven development. MDD educators and trainers can influence the practices in industry by producing an increasing number of graduates with deep understanding of MDD principles, technologies and challenges.

The Educators' Symposium at MODELS 2009 will include paper presentations and discussions as well as panels and invited statements on the symposium topics by teachers from acedemia and industry.

2 Themes

In this fifth version of the symposium we focus discussions on the resources needed to effectively educate future MDD practitioners. In particular, we will

A. Schürr and B. Selic (Eds.): MODELS 2009, LNCS 5795, pp. 753–754, 2009.

hear about efforts on developing community-based MDD education resources, that is, resources that allow educators in the MDD community to share, evaluate, and evolve education artifacts. These artifacts should be based upon synergies between industrial needs and academic education and research goals. Therefore papers on the following topics were expected:

- Education artifacts that can be effectively shared through a community-based MDD resource.
- Descriptions of existing community-based MDD education resources.
- Plans for developing and maintaining community-based education resources.

Also encouraged were contributions discussing general questions and topics of more broader interest as for example:

- Designing university courses at various levels with industrial needs in mind.
- How to include industrial experiences into teaching modeling and MDD.
- How to ensure and assess industrial relevance of the contents of modeling courses.
- How to assess industrial relevance of the teaching and learning process.
- How the teaching of modeling techniques influences industrial practices.
- Methodology issues (how to teach modeling or MDD) with industry in mind.
- Integrating modeling and MDD into the software engineering curriculum.
- Teaching modeling and MDD and associated tools (requirements, available tools).
- Experience reports from designing university courses in modeling with industrial focus.
- Requirements from industry for university education in MDD.
- Experiences from industry about university education in MDD.
- Case studies on required skills for realizing the vision of MDD.

3 Program Committee

The paper selection was carried out by an international Program Committee.

- Jordi Cabot, University of Toronto, Canada
- Peter Clarke, Florida International University, USA
- Jeff Gray, University of Alabama at Birmingham
- Oystein Haugen, SINTEF and University of Oslo, Norway
- Ludwik Kuzniarz, Blekinge Institute of Technology, Sweden
- Timothy Lethbridge, University of Ottawa, Canada
- Michal Smialk, Warsaw University of Technology, Poland

Author Index